ANCIENT WORLD

HOLT
World History

The Human Journey

HOLT, RINEHART AND WINSTON

A Harcourt Education Company

Austin • Orlando • Chicago • New York • Toronto • London • San Diego

Content Reviewers

Dr. Jack Balcer
Ohio State University
Ancient Greece

Dr. Lenard Berlanstein
University of Virginia
European social, modern France

Dr. Pierre Cagniart
Southwest Texas State U.
Ancient

Dr. Elton Daniel
University of Hawaii at Manoa
Islamic, West Asia, Iran

Dr. Toyin Falala
University of Texas at Austin
West Africa

Dr. Michael Hall
University of Texas at Austin
Colonial America

Dr. Arnold Krammer
Texas A&M University
Modern Europe, Germany

Dr. Julian Martin
University of Alberta
Science and medicine, early modern Britain

Dr. Alida Metcalf
Trinity University
Latin America, Brazil

Dr. Mark Parillo
Kansas State University
United States military, diplomatic, Japan

Dr. E. Bruce Reynolds
San Jose State University
Japan, China, Southeast Asia

Dr. Richard Saller
University of Chicago
Ancient, Roman

Dr. Lynn Struve
Indiana University
Premodern China, Chinese political and intellectual

Dr. Gerhard L. Weinberg
Emeritus, University of North Carolina—Chapel Hill
Modern Germany, WW I and WW II

Educational Reviewers

Peggy Altoff, Supervisor
Carroll County Public Schools
Westminster, Maryland

Laura L. Boelter
Shepherd Junior High School
Mesa, Arizona

Margaret Elaine Cox
Retired, Manatee High School
Bradenton, Florida

Alfred J. Hamel
South High Community School
Worcester, Massachusetts

Jay Harmon
Catholic High School
Baton Rouge, Louisiana

Paul Horne
Education Oversight Committee
Columbia, South Carolina

David Olson
Angola High School
Angola, Indiana

Madeleine Schmitt
St. Louis Public Schools
St. Louis, Missouri

Deanna Spring
Cincinnati Public Schools
Cincinnati, Ohio

Andy Turay
Bronx High School
Bronx, New York

Scott Whitlow
Round Rock High School
Round Rock, Texas

Laura Watkins
Acton Boxborough Regional High School
Acton, Massachusetts

It's All About

The first step to success in the social studies classroom is capturing and sustaining the interest of your students. *HOLT WORLD HISTORY: THE HUMAN JOURNEY* is designed to be open and friendly to all students, so that they develop an enthusiasm for learning and an appreciation for their world.

HOLT WORLD HISTORY: THE HUMAN JOURNEY offers
- Built-in Reading Support
- Technology with Instructional Value
- Standardized Testing and Skill Building
- The Best Teacher Management System in the Industry

RELEVANCE

CNNfyi.com™ is designed to give students in grades 6–12 access to the news about people, places, and environments around the globe while offering "real-world" articles, career and college resources, and online activities.

In-Text Features that Put History into Perspective

- Connecting to Civics
- Connecting to Economics
- Connecting to Geography
- Connecting to Science and Technology
- Connecting to the Arts
- Cross-Cultural Connections
- Daily Life

- History Maker
- History Through the Arts
- Skill-Building Strategies
- Then and Now
- What If?
- Why it Matters Today
- Young People in History

M1

Reading for

At Holt, we don't assume that students know how or have any desire to make sense of what they're reading, and we develop our programs based on that assumption. We don't just ask students questions about content, we give them strategies to get to that content. Through design, research, and the help of experts like Dr. Judith Irvin, we make sure students' reading needs are covered with our programs.

Helping Students Make Sense of What They're Reading

An Essay by Dr. Judith Irvin, Ph.D.

Who in middle and high schools helps students become more successful at reading and writing informational text? When I ask this question of a school faculty, the Language Arts/English teachers point to the social studies and science teachers because they are the ones with this type of textbook. The social studies and science teachers point to the Language Arts/English teachers because they are the ones that "do" words.

I advocate teachers taking an active role in helping students learn how to use text structure and context to understand what they read. Through consistent and systematic instruction that includes modeling of effective reading behavior, teachers can assist students in becoming better readers while at the same time helping them learn more content material.

The strategies in this book are designed to assist students with getting started, maintaining focus with reading, and organizing information for later retrieval. They engage students in learning material, provide the vehicle for them to organize and reorganize concepts, and extend their understanding through writing.

When teachers combine the teaching of reading and the teaching of content together into meaningful, systematic, and corrected instruction, students can apply what they have learned to understanding increasingly more difficult and complex texts as they progress through the school years.

READING STRATEGIES FOR THE SOCIAL STUDIES CLASSROOM

by Dr. Judith Irvin,
Ph.D. Reading Education

HOLT, RINEHART AND WINSTON

Reading Strategies
for the
Social Studies Classroom
Dr. Judith Irvin

Additional Reading Support

- **Main Idea Activities**
- **Graphic Organizer Activities**
- **Audio CD Program**
- **Guided Reading Strategies**

MEANING

SECTION 4

Roman Society and Culture

READ TO DISCOVER
1. How did the Romans build a strong and unified empire?
2. How did citizens of the Roman Empire make a living and lead their daily lives?
3. What part did science and the arts play in the empire?

DEFINE
gladiators
aqueducts

IDENTIFY
Galen
Ptolemy
Virgil
Horace
Ovid
Tacitus
Plutarch

WHY IT MATTERS TODAY
European and American cultures have borrowed heavily from the culture of the early Romans. Use **CNNfyi.com** or other **current event** sources to find a current example of an idea or object that is based on Roman culture. Record your findings in your journal.

The Main Idea
Over the course of centuries, the Romans built a cultural heritage that continues to influence us today.

The Story Continues *The Pax Romana was one of the longest periods of peace and stability the world has ever known. As a result, the Romans made great advances, many of which affect people even today. If you were to travel to Europe today, for example, you could find your way by using the same road system built by the Romans two thousand years ago.*

Building a Strong Empire

Several factors helped the Romans build their empire and maintain order. First, the Romans organized a strong government and revised their laws. Second, widespread trade and good transportation strengthened the economy and unified the empire. Finally, a strong army defended the frontiers and controlled the provinces.

Government and law. The Roman government was the strongest unifying force in the empire. It helped keep order and enforce the laws. The emperor ran the government, made all policy decisions, and appointed officials of the provinces, including the provincial governors. These officials were responsible to the government in Rome for the effective, peaceful, and profitable administration of the provinces.

Roman law also helped unify the empire. To fit the needs of their huge empire, the Romans changed the laws—the code of the Twelve Tables—in two important ways. First, the government passed new laws as needed. Second, judges interpreted the old laws to fit new circumstances. Roman judges helped develop the belief that certain basic legal principles should apply to all humans. This idea came from the Greek view that law was dictated by nature and therefore common to all people.

Trade and transportation. Widespread trade of farm goods and other products also helped unify the empire. The Roman government developed policies that were designed to encourage trade and commerce. Throughout the time of the Pax Romana, agriculture was the most important occupation in the empire. In Italy many farmers worked on large estates. In the provinces, small farms were fairly common.

Most trade within the empire centered around grain, wine, oil, other food items, and everyday items such as cloth, pottery, and glassware. Foreign trade often included luxury goods such as African ivory, Chinese silk, and Indian pepper. Most of these goods ended up in Rome. From there, they could be carried to wealthy customers throughout the sprawling empire along its overland and seagoing trade routes.

During the Pax Romana, the Romans imported silk, linen, glassware, jewelry, and furniture from East Asia. From India came spices, cotton, and many luxuries new to the Romans.

162 CHAPTER 7

Trade in the Roman Empire, A.D. 117
Interpreting Maps Although an improved system of roads made it easier to transport goods across land, most goods still traveled by sea or river in the A.D. 100s. Historians estimate that it was 28 times more expensive to move goods by land than by sea.
■ **Skills Assessment:**
1. **The World in Spatial Terms** How far would it have been to move goods from Rome to Alexandria by sea? By land? 2. **Drawing Conclusions** Why might the land route have been more expensive?

Nearly everywhere it went during the Pax Romana, the Roman army built roads and bridges. These well-constructed road systems served to move reinforcements and supplies quickly. They also promoted trade, travel, and communication throughout the empire. About 60,000 miles of paved highways extended to army outposts. Bridges spanned rivers, and highways linked all provincial cities to Rome. These roads were built to last. The top pavement rested on several layers of broken stone and crushed chalk. The good surfaces made travel fast. This was especially true of Rome's major road systems, which were designed to carry heavy military and trade traffic.

The Roman army. The Roman army, too, helped strengthen the empire by keeping peace. Citizen soldiers served for 16 to 20 years in the Roman legions. They were stationed in large fortified camps along the frontiers. People often settled around these camps, which eventually grew into cities. Often men from the provinces or from border areas enlisted in the Roman army. In return they were promised Roman citizenship at the end of their enlistment. Thus a vast army of veterans guarded the frontiers.

If necessary, the army used force to maintain peace in the provinces. In A.D. 60, for example, an uprising in Britain left some 70,000 Romans and their allies dead. The army soon crushed the rebels and destroyed their lands. More often, however, provincial governors aligned themselves with local leaders. This helped ensure that the locals would work to keep the peace.

✔ **READING CHECK: Summarizing** What aspects of Roman rule helped unify and strengthen the Roman Empire?

THE ROMAN WORLD 163

Successful Readers must have:

1 AN ENGAGING NARRATIVE

Great care is taken in selecting and presenting content in a way that students will find motivating and engaging. Features such as **Young People in History** help students connect their own lives to those who have played a role in the development of our nation.

2 A FORECAST OF WHAT THEY WILL LEARN

Read to Discover questions give students insight into the content they will cover in the chapter to come. In features such as **What's Your Opinion?** students are encouraged to give their opinions, thus helping them develop an ownership of the material.

3 OPPORTUNITIES TO ACTIVATE PRIOR KNOWLEDGE

In the pre-reading features **Build on What You Know** and **Chapter Timelines,** students are encouraged to connect content they have covered in previous chapters or other courses to the material they will learn about in the upcoming chapter.

4 VOCABULARY DEFINED IN CONTEXT

Important new terms are identified at the beginning of every section and are defined in context so students will develop an understanding of the contextual meaning of all terms.

5 STRATEGIES FOR UNDERSTANDING WHAT THEY READ

Through the design of the text, students are led through the content using built-in reading strategies. For example, **Reading Checks** in the text are used as a comprehension tool. The checks remind students to stop and engage with what they have read, functioning as a "Tutor in the Text."

M3

Get Your Students

Your students love activities that get them involved with the content. That's why Holt offers active-learning resources that link directly to program content and provide a multitude of different lessons for large-group, small-group, and individual projects.

CREATIVE TEACHING STRATEGIES

Customize these innovative teaching strategies and use them at various points in your lessons to motivate your students by getting them actively involved in the learning process.

ACTIVE LEARNING AND GEOGRAPHY SUPPORT

Hands-on History Activities: Classroom to Community will get your students out of their seats for group-oriented, active-learning projects that offer specific links between history and your local community.

Geography Activities help your students understand the role geography plays in history through mapping and skill-related activities.

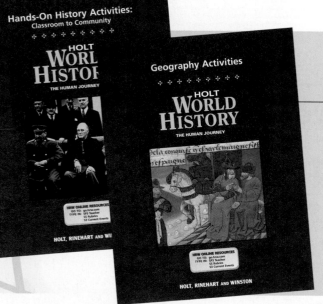

PRIMARY SOURCES

World History and Geography Document-Based Questions Activities offers your students rich content allowing them to make intelligent, formed opinions based on their observations of a diverse range of primary sources. Important historical themes are grouped together, allowing for scaffolded instruction.

Readings in World History presents primary and secondary-source historical readings, discussing the political, cultural, social, and intellectual significance of events.

Involved
in Learning

Skill-Based Ancillaries

- **Guided Reading Strategies**
- **Visual Resources**
- **The Complete School Atlas**
- **Creative Teaching Strategies**
- **Hands-on History Activities: Classroom to Community**
- **Geography Activities**
- **World History and Geography Document-Based Questions Activities**
- **Readings in World History**

Joining Forces

to Enrich your Classroom

CNNfyi.com

At **CNNfyi.com**, students will love exploring news stories written by experienced journalists as well as student bureau reporters complete with links to homework help and lesson plans.

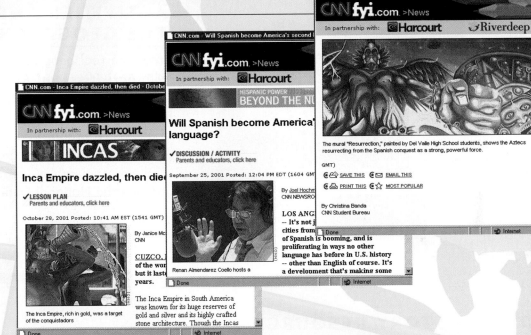

CNN PRESENTS VIDEO LIBRARY

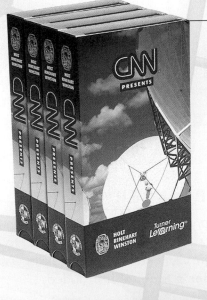

The **CNN PRESENTS** video collection tackles the issue of making content relevant to students head on. Real-world news stories enable students to see the connections between classroom curriculum and today's issues and events around the nation and the world.

CNN PRESENTS...

- **America: Yesterday and Today, Beginnings to 1914**
- **America: Yesterday and Today, 1850 to Present**
- **America: Yesterday and Today, Modern Times**
- **Geography: Yesterday and Today**
- **World Cultures: Yesterday and Today**
- **American Government**
- **Economics**
- **September 11, 2001: Part One**
- **September 11, 2001: Part Two**

Holt is proud to team up with CNN/TURNER LEARNING® to provide you and your students with exceptional current and historical news videos and online resources that add depth and relevance to your daily instruction. This information collection takes your classroom to the far corners of the globe without students ever leaving their desks!

Your Multi-talented Classroom

ACTIVITIES AND READINGS IN THE GEOGRAPHY OF THE WORLD

Integrate real geography into the topic you're studying with **Activities and Readings in the Geography of the World (ARGWorld).** This CD-ROM features world geography case studies with a multitude of activities that focus around geographical themes, population geography, economic geography, political geography, and environmental issues. Case studies will help teachers address the **National Geography Standards**.

GLOBAL HISTORY RESOURCE CENTER CD-ROM

This comprehensive database includes audio and video clips, maps, photographs, and readings to be integrated with the textbook for additional study.

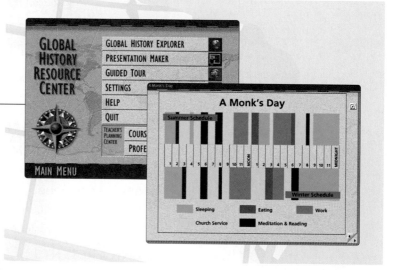

GLOBAL SKILL BUILDER CD-ROM

This CD-ROM is a comprehensive program containing interactive lessons that motivate your students to strengthen their map, graph, and computer skills. A **User's Guide and Teacher's Manual** is included.

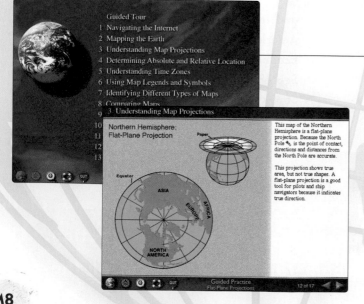

needs Multimedia Tools

THE WORLD TODAY VIDEODISC PROGRAM

This unique resource offers a stimulating outlook on world geography by showing your students the different ways geographers organize the world, and challenging them to contemplate and discuss significant world issues. Compelling video segments with in-depth content cover contemporary culture in every major world region.

HOLT WORLD HISTORY AUDIO CD PROGRAM

The *Audio CD Program* provides in-depth audio section summaries and self-check activity sheets to help those students who respond to auditory learning. Available in English and Spanish.

Other Multimedia Products

- CNN Presents Geography: Yesterday and Today
- CNN Presents World Cultures: Yesterday and Today
- Holt Researcher Online: World History and Cultures
- World History and Cultures Video Program, English
- World History and Cultures Video Program, Spanish
- World History and Cultures Videodisc Program

Technology with

go.hrw.com FOR TEACHERS

Throughout the *Annotated Teacher's Edition*, you'll find **Internet Connect** boxes that take you to specific chapter activities, links, current events, and more that correlate directly to the section you are teaching. Through **go.hrw.com** you'll find a wealth of teaching resources at your fingertips for fun, interactive lessons.

...ut materials for your students
...th **Test Generator**.

Reinforcement, Review, and Assessment

Daily Quiz 7.1
Main Idea Activity 7.1
English Audio Summary 7.1
Spanish Audio Summary 7.1
REV Section 1 Review, p. 154

Daily Quiz 7.2
Main Idea Activity 7.2
English Audio Summary 7.2
Spanish Audio Summary 7.2
REV Section 2 Review, p. 157

Daily Quiz 7.3
Main Idea Activity 7.3
English Audio Summary 7.3
Spanish Audio Summary 7.3
REV Section 3 Review, p. 161

Daily Quiz 7.4
Main Idea Activity 7.4
English Audio Summary 7.4
Spanish Audio Summary 7.4
REV Section 4 Review, p. 167

Daily Quiz 7.5
Main Idea Activity 7.5
English Audio Summary 7.5
Spanish Audio Summary 7.5
REV Section 5 Review, p. 171

Daily Quiz 7.6
Main Idea Activity 7.6
English Audio Summary 7.6
Spanish Audio Summary 7.6
REV Section 6 Review, p. 177

internet connect

HRW ONLINE RESOURCES
  GO TO: go.hrw.com
  Then type in a keyword.

TEACHER HOME PAGE
  KEYWORD: SP3 Teacher

CHAPTER INTERNET ACTIVITIES
  KEYWORD: SP3 WH7
Choose an activity to:
- analyze the *Aeneid* to learn the connection between ancient Troy and Roman culture.
- create a model or structure that employs Roman architectural, artistic, or decorative styles.
- research the destruction of Pompeii and review the tectonic causes of volcanoes.

CHAPTER ENRICHMENT LINKS
  KEYWORD: SP3 CH7

ONLINE ASSESSMENT
  Homework Practice
  KEYWORD: SP3 HP7

  Standardized Test Prep
  KEYWORD: SP3 STP7

  Rubrics
  KEYWORD: SS Rubrics

ONLINE MAPS, CHARTS, AND GRAPHS
  KEYWORD: SP3 MCG

CONTENT UPDATES
  KEYWORD: SS Content Updates

HOLT PRESENTATION MAKER
  KEYWORD: SP3 PPT7

ONLINE READING SUPPORT
  KEYWORD: SS Strategies

CURRENT EVENTS
  KEYWORD: S3 Current Events

DIRECT LAUNCH TO CHAPTER ACTIVITIES

GUIDED ONLINE ACTIVITIES

LINKS FOR EVERY SECTION

INTERACTIVE PRACTICE AND REVIEW

RUBRICS FOR SUBJECTIVE GRADING

MAPS AND CHARTS

UP-TO-DATE INFORMATION

CLASSROOM PRESENTATION SUPPORT

PRACTICE FOR READING SUCCESS

WEB RESOURCES FOR CURRENT ISSUES

Chapter Review and Assessment

IC   Vocabulary Activity 7
     Global Skill Builder CD–ROM
     HRW Web Site
REV Chapter 7 Tutorial for Students, Parents, Mentors, and Peers
REV Chapter 7 Review, pp. 178–179
A   Chapter 7 Test Generator (on the One-Stop Planner)
A   Chapter 7 Test (Form A or B)
A   Alternative Assessment Handbook
A   Chapter 7 Test for English Language Learners and Special-Needs Students

147b

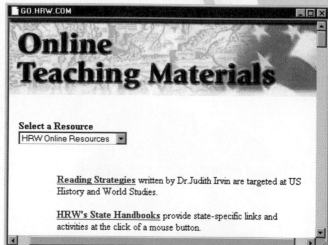

GO.HRW.COM

Online Teaching Materials

Select a Resource
[HRW Online Resources ▼]

Reading Strategies written by Dr. Judith Irvin are targeted at US History and World Studies.

HRW's State Handbooks provide state-specific links and activities at the click of a mouse button.

Instructional Value

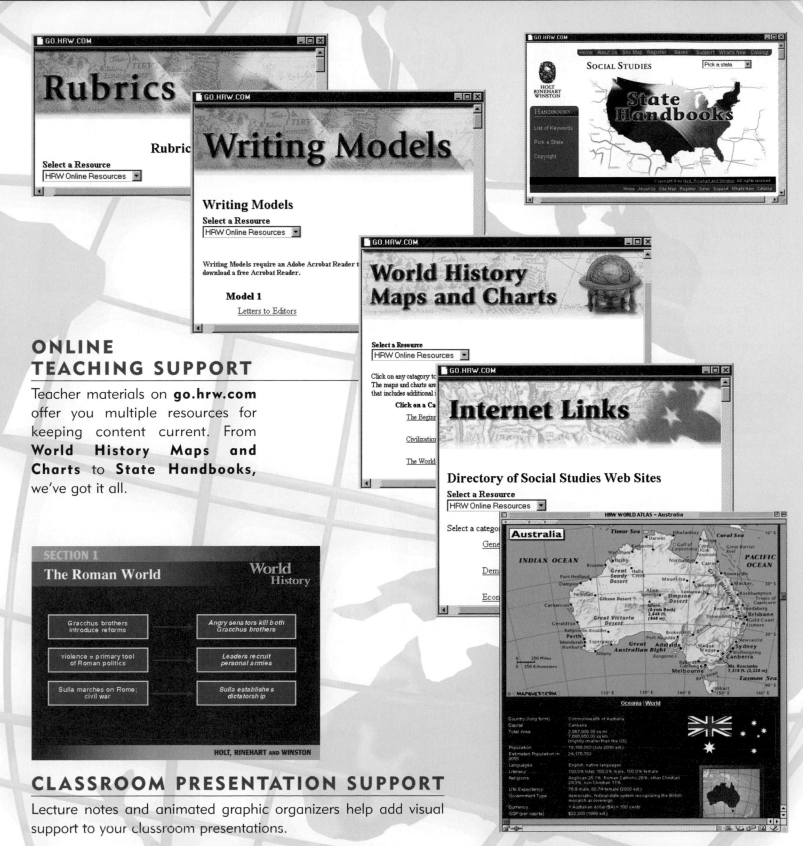

ONLINE TEACHING SUPPORT

Teacher materials on **go.hrw.com** offer you multiple resources for keeping content current. From **World History Maps and Charts** to **State Handbooks,** we've got it all.

CLASSROOM PRESENTATION SUPPORT

Lecture notes and animated graphic organizers help add visual support to your classroom presentations.

Technology that

go.hrw.com FOR STUDENTS

Your students can access interactive activities, homework help, up-to-date maps, and more when they visit **go.hrw.com** and type in the keywords they find in their text.

ONLINE WORLD TRAVEL

When you log on to **go.hrw.com**, you and your students gain passage to **GeoTreks**—a site with guided Internet activities that integrate program content, spark imaginations, and promote online research skills. You'll find:

Interactive templates for creating newspapers, postcards, travel brochures, guided research reports, and more

GeoMaps—Interactive satellite maps of the world's regions for content review

Drag-and-drop exercises to review chapter content in short, fun activities

Chapter Web Links for prescreened, age-appropriate Web sites and current events

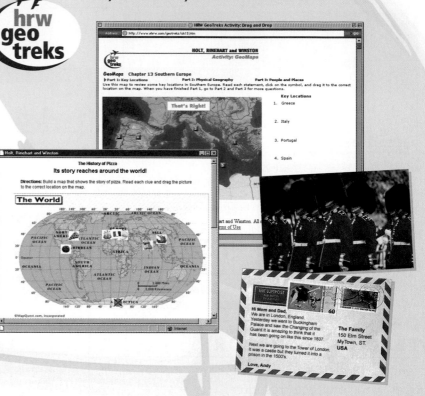

HOMEWORK PRACTICE

This helpful tool allows students to practice and review content by chapter anywhere there is a computer.

HRW ONLINE ATLAS AND HISTORICAL MAPS

The helpful online atlas contains over 300 well-rendered and clearly labeled country and state maps. Available in English and Spanish, these maps are continually updated so you can rest assured that you and your students have the latest and most accurate geographical content.

Online historical maps provide fascinating visual "snapshots" of the past. Students will relish the chance to explore medieval European trade routes, explorers' routes, ancient African kingdoms, and more.

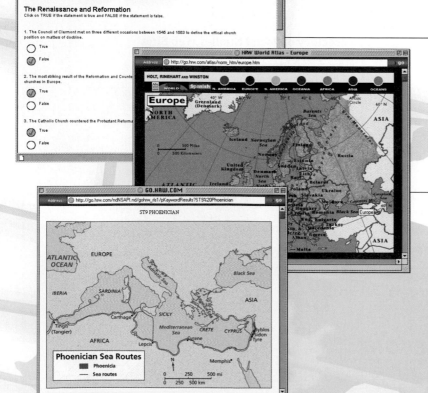

Delivers Content

New Online Textbook

You'll know what to do when you see it!

Finally, an online textbook that takes full advantage of Web technology in a way that makes sense—***HOLT WORLD HISTORY: THE HUMAN JOURNEY ONLINE EDITION.***

- **Entire student edition online formatted to match printed text**
- **User-friendly navigation**
- **Hot links to interactive activities, practice, and assessment**
- **Student Notebook for online responses**

Unique Teacher's

In-Text Chapter Planning

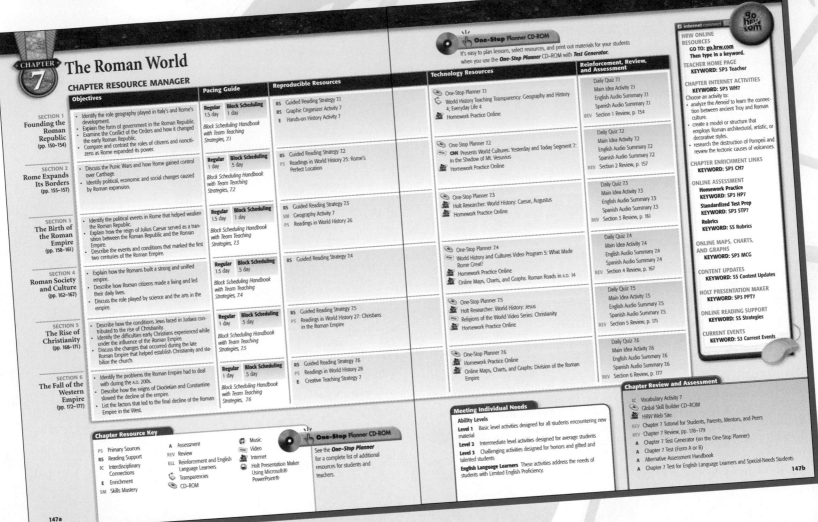

Program Resources at Your Fingertips

READING SUPPORT

- Graphic Organizer Activities
- Guided Reading Strategies
- Main Idea Activities for English Language Learners and Special-Needs Students
- Reading Strategies for the Social Studies Classroom

PRIMARY SOURCES

- Readings in World History
- Visual Resources
- World History and Geography Document-Based Questions Activities
- Visual Resources Transparency Directory

GEOGRAPHY SUPPORT

- The Complete School Atlas
- Geography Activities
- World and Regional Outline Maps

ACTIVE-LEARNING SUPPORT

- Block Scheduling Handbook with Team Teaching Strategies
- Creative Teaching Strategies
- Hands-on History Activities: Classroom to Community

REVIEW AND ASSESSMENT

- Daily Quizzes
- Chapter Tutorials for Students, Parents, Mentors, and Peers
- Chapter and Unit Tests
- Chapter and Unit Tests for English Language Learners and Special-Needs Students
- Alternative Assessment Handbook
- Social Studies Skills Review

Management System

One-Stop Planner
with Test Generator

ONE-STOP PLANNER® CD-ROM WITH TEST GENERATOR

Holt brings you the most user-friendly management system in the industry with the ***One-Stop Planner CD-ROM with Test Generator.*** Plan and manage your lessons from this single disc containing all the teaching resources for ***Holt World History: The Human Journey,*** valuable planning and assessment tools, and more.

- **Editable lesson plans**
- **Classroom Lecture Notes and Animated Graphic Organizers**
- **Easy-to-use test generator**
- **Previews of all teaching and video resources**
- **Easy printing feature**
- **Direct launch to go.hrw.com**

Everything you need is on one disc!

BLOCK SCHEDULING HANDBOOK WITH TEAM TEACHING STRATEGIES

This is more than a pacing guide—it provides daily lesson plans that suggest practical ways to cover more than one textbook section in an extended class period and ways to make interdisciplinary connections.

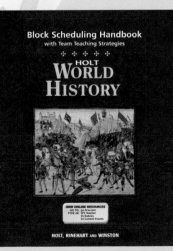

Block Scheduling Handbook
with Team Teaching Strategies

HOLT
WORLD
HISTORY

HRW ONLINE RESOURCES
GO TO: go.hrw.com
TYPE IN: SF1 Teacher
SF4 Rubrics
S3 Current Events

HOLT, RINEHART AND WINSTON

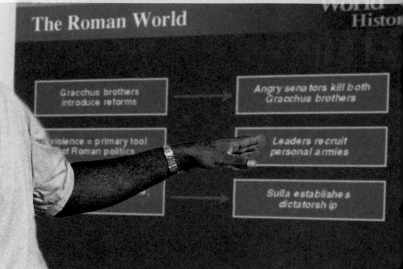

Energize

Presentations That Benefit Learning

Classroom presentations and lecture notes can be accessed with ease when you use Holt's **Presentation** tool found on the *One-Stop Planner CD-ROM.* This resource helps you spice up your presentations and gives you ideas to build on. You'll find Microsoft® PowerPoint® presentations that include lecture notes and animated graphic organizers for each chapter and section of your text.

Your Classroom Presentations

OBJECTIVE-BASED LESSON CYCLE

With lively activities and presentation strategies such as **Let's Get Started, Building Vocabulary,** and **Graphic Organizers,** your step-by-step lesson cycle makes planning your lessons easy and productive.

SECTION 3

OBJECTIVES

1 **Identify the political events in Rome during the first century B.C. that helped weaken the Roman Republic.**

2 **Explain how the reign of Julius Caesar served as a transition between the Roman Republic and the Roman Empire.**

3 **Describe the events and conditions that marked the first two centuries of the Roman Empire.**

LET'S GET STARTED!

As students enter the classroom, ask them to write a list of the challenges that faced Rome as it expanded after the Punic Wars. *(government corruption, changes in agriculture, loss of discipline and devotion to the state)* Ask students how they think these problems might have weakened the Roman Republic. Tell students that in Section 3 they will learn that these challenges ultimately brought about the end of the Roman Republic and the rise of the Roman Empire.

TEACHER TO TEACHER

These strategies are offered in the columns of your *Annotated Teacher's Edition* and provide you with valuable, classroom-tested ideas and activities that have been developed and successfully applied by your peers.

TEACH OBJECTIVE 1

LEVEL 1: Copy the following cause-and-effect chart on the board, omitting the italicized answers, and have students complete after reading Section 3.
ENGLISH LANGUAGE LEARNERS

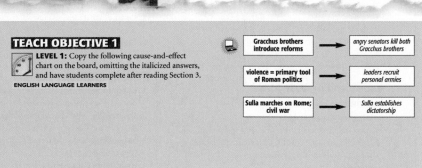

Gracchus brothers introduce reforms	→	angry senators kill both Gracchus brothers
violence = primary tool of Roman politics	→	leaders recruit personal armies
Sulla marches on Rome; civil war	→	Sulla establishes dictatorship

TEACH OBJECTIVE 2

ALL LEVELS: As students read the section "Caesar in Power" on page 159, have them complete a web diagram that includes characteristics and events related to Caesar. Then draw a web on the board and fill it in with students' responses.
ENGLISH LANGUAGE LEARNERS

HOMEWORK Write an essay explaining how Julius Caesar's reign was a transition between the Roman Republic and the Roman Empire. Use standard grammar, spelling, sentence structure, and punctuation.

TEACH OBJECTIVE 3

LEVEL 3: Assign pairs of students to study a Roman leader of this time and to write a profile that explains the leader's significance. Encourage students to use their textbooks, the library, the Internet, and other sources. Invite students to read their profiles aloud.

CLOSE

List characteristics of Roman politics before, during, and after the rule of Julius Caesar.

In-Text Features that put History into Perspective

- **Connecting to Civics**
- **Connecting to Economics**
- **Connecting to Geography**
- **Connecting to Science and Technology**
- **Connecting to the Arts**
- **Cross-Cultural Connections**
- **Daily Life**
- **History Maker**
- **History Through the Arts**
- **Skill-Building Strategies**
- **Then and Now**
- **What If?**
- **Why it Matters Today**
- **Young People in History**

REVIEW
Have students complete the Section 3 Review on page 161.

ASSESS
Have students complete Daily Quiz 7.3. As Alternative Assessment, have students complete the cause-and-effect chart or Caesar web diagram in this section's lessons.

RETEACH
Have students complete Main Idea Activity for English Language Learners and Special-Needs Students 7.3. Have students identify three events during the time the republic fell that changed the course of Roman history.
ENGLISH LANGUAGE LEARNERS

EXTEND
Have students write a brief script and stage a mock trial of Caesar's assassins. Students should take the roles of judge, prosecutor, defense attorney, and conspirators. **BLOCK SCHEDULING**

Assessment for

SECTION 4 REVIEW

1. **Define** and explain the significance:
   gladiators
   aqueducts

2. **Identify** and explain the significance:
   Galen
   Ptolemy
   Virgil
   Horace
   Ovid
   Tacitus
   Plutarch

3. **Summarizing** Make a chart like this to summarize the lives of the Romans.

	Description
Daily Life	
Slavery	
Roles of men and women	
Religion	
Entertainment	

4. **Finding the Main Idea**
   a. What factors contributed to the strength of the Roman Empire? How?
   b. What do you think are the five most important contributions the Romans made to law and government, engineering and architecture, and literature and language? Explain your answers.

Writing and Critical Thinking
Making Generalizations Imagine that you are a teenager belonging to the upper class and living in the Roman Empire during the Pax Romana. Write a short diary entry recounting the events of a typical day.
Consider:
• the importance of your family
• the kind of schooling and education you receive
• how being a boy or a girl influences your life

Homework Practice Online
keyword: SP3 HP7

M18

CHAPTER 7 Review

Creating a Time Line
Copy the time line below onto a sheet of paper. Complete the time line by filling in the events, individuals, and dates from the chapter that you think were significant. Pick three events and explain why you think they were significant.

| 1000 B.C. | 500 B.C. | A.D. 1 | A.D. 500 |

Writing a Summary
Using standard grammar, spelling, sentence structure, and punctuation, write an overview of the events in the chapter.

Identifying People and Ideas
Identify the following terms or individuals and explain their significance:

1. republic
2. checks and balances
3. dictator
4. Punic Wars
5. Pax Romana
6. Julius Caesar
7. Augustus (Octavian)
8. aqueducts
9. Jesus
10. Constantine

Understanding Main Ideas

SECTION 1 (pp. 150–154)
Founding the Roman Republic
1. How was the Roman Republic's government organized?
2. How did the Conflict of the Orders change how the Roman Republic was governed?

SECTION (pp. 155–157)
Rome Expands Its Borders
3. What was the outcome of the Punic Wars?
4. What problems occurred as a result of Rome's expansion?

SECTION 3 (pp. 158–161)
The Birth of the Roman Empire
How did Julius Caesar rise to power?
How did the republic become the Roman Empire?

SECTION 4 (pp. 162–167)
Roman Society and Culture
7. What was the economy of the Roman Empire like?
8. In what areas did Rome make great contributions to the world? Give examples to support your answers.

SECTION 5 (pp. 168–171)
The Rise of Christianity
9. How did Christianity begin and what was unique about it?
10. What factors helped Christianity gain acceptance in the Roman Empire?

SECTION 6 (pp. 172–177)
The Fall of the Western Empire
11. How did Diocletian and Constantine try to strengthen the Roman Empire?
12. What were some causes of Rome's decline?

Reviewing Themes
1. **Government** What two major factors helped Rome unify its empire and maintain peace?
2. **Culture** What ideas and inventions did the Romans borrow and adapt from the Greeks?
3. **Global Relations** How did Rome's relationship with the people it conquered change over time?

Thinking Critically
1. **Comparing** Compare the role of citizens in Athenian democracy with that of citizens in Rome's republic.
2. **Contrasting** How did the governments of the Roman Republic and the Roman Empire differ?
3. **Sequencing** Trace the spread of Christianity in the Roman world.
4. **Identifying Cause and Effect** How did the use of written law strengthen Rome's government?

Writing About History
Analyzing Information Romans were skilled builders who developed many new ideas. Write a description of how Roman engineering ideas are used today. Use the following chart to organize your thoughts before you begin writing.

	Roman Examples	Examples Today
Ideas and Innovations in Architecture and Engineering		

178 CHAPTER 7

Every Student

WORLD HISTORY AND GEOGRAPHY DOCUMENT-BASED QUESTIONS ACTIVITIES

This resource provides a wide variety of primary sources and thought-provoking questions to help students develop intelligent, formed opinions. Important historical and geographical themes are grouped together, allowing for scaffolded instruction.

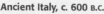

Building Social Studies Skills

Interpreting Maps

Study the map below. Then use the information on the map to help you answer the questions that follow.

Ancient Italy, c. 600 B.C.

Etruscan
Latin
Greek

1. Which of the following statements correctly describes how geographic factors influenced Rome's rise to power?
   a. The Alps protected Italy from invasion from the north.
   b. The rugged Apennine Mountains made it difficult to unify Italy.
   c. Italy's location helped Rome control the eastern and western Mediterranean.
   d. Italy's rugged coast discouraged sea trade.

2. Using information from the map, support your choice of statements in question 1.

Analyzing Primary Sources

Read the following quote by the historian Polybius, who lived in Rome during the 100s B.C., then answer the questions.

"Having then got rid of these rulers by assassination or exile, they do not venture to set up a king again, being still in terror of the injustice to which this led before; nor dare they intrust the common interests again to more than one, considering the recent example of their misconduct: and therefore, as the only sound hope left them is that which depends upon themselves, they are driven to take refuge in that; and so changed the constitution from an oligarchy to a democracy."

3. Which of the following statements best describes the author's point of view?
   a. People cannot pick good leaders.
   b. People have no control over their leaders.
   c. Power should be limited to a few people.
   d. Democracy is a response to past abuses.

4. When interpreting a primary source, historians examine the historical context in which the source was written. What events in Rome's history might have influenced Polybius's point of view? Give specific examples.

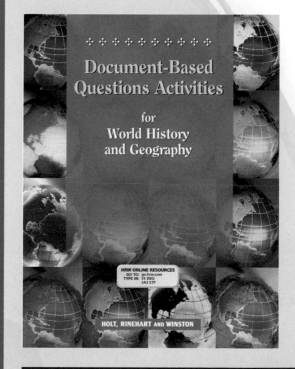

✦ ✦ ✦ ✦ ✦ ✦ ✦ ✦ ✦ ✦ ✦

Document-Based Questions Activities

for

World History and Geography

HRW ONLINE RESOURCES
GO TO: go.hrw.com
TYPE IN: SS DBQ
SA3 STP

HOLT, RINEHART AND WINSTON

Alternative Assessment

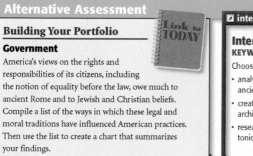

Building Your Portfolio

Link to TODAY

Government

America's views on the rights and responsibilities of its citizens, including the notion of equality before the law, owe much to ancient Rome and to Jewish and Christian beliefs. Compile a list of the ways in which these legal and moral traditions have influenced American practices. Then use the list to create a chart that summarizes your findings.

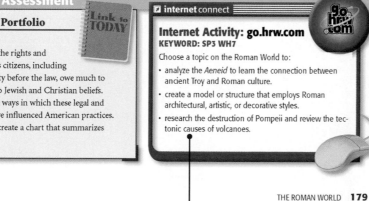

✎ **internet** connect

Internet Activity: go.hrw.com
KEYWORD: SP3 WH7

Choose a topic on the Roman World to:
- analyze the *Aeneid* to learn the connection between ancient Troy and Roman culture.
- create a model or structure that employs Roman architectural, artistic, or decorative styles.
- research the destruction of Pompeii and review the tectonic causes of volcanoes.

THE ROMAN WORLD **179**

ACCESS ONLINE RUBRICS FOR GRADING PROJECTS AND PORTFOLIO ASSIGNMENTS

Additional Print and Technology Assessment Resources

- **Alternative Assessment Handbook**
- **Audio CD Program**
- **Chapter and Unit Tests**
- **Chapter and Unit Tests for English Language Learners and Special-Needs Students**
- **Chapter Tutorials for Students, Parents, Mentors, and Peers**
- **Daily Quizzes**
- **Document-Based Questions Activities for World History and Geography**
- **Main Idea Activities**
- **Test Generator (located on the One-Stop Planner CD-ROM)**

Contents

UNIT 1 — The Beginnings of Civilization xxvii

Early castings of horseriders

Indus valley pictographic seals

The Parthenon of Athens

Carved mask from the African kingdom of Benin

Buffalo on the American Plains

Early Arab navigational instrument

The throne of Charlemagne

*Copernican model showing
planetary revolutions*

*The papal palace
at Avignon*

Glazeware from Safavid Persia

The Great Wall of China

The golden fountain at Versailles

Primary Sources

Singer and musicians from the Tokugawa period

Niccolò Machiavelli

Primary Sources continued

History and Your World

YOUNG PEOPLE IN HISTORY

Cuneiform writing from early Sumeria

▶ WHY IT MATTERS TODAY
CNN fyi.com

History and Your World *continued*

View of the Deccan, in India

Cross–Cultural Connections

*Islamic calligraphy and box of
calligrapher's tools*

CROSS-CULTURAL CONNECTIONS *Literature*

William Shakespeare

Illustration from Chaucer's The
Canterbury Tales

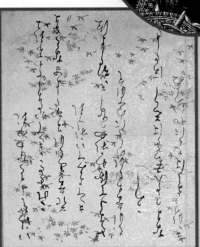

Japanese haiku

Interdisciplinary Activities

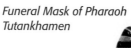

Funeral Mask of Pharaoh Tutankhamen

Historical Highlights

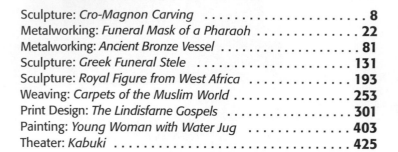

Early American stone-tipped spears

DAILY LIFE

What If?

Historical Highlights *continued*

Technology Activities

Holt Researcher go.hrw.com

internet connect go.hrw.com

Skill-Building Activities

SKILL-BUILDING STRATEGIES

TIME LINES

Charts and Graphs

Skill-Building Activities *continued*

Maps

Renaissance Italy, c. 1500

Interpreting Maps During the Renaissance, Italy was a patchwork of states.

■ **Skills Assessment: Human Systems** What commercial cities became the centers of city-states?

How to Use Your Textbook

Use the chapter opener to get an overview of the time period.

The Chapter Time Line shows you selected events in world history within the timeframe of the chapter.

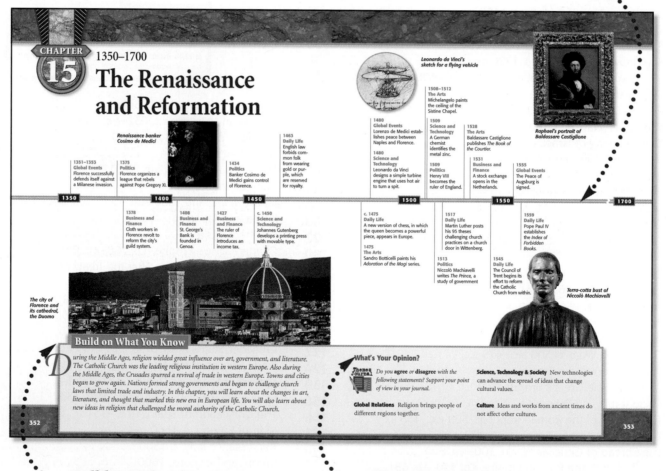

Build on What You Know bridges the material you have studied in previous chapters with the material you are about to begin. As you read the Build on What You Know feature, take a few minutes to think about the topics that might apply to the chapter you are starting.

What's Your Opinion puts you in the place of the historian looking at the past. In this section, you will be asked to respond to three general statements about the chapter. Each statement is tied to one of the key themes of the program. You should respond based on your own knowledge, and record your responses in your journal. There are no right or wrong answers, just your informed opinion.

Use these built-in tools to read for understanding.

Read to Discover questions begin each section of *The Human Journey.* These questions serve as your guide as you read through the section. Keep them in mind as you explore the section content.

Define and Identify terms are introduced at the beginning of each section. The terms will be defined in context throughout the section.

Why It Matters Today is an exciting way for you to make connections between what you are reading in your history book and the world around you. In each section, you will be invited to explore a topic that is relevant to our lives today by using **CNNfyi.com** connections.

Interpreting the Visual Record features accompany many of the book's rich images. Pictures are one of the most important primary sources historians can use to help analyze the past. These features invite you to examine the images and make predictions about their content.

Reading Check questions appear throughout the book to allow you to check your comprehension while you are reading. As you read each section, pause for a moment to consider each Reading Check. If you have trouble answering the question, go back and examine the material you just read.

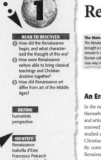

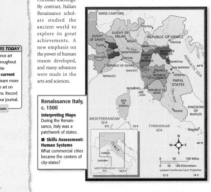

The Story Continues features an interesting episode from world history that shows you that history is not just a collection of facts, but a blend of many individual stories and adventures.

History Makers Speak quotations appear frequently throughout the book. These exciting primary source quotations give you a glimpse into the lives of the actual people who made history. Many of these quotations are accompanied by an **Analyzing Primary Sources** question to help you better interpret the sources and draw inferences about their importance.

Use these built-in tools to read for understanding.

Homework Practice Online lets you log on to the **GO.hrw.com** Web site to complete an interactive self-check.

Finding the Main Idea questions help review the main points you have studied in the section.

Writing and Critical Thinking activities allow you to explore a section topic in greater depth and build your skills.

Graphic Organizers will help you pull together important information from the section. You can complete the graphic organizer as a study tool to prepare for a test or writing assignment.

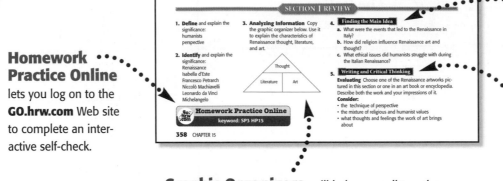

Creating a Time Line and **Writing a Summary** activities help you to organize, sequence, and synthesize the chapter discussion and place major events and individuals into the historical chronology.

Reviewing Themes, Thinking Critically, and **Writing About History** activities help you to focus on key chapter ideas and enhance critical thinking and writing skills as you explore major chapter topics.

Identifying People and Ideas and **Understanding Main Ideas** reinforce learning by extending your understanding and comprehension of history–shaping people and concepts.

Building Social Studies Skills and **Building Your Portfolio** activities create exciting opportunities to practice social studies skills, to use interesting primary and secondary source materials, and to develop understanding of the connections between past and present.

Use these review tools to pull together all the information you have learned.

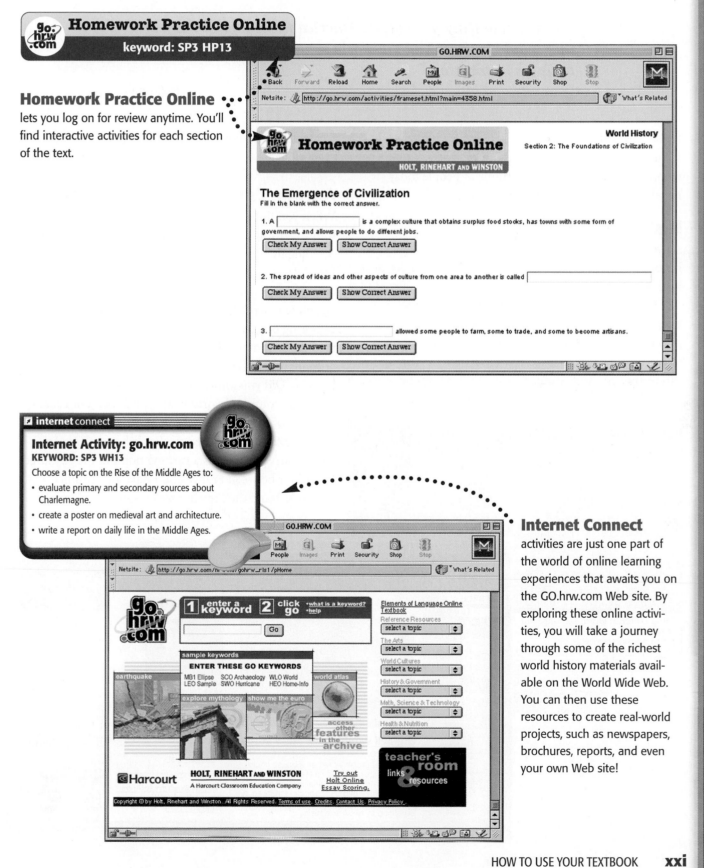

Homework Practice Online
keyword: SP3 HP13

Homework Practice Online lets you log on for review anytime. You'll find interactive activities for each section of the text.

Internet Connect activities are just one part of the world of online learning experiences that awaits you on the GO.hrw.com Web site. By exploring these online activities, you will take a journey through some of the richest world history materials available on the World Wide Web. You can then use these resources to create real-world projects, such as newspapers, brochures, reports, and even your own Web site!

Why History Matters Today

"History and destiny have made America the leader of the world that would be free. And the world that would be free is looking to us for inspiration."

Colin Powell

Right now, at this very second, somewhere in the world, someone is making history. It is impossible to know who, or in what way, but the actions of people today may become the history of tomorrow.

History and Your World

All you need to do is watch or read the news to see history unfolding. How many news stories do you see or hear about ordinary people doing extraordinary things? The Why It Matters Today feature beginning every section of *The Human Journey* invites you to use the vast resources of **CNNfyi.com** or other current event sources to examine the links between past and present. Through this feature you will be able to draw connections between what you are studying in your history book and the events that are taking place in our world today.

Anyone Can Be a History Maker

When you think of the word history, what comes to mind? Do you picture politicians sitting around a table deciding the future of the world? Or do you see a long list of dates and boring facts to be memorized? Of course, politicians, dates, and facts are part of history, but there is actually much more to understanding and exploring our past. Our world has developed through the efforts of many different people, from all backgrounds and walks of life. Many of them were teenagers like you. Did you know that teenagers have helped to shape the course of world history? It's true. For example, Joan of Arc was only about 17 when she led the French army that defeated the English at Orléans in 1429. Joan's victory was a turning point in the Hundred Years' War between France and England, a conflict that helped to build the French nation. Anne Frank, whose

haunting account of Nazi persecution during World War II is an eloquent and timeless attack on all forms of political repression, was 16 years old when she died at Belsen concentration camp in 1945. Her tragic yet triumphant story has inspired people around the world. You might also be interested to know that young people in their teens helped to open and settle our own nation's frontiers long before there was a United States of America. These are just a few of the many examples of how people in their teens—people your age—have helped to shape our world's past. What contributions do you think your generation will make to world history?

History Makes Us Who We Are

There is no one single "story" in history. Instead, the combined experiences of millions of people across time have come together to form the societies and cultures of today's world.

Although the World War II Memorial was under construction when we visited, it was an awesome and inspiring sight.

So when someone asks you, "Why does history matter today?," you might answer, "Because in our past, we see a reflection of ourselves."

Students of today dressed in Renaissance-era garb

Themes in World History

A Hindu religious sculpture from early India

The Human Journey begins every chapter with a set of theme statements under the heading "What's Your Opinion?" These statements are drawn from several broad themes central to world history: Geography, Economics, Government, Citizenship, Culture, Science, Technology & Society, Constitutional Heritage, and Global Relations. As you begin each chapter of *The Human Journey,* you will be asked to respond to the theme statements in a general way on the basis of your own knowledge. At the end of the chapter, you will be asked to respond to more specific questions about the themes, based on the chapter content.

Geography

The Geography theme explores ways in which our world's vast and diverse geography has played an important role in world history. The theme examines how the development of the world's resources has

The Astronomer, by Jan Vermeer

helped shape world economies, societies, and political structures. In addition, the Geography theme traces how public and government attitudes about resources and the environment have changed over time.

Economics

The Economics theme asks you to explore the relationship between history and economics over the course of human development. The theme examines how various, often very different economic systems have developed to address changing human needs and how they have influenced the world's political and social growth.

Gold Byzantine goblet

Government

The Government theme asks you to explore the workings of different systems of government—from the earliest forms of community organization to the complex structures of the present. This theme also examines the various aspects of different types of governments utilized by various societies throughout history and how different governmental systems affect societies in different ways.

Scene of Japanese Kabuki theater

Citizenship

Throughout history, people have struggled to define the rights and responsibilities of citizenship in their societies. The Citizenship theme explores how changing social, economic, and political conditions have influenced different societies and how those societies have perceived and addressed the ideas of citizenship.

Culture

The rich, unique, and diverse cultures that have developed over the course of history have emerged from our world's many ethnic, racial, and religious groups. The Culture theme examines how people have built their diverse cultures from earliest times to the present. It also investigates how various aspects of culture, including religion, rituals and shared traditions, art, music, and literature, have influenced social and political events throughout history.

Science, Technology & Society

From the building of the Egyptian pyramids and the irrigation systems of the earliest farming peoples to the development of advanced computers and the advent of the information age, science and technology have influenced every aspect of our world's cultures and societies. The Science, Technology & Society theme explores scientific and technological developments and their impacts on economic, political, and social developments around the world.

Constitutional Heritage

No study of world history would be complete without examining how the idea of constitutionalism developed over time. This includes influences on the United States Constitution, as well as comparisons of different constitutional systems as they developed over time.

Global Relations

The Global Relations theme invites you to trace ways in which different nations, cultures, and peoples around the world and throughout history have interacted with one another. It also explores issues and events that affect large segments of the world, not just one particular country.

Essential Elements of Geography

History and geography share many elements. History describes important events that have taken place from ancient times until the present day. Geography describes how physical environments affect human events. It also examines how people's actions influence the environment around them. One way to look at geography is to identify essential elements of its study. The following six essential elements, developed as part of the National Geography Standards, will be used throughout The Human Journey:

▶ **The World in Spatial Terms** This essential element refers to the way geographers view the world. They look at where things are and how they are arranged on Earth's surface. For example, geographers might be interested to learn why certain cities developed where they did.

▶ **Places and Regions** Geographers often focus on the physical and human characteristics that make particular parts of Earth special. A region is an area with common characteristics that make it different from surrounding areas. People create regions as a convenient way to study the world. Regions can be large like Asia, or small like a neighborhood.

Early Egyptian pyramids at Giza

▶ **Physical Systems** Geographers study the physical processes and interactions among four physical systems—Earth's atmosphere, land, water, and life. Physical processes shape and change Earth's physical features and environments.

▶ **Human Systems** As with physical systems, studying human systems can tell geographers much about the world around us. For example, studying population growth, distribution, and movement helps in understanding human events and their effect on the environment.

▶ **Environment and Society** One of the most important topics in geography is how people interact with the environment. Human activities can have both positive and negative effects on Earth's environment. However, people depend on the environment's natural resources for survival.

▶ **The Uses of Geography** Historians use geography to understand the past. They look not only at when things happened but at where and why they happened. But geography is also important to the present as well as the past. People use geography every day to determine how to use Earth's limited resources, such as water and minerals, more effectively and in ways that ensure the success of future generations.

Skills Handbook

Critical Thinking and the Study of History

Throughout *The Human Journey*, you are asked to think critically about the events and issues that have shaped world history. Critical thinking is the reasoned judgment of information and ideas. The development of critical thinking skills is essential to effective citizenship. Such skills empower you to exercise your civic rights and responsibilities. Helping you develop critical thinking skills is an important goal of *The Human Journey*. The following critical thinking skills appear in the section reviews and chapter reviews of the book.

Link to TODAY

◆ **Analyzing Information** is the process of breaking something down into its parts and examining the relationships between them. Analyzing enables you to better understand the whole. For example, to analyze the outcome of the Norman invasion of England in 1066, you might study the basis for Duke William of Normandy's claims to the English throne, why Harold Godwinson opposed those claims, and how the English people viewed the issues.

Emperor Maximilian I

◆ **Sequencing** is the process of placing events in correct chronological order to better understand the historical relationships among these events. You can sequence events in two basic ways: according to *absolute* or *relative* chronology. Absolute chronology means that you pay close attention to the actual dates events took place. Placing events on a time line would be an example of absolute chronology. Relative chronology refers to the way events relate to one another. To put events in relative order, you need to know which one happened, which came next, and so forth.

A sailor's astrolabe, an early navigational instrument

◆ **Categorizing** is the process by which you group things together by the characteristics they have in common. By putting things or events into categories, it is easier to make comparisons and see differences among them.

◆ **Identifying Cause and Effect** is a part of interpreting the relationships between historical events. A *cause* is an action that leads to an event. The outcome of the action is an *effect*. To explain historical events, historians often point out multiple causes and effects. For example, economic and political differences between the United States and the

Soviet Union led to the "cold war" that characterized the post-World War II era. These differences also resulted in an arms race that posed serious threats to world peace and development.

◆ Comparing and Contrasting

is the process of examining events, situations, or points of view for their similarities and differences. *Comparing* focuses on both similarities and the differences. *Contrasting* focuses only on differences. For example, a comparison of the development of civilization in the Indus River valley or northern India and the Hwang River valley of east-central China shows that certain factors were shared by each group of early people, while other factors were unique to one emerging civilization or the other.

Stone relief from early India

◆ Finding the Main Idea

is combining and sifting through information to determine what is most important. Historical writing often uses many examples and details to support the author's main ideas. Throughout *The Human Journey*, you will find numerous Reading Checks and questions in section reviews to help you focus on the main ideas in the text.

◆ Summarizing

is the process of taking a large amount of information and boiling it down into a short and clear statement. Summarizing is particularly useful when you need to give a brief account of a longer story or event. For example, Alexander the Great's conquest of the Persian Empire is an exciting but detailed story consisting of a complex chain of conditions, actions, and situations. Many different events came together to make up this story. You could summarize these events by saying something like, "Between 334 B.C. and 333 B.C., Alexander won major victories against the Persians at Granicus and then at Issus, where he defeated the Persian emperor, Darius III. Alexander then conquered the Persian-held lands of Syria, Egypt, and Mesopotamia. He met Darius again in 331 B.C., defeated him in the Battle of Gaugamela, and won control of the once-mighty Persian Empire."

◆ Making Generalizations and Predictions

is the process of interpreting information to form more general statements and guess about what will happen next. A *generalization* is a broad statement that holds true for a variety of historical events or situations. Making generalizations can help you see the "big picture" of historical events, rather than just focusing on details. It is very important, however, that when making generalizations you try not to include situations that do not fit the statement. When this occurs, you run the risk of creating a stereotype, or overgeneralization. A *prediction* is an educated guess about an outcome. When you read history, you should always be asking yourself questions like, "What will happen next? If this person does this, what will that mean for . . . ?", and so on. These types of questions help you draw on information you already know to see patterns throughout history

◆ Drawing Inferences and Conclusions

is forming possible explanations for an event, a situation, or a problem. When you make an *inference,* you take the information you know to be true and come up with an educated guess about what else you think is true about that situation. A *conclusion* is a prediction about the outcome of a situation based on what you already know. Often, you must be prepared to test your inferences and conclu-

Cover from Upton Sinclair's The Jungle

sions against new evidence or arguments. For example, a historian might conclude that women's leadership roles in the abolition movement led to the development of the early women's movement. The historian would then organize the evidence needed to support this conclusion and challenge other arguments.

◆ Identifying Points of View

is the process of identifying factors that influence the outlook of an individual or group. A person's point of view includes beliefs and attitudes that are shaped by factors such as age, gender, religion, race, and economic status. This critical thinking skill helps you examine why people see things as they do and reinforce the realization that people's views may change over time or with a change in circumstances.

◆ **Supporting a Point of View** involves choosing a viewpoint on a particular event or issue and arguing persuasively for that position. Your argument should be well organized and based on specific evidence that supports the point of view you have chosen. Supporting a point of view often involves working with controversial or emotional issues. For example, you might consider the points of view involved in the struggles between labor unions and business owners in Great Britain and the United States during the late 1800s. Whether you choose a position in favor of labor unions or in favor of business owners, you should state your opinion clearly and give reasons to support it.

◆ **Identifying Bias** is the process of evaluating the opinions of others about events or situations. *Bias* is an opinion based on prejudice or strong emotions, rather that fact. It is important to identify bias when looking at historical sources because biased sources often give you a false sense of what really happened. When looking at both primary and secondary sources, it is always important to keep the author's or speaker's point of view in mind and to adjust your interpretation of the source based on any bias you might detect.

The first step towards lightening
The White Man's Burden
is through teaching the virtues of cleanliness.
Pears' Soap
is a potent factor in brightening the dark corners of the earth as civilization advances, while amongst the cultured of all nations it holds the highest place—it is the ideal toilet soap.

Soap advertisement reflecting a widespread bias of the late 1800s

◆ **Evaluating** is assessing the significance or overall importance of something, such as the success of a reform movement, the actions of a president, or the results of a major conflict. You should base your judgment on standards that others will understand and are likely to share. For example, you might consider the outcomes of the Spanish conquests of the Aztec and Inca empires and evaluate their importance

Aztec dishware

relative to the development of Spain as a major European power. You could also evaluate the effect of the conquests on Native American peoples and civilizations.

◆ **Problem Solving** is the process by which you pose workable solutions to difficult situations. The first step in the process is to identify a problem. Next you will need to gather information about the problem, such as its history and the various factors that contribute to the problem. Once you have gathered information, you should list and consider the options for solving the problem. For each of the possible solutions, weigh their advantages and disadvantages and, based on your evaluation, choose and implement a solution. Once the solution is in place, go back and evaluate the effectiveness of the solution you selected.

◆ **Decision Making** is the process of reviewing a situation and then making decisions or recommendations for the best possible outcome. To complete the process, first identify a situation that requires a solution. Next, gather information that will help you reach a decision. You may need to do some background research to study the history of the situation, or carefully consider the points of view of the individuals involved. Once you have done your research, identify options that might resolve the situation. For each option, predict what the possible consequences might be if that option were followed. Once you have identified the best option, take action by making a recommendation and following through on any tasks that option requires.

Becoming a Strategic Reader

by Dr. Judith Irvin

Everywhere you look, print is all around us. In fact, you would have a hard time stopping yourself from reading. In a normal day, you might read cereal boxes, movie posters, notes from friends, T-shirts, instructions for video games, song lyrics, catalogs, billboards, information on the Internet, magazines, the newspaper, and much, much more. Each form of print is read differently depending on your purpose for reading. You read a menu differently from poetry, and a motorcycle magazine is read differently than a letter from a friend. Good readers switch easily from one type of text to another. In fact, they probably do not even think about it, they just do it.

When you read, it is helpful to use a strategy to remember the most important ideas. You can use a strategy before you read to help connect information you already know to the new information you will encounter. Before you read, you can also predict what a text will be about by using a previewing strategy. During the reading you can use a strategy to help you focus on main ideas, and after reading you can use a strategy to help you organize what you learned so that you can remember it later. *The Human Journey* was designed to help you more easily understand the ideas you read. Important reading strategies employed in *The Human Journey* include:

1 Methods to help you **anticipate** what is to come

2 Tools to help you **preview and predict** what the text will be about

3 Ways to help you **use and analyze visual information**

4 Ideas to help you **organize the information** you have learned

1. Anticipating Information

How can I use information I already know to help me understand what a new chapter will be about?

Anticipating what a new chapter will be about helps you connect the upcoming information to what you already know. By drawing on your background knowledge, you can build a bridge to the new material.

1 Each chapter of *The Human Journey* asks you to explore the main themes of the chapter before you start reading by forming opinions based on your current knowledge.

What's Your Opinion?

Do you **agree** *or* **disagree** *with the following statements? Support your point of view in your journal.*

Government A strong army and government are necessary to maintain an empire.

Culture Great civilizations build on the discoveries, developments, and contributions of earlier cultures.

Global Relations An empire that enslaves conquered peoples is destined to fall.

Create a chart like this one to help you analyze the statements.

A Before Reading Agree/Disagree		B After Reading Agree/Disagree
2	Government—A strong army and government are necessary to maintain an empire.	**4**
	Culture—Great civilizations build on the discoveries, developments, and contributions of earlier cultures.	
	Global Relations—An empire that enslaves conquered peoples is destined to fall.	

3 Read the text and discuss with classmates.

5 You can also refine your knowledge by answering the Reviewing Themes questions in the chapter review.

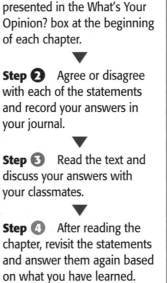

Anticipating Information

Step 1 Identify the major concepts of the chapter. In *The Human Journey*, these are presented in the What's Your Opinion? box at the beginning of each chapter.

▼

Step 2 Agree or disagree with each of the statements and record your answers in your journal.

▼

Step 3 Read the text and discuss your answers with your classmates.

▼

Step 4 After reading the chapter, revisit the statements and answer them again based on what you have learned.

Reviewing Themes

1. **Government** What two major factors helped Rome unify its empire and maintain peace?
2. **Culture** What ideas and inventions did the Romans borrow and adapt from the Greeks?
3. **Global Relations** How did Rome's relationship with the people it conquered change over time?

2. Previewing and Predicting

How can I figure out what the text is about before I even start reading a section?

Previewing and Predicting

Step 1 Identify your purpose for reading. Ask yourself what you will do with this information after you have finished reading.

▼

Step 2 Determine the main idea of the text and the key vocabulary words you need to know.

▼

Step 3 Use signal words to help identify the structure of the text.

▼

Step 4 Connect the information to what you already know.

Previewing and **predicting** are good methods to help you understand the text. If you take the time to preview and predict before you read, the text will make more sense to you during your reading.

1 Usually, your teacher will set the purpose for reading. After reading some new information, you may be asked to write a summary, take a test, or complete some other type of activity.

"After reading about the English Civil War, you will work with a partner to create a historical museum exhibit describing . . .".

2 As you preview the text, use graphic signals such as headings, subheadings, and boldface type to help you determine what is important in the text. Each section of *The Human Journey* opens by giving you important clues to help you preview the material.

Read to Discover questions give you clues as to the section's main ideas.

Define and Identify terms let you know the key vocabulary you will encounter in the section.

Looking at the section's **main heading** and **subheadings** can give you an idea of what is to come.

3 Other tools that can help you in previewing are **signal words**. These words prepare you to think in a certain way. For example, when you see words such as *similar to*, *same as*, or *different from*, you know that the text will probably compare and contrast two or more ideas. Signal words indicate how the ideas in the text relate to each other. Look at the list below of some of the most common signal words grouped by the type of text structures they include.

Cause and Effect	Compare and Contrast	Description	Problem and Solution	Sequence or Chronological Order
because	different from	for instance	problem	not long after
since	same as	for example	the question is	next
consequently	similar to	such as	a solution	then
this led to . . . so	as opposed to	to illustrate	one answer is	initially
if . . . then	instead of	in addition		before
nevertheless	although	most		after
accordingly	however	importantly		finally
because of	compared with	another		preceding
as a result of	as well as	furthermore		following
in order to	either . . . or	first, second . . .		on (date)
may be due to	but			over the years
for this reason	on the other hand			today
not only . . . but	unless			when

4 Learning something new requires that you connect it in some way with something you already know. This means you have to think before you read and while you read. You may want to use a chart like this one to remind yourself of the information already familiar to you and to come up with questions you want answered in your reading. The chart will also help you organize your ideas after you have finished reading.

What I know	What I want to know	What I learned

3. Use and Analyze Visual Information

How can all the pictures, maps, graphs, and time lines with the text help me be a stronger reader?

Analyzing Information

Step ❶ As you preview the text, ask yourself how the visual information relates to the text.

▼

Step ❷ Generate questions based on the visual information.

▼

Step ❸ After reading the text, go back and review the visual information again.

Using visual information can help you understand and remember the information presented in *The Human Journey*. Good readers make a picture in their mind when they read. The pictures, charts, graphs, cartoons, time lines, and diagrams included throughout *The Human Journey* are placed strategically to increase your understanding.

❶ You might ask yourself questions like:

"Why did the author include this image with the text?"

"What details about this visual are mentioned in the text?"

After you have read the text, see if you can answer your own questions.

❷ *"What seems to be happening in this illustration?"*

"Why are the people, their styles of dress, and their surroundings important?"

"How does this illustration reflect the social and political conditions of the era it portrays?"

Scene from the court of King Philip IV of France

❸ After reading, take another look at the visual information.

❹ Try to make connections to what you already know.

4. Organize Information

Once I learn new information, how do I keep it all straight so that I will remember it?

To help you remember what you have read, you need to find a way of **organizing information**. Two good ways of doing this are by using graphic organizers and concept maps. **Graphic organizers** help you understand important relationships—such as cause-and-effect, compare/contrast, sequence or events, and problem/solution—within the test. **Concept maps** provide a useful tool to help you focus on the text's main ideas and organize supporting details.

Identifying Relationships

Using graphic organizers will help you recall important ideas from the section and give you a study tool you can use to prepare for a quiz or test or to help with a writing assignment. Some of the most common types of graphic organizers are shown below.

Cause and Effect Events in history cause people to react in a certain way. Cause-and-effect patterns show the relationship between results and the ideas or events that made the results occur. You may want to represent cause-and-effect relationships as one cause leading to multiple effects, or as a chain of cause-and-effect relationships.

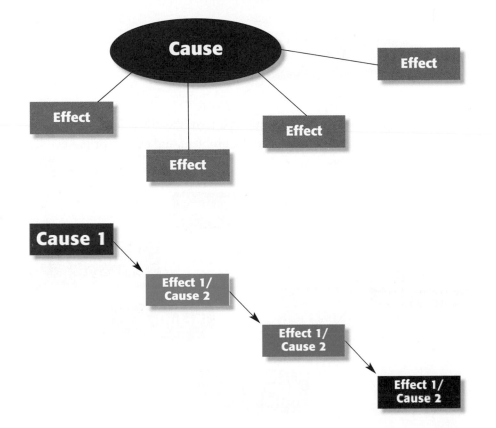

Comparing and Contrasting Graphic Organizers are often useful when you are comparing or contrasting information. Compare-and-contrast diagrams point out similarities and differences between two concepts or ideas.

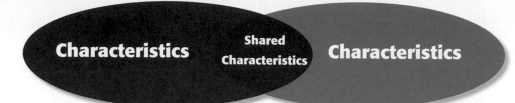

Sequencing Keeping track of dates and the order in which events took place is essential to understanding history. Sequence or chronological-order diagrams show events or ideas in the order in which they happened.

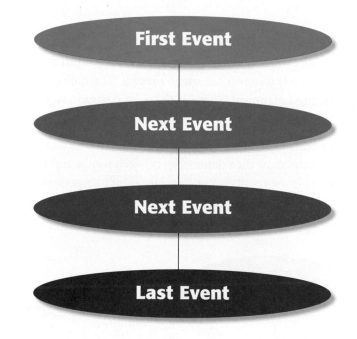

Problem and Solution Problem-solution patterns identify at least one problem, offer one or more solutions to the problem, and explain or predict outcomes of the solutions.

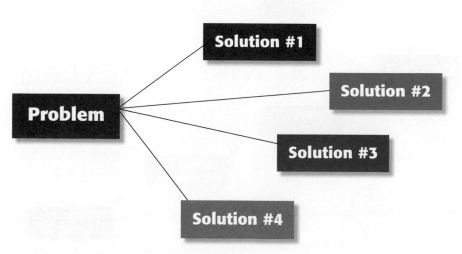

Identifying Main Ideas and Supporting Details

One special type of graphic organizer is the concept map. A concept map, sometimes called a semantic map, allows you to zero in on the most important points of the text. The map is made up of lines, boxes, circles, and/or arrows. It can be as simple or as complex as you need it to be to accurately represent the text.

Here are a few examples of concept maps you might use.

Constructing Concept Maps

Step ① Preview the text looking at what type of structure might be appropriate to display a concept map.

▼

Step ② Taking note of the headings, bold-faced type, and text structure, sketch a concept map you think could best illustrate the text.

▼

Step ③ Using boxes, lines, arrows, circles, or any shapes you like, display the ideas of the text in the concept map.

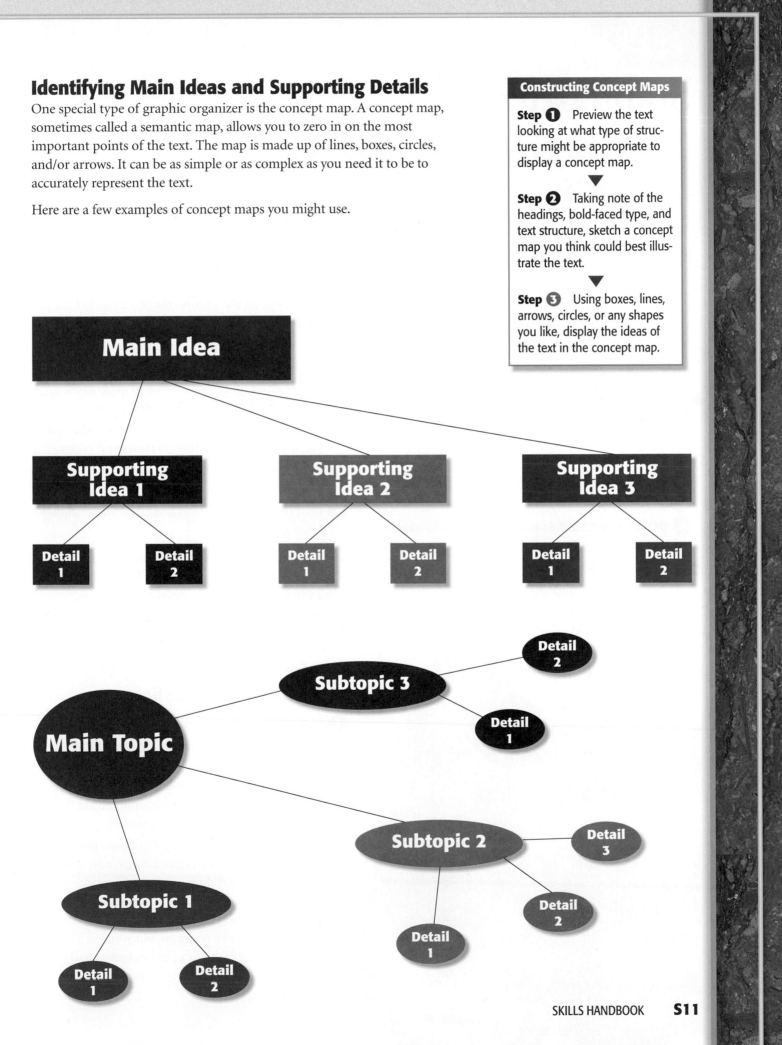

Standardized Test-Taking Strategies

A number of times throughout your school career, you may be asked to take standardized tests. These tests are designed to demonstrate the content and skills you have learned. It is important to keep in mind that in most cases the best way to prepare for these tests is to pay close attention in class and take every opportunity to improve you general social studies, reading, writing, and mathematical skills.

Tips for Taking the Test

1 Be sure that you are well rested.

2 Be on time, and be sure that you have the necessary materials.

3 Listen to the instructions of the teacher.

4 Read directions and questions carefully.

5 **DON'T STRESS!** Just remember what you have learned in class, and you should do well.

Practice the Strategies at go.hrw.com

Tackling Social Studies

The social studies portions of many standardized tests are designed to test your knowledge of the content and skills that you have been studying in one or more of your social studies classes. Specific objectives for the test vary, but some of the most common include:

1 Demonstrate an understanding of issues and events in history.

2 Demonstrate an understanding of geographic influences on historical issues and events.

3 Demonstrate an understanding of economic and social influences on historical issues and events.

4 Demonstrate an understanding of political influences on historical issues and events.

5 Use critical thinking skills to analyze social studies information.

Standardized tests usually contain multiple-choice and, sometimes, open-ended questions. The multiple-choice items will often be based on maps, tables, charts, graphs, pictures, cartoons, and/or reading passages and documents.

Tips for Answering Multiple-Choice Questions

1 If there is a written or visual piece accompanying the multiple-choice question, pay careful attention to the title, author, and date.

2 Then, read through or glance over the content of the written or visual piece accompanying the question to familiarize yourself with it.

3 Next, read the multiple-choice question first for its general intent and then reread it carefully, looking for words that give clues or can limit possible answers to the question. For example, words such as *most* or *best* tell you that there may be several correct answers to a question, but you will look for the one that is the most important or had the most effect.

4 Read through the answer choices. Always read all of the possible answer choices even if the first one seems like the correct answer. There may be a better choice farther down in the list.

5 Reread the accompanying information (if any is included) carefully to determine the answer to the question. Again, note the title, author, and date of primary-source selections. The answer will rarely be stated exactly as it appears in the primary source, so you will need to use your critical thinking skills to read between the lines.

6 Think of what you already know about the time in history or person involved and use that to help limit the answer choices.

7 Finally, reread the question and selected answer to be sure that you made the best choice and that you marked it correctly on the answer sheet.

Strategies for Success

There are a variety of strategies you can prepare ahead of time to help you feel more confident about answering questions on social studies standardized tests. Here are a few suggestions:

1 Adopt an acronym—a word formed from the first letters of other words—that you will use for analyzing a document or visual that accompanies a question.

Helpful Acronyms			
For a document, use **SOAPS** *which stands for:*		*For a picture, cartoon, map, or other visual piece of information, use* **OPTIC***, which stands for:*	
S	**S**ubject	**O**	**O**verview
O	**O**ccasion (or time)	**P**	**P**arts (labels or details of the visual)
A	**A**udience	**T**	**T**itle
P	**P**urpose	**I**	**I**nterrelations (how the different parts of the visual work together)
S	**S**peaker/author	**C**	**C**onclusion (what the visual means)

2 Form visual images of maps and try to draw them from memory. The standardized test will most likely include important maps from the time period and subjects you have been studying. For example, in early Chinese history, be able to see in your mind's eye such things as the location and geographic outline of China Proper, the area's major land forms, rivers, and sea coasts, and the general geography of surrounding lands. Understand patterns of population distribution and ways in which humans interacted with the environment. Know major physical features, such as river and mountain systems, other topographic characteristics of the region, and the locations of important human systems, such as transportation routes and areas of major settlement.

3 When you have finished studying any historical era, try to think of who or what might be important enough for the test. You may want to keep your ideas in a notebook to refer to when it is almost time for the test.

4 Pay particular attention to the concept of constitutionalism. Many standardized tests contain questions dealing with this all-important idea and its historical development. Questions may test your understanding of Magna Carta, the English Bill of Rights, the American Declaration of Independence, the United States Constitution, as well as many other important historical documents. Questions may also cover the roles of various political thinkers and philosophers, such as the French *philosophes*.

5 For the skills area of the tests, practice putting major events and personalities in order in your mind. Sequencing people and events by dates can become a game you play with a friend who also has to take the test. Always ask yourself why this event is important.

6 Follow the tips under "Ready for Reading" on the next page when you encounter a reading passage in social studies, but remember that what you have learned about history can help you in answering reading comprehension questions.

Ready for Reading

The main goal of the Reading sections of most standardized tests is to determine your understanding of different aspects of a reading passage. Basically, if you can grasp the main idea and the author's purpose, and then pay attention to the details and vocabulary so that you are able to draw inferences and conclusions, you will do well on the test.

Tips for Answering Multiple-Choice Questions

1. Read the passage as if you were not taking a test.
2. Look at the big picture. Ask yourself questions like, "What is the title? What do the illustrations or pictures tell me?" and "What is the author's purpose?"
3. Read the questions. This will help you know what information to look for.
4. Reread the passage, underlining information related to the questions.
5. Go back to the questions and try to answer each one in your mind before looking at the answers.
6. Read all the answer choices and eliminate the ones that are obviously incorrect.

Types of Multiple-Choice Questions	
Main Idea	This is the most important point of the passage. After reading the passage, locate and underline the main idea.
Significant Details	You will often be asked to recall details from the passage. Read the question, and underline the details as you read, but remember that the correct answers do not always match the wording of the passage precisely.
Vocabulary	You will often need to define a word within the context of the passage. Read the answer choices and plug them into the sentence to see what fits best.
Conclusion and Inference	There are often important ideas in the passage that the author does not state directly. Sometimes you must consider multiple parts of the passage to answer the question. If answers refer to only one or two sentences or details in the passage, they are probably incorrect.

Tips for Answering Short-Answer Questions

1. Read the passage in its entirety, paying close attention to the main events and characters. Jot down information you think is important.
2. If you can't answer a question, skip it and come back later.
3. Words such as compare, contrast, interpret, discuss, and summarize appear often in short answer questions. Be sure you have a complete understanding of each of these words.
4. To help support your answer, return to the passage and skim the parts you underlined.
5. Organize your thoughts on a separate sheet of paper. Write a general statement with which to begin. This will be your topic statement.
6. When writing your answer, be precise but brief. Be sure to refer to details in the passage in your answer.

Targeting Writing

On many standardized tests, you will occasionally be asked to write an essay. In order to write a concise essay, you must learn to organize you thoughts before you begin writing the actual composition. This keeps you from straying too far from the essay's topic.

Tips for Answering Composition Questions

1. Read the question carefully.

2. Decide what kind of essay you are being asked to write. Essays usually fall into one of the following types: persuasive, classificatory, compare/contrast, or "how to." To determine the type of essay, ask yourself questions like, "Am I trying to persuade my audience? Am I comparing or contrasting ideas?," or "Am I trying to show the reader how to do something?"

3. Pay attention to keywords, such as compare, contrast, describe, advantages, disadvantages, classify, or speculate. They will give you clues as to the structure that your essay should follow.

4. Organize your thoughts on a separate sheet of paper. You will want to come up with a general topic sentence that expresses your main idea. Make sure this sentence addresses the question. You should then create an outline or some type of graphic organizer to help you organize the points that support your topic sentence.

5. Write your composition using complete sentences. Also be sure to use correct grammar, spelling, punctuation, and sentence structure.

6. Be sure to proofread your essay once you have finished writing.

Gearing Up for Math

On most standardized tests you will be asked to solve a variety of mathematical problems that draw on the skills and information you have learned in class. If math problems sometimes give you difficulty, have a look at the tips below to help you work through the problems.

Tips for Solving Math Problems

1. Determine the goal of the question. Read or study the problem carefully and determine what information must be found.

2. Locate the factual information. Decide what information represents key facts—the ones you must have to solve the problem. You may also find facts you do not need to reach your solution. In some cases, you may determine that more information is needed to solve the problem. If so, ask yourself, "What assumptions can I make about this problem?" or "Do I need a formula to help solve this problem?"

3. Decide what strategies you might use to solve the problem, how you might use them, and what form your solution will be in. For example, will you need to create a graph or chart? Will you need to solve an equation? Will your answer be in words or numbers? By knowing what type of solution you should reach, you may be able to eliminate some of the choices.

4. Apply your strategy to solve the problem and compare your answer to the choices.

5. If the answer is still not clear, read the problem again. If you had to make calculations to reach your answer, use estimation to see if your answer makes sense.

The Geographer's Tool Kit

A map is an illustration drawn to scale of all or part of Earth's surface. Knowing how to read and interpret maps is one of the most valuable tools you can use to study history.

Types of Maps

Types of maps include physical maps, political maps, and thematic (special-purpose) maps.

Physical maps illustrate the natural landscape of an area—the landforms that mark Earth's surface. Physical maps often use shading to show relief—the existence of mountains, hills, and valleys—and colors to show elevation, or the height above sea level. The map of the World on pages A2–A3 is strictly a physical map.

Political maps illustrate political units, such as states and nations, and use color variations and lines to mark boundaries, dots for major cities, and stars or stars within circles for capitals. Political maps show information such as territorial changes or military alliances. The map of the United States on page A4 is a political map.

Thematic (special-purpose) maps present specific information, such as the route of an explorer or the outcome of an election. The maps shown on page 56 ("Indo-European Migrations") and page 188 ("Trading States of Africa, c. 1230–1591") of *The Human Journey*, for example, are thematic maps.

Map Features

Most maps have a number of features in common. Familiarity with these elements makes reading maps easier.

Titles, legends, and labels A map's title tells you what the map is about, what areas are shown, and usually what time period is being represented. The legend, or key, explains any special symbols, colors, or shadings used on the map. Labels designate political and geographic

place-names, and physical features like mountain ranges, oceans, and rivers.

The global grid The absolute location of any place on Earth is given in terms of latitude (degrees north or south of the equator) and longitude (degrees east or west of the prime meridian). The symbol for a degree is °. Degrees are divided into 60 equal parts called minutes, which are represented by the symbol ´. The global grid is created by the intersecting lines of latitude (parallels) and lines of longitude (meridians). Lines of latitude and longitude may sometimes be indicated by tick marks near the edge of the map, or by lines across an entire map. Many maps also have locator maps, which place the area of focus in a larger context, showing it in relation to a continent or to the entire world.

Directions and distance Most maps in this textbook have a compass rose, or directional indicator. The compass rose indicates the four cardinal points—*N* for north, *S* for south, *E* for east, and *W* for west. You can also find intermediate directions—northeast, southeast, southwest, and northwest—using the compass rose. This helps in

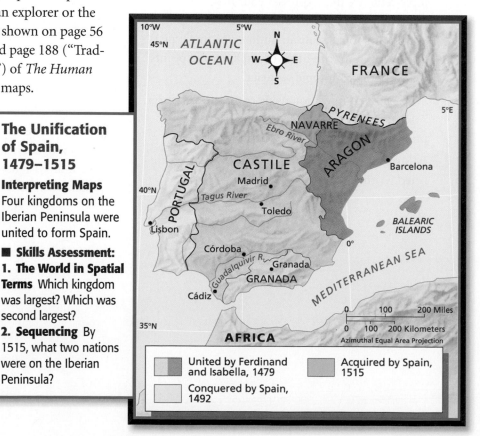

The Unification of Spain, 1479–1515

Interpreting Maps
Four kingdoms on the Iberian Peninsula were united to form Spain.

■ **Skills Assessment:**
1. The World in Spatial Terms Which kingdom was largest? Which was second largest?
2. Sequencing By 1515, what two nations were on the Iberian Peninsula?

describing the relative location of a place. (If a map has no compass rose, assume that north is at the top, east is to the right, and so on.) Many maps in this textbook include a scale, showing both miles and kilometers, to help you relate distances on the map to actual distances on Earth's surface.

Map projections Because Earth is a sphere, it is best represented by a three-dimensional globe. Although a flat map is an imperfect representation of Earth's surface, mapmakers have devised various ways of showing Earth two dimensionally. These different flat views of Earth's surface are called projections.

Every map projection, and therefore every map, distorts to some extent at least one of the following aspects: (1) the shape of land areas, (2) their relative sizes, (3) directions, or (4) distances. Mapmakers choose the projection that least distorts what they wish to show. For example, an equal-area projection shows the relative sizes of different countries or continents quite accurately but distorts shapes somewhat.

How to Read a Map

1 Determine the focus of the map. Read the map's title and labels to determine the map's focus—its subject and the geographic area it covers.

2 Study the map legend. Read the legend and become familiar with any special symbols, lines, colors, and shadings used in the map.

3 Check directions and distance. Use the directional indicator and scale as needed to determine direction, location, and distance between various points on the map.

4 Check the grid lines. Refer to lines of longitude and latitude, or to a locator map, to place the area on the map in a larger context.

5 Study the map. Study the map's basic features and details, keeping its purpose in mind. If it is a special-purpose map, study the specific information being presented.

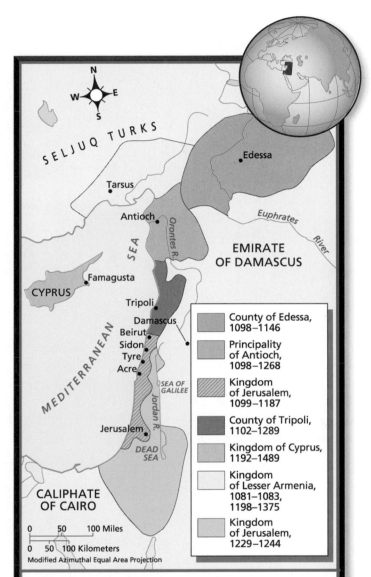

County of Edessa, 1098–1146

Principality of Antioch, 1098–1268

Kingdom of Jerusalem, 1099–1187

County of Tripoli, 1102–1289

Kingdom of Cyprus, 1192–1489

Kingdom of Lesser Armenia, 1081–1083, 1198–1375

Kingdom of Jerusalem, 1229–1244

0   50   100 Miles
0   50   100 Kilometers
Modified Azimuthal Equal Area Projection

Crusader States from 1098

Interpreting Maps During and after the First Crusade, crusaders set up small states in the Middle East.

■ **Skills Assessment: 1. Places and Regions** Name the four states set up by crusaders between 1098 and 1102. How long did each state stay under the crusaders' control?

2. Drawing Conclusions Compare this map with the map on page 319. Why might it have been difficult for the crusaders to maintain control of these states?

ATLAS

World: Political

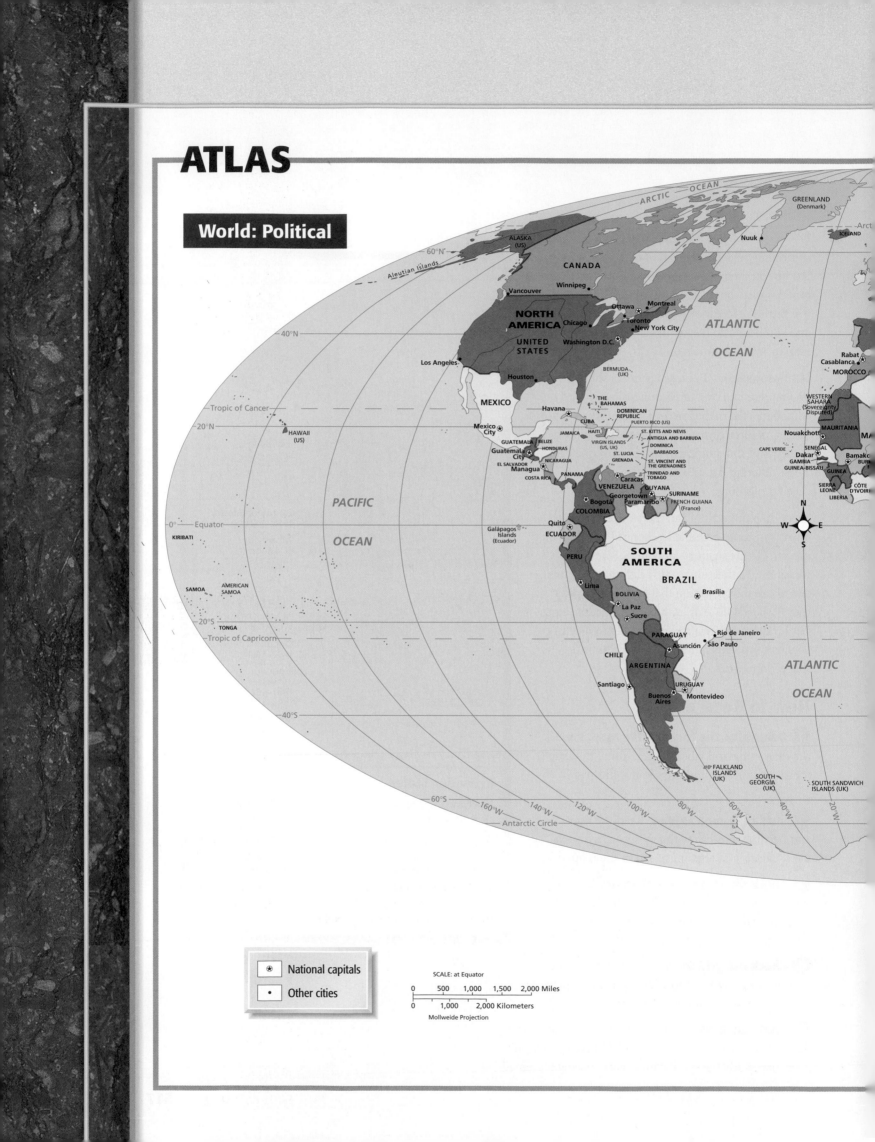

ARCTIC OCEAN

GREENLAND (Denmark)

ICELAND

ALASKA (US)

60°N

CANADA

Nuuk

Arct

Aleutian Islands

Vancouver

Winnipeg

NORTH AMERICA

Ottawa

Montreal

Toronto

New York City

ATLANTIC

UNITED STATES

Chicago

Washington D.C.

OCEAN

40°N

Los Angeles

Houston

BERMUDA (UK)

Rabat

Casablanca

MOROCCO

Tropic of Cancer

MEXICO

THE BAHAMAS

Havana

DOMINICAN REPUBLIC

WESTERN SAHARA (Sovereignty Disputed)

20°N

HAWAII (US)

CUBA

Mexico City

PUERTO RICO (US)

Nouakchott

MAURITANIA

MA

GUATEMALA

BELIZE

JAMAICA

HAITI

ST. KITTS AND NEVIS

ANTIGUA AND BARBUDA

CAPE VERDE

SENEGAL

Guatemala City

HONDURAS

VIRGIN ISLANDS (US, UK)

DOMINICA

Dakar

Bamako

ST. LUCIA

BARBADOS

GAMBIA

EL SALVADOR

NICARAGUA

GRENADA

ST. VINCENT AND THE GRENADINES

GUINEA-BISSAU

GUINEA

BURI

Managua

COSTA RICA

PANAMA

TRINIDAD AND TOBAGO

SIERRA LEONE

CÔTE D'IVOIRE

VENEZUELA

Caracas

GUYANA

LIBERIA

PACIFIC

Bogotá

Georgetown

Paramaribo

SURINAME

COLOMBIA

FRENCH GUIANA (France)

N

OCEAN

0°

Equator

Quito

ECUADOR

W

E

KIRIBATI

Galápagos Islands (Ecuador)

S

PERU

SOUTH AMERICA

SAMOA

AMERICAN SAMOA

BRAZIL

Lima

Brasília

BOLIVIA

20°S

TONGA

La Paz

Sucre

Tropic of Capricorn

PARAGUAY

Río de Janeiro

São Paulo

CHILE

Asunción

ATLANTIC

ARGENTINA

URUGUAY

OCEAN

Santiago

Buenos Aires

Montevideo

40°S

FALKLAND ISLANDS (UK)

SOUTH GEORGIA (UK)

SOUTH SANDWICH ISLANDS (UK)

60°S

160°W

140°W

120°W

100°W

80°W

60°W

40°W

20°W

Antarctic Circle

Legend

⊛ National capitals

• Other cities

SCALE: at Equator

0   500   1,000   1,500   2,000 Miles

0   1,000   2,000 Kilometers

Mollweide Projection

COUNTRY

1 Czech Republic
2 Slovakia
3 Slovenia
4 Croatia
5 Bosnia and Herzegovina
6 Macedonia
7 Serbia and Montenegro
8 Lithuania
9 Latvia
10 Estonia

CAPITAL

Prague
Bratislava
Ljubljana
Zagreb
Sarajevo
Skopje
Belgrade
Vilnius
Riga
Tallinn

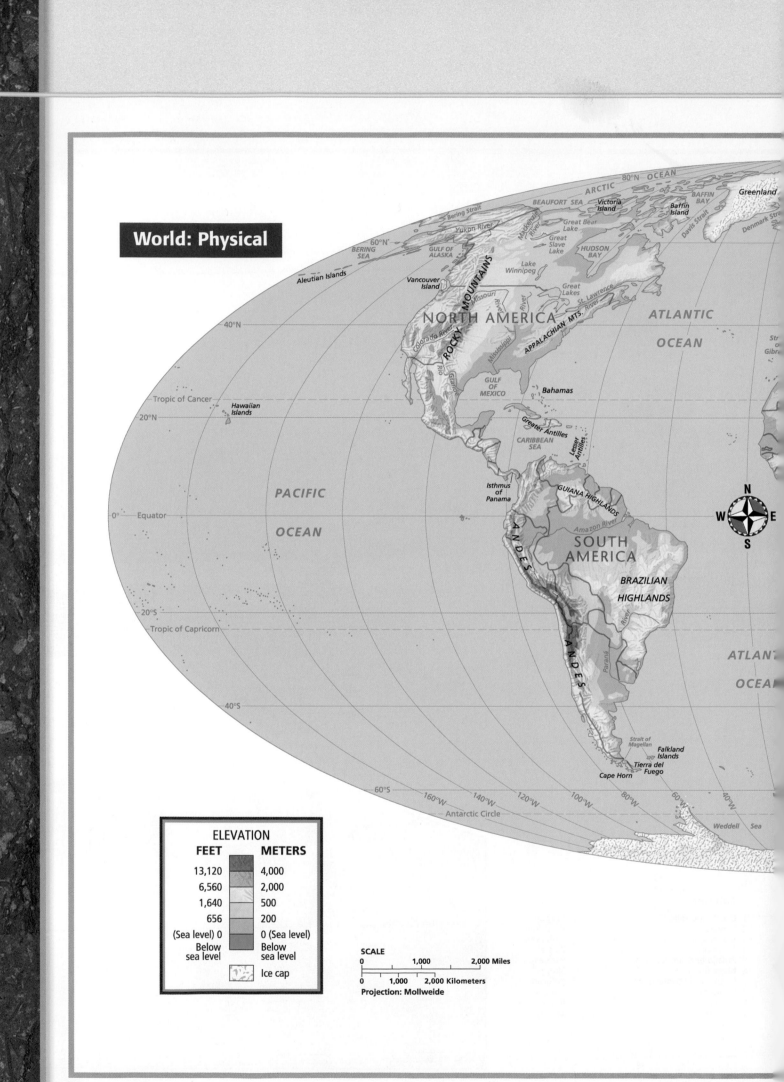

World: Physical

ARCTIC OCEAN
80°N
BAFFIN BAY
Greenland
BEAUFORT SEA
Victoria Island
Baffin Island
Bering Strait
Davis Strait
Denmark Str
60°N
Yukon River
Mackenzie River
Great Bear Lake
Great Slave Lake
HUDSON BAY
BERING SEA
GULF OF ALASKA
Lake Winnipeg
Great Lakes
St. Lawrence River
ATLANTIC OCEAN
Aleutian Islands
Vancouver Island
ROCKY MOUNTAINS
NORTH AMERICA
40°N
Missouri River
APPALACHIAN MTS.
Str Gibr
Colorado River
Mississippi
Rio Grande
Tropic of Cancer
Hawaiian Islands
20°N
GULF OF MEXICO
Bahamas
Greater Antilles
CARIBBEAN SEA
Lesser Antilles
PACIFIC
Isthmus of Panama
GUIANA HIGHLANDS
0° Equator
OCEAN
Amazon River
ANDES
SOUTH AMERICA
BRAZILIAN HIGHLANDS
20°S
Tropic of Capricorn
Parana River
ATLANT
OCEA
ANDES
40°S
Strait of Magellan
Falkland Islands
Tierra del Fuego
Cape Horn
60°S
160°W 140°W 120°W 100°W 80°W 60°W 40°W
Antarctic Circle
Weddell Sea

N
W E
S

ELEVATION

FEET		METERS
13,120		4,000
6,560		2,000
1,640		500
656		200
(Sea level) 0		0 (Sea level)
Below sea level		Below sea level
		Ice cap

SCALE
0   1,000   2,000 Miles
0   1,000   2,000 Kilometers
Projection: Mollweide

ARCTIC 80°N OCEAN
North Cape
BARENTS SEA
KARA SEA
LAPTEV SEA
EAST SIBERIAN SEA
BALTIC SEA
UROPE
URAL MOUNTAINS
Yenisey River
Ob River
Lena River
Kolyma River
60°N
SEA OF OKHOTSK
KAMCHATKA PENINSULA
Volga River
Lake Baikal
ALTAY SHAN
Amur River
Sakhalin
BLACK SEA
CASPIAN SEA
ARAL SEA
Lake Balkhash
ASIA
GOBI
Yellow River
40°N
Hokkaidō
Honshū
SEA OF JAPAN
MEDITERRANEAN SEA
Tigris River
Euphrates River
Jordan River
Persian Gulf
HIMALAYAS
Brahmaputra River
Chang (Yangtze) River
Shikoku
Kyūshū
EAST CHINA SEA
ARA
Nile River
ARABIAN PENINSULA
Indus River
THAR DESERT
Ganges River
Mekong River
Taiwan
Tropic of Cancer
AFRICA
RED SEA
ARABIAN SEA
Bay of Bengal
20°N
PACIFIC
Sri Lanka
Strait of Malacca
SOUTH CHINA SEA
Philippine Islands
OCEAN
Congo River
MALAY PENINSULA
Lake Tanganyika
Lake Victoria
Borneo
Equator 0°
Sumatra
Sulawesi (Celebes)
New Guinea
Solomon Islands
Java
INDIAN OCEAN
Madagascar
Mozambique Channel
CORAL SEA
GREAT SANDY DESERT
New Caledonia
20°S
KALAHARI DESERT
AUSTRALIA
Tropic of Capricorn
GREAT VICTORIA DESERT
Darling River
GREAT DIVIDING RANGE
North Island
ape of d Hope
TASMAN SEA
Tasmania
South Island
20°E 40°E 60°E 80°E 100°E 120°E 140°E 160°E 60°S
ARCTICA

Denmark Strait
Iceland
10°E
North Cape
20°E
40°E
50°E
60°E
KARA SEA
80°E
BARENTS SEA
SCANDINAVIAN MTS.
URAL MTS.
N
W E
S
60°N
NORTH SEA
BALTIC SEA
Volga River
EUROPE
British Isles
SCALE
0   250   500   750 Miles
0 250 500 750 Kilometers
Projection: Mollweide
50°N
ATLANTIC
OCEAN
Bay of Biscay
Rhine River
Danube River
ALPS
BLACK SEA
40°N
Tigris R.
Euphrates R.
Strait of Gibraltar
MEDITERRANEAN SEA
Crete

United States of America: Political

To understand the relative locations of Alaska and Hawaii, as well as the vast distances separating them from the rest of the United States, see the world map.

Projection: Albers Equal Area

CANADA

NESOTA
Duluth
• Superior   • Marquette   • Sault Ste. Marie

Minneapolis
★ St. Paul

Green Bay
WISCONSIN

Madison ★
• Milwaukee

Lake Superior

Lake Michigan

Lake Huron

MICHIGAN
Grand Rapids
• Saginaw
Lansing ★

MAINE
Augusta ★

Lake Champlain
• Burlington
★ Montpelier
VT   NH
Concord
★ Manchester

• Portland

YA
Cedar Rapids
Davenport
es Moines

• Rockford
Chicago
Gary • South Bend
Fort Wayne

Ann Arbor
• Detroit
Lake Erie
Cleveland
Toledo Youngstown
Akron

NEW YORK
• Buffalo • Rochester • Syracuse
Albany ★
Springfield ★
Hartford ★ CT RI
Bridgeport • New Haven
LONG ISLAND SOUND
Yonkers
New York City
Newark • Jersey City

MA
Boston
★ Worcester
★ Providence
Cape Cod

Lake Ontario

Hudson River

ILLINOIS
• Peoria

★ Springfield
Indianapolis ★
INDIANA

OHIO
• Columbus
• Dayton
• Cincinnati

PENNSYLVANIA
Susquehanna River
• Allentown
Harrisburg ★
• Pittsburgh   Philadelphia •
Baltimore •
MD
⊗ Annapolis ★
Washington, D.C.

• Trenton
• Camden
NJ
Atlantic City
DE
★ Dover
DELAWARE BAY

St. Louis •
East St. Louis
Jefferson City ★

MISSOURI
• Springfield

WEST VIRGINIA
Charleston ★

VIRGINIA
Richmond ★

CHESAPEAKE

ATLANTIC OCEAN

Louisville •
Evansville •
Ohio River
Frankfort ★
• Lexington

KENTUCKY

Lake Barkley

Newport News •
Norfolk
• Virginia Beach

Cape Hatteras

tteville

Kentucky Lake

• Nashville
Knoxville •

Winston-Salem •
• Greensboro
Durham
★ Raleigh

TENNESSEE
Chattanooga •

Asheville •
NORTH CAROLINA
• Charlotte

ARKANSAS
e Rock
ine Bluff

• Memphis

Mississippi River

• Greenville

SOUTH CAROLINA
Columbia ★

MISSISSIPPI

• Huntsville

ALABAMA
• Birmingham

Atlanta ★
GEORGIA
• Macon
Columbus •

• Charleston

Savannah River

Savannah •
SEA ISLANDS

National capital ⊗
State capitals ★
Other cities •

reveport

Vicksburg •
★ Jackson

Meridian •
Montgomery ★

Chattahoochee River

LOUISIANA
emont

• Baton Rouge
• Mobile • Pensacola
• Biloxi
CHANDELEUR ISLANDS

New Orleans •

★ Tallahassee

Gainesville •

Jacksonville •

FLORIDA

Cape Canaveral

ARCTIC OCEAN
NORTH AMERICA   EUROPE   ASIA
ATLANTIC OCEAN   AFRICA
Equator
PACIFIC OCEAN   SOUTH AMERICA   INDIAN OCEAN
AUSTRALIA
ANTARCTICA
Robinson Projection

GULF OF MEXICO

N
W ⊕ E
S

Orlando •
Tampa •
St. Petersburg •
Lake Okeechobee

• Fort Myers

Fort Lauderdale •
THE BAHAMAS

• Miami

Cape Sable
FLORIDA KEYS
Straits of Florida

0   250   500 Miles
0   250   500 Kilometers
Projection: Albers Equal Area

CUBA

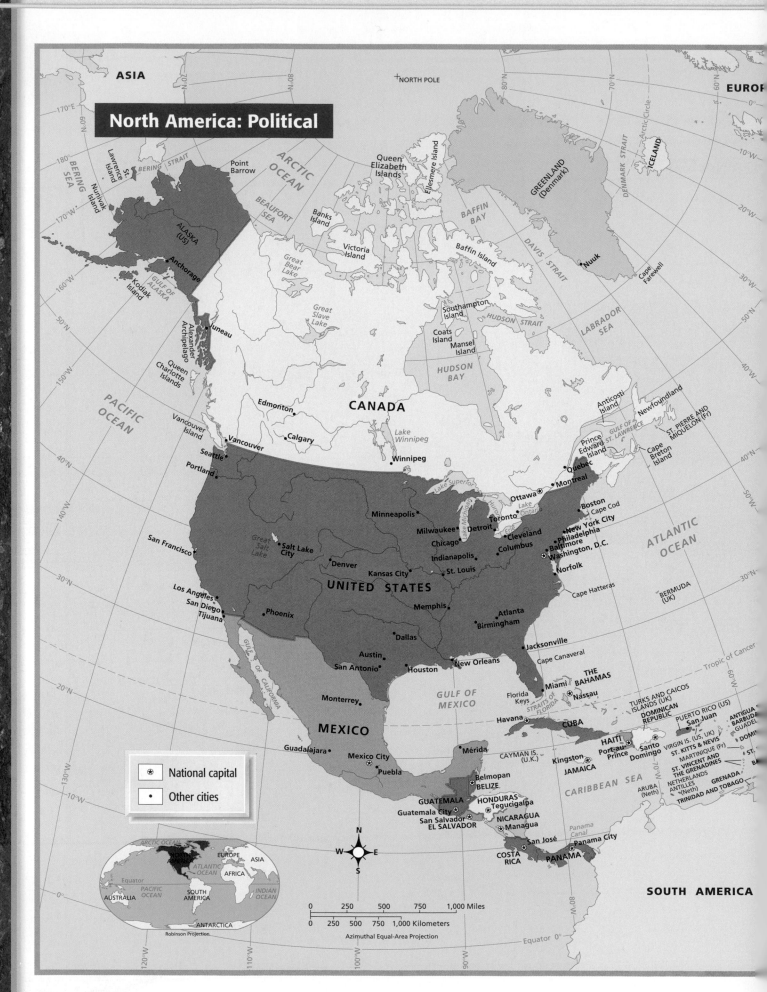

North America: Political

ASIA

+NORTH POLE

EUROP

170°E

180°

ARCTIC OCEAN

BERING SEA

St. Lawrence Island

Nunivak Island

Point Barrow

BEAUFORT SEA

Queen Elizabeth Islands

Ellesmere Island

BAFFIN BAY

GREENLAND (Denmark)

DENMARK STRAIT

ICELAND

BERING STRAIT

170°W

160°W

ALASKA (US)

Anchorage

GULF OF ALASKA

Kodiak Island

Banks Island

Victoria Island

Great Bear Lake

Baffin Island

DAVIS STRAIT

Nuuk

Cape Farewell

LABRADOR SEA

Arctic Circle

10°W

20°W

30°W

Juneau

Alexander Archipelago

Queen Charlotte Islands

Great Slave Lake

Southampton Island

Coats Island

Mansel Island

HUDSON STRAIT

60°N

50°N

PACIFIC OCEAN

150°W

Vancouver Island

Edmonton

CANADA

HUDSON BAY

Anticosti Island

Newfoundland

ST. PIERRE AND MIQUELON (Fr)

40°W

Vancouver

Calgary

Lake Winnipeg

Prince Edward Island

GULF OF ST. LAWRENCE

Cape Breton Island

40°N

Seattle

Portland

Winnipeg

Lake Superior

Quebec

Montreal

50°N

140°W

Minneapolis

Milwaukee

Detroit

Lake Michigan

Lake Huron

Ottawa

Toronto

Lake Ontario

Lake Erie

Boston

Cape Cod

New York City

ATLANTIC OCEAN

San Francisco

Great Salt Lake

Salt Lake City

Chicago

Cleveland

Columbus

Philadelphia

Baltimore

Washington, D.C.

30°N

Denver

Kansas City

Indianapolis

St. Louis

UNITED STATES

Norfolk

BERMUDA (UK)

Los Angeles

San Diego

Tijuana

Phoenix

Memphis

Atlanta

Birmingham

Cape Hatteras

30°N

Dallas

Jacksonville

Austin

San Antonio

Houston

New Orleans

Cape Canaveral

Tropic of Cancer

20°N

Monterrey

GULF OF MEXICO

Miami

Florida Keys

THE BAHAMAS

Nassau

60°W

GULF OF CALIFORNIA

MEXICO

Havana

STRAITS OF FLORIDA

CUBA

TURKS AND CAICOS ISLANDS (UK)

DOMINICAN REPUBLIC

PUERTO RICO (US)

San Juan

ANTIGUA

BARBUD

GUADEL

Guadalajara

Mexico City

Mérida

CAYMAN IS. (U.K.)

Kingston

JAMAICA

HAITI

Port-au-Prince

Santo Domingo

VIRGIN IS. (US, UK)

ST. KITTS & NEVIS

MARTINIQUE (Fr)

DOMI

ST

⊛ National capital

• Other cities

Puebla

Belmopan

BELIZE

ST. VINCENT AND THE GRENADINES

NETHERLANDS ANTILLES (Neth)

GRENADA

TRINIDAD AND TOBAGO

10°W

GUATEMALA

HONDURAS

Tegucigalpa

CARIBBEAN SEA

ARUBA (Neth)

Guatemala City

San Salvador

EL SALVADOR

NICARAGUA

Managua

Panama Canal

ARCTIC OCEAN

EUROPE

ASIA

NORTH AMERICA

ATLANTIC OCEAN

AFRICA

N

W   E

S

San José

Panama City

PACIFIC OCEAN

Equator

SOUTH AMERICA

INDIAN OCEAN

COSTA RICA

PANAMA

AUSTRALIA

SOUTH AMERICA

SOUTH AMERICA

ANTARCTICA

Robinson Projection

0   250   500   750   1,000 Miles

0   250   500   750   1,000 Kilometers

Azimuthal Equal-Area Projection

Equator 0°

120°W

110°W

100°W

90°W

South America: Political

CENTRAL
AMERICA

CARIBBEAN SEA

Barranquilla
Cartagena

Caracas

Lake
Maracaibo

VENEZUELA

Georgetown
Paramaribo

GUYANA

Cayenne

Medellín

SURINAME

FRENCH
GUIANA
(Fr)

Bogotá

ATLANTIC
OCEAN

COLOMBIA

Malpelo
Island
(Colombia)

Cali

Orinoco River

Rio Negro

Amazon River

Quito

Equator

ECUADOR

Belém

Equator 0°

Guayaquil

Amazon River

BRAZIL

PERU

Marañón River

Trujillo

Ucayali River

Recife

Callao
Lima

São Francisco River

10°S

PACIFIC
OCEAN

Lake
Titicaca

Salvador

Arequipa

BOLIVIA

La Paz

Brasília

Lake
Poopó

Sucre

Belo Horizonte

San Ambrosio
Island
(Chile)

PARAGUAY

Campinas

São Paulo

20°S

Tropic of Capricorn

San Félix Island
(Chile)

Asunción

Curitiba

Rio de Janeiro

Tropic of Capricorn

N

CHILE

Paraguay River

W   E

Paraná River

S

Pôrto Alegre

Córdoba

Uruguay River

ATLANTIC
OCEAN

30°S

Juan Fernández
Islands
(Chile)

Rosario

URUGUAY

Valparaíso
Santiago

Buenos Aires
Morón
San Justo
Lomas de Zamora

Montevideo

RIO DE LA PLATA

ARGENTINA

National capital

Other cities

ARCTIC OCEAN

NORTH
AMERICA

EUROPE

ASIA

ATLANTIC
OCEAN

AFRICA

Equator

40°S

PACIFIC
OCEAN

INDIAN
OCEAN

AUSTRALIA

SOUTH
AMERICA

ANTARCTICA

Robinson Projection

0   250   500   750   1,000 Miles

0   250   500   750   1,000 Kilometers

Azimuthal Equal-Area Projection

STRAIT OF
MAGELLAN

FALKLAND
ISLANDS (UK)

Tierra del
Fuego

SOUTH GEORGIA
ISLAND
(UK)

50°S

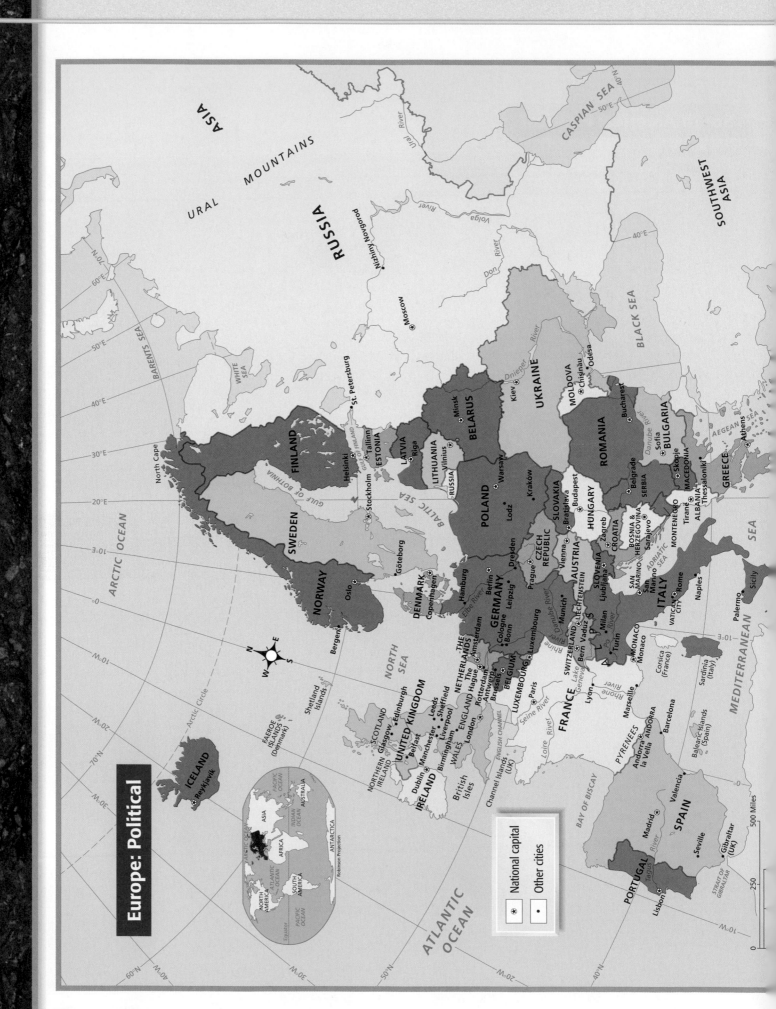

Europe: Political

ASIA

URAL MOUNTAINS

RUSSIA

CASPIAN SEA

SOUTHWEST ASIA

BARENTS SEA

WHITE SEA

Nizhniy Novgorod

Volga River

Moscow

Don River

BLACK SEA

St. Petersburg

North Cape

FINLAND

Helsinki

GULF OF FINLAND

Tallinn

ESTONIA

LATVIA

Riga

Minsk

BELARUS

Kiev

UKRAINE

MOLDOVA

Chişinău

Odesa

Bucharest

ROMANIA

BULGARIA

Sofia

Danube River

AEGEAN SEA

Athens

GREECE

SWEDEN

Stockholm

GULF OF BOTHNIA

LITHUANIA

Vilnius

RUSSIA

BALTIC SEA

POLAND

Warsaw

Łódź

Kraków

SLOVAKIA

Bratislava

HUNGARY

Budapest

Belgrade

SERBIA

Skopje

MACEDONIA

Tiranë

Thessaloníki

ALBANIA

NORWAY

Oslo

Göteborg

DENMARK

Copenhagen

Hamburg

Berlin

Elbe River

Leipzig

Dresden

Prague

CZECH REPUBLIC

Vienna

AUSTRIA

Zagreb

CROATIA

Ljubljana

SLOVENIA

BOSNIA & HERZEGOVINA

Sarajevo

MONTENEGRO

ADRIATIC SEA

SAN MARINO

San Marino

ITALY

Rome

VATICAN CITY

Naples

Sicily

Palermo

SEA

Bergen

NORTH SEA

ARCTIC OCEAN

ATLANTIC OCEAN

Arctic Circle

Shetland Islands

FAEROE ISLANDS (Denmark)

SCOTLAND

Edinburgh

Glasgow

Belfast

NORTHERN IRELAND

IRELAND

Dublin

UNITED KINGDOM

Leeds

Manchester

Sheffield

Liverpool

Birmingham

WALES

ENGLAND

London

ENGLISH CHANNEL

British Isles

Channel Islands (UK)

THE NETHERLANDS

Amsterdam

The Hague

Rotterdam

Antwerp

BELGIUM

Brussels

LUXEMBOURG

Luxembourg

GERMANY

Cologne

Bonn

Munich

Rhine River

SWITZERLAND

Bern

Vaduz

LIECHTENSTEIN

Danube River

ALPS

Lake Geneva

Milan

Turin

Po River

MONACO

Monaco

Corsica (France)

Sardinia (Italy)

MEDITERRANEAN SEA

Paris

Seine River

FRANCE

Lyon

Rhône River

Marseille

Loire River

BAY OF BISCAY

PYRENEES

ANDORRA

Andorra la Vella

Barcelona

Balearic Islands (Spain)

SPAIN

Madrid

Valencia

Seville

Gibraltar (UK)

STRAIT OF GIBRALTAR

PORTUGAL

Lisbon

Tagus River

ICELAND

Reykjavík

Legend

National capital

Other cities

ARCTIC OCEAN

ASIA

PACIFIC OCEAN

AUSTRALIA

INDIAN OCEAN

NORTH AMERICA

ATLANTIC OCEAN

AFRICA

SOUTH AMERICA

PACIFIC OCEAN

Equator

ANTARCTICA

Robinson Projection

ATLANTIC OCEAN

N E S W

0   250   500 Miles

80°N

70°N

60°N

50°N

40°N

30°N

10°W 0° 10°E 20°E 30°E 40°E 50°E

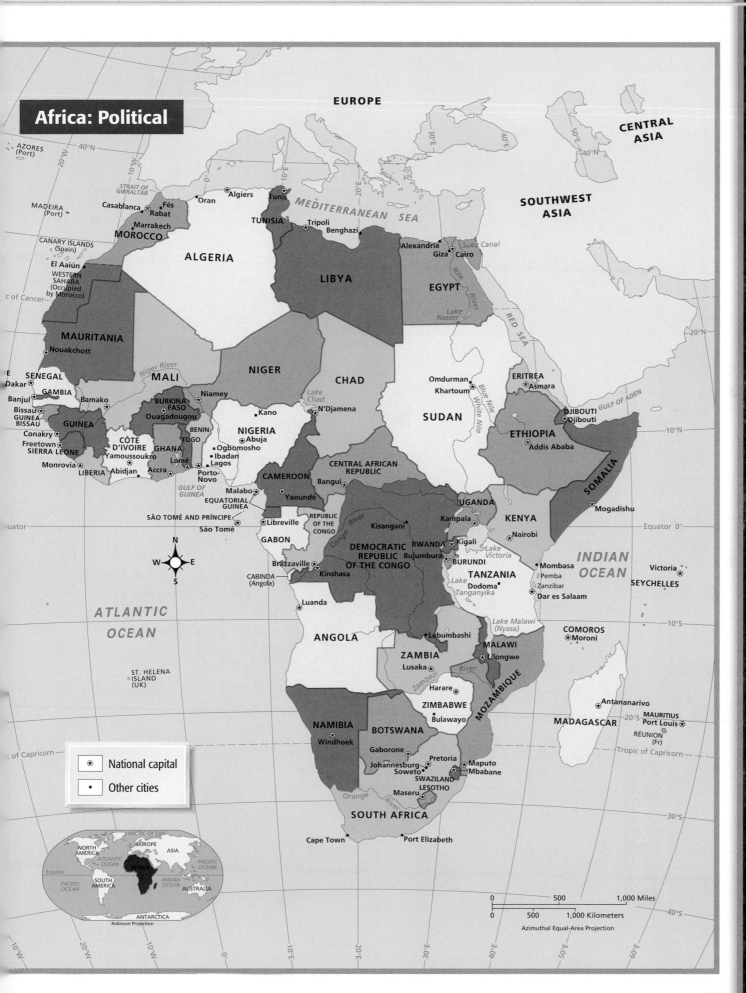

Africa: Political

EUROPE

CENTRAL ASIA

SOUTHWEST ASIA

AZORES (Port)

MADEIRA (Port)

STRAIT OF GIBRALTAR

Casablanca · Fés · Rabat · Marrakech

Oran · Algiers · Tunis

MEDITERRANEAN SEA

Tripoli · Benghazi

Suez Canal

Alexandria · Giza · Cairo

MOROCCO

CANARY ISLANDS (Spain)

ALGERIA

LIBYA

EGYPT

El Aaiún

WESTERN SAHARA (Occupied by Morocco)

c of Cancer

Lake Nasser

Nile River

RED SEA

MAURITANIA

Nouakchott

E Dakar

SENEGAL

Banjul · **GAMBIA**

Bissau · **GUINEA-BISSAU**

Bamako

MALI

NIGER

Niamey

CHAD

Omdurman · Khartoum

Blue Nile · White Nile

ERITREA

Asmara

Niger River

Lake Chad

N'Djamena

SUDAN

DJIBOUTI · Djibouti

GULF OF ADEN

Conakry · **GUINEA**

Freetown · **SIERRA LEONE**

BURKINA FASO

Ouagadougou · Kano

NIGERIA

Abuja

ETHIOPIA

Addis Ababa

Monrovia · **LIBERIA**

CÔTE D'IVOIRE

Yamoussoukro · **GHANA**

Abidjan · Accra

BENIN · **TOGO**

Lomé · Porto-Novo

· Ogbomosho · Ibadan · Lagos

CENTRAL AFRICAN REPUBLIC

Bangui

CAMEROON

GULF OF GUINEA

Malabo

EQUATORIAL GUINEA

Yaoundé

UGANDA

Kampala

SOMALIA

Mogadishu

SÃO TOMÉ AND PRÍNCIPE

São Tomé

Libreville

REPUBLIC OF THE CONGO

Congo River

Kisangani

KENYA

Nairobi

Equator 0°

uator

GABON

Brazzaville

DEMOCRATIC REPUBLIC OF THE CONGO

Kinshasa

RWANDA · Kigali

Bujumbura · **BURUNDI**

Lake Victoria

Mombasa

Pemba · Zanzibar

INDIAN OCEAN

Victoria

SEYCHELLES

CABINDA (Angola)

TANZANIA

Dodoma

Dar es Salaam

Lake Tanganyika

ATLANTIC OCEAN

Luanda

Lubumbashi

Lake Malawi (Nyasa)

COMOROS

Moroni

ANGOLA

ZAMBIA

Lusaka

MALAWI

Lilongwe

ST. HELENA ISLAND (UK)

River

Zambezi

Harare

MOZAMBIQUE

Antananarivo

ZIMBABWE

Bulawayo

MADAGASCAR

MAURITIUS Port Louis

RÉUNION (Fr)

of Capricorn

NAMIBIA

Windhoek

BOTSWANA

Gaborone

Tropic of Capricorn

Pretoria

Maputo

Johannesburg · Soweto · Mbabane

SWAZILAND

Maseru · **LESOTHO**

Orange River

SOUTH AFRICA

Cape Town

Port Elizabeth

Legend:
⊛ National capital
· Other cities

N / W–E / S

NORTH AMERICA · **EUROPE** · **ASIA**

ARCTIC OCEAN

ATLANTIC OCEAN · PACIFIC OCEAN

Equator

AFRICA · INDIAN OCEAN

PACIFIC OCEAN

SOUTH AMERICA · AUSTRALIA

ANTARCTICA

Robinson Projection

0 / 500 / 1,000 Miles
0 / 500 / 1,000 Kilometers

Azimuthal Equal-Area Projection

Asia: Political

Legend
- ⊛ National capital
- • Other cities

Australia, New Zealand, and the Pacific Islands: Political

Scale: At Equator

Miller Cylindrical Projection

Legend:
- ⊛ National capital
- • Other cities

Robinson Projection

UNIT 1

The Beginnings of Civilization

 CHAPTER 1 The Emergence of Civilization

Scholars study prehistoric peoples, such as Neanderthals and Cro-Magnons, by examining the objects they left behind. During the Stone Age, humans discovered how to make and use primitive tools, plant and grow food, and domesticate animals. The development of agriculture allowed the first civilizations to begin in four great river valleys in Asia and Africa.

CHAPTER 2 The First Civilizations

The first civilizations developed more than 5,000 years ago around two river valleys—the Nile and the Tigris-Euphrates. Due to geographic differences, Egyptian civilization lasted thousands of years, while Mesopotamia rose and fell in a series of empires. These early civilizations developed complex societies with religious beliefs, systems of law and education, and artistic traditions. They also made important technological and scientific discoveries.

CHAPTER 3 Ancient Indian Civilizations

The Harappan civilization developed in the Indus Valley about 2500 B.C. and lasted about 1,000 years,

---

EXAMINING THE VISUAL RECORD

❶ *How do you think these paintings survived for more than 17,000 years?*

ANSWER: not exposed to outside air

Four teenagers discovered the Lascaux cave in 1940. While exploring a hole left by a large fallen pine tree, the boys suddenly found themselves in a large cavern filled with magnificent prehistoric paintings. The paintings had been naturally preserved when soil built up and sealed the entrance to the cave. Lack of exposure to outside air kept the paintings in perfect condition. The chambers of the Lascaux cave contain some 600 painted and drawn animals and symbols, as well as nearly 1,500 engravings.

❷ *What do these paintings suggest about Cro-Magnons' spiritual world?*

ANSWER: celebration of animals

Archaeologists believe that Lascaux served as a ceremonial space. Early humans probably performed hunting and magical rites here over a long period of time. Lascaux is one of 130 prehistoric caves located on the northern slopes of the Pyrenees Mountains in France.

ACTIVITY: Ask students to think about the most meaningful aspects of their physical and spiritual worlds. Then have students create a visual expression of these characteristics, using symbols or other representations. Display students' artwork in the classroom.

UNIT 1

The Beginnings of Civilization

c. 3,700,000 B.C.–A.D. 589

until Aryans invaded India. During the Vedic Age, Indo-Aryans followed the Vedas, a religious text that defined Indian life for centuries. Hinduism and Buddhism eventually replaced the Vedic religion in India. Indian civilization developed distinctive styles of art, architecture, and literature under the Mauryan and Gupta Empires. Indian scientists also excelled in mathematics, astronomy, and medicine.

large and powerful empire. Important philosophies, including Daoism, Legalism, and Confucianism, appeared in China. In addition, Buddhism was introduced from India. Chinese literature, medicine, science, and technology also flourished during this time.

CHAPTER 4 Ancient Chinese Civilization

Chinese civilization developed in the Huang River valley. Under the first dynasty, the Shang, irrigation and flood-control systems were introduced. During the three succeeding dynasties—the Zhou, Qin, and Han—China grew into a

Main Events
- The beginnings of human development
- The growth of earliest civilizations
- The development of Indus Valley culture
- The rise of Chinese civilization

Main Ideas
- How did early human societies become the first civilizations?
- In what ways were the first civilizations similar? In what ways did they differ?
- How did the philosophies of Hinduism and Buddhism influence ancient Indian civilization?
- How did China's early dynasties affect the continuing development of its civilization?

Harappan metal and stone board game

These Cro-Magnon cave paintings from Lascaux Cave in present-day France date from about 15,000 B.C.

Main Events
Ask students to select two Main Events and list questions they would like to have answered about the topics. Later, when you have completed Unit 1, ask students to return to their original questions and write an answer using the information they learned in the unit.

Main Ideas
Ask each student to read the Main Ideas and write brief answers to the questions. Share the *Consider* points with students as necessary. Later, when you have completed Unit 1, ask students to analyze their original answers by comparing them to information they learned in the unit. Tell them to revise or expand their answers as necessary.

Development of the First Civilizations
Consider:
- the effects of the Neolithic agricultural revolution
- the characteristics of civilization

Characteristics of Ancient Civilizations in India and China
Consider:
- the role of religion in ancient civilization
- the influence of China's early dynasties

CROSS-CULTURAL CONNECTIONS

Focus On: Geography

 LET'S GET STARTED!

As students enter the classroom, have them study the map on page 12 and ask them to locate and name the four river valley civilizations. Explain that these civilizations will be the focus of this unit. Tell students that in this unit they will learn about the important changes in human life brought about by the Neolithic agricultural revolution, as well as the economic, social, and geographic factors that led to the development of the first civilizations.

TEACH

ALL LEVELS: Help students fill out the graphic organizer below with the information shown in italics. Then ask students to give examples of each influence from the text and from contemporary society.

ENGLISH LANGUAGE LEARNERS

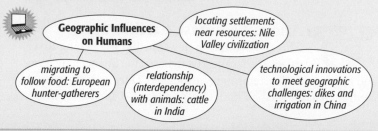

Geographic Influences on Humans
- locating settlements near resources: Nile Valley civilization
- migrating to follow food: European hunter-gatherers
- relationship (interdependency) with animals: cattle in India
- technological innovations to meet geographic challenges: dikes and irrigation in China

---

History Maker

HOWARD CARTER. One of the most famous scholars to study ancient Egypt was the British archaeologist Howard Carter (1873–1939). In 1922 Carter and his team discovered the untouched tomb of the Egyptian king, or pharaoh, Tutankhamen. King Tut—who died when he was only 18 years old—ruled Egypt about 3,300 years ago. Within the tomb, 5000 artifacts were discovered. These included a golden throne, parts of a chariot, life-sized wooden statues of King Tut, cups, jars, furniture, and a golden funeral mask that covered the king's head and shoulders. Previously, Carter had discovered the tombs of Egyptian Queen Hatshepsut and King Thutmose IV.

Critical Thinking

What do you think scholars learned from the artifacts found in King Tutankhamen's tomb?

ANSWER: Answers will vary. Students might suggest religious practices, daily life, use of local resources, and scientific achievements.

CROSS-CULTURAL CONNECTIONS

Focus On: Geography

Main Idea How did geography affect early societies? The early history of human beings was greatly shaped by geography. Early hunter-gatherers migrated in search of food, Egyptians relied on the mighty Nile River, Indians domesticated animals that could manage their rough terrain, and the Chinese built dikes to control annual flooding.

	Cro-Magnon		Egypt	India	China	

c. 33,000 B.C.   c. 8000 B.C.   c. 3200 B.C.   c. 1500 B.C.   c. 2500 B.C.   c. 300 B.C.   A.D. 550   A.D. 589

Hunter-gatherers Early hunter-gatherers traveled in search of food. In the northeastern region of Europe, where timber was scarce, people used the bones of giant mammoths to build shelters similar to the museum model shown here. Hunter-gatherer groups moved to different sites throughout the year, returning to these shelters on a regular basis. They dug oval holes in the ground and carefully arranged the bones above the holes to create a strong frame. The frames were then covered with mammoth skins. These mammoth-bone houses probably took ten people between five and six days to build.

Cro-Magnon, c. 33,000 B.C.–c. 8000 B.C.

Egyptian Civilization The presence of natural resources often determined patterns and distributions of early human settlement and activity. The annual flood cycle of Egypt's Nile River, for example, produced rich deposits of topsoil and created an excellent farming and herding environment. The river itself, moreover, provided a natural transportation highway. Early farming settlements grew along the river. Over time, some of these communities developed into religious and political centers as well as sources of food, trade, and transportation.

Egypt, c. 3200 B.C.–300 B.C.

Have students review the information about geographic influences on civilizations. Ask them to use standard grammar, spelling, sentence structure, and punctuation to answer the question in "Why it Matters Today" and to share their answers with the class.

ASSESS

Have students complete their answer to the question in "Why It Matters Today" and add it to their portfolio. As Alternative Assessment, you may want to use the graphic organizer in this lesson.

EXTEND

Have students choose one of the four river valley civilizations and research its geography. Tell students to use information from their textbooks, the library, computer software, and any other available resources to determine how geographic factors influenced that particular civilization. Have students present their findings in an oral report to the class. **BLOCK SCHEDULING**

Interdependence in Early India India is a land of great geographic variety. Rugged mountains, arid deserts, humid jungles, and fertile plains share the sub-continent. India's early people relied for food and labor upon strong animals that could survive the region's geographic challenges. Whether herded through rocky mountain passes or grazed on plains grasslands, cattle were a valuable resource. Cow's milk was a staple of the early Indian diet. Early farmers used cattle to pull carts and plows. Cattle became so valuable to early Indian civilization that they were used as money and were viewed as sacred beings.

India, c. 2500 B.C.—A.D. 550

Carved stone bull image, c. 2500 B.C.—1700 B.C.

Chinese Dikes and Tools The availability and use of natural resources often affects the way people live. In ancient China, people responded to the challenges of their surrounding geography by developing effective flood-control and irrigation systems. Dikes held back damaging floodwaters, while canals linked river systems and improved trade and transportation. Irrigation systems turned arid soil into rich farmland. China's early people also used other natural resources to improve their living conditions. For example, the Chinese used iron to make tools, weapons, and equipment.

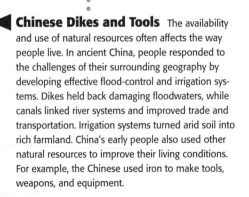

China, c. 1500 B.C.—A.D. 589

Chinese iron-casting mold, c. 500—300 B.C.

Why It Matters Today

People and societies of today, like early people and civilizations, are strongly influenced by geographic factors such as landforms, weather patterns, and the availability of natural resources. **How does the influence of geography today compare with its influence on early peoples and civilizations?**

Culture

The religions that developed in early Indian civilization taught respect and even reverence for animals. Hindus and Buddhists believed all forms of life are equally important and that each creature is an incarnation of a single energy or life force. They believed that when a being died, this energy was reincarnated in another life form. Therefore, killing any other being was inconceivable, because it might be the soul of an ancestor or a friend.

Critical Thinking

How might religious beliefs have affected Indians' diets?

ANSWER: Indians following these religions probably would have been vegetarians because killing animals went against their religious beliefs.

WHY IT MATTERS TODAY ANSWER

Answers will vary, but students might say most people today do not have to migrate to find their food; geographic factors continue to influence the economic development of places and regions today; people now rely more on machines than on animals to overcome geographic obstacles; and people continue to modify their environment with mechanisms such as dikes and irrigation.

The Emergence of Civilization

CHAPTER RESOURCE MANAGER

Objectives	Pacing Guide	Reproducible Resources
SECTION 1 **Prehistoric Peoples** (pp. 6–10) • Describe how anthropologists, archaeologists, historians, and geographers study prehistory. • Identify the major achievements of Neanderthal and Cro-Magnon peoples. • Explain the important changes caused by the Neolithic agricultural revolution.	**Regular** 1.5 day **Block Scheduling** 1 day *Block Scheduling Handbook with Team Teaching Strategies, 1.1*	**RS** Guided Reading Strategy 1.1 **RS** Graphic Organizer Activity 1: The Prehistoric **SM** Geography Activity 1: Anthropology and Geology **PS** Readings in World History 1: The Task of the Archaeologist **PS** Readings in World History 2: The Nomadic Life **PS** Readings in World History 3: The First Painters **PS** Readings in World History 4: An Early Agricultural Village **E** Hands-on History Activity 1: On the Archaeological Trail **E** Creative Teaching Strategy 1: Time Lines of Prehistoric Peoples
SECTION 2 **The Foundations of Civilization** (pp. 11–15) • Identify the three main characteristics shared by civilizations. • Explain what other two characteristics may be shared by civilizations. • Describe the other characteristics and achievements that marked the first river valley civilizations.	**Regular** 1.5 day **Block Scheduling** 1 day *Block Scheduling Handbook with Team Teaching Strategies, 1.2*	**RS** Guided Reading Strategy 1.2

Chapter Resource Key

PS Primary Sources
RS Reading Support
IC Interdisciplinary Connections
E Enrichment
SM Skills Mastery
A Assessment

REV Review
ELL Reinforcement and English Language Learners
 Transparencies
 CD-ROM
 Music

 Video
 Internet
 Holt Presentation Maker Using Microsoft® PowerPoint®

 One-Stop Planner CD-ROM

See the **One-Stop Planner** for a complete list of additional resources for students and teachers.

One-Stop Planner CD-ROM

It's easy to plan lessons, select resources, and print out materials for your students when you use the *One-Stop Planner* CD–ROM with *Test Generator.*

Technology Resources

- One-Stop Planner 1.1
- Holt Researcher: World History: Mary Leakey
- CNN Presents World Cultures: Yesterday and Today Segment 1: The Kennewick Man
- World History Teaching Transparencies: Geography and History 1: World Domestication
- World History Teaching Transparencies: Art and History 1: Hall of the Bulls, Lascaux Cave
- Online Maps, Charts, and Graphs: Early Agriculture in Asia

- One-Stop Planner 1.2
- World History and Cultures Video Program 1: The Rise of Civilization
- Homework Practice Online

Reinforcement, Review, and Assessment

Daily Quiz 1.1

Main Idea Activity 1.1

English Audio Summary 1.1

Spanish Audio Summary 1.1

REV Section 1 Review, p. 10

Daily Quiz 1.2

Main Idea Activity 1.2

English Audio Summary 1.2

Spanish Audio Summary 1.2

REV Section 2 Review, p. 15

internet connect

HRW ONLINE RESOURCES
GO TO: go.hrw.com
Then type in a keyword.

TEACHER HOME PAGE
KEYWORD: SP3 Teacher

CHAPTER INTERNET ACTIVITIES
KEYWORD: SP3 WH1
Choose an activity to:
- analyze artifacts from an archaeological site.
- compare and contrast a modern calendar used in the United States with calendars of different cultures.
- list different divisions of labor in modern society.

CHAPTER ENRICHMENT LINKS
KEYWORD: SP3 CH1

ONLINE ASSESSMENT
Homework Practice
KEYWORD: SP3 HP1
Standardized Test Prep
KEYWORD: SP3 STP1
Rubrics
KEYWORD: SS Rubrics

ONLINE MAPS, CHARTS, AND GRAPHS
KEYWORD: SP3 MCG

CONTENT UPDATES
KEYWORD: SS Content Updates

HOLT PRESENTATION MAKER
KEYWORD: SP3 PPT1

ONLINE READING SUPPORT
KEYWORD: SS Strategies

CURRENT EVENTS
KEYWORD: S3 Current Events

Meeting Individual Needs

Ability Levels

Level 1 Basic level activities designed for all students encountering new material

Level 2 Intermediate level activities designed for average students

Level 3 Challenging activities designed for honors and gifted and talented students

English Language Learners These activities address the needs of students with Limited English Proficiency.

Chapter Review and Assessment

IC Vocabulary Activity 1

Global Skill Builder CD–ROM

HRW Web Site

REV Chapter 1 Tutorial for Students, Parents, Mentors, and Peers

REV Chapter 1 Review, pp. 16–17

A Chapter 1 Test Generator (on the One-Stop Planner)

A Chapter 1 Test (Form A or B)

A Alternative Assessment Handbook

A Chapter 1 Test for English Language Learners and Special-Needs Students

Build on What You Know

Ask students to answer the following questions:

What basic things do all humans share? What do people need to advance beyond simple survival?
Consider:

- the necessities of life
- the reasons that people form groups
- the role of technology in human survival and progress

How might early humans have met these needs?
Consider:

- the interaction between humans and their environments
- geographic factors that help to shape human standards of living
- scientific discoveries and technological innovations that enable humans to gain control of their surroundings

---

EXPLORING THE TIME LINE
GLOBAL EVENTS

internet connect

TOPIC: Early Human Settlement

GO TO: go.hrw.com

KEYWORD: SP3 WH1

Have students access the Internet through the HRW Go site to conduct research on the geographic patterns and factors of early human settlement. Then ask students to compose an informative report that details how geographic conditions influenced where early humans settled and how they met basic needs such as food and shelter. Students' reports should include appropriate examples and evidence drawn from their research.

CHAPTER 1

3,700,000 B.C.–1200 B.C.

The Emergence of Civilization

Prehistoric cave painting from Lascaux Cave, France

c. 3,400,000 B.C.
Global Events
The Isthmus of Panama forms as a land bridge linking the Americas.

c. 1,800,000 B.C.
Global Events
Early humans migrate from Africa to Asia.

c. 500,000 B.C.–300,000 B.C.
Science and Technology
People are using fire.

c. 33,000 B.C.
The Arts
Cro-Magnon people create cave paintings.

4,000,000 B.C.		500,000 B.C.	30,000 B.C.

c. 3,700,000 B.C.
Daily Life
Wandering Australopithecus leave footprints in volcanic ash, proving to modern anthropologists that early hominids walked upright.

c. 2,500,000 B.C.
Science and Technology
The first stone tools appear.

c. 400,000 B.C.–100,000 B.C.
Daily Life
The first *Homo sapiens* appear.

Anthropologist Mary Leakey measures prehistoric footprints near Olduvai Gorge, Tanzania.

Neolithic stone axes and carved ivory tool

Build on What You Know

H istory is the record of events since people first developed writing, about 5,000 years ago. People, however, have lived on earth for far more than 5,000 years. The period of time before writing was developed is called prehistory. In this chapter, you will learn about prehistory— how and why we study it, how the prehistoric record has helped to shape the present, and how prehistoric humans gradually developed the first civilized societies. You will learn, too, how and why our understanding of prehistory is continually changing as a result of scientific discoveries, new tools, and new ways of thinking about the past.

What's Your Opinion?

To help students create their Themes Journal entries, provide the following examples of appropriate **agree**/**disagree** *statements.*

Culture

Agree The development of culture enables people to live and work together based on cooperation and shared values.

Disagree Biological and physical differences and the human brain do more than culture to set humans apart from other creatures.

Geography

Agree When humans seek a place to settle, geography and climate are not of primary importance.

Disagree Physical environment is the most important factor in determining whether a civilization develops.

Economics

Agree Farming is an economic activity fundamental to all civilizations.

Disagree Manufacturing and trade form the basis of all human economies.

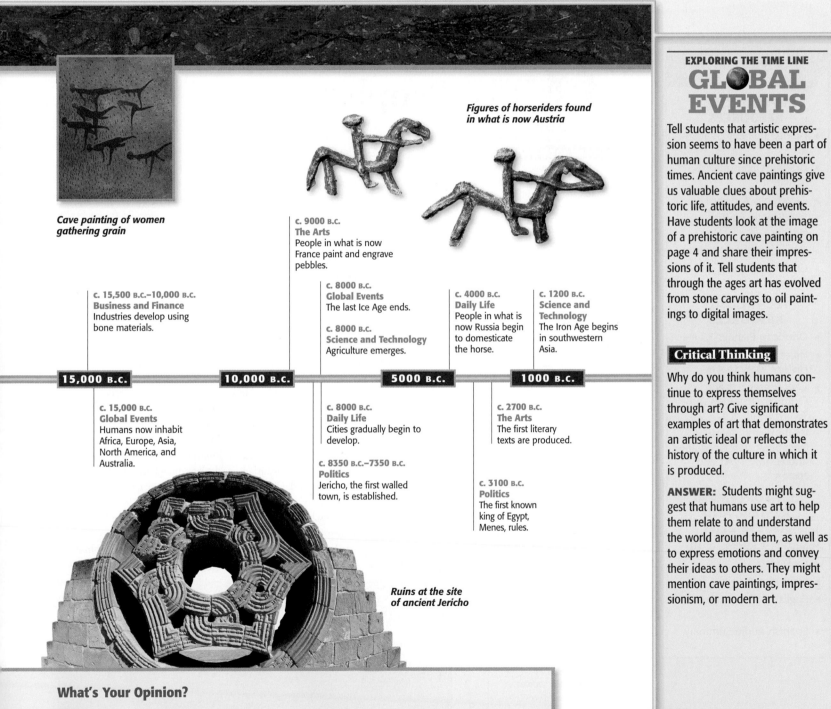

Figures of horseriders found in what is now Austria

Cave painting of women gathering grain

c. 9000 B.C.
The Arts
People in what is now France paint and engrave pebbles.

c. 15,500 B.C.–10,000 B.C.
Business and Finance
Industries develop using bone materials.

c. 8000 B.C.
Global Events
The last Ice Age ends.

c. 8000 B.C.
Science and Technology
Agriculture emerges.

c. 4000 B.C.
Daily Life
People in what is now Russia begin to domesticate the horse.

c. 1200 B.C.
Science and Technology
The Iron Age begins in southwestern Asia.

| 15,000 B.C. | 10,000 B.C. | 5000 B.C. | 1000 B.C. |

c. 15,000 B.C.
Global Events
Humans now inhabit Africa, Europe, Asia, North America, and Australia.

c. 8000 B.C.
Daily Life
Cities gradually begin to develop.

c. 8350 B.C.–7350 B.C.
Politics
Jericho, the first walled town, is established.

c. 2700 B.C.
The Arts
The first literary texts are produced.

c. 3100 B.C.
Politics
The first known king of Egypt, Menes, rules.

Ruins at the site of ancient Jericho

EXPLORING THE TIME LINE
GLOBAL EVENTS

Tell students that artistic expression seems to have been a part of human culture since prehistoric times. Ancient cave paintings give us valuable clues about prehistoric life, attitudes, and events. Have students look at the image of a prehistoric cave painting on page 4 and share their impressions of it. Tell students that through the ages art has evolved from stone carvings to oil paintings to digital images.

Critical Thinking

Why do you think humans continue to express themselves through art? Give significant examples of art that demonstrates an artistic ideal or reflects the history of the culture in which it is produced.

ANSWER: Students might suggest that humans use art to help them relate to and understand the world around them, as well as to express emotions and convey their ideas to others. They might mention cave paintings, impressionism, or modern art.

What's Your Opinion?

Do you **agree** *or* **disagree** *with the following statements? Support your point of view in your journal.*

Culture The most important factor that sets humans apart from other creatures is the development of culture.

Geography Physical environment has little, if any, influence on the development of a civilization.

Economics Farming and the domestication of animals are the most basic of human economic activities.

OBJECTIVES

1 **Describe how anthropologists, archaeologists, historians, and geographers study prehistory.**

2 **Identify the major achievements of Neanderthal and Cro-Magnon peoples.**

3 **Explain the important changes caused by the Neolithic agricultural revolution.**

SECTION 1

READ TO DISCOVER

❶ How do anthropologists, archaeologists, historians, and geographers study prehistory?
❷ What were the achievements of Neanderthal and Cro-Magnon peoples?
❸ What important changes did the Neolithic agricultural revolution cause?

DEFINE

hominids
artifacts
culture
limited evidence
nomads
agriculture
domestication
hunter-gatherers

IDENTIFY

Donald Johanson
Lucy
Mary Leakey
Neanderthals
Cro-Magnons
Neolithic agricultural revolution

WHY IT MATTERS TODAY

How scientists study and draw conclusions from prehistoric remains and artifacts affects our understanding of humans and of our place on Earth. Use CNNfyi.com or other **current event** sources to explore recent discoveries by anthropologists, archaeologists, historians, and geographers. Record your findings in your journal.

CNNfyi.com

Prehistoric Peoples

The Main Idea
The cultures of early peoples gradually changed as humans adapted to environmental shifts.

The Story Continues *Many researchers have long believed that human beings originated in Africa. In 1974 a team of researchers went out seeking evidence that might support this claim. In November of that year, in a place called Hadar in Ethiopia, the team found some very convincing evidence—the oldest humanlike skeleton discovered up to that time.*

Exploring Prehistory

Scientists have discovered much about prehistory by using scientific methods. For example, scientists called anthropologists study the remains of the skeletons of **hominids.** Hominids include humans as well as earlier humanlike creatures. By studying their remains, anthropologists can figure out what early hominids looked like. They can also determine how long the hominids lived.

Other scientists, called archaeologists, dig into ancient settlements to find objects made and used by early hominids. These objects—including tools, clothing, works of art, weapons, and toys—are **artifacts.** By studying artifacts, archaeologists learn about early peoples and their cultures. **Culture** is the set of beliefs, knowledge, and patterns of living that a group of people develops. Anthropologists and archaeologists use advanced technology to date remains and artifacts. Because artifacts give **limited evidence,** however, anthropologists, archaeologists, historians, and geographers must make educated guesses about the prehistoric world. Using their knowledge of geography and climate, scientists draw conclusions. They make judgments about changes that took place many thousands of years ago to describe some of the ways the first human beings lived.

Anthropologists have found evidence that humanlike creatures appeared on Earth millions of years ago. In 1974 in Ethiopia, a team led by **Donald Johanson** found the remains of a hominid skeleton.

Archaeologists carefully unearth artifacts in "digs" such as this one.

TEACH OBJECTIVE 1

LEVEL 1: Ask a volunteer to read aloud the first two paragraphs under "Exploring Prehistory" on page 6. Then ask students to explain what anthropologists and archaeologists do. *(Anthropologists study the remains of the skeletons of hominids. Archaeologists dig into ancient settlements and study the artifacts they find.)* Have another volunteer read the next paragraph before asking students to describe how scientists date remains and artifacts. *(They use advanced technology but must also make educated guesses because artifacts give limited evidence.)* **ENGLISH LANGUAGE LEARNERS**

⏩ internet connect

Internet Activity: go.hrw.com
TOPIC: Archaeology **KEYWORD: SP3 WH1**

Have students access the Internet through the HRW Go site to learn more about archaeological finds. Have students select artifacts or archaeological sites that interest them and write a short informative article that could be published in the student science magazine. Have them describe their topic in detail: What is it? Where is it located? Who created it? If possible, have students include illustrations with their article.

The bones Johanson found belonged to a female hominid who may have lived 3 million years ago. Johanson and his team named the skeleton **Lucy** after the Beatles song "Lucy in the Sky with Diamonds." Johanson later described his remarkable discovery.

> **❝I spent the morning of November 30 scanning the ground for fossils . . . At midday, under a murderous sun and in temperatures topping 100 degrees, we reluctantly headed back toward camp. Along the way I glanced over my right shoulder. Light glinted off a bone. I knelt down for a closer look. This time I knew at once I was looking at a hominid elbow. . . . Everywhere we looked on the slope around us we saw more bones lying on the surface. Here was the hominid skeleton . . .❞**
>
> Donald Johanson, from *Ancestors: In Search of Human Origins*, by Donald Johanson, Lenora Johanson, and Blake Edgar

Other researchers added to the findings of Johanson's team. In the late 1970s in Tanzania, anthropologist **Mary Leakey** found parts of a skeleton dating back about 3.7 million years. Like Lucy, this hominid belonged to a group called Australopithecus (aw·stray·lo·PI·thuh·kuhs), or "southern ape." These hominids walked upright, like humans. Other hominids lived in East Africa 2 million years ago. Tools made from chipped stone have been found near their remains.

The period of prehistory that begins with the development of stone tools is called the Stone Age. It began about 2.5 million years ago. Almost all the artifacts that have been found from this time were made of stone. The oldest part is called the Old Stone, or Paleolithic (pay·lee·uh·LI·thik), Age. The word *paleolithic* comes from two Greek words: *palaios* ("ancient") and *lithos* ("stone"). The Old Stone Age lasted for more than 2 million years—until about 12,000 years ago.

✔ **READING CHECK: Finding the Main Idea** What limited evidence did Donald Johanson and Mary Leakey examine to learn about early hominids? *skeletal remains, artifacts*

Early Humans

There is limited evidence from prehistory about early humans. Therefore, many scientists disagree about what conclusions can be drawn about them. Future discoveries may change the ideas that many scientists hold today.

The first people. From studying bones, anthropologists can describe what the first humans looked like. These individuals had powerful jaws, receding chins, low foreheads, and heavy eyebrow ridges. Scientists believe they sometimes used caves as shelters. They probably ate seeds, fruits, nuts, and other plants. Eventually, they hunted—first small and then large animals. To hunt successfully, they had to make tools, work together, and communicate.

As humans became successful hunters, they migrated, or moved over great distances, in search of food. Over many generations, early people migrated from Africa to Asia. At some point, probably between 100,000 and 400,000 years ago, a new human species, *Homo sapiens,* appeared. *Homo sapiens* may have developed first in Africa, then spread to Europe and Asia. All people living today belong to this species.

The Ice Age. Several times within the last 1.7 million years, Earth has had periods of extremely cold weather. Each cold period lasted from 20,000 to about 140,000 years. Together these periods are called the Ice Age. Scientists believe we live in a warm era that began about 10,000 years ago. That is when the last period of the Ice Age ended.

Analyzing Primary Sources

Drawing Conclusions What evidence might Donald Johanson have used to draw his conclusion that the bones were those of a hominid? *skeletal remains*

HISTORY MAKER
Lucy
(c. 3,000,000 B.C.)

After examining the hominid skeleton called Lucy, researchers concluded that the young female had walked upright, like humans do. Scientists are still not certain whether modern humans are related to Lucy and Australopithecines. An upright posture, however, leaves the hands free to use tools. Many scientists believe that this was a major step in early human development. **What evidence indicates Lucy might be related to modern humans?**

History Maker

MARY LEAKEY. Mary Leakey knew she wanted to be an anthropologist at age 11 when she visited a Cro-Magnon rock shelter containing early modern human fossils. As an adult, Leakey became an expert in early human technology and stone tools. She participated in numerous pioneering excavations in East Africa and elsewhere.

ACTIVITY: Have students find out more about Mary Leakey. Ask them to create a time line that shows her major finds.

Interdisciplinary Connection

STRATIGRAPHY. One way to verify artifacts' ages is through stratigraphy. It assumes that objects found in deeper layers of earth are older than those found above them. Stratigraphy is not very exact, however. Layers of earth can shift, and objects within them could range in age.

Critical Thinking

How might an archaeologist rely on stratigraphy to date a site or an artifact?

ANSWER: Archaeologists could use their knowledge about the age of layers of earth to guide them in their digging.

HISTORY MAKER ANSWER
her upright posture, structure of hands, feet, skull

ALL LEVELS: Tell students that a significant part of trying to understand the lives of prehistoric people is understanding the environment in which they probably lived. Using the information under "The Ice Age" on pages 7–8, point out the extreme challenges presented by the environment for many thousands of years. Help students further explore what scientists have learned about prehistoric peoples by having them complete a Venn diagram comparing and contrasting the Neanderthal and Cro-Magnon peoples. **ENGLISH LANGUAGE LEARNERS**

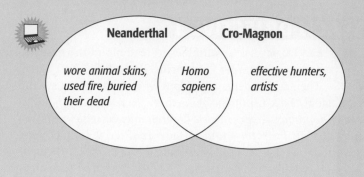

Neanderthal — *wore animal skins, used fire, buried their dead* — Homo sapiens — Cro-Magnon — *effective hunters, artists*

Science, Technology & Society

Hearths have been discovered with the remains of Peking man, who lived approximately 500,000 years ago. With the advent of controlled fire, prehistoric people apparently learned to cook their meat, making it easier to chew and eliminating the need for a powerful jaw and large teeth. The mastery of fire also allowed people to live in colder parts of the world.

Critical Thinking

Ask students how hominids may have learned to master fire.

ANSWER: Lightning may have started a fire, and hominids learned how to keep it burning.

WHAT IF? ANSWER

People and animals might not have migrated to the Americas. Prehistoric species of animals might have survived, and humans might not have learned to use fire or other survival techniques as quickly. Finally, Earth's geography would have been vastly different without the chiseling and grinding effects of glaciers.

CONNECTING TO ART ANSWER

Some prehistoric peoples had an appreciation of beauty similar to ours, and some groups had time for artistic creation.

What If? If there had been no Ice Age, how might prehistory have been different?

Holt Researcher
go.hrw.com
KEYWORD: Holt Researcher
FreeFind: Mary Leakey
After reading more about Mary Leakey on the Holt Researcher, draw a sketch of one of her findings and explain what conclusions she reached from it.

CONNECTING TO Art

Sculpture: Cro-Magnon Carving

A Cro-Magnon artist in what is now France carved this ivory head of a woman thousands of years ago, during the Old Stone Age. From artifacts such as this, we learn that some prehistoric peoples had an appreciation of beauty, as we do. We also learn that some groups had time for activities other than looking for food and making tools.

Understanding the Arts

What can we learn from this Cro-Magnon art?

During the cold periods, ice covered a large part of Earth's surface. Sea levels dropped because so much seawater was locked in large ice caps. As sea levels fell, ridges that had been underwater were uncovered, forming land bridges between some regions that are today separated by water. Humans and animals migrated over some of these land bridges. However, only when prehistoric people learned to make fire and clothing could they settle in colder regions.

Neanderthal people. In caves in Europe and Southwest Asia, anthropologists have found remains of early *Homo sapiens* called **Neanderthals** (nee·AN·duhr·tawls). Neanderthals lived about 35,000 to 130,000 years ago, during the Old Stone Age. They wore animal skins as clothing and used fire for warmth and for cooking. Their tools were more efficient than the tools of earlier hominids.

Neanderthals also differed from earlier hominids in another important way—they buried their dead. What is more, they buried meat and tools with the dead. Scientists think this shows that Neanderthals believed in some form of life after death. Belief in an afterlife is basic to many of the world's religions.

Like earlier hominids, Neanderthals disappeared. No one knows why. Perhaps a new period of the Ice Age began, producing a cold, hostile environment. Or perhaps another group of *Homo sapiens*—stronger or more mentally alert—destroyed or interbred with them.

Cro-Magnon people. About 35,000 years ago, another kind of *Homo sapiens*—the **Cro-Magnons**—appeared in Europe. These new people made even better tools and weapons. Their spear-throwers, for example, made them effective hunters. Cro-Magnons were thus well equipped to survive.

Scientists know something about Cro-Magnons from their artwork. Paintings of the animals they hunted have been found. On cave walls in Spain and southern France, bulls toss their heads. Wounded bison chase a hunter. Long horses leap majestically. Scientists are not sure, however, why Cro-Magnons painted such scenes. The art might be the story of a hunt. It could be a "textbook" to teach young hunters. Or it may be a creation myth.

By about 20,000 years ago, humans had migrated to northern Asia and Australia. This movement of people into new areas marks humans' ability to adapt—to live and succeed in many different environments.

The Cro-Magnons lived on Earth for many thousands of years. By about 10,000 years ago, however, Cro-Magnons as distinct types of humans no longer existed. In appearance, people looked basically like they do today.

✔ **READING CHECK: Summarizing** What important advances did Neanderthal and Cro-Magnon peoples make? fire, clothing, better tools, artwork

The Agricultural Revolution

The Middle Stone Age and the New Stone Age followed the Old Stone Age. The dates for each age vary in different regions of the world. Generally, however, the Middle Stone Age lasted until about 10,000 years ago. The New Stone Age lasted to about 4,000 years ago. Each age is marked by a new level of tools and other artifacts. In addition, the New Stone Age is marked by a revolutionary human activity.

LEVEL 3: Have students create illustrated time lines with known facts about life during the Paleolithic, Mesolithic, and Neolithic time periods. They should include several appropriate illustrations to help clarify advancements in the lives of early humans during each time period. Have several volunteers share their time lines. Point out that the Neolithic agricultural revolution was one of the most significant turning points in human history. Ask students to explain why the rise of agriculture was so important to human development. *(It allowed people to establish permanent settlements and produce a surplus of food, paving the way for the development of civilizations.)*

HOMEWORK Assign each student to one time period: Paleolithic, Mesolithic, or Neolithic. Have each student develop a brief oral presentation about his or her time period. Encourage students to include environmental and physical challenges faced by people of their time periods and to describe the technological advances made during the era to meet these challenges.

CLOSE

Discuss the change from hunting and gathering to agriculture, including economic, social, and geographic factors. How did a hunter-gatherer society differ from an agricultural society?

The Middle Stone Age is also called the Mesolithic Age (from the Greek word *mesos,* meaning "middle"). During the Mesolithic Age, the use of the bow and arrow, fishhooks, fish spears, and harpoons made from bones and antlers was widespread. People tamed dogs, which were useful in hunting smaller animals. Humans also hollowed out logs to make dugout canoes so they could fish in deep water and cross rivers.

The New Stone Age is also called the Neolithic Age (from the Greek word *neos,* meaning "new"). During the Neolithic Age, technology continued to improve. In earlier ages, people chipped stone to produce an edge or a point. In the Neolithic Age, people shaped stone tools by polishing or grinding. They also discovered ways to make tools from many kinds of stone as well as from wood. With such new methods and materials, people were able to make more specialized tools. Even more important changes occurred during the New Stone Age. Earlier people had been **nomads,** wandering from place to place in search of food. Some Neolithic people, however, began settling in permanent villages. They began to develop **agriculture**—the raising of crops for food. They practiced **domestication**—the taming of animals such as cattle, goats, sheep, and pigs.

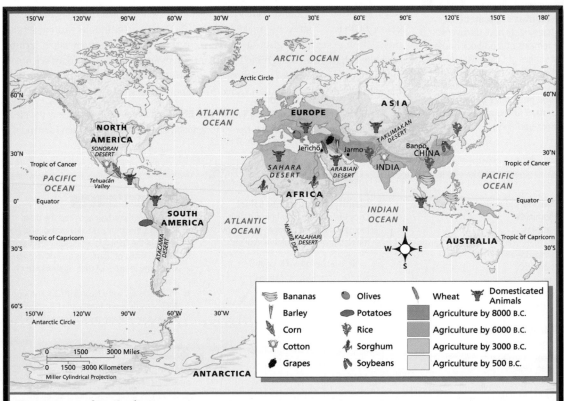

Emergence of Agriculture

Interpreting Maps Agricultural techniques spread throughout early human societies over a period of thousands of years.

■ **Skills Assessment: Human Systems** What crops did the earliest farmers grow? What crops did later farmers grow?

Culture

Many cultures throughout history—including some American Indian and African cultures—have held beliefs about life after death, as evidenced by their burial rituals. Like the Neanderthal, people of such cultures buried food, tools, and luxury items with their dead, presumably for use by the deceased in the afterlife. In modern American society, the majority of people are buried or cremated following religious or secular ceremonies of farewell.

Critical Thinking

Ask students to consider modern American burial customs. What parts, if any, of the typical American burial ritual may have been practiced by our ancestors?

ANSWER: Students might point out that we tend to bury our dead dressed in their best, with jewelry and beloved objects to accompany them into the grave.

MAP ANSWER
earliest farmers: rice, barley
later farmers: potatoes, corn

Technology Resources
go. hrw .com Online Maps, Charts, and Graphs: Early Agriculture in Asia

REVIEW

Have students complete the Section 1 Review on p. 10.

ASSESS

Have students complete Daily Quiz 1.1. As Alternative Assessment, you may want to use the Venn diagram or time line exercise in this section's lessons.

RETEACH

Have students complete Main Idea Activity for English Language Learners and Special-Needs Students 1.1. Then have students list the main ideas of each heading and subheading in the section. **ENGLISH LANGUAGE LEARNERS**

EXTEND

Organize the class into four groups and have each group use the process of historical inquiry to research a method of dating archaeological finds: radiocarbon dating, potassium-argon dating, dendrochronology, or stratigraphy. Have each group teach the rest of the students about the method it researched, using a visual based on written or statistical information. **BLOCK SCHEDULING, COOPERATIVE LEARNING**

VISUAL RECORD ANSWER

Students might point out that hunter-gatherers moved around; therefore they had no permanent villages.

SECTION 1 REVIEW ANSWERS

❶ Define
- hominids, p. 6
- artifacts, p. 6
- culture, p. 6
- limited evidence, p. 6
- nomads, p. 9
- agriculture, p. 9
- domestication, p. 9
- hunter-gatherers, p. 10

❷ Identify
- Donald Johanson, p. 6
- Lucy, p. 7
- Mary Leakey, p. 7
- Neanderthals, p. 8
- Cro-Magnons, p. 8
- Neolithic agricultural revolution, p. 10

❸ hunter-gatherers turned to farming; hunting-and-gathering settlements became farming settlements; development of cities

❹ a. advantages: shift from food gathering to food producing, growth of cities; disadvantages: dependence on weather, threats of crop failure

b. Australopithecus, Neanderthal, Cro-Magnon

c. They buried their dead. Cro-Magnons had more advanced tools and weapons, fire, and clothing.

❺ Scientists use technology to date artifacts. They must make educated guesses and draw conclusions.

INTERPRETING THE VISUAL RECORD

A Neolithic settlement
Archaeologists have discovered the remains of mud-brick houses and shrines at Çatalhüyük in Turkey. *What evidence would tell archaeologists that such a village must have been home to settled farmers rather than hunter-gatherers?*

The development of agriculture changed the basic way people lived. In prehistoric times people were **hunter-gatherers.** Men went out to hunt animals. Women remained near the campsite to care for children. Women and children gathered plants and fruit for food. Perhaps it was a woman who first realized that seeds could be planted and grown. The knowledge that grains and other plants grew from seeds was a major breakthrough in human progress.

Over time people learned to raise wheat, barley, rice, and millet. They learned to make furrows in the earth—probably first using sharpened sticks—in which to plant seeds. The invention of the plow and the use of fertilizer marked major steps in the human record. The shift from food gathering to food producing was an achievement of the greatest importance. It revolutionized human life, which is why we call this long process the **Neolithic agricultural revolution.**

Between about 9000 B.C. and about 5000 B.C., many hunting-and-gathering settlements throughout the world turned to farming. Some grew larger and more complex. In fact, many Neolithic villages developed into small cities. For example, in Jericho, on the west bank of the Jordan River, scientists have found evidence of a Neolithic walled town that may date from before 8000 B.C. That would make it one of the earliest continuous human settlements. In Iraq, archaeologists have discovered the remains of a town called Jarmo, which may have had 100 or more inhabitants in about 6500 B.C. In Turkey, scientists have dug out Çatalhüyük (chah·TUHL·hoo·YOOHK). This town, which may have had many hundreds of residents, flourished from about 6700 B.C. to about 5600 B.C.

✔ **READING CHECK: Identifying Cause and Effect** What advances were early peoples able to make as a result of the Neolithic agricultural revolution? shift from food gathering to food producing; growth of cities

---

SECTION 1 REVIEW

1. **Define** and explain the significance:
   hominids
   artifacts
   culture
   limited evidence
   nomads
   agriculture
   domestication
   hunter-gatherers

2. **Identify** and explain the significance:
   Donald Johanson
   Lucy
   Mary Leakey
   Neanderthals
   Cro-Magnons
   Neolithic agricultural revolution

3. **Identifying Cause and Effect**
   Copy the concept web below. Use it to show the main changes caused by the Neolithic agricultural revolution.

   Neolithic Agricultural Revolution

4. **Finding the Main Idea**
   a. What were the advantages and the disadvantages that humans experienced as a result of the Neolithic agricultural revolution?
   b. List the kinds of hominids that developed over time in order of their appearance on Earth.
   c. In what ways were Neanderthals and Cro-Magnons different from earlier hominids? In what ways were they different from each other?

5. **Writing and Critical Thinking**
   Drawing Conclusions How do anthropologists, archaeologists, historians, and geographers draw conclusions about the prehistoric world from limited evidence?
   Consider:
   - the evidence researchers use
   - the limits of that evidence
   - the information such evidence provides

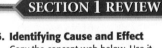
Homework Practice Online
keyword: SP3 HP1

OBJECTIVES

1 Identify the three main characteristics shared by civilizations.

2 Explain what other two characteristics may be shared by civilizations.

3 Describe the other characteristics and achievements that marked the first river valley civilizations.

SECTION 2

The Foundations of Civilization

READ TO DISCOVER

❶ What three main characteristics are shared by civilizations?

❷ What two other characteristics may be shared by civilizations?

❸ What other characteristics and achievements marked the first river valley civilizations?

DEFINE

civilization
irrigation
division of labor
artisans
cultural diffusion

WHY IT MATTERS TODAY

Civilizations today share basic characteristics with the first civilizations. Use **CNNfyi.com** or other **current event** sources to explore a modern civilization. Record your findings in your journal.

CNNfyi.com

The Main Idea
As early settlements grew, they began to show the characteristics of major civilizations.

The Story Continues *By the end of the New Stone Age, people had learned to make tools and weapons, use fire, create works of art, tame animals, and grow food. Many had established permanent settlements. The stage was set for the next level of development.*

Characteristics of a Civilization

Not all people had established permanent settlements by the end of the New Stone Age. Those who lived in climates unsuitable for farming continued their old ways of hunting and gathering. Those in permanent settlements, however, began to advance more rapidly. The settlements in four specific regions were particularly important for later human development. These four regions were (1) the Nile River valley in Africa, (2) the valley of the Tigris and Euphrates (yoo·FRAY·teez) Rivers in southwestern Asia, (3) the Indus River valley in southern Asia, and (4) the Huang, or Yellow, River valley in eastern Asia.

In these four river valleys, civilizations first developed. A **civilization** is a complex culture that has at least three characteristics. The first is that people are able to produce surplus, or extra, food. The second is that people establish large towns or cities with some form of government. The third is that people perform different jobs, instead of each person doing all kinds of work.

Surplus food and irrigation. The valleys of the Nile, Tigris and Euphrates, Indus, and Huang share a common feature. Their rivers rise and flood the valleys during periods of heavy rain. Except for these rainy periods, little if any rain falls. During much of the year, the climate is warm or hot.

The yearly flooding of the Nile River was actually a factor in the rise of civilization.

SECTION 2 RESOURCES

REPRODUCIBLE RESOURCES

▶ Guided Reading Strategy 1.2

TECHNOLOGY RESOURCES

▶ One-Stop Planner 1.2

▶ World History and Cultures Video Program 1: The Rise of Civilization

▶ Homework Practice Online

REINFORCEMENT, REVIEW, AND ASSESSMENT

▶ Section 2 Review, p. 15

▶ Daily Quiz 1.2

▶ Main Idea Activity 1.2

▶ English Audio Summary 1.2

▶ Spanish Audio Summary 1.2

TEACH OBJECTIVE 1

LEVEL 1: Have students list the three main characteristics shared by civilizations. *(surplus food, government, division of labor)* Ask students to write a short paragraph explaining why each characteristic is necessary. *(Answers will vary. Surplus food allows the population to grow. Government regulates people's behavior and helps to ensure order and security. A division of labor allows people to specialize in different jobs.)* **ENGLISH LANGUAGE LEARNERS**

TEACH OBJECTIVE 2

ALL LEVELS: Ask students what other two accomplishments are characteristic of civilizations. *(a calendar and some form of writing)* Have students draw a two-column chart, with one of these characteristics at the top of each column. Then, ask students to list the reasons why each characteristic is important in a civilization. *(Students might mention that a calendar was important to river valley civilizations because it told people when the yearly floods would occur. A system of writing allowed people to communicate and pass on ideas more easily.)* **ENGLISH LANGUAGE LEARNERS**

Geography

The climate around the Nile provided early Egyptians with ideal conditions for farming. The two main tributaries of the Nile, the Blue Nile and the White Nile, received heavy rainfall during the summer. When the Nile overflowed its banks, it flooded the Nile Valley and Delta. In October and November the water receded and the remaining moisture in the soil sustained the crops until harvest.

Critical Thinking

Ask students why the seasonal cycle of the Nile was ideal for farming.

ANSWER: Students might note that the Nile floods brought essential water to growing crops, yet receded in time to allow harvest.

MAP ANSWERS

1. 20° N and 40° N

2. They were located along rivers.

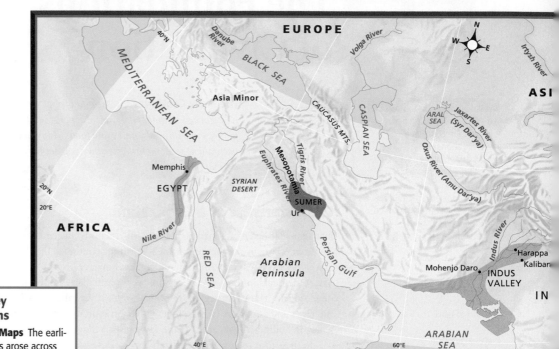

River Valley Civilizations

Interpreting Maps The earliest civilizations arose across Asia and Africa.

■ **Skills Assessment:**
1. Locate Between which degrees of latitude did the Indus, Nile, Tigris-Euphrates, and Huang river valleys lie?
2. Human Systems What geographic features did the four major civilization areas share?

The climate and flooding greatly influenced the development of civilizations in these river valleys. Somehow farmers had to get water to their crops during the dry season. At some point, farmers in each valley learned to dig ditches and canals to move water from the river to their fields. Thus they developed the first systems of **irrigation.** Farmers also built dikes to keep the rivers within their banks during the rainy season. These improved farming techniques led to more and better food, which then led to increases in population. As the population grew, some of the villages became cities.

Cities, government, and labor. The large number of people in the cities provided labor to build great palaces, temples, and other public buildings. Also, improved farming techniques such as irrigation and flood-control systems required a high level of cooperation. Different forms of leadership emerged to help societies run. These were the first governments. Governments made rules to guide people's behavior. Having rules helped people plan, direct, and regulate their work. Government leaders made and enforced the rules.

As methods of farming improved, fewer people had to work the fields. Some people could specialize in other kinds of work. In other words, there was a **division of labor.** For example, people skilled in making tools could devote their time to such work. They would then trade their products for food. Soon a class of skilled workers, called **artisans,** developed. Other people became merchants and traders. They made their living by buying goods from farmers or artisans and then selling them. Traders not only transported goods to be sold, but also passed along ideas. The spread of ideas and other aspects of culture from one area to another is called **cultural diffusion.**

✔ **READING CHECK: Making Generalizations** In what ways are surplus food, government, and division of labor necessary for advanced civilization? allow improved cooperation and leadership, appearance of skilled workers and trades

LEVEL 3: Organize students into four or five groups to take on the role of a museum committee that is planning an exhibit called "The Dawn of Civilization." Their job is to come up with a list of the types of artifacts they would like to display. Their exhibit should identify and explain the following:

- advances in farming and metalworking
- the rise of governments
- division of labor
- the development of calendars and alphabets

(Students' lists will vary but should include items such as tools and written documents that demonstrate the achievements of early civilizations.) **COOPERATIVE LEARNING**

HOMEWORK Have students use their textbooks to make a list of facts about the Neolithic agricultural revolution and the economic, social, and geographic factors that led to the growth of the first civilizations in one column of a two-column chart. In the other column, tell them to write any logical conclusion they can draw regarding the significance of each fact in the first column.

Fact	Significance
People began making tools and weapons out of bronze.	*They could work more efficiently with stronger tools, produce surplus food, and make division of labor possible.*

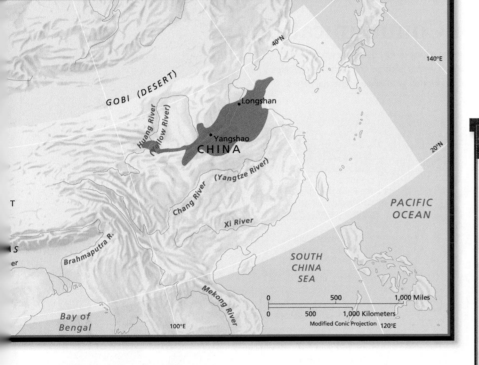

Daily Life

Pottery discovered by scientists at Mohenjo Daro on the Indus indicates skillful artists capable of showing great detail. Most pottery varied in shape. Pieces were made of pinkish clay with a red slip, and black paint stylized features. Usual themes for pottery included animals, plants, and geometric motifs of intersecting circles and scales. Because scientists have found Indus objects on Mesopotamian sites, they believe trade existed between the two civilizations and have compared the pottery created by both populations.

Critical Thinking

Ask students why a civilization would have developed that was located beyond the flood plain of the Indus River.

ANSWER: Students should suggest that such a location would avoid flooding and destruction of crops and buildings.

INTERPRETING THE CHART ANSWER
It suggests that the characters of a written language evolve from pictures.

Other Characteristics

In addition to food supply, cities and government, and division of labor, some historians consider two more accomplishments to be characteristics of civilization: a calendar and some form of writing.

Early in their histories, river valley civilizations developed calendars. Because these people farmed, they needed to know when the yearly floods would start and stop. One way was to regard the time from flood to flood as a year. That year was divided according to the phases of the moon. The time from one full moon to the next full moon was a month. This system presented a major problem, however. A lunar month lasts only about 29 ½ days. Thus, 12 lunar months equal 354 days. A solar year, however, has approximately 365 ¼ days. Therefore, the moon-based calendars of the river valley civilizations fell about 11 days short of the time it took Earth to rotate around the sun. As you read about the river valley civilizations in following chapters, you will see how they coped with this problem.

Life in a civilized society is complex. Civilizations in the river valleys were trading goods and developing rules for living and working together. These developments required new forms of communication. People needed a written language to keep and pass on information and ideas. What we now define as writing began around 3000 B.C. The development of writing was a long and complex process. By developing written languages, the early river valley civilizations created records of their cultures and societies. In other words, history had begun.

✔ **READING CHECK: Identifying Cause and Effect** How did the needs of early civilizations lead to the development of calendars and systems of writing? calendar was necessary for agriculture, writing was necessary for increased communication

Development of Writing: One Theory

Pictures represent things.

Pictures symbolize ideas.

Pictures stand for sounds.

Signs represent sounds.

Interpreting the Chart
This flowchart of the possible development of the letter T is meant to illustrate how letters of alphabets may have been invented. *What does this chart indicate about the development of written language?*

Ancient people sometimes went to war to win herds of animals or more farmland to feed their communities and to provide economic stability. Throughout history land rights have been one of the primary causes of wars. In modern times, however, though people still fight over land, many wars are fought primarily over ideas such as liberty, justice, or economic systems. Have students identify and explain the economic effects of wars in which the United States has been involved. *(Students might mention that the American Revolution was fought over the idea of independence and freedom from excessive taxation; the Vietnam War was fought to halt the spread of communism.)* **BLOCK SCHEDULING**

Teacher to Teacher

Deanna Spring of Cincinnati, Ohio, suggested the following activity: Have students form groups, with each group picking a type of implement—stone, copper, bronze, or iron. Have each group prepare and perform a skit about how ancient peoples made tools from these materials and used these tools. The skits should be framed with a prologue and epilogue that discusses the era.

---

internet connect

go.hrw.com

TOPIC: Calendar
GO TO: go.hrw.com
KEYWORD: SP3 WH1

Have students access the Internet through the HRW Go site to research different types of calendars. Have them select a calendar to study. Ask students to find information that explains how the calendar calculates a month, how this period compares with one month on the Christian (or western, or Gregorian) calendar, and why the calendar they have selected begins the year as it does. After students have completed their research, have them write a short report about their calendar.

SKILLS PRACTICE ANSWERS

1. 2,300 years

2. It implies that the development of communication is a long process and that it occurs at different times among different cultures.

3. Students' time lines will vary but might include food supply, cities and government, division of labor, or a calendar.

SKILL-BUILDING STRATEGIES   **Using a Time Line**

The History of Communication

The invention of writing was just one step in a long history of changes in the way people communicate. Reading a time line of events in communications history helps us to understand the absolute and relative chronology of when events happened.

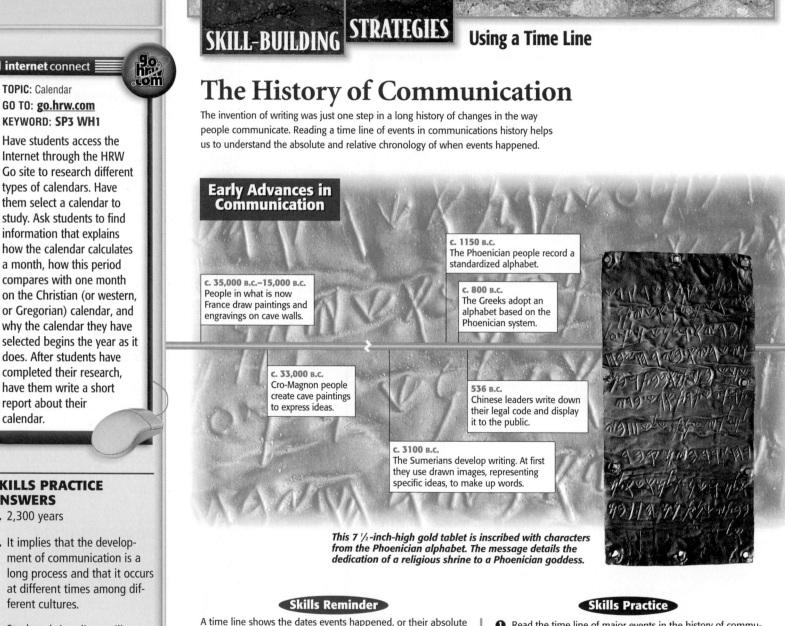

Early Advances in Communication

c. 1150 B.C.
The Phoenician people record a standardized alphabet.

c. 35,000 B.C.–15,000 B.C.
People in what is now France draw paintings and engravings on cave walls.

c. 800 B.C.
The Greeks adopt an alphabet based on the Phoenician system.

c. 33,000 B.C.
Cro-Magnon people create cave paintings to express ideas.

536 B.C.
Chinese leaders write down their legal code and display it to the public.

c. 3100 B.C.
The Sumerians develop writing. At first they use drawn images, representing specific ideas, to make up words.

This 7 ½-inch-high gold tablet is inscribed with characters from the Phoenician alphabet. The message details the dedication of a religious shrine to a Phoenician goddess.

Skills Reminder

A time line shows the dates events happened, or their absolute chronology, as well as when events happened relative to each other, or their relative chronology. This book follows a system of dating years based on the traditional date of birth of Jesus Christ. The Muslim, Chinese, Jewish, and Hindu calendars all count the years differently. Years following Jesus's birth are numbered in order. They start with A.D., which stands for the Latin phrase *Anno Domini* ("in the year of the Lord" or "since the birth of Christ"). Years before Jesus's birth are numbered in reverse order. They are followed by B.C. ("Before Christ"). The initial c. (for "circa," meaning "approximately") indicates that the exact date is unknown and that the one given is a good estimate.

Skills Practice

❶ Read the time line of major events in the history of communication. Approximately how many years passed between the invention of writing by the Sumerians and the Greek adoption of an alphabet?

❷ What does the passage of time between these two events imply about the development of communication? Based on the other information given, what else does the time line imply about the development of communication?

❸ Using information in your textbook and from other sources, create your own time line of events reflecting a characteristic other than writing that was crucial to the development of early civilizations.

The River Valley Civilizations

The river valley civilizations moved humans out of the Stone Age. People developed family roles and religious beliefs that related to their farming-based cultures.

The use of metals. More than 6,000 years ago, people in both the Nile and the Tigris-Euphrates river valleys were using copper to make tools and jewelry. In time people learned to make a more useful metal—bronze. A mixture of copper and tin, bronze is harder than copper. People in the Nile and the Tigris-Euphrates river valleys made objects of bronze as early as 5,000 years ago. People in India and China also used bronze at an early date. The invention of bronze tools marked the end of the Stone Age and the beginning of the Bronze Age.

Iron is stronger than copper or bronze. Making iron is a long, difficult process. We do not know when people discovered how to use iron. It may have been discovered separately in several different areas. We do know, however, that about 3,200 years ago people in southwestern Asia had learned to make iron. The Iron Age began.

Family and religion. Women managed the family. They cared for children, prepared food, made clothing, and probably invented pottery and weaving. When agriculture initially developed, women did much of the farming. The rise of goddesses during this time suggests that responsibility for the food supply increased women's authority and independence. However, when the plow was invented and animals were harnessed to pull it, men again became the primary food providers. This change shifted the power women had gained back to men, who continued to be the primary authorities in society.

People believed in many gods and goddesses and in unseen forces of nature. These controlled all aspects of human life. People worried that the rains would not come and their crops would not grow. They prayed to their gods and goddesses to provide water. Often they offered sacrifices. They gave thanks when they believed their prayers had been answered.

✔ **READING CHECK: Summarizing** What technologies and patterns of home life did the first river valley civilizations share? bronze and iron tools, women in charge of family and agriculture

This small figure represents the mother goddess of the Indus River valley civilization.

SECTION 2 REVIEW

1. **Define** and explain the significance:
   civilization
   irrigation
   division of labor
   artisans
   cultural diffusion

2. **Drawing Conclusions** Make a flowchart like the one below. Add to it to show how a food surplus led people in four river valleys to develop other characteristics of civilization.

Food Surplus	→	Increase in Population
	→	
	→	

3. **Finding the Main Idea**
   a. What did the four main early civilizations have in common geographically and culturally?
   b. What problems did a calendar and a system of writing help solve?
   c. Identify aspects of the following eras and list them according to their relative chronology: Iron Age, Stone Age, Bronze Age.

4. **Writing and Critical Thinking**
   Making Generalizations Imagine you are living in a culture before it has developed a system of writing. Describe what everyday life would be like.
   Consider:
   • what human activities can make use of writing
   • how those same activities would be handled without writing

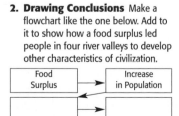

Homework Practice Online

keyword: SP3 HP1

THE EMERGENCE OF CIVILIZATION **15**

REVIEW AND ASSESSMENT RESOURCES

REPRODUCIBLE RESOURCES
▶ Vocabulary Activity 1

TECHNOLOGY RESOURCES
▶ Chapter 1 Test Generator (on the One-Stop Planner)
▶ Global Skill Builder CD–ROM
▶ HRW Web Site

REINFORCEMENT, REVIEW, and ASSESSMENT
▶ Chapter 1 Review, pp. 16–17
▶ Chapter 1 Tutorial for Students, Parents, Mentors, and Peers
▶ Chapter 1 Test (Form A or B)
▶ Alternative Assessment Handbook
▶ Chapter 1 Test for English Language Learners and Special-Needs Students

REVIEW
Have students complete the Chapter 1 Review on pages 16–17.

ASSESS
Use one of the chapter tests to assess students' understanding of the content. For Alternative Assessment, see the Portfolio Activities and Alternative Assessment Handbook.

CHAPTER 1 REVIEW ANSWERS

Understanding Main Ideas
1. They use advanced technology to date remains and artifacts. They also use educated guesses and assumptions to determine information about the artifacts they find.

2. wore animal skins as clothing; used fire for warmth and cooking; buried their dead with meat and tools

3. more advanced tools and weapons; better hunters; art on cave walls

4. More permanent farming settlements developed.

5. People are able to produce surplus food. People establish large towns or cities with some form of government. Division of labor occurs.

6. As cities develop, government is needed to make rules to guide people's behavior.

7. a calendar, a system of writing

8. They invented bronze and iron tools.

Reviewing Themes
1. They became successful hunters and migrated great distances in search of food.

2. They developed along rivers.

3. It resulted in food surpluses which caused an increase in population and the development of cities.

CHAPTER 1 Review

Creating a Time Line
Copy the time line below onto a sheet of paper. Complete the time line by filling in the events, individuals, and dates from the chapter that you think were significant. Pick three events and explain why you think they were significant.

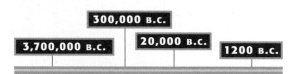

| 3,700,000 B.C. | 300,000 B.C. | 20,000 B.C. | 1200 B.C. |

Writing a Summary
Using standard grammar, spelling, sentence structure, and punctuation, write an overview of the events in the chapter.

Identifying People and Ideas
Identify the following terms or individuals and explain their significance:

1. hominids
2. artifacts
3. culture
4. limited evidence
5. Lucy
6. Neanderthals
7. Cro-Magnons
8. Neolithic agricultural revolution
9. civilization
10. division of labor

Understanding Main Ideas
SECTION 1 *(pp. 6–10)*
Prehistoric Peoples
1. What methods do anthropologists, archaeologists, historians, and geographers use to explore prehistory?
2. What were some important characteristics of Neanderthal people?
3. What were some important characteristics of Cro-Magnon people?
4. What effect did the Neolithic agricultural revolution have on people's lives?

SECTION 2 *(pp. 11–15)*
The Foundations of Civilization
5. What are the three major characteristics of a civilization?
6. How are the development of cities and government related?
7. What other two characteristics usually mark civilizations?
8. What advances in metalworking did early river civilizations make?

Reviewing Themes
1. **Culture** What characteristics of early *Homo sapiens* most set them apart from earlier hominids?
2. **Geography** What similarities in physical environment did the first civilizations share?
3. **Economics** How did improved farming lead to the development of civilization?

Thinking Critically
1. **Comparing** Explain the economic, social, and geographic factors that led to the first civilizations.
2. **Drawing Conclusions** How did the development of towns and cities affect prehistoric peoples?
3. **Evaluating** Why was the development of bronze and iron important?
4. **Identifying Cause and Effect** How did the development of agriculture in the river valley civilizations affect the roles and influence of women?

Writing About History
Analyzing Information Imagine you are an archaeologist. You have dug up the site of one of the first human civilizations. Write a description of the artifacts you might find and what they reveal about the culture. Use the following chart to organize your thoughts before you begin writing.

Artifact	What this suggests about the culture

CLOSE

Ask students to name the three major characteristics of civilizations. Have them explain how life in the United States today meets each of these characteristics.

RETEACH

Group students who had trouble with the test into pairs. Have them use their textbook to correct their tests. Ask them to create flash cards and then quiz each other on the chapter content. Then have students take the Form B test to assess their mastery of the material. **ENGLISH LANGUAGE LEARNERS, COOPERATIVE LEARNING**

Portfolio Extensions

Link to TODAY

1. Ask students to imagine they are archaeologists excavating the site of an ancient civilization. Have them create a list of artifacts that might indicate what farming techniques people used. Have students write an explanation of each item.

2. Assign groups of students a major crop such as corn, wheat, or rice. Then have group members research where their crop is grown and identify major producers. Have groups prepare maps and/or graphs showing the results of their research.

3. Have students locate and use web sites, media and news services, and interviews to collect information about recent archaeological finds. Have them use this information to write articles on the development of agriculture.

Building Social Studies Skills

Using Art to Understand History

Study the painting below. Then answer the questions that follow.

Cro-Magnon cave painting, Lascaux Cave, France.

1. Which statement best describes what you can infer about the artist who drew this painting?

  a. The artist hunted animals like this for food.

  b. The artist was intelligent, was able to mix paints and use tools, and had carefully observed the environment.

  c. Huge herds of animals were in existence at the time the artist drew the painting.

  d. The artist drew the animal to decorate the walls of the cave.

2. Art helps historians understand the people who created it. What conclusions regarding the Cro-Magnon people can you reach on the basis of this illustration?

Analyzing a Primary Source

Read the following description by anthropologists Alan Walker and Pat Shipman. Then answer the questions.

> "First we had to clear every twig, leaf, and rock from a large area where Kamoya found the fossil. Then the whole gang would take Olduvai picks—six-inch nails embedded in curved, hand-carved wooden handles—and break up the top few inches of the surface layer of pebbles and disturbed sediment. How deep we had to go depended on how loose or consolidated the sediment was and whether or not any more pieces were recovered in the process."

3. Which of the following statements best summarizes the excerpt?

  a. Anthropologists use a tool called an Olduvai pick.

  b. The diggers cleared twigs, leaves, and rocks from a large area.

  c. Anthropologists break up the soil around an area where a fossil has been found.

  d. The diggers cleared the ground around the fossil site and carefully broke up the soil to look for more fossils.

4. Reread the excerpt. Then decide whether you would want to take part in an anthropological dig. Give specific reasons.

Alternative Assessment

Building Your Portfolio

Link to TODAY

Economics

Agriculture was a significant development in human history. The ability to produce food surpluses led to the development of early civilizations. Using your textbook and other sources, gather data about the agricultural production of the United States today. Make a graph of the data. Then write an explanation of how the food production of the United States affects its economy as well as its culture. Consider what the country would be like if it did not produce the amount of food that it does.

⊡ internet connect

go.hrw.com

Internet Activity: go.hrw.com
KEYWORD: SP3 WH1

Choose a topic on the Emergence of Civilization to:

• analyze artifacts from an archaeological site.

• compare and contrast a modern calendar used in the United States with calendars of different cultures.

• list different divisions of labor in modern society.

Thinking Critically

1. Climate and flooding in river valleys produced a food surplus; population increased; villages became cities.

2. Governments emerged.

3. improved tools and weapons

4. Women initially did much of the farming. After the invention of the plow, men again became the primary food providers. The power women had gained shifted back to men.

Writing About History

Answers will vary but might include items such as jewelry, pottery, and tools. Students should describe what each item reveals about the culture.

Building Social Studies Skills

1. b

2. skilled artists, hunters

3. d

4. Answers will vary.

Building Your Portfolio

Students should describe how economy and culture are affected by the ability of the United States to produce the amount of food it does.

The First Civilizations

CHAPTER RESOURCE MANAGER

Objectives	Pacing Guide	Reproducible Resources
SECTION 1 **Ancient Kingdoms of the Nile** (pp. 20–25)	• Explore how geography affected the development of ancient Egypt. • Identify the events and discoveries that marked the development of Egyptian civilization. • Explain how Egyptian kingdoms developed and why they collapsed.	**Regular** 1.5 day **Block Scheduling** 1 day *Block Scheduling Handbook with Team Teaching Strategies 2.1*	**RS** Guided Reading Strategy 2.1
SECTION 2 **Egyptian Life and Culture** (pp. 26–29)	• Describe Egyptian achievements in the arts and architecture. • Examine how the Egyptians expressed their religious beliefs. • Explain how farming and trade were carried on in Egypt.	**Regular** 1 day **Block Scheduling** .5 day *Block Scheduling Handbook with Team Teaching Strategies 2.2*	**RS** Guided Reading Strategy 2.2 **PS** Readings in World History 5 **E** Hands-on History Activity 2
SECTION 3 **Sumerian Civilization** (pp. 30–34)	• Explore how geography affected the development of the Sumerian civilization. • Identify the achievements of the Sumerian people. • Describe what life was like in Sumerian society.	**Regular** 1.5 day **Block Scheduling** 1 day *Block Scheduling Handbook with Team Teaching Strategies 2.3*	**RS** Guided Reading Strategy 2.3 **PS** Readings in World History 6: An Early City in the Tigris-Euphrates Valley
SECTION 4 **Empires of the Fertile Crescent** (pp. 35–40)	• Explain why Sumerians were attacked by outsiders. • Examine the characteristics of Babylonian society. • Investigate which invaders conquered Babylon and why they failed to control it. • Describe the achievements of the Persians.	**Regular** 1.5 day **Block Scheduling** .5 day *Block Scheduling Handbook with Team Teaching Strategies 2.4*	**RS** Guided Reading Strategy 2.4 **RS** Graphic Organizer Activity 2 **PS** Readings in World History 7, 8
SECTION 5 **The Phoenicians and the Lydians** (pp. 41–43)	• Examine how trade influenced Phoenician culture. • Describe how a money economy developed in Lydia.	**Regular** 1 day **Block Scheduling** .5 day *Block Scheduling Handbook with Team Teaching Strategies 2.5*	**RS** Guided Reading Strategy 2.5 **SM** Geography Activity 2: The End of an Island Civilization
SECTION 6 **The Origins of Judaism** (pp. 44–47)	• Explain how the migrating Hebrews found a homeland. • Explore how religious views affected Hebrew culture.	**Regular** 1 day **Block Scheduling** .5 day *Block Scheduling Handbook with Team Teaching Strategies 2.6*	**RS** Guided Reading Strategy 2.6 **E** Creative Teaching Strategy 2: Time Capsules from the Ancient World

Chapter Resource Key

PS Primary Sources	**A** Assessment	🎵 Music	
RS Reading Support	**REV** Review	📼 Video	**One-Stop** Planner CD-ROM
IC Interdisciplinary Connections	**ELL** Reinforcement and English Language Learners	🌐 Internet	See the *One-Stop Planner* for a complete list of additional resources for students and teachers.
E Enrichment	💾 Transparencies	💻 Holt Presentation Maker Using Microsoft® PowerPoint®	
SM Skills Mastery	💿 CD-ROM		

One-Stop Planner CD-ROM

It's easy to plan lessons, select resources, and print out materials for your students when you use the *One-Stop Planner* CD–ROM with *Test Generator.*

Technology Resources

One-Stop Planner 2.1
Holt Researcher: World History: Ramses II
World History Teaching Transparency: Everyday Life 1: Irrigation in Ancient Egypt
Homework Practice Online

One-Stop Planner 2.2
CNN Presents World Cultures: Yesterday and Today Segment 2: Restoring the Sphinx
World History Teaching Transparency: Everyday Life 2
Homework Practice Online

One-Stop Planner 2.3
Homework Practice Online
Online Maps, Charts, and Graphs: Development of Cuneiform, 3000 B.C.– 600 B.C.

One-Stop Planner 2.4
Holt Researcher: World History: Cyrus, Darius I, Zoroaster
World History and Cultures Video Program 2: The First Empires
Homework Practice Online

One-Stop Planner 2.5
World History Teaching Transparency: Geography and History 2: The Eastern Mediterranean
Homework Practice Online
Online Maps, Charts, and Graphs: Phoenician Sea Routes

One-Stop Planner 2.6
Holt Researcher: World History: David, Solomon
Religions of the World Video Series: Judaism
Homework Practice Online

Reinforcement, Review, and Assessment

Daily Quiz 2.1
Main Idea Activity 2.1
English Audio Summary 2.1
Spanish Audio Summary 2.1
REV Section 1 Review, p. 25

Daily Quiz 2.2
Main Idea Activity 2.2
English Audio Summary 2.2
Spanish Audio Summary 2.2
REV Section 2 Review, p. 29

Daily Quiz 2.3
Main Idea Activity 2.3
English Audio Summary 2.3
Spanish Audio Summary 2.3
REV Section 3 Review, p. 34

Daily Quiz 2.4
Main Idea Activity 2.4
English Audio Summary 2.4
Spanish Audio Summary 2.4
REV Section 4 Review, p. 40

Daily Quiz 2.5
Main Idea Activity 2.5
English Audio Summary 2.5
Spanish Audio Summary 2.5
REV Section 5 Review, p. 43

Daily Quiz 2.6
Main Idea Activity 2.6
English Audio Summary 2.6
Spanish Audio Summary 2.6
REV Section 6 Review, p. 47

internet connect

HRW ONLINE RESOURCES
GO TO: go.hrw.com
Then type in a keyword.

TEACHER HOME PAGE
KEYWORD: SP3 Teacher

CHAPTER INTERNET ACTIVITIES
KEYWORD: SP3 WH2
Choose an activity to:
• explore Egyptian pyramids and create an illustrated brochure.
• interview the leader of an ancient civilization.
• write about ancient and modern structures in Egypt.

CHAPTER ENRICHMENT LINKS
KEYWORD: SP3 CH2

ONLINE ASSESSMENT
Homework Practice
KEYWORD: SP3 HP2
Standardized Test Prep
KEYWORD: SP3 STP2
Rubrics
KEYWORD: SS Rubrics

ONLINE MAPS, CHARTS, AND GRAPHS
KEYWORD: SP3 MCG

CONTENT UPDATES
KEYWORD: SS Content Updates

HOLT PRESENTATION MAKER
KEYWORD: SP3 PPT2

ONLINE READING SUPPORT
KEYWORD: SS Strategies

CURRENT EVENTS
KEYWORD: S3 Current Events

Meeting Individual Needs

Ability Levels

Level 1   Basic level activities designed for all students encountering new material

Level 2   Intermediate level activities designed for average students

Level 3   Challenging activities designed for honors and gifted and talented students

English Language Learners   These activities address the needs of students with Limited English Proficiency.

Chapter Review and Assessment

IC   Vocabulary Activity 2
Global Skill Builder CD–ROM
HRW Web Site
REV   Chapter 2 Tutorial for Students, Parents, Mentors, and Peers
REV   Chapter 2 Review, pp. 48–49
A   Chapter 2 Test Generator (on the One-Stop Planner)
A   Chapter 2 Test (Form A or B)
A   Alternative Assessment Handbook
A   Chapter 2 Test for English Language Learners and Special-Needs Students

Build on What You Know

Ask students to answer the following questions:

What were some of the developments of prehistoric peoples?

Consider:

- agriculture
- government
- science and technology

Where are civilizations likely to develop?

Consider:

- geography
- climate
- science and technology

EXPLORING THE TIME LINE

GLOBAL EVENTS

CHAPTER

2

C. 6000 B.C.–587 B.C.

The First Civilizations

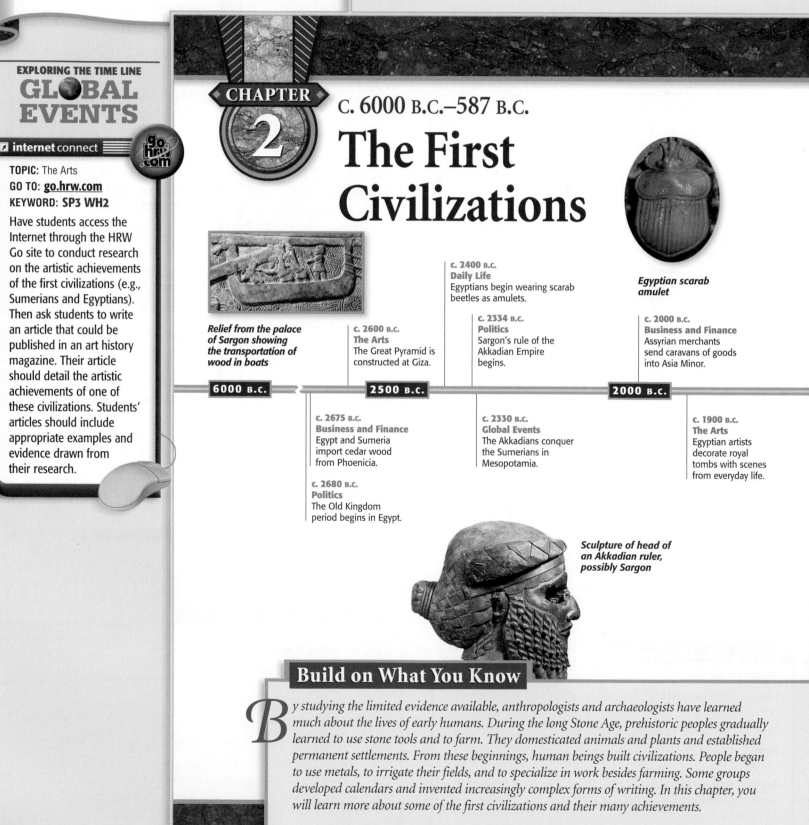

Relief from the palace of Sargon showing the transportation of wood in boats

c. 2600 B.C.
The Arts
The Great Pyramid is constructed at Giza.

c. 2400 B.C.
Daily Life
Egyptians begin wearing scarab beetles as amulets.

Egyptian scarab amulet

c. 2334 B.C.
Politics
Sargon's rule of the Akkadian Empire begins.

c. 2000 B.C.
Business and Finance
Assyrian merchants send caravans of goods into Asia Minor.

6000 B.C.   2500 B.C.   2000 B.C.

c. 2675 B.C.
Business and Finance
Egypt and Sumeria import cedar wood from Phoenicia.

c. 2680 B.C.
Politics
The Old Kingdom period begins in Egypt.

c. 2330 B.C.
Global Events
The Akkadians conquer the Sumerians in Mesopotamia.

c. 1900 B.C.
The Arts
Egyptian artists decorate royal tombs with scenes from everyday life.

Sculpture of head of an Akkadian ruler, possibly Sargon

Build on What You Know

By studying the limited evidence available, anthropologists and archaeologists have learned much about the lives of early humans. During the long Stone Age, prehistoric peoples gradually learned to use stone tools and to farm. They domesticated animals and plants and established permanent settlements. From these beginnings, human beings built civilizations. People began to use metals, to irrigate their fields, and to specialize in work besides farming. Some groups developed calendars and invented increasingly complex forms of writing. In this chapter, you will learn more about some of the first civilizations and their many achievements.

What's Your Opinion?

To help students create their Themes Journal entries, provide the following examples of appropriate agree/disagree statements.

Global Relations

Agree Trade can promote the exchange of cultural beliefs and ideas between civilizations.

Disagree Cultural beliefs and ideas are not exchanged between civilizations through trade.

Geography

Agree Civilizations cannot survive if they are geographically isolated.

Disagree Civilizations that are geographically isolated can survive.

Government

Agree A civilization needs strong rulers to survive.

Disagree To survive, a civilization does not need strong rulers.

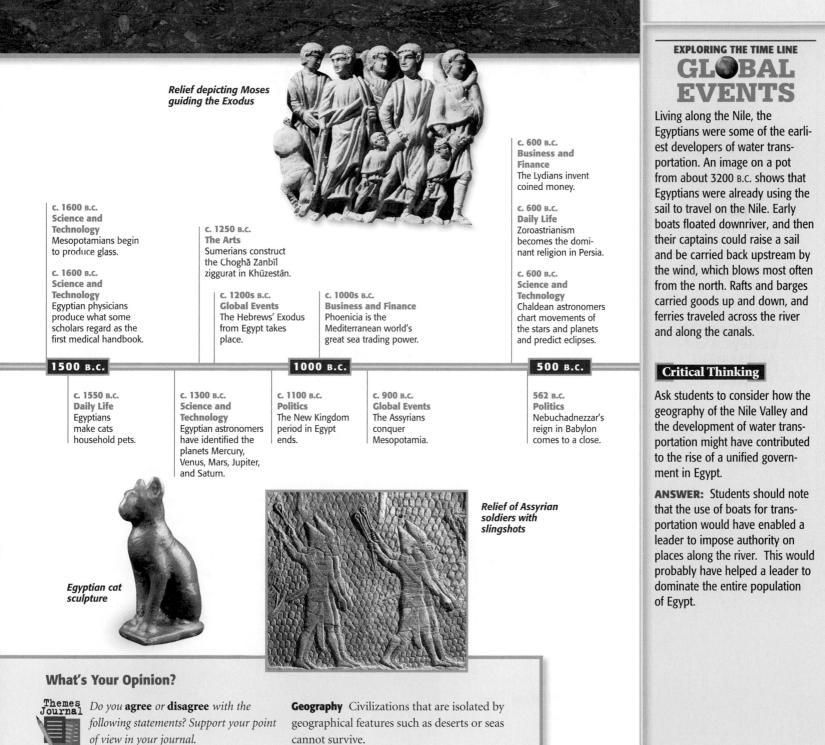

Relief depicting Moses guiding the Exodus

c. 1600 B.C.
Science and Technology
Mesopotamians begin to produce glass.

c. 1600 B.C.
Science and Technology
Egyptian physicians produce what some scholars regard as the first medical handbook.

c. 1250 B.C.
The Arts
Sumerians construct the Choghã Zanbīl ziggurat in Khūzestān.

c. 1200s B.C.
Global Events
The Hebrews' Exodus from Egypt takes place.

c. 1000s B.C.
Business and Finance
Phoenicia is the Mediterranean world's great sea trading power.

c. 600 B.C.
Business and Finance
The Lydians invent coined money.

c. 600 B.C.
Daily Life
Zoroastrianism becomes the dominant religion in Persia.

c. 600 B.C.
Science and Technology
Chaldean astronomers chart movements of the stars and planets and predict eclipses.

1500 B.C.	**1000 B.C.**	**500 B.C.**

c. 1550 B.C.
Daily Life
Egyptians make cats household pets.

c. 1300 B.C.
Science and Technology
Egyptian astronomers have identified the planets Mercury, Venus, Mars, Jupiter, and Saturn.

c. 1100 B.C.
Politics
The New Kingdom period in Egypt ends.

c. 900 B.C.
Global Events
The Assyrians conquer Mesopotamia.

562 B.C.
Politics
Nebuchadnezzar's reign in Babylon comes to a close.

Egyptian cat sculpture

Relief of Assyrian soldiers with slingshots

What's Your Opinion?

Do you agree or disagree with the following statements? Support your point of view in your journal.

Global Relations Trade between civilizations can be a way to exchange cultural beliefs and ideas.

Geography Civilizations that are isolated by geographical features such as deserts or seas cannot survive.

Government Strong rulers are needed to help a civilization survive.

GLOBAL EVENTS

Living along the Nile, the Egyptians were some of the earliest developers of water transportation. An image on a pot from about 3200 B.C. shows that Egyptians were already using the sail to travel on the Nile. Early boats floated downriver, and then their captains could raise a sail and be carried back upstream by the wind, which blows most often from the north. Rafts and barges carried goods up and down, and ferries traveled across the river and along the canals.

Critical Thinking

Ask students to consider how the geography of the Nile Valley and the development of water transportation might have contributed to the rise of a unified government in Egypt.

ANSWER: Students should note that the use of boats for transportation would have enabled a leader to impose authority on places along the river. This would probably have helped a leader to dominate the entire population of Egypt.

OBJECTIVES

1 **Explore how geography affected the development of ancient Egypt.**

2 **Identify the events and discoveries that marked the development of Egyptian civilization.**

3 **Explain how Egyptian kingdoms developed and why they collapsed.**

SECTION
1

▶ **READ TO DISCOVER**

❶ How did geography affect the development of ancient Egypt?

❷ What events and discoveries marked the development of Egyptian civilization?

❸ How did Egyptian kingdoms develop and why did they collapse?

▶ **DEFINE**

hieroglyphics
papyrus
dynasty
pharaoh
empire
polytheism
monotheism

▶ **IDENTIFY**

Rosetta Stone
Menes
Hyksos
Hatshepsut
Thutmose III
Amenhotep IV
Ramses II

▶ **WHY IT MATTERS TODAY**

Water is necessary for a community to develop. Use CNNfyi.com or other **current event** sources to find information about a country or a community dealing with a water shortage. Record your findings in your journal.

CNNfyi.com

Ancient Kingdoms of the Nile

The Main Idea
Patterns of daily life and culture in early Egyptian empires were shaped by the features of the Nile River.

The Story Continues *"Hail to thee, O Nile! Who manifests thyself over this land, and comes to give life to Egypt!" These lines begin "Hymn to the Nile," an ancient poem celebrating the river that gave birth to and sustained the culture of the Egyptians. Without the Nile, there would be no Egypt as we know it.*

The Land: Its Geography and Importance

Today desert covers large areas of Egypt. In ancient times, however, the landscape was quite different. Some 12,000 years ago, much of the area was covered by swampland that probably supported large populations of animals such as the hippopotamus and the crocodile. Even so, for the last 5,000 years one physical feature has dominated the region: the Nile River. Without this important river, the land could not have supported the great civilization that appeared in Egypt. This civilization developed in the fertile valley provided by the Nile.

The Nile River. For many thousands of years, the geography of Egypt has been dominated by the mighty Nile River. The Nile is the longest river in the world, stretching about 4,160 miles. Its main sources are the White Nile, which begins near Lake Victoria in eastern Africa, and the Blue Nile, which runs from the Ethiopian highlands. The river flows from south to north, eventually branching into a fan-shaped delta and emptying into the southern Mediterranean Sea. During ancient times, the long course of the Nile was broken by a series of six great cataracts, or rapids. At each cataract, the river was forced into a narrow channel cut through rock. The white-water rapids driving through the cataracts were difficult or nearly impossible to navigate.

The mighty Nile River gave birth to one of history's earliest and richest civilizations.

LEVEL 1: Tell students to imagine that they are members of an agricultural community and are searching for a new home. Ask students what kind of geographical features they would look for. *(rich soil, fair climate, natural resources, access to water, natural protection from invaders)* Have students identify geographical factors of the Nile River valley that meet any of these needs. *(fertile soil; a sunny, frost-free climate; deposits of minerals; the Nile River; deserts and seas)* Discuss how each geographic factor contributed to the success of the Egyptian civilization. **ENGLISH LANGUAGE LEARNERS, COOPERATIVE LEARNING**

Teacher to Teacher

Laura Watkins of Acton, Massachusetts, suggested the following activity: Create a chart listing four key characteristics of the natural environment of Egypt, with examples of how each characteristic affected the culture of Egypt. Then create a similar chart reflecting how the natural environment of your town or region has affected your local culture.

Along most of its course, however, the Nile's smooth, steady flow provided a natural route for transportation, as well as a seemingly endless supply of life-giving water.

The ancient Egyptians built their civilization along a 750-mile stretch of the Nile, roughly between the first great cataract and the delta. The Nile's south-to-north flow made it possible for early people to move goods upland. At the same time, prevailing winds blowing from north to south enabled boats to sail southward on the river. In the 400s B.C. the Greek historian Herodotus (hih·RAHD·uh·tuhs) described another remarkable feature of the Nile River—its annual cycle of months-long flooding.

History Makers Speak ❝When the Nile overflows, it floods both its banks to an average distance of forty miles. But why it does so I find it impossible to discover . . . I would particularly like to know why it starts flooding in mid-summer, of all times, and goes on doing so for over three months before sinking back to its original level. . . .❞

Herodotus, from *The Histories*

Analyzing Primary Sources
Evaluating What puzzled Herodotus about the Nile? why the Nile flooded in mid-summer

We know now that heavy summer rains at the Nile's source cause the summer floods. Although Egyptian farmers could not explain the floods, they planned their work around them. They harvested crops before the floods came. When the waters receded, fertile soil was left behind.

By digging short canals to carry river water to their fields, farmers could grow two or even three crops a year. With several crops a year, the farmers could feed a large population. The planning of irrigation systems promoted cooperation among the people.

Other natural advantages. The Nile Valley offered other natural resources besides its fertile soil. Its sunny, frost-free climate made it easy to grow many kinds of crops. Another important feature of the climate was, and still is, the north wind that blows from the Mediterranean Sea upstream into the Nile Valley. Boats on the Nile can either travel upstream with the wind or row downstream with the current. This fact allowed the ancient Egyptians to use the Nile River as a pathway of travel and trade linking all parts of the Nile Valley. It also helped the ancient Egyptians unite the region into one kingdom.

The Nile Valley contains deposits of granite, sandstone, and limestone. The Egyptians used these minerals as building materials. Finally, the valley's location also created an advantage. The deserts and seas that surrounded the Nile Valley provided a natural protection against invaders. Only the Isthmus of Suez broke these natural barriers. The isthmus forms a land bridge between Africa and Asia. This land bridge provided a route for trade and for the exchange of ideas between the Egyptians and their neighbors to the east.

✔ **READING CHECK: Finding the Main Idea** How did the Nile River contribute to the development of Egyptian civilization? provided route for trade and travel, aided farming

Map:

MEDITERRANEAN SEA
25°E 30°E 35°E
Nile Delta
ASIA
LIBYAN DESERT
LOWER EGYPT
Isthmus of Suez
Memphis
Sinai Peninsula
UPPER EGYPT
ARABIAN DESERT
AFRICA
25°N
SAHARA
RED SEA
Nile River
20°N

Key:
Nile floodplain
Northern winds

0   150   300 Miles
0 150 300 Kilometers
Lambert Conformal Conic Projection

Ancient Egypt, c. 3000 B.C.

Interpreting Maps The Nile is the longest river in the world.

■ **Skills Assessment: 1. Physical Systems** Into which body of water does the Nile River flow? **2. Drawing Conclusions** How might the ability to travel both north and south along the Nile have helped early Egyptian civilizations?

Linking Past to Present

The Aswan High Dam was built to hold back the floodwaters of the Nile River, generate electricity, and to provide year-round irrigation for Egypt's agricultural fields. In these respects, the dam has been remarkably successful. Since its construction, the dam has increased the amount of land irrigated each year by about 2.25 million acres and enabled Egypt to double its agricultural production. This advancement, however, has not come without cost. The dam has had serious negative side effects on the environment, including the once fertile soil of the Nile River valley. Without the annual flooding, the land no longer is naturally fertilized by silt. Modern farmers must resort to applying millions of tons of expensive artificial fertilizers on their farmland. The absence of silt has also caused greater erosion of land along the Mediterranean coast.

ACTIVITY: Have groups of students discuss other technological advances that have produced both benefits and costs.

MAP ANSWERS
1. the Mediterranean Sea

2. Students might suggest that it made trading goods easier.

History Maker

TUTANKHAMEN. Pharaoh Tutankhamen was just nine years old when he came to the throne. He died in his late teens. Since pharaohs were buried with all the things they might need in the afterlife, scholars and historians analyzed evidence from the tomb to create a detailed picture of this "boy king." The contents of his tomb included mirror holders, elaborate shaving tools, and an array of boxes that had once contained various oils and ointments. Although much of the clothing had decayed over time, it was obvious that Tutankhamen had an extensive wardrobe. Some of the clothes were brightly colored and decorated with gold and precious stones. Many pieces of jewelry were also found in the tomb.

Critical Thinking

What do the contents of Tutankhamen's tomb say about him?

ANSWER: Students may point out that he seems to have taken great care of his personal appearance.

CONNECTING TO ART ANSWER
The beard links the pharaoh with the god Osiris; the vulture and cobra symbolize power over Upper and Lower Egypt.

CONNECTING TO
Art

Metalworking: Funeral Mask of a Pharaoh
One of the world's most beautiful treasures is this life-size funeral mask of Pharaoh Tutankhamen. The mask shows the pharaoh as he was when he died in his late teens. It is made of beaten gold, with blue glass and beads. The beard is a symbol of the god Osiris, who judged the dead. The vulture and cobra on the headdress represent the pharaoh's power over Upper and Lower Egypt.

Understanding the Arts

How does the mask show the power of the pharaoh in Egyptian life?

Early Steps Toward Civilization

Archaeological finds suggest that other ancient cultures influenced early Nile Valley civilization. Hunter-gatherer groups had moved into the Nile River valley by 12,000 B.C. or earlier. Over time, these people formed farming settlements. A Neolithic culture developed in the valley probably by about 6000 B.C. By about 3800 B.C. Nile River valley people had taken other important steps along the road to civilization. They mined copper, perhaps to make tools and jewelry. They discovered how to make bronze, a mixture of copper and tin. They may also have learned to glaze pottery.

By about 3000 B.C. Nile River valley people had developed **hieroglyphics** (hy·ruh·GLI·fiks), a form of writing. Hieroglyphic writing used more than 600 signs, pictures, or symbols to represent words and sounds. At first Egyptians carved hieroglyphics in stone or other hard materials. Carving was a long and difficult process, however, and soon the Egyptians discovered a way to make a kind of paper. They used the papyrus plant that grew in marshes near the Nile. They cut the plant stem into long, thin slices. They then moistened the strips and pressed them together to make **papyrus,** from which we get our word *paper*. Egyptians wrote on papyrus with ink made from soot, water, and plant juice, using a brush made from a rush.

Thousands of years later, scholars learned to read hieroglyphic writing. In A.D. 1798 a French army invaded Egypt. The next year a French officer discovered an unusual stone. It became known as the **Rosetta Stone** because it was found in the village of Rosetta. Carved on this stone were passages written in Greek, hieroglyphics, and an Egyptian writing style called *demotic*. Some 23 years later, a French language expert used the Rosetta Stone to solve the mystery of hieroglyphics. Modern scholars could read the Greek text, which stated that all three passages said the same thing. The language expert used the Greek text to decode the hieroglyphics. He also figured out rules for understanding all other hieroglyphics. Scholars could now read eyewitness accounts of Egypt's history.

✔ **READING CHECK: Analyzing Information** What evidence indicates that Egyptians were creating a civilization? mining metals, making alloys and pottery, writing

The Egyptian Kingdoms

Over the centuries, two distinct cultures developed along the Nile. They formed two kingdoms, Lower Egypt and Upper Egypt. Lower Egypt lay to the north in the Nile River delta. Upper Egypt lay farther south, away from the Mediterranean Sea.

Sometime after 3200 B.C., **Menes** (MEE·neez), a king of Upper Egypt, united all of Egypt into one kingdom. Menes founded a **dynasty,** or family of rulers. In a dynasty the right to rule passes on within the family, usually from father to son or daughter. A dynasty's rule ends when the family is driven from power or when no family member is left to become ruler. Menes and his successors gained new territory. They also improved irrigation and trade, making Egypt wealthier. Egypt's dynastic rulers were religious and political leaders. The people regarded them as gods, and built great temples and tombs to honor them. In later years the rulers took the title **pharaoh,** which means "great house." Pharaohs held absolute, or unlimited, power. They not only led the government, but also served as judges, high priests, and generals of the armies.

LEVEL 3: Draw a time line beginning with the date 2650 B.C. and ending with 200 B.C. and have the periods of the Old Kingdom (2650 to 2180 B.C.), Middle Kingdom (2040 to 1650 B.C.), and New Kingdom (1570 to 1100 B.C.) marked on it. Have students fill in the time line with important events in Egypt's history during each time period. *(Possible answers: Old Kingdom—pyramids, science, art, civil war; Middle Kingdom—Hyksos rule Egypt, falls into disorder; New Kingdom—empire, strict government, army, conquering of new territories)*

HOMEWORK Have each student construct a chart with these column headings: *Old Kingdom, Middle Kingdom, New Kingdom;* and these row headings: *Duration, Global Relations, Internal Power Structure, Technological Developments.* Have students use information from the text to complete the chart.

From the time of Menes until almost 300 B.C., some 30 dynasties ruled Egypt. Historians divide this time span into three kingdoms: the Old Kingdom, the Middle Kingdom, and the New Kingdom.

The Old Kingdom. The Old Kingdom existed from about 2680 B.C. to about 2180 B.C. Many important developments in science and the arts took place during this time. For example, Egyptians of the Old Kingdom built the Great Sphinx and the largest pyramids. These structures still stand as symbols of the glory of Egyptian civilization.

Egyptian society in the Old Kingdom was split into two classes. The lower class included peasants and farmers. These people owed the pharaoh certain services. They served in the army and worked on building projects, such as irrigation canals and pyramids. The upper class included the pharaoh, the royal family, priests, scribes, and government officials. As time passed, these upper-class officials gradually became a small but powerful hereditary group of nobles.

Toward the end of the Old Kingdom, the pharaohs grew weaker and the nobles grew stronger. For more than 100 years after the end of the Old Kingdom, civil wars divided Egypt as rivals battled for control of the land. Historians call this period of internal strife before a new line of pharaohs came to power the First Intermediate Period.

The Middle Kingdom. In about 2050 B.C. this new line of pharaohs reunited Egypt and ushered in the Middle Kingdom. Overall, this was the "golden age" for the Egyptians, marked by stability and prosperity. During the Middle Kingdom, however, nobles and priests again began to weaken the power of the pharaoh. By 1780 B.C. the Middle Kingdom was becoming unstable.

At this time a people called the **Hyksos** (HIK·sos), meaning "foreigners," arrived in Egypt from Asia, introducing new war tools such as the chariot and the compound bow. Historians disagree greatly about the history of the Hyksos. In about the 200s B.C. an Egyptian priest, Manetho, wrote an account of Egyptian history that described how people from the east had invaded Egypt. Manetho claimed that these people destroyed cities and temples, murdered Egyptians, and made women and children slaves. Based on Manetho's account and other stories, some historians believe that the Hyksos invaded and conquered Egypt.

Other historians, however, disagree. They point out that there is little evidence that Egyptian cities and temples were destroyed. They claim that tales of the Hyksos' brutality were made up. Egyptians needed an excuse to explain why foreigners were able to take over Egypt. After all, how could a land ruled by a god fall under foreign rule unless the foreigners had mighty armies? These historians believe that the nomadic Hyksos migrated to the Nile Delta in the 1700s B.C. In the confusion following the collapse of the Middle Kingdom, they became powerful. The Hyksos ruled most of Lower Egypt for more than 100 years. In about 1650 B.C. much of Egypt fell under the rule of their horse-drawn chariots, ushering in a Second Intermediate Period before the Egyptians rose to power again.

INTERPRETING THE VISUAL RECORD

The Sphinx The Great Sphinx at Giza was probably constructed during the reign of the pharaoh Khafre, c. 2540 B.C.–c. 2514 B.C. The head of the Sphinx may have portrayed Khafre. *What characteristics of Egypt's ruler does the Sphinx reflect?*

Government

Explain to students that Egypt was a monarchy when it was ruled by pharaohs. In a monarchy, there is one ruler who has absolute power. Ask students which present-day countries are monarchies. Have students discuss the problems that this type of government can cause. Then have students compare a monarchy to a democracy.

ACTIVITY: Ask students to create a chart comparing the government of ancient Egypt to the U.S. government. After students have completed their comparison chart, go over their responses as a class.

VISUAL RECORD ANSWER

Students may note that it reflects the ruler's majesty and power.

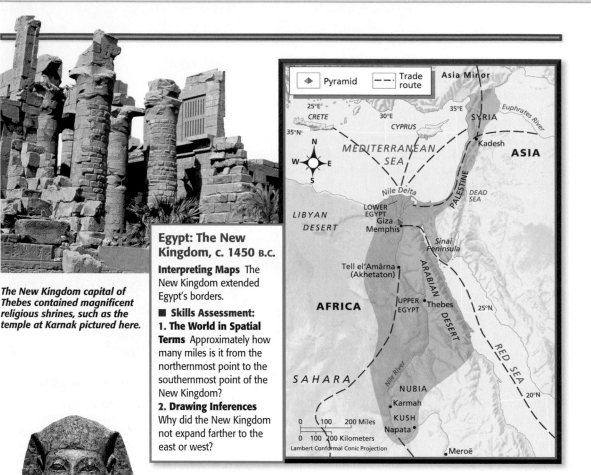

Spotlight on CULTURE

Akhenaton is considered one of the first monotheists in history because he promoted the worship of only one god—Aton. In his effort to eradicate all of the old gods, he commanded his servants to climb to the top of towering structures to erase images that were not even visible from the ground. Akhenaton's reforms failed, however, partly because of his religion's focus on the afterlife, instead of life on Earth, and its lack of traditional lavish ceremonies.

CLOSE

Organize the class into three groups representing priests of Akhenaton who want to spread the religious belief of monotheism, priests who want to maintain a polytheistic Egyptian religion, and critics of Egyptian religious society. Have the first two groups prepare and present speeches trying to convince their audience that their religious beliefs are correct. The third group should note problems with the beliefs and practices of both groups of priests. Finally, have the class discuss the ideas and critiques presented. **BLOCK SCHEDULING, COOPERATIVE LEARNING**

Geography

After the Hyksos were driven from Egypt, a new warrior tradition arose. It became the duty of Egyptian kings to lead their armies into battle. The most famous of these warrior-kings was Thutmose III, who has been called the Napoléon of Egypt. Through Thutmose's military expertise and courage, Egypt conquered land in Southwest Asia and established it as a part of the New Kingdom.

Critical Thinking

Ask students if they think the concept of a "warrior-king" applies to present-day national leaders.

ANSWER: Modern national leaders do not usually lead battles, but they must decide when military action is necessary.

MAP ANSWERS

1. approximately 1,500 miles

2. The New Kingdom did not expand far beyond the fertility of the Nile.

HISTORY MAKER ANSWER

Students might suggest that she wanted to command the same respect as her male predecessors.

The New Kingdom capital of Thebes contained magnificent religious shrines, such as the temple at Karnak pictured here.

Egypt: The New Kingdom, c. 1450 B.C.

Interpreting Maps The New Kingdom extended Egypt's borders.

■ **Skills Assessment:**
1. The World in Spatial Terms Approximately how many miles is it from the northernmost point to the southernmost point of the New Kingdom?
2. Drawing Inferences Why did the New Kingdom not expand farther to the east or west?

HISTORY MAKER

Hatshepsut
(c. 1503 B.C.–1482 B.C.)

Sometime after her husband's death, Hatshepsut became pharaoh of Egypt. This was a bold move, for no woman had ever dared to take such complete power before.

Hatshepsut ruled as a male pharaoh would. She dressed like a pharaoh, too, even wearing the false beard that only kings could wear. **Why might Hatshepsut have dressed like a male pharaoh?**

The New Kingdom. Most historians agree on one thing about the Hyksos: they remained outsiders in Egypt. Eventually leaders in Upper Egypt drove the Hyksos out of the country. A line of strong pharaohs began to rule a reunited Egypt. Their base was the city of Thebes. The period in which they ruled—from about 1570 B.C. to about 1080 B.C.—is called the New Kingdom.

For a time, the pharaohs once again had absolute power. They kept strict control over the government. Adopting the horse-drawn chariots of the Hyksos, the pharaohs created a strong army. They gained land along the eastern end of the Mediterranean Sea and south into Nubia. In doing so, the New Kingdom pharaohs built an **empire,** a form of government in which an individual or a single people rules over many other peoples and their territories. Only the strongest pharaohs could hold the empire together. When weaker pharaohs ruled, some parts of the empire tried to break away.

One of the New Kingdom pharaohs was also one of the first known female rulers. After the death of her husband, **Hatshepsut** (hat·SHEP·soot) reigned as pharaoh from about 1503 B.C. to about 1482 B.C. Although technically a co-pharaoh with her young stepson, Hatshepsut was a strong ruler who kept Egypt's borders secure and built trade with other lands. Her stepson **Thutmose III** continued this trend, bringing Egypt to the height of its power through conquest and trade until his death in 1450 B.C.

From about 1380 B.C. to 1362 B.C. Egypt was ruled by the pharaoh **Amenhotep IV** (ahm·en·HOH·tep). Amenhotep tried to bring about social and religious change in Egypt. Before Amenhotep became pharaoh, Egyptians believed that many gods

REVIEW

Have students complete the Section 1 Review on p. 25.

ASSESS

Have students complete Daily Quiz 2.1. As Alternative Assessment, use the time line exercises in this section's lessons.

RETEACH

Have students complete Main Idea Activity for English Language Learners and Special-Needs Students 2.1. Then have students write the section's headings and subheadings on a sheet of paper and list the main ideas. **ENGLISH LANGUAGE LEARNERS**

internet connect

Internet Activity: go.hrw.com
TOPIC: Egyptian Structures KEYWORD: **SP3 WH2**

Have students access the Internet through the HRW Go site to research both ancient Egyptian structures and modern structures. Then tell students to find examples of a modern and ancient structure and write a paragraph contrasting these ancient and modern styles.

Eras of Egyptian History					
Old Kingdom c. 2680 B.C. to c. 2180 B.C.	**1st Intermediate Period** c. 2180 B.C. to c. 2050 B.C.	**Middle Kingdom** c. 2050 B.C. to c. 1650 B.C.	**2nd Intermediate Period** c. 1650 B.C. to c. 1570 B.C.	**New Kingdom** c. 1570 B.C. to c. 1080 B.C.	**Post-Imperial Era** c. 1080 B.C. to c. 300s B.C.

existed. This belief is called **polytheism.** Amenhotep believed in only one god—a belief called **monotheism.** For Amenhotep, the one god was the sun, symbolized by a disk called the Aton. To honor Aton, the pharaoh changed his name to Akhenaton (ahk-NAHT-uhn), which means "he who is pleasing to Aton."

Akhenaton, however, could not change his people's religious beliefs. The pharaoh struggled with Egyptian priests, who did not want to lose their power and wealth. After the death of Akhenaton, the priests regained power and Egyptians returned to the old polytheistic religion.

Egypt's decline. After the death of Akhenaton, few strong pharaohs ruled Egypt. **Ramses II** was among those leaders. Ramses, who ruled from 1279 B.C. to 1213 B.C., kept the Egyptian empire together and ordered the construction of many temples and monuments. He is sometimes called Ramses the Great. The pharaohs who followed Ramses were not as successful. A series of invasions from groups called the Sea Peoples weakened Egypt. Eventually foreign empires such as the Assyrians, the Nubians, and the Persians attacked Egypt. It was no longer an imperial power. By the 300s B.C. rule in Egypt by Egyptians came to an end.

✔ **READING CHECK: Making Generalizations** What kind of rule characterized the height of each Egyptian kingdom?
strong rule by pharaohs

Holt Researcher
go.hrw.com
KEYWORD: Holt Researcher
FreeFind: Ramses II
After reading more about Ramses II on the Holt Researcher, write an essay evaluating whether he deserved the title "Ramses the Great."

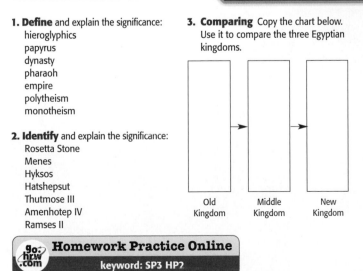

This black granite statue of Ramses II dates from between about 1300 B.C. and about 1200 B.C.

SECTION 1 REVIEW

1. Define and explain the significance:
hieroglyphics
papyrus
dynasty
pharaoh
empire
polytheism
monotheism

2. Identify and explain the significance:
Rosetta Stone
Menes
Hyksos
Hatshepsut
Thutmose III
Amenhotep IV
Ramses II

3. Comparing Copy the chart below. Use it to compare the three Egyptian kingdoms.

Old Kingdom → Middle Kingdom → New Kingdom

4. ▸ **Finding the Main Idea**
a. What physical features of the Nile River valley contributed to the rise of civilization there?
b. What factors within Egyptian society contributed to the disruption of the Old Kingdom and the beginning of the First Intermediate Period between kingdoms?
c. What benefits did strong pharaohs bring to the Egyptian kingdoms?

5. ▸ **Writing and Critical Thinking**
Summarizing Write a paragraph for a travel brochure that discusses the importance of the Nile River in Egyptian history.
Consider:
• the geography and climate of the Nile River valley
• the annual Nile flood
• the natural advantages provided by the location of the Egyptian kingdoms

Homework Practice Online
keyword: SP3 HP2

❶ Define
• hieroglyphics, p. 22
• papyrus, p. 22
• dynasty, p. 22
• pharaoh, p. 22
• empire, p. 24
• polytheism, p. 25
• monotheism, p. 25

❷ Identify
• Rosetta Stone, p. 22
• Menes, p. 22
• Hyksos, p. 23
• Hatshepsut, p. 24
• Thutmose III, p. 24
• Amenhotep IV, p. 24
• Ramses II, p. 25

❸ Old Kingdom: development of noble class, building of the Great Sphinx and pyramids; Middle Kingdom: pharaohs reunited Egypt; New Kingdom: Egypt became an empire

❹ a. sunny, frost-free climate; north wind enabled boats to sail upstream; deposits of granite, sandstone, and limestone; natural protection of deserts and seas

b. Pharaohs grew weaker and nobles grew stronger.

c. strict control of government, strong army, expansion

❺ Students may suggest that the annual flooding of the Nile made the surrounding land fertile, that Egyptian farmers used water from the Nile to irrigate their fields, and that the Nile also provided a natural transportation route.

OBJECTIVES

1 Describe Egyptian achievements in the arts and architecture.

2 Examine how the Egyptians expressed their religious beliefs.

3 Explain how farming and trade were carried on in Egypt.

📡 LET'S GET STARTED!

As students enter the classroom, ask them to list some of the technological and scientific achievements of the United States during the past 100 years. Have them circle the three they consider most important to American life and culture. Tell students that in Section 2 they will learn about the achievements of ancient Egypt.

SECTION 2

Egyptian Life and Culture

READ TO DISCOVER

❶ What did the Egyptians achieve in the arts and architecture?

❷ How did the Egyptians express their religious beliefs?

❸ How were farming and trade carried on in Egypt?

DEFINE

scribes
mummification
caravans

WHY IT MATTERS TODAY

People still build large buildings for many reasons. Use **CNNfyi.com** or other **current event** sources to explore the construction of a new government building, stadium, or skyscraper. Record your findings in your journal.

CNNfyi.com

The Main Idea
Egyptian culture was marked by long periods of stability built around their religion and geography.

The Story Continues *According to myth, Osiris was a king of Egypt murdered by his evil brother. Osiris's wife, Isis, turned into a bird and flapped her wings until the breeze breathed life back into Osiris's body. This story reflects many of the beliefs the Egyptians held about their religion and culture. For example, many Egyptian coffins showed the wings of Isis, which bring life to the souls of the dead.*

The Achievements of Ancient Egypt

Although dynasties rose and fell, Nile Valley civilization lasted for many centuries. Ancient Egyptians lived in a stable world based on the dependability of the annual Nile floods and Egypt's geographic isolation, which protected it from frequent invasions. This stability allowed the Egyptians to create a remarkable culture.

Architecture and the arts. When people today think of Egypt, they often picture the huge stone figure of the Great Sphinx and the pyramids. The Egyptians built the pyramids as tombs for the pharaohs. About 80 pyramids still stand, most of which are clustered in groups along the west bank of the Nile. The best-known pyramids, including the Great Pyramid, tower above the sands at Giza. Built in about 2600 B.C., the Great Pyramid covers about 13 acres at its base. It was originally about 480 feet high and was constructed with more than 2 million blocks of stone, each weighing about 5,000 pounds.

The pyramids at Giza were built during the reigns of several Old Kingdom pharaohs.

TEACH OBJECTIVE 1

ALL LEVELS: On the board draw a chart like the one shown. Have students fill in the columns with achievements of ancient Egypt and comparable modern-day achievements. Possible answers are listed in italics.
ENGLISH LANGUAGE LEARNERS, COOPERATIVE LEARNING

	Then	Now
Architecture	*pyramids*	*skyscrapers*
The Arts	*Great Sphinx*	*monuments*
Science	*calendar*	*X-rays*
Mathematics	*number system*	*computer math programs*
Medicine	*herbal and medicinal treatments for illnesses*	*penicillin, antibiotics, vaccines, organ transplants, artificial organs*

ENGLISH LANGUAGE LEARNERS

Building the pyramids required great skill. Egyptian architects and engineers ranked among the best in the ancient world. Historians believe the engineers built ramps and levers, which were used by thousands of workers to move the heavy stones.

The Egyptians perfected other art forms as well. Sculptors crafted small, lifelike statues of rulers and animals. Buildings were decorated with paintings of everyday life. The paintings show farmers in their fields, artisans at work, and people at banquets. They provide us with colorful examples of the Egyptian way of life.

Science, math, and medicine. Early in their history the Egyptians invented a calendar based on the movements of the moon. As discussed in Chapter 1, such a calendar does not fill the entire year. Some time later, the Egyptians realized that a bright star appeared above the horizon right before the Nile floods. The time between one rising of this star and the next is 365 days. The Egyptians based their calendar on this cycle. This calendar had 12 months of 30 days each. The remaining five days were used for holidays and feasting. To keep track of the years, Egyptians counted the years of the pharaohs' reigns. For example, they might refer to the first, second, or tenth years of the reign of a certain pharaoh.

In addition to developing a calendar, the Egyptians used a number system based on ten. This system is similar to the decimal system used today. The Egyptians used fractions and whole numbers. They also used geometry to build pyramids and rebuild fields after floods.

The Egyptians made important discoveries in medicine. They knew a good deal about the human body. They used their knowledge to treat illnesses and to preserve bodies after death. Although Egyptian treatments included "magic spells," they also often involved herbs and medicines.

✔ **READING CHECK: Categorizing** What accomplishments did the Egyptians make in architecture, the arts, science, math, and medicine? pyramids, sculptures, calendar, number system and geometry, herbal medicines

Education and Religion

To pass on their knowledge, Egyptians developed an educational system. Education focused mainly on an elite group of people called **scribes,** or clerks. Scribes learned to read and write so that they could work for the government. Religious instruction formed an important part of Egyptian education. Schools were usually attached to temples. In fact, religion played a major role in Egyptian life.

The gods. In the early days of Egyptian civilization, many villages had their own local god or gods. These gods often had an animal symbol that people considered sacred. Sacred animals included the cat, the bull, the crocodile, and the scarab beetle.

In time, some of these gods came to be worshiped by people throughout Egypt. The most important god was Amon, or Amon-Re, the creator, identified with the sun. Osiris, who judged people after death, was also associated with the Nile River—just as

INTERPRETING THE VISUAL RECORD

Rituals Wealthy Egyptians used many herbs and ointments to protect their bodies. In this scene from the back of the ornate chair pictured below it, a wife is anointing her husband. ***What does this image imply about Egyptian views toward the human body?***

Interdisciplinary Connection

ARCHITECTURE. Around the time of the first dynasties, Egyptians began building tombs in which to bury their dead. Called *mastaba* in Arabic, these tombs had flat tops and sloped sides and were made of mud bricks. Within the tomb, and usually below the ground, were a chamber for the body and other chambers for burial goods. Over time, people began to build larger tombs, some with as many as 30 chambers.

Critical Thinking

Ask students to compare American monuments built to honor dead leaders, such as the Washington Monument with Egyptian pyramids. Do they reflect similar concepts of death and leadership?

ANSWER: Students might point out that, although American monuments are built to honor leaders, they are not tombs and have no religious significance.

VISUAL RECORD ANSWER

Students might conclude that the body was very important to the Egyptians, and they believed it should be preserved and protected.

Technology Resources

World History Teaching Transparency: Everyday Life 2: Egyptian Tomb Painting

TEACH OBJECTIVE 2

LEVEL 3: Tell students that the Egyptians did not believe that their life cycle ended with death. The Egyptians felt the body needed to be preserved to make existence after death possible. Ask students what objects people with such beliefs might also consider to be important in the afterlife and why.

 HOMEWORK Have each student write a paragraph that describes ancient Egyptian religious beliefs and how these beliefs influenced Egyptian burial practices.

TEACH OBJECTIVE 3

LEVEL 1: Tell students that in ancient Egypt most people were farmers, but the pharaohs directed and profited from their labor. Remind students that farmers grew more crops than they could use in order to have items to trade with other civilizations. Have students look at the map on page 24. Ask them how Egypt might have conducted trade with people in Europe and western and central Africa. *(build ships that would carry them across the Mediterranean, sail ships down the Red Sea, cross the desert)*
ENGLISH LANGUAGE LEARNERS

That's Interesting!

Women had economic power in ancient Egypt. Women could write their own wills, and one woman, displeased with four of her children, disinherited them. Another court document records that a wife loaned some of her silver to her husband. The contract stated that he was required to repay it over three years at a 30 percent interest rate.

VISUAL RECORD ANSWER

They were able to communicate their beliefs visually.

internet connect

TOPIC: Pyramids
GO TO: go.hrw.com
KEYWORD: SP3 WH2

Have students access the Internet through the HRW Go site to research the Egyptian Pyramids. Then have them write detailed paragraphs about the pyramids that they will use in an illustrated brochure. Tell students to include information in their brochure that gives historical background on the pyramids, how they were built, what is inside them, and how they were excavated.

INTERPRETING THE VISUAL RECORD

The ankh The ankh was a powerful religious and spiritual image in ancient Egypt. It was used to symbolize the idea of life. *What do objects such as this ankh tell us about the Egyptians' ability to communicate their beliefs?*

the Nile River regularly flooded and receded, Osiris periodically died and was reborn. Isis was Osiris's wife and the goddess of the royal throne.

The afterlife. At first, Egyptians believed that only pharaohs had an afterlife, or life after death. Later, Egyptians believed that everyone, including animals, had an afterlife. They believed that in the afterlife a person was judged. The person's heart, which would tell whether the person had lied, murdered, or been too proud, was weighed on a great scale against a sacred feather, the symbol of truth. If the scale balanced, the heart had told the truth. It could then enter a place of eternal happiness. If the scale did not balance, the heart was thrown to a horrible monster called the Eater of the Dead.

Egyptians believed that the body had to be preserved to make life after death possible. To do this, they developed a process called **mummification.** Organs were removed from the body, which was then treated with chemicals. This process preserved the body for centuries. Workers placed the mummy in a tomb stocked with clothing, food, tools, and weapons. They even included painted figures that represented servants. The number and value of the objects in the tomb depended on the importance of the dead person. The Egyptians considered the objects necessary for use in the afterlife. In later years, scrolls known as the *Book of the Dead* were placed in the tomb to serve as a kind of guide to the afterlife.

✔ **READING CHECK: Drawing Inferences** In what way can burial sites reveal information about ancient Egyptian religious beliefs? artifacts were meant for use in afterlife

Society and Economy

The pyramids reflected the greatness of the pharaohs. Most Egyptians, however, could never hope for wealth or power. Egyptian social classes were rigidly divided. People in the lower class could improve their status, but they almost never entered the ranks of the upper class. Women, however, enjoyed many legal rights. They ranked as the equals of their husbands in social and business affairs. An Egyptian woman could own property in her own right. She could leave that property to her daughter. In many ways, Egyptian women had more freedom and power than women of other cultures in the region.

Farming. Farmland in Egypt was divided into large estates. Peasants did most of the farming, using crude hoes or wooden plows. Wheat and barley were the chief grain crops. Flax was grown and then spun and woven into linen. Farmers also grew cotton—just as important to Egypt in ancient times as it is today—for weaving into cloth.

CLOSE

Ask students to list the accomplishments of the Egyptians in architecture, the arts, science, mathematics, and medicine and tell which accomplishments were the most important.

REVIEW

Have students complete the Section 2 Review on p. 29.

ASSESS

Have students complete Daily Quiz 2.2. As Alternative Assessment, use the achievements exercise in this section's lesson.

RETEACH

Have students complete Main Idea Activity for English Language Learners and Special-Needs Students 2.2. Then ask students to write a question and answer that covers the main idea for each subsection in the section. **ENGLISH LANGUAGE LEARNERS**

EXTEND

Have students work in groups to build a pyramid. They may use a problem-solving process to create a pyramid modeled after one that exists in Egypt or create a new pyramid with whatever type of materials they choose. **BLOCK SCHEDULING, COOPERATIVE LEARNING**

This mural shows Egyptian farmers processing grain.

The peasants, however, could keep just part of the crop. The rest went to the pharaoh, who legally owned all land, as rents and taxes. The life of a farmer was difficult. One Egyptian described the farmer's day:

> **Primary Source**
>
> **❝Let me set out for you the farmer's state—that other hard calling. . . . He spends the day cutting tools for cultivating barley and the night twisting ropes. His midday hour even he is in the habit of spending in farmer's work. He sets about equipping himself to sally forth in the field like any warrior [that is, the farmer is burdened with many heavy tools]. The field is parched . . .❞**
>
> Lansing Papyrus, from *Pharaoh's People*

Analyzing Primary Sources

Drawing Conclusions Why does the writer claim that farmers have a "hard calling"? farm work was labor-intensive and time-consuming

Trade. Trade was also tightly controlled by the government. Since the peasants of ancient Egypt grew more food than the country needed, Egyptians traded the extra food with other peoples. As trade developed it offered new opportunities to the growing merchant class. Merchants riding donkeys and later camels formed **caravans**— groups of people traveling together for safety over long distances. Caravans traveled from Egypt to western Asia and deep into Africa. Egyptians also traded by sea. They were among the first people to build seagoing ships. Egyptian ships sailed the Mediterranean and Red Seas and traveled the African coast.

✔ **READING CHECK: Making Predictions** How might trade affect the spread of Egyptian culture? could expose people in far-off places to Egyptian ideas

SECTION
2 REVIEW ANSWERS

❶ Define
- scribes, p. 27
- mummification, p. 28
- caravans, p. 29

❷ Architecture: pyramids; The Arts: Great Sphinx, sculpture, painting; Education: education system for the elite; Mathematics: a number system; Medicine: treatments, ways to preserve bodies after death; Science: a calendar based on 365 days

❸ a. Egyptians based their calendar on a star that appeared near the beginning of the flood cycle.

b. They believed a good character was important for having a good afterlife.

c. Because they grew more food than the country needed, they began trading with other peoples.

❹ Students might suggest that burying people in tombs allowed them to be buried with all they would need in the afterlife.

SECTION 2 REVIEW

1. **Define** and explain the significance:
   scribes
   mummification
   caravans

2. **Categorizing** Copy the concept web below. Use it to record Egyptian achievements in architecture, the arts, education, mathematics, medicine, and the sciences.

   Architecture — Mathematics
   The Arts — Egypt — Medicine
   Education — Science

3. **Finding the Main Idea**
   a. How did the Nile floods influence the development of the Egyptian calendar?
   b. What does the Egyptian belief in an afterlife tell about the importance they placed on having a good character?
   c. How did Egyptian success at farming lead to contact with other peoples and cultures?

4. **Writing and Critical Thinking**
   Summarizing Explain why the Egyptians buried mummies in tombs.
   Consider:
   - Egyptian beliefs regarding the afterlife
   - the process of mummification
   - the goods placed in the tombs

Homework Practice Online
keyword: SP3 HP2

OBJECTIVES

1 Explore how geography affected the development of the Sumerian civilization.

2 Identify the achievements of the Sumerian people.

3 Describe what life was like in Sumerian society.

REPRODUCIBLE RESOURCES

▸ Guided Reading Strategy 2.3

▸ Readings in World History 6: An Early City in the Tigris-Euphrates Valley

TECHNOLOGY RESOURCES

▸ One-Stop Planner 2.3

▸ Homework Practice Online

▸ Online Maps, Charts, and Graphs: Development of Cuneiform, 3000 B.C.– 600 B.C.

REINFORCEMENT, REVIEW, AND ASSESSMENT

▸ Section 3 Review, p. 34

▸ Daily Quiz 2.3

▸ Main Idea Activity 2.3

▸ English Audio Summary 2.3

▸ Spanish Audio Summary 2.3

MAP ANSWER

rivers

🔴 LET'S GET STARTED!

As students enter the classroom, remind them that Egypt was geographically isolated. Ask them why that was important to the success of Egyptian civilization. (*Students should point out that it lessened the threat of outside invasions.*) Have them predict the difficulties a civilization that was not geographically isolated might have faced. (*Students might note that outsiders could attack more frequently.*) Tell students that in Section 3 they will learn about the effect geography had on Sumerian civilization.

SECTION 3

READ TO DISCOVER

❶ How did geography affect the development of the Sumerian civilization?

❷ What were the achievements of the Sumerian people?

❸ What was life like in Sumerian society?

DEFINE

cuneiform
arch
ziggurats
city-state

WHY IT MATTERS TODAY

The Fertile Crescent remains an area of conflict today. Use **CNNfyi.com** or other **current event** sources to explore conflicts between present-day nations in that region. Record your findings in your journal.

CNNfyi.com

Sumerian Civilization

The Main Idea
The Fertile Crescent gave rise to the Sumerian civilization in the Tigris-Euphrates Valley.

The Story Continues *Almost 4,000 years ago in the town of Sumer, a father gave his son the advice that would be repeated by fathers throughout history: "Go to school, stand before your 'school-father,' recite your assignment . . . After you have finished your assignment . . . come to me. . . . Don't stand about in the public square, or wander about the boulevard." The story of the Sumerians shows how early peoples of the Fertile Crescent passed their cultures on to future generations.*

The Land: Its Geography and Importance

The story of ancient Egypt describes one people living in one place for centuries. A very different story developed in southwestern Asia, another cradle of early civilization. Unlike Egypt, this area was not geographically isolated. Wave upon wave of invaders crisscrossed the land.

A strip of fertile land begins at the Isthmus of Suez and arcs through Southwest Asia to the Persian Gulf. The land within this crescent-shaped area is so well suited to farming that it is known as the Fertile Crescent. Between 5000 B.C. and 4000 B.C., Neolithic farmers began to build an identifiable civilization in the Fertile Crescent. Their society was built around the cooperation necessary to control floodwaters and to irrigate fields.

The Fertile Crescent, c. 3000 B.C.

Interpreting Maps Early civilizations thrived in Mesopotamia, in the heart of the Fertile Crescent.

■ **Skills Assessment: Physical Systems** According to the map, what type of geographic feature was common to the locations of the earliest Mesopotamian cities?

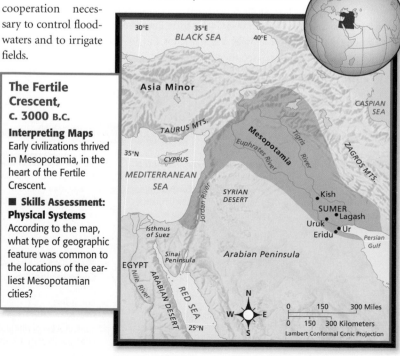

TEACH OBJECTIVE 1

ALL LEVELS: Have students compare the map of ancient Egypt on page 24 with the map of the Fertile Crescent on page 30. Ask them what similarities they find in the geography of the two civilizations. *(Both civilizations have some natural protections, such as mountains, seas, and desert.)* Then have students make up questions about the geographic distribution of peoples in these regions. Use the questions for class discussion. **ENGLISH LANGUAGE LEARNERS**

HOMEWORK Tell students that they are journalists who write for the newspaper *Sumer Today.* Their assignment is to write an article summarizing why the Fertile Crescent experienced so many invasions, what happened to the newcomers, and the result for Sumer of these invasions. Instead of writing an article, some students may draw illustrations for the newspaper and write short captions.

The Tigris and Euphrates Rivers are major geographical features of the Fertile Crescent. Both rivers begin in the hills of what is now Turkey and flow southeast. At one point the two rivers lie within 30 miles of each other. They then spread apart until the valley between them—the Tigris-Euphrates Valley—widens to about 250 miles. The Tigris-Euphrates Valley has been known by many names, including Mesopotamia. The southeastern part of the valley has usually been called Babylonia.

Both the Tigris and the Euphrates overflow often, sending floodwaters swirling over the surrounding land. People must build canals and dikes to bring water to their fields and to return water to the river after floods. Unlike the Nile flood, the flooding of the Tigris and Euphrates cannot be easily predicted. It may come anytime between the beginning of March and the end of June. The size of the flood also varies. Not surprisingly, the early people of the valley viewed nature and the gods as harsh and unpredictable.

As with the Nile Valley, the Fertile Crescent was surrounded by dry lands and mountains. They were not as barren as those around Egypt, however. Tribes of wandering herders lived off the grasses and other plant life there. They often invaded the valley, conquered it, and established empires. Over time, these invaders grew weak and new waves of invaders conquered them. This pattern makes the history of the Fertile Crescent a story of repeated migration and conquest. A priest described the results of one such invasion.

Primary Source
❝The [invading herders] have set fire to the [crop lands surrounding several Sumerian villages]. They have carried away the silver and precious stones. They have shed blood in the palace of [the local Sumerian ruler]. . . . They have removed the grain from [Sumerian fields and villages], all of it that was under cultivation.❞

Priest of Lagash, from *The Sumerians*

✔ **READING CHECK: Contrasting** How did the geography of the Fertile Crescent differ from that of ancient Egypt? not isolated by natural barriers

Sumer and Its Achievements

As the Tigris and Euphrates flow to the Persian Gulf, they carry rich soil. In ancient times, particularly fertile soil covered the lower part of the Tigris-Euphrates Valley. Neolithic people settled in this area, called Sumer (SOO·muhr), and grew crops. Over time, they created what we call Sumerian culture. We do not know much about the origins of the Sumerians. A group of nomadic people probably migrated to Sumer and mingled with the people already there. By 3000 B.C. these people used metal and had developed a kind of writing called pictographs, or picture writing. Sumerian pictographs are one of the earliest known forms of writing.

Sumerian writing. Sumerian writing was different from Egyptian writing. Egyptian hieroglyphics were symbols carved on stone or written on paper. The papyrus reed that Egyptians used to make paper did not grow in Sumer, however. Sumerians wrote by pressing marks into clay tablets. Writers used a wedge-shaped tool called a stylus. As a result, most signs were wedge shapes. Today we call Sumerian writing **cuneiform** (kyooh·NEE·uh·fawrm), from the Latin word for wedge, *cuneus.* Cuneiform writing developed from pictographic writing. Sumerians had about 600 cuneiform signs.

Analyzing Primary Sources

Identifying Cause and Effect
How might their fear of the destruction described by the priest have affected the river valley people? might have made them suspicious of outsiders or foreigners

INTERPRETING THE VISUAL RECORD
Sumerian writing The cuneiform above, carved on a clay tablet with a stylus, dates from about 2400 B.C. *In what way does this writing reflect the tools used by the Sumerians?*

LEVEL 3: Tell students that, like the Egyptians, the Sumerians created a successful civilization. Ask students to use their knowledge of early civilizations to predict Sumerian achievements.

As a class, have students create a set of 26 cuneiform-style wedge shapes to represent all the letters of the alphabet. Draw these shapes on the chalkboard so that students can copy them. Have each student write a word or phrase in the new alphabet that relates to an aspect of Sumerian society. Have students exchange papers and translate each other's work.
BLOCK SCHEDULING, COOPERATIVE LEARNING

Economics

Economic wealth often shifted between the major city-states throughout the history of Sumer. Just before 3000 B.C. the city-state of Uruk was extremely prosperous. During this period, Sumerians built major temples and shrines in Uruk, which were large and elaborately decorated. When archaeologists uncovered the ruins of these temples, they discovered silver and copper figurines, bowls inlaid with stones, and other carved stone objects. A three-foot-tall vase, with sculpted decorations of a religious procession, as well as a realistic sculpted head of a woman, were also found. Other objects found include the first preserved written records, which were primitive pictographs.

Critical Thinking

Ask students to suggest what the size and wealth of the temples of Uruk may tell us about the role of religion in Sumerian society.

ANSWER: Students should note that religion was important enough to control large amounts of wealth and labor. This would be consistent with the priests' great influence on the Sumerian city-states.

Builders constructed the Choghā Zanbīl ziggurat in the Khūzestān province of present-day Iran in about 1250 B.C.

Architecture and science. The Sumerians may also have invented several important architectural designs. The **arch,** a curved structure over an opening, is one of the strongest forms in building. By combining several arches, the Sumerians built rounded roofs in the shape of domes or vaults.

The most striking Sumerian buildings were the temples, known as **ziggurats.** Like other Sumerian buildings, ziggurats were made of baked brick placed in layers. The ziggurats looked something like a wedding cake. Each could be up to 150 feet high. The top served as a shrine to a Sumerian god.

The Sumerians may have been the first people to develop and use the wheel. In mathematics, they used a system of numbers based on 60. For example, Sumerians divided a circle into 360 degrees (six 60s). Each degree was divided into 60 minutes, and each minute into 60 seconds. Today, when you look at a compass or a watch, you are using a system that the Sumerians developed thousands of years ago.

Like other early civilizations, the Sumerians created a lunar calendar. To keep it accurate, they added a month every few years.

✔ **READING CHECK: Finding the Main Idea** What were the main achievements of the Sumerian civilization? cuneiform writing, the arch, the wheel, math

Sumerian Society

Early in their history, Sumerians developed a form of community called the **city-state.** A city-state included a town or city and the surrounding land controlled by it. Major Sumerian city-states—such as Ur, Erech, and Kish—had thousands of residents.

Government and society. The many Sumerian city-states rarely united under a single government. The people believed that much of the land in each city-state belonged to one or more gods. Not surprisingly, priests were important figures. As city-states competed for water and land, however, war leaders became more important. Eventually these leaders ruled as kings.

Kings, high priests, and nobles were at the top of Sumerian society, followed by lower priests, merchants, and scholars. Below them were peasant farmers, then slaves who had been kidnapped from other regions or captured in war.

LEVEL 1: Distribute sheets of drawing paper to students. Tell students to draw a map of a Sumerian city-state. Explain that the maps should include symbols for places such as homes, schools, government buildings, markets, ziggurats, and farms. Students should include a map key to explain the symbols.
ENGLISH LANGUAGE LEARNERS

CLOSE

Have students create a chart or a Venn diagram to compare the religious beliefs of the Sumerians and the Egyptians. *(similarities: polytheism, gods identified with forces of nature and heavenly bodies, gods guarded cities, belief in afterlife; differences: Sumerians did not believe in rewards and punishments after death; Egyptians believed that people were judged after death.)*

SKILL-BUILDING STRATEGIES Evaluating Sources of Evidence

Ancient Discoveries

To learn about ancient civilizations such as the Sumerians or Egyptians, we can study both primary and secondary sources. Primary sources include items such as artifacts, diaries, letters, official documents, and eyewitness accounts. Secondary sources are accounts or histories written after the events by people who did not take part in those events. Each type of evidence offers different information. Sometimes a piece of evidence can be both a primary and a secondary source of evidence.

Howard Carter (top) and colleagues open Tutankhamen's tomb at Luxor, Egypt, 1922.

An Archaeologist's View:

Archaeologist Howard Carter found many artifacts in his lifetime. His greatest discovery was the tomb of the Egyptian pharaoh Tutankhamen. Carter described his find:

"With suppressed excitement I carefully cut the cord, removed that precious seal, drew back the bolts, and opened the doors, when a fourth shrine was revealed . . . There, filling the entire area within stood an immense yellow quartzite sarcophagus [stone coffin]. . . . The lid being suspended in mid-air, we rolled back those covering shrouds, one by one . . . so gorgeous was the sight that met our eyes: a golden effigy [image] of the young boy king.

"The hands, crossed over the breast, held the royal emblems—the Crook and the Flail. Upon the forehead of this recumbent figure . . . were two emblems delicately worked in brilliant inlay—the Cobra and the Vulture—symbols of Upper and Lower Egypt."

The Standard of Ur was found in a Sumerian royal cemetery. It is a mosaic from about 2500 B.C., made of shells and colored stones. The panel is double-sided, showing scenes of war on one side and scenes of peace (right) on the other.

Skills Reminder

To evaluate sources of evidence, you must first identify the source. For example, is it a biography, a diary, a government record, or a work of art? Then review the definitions of primary and secondary sources to determine what type of source it is. The language of a written source, comparison with other sources, and information about the origins or author of the source will also help you determine its usefulness.

Skills Practice

❶ What kind of source is *The Standard of Ur*? What does it reveal about Sumerian society?
❷ How might Howard Carter's description of the opening of King Tutankhamen's tomb be considered both a primary and a secondary source?
❸ Is a primary source always more reliable than a secondary source? Why or why not?

That's Interesting!

Artistic innovations can be found in several Sumerian temples. At the Eanna temple, builders found an innovative way to decorate the walls. Artists took tens of thousands of small clay cones with red, black, or buff tips. They then inserted these cones into the mud plaster of the walls to form triangles, zigzags, and other geometric designs.

SKILLS PRACTICE ANSWERS

1. It is a primary source. It reveals the various activities of Sumerian society.

2. The description would be considered a primary source when used to answer questions about the opening of the tomb, and it would be considered a secondary source when used to answer questions about the burial of King Tut.

3. Students might answer yes, because the writer was present during the event, or no, because the accounts may be subjective.

REVIEW

Have students complete the Section 3 Review on p. 34.

ASSESS

Have students complete Daily Quiz 2.3. As Alternative Assessment, have students complete either of the map exercises in this section's lessons.

RETEACH

Have students complete Main Idea Activity for English Language Learners and Special-Needs Students 2.3. Have students

write three important Sumerian achievements and describe why each was important. *(Students may mention cuneiform, arches, ziggurats, the wheel, the city-state. Encourage students to expand on their descriptions of why each was important.)*
ENGLISH LANGUAGE LEARNERS

EXTEND

Tell students to imagine that they are social studies schoolteachers in ancient Sumer. Using social studies terminology, have them prepare a lesson to present to the class about Sumerian history, contemporary civilization, or any aspect of Sumerian society.
BLOCK SCHEDULING

YOUNG PEOPLE IN HISTORY ANSWER

Students might suggest that the Sumerians believed only intelligent and skillful boys could learn to be scribes.

SECTION 3 REVIEW ANSWERS

❶ **Define**
- cuneiform, p. 31
- arch, p. 32
- ziggurats, p. 32
- city-state, p. 32

❷ Writing: cuneiform; Religion: polytheism, did not believe in rewards and punishment after death; Architecture/Science: arches, ziggurats, the wheel, number system, calendar; Government/Society: city-state, trade, education

❸ **a.** It was not geographically isolated, making invasions easy.

b. They considered learning very important for intelligent, upper-class males.

c. The Sumerians did not believe in an afterlife or in rewards or punishments after death.

❹ Students should mention achievements such as cuneiform writing, ziggurats, the wheel, a number system, a calendar, and successful trade with other peoples.

YOUNG PEOPLE IN HISTORY

Ancient Schools
Sumerian boys who showed intelligence and skill were trained to be scribes. They learned to read and write in cuneiform. They also learned basic mathematics. Teachers often punished poor performance with beatings.

Schoolboys who were late for class were also punished harshly. One Sumerian boy wrote, "In school the monitor in charge said to me: 'Why are you late?' Afraid and with pounding heart, I entered before my teacher and made a respectful [bow]." History does not record the outcome of the boy's tardiness. **Why might just some Sumerian boys have been allowed to receive an education?**

Farming and trade. Most Sumerians farmed. They grew dates, grains, and vegetables, and raised domestic animals. They also grew flax for linen and wove woolen goods.

Sumerian farmers grew enough food to allow many people to work as artisans and traders. Before 3000 B.C., Sumerians had begun trading with other peoples of Southwest Asia. Some merchants had agents in faraway places. Others traveled by land or boat to sell Sumerian goods.

Education and religion. The Sumerians considered education very important. However, only upper-class boys—and no girls—attended school. Students learned to write and spell by copying religious books and songs. They also studied drawing and arithmetic.

Like the Egyptians, the Sumerians practiced polytheism. The Sumerian gods were identified with forces of nature and heavenly bodies, such as the sun and the moon. Important gods included An (lord of heaven), Enlil (god of air and storms), and Enki (god of water and wisdom). Sumerian gods and goddesses also guarded individual cities. The city of Nippur, for example, was overseen by the god Enlil, while his son Nanna, god of the moon, guarded the city of Ur.

The Sumerians buried food and tools with their dead. Unlike the Egyptians, however, the Sumerians did not imagine the afterlife in detail. Instead, the Sumerians believed in a kind of shadowy lower world. They did not believe in rewards and punishments after death.

✔ **READING CHECK: Identifying Bias** What did the structure of their educational system reveal about the biases in Sumerian society? only upper-class males were educated

Sheep provided wool and meat for early Sumerians. This sheep's head sculpture was crafted in Sumeria about 5,200 years ago.

SECTION 3 REVIEW

1. Define and explain the significance:
cuneiform
arch
ziggurats
city-state

2. Summarizing Copy the chart below. Use it to show the major characteristics of Sumerian civilization.

Sumer
- Writing
- Religion
- Architecture/Science
- Government/Society

3. **Finding the Main Idea**
a. How did geography shape life in the Fertile Crescent?
b. What did their focus on education reveal about Sumerian values?
c. How was society in Sumer different from society in Egypt?

4. **Writing and Critical Thinking**
Supporting a Point of View Write a report that persuades readers that Sumerians created a successful civilization.
Consider:
- Sumerian achievements in math and writing
- trade with other peoples
- construction of large temples

Homework Practice Online
keyword: SP3 HP2

OBJECTIVES

1 Explain why Sumerians were attacked by outsiders.

2 Examine the characteristics of Babylonian society.

3 Investigate which invaders conquered Babylon and why they failed to control it.

4 Describe the achievements of the Persians.

🔊 **LET'S GET STARTED!**

As students enter the classroom, ask them to write a short description of what they think happened to the Sumerians. (*Students might guess that their geographic vulnerability led to many attacks on them and eventually they were conquered.*) Tell students that in Section 4 they will learn about the empires of the Fertile Crescent that developed after the Sumerians were conquered.

SECTION 4

Empires of the Fertile Crescent

READ TO DISCOVER

❶ Why were Sumerians attacked by outsiders?

❷ What characterized Babylonian society?

❸ What invaders conquered Babylon and why did they fail to control it?

❹ What were the achievements of the Persians?

IDENTIFY

Sargon
Hammurabi
Nebuchadnezzar
Cyrus
Zoroaster

WHY IT MATTERS TODAY

The people who lived in the Fertile Crescent developed different legal systems. Use CNNfyi.com or other **current event** sources to find information about a law being proposed in the United States today and why people oppose or support it. Record your findings in your journal.

CNNfyi.com

The Main Idea
A series of invaders from both within and outside of Mesopotamia controlled the Fertile Crescent.

The Story Continues *"You dolt, numskull, school pest, you illiterate, you Sumerian ignoramus, your hand is terrible; it cannot even hold the stylus properly; it is unfit for dictation."* So wrote one Sumerian scribe about another, criticizing his writing skills. More serious infighting so weakened the Sumerians that they were left vulnerable to attack.

The Akkadians

In about 2330 B.C. the Akkadians, a people who lived in Mesopotamia, attacked and conquered the Sumerians. The Akkadians spoke a Semitic language related to modern Arabic and Hebrew. **Sargon,** who ruled from about 2334 B.C. to 2279 B.C., was the most powerful Akkadian king. He established a great empire that reached as far west as the Mediterranean Sea.

The Akkadian Empire lasted about 150 years. When it ended, Sumerian city-states once again prospered, including the important city of Ur. However, new waves of invaders swept through the eastern Fertile Crescent. Another powerful state of Semitic-speaking people arose. It was centered at a large new city called Babylon.

✔ **READING CHECK: Problem Solving** What actions might the Sumerians have taken to help fight off invaders like the Akkadians? unite city-states

Akkadian Empire, c. 2330 B.C.

Interpreting Maps The Akkadian king Sargon first came to power in the city of Kish. Later, Sargon moved his capital to Akkad.

■ **Skills Assessment: Environment and Society** Why might the city of Ur have been an important center of Mesopotamian trade?

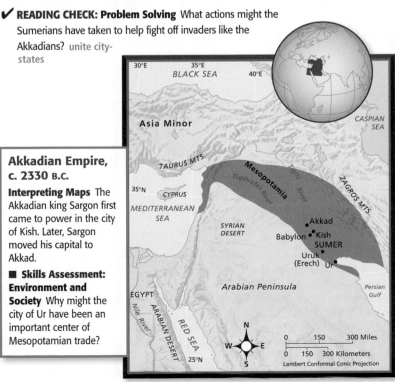

SECTION 4 RESOURCES

REPRODUCIBLE RESOURCES

▸ Guided Reading Strategy 2.4

▸ Graphic Organizer Activity 2

▸ Readings in World History 7, 8

TECHNOLOGY RESOURCES

▸ One-Stop Planner 2.4

▸ Holt Researcher: World History: Cyrus, Darius I, Zoroaster

▸ Homework Practice Online

REINFORCEMENT, REVIEW, AND ASSESSMENT

▸ Section 4 Review, p. 40

▸ Daily Quiz 2.4

▸ Main Idea Activity 2.4

▸ English Audio Summary 2.4

▸ Spanish Audio Summary 2.4

MAP ANSWER

Students might point out that it was located near other cities.

LEVEL 3: Tell students to imagine they are Sumerians preparing for an attack by outside invaders. Have students use a problem-solving process to determine why outside invaders attack and to develop a method for defending their city-state. Ask them to develop a plan for governing the area that would unite all the city-states and prevent outside invaders from conquering them. Have students share their plans with the class.

Government

The Code of Hammurabi covered all sorts of legal issues and dealings between individuals. One important aspect of the code was that it made people think twice about bringing false charges against a neighbor. The code stated: "If a seignior came forward with false testimony in a case, and has not proved the word which he spoke, if that case was a case involving life, that seignior shall be put to death."

Critical Thinking

Ask if students see any disadvantage to this aspect of the Code of Hammurabi.

ANSWER: This rule might have discouraged people from testifying, out of fear for their own lives.

HISTORY MAKER ANSWER
his code of laws

MAP ANSWER
the mountains

Technology Resources
World History and Cultures Video Program 2: The First Empires

HISTORY MAKER
**Hammurabi
(d. 1750 B.C.)**

Hammurabi was originally a king of the Amorite people, who migrated into Mesopotamia. As ruler Hammurabi built on the civilization that had begun in Sumer. Today he is best remembered for his code of laws. **What is Hammurabi best known for?**

The Babylonians

In about 1792 B.C. a strong ruler named **Hammurabi** (ham·uh·RAHB·ee) came to power in Babylon. He conquered most of the Tigris-Euphrates Valley. More than just a great military leader, Hammurabi was also an outstanding political leader and lawmaker. He is best known for the Code of Hammurabi. This collection of about 282 laws was compiled under his direction. It contained some ideas that are still found in law codes today.

Code of Hammurabi. The Code of Hammurabi concerned all aspects of life in Babylon. Some laws dealt with commerce and industry, while others regulated wages, hours, working conditions, and property rights. Punishment was harsh, based as it was on the idea of "an eye for an eye."

> **History Makers Speak**
> **"[1] If a man bring[s] an accusation against a man, and charge[s] him with a [major] crime, but cannot prove it, he, the accuser, shall be put to death. [229–30] If a builder build[s] a house for a man and [does] not make its construction firm, and the house which he has built collapse[s] and cause[s] the death of the owner of the house, that builder shall be put to death."**
>
> Hammurabi, from *Code of Hammurabi*

Punishment varied according to status, however. If a wealthy man destroyed the eye of a poor man, the wealthy man did not lose his eye. Instead, he paid a fine.

Babylonian culture. In some ways Babylonian culture resembled that of the Sumerians. Most Babylonians farmed. They kept domestic animals and grew a wide variety of food crops. They also wove cotton and wool cloth. The Babylonians were very active traders. Their merchants exchanged goods with distant parts of the Fertile Crescent and with Egypt and India.

Babylonian women had some legal and economic rights, including property rights. Women could be merchants, traders, or even scribes. On the other hand, husbands could divorce their wives, but wives could not divorce their husbands. If a husband was cruel, however, a woman could leave him and take her property with her.

Religion. The Babylonians adopted many Sumerian religious beliefs. The Babylonians made sacrifices to their gods for favors like good harvests or success in business. Like the Sumerians, they believed in a shadowy life after death. Their religious practices were directed toward a successful life on Earth. Babylonians also believed that their priests could foretell the future. Therefore, Babylonian priests held great power and wealth.

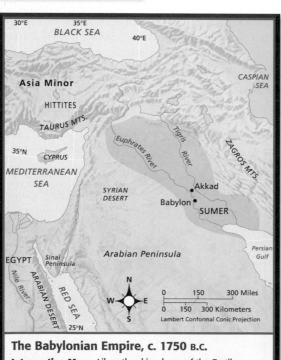

The Babylonian Empire, c. 1750 B.C.
Interpreting Maps Like other kingdoms of the Fertile Crescent, the Babylonian Empire was centered on the Tigris and Euphrates Rivers.

■ **Skills Assessment: Using Geography** What major geographic feature may have prevented the expansion of the Babylonian Empire northward?

✔ **READING CHECK: Drawing Conclusions** How do you think the Code of Hammurabi affected Babylonian society? people probably feared breaking the law

Other Conquerors

Many times throughout history, conquerors adopted the culture of the people they conquered. This was certainly true of the Babylonians after they conquered the Sumerians. Some conquerors, however, kept their own cultural values. This was the case with the Hittites.

The Hittites. The Hittites were a warlike people who invaded the Tigris-Euphrates Valley from Asia Minor sometime in the 1600s B.C. The Hittites were among the first people to smelt iron. Their most important achievement, however, may have been their laws and government. Under Hittite law, only major crimes received the death penalty. Hittite law called for a person to pay a fine, rather than experience retaliation, for causing damage or injury. As in some other empires of the time, the Hittite kings were regarded as chief-priests, although they allowed significant religious freedom.

When the Hittites invaded the Tigris-Euphrates Valley, they conquered and looted the city of Babylon. The Hittites were too far from their homeland to control Babylon permanently, however. They soon withdrew to the western part of the Fertile Crescent. They remained a powerful force there until about 1200 B.C., when the entire region began to be hit by invasions from the Sea Peoples.

The Assyrians. The Assyrians were a Semitic-speaking people from northern Mesopotamia. As early as the 2000s B.C. they had settled the city of Ashur on the upper Tigris River and adopted many elements of Sumerian culture. For centuries they had been dominated by others. The Assyrians briefly established an empire of their own in the 1300s B.C., but it was soon overrun by nomadic migrations. They gradually recovered, however, and began to dominate the area of southwest Asia. Between about 900 B.C. and about 650 B.C., the Assyrians expanded their power across the Fertile Crescent and into Egypt. At its height, the mighty empire included all of Mesopotamia, Syria, Palestine, and the Nile Valley.

The Assyrians were fierce, effective warriors. Not only did they use chariots in battle, but they also were the first to use cavalry—soldiers on horseback. They used terror to control their enemies. They frequently enslaved the people they conquered and killed captured enemy soldiers. Sometimes they deported whole populations to other regions. By these methods, the Assyrians added land to their empire and gained many slaves. About 700 B.C. the Assyrians captured Babylon, looted it, and then destroyed it completely.

Hittite and Assyrian Empires, c. 1250 B.C.–650 B.C.

Interpreting Maps Assyrian rulers used their powerful, well-trained army to conquer new lands and to expand their empire. Captive peoples were forced by the Assyrians to work on various construction projects.

■ **Skills Assessment: The World in Spatial Terms** In terms of size, how did the Assyrian Empire compare to the earlier empires of Akkad and Babylonia?

Map legend:
- Hittite Empire, c. 1250 B.C.
- Assyrian Empire, c. 650 B.C.

INTERPRETING THE VISUAL RECORD

Epic of Gilgamesh Preserved by the Assyrians, the *Epic of Gilgamesh* is the story of a mythical Sumerian king. It reflects Sumerians' beliefs about life and death. Here Gilgamesh is pictured wrestling with a lion. *In what way does this ancient relief portray Gilgamesh as a heroic, larger-than-life figure?*

Culture

A Hittite king was also the chief priest of the kingdom. On occasion, a king might even return from a military campaign to perform his religious duties. Indeed, when a Hittite king died, it was believed that he became a god. This supposed transformation, along with the Hittite custom of adopting the gods of their conquered subjects, meant that the number of Hittite gods continued to grow. At the height of their power, it is believed that the Hittites worshipped over 600 gods. Arinna, the sun goddess, was the most powerful of the deities, while Tarhunnas, the weather god, stood at her side.

Critical Thinking

Ask students why the Hittites might have adopted the gods of their conquered subjects.

ANSWER: Students might suggest that the Hittites wanted to win some acceptance from the peoples they conquered.

LEVEL 1: Have students write their definition of the word *empire. (a government that unites different territories and people under one rule)* Then ask students what systems and skills are necessary to run an empire. *(Students might answer: strong army, good communication and transportation system, efficient government, common language, legal system.)* Then tell students to make a chart with the headings *Pros* and *Cons*. Have students list the following empires along the left side of the chart: *Akkadians, Babylonians, Hittites, Assyrians, Chaldeans, Persians.* Tell students to fill in their charts as they read the section. The *Pros* column includes characteristics that contributed to the empire's continuation, and the *Cons* column includes characteristics that contributed to its downfall.

ENGLISH LANGUAGE LEARNERS

Empire	Pros	Cons
Akkadians		
Babylonians		
Hittites		
Assyrians		
Chaldeans		
Persians		

Interdisciplinary Connection

LITERATURE. In the *Epic of Gilgamesh* the hero travels to the Land of the Dead to search out immortality. His first advice comes from a wine maiden in the Land of the Dead. To his confession that he fears death and cannot rest, she replies: "Gilgamesh, where are you hurrying to? You will never find that life for which you are looking. When the gods created man they allotted to him death, but life they retained in their own keeping. As for you, Gilgamesh, fill your belly with good things; day and night, night and day, dance and be merry, feast and rejoice. . ." An ancestor to whom Gilgamesh goes for advice on obtaining immortality replies: "There is no permanence. Do we build a house to stand for ever, do we seal a contract to hold for all time? Do brothers divide an inheritance to keep for ever, does the flood-time of the rivers endure?"

Critical Thinking

Ask students what this myth indicates about Mesopotamians' view of life and death.

ANSWER: Mesopotamians seemed to believe that there was little permanence in life and it was better to enjoy life while it lasted.

MAP ANSWERS

1. the Euphrates

2. They could transport goods easily by boat.

The Assyrians were one of the first peoples to effectively govern a large empire. The Assyrian king had absolute, or total, power. He was responsible only to the god Ashur. Priests and government officials took orders from the king and answered to him. Governors ruled conquered lands and made regular reports to the king.

After the Assyrians rose to power, they made the city of Nineveh their capital. Attempting to fortify the city as strongly as possible, they constructed a huge double wall around it. The wall was more than 70 feet high and stretched for 7.5 miles around the city. In places, it was as much as 148 feet wide and it had 15 decorated gates.

Nineveh contained a great library in which Assyrian scholars kept clay tablets filled with literature and other works collected from all over the empire. This library helped to preserve learning for future generations. Among the many texts it contained was the great *Epic of Gilgamesh*, the story of a Sumerian king and one of the oldest works of literature known. Today's historians have learned much about Sumerian beliefs and lifestyles by studying the *Epic of Gilgamesh*.

Powerful Assyria and its great capital eventually fell. In about 635 B.C. civil war broke out, weakening Assyria so that it could not resist outside invaders. Finally in 612 B.C., a group of enemies led by the Chaldeans and the Medes captured and destroyed Nineveh.

The Chaldeans. The Chaldeans took control of much of the territory that the Assyrians had ruled. Under the leadership of **Nebuchadnezzar** (neb·uh·kuhd-NEZ·uhr), the Chaldeans conquered most of the Fertile Crescent. Nebuchadnezzar governed from the rebuilt city of Babylon from 605 B.C. until his death in 562 B.C.

Under Nebuchadnezzar, Babylon once again became a large and wealthy city. Trade flourished, and within the city were impressive canals and magnificent buildings. The king's palace included beautiful terraced gardens, known as the Hanging Gardens. According to legend, Amytis, one of Nebuchadnezzar's wives, had lived in the mountains. Now, living on the drier plains of Babylonia, she missed the greenery of her homeland. To please her, the king planted thousands of brightly colored tropical trees and flowers on the palace grounds. The Greeks and other peoples of the ancient world regarded the Hanging Gardens of Babylon as one of the Seven Wonders of the World.

The Chaldeans were skilled astronomers. They kept careful records of the apparent movement of the stars and planets and could predict solar and lunar eclipses. The Chaldeans also made advances in mathematics. They calculated the length of a year with a very high degree of accuracy.

All the strength of the Chaldeans, however, lay in the leadership of Nebuchadnezzar. After he died the Chaldeans had difficulties. One of his successors quarreled with the priests, who then betrayed the city to enemies. Within 30 years of Nebuchadnezzar's death, the Chaldean empire fell.

Chaldean Empire, c. 600 B.C.

Interpreting Maps The Chaldeans under Nebuchadnezzar conquered a large part of the Assyrians' far-flung empire.

■ **Skills Assessment: 1. Locate** On what river was Babylon located? **2. Drawing Conclusions** How would this location have helped the Chaldeans improve trade?

✔ **READING CHECK: Evaluating** In what ways did the great Assyrian library at Nineveh contribute to the ancient world's store of knowledge? preserved learning from many regions for future generations

TEACH OBJECTIVES 2 and 4

LEVEL 2: Have students complete a list of the accomplishments of the empires of the Fertile Crescent. (*Babylonians: Code of Hammurabi; Hittites: less brutal system of law than the Babylonians; Assyrians: built a large library, encouraged scholarship and literature; Chaldeans: advances in astronomy; Persians: developed an effective government, developed Zoroastrianism*) You may choose to extend this activity by organizing the class into three groups: Assyrians, Chaldeans, and Persians. Tell the members of each group to prepare a debate speech explaining why their accomplishments demonstrate that they are the most advanced Fertile Crescent society. Members of the opposing groups should ask questions. **COOPERATIVE LEARNING**

 HOMEWORK Have students read the section under "Persian religion" on page 40. Ask students to list similarities and differences between Zoroastrianism and the religions of ancient Egypt and Babylon. Then ask them to list similarities between Zoroastrianism and Judaism.

CLOSE

Have students write a brief summary of the achievements and political systems of the Akkadians, Babylonians, Hittites, Assyrians, Chaldeans, and Persians.

REVIEW

Have students complete the Section 4 Review on p. 40.

The Persians

The Persians conquered Babylon in 539 B.C. Like the Hittites, the Persians spoke an Indo-European language. They and another group, the Medes, had migrated into what is now Iran by about 850 B.C. The region became known as Persia and Media.

At first the Medes ruled over the Persians. In about 550 B.C., however, the Persian ruler **Cyrus** the Great rebelled against the Medes. Cyrus then captured Babylon and took over the rest of the Fertile Crescent and Asia Minor.

Cyrus and later rulers, including Darius I and his son Xerxes I (ZUHRK·seez), expanded Persian rule even more. The Persian Empire stretched between the Indus River and parts of southeastern Europe. Both Darius and Xerxes invaded Greece in the 400s B.C., but failed to conquer it. Nevertheless, the Persians still ruled the mightiest empire in history up to that time.

Government. The early Persian kings were effective rulers as well as great generals. Although all-powerful, they showed great concern for justice. They collected taxes and administered the law fairly. The Persians also treated the people they conquered better than earlier empires had. They allowed conquered peoples to keep their own religions and laws. Secret agents known as "the King's Eyes and Ears" kept the king informed. As a result, regional governors and military leaders appointed by the ruler were held in check.

Holt Researcher
go.hrw.com
KEYWORD: Holt Researcher
FreeFind: Cyrus
Darius I
After reading more about Cyrus and Darius I on the Holt Researcher, create a chart comparing and contrasting their reigns.

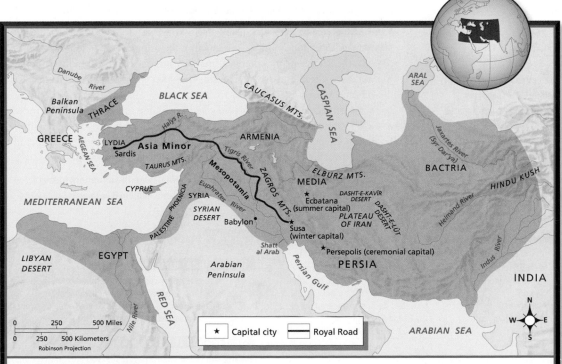

Persian Empire, c. 500 B.C.
Interpreting Maps At its height, the mighty Persian Empire stretched from southeastern Europe to the Hindu Kush plateau and the Indus River in southwestern Asia.
■ **Skills Assessment: 1. Human Systems** What road ran through the Persian Empire? **2. Drawing Inferences** How might this road have helped Persian rulers control their huge empire?

Government

Before weights and measures were standardized, different methods were used across the Persian Empire. This made trade difficult. To determine volume, Darius established the king's measure, which was similar to the modern bushel. The unit of length was the royal cubit, measuring 18 inches, and the standard for weight was the karsha, which equaled about one-fifth of a pound.

Critical Thinking

Ask students to imagine why standardized measures would have made trade easier.

ANSWER: Students should suggest that standardized measures would have allowed people to easily know the cost of the product, without having to convert units of measure.

MAP ANSWERS
1. Royal Road

2. It connected the widely separated cities of the realm, allowing rulers to travel between them more easily.

ASSESS

Have students complete Daily Quiz 2.4. As Alternative Assessment, you may want to use the empires or accomplishments exercises in this section's lessons.

RETEACH

Have students complete Main Idea Activity for English Language Learners and Special-Needs Students 2.4. Then ask them to think about what they have learned about each of the empires of the Fertile Crescent. Have them write brief journal entries describing a day in the life of a teenager in the Fertile Crescent. **ENGLISH LANGUAGE LEARNERS**

EXTEND

Divide students into six groups and assign one of the empires discussed in the section to each group. Tell students that they are to use sources such as computer software, biographies, and artifacts to produce a contemporary magazine about their empire.
BLOCK SCHEDULING, COOPERATIVE LEARNING

SECTION 4 REVIEW ANSWERS

❶ **Identify**
• Sargon, p. 35
• Hammurabi, p. 36
• Nebuchadnezzar, p. 38
• Cyrus, p. 39
• Zoroaster, p. 40

❷ Akkadians: conquered Sumerians, established a great empire; invaders; Babylonians: Code of Hammurabi, cotton and wool, trade, property rights for women; conquered by Hittites; Hittites: iron, legal system; too far from homeland to control Babylon, invasion from the Sea Peoples; Assyrians: chariots, cavalry, library; civil war led to invasions from outside; Chaldeans: trade, canals, buildings, advances in astronomy, sciences and mathematics; death of Nebuchadnezzar; Persians: just government, roads, Zoroaster; weak rulers

❸ **a.** Akkadians, Babylonians, Hittites, Assyrians, Chaldeans, Persians

b. Students answers will vary and should be supported.

❹ Students should mention the Code of Hammurabi, the legal and economic rights of women, and the focus on a successful life on Earth rather than in an afterlife.

The Persians built roads to connect the cities within their empire. The Royal Road, for example, stretched more than 1,250 miles. It connected Sardis in western Asia Minor with Susa, one of the imperial capitals. The Persians built these roads mainly for the army and postal riders. Some historians think that later civilizations, such as the Romans, borrowed this idea. The Persian road system helped to link the sprawling empire together. The roads also allowed different cultures in the empire to exchange customs, goods, and ideas.

Persian religion. Perhaps the greatest cultural contribution of the Persians concerned religion. At first, like other early peoples, the Persians worshiped many gods. Then, in about 600 B.C., the teachings of a great prophet named **Zoroaster** (ZOHR·uh·was·tuhr), or Zarathushtra, changed their religious outlook.

Zoroaster taught that on Earth people receive training for a future life. He said that in the world the forces of good and evil battle one another. People must choose between them. Those who chose good would be rewarded with eternal blessings; those who chose evil would face punishment. In the distant future, the forces of good would triumph. Then Earth would disappear.

The teachings of Zoroaster are known as Zoroastrianism. The central beliefs of this religion—the universal struggle between good and evil and the idea of final judgment—have had a great impact on history. Among the many great religions that Zoroastrianism probably influenced were Judaism and, later, Christianity.

The decline of the Persians. The Persian kings who followed Darius and Xerxes lacked their leadership abilities. Consequently, the empire began to lose its strength. In 331 B.C., the Persian Army suffered a final defeat at the hands of the Greek forces of Alexander the Great. Thus, more than 200 years after Cyrus's revolt against the Medes, the Persian empire was conquered.

Centuries later, Persian power revived for a time under a dynasty founded in A.D. 226 by a ruler named Ardashir, who saw himself as following in the tradition of Darius and Xerxes. Ardashir worked to rid Persia of foreign influences, including those left from the Greeks. He also revived the practice of Zoroastrianism.

✔ **READING CHECK: Finding the Main Idea** What were the important ideas of Zoroaster's teachings? struggle between good and evil, final judgment

The Persian prophet and teacher Zoroaster developed an influential religious philosophy during the 600s B.C.

Holt Researcher go.hrw.com
KEYWORD: Holt Researcher
FreeFind: Zoroaster
After reading more about Zoroaster on the Holt Researcher, make a list of the ways in which Zoroastrianism influenced world events.

SECTION 4 REVIEW

1. **Identify** and explain the significance:
   Sargon
   Hammurabi
   Nebuchadnezzar
   Cyrus
   Zoroaster

2. **Sequencing** Copy the graphic organizer below six times. Use it to plot the main achievements and causes of decline of the empires of the Fertile Crescent.

   Empire

   Achievements   Decline

3. **Finding the Main Idea**
   a. List the names of the various peoples who ruled the Fertile Crescent in the order in which they ruled.
   b. Which achievement of the empires of the Fertile Crescent do you believe was most important? Why?

4. **Writing and Critical Thinking**
   Finding the Main Idea Imagine that you are a traveler in the ancient world who is visiting the Tigris-Euphrates Valley from another land. Write a brief description of Babylonian society.
   Consider:
   • how society was organized
   • how people were treated under Babylonian law and the Code of Hammurabi
   • how religion affected the way people acted

Homework Practice Online
keyword: SP3 HP2

OBJECTIVES

1 **Examine how trade influenced Phoenician culture.**

2 **Describe how a money economy developed in Lydia.**

🔊 LET'S GET STARTED!

🔊 LET'S GET STARTED!

As students enter the classroom, ask them what caused elements of culture to spread between ancient civilizations. *(traveling to other areas for trade)* Tell students that in Section 5 they will learn about Phoenician trade and the cultural diffusion that resulted.

TEACH OBJECTIVE 1

ALL LEVELS: Have students work in pairs to conduct a business transaction, replacing written words with visuals. Then discuss how the development of an alphabet influenced the spread of Phoenician culture. *(Other peoples learned the alphabet from Phoenician traders who used written contracts.)*
ENGLISH LANGUAGE LEARNERS, COOPERATIVE LEARNING

SECTION 5

READ TO DISCOVER

❶ How did trade influence Phoenician culture?
❷ How did a money economy develop in Lydia?

DEFINE

barter
commodities
money economy

IDENTIFY

Phoenician alphabet

WHY IT MATTERS TODAY

Trade remains an important activity in the world today. Use **CNN fyi.com** or other **current event** sources to find information about international trade. Record your findings in your journal.

CNN fyi.com

The Phoenicians and the Lydians

The Main Idea
The societies of Phoenicia and Lydia made important contributions to other Mediterranean cultures.

The Story Continues *"Who was ever silenced like Tyre . . . ? When your merchandise went out on the seas, you satisfied many nations; with your great wealth and your wares you enriched the kings of the earth."* This passage from the Bible evokes the splendor of the Phoenician city-state of Tyre at its height.

The Phoenicians

The peoples in the western end of the Fertile Crescent did not create large empires, but they still had a great influence on the modern world. Today this region forms the nations of Israel, Lebanon, and Syria. In ancient times, people called part of this region Phoenicia (fi·NI·shuh).

Phoenicia consisted of a loose union of city-states, each governed by a different king. Phoenicia had little fertile land and the Lebanon Mountains made migration to the east difficult. Thus, the Phoenicians turned to trading on the sea. The Phoenician seaports of Tyre and Sidon (SYD·uhn) became world famous.

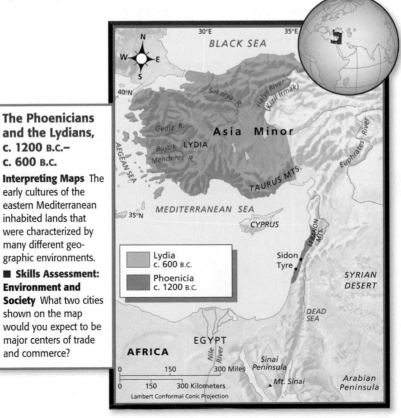

The Phoenicians and the Lydians, c. 1200 B.C.– c. 600 B.C.

Interpreting Maps The early cultures of the eastern Mediterranean inhabited lands that were characterized by many different geographic environments.

■ **Skills Assessment: Environment and Society** What two cities shown on the map would you expect to be major centers of trade and commerce?

SECTION 5 RESOURCES

REPRODUCIBLE RESOURCES

▸ Guided Reading Strategy 2.5
▸ Geography Activity 2: The End of an Island Civilization

TECHNOLOGY RESOURCES

▸ One-Stop Planner 2.5
▸ World History Teaching Transparency: Geography and History 2: The Eastern Mediterranean
▸ Homework Practice Online

REINFORCEMENT, REVIEW, AND ASSESSMENT

▸ Section 5 Review, p. 43
▸ Daily Quiz 2.5
▸ Main Idea Activity 2.5
▸ English Audio Summary 2.5
▸ Spanish Audio Summary 2.5

MAP ANSWER

Sidon, Tyre

TEACH OBJECTIVE 2

LEVEL 1: Organize students into groups and assign each group a different product. Then have groups negotiate with one another to trade their goods. Discuss how the use of coined money simplifies trade.

ENGLISH LANGUAGE LEARNERS, COOPERATIVE LEARNING

HOMEWORK Ask students to write a short report about how salespeople conduct business today. How do these methods compare with those used by Phoenicians and Lydians?

TEACH OBJECTIVE 2

LEVEL 3: Have students work in groups to design coins and determine their values. Students should use the following chart to illustrate their money systems.

Coins	Values

COOPERATIVE LEARNING

That's Interesting!

It took about 60,000 murices to make one pound of royal purple dye. The dye came from a small gland in the murex, but each gland yielded only a drop or two of the yellowish liquid that would darken into purple when exposed to sun and air.

VISUAL RECORD ANSWER

It was far-reaching.

WHAT IF? ANSWER

Europeans might have developed an alphabet later in history, and they might have been influenced by other cultures, such as Arabic or Chinese cultures.

Technology Resources

 Online Maps, Charts, and Graphs: Phoenician Sea Routes

INTERPRETING THE VISUAL RECORD

Ivory carving Ivory—the material from which this Phoenician sculpture was carved—was highly prized in the ancient world. Phoenician merchants imported ivory from coastal North and East Africa. *What evidence does this carving provide about the extent of the Phoenicians' trading empire?*

What If? Phoenician trade helped spread the use of the alphabet throughout the Mediterranean region. **How might the history of writing have been different if the Phoenicians had not been traders?**

Phoenician trade. The Phoenicians sailed in ships that today would seem small and frail, but their sailors were highly skilled. Using sails and oars, the Phoenicians took their ships throughout the Mediterranean and beyond. Some historians believe that the Phoenicians sailed as far as Britain. They might even have sailed around the western coast of Africa. In time the Phoenicians became the greatest traders in the ancient world.

Phoenicia reached its peak as a great sea trading power in the centuries after 1000 B.C. Phoenician colonies were established throughout the Mediterranean region. The Phoenician city of Carthage in North Africa became a major regional power. Other important colonies could be found on the islands of Sicily, Sardinia, and Malta. Farther west, the Phoenicians established a colony in what is now Spain. These colonies themselves became centers for trade.

Phoenicia had one particularly important natural resource—lumber. The Lebanon Mountains had beautiful cedar forests and other trees. Many ancient peoples used this lumber for building.

The Phoenicians developed several other valuable exports as well. They became skilled workers in metal and created beautiful objects of gold and silver. To do so, the Phoenicians used methods they learned from the Egyptians. They probably imported the materials they used as well. The Phoenicians invented the art of glassblowing and made exquisite glass objects. The city of Sidon became the home of a well-known glass industry.

On their coast the Phoenicians gathered a shellfish called murex. They used the murex to make a purple dye. Sidon and Tyre became the centers of the dyeing trade. People throughout the ancient world prized cloth dyed with this purple. A favorite of the rich and of royalty, the color became known as royal purple. The Phoenicians also exported dried fish, linen, olive oil, and wine.

Phoenician culture. The Phoenicians imitated the cultures of other peoples. Their government and customs resembled those of the Egyptians and Babylonians. Through trading, the Phoenicians spread Egyptian and Babylonian culture throughout the Mediterranean area.

The religion of the Phoenician people offered few comforts. While the Phoenicians believed in an afterlife, their efforts were focused on winning the favor of one of the many gods they worshiped, sometimes going so far as to sacrifice their own children. Some scholars believe this was done just in a few places and just under extreme circumstances. Sacrifices might have taken place, for example, if a natural disaster convinced people that the gods were very angry with them.

The Phoenicians never established a major empire. Eventually, their cities were conquered by the Assyrians. The Phoenicians did, however, make one major contribution to the world: the **Phoenician alphabet.** Writing systems had been developed earlier in both Egypt and Mesopotamia. The Phoenicians, however, developed the alphabet that became the model for later Western alphabets.

The spread of the alphabet is a good example of how commerce can speed cultural diffusion. Phoenicians used writing in their businesses to draw up contracts and record bills. Their trading partners saw these written records. They probably also saw the advantages of them. Phoenician traders spread the knowledge of alphabetical writing throughout the Mediterranean world.

Relief of a Phoenician trading ship

CLOSE

Ask students how the invention of coined money made trade easier. Lead a class discussion about the benefits of coined money.

REVIEW

Have students complete the Section 5 Review on p. 43.

ASSESS

Have students complete Daily Quiz 2.5. As Alternative Assessment, you may want to use either of the coined money exercises in this section's lessons.

RETEACH

Have students complete Main Idea Activity for English Language Learners and Special-Needs Students 2.5. Ask students to summarize the achievements of the Phoenicians and Lydians.
ENGLISH LANGUAGE LEARNERS

EXTEND

Have students draw a map to show the extent of the Phoenician trading network. **BLOCK SCHEDULING**

The Greeks adopted the Phoenician alphabet. They improved it by adding signs for vowel sounds. Later, the Etruscans and then the Romans copied this alphabet from the Greeks. Eventually, the Romans developed the alphabet we use now.

✔ **READING CHECK: Drawing Inferences** Why were the Phoenicians more likely than some ancient peoples to spread and borrow from other cultures? **as traders they had more contact with other peoples**

Lydians

Today Asia Minor makes up the greater part of the nation of Turkey. In ancient times the western portion of Asia Minor was called Lydia (LI·dee·uh). Like the Phoenicians, the Lydians did not create an empire. Also like the Phoenicians, however, they made an extremely important contribution. Today Lydians are remembered as the first people to use coined money. They began issuing small kidney-bean-shaped pieces of money made out of a mixture of gold and silver.

Before coins were invented in about 600 B.C., traders had to rely on barter. **Barter** is the exchange of one good or service for another; goods that have value are called **commodities.** In bartering, for example, a fisherman might trade a commodity such as a basket of fish for a farmer's extra vegetables. Barter, however, limited trade. Two people could strike a bargain only if each could offer goods or services that the other wanted.

In contrast, the use of money allowed traders to set prices for goods and services. Lydian traders developed a **money economy.** This economic system is based on the use of money as a measure of value and a unit of account. Through trade, the Lydians passed on the concept of a money economy to the Greeks and Persians. They, in turn, helped spread this concept to other parts of the world.

✔ **READING CHECK: Contrasting** How does a money economy differ from barter? **in barter, goods are traded directly; in a money economy, prices are set for goods**

These Greek coins show the influence of the Lydians' development of a money economy.

DAILY LIFE

Money

Money can be any object that people are willing to accept as payment for goods or services. The first form of money was called commodity money. Salt, shells, and special stones were all used as commodity money.

Later, Mediterranean countries began making coins from precious metals. These ancient coins often were stamped with images of gods or rulers. Today, coins and paper notes still bear images, but the materials themselves have little actual value. Instead, they represent a value that everyone agrees upon. **What might be some advantages of a money economy?**

DAILY LIFE ANSWER
Students should note that you don't have to have the specific good someone else wants in order to trade.

SECTION 5 REVIEW ANSWERS

❶ Define
• barter, p. 43
• commodities, p. 43
• money economy, p. 43

❷ Identify
• Phoenician alphabet, p. 42

❸ Students should include: cultural diffusion, imitation of other cultures, and imported materials.

❹ a. Trade helped Mediterranean peoples exchange goods and ideas, including the use of the alphabet.

b. They became centers for trade.

c. It made trade easier because it allowed traders to set prices for goods and services and enabled more people to obtain the goods and services they needed.

❺ Students should mention what goods they are trading and their method of transport.

SECTION 5 REVIEW

1. Define and explain the significance:
   barter
   commodities
   money economy

2. Identify and explain the significance:
   Phoenician alphabet

3. Identifying Cause and Effect
   Copy the chart below. Use it to illustrate the ways in which trade influenced life in Phoenicia.

   Trade → ☐
         → ☐
         → ☐

4. **Finding the Main Idea**
   a. What effect did the trading civilization of Phoenicia have on the ancient world?
   b. What role did colonies fill for Phoenicia?
   c. What effect would the Lydians' development of a money economy have on ancient civilizations?

5. **Writing and Critical Thinking**
   Summarizing Imagine that you are a Phoenician trader. Write a journal account about traveling to a foreign land to trade.
   Consider:
   • the goods the Phoenicians traded
   • how they transported goods to other lands

go. hrw. com **Homework Practice Online**
keyword: SP3 HP2

OBJECTIVES

1 **Explain how the migrating Hebrews found a homeland.**

2 **Explore how religious views affected Hebrew culture.**

SECTION 6

▶ READ TO DISCOVER

❶ How did the migrating Hebrews find a homeland?

❷ How did religious views affect Hebrew culture?

▶ DEFINE

covenant
ethical monotheism

▶ IDENTIFY

Abraham
Twelve Tribes of Israel
Moses
Exodus
Saul
David
Solomon
Torah
Judeo-Christian ethics

▶ WHY IT MATTERS TODAY

The ethical laws of Judaism, many of which were later adopted by Christians, still influence the beliefs of many Americans today. Use **CNNfyi.com** or other **current event** sources to find recent news stories about the Ten Commandments and the impact of Judeo-Christian ethics on society today. Record your findings in your journal.

CNNfyi.com

The Origins of Judaism

The Main Idea
The Hebrews established a unique and influential religion based on ethical monotheism.

The Story Continues *"You shall not ill-treat any widow or orphan. . . . You shall not commit robbery. . . . Love your fellow [countryman] as yourself. . . You . . . must befriend the stranger . . . [Do] not harden your heart and shut your hand against your needy kinsman." These and other holy laws from the ancient culture of the Hebrews were to have a profound effect on Western civilization.*

The Hebrews

To the south of Phoenicia lay a small strip of land known as Canaan. Just as in the eastern part of the Fertile Crescent, a series of peoples inhabited Canaan. At different times the Assyrians, Babylonians, Egyptians, Persians, Syrians, and other groups all conquered this area. One group of people who lived in Canaan were the Hebrews—the ancestors of modern Jews. They had a great influence on the region and on the history of the world.

According to the Bible, the founder of the Hebrew people was **Abraham.** Abraham once lived in Sumer. He left there and led his people through the desert to the borders of northern Canaan. Modern Jews trace their heritage through Abraham's grandson Jacob (also called Israel), whose twelve sons each established a tribe. These groups were known as the **Twelve Tribes of Israel.**

The Exodus. The descendants of Abraham left Canaan and traveled west into Egypt, probably to escape drought and famine. These Hebrews lived peacefully in Egypt for some time. Eventually, however, they fell from favor with the Egyptians. Some scholars believe that one group of Hebrews may have entered Egypt with the Hyksos in the 1700s B.C. When the Egyptians expelled the Hyksos in the 1200s B.C. they enslaved the Hebrews. The Hebrews were held as slaves for 400 years, during which time they suffered greatly.

The Hebrews were led out of slavery by a great leader, **Moses.** The biblical books of Exodus, Numbers, and Deuteronomy tell the story of Moses. According to the Bible, Moses led the **Exodus,** the escape of the Hebrews from Egypt. The Hebrews fled into the deserts of the Sinai Peninsula, where they wandered in the wilderness.

INTERPRETING THE VISUAL RECORD

Mount Sinai Mount Sinai is located in the southern Sinai Peninsula. According to the Bible, this is where Moses received the written words that established the principles and beliefs of Judaism. It remains a biblical landmark today.

Link to Today Why might Mount Sinai be an important place for followers of Judaism today?

TEACH OBJECTIVE 1

LEVEL 1: Have students complete the following graphic organizer to show how the migrating Hebrews found a homeland.

Journey to Egypt

(Students should include their journey to Canaan, their journey to Egypt, the Exodus from Egypt, and their journey back to Canaan.)
ENGLISH LANGUAGE LEARNERS

TEACH OBJECTIVE 2

ALL LEVELS: Ask students to think of instances in history in which people held other humans as slaves. Discuss with students how these enslaved persons reacted to this situation. Ask students how some slaves and other people who were against slavery tried to free the slaves. Close by asking students to imagine how the Hebrews felt about leaving Egypt and what their expectations for the future were. **ENGLISH LANGUAGE LEARNERS**

The Ten Commandments. As the Bible tells it, Moses climbed to the top of Mount Sinai. When he returned to the Hebrews, he carried tablets bearing the Ten Commandments. These commandments were the moral laws that the Hebrew god, Yahweh (YAH·way), had revealed to Moses.

The first four commandments establish the Hebrews' relationship with Yahweh. The rest of the commandments emphasize self-restraint and underscore the importance of family and human life. When the Hebrews agreed to follow these commandments, they entered into a **covenant,** or solemn agreement, with Yahweh.

Moses announced that Canaan was a land promised to his ancestors. He also said that Yahweh had sent him to found a holy nation. Inspired by his words, the Hebrews set out for Canaan. They wandered in the desert for many years, however, before finally entering the "promised land." They expected to find a land "flowing with milk and honey."

The founding of Israel. The Hebrews who had come from Egypt joined those who had lived on the borders of northern Canaan. They remained a loose confederation of tribes bound together in part by the need to maintain a strong central shrine for the Ark of the Covenant—the container of Moses's tablets. Leaders known as Judges ruled the various tribes in these years. Their task was to enforce God's laws and settle disputes among the tribes. The Hebrews also sometimes acknowledged the authority of holy men known as prophets, who appeared from time to time to warn people that they were incurring God's anger by straying from the terms of the covenant.

The harsh wilderness life had hardened the Hebrews into tough desert tribes. However, establishing a homeland in Canaan nonetheless proved difficult for the Hebrews. People known as Canaanites held the northern Jordan Valley. Another group, the Philistines, lived along the southern coast. Both groups resisted the Hebrews and defended their lands in a struggle that lasted more than 200 years. The Hebrews first conquered the Canaanites. The Philistines, however, proved far more difficult to overcome. Over time, the Hebrews drove them closer to the seacoast, but they never succeeded in conquering the Philistines completely.

As nomads, the Hebrews had been divided into 12 tribes. During the years of fighting, the tribes united under one king. The first king of this united kingdom called Israel was **Saul.** Saul was succeeded by **David,** who formed a new dynasty. David occupied the city of Jerusalem, making it a capital and religious center.

THE TEN COMMANDMENTS

According to the Bible, "God spoke, and these were his words:

1. I am the Lord your God who brought you out of Egypt. You shall have no other gods.*
2. You shall not make or worship idols.
3. You shall not swear falsely by the name of the Lord your God.
4. Remember the Sabbath and keep it holy.
5. Honor your father and mother.
6. You shall not murder.
7. You shall not commit adultery.
8. You shall not steal.
9. You shall not bear false witness against your neighbor.
10. You shall not covet your neighbor's belongings."

*Some translations include this sentence in the second commandment.

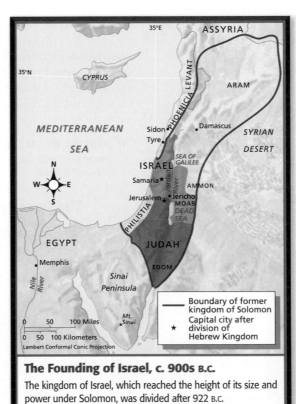

The Founding of Israel, c. 900s B.C.

The kingdom of Israel, which reached the height of its size and power under Solomon, was divided after 922 B.C.

■ **Skills Assessment: Places and Regions** After the mid-900s B.C., which of the Hebrew kingdoms probably had great access to seagoing trade and commerce?

Geography

The geography of the Fertile Crescent greatly affected the coastal towns of Canaan. To the east of Canaan were the Assyrian and Babylonian Empires (at different times), to the south was the Egyptian Empire, and to the north was the Hittite Empire, which were separated by deserts. These empires had powerful, large armies but no naval fleets. In order to attack each other, the armies of these empires could only travel by land through a few mountain passes or along the Mediterranean coast. Thus Canaan's port towns were constantly fought over, destroyed, burned, and built up again.

Critical Thinking

Ask students what one consequence of Canaan's location could be for archaeologists.

ANSWER: Answers may vary but students might suggest that there are fewer artifacts left from Canaan, making it hard to learn about its culture.

MAP ANSWER
Israel

HOMEWORK Have students carefully read through the Ten Commandments on page 45. Ask students to write a response to each commandment, explaining why such a rule would help to preserve the Hebrew community.

TEACH OBJECTIVE 2

LEVEL 3: Review with students the meaning of the word *ethics.* Have students brainstorm actions that are ethical and actions that are not ethical. Ask students how ethical they feel the laws of the Egyptians, Babylonians, Hittites, Assyrians, and Persians were. Have students discuss how ethical these civilizations' laws seem compared to those of the Hebrews. Then have students describe how basic elements of the Hebrew religion can be seen in modern religious thought. Close by having students brainstorm how Judeo-Christian ethics influence societies and institutions today.

Culture

It is likely that Solomon's royal scribes first recorded the Hebrew narratives that would evolve into the Torah. Today, scribes still scrupulously follow a carefully defined ritual when preparing a new Torah scroll. Using ritually cleaned parchment, pen, and ink, the scribe copies from an authorized guide. The scribe will work for about 18 months to complete a single handwritten Torah.

Critical Thinking

Ask students to think of reasons why the old methods are still used to make new Torah scrolls.

ANSWER: Students might suggest that members of a religious or cultural group might preserve ancient traditions and rituals because they are part of the rules of their religion, or to strengthen their sense of group identity.

Technology Resources

Religions of the World Video Series: Judaism

Analyzing Primary Sources

Identifying Cause and Effect
How might the covenant between the Hebrew kings and their people have helped the kings to rule? *states that they both share a common faith*

Holt Researcher
go.hrw.com
KEYWORD: Holt Researcher
FreeFind: David
Solomon
After reading more about David and Solomon on the Holt Researcher, use a problem-solving process to evaluate how well they handled problems during their reigns.

The Torah consists of the Hebrews' most sacred writings.

Also beginning with David, the kings of Israel established a tradition of making a covenant with their people as well as with God. According to a biblical account of one king's coronation,

Primary Source
"Jehoida [the priest] solemnized the covenant between the Lord, on the one hand, and the king and the people, on the other—as well as between the king and the people—that they should be the people of the Lord."

Benjamin Mazer, *Biblical Israel: State and People*

Under the rule of David's son and successor, **Solomon,** Israel reached the height of its wealth and power. Solomon sought to build peaceful, cooperative relations with the other leading powers of the region. One of his wives, for example, was a daughter of Egypt's pharaoh. Solomon vastly increased Israel's wealth through favorable trade policies with Arabia. The king used the riches gained from this trade to build a magnificent temple to God in Jerusalem. The temple became both the center of religious life in Israel and a symbol of the Israelite state.

Following Solomon's death, unity within the Israelite kingdom was disrupted by struggles for political power. In the late 900s B.C. the 10 northern tribes revolted, and the kingdom split in two. The northern part remained the kingdom of Israel, with its capital at Samaria. The southern part, located around the Dead Sea, became the kingdom of Judah. Its capital was Jerusalem.

These two Hebrew kingdoms lacked the strength to withstand invasions from the east. In about 722 B.C. the Assyrians conquered Israel. They captured and enslaved many Hebrews. Later, in 587 B.C., the Chaldeans conquered Judah and destroyed Jerusalem. They destroyed Solomon's temple and took the southern Hebrews captive. When Cyrus, the Persian king, conquered the Chaldeans, he allowed the Hebrews to return to their homeland. The Hebrews then rebuilt the temple in Jerusalem.

✔ **READING CHECK: Sequencing** What events led to the Hebrews making Canaan their homeland? *conquest of Hebrew kingdoms by Assyrians and Chaldeans, then freeing by Cyrus*

The Development of Judaism

The Hebrew scriptures tell of the creation of the world and the special mission of the Hebrews. About one third of these scriptures—also known as the Old Testament of the Christian Bible—is Hebrew history. The remaining scriptures include laws, poetry, prophecy, and religious instruction.

Law and ethics. The first five books of the Old Testament are known as the **Torah.** They include the Hebrew code of laws. This Mosaic law—named for Moses—includes the Ten Commandments. Like the Code of Hammurabi, it demanded an "eye for an eye." Mosaic law, however, placed a higher value on human life. The law demanded kindness toward the poor and toward slaves. It reserved the death sentence for severe crimes, such as adultery, kidnapping, treason, and sacrifices to idols. This system of law reflected the belief that all people deserved kindness and respect.

For the Hebrews, prophets were messengers sent to reveal the will of Yahweh. The prophets' messages often formed the basis for Jewish moral and ethical behavior.

CLOSE

Ask volunteers to sequence on the board the events that led up to the Hebrews settling in Canaan.

REVIEW

Have students complete the Section 6 Review on p. 47.

ASSESS

Have students complete Daily Quiz 2.6. As Alternative Assessment, you may want to have students complete the slavery or ethics exercises in this section's lessons.

RETEACH

Have students complete Main Idea Activity for English Language Learners and Special-Needs Students 2.6. Then ask each student to create an annotated time line of Hebrew history.

ENGLISH LANGUAGE LEARNERS

EXTEND

Have students create a map like the one on page 41. First, have them shade the Jordan Valley and the regions where the Canaanites and Philistines lived. Tell students to use lines and arrows to show the movement of the Hebrews from the days of Abraham up through the 500s B.C., and to label locations with dates.

BLOCK SCHEDULING

Religion. The early Hebrews worshiped Yahweh as their only god. They believed that Yahweh protected them from enemies and provided them with food and water. Those who sinned against Yahweh would suffer, and so would their children and succeeding generations. The early Hebrews therefore viewed Yahweh as a god to fear.

This understanding of Yahweh slowly changed. The Hebrews came to believe that people had a choice between good and evil. Yahweh held them responsible for their choices, but he allowed them the freedom to make those choices for themselves. The Hebrews came to think of Yahweh as a god who lived in the hearts of worshippers. Humans were not intended to be Yahweh's slaves, but to serve him out of love.

Other ancient peoples thought of their gods as being more powerful than humans but still having human qualities. In contrast, the Hebrews viewed Yahweh as a spiritual force, not as a glorified human being or part of nature. Moreover, other ancient cultures sometimes viewed their kings as gods or the representatives of gods. Among the Hebrews, however, earthly political rulers had no claims to divinity. As stated in the Ten Commandments, only Yahweh was divine.

The Hebrew religion was monotheistic based on belief in a single god. Because it emphasized ethics, or proper conduct, it is often called **ethical monotheism.** The Jewish system of ethics carried over into the founding of Christianity. Thus today many people refer to the values first established by the Hebrews as **Judeo-Christian ethics.** These ideas rank among the Hebrews' most important contributions to Western civilization.

✔ **READING CHECK: Contrasting** How did the Hebrews' idea of God differ from those of other ancient civilizations? viewed Yahweh as a spiritual force, not as a glorified human being or force of nature

Dating from about the 100s B.C., the Dead Sea Scrolls contain ancient manuscripts detailing the history and principles of Judaism.

SECTION 6 REVIEW

1. **Define** and explain the significance:
   covenant
   ethical monotheism

2. **Identify** and explain the significance:
   Abraham
   Twelve Tribes of Israel
   Moses
   Exodus
   Saul
   David
   Solomon
   Torah
   Judeo-Christian ethics

Homework Practice Online
keyword: SP3 HP2

3. **Sequencing** Copy the time line below. Use it to organize the history of the Hebrew people.

1500 B.C.	500 B.C.
2000 B.C.	1000 B.C.

4. **Finding the Main Idea**
   a. In what way is the history of the land of Canaan typical of the Fertile Crescent region?
   b. If you had been one of the ancient Hebrews, would you have fought to stay in Canaan or would you have moved elsewhere? Explain your answer.
   c. How did the Hebrews' ideas about people's rights, such as fair treatment before the law, differ from other ancient groups?
   d. Explain why the Hebrew or Jewish religion can be called ethical monotheism.

5. **Writing and Critical Thinking**
   Analyzing Information Why do you think that many people consider the values that came to be known as Judeo-Christian ethics to be among the Hebrews' most important contributions to Western civilization?
   Consider:
   • the meaning of those values
   • the effect they had on Jewish society
   • how they are evident in societies and institutions today

REVIEW AND ASSESSMENT RESOURCES

REPRODUCIBLE RESOURCES
▶ Vocabulary Activity 2

TECHNOLOGY RESOURCES
▶ Chapter 2 Test Generator (on the One-Stop Planner)
▶ Global Skill Builder CD–ROM
▶ HRW Web Site

REINFORCEMENT, REVIEW, and ASSESSMENT
▶ Chapter 2 Review, pp. 48–49
▶ Chapter 2 Tutorial for Students, Parents, Mentors, and Peers
▶ Chapter 2 Test (Form A or B)
▶ Alternative Assessment Handbook
▶ Chapter 2 Test for English Language Learners and Special-Needs Students

REVIEW
Have students complete the Chapter 2 Review on pages 48–49.

ASSESS
Use one of the chapter tests to assess students' understanding of the content. For Alternative Assessment, see the Portfolio Activities and Alternative Assessment Handbook.

CHAPTER 2 REVIEW ANSWERS

Understanding Main Ideas

1. It provided a transportation route, a supply of water, and fertile soil.

2. Old Kingdom: nobles grew stronger than the pharaohs, civil war; Middle Kingdom: weakening of pharaohs' power by nobles and priests; New Kingdom: weaker pharaohs and outside invasions

3. as tombs for pharaohs

4. The soul was judged and entered either a place of eternal happiness or was thrown to a horrible monster called the Eater of the Dead.

5. They were not geographically isolated.

6. It regulated all aspects of life in Babylon.

7. Akkadians, Babylonians, Hittites, Assyrians, Chaldeans, Persians

8. They lacked fertile land and the Lebanon Mountains made migration to the east difficult.

9. It viewed Yahweh as a spiritual force rather than as a glorified human or a part of nature. Earthly political rulers had no claims to divinity.

Reviewing Themes

1. Peoples often adopted aspects of the cultures of those they had contact with.

2. Egyptians could focus on developing culture because they had less chance of invasion.

48

Review

Creating a Time Line

Copy the time line below onto a sheet of paper. Complete the time line by filling in the events, individuals, and dates from the chapter that you think were significant. Pick three events and explain why you think they were significant.

```
                    2000 B.C.
  3000 B.C.                    1000 B.C.
                                          1 B.C.
```

Writing a Summary

Using standard grammar, spelling, sentence structure, and punctuation, write an overview of the events in the chapter.

Identifying People and Ideas

Identify the following terms or individuals and explain their significance:

1. hieroglyphics
2. dynasty
3. empire
4. ziggurats
5. city-state
6. Hammurabi
7. Zoroaster
8. money economy
9. Moses
10. ethical monotheism

Understanding Main Ideas

Section 1 (pp. 20–25)

Ancient Kingdoms of the Nile

1. How did the Nile River contribute to the development of ancient Egypt?
2. Why did each of the three kingdoms of ancient Egypt collapse?

Section 2 (pp. 26–29)

Egyptian Life and Culture

3. Why did the Egyptians build pyramids?
4. What were some Egyptian beliefs about the afterlife?

Section 3 (pp. 30–34)

Sumerian Civilization

5. Why were civilizations in the Fertile Crescent frequently invaded?

Section 4 (pp. 35–40)

Empires of the Fertile Crescent

6. What was the impact of the Code of Hammurabi?
7. Which peoples established empires in the Fertile Crescent?

Section 5 (pp. 41–43)

The Phoenicians and the Lydians

8. Why did the Phoenicians become traders?

Section 6 (pp. 44–47)

The Origins of Judaism

9. In what ways was Judaism different from the religions of other ancient civilizations?

Reviewing Themes

1. **Global Relations** How did trade promote cultural exchanges between ancient civilizations?
2. **Geography** How did geographic isolation contribute to the development of Egyptian culture?
3. **Government** Why did civilizations with strong rulers typically survive longer than other civilizations with weak rulers?

Thinking Critically

1. **Comparing** What did the governments of Babylon, Egypt, and Israel have in common?
2. **Contrasting** How did life in the Nile River valley differ from life in the Tigris-Euphrates Valley?
3. **Evaluating** What aspects of the Code of Hammurabi and of the Hebrews' laws are evident in our legal system today?
4. **Summarizing** How did slavery affect people and civilizations in the ancient world?

Writing About History

Comparing and Contrasting Write a report describing the most important similarities and differences among Egyptian, Sumerian, and Hebrew beliefs. Use the chart below to organize your thoughts before writing.

Religious beliefs	Egyptian	Sumerian	Hebrew
Number of gods			
Role of gods			
Behavior on Earth			
Belief in afterlife			

CLOSE

Have students choose two groups of people in the chapter and explain how the environment affected their ways of living.

RETEACH

Have students who had difficulty with the test compile a chapter glossary of important places, people, and concepts. Then have students take the Form B Test to assess their mastery of the material.

ENGLISH LANGUAGE LEARNERS

Portfolio Extensions

1. Ask students to imagine they are Mesopotamian travelers in the year 1500 B.C. Have them write a journal that describes the geography of the lands they visit, the people they meet, the difficulties they face, and the ideas that they will take back to Mesopotamia. Students should include a map of their routes, showing the major geographical features and civilizations they encounter.

2. Have students use encyclopedias to write a report comparing Judaism, Zoroastrianism, and the religion of ancient Egypt. Ask them to focus on beliefs about the struggle between good and evil. Tell students to discuss why the conflict between good and evil is a theme in most religions.

3. The pyramids are among the most impressive structures left by any civilization. Have students research and write a report on techniques of ancient Egyptian building. Ask them to include illustrations in their report.

Building Social Studies Skills

Using a Model

Analyze the model below. Then use the conclusions you have reached to answer the questions that follow.

The Great Pyramid at Giza, c. 2600 B.C.

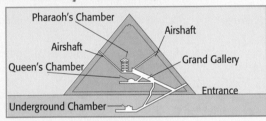

Interior of the Great Pyramid at Giza

1. Which statement best describes the information provided by the model?
   a. The Great Pyramid was constructed of limestone blocks.
   b. Each of the blocks used in the pyramid's construction weighed about 3,000 pounds.
   c. A single entrance opened from one side of the pyramid.
   d. The pyramid's builders used log rollers to move and position its blocks.

2. Using information from the model, describe the interior of the Great Pyramid at Giza.

Sequencing

Read the sentences below about the city of Babylon. Then answer the questions that follow.

   A. Even before the Persians captured it in 539 B.C., Babylon was the target of conquerors.
   B. Hammurabi came to power in Babylon in about 1792 B.C.
   C. It was not until Nebuchadnezzar's time (605 B.C. to 562 B.C.) that the Hanging Gardens of Babylon were built.
   D. Babylon was conquered and destroyed by the Assyrians in about 700 B.C. It was later rebuilt.
   E. In the 1600s B.C. the powerful Hittites, expanding their empire from Anatolia, captured Babylon.

3. Which of the following lists shows the events in the order in which they occurred?
   a. D, E, B, C, A
   b. B, E, D, C, A
   c. A, C, D, E, B
   d. B, D, E, A, C

4. According to the information provided, which group of conquerors was the first to capture Babylon? Which group was the last?

Alternative Assessment

Building Your Portfolio

Global Relations

Just as world leaders today make important decisions about global events, early civilizations had rulers whose influence was felt throughout the ancient world. Locate and use biographies of these rulers to write a brief summary of their impact. Then locate and use interviews to learn about the activities and influence of some current world leaders. Create a chart to summarize your findings.

🔲 internet connect

Internet Activity: go.hrw.com
KEYWORD: SP3 WH2

Choose a topic on the First Civilizations to:
- explore Egyptian pyramids and create an illustrated brochure.
- interview the leader of an ancient civilization.
- write about ancient and modern structures in Egypt.

---

3. Strong rulers were often able to unify their civilizations.

Thinking Critically

1. They were monarchies.

2. The Nile River valley was geographically isolated and thus less prone to attack than the Tigris-Euphrates Valley was.

3. Laws deal with many aspects of life; death sentence is reserved for severe crimes.

4. Hebrews, who had been held as slaves for 400 years, developed a great civilization.

Writing About History

Answers should compare and contrast the beliefs of each civilization.

Building Social Studies Skills

1. c

2. The Great Pyramid contained a Pharaoh's chamber, a Queen's chamber, an underground chamber, and a grand gallery. The interior was connected to the outside through one entrance and two airshafts.

3. b

4. Babylonians; Persians

Building Your Portfolio

Charts should show similarities and differences among leaders.

Ancient Indian Civilizations

CHAPTER RESOURCE MANAGER

Objectives	Pacing Guide	Reproducible Resources
SECTION 1 **Indus River Valley Civilizations** (pp. 52–55) • Examine the role geography and climate played in the settlement of the Indian subcontinent. • Investigate how people in the first Indus River valley civilization lived.	**Regular** 1 day **Block Scheduling** .5 day *Block Scheduling Handbook with Team Teaching Strategies, 3.1*	**RS** Guided Reading Strategy 3.1 **SM** Geography Activity 3: Indian Trade **PS** Readings in World History 4: Everyday Life in Mohenjo-Daro and Harappa
SECTION 2 **Indo-Aryan Migrants** (pp. 56–59) • Explain how life in northern India changed with the coming of the Indo-Aryans. • Identify the major contributions of the Indo-Aryans to ancient Indian society.	**Regular** 1 day **Block Scheduling** .5 day *Block Scheduling Handbook with Team Teaching Strategies, 3.2*	**RS** Guided Reading Strategy 3.2 **E** Creative Teaching Strategy 3: Telling the Story of India
SECTION 3 **Hinduism and Buddhism** (pp. 60–65) • Describe the importance of religion in ancient Indian society. • Identify the principal elements of Hinduism. • Identify the basic beliefs of Buddhism.	**Regular** 1.5 day **Block Scheduling** 1 day *Block Scheduling Handbook with Team Teaching Strategies, 3.3*	**RS** Guided Reading Strategy 3.3 **RS** Graphic Organizer Activity 3: Buddhism and Hinduism **PS** Readings in World History 10: Buddhism and Equality **E** Hands-on History Activity 3: Hinduism in Indian Life
SECTION 4 **Ancient Indian Dynasties and Empires** (pp. 66–68) • Explain how the Mauryan rulers increased their power. • Examine the reasons for the decline of Gupta rule.	**Regular** 1 day **Block Scheduling** .5 day *Block Scheduling Handbook with Team Teaching Strategies, 3.4*	**RS** Guided Reading Strategy 3.4 **PS** Readings in World History 11: Aśoka's Edicts
SECTION 5 **Ancient Indian Life and Culture** (pp. 69–71) • Describe how women's rights were limited in ancient Indian society. • Identify the most important achievements of the Gupta period.	**Regular** 1 day **Block Scheduling** .5 day *Block Scheduling Handbook with Team Teaching Strategies, 3.5*	**RS** Guided Reading Strategy 3.5 **PS** Readings in World History 12: The Place of Women in Hindu Society

Chapter Resource Key

PS Primary Sources	**A** Assessment	🎵 Music	
RS Reading Support	**REV** Review	📼 Video	
IC Interdisciplinary Connections	**ELL** Reinforcement and English Language Learners	🌐 Internet	
E Enrichment	✏️ Transparencies	💻 Holt Presentation Maker Using Microsoft® PowerPoint®	
SM Skills Mastery	💿 CD-ROM		

🖐 **One-Stop** Planner CD-ROM

See the **One-Stop Planner** for a complete list of additional resources for students and teachers.

One-Stop Planner CD-ROM

It's easy to plan lessons, select resources, and print out materials for your students when you use the *One-Stop Planner* CD–ROM with *Test Generator.*

Technology Resources

- One-Stop Planner 3.1
- Homework Practice Online
- Online Maps, Charts, and Graphs: Mohenjo-Daro
- Online Maps, Charts, and Graphs: Sites of Harappan Civilization

- One-Stop Planner 3.2
- Homework Practice Online
- Online Maps, Charts, and Graphs: Indo-Aryan Migration into India, c. 1750 B.C.

- One-Stop Planner 3.3
- CNN. Presents World Cultures: Yesterday and Today Segment 3: The Sacred Ganges
- World History Teaching Transparency: Everyday Life 6: Ganesha, Hindu Deity
- World History Teaching Transparency: Art and History 12: Seated Buddha Preaching the First Sermon
- Religions of the World Video Series: Hinduism
- Religions of the World Video Series: Buddhism
- Homework Practice Online
- Online Maps, Charts, and Graphs: The Spread of Buddhism, 500s B.C.–A.D. 600s

- One-Stop Planner 3.4
- Holt Researcher: World History: Chandragupta Maurya
- Homework Practice Online

- One-Stop Planner 3.5
- Regions of the World Music Audio CD Program 17: India: Ragas: Songs from India
- Homework Practice Online

Reinforcement, Review, and Assessment

- Daily Quiz 3.1
- Main Idea Activity 3.1
- English Audio Summary 3.1
- Spanish Audio Summary 3.1
- REV Section 1 Review, p. 55

- Daily Quiz 3.2
- Main Idea Activity 3.2
- English Audio Summary 3.2
- Spanish Audio Summary 3.2
- REV Section 2 Review, p. 59

- Daily Quiz 3.3
- Main Idea Activity 3.3
- English Audio Summary 3.3
- Spanish Audio Summary 3.3
- REV Section 3 Review, p. 65

- Daily Quiz 3.4
- Main Idea Activity 3.4
- English Audio Summary 3.4
- Spanish Audio Summary 3.4
- REV Section 4 Review, p. 68

- Daily Quiz 3.5
- Main Idea Activity 3.5
- English Audio Summary 3.5
- Spanish Audio Summary 3.5
- REV Section 5 Review, p. 71

internet connect

HRW ONLINE RESOURCES
GO TO: go.hrw.com
Then type in a keyword.

TEACHER HOME PAGE
KEYWORD: SP3 TEACHER

CHAPTER INTERNET ACTIVITIES
KEYWORD: SP3 WH3
Choose an activity to:
- study ancient India and create a travel poster.
- write a biography of a leader of the Mauryan Empire.
- explore the geographic regions of India and create a brochure.

CHAPTER ENRICHMENT LINKS
KEYWORD: SP3 CH3

ONLINE ASSESSMENT
Homework Practice
KEYWORD: SP3 HP3

Standardized Test Prep
KEYWORD: SP3 STP3

Rubrics
KEYWORD: SS Rubrics

ONLINE MAPS, CHARTS, AND GRAPHS
KEYWORD: SP3 MCG

CONTENT UPDATES
KEYWORD: SS Content Updates

HOLT PRESENTATION MAKER
KEYWORD: SP3 PPT3

ONLINE READING SUPPORT
KEYWORD: SS Strategies

CURRENT EVENTS
KEYWORD: S3 Current Events

Meeting Individual Needs

Ability Levels

Level 1 Basic level activities designed for all students encountering new material

Level 2 Intermediate level activities designed for average students

Level 3 Challenging activities designed for honors and gifted and talented students

English Language Learners These activities address the needs of students with Limited English Proficiency.

Chapter Review and Assessment

- IC Vocabulary Activity 3
- Global Skill Builder CD–ROM
- HRW Web Site
- REV Chapter 3 Tutorial for Students, Parents, Mentors, and Peers
- REV Chapter 3 Review, pp. 72–73
- A Chapter 3 Test Generator (on the One-Stop Planner)
- A Chapter 3 Test (Form A or B)
- A Alternative Assessment Handbook
- A Chapter 3 Test for English Language Learners and Special-Needs Students

Build on What You Know

Ask students to answer the following questions:

What were some of the developments of the first civilizations?

Consider:

- **art**
- **agriculture**
- **science and technology**
- **government**

List some characteristics of the early empires of the Fertile Crescent and describe the reasons for the empires' collapse.

Consider:

- **the Akkadians**
- **the Babylonians**
- **the Persians**

EXPLORING THE TIME LINE

GLOBAL EVENTS

internet connect

TOPIC: Ancient Indian
Civilization

GO TO: go.hrw.com

KEYWORD: SP3 WH3

Have students access the Internet through the HRW Go site to conduct research on the ways in which geography and climate affected the development of Indian civilization. Then ask students to compose an informative report that details how geographic and climactic conditions influenced where civilizations developed on the Indian subcontinent. Students' reports should include appropriate examples and evidence drawn from their research.

CHAPTER 3

c. 2500 B.C.–A.D. 550

Ancient Indian Civilizations

Harappan animal sculptures

c. 2500 B.C.
Politics
The Harappan civilization appears in the Indus Valley.

c. 1500 B.C.
Global Events
The Rig-Veda is compiled.

| 2500 B.C. | 2000 B.C. | 1500 B.C. |

c. 2300 B.C.
The Arts
Indus River valley people use pictographs.

c. 2300 B.C.
Business and Finance
Indus River valley people trade with people of the Tigris and Euphrates River valleys.

c. 2000 B.C.
Science and Technology
Harappans use extensive irrigation and drainage systems.

c. 1750 B.C.
Global Events
Indo-Aryans begin migrating into the Indian subcontinent.

c. 1750 B.C.
Daily Life
The city of Mohenjo Daro begins to decline.

Dome of the Sanchi Stupa

Gemstone necklace from Mohenjo Daro

Build on What You Know

Scientists have learned much about the early peoples of the world. From artifacts we know that early peoples invented tools, produced beautiful art, built cities, and developed governments. Gradually the first civilizations arose in northeastern Africa and southwestern Asia. Civilizations were defined by the ability to produce food, the creation of towns with governments, and a division of labor. In this chapter, you will learn how civilizations in ancient India not only fulfilled these conditions but also went on to develop complex social and religious systems and make great advances in science and culture.

What's Your Opinion?

Geography

Agree A region's physical geography and climate greatly affect a civilization's ability to engage in successful farming, trade, and cultural development.

Disagree A civilization can develop despite a treacherous physical geography and harsh climate.

Science, Technology & Society

Agree In order for a civilization to survive, it must make many advances in science and technology.

Disagree Cultural achievements, such as religion and art, are more important than a society's scientific and technological advances.

Culture

Agree A people's culture and religion are interwoven with the activities of their daily lives.

Disagree People are generally not affected by their society's cultural and religious developments during their daily lives.

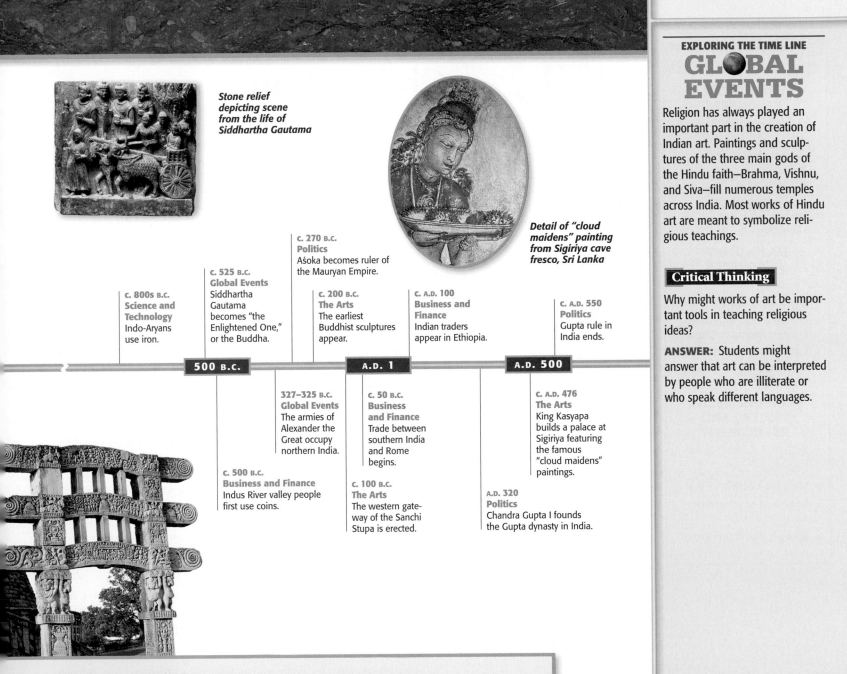

Stone relief depicting scene from the life of Siddhartha Gautama

Detail of "cloud maidens" painting from Sigiriya cave fresco, Sri Lanka

c. 800s B.C.
Science and Technology
Indo-Aryans use iron.

c. 525 B.C.
Global Events
Siddhartha Gautama becomes "the Enlightened One," or the Buddha.

c. 270 B.C.
Politics
Aśoka becomes ruler of the Mauryan Empire.

c. 200 B.C.
The Arts
The earliest Buddhist sculptures appear.

C. A.D. 100
Business and Finance
Indian traders appear in Ethiopia.

C. A.D. 550
Politics
Gupta rule in India ends.

500 B.C.

A.D. 1

A.D. 500

327–325 B.C.
Global Events
The armies of Alexander the Great occupy northern India.

c. 50 B.C.
Business and Finance
Trade between southern India and Rome begins.

C. A.D. 476
The Arts
King Kasyapa builds a palace at Sigiriya featuring the famous "cloud maidens" paintings.

c. 500 B.C.
Business and Finance
Indus River valley people first use coins.

c. 100 B.C.
The Arts
The western gateway of the Sanchi Stupa is erected.

A.D. 320
Politics
Chandra Gupta I founds the Gupta dynasty in India.

What's Your Opinion?

 Do you **agree** *or* **disagree** *with the following statements? Support your point of view in your journal.*

Geography The physical geography and climate of a region strongly affect the development of civilization there.

Science, Technology & Society A society's scientific and technological achievements are its greatest contribution to human civilization.

Culture In general, cultural and religious developments have a major influence on people's daily lives.

OBJECTIVES

1 Examine the role geography and climate played in the settlement of the Indian subcontinent.

2 Investigate how people in the first Indus River valley civilization lived.

SECTION ①

READ TO DISCOVER

❶ What role did geography and climate play in the settlement of the Indian subcontinent?

❷ How did people in the first Indus River valley civilization live?

DEFINE

monsoons
citadel

WHY IT MATTERS TODAY

Despite our advanced technology, geography and climate still affect the way we live. Use **CNNfyi**.com or other **current event** sources to explore how the geography and climate of your region influence the way people live and work. Record your findings in your journal.

CNNfyi.com

Indus River Valley Civilization

The Main Idea
The Indus River valley in the Indian subcontinent gave rise to the earliest Indian civilizations.

The Story Continues *Thousands of years ago near the Indus River valley there existed a village called Amri, whose citizens were makers of fine pottery. Indus River valley people like those in Amri helped lay the foundation for cultures in the modern countries of Bangladesh, Bhutan, India, Nepal, Pakistan, and Sri Lanka.*

The Importance of Geography and Climate

The first Indian civilization developed in the Indus River valley, in the northwestern part of the Indian subcontinent, about 4,500 years ago. Geography and climate played important roles in the development of civilization on the subcontinent.

Physical geography. The Indian subcontinent extends southward from central Asia into the Indian Ocean. It is separated in the north from the rest of Asia by towering mountain ranges. The greatest of these ranges is the Himalayas, which include the highest peaks in the world. These mountains made it difficult for immigrants and invaders to enter India by land. The famous Khyber Pass was one of a few paths that permitted people to cross the mountains into India.

Two great rivers lie south of the northern mountains. The Ganges River flows to the southeast through a fertile valley. In the west the Indus River flows southwest across a drier plain. The region drained by these two rivers is called the Indo-Gangetic Plain. To the south of these great river systems lies a high plateau called the Deccan. It makes up much of the interior of the subcontinent. To the west of the Deccan stand the Western Ghats. This mountain range rises abruptly from a narrow coastal plain along the Arabian Sea. A lower mountain range called the Eastern Ghats marks the eastern edge of the Deccan. On the eastern coast of India, another and broader coastal plain faces the Bay of Bengal. The inhabitants of the coastal plains became sea traders very early in their history.

The climate. Two features dominate India's climate: monsoons and high temperatures. **Monsoons** are winds that mark the seasons in India. Generally from November until the following March, monsoons blow from the north and northeast. Any moisture they carry falls onto the northern slopes of the Himalayas. Little rain falls on India during this season.

The wet season, called the southwest monsoon, occurs from mid-June through October, when southwesterly winds carry warm, moist air from the Indian Ocean. Water vapor in the air condenses to form clouds and rain. Heavy rains fall along the coastal plains, but sparse rainfall is typical of the land behind the Western Ghats. The lower Ganges Valley and the eastern Himalayas receive the heaviest rainfall. These regions lie directly in the path of the monsoon.

In most of India, much of the year's rainfall comes with the southwest monsoon. The timing of the monsoon is important. If it arrives late or brings little rain, crops fail. If the monsoon brings too much rain, floods may wash across the countryside.

TEACH OBJECTIVE 1

LEVEL 1: Ask students to summarize India's climate. *(They should note the seasonal monsoons and the potential for extreme heat.)* Remind the class that the first civilizations arose in four great river valleys; point out that one of these four valleys was the Indus River valley and help students locate the region on a map. Ask students why they think this civilization arose in the Indus Valley rather than in the Ganges Valley. *(Students should note that the Ganges Valley receives the heaviest rainfall during the monsoon.)* **ENGLISH LANGUAGE LEARNERS**

TEACH OBJECTIVE 2

LEVEL 3: Have students make a chart that lists 10 to 15 facts about the Harappan civilization, using the information on pages 53–55. Have them organize their charts into four columns labeled: *government, religion, technology,* and *economy.* Call on each student to share one fact from his or her chart. Ask students what causes, other than an earthquake or flood, might explain the unburied skeletons and abandoned homes at Mohenjo Daro. *(Students might suggest a plague, a drought, a deadly heat wave, and so on.)*

The other important feature of India's climate is the range of temperatures. Along the coast or on the Deccan, summers are fairly mild. In the Indo-Gangetic Plain, however, summer temperatures can reach 120°F.

✔ **READING CHECK: Making Predictions** How might geography and climate have affected early settlement in the Indian subcontinent? mountains slowed entry into India; monsoons and high temperatures made settlement difficult

Early Civilization in the Indus River Valley

A great civilization arose in the Indus River valley in about 2500 B.C. and lasted until about 1500 B.C. Much of what we know of this civilization comes from the ruins of two ancient cities, Harappa and Mohenjo Daro. Scholars have named it the Harappan civilization after the first of these cities.

Extensive archaeological digs at Harappa and Mohenjo Daro have revealed much about this early civilization. We know, for example, that both cities were large and carefully planned. Wide streets crossed at right angles. Each city had a water system with public baths and brick sewers. Some Harappans lived in two-story brick homes, some of which had bathrooms and garbage chutes. Each city had a strong central fortress, or **citadel,** built on a brick platform. There were also storehouses for grain. At Harappa the storehouses could hold enough to feed about 35,000 people.

The ability of Harappan leaders to store and distribute surplus food provides added evidence of careful, long-range planning. It may also suggest that Harappans were threatened by invaders or by crop-destroying floods. In any case, similar findings at Harappa, Mohenjo Daro, and other Harappan sites indicate that the civilization was probably organized around a strong central government.

Excavations at the site of Mohenjo Daro have revealed a large, well-planned city and a fortified citadel.

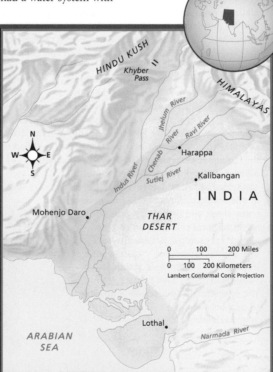

Harappan Civilization, c. 1700 B.C.
Interpreting Maps Rivers formed natural highways that encouraged exchange as well as unity in the Harappan civilization.
■ **Skills Assessment: 1. Locate** Identify the major waterways in the Indus River valley. **2. Drawing Conclusions** How might the location of Harappa and Mohenjo Daro have affected their relationship? Why?

ALL LEVELS: Have students look at the chart they created about Harappan achievements. Have them draw at least one other type of graphic organizer that could convey this information effectively. *(Students might draw cluster diagrams, branching or webbing organizers, horizontal or vertical lists, circular [pie] charts, concentric circles in a "bulls-eye" formation, and so on.)*

 HOMEWORK Have students draw a map of the Indian subcontinent showing the Indus River valley and Ganges River valley.

Teacher to Teacher

Mary Catherine Rahman of Chicago, Illinois, suggested the following activity: Give students an outline map of India. Have them locate and label the major landforms and rivers of India, as well as the two famous Harappan cities. Then have them explain what geographic factors might have helped or hurt early civilizations in India.

That's Interesting!

The Ganges River is considered sacred by the Hindus. Its soil is rich, and the crops along the Ganges have always been plentiful, irrigated by the river and the seasonal monsoons. Earthly sins are thought to be washed away by a bath in the waters of the Ganges. Many Hindus hope to make a pilgrimage to the river at some point in their lives to experience its purification.

SKILLS PRACTICE ANSWERS

1. Students might conclude that Harappan cities were planned carefully and the people were very resourceful.

2. Check students' charts to make sure they have categorized information accurately.

SKILL-BUILDING STRATEGIES   Categorizing Historical Information

Harappan Civilization

There are many different aspects to early civilizations like that of the Harappans. To help understand all of these different aspects, it sometimes helps to classify information. This involves grouping facts into categories according to the characteristics they share.

A Historian's View

Read the following description of Harappa and Mohenjo Daro by a historian who has studied the region:

"At Harappa and Mohenjo Daro the basic form of the ideal Indus city was achieved. . . . on the west a citadel mound built on a high podium of mud brick. . . and to the east, dominated by the citadel, a lower city. . . . The architects of the citadel platform were . . . troubled by the prospects of flooding and to counter this danger they protected the citadel by a mud-brick embankment. . . . [The Great Bath] occupied a central area in the citadel. . . . The Great Bath may have been part of a religious and ceremonial center, offering ritual immersion and perhaps the services of resident priesthood. . . . To the north and east of the Great Bath were other large and prestigious [important] buildings, which may have been the offices or quarters of administrators. . . . Divided into rectangular blocks by the street pattern, the individual buildings of the lower city differed considerably in size and function. . . . Nearly all the larger houses were equipped with wells, indoor bathroom platforms and seated latrines connected to sewers underneath the streets. . . . In addition to residential areas, there were many shops and workshops, producing wares for local consumption and for export: for example, potteries, dyers' vats and metalworkers', shell-ornament makers' and beadmakers' shops. . . . Wheat and barley were two staple crops. . . . The agricultural surplus made it possible to support a number of crafts and specialists. . . ."

Categories of Progress

Economic
division of labor
specialization of crafts
variety of services
products made for export
crop surplus

Technological
architectural skill
city planning
flood protection
   and water drainage system

This baked-clay sculpture from Mohenjo Daro shows well-developed artistic techniques.

Skills Reminder

To classify information, first read the information and sort it into groups of related data. Assign a category name to each group to indicate the topic to which the data in that group refers. Then, place the groups into broader categories if possible. Finally, compose a statement relating the categories to each other. This should help you to clearly establish the meaning of the information.

Skills Practice

Study the chart above to see how the information in the quote about Harappan civilization can be grouped into categories.

❶ What conclusions can you draw about Harappan civilization based on this information?

❷ Build a similar chart to classify evidence of economic and technological progress in your town or city.

CLOSE

Have students explain how geography and climate affected the growth of civilization in the Indus River valley.

REVIEW

Have students complete the Section 1 Review on p. 55.

ASSESS

Have students complete Daily Quiz 3.1. As Alternative Assessment, you may want to use the map or chart exercises in this section's lessons.

RETEACH

Have students complete Main Idea Activity for English Language Learners and Special-Needs Students 3.1. Then have them write a question about the main idea for each subsection in the section.

ENGLISH LANGUAGE LEARNERS

EXTEND

Have students use primary and secondary sources, such as computer software, to conduct research on monsoons. Have them write a report explaining how monsoons affected Indian civilization.

Rich farmlands surrounded Harappa and Mohenjo Daro. Harappan farmers grew cotton, wheat, barley, and rice. They also raised cattle, sheep, pigs, and goats. To irrigate their fields, the farmers built canals and ditches. Successful farming practices allowed Harappan farmers to raise surplus crops for storage and trade.

City dwellers were involved in the production or trade of goods. As early as 2300 B.C. they traded with people of the Tigris-Euphrates River valley. Indus River valley craft workers made fine goods. Products included cotton cloth, pottery, bronze items, and gold and silver jewelry.

The early Indus River valley people also developed a written language, as evidenced by pictographs dating from about 2300 B.C. Scholars have not yet been able to read these, however. This is because most of the pictographs that have been found are personal seals that may bear the names of individuals. Writing has also been found on clay pots and fragments, but scholars have been unable to connect this writing to any other language.

No Harappan temples, shrines, or religious writings have been found. Scholars believe, however, that people of the Indus River valley worshiped a great god and used images of certain animals, such as the bull, the buffalo, and the tiger, in religious rituals. Evidence indicates that a mother goddess symbolized fertility. Harappans may have held religious ceremonies in their homes or in outdoor locations, such as around sacred trees.

We do not know why the Indus River valley civilization disappeared. There are several possible reasons. Scientists do know that the waters of the Indus River valley have changed course in the past. Floods caused by these shifts destroyed settlements and would have made life difficult for farmers. Some evidence suggests possible violence from invading forces. There is also evidence of a major earthquake striking the region in about 1700 B.C. Several unburied skeletons were found at Mohenjo Daro, and people appear to have abandoned their homes and possessions. This seems to indicate that some disastrous event occurred at Mohenjo Daro, but evidence to verify this theory has not been found.

✔ **READING CHECK: Drawing Inferences**
What does the size of Harappa's grain storehouses tell us about the city's population?
numbered in the thousands

The pictographs on these Harappan seals may symbolize individuals' names.

CONNECTING TO Economics

Industry and Trade in the Indus River Valley

Trade was an important part of life in the Indus River valley. Artisans made both decorative and practical goods to trade. Decorative articles included ceramic beads, ornaments, and gold and silver jewelry. Useful goods included bronze and copper tools, pots and pans, and stone tools.

Among the most interesting art objects are seals like the ones shown below. These Harappan seals have been found in the Tigris-Euphrates region near Sumerian sites.

Understanding Economics

What might explain the appearance of these seals so far from the Indus River valley?

CONNECTING TO ECONOMICS ANSWER

Students might suggest that the Harappans traded with civilizations in the Tigris-Euphrates region.

🖳 **internet** connect

TOPIC: Ancient India
GO TO: go.hrw.com
KEYWORD: SP3 WH3

Have students access the Internet through the HRW Go site to research ancient India. Then have them make a poster "advertisement" on ancient India that promotes it as a vacation spot.

SECTION 1 REVIEW ANSWERS

❶ **Define**
- monsoons, p. 52
- citadel, p. 53

❷ Students should mention that the civilization's location near waterways led to sea trade, and that farmers had to adapt their practices to the monsoon climate.

❸ **a.** It allowed easy trade and successful farming.

b. Harappan seals have been found in the Tigris-Euphrates region.

❹ Students' paragraphs should discuss the things that were important to Harappans and the occupations of the people.

SECTION 1 REVIEW

1. **Define** and explain the significance:
   monsoons
   citadel

2. **Analyzing Information** Copy the graphic organizer below. Use it to analyze the influence of geography and climate on early Indus River valley civilization.

   Geography → Indus River Valley Civilization ← Climate

3. **Finding the Main Idea**
   a. In what ways did the physical setting of the Indus River valley encourage the growth of civilization?
   b. What evidence suggests that people of the Indus River valley had contact with other early civilizations?

4. **Writing and Critical Thinking**
   Supporting a Point of View Write a paragraph from the point of view of a young person in Harappa describing what you like most about life in your city.
   Consider:
   • what seemed important to the people of the city
   • how the people of the city made their livings

Homework Practice Online
keyword: SP3 HP3

OBJECTIVES

1 **Explain how life in northern India changed with the coming of the Indo-Aryans.**

2 **Identify the major contributions of the Indo-Aryans to ancient Indian society.**

MAP ANSWER

mountains

READ TO DISCOVER

❶ How did life in northern India change with the coming of the Indo-Aryans?

❷ What were the major contributions of the Indo-Aryans to ancient Indian society?

DEFINE

raja

IDENTIFY

Indo-Aryans
Vedas
Sanskrit
Vedic Age
Brahmins

WHY IT MATTERS TODAY

Human migration plays a key role in our society. Use CNNfyi.com or other **current event** sources to explore how immigrants have influenced American society. Record your findings in your journal.

CNNfyi.com

Indo-Aryan Migrants

The Main Idea
The Vedic Age of early Indian civilization was marked by Indo-Aryan migration and cultural development.

The Story Continues *As the Harappan civilization was declining, a new warrior civilization was entering India. It is possible that this group destroyed what was left of the Harappan civilization. Whether or not they did, we know that these warriors soon came to dominate the region.*

The Nomadic Indo-Aryans

In about 1750 B.C. tribes of Indo-European peoples began to cross the Hindu Kush Mountains into northwestern India. They came from north of the Black and Caspian Seas. We call these nomadic people the **Indo-Aryans.**

The Vedic Age. The Indo-Aryans, sheep and cattle herders as well as skilled warriors, were drawn into northern India by the region's rich pasturelands. In fact, the Indo-Aryan word for war meant "a desire for more cows." Their armies of archers and charioteers enabled the Indo-Aryans to conquer all of northern India.

Most of what we know of these people comes from the **Vedas.** These are the Indo-Aryans' great works of religious literature. For centuries people memorized the Vedas and retold them to their children. Later the Indo-Aryans developed writing. Scholars recorded the Vedas in **Sanskrit,** the Indo-Aryan language. We call the period of India's history from 1500 B.C. to 1000 B.C. the **Vedic Age.**

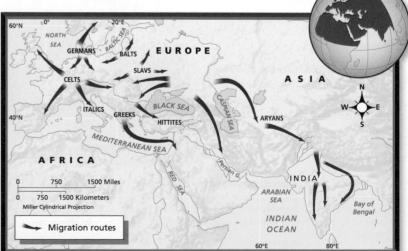

Indo-European Migrations and Indo-Aryan Invasions
Interpreting Maps The Indo-Aryan invaders of northern India were part of a larger movement of peoples westward from central Asia.

■ **Skills Assessment: Physical Systems** What geographic features determined the routes taken by the Indo-Aryans into northern India?

TEACH OBJECTIVE 1

LEVEL 1: Have students read Section 2 and then list some of the ways life in northern India changed with the coming of the Indo-Aryans, including major political, economic, and cultural developments. *(Students should mention the Vedas, Indo-Aryan religion, the formation of states, and the spread of Sanskrit.)* **ENGLISH LANGUAGE LEARNERS**

LEVEL 3: Tell students that throughout history urban societies have often come into conflict with their nomadic neighbors. Although the Harappan civilization was well-protected by the natural barrier presented by the northern mountains, the Khyber Pass through the Hindu Kush Mountains provided a means for the Indo-Aryans to invade India after about 1750 B.C. Ask students why they think the Indo-Aryans invaded India. If students guess that the Indo-Aryans were interested in the cities, tell them that they ignored the cities, leaving them to decay.

Indo-Aryan religion. The earliest gods mentioned in the Vedas were drawn from nature. Earth, fire, light, rain, sky, storms, sun, and water were personified. Thus the sky became a father, Earth a mother. Although the Vedas mention gods and goddesses, they also refer to one supreme god. An important hymn celebrates "That One," who created order in the universe. As Indo-Aryan views developed, the Vedic gods were portrayed as having particular characteristics. Varuna, for example, was the guardian of cosmic order. He lived in a great palace in the sky. Over time Varuna became the divine judge who punished sin. Other gods had different characteristics.

It appears that there were no temples in the early Vedic religion. Ceremonies were performed in open spaces chosen for important occasions. Fires were lit on special altars. Foods such as meat, butter, milk, and barley cakes were offered as ritual sacrifices. The juice of the soma plant was poured into the sacred fire as a special offering. The plant's juice was thought to be the drink of immortality.

It was important to the Indo-Aryans that religious ceremonies be performed properly. As time passed, their religious rituals became more and more complicated. Special priests called **Brahmins** knew the proper forms and rules. Brahmins became very important in Indo-Aryan society. No longer the language of everyday speech, Sanskrit became the language used by priests in their rituals.

✔ **READING CHECK: Finding the Main Idea** Why were Brahmins important members of Indo-Aryan society? They had specialized religious training.

Early Indo-Aryan Society

As Indo-Aryans settled in villages, they gave up the way of nomadic wanderers. They continued to herd animals, but they planted crops as well. In time Indo-Aryan settlements joined to form small independent states or territories, each of which was governed by a **raja,** or chief. The raja acted as the military leader, lawmaker, and judge. A royal council assisted him. At times states or territories would go to war against one another. Most often, however, Indo-Aryans lived in peace with neighboring groups.

Indo-Aryan society. Physical and social differences existed between the Indo-Aryan migrants and the earlier inhabitants of the Indo-Gangetic Plain. These differences were the source of the complex system of social orders that over time became very important in Indian society. The Indo-Aryans were light skinned, whereas the earlier settlers were dark skinned. The Indo-Aryans had been a nomadic people, while Indus Valley peoples lived in settled communities. Warriors, and later priests, were at the top of the Indo-Aryan social structure, with merchants, traders, farmers, and servants below them.

In addition to providing information about Indo-Aryan religion, the Vedas tell us a great deal about family life in the Vedic Age. Marriage was an important Indo-Aryan institution, and rules governed—and later limited—marriage among the social orders. Other rules outlined complicated marriage ceremonies. Parents usually arranged marriages, but marriage by purchase or capture and marriage for love were

In this relief from Gandhara, two young Brahmins raise their right hands to perform a religious gesture.

Culture

Throughout their history, the people of India have respected and revered animals. The ancient Indus Valley dwellers carved the likenesses of animals, particularly bulls, on their beautiful trading seals. The Indo-Aryans, with nomadic herding roots, valued cattle so highly that they considered them to be the basic unit of wealth and used cattle as currency to purchase items of great value. Eventually the Hindus declared cows to be sacred and forbade killing them. The Hindus believed that souls could be reincarnated as humans or animals. Killing any creature—even an insect—was forbidden because any creature might house the soul of an ancestor or friend. Other animals that were highly revered in India include birds, monkeys, and elephants.

Critical Thinking

Ask students why they think the cow has been valued so highly by Indian peoples from the earliest civilizations to the present.

ANSWER: Students might mention that the cow was a source of food and fuel, and was even used as currency by the earliest Indians. They might also point out that cow's milk was likely a major source of nutrition for Indians throughout history. They should also mention the Hindu belief that the cow is a sacred animal.

ALL LEVELS: Tell students that most of what we know about the Indo-Aryans comes from the Vedas. These are the great literature of the Indo-Aryan religion, memorized and passed on for centuries. After the development of writing, scholars wrote them in the Indo-Aryan language. Draw a three-column chart on the board. Title it *Characteristics of Indo-Aryan Society,* and label its three columns *Government, Social Life,* and *Economy.* Have students copy this chart and categorize the information as they read Section 2. **ENGLISH LANGUAGE LEARNERS**

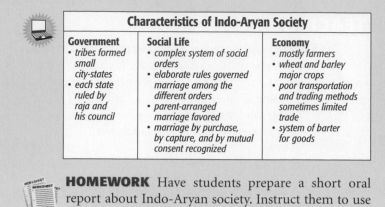

Characteristics of Indo-Aryan Society		
Government	**Social Life**	**Economy**
• tribes formed small city-states • each state ruled by raja and his council	• complex system of social orders • elaborate rules governed marriage among the different orders • parent-arranged marriage favored • marriage by purchase, by capture, and by mutual consent recognized	• mostly farmers • wheat and barley major crops • poor transportation and trading methods sometimes limited trade • system of barter for goods

HOMEWORK Have students prepare a short oral report about Indo-Aryan society. Instruct them to use correct social studies terminology to describe the society.

Daily Life

Life in Indo-Aryan clans and families was somewhat freer and more open than in other societies. Although the Indo-Aryans were a patriarchal society, tribal chiefs did not have the absolute authority over the affairs of the group. Indo-Aryan customs and laws governed the chief's actions. When the Aryans first came to India, women were also freer to choose their own husbands, rather than being told whom they must marry. This practice, however, changed over time.

Critical Thinking

Ask students to suggest possible reasons why this freedom for women might have been taken away over time.

ANSWER: Cultural attitudes toward women might have changed, or families might have begun arranging women's marriages as a way of gaining power through family alliances.

SCIENCE AND TECHNOLOGY ANSWER

shovels, trowels, brushes, aerial photography, magnetometers, sonar scanners, computers, particle accelerators, potassium-argon dating

CONNECTING TO
Science and Technology

The Tools of Archaeology

Archaeologists have a number of tools that they use to understand ancient peoples like the Indo-Aryans. Many are simple tools, such as shovels, trowels, and brushes. Archaeologists use these and other tools to carefully uncover and preserve artifacts. Aerial photographs, magnetometers, and sonar scanners also help archaeologists find sites both visible and buried under earth or water. Once a site is found; computers aid in cataloging and classifying uncovered objects.

Since the development in the late 1940s of carbon-14 dating, archaeologists have been able to date the remains of living things from up to 50,000 years ago. A machine measures the amount of radiocarbon in the remains. This tells scientists how long ago the person, animal, or plant died.

Archaeologists have other tools for measuring the age of artifacts. Some instruments help to determine the age of tiny objects up to 60,000 years old. Recently potassium-argon dating has been used to date rock formations that are millions of years old.

Understanding Science and Technology

What are some of the scientific tools that archaeologists use?

Grid system for keeping track of location of artifacts

Screen for sifting soil samples

Brushing dirt from the artifact

Analyzing Primary Sources

Drawing Inferences What do you think the writer meant by the last line of this chant? *that they strengthened their social values by following tradition*

also recognized. Indo-Aryan society strongly emphasized the value of sacrificing, as this passage from the Vedas reveals:

Primary Source

❝All power to our life through sacrifice!
All power to our lungs through sacrifice!
All power to our eyes through sacrifice!
All power to our ears through sacrifice!
All power to our backs through sacrifice!
All power to Sacrifice through sacrifice!❞

Yajur-Veda IX, 21

The Indo-Aryan Economy. The Indo-Aryans began raising wheat and barley on the rich plains of the Indus and Ganges Rivers. Irrigation was used to grow rice. Other crops included sugarcane, leafy vegetables, gourds, peas, beans, and lentils. Although villages traded with one another, poor transportation made continuous trade difficult. Early traders bartered, since coins were not widely used in Indo-Aryan society until about 500 B.C.

The Indo-Aryan migrants had a significant impact on the civilization of northern India. They brought with them a new social order. Their language, an early form of Sanskrit, soon spread over much of India. They contributed new religious ideas of how the world works, involving many gods associated with forces of nature. Archaeologists believe that over time these migrants blended into the existing civilization of the Indus River valley people. Religious values changed as social classes became more rigid and closely identified with ritual purity. The result was a new society.

CLOSE

Ask students to explain who the Indo-Aryans were. Then have them describe how the Indo-Aryans influenced political, economic, and cultural developments in Indian civilization.

REVIEW

Have students complete the Section 2 Review on p. 59.

ASSESS

Have students complete Daily Quiz 3.2. As Alternative Assessment, you may want to use the chart exercise in this section's lessons.

RETEACH

Have students complete Main Idea Activity for English Language Learners and Special-Needs Students 3.2. Then have them write a paragraph that describes the developments of Indo-Aryan society, using standard grammar, spelling, sentence structure, and punctuation. **ENGLISH LANGUAGE LEARNERS**

EXTEND

Ask students to use computer software to locate an excerpt from the Vedas in English translation. Encourage them to make a dramatic reading from the Vedas. **BLOCK SCHEDULING**

Southern India. Early civilization in the southern portion of the Indian subcontinent followed different patterns of development. The southern part of the subcontinent was protected from invasion from the north by mountains. The rugged, forest-covered Vindhya Range separates the southern region of the subcontinent from the Indo-Gangetic Plain. The people of the south were able to hold on to their distinct ways of life. The hilly landscape of southern India made unification of its peoples difficult. As a result, people there remained divided into diverse social groups. Many of these divisions still exist today.

Many southern Indians lived as farmers, while others were hunter-gatherers. Others, living along the subcontinent's southern coastal areas, turned to trade to make a living. A few became wealthy trading cotton, spices, and ivory. Through coastal ports, southern Indians eventually made contact with the peoples of other civilizations in Southeast Asia.

✔ **READING CHECK: Summarizing** What were the major contributions of the Indo-Aryans to ancient Indian society? established a new social order, language, and religion

The rough terrain of the Deccan and the Vindhya Range slowed the flow of goods and ideas between northern and southern India.

SECTION 2 REVIEW ANSWERS

❶ **Define**
• raja, p. 57

❷ **Identify**
• Indo-Aryans, p. 56
• Vedas, p. 56
• Sanskrit, p. 56
• Vedic Age, p. 56
• Brahmins, p. 57

❸ Students' analyses should include the following: gods were drawn from nature, natural elements were personified, ceremonies were performed in open spaces.

❹ **a.** Their language and new religious ideas resulted in a new society.

b. Students might guess that it was to prevent intermarriage between social orders.

❺ Students should contrast the social order created by the Indo-Aryans to what they know about Indian civilizations before the arrival of the Indo-Aryans.

SECTION 2 REVIEW

1. **Define** and explain the significance:
   raja

2. **Identify** and explain the significance:
   Indo-Aryans
   Vedas
   Sanskrit
   Vedic Age
   Brahmins

3. **Analyzing Information** Copy the concept web below. Use it to analyze how early Indo-Aryan religious beliefs reflected the natural world.

   The Natural World

4. **Finding the Main Idea**
   a. How did the early Indo-Aryans' nomadic lifestyle help them to win control of northern India?
   b. Why might the Indo-Aryans have created strict rules governing marriage among the different social orders?

5. **Writing and Critical Thinking**
   Summarizing Write a paragraph explaining the changes in ancient Indian civilization as a result of Indo-Aryan migration.
   Consider:
   • what you know about Indian civilization before the arrival of the Indo-Aryans
   • what you know about the new social order the Indo-Aryans created

Homework Practice Online
keyword: SP3 HP3

ANCIENT INDIAN CIVILIZATIONS **59**

59

OBJECTIVES

1 Describe the importance of religion in ancient Indian society.

2 Identify the principal elements of Hinduism.

3 Identify the basic beliefs of Buddhism.

LET'S GET STARTED!

As students enter the classroom, have them think about social divisions in American society today. Ask them how structured they believe American social classes are and if it is possible for a person to move to a higher social class. *(Students might mention examples of people achieving a higher social class.)* Tell students that in Section 3 they will learn about the structure of social classes in ancient India.

SECTION 3

READ TO DISCOVER

❶ How important was religion in ancient Indian society?

❷ What were the principal elements of Hinduism?

❸ What were the basic beliefs of Buddhism?

DEFINE

epics
caste system
varnas
monism
maya
reincarnation
nirvana
polytheistic

IDENTIFY

Upanishads
Bhagavad Gita
Siddhartha Gautama

WHY IT MATTERS TODAY

Religion plays an important role in world affairs today. Use CNNfyi.com or other **current event** sources to identify news stories with religious elements. Record your findings in your journal.

CNNfyi.com

Hinduism and Buddhism

The Main Idea
Hinduism and Buddhism became the dominant spiritual philosophies of ancient India.

The Story Continues *"From the unreal lead me to the real. From darkness lead me to light! From death lead me to immortality!" These verses from a religious text reflect a growing focus on spiritualism in ancient India. Enlightenment became the goal for many Indian believers.*

The Upanishads and the Epics

By the end of the Vedic Age, the social structure of India had taken shape. Over the next thousand years, many great works of religious literature were written, based on earlier Indo-Aryan religious stories and traditions. During this time two of the world's great religions—Hinduism and Buddhism—developed in India.

In about 700 B.C. several Indian religious thinkers began to question the authority of the Brahmins. These thinkers became wanderers who taught their messages in the forests of the Ganges Plain. The school of thought that grew from their teachings was known as Vedanta, or "end of the Vedas." These teachings were collected in the **Upanishads** (oo·PAH·ni·shahdz). They were the written explanations of the Vedic religion.

Ordinary people, who could neither read nor write, could not use the Upanishads. Instead they listened to religious stories that helped to explain the ideas of Vedanta. These exciting stories used tales of heroes and great events to pass along religious traditions. After generations of retelling, the stories were combined into two **epics**—long poems based on historical or religious themes. They became known as the Mahabharata (muh·HAH·BAHR·uh·tuh) and the Ramayana.

The Mahabharata tells the story of a great battle in a kingdom in what is now northern India. Part of this epic is known as the **Bhagavad Gita.** It is the most famous of Hindu scriptures. The Ramayana tells the story of Rama, a prince and an incarnation of the god Vishnu, and his wife Sita. When Sita was kidnapped by a demon, Rama rescued her and became king. Rama and Sita became role models for men and women in Indian society.

✔ **READING CHECK: Identifying Cause and Effect** In what way did the epics help to spread religious understanding among India's ordinary people? Illiterate people could still listen to the epics.

The god Vishnu is depicted in this striking Indian sculpture.

TEACH OBJECTIVE 1

LEVEL 3: Have students study the information in the sections titled "A Changing Society" and "Hinduism." Ask students to describe how the Indian caste system and Hinduism were related. *(According to Hinduism, people who fulfill their dharma gain good karma and are born into a higher social group in the next life. People who do not live moral lives will be born as members of lower groups.)*

Spotlight on CULTURE

The Puranas are a group of 18 epics made up of many myths and legends. Their plots are taken from the Mahabharata. Narratives from the Puranas have been used to teach Hindu religious ideals to the public. Ask students to list examples of stories from the Bible that have been popularized in American culture. *(Students might list stories such as creation, Adam and Eve, Noah and the Ark, and Moses.)*

A Changing Society

Two developments transformed Indian society between 1500 B.C. and A.D. 500. One of these was the establishment of the **caste system,** a complex form of social organization that began to take shape after the Indo-Aryan migration. Four distinct **varnas,** or social classes, appeared in Indian society. At the top of the social scale were the rulers and warriors. The second varna was the Brahmins, the priests and scholars. Over the centuries the Brahmins became the first varna because of their important role in society. The third class included merchants, traders, and farmers. Peasants who worked in fields owned by others, or who did menial labor, made up the fourth varna.

People in a fifth group were called Pariahs, or "untouchables." Pariahs were viewed as being outside of varnas, although still a part of the caste system. They were allowed to perform only jobs that were considered unclean, such as skinning animals or preparing the dead for funerals. According to the Indian law of the time,

Primary Source **❝**Not only does one not take water from them [the untouchables], they may not even take water from the same well. . . . Not only does one not marry them, they may not even enter the temple or the house or stroll on the main village streets. Even their cattle may often not drink from the same pool as [others.]**❞**

Taya Zinkin, *Caste Today*

Over time the four varnas divided into smaller subgroups, called jati. Eventually there were some 3,000 different jati. Strict rules developed. A person was born into the jati of his or her parents and could marry only within that subgroup. People's jatis determined what jobs they could hold and who they could eat with. This complex caste system remained a part of Indian society for centuries. The constitution of today's India has abolished the caste system, but its influence remains strong in parts of Indian society.

✔ **READING CHECK: Analyzing Information** How did the caste system affect Indian society? separated people into classes

Hinduism

The other major development in ancient Indian society was the growth of Hinduism, which became deeply interwoven with the caste system. Hinduism gradually spread to become India's major religion. It developed through the Brahmin priests' explanations of the Vedas. According to the Upanishads, a divine essence called Brahman fills everything in the world. People have an individual essence, called Self or Atman. Hinduism teaches that Brahman and Atman are one and the same. This reflects the belief that all things in the universe are of the same essence as God. This belief in the unity of God and creation is called **monism** (not to be confused with *monotheism,* the belief in one god).

Hindu beliefs. Hinduism teaches that the world we see is an illusion. If people accept this illusion, called **maya,** they cannot be saved. People can gain salvation only if they learn to recognize and reject maya, but this is not easy to do. According to Hinduism it can take many lifetimes to fully recognize maya. As a result, souls must be reborn over and over again. The experience they gain as they pass through life helps them to identify maya. This belief in the rebirth of souls is called **reincarnation.** Hindus believe that the soul does not die, but rather can be reborn in the body of another human being or even an animal.

Link to Today This Indian woman's caste can be determined by her traditional clothing and facial decoration.

Analyzing Primary Sources

Identifying Bias How do the instructions regarding the treatment of untouchables reflect the view of others towards them? The instructions set them apart.

Linking Past to Present

Only in the past few decades has the system of jati begun to change. In 1950 the Indian government adopted a new constitution outlawing untouchability. It took several more years, however, before punishment for discrimination against the untouchables began to be enforced. Since the 1950s the Indian government has tried to broaden opportunities for former untouchables. Today the children of former untouchables also receive benefits, such as special scholarships to Indian universities.

Critical Thinking

Ask students why they think a society might develop a system of jati.

ANSWER: Students might suggest that a system of jati would likely provide order and stability within a society.

Technology Resources
Religions of the World Video Series: Hinduism

LEVEL 1: Remind students of the connection between Hinduism and the Indian caste system. Tell them to create a graphic organizer that clearly shows how the classes were categorized and ranked in early India. Here is one acceptable way to accomplish this:

Point out to students that these classes eventually were divided into thousands of smaller groups called jati.
ENGLISH LANGUAGE LEARNERS

Class System in Early India	
Upper Class	*Brahmins: priests, scholars*
	rulers, warriors
Middle Class	*merchants, traders, farmers*
Lower Class	*peasants bound to the land*
	Pariahs: untouchables

That's Interesting!

Many of the most beautiful buildings in early India were religious buildings such as Buddhist sanctuaries and Hindu temples. These buildings were frequently covered with carvings of religious symbols; images of gods, animals, and beautiful men and women; and elaborate ornamentation. Sometimes not an inch of such structures remained unadorned. Some scholars believe that the temple builders carved such images and scenes into their buildings because worshipers frequently were illiterate; the building itself therefore became a teaching tool since its images told the story of religious beliefs.

VISUAL RECORD ANSWER

The image shows three different aspects of one Hindu god.

Technology Resources

World History Teaching Transparency: Everyday Life 6: Ganesha, Hindu Deity

INTERPRETING THE VISUAL RECORD

The Hindu god This sculpture represents Brahma, Vishnu, and Siva as a three-headed creature. *How does this image reflect the Hindu belief in the oneness of the universe?*

Two important principles of Hinduism are dharma and karma. Dharma means doing one's moral duty in this life so that the soul can advance in the next life. Karma is the good or bad force created by a person's actions. According to Hinduism, people who fulfill their dharma gain good karma and are born into a higher social group in the next life. People who do not live moral lives will be born as members of lower groups or as animals. In time, souls who grow spiritually can reach **nirvana**, a perfect peace. At that point the cycle of reincarnation is complete and the individual's soul unites with Brahman.

The Hindu god Brahma can be represented as a number of gods. Brahma the Creator, Vishnu the Preserver, and Siva the Destroyer can be forms of Brahma. Other gods are represented in the spirits of trees, animals, or people, but each is a part of Brahman. For this reason, Hindus must respect all forms of life. To many outsiders, Hinduism appears **polytheistic**—based on a belief in many gods. Hindus point out, however, that their gods simply represent different aspects of creation. Thus Hinduism is actually a monistic faith.

Hindu religious practices. Hindus often practice yoga, a set of mental and physical exercises designed to bring the body and soul together. In one form of yoga, a person might sit for hours in the same position. Over time, this frees the mind of thoughts about the body.

Hindu festivals combine religious ceremonies, rituals, music, dancing, eating, and drinking. Celebrations might last for days. These festivals represent the seasonal course of nature. Originally it was believed that such festivals helped to promote the return of the seasons. Many ancient festivals are celebrated throughout India today.

Some Hindus see certain animals as particularly sacred. Cows are special because they traditionally provided power for plows and carts. They also produce milk and butter for food. For these reasons cows are protected by law.

✔ **READING CHECK: Drawing Conclusions** Why is Hinduism considered to be a monistic faith? holds that all things are of the same essence as God

There are many festivals and celebrations in the Hindu calendar. This image shows Hindu women celebrating the Chaat Puja festival in early November.

ALL LEVELS : Have students create a Venn diagram to compare Hinduism and Buddhism. The diagram should include elements that are unique to each religion as well as elements they have in common. *(Hinduism: belief in dharma and karma, belief that the sensory world is an illusion; Buddhism: belief in the way to enlightenment, ethical guidelines—Four Noble Truths and Eightfold Path; both: belief in reincarnation, belief that progress of soul depends on life led, belief in nirvana)* **ENGLISH LANGUAGE LEARNERS**

Buddhism

Buddhism, another of the world's great religions, also arose in India. Its founder was **Siddhartha Gautama.** He became known as the Buddha, or "the Enlightened One." Born in about 563 B.C. in northern India, Siddhartha Gautama was the son of a wealthy prince of the region. During his youth he received every advantage of luxury, education, and comfort. His royal lifestyle shielded him from the harsh realities of everyday life. He knew nothing, for example, of disease, poverty, fear, or other aspects of life among ordinary people.

At the age of 29, Siddhartha Gautama ventured out of his palace and was shocked to learn of the challenges and tragedies common to everyday life. He vowed to discover the reasons for human suffering. In what is now called the Great Renunciation, he left his family and his lifestyle in search of truth and meaning. He tried many methods to discover wisdom, practicing yoga and meditation and fasting so strictly that he nearly died. None of these approaches, however, gave Siddhartha Gautama the answers that he sought.

One day, after six years of searching, Siddhartha Gautama sat meditating under a tree. Suddenly, he felt that he understood the truth that forms the basis of life. In that moment, according to his followers, Siddhartha Gautama became the Buddha. He spent the remainder of his life teaching his followers to pursue the way to enlightenment, the Way of Life.

Holt Researcher
go.hrw.com
KEYWORD: Holt Researcher
FreeFind:
   Siddhartha Gautama
After reading more about Siddhartha Gautama on the Holt Researcher, write a series of interview questions that you would ask the Buddha if you could meet him.

Culture

A religion called Jainism arose from the questioning of the Vedas. Its founder, Varadhamana, was later called Mahavira, the "Great Hero." Mahavira accepted the ideas of karma and reincarnation as well as the concepts of Atman and Brahman. But he believed that, in order to cleanse the soul, one must abstain from any activities that would add to the impurities clinging to the soul like barnacles. This belief led to an ascetic lifestyle in which Jainists did not eat meat and avoided causing harm to other souls, including those of insects. The supreme accomplishment of a Jain was to commit suicide by starvation, which is how Mahavira died at the age of 72.

Critical Thinking

Ask students how Jainism is similar to Hinduism.

ANSWER: It embraces the ideas of karma, reincarnation, and Atman and Brahman. Students might also point out that it has its foundation in the Vedas.

MAP ANSWER
to Japan, Burma, and Siam

Technology Resources
   Religions of the World Video Series: Buddhism

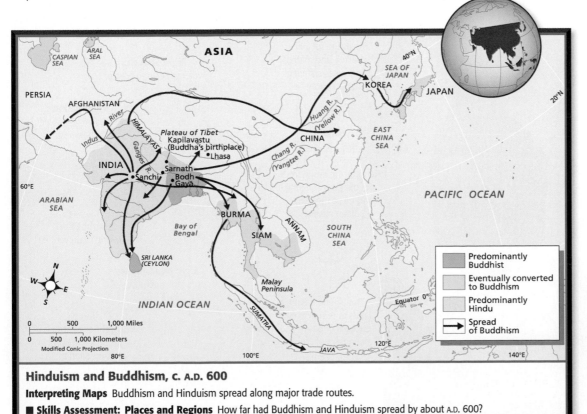

Hinduism and Buddhism, c. A.D. 600
Interpreting Maps Buddhism and Hinduism spread along major trade routes.
■ **Skills Assessment: Places and Regions** How far had Buddhism and Hinduism spread by about A.D. 600?

CLOSE

Organize the class into small groups. Have each group discuss the Four Noble Truths and the principles of the Eightfold Path.

The Buddha's teachings. The Buddha accepted some Hindu ideas, including reincarnation. He believed that the progress of the soul depends on the life a person leads—good is rewarded and evil punished. However, he taught that salvation comes from knowing the "Four Noble Truths" and following the "Eightfold Path."

The Buddha taught ethics—a code of morals and conduct—more than ceremonies. He believed that desire causes suffering. As a result, he stressed the importance of selflessness. The Buddha did not accept the Hindu gods, but rather taught that priests should live peaceful and moral lives of poverty. He did not attack the Hindu caste system openly, but denied its importance. According to Buddhism, any person, regardless of caste, could reach nirvana. This gave Buddhism a broad appeal. Powerful Brahmins opposed these teachings.

THE FOUR NOBLE TRUTHS

All human life involves suffering and sorrow.

The desire for a life of pleasure and material gain causes suffering and sorrow.

Renouncing desire frees people from suffering and helps their souls attain nirvana.

The Eightfold Path leads to renunciation, or denial of desire and attainment of nirvana.

THE EIGHTFOLD PATH

Right Views
seeing life as it really is

Right Intentions
living a life of good will; striving toward perfection

Right Speech
avoiding lies and gossip

Right Action
trying to be law-abiding and honest

Right Living
avoiding work that harms others

Right Effort
seeking to prevent evil

Right Mindfulness
constant awareness of one's self

Right Concentration
directing the mind in meditation

Traditional stone sculpture of the Buddha near the Japanese city of Tokyo

REVIEW

Have students complete the Section 3 Review on p. 65.

ASSESS

Have students complete Daily Quiz 3.3. As Alternative Assessment, you may want to use the Venn diagram exercise in this section's lessons.

RETEACH

Have students complete Main Idea Activity for English Language Learners and Special-Needs Students 3.3. Ask students to list the main ideas of each heading and subheading in this section.
ENGLISH LANGUAGE LEARNERS

EXTEND

Organize students into two groups to study Hinduism and Buddhism. Have students use computer software to acquire information about how the respective religions spread throughout Asia. Finally, have students from each group teach each other about the religion they studied. **BLOCK SCHEDULING,**
COOPERATIVE LEARNING

The Buddha taught that the Vedas—the great works of Hindu religious literature—were not actually sacred writings. He believed that virtue could not be inherited and that all people should practice virtuous conduct, nonviolence, and poverty. He explained the cycle through which one passed to achieve wisdom and, ultimately, the state of nirvana:

History Makers Speak

❝A learned, noble hearer of the word becomes weary of body, weary of sensation, weary of perception . . . weary of consciousness. Becoming weary of all that, he divests [rids] himself of passion; by absence of passion he is made free; when he is free, he becomes aware that he is free; and he realizes that re-birth is exhausted; that holiness is completed; that duty is fulfilled; and there is no further return to this world.❞

The Buddha, from Max Mueller, ed., *The Sacred Books of the East*

The spread of Buddhism. The Buddha gained only a few followers in his lifetime. Over several centuries, however, his teachings won wide acceptance in Asia. Between about 200 B.C. and A.D. 200, Buddhism split into two branches. Theravada followed the traditional beliefs of Buddhism. Its followers believed that the Buddha was a great teacher and spiritual leader. Theravada Buddhism was widely accepted in Burma (now Myanmar), Siam (now Thailand), Ceylon (now Sri Lanka), Laos, and other countries. Followers of Mahayana Buddhism, on the other hand, regarded the Buddha as a god and savior. Mahayana Buddhism, which uses more elaborate ceremonies than Theravada, took hold in China, Vietnam, Korea, and Japan.

As contacts increased between India and central Asia, Buddhism developed and spread. In India it began to gain more followers, but it was strongly opposed by the Brahmins. Over time Buddhism declined in India. It was in other parts of Asia that Buddhism reached its greatest strength.

✔ **READING CHECK: Contrasting** In what way did the two branches of Buddhism that formed after about 200 B.C. differ from one another? Theravada was traditional; Mahayana viewed the Buddha as a deity

SECTION 3 REVIEW

1. **Define** and explain the significance:
   epics
   caste system
   varnas
   monism
   maya
   reincarnation
   nirvana
   polytheistic

2. **Identify** and explain the significance:
   Upanishads
   Bhagavad Gita
   Siddhartha Gautama

Homework Practice Online
keyword: SP3 HP3

3. **Comparing and Contrasting**
   Build a Venn diagram like the one shown below. Use it to explain the differences and similarities between the two branches of Buddhism.

   Mahayana Buddhism / Theravada Buddhism

4. **Finding the Main Idea**
   a. Which elements of Indian religion seem most clearly reflected in the Indian social structure?
   b. In what ways can Hinduism be considered monistic?

5. **Writing and Critical Thinking**
   Identifying a Point of View Imagine that you are Siddhartha Gautama. Write a song or a poem that reflects the beliefs that you formed after experiencing enlightenment.
   Consider:
   • the early life that Siddhartha Gautama led as a wealthy prince
   • the conditions that led him to begin his search for the causes of human suffering
   • his later teachings

❶ **Define**
• epics, p. 60
• caste system, p. 61
• varnas, p. 61
• monism, p. 61
• maya, p. 61
• reincarnation, p. 61
• nirvana, p. 62
• polytheistic, p. 62

❷ **Identify**
• Upanishads, p. 60
• Bhagavad Gita, p. 60
• Siddhartha Gautama, p. 63

❸ similarities: based on teachings of the Buddha; declined in India; differences: Mahayana—regarded the Buddha as a god; used elaborate ceremonies; spread in China, Vietnam, Korea, Japan; Theravada—considered the Buddha a great teacher; spread in Burma, Siam, Ceylon, Laos

❹ a. caste system and Hinduism are deeply interwoven; belief in the unity of God and creation

b. Hinduism holds that all things in the universe are of the same essence as God.

❺ Students' poems and songs should reflect the Buddha's teachings.

OBJECTIVES

1 **Explain how the Mauryan rulers increased their power.**

2 **Examine the reasons for the decline of Gupta rule.**

 **LET'S GET STARTED!**

As students enter the classroom, ask them to imagine life under imperial rule, a life in which one very powerful person's attitudes and actions can change their lives. How would living under a warlike ruler affect them? Under a cruel ruler? Under a ruler who believes strongly in education? Tell students that in Section 4 they will learn about the rulers of ancient Indian dynasties and empires.

MAP ANSWERS

1. Hindu Kush, Karakoram, or Himalayas

2. Students might ask how mountains affected expansion of the Mauryan Empire.

SECTION 4

READ TO DISCOVER

❶ How did the Mauryan rulers increase their power?

❷ What were the reasons for the decline of Gupta rule?

IDENTIFY

Chandragupta Maurya
Aśoka
Chandra Gupta II

▶ WHY IT MATTERS TODAY

National boundaries are the location of many conflicts today. Use CNNfyi.com or other **current event** sources to identify locations where a boundary dispute is ongoing. Record your findings in your journal.

CNNfyi.com

Ancient Indian Dynasties and Empires

The Main Idea
The Mauryans and Guptas established the first Indian empires to control most of the subcontinent.

The Story Continues *Geography helped protect the Indian kingdoms from foreign invaders. Yet India was not a unified country. By the early 500s B.C., some 16 kingdoms existed in northern India alone. The most powerful kingdom was that of Magadha.*

Rise of the Mauryan Empire

The rulers of the Magadha kingdom were the first to try to unify much of India. Their efforts helped protect India from a new round of invasions. The kingdom of Magadha was at its most powerful in 540 B.C., under King Bimbisara. Sometime between about 520 B.C. and 510 B.C., the Persian ruler Darius the Great sent an army to invade the Indus River valley. Darius held the area for a time as part of the Persian Empire, but Magadha soon regained control and held the area until its rule ended in about 320 B.C.

Chandragupta Maurya. As Magadha was declining, a powerful young adventurer named **Chandragupta Maurya** appeared on the scene. He established the Mauryan Empire. The Mauryans ruled for almost 150 years.

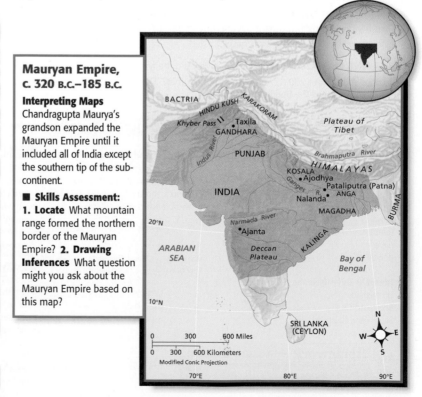

Mauryan Empire, c. 320 B.C.–185 B.C.

Interpreting Maps
Chandragupta Maurya's grandson expanded the Mauryan Empire until it included all of India except the southern tip of the subcontinent.

■ **Skills Assessment:**
1. Locate What mountain range formed the northern border of the Mauryan Empire? **2. Drawing Inferences** What question might you ask about the Mauryan Empire based on this map?

TEACH OBJECTIVES 1 and 2

LEVEL 1: Have students fill in the following chart to categorize the information in Section 4.
ENGLISH LANGUAGE LEARNERS

Mauryan and Gupta Rulers	
Mauryan	**Examples:**
Chandragupta Maurya	• *made Patalipura into a beautiful city* • *united northern India*
Aśoka	• *enlarged empire to include all but the southern tip of India* • *converted to Buddhism*
Gupta	
Chandra Gupta II	• *favored Hinduism* • *society and the arts prospered*
Skanda Gupta	• *last Gupta ruler* • *empire was weakened under his rule*

TEACH OBJECTIVES 1 and 2

ALL LEVELS: Have students create a time line that shows the approximate length of time each ruler controlled India. Tell them to include Chandragupta Maurya, Aśoka, and Chandra Gupta II. Ask students which ruler mentioned in this section they think was probably the most effective leader. Encourage volunteers to justify their choices. **ENGLISH LANGUAGE LEARNERS**

HOMEWORK Ask students to write a paragraph explaining how the Gupta Empire was created.

Because a Greek diplomat at the Mauryan court kept a detailed record of his experiences, we know much about Chandragupta Maurya's rule. Chandragupta built a grand palace at Pataliputra on the Ganges River. He raised an army of 600,000 soldiers who were equipped with thousands of chariots and elephants. His army united northern India from the Ganges River to the region west of the Indus. Chandragupta conquered all of northwestern India up to the Hindu Kush.

Chandragupta Maurya was an able ruler who established a rigid bureaucracy to carry out his commands. Under his rule workers dug mines and built centers for spinning and weaving. Chandragupta standardized weights and measures throughout the empire and established standards for physicians.

Chandragupta also made many enemies. The Greek diplomat wrote that the ruler slept in a different room each night for fear of attempts on his life. Because of the dangers of assassination, strong precautions were taken for the ruler's safety. In about 300 B.C. he gave up his throne to his son, Bindusāra.

Aśoka. Chandragupta's grandson, **Aśoka,** came to power in about 270 B.C. Aśoka proved to be an even greater ruler than his grandfather. Early in his rule, Aśoka fought bloody wars to increase the size of his kingdom. He enlarged the Mauryan Empire until it included all of India except the southern tip of the subcontinent. Thus the Mauryans became the first imperial dynasty to hold nearly all of India.

In time Aśoka became sickened by the bloody battles he had fought. He ordered an end to the killing and became a Buddhist. Many other Indian people also became Buddhists about this time. Aśoka sent a relative as a missionary to Ceylon. He also sent missionaries to other countries, thus spreading the Buddhist faith. Aśoka reversed many of the policies of his father and grandfather. His laws were carved into stone pillars set up in public places. On one pillar he carved this quote reflecting his views about religious tolerance:

History Makers Speak

❝ **The Beloved of the Gods. . . honors members of all sects. . . . Whoever honors his own sect and disparages [speaks ill of] another man's . . . does his own sect the greatest possible harm. Concord [harmony] is best, with each hearing and respecting each other's teachings.** ❞

Aśoka, from William Theodore de Bary et al., *Sources of Indian Tradition*

The Mauryan conquests brought many different peoples and states under imperial control. In an effort to unite his diverse empire, Aśoka worked to improve living conditions throughout the subcontinent. He explained, "On the roads I have had banyan trees planted which will give shade to beasts and men." He also ordered wells to be dug and had rest houses built along trade routes. The later years of Aśoka's rule were remembered as a time of cultural and political advance in India.

Aśoka died in about 232 B.C. and the strength of the Mauryan Empire began a slow decline. His sons battled one another for control of the throne, and invaders from the north and east attacked the empire's northern provinces. Finally, in 184 B.C., the last Mauryan emperor was killed by one of his Brahmin generals, who declared the beginning of a new imperial dynasty. After some 140 years, the once mighty Mauryan Empire collapsed.

✔ **READING CHECK: Making Generalizations** In general, how did the Mauryan rulers increase the power and size of their empire? military conquest

Holt Researcher

go.hrw.com
KEYWORD: Holt Researcher
FreeFind:
    Chandragupta Maurya
After reading more about Chandragupta Maurya on the Holt Researcher, evaluate how his political rule changed India.

HISTORY MAKER

**Aśoka
(unknown–c. 232 B.C.)**

Aśoka became a dedicated Buddhist late in his life. His great reputation and authority helped to spread Buddhism throughout India. However, as ruler of India, Aśoka supported religious freedom for all people.

Aśoka also carried out a number of good works. For example, he built animal hospitals and passed laws punishing those who were cruel to animals. **How did Aśoka show his respect for all life?**

Government

After Aśoka enlarged the Mauryan Empire, his conversion to Buddhism and his policy of nonviolence led him to abandon military conquest. To help ensure peace, Aśoka established a group of "High Commissioners of Equity," who traveled his empire and addressed the complaints and needs of minorities and other groups. Aśoka is so revered in Indian history that today the official Indian government seal features the top of one of the pillars he erected.

🖥 internet connect

TOPIC: Mauryan Leaders
GO TO: go.hrw.com
KEYWORD: SP3 WH3

Have students access the Internet through the HRW Go site to research the leaders of the Mauryan Empire, especially the rulers Chandragupta Maurya and Aśoka. Ask students to think about what it takes to build an empire. Then ask them to choose one of these historical leaders of India and write a biography on the life and accomplishments of that leader. Instruct students to use standard grammar, spelling, sentence structure, and punctuation.

HISTORY MAKER ANSWER
He enacted changes that respected animal life.

CLOSE

Have students make a list to summarize the accomplishments of each: Chandragupta Maurya, Aśoka, Chandra Gupta I, and Chandra Gupta II.

REVIEW

Have students complete the Section 4 Review on p. 68.

ASSESS

Have students complete Daily Quiz 3.4. As Alternative Assessment, you may want to use the chart or time line exercises in this section's lessons.

RETEACH

Have students complete Main Idea Activity for English Language Learners and Special-Needs Students 3.4. Then have them write a question about the main idea for each subsection in the section. Have volunteers read their questions for the class to answer.
ENGLISH LANGUAGE LEARNERS

EXTEND

Have students imagine that they are policy advisors in an ancient Indian kingdom. Have them use a decision-making process to compile a list of policies they would recommend to their ruler to help establish a strong, stable government. **BLOCK SCHEDULING**

MAP ANSWER
Arabian Sea, Bay of Bengal

SECTION 4 REVIEW ANSWERS

❶ **Identify**
- Chandragupta Maurya, p. 66
- Aśoka, p. 67
- Chandra Gupta II, p. 68

❷ Hinduism: Chandragupta Maurya; Buddhism: Aśoka; Both: Chandra Gupta

❸ **a.** It was the first imperial dynasty to hold nearly all of India.

b. Society prospered and great progress was made in the arts.

❹ Students' paragraphs should consider Chandragupta Maurya's rigid bureaucracy and Aśoka's wide popular appeal. Students should also imagine how the Gupta rulers may have responded to invaders from central Asia.

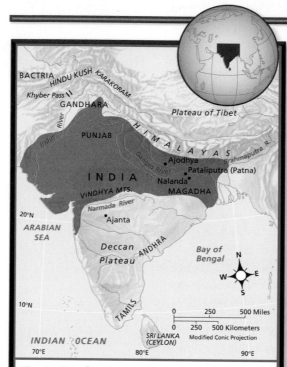

Gupta Empire, c. A.D. 400

Interpreting Maps The Gupta rulers united northern India, where they built temples to Hindu gods.

■ **Skills Assessment: The World in Spatial Terms** What major bodies of water bordered the Gupta Empire on the east and west?

The Gupta Rulers

The rise of a new dynasty also contributed to the relative decline of Buddhism and the growth of Hinduism in India. In the A.D. 300s the Gupta family came to power in Magadha, the old capital of the Mauryans. Chandra Gupta I, the founder of the Gupta Empire, took power in A.D. 320. The Gupta family then began to expand their territory through conquest and intermarriage. By A.D. 400 the Gupta Empire reached from the Bay of Bengal to the Arabian Sea. Eventually it included all of the northern part of India.

Under the early Gupta rulers, Indian civilization flourished. The Guptas favored Hinduism, but they also supported Buddhism. During Gupta rule Hinduism became the dominant religion of India. It remains so today.

The early years of Gupta rule have been called a golden age. Indian civilization flourished under their leadership. During the reign of **Chandra Gupta II** (A.D. 374–415) society prospered. Great progress was made in the arts as well. Under later rulers, however, this great empire became weakened. The Gupta political system was less centralized than the Mauryan government had been, and gave much power to local leaders.

Invaders from central Asia crossed into India in the late A.D. 400s. During the next century they began to take control of northern India. The last great Gupta king, Skanda Gupta, drained the treasury in an attempt to defend the empire. Gupta rule ended by about A.D. 550.

✔ **READING CHECK: Evaluating** In what way did the Guptas allow religious freedom in their empire? supported both Hinduism and Buddhism

---

SECTION 4 REVIEW

1. **Identify** and explain the significance:
   Chandragupta Maurya
   Aśoka
   Chandra Gupta II

2. **Categorizing** Copy the chart below. Use it to identify which rulers supported Hinduism, which supported Buddhism, and which supported both religions.

Hinduism	Both	Buddhism

3. **Finding the Main Idea**

   a. In what ways did the Mauryan Empire differ from previous empires and kingdoms in ancient India?

   b. Why might the period of early Gupta rule be called a "golden age" in India?

4. **Writing and Critical Thinking**

   Analyzing Information Write a paragraph explaining how the Mauryan and Gupta rulers persuaded people to support them in power.
   Consider:
   - what Chandragupta Maurya and his successors did to consolidate their power
   - how the Gupta rulers may have responded to invaders from central Asia

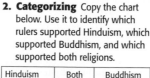
Homework Practice Online
keyword: SP3 HP3

SECTION 5

OBJECTIVES

1 Describe how women's rights were limited in ancient Indian society.

2 Identify the most important achievements of the Gupta period.

📀 LET'S GET STARTED!

As students enter the classroom, ask them if they think cultural advances are a good way to measure the historical significance of a nation. Have them make a list of ten achievements for which they predict the United States will be remembered in the future. *(Students might mention achievements in technology, science, or medicine.)* Tell students that in Section 5 they will learn about ancient Indian cultural achievements.

SECTION 5

READ TO DISCOVER

❶ In what ways were women's rights limited in ancient Indian society?

❷ What were the most important cultural achievements of the Gupta period?

DEFINE

polygyny
suttee
inoculation

IDENTIFY

Panchatantra
Nalanda
Aryabhata

▶ WHY IT MATTERS TODAY

Cultural advances are still an important way to measure the historical significance of a nation. Use **CNNfyi**.com or other **current event** sources to identify recent advances in art, medicine, science, and education. Record your findings in your journal.

CNNfyi.com

Ancient Indian Life and Culture

The Main Idea
Early Indian cultures made many significant advances in economics, arts, and sciences.

The Story Continues *"It is a day of festival. . . . the streets are broad rivers of people, folk of every race, buying and selling in the marketplace or singing to the music of wandering minstrels." This account recalls a day of celebration during the Gupta Empire, an era in which Indian culture and achievements flourished.*

Economy and Society

From ancient times, the land provided a living for almost all the people of northern India. Although a few members of the highest social classes enjoyed great luxury, most people barely got by. During the Indo-Aryan period, the rajas controlled the land and drew much of their wealth from farmers who worked their fields. During the time of the Mauryans, the rulers claimed one-fourth of each harvest in taxes.

In southern India many people made their living through trade with foreign nations. Foreign trade expanded to northern India under the Guptas. Traders sold silks, cottons, wool, ivory, spices, and precious gems. Indian goods appeared in the Far East, Southwest Asia, Africa, and Europe.

Hindu custom gave women in ancient Indian society some protections. Under the law, however, women did not have the same rights as men. The Hindu Laws of Manu were written between 200 B.C. and A.D. 200. According to these laws, girls were required to obey their fathers. When they married, women were forced to obey their husbands. If their husbands died, widows were supposed to obey their sons. The Laws of Manu also prohibited women from owning property or from studying sacred writings such as the Vedas.

Men were allowed to have more than one wife in ancient India. This practice, called **polygyny,** became widespread during the Gupta period. Another practice that became common later was **suttee.** Widows committed suicide by throwing themselves on top of their husbands' flaming funeral pyres. Suttee was sometimes required among the upper castes.

✔ **READING CHECK: Drawing Inferences** How much independence did women have in ancient Indian society? very little

This image from the 1600s depicts women practicing suttee.

ALL LEVELS: Ask students to imagine they are women in ancient India. Have each student write a letter to a friend explaining what life is like in Indian society.
ENGLISH LANGUAGE LEARNERS

TEACH OBJECTIVE 2

LEVEL 1: Have students draw a four-column chart in their notes with the columns labeled *Art and Architecture, Education, Mathematics and Astronomy,* and *Medicine.* Have them fill in their charts with cultural achievements during the Gupta period. *(Students' charts should include the* Panchatantra, *stu-*pas, Nalanda, algebra and Arabic numerals, astronomy, and inoculation.) **ENGLISH LANGUAGE LEARNERS**

HOMEWORK Ask students to reflect on the advances in mathematics, science, and technology made by ancient Indians. Have them list some of the Indian achievements and trace the spread of these ideas to other civilizations.

Interdisciplinary Connection

LITERATURE. The *Panchatantra* is an anonymous collection of Buddhistic fables most likely compiled sometime before A.D. 500. The framework of the *Panchatantra* consists of one narrative thread that holds together several different stories. The stories, which combine both prose and verse, were originally intended for the instruction of the sons of royalty.

Critical Thinking

Ask students why the author of the *Panchatantra* might have used one narrative theme for several stories.

ANSWER: Students might suggest that the author used multiple stories to tell a broad, moral idea from different perspectives.

THEN AND NOW ANSWER

Students might suggest that they communicate human concerns that are similar in many different cultures.

VISUAL RECORD ANSWER

Students might suggest that its towering structure represents the quest for nirvana.

Fairy Tales

"Once upon a time . . ." is a phrase that we all recognize from the fairy tales that we read as children. The stories that we call fairy tales occur in many cultures around the world. Often the same basic tales can be found in several cultures.

The Jataka tales are popular Indian stories taken from Buddhist writings. They use animals as characters to teach lessons about kindness. Their theme is good versus evil. The same theme underlies the story of Cinderella. There are at least 500 different versions of the tale from various cultures. **Why do you think similar themes are found in fairy tales from different cultures?**

Cultural Achievements

In addition to the religious epics, people enjoyed the stories of the **Panchatantra,** or "Five Books." These were fables from the Gupta period—stories with morals that taught such traits as adaptability, shrewdness, and determination. They influenced stories that were already popular in other parts of the world. The *Panchatantra* has been translated into more languages than any other book except the Bible.

Indian drama developed greatly in the Gupta period. The plays might contain tragic scenes, but they always ended happily. Plays were performed in the open air. They made little use of scenery, since there were no regular theaters.

Art and architecture. Mural paintings in caves tell us something about early Indian painters. They also offer clues about daily life in ancient India. The cave paintings at Ajanta, from the Gupta period, depict the Buddha and his followers. Less is known about other types of painting. The wood and cloth that artists used have not survived.

Early images of the Buddha show the influence of Greek and Roman art. The styles began to change during the Gupta period. Sculpture became more rigid and formal. As Hinduism grew in importance, architects designed great temples. Hindu temples were built square with heavy walls surrounding a statue of a god. The great Mauryan ruler Aśoka, who had carved his laws on stone pillars, also built thousands of stupas. A stupa was a dome-shaped shrine. Artifacts and objects associated with the Buddha were placed inside.

INTERPRETING THE VISUAL RECORD

The great dome of the Boudha Stupa in Nepal is an inspiring symbol of Buddhism. *How does the Boudha Stupa serve to inspire a spiritual response from believers?*

CLOSE

Have students describe what the early Indians achieved in the fields of literature, mathematics, astronomy, and medicine.

REVIEW

Have students complete the Section 5 Review on p. 71.

ASSESS

Have students complete Daily Quiz 3.5. As Alternative Assessment, you may want to use the letter or chart exercises in this section's lessons.

RETEACH

Have students complete Main Idea Activity for English Language Learners and Special-Needs Students 3.5. Have students identify three important Indian cultural achievements and describe why each was important. **ENGLISH LANGUAGE LEARNERS**

EXTEND

Have students use a decision-making process to plan attractions that promote an understanding and appreciation of Indian culture during the Gupta Empire. **BLOCK SCHEDULING**, **COOPERATIVE LEARNING**

Education. Education was very advanced for some in ancient India. Children of the higher castes received formal education in many subjects. They studied the Vedas and other literature, including the great epics. They also learned astronomy, mathematics, warfare, and government. Children of lower castes learned only crafts or trades.

Nalanda was a famous Buddhist university located in the eastern Ganges Valley. It became the center of higher learning in India during the time of the Guptas. Thousands of students attended for free. Although it was a Buddhist university, students also studied the Vedas and Hindu philosophy, along with logic, grammar, and medicine.

Mathematics and astronomy. Indian scientists were highly skilled. Mathematicians understood abstract numbers and negative numbers, without which algebra could not exist. They also understood the concepts of zero and infinity. **Aryabhata** was a mathematician born in the late A.D. 400s. He was one of the first people known to have used algebra and to have solved quadratic equations. Today we call the digits 1 through 9 "Arabic." However, they probably were invented by Indian mathematicians. Other scientists studied the stars. Indian astronomers identified the seven planets visible to the naked eye. They also understood the rotation of the earth and accurately predicted eclipses of the sun and moon.

Medicine. Indian medicine was very advanced. Indian physicians understood the importance of the spinal cord. Their surgical procedures included bone setting and plastic surgery. They developed the technique of **inoculation**—the practice of infecting a person with a mild form of a disease so that he or she will not become ill with the more serious form. Early Indian physicians successfully inoculated people against smallpox. Smallpox vaccines were unknown in the Western world until the 1700s. Indian rulers built free hospitals in the A.D. 400s. Physicians practiced cleanliness before an operation and also disinfected wounds, another procedure not known in the West until modern times.

✔ **READING CHECK: Summarizing** What were the main cultural achievements of the Gupta Period? *Panchatantra*, stupas, Nalanda, algebra and Arabic numerals, astronomy, medicine

The remains of the great university at Nalanda (above) reflect the importance of this ancient center of learning. An Indian educator of today provides an important learning experience.

Link to Today What do these images tell us about educational traditions in Indian culture?

LINK TO TODAY ANSWER
India has a strong educational tradition.

SECTION 5 REVIEW ANSWERS

❶ **Define**
• polygyny, p. 69
• suttee, p. 69
• inoculation, p. 71

❷ **Identify**
• *Panchatantra*, p. 70
• Nalanda, p. 71
• Aryabhata, p. 71

❸ Mauryan cultural achievements: standardized weights and measures, roads, built centers for spinning and weaving; Mauryan artistic achievements: stupas; Gupta cultural achievements: *Panchatantra*, Nalanda, algebra and Arabic numerals, astronomy, medicine, drama; Gupta artistic achievements: cave paintings, temples

❹ **a.** Women were forced to obey men and some were expected to commit suicide when their husbands died.

b. *Panchatantra*, drama

❺ Students should mention the *Panchatantra*, temples, Nalanda, algebra and Arabic numerals, astronomy, medicine and indicate which they believe was most important.

SECTION 5 REVIEW

1. **Define** and explain the significance:
   polygyny
   suttee
   inoculation

2. **Identify** and explain the significance:
   Panchatantra
   Nalanda
   Aryabhata

3. **Summarizing** Copy the table below. Use it to illustrate the cultural and artistic achievements made during the Mauryan and Gupta periods.

	Mauryan Period	Gupta Period
Cultural Achievements	• • •	• • •
Artistic Achievements	• • •	• • •

4. **Finding the Main Idea**
   a. What limitations were imposed on Indian women during the Gupta period?
   b. Describe the major literary contributions of the Gupta period.

5. **Writing and Critical Thinking**
   Drawing Conclusions Write a paragraph detailing the cultural advances of the Gupta period. Indicate which you believe to be most important.
   Consider:
   • the advances in various fields
   • how these advances may have affected people's lives

Homework Practice Online
keyword: SP3 HP3

REVIEW AND ASSESSMENT RESOURCES

REPRODUCIBLE RESOURCES
▸ Vocabulary Activity 3

TECHNOLOGY RESOURCES
▸ Chapter 3 Test Generator (on the One-Stop Planner)
▸ Global Skill Builder CD–ROM
▸ HRW Web Site

REINFORCEMENT, REVIEW, and ASSESSMENT
▸ Chapter 3 Review, pp. 72–73
▸ Chapter 3 Tutorial for Students, Parents, Mentors, and Peers
▸ Chapter 3 Test (Form A or B)
▸ Alternative Assessment Handbook
▸ Chapter 3 Test for English Language Learners and Special-Needs Students

REVIEW
Have students complete the Chapter 3 Review on pages 72–73.

ASSESS
Use one of the chapter tests to assess students' understanding of the content. For Alternative Assessment, see the Portfolio Activities and Alternative Assessment Handbook.

Understanding Main Ideas

1. Students should mention that it allowed easy trade and successful farming.

2. Farmers raised crops for storage and trade while city dwellers were involved in the production or trade of goods.

3. Students should discuss the religion, society, and economy of the Indo-Aryans.

4. The caste system was supported by the Hindu belief in reincarnation.

5. retained: belief in reincarnation, nirvana; rejected: ceremonies, Hindu gods, caste system, the Vedas

6. All were successful in consolidating power, but each empire eventually collapsed.

7. very few

8. Society prospered and great progress was made in the arts.

Reviewing Themes

1. Waterways allowed easy trade and the climate allowed successful farming after the farmers adapted to the monsoons.

2. algebra and Arabic numerals, astronomy, medicine

3. Hinduism was reflected in India's caste system; Buddhism denied the caste system; both emphasized living a moral life.

Review

Creating a Time Line

Copy the time line below onto a sheet of paper. Complete the time line by filling in the events, individuals, and dates from the chapter that you think were significant. Pick three events and explain why you think they were significant.

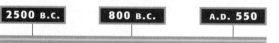

2500 B.C.   **800 B.C.**   **A.D. 550**

Writing a Summary

Using standard grammar, spelling, sentence structure, and punctuation, write an overview of the events in the chapter.

Identifying People and Ideas

1. Indo-Aryans
2. Vedas
3. Sanskrit
4. Brahmins
5. Upanishads
6. Bhagavad Gita
7. Siddhartha Gautama
8. Aśoka
9. Chandra Gupta II
10. inoculation

Understanding Main Ideas

SECTION 1 (pp. 52–55)
Indus River Valley Civilizations
1. How did the geography and climate of the Indian subcontinent influence the development of early civilizations there?
2. What was daily life like for the people of the first Indus River valley civilization?

SECTION 2 (pp. 56–59)
Indo-Aryan Migrants
3. Compare and contrast the society of the first Indus River valley civilization with that of the Indo-Aryans.

SECTION 3 (pp. 60–65)
Hinduism and Buddhism
4. In what ways did life in ancient Indian society reflect the beliefs of Hinduism?
5. Which elements of Hinduism did the Buddha retain? Which did he reject?

SECTION 4 (pp. 66–68)
Ancient Indian Dynasties and Empires
6. How successful were the Mauryan and Gupta rulers in consolidating and holding on to power?

SECTION 5 (pp. 69–71)
Ancient Indian Life and Culture
7. What rights did women have in ancient Indian society?
8. Why was the period of Gupta rule known as a "golden age" in Indian history?

Reviewing Themes

1. Geography How did the physical geography and climate of the Indian subcontinent help lead to the development of a unique civilization?
2. Science, Technology & Society What were the particular scientific and technological achievements of ancient Indian civilization?
3. Culture In what ways did Hinduism and Buddhism influence daily life in ancient India?

Thinking Critically

1. Evaluating What sources do scholars use to find out about daily life in ancient Indian society?
2. Supporting a Point of View Explain why you agree or disagree with the following statement: The ancient Indus River valley civilization was superior to the Indo-Aryan society that replaced it.
3. Drawing Inferences How might Siddhartha Gautama's observations of the world have influenced his religious philosophy?
4. Analyzing Information How did Buddhism and Hinduism change the course of Indian history?

Writing About History

Evaluating The "golden age" of Gupta rule saw important advances in science, medicine, and mathematics, many of which are still valid today. Write an essay explaining how achievements in Indian science still have uses in modern life. Use the following table to organize your ideas.

	Ancient India	Today
Mathematics		
Science		
Medicine		

CLOSE

Ask students to make a chart showing the major accomplishments of the Indus River valley civilization and the Indo-Aryan society.

RETEACH

Have students who had difficulty with the test develop several questions about the information in a section of the chapter. Have them trade questions with a partner and answer them. Then assign Form B Test to assess students' mastery of the material.

ENGLISH LANGUAGE LEARNERS, COOPERATIVE LEARNING

Portfolio Extensions

1. Have students work in groups to create collages depicting the importance of water as a resource. Have group members write a poem or a paragraph summarizing the ideas shown in their collage.

2. Have students research their city's water system. They should find out about the source of water, methods of storage and purification, and sewage systems. Students might create diagrams such as charts and graphs to illustrate their findings.

3. Have students use media and news services to acquire information about public health concerns related to water systems in India today.

Building Social Studies Skills

Connecting Architecture to History

Study the photograph below of the ruins of a city in the Indus Valley. Then answer the questions that follow.

Mohenjo Daro, from c. 2500–1500 B.C., Indus Valley, Pakistan

1. Which is the best general statement about the people who built this city?
  a. They took pride in a well-planned, orderly city.
  b. They valued large open spaces around their homes.
  c. They preferred architecture that used many different geometric forms.
  d. They preferred to build with materials that could be dismantled and moved quickly.
  e. Their city was constructed in a haphazard and poorly planned fashion.

2. Explain your choice of statements in question 1. Give specific examples to support your point of view.

Using Biographies

Read the following quote from *Siddhartha,* a novel about the early life of the Buddha. It was published in 1922 by Hermann Hesse. Then answer the questions.

> **"Siddhartha went into the room where his father was sitting on a mat made of bast. He went up behind his father and remained standing there until his father felt his presence. . . . Siddhartha said: 'With your permission, Father, I have come to tell you that I wish to leave your house tomorrow and join the ascetics [holy men]. . . . I trust my father will not object.'"**

3. Which statement best describes the main point the author is making about Siddhartha in this passage?
  a. Siddhartha wanted his father's opinion of his plan.
  b. Neither Siddhartha nor his father were ascetics.
  c. Siddhartha was a respectful and obedient son.
  d. Siddhartha's father was a kind man.
  e. Siddhartha's father was violently opposed to his son's plan to join the ascetics.
  f. Siddhartha was fearful of his father, who was harsh and heavy-handed toward his son.

4. Based on this passage, why did Siddhartha wish to leave his father's house?

Alternative Assessment

Building Your Portfolio

Science, Technology & Society

Like the people of ancient India, Americans today recognize the importance of water as a resource. Using your textbook and other sources, show how modern people have developed technologies similar to those found in the early Indus River valley. Create a chart to summarize your findings.

internet connect

Internet Activity: go.hrw.com
KEYWORD: SP3 WH3

Choose a topic on Ancient Indian Civilizations to:
• study ancient India and create a travel poster.
• write a biography of a leader of the Mauryan Empire.
• explore the geographic regions of India and create a brochure.

Thinking Critically

1. artifacts discovered during archaeological digs

2. Students may agree or disagree, but should support their position.

3. Students might answer that leaving his life of luxury to observe poverty and suffering compelled him to create a religion with broad appeal.

4. Answers will vary but should include an emphasis on moral conduct.

Writing About History

Check students' tables to ensure they mention algebra and Arabic numerals, astronomy, and inoculation.

Building Social Studies Skills

1. a

2. Students might note the orderly arrangement of buildings grouped closely together, the use of brick or stone building materials, and the geometric style of the structures.

3. c

4. to become an ascetic

Building Your Portfolio

Charts will vary.

Ancient Chinese Civilization

CHAPTER RESOURCE MANAGER

Objectives	Pacing Guide	Reproducible Resources
SECTION 1 **Geographic and Cultural Influences** (pp. 76–79)	• Explore the role that rivers played in Chinese life. • Investigate how geography influenced the development of Chinese culture.	**Regular** 1 day **Block Scheduling** .5 day *Block Scheduling Handbook with Team Teaching Strategies, 4.1*	RS Guided Reading Strategy 4.1
SECTION 2 **The Shang Dynasty** (pp. 80–83)	• Examine how the Chinese explained their early history. • Describe how the Shang government and economy were organized. • Identify the religious beliefs held by the Shang. • Explain why the Shang dynasty collapsed.	**Regular** 1 day **Block Scheduling** .5 day *Block Scheduling Handbook with Team Teaching Strategies, 4.2*	RS Guided Reading Strategy 4.2
SECTION 3 **The Zhou, Qin, and Han Dynasties** (pp. 84–88)	• Explain why the Zhou fell from power. • Describe how the Qin dynasty used power to maintain its authority. • Identify the achievements of the Han emperors.	**Regular** 1.5 day **Block Scheduling** 1 day *Block Scheduling Handbook with Team Teaching Strategies, 4.3*	RS Guided Reading Strategy 4.3 SM Graphic Organizer Activity 4 E Hands-on History Activity 4
SECTION 4 **Philosophies of Ancient China** (pp. 89–92)	• Examine why the Chinese valued the concept of balance. • Explore what the Chinese philosopher Confucius taught. • Analyze how Daoism and Confucianism worked together in Chinese society. • Investigate how beliefs such as Legalism and Buddhism influenced Chinese history.	**Regular** 1.5 day **Block Scheduling** .5 day *Block Scheduling Handbook with Team Teaching Strategies, 4.4*	RS Guided Reading Strategy 4.4 PS Readings in World History 13, 14, 15: The Wisdom of Confucius; The *Dao De Ching* of Laozi; Mo Tzu on Universal Love E Creative Teaching Strategy 4
SECTION 5 **Chinese Life and Culture** (pp. 93–95)	• Explain why the family was a central institution in Chinese society. • Describe how farmers lived in ancient China. • Identify the artistic and scientific achievements of the Chinese.	**Regular** 1 day **Block Scheduling** .5 day *Block Scheduling Handbook with Team Teaching Strategies, 4.5*	RS Guided Reading Strategy 4.5 RS Graphic Organizer Activity 4 PS Readings in World History 16

Chapter Resource Key

PS Primary Sources	**A** Assessment	Music	
RS Reading Support	**REV** Review	Video	
IC Interdisciplinary Connections	**ELL** Reinforcement and English Language Learners	Internet	
E Enrichment	Transparencies	Holt Presentation Maker Using Microsoft® PowerPoint®	
SM Skills Mastery	CD-ROM		

One-Stop Planner CD-ROM

See the ***One-Stop Planner*** for a complete list of additional resources for students and teachers.

One-Stop Planner CD-ROM

It's easy to plan lessons, select resources, and print out materials for your students when you use the **One-Stop Planner** CD–ROM with *Test Generator.*

Technology Resources

- One-Stop Planner 4.1
- World History and Cultures Video Program 6: Confucius, Laozi, and the Buddha
- Homework Practice Online

- One-Stop Planner 4.2
- CNN. Presents World Cultures: Yesterday and Today Segment 4: Treasures from China
- Homework Practice Online

- One-Stop Planner 4.3
- World History Teaching Transparency: Art and History 6: Han Dynasty
- Homework Practice Online

- One-Stop Planner 4.4
- Holt Researcher: World History: Confucius, Laozi
- World History Teaching Transparency: Geography and History 6: The Rise of Buddhism and Daoism
- Religions of the World Video Series: Buddhism
- Homework Practice Online
- Online Maps, Charts, and Graphs: Early Confucianism c. 200 B.C.

- One-Stop Planner 4.5
- Homework Practice Online

Reinforcement, Review, and Assessment

Daily Quiz 4.1
Main Idea Activity 4.1
English Audio Summary 4.1
Spanish Audio Summary 4.1
REV Section 1 Review, p. 79

Daily Quiz 4.2
Main Idea Activity 4.2
English Audio Summary 4.2
Spanish Audio Summary 4.2
REV Section 2 Review, p. 83

Daily Quiz 4.3
Main Idea Activity 4.3
English Audio Summary 4.3
Spanish Audio Summary 4.3
REV Section 3 Review, p. 88

Daily Quiz 4.4
Main Idea Activity 4.4
English Audio Summary 4.4
Spanish Audio Summary 4.4
REV Section 4 Review, p. 92

Daily Quiz 4.5
Main Idea Activity 4.5
English Audio Summary 4.5
Spanish Audio Summary 4.5
REV Section 5 Review, p. 95

internet connect

HRW ONLINE RESOURCES
GO TO: go.hrw.com
Then type in a keyword.

TEACHER HOME PAGE
KEYWORD: SP3 Teacher

CHAPTER INTERNET ACTIVITIES
KEYWORD: SP3 WH4
Choose an activity to:
- compare and contrast Western, Arabic, and Chinese calligraphy.
- research the Qin dynasty and create a brochure on the Great Wall.
- write a report on Chinese philosophy or Chinese contributions to science.

CHAPTER ENRICHMENT LINKS
KEYWORD: SP3 CH4

ONLINE ASSESSMENT
Homework Practice
KEYWORD: SP3 HP4
Standardized Test Prep
KEYWORD: SP3 STP4
Rubrics
KEYWORD: SS Rubrics

ONLINE MAPS, CHARTS, AND GRAPHS
KEYWORD: SP3 MCG

CONTENT UPDATES
KEYWORD: SS Content Updates

HOLT PRESENTATION MAKER
KEYWORD: SP3 PPT4

ONLINE READING SUPPORT
KEYWORD: SS Strategies

CURRENT EVENTS
KEYWORD: S3 Current Events

Meeting Individual Needs

Ability Levels

Level 1   Basic level activities designed for all students encountering new material

Level 2   Intermediate level activities designed for average students

Level 3   Challenging activities designed for honors and gifted and talented students

English Language Learners   These activities address the needs of students with Limited English Proficiency.

Chapter Review and Assessment

- IC   Vocabulary Activity 4
- Global Skill Builder CD–ROM
- HRW Web Site
- REV   Chapter 4 Tutorial for Students, Parents, Mentors, and Peers
- REV   Chapter 4 Review, pp. 96–97
- A   Chapter 4 Test Generator (on the One-Stop Planner)
- A   Chapter 4 Test (Form A or B)
- A   Alternative Assessment Handbook
- A   Chapter 4 Test for English Language Learners and Special-Needs Students

Build on What You Know

Ask students to answer the following questions:

How did religion affect ancient Indian society?

Consider:

- **Hinduism**
- **Buddhism**

How was power transferred from one government to another in ancient India?

Consider:

- **the Indo-Aryans**
- **the Mauryans**
- **the Guptas**

EXPLORING THE TIME LINE
GL⊘BAL EVENTS

internet connect

TOPIC: Ancient Chinese Culture

GO TO: go.hrw.com
KEYWORD: SP3 WH12

Have students access the Internet through the HRW Go site to conduct research on the "Warring States" of ancient China. Then have students write an informative report on the progression of dynasties that evolved from the Warring States. Have students focus on the significant political and cultural developments of each dynasty. Encourage students to enhance their reports with illustrations.

CHAPTER 4

c. 1500 B.C.–A.D. 589

Ancient Chinese Civilization

Wall hanging depicting a giraffe given in tribute to China's emperor

c. 1000 B.C.
Daily Life
Emperor Wen Wang establishes a zoo in China.

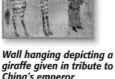

Early Chinese coin

c. 1000 B.C.–700 B.C.
Science and Technology
Iron is in widespread use in China.

c. 500 B.C.
Business and Finance
The Chinese begin using coined money.

| 1500 B.C. | 1000 B.C. | 500 B.C. |

c. 1300 B.C.
Daily Life
According to tradition, the Chinese found the city of Anyang.

c. Late 1000s B.C.
Politics
The Zhou dynasty begins in China.

771 B.C.
Global Events
Invaders destroy the Zhou capital.

c. 1500 B.C.
The Arts
Chinese potters create leak-proof stoneware pottery.

Life-size terra-cotta figures from the tomb of Emperor Cheng

Build on What You Know

The earliest civilizations grew along major rivers, slowly rising from Neolithic farming villages. The fertile valleys of the Nile, Tigris, Euphrates, and Indus rivers each gave birth to early cultures. The societies that grew along these great river systems shared many key characteristics, while at the same time developing their own distinct cultures and patterns of life. The river valleys of China also nurtured early civilizations. In this chapter, you will learn how China's earliest civilizations developed and how they compare with other ancient cultures.

What's Your Opinion?

 To help students create their Themes Journal entries, provide the following examples of appropriate **agree**/**disagree** *statements.*

Culture

Agree In order to develop new ideas, a culture must be exposed to and influenced by many other cultures.

Disagree Isolated cultures can develop new and unique ideas independently.

Global Relations

Agree The development of philosophies, art, and government has little to do with unsuccessful foreign invasions.

Disagree Unsuccessful attacks from outsiders influence the ideas and values of a culture.

Government

Agree Rulers are successful only if they assert absolute authority in order to help their people.

Disagree Moderation is the key to becoming a successful ruler.

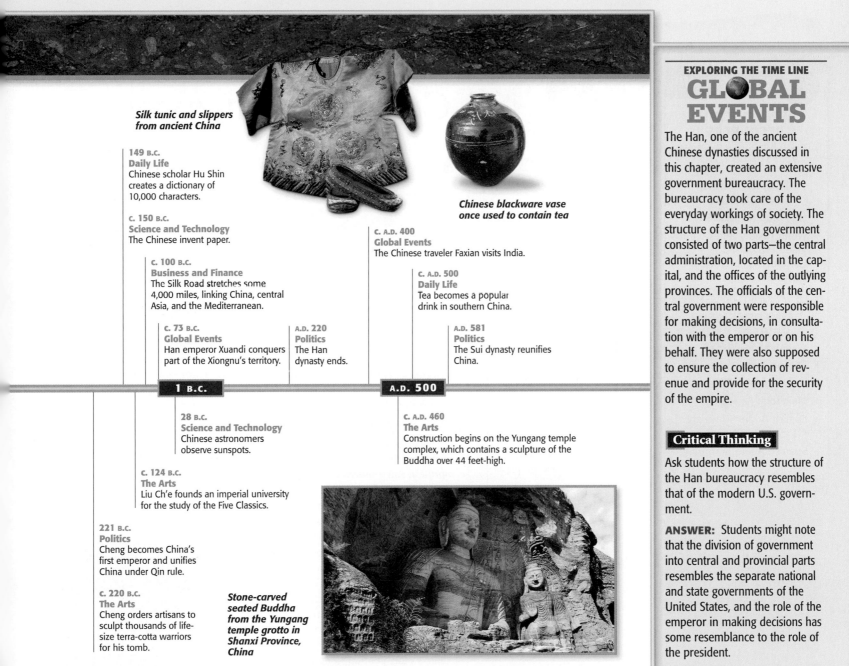

Silk tunic and slippers from ancient China

149 B.C.
Daily Life
Chinese scholar Hu Shin creates a dictionary of 10,000 characters.

c. 150 B.C.
Science and Technology
The Chinese invent paper.

c. 100 B.C.
Business and Finance
The Silk Road stretches some 4,000 miles, linking China, central Asia, and the Mediterranean.

c. 73 B.C.
Global Events
Han emperor Xuandi conquers part of the Xiongnu's territory.

A.D. 220
Politics
The Han dynasty ends.

Chinese blackware vase once used to contain tea

C. A.D. 400
Global Events
The Chinese traveler Faxian visits India.

C. A.D. 500
Daily Life
Tea becomes a popular drink in southern China.

A.D. 581
Politics
The Sui dynasty reunifies China.

1 B.C.

A.D. 500

28 B.C.
Science and Technology
Chinese astronomers observe sunspots.

c. 124 B.C.
The Arts
Liu Ch'e founds an imperial university for the study of the Five Classics.

221 B.C.
Politics
Cheng becomes China's first emperor and unifies China under Qin rule.

c. 220 B.C.
The Arts
Cheng orders artisans to sculpt thousands of life-size terra-cotta warriors for his tomb.

C. A.D. 460
The Arts
Construction begins on the Yungang temple complex, which contains a sculpture of the Buddha over 44 feet-high.

Stone-carved seated Buddha from the Yungang temple grotto in Shanxi Province, China

EXPLORING THE TIME LINE

GLOBAL EVENTS

The Han, one of the ancient Chinese dynasties discussed in this chapter, created an extensive government bureaucracy. The bureaucracy took care of the everyday workings of society. The structure of the Han government consisted of two parts—the central administration, located in the capital, and the offices of the outlying provinces. The officials of the central government were responsible for making decisions, in consultation with the emperor or on his behalf. They were also supposed to ensure the collection of revenue and provide for the security of the empire.

Critical Thinking

Ask students how the structure of the Han bureaucracy resembles that of the modern U.S. government.

ANSWER: Students might note that the division of government into central and provincial parts resembles the separate national and state governments of the United States, and the role of the emperor in making decisions has some resemblance to the role of the president.

What's Your Opinion?

 Do you **agree** *or* **disagree** *with the following statements? Support your point of view in your journal.*

Culture Cultures that grow in isolation from other cultures generally do not develop new ideas, nor do they emphasize inquiry and innovation.

Global Relations Unsuccessful foreign invasions have little or no effect on the way that a culture grows and develops.

Government Leaders who combine harsh rule with actions to help their people are often successful.

SECTION ①

OBJECTIVES

1 Explore the role that rivers played in Chinese life.

2 Investigate how geography influenced the development of Chinese culture.

🔔 *LET'S GET STARTED!*

As students enter the classroom, have them think about how interaction with other societies influences the development of a society's culture. Ask students what a society's culture might be like if the people had no contact with foreigners. *(Students may answer that it might be very unique.)* Tell students that in Section 1 they will learn about the geographic isolation of China and how it influenced Chinese culture.

SECTION ①

▶ READ TO DISCOVER

❶ What role did rivers play in Chinese life?

❷ How did geography influence the development of Chinese culture?

▶ DEFINE

loess
dikes

▶ WHY IT MATTERS TODAY

Every year, river floods devastate different regions of the world. Use **CNNfyi.com** or other **current event** sources to find information about a country or a community that has recently faced severe flooding. Record your findings in your journal.

CNNfyi.com

Geographic and Cultural Influences

The Main Idea
China's rivers, and isolation caused by mountains and deserts, shaped early Chinese culture.

The Story Continues *"Floodwater dashed up against the skies. . . . God issued a command allowing Yü to spread out the self-replacing soil so as to quell the floods in the Nine Provinces." This myth from China's remote past may reflect stories about the efforts of early rulers to control the floodwaters of the Huang River—the mighty river that has been central to Chinese civilization since earliest times.*

The Physical Setting

China is a land of enormous size, great geographic variety, and widely contrasting climate patterns. Rugged, snow-capped mountains range across the country's west, northwest, and southwest. These towering mountains, including some of the world's tallest and most forbidding, slope down to high, wind-swept desert or semi-desert plateaus. Moving south the plateaus give way to rolling country of low hills and valleys. In the north the plateaus slope gently down to the North China Plain, a coastal area along the Yellow Sea.

Different regions. The mountain range that cuts from west to east across China is called the Qinling (CHIN·LING) Shandi. This range separates the valleys of two great rivers—the Huang and the Chang, or Yangtze. The Qinling Shandi also marks the boundary between northern and southern China. Compared to central and southern China, the north receives less rain. Temperatures are more extreme in the north, and the growing season is shorter. Wheat is the principal crop there. In China's central and southern areas, where rainfall is more plentiful, rice is the leading farm product.

What we call China has consisted of many different geographic and political sections over time. The smaller but most historically significant section—the heart of China—is called China Proper. It stretches from the eastern seacoast inland. Three great river systems wind through China Proper. These include the Huang, Chang, and Xi (SHEE). China's other political sections have at various times included Tibet, Xinjiang (SHIN·JYAHNG), Mongolia, Manchuria, and northern Korea. These regions form a semicircle around China Proper. At different times throughout their history, the Chinese conquered and ruled these regions. On other occasions, nomads from one or another of these outlying regions conquered and ruled China's heartland.

This Chinese animal-pattern bronze plate dates from c. 2100 B.C.–1600 B.C.

ALL LEVELS: Draw a three-column chart on the chalkboard. Label the columns with the following river names: *Huang, Chang,* and *Xi.* Ask students to explain how the Chinese used each river and fill in the chart as students give their answers. (*Huang: fertile farming; Chang and Xi: commercial waterways*) Ask class members what other geographic features of China played a part in shaping its development and how they were important. (*isolating influence of mountains, deserts, vastness*) **ENGLISH LANGUAGE LEARNERS**

Huang	Chang	Xi
fertile farming	*commercial waterway*	*commercial waterway*

HOMEWORK Have students read History Makers Speak on page 78 and write a short paragraph that explains why they think the Chinese did not follow Chang Jung's advice. Remind students to use standard grammar, spelling, sentence structure, and punctuation.

SKILL-BUILDING STRATEGIES

Reviewing Map Basics

China's Geography

To understand the history of China, one must understand its geography. One of the best ways to learn about China's geography is by studying maps of the country. Maps show many different types of information, from political boundaries to military battles to climate patterns. Most maps share several characteristics, and familiarity with these elements makes reading a map easier. The map's title explains its subject or focus. The legend, or key, explains any special symbols, colors, or shadings used on a map. The directional indicator, or compass rose, indicates direction on a map——the map's "orientation." The scale compares distances on the map to actual distances on the earth's surface. Grid lines provide a frame of reference for a map in terms of latitude and longitude.

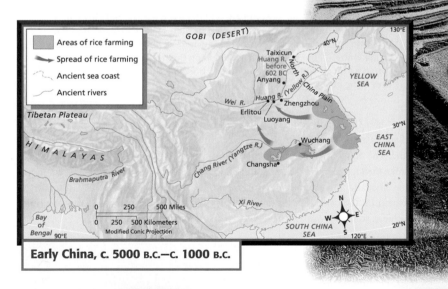

Early China, c. 5000 B.C.—C. 1000 B.C.

Geography

In early China, two patterns of agricultural development emerged as early as 5000 B.C. In northern China, people relied on drought-resistant crops like millet, and supplemented their diets with fruits and nuts. In southern China, people grew rice.

Critical Thinking

Ask students to speculate how the climates of northern and southern China might be different.

ANSWER: Based on the crops, students might suggest that southern China has a wetter climate, while northern China is drier and subject to droughts.

SKILLS PRACTICE ANSWERS

1. early China, c. 5000 B.C.– 1000 B.C.

2. rivers, which provided water and transportation

3. It spread from the coast to the river valleys.

4. about 300 miles

5. Students' maps should use appropriate labels, symbols, and a legend.

Skills Reminder

A map is a drawn or printed representation of all or part of the earth's surface. To accurately interpret a map's information, read the map's title and labels to determine its focus. Then study the legend to become familiar with the map's symbols, colors, and shadings. Different colors and shadings can indicate features of the landscape, such as height above sea level or climate and rainfall. Consult the directional indicator and scale to determine the map's direction and distances. You may also need to use math skills to determine distances. Analyze the map's features and details, including the location of rivers, mountains, and human settlements. Use this information to form generalizations and draw conclusions, particularly about distribution of geographic features and patterns in human history.

Skills Practice

❶ Study the map shown above. What is the subject of the map?

❷ Around what geographic feature were most of the cities built? Why might this have been so?

❸ What does the activity of rice farming shown on the map demonstrate about the geographic distribution of agriculture in early east Asia?

❹ Approximately how much farther is the trip from Wuchang to Taixicun than Wuchang to Erlitou?

❺ Trace the map above. Use an atlas to create an outline map of modern China. Locate and label important land forms and features such as major cities, rivers, and elevations. Include other items, such as types of crop, dams, weather patterns, and resources.

LEVEL 1: Have students read the material under the heading "The rivers of China." Ask for a volunteer to describe what purpose the earthen walls around the Huang River were supposed to serve. *(prevent flooding)* What was the result of building ever-higher dikes along the Huang River? *(The river now flows at least 12 feet above the surrounding land.)* Did the dikes stop the Huang River from flooding? *(No)*
ENGLISH LANGUAGE LEARNERS

LEVEL 3: Tell students that early Chinese called the region in which they lived "All under Heaven." Ask the class what clues this name provides about how the Chinese regarded their culture. *(Students should suggest feelings of cultural superiority, a link with the divine, a blessed land and people.)* Ask students what other name the Chinese had for their land that indicates they felt culturally superior. *(Middle Kingdom)* Then discuss what caused these feelings of superiority. *(China's geographic isolation and lack of contact with foreigners)*

Economics

The Chang is the world's third-longest river (after the Amazon and the Nile). It carries about 75 percent of China's domestic water-borne commerce and irrigates more than a third of the nation's agriculture. In addition, the river's watershed covers some 700,000 square miles, about a fifth of China's total land area.

Critical Thinking

Ask students why water transportation would be especially important to the economic development of civilizations in China.

ANSWER: Students should recognize that developing nations generally lack the sophisticated infrastructure, such as highways and railroads, of more developed nations.

That's Interesting!

The Chinese do not call their nation "China." Foreigners use this name. Instead the Chinese use the name Zhongguo (chung-kou), meaning "Middle Kingdom," a reference to the early Chinese belief that their country was at the center of the world.

VISUAL RECORD ANSWER

It is navigable.

The rivers of China. The Huang, the Chang, and the Xi rivers have played major roles in Chinese history. The Huang River flows some 2,900 miles across China before emptying into an arm of the Yellow Sea. The Huang River valley has a fertile yellow soil called **loess** (LES). So much loess washes into the Huang River that it gives the river a yellow tint. That is why the Chinese named it the Huang River, which means "Yellow River."

The Huang River has also been prone to devastating floods. These floods led the ancient Chinese to nickname the river "China's Sorrow." Early farmers built earthen **dikes**, or walls, along the Huang to protect crops from floods. The dikes had the unintended effect, however, of slowing the river's flow. This in turn caused the Huang to deposit silt on the river bottom. Over the years, the silt grew deeper, forcing the river level higher. The river level finally reached the tops of the dikes, so that even moderate rains caused the river to wash over the dikes and into the surrounding fields. In about 1 B.C., a Chinese engineer, Chang Jung, proposed a new solution to this problem.

Analyzing Primary Sources

Problem Solving What solution did Chang Jung offer to reduce flooding along the Huang River?
to stop building dikes

INTERPRETING THE VISUAL RECORD

The Huang River The Huang River in northeastern China has shifted course many times over the centuries. These shifts have affected millions of acres of rich farmland. ***What does the deep channel of the Huang River tell us about the river?***

History Makers Speak `❝` . . . the government and the people go on building dykes until the level [of the river] becomes slightly higher than the surrounding country. . . . It would be better to follow the nature of the water . . . the water-ways would keep themselves in order and there would be much less danger from floods breaking through, with all the harm they bring about. `❞`

Chang Jung, from *Science and Civilisation in China*

Chang Jung's advice was mostly ignored, however. The Chinese built ever-higher dikes. As a result, today the Huang River flows at least 12 feet above the surrounding land. The higher dikes, however, did not end the flooding. Every few years the Huang broke through the dikes. The resulting floods destroyed crops and caused great loss of life. Since the floodwater could not drain back into the higher riverbed, it tended to remain on the land until it evaporated. Moreover, rainfall in the region was unpredictable, so that floods alternated with periods of drought and famine.

The Chang River, in central China, flows for 3,434 miles. The river cuts a deep channel through its valley. In modern times, large ocean-going ships have been able to navigate nearly 600 miles upstream. Smaller ships can travel about 1,700 miles upriver. The Xi River, in southern China, is about 1,200 miles long. Like the Chang, it forms an important commercial waterway. Large ships can navigate about one third of its length.

✔ **READING CHECK: Summarizing** What benefits do the Huang River, the Chang River, and the Xi River bring to the Chinese people? fertile soil, commercial waterways

China's Isolation

Great distances, rugged mountains, and harsh deserts, such as the Gobi, isolated China from the civilizations of India and the West. As a result, China developed its own distinctive culture. The Chinese did adopt some ideas and skills from other peoples. However, they were probably influenced less by other cultures than any other people in ancient times.

Along their northern and northwestern borders, the Chinese had regular contact with nomadic and semi-nomadic peoples. These peoples spoke their own languages and had their own cultures. Usually they traded peacefully with the Chinese. Sometimes, however, they organized bands of mounted warriors and attacked Chinese settlements. The Chinese considered these people culturally inferior and called them barbarians.

Infrequent contact with foreigners helped give the Chinese a strong sense of identity and superiority. They regarded China as the only civilized land, calling it *Zhongguo,* or "Middle Kingdom," meaning the center of the world. They believed that other people became fully civilized only by learning the Chinese language and adopting Chinese customs. In many cases, even when outsiders overran parts of China, as sometimes happened, the invaders would lose their identity over time and be absorbed into China's population.

✔ **READING CHECK: Identifying Bias** Why did the Chinese regard other peoples as inferior? lack of contact with foreigners

In parts of Mongolia, north of China, nomadic lifestyles continue today.

REVIEW ANSWERS

❶ **Define**
• loess, p. 78
• dikes, p. 78

❷ Huang: fertile farming; Chang: commercial waterway; Xi: commercial waterway

❸ **a.** northern: less rain, more extreme temperatures, shorter growing season; southern: more rainfall; China Proper: most historically significant; outlying regions (Tibet, Xinjiang, Mongolia, Manchuria, northern Korea): sometimes conquered by China, sometimes ruled China

b. China's isolation led to the development of a distinctive culture.

❹ Students' outlines will vary but should include a discussion of flooding and dikes.

SECTION 1 REVIEW

1. Define and explain the significance:
loess
dikes

2. Comparing Copy the web diagram below. Use it to compare the uses that the Chinese have made of the Huang, the Chang, and the Xi rivers.

```
    Chang                Xi
    River               River

            Huang
            River
```

3. **Finding the Main Idea**
a. How do the northern and southern regions of China differ geographically and politically?
b. How did geography contribute to the Chinese sense of identity?

4. **Writing and Critical Thinking**
Summarizing Imagine you are a university professor teaching a class on the history of China. Prepare an outline for a lecture in which you teach students about the role the Huang River has played in Chinese history.
Consider:
• the characteristics of the river and its surrounding lands
• the problem of flooding
• the effects of dikes on the river

Homework Practice Online
keyword: SP3 HP4

OBJECTIVES

1 Examine how the Chinese explained their early history.

2 Describe how the Shang government and economy were organized.

3 Identify the religious beliefs held by the Shang.

4 Explain why the Shang dynasty collapsed.

🔊 *LET'S GET STARTED!*

As students enter the classroom, ask them to name several legends with which they are familiar. Have them state some reasons why legends are important to many cultures. (*Students might answer that legends often explain events of the past.*) Tell students that in Section 2 they will learn about some legends of ancient China.

SECTION 2 RESOURCES

REPRODUCIBLE RESOURCES

▶ Guided Reading Strategy 4.2

TECHNOLOGY RESOURCES

▶ One-Stop Planner 4.2

▶ CNN Presents World Cultures: Yesterday and Today Segment 4: Treasures from China

▶ Homework Practice Online

REINFORCEMENT, REVIEW, AND ASSESSMENT

▶ Section 2 Review, p. 83

▶ Daily Quiz 4.2

▶ Main Idea Activity 4.2

▶ English Audio Summary 4.2

▶ Spanish Audio Summary 4.2

MAP ANSWER

desert to the north and mountains to the west

SECTION 2

READ TO DISCOVER

❶ How did the Chinese explain their early history?

❷ How was the Shang government and economy organized?

❸ What religious beliefs did the Shang hold?

❹ Why did the Shang dynasty collapse?

DEFINE

bureaucracy
animism
oracle bones
dialects
calligraphy

IDENTIFY

Xia
Shang
Zhou

▶ WHY IT MATTERS TODAY

Myths and legends still play an important role in today's world. Use **CNNfyi.com** or other **current event** sources to find information regarding a myth or legend that remains influential today. Record your findings in your journal.

CNNfyi.com

The Shang Dynasty

The Main Idea
The Shang dynasty established a model that shaped future governments of China.

The Story Continues *"To give continuance to foremothers and forefathers / We build a house, many hundred cubits of wall; . . . / Here we shall live, here rest, / Here laugh, here talk."* This ancient Shang poem—*celebrating the building of a house—reflects the values of those people who gave China its first great dynasty.*

Legends of Ancient China

The early Chinese placed great importance on explaining the distant past and on China's role in history. They passed on many legends about the beginnings of the world and about the origins of ancient China. For example, an early Chinese story tells of Pangu, the first man, who awoke from 18,000 years of sleep to create the universe. Another Chinese legend describes the labors of Yu, a mythological figure who drained away floodwaters so people could live in China. Yu established a line of kings called the **Xia** (SHAH). The Xia ruled over a late Neolithic people who lived in the Huang River region starting in about 2200 B.C.

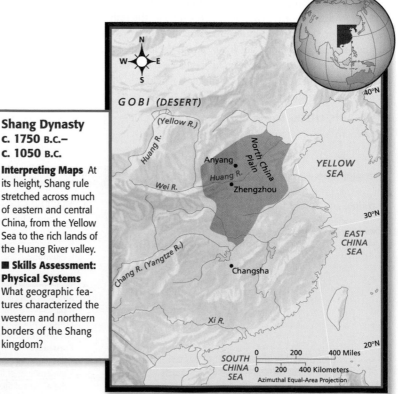

Shang Dynasty
c. 1750 B.C.–
c. 1050 B.C.

Interpreting Maps At its height, Shang rule stretched across much of eastern and central China, from the Yellow Sea to the rich lands of the Huang River valley.

■ **Skills Assessment: Physical Systems** What geographic features characterized the western and northern borders of the Shang kingdom?

TEACH OBJECTIVE 1

LEVEL 3: Explain that in cultures without writing, history depends on stories passed from one generation to the next. Have students write a short legend about Xia's rule. Form small groups and have one member tell his or her legend to another. That student should repeat it to a third, and so on, until it has passed through the group. Have the last person in each group tell the legend to the class. Ask the class to assess the value of legends as historical sources. Then discuss what the accuracy of China's legends suggests about the importance its people put on their past. **COOPERATIVE LEARNING**

HOMEWORK Create a chart titled *Developments under the Shang.* Head the columns *Farming Advances,* *Crafts Advances,* and *Government Accomplishments.* Have students copy the chart and categorize the information on their own.

Developments under the Shang		
Farming Advances	Crafts Advances	Government Accomplishments

There is little evidence to support most of these legends. Scholars agree, however, that the Xia people existed and that they made great advances over time. For example, they developed improved methods of agriculture and may have begun to use written symbols. The people lived well in good times, but may have had little centralized control over irrigation and flood-prevention measures. The early Chinese, then, could do little in the face of droughts and floods.

At some point between 1750 B.C. and 1500 B.C., invaders called the **Shang** swept into the Huang River valley. Many scholars believe that the Shang introduced simple irrigation and flood-control systems to the region. This may have strengthened Shang rule. By controlling these systems, the Shang could more easily control the region's people.

The Shang created China's first historic dynasty. Later Chinese writers wrote an account in which Tang, a Shang leader, asks the Xia people to reject their king and to follow him.

History Makers Speak

❝I would have you stand by my side . . . to bring upon him [the Xia ruler] Heaven's punishment. I will greatly reward you. Do not ye disbelieve me. I do not eat my words. If you do not follow the words of this vow, I will slay you and all your offspring and none will be forgiven.❞

Tang, from *An Anthology of Chinese Literature*

✔ **READING CHECK: Drawing Inferences** Why would people use legends to explain their past? They placed importance on explaining their own role in history.

Government and Culture

At its height, the Shang kingdom stretched across 40,000 square miles. Apparently the Shang moved their capital several times, probably for defensive reasons or to avoid floods. During the last centuries of Shang rule, the capital was near what is today the city of Anyang.

Shang rulers created a complex **bureaucracy**—a government organized into different levels and tasks. A hereditary king ruled over all land in the kingdom. The Shang army used war chariots and bronze weapons to defend against the peoples on the kingdom's borders. Their military might and well-organized government allowed the Shang to gain territory and to spread their culture.

Economy and handicrafts. The Shang economy was based mainly on agriculture. Crops included millet and rice. Domestic animals included pigs and chickens for meat and horses for labor. During the Shang dynasty, the Chinese knew how to raise silkworms. They spun thread from the silkworms' cocoons and wove silk cloth from the thread.

Not all Chinese of the Shang period were farmers. Many merchants and artisans lived in the capital and in the towns of the Shang realm. Artisans worked in bone, ivory, and jade. Shang artisans also established the foundation for later Chinese ceramic art. They developed the forms and shapes used in Chinese ceremonial vases. Shang potters used *kaolin,* a fine white clay, and could glaze pottery to give it a shiny finish. This made the pottery more durable.

Analyzing Primary Sources

Evaluating How did Tang appeal to the people's spiritual and moral sense in his effort to overthrow the Xia ruler? by claiming that he was acting on behalf of Heaven

CONNECTING TO

Metalworking: Ancient Bronze Vessel
This small vessel—just over a foot long—shows animal designs that were common in Shang dynasty bronzes. The tiger at the left becomes an owl in the middle and yet another bird on the right. The vessel was probably used for mixing and pouring wine. The head of the tiger serves as a lid. The neck of the bird at the right provides a handle for pouring.

Understanding the Arts

How was this bronze casting multi-functional?

Science, Technology & Society

Silkworms are not worms at all. Instead they are caterpillars in a family belonging to the biological order of Lepidoptera—butterflies and moths. The most commonly raised silkworms eat only the leaves of mulberry trees. The silk comes from the cocoons they spin and live in when they grow large enough to metamorphasize into moths. In the silk-making process, heat is used to kill the caterpillar inside the cocoon. Next the cocoon is carefully unwound, producing a continuous silk thread. These threads are then spun into silk cloth. About 100 cocoons are needed to make a silk tie, and more than 600 for a blouse. A silk kimono can require 3,000 silkworms, which will eat about 135 pounds of mulberry leaves before they spin their cocoons.

Critical Thinking

Garments made of silk generally cost more than similar items made of cotton, wool, or polyester. Ask students why this would be so.

ANSWER: Students should recognize the high costs involved in producing silk thread and enough cloth to make an item.

CONNECTING TO ART ANSWER
It is both beautiful and practical.

TEACH OBJECTIVE 2

ALL LEVELS: Ask students to identify two ways that the Shang dynasty maintained its power. (*force of arms, such as war chariots and bronze weapons; public works systems, such as irrigation and flood control*) Ask them to deduce the role that technology played in sustaining the dynasty. (*Both examples are technology-related.*) **ENGLISH LANGUAGE LEARNERS**

TEACH OBJECTIVE 3

LEVEL 1: Call on volunteers to name some of the religious beliefs held by the Shang. (*combination of animism and ancestor worship, Shangdi, interpretation of oracle bones*) Ask students how Shang rulers used the religious beliefs of the early Chinese to legitimize their rule. (*They claimed that their decisions were the will of Shangdi.*) **ENGLISH LANGUAGE LEARNERS**

TEACH OBJECTIVE 4

LEVEL 1: Ask students why the Shang dynasty collapsed. (*It could not defend against the constant attacks from peoples on its borders.*) Have students explain who conquered the Shang dynasty and how they justified their conquest. (*the Zhou; claimed that the Shang were corrupt and unfit to rule*)
ENGLISH LANGUAGE LEARNERS

Government

The belief system of the Shang religion legitimized the power of the ruling king. According to this religion, the god Shangdi could bestow bountiful harvests and victory in battle on the Shang people, and the king's ancestors could supposedly influence Shangdi in these matters. Through prayer and sacrifice, the king was believed to be able to communicate with his ancestors and ask them to intercede with Shangdi on behalf of the Shang people. Therefore it was the king himself who could produce abundant crops and ensure military triumphs, and consequently, religious and political powers were concentrated in his hands.

Critical Thinking

Ask students how the Shang beliefs about their kings could turn out to be a disadvantage for a ruler.

ANSWER: Students might suggest that a random event such as a drought could discredit a ruler.

VISUAL RECORD ANSWER

They recorded the answers in writing on the bones.

INTERPRETING THE VISUAL RECORD

Oracle bones The Shang believed that they could receive answers and advice from the spirit world through the use of oracle bones like the one shown here. *What does the writing on this bone suggest about the Shang system for interpreting these messages?*

Astronomy and the calendar. The Chinese primarily used two calendars, one based on the sun and one based on the movements of the moon. The lunar, or moon-based, calendar was probably used to record private and public events, such as the birth of a child or the death of a ruler. Each lunar month began with a new moon and was about 29 days long. Twelve lunar months made one year. To include enough days for a full 365-day year, skilled priest-astronomers employed by the government were responsible for adding days as needed. The king's popularity depended upon the success of the harvest, which in turn depended in part on the time of planting as determined by the calendar. Therefore the priest-astronomers played a very important role.

✔ **READING CHECK: Analyzing Information** What factors enabled the Shang to build and extend their kingdom? military strength, well-organized government

Religion in the Shang Period

The religion that developed during the Shang period combined **animism**—the belief that spirits inhabit everything—with ancestor worship. People believed in an all-powerful and kindly dragon that lived in the seas and rivers and that could rise into the clouds. In time, this dragon became the symbol of Chinese rulers.

The Chinese also worshiped gods of the wind, sun, clouds, and moon. Some of these gods were honored by festivals. The people held a great religious festival in the spring to ensure good crops. In an autumn religious festival, the people thanked the moon god for the harvest.

The Shang also believed in Shangdi, a great god who controlled human destiny and the forces of nature. Rulers often asked the spirits of their ancestors to plead on their behalf with Shangdi, offering them sacrifices. Rulers used Shangdi's control over destiny to justify their decisions.

Priests played an important role in Chinese religion. Some tried to predict future events or interpret divine messages, especially messages from the spirits of ancestors. The priests wrote questions on **oracle bones**—the shoulder bones of cattle or tortoise shells. The priests heated the bones and interpreted the cracks that would then appear. They marked their interpretations on the bone or shell. Some think the name of the ruler who asked the questions was also often scratched onto the bone. Thus the markings on oracle bones have helped scholars learn more about the Shang.

✔ **READING CHECK: Drawing Conclusions** How did Shang leaders use religious beliefs to build support for their rule? claimed that their decisions were the will of Shangdi

Language and Writing

The Chinese of the Shang period were among the few early peoples to develop a written language. The early Chinese—like the Chinese of today—spoke many **dialects,** or variations of their language. The Chinese developed a written language that could be used for all these dialects. They assigned special symbols, or characters, to the words in their language. At first these characters were pictographs, or drawings of objects. Later, as their language became more complex, the Chinese developed ideographs. Many ideographs consisted of two parts—a signifier, or idea sign, and a phonetic sound sign. The signifier showed the meaning of the character and the phonetic sign told how to pronounce it.

CLOSE

Ask students to name the major cultural achievements that occurred under the Shang dynasty.

REVIEW

Have students complete the Section 2 Review on p. 83.

ASSESS

Have students complete Daily Quiz 4.2. As Alternative Assessment, you may want to use the legend or religion exercises in this section's lessons.

RETEACH

Have students complete Main Idea Activity for English Language Learners and Special-Needs Students 4.2. Then ask students to use correct social studies terminology to write a question that covers the main idea for each subsection in the section.
ENGLISH LANGUAGE LEARNERS

EXTEND

Have students research and report on bronze casting and a writing system, two important technological breakthroughs that took place in Shang China. Have them create visuals such as charts and graphs to illustrate their reports. **BLOCK SCHEDULING**

This system of writing allowed the Shang to invent new characters by combining existing signs. Each character, however, had to be memorized. For many centuries the ability to read and write was limited to a small number of specialists. These people generally served the Shang rulers as clerks, scribes, and teachers. Scribes recorded special events and composed literary works. They wrote characters in lines that ran from the top to the bottom of the page, beginning on the right side. Eventually, writing became an art called **calligraphy.** Artists used the same kind of brush for calligraphy as for painting.

✔ **READING CHECK: Identifying Cause and Effect** Why were reading and writing limited to specialists in early China? required long study

Fall of the Shang Dynasty

By about 1200 B.C. herders from the harsh Gobi Desert and the Tian Shan foothills had begun to edge toward the Huang valley. These peoples were probably attracted by the wealth and lifestyles of China Proper. Over time, some seem to have begun to settle along the borders of Shang China.

During the 1100s B.C. the Shang almost continuously battled these warlike neighboring states. Their extended military efforts finally exhausted the Shang rulers. The last Shang king, Di-xin, could not protect the kingdom's northwest borders. In about 1050 B.C. a people called the **Zhou** (JOH) formed an alliance with nearby tribes and overthrew the dynasty. The Zhou justified their conquest by claiming that the Shang were corrupt and unfit to rule. This explanation for the overthrow of one dynasty by another has been used throughout China's long history.

✔ **READING CHECK: Identifying Cause and Effect** Why did the Shang dynasty collapse? constant attacks from peoples on their border

Mastery of the traditional Chinese written language demanded much study and practice. Thus most ancient Chinese people, whose working lifestyles left little time for study, were prevented from learning to write or to read.

SECTION 2 REVIEW ANSWERS

❶ **Define**
• bureaucracy, p. 81
• animism, p. 82
• oracle bones, p. 82
• dialects, p. 82
• calligraphy, p. 83

❷ **Identify**
• Xia, p. 80
• Shang, p. 81
• Zhou, p. 83

❸ Students' answers should include descriptions of the lunar calendar, the agricultural economy, bureaucracy, animism, oracle bones, and calligraphy.

❹ **a.** They used legends to explain how Yu drained away floodwaters in China so people could live there.

b. centralized rule under a king

c. They were under constant attack from peoples on their borders.

❺ Students' descriptions will vary but should include a discussion of Shangdi, oracle bones, and the role of priests in Shang society.

SECTION 2 REVIEW

1. **Define** and explain the significance:
   bureaucracy
   animism
   oracle bones
   dialects
   calligraphy

2. **Identify** and explain the significance:
   Xia
   Shang
   Zhou

3. **Summarizing** Copy the chart below. Use it to create a written description of the calendars, economy, government, religion, and forms of writing that developed during the Shang dynasty.

   Calendars
   Economy
   Government → Shang Dynasty Achievements
   Religion
   Writing

4. **Finding the Main Idea**
   a. How did the Xia use legends about early Chinese history to explain their origins as a people?
   b. How did the Shang rulers maintain control over their large kingdom?
   c. How did poor relations with neighboring peoples help contribute to the ultimate collapse of the Shang dynasty?

5. **Writing and Critical Thinking**
   Analyzing Information The Shang believed that spirits, including those of their ancestors, continued to play an important role in daily life. Describe the method of communicating with the spirit world that was developed during the Shang dynasty.
   Consider:
   • the Shang belief in Shang di
   • the meaning and use of oracle bones
   • the role of priests in Shang society

Homework Practice Online
keyword: SP3 HP4

OBJECTIVES

1 Explain why the Zhou fell from power.

2 Describe how the Qin dynasty used power to maintain its authority.

3 Identify the achievements of the Han emperors.

SECTION **3**

READ TO DISCOVER

❶ Why did the Zhou fall from power?

❷ How did the Qin dynasty use power to maintain its authority?

❸ What did the Han emperors achieve?

DEFINE

autocracy
civil service
leveling

IDENTIFY

Qin
Han
Cheng
Great Wall of China
Liu Bang
Liu Ch'e
Silk Road

▶ **WHY IT MATTERS TODAY**

Some governments today still use harsh methods to control their people. Use **CNNfyi.com** or other **current event** sources to explore repressive governments. Record your findings in your journal.

CNNfyi.com

The Zhou, Qin, and Han Dynasties

The Main Idea
Three major dynasties—the Zhou, the Qin, and the Han—built China into a powerful country.

The Story Continues *"Nothing is so strong as goodness; / On all sides men will take their lesson from it. . . . / But those that rule today / Have brought confusion and disorder into government; / . . . / Therefore mighty Heaven is displeased."* These verses appear in the Book of Poetry, *one of the ancient Five Classics. During the time of China's great dynasties, these works served as a guide to good government.*

The Zhou Dynasty

The Zhou conquest of China in about 1050 B.C. marked the beginning of a dynamic era in Chinese history. Under the rule of three successive dynasties—the Zhou, the **Qin** (CHIN), and the **Han**—China gradually became a large and powerful state. The longest-lasting of the three dynasties was the Zhou, which ruled China from about 1050 B.C. until about 256 B.C.

The Zhou rulers did not create a centralized form of government following their conquest of the Shang kingdom. Instead, they granted territories to members of the royal family and their allies. The rulers of the territories had to give military service and tribute to the Zhou kings. Their positions were hereditary, but each generation had to renew its pledge of loyalty. Zhou rulers believed that the god of Heaven determined who should rule China, a right known as the "Mandate of Heaven." Throughout Chinese history, when rebels overthrew a dynasty, they claimed that the old dynasty had lost the Mandate of Heaven.

By the 700s B.C. Zhou kings were losing control as local leaders began to fight among themselves. In addition, Zhou lands were often attacked by outsiders. Chinese tradition has it that the quality of the Zhou kings also declined at this time. One legend claims that wicked King Yu abandoned his wife for another woman, Pao-Szu. To entertain themselves, Yu and Pao-Szu signaled that nomadic raiders were attacking. The false alarm led Zhou soldiers to rush to defend their capital. Later, angry troops ignored warnings when a real army attacked. Whether or not the legend is true, an invading force actually did destroy the Zhou

This bronze vessel of the Zhou dynasty reflects a high standard of technology and artistry.

TEACH OBJECTIVE 1

LEVEL 1: Ask students to explain why the Zhou fell from power. *(internal fighting and attacks by outsiders)* Then have students create an annotated time line showing significant events in the Zhou dynasty. Ask volunteers to present their time lines to the class. **ENGLISH LANGUAGE LEARNERS**

Zhou Dynasty

771 B.C. Zhou capital is destroyed

256 B.C. the Zhou fall from power

1200 B.C. 1000 B.C. 800 B.C. 600 B.C. 400 B.C. 200 B.C.

1050 B.C. the Zhou seize power

700 B.C. Zhou kings begin to lose control

400 B.C. the Zhou lose all power except within their own city-state

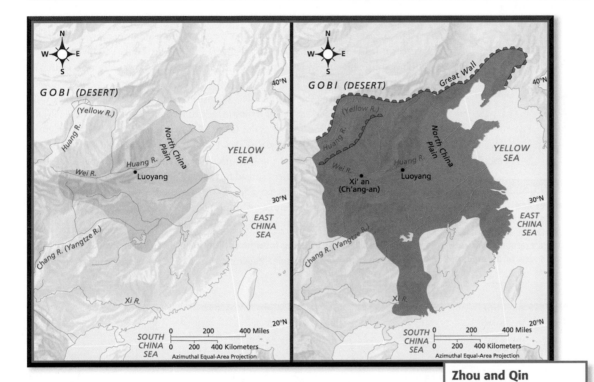

Zhou and Qin Dynasties

Interpreting Maps The Zhou Dynasty (left) relied heavily upon the kingdom's great river systems. Cheng extended Qin rule (right) even farther.

■ **Skills Assessment:**
1. Places and Regions What were the main rivers in the Zhou Dynasty? **2. Comparing** How did the size of the Qin Dynasty compare to that of the Zhou?

capital in 771 B.C. The Zhou ruler fled eastward and established a new capital. The Zhou dynasty lasted for 500 more years but had lost much of its former power. New powers, known as the Warring States, began to compete for control of China. By the 400s B.C. the Zhou had no real power outside their own city-state. Instead, local rulers ran things. One of the Warring States, the Qin, emerged victorious.

✔ **READING CHECK: Identifying Cause and Effect** What factors led to the decline of the Zhou dynasty? fought among themselves, attacked by outsiders

The Qin Dynasty

The Qin dynasty came to power in 221 B.C. through their military might. The ruler **Cheng** founded this new dynasty, taking for himself the title Shih Huang Ti, which means "first emperor." The Qin dynasty lasted only 15 years but produced many lasting changes in Chinese life. In fact, the Western name for "China" is derived from the name of the Qin dynasty. Cheng claimed that the founding of his dynasty marked a turning point in China's history.

History Makers Speak

❝In the . . . years of his reign
A new age is opened by [Cheng].
Rules and measures are corrected,
Everything is set in order,
Human affairs are clarified
And there is harmony between fathers and sons.❞

Cheng, from *The First Emperor*

Analyzing Primary Sources

Evaluating What benefits did Cheng claim his rule would bring to China? improved social order and family harmony

EXPLORING THE TIME LINE
GLOBAL EVENTS

Initially the Zhou were merely a minor satellite state of the powerful Shang dynasty. In about 1100 B.C., however, the Zhou began to form alliances with several smaller states to the south and the west of the Shang. In 1122 B.C., the Zhou and their allies decisively defeated the demoralized Shang. The former subjects had triumphed over the most dominant empire in ancient China.

Critical Thinking

Ask students to list the ways the Zhou, a minor power, were able to defeat the Shang.

ANSWER: Students should note that the Zhou formed alliances with other states and waited until the military power of the Shang was weakened.

MAP ANSWERS
1. Huang, Wei, and Chang

2. It was much larger.

ALL LEVELS: Tell students to imagine they are newspaper editors during the Qin dynasty and to write an editorial about the emperor. Editorials should either charge that the emperor has lost the Mandate of Heaven or defend him as having it. Remind students that editorials explain to readers the reasons for the writer's point of view. *(has lost mandate: Qin's harsh rule, popular unrest; has mandate: dynasty's accomplishments, maintains strong power)* Have students read their editorials to the class. Then hold a discussion on whether the Qin had the Mandate of Heaven. **ENGLISH LANGUAGE LEARNERS**

✈ internet connect

Internet Activity: go.hrw.com
TOPIC: The Great Wall of China **KEYWORD: SP3 WH4**

Have students access the Internet through the HRW Go site to do research on the Qin Dynasty and the Great Wall of China. Then have students write four paragraphs about the history of the wall, hiking along the Great Wall, interesting facts, and the myths and legends that surround the wall. Students may wish to use the interactive template provided to create an illustrated brochure on the Great Wall of China.

History Maker

QU YAN. Each year Chinese Americans gather in New York City for the Dragon Boat Festival. The event commemorates the death of Qu Yan, a poet from the 300s B.C. who drowned in China's Milo River. Dragon boat races reenact the attempt to reach Qu Yan and rescue him. The boats, each of which holds 20 paddlers, are 40 feet long and are adorned at bow and stern by a dragon's head and tail. The Dragon Boat Festival in Great Britain attracts some 20,000 participants each year.

ACTIVITY: Organize students into groups and have them write a plan for a festival that commemorates an important person from their community. Have them describe the kinds of activities they want to include in the festival as well as why the person they choose to commemorate is important.

VISUAL RECORD ANSWER

negative

MAP ANSWER
Answers should include two of the following: Kashi, Dunhuang, Xi'an

INTERPRETING THE VISUAL RECORD

Qin oppression Cheng maintained rigid control over his subjects. Here he watches as scholars are executed. *What was the artist's view of the emperor?*

From their capital near Ch'ang-an—now called Xi'an (shee·AHN)—the Qin ruled over a huge area. They maintained order by establishing an **autocracy,** in which the emperor held total power. Cheng saw dangers in allowing scholars to investigate and discuss problems freely. He suppressed and even executed scholars who criticized the government.

Like earlier rulers, the Qin guarded against invasion by building defensive walls along parts of their borders. Later dynasties added to these structures. Eventually, the connected walls became known as the **Great Wall of China.** This massive structure, much of which still stands today, was about 1,500 miles long during Qin times. The Qin employed forced labor for public works projects like the Great Wall. This policy angered many people. Discontent spread further as a great gap arose between the ruler and the mass of people. In 206 B.C. a rebel army revolted against the dynasty. In that same year **Liu Bang,** a commoner who had become a Qin general, overthrew the empire. Liu Bang founded a new dynasty known as the Han.

✔ **READING CHECK: Drawing Inferences** Why might Cheng have felt that free discussion was dangerous to his rule? Public criticism might have weakened his total power.

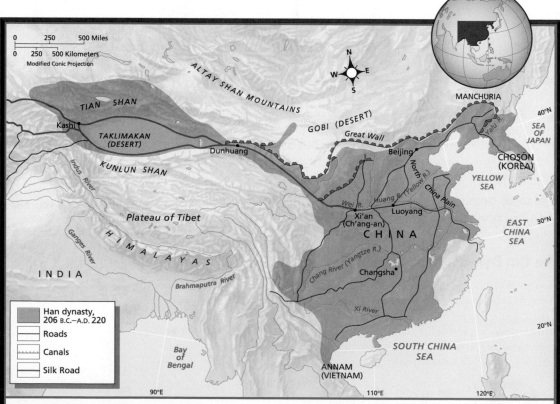

Han Dynasty, c. 206 B.C.–A.D. 220

Interpreting Maps Trade and commerce helped the Han to extend their control far to the west of earlier Chinese dynasties.

■ **Skills Assessment: Human Systems** Name two cities through which a merchant would have to pass while traveling along the Silk Road.

TEACH OBJECTIVE 3

LEVEL 3: Have small groups conduct short interviews with Hsiao Yen, focusing on some aspect of his rule, such as conquest of the Xiongnu. One student takes the role of the interviewer and another of Hsiao Yen. The third student plays an imperial assistant such as a general. Have groups present their interviews to the class. **COOPERATIVE LEARNING**

HOMEWORK Ask students to decide whether they would have preferred to live under Zhou, Qin, or Han rule. Have students write a paragraph that supports their point of view.

Teacher to Teacher

Rudy Martinez of San Antonio, Texas, suggested the following activity: Have students, either individually or in groups, write papers or create visual presentations comparing the tombs of ancient Egyptians with those of ancient Chinese leaders. Presentations should assess how these comparisons reflect cultural differences and similarities.

The Han Dynasty

The new dynasty received its name from the title that Liu Bang took—King of Han. Like the Qin, the Han ruled a centralized and growing empire. The Han were more moderate rulers than the Qin, however, and kept power for about 400 years. Han rulers had so much influence over the development of China that many Chinese today call themselves "People of Han." The longest-ruling Han emperor was **Liu Ch'e,** commonly known as Wu Ti, who ruled from about 140 B.C. to 87 B.C. From his capital at Ch'ang-an, Liu Ch'e extended Han rule north into present-day Manchuria and Korea, south into Southeast Asia, and west into central Asia. The Han ruled over an area larger than the Roman Empire.

The civil service system. Building on a foundation laid by the Qin, the Han dynasty established a centralized civil service system to govern China. A **civil service** system runs the day-to-day business of government. At first government officials recommended candidates for civil service positions on the basis of family connections. Eventually, however, the Han created a system of examinations to select the most qualified candidates. Liu Ch'e also established an imperial university to train people for government service. Theoretically the civil service was open to anyone. In practice, however, usually only those with family connections and money for schooling and books could train. The civil service was improved over the centuries and during the course of many Chinese dynasties. Over generations, it produced many effective, well-trained government workers who helped the emperors rule China's growing, increasingly complex society. The system remained important to China's government until the early A.D. 1900s.

Other accomplishments. Under earlier rulers, rising and falling prices for farm products had caused much hardship for peasants. Liu Ch'e began an economic policy, which some scholars call **leveling,** to solve this problem. Under the leveling system, the

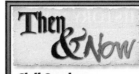

Civil Service

The Chinese civil service was created to help run the government. The system was designed to be fair and to reward ability. Citizens had to pass a written test in order to hold civil service jobs. Those who showed strong ability were promoted to higher positions.

In today's China, entry into the civil service is based upon loyalty to the ruling political party as well as on ability. In the United States, most civil service jobs are gained by passing a written test. American laws forbid the selection of civil service workers based upon political ties.

Why might some people today consider civil service exams to be unfair?

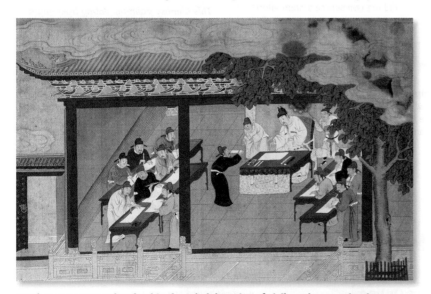

Much ceremony was involved in the administration of civil service examinations. Candidates for government positions had to thoroughly prepare for the test, which often involved years of study and training. Failure was considered a disgrace.

TEACH OBJECTIVE 1

LEVEL 1: Ask students why the Chinese valued the concept of balance. (*They believed that everything in the world resulted from a balance between two forces.*) Draw a two-column chart with one column labeled *yin* and the other labeled *yang.* Have students list the characteristics of each in the chart. **ENGLISH LANGUAGE LEARNERS**

Yin	Yang
female	male
dark	bright
passive	active

TEACH OBJECTIVE 2

ALL LEVELS: Write the following passage from the *Analects* on the chalkboard: "*To see what is right and not to do it is want of courage.*" Tell students that the passage is a teaching of Confucius. Ask the class what the saying means and what effect following it would have had on the government of China. (*Students should restate the adage in their own words and realize that it would encourage good government.*) Discuss whether these are words to live by today. **ENGLISH LANGUAGE LEARNERS**

📡 **internet** connect

TOPIC: Chinese Philosophy and Science
GO TO: go.hrw.com
KEYWORD: SP3 WH4

Have students access the Internet through the HRW Go site to conduct research on Chinese philosophy or Chinese contributions to science. Ask students to take notes on the topic they choose and then write a report. Students may wish to use the interactive report template. Students should use standard grammar, punctuation, and sentence structure in their reports.

VISUAL RECORD ANSWER

The scrolls he is carrying show that learning was very important to him.

WHAT IF? ANSWER

Answers will vary, but students should recognize that the teachings of Confucius reinforced the importance of ancestors, family, individual responsibility to society, and good government. Without Confucius, these cultural forces might have been weaker or nonexistent.

Technology Resources

Online Maps, Charts, and Graphs: Early Confucianism c. 200 B.C.

INTERPRETING THE VISUAL RECORD

Confucius The death of his father left Confucius in poverty at the age of three. Largely self-educated, Confucius became a symbol of wisdom, learning, and great moral strength. *What clues does this picture provide about the focus of Confucius's life?*

What If? **What if Confucius had never lived? How might the history of China have been different?**

Holt Researcher
go.hrw.com
KEYWORD: Holt Researcher
FreeFind: Confucius
Laozi
After reading more about Confucius and Laozi on the Holt Researcher, write an imaginary dialogue between the two comparing their ideas.

Confucius and Laozi

Chinese philosophers developed new ideas and theories to explain economic, political, and social change during the Zhou era. A leading philosopher of the period was **Confucius.** He lived from 551 B.C. to 479 B.C. Confucius's followers collected his ideas and teachings in a work called the **Analects.** In time, Confucius's teachings became known as Confucianism.

Confucianism. The philosophy of Confucianism had more influence on Chinese life than any other philosophy. Confucius taught about the importance of family, respect for one's elders, and reverence for the past and one's ancestors. These three concepts form the basis of Confucian philosophy.

Confucius sought to end the political disorder of his time. He was not a religious prophet, and he had little to say about gods or about purely religious ideas. Confucius's teachings were not concerned with the meaning of death, ideas about life after death, or issues of faith. Instead, Confucius was concerned with the causes of political and social unrest and with how moral and ethical leadership could solve those problems.

Confucius aimed to encourage strong, positive behavior on the part of China's leaders. He believed that this could be accomplished in two ways. First, every person should willingly accept his or her role in society and should perform the duties of that role. Second, the government and its leaders should be virtuous. Virtue, according to Confucius, involved correct behavior toward others. Instead of seeking wealth and power, rulers should be honest and honorable toward those they lead. Their greatest interest should be the welfare and happiness of their people. Confucius encouraged only moral, well-educated officials to be appointed to lead the government and to administer its laws. In this way rulers would set a good example for all. The people, moreover, would willingly follow leaders who lived and governed according to these virtuous guidelines.

Over time, many of Confucius's ideas and values were adopted by other Chinese thinkers. One of the most influential of these was Mencius, who lived between about 372 B.C. and about 289 B.C. Mencius was a strong supporter of the Confucian philosophy. He taught that individuals contained much goodness. In the proper environment, Mencius argued, the best characteristics of the individual would strengthen and would benefit others.

Like Confucius, Mencius believed that rulers who governed according to strong moral and ethical guidelines would receive the willing support of their people. Mencius also believed that people had a right to rebel against weak or harsh rulers. He held that unjust rulers who oppressed their people surrendered their right to rule and should be overthrown, by force if necessary. Mencius's teachings, like those of Confucius, became part of China's classical tradition over time.

✔ **READING CHECK: Identifying a Point of View** What were Confucius's views on politics? *favored strong but moral government*

Daoism. At about the same time that Confucius lived and taught, another important Chinese philosophy appeared. According to legend, **Laozi** (LOWD·ZOO) founded the philosophy called Daoism (DOW·ih·zuhm). Daoism took its name from its central idea, the Dao, which is defined as "The Way." Laozi saw the Dao as an indescribable force that governed the universe and all of nature. He taught that people should withdraw from the world and contemplate nature. In this way, they could understand the Dao and live with it in harmony.

TEACH OBJECTIVES 3 and 4

LEVEL 3: Organize groups of three students with each taking one role: a Daoist, a Legalist, or a Confucian. Have them debate, in their roles, one of the following questions: (1) What should be the main goal in life? (2) Are people basically bad or good? (3) What is the best kind of government? After their discussion, ask members to describe their positions. Then have the class predict the consequences of following each philosophy.

COOPERATIVE LEARNING

HOMEWORK Present the class with the following situation: A weak, inefficient, and corrupt ruler is governing their country. Crime and disorder are rampant and a revolt is likely. Have students write the solutions a Confucian, a Daoist, and a Legalist might offer in this situation.

TEACH OBJECTIVE 4

LEVEL 2: Explain that a maxim is a saying that sets out a truth or rule of conduct. Then have pairs of students write a maxim for Buddhism with the purpose of attracting Chinese converts to the faith. Have pairs read their maxims to the class. Have the class discuss whether each maxim accurately represents Buddhism.

COOPERATIVE LEARNING

According to Laozi, people should not strive for material wealth. Unlike Confucius, Laozi shunned politics. He advised people not to seek power. Rather, they should work to bring themselves into harmony with the Dao by being humble, quiet, and thoughtful. This advice could be found in the **Dao De Jing,** a compilation of Laozi's teachings.

History Makers Speak

❝They know the world without even going out the door. They see the sky and its pattern without even looking out the window. The further out it goes, the less knowledge is; therefore sages know without going, name without seeing, complete without striving.❞

Laozi, from *Dao De Jing*

Daoism became second only to Confucianism in importance to Chinese life. The Daoist ideal appealed to many peasants because of its concern with natural forces. It appealed to many artists and poets because it valued the spontaneity and freedom of artistic expression. Daoism appealed to many Confucianists as well because it encouraged balance in life. Some Confucianists believed that concerning oneself only with education, politics, and social problems was frustrating and pointless. In the Daoist contemplation of nature, officials and rulers found a way to put the pressures of governing in perspective. Like yin and yang, Daoism and Confucianism provided balance to Chinese culture; each supplied what the other lacked.

✔ **READING CHECK: Finding the Main Idea** What were the main beliefs of the Daoists?
appreciation of nature, harmony, balance

Legalism and Buddhism

Like Confucianism, the school of Chinese philosophy called **Legalism** concerned itself with politics. It differed from Confucianism, however, in that Legalists believed in power—not virtue—and in harsh laws. In their view, people were by nature selfish and untrustworthy. Peace and prosperity could be achieved only by threatening severe punishment if people did not obey the laws. One Legalist philosopher noted,

Primary Source

❝Men have likes and dislikes; thus they can be controlled by means of rewards and punishments. . . . The ruler need only hold these handles [rewards and punishments] firmly, in order to maintain his supremacy. . . . Force is the stuff that keeps the masses in subjection [under control].❞

Han-fei-tzu, quoted in *Chinese Thought from Confucius to Mao Tse-tung*

Legalism in practice. The first Qin emperor, Cheng, followed the ideas of Legalism. He succeeded in creating a very powerful empire. His dynasty ruled, however, for only a very short period. Later Chinese philosophers claimed that the Qin dynasty failed because of its cruel methods.

The government of the Han dynasty accepted many of the Legalist principles of the Qin dynasty. Han rulers, however, also followed the more moderate principles of Confucianism. Many later scholars agreed that the Han dynasty possibly lasted so long because it achieved a balance between Legalism and Confucianism.

INTERPRETING THE VISUAL RECORD

Laozi Laozi and the Daoists believed that, left to itself, the universe would proceed along a harmonious course. *What conclusions might the creator of this sculpture have wanted viewers to draw about the character of Laozi?*

Government

Cheng ruled his state on the Legalist principles of reward and punishment. As Shang Yang, his adviser, put it: "To club together and keep your mouth shut is to be good; to be alienated from and spy on each other is to be a scoundrel. If you glorify the good, errors will be hidden; if you put scoundrels in charge, crime will be punished."

Critical Thinking

Ask students to describe what it might be like to live in a society based on Legalist principles.

ANSWER: Students' answers will vary, but they might include a concentration of power in the government, laws enforced by the threat of violence, and rewards given to encourage cooperation.

VISUAL RECORD ANSWER
He was in harmony with nature.

Technology Resources

World History Teaching Transparency: Geography and History 6: The Rise of Buddhism and Daoism

CLOSE

Have students work in groups to summarize the fundamental ideas of Confucianism, Daoism, or Legalism.

REVIEW

Have students complete the Section 4 Review on p. 92.

ASSESS

Have students complete Daily Quiz 4.4. As Alternative Assessment, you may want to use the Confucianism or maxim exercises in this section's lessons.

RETEACH

Have students complete Main Idea Activity for English Language Learners and Special-Needs Students 4.4. Then have students write one question and answer for each Chinese philosophy.
ENGLISH LANGUAGE LEARNERS

EXTEND

Have students use a problem-solving process to devise a plan of government for their community based on a Chinese philosophical tradition. **BLOCK SCHEDULING**

VISUAL RECORD ANSWER

charity and compassion

SECTION 4 REVIEW ANSWERS

❶ **Define**
- yin, p. 89
- yang, p. 89

❷ **Identify**
- Confucius, p. 90
- *Analects*, p. 90
- Laozi, p. 90
- *Dao De Jing*, p. 91
- Legalism, p. 91

❸ Legalism: power without moral virtue, people naturally selfish and untrustworthy; Daoism: people should withdraw from the world and contemplate nature; Buddhism: universal charity and compassion; Confucianism: importance of family, respect for elders, reverence for past and ancestors

❹ **a.** The government might have been corrupt and the people rebellious.

b. The turmoil caused philosophers to look for ways to restore harmony, which led to the development of their philosophies.

c. Its teachings, temples, and ceremonies offered a sense of comfort, tranquility, and a vision for dealing with worldly problems during turbulent times.

❺ Students' poems will vary but should demonstrate an understanding of Daoist belief.

INTERPRETING THE VISUAL RECORD

Buddhism Mahayana Buddhism emphasizes the heavenly qualities of the Buddha. The figure shown here is found in the Jade Buddha Temple in Shanghai. *What aspects of the Buddha's personality and teachings do these images emphasize?*

Buddhism in China. Buddhism was another great influence on Chinese thought and religious belief. Missionaries from India first brought Buddhism to China during the Han dynasty.

Throughout the later years of the dynasty, violence and lawlessness became increasingly common in many parts of China. Military leaders, competing with one another for power, led destructive raids through many areas of the once-peaceful land. The traditional Chinese emphasis upon order and family-centered security seemed to be threatened. When the Han dynasty finally fell, many Chinese, especially peasants, turned to Buddhism. They felt that the teachings of the Buddha helped to explain the widespread disruption that accompanied the Han collapse. They found comfort, as well, in the values that Buddhism championed. Buddhist temples and ceremonies offered a sense of peace and safety during turbulent times. In addition, Buddhism emphasized universal charity and compassion, ideals that Chinese philosophy had largely overlooked. The branch of Buddhism called Mahayana Buddhism became popular in China, Japan, and Korea. Mahayana Buddhists worship the Buddha as a savior. They believe that he is committed to helping all human beings escape from the miseries of the world.

The teachings of the Buddha, Confucius, Laozi, and the Legalists had a lasting effect on Chinese attitudes. Eventually the northern nomads established kingdoms and adopted Chinese ways. Buddhism, Confucianism, and Daoism provided moral and ethical guides to right living. They strongly influenced Chinese social ideals, attitudes, and individual and group behavior. The centralizing political ideas of Legalism provided a strong foundation for Chinese government. Confucianism, with reverence for the past and emphasis on the family, won the most followers. The Chinese also absorbed Daoist and Buddhist ideas regarding values such as contentment, justice, loyalty, obedience, and wisdom.

✔ **READING CHECK: Contrasting** In what major way did Legalism differ from the teachings of Confucius? believed in power without moral virtue

---

SECTION 4 REVIEW

1. **Define** and explain the significance:
   yin
   yang

2. **Identify** and explain the significance:
   Confucius
   Analects
   Laozi
   Dao De Jing
   Legalism

3. **Categorizing** Copy the web diagram below. Use it to illustrate the main concepts of Buddhism, Confucianism, Daoism, and Legalism.

Legalism		Daoism
Buddhism		Confucianism

4. **Finding the Main Idea**

   a. What might have happened had the rulers of the Han dynasty not included Confucian philosophy in their style of governing?

   b. How did the turmoil of the Zhou dynasty influence Confucianism and Daoism?

   c. What factors contributed to the increased popularity of Buddhism among Chinese peasants after the fall of the Han dynasty?

5. **Writing and Critical Thinking**

   Summarizing Write a poem that expresses a Daoist belief.
   Consider:
   - the meaning of the Dao
   - Daoist attitudes toward wealth and power
   - how Daoists sought to understand the Dao

Homework Practice Online

keyword: SP3 HP4

OBJECTIVES

1 Explain why the family was a central institution in Chinese society.

2 Describe how farmers lived in ancient China.

3 Identify the artistic and scientific achievements of the Chinese.

SECTION 5

Chinese Life and Culture

READ TO DISCOVER

❶ Why was the family a central institution in Chinese society?

❷ How did farmers live in ancient China?

❸ What did the Chinese achieve in the arts and sciences?

DEFINE

genealogy
acupuncture

IDENTIFY

Five Classics

WHY IT MATTERS TODAY

Ancient Chinese medical practices, including the use of herbs and acupuncture, have received attention in modern America. Use **CNNfyi.com** or other **current event** sources to gather information about the use of an ancient Chinese medical practice. Record your findings in your journal.

CNNfyi.com

The Main Idea
The family, farming, and educational pursuits for government officials marked daily life in China.

The Story Continues *"As Yin and Yang are not of the same nature, so man and woman have different characteristics,"* wrote a first-century Chinese woman named Ban Zhao. *"Man is honored for strength; a woman is beautiful on account of her gentleness. . . . The correct relationship is based upon harmony and . . . love is grounded in proper union."* This idea greatly influenced the Chinese approach to family life.

Family and Social Life

The ancient Chinese believed that the well-being of the state rested upon the well-being of the family. Values that governed family life included reverence for one's family, respect for age, and acceptance of decisions made by one's superiors. These values also shaped China's social and cultural life, including economics, education, literature, and science.

The family, not the individual, was the most important factor in Chinese society. Each upper-class family probably kept a careful **genealogy,** or record of its family tree. When family members died, they became honored ancestors. The Chinese expressed reverence for their ancestors as links between the family's past, present, and future. Most families constructed altars in honor of their ancestors.

Typically, an upper-class family included a father, his wife, sons with their wives and children, and unmarried daughters. Often all members of the family lived in the same house. The father ruled the family. He arranged his children's and his grandchildren's marriages. He decided how much education his sons would receive. He even chose his sons' careers.

Chinese women had fewer rights and powers than did men. They usually had no property rights of their own. On the other hand, Chinese society taught great respect for mothers and mothers-in-law. Within the household these women held much power. After she married, a young woman sometimes became almost a servant in the household of her husband's family. However, she became an important family figure after bearing children, especially sons.

✔ **READING CHECK: Comparing and Contrasting** What roles did men and women play in the family life of traditional China? men: ruled family, decided on marriages and careers; women: gained power by bearing children

INTERPRETING THE VISUAL RECORD

The ideal of the extended family was of great importance in ancient China. Traditional households often included parents, grandparents, children, and grandchildren.

Link to Today How does the modern Chinese family pictured here reflect the concept of "family" in traditional Chinese society?

TEACH OBJECTIVE 1

ALL LEVELS: Develop a list with the class that describes a typical family in ancient China. Then ask them to cite ways in which this family illustrates the philosophy of Confucianism. (*importance of family, respect for elders, members' acceptance and fulfillment of their roles*) **ENGLISH LANGUAGE LEARNERS**

TEACH OBJECTIVE 2

LEVEL 3: Organize the class into small groups to discuss how rural life in ancient China compares to rural life in the United States today. (*similarities: most people farmed, paid taxes, con-*

tended with nature; differences: most Chinese lived in rural areas, Chinese farmers lived in villages, often worked fields in common, had to perform public services) **COOPERATIVE LEARNING**

TEACH OBJECTIVES 3 and 4

LEVEL 1: Have students draw a chart listing Chinese achievements in the arts and sciences. **ENGLISH LANGUAGE LEARNERS**

Artistic Achievements	Scientific Achievements
Book of Poems	*astronomy*
Book of History	*seismography*

Daily Life

Grass fibers, hemp, and silk were the most common fabrics in use during the Han dynasty. While few examples of hemp cloth exist today, historians assume that the majority of the population used hemp or other fibers for clothes. Silk was very expensive and is known to have been used for imperial robes.

Critical Thinking

Ask students to suggest reasons why soldiers' uniforms might have been made from a luxury fabric like silk.

ANSWER: Students might suggest that soldiers can be considered representatives of the government, and silk uniforms would emphasize the wealth and power of the state.

LINK TO TODAY ANSWER

The design is similar to an ancient Chinese junk.

INTERPRETING THE VISUAL RECORD

Junks The early Chinese used sailboats called junks to trade throughout East Asia. The basic design of junks that sail China's rivers and coastlines today has changed little from the design of ancient Chinese junks.

Link to Today In what way does the junk pictured here reflect the importance of tradition in Chinese culture?

Analyzing Primary Sources

Finding the Main Idea What does this poem reveal about ancient Chinese courtship practices? men courted women, not vice versa

The Economy

Although Chinese towns grew in size and number, most Chinese people lived as small village farmers. Farm life was difficult. A group of families might work fields in common, using ox-drawn plows and complex systems of irrigation and flood control. If too much or too little rain fell, crops could be ruined. Also, the government required peasants to pay taxes and to perform labor on canals, roads, and other local construction projects.

Trade was not an important factor in the economy of earliest China. Trade and commerce grew quickly, however, during the Qin dynasty. Qin leaders brought many important reforms to China's economy. They standardized the currency and the system of weights and measures. Trade also increased during the Han dynasty when the Silk Road linked China with the Mediterranean region.

✔ **READING CHECK: Categorizing** What reforms helped to encourage the growth of trade during the Qin dynasty? Qin standardized currency, weights, and measures

Arts and Sciences

The Chinese education system relied upon a small number of texts to train scholars and civil servants, who tended to be dedicated and reliable. By using these books, the system emphasized respect for tradition. At the same time, the use of the same books created a common culture all across China.

The Five Classics. The texts used to train scholars and civil servants in ancient China were known as the **Five Classics.** We do not know who wrote these works or exactly when they were written. We do know, however, that they had started to become important in the time of the Zhou dynasty. The *Book of Poems* contains more than 300 songs about domestic life, joy, love, and politics. For example, the second poem of the collection is about courtship.

Primary Source

> **"Plop fall the plums; but there are still seven.**
> **Let those gentlemen who would court me**
> **Come while it is still lucky!**
> **Plop fall the plums; there are still three.**
> **Let any gentleman who would court me**
> **Come before it is too late!**
> **Plop fall the plums; in shallow baskets we lay them.**
> **Any gentleman who would court me**
> **Had better speak while there is time."**

The *Book of Poems*, from *An Anthology of Chinese Literature*

The *Book of History* contains speeches and documents about government. The *Book of Changes* is about the art of predicting the future. The *Spring and Autumn Annals* is a record of events in the city-state of Lu from 722 B.C. to 481 B.C. The *Book of Rites* deals with manners and ceremonies. Study of the Five Classics became essential for every well-educated young man in China, along with the *Analects* of Confucius.

HOMEWORK Review China's accomplishments under the Shan, Zhou, Qin, and Han rulers. Then have students write an answer to the following question: How did strong rulers encourage the development of Chinese civilization?

CLOSE

Ask students to list some of the major Chinese contributions to science, technology, and math.

REVIEW

Have students complete the Section 5 Review on p. 95.

ASSESS

Have students complete Daily Quiz 4.5. As Alternative Assessment, you may use the family exercises in this section's lessons.

RETEACH

Have students complete Main Idea Activity for English Language Learners and Special-Needs Students 4.5. Ask students to list the main ideas of each heading. **ENGLISH LANGUAGE LEARNERS**

EXTEND

Have students find out about ancient Chinese achievements in science and technology. **BLOCK SCHEDULING**

Science and technology. Education was available only to a privileged few in ancient China. However, the Qin and Han periods still saw dramatic developments in science and technology. Early Chinese astronomers learned that the year was slightly longer than 365 days. Han dynasty astronomers further refined these calculations. In 28 B.C. astronomers in China first observed sunspots; Europeans did not make similar observations until the A.D. 1600s. Sometime before A.D. 100 Chinese astronomers built instruments to track the movements of planets.

The Chinese invented a seismograph that registered even the faintest of earthquakes. They also invented paper, which was first produced in about 150 B.C. The earliest paper was made from fishing nets, hemp, old rags, and tree bark. By the middle of the A.D. 700s, the use of paper had spread throughout Central Asia and the Middle East, where it replaced papyrus as the main writing material. The Chinese also invented the sundial, the water clock, and the process of printing.

Chinese scholars, especially the Daoists, were very interested in chemistry. They discovered substances for dyeing cloth and glazing pottery. They also developed medicines based on herbs and minerals. Perhaps the most widely known Chinese contribution to medicine is the therapy known as **acupuncture.** Its development stemmed from the Daoist belief that good health depends on the movement of a life-force energy through the body. Illness or pain results when something interferes with that movement.

In acupuncture the doctor inserts needles into certain points of the body to enable the life-force energy to move properly. Some modern researchers believe that these needle insertion points may have less electrical resistance than other parts of the body and thus may affect the nervous system. Today the Chinese use acupuncture as an anesthetic in many types of surgery. Many Americans use it to relieve pains from ailments such as arthritis or cancer.

✔ **READING CHECK: Contrasting** In what areas did Chinese scientists of ancient times surpass their European counterparts? astronomy, seismography, clocks, paper-making, and printing

This device, developed in A.D. 132, warned of earthquakes. Ground tremors would cause metal balls to drop from the dragons' mouths to the frogs below.

SECTION 5 REVIEW

1. **Define** and explain the significance:
   genealogy
   acupuncture

2. **Identify** and explain the significance:
   Five Classics

3. **Making Generalizations** Copy the chart below. Use it to illustrate the different roles of men, women, and children in the Chinese family.

   | Male Family Members | Female Family Members |

Finding the Main Idea

4.
a. What effect did Chinese philosophy have on Chinese medicine?
b. How might the limited role of trade in ancient China have affected the development of Chinese culture?

Writing and Critical Thinking

5.
Evaluating Write a brief report that evaluates the different aspects of family life in ancient China.
Consider:
• the importance of family to the Chinese
• respect paid to various family members
• the roles of men and women in the traditional families of ancient China

Homework Practice Online
keyword: SP3 HP4

SECTION 5 REVIEW ANSWERS

❶ **Define**
• genealogy, p. 93
• acupuncture, p. 95

❷ **Identify**
• Five Classics, p. 94

❸ males: ruled family, decided on marriages and careers; females: fewer rights and powers, gained power by bearing children

❹ a. Acupuncture was developed because of the Daoist belief that good health depends on the movement of a life-force energy through the body.

b. It may have caused China to be fairly culturally isolated.

❺ Students' reports will vary but should discuss the Chinese family, respect, and the roles of men and women.

CHAPTER 4

REVIEW AND ASSESSMENT RESOURCES

REPRODUCIBLE RESOURCES

▶ Vocabulary Activity 4

TECHNOLOGY RESOURCES

▶ Chapter 4 Test Generator (on the One-Stop Planner)
▶ Global Skill Builder CD–ROM
▶ HRW Web Site

REINFORCEMENT, REVIEW, and ASSESSMENT

▶ Chapter 4 Review, pp. 96–97
▶ Chapter 4 Tutorial for Students, Parents, Mentors, and Peers
▶ Chapter 4 Test (Form A or B)
▶ Alternative Assessment Handbook
▶ Chapter 4 Test for English Language Learners and Special-Needs Students

REVIEW

Have students complete the Chapter 4 Review on pages 96–97.

ASSESS

Use one of the chapter tests to assess students' understanding of the content. For Alternative Assessment, see the Portfolio Activities and Alternative Assessment Handbook.

CHAPTER 4 REVIEW ANSWERS

Understanding Main Ideas

1. problems: flooding; benefits: fertile soil

2. great distances, rugged mountains, harsh deserts

3. combination of animism and animal worship; belief in Shangdi; interpretation of oracle bones

4. consists of ideographs

5. fought among themselves; attacked by outsiders

6. civil service system, leveling, peace

7. Everything in the world results from a balance between two forces, yin and yang.

8. power without virtue; harsh laws

9. discoveries in astronomy, inventions, chemistry, medicine, acupuncture

Reviewing Themes

1. Great distances, rugged mountains, and harsh deserts isolated China geographically.

2. Some of the dynasties collapsed because of attacks from outsiders.

3. They were more moderate rulers than their predecessors.

CHAPTER 4 Review

Creating a Time Line

Copy the time line below onto a sheet of paper. Complete the time line by filling in the events, individuals, and dates from the chapter that you think were significant. Pick three events and explain why you think they were significant.

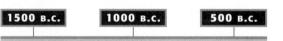

| 1500 B.C. | 1000 B.C. | 500 B.C. |

Writing a Summary

Using standard grammar, spelling, sentence structure, and punctuation, write an overview of the events in the chapter.

Identifying People and Ideas

Identify the following terms or individuals and explain their significance:

1. loess
2. dike
3. animism
4. calligraphy
5. Cheng

6. Liu Ch'e
7. Confucius
8. *Dao De Jing*
9. Five Classics
10. acupuncture

Understanding Main Ideas

Section 1 *(pp. 76–79)*

Geographic and Cultural Influences

1. What problems and benefits did the Huang River bring to the Chinese people?

2. What geographic features contributed to Chinese isolation?

Section 2 *(pp. 80–83)*

The Shang Dynasty

3. What were the main features of Shang religious beliefs?

4. How is Chinese writing different from the Western alphabet?

Section 3 *(pp. 84–88)*

The Zhou, Qin, and Han Dynasties

5. Why did the Zhou dynasty collapse?

6. What were the main achievements of Han emperor Liu Ch'e?

Section 4 *(pp. 89–92)*

Philosophies of Ancient China

7. What was the ancient Chinese belief concerning the dualism of nature?

8. What did the Legalists teach?

Section 5 *(pp. 93–95)*

Chinese Life and Culture

9. What did the ancient Chinese achieve in science and technology?

Reviewing Themes

1. Culture Why did Chinese culture develop in isolation?

2. Global Relations What effect did foreign peoples have on the success or failure of Chinese dynasties?

3. Government Why were Liu Ch'e and other Han dynasty rulers more effective than earlier Chinese rulers?

Thinking Critically

1. Analyzing Information How did the idea of the Mandate of Heaven influence Chinese government?

2. Contrasting How did the teachings of Confucius differ from those of Laozi?

3. Evaluating How did the geography of China affect the governments and dynasties in the region?

4. Drawing Conclusions How did literature shape Chinese thought and education?

Writing About History

Summarizing Write a report summarizing the similarities and differences between the Zhou, Qin, and Han dynasties. Use the chart below to organize your thoughts before writing.

	Zhou	Qin	Han
Period of rule			
Achievements			
Causes of decline			

CLOSE

Ask students which dynasty—the Zhou, the Qin, or the Han—did the most to advance Chinese culture. Have each student write a short paragraph that gives evidence to support his or her response.

RETEACH

Organize students who had difficulty with the test into five small groups. Have each group use correct social studies terminology to answer the Read to Discover questions in one section. Have students take the Form B Test to assess their mastery of the material.

ENGLISH LANGUAGE LEARNERS

Portfolio Extensions

1. Have students choose one of the three main Chinese philosophical traditions—Confucianism, Daoism, or Legalism—learn more about it, and use a decision-making process to devise a plan of student government for their school that is based on the tenets of this philosophy.

2. Have students use the process of historical inquiry to research pictures of bronze items from the Shang dynasty. Ask them to study the pictures to determine the religious functions and the aesthetic value of the bronzes. Have them write a report that describes their findings.

3. Have students use media and news services to find out about philosophies and beliefs in China today. Have them report on the similarities and differences between ancient and modern Chinese culture.

Building Social Studies Skills

Reading a Chart

Study the chart below. Then answer the questions that follow.

Chinese Dynasty	When	Achievements
Shang	c. 1750 B.C.–1122 B.C.	Calendar, astronomy, writing
Zhou	c. 1050 B.C.–c. 256 B.C.	Copper coins, iron tools, canals, dikes, reservoirs
Qin	c. 221 B.C.–c. 206 B.C.	Standard weights, measures, and coins, uniform writing system
Han	c. 206 B.C.–A.D. 220	Civil service system, paper

1. Which statement correctly describes a relationship shown on the chart?
   a. The Shang Dynasty did not last as long as the Han Dynasty.
   b. Iron tools came into use before the calendar.
   c. Although writing began before 1100 B.C., paper was not invented until more than 900 years later.
   d. The Zhou Dynasty adopted the uniform writing system developed during the Qin Dynasty.

2. In your opinion, which dynasty made the most important contributions? Give specific reasons for your choice.

Making Generalizations

Read the excerpt from the *Analects* by Confucius. Then answer the questions that follow.

> "If you govern the people by laws, and keep them in order by penalties, they will avoid the penalties, yet lose their sense of shame. But if you govern them by your moral excellence, and keep them in order by your dutiful conduct, they will retain their sense of shame, and also live up to this standard [that is, to the ruler's standard of moral excellence and dutiful conduct]."

3. Which of the following is the best general statement of the ideas in this excerpt?
   a. A ruler should lead by example.
   b. People should lose their sense of shame.
   c. Laws are not necessary to keep order.
   d. A ruler should be moral.
   e. A ruler should impose harsh laws and strict penalties to maintain order.
   f. A ruler's conduct has little or no real impact on the behavior of the people.

4. In your opinion, what would be the effect on a society if a ruler did what Confucius suggested in this excerpt? Give examples.

Alternative Assessment

Building Your Portfolio

Culture

Chinese philosophy and religion remain an important influence on thought today. Using your textbook and other sources, compile a list of different Chinese philosophies and beliefs. Then prepare a pamphlet that illustrates the philosophical and religious ideas that you have studied.

internet connect

Internet Activity: go.hrw.com
KEYWORD: SP3 WH4

Choose a topic on Ancient Chinese Civilization to:
• compare and contrast Western, Arabic, and Chinese calligraphy.
• research the Qin dynasty and create a brochure on the Great Wall.
• write a report on Chinese philosophy or Chinese contributions to science.

Thinking Critically

1. Rulers believed that the gods determined who should rule.

2. Unlike Confucius, Laozi shunned politics and advised people not to seek power.

3. Isolation from India and the West caused the government to develop independently; proximity to neighboring states resulted in attack from outsiders and the fall of some dynasties.

4. The educational system emphasized respect for tradition and created a common culture.

Writing About History

Students' reports should include the information that follows. Zhou: c. 1050–256 B.C.; Mandate of Heaven; internal fighting, outside attack; Qin: 221–206 B.C.; autocracy, defensive walls; people's revolt; Han: 206 B.C.–A.D. 220; civil service system, leveling, peace; attack from nomads

Building Social Studies Skills

1. c

2. Students' answers should demonstrate knowledge of contributions and logical reasoning.

3. a

4. Students' answers will vary.

Building Your Portfolio

Students' pamphlets should include a discussion of Confucianism, Daoism, Legalism, and Buddhism.

Spotlight on LITERATURE

Cultural epics originated as oral traditions. During ancient times, aristocratic families would recite the heroic deeds of their ancestors. In Japan, families of reciters known as *katari-be* handed down myths and legends by word of mouth. As more people became literate, oral epics were transferred to written form. Have students research the history of a cultural epic.

Spotlight on LITERATURE

The universal themes expressed in the *Epic of Gilgamesh* (c. 3000 B.C.) and the *Ramayana* (c. 300 B.C.) have made these epics meaningful far beyond the historical periods that produced them. For example, the *Odyssey*, written in the 900s or 800s B.C., contains many parallels with the *Epic of Gilgamesh*. Today, the Ramayana continues to be very popular in India, and recitation of the poem is considered an honored accomplishment. Have students research the literary and/or cultural influence of either the *Epic of Gilgamesh* or the Ramayana. Ask them to find modern references to the epics if possible.

Daily Life

After his friend Enkidu dies, Gilgamesh, in the *Epic of Gilgamesh,* wanders through the wilderness searching for immortality. Gilgamesh is told several times that it is no use trying to avoid death–everyone must die sooner or later. He is advised to live his life to the fullest–to eat well, to care for himself, and to enjoy life. This advice reflects the culture's live-for-the-day attitude. Mesopotamians did not believe in life after death. In contrast, the Hindu epic, the Ramayana, tells of Sita freely giving herself over to death to prove her love and faithfulness to her husband.

Critical Thinking

Why do you think Sita was able to die so willingly?

ANSWER: Students might suggest that the Hindu belief in reincarnation allowed Sita to die; knowing that she was innocent, she believed that she would come back to earth with a higher status.

UNDERSTANDING LITERATURE ANSWER

Answers will vary. Students might cite, "Then Gilgamesh wept some more for his dead friend," as expressing the value of friendship; or, "For that moment, everywhere in the whole universe, there was harmony," from the Ramayana, as showing how important peace, even for a moment, is in Hindu culture.

CROSS-CULTURAL CONNECTIONS *Literature*

Ancient Worldviews

Cultural epics are ancient stories—often myths or legends—that describe and explain a culture's origins and that shape its values. They help to express a culture's view of life and the world, and they emphasize the culture's most basic ideals. The Babylonian cultural epic, The Epic of Gilgamesh, *describes how early Mesopotamians viewed such concepts as loyalty, friendship, and death. These same theses are echoed in different ways in the Ramayana, one of ancient India's great cultural epics.*

Stone relief of Gilgamesh between two gods

The Epic of Gilgamesh

[Enkidu] is the friend who, wild heart for wild heart, will equal you and be your second self, to guard your back in battle and in peace sit by your side; to laugh when you laugh and to share your grief. He will not forsake you. . . .

[Following Enkidu's tragic death]. . . Gilgamesh wept . . . for his dead friend. He wandered over barren hills, mumbling to his own spirit: "Will you too die as Enkidu did? Will grief become your food? Will we both fear the lonely hills, so vacant? I now race from place to place, dissatisfied with wherever I am . . .

As if in sleep I come upon the mountain door at midnight where I face wild-eyed lions, and I am afraid. Then to Sin, the god of mighty light, I raise my solemn chant to beg: 'Save me, please, my god.' " [He] wandered through the woods so like a savage beast just then did he bring death again and again upon the lions' heads with an ax he drew from off his belt.

The Ramayana

[A trusted friend tells Sita,] "All the universe is a sign to be read rightly. War and peace, love and separation/ Are hidden gateways we must pass [through]/ To reach other worlds. Let us not grow old thinking that truth Is what most people see or say it is."

. . . This world is like a breath on a mirror. It does not last. Have patience.

. . . Sita approached Rama and said, "Let me prove my innocence before you/ Once and for all."

. . . Then Sita took a step back and said, "Mother earth, if I have been faithful to my husband,/ Take me home." . . . The ground rolled and moved/ Beneath Sita. With a great noise/ The ground opened and took Sita back.

. . . For that moment, everywhere in the whole universe,/ There was harmony.

Scene from the Ramayana

Understanding Literature

Explain how a cultural epic expresses the values and worldview of its culture, using examples from *The Epic of Gilgamesh* and the Ramayana.

Science, Technology & Society

Copy the following graphic organizer on the board. Ask students to work together in pairs, using their textbooks and other available resources, to fill in the graphic organizer with examples, including the appropriate dynasty. *(Possible answers include math—calendar [Shang], economic "leveling" [Han]; science—paper [Han]; technology—irrigation and flood control [Shang], sophisticated bronzework [Shang], defensive walls [Qin])*

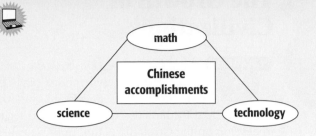

BUILDING YOUR Portfolio

Science, Technology & Society

Social scientists learn much about ancient civilizations by studying the artifacts—or material remains— they have left behind. In many cases, works of art are especially useful in helping researchers to understand what an early civilization was like during a particular time. Imagine that you are an ancient Chinese artist. Your task is to create a series of line drawings or paintings meant to illustrate Chinese discoveries in math, science, and technology, especially ones that came to affect later cultures. What kinds of images would you show, and what would they reveal about life in China?

Han dynasty line painting

Egyptian tools, shards, and weapons, dating from Old or Middle Kingdom dynasties

Culture

To find out how ancient civilizations such Egypt interacted with other cultures, scientists often pose and answer questions from information revealed on maps, graphs, charts, models, and databases. Write a series of questions about geographic distribution and patterns that a scientist might pose about early Egyptian culture. Then, using resources on the bibliography below, as well as any maps, graphs, charts, models, or databases referenced in this unit, record any answers to your questions that you find.

Further Reading

Dersin, Denise, ed. *What Life Was Like: On the Banks of the Nile, Egypt 3050–30 B.C.* Alexandria, Virginia: Time-Life Books, 1999. A survey of daily life in ancient Egypt.

Gowlett, John A. *Ascent to Civilization: The Archaeology of Early Humans.* New York: McGraw-Hill, 1993. An overview of historical developments in the art, agriculture, and technology of early humans.

Oliphant, Margaret. *The Atlas of the Ancient World: Charting the Great Civilizations of the Past.* New York: Simon and Schuster, 1992. A comprehensive and descriptive overview of nine ancient world civilizations.

Starr, Chester G. *A History of the Ancient World.* New York: Oxford University Press, 1991. A survey of Chinese, Indian, Greek, and Mesopotamian cultures.

🖳 internet connect

Internet Activity
KEYWORD: SP3 U1

In assigned groups, develop a multimedia presentation about early people and civilizations between about 3,700,000 B.C. and A.D. 589. Choose information from the chapter Internet Connect activities and the Holt Researcher that best reflects the major topics of the period. Write an outline and a script for your presentation, which may be shown to the class.

go hrw .com

Culture

Ask students to research geographic distributions during one period in ancient Egyptian history. Have them create a thematic map that illustrates their research findings. Have students present their maps to the class and explain the physical and human characteristics of their chosen period.

Interdisciplinary Connection

ARCHAEOLOGY. In 1968 archaeologists excavated the tomb of Liu Sheng, who was king of Zhongshan province during the Han dynasty. The more than 2,800 objects in Liu Sheng's tomb offer clues into his luxurious lifestyle. Members of the Liu family—ancestors of the Han emperors—were often buried with full-body jade coverings. For Liu Sheng's body, 2,498 small plaques of the precious stone were sewn together with gold wire and his head was placed on an elaborate headrest of gilt bronze with jade inlay. The Han believed jade's durable properties could be transferred to humans to ensure immortality.

Critical Thinking

Ask students why the Han might have buried family members in jade shrouds.

ANSWER: The shroud may have been an immortal replacement of Liu Sheng's body, or a type of "armor" to protect him from evil spirits.

EXAMINING THE VISUAL RECORD

❶ What is the main architectural element of the building in the center of the painting?

ANSWER: marble columns

Marble columns support the roof of the Temple of Castor and Pollux in the Roman Forum. The Greeks had three styles for the capital, or top, of their columns: Doric (see Parthenon, page 130), Ionic (see Temple of Saturn, page 152), and Corinthian (this temple). The Romans added another style—Composite—that combined the curved corners of the Ionic with the leaf designs of the Corinthian. These styles of columns are still used in classical or Neoclassical architecture today.

❷ What architectural element did the designers use in the building to the right of the Temple of Castor and Pollux?

ANSWER: arches

The Romans' greatest contribution to architecture was perfecting the use of the arch. This marble building, the Basilica Julia, housed the civil courts. The U.S. Capitol, with its columns and arches, has many elements from Greco-Roman buildings.

ACTIVITY: Ask students to use primary and secondary sources, including computer software, to identify public buildings in the United States and around the world that have examples of columns and arches in their designs.

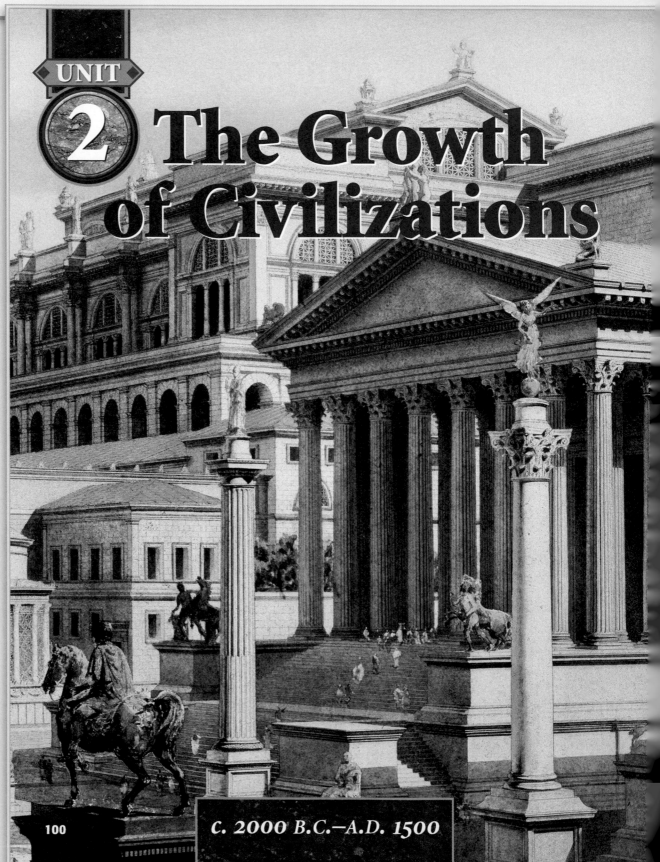

UNIT 2 The Growth of Civilizations

c. 2000 B.C.–A.D. 1500

empire, Rome's power spread throughout the Mediterranean and into northern Europe. Christianity spread throughout the empire and became the leading religion. In the late A.D. 400s, internal problems and invasions from Germanic tribes caused the decline and collapse of the Roman Empire in the West.

CHAPTER 8 Africa

Trading kingdoms of Kush and Aksum grew in the interior of eastern Africa. Swahili-speaking city-states developed on the East Coast. The Shona people of Great Zimbabwe controlled the gold trade. Control of the salt-for-gold trade in West Africa resulted in the rise and fall of the kingdoms of Ghana, Mali, and Songhai.

CHAPTER 9 The Americas

People began migrating from Asia to the Americas about 50,000 years ago. In North America many different cultures developed because of the variety of geography and climate. The Maya and the Aztecs developed advanced cultures in Mesoamerica, and the Incas controlled much of Andean South America.

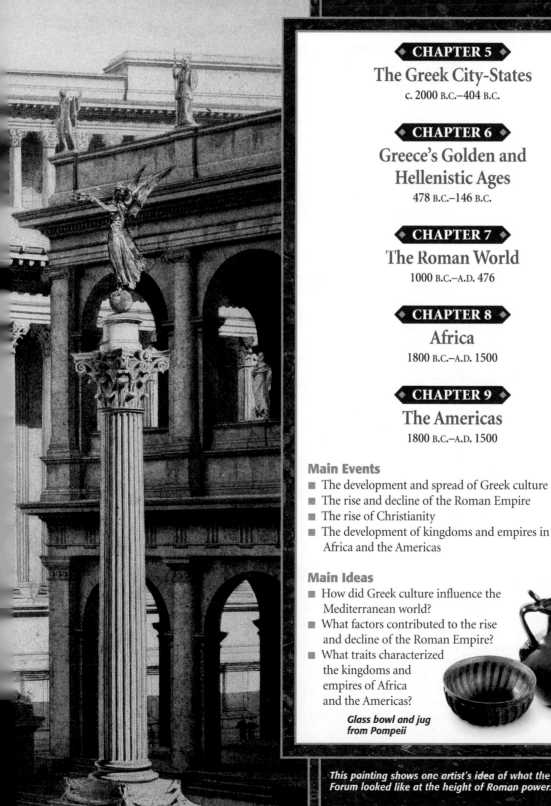

◆ CHAPTER 5 ◆
The Greek City-States
c. 2000 B.C.–404 B.C.

◆ CHAPTER 6 ◆
Greece's Golden and Hellenistic Ages
478 B.C.–146 B.C.

◆ CHAPTER 7 ◆
The Roman World
1000 B.C.–A.D. 476

◆ CHAPTER 8 ◆
Africa
1800 B.C.–A.D. 1500

◆ CHAPTER 9 ◆
The Americas
1800 B.C.–A.D. 1500

Main Events
- The development and spread of Greek culture
- The rise and decline of the Roman Empire
- The rise of Christianity
- The development of kingdoms and empires in Africa and the Americas

Main Ideas
- How did Greek culture influence the Mediterranean world?
- What factors contributed to the rise and decline of the Roman Empire?
- What traits characterized the kingdoms and empires of Africa and the Americas?

Glass bowl and jug from Pompeii

This painting shows one artist's idea of what the Forum looked like at the height of Roman power. **101**

CROSS-CULTURAL CONNECTIONS

Focus On Government

📡 LET'S GET STARTED!

As students enter the classroom, ask them to write definitions of *democracy* and *republic*. Have students keep their definitions to revise as they read Cross-Cultural Connections. Tell students that in this unit they will learn how democratic-republican government began in classical Greece and Rome. In later units they will trace the process by which this kind of government evolved in England and during the Enlightenment.

TEACH

 ALL LEVELS: Help students fill in the chart below with information about these governments.

ENGLISH LANGUAGE LEARNERS

	Athens	Rome	Kush	Maya
Government/ Dates	Democracy 570–322 B.C.	Republic 509–27 B.C.	Monarchy 250 B.C.– A.D. 150	Monarchy A.D. 250–900
Who ruled	all male citizens	elected officials	king or queen	kings helped by military
Power of women	none	none	queens	none

Daily Life

The toga, a distinctive white-woolen cloth garment, could be worn only by Romans. During early Roman times before the use of military uniforms, the toga was worn into battle. Men, boys, and girls wore togas. When girls married, they turned in their togas for the stola, the dress of a married woman.

Members of the upper classes and later emperors wore white togas. The lower classes wore dark colors. Colored stripes on togas symbolized various offices. A broad purple stripe was woven into the front of senators' togas. Generals wore togas with a red stripe and gold embroidery to special ceremonies. Eventually, only emperors could wear that special toga.

Critical Thinking

Compare how the use of stripes on a toga in Rome and on a U.S. military uniform reflect social and political order.

ANSWER: The colored stripes on a toga showed a man's position of power. In the same way, the number of stripes on a military uniform indicates a position of authority.

CROSS-CULTURAL CONNECTIONS

Focus On: Government

Main Idea Who participated in government? Within the great city-states and empires of early history, levels of public participation in government varied. Some societies were led exclusively by kings and queens, others by small groups of wealthy men. Some experimented with democracy, helping lay the foundation for the democratic systems we enjoy today.

Greece — The Americas — Africa — Rome

2000 B.C. 1800 B.C. 1000 B.C. 146 B.C. A.D. 476 A.D. 1500

Greece, c. 2000 B.C.–146 B.C.

Democracy in Athens This stone carving shows Democracy, represented by a woman, crowning the people of Athens. From about 570 B.C. to 322 B.C. Athens ruled itself as a democracy. All full citizens had an equal vote in the assembly, regardless of their wealth or education. Not everyone was a citizen, however. It is estimated that at its height, Athens had approximately 50,000 full citizens out of a population of about 350,000 people. To be a full citizen you had to be a male over the age of 18 born of a citizen family.

The Roman Republic In 509 B.C. wealthy Roman landowners overthrew the king and established a republic. In a republic, voters elect officials to run the government. As in Greece, only adult male citizens could vote. Unlike in Greece, however, a person did not have to be born into a citizen family to become a citizen. Even the sons of freed slaves became citizens. Nevertheless, the first ordinary citizen was not elected to the government until 409 B.C. Even after this date, the Senate and other key parts of Rome's government remained firmly in the hands of the wealthiest members of society. This image shows the Roman Senate.

Rome, 1000 B.C.–A.D. 476

REVIEW

Have students review the information about the different groups that participated in government in Athens, Rome, Kush, and the Maya Empire. Ask them to use standard grammar, spelling, sentence structure, and punctuation to answer the question in "Why It Matters Today" and to share their answers with the class.

ASSESS

Have students complete their answer to the question in "Why It Matters Today" and add it to their portfolio. As Alternative Assessment, you may want to use the chart exercise in this lesson.

EXTEND

Have students work in groups of three or four to propose a new student government for their school. Tell students to use information from their textbooks, the library, computer software, and any other available resources to determine the structure of the government and who will participate directly and indirectly in it. Allow time for students to demonstrate how their various governments would work. **BLOCK SCHEDULING, COOPERATIVE LEARNING**

The Kingdom of Kush   Located south of Egypt, the wealthy African trading kingdom of Kush reached its height between about 250 B.C. and A.D. 150. Kush patterned its government after that of the Egyptians, who were ruled by a powerful royal family. There were key differences, though. The kings and queens of Kush were not all-powerful. Rather than make laws, they followed and enforced laws established by priests. Also, when one king died, his son did not automatically inherit the throne. New monarchs were elected from among the royal family. Because the royal family traced its heritage through women and elected its rulers, more queens (like the one pictured here) ruled Kush than any other major early civilization.

Africa, 1800 B.C.–A.D. 1500

The Americas, c. 1800 B.C.–A.D. 1500

The Maya   The Yucatán Peninsula was home to the great city-states of the Maya. During the Classic Period (c. A.D. 250–A.D. 900), kings ruled the Maya with assistance from military leaders and royal priests. The empire was divided into provinces, each ruled by a governor chosen from among four royal families. The governors were all-powerful, running their provinces like mini-kingdoms. Below the governors were leaders of small towns and provinces. These leaders were not members of the royal family; they were usually members of the society who had distinguished themselves somehow. The stone temple relief to the left, dating from c. A.D. 725, shows a possibly mythical Mayan ruler and his wife.

Mayan plate from A.D. 900–A.D. 1500

Why It Matters Today

Today most countries practice some form of democracy. In the United States, almost all adult citizens are allowed to vote, regardless of income, gender, or race. **How does our system of government today compare to those of ancient Greece, Rome, Africa, and the Americas?**

History Maker

PACEL. Pacel, one of the greatest Mayan leaders, ruled the city of Palenque from A.D. 615 to 683. At the age of 12, he inherited his throne from his mother, Lady Zac-Kuk. One of Pacel's important contributions was construction of the Temple of the Inscriptions. Its corridors displayed lists of the past kings and their reigns. Some scholars think that Lady Zac-Kuk held actual power until her death in 640 because Pacel did not commission inscriptions relating to his rule until after her death.

Critical Thinking

How did scholars use information from the Temple of Inscriptions to interpret Mayan political history?

ANSWER: Students might suggest that scholars could trace Mayan history through the list of kings and infer that Lady Zac-Kuk held power until her death.

WHY IT MATTERS TODAY ANSWER

Answers will vary but might include that New England town meetings are somewhat like the Assembly in Athens; that the U.S. Senate and state senates are based on the Roman Senate; that the way U.S. presidents are elected and the way they carry out laws made by Congress is similar to the government in Kush; and that the levels of U.S. government show some similarity to the levels of government of Mayan city-states.

The Greek City-States

CHAPTER RESOURCE MANAGER

	Objectives	Pacing Guide	Reproducible Resources
SECTION 1 **Early Greeks and the Rise of City-States** (pp. 106–109)	• Analyze the role that geography played in early Greek history. • Explain the influence that Minoan and Mycenaean civilizations had on Greek civilization. • Describe the development of the Greek city-states.	**Regular** 1.5 day / **Block Scheduling** 1 day *Block Scheduling Handbook with Team Teaching Strategies, 5.1*	**RS** Guided Reading Strategy 5.1 **E** Hands-on History Activity 5: The Greek City-States
SECTION 2 **Greek Government and Society** (pp. 110–112)	• Explain the importance of Homer's works. • Identify major religious beliefs and practices of the ancient Greeks. • Describe changes that occurred in the governments of the Greek city-states.	**Regular** 1.5 day / **Block Scheduling** 1 day *Block Scheduling Handbook with Team Teaching Strategies, 5.2*	**RS** Guided Reading Strategy 5.2 **RS** Graphic Organizer Activity 5 **PS** Readings in World History 17
SECTION 3 **Sparta and Athens** (pp. 113–117)	• Analyze the society of Sparta. • Explain the development of democracy in Athens.	**Regular** 1.5 day / **Block Scheduling** 1 day *Block Scheduling Handbook with Team Teaching Strategies, 5.3*	**RS** Guided Reading Strategy 5.3 **PS** Readings in World History 18: The Making of Spartan Soldiers **PS** Readings in World History 19: A Plea for Eunomy
SECTION 4 **Daily Life in Athens** (pp. 118–120)	• Explain the basis of Athens's economy. • Describe the family life and education in Athens.	**Regular** 1.5 day / **Block Scheduling** 1 day *Block Scheduling Handbook with Team Teaching Strategies, 5.4*	**RS** Guided Reading Strategy 5.4 **E** Creative Teaching Strategy 5: Athens Today!
SECTION 5 **The Expansion of Greece** (pp. 121–125)	• Explain how the Persian Wars began and what the results of those wars were. • Analyze the effects of Pericles's leadership on Athens. • Explain how the Peloponnesian War began and its results.	**Regular** 1.5 day / **Block Scheduling** 1 day *Block Scheduling Handbook with Team Teaching Strategies, 5.5*	**RS** Guided Reading Strategy 5.5 **SM** Geography Activity 5: Greek Alliances **PS** Readings in World History 20: The Greatness of Athens

Chapter Resource Key

PS	Primary Sources	**A**	Assessment	🎵	Music
RS	Reading Support	**REV**	Review	📼	Video
IC	Interdisciplinary Connections	**ELL**	Reinforcement and English Language Learners	🌐	Internet
E	Enrichment			💻	Holt Presentation Maker Using Microsoft® PowerPoint®
SM	Skills Mastery	📄	Transparencies		
		💿	CD–ROM		

One-Stop Planner CD-ROM

See the *One–Stop Planner* for a complete list of additional resources for students and teachers.

One-Stop Planner CD-ROM

It's easy to plan lessons, select resources, and print out materials for your students when you use the **One-Stop Planner CD–ROM with Test Generator.**

Technology Resources

- One-Stop Planner 5.1
- CNN. Presents World Cultures: Yesterday and Today Segment 5: Crete: Past and Present
- Homework Practice Online
- Online Maps, Charts, and Graphs: Turmoil in the Aegean Lands, c. 1250–1100 B.C.

- One-Stop Planner 5.2
- Holt Researcher: World History: Homer
- World History Teaching Transparency: Art and History 3: Dipylonvase
- Homework Practice Online

- One-Stop Planner 5.3
- Holt Researcher: World History: Solon
- World History and Cultures Video Program 3
- Homework Practice Online
- Online Maps, Charts, and Graphs: The Long Walls of Athens

- One-Stop Planner 5.4
- World History Teaching Transparency: Geography and History 3: The Peloponnesian War
- Homework Practice Online

- One-Stop Planner 5.5
- Holt Researcher: World History: Xerxes
- Homework Practice Online
- Online Maps, Charts, and Graphs: The Battle of Salamis
- Online Maps, Charts, and Graphs: The Battle of Thermopylae

Reinforcement, Review, and Assessment

Daily Quiz 5.1
Main Idea Activity 5.1
English Audio Summary 5.1
Spanish Audio Summary 5.1
REV Section 1 Review, p. 109

Daily Quiz 5.2
Main Idea Activity 5.2
English Audio Summary 5.2
Spanish Audio Summary 5.2
REV Section 2 Review, p. 112

Daily Quiz 5.3
Main Idea Activity 5.3
English Audio Summary 5.3
Spanish Audio Summary 5.3
REV Section 3 Review, p. 117

Daily Quiz 5.4
Main Idea Activity 5.4
English Audio Summary 5.4
Spanish Audio Summary 5.4
REV Section 4 Review, p. 120

Daily Quiz 5.5
Main Idea Activity 5.5
English Audio Summary 5.5
Spanish Audio Summary 5.5
REV Section 5 Review, p. 125

internet connect

HRW ONLINE RESOURCES
GO TO: go.hrw.com
Then type in a keyword.

TEACHER HOME PAGE
KEYWORD: SP3 Teacher

CHAPTER INTERNET ACTIVITIES
KEYWORD: SP3 WH5
Choose an activity to:
- model ancient writing systems of the Mediterranean.
- build a map that connects modern and ancient Mediterranean cultures with pizza.
- report on Minoan civilization.

CHAPTER ENRICHMENT LINKS
KEYWORD: SP3 CH5

ONLINE ASSESSMENT
Homework Practice
KEYWORD: SP3 HP5
Standardized Test Prep
KEYWORD: SP3 STP5
Rubrics
KEYWORD: SS Rubrics

ONLINE MAPS, CHARTS, AND GRAPHS
KEYWORD: SP3 MCG

CONTENT UPDATES
KEYWORD: SS Content Updates

HOLT PRESENTATION MAKER
KEYWORD: SP3 PPT5

ONLINE READING SUPPORT
KEYWORD: SS Strategies

CURRENT EVENTS
KEYWORD: S3 Current Events

Meeting Individual Needs

Ability Levels

Level 1 Basic level activities designed for all students encountering new material

Level 2 Intermediate level activities designed for average students

Level 3 Challenging activities designed for honors and gifted and talented students

English Language Learners These activities address the needs of students with Limited English Proficiency.

Chapter Review and Assessment

IC Vocabulary Activity 5
Global Skill Builder CD-ROM
HRW Web Site
REV Chapter 5 Tutorial for Students, Parents, Mentors, and Peers
REV Chapter 5 Review, pp. 126–127

A Chapter 5 Test Generator (on the One-Stop Planner)
A Chapter 5 Test (Form A or B)
A Alternative Assessment Handbook
A Chapter 5 Test for English Language Learners and Special-Needs Students

Build on What You Know

Ask students to answer the following questions:

How might other civilizations have influenced the development of Greek civilization?

Consider:

• the location of early civilizations

• how ideas would spread along the trade routes

• the examples that early civilizations set of what people could do

What might the Greeks have learned from China, India, Egypt, and Mesopotamia?

Consider:

• new ideas in religion, art, and science

• advances in manufacturing, ship-building, and trade

• ways in which the governments of these civilizations developed

---

internet connect

TOPIC: The First Olympic Games

GO TO: go.hrw.com

KEYWORD: SP3 WH5

Have students access the Internet through the HRW Go site to conduct research on the first Olympic Games in 776 B.C. Then ask students to compose an informative report that details the origin and history of the games, what types of sports were played, and the similarities and differences between ancient Olympic games and the Olympics of today. Students' reports should include appropriate examples and evidence drawn from their research. Instruct students to use standard grammar, spelling, sentence structure, and punctuation.

◆ **CHAPTER** ◆

5

C. 2000 B.C.–404 B.C.

The Greek City-States

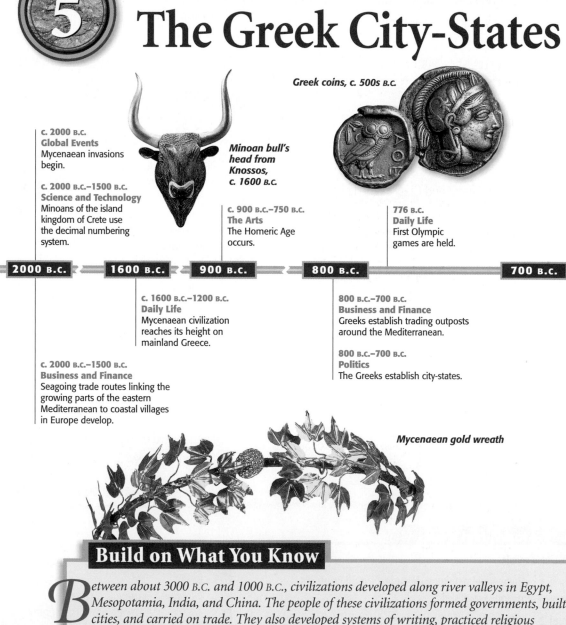

Greek coins, c. 500s B.C.

Minoan bull's head from Knossos, c. 1600 B.C.

c. 2000 B.C.
Global Events
Mycenaean invasions begin.

c. 2000 B.C.–1500 B.C.
Science and Technology
Minoans of the island kingdom of Crete use the decimal numbering system.

c. 900 B.C.–750 B.C.
The Arts
The Homeric Age occurs.

776 B.C.
Daily Life
First Olympic games are held.

| 2000 B.C. | 1600 B.C. | 900 B.C. | 800 B.C. | 700 B.C. |

c. 1600 B.C.–1200 B.C.
Daily Life
Mycenaean civilization reaches its height on mainland Greece.

c. 2000 B.C.–1500 B.C.
Business and Finance
Seagoing trade routes linking the growing parts of the eastern Mediterranean to coastal villages in Europe develop.

800 B.C.–700 B.C.
Business and Finance
Greeks establish trading outposts around the Mediterranean.

800 B.C.–700 B.C.
Politics
The Greeks establish city-states.

Mycenaean gold wreath

Build on What You Know

Between about 3000 B.C. and 1000 B.C., civilizations developed along river valleys in Egypt, Mesopotamia, India, and China. The people of these civilizations formed governments, built cities, and carried on trade. They also developed systems of writing, practiced religious beliefs, and invented new ways of making things. Some ideas from these early civilizations were passed on to the Greeks who lived along the eastern Mediterranean Sea. In this chapter, you will learn about early Greek history and the various forms of government that the ancient Greeks developed.

What's Your Opinion?

Geography

Agree The geography of a region must allow for good transportation and communication in order for civilizations to develop.

Disagree A civilization can develop even if the terrain isolates towns and cities.

Citizenship

Agree A government can rule best if decisions are made by only a limited number of citizens.

Disagree A government rules best when all members of society are invited to participate as citizens.

Global Relations

Agree The development of an advanced and respected civilization often requires military dominance.

Disagree War-mongering societies are often seen as barbarians not worthy of respect.

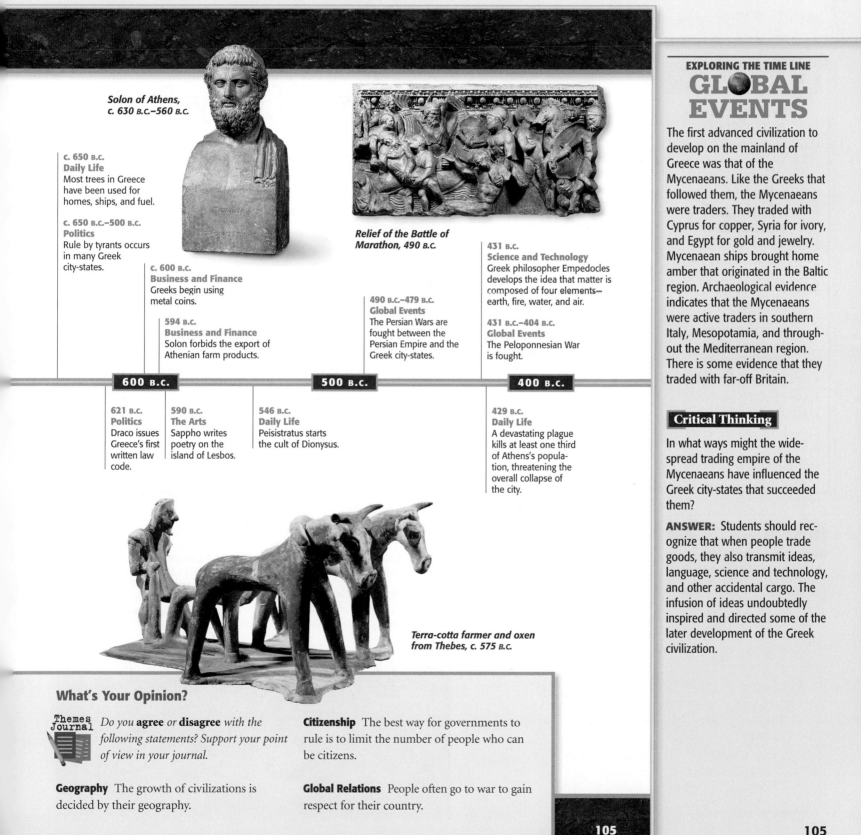

Solon of Athens, c. 630 B.C.–560 B.C.

c. 650 B.C.
Daily Life
Most trees in Greece have been used for homes, ships, and fuel.

c. 650 B.C.–500 B.C.
Politics
Rule by tyrants occurs in many Greek city-states.

c. 600 B.C.
Business and Finance
Greeks begin using metal coins.

594 B.C.
Business and Finance
Solon forbids the export of Athenian farm products.

Relief of the Battle of Marathon, 490 B.C.

490 B.C.–479 B.C.
Global Events
The Persian Wars are fought between the Persian Empire and the Greek city-states.

431 B.C.
Science and Technology
Greek philosopher Empedocles develops the idea that matter is composed of four elements—earth, fire, water, and air.

431 B.C.–404 B.C.
Global Events
The Peloponnesian War is fought.

600 B.C.   **500 B.C.**   **400 B.C.**

621 B.C.
Politics
Draco issues Greece's first written law code.

590 B.C.
The Arts
Sappho writes poetry on the island of Lesbos.

546 B.C.
Daily Life
Peisistratus starts the cult of Dionysus.

429 B.C.
Daily Life
A devastating plague kills at least one third of Athens's population, threatening the overall collapse of the city.

Terra-cotta farmer and oxen from Thebes, c. 575 B.C.

EXPLORING THE TIME LINE
GLOBAL EVENTS

The first advanced civilization to develop on the mainland of Greece was that of the Mycenaeans. Like the Greeks that followed them, the Mycenaeans were traders. They traded with Cyprus for copper, Syria for ivory, and Egypt for gold and jewelry. Mycenaean ships brought home amber that originated in the Baltic region. Archaeological evidence indicates that the Mycenaeans were active traders in southern Italy, Mesopotamia, and throughout the Mediterranean region. There is some evidence that they traded with far-off Britain.

Critical Thinking

In what ways might the widespread trading empire of the Mycenaeans have influenced the Greek city-states that succeeded them?

ANSWER: Students should recognize that when people trade goods, they also transmit ideas, language, science and technology, and other accidental cargo. The infusion of ideas undoubtedly inspired and directed some of the later development of the Greek civilization.

What's Your Opinion?

 *Do you **agree** or **disagree** with the following statements? Support your point of view in your journal.*

Geography The growth of civilizations is decided by their geography.

Citizenship The best way for governments to rule is to limit the number of people who can be citizens.

Global Relations People often go to war to gain respect for their country.

OBJECTIVES

1 **Analyze the role that geography played in early Greek history.**

2 **Explain the influence that Minoan and Mycenaean civilizations had on Greek civilization.**

3 **Describe the development of the Greek city-states.**

As students enter the classroom, ask them to list some advances made by civilizations they have studied. (*metalworking, calendars, religions, Arabic numerals, astronomy, writing*) Ask what basic qualities a society needs in order to grow into a civilization. (*Students might suggest a common language and religion, an interest in education and art, a common ancestry, and an economic system.*) Tell students that in Section 1 they will learn about the early Greek people and the rise of the Greek city-states.

REPRODUCIBLE RESOURCES

▸ Guided Reading Strategy 5.1

▸ Hands-on History Activity 5: The Greek City-States

TECHNOLOGY RESOURCES

▸ One-Stop Planner 5.1

▸ Homework Practice Online

▸ Online Maps: Turmoil in the Aegean Lands, c. 1250–1100 B.C.

REINFORCEMENT, REVIEW, AND ASSESSMENT

▸ Section 1 Review, p. 109

▸ Daily Quiz 5.1

▸ Main Idea Activity 5.1

▸ English Audio Summary 5.1

▸ Spanish Audio Summary 5.1

VISUAL RECORD ANSWER

Women were active athletes and participants in Minoan practices.

SECTION 1

READ TO DISCOVER

❶ How did geography influence Greek history?

❷ How did the Minoans and Mycenaeans affect Greek civilization?

❸ How did Greek city-states develop?

DEFINE

frescoes
polis
acropolis
agora

IDENTIFY

Minoans
Mycenaeans

WHY IT MATTERS TODAY

The United States and other democratic countries have adopted the Greek idea that citizens can govern themselves. Use **CNNfyi.com** or other **current event** sources to find examples of how citizens in the United States and in other countries take part in government. Record your findings in your journal.

CNNfyi.com

Early Greeks and the Rise of City-States

The Main Idea
The geography of Greece isolated settlements and strongpoints from one another, leading to the rise of city-states.

The Story Continues *According to legend, primitive Greeks called Dorians moved into Asia Minor, Crete, and the Peloponnesus about 1100 B.C. Modern historians now believe the Dorians never really existed. They do know, however, that some invaders did arrive at about this time, and that they influenced the development of certain Greek city-states.*

The Sea and the Land

The geography of Greece had much to do with the way the early Greeks lived. Mainland Greece lies on the southern part of the Balkan Peninsula. This peninsula is at the northeastern end of the Mediterranean Sea. The Aegean Sea to the east separates Greece from Asia Minor. To the west, the Ionian Sea divides Greece from the Italian Peninsula. Small islands dot the Aegean and Ionian Seas. Many of them are also part of Greece.

Greece's long, uneven coastline brought every part of the mainland close to the sea. The sea came to play an important part in the lives of the Greeks, many of whom became fishers, sailors, and traders. People from Egypt and the Fertile Crescent also traveled to Greece, bringing with them goods and ideas. Later, the Greeks set up colonies in other parts of the Mediterranean.

Greece's geography made it hard for its early people to develop a sense of unity. Short mountain ranges cut up the Greek mainland. These mountains kept villages apart. They also allowed invaders to enter Greece from the north. Unlike the great rivers of Egypt and Mesopotamia, rivers in Greece were short and did not aid travel and trade between villages. Instead of a large kingdom or empire forming in Greece, separate city-states arose.

✔ **READING CHECK: Identifying Cause and Effect** How did geography affect the development of ancient Greece? *groups developed in isolation*

INTERPRETING THE VISUAL RECORD

Early Greek frescoes *The Toreador Fresco* (c. 1500 B.C.) is the largest Minoan mural in existence. It shows athletes jumping over a bull, a Minoan religious practice. The figures with the lighter skin tones are women. ***What does this fresco imply about the role women played in Greek society?***

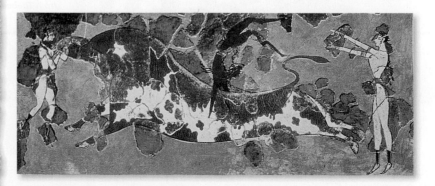

TEACH OBJECTIVE 1

LEVEL 1: Before students read "The Sea and the Land," have them examine the maps on pages 107 and 108. Ask students what geographical features they notice on the Balkan Peninsula. (*Students should mention the numerous mountain ranges, the lack of long rivers, the long irregular coastline, and many islands.*) Guide a discussion of the advantages and disadvantages these features posed for people living in the region.

TEACH OBJECTIVE 2

ALL LEVELS: Draw a compare-and-contrast chart on the chalkboard. Guide students in filling in the chart. Then have students pose and answer questions about the influence of the Minoans and Mycenaeans on Greek civilization.

ENGLISH LANGUAGE LEARNERS , COOPERATIVE LEARNING

	Minoans	Mycenaeans
Location	Crete	Greek mainland, Crete
Dates	c. 2000 B.C.–1500 B.C.	c. 1600 B.C.–1200 B.C.
Achievements	indoor running water, art, traded network, navy, written language	built fort-like cities throughout Greece, kept written records
Reasons for collapse	volcanic eruption, tidal waves	earthquakes, war

Early Greek Peoples

People first lived in Greece about 55,000 years ago. Not until about A.D. 1900, however, did archaeologists find evidence of the earliest Greek civilization. This was the Minoan civilization. It had developed on the island of Crete by 2000 B.C. About that same time, Indo-European people entered the Greek mainland from the north.

The Minoans. The Minoan civilization was named after the legendary king of Crete, King Minos. Minos had his palace in the city of Knossos (NAHS·uhs). There the **Minoans** built a great civilization. The palace and the homes of nobles had running water. Minoan artists covered the palace walls with colorful **frescoes**—paintings made on wet plaster walls. Other artists carved beautiful figures from bronze, gold, ivory, silver, and stone. Some of the figures show the Minoans worshipping a bull and an Earth goddess.

Many Minoans became sailors and traders. They traded for food because Crete's soil was poor. It could not grow many kinds of crops. These Minoans set up trading posts on islands in the Aegean Sea and in Asia Minor. The kings of Crete maintained strong navies to support Minoan trade.

In about 1628 B.C. a volcano erupted on a nearby island. Tidal waves caused by the eruption destroyed many coastal settlements on Crete. From that time on Minoan civilization grew weak. In about 1400 B.C. **Mycenaeans** (my·suh·NEE·uhnz) from the Greek mainland conquered central Crete.

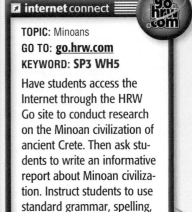

TOPIC: Minoans
GO TO: go.hrw.com
KEYWORD: SP3 WH5

Have students access the Internet through the HRW Go site to conduct research on the Minoan civilization of ancient Crete. Then ask students to write an informative report about Minoan civilization. Instruct students to use standard grammar, spelling, sentence structure, and punctuation.

That's Interesting!

Although human habitation first began in present-day Greece about 55,000 years ago, the first people to speak the language we know as Greek were the Mycenaeans.

MAP ANSWER

Greece was in a central location with access to sea trade with Europe, Asia, and Africa.

Technology Resources

CNN Presents World Cultures: Yesterday and Today Segment 5: Crete: Past and Present

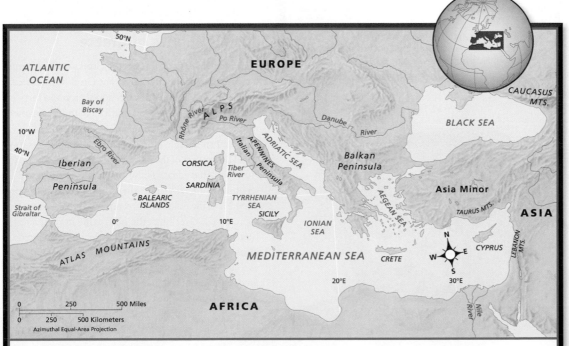

The Mediterranean Region
Interpreting Maps The geography of the Balkan Peninsula placed the Greeks in a central location in the Mediterranean, encouraging trade, colonization, and communication.

■ **Skills Assessment: Physical Systems** In what ways did the location of Greece encourage commerce and trade?

LEVEL 3: After students read the paragraphs under "The City-States of Greece," create a chart with four columns on the chalkboard. Label each column with these key features of the city-state: *small size, small population, setting on a hill,* and *public meeting place.* Have students copy the chart and list details about each key feature as it relates to the development of city-states. Then have students write details about each feature as it applies to their city or town.

HOMEWORK Have students draw a large map of the Balkan Peninsula and illustrate it with the geographic factors they have read about and discussed. Then have them make icons or models to represent how people made a living in ancient Greece and place the icons or models on the map.

CLOSE

Ask students to list ways in which all ancient Greeks were alike.

REVIEW

Have students complete the Section 1 Review on p. 109.

Interdisciplinary Connection

ARCHITECTURE. Although little is known about the earliest palaces, the later palaces of the Minoans and Mycenaeans are distinctive for the quality of their workmanship and the sophistication of their designs. The carefully laid-out palaces had wide staircases, multiple stories, vistas and facades, and storage rooms for goods and crops. Artisans painted the interior walls with scenes of everyday life. Built-in bathtubs and running water could be found inside the palaces.

Critical Thinking

Ask students what the remains of the palaces show about the societies that built them.

ANSWER: The palaces show that the societies were concerned with practical function as well as aesthetics.

MAP ANSWERS

1. Athens, Mycenae, Tiryns, Pylos, Troy, Knossos

2. They were traders. Transportation and commerce were easier by sea than across the mountains.

VISUAL RECORD ANSWER

Mycenaean artisans had highly developed, sophisticated skills.

Aegean Civilization, c. 1450 B.C.–700 B.C.
Interpreting Maps The early Greeks were great traders and warriors alike.

■ **Skills Assessment: 1. Locate** Locate cities on the Greek mainland and on Crete. **2. Drawing Conclusions** Why did the Greeks build their cities near the sea?

The Mycenaeans. The Mycenaeans controlled mainland Greece from about 1600 B.C. to about 1200 B.C. They were a warring people who grouped themselves into clans and tribes. Several related families formed a clan that was headed by a warrior. A number of clans made up a tribe that had its own chief. The Mycenaeans built fort-like cities in the Peloponnesus (pel·uh·puh·NEE·suhs), the southern part of Greece, as well as in north-central Greece. The Mycenaeans carried out raids throughout the eastern Mediterranean. However, by 1200 B.C. earthquakes and warfare had destroyed most of the Mycenaean cities.

The Mycenaeans made important contributions to the development of Greek civilization. After conquering Crete, the Mycenaeans adopted many elements of Minoan civilization. For instance, they used the Minoan system of writing. Called linear B, this writing system was an early form of Greek writing. The Mycenaeans kept records in linear B.

✔ **READING CHECK: Summarizing** In what ways did the Minoans and Mycenaeans influence Greek civilization?
Minoans made advances that the Mycenaeans passed on.

The City-States of Greece

During the 800s and 700s B.C. the Greeks formed a number of independent city-states. The Greek word for city-state is **polis.** A polis usually developed around a fort. As a city grew up around the fort, the idea of the polis came to mean the fort, its city, and the lands and small farming villages that surrounded the city and that supplied its food.

The concept of the polis was based on three basic and closely related ideas. These included the geographical territory of the city-state; the community that it represented; and the political and economic independence that it produced. Over time, the polis came to represent the center of Greek identity and its inhabitants were intensely loyal to it. The Greeks also understood the polis as an absolutely independent and self-sufficient community. Frequently, economic and political competition separated one polis from another.

INTERPRETING THE VISUAL RECORD
Mycenaean artifacts The Mycenaeans buried their dead in cone-shaped stone chambers. Silver and gold masks, cups, jewelry, and weapons were also placed in these tombs. *What do these artifacts reveal about the skills of Mycenaean artisans?*

ASSESS

Have students complete Daily Quiz 5.1. As Alternative Assessment, you may want to use the charts in this section's lessons.

RETEACH

Have students complete Main Idea Activity for English Language Learners and Special-Needs Students 5.1. Then have students create a web diagram for each section.

ENGLISH LANGUAGE LEARNERS

EXTEND

⚡ internet connect

Internet Activity: go.hrw.com
TOPIC: Ancient Writings **KEYWORD: SP3 WH5**

Have students access the Internet through the HRW Go site to conduct research about the writing systems of the Mediterranean. These can include linear B, cuneiform, hieroglyphics, and the early alphabet. Then ask students to construct their own model of a writing system. Ask them to create a few sentences for the class to decipher.

The Greek city-states were alike in many ways. First, they covered a small area of land. For example, Athens was smaller than the state of Rhode Island. Sparta was smaller than Connecticut. Yet these two city-states were very large compared to the others. Second, most city-states had a population of fewer than 10,000 people, most of whom were slaves and other non-citizens. Only free adult males had citizenship rights. Third, in most city-states the original fort was built on an **acropolis,** or hill. Temples and other public buildings also stood on the acropolis. Finally, each city-state had an **agora,** or marketplace. The agora also served as the main public meeting place. Citizens met in the agora to discuss common issues.

The polis gave ancient Greeks a sense of identity. Greek citizens believed that they owed loyalty to their polis. They loved their city-state and often were willing to die for it.

The Greeks placed great value on the political independence of each polis. Each city-state formed its own kind of government and laws. Each city-state also had its own calendar, money, and system of weights and measures.

However, all ancient Greeks had certain things in common. They spoke the same language; they tended to regard people who did not speak Greek as barbarians; and they shared many religious ideas, cultural characteristics, and social patterns. Great festivals also brought the Greeks together.

✔ **READING CHECK: Comparing and Contrasting** In what ways were the Greek city-states alike and different? all had a polis and agora, most had an acropolis; each formed its own government and laws

The agora of Corinth once bustled with marketplace and religious activity.

SECTION 1 REVIEW

1. **Define** and explain the significance:
   frescoes
   polis
   acropolis
   agora

2. **Identify** and explain the significance:
   Minoans
   Mycenaeans

Homework Practice Online
keyword: SP3 HP5

3. **Analyzing Information** Copy the outline map of ancient Greece below. Fill in and label the geographic features that made it hard for the ancient Greeks to become united.

4. **Finding the Main Idea**
   a. How did life in ancient Greece change after the fall of the Mycenaeans?
   b. Why was the development of the polis important in ancient Greece?

5. **Writing and Critical Thinking**
   Supporting a Point of View Imagine you are a citizen of a Greek city-state. Write a letter to a Greek leader explaining your reasons for wanting to open citizenship to all people in the city-state.
   Consider:
   • the qualifications for citizenship in ancient Greece
   • how Greek citizens felt about their polis
   • the things ancient Greeks had in common

SECTION 1 REVIEW ANSWERS

❶ **Define**
• frescoes, p. 107
• polis, p. 108
• acropolis, p. 109
• agora, p. 109

❷ **Identify**
• Minoans, p. 107
• Mycenaeans, p. 107

❸ Students' maps should show the mountains that divided the Greek mainland and kept villages apart.

❹ a. After the fall of the Mycenaeans, the Greeks formed independent city-states. These were built around forts that were often on hilltops. They also had an agora, which was both a marketplace and a meeting place where citizens discussed common issues.

b. The polis gave Greeks a sense of identity and pride.

❺ Students' letters should express an understanding that only adult free males could vote. Slaves and women were excluded from citizenship. People of the city-states had great loyalty to their cities. They also had a great deal in common, including language, religion, and festivals, and a general arrogance toward outsiders. Students should use these details to support an argument for granting citizenship to all people in the city-state.

OBJECTIVES

1 Explain the importance of Homer's works.

2 Identify major religious beliefs and practices of the ancient Greeks.

3 Describe changes that occurred in the governments of the Greek city-states.

SECTION 2

READ TO DISCOVER

❶ Why was the work of the poet Homer important?

❷ What were the main religious beliefs and practices of the ancient Greeks?

❸ How did the governments of the Greek city-states change over time?

DEFINE

myths
oracles
aristocracies
hoplite
tyrants
popular government
democracy

IDENTIFY

Iliad
Odyssey
Homer
Olympic Games

WHY IT MATTERS TODAY

Several nations in Europe and the Middle East have democratic monarchies somewhat like those in later Greek city-states. Use **CNNfyi**.com or other **current event** sources to discover which nations still have kings and queens, as well as elected assemblies. Record your findings in your journal.

CNNfyi.com

Greek Government and Society

The Main Idea
Greeks sought to improve their lives through religious practices and experiments in government.

The Story Continues *Between 1000 B.C. and 700 B.C., the Greeks based their governments on the old system of tribes and chiefs. These tribal systems gradually developed into small kingdoms that were often at war with one another. By 700 B.C., however, many city-states had overthrown their kings. New forms of government began to evolve.*

Greek Culture in the Homeric Age

The Greeks of this period did not have a very advanced civilization. Few people could write, so most communication was oral, or spoken. Traveling poets sang or recited folk songs, ballads, or epics. An epic is a long poem about heroes and great events.

The *Iliad* and the *Odyssey*. Sometime during the 700s B.C. much of this oral poetry was gathered into two great epics, the *Iliad* and the *Odyssey*. According to tradition, the blind poet **Homer** wrote these epics. However, we do not really know who the author or authors were. Nevertheless, this period is often called the Homeric Age.

The *Iliad* tells the legend of the Trojan War. The story begins when a Trojan prince named Paris falls in love with Helen, the wife of a Mycenaean king. Paris kidnaps Helen and takes her with him to Troy. The Mycenaeans lay siege to Troy for 10 years but cannot capture the city. Finally, the Mycenaeans win by building a wooden horse so huge that all their best soldiers can hide inside. They give the horse to the Trojans as a "gift." Thinking they have won, the Trojans bring the horse into the city. That night the Mycenaean soldiers leap out of the horse and conquer Troy.

The *Odyssey* tells what happened after the Trojan War. It describes the adventures of the Mycenaean king Odysseus on his way home from the war. Along the way he encounters many dangers as well as interference from the gods. In the story it takes Odysseus 10 years to reach his home city-state of Ithaca. Today we use the word *odyssey* to refer to any long, adventure-filled journey.

Greek religious beliefs. The religion that the Greeks developed during the Homeric Age differed from that of the Egyptians, Hebrews, and Persians. For the most part, Greek religion did not emphasize high standards of personal morality. Instead, the ancient Greeks looked to religion for three things. First, they wanted religion to explain nature. For example, they wanted to know what caused lightning, thunder, and the change of seasons. Second, they wanted religion to explain the emotions that sometimes cause people to lose self-control. The Greeks considered self-control very important. Third, they believed religion could bring them certain benefits

Holt Researcher

go.hrw.com
KEYWORD: Holt Researcher
FreeFind: Homer
After reading more about Homer on the Holt Researcher, identify how his works transcend Greek culture to convey universal themes.

TEACH OBJECTIVE 1

ALL LEVELS: Ask students why the poems of Homer were important to the ancient Greeks. *(told about the Trojan War; form of entertainment; told about Greek history and heroes)* Then ask what modern scholars might learn about ancient Greeks from these epics. *(They would learn about the history and culture of the Greeks in the Homeric Age.)*

TEACH OBJECTIVE 2

LEVEL 3: Ask students to read a short Greek myth, such as one in Edith Hamilton's *Mythology*. Have students write a brief essay that explains Greek beliefs about natural phenomena.

HOMEWORK Have students read a myth and list the characteristics of the myth. Later, students may compare their lists to determine common characteristics of myths.

TEACH OBJECTIVE 3

LEVEL 1: Tell students that between about 700 and 500 B.C., the Greek city-states had a number of different types of government. Have students fill in a chart with heads as shown below.

ENGLISH LANGUAGE LEARNERS

Government	Who ruled	Why rulers lost power
kingdoms	*kings*	*overthrown by nobles*
aristocracies	*aristocrats*	*overthrown by tyrants*

here and now, such as long life, good luck, or a good harvest. The Greeks did not expect their religion to save them from sin. Also, Greeks of the Homeric Age were not as concerned as other ancient peoples about what happened after death. They believed that the spirits of almost all people went to a gray, gloomy underworld ruled by the god Hades. It was not viewed as a place of either punishment or reward.

To explain their world, the Greeks created myths. **Myths** are traditional stories about gods, goddesses, and heroes. The Greeks gave human qualities and personalities to their gods, who were said to live on Mount Olympus in northern Greece. Zeus was the king of the gods. One of his daughters was the goddess Athena, protector of wisdom and womanly goodness. She was also the special protector of the great city-states. Athens was named in her honor. Apollo, one of Zeus's sons, was the god of light, music, and poetry. Dionysus was the god of fertility and wine. The Greeks believed that the gods spoke through priests and priestesses at special places called **oracles.** Greeks would often travel to oracles to ask questions about the future.

Pleasing the gods was an important part of Greek life. Showing strength and bravery in athletic contests was one way to do this. The most important contests were the **Olympic Games,** held every four years in honor of Zeus. Only men could watch or compete in these games. The Olympics were probably held for the first time in 776 B.C. Events included boxing, foot races, javelin and discus throwing, and wrestling. At the end of the games, the winners received wreaths of wild olive branches. There were no second or third prizes.

✔ **READING CHECK: Finding the Main Idea** What were the main aspects of Greek culture? epic poems, religion, myths, oracles, athletic contests

Greek Government: From Kings to Democracy

The city-states of Greece had originated as small kingdoms ruled by warrior chieftains from their hilltop fortresses. These chieftains had in turn relied on wealthy landowners to support their rule and to form their armies. This was because only wealthy landowners could afford the expensive horses, chariots, and bronze weapons necessary to discourage raiders and to maintain each kingdom's security. Over time, the small group of landowners, known as *aristocrats,* or "best men" in Greek, came to represent each city-state's noble class. Little by little, the nobles gained more land and power. By about 700 B.C. nobles in many of the Greek city-states had overthrown their kings and had taken power themselves.

Greek city-states that were controlled by nobles were known as **aristocracies.** Originally, the word *aristocracy* meant "rule by the best." Over time, however, the term came to describe a privileged social class, usually composed of the wealthiest landowners in the city-state. Aristocrats controlled virtually every aspect of Greek society during these years. They held a monopoly over the military and, as major landowners, they controlled the economy. Aristocrats acted

Then & Now

Stadiums

Throughout the world, millions of people fill stadiums to watch sporting events. Ancient Greeks built the first stadiums about 2,500 years ago. The first Olympic Games were held in a stadium especially built for them.

Today, stadiums also have more than one use. For example, Yankee Stadium in New York City has baseball games and music events. Of course, most modern stadiums are larger than the ancient ones. **How do stadiums reflect Greek influences on modern architecture?**

Culture

Women also participated in their own Olympic Games. This competition was held in honor of Hera, wife of Zeus. It took place at a different time than the men's games. Little is known about these games, but one Greek reported that unmarried women competed in a footrace that was five-sixths as long as the men's race.

Critical Thinking

Ask students if they think the winners of the women's games were treated as enthusiastically as the winners of the men's games. Have them support their point of view.

ANSWER: No, women were not considered to be men's equals, so they most likely would not have been treated as enthusiastically.

CLOSE

Have students representing nonaristocratic male citizens, women, and slaves in Greek city-states describe how changes in government between 650 B.C. and 500 B.C. affected them.

REVIEW

Have students complete the Section 2 Review on p. 112.

ASSESS

Have students complete Daily Quiz 5.2. As Alternative Assessment, use the chart or the essay in this section's lessons.

RETEACH

Have students complete Main Idea Activity for English Language Learners and Special-Needs Students 5.2. Then ask students to create a web diagram for each of the section's main ideas.
ENGLISH LANGUAGE LEARNERS

EXTEND

Have students select a passage from the *Odyssey* to present orally. Discuss the universal themes presented in this epic.
COOPERATIVE LEARNING, BLOCK SCHEDULING

SECTION 2 REVIEW ANSWERS

❶ Define
• myths, p. 111
• oracles, p. 111
• aristocracies, p. 111
• hoplite, p. 112
• tyrants, p. 112
• popular government, p. 112
• democracy, p. 112

❷ Identify
• *Iliad*, p. 110
• *Odyssey*, p. 110
• Homer, p. 110
• Olympic Games, p. 111

❸ Government: kingdoms, aristocracies, tyrannies, democracies; Writings: *Iliad, Odyssey*; Religious Events: visits to oracles, Olympic Games

❹ a. Kings fell because the aristocrats became too strong. The aristocrats fell because nonaristocrats acquired weapons and overthrew them. Tyrants fell because they abused power.

b. Homer's work was great literature and recorded the values and history of the Greeks.

c. They used religion to explain natural events and people's emotions and to bring them benefits.

❺ A tyrant needed courage and boldness to seize power, sound business judgment, and fairness in order to keep the support of the people.

The rise of the heavily armed, well-trained Greek infantry soldier known as the hoplite did much to weaken the power of the aristocrats.

as judges and determined the city-state's laws and punishments. They even held control over religion, since the gods supposedly would not listen to commoners. Before the 600s B.C. aristocrats were the only people who participated in politics.

In time, social and economic changes took place that weakened the power of the aristocrats. By the 600s B.C. some wealthy nonaristocrats could afford the costly weapons and armor needed by the soldiers of the times. A new kind of nonaristocratic soldier called the **hoplite** emerged in many parts of Greece. Hoplites were heavy infantry who carried long spears and who fought in closely spaced rows. The cavalry and chariots of the aristocrats were no match for the powerful hoplite formations. As hoplites became more important to the defense of the city-state, they demanded more say in its daily government. Poor citizens, especially farmers, were also unhappy with the rule of the nobles. Many citizens began to look for leaders who could provide a better life.

The leaders who were able to bring a better life to the people were the **tyrants.** A tyrant was someone who illegally took power but had the people's support. Between 650 B.C. and 500 B.C. tyrants ruled many city-states. At first, many tyrants ruled well. They ended the nobles' fights for power and promoted more trade. In some cases, however, these powerful rulers became unjust. The word *tyrant* came to mean someone who uses absolute power brutally.

During the 150 years after about 650 B.C., many Greek city-states overthrew their tyrants. In some of these city-states, the idea of **popular government** began to take root. This is the idea that people can and should rule themselves. Some city-states, such as Athens, developed forms of **democracy,** or government in which citizens take part. Even in these developing democracies, however, full political rights were allowed to only a small part of the population. Women, for example, did not have political rights. Slaves, who often represented a large part of the city-state's population, also lacked political rights. Other Greek city-states, including the powerful Sparta, either maintained their aristocratic forms of government or restored rule by kings or nobles. Even in monarchies and aristocracies, however, a council of citizens now limited the individual ruler's power.

✔ **READING CHECK: Analyzing Information** How did Greek government change between the 700s B.C. and the late 500s B.C.? passed from monarchy through aristocracy and tyrants to democracy

---

SECTION 2 REVIEW

1. **Define** and explain the significance:
   myths   hoplite
   oracles   tyrants
   aristocracies popular government
                democracy

2. **Identify** and explain the significance:
   Iliad
   Odyssey
   Homer
   Olympic Games

   Homework Practice Online
   keyword: SP3 HP5

3. **Categorizing** Copy the web diagram below. Use it to name the type of government, important pieces of writing, and religious events that were part of the Homeric Age (c. 900 B.C. to 750 B.C.).

   Government   Writings
           Homeric Age
                Religious
                Events

4. **Finding the Main Idea**
   a. Why did the rulers of governments in the Greek city-states change?
   b. Why might Homer's work have been important to later generations?
   c. How did the Greeks view the role of religion in their lives?

5. **Writing and Critical Thinking**
   Making Generalizations In a paragraph, describe the qualities a tyrant needed to be successful.
   Consider:
   • how the tyrants came to power
   • what some tyrants were able to accomplish
   • the importance of the support of the public to a tyrant's rule

SECTION 3

OBJECTIVES

1 Analyze the society of Sparta.

2 Explain the development of democracy in Athens.

🔊 **LET'S GET STARTED!**

As students enter the classroom, ask them to describe the types of government that developed in the Greek city-states. (*First Greek city-states were governed by kings. The kings were overthrown by aristocrats. Eventually the aristocrats were overthrown by tyrants who, in turn, were overthrown by citizens who set up popular governments.*) Explain to students that in Section 3 they will learn about the government and society of two of the most important city-states: Sparta and Athens.

SECTION 3

READ TO DISCOVER

❶ What kind of society developed in Sparta?

❷ How did democracy develop in Athens?

DEFINE

helots
ephors
metics
archons
direct democracy
representative democracy

IDENTIFY

Draco
Solon
Peisistratus
Cleisthenes

WHY IT MATTERS TODAY

The United States and other democracies trace the idea of government and people working together from Athenian democracy. Use CNNfyi.com or other **current event** sources to discover ways in which the United States government and ordinary citizens work together. Record your findings in your journal.

CNNfyi.com

Sparta and Athens

The Main Idea
Sparta and Athens developed very different societies and systems of government.

The Story Continues *Greek city-states were both similar and different. The two most important city-states, Athens and Sparta, showed great differences. While Athens was known for its laws and government, Sparta was known for the physical strength and discipline of its people. According to legend, Spartan laws were intentionally not written down so that people would have to memorize them as a further test of discipline.*

Sparta: The Military Ideal

By the late 1100s B.C., invaders from the north had overrun most of the Peloponnesus and forced many of the people they conquered to work for them. They called these conquered people **helots.** The invaders conquered the village that became their capital, Sparta. Unlike other city-states, Sparta was located in a valley, not on a hill. Moreover, it was not surrounded by walls for defense. The Peloponnesus was isolated and mountainous. This may help to explain why Sparta developed very differently from Athens, becoming a rigid and highly militarized society.

Spartan society. Sparta had three social groups. Members of the first group, known as the equals, were descended from the invaders. They controlled the city-state. Land was divided equally among these citizens and their families. Along with the land went helots to work it. Sparta's second group was made up of half-citizens. They were free, paid taxes, and served in the army. Half-citizens, however, had no political power. Some half-citizens farmed. Others lived in the towns, where they worked in trade and industry. Some half-citizens even became rich.

Helots made up the third and lowest group in Sparta. The helots became the slaves of the Spartan city-state. The Spartans decided how the helots should work and live. However, the helots greatly outnumbered the Spartans. Therefore, the Spartans had to use force to control them. Fear of a helot uprising was one reason the Spartans created a military society. The Spartans systematically terrorized the helots to keep them from rebelling. Not surprisingly, the helots hated the Spartans.

INTERPRETING THE VISUAL RECORD

A Spartan soldier Some of Sparta's half-citizens became artisans. Much of their work also focused on Sparta's military. *How does this bronze figure of a Spartan soldier show that artisans were also involved in Sparta's military society?*

SECTION 3 RESOURCES

REPRODUCIBLE RESOURCES

▶ Guided Reading Strategy 5.3

▶ Readings in World History 18, 19

TECHNOLOGY RESOURCES

▶ One-Stop Planner 5.3

▶ Holt Researcher: World History: Solon

▶ World History and Cultures Video Program 3

▶ Homework Practice Online

▶ Online Maps, Charts, and Graphs: The Long Walls of Athens

REINFORCEMENT, REVIEW, AND ASSESSMENT

▶ Section 3 Review, p. 117

▶ Daily Quiz 5.3

▶ Main Idea Activity 5.3

▶ English Audio Summary 5.3

▶ Spanish Audio Summary 5.3

VISUAL RECORD ANSWER

Artisans helped to promote the respect for and tradition of military excellence.

LEVEL 1: Assign students to one of the following categories of Sparta's inhabitants: half-citizens, helots, equals, ephors, boy soldiers, Spartan girls. Have students write a journal entry in the role of their assigned character, describing daily life, Sparta, their role in Spartan society, and what the character thinks about that role.

HOMEWORK Have students reread the quote from Lycurgus on page 114. Then ask them to write a paragraph describing how most Americans today would react to such treatment of children.

History Maker

LYCURGUS. Scholars are not certain whether Lycurgus was a historical or mythical figure. If he was a real person, he probably lived in the 700s or 800s B.C. According to legend, Lycurgus developed Sparta's laws and government. Legend held that Lycurgus and the Spartan people were descended from Hercules, a mythical hero of incredible strength. Lycurgus passed laws that eliminated inequalities and luxuries from Spartan life. He emphasized discipline and obedience. He banned the use of money in Sparta and redistributed land. He is most famous for creating the Spartan system of communal education for men. Laws were taught in schools so that every citizen would memorize them.

Critical Thinking

Ask students why scholars know more about the government and society of Athens than they do about Sparta.

ANSWER: Students should suggest that because Spartans emphasized military preparedness, they did not leave the large body of political, philosophical, and historical writings that the Athenians left behind.

LINK TO TODAY ANSWER
Because scholars have few ruins to study, they have little evidence of how Spartans lived or how they organized their households, businesses, government, and society in general.

114

Government in Sparta. Sparta's government had several parts. Two kings were at the head of the government. One king led the army, while the other took care of matters at home. A Council of Elders was made up of 28 male citizens over the age of 60. These were usually wealthy, aristocratic men. The council proposed laws and served as a criminal court. The final part of Sparta's government was an assembly that included all male citizens over 30 years old. The assembly voted to accept or reject laws proposed by the Council of Elders. The assembly also elected five **ephors** for one-year terms. The ephors made sure that the kings stayed within the law. They also had complete control over the education of young Spartans.

Life in Sparta's military society. Sparta controlled the lives of its citizens from birth to death. The goal was to make every adult male citizen part of the military machine. The Spartan military worked to control the helots and to expand Spartan power.

The development of Spartan fighting men began at birth. A group of officials examined newborn babies. Any child who seemed unhealthy was left to die. One Spartan lawmaker, Lycurgus, ordered the following practices:

Analyzing Primary Sources

Identifying a Point of View How did the treatment of children in Sparta reflect Spartan ideals? harsh discipline

 Primary Source **«The Spartans bathed their infants in wine rather than water, to test and toughen their bodies. Children were subject to strict discipline from the start, and were taught not to be afraid in the dark, not to be finicky about their food, and not to be peevish [moody] and tearful.»**

Lycurgus, as quoted by Plutarch in *Parallel Lives*

Link to Today These ruins are all that is left of the once-thriving city-state of Sparta. How might having few ruins today limit our knowledge of Spartan society?

At the age of seven, boys left home to live in military barracks. Military training formed the basis of their education, along with reading and writing. From ages 18 to 20, they trained specifically for war.

At the age of 20, Spartan male citizens began their military service. They could now marry but could not live at home until they were 30. They were not allowed to engage in any trade or business. The authorities believed that the love of money interfered with military discipline. Men remained available for military service until they were 60 years old. Older men were expected to work for the public good rather than focus on their private lives.

As the future wives and mothers of Spartan soldiers, Spartan girls also had to be strong and healthy. They received strict physical training and were taught to be devoted to the city-state. Both boys and girls studied music in order to learn discipline and coordination.

This training by the Spartan state led to a strong government and an almost unbeatable army. The Spartans, however, paid a high price for their power—they gave up their individual freedom. In addition, Spartan society created little in art, literature, philosophy, or science.

✔ **READING CHECK: Identifying Bias** How did the need for defense influence the way the Spartan government ruled its people? emphasized militarism

TEACH OBJECTIVE 2

ALL LEVELS: Have students match each of the following reforms with the Athenian who enacted them.

Descriptions	Identifications
1. developed a form of direct democracy	a. Draco
2. improved Athens's economy but clashed with nobles	b. Cleisthenes
3. created Athens's first written law code	c. Solon
4. set up a court system with citizen jurors	d. Peisistratus

(1: b, 2: d, 3: a, 4: c)

LEVEL 3: Ask students to compare the basic features of direct and representative democracies. *(All citizens participate in making the decisions in a direct democracy, while citizens elect representatives to run the government for them in a representative democracy.)* Ask students if they think a direct democracy would work well in the United States, and why or why not.

Athens: The Birth of Democracy

Athens developed very differently from Sparta. Athens is located on the Attic peninsula, one of the least fertile areas in Greece. Thus the Athenians turned to the sea, and many became sea traders. The introduction of coined money in the 600s B.C. also stimulated trade by making it easier to buy and sell goods. The Athenians built their city inland, perhaps to protect it from pirates, and constructed Piraeus (py·REE·uhs) as its special port. Athens itself was a typical polis built around the rocky hill of the Acropolis. In times of war, people took refuge inside the city's strong walls.

Athenian society. Citizens formed the top group in Athenian society. Citizens might be rich aristocrats or poor farmers. Only Athenian-born men, however, had full political rights. Female citizens could not vote or hold office.

The next group in Athenian society was the **metics.** These people were non-citizens because they had been born outside Athens. Metics usually worked as merchants or artisans. They were free and paid the same taxes as citizens. Metics, however, could not take part in government or own land.

Slaves stood at the bottom of Athenian society. Like all Greeks, Athenians considered slavery natural and necessary. Slaves were people captured in war. They were owned by masters and treated as property. Sometimes masters freed slaves, who then became metics. In time, slaves and metics made up more than half of Athens's population.

Early government in Athens. After Athens's monarchy ended, the city-state had an aristocratic government. Only citizens who owned land held office. All adult male citizens, however, met in an assembly. They elected generals in time of war. They also elected nine **archons,** rulers who served one-year terms.

At first, Athens's laws were not written down. In the late 600s B.C., many non-aristocrats complained about this. An archon named **Draco** is believed to have created Athens's first written law code around 621 B.C. Draco's laws were so harsh and severe that today we call a harsh law a Draconian law.

As time passed, nobles and metics became wealthy from trade but many farmers grew poorer. More and more citizens were sold into slavery to pay their debts. Discontent and anger spread among the poor. **Solon,** who became an archon in 594 B.C., settled the disputes between creditors and debtors by erasing the debts of the poor and outlawing slavery for debt. He freed people who had become slaves to pay their debts. Solon believed that this was the best way to help the city. He once wrote,

History Makers Speak

❝These are the evils loosed upon the people:
Of the poor, many, sold, in shameful chains,
Take the road leading to a foreign land. . . .
Thus the public evil reaches each man at home.❞

Solon, *Eunomy*

This juror's token from the 300s B.C. symbolizes the importance of the individual citizen in the Athenian judicial system.

CONNECTING TO

Civics

Rights and Responsibilities in Ancient Greece

The ancient Athenians took their duties seriously. All free men over the age of 18 were members of the assembly, which met regularly to make decisions and solve problems. Men could speak, make motions, and vote. The decisions of the assembly were law.

Each year 500 men were chosen by lot to serve on the Council, which attended to state business. Athenian trials were judged by juries of 101 to 1,001 people, and each year 6,000 citizens were chosen by lot to serve on the juries, whose decisions were final.

Understanding Civics

Why would the Athenian form of government be difficult to use today?

Analyzing Primary Sources

Evaluating According to Solon, how did slavery affect all Athenians, even those who were not themselves slaves? removes citizens from the community

---

Government

In addition to erasing debt and outlawing slavery for debt, Solon also wanted to eliminate social pressures in Athenian society by basing citizenship on wealth rather than birth into the aristocracy.

Critical Thinking

Ask students why basing citizenship on wealth might relieve some of the social tensions in Athens. Have them support their point of view.

ANSWER: Students should note that some nonaristocrats—the metics—had become wealthy, but since they were not citizens they could neither vote nor hold office. When they were allowed to hold political office, they had less reason to resent the aristocrats' power.

CONNECTING TO CIVICS ANSWER
Students should recognize that populations are too large and society is too complex now for direct democracy to work well.

That's Interesting!

U.S. bankruptcy laws say that a person who has legally declared bankruptcy cannot be held responsible for debts previously incurred. The source of these laws is Solon's ordinance canceling the burdens of Greek debtors.

Pericles was one of the great leaders in Athenian history. In fact, the 30-year period of his rule became known as the Age of Pericles. He fought wars to expand Athens's power and influence. He restored democracy that had been lost after the death of Cleisthenes. He built Athens's navy and beautified the city with new buildings and sculptures. But his rule was not without controversy. Have students work in pairs to investigate the Age of Pericles. Urge them to assess Pericles's accomplishments both in light of the time in which he lived and of the legacy he left to Greece and Western civilization. Have students share their findings with the class. Encourage them to use visuals such as charts and time lines to enhance their presentation.

COOPERATIVE LEARNING, BLOCK SCHEDULING

CLOSE

Have students write a paragraph explaining whether they would rather have lived in Sparta or Athens. Ask them to provide at least three reasons to support their point of view.

REVIEW

Have students complete the Section 3 Review on p. 117.

Interdisciplinary Connection

LITERATURE. The poet Terpandros spent most of his life in Sparta. According to the *Suda Lexicon,* an ancient Greek work, "The Spartans were fighting amongst themselves and sent to Lesbos for the musician Terpandros; he came and made their minds tranquil and stopped the quarrel."

Critical Thinking

Ask students what they learned about Spartans from this excerpt from the *Suda Lexicon.*

ANSWER: Spartans valued music and found creative ways to manage conflict.

SKILLS PRACTICE ANSWERS

1. favors the many instead of the few; laws provide equal justice; leadership based on ability

2. Athenian democracy: equal rights to all citizens; Spartan government: most power to aristocrats; Athens: could pursue private interests; Sparta: interests of city-state above private interests

3. United States: representative; Athens: direct

4. Athenian government was advanced; citizens of surrounding city-states probably had less freedom, no participation in government

SKILL-BUILDING STRATEGIES Analyzing Historical Context

Athenian Democracy

Analyzing historical context involves trying to understand events and people within the context, or circumstances, of their times. Historians take up this task because ideas and notions have meant different things at various times in history. For example, today, many people would probably consider Athenian democracy limited since it did not include women, slaves, or those born outside Athens. In analyzing historical context, historians seek to identify the beliefs and values of a particular group during a specific era. This helps them to evaluate and understand the choices and decisions that people have made throughout the different periods of history.

A Historian's View

The Greek historian Thucydides is often called the first true historian because he took a critical look at historical evidence. Partly for this reason, he is widely recognized as the greatest historian of ancient times, even though he wrote only one work. The following excerpt is his account of a speech given by Pericles about Athenian democracy.

"Our constitution does not copy the laws of neighbouring states; we are rather a pattern to others than imitators ourselves. Its administration favours the many instead of the few; this is why it is called a democracy. If we look to the laws, they afford equal justice to all in their private differences; if to social standing, advancement in public life falls to reputation for capacity [ability], class considerations not being allowed to interfere with merit. . . . The freedom which we enjoy in our government extends also to our ordinary life. There, far from exercising a jealous surveillance [secret observation] over each other, we do not feel called upon to be angry with our neighbor for doing what he likes. . . . But all this ease in our private relations does not make us lawless as citizens. Against this fear is our chief safeguard, teaching us to obey the magistrates and the laws."

Although Athens was named after a woman—the goddess Athena—women could not participate in its government. This temple to Athena, the Erechtheion, was built between about 421 B.C. and 405 B.C.

Skills Reminder

To analyze historical context, identify the topic by determining the person or group as well as the time period you are examining. Recognize clues that explain attitudes and beliefs. Look for words, phrases, or quotes that provide reasons for a person's or group's choices and decisions. This will help you establish the historical context. Then formulate a comparison. Evaluate how the group's actions and decisions differ from those of later or present-day societies.

Skills Practice

❶ According to Pericles, what were the advantages of Athenian democracy?

❷ How did the Athenian government differ from that of Sparta?

❸ How did Athenian democracy differ from democracy in the United States today?

❹ Given the historical context of the time, was the Athenian form of government advanced? Explain your answer.

ASSESS

Have students complete Daily Quiz 5.3. As Alternative Assessment, have students complete the role-playing or the matching exercises in this section's lessons.

RETEACH

Have students complete Main Idea Activity for English Language Learners and Special-Needs Students 5.3. Instruct students to create a Venn diagram in which they use correct social studies terminology to compare and contrast the society and government of Sparta and Athens. They should use the later Athens government. (*Alike—three social groups: equals/citizens, half-citizens/metics,*

EXTEND

Organize students into groups of five and direct them to prepare a live TV broadcast about government or social conditions in Sparta or Athens. Are people satisfied? What should be changed? Who benefits? Is it fair? Students should take the roles of reporters, news anchor, and citizens and half-citizens.
COOPERATIVE LEARNING, BLOCK SCHEDULING

Democracy in Athens

621 B.C.	594 B.C.	546 B.C.–527 B.C.	508 B.C.	461 B.C.–429 B.C.
Law code attributed to Draco was drawn up.	Solon abolished enslavement for debt, defined political rights in terms of wealth rather than birth, and established court of appeals.	Peisistratus, tyrant who ruled with support of lower classes, may have divided nobles' estates among poor farmers.	Cleisthenes broke up power of aristocrats and created the Council of Five Hundred, chosen from local government units, with wide power.	Pericles opened offices to all male citizens and provided that officeholders be paid.

Solon also made changes in Athens's government. He divided all citizens into four groups based on wealth. The two richest groups could hold public office. All citizens, however, could sit in the assembly that elected those officials. Solon set up a court made up of citizen jurors. Solon's changes did not end Athens's problems, however. Between about 546 B.C. and 527 B.C., **Peisistratus** (py·SIS·truh·tuhs) ruled over Athens as a tyrant. Although Peisistratus improved Athens's economy, he clashed with the nobles. After the rule of Peisistratus's sons, the nobles returned to power.

Athenian democracy. In about 507 B.C., **Cleisthenes** (KLYS·thuh·neez) seized power in Athens and turned it into a democracy. First, he divided Athens's citizens into 10 tribes. Then he had each tribe choose 50 men. These men formed the Council of Five Hundred. Members served for one year and could not be chosen more than twice. The council proposed laws to the assembly, but the assembly had final authority. Athens's courts also became more democratic. Jurors were citizens chosen by lot. Each man could plead his own case to the jury. The jury voted on each case by secret ballot. The form of democracy Athens had under Cleisthenes is called **direct democracy.** That is, all citizens participated directly in making decisions. Present-day democracies such as the United States use **representative democracy.** That is, citizens elect representatives to govern for them.

Holt Researcher
go.hrw.com
KEYWORD: Holt Researcher
FreeFind: Solon
After reading more about Solon on the Holt Researcher, make a chart comparing Solon's government to the U.S. government today.

✔ **READING CHECK: Supporting a Point of View** Which leader did the most to help lead Athens to democracy? Cleisthenes

SECTION 3 REVIEW

1. **Define** and explain the significance:
   helots
   ephors
   metics
   archons
   direct democracy
   representative democracy

2. **Identify** and explain the significance:
   Draco
   Solon
   Peisistratus
   Cleisthenes

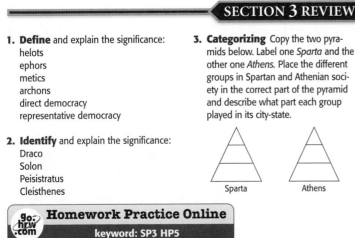

Homework Practice Online
keyword: SP3 HP5

3. **Categorizing** Copy the two pyramids below. Label one *Sparta* and the other one *Athens*. Place the different groups in Spartan and Athenian society in the correct part of the pyramid and describe what part each group played in its city-state.

Sparta   Athens

4. **Finding the Main Idea**
   a. How did Sparta build its military society?
   b. What changes led to Athens's aristocratic government becoming a democracy?
   c. How does direct democracy differ from representative democracy?

5. **Writing and Critical Thinking**
   Making Predictions Explain what the results might have been if Solon had not changed the way citizens in debt were treated and the way citizens could receive a hearing in court.
   Consider:
   • how those citizens were treated before Solon's changes
   • what effect Solon's changes had

SECTION 3 REVIEW ANSWERS

❶ **Define**
• helots, p. 113
• ephors, p. 114
• metics, p. 115
• archons, p. 115
• direct democracy, p. 117
• representative democracy, p. 117

❷ **Identify**
• Draco, p. 115
• Solon, p. 115
• Peisistratus, p. 117
• Cleisthenes, p. 117

❸ Answers given in top to bottom order. Sparta: equals, half-citizens, helots; Athens: citizens, metics, slaves

❹ **a.** Young boys began military training at age 7 and served in the military until age 60.

b. Cleisthenes broke up the power of the aristocrats and created the Council of Five Hundred, comprised of citizens elected by their tribe. The council proposed laws, which were approved or vetoed by the Assembly made up of all citizens.

c. In a direct democracy, all citizens vote on all issues and laws. In a representative democracy, citizens vote for representatives who govern for them.

❺ If Solon had not changed the way citizens who were in debt were treated, the society would have been depleted as more and more citizens became slaves. The old policy might also have pushed poorer citizens to revolt and overthrow their government.

OBJECTIVES

1 Explain the basis of Athens's economy.

2 Describe the family life and education of Athenians.

SECTION 4

READ TO DISCOVER

❶ What activities formed the basis of Athens's economy?

❷ What were Athenian family life and education like?

DEFINE

terracing
import
export
pedagogue
ethics
rhetoric

IDENTIFY

Sappho
Sophists

Daily Life in Athens

The Main Idea
Daily life in Athens consisted of simple economic and educational pursuits, and family concerns.

The Story Continues *In most city-states, private and public life were carefully balanced. As far as we know, citizens of most Greek city-states, except Sparta, lived their daily lives in much the same way as the people of Athens. Their days were filled with work, family, and educational pursuits.*

The Athenian Economy

Most Athenian citizens were farmers who grew olives, grapes, and figs, which they planted on terraced hillsides. **Terracing** means carving small, flat plots of land from hillsides.

The Athenian assembly voted to send farmers and workers to set up overseas colonies. This spread Greek culture throughout the Mediterranean and promoted trade. Colonies imported goods from, and exported goods to, Greece. An **import** is a good or service bought from another country or region. An **export** is a good or service sold to another country or region.

Trade was the mainstay of Athens's economy. The Athenians exported olive oil, wine, and household items, and imported grain and other foodstuffs. Athenian ships sailed throughout the Mediterranean world.

✔ **READING CHECK: Categorizing** What goods did Athenian farmers, metics, and traders produce or handle? vases, olives, grapes, wine

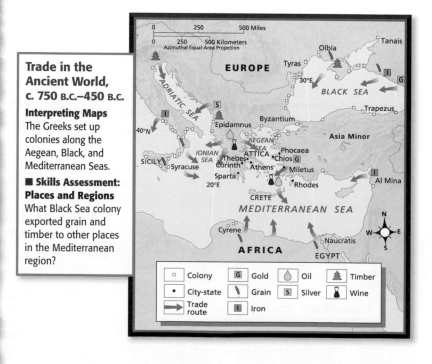

Trade in the Ancient World, c. 750 B.C.–450 B.C.

Interpreting Maps The Greeks set up colonies along the Aegean, Black, and Mediterranean Seas.

■ **Skills Assessment: Places and Regions** What Black Sea colony exported grain and timber to other places in the Mediterranean region?

Legend		
▢ Colony	G Gold	◊ Oil	▲ Timber
• City-state	\ Grain	S Silver	⚱ Wine
→ Trade route	I Iron		

TEACH OBJECTIVE 1

ALL LEVELS: Make a web diagram on the chalkboard with *Athenian Economy* at the center. Then write *Agriculture* and *Trade*, circle each, and connect them to the first circle. Have students read the paragraphs on the Athenian economy and complete the web. *(Agriculture: poor soil; terracing; olives, grapes, figs, olive oil, wine. Trade: set up colonies; imported grain and foodstuffs; exported vases and household items)*
ENGLISH LANGUAGE LEARNERS

TEACH OBJECTIVE 2

LEVEL 3: Have students create a chart with two headings: *Female* and *Male*. Then have them fill in the columns with equivalent facts about the lives and duties of females and males in Athens. Have students combine their ideas in a class chart to be used for discussion. **COOPERATIVE LEARNING**

HOMEWORK Have students identify subjects that Greek boys learned in school at different ages and discuss why the subjects differed.

INTERPRETING THE VISUAL RECORD

Scenes of daily life Greek artisans showed scenes from everyday life in small sculptures. *What are the women in this sculpture doing?*

Home and Family Life

Athenians built magnificent temples and other public buildings. However, most Athenian families lived in simple homes. Generally, most Athenians believed that money should be spent on buildings to benefit the whole community, not on private homes. Their one-story houses, made of sun-dried brick, sat close to the street. The door to the home opened from the street into a courtyard. From the courtyard, doors opened into other parts of the home. These included the living room, dining room, bedrooms, storerooms, and kitchen. Lamps that burned olive oil provided dim light. The houses had no plumbing. Residents had to fill jars with water at the fountain near the agora.

Marriage and family life were very important to Athenians. Parents always arranged marriages. Girls married young, at age 13 or 14. A girl's husband might be twice her age or older. The main purpose of marriage was to have children. Sometimes, however, a family could not afford to raise a child. Then the baby was left to die, especially if it was a girl. This is not to say that Greek parents did not love their daughters. One of the most touching poems written by the ancient Greek poet **Sappho** was "Sleep, Darling," an ode to her daughter.

> **Primary Source**
>
> ❝Sleep, darling
> I have a small daughter called Cleis, who is
> like a golden flower
> I wouldn't take all Croesus' kingdom with love thrown in, for her❞
>
> Sappho, "Sleep, Darling," from *Sappho: A New Translation* by Mary Barnard

Despite such personal feelings, legally and socially Athenian women were considered inferior to men. They were citizens but could not own or inherit property. Even at home, women were expected to stay in the background. For example, they stayed out of sight when their husbands had guests. They could appear in public only with their husbands' permission. Women's duties included managing the household and slaves and raising children.

In many Athenian households, the mother took care of all children until the age of six. At about age seven, boys came under the care of their **pedagogue.** This was a male slave who taught the boy manners. The pedagogue went everywhere with the boy, including to school. Athenian girls stayed at home. They learned to run a household but usually received no other education. Some daughters of wealthy families, however, were taught to read and write.

✔ **READING CHECK: Contrasting** How did life differ for men and women and for boys and girls in Athens? men participated in public life, women were kept in the home; boys got an education, girls were trained for household

HISTORY MAKER

Sappho
(c. 610 B.C.–c. 580 B.C.)

The daughter of a wealthy Greek family, Sappho became famous for her poetry. She often described everyday scenes from Greek life. Among her themes were rural life and celebrations such as weddings.

Sappho also wrote about the personal lives and feelings of women. In the area where Sappho lived, women used to gather together to write and recite poetry. Sappho led one such group. Although at one point up to nine volumes of her poetry existed, today only a few poems and fragments by Sappho have survived. **What can Sappho's writings teach us about the lives of women in the ancient Greek world?**

That's Interesting!

The standardized form of the Athenian dialect was known as *koine,* which means "common Greek." For centuries *koine* was the language of commerce throughout the eastern Mediterranean world.

Culture

In ancient Greece, men held all legal rights, and a woman who wished to be respectable would not even leave her house. Marriage was largely a financial agreement. Women played such a minor role in Greek society that they were often not named publicly until their death. As a result, historians have very little evidence about Athenian women.

Critical Thinking

Ask students to suggest ways that modern scholars have learned about the ancient Greeks' attitudes toward women.

ANSWER: Students should suggest that scholars have probably learned about ancient Greek attitudes from written accounts from the time.

VISUAL RECORD ANSWER

They appear to be kneading dough.

HISTORY MAKER ANSWER
Her writings reveal women's lives and feelings.

As part of their gymnastics training, young boys learned how to box.

Education and Military Service

Most Greeks were poor and hardworking. They labored long hours and had little leisure time. Wealthy men spent their time in the pursuit of intellectual and physical excellence. They engaged in politics, gossip in the marketplace, conversations with friends, and athletic activities.

Athenians placed great value on literacy and education. They sent their sons to elementary schools, which charged a small fee. Athenian boys studied reading, writing, grammar, poetry, music, and gymnastics. They learned poetry by heart, including Homer's *Iliad* and *Odyssey*.

The Athenian ideal stressed a sound mind in a healthy body. Grammar and music were meant to develop the minds and emotions of students. Gymnastics developed the body. In open fields at the edge of the city, boys practiced running, jumping, boxing, and throwing the discus and javelin.

In the 400s B.C. men called **Sophists** opened schools for older boys. The Sophists took their name from the Greek word *sophos*, meaning "wise." At these schools boys studied government, mathematics, ethics, and rhetoric. **Ethics** deals with what is good and bad, and moral duty. **Rhetoric** was the study of oratory, or public speaking, and debating.

Education helped spread the Greek language and civilization throughout the Mediterranean world. Greek was a second language for educated people everywhere. Even today we use many words that are derived from Greek.

At age 18 Athenian males received a year of military training. Young men who could afford armor and weapons then became hoplites and served in the army for a year. Hoplites formed the center of the infantry. Poorer men, who could not afford good equipment, served on the army's flanks. Citizens also rowed the warships in the Athenian fleet.

✔ **READING CHECK: Summarizing** How did Athenian education fulfill the Greek ideal of a sound mind in a healthy body? students exercised physically and mentally

SECTION 4 REVIEW

1. **Define** and explain the significance:
   terracing
   import
   export
   pedagogue
   ethics
   rhetoric

2. **Identify** and explain the significance:
   Sappho
   Sophists

3. **Sequencing** Copy the graphic organizer below. Use it to show what Athenian boys and young men learned at each stage of their educations.

```
        Pedagogue        Elementary
                           School
              Athenian
             Education
        Military          Sophist
        Training          School
```

4. **Finding the Main Idea**
   a. Why did trade become the most important part of the Greek economy?
   b. What role did colonies play in the rise of Greek trade?
   c. In what ways did Greek society show the attitude that women were valued less than men?

5. **Writing and Critical Thinking**
   Summarizing In a diary entry, describe a day in the life of a young Athenian boy or girl.
   Consider:
   - how Athenians made their livings
   - what Athenian home and family life was like
   - what place education had in Athenian life

Homework Practice Online
keyword: SP3 HP5

OBJECTIVES

1 Explain how the Persian Wars began and what the results of those wars were.

2 Analyze the effects of Pericles's leadership on Athens.

3 Explain how the Peloponnesian War began and its results.

SECTION 5

The Expansion of Greece

READ TO DISCOVER

❶ How did the Persian Wars begin and what were their results?

❷ What effect did Pericles's leadership have on Athens?

❸ Why did the Peloponnesian War begin and what were its results?

IDENTIFY

Persian Wars
Battle of Marathon
Battle of Thermopylae
Themistocles
Delian League
Pericles
Peloponnesian War

▶ WHY IT MATTERS TODAY

The United Nations today works much like the Delian League in ancient Greece. Member nations contribute money and promise to send troops to trouble spots around the world. Use CNNfyi.com or other **current event** sources to find examples of activities in which the United Nations is involved. Record your findings in your journal.

CNNfyi.com

The Main Idea
Destructive wars that pitted Greeks against other powers and city-state against city-state weakened Greece.

The Story Continues *At first, the Greek city-states developed without interference from the nearby empires of Southwest Asia. Eventually, however, the mighty Persian Empire entered into Greek affairs. In 546 B.C. King Cyrus of Persia conquered the Greek colonies on the western coast of Asia Minor. Cyrus permitted these Greeks to keep their local governments. Later rulers, however, tightened Persian rule and raised taxes.*

The Persian Wars

In about 500 B.C. Greeks in Asia Minor rebelled against the Persians. Athens helped these city-states in their uprisings. This began a series of conflicts between Greece and Persia that lasted until 479 B.C. These conflicts are known as the **Persian Wars.**

The wars under Darius and Xerxes. Persian ruler Darius easily crushed the Greek revolts in Asia Minor. However, he also wanted to punish Athens for helping the rebels. Darius hoped to gain control of the Greek mainland. In 492 B.C. his forces conquered Thrace and Macedonia. Two years later, the Persians invaded Greece itself. The Athenians, although outnumbered, defeated the Persians at the **Battle of Marathon.** The Persians withdrew, and an uneasy peace lasted for 10 years.

In 480 B.C. Darius's son Xerxes led another huge Persian army and fleet against Greece. This time, several Greek city-states united to stop the Persians. The Persians had to advance through the narrow mountain pass of Thermopylae (thuhr·MAH·puh·lee). A small force led by 300 Spartans met them there. The Greeks held the pass for three days. Then the Persians found another way  through the mountains and surrounded the Greeks. The Spartans, although badly outnumbered, refused to surrender. Instead, they fought until they were all killed. The Spartans' courage at the **Battle of Thermopylae** bought the other city-states time to prepare their forces.

INTERPRETING THE VISUAL RECORD

War memorial This present-day memorial honors the Greek soldiers who fought to the death at Thermopylae. Even today, the battle symbolizes resistance against huge odds.

Link to Today What does this memorial tell us about how modern Greeks feel about the Battle of Thermopylae?

LEVEL 3: Have students create an illustrated time line showing the significant events of the Persian Wars. (*546 B.C.: Persia conquers Greek colonies in Asia Minor; c. 500 B.C.: Greek colonies rebel/Athens becomes involved; 492 B.C.: Persia conquers Thrace and Macedonia; 490 B.C.: Athens defeats Persians at Battle of Marathon; 480 B.C.: Spartans inspire Greeks in loss of Battle of Thermopylae; Persians destroy Athens; 479 B.C.: Athens and Sparta defeat Persia.*) Tell students that they should try to make their time line self-explanatory so that someone looking at it can understand the events of the Persian Wars and who took part in them.

ENGLISH LANGUAGE LEARNERS

ALL LEVELS: Ask students if the final Greek victory successfully ended the conflict with Persia. (*Students should recognize that the victory was incomplete because the threat from Persia continued.*) Have students identify the effects of the ongoing tensions between Greece and Persia. (*Greek city-states worked toward unity; Athens and other city-states formed Delian League.*)

COOPERATIVE LEARNING

Global Relations

The Persian army drew soldiers and fleets from their conquered territories, among them Phoenicia. The Phoenicians may have contributed as many as 300 ships to the Persian fleet total of about 1,000. Phoenician sailors served in the Persian army. These sailors, who were more skilled than the Persians and the Greeks at naval maneuvers, bore the brunt of the Persian defeat at Salamis.

Critical Thinking

Why do you think the Phoenician sailors served in the Persian fleet? How do you think they felt about it? Support your point of view.

ANSWER: The Phoenicians may have been forced to serve in the fleet and resented it. Some may have liked serving in a powerful army.

MAP ANSWERS

1. The valleys between the mountain ranges run in a north-south direction, so the invading Persians would not have had to cross high mountain passes.

2. Some Greek city-states may have resented the power of Athens and Sparta.

Technology Resources

go.hrw.com Online Maps, Charts, and Graphs: The Battle of Salamis; The Battle of Thermopylae

Holt Researcher
go.hrw.com
KEYWORD: Holt Researcher
FreeFind: Xerxes
After reading more about Xerxes on the Holt Researcher, write a paragraph summarizing his successes and failures as a leader.

The Persians then marched toward Athens. **Themistocles** (thuh·MIS·tuh·kleez), Athens's leader, told the Athenians to leave the city and escape. Xerxes's army entered Athens and destroyed it. However, Themistocles tricked Xerxes into attacking the Athenian fleet in the narrow Salamis Strait. The Persian navy was larger than the Greek navy, but the Greek ships were more maneuverable. In the narrow waters of the strait, the Greeks sank much of the Persian fleet. In 479 B.C. the Athenians and Spartans joined forces to defeat the Persians at Plataea, northwest of Athens. This ended the Persian Wars.

Results of the Persian Wars. Although Greek city-states in Asia Minor were now free from Persian rule, the Persian Empire still remained powerful. The Persians still meddled

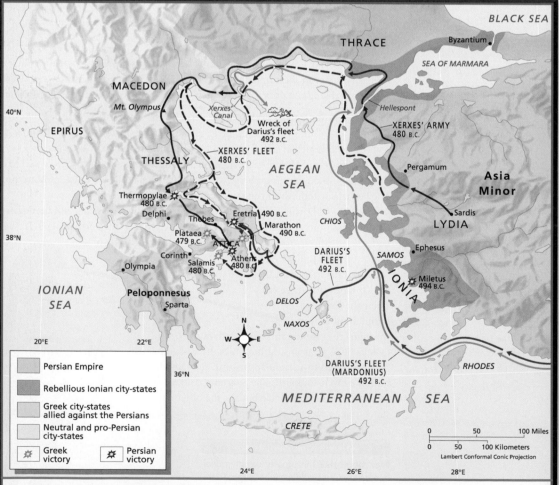

The Persian Wars, c. 500 B.C.–479 B.C.
Interpreting Maps Some of the Greek city-states supported Persia or took no side in the Persian Wars.
■ **Skills Assessment: 1. Using Geography** Why was the Persian army able to march easily through northern Greece?
2. Drawing Inferences Why might some Greek city-states have remained neutral or favored Persia?

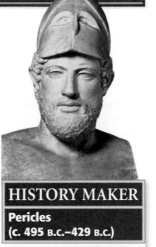

Teacher to Teacher

Peggy Altoff of Baltimore, Maryland, suggested the following activity: Have students analyze the images of ancient Greek buildings in this chapter and list some of their notable features. Then have students compare these images to public buildings in their own town. They should write a short summary of the similarities and differences between public buildings then and now.

HOMEWORK Ask students to imagine that they are members of a Greek family who have lived through the Persian Wars. They want to leave behind a time capsule for their ancestors that will explain what the Persian Wars were like, how they affected the lives of Greek women and children, how the Greek soldiers defeated the Persians, and the effects of the victory. Tell students that they may create any type of objects for their time capsules, such as written documentation, illustrations, or artifacts. Have students present their collection to the class and explain how the items in the time capsules tell the story of the Persian Wars. **COOPERATIVE LEARNING**

in Greek affairs and worked to prevent Greek unity. However, success against the Persians gave the Greeks confidence. The Athenians rebuilt their city and entered a period of great cultural achievement. Athens began to create its own empire in the Aegean Sea.

Although the Persians had been defeated, the threat of invasion from the Persian Empire continued. Unity among the Greek city-states seemed necessary for survival. Sparta wanted Greek unity under its own leadership, but fear of helot revolt kept the Spartans from sending troops far from home for very long. Athens was more successful, using diplomacy to form the **Delian League,** an alliance of city-states with Athens as leader. Eventually the league included 140 other city-states, who each contributed money or ships. The money was kept on the island of Delos, from which the name Delian is derived. By the 450s B.C. Athens had built an empire based on the Delian League.

✔ **READING CHECK: Drawing Conclusions** Why did the Greek city-states unite during and after the Persian Wars? to face the Persian threat

The Age of Pericles

During this time, Pericles was the leader in Athens. **Pericles** was a great general, orator, and statesman who held public office or was active in public life from 461 B.C. to 429 B.C. During those years, Athens reached its peak of power and wealth. Pericles's leadership was so important to Athenian success that this period is called the Age of Pericles.

Under Pericles, Athenian democracy reached its height. All male citizens except for the lowest class could hold public office. Officeholders were paid a salary and were chosen by lot so that no one had an advantage. Athens achieved probably the most completely democratic government in history. Remember, however, that women rarely took part in public life. Also, many other residents were not citizens or were slaves.

Pericles strengthened and extended the empire that Athens had built. He established colonies of Athenian citizens in important or rebellious areas. He used the Athenian navy to keep the Persians out of the Aegean Sea. The Athenian system of weights and measures became standard throughout the empire. The rule of Pericles brought stability and prosperity to the eastern Mediterranean region. The members of the Delian League received these benefits but lost their independence.

HISTORY MAKER

Pericles
(c. 495 B.C.–429 B.C.)

Pericles was one of the greatest Greek statesmen. He was responsible for building the Parthenon and the Acropolis. He made Athens the cultural and political capital of Greece.

Pericles came of age at a time when Greeks first used the popular vote to change politics. He defeated his enemies in war, but used trade to build unity among the Greek city-states. **How did Pericles help make Athens the center of Greece?**

INTERPRETING THE VISUAL RECORD

The Acropolis Pericles rebuilt the buildings on the Acropolis after the Persian Wars. All Athenians took pride in the new look of the Acropolis. *How did the Acropolis reflect Athenian pride?*

Government

At first, members of the Delian League were independent and on equal terms with other members. Soon, however, Athens turned the alliance into its own empire, changing allies into subjects, and forbidding any city from withdrawing from the League. Athens first demonstrated its power over the League when the island of Naxos tried to withdraw in about 470 B.C. Athens took control and forced Naxos to remain in the League. About seven years later, Thasos withdrew from the League and was quickly subdued. In 454 B.C. the League's treasury was moved from Delos to Athens.

Critical Thinking

Ask students if they think Athens's control of the treasury gave it an advantage in controlling the League. Have them support their point of view.

ANSWER: Students might suggest that control of the treasury allowed Athens to use money for its own benefit.

HISTORY MAKER ANSWER

Pericles extended Athens's empire and strengthened its navy. He used Athens's power to ensure prosperity and stability in the region.

VISUAL RECORD ANSWER

buildings were large and stately; clearly dominated the landscape

TEACH OBJECTIVE 2

LEVEL 2: Write *Age of Pericles* on the chalkboard and circle it. Have students use this beginning to create a web summarizing the achievements of this period. *(Athens at peak of power and wealth; officeholders were paid; Athenian empire extended; Athenian navy kept Persians from Aegean Sea; Athenian weights and measures became Greek standard; stability and prosperity; Delian League cities received benefits but lost independence)*
ENGLISH LANGUAGE LEARNERS

TEACH OBJECTIVE 3

LEVEL 1: Before students read about the Peloponnesian War, discuss with them the quotation by Thucydides on page 124. Ask students if they can think of other reasons that young Greeks might be eager to go to war. Then tell students that war finally broke out between Athens and Sparta. Lead a discussion about who students think will win the Peloponnesian War. Close by having them read about the war.

Interdisciplinary Connection

SCIENCE. The plague that broke out in Athens was devastating. Thucydides was himself a victim of it, although he survived. He gave a detailed account of the disease. Modern scientists have not been able to positively identify it from his description, however. They know it was not the bubonic plague, which rampaged through Europe in the 1300s. The strongest candidate is typhus, a disease characterized by fever, rash, and mental confusion. The plague may have killed about one-third of the Athenians and left the rest badly demoralized.

ACTIVITY: Have students use their textbooks, the library, computer software, and other available resources to research other plagues throughout history. Students should transfer any statistical information to a written or visual form.

MAP ANSWERS

1. Athens: Ionia, Rhodes, Chalcidice, Thessaly, Euboea, Attica; Sparta: Macedon

2. Sparta's allies included a major land power.

Although government in Athens was democratic, the Delian League was not. Athens made all the decisions. According to the historian Thucydides (thoo·SID·uh·deez), one citizen gave the following advice to his fellow Athenians:

> **Primary Source**
>
> ❝Your empire is a tyranny . . . over subjects who do not like it and who are always plotting against you; you will not make them obey you by injuring your own interests . . . ; your leadership depends on superior strength and not on any goodwill of theirs.❞
>
> Thucydides, *History of the Peloponnesian War*

Analyzing Primary Sources

Identifying Points of View
According to this passage, how did some Athenians feel about Pericles's policies? opposed them

Pericles moved the league's treasury from Delos to Athens. He used the money for the good of Athens. Pericles also forced more city-states to join the league. Sometimes Athenian forces had to put down revolts by other city-states.

✔ **READING CHECK: Summarizing** What changes did Pericles bring to Athens and to the rest of Greece? strengthened Delian League, made other city-states subordinate to Athens

The Peloponnesian War

Pericles failed to unite Greece under Athens. Discontent grew. Quarrels over trade divided Athens and Corinth. Tensions grew between Athens and Sparta until war broke out in 431 B.C. This war is called the **Peloponnesian War.** Athens and Sparta shared responsibility for the Peloponnesian War. The city-states had been rivals for years. As Thucydides wrote, "The Peloponnesus [Sparta] and Athens were both full of young men whose inexperience made them eager to take up arms."

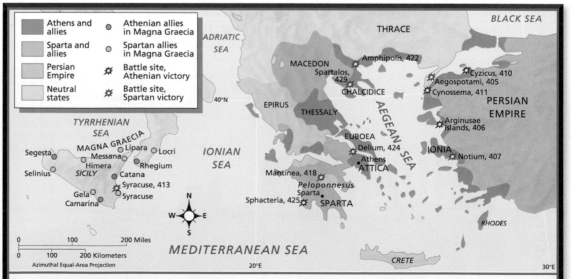

The Peloponnesian War

Interpreting Maps At the beginning of the Peloponnesian War, both Athens and Sparta had help from other city-states.

■ **Skills Assessment: 1. Locate** Locate the main allies of Athens and Sparta. **2. Drawing Conclusions** Why might Sparta be better able to win the Peloponnesian War?

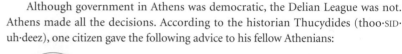

CLOSE

Have students write an epitaph for Pericles. Ask them to include a summary of his major accomplishments.

REVIEW

Have students complete the Section 5 Review on p. 125.

ASSESS

Have students complete Daily Quiz 5.5. As Alternative Assessment, use the time line of the Persian Wars or the web diagram about the Age of Pericles in this section's lessons.

RETEACH

Have students complete Main Idea Activity for English Language Learners and Special-Needs Students 5.5. Have groups write the main idea and six supporting details for each of the main subheadings of the section.

EXTEND

Organize students into groups representing Athenians and Spartans or other members of the Delian League. Have groups discuss ways to settle the disagreements among city-states and present their solutions to the class. **COOPERATIVE LEARNING**, **BLOCK SCHEDULING**

The Spartans had the stronger army. They started the fighting by invading the Attic peninsula, destroying fields and villages. The Athenians withdrew behind the city walls of Athens. Because Athens had the better navy and could bring in food by ship, the Spartans could not starve the Athenians out. The siege of Athens continued for years. During this time a plague broke out in Athens, killing many people, including Pericles.

The war continued for 27 years, punctuated by periods of truce and armed peace. The struggle even spilled over into the rest of the Greek world. During one truce in 415 B.C., Athens attacked the Greek city-state of Syracuse in Sicily. Syracuse was friendly to Sparta. The Athenians were driven back with great losses, which weakened the government of Athens. For a time aristocrats seized power. The Athenian people overthrew the aristocrats and restored their democracy, but the internal fighting further weakened Athens. Sparta, with the help of Persia, finally managed to block Athens's food supply. The starving Athenians finally surrendered to Sparta in 404 B.C. Athens was reduced for a time to being a second-rate power in Greece.

After the Peloponnesian War, Greece was politically unstable. First Sparta and then Thebes tried to control all of Greece. They were defeated and wars between the city-states continued. Many Greeks felt that only a foreign power could unite Greece. It would be many years before this would come to pass. However, Greek civilization still made great advances during this time.

During the Peloponnesian War, Athenians erected monuments to soldiers killed in battle.

✔ **READING CHECK: Identifying Cause and Effect** Why did the Peloponnesian War begin? old rivalries, Athenian control of Delian League

SECTION 5 REVIEW

1. **Identify** and explain the significance:
   Persian Wars
   Battle of Marathon
   Battle of Thermopylae
   Themistocles
   Delian League
   Pericles
   Peloponnesian War

2. **Comparing** Copy the graphic organizer below. Use it to write a brief comparison of the relationship between Athens and Sparta during the Persian Wars and the Peloponnesian War.

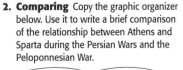
Persian Wars

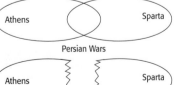
Peloponnesian War

Homework Practice Online
keyword: SP3 HP5

3. **Finding the Main Idea**
   a. How did the Greek victory over the Persians help bring about an Athenian empire?
   b. Why did paying officeholders a salary widen Athenian democracy during the Age of Pericles?
   c. How did the many differences between Sparta and Athens lead to the Peloponnesian War?

4. **Writing and Critical Thinking**
   Supporting a Point of View Write a letter to a friend in which you share your thoughts and feelings about Pericles's policies toward the Delian League.
   Consider:
   • why the Delian League was set up
   • how Pericles affected the Delian League

SECTION 5 REVIEW ANSWERS

❶ **Identify**
• Persian Wars, p. 121
• Battle of Marathon, p. 121
• Battle of Thermopylae, p. 121
• Themistocles, p. 122
• Delian League, p. 123
• Pericles, p. 123
• Peloponnesian War, p. 124

❷ Students' comparisons should note that during the Persian Wars, Athens and Sparta were allies against the Persians. In the Peloponnesian War, the two cities were enemies who fought for control of Greece.

❸ **a.** The Greek victory was incomplete, leaving the Persians as a constant threat. As a result, the Greek city-states were willing to form an alliance, and Athens became dominant, turning the other city-states into an Athenian empire.

b. Paying officeholders a salary allowed poor people as well as wealthy aristocrats to hold public office.

c. Sparta and Athens were natural rivals. Discontent in Greece grew. Quarrels over trade divided cities. Young men were eager to take up arms. One had a strong army, one a strong navy. Sparta was a kingdom; Athens was a democracy. Both sought leadership of Greece.

❹ Letters will vary, but students should explain the impetus for forming the Delian League as well as how people would have responded to Pericles's strong leadership abilities.

REVIEW AND ASSESSMENT RESOURCES

REPRODUCIBLE RESOURCES

▶ Vocabulary Activity 5

TECHNOLOGY RESOURCES

▶ Chapter 5 Test Generator (on the One-Stop Planner)
▶ Global Skill Builder CD–ROM
▶ HRW Web Site

REINFORCEMENT, REVIEW, and ASSESSMENT

▶ Chapter 5 Review, pp. 126–127
▶ Chapter 5 Tutorial for Students, Parents, Mentors, and Peers
▶ Chapter 5 Test (Form A or B)
▶ Alternative Assessment Handbook
▶ Chapter 5 Test for English Language Learners and Special-Needs Students

REVIEW

Have students complete the Chapter 5 Review on pages 126–127.

CLOSE

Ask students to write an outline for an encyclopedia article on the Greek city-states. Main headings and subheadings should indicate what topics the article would include.

Understanding Main Ideas

1. Mountains isolated the early civilizations; communication and travel were difficult; people focused on the sea and trading.

2. Everything the people needed was in their polis.

3. Governments evolved from kingdoms to aristocracies to democracies.

4. *Iliad:* story of the Trojan War; *Odyssey:* tells of Odysseus's adventures as he returns home from the Trojan War

5. to be good soldiers and to defend their city-state

6. Cleisthenes made Athens a direct democracy. Solon allowed more citizens to hold office.

7. men: farmed, produced goods, engaged in trade, participated in public life; women: managed household, raised children; boys: attended school; girls: learned to run a household

8. defended the pass at Thermopylae

9. Greece became politically unstable and wars continued.

Reviewing Themes

1. Mountains isolated cities; people became sailors and traders.

2. only free, adult men

3. Both wanted to control Greece.

CHAPTER
5 Review

Creating a Time Line

Copy the time line below onto a sheet of paper. Complete the time line by filling in the events, individuals, and dates from the chapter that you think were significant. Pick three events and explain why you think they were significant.

| 2000 B.C. | 700s B.C. | 594 B.C. | 404 B.C. |
| | | 500 B.C. | |

Writing a Summary

Using standard grammar, spelling, sentence structure, and punctuation, write an overview of the events in the chapter.

Identifying People and Ideas

Identify the following terms or individuals and explain their significance:

1. polis
2. Homer
3. myths
4. aristocracies
5. Solon
6. direct democracy
7. Sophists
8. Battle of Thermopylae
9. Delian League
10. Pericles

Understanding Main Ideas

SECTION 1 *(pp. 106–109)*

Early Greeks and the Rise of City-States

1. How did the geography of Greece affect the way its early civilizations grew?
2. Why was the polis such an important part of Greek life?

SECTION 2 *(pp. 110–112)*

Greek Government and Society

3. What kinds of governments did Greek city-states have between the 700s B.C. and the late 500s B.C.?
4. What kinds of information did Homer provide in the *Iliad* and the *Odyssey*?

SECTION 3 *(pp. 113–117)*

Sparta and Athens

5. From the Spartans' point of view, what was the purpose of life?
6. What conditions or developments helped to promote the rise of democracy in Athens?

SECTION 4 *(pp. 118–120)*

Daily Life in Athens

7. What were the main activities for men, for women, and for children in Athens?

SECTION 5 *(pp. 121–125)*

The Expansion of Greece

8. How did Sparta help Athens during the Persian Wars?
9. What happened in Greece after the Peloponnesian War?

Reviewing Themes

1. **Geography** How did Greece's landscape help determine the growth of the polis and of Greek trade?
2. **Citizenship** Who were allowed to be citizens in Athens and in Sparta?
3. **Global Relations** Why did Sparta go to war with Athens?

Thinking Critically

1. **Comparing** Compare the social classes in Spartan society with those in Athenian society.
2. **Contrasting** How did life in the city-states of Sparta and Athens differ?
3. **Sequencing** Trace the growth of Athenian democracy from Draco to Pericles.
4. **Categorizing** What were the outcomes of the Persian Wars and of the Peloponnesian War?

Writing About History

Evaluating Over a period of many years, the Athenians formed the world's first democracy. Write an explanation of how basic ideals from Athenian democracy, rules of law, and rights and responsibilities of citizens, including equality before the law, have become part of life in the United States today. Use the following chart to organize your thoughts before you begin writing.

Ideals of Democracy	
In Athens	In the United States

Use one of the chapter tests to assess students' understanding of the content. For Alternative Assessment, see the Portfolio Activities and Alternative Assessment Handbook.

RETEACH

Organize students into small groups and ask them to plan a children's book on the Greek city-states. Have each group develop an outline that contains chapter headings. Groups should also prepare a two-paragraph mar-

keting statement that summarizes the book in an engaging way. Then have students take the Form B Test to assess their mastery of the material. **ENGLISH LANGUAGE LEARNERS, COOPERATIVE LEARNING**

Portfolio Extensions

1. Have the students make a brochure describing the qualifications for citizenship in ancient Greece.
2. Have students work in groups of two or three and use their textbooks and other

sources to trace the process of the democratic-republican form of government from its beginnings in classical Greece and Rome through its developments in England and during the Enlightenment. Ask students to pay particular attention to how citizens were defined and the privileges they had. Then have each group create a chart to summarize its findings.
3. Have students write a newspaper editorial explaining whether they feel that requirements for citizenship in the United States today are fair or unfair.

Building Social Studies Skills

Interpreting Artifacts

The Greek coins below date from the 500s B.C. Study the coins and consider what they reveal about the culture that made and used them. Then answer the questions that follow.

1. Using only the information that can be inferred from the image above, select the statement that best describes early Greek society and culture.
   a. The Greek city-states differed greatly from one another in terms of technological development.
   b. These coins reflect a relatively high level of technological development.
   c. There was much economic competition among the Greek city-states.
   d. The Greeks colonized and traded throughout the Mediterranean region during the 500s B.C.

2. In what ways might coined money help to promote trade and commerce across a culture?

Identifying Bias

Read the following excerpt from the work of Thucydides, an Athenian who wrote a history of the Peloponnesian War. Then answer the questions.

> **"As for this present war, . . . if one looks at the facts themselves, one will see that this was the greatest war of all. . . . And with regard to my factual reporting of the events of the war . . . either I was present myself at the events which I have described or else I heard of them from eye-witnesses whose reports I have checked with as much thoroughness as possible."**

3. Which of the following statements drawn from the excerpt above represents the author's opinion?
   a. "I was present myself at the events."
   b. "I heard of them [the events] from eye-witnesses whose reports I have checked."
   c. "This was the greatest war of all."
   d. "my factual reporting of the events of the war."

4. Use the information you have gained from Chapter 5 to identify important events that an Athenian such as Thucydides might have experienced during the Peloponnesian War? Give specific examples.

Alternative Assessment

Building Your Portfolio

Citizenship

The ancient Greeks set up qualifications for citizenship. Today, most nations also have certain requirements that people must meet to become citizens. Using your textbook and other sources, find information about requirements for citizenship in the United States, Russia, and modern Greece. Create a chart comparing the three.

▸ internet connect

Internet Activity: go.hrw.com
KEYWORD: SP3 WH5

Choose a topic on the Greek City-States to:
- model ancient writing systems of the Mediterranean.
- build a map that connects modern and ancient Mediterranean cultures with pizza.
- report on Minoan civilization.

Thinking Critically

1. Citizens in Athens and equals in Sparta were males who could vote and own property. Metics in Athens and half-citizens in Sparta were free and paid taxes but could not take part in government or own land. Athens's slaves and Sparta's helots had no political rights.

2. Sparta: focused on military training; Athens: centered on education and culture

3. Draco: first written law; Solon: abolished enslavement for debt and established a court of appeals; Peisistratus: ruled with support of lower classes; Cleisthenes: broke up the power of aristocrats, created the Council of Five Hundred; Pericles: opened offices to all male citizens

4. Persian Wars: ended conflict with but not threat of Persia; Peloponnesian War: Athens defeated; conflicts between city-states persisted

Writing About History

Students might include individuals' rights.

Building Social Studies Skills

1. b

2. Coins could be traded instead of goods.

3. c

4. Answers will vary.

Building Your Portfolio

Students should include reasons for a country's requirements.

Greece's Golden and Hellenistic Ages

CHAPTER RESOURCE MANAGER

Objectives	Pacing Guide		Reproducible Resources
SECTION 1 **Greek Art of the Golden Age** (pp. 130–132) • Explain why the 400s B.C. are considered the golden age of Greek art and architecture. • Examine how Greek art of the golden age reflected the Greeks' view of themselves and the world.	**Regular** 1.5 day *Block Scheduling Handbook with Team Teaching Strategies, 6.1*	**Block Scheduling** 1 day	**RS** Guided Reading Strategy 6.1 **RS** Graphic Organizer Activity 6: Greek Arts
SECTION 2 **Philosophers and Writers of the Golden Age** (pp. 133–137) • Explain the basic ideas of Socrates, Plato, and Aristotle. • Identify the achievements of Greek mathematicians and scientists of the golden age. • Identify the important literary forms that originated or flourished during Greece's golden age.	**Regular** 1.5 day *Block Scheduling Handbook with Team Teaching Strategies, 6.2*	**Block Scheduling** 1 day	**RS** Guided Reading Strategy 6.2 **PS** Readings in World History 21: The Death of Socrates **PS** Readings in World History 22: Aristotle's Views on Education **PS** Readings in World History 23: The Medical Aphorisms of Hippocrates
SECTION 3 **Alexander the Great** (pp. 138–141) • Detail how Philip II of Macedon paved the way for cultural change. • Examine what Alexander the Great accomplished. • Identify the factors that contributed to the breakup of Alexander's empire.	**Regular** 1.5 day *Block Scheduling Handbook with Team Teaching Strategies, 6.3*	**Block Scheduling** 1 day	**RS** Guided Reading Strategy 6.3 **SM** Graphic Activity 6 **PS** Readings in World History 24 **E** Creative Teaching Strategy 6
SECTION 4 **The Spread of Hellenistic Culture** (pp. 142–145) • Describe how society changed during the Hellenistic Age. • Explain how philosophers of the Hellenistic Age viewed ethics. • Identify how Hellenistic scientists added to the existing body of knowledge.	**Regular** 1.5 day *Block Scheduling Handbook with Team Teaching Strategies, 6.4*	**Block Scheduling** 1 day	**RS** Guided Reading Strategy 6.4 **E** Hands-on History Activity 6: A Hellenistic Family

Chapter Resource Key

PS	Primary Sources	**A**	Assessment	🎵	Music
RS	Reading Support	**REV**	Review	📼	Video
IC	Interdisciplinary Connections	**ELL**	Reinforcement and English Language Learners	🌐	Internet
E	Enrichment		Transparencies	💻	Holt Presentation Maker Using Microsoft® PowerPoint®
SM	Skills Mastery		CD-ROM		

One-Stop Planner CD-ROM

See the **One-Stop Planner** for a complete list of additional resources for students and teachers.

One-Stop Planner CD-ROM

It's easy to plan lessons, select resources, and print out materials for your students when you use the *One-Stop Planner* CD–ROM with *Test Generator*.

Technology Resources	Reinforcement, Review, and Assessment
One-Stop Planner 6.1	Daily Quiz 6.1
World History teaching Transparency: Everyday Life 3: Greek Architecture	Main Idea Activity 6.1
Homework Practice Online	English Audio Summary 6.1
	Spanish Audio Summary 6.1
	REV Section 1 Review, p. 132
One-Stop Planner 6.2	Daily Quiz 6.2
Holt Researcher: World History: Pythagoras	Main Idea Activity 6.2
Holt Researcher: World History: Thucydides	English Audio Summary 6.2
World History and Cultures Video Program 4: A Socratic Education	Spanish Audio Summary 6.2
CNN Presents World Cultures: Yesterday and Today Segment 6: The Ancient Theaters of Epidaurus	REV Section 2 Review, p. 137
Homework Practice Online	
One-Stop Planner 6.3	Daily Quiz 6.3
Homework Practice Online	Main Idea Activity 6.3
Online Maps, Charts, and Graphs: Division of Alexander's Empire, 303 B.C.	English Audio Summary 6.3
	Spanish Audio Summary 6.3
	REV Section 3 Review, p. 141
One-Stop Planner 6.4	Daily Quiz 6.4
Holt Researcher: World History: Archimedes	Main Idea Activity 6.4
Holt Researcher: World History: Erastosthenes	English Audio Summary 6.4
World History Teaching Transparency: Art and History 3	Spanish Audio Summary 6.4
Homework Practice Online	REV Section 4 Review, p. 145
Online Maps, Charts, and Graphs: The Hellenization of Asia	
Online Maps, Charts, and Graphs: The Economy of the Hellenistic Era	

internet connect

HRW ONLINE RESOURCES
   GO TO: go.hrw.com
   Then type in a keyword.

TEACHER HOME PAGE
   KEYWORD: SP3 Teacher

CHAPTER INTERNET ACTIVITIES
   KEYWORD: SP3 WH6
Choose an activity to:
- research Athens's golden age and create a newspaper article describing a representative political development.
- identify currents of Greek thought in art from different time periods.
- report on the scientific contributions of the ancient Greeks.

CHAPTER ENRICHMENT LINKS
   KEYWORD: SP3 CH6

ONLINE ASSESSMENT
   Homework Practice
   KEYWORD: SP3 HP6
   Standardized Test Prep
   KEYWORD: SP3 STP6
   Rubrics
   KEYWORD: SS Rubrics

ONLINE MAPS, CHARTS, AND GRAPHS
   KEYWORD: SP3 MCG

CONTENT UPDATES
   KEYWORD: SS Content Updates

HOLT PRESENTATION MAKER
   KEYWORD: SP3 PPT6

ONLINE READING SUPPORT
   KEYWORD: SS Strategies

CURRENT EVENTS
   KEYWORD: S3 Current Events

Meeting Individual Needs

Ability Levels

Level 1 Basic level activities designed for all students encountering new material

Level 2 Intermediate level activities designed for average students

Level 3 Challenging activities designed for honors and gifted and talented students

English Language Learners These activities address the needs of students with Limited English Proficiency.

Chapter Review and Assessment

IC	Vocabulary Activity 6
	Global Skill Builder CD–ROM
	HRW Web Site
REV	Chapter 6 Tutorial for Students, Parents, Mentors, and Peers
REV	Chapter 6 Review, pp. 146–147
A	Chapter 6 Test Generator (on the One-Stop Planner)
A	Chapter 6 Test (Form A or B)
A	Alternative Assessment Handbook
A	Chapter 6 Test for English Language Learners and Special-Needs Students

Build on What You Know

Ask students to answer the following questions:

What characteristics distinguished Greece from other early civilizations?

Consider:

- **the rise of the city-states**
- **democratic rule**
- **religion and myths with humanlike gods and goddesses**

How might the Greeks' victory over the Persians have affected Greek culture?

Consider:

- **the confidence and sense of security it gave the Greeks**
- **the rise of Athens after the victory**
- **the strong leadership of Pericles**

EXPLORING THE TIME LINE
GLOBAL EVENTS

internet connect

go.hrw.com

TOPIC: Golden Age of Greece
GO TO: go.hrw.com
KEYWORD: SP3 WH6

Have students access the Internet through the HRW Go site to conduct research on ancient art of Greece. Remind them that these achievements in art are the works of ancient people from thousands of years ago. Ask them to write poems, music, or raps that express the emotions evoked by these works. Select volunteers to deliver their compositions to the class.

CHAPTER 6

478 B.C.–146 B.C.

Greece's Golden and Hellenistic Ages

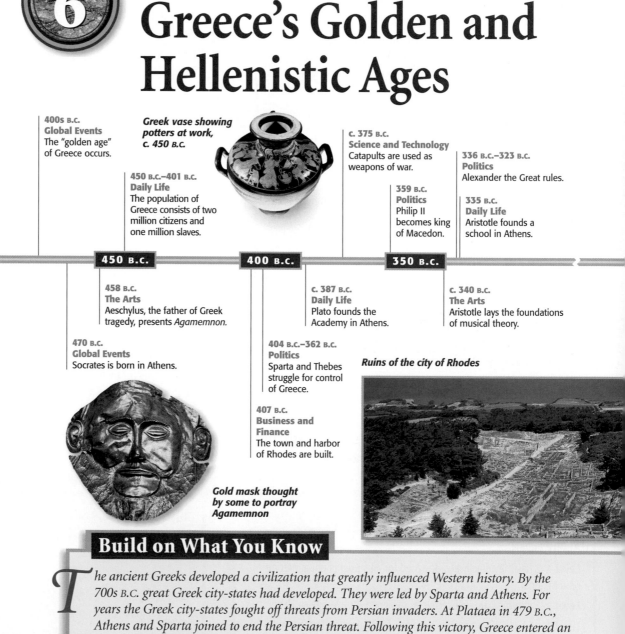

400s B.C.
Global Events
The "golden age" of Greece occurs.

Greek vase showing potters at work, c. 450 B.C.

c. 375 B.C.
Science and Technology
Catapults are used as weapons of war.

336 B.C.–323 B.C.
Politics
Alexander the Great rules.

450 B.C.–401 B.C.
Daily Life
The population of Greece consists of two million citizens and one million slaves.

359 B.C.
Politics
Philip II becomes king of Macedon.

335 B.C.
Daily Life
Aristotle founds a school in Athens.

450 B.C.   **400 B.C.**   **350 B.C.**

458 B.C.
The Arts
Aeschylus, the father of Greek tragedy, presents *Agamemnon*.

c. 387 B.C.
Daily Life
Plato founds the Academy in Athens.

c. 340 B.C.
The Arts
Aristotle lays the foundations of musical theory.

470 B.C.
Global Events
Socrates is born in Athens.

404 B.C.–362 B.C.
Politics
Sparta and Thebes struggle for control of Greece.

Ruins of the city of Rhodes

407 B.C.
Business and Finance
The town and harbor of Rhodes are built.

Gold mask thought by some to portray Agamemnon

Build on What You Know

*T*he ancient Greeks developed a civilization that greatly influenced Western history. By the 700s B.C. great Greek city-states had developed. They were led by Sparta and Athens. For years the Greek city-states fought off threats from Persian invaders. At Plataea in 479 B.C., Athens and Sparta joined to end the Persian threat. Following this victory, Greece entered an era of great cultural progress. In this chapter, you will learn about the development of Greek culture and how a rising power from outside of Greece helped to spread Greek achievements throughout the ancient world.

What's Your Opinion?

Government

Agree A powerful leader can stress common characteristics and show how unity brings strength.

Disagree A powerful leader can stir resentment and the desire for independence.

Culture

Agree A strong sense of cultural unity helps people put aside their differences and work for the common good.

Disagree A strong sense of cultural unity is not really possible when many diverse groups live in one nation.

Economics

Agree Contact with different lands introduces people to new goods and services and to the means of producing or trading for them.

Disagree Contact with different lands can make a people feel threatened and want to protect their culture and economy from outside influences.

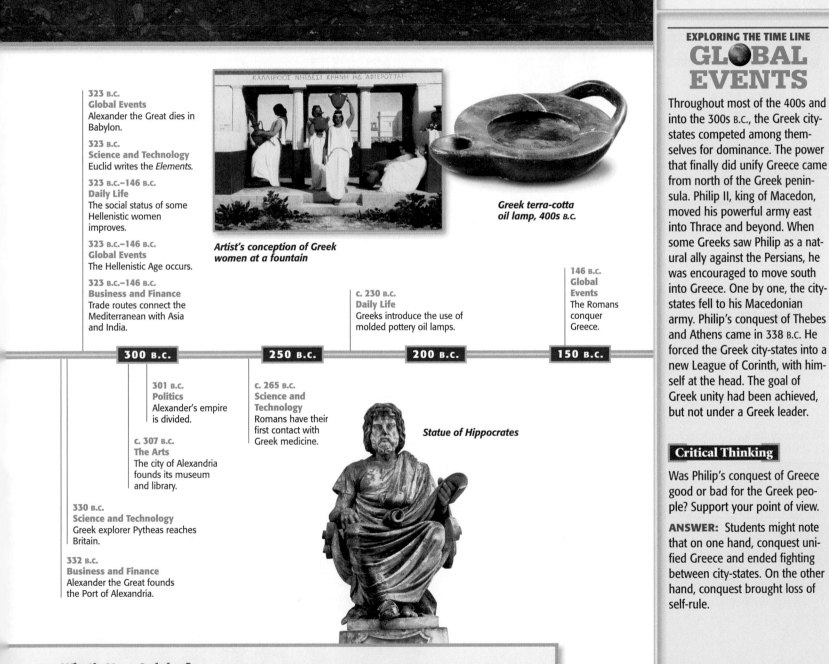

323 B.C.
Global Events
Alexander the Great dies in Babylon.

323 B.C.
Science and Technology
Euclid writes the *Elements*.

323 B.C.–146 B.C.
Daily Life
The social status of some Hellenistic women improves.

323 B.C.–146 B.C.
Global Events
The Hellenistic Age occurs.

323 B.C.–146 B.C.
Business and Finance
Trade routes connect the Mediterranean with Asia and India.

Artist's conception of Greek women at a fountain

Greek terra-cotta oil lamp, 400s B.C.

c. 230 B.C.
Daily Life
Greeks introduce the use of molded pottery oil lamps.

146 B.C.
Global Events
The Romans conquer Greece.

300 B.C.   **250 B.C.**   **200 B.C.**   **150 B.C.**

301 B.C.
Politics
Alexander's empire is divided.

c. 265 B.C.
Science and Technology
Romans have their first contact with Greek medicine.

Statue of Hippocrates

c. 307 B.C.
The Arts
The city of Alexandria founds its museum and library.

330 B.C.
Science and Technology
Greek explorer Pytheas reaches Britain.

332 B.C.
Business and Finance
Alexander the Great founds the Port of Alexandria.

What's Your Opinion?

 Do you **agree** *or* **disagree** *with the following statements? Support your point of view in your journal.*

Government A powerful national leader can unite local governments.

Culture A strong sense of cultural unity can help a nation that includes diverse groups of people grow.

Economics Contact with people in distant lands helps to strengthen a country's economy.

OBJECTIVES

1 Explain why the 400s B.C. are considered the golden age of Greek art and architecture.

2 Examine how Greek art of the golden age reflected the Greeks' view of themselves and the world.

SECTION 1 RESOURCES

REPRODUCIBLE RESOURCES

▸ Guided Reading Strategy 6.1

▸ Graphic Organizer Activity 6: Greek Arts

TECHNOLOGY RESOURCES

▸ One-Stop Planner 6.1

▸ World History Teaching Transparency: Everyday Life 3: Greek Architecture

▸ Homework Practice Online

REINFORCEMENT, REVIEW, AND ASSESSMENT

▸ Section 1 Review, p. 132

▸ Daily Quiz 6.1

▸ Main Idea Activity 6.1

▸ English Audio Summary 6.1

▸ Spanish Audio Summary 6.1

SECTION 1

READ TO DISCOVER

❶ Why are the 400s B.C. considered the golden age of Greek art and architecture?

❷ How did Greek art of the golden age reflect the Greeks' view of themselves and the world?

DEFINE

golden age

IDENTIFY

Acropolis
Parthenon
Myron
Phidias
Praxiteles

▶ WHY IT MATTERS TODAY

Greek art and architecture had a lasting influence on Western culture. Use CNNfyi.com or other **current event** sources to find a current example of a building or object that is based on Greek styles. Record your findings in your journal.

CNNfyi.com

Greek Art of the Golden Age

The Main Idea
Greek artists of the golden age expressed their society's ideals in styles that combined beauty and usefulness.

The Story Continues *After the Persian Wars, the wealth and power of Athens drew artists and teachers from across Greece. These people worked to make Athens a center of learning and artistic achievement. As Pericles said to his fellow Athenians, "We are lovers of the beautiful, yet with economy, and we cultivate the mind without loss of manliness. . . . To sum up: I say that Athens is the school of Hellas [Greece]."*

The Arts of the Golden Age

In the 400s B.C. Greece entered a new era of cultural progress. Thus, we call this period the **golden age** of Greek culture. Athens stood as the symbol of Greece's golden age. The city's wealth and power drew artists and teachers from across Greece. These people worked to make Athens a center of learning and artistic achievement.

Architecture. The Athenians surrounded themselves with beauty. They showed their pride in Athens by building temples, gymnasiums, and theaters. Artists decorated these structures with their finest work, especially sculpture.

A high hill called the **Acropolis** was the center of the original city-state. This hill offered a perfect setting for special artistic creations. A magnificent gate marked the entrance to a path up the hill. Nearby stood a towering bronze statue of the goddess Athena.

At the top of the Acropolis stood the **Parthenon,** a white marble temple built in honor of Athena. The Parthenon is considered the finest example of Greek architecture. People admire it most for its perfectly balanced proportions—that is, the relation of length to width, and of length and width to height.

Construction of the Parthenon began in 447 B.C. and was completed about 15 years later.

TEACH OBJECTIVE 1

ALL LEVELS: Copy the following graphic organizer on the board, omitting the italicized answers. Ask each student to complete it. **ENGLISH LANGUAGE LEARNERS**

Examples/Artists	Characteristics
Architecture: *Parthenon*	*balanced proportions; columns; statues*
Painting: *vases*	*everyday life and myths; graceful, natural movement; light, shade show contour, depth*
Sculpture: *steles; Myron's The Discus Thrower; statues by Phidias; Praxiteles*	*showed how people lived and worked; early figures were stiff and unnatural; later figures were lifelike, natural*

TEACH OBJECTIVE 2

LEVEL 1: Have students discuss the ideals expressed in the Parthenon. **ENGLISH LANGUAGE LEARNERS**

LEVEL 3: Have each student select a piece of Greek art and explain how it expresses the four basic Greek ideals.

HOMEWORK Have students explain how the art in this section exhibits Greek characteristics.

CLOSE

Have students write a letter to Myron, Phidias, or Praxiteles explaining why they admire his work.

The Parthenon had doors but probably had few windows. This is because Greek temples were built as shrines to honor Greek gods, not as meeting places for worshippers. A series of columns, called a colonnade, surrounded the structure. Large, sculpted figures painted in bright colors decorated the marble above the columns. Inside the Parthenon stood an even larger statue of Athena. Made of ivory and gold, it rose to about 38 feet high. Today many people consider the Parthenon and its sculpture to be among the Greeks' greatest achievements.

Painting. Painting was an important form of art in ancient Greece. Unfortunately, most original artwork has been lost or badly damaged. Knowledge of Greek painting comes mainly from written descriptions and from later Roman copies. The best-preserved Greek paintings are found on vases. Greek vase painters illustrated scenes from everyday life as well as mythological events. These artists delighted in showing graceful and natural movements of their subjects. Some vase painters used light and shade on the pottery to show contour and depth.

The Greeks initially adopted styles of painting from other cultures, then transformed them into their own. Researchers believe that Greek traders were impressed by the animals they found painted on pottery in places such as Egypt. Greek artists adopted this style, but over a few centuries began to replace the animals with human figures.

Sculpture. Original works of Greek sculpture, like Greek paintings, are rare today. We know about Greek sculpture chiefly from studying copies made during Roman times. Like Greek paintings, Greek sculpture shows Egyptian influences. Early Greek sculpture was highly structured. Figures were shown in stiff, unnatural poses. Men and women were often portrayed standing with their arms straight down by their sides. By the 400s B.C., however, Greek sculptors were creating figures that were more lifelike. Many used mathematical proportions to make their works look realistic.

Myron and **Phidias** (FID·ee·uhs) were two of history's greatest sculptors. They both lived during the golden age. Myron sculpted the famous figure *The Discus Thrower.* Phidias created the statues of Athena that decorated the Acropolis and the Parthenon. His greatest work, however, was the statue of Zeus at the Temple of Olympia. In ancient times people considered this statue, which stood almost 40 feet high, to be one of the Seven Wonders of the World.

Praxiteles (prak·SIT·uhl·eez) lived about 100 years after Phidias. He created a very different kind of sculpture. Phidias had made large, formal works appropriate for the gods. Praxiteles, on the other hand, sculpted figures that were more lifelike and natural in form and size. Above all, Praxiteles expressed the Greek admiration for the beauty of the human body.

✔ **READING CHECK: Analyzing Information** What qualities defined Greek architecture, painting, and sculpture? balanced proportions; scenes from everyday life; admiration for the human form

CONNECTING TO Art

Sculpture: Greek Funeral Stele

The ancient Greeks believed in a sort of "shadowy" existence after death. They carved steles (STEE·leez), or stone slabs, to commemorate their dead. Many steles showed how the dead person had lived and worked. The *Grave Stele of Hegeso* is from the late 400s B.C. It shows Hegeso, an Athenian woman. Hegeso is choosing a jewel from a box held by her servant.

Understanding the Arts

How does the *Grave Stele of Hegeso* show major characteristics of Greek art?

The Grave Stele of Hegeso

Interdisciplinary Connection

MATHEMATICS. The visual appeal of the Parthenon and other Greek temples results from the application of mathematical principles of proportion. The Parthenon is constructed in a ratio of 4:9, which the Greeks believed to be the ideal relationship of width to length. This ratio holds throughout the structure of the temple, from the arrangement of the columns along the ends and sides to the size and spacing of the columns themselves. Although the columns of the Parthenon are of different thicknesses, the diameter of each column is four-ninths of the space between any two of them.

ACTIVITY: Have students draw diagrams of the Parthenon in scale with its actual proportions, including 8 columns on the ends and 17 on the sides, and discuss the visual appeal of these dimensions. Discuss how this style of architecture influenced other cultures.

CONNECTING TO ART ANSWER

relief figures are physically beautiful, graceful; scene is taken from daily life

131

INTERPRETING THE VISUAL RECORD

Greek sculpture This marble statue, entitled *The Discus Thrower*, was crafted by Myron during the mid-400s B.C. *What qualities in this statue show the artist's admiration for the human form?*

The Nature of Greek Art

Greek architecture, painting, and sculpture reflected the Greeks' view of themselves and the world. Artistic styles of the golden age expressed Greek ideals in four main ways. First, Greek art glorified human beings. Much of Greek painting and sculpture portrayed gods and goddesses. However, the Greeks also placed great importance on human qualities and actions. By the time of the golden age, Greek sculptors had begun to create detailed statues of athletes, warriors, and even ordinary citizens. Greek painters and sculptors idealized their human subjects. In other words, the faces and figures of men and women represented the Greek ideal of beauty. The statues also suggested other traits admired by the Greeks. These included strength, intelligence, pride, grace, and courage.

Second, the art of the golden age symbolized Greeks' pride in their city-states. Art was meant for public enjoyment, and the architecture of public buildings was meant to be a monument to the power and glory of the polis. Through their art the Greeks honored and thanked the gods and tried to win their favor. For example, the Athenians built the Parthenon as a beautiful shrine for Athena. This showed their love for their city and their hope for its continued good fortune.

Third, Greek art expressed Greek beliefs in harmony, balance, order, and moderation. By moderation, the Greeks meant simplicity and restraint, qualities that they emphasized in their day-to-day lives. In art and architecture these principles resulted in a search for calmness, clarity, and freedom from any details not absolutely necessary to the work.

Finally, Greek art expressed the Greek belief in combining beauty and usefulness. In Greek culture the useful, the beautiful, and the good were closely bound together. Most Greek art was functional and had a clearly defined purpose. For example, the Greeks designed vases with different shapes intended for different functions. The potters and artists adapted their decorations to the curves and shapes of their vases.

✔ **READING CHECK: Making Generalizations** How did Greeks of the golden age use art to express their ideals? used art to express ideals of harmony, order, and balance; art combined beauty and usefulness

SECTION 1 REVIEW

1. **Define** and explain the significance:
   golden age

2. **Identify** and explain the significance:
   Acropolis
   Parthenon
   Myron
   Phidias
   Praxiteles

3. **Categorizing** Copy the web below. Use it to list examples of Greek artistic achievements during the golden age.

   Sculpture — Painting — Architecture — Greek Art

4. **Finding the Main Idea**

   a. Briefly explain how the following quotation can be applied to Greek architecture: "Nothing in excess, and everything in proportion."
   b. How did the style of Phidias differ from that of Praxiteles?
   c. List four characteristics of Greek art and explain how each reflected Greek ideals.

5. **Writing and Critical Thinking**

   Supporting a Point of View Imagine you are a citizen of Athens during Greece's golden age. Write a letter to your fellow citizens describing what types of buildings or public works of art you feel should be added to the city.
   Consider:
   • the purpose or use of any new buildings, statues, or paintings
   • the religious beliefs of you and your fellow citizens
   • the daily activities or entertainment needs of Athenians

Homework Practice Online
keyword: SP3 HP6

OBJECTIVES

1 **Explain the basic ideas of Socrates, Plato, and Aristotle.**

2 **Identify the achievements of Greek mathematicians and scientists of the golden age.**

3 **Identify the literary forms that originated or flourished during Greece's golden age.**

SECTION 2

READ TO DISCOVER

❶ What basic ideas did Socrates, Plato, and Aristotle express?

❷ What were the achievements of Greek mathematicians and scientists of the golden age?

❸ What important literary forms originated or flourished during Greece's golden age?

DEFINE

philosophy
aristocracy
dramas
tragedies

IDENTIFY

Socrates
Plato
Aristotle
Pythagoras
Hippocrates
Herodotus
Sophocles
Euripides
Aristophanes

▶WHY IT MATTERS TODAY

Greek writers often used drama to comment on aspects of Greek society such as war or politics. Use **CNNfyi.com** or other **current event** sources to find examples of writers or artists today who comment on social or political issues through their work. Record your findings in your journal.

CNNfyi.com

Philosophers and Writers of the Golden Age

The Main Idea
Greeks of the golden age made great advances in philosophy, the sciences, and literature.

The Story Continues *As Greece entered its golden age, philosophers and writers began to think about the nature of the universe and of human life. While the Greeks still honored the old gods, they took pride in human accomplishments. As the playwright Sophocles wrote, "Many are the wonders, none is more wonderful than what is man."*

The Rise of Philosophy

One of the Greeks' greatest achievements was the development of **philosophy,** the study of basic questions of reality and human existence. The Greeks used philosophy to better understand themselves and the world around them. (The word *philosopher* means "lover of wisdom.") Philosophers often disagreed with one another, but most believed that all of nature is based upon certain natural laws, or truths. They believed they could discover these truths through reason.

According to tradition, the first Greek philosopher was Thales of Miletus. Thales and others like him wanted to understand the nature of the cosmos, or universe. Thus they are known as cosmologists. Parmenides of Elea set up formal rules of logic for philosophical arguments. Another cosmologist, Democritus, developed atomic theory by using logic and mathematics. Democritus stated that everything is made up of tiny bits of matter called atoms.

Socrates. One of the most important thinkers of the new era was an Athenian, **Socrates** (SAHK·ruh·teez). He taught that education was the key to personal growth. Unlike other teachers, Socrates did not use memorization as a teaching tool. Instead, he insisted that students be trained to think for themselves. He asked questions that forced students to test their own values and ideas. Socrates's way of teaching through questioning has become known as the Socratic Method.

Although greatly loved, Socrates had powerful enemies. His questions often made public officials look foolish. He criticized democracy, saying that unskilled people should not hold positions of power. Finally, Socrates came into conflict with the Sophists, a group of Athenian teachers. He mocked their teachings as little more than untested assumptions.

Socrates's enemies falsely accused him of denying the existence of many Greek gods. They also said his teachings corrupted the minds of Athenian youth. The leaders of Athens brought Socrates to trial. Socrates did little to defend himself. He refused to deny his teachings, although this could possibly have saved his life. Socrates was found guilty and executed.

Plato. Socrates never recorded his ideas. Later generations learned of them from the writings of **Plato,** a wealthy young aristocrat and the greatest of Socrates's students. After the death of Socrates, Plato founded the Academy, a special school in Athens for teaching philosophy.

HISTORY MAKER

Socrates
(470 B.C.–399 B.C.)

Born in Athens, Socrates was one of the leading teachers and philosophers in Greece. His ideas and teaching methods helped to shape Western thought and education.

One of Socrates's greatest contributions was his study of ethics or "right living." Socrates felt that values such as duty and honesty should be studied and taught. "The unexamined life," Socrates held, "is not worth living." He trained his students to follow the motto "Know thyself." Socrates encouraged people to think about the personal meaning of common values. **What do you think Socrates meant by saying, "The unexamined life is not worth living"?**

Plato wrote dialogues, or imaginary discussions among several people. He dealt with government, education, justice, and religion. Most of the dialogues featured Socrates teaching and asking questions, but they also expressed many of Plato's own theories. Perhaps Plato's most important idea was the "Theory of Forms." Plato believed that all material things were imperfect expressions of perfect and universal ideas, or "forms." He felt that perfection could never be reached in the physical world. Because the human senses could be fooled, Plato argued, a true philosopher pursued knowledge of the perfect form that lay beyond the senses. For example, an ideal geometrical figure, such as a square, could be expressed perfectly as a mathematical formula. But in practical terms, it was almost impossible to make a perfect physical square.

For Plato, the realm of perfect forms had been conceived by the "divine worker," or God. This realm of perfection, he believed, existed apart from the physical examples of forms. Plato also saw human beings as consisting of two parts—the soul and the body. The soul, he taught, was the creation of God. Plato believed that through reincarnation, soul and form would eventually unite.

Plato was also interested in politics. The *Republic* is a long dialogue describing Plato's view of the perfect society. Plato's ideal government was an **aristocracy**—a government ruled by an upper class. However, this would not be an aristocracy of birth or of wealth. Instead, Plato's ideal rulers were philosophers, chosen for their wisdom, ability, and high ideals.

Aristotle. One of Plato's students in the Academy was a young man named **Aristotle.** Aristotle founded his own school in Athens in 335 B.C. Aristotle believed that every field of knowledge had to be studied logically. He collected as many facts as possible and organized them into systems. Aristotle had a special skill for defining and classifying things. This process of organization is an important part of modern science.

Aristotle investigated almost every field of study known during his time. He collected, described, and classified plants and animals. In his book *Ethics*, Aristotle tried to learn what brings people happiness. In *Poetics*, he analyzed Greek drama to show what makes a good or bad play.

INTERPRETING THE VISUAL RECORD

The teaching of philosophy This mosaic depicts Plato's Academy, founded about 387 B.C. to instruct students in philosophy and science. *What does this scene tell you about styles of teaching and learning at the Academy?*

TEACH OBJECTIVE 2

ALL LEVELS: Copy the following graphic organizer on the board, omitting the italicized answers. Ask each student to complete it. **ENGLISH LANGUAGE LEARNERS**

Greek Science and Medicine	
Scientists	**Contribution**
Pythagoras	*Pythagorean theorem*
Aristotle	*foundations for anatomy, botany, zoology; classification*
Hippocrates	*medical studies, cures*

Spotlight on CULTURE

Engage students in a dialogue by asking such questions as: What is philosophy? With what questions is a philosopher concerned? What is the difference between philosophy and science? Tell students they have just taken part in the Socratic Method of teaching. Challenge them to carry on a short lesson on a particular theme, such as honesty or happiness, using the Socratic Method. They should take turns playing the role of Socrates.

Aristotle's political views reflected his study of Greek culture. He believed that monarchy, aristocracy, and democracy were equally good forms of government. However, he felt that they could easily be corrupted. Aristotle wanted to combine the best of all three types of government to create a limited democracy.

✔ **READING CHECK: Comparing and Contrasting** What common issues did Socrates, Plato, and Aristotle study? How did their ideas about government differ? studied social and individual values; differed on democracy

Mathematics, Medicine, and Science

For the Greeks, philosophy covered all areas of knowledge, including the fields of mathematics and science. For example, **Pythagoras** (pih·THAG·uhr·uhs) was a philosopher who believed that everything could be explained in terms of mathematics. He is best remembered for his development of the Pythagorean theorem. According to the Pythagorean theorem, the length of the longest side of a right triangle can be found if the lengths of the two shorter sides are known.

Greek philosophers did not specialize in any one field of study. This kept them from fully developing practical scientific knowledge until much later. Aristotle, for example, did little more than lay the foundations for anatomy, botany, and zoology. He also helped to pioneer important classification practices, used to group similar things together and to describe and compare them. The Greek approach to scientific thought, however, differed in very important ways from the work of the Egyptians and Mesopotamians. These earlier thinkers made little distinction between the natural and the supernatural worlds. They tended to explain natural events as the work of gods and other supernatural forces. The Greeks, in contrast, believed that the natural world could be explained in terms of natural laws. They held, too, that the rules that govern our universe could be identified, observed, and defined. This approach depended on objectivity and reason, rather than on superstition, and did much to advance scientific thought.

The Greeks excelled in medicine. **Hippocrates** (hip·AHK·ruh·teez), who lived between about 460 B.C. and about 377 B.C., is considered to be the founder of medical science. Many historians believe that Hippocrates wrote between 60 and 70 medical studies. These studies were based on observation, experiment, and experience and helped to collect medical knowledge in a usable form. Hippocrates taught that disease comes from natural causes, not as punishment from the gods. He believed that rest, fresh air, and a proper diet made the best cures. Hippocrates's ideals were passed along to other Greek physicians. Doctors who were trained in Hippocrates's methods accepted his philosophy that medical treatment should be based on reason, rather than on magic. Today, medical doctors still take the Hippocratic oath. They pledge to follow a code of ethics based on Hippocrates's teachings.

> **Primary Source** ❝I swear . . . that I will carry out, according to my ability and judgment, this oath and this indenture [contract]. . . . I will use treatment to help the sick according to my ability and judgment, but never with a view to injury and wrongdoing.❞

✔ **READING CHECK: Contrasting** How did the Greeks' approach to medical science differ from their approach to other sciences? developed practical applications

CONNECTING TO Math

The Pythagorean Theorem

The Pythagorean theorem is one of the basic tools of geometry. Although it is named after Pythagoras, he actually built on ideas developed earlier by the Egyptians and others.

The theorem states that by squaring (multiplying by itself) the lengths of the two shorter sides of a right triangle and adding those numbers together, the sum will equal the square of the longest side.

This knowledge is useful in many fields, including architecture, engineering, manufacturing, navigation, and surveying.

$$c^2 = a^2 + b^2$$

Understanding Math

What does the development of the Pythagorean theorem tell us about the exchange of ideas in the ancient world?

Holt Researcher

go.hrw.com
KEYWORD: Holt Researcher
FreeFind: Pythagoras
After reading more about Pythagoras on the Holt Researcher, assess his contributions to science, noting how his ideas are still used today.

Linking Past to Present

Modern scientists use various methods in their research. These methods include observing, collecting and classifying data, applying logical reasoning, experimenting, hypothesizing, and expressing their findings mathematically.

Critical Thinking

How do modern scientific methods relate to the beliefs of ancient Greeks?

ANSWER: Aristotle helped pioneer classification principles. Pythagoras believed the world could be explained mathematically.

CONNECTING TO MATH ANSWER

implies that knowledge was transmitted from culture to culture throughout the ancient world

internet connect

TOPIC: Greek Scientist
GO TO: go.hrw.com
KEYWORD: SP3 WH6

Have students access the Internet through the HRW Go site to find information about Greek contributions to science. Have them summarize their findings in a report.

HOMEWORK Have students write paragraphs about what scientific knowledge in Greece might have been like before the golden age compared to changes produced by scientific discovery during the golden age. *(unsystematic and tied to religion)* Remind them to use standard grammar, spelling, sentence structure, and punctuation.

TEACH OBJECTIVE 3

LEVEL 1: Write the following literary genres on the board: *History, Tragedy, Comedy.* Ask students what the Greeks contributed to the development of each. Conclude by asking how all three contribute to our knowledge and understanding of ancient Greece. *(Histories record important events; tragedies and comedies give insights into values.)*

ENGLISH LANGUAGE LEARNERS

LEVEL 3: Ask students to choose and read a play written by one of the Greek dramatists discussed in this section, and report to the class on its theme, plot, and characters.

CLOSE

Have students design a chart that lists each philosopher, scientist, historian, and dramatist, and each person's major ideas, works, and/or contributions.

History Maker

THUCYDIDES. Born about 460 B.C. into a wealthy Athenian family, Thucydides served as a general for his city-state against Sparta in the Peloponnesian War. After failing to stop the Spartans from taking the city of Amphipolis in 424 B.C., he was exiled from Athens. Thucydides drew on his military experiences to write his *History of the Peloponnesian War.* He focused on how human choices and actions affected the course of the war.

Critical Thinking

How might the experiences of Thucydides have affected his writing?

ANSWER: His first-hand knowledge of the war would enable him to make the connection between human choices and outcomes. His experience might also have given him the desire to report events accurately.

VISUAL RECORD ANSWER

Students may note the theater is an open-air amphitheater with stage at bottom. Most theaters today are indoors with raised stages. Also they may note the stone seats and narrow aisles.

Technology Resources

CNN Presents World Cultures: Yesterday and Today Segment 6: The Ancient Theaters of Epidaurus

---

Holt Researcher
go.hrw.com
KEYWORD: Holt Researcher
FreeFind: Thucydides
After reading more about Thucydides on the Holt Researcher, identify what evidence Thucydides analyzed to make his historical study more accurate.

INTERPRETING THE VISUAL RECORD

Greek theaters The theater at Epidaurus, which dates from the mid-300s B.C., is one of the best-preserved Greek theaters. Its many rows of benches seat about 12,000 people. *How does this theater differ from present-day theaters?*

History

The Greeks became the first people to take the writing of history seriously. **Herodotus** (hih·RAHD·uh·tuhs) was the first historian of the Western world. Herodotus traveled to Babylonia, Phoenicia, and Egypt. He included his views of these countries and their people in his histories.

Herodotus was an interesting writer and a wonderful storyteller. He exaggerated at times. However, Herodotus was careful to note whether he had seen something for himself or had only been told about it. Historians still consult his writings for information about the world during his time. Herodotus is often called the Father of History.

Another Greek historian, Thucydides (thoo·SID·uh·deez), became famous for his *History of the Peloponnesian War.* Thucydides believed that studying the past helps us to understand human nature. He tried to make his own work reflect this belief. Thus, Thucydides worked to make his history accurate and fair.

✔ **READING CHECK: Drawing Inferences** Why was the approach to history developed by Herodotus and Thucydides important? This approach led to improved accuracy and objectivity.

Greek Theater

Athenian writers produced many of the world's greatest works of literature. Many of today's literary styles were first developed by the Greeks.

Drama. The Greeks were the first people to write **dramas**—plays containing action or dialogue and involving conflict and emotion. The Greeks always wrote plays in poetic form. Two or three actors spoke or sang the lines for an audience. Male actors with trained voices played women's roles. A group of singers, called the chorus, described the scene and commented on the action.

The Greeks carved outdoor theaters into hillsides. At the bottom of the hill they created a flat area called the *orchestra,* where the chorus and actors performed. Unlike many plays of today, Greek dramas featured little scenery. Instead, audiences relied on the chorus to describe the time and place.

Greek dramas were often performed in connection with religious festivals. Each spring three playwrights were invited to compete at the annual festival of Dionysus, the Greek god of fertility and wine. This festival, called the Great Dionysia, became Athens's major dramatic

competition. The competition's judges were ordinary citizens chosen by lottery. They awarded prizes based on the beauty or wisdom of each play.

Tragedies. In Greek **tragedies** the main character struggled against fate, or events. Usually a combination of outside forces defeated the main character. Often, tragic heroes were punished for displaying *hubris* (HYOO·bruhs)—the sin of pride. Hubris offended the gods and doomed the hero to a tragic end.

Three well-known writers of tragedies lived during the 400s B.C. Aeschylus (ES·ke·luhs) wrote about religion and the relationship between gods and people. His three most famous plays centered on the murder of Agamemnon, the king who had led the Greeks against Troy. Another writer of tragedies, **Sophocles** (SAHF·uh·kleez), defended many traditional Greek values. Aristotle called Sophocles's most famous play, *Oedipus Rex*, a perfect example of tragedy.

The third great playwright of the golden age was **Euripides** (yoo·RIP·uh·deez). He was more of a realist than Aeschylus or Sophocles. Like Socrates, he questioned many old beliefs and ideas. Earlier writers had often honored war for its deeds of courage and heroism. In *The Trojan Women*, Euripides showed the pain and misery of war.

Comedies. Greek comedies also originated at the Great Dionysia festival. These plays made fun of ideas and people. Comedies usually included both tragic and humorous figures. Unlike characters in tragedies, however, the main characters in comedies solved their problems.

The finest writer of Greek comedies, **Aristophanes** (ar·uh·STAHF·uh·neez), was known for his sharp wit. In *Clouds* he poked fun at Socrates for his theories about education. Aristophanes also disliked war. He used comedy to make Athenians think about the causes and effects of war.

Greek actors wore masks, such as this one, to represent various characters and emotions.

✔ **READING CHECK: Analyzing Information** How did the Greeks' style of playwriting reflect their society? reflected belief in the gods, commented on social issues

---

SECTION 2 REVIEW

1. Define and explain the significance:
philosophy
aristocracy
dramas
tragedies

2. Identify and explain the significance:
Socrates
Plato
Aristotle
Pythagoras
Hippocrates
Herodotus
Sophocles
Euripides
Aristophanes

3. Comparing and Contrasting Copy the following graphic organizer. Use it to list the ideas of Socrates and Plato that differed from those of Aristotle. Then list areas in which all three agreed.

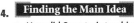
Socrates, Plato ⟨ ⟩ Aristotle

4. **Finding the Main Idea**

a. How did Socrates's teaching method help him accomplish his purpose?
b. What were the main characteristics of the ideal government described in Plato's *Republic*?
c. In what ways did Aristotle's view of the principles of government differ from Plato's view?
d. What view did the Greeks take toward the development of practical scientific knowledge?
e. What do the dramatic styles developed by the Greeks reveal about their culture?

5. **Writing and Critical Thinking**

Summarizing Describe how Greek ideas of good government and citizenship developed and changed during the golden age.
Consider:
• the different theories of government of Socrates, Plato, and Aristotle
• public reaction to Socrates's teachings
• the opinions about leaders expressed by Greek playwrights

Homework Practice Online
keyword: SP3 HP6

LEVEL 1: Have students work in pairs to note the various scientists discussed in the text and the accomplishments of each. You might also want students to prepare questions for the presenters in the Level 3 activity for this objective.
ENGLISH LANGUAGE LEARNERS, COOPERATIVE LEARNING

LEVEL 2: Ask students to discuss or write a paragraph describing Hellenistic science as largely "knowledge for knowledge's sake." Then have them discuss or write a second paragraph predicting how this concept might have changed if slavery were not so prevalent in the empire. Students should support their point of view.

LEVEL 3: Have students play the roles of Euclid, Archimedes, Aristarchus, Hipparchus, or Eratosthenes. Ask each to explain the scientist's work to the class and discuss how it spread to other cultures. **COOPERATIVE LEARNING**

CLOSE

Ask students to imagine they are elderly Greeks in Hellenistic society. Ask them to describe changes in the economy, society, and ways of thinking during their lifetime.

SKILLS PRACTICE ANSWERS

1. The size of the tool affects the volume of water it can move.
2. less time and manual labor spent bringing water to and away from fields
3. were spread and used hundreds of miles away and hundreds of years later
4. Answers will vary.

SKILL-BUILDING STRATEGIES — Using Models to Understand History

The Archimedes Screw

Many of Archimedes's inventions are still in use today. One of these is the Archimedes screw. It can be used in drainage, irrigation, and pump systems. Although Archimedes himself left no sketches or models of his invention, knowledge of its use became well known by word of mouth and through the writings of others. A Roman engineer named Vitruvius described the Archimedes screw in an architectural guide he wrote in the first century B.C. He provided some of the first known sketches of the device.

Historians often use models to help us understand past events or eras. In most common uses, a model is a representation of something. A scale model of a ship or a building is one example. Some researchers use models to illustrate what ancient cities once looked like. Others use models of geographic areas, such as three-dimensional maps, to illustrate conclusions regarding geographic distribution, land use, or other geography-related factors.

circular treadmill to drive screw

enclosed, water-tight outer tube

continuously revolving spiral threads

spiral threads draw water upward above original level

Skills Reminder

To use a model to understand historical developments, first identify what the model is designed to represent. If the model has been made to scale, use your mathematics skills to determine the actual size of the item represented. Make sure you understand the time frame during which the item would have been created and used. Ask yourself questions about the various ways in which the item represented by the model might have been used. Try to imagine why such an item might have been important for the daily life or work of people at the time. This will indicate what needs the item was designed to meet and will help you to evaluate what the model reveals about an event or era.

Skills Practice

Study the illustration above, picturing the use of an Archimedes screw in Europe in the 1500s.

❶ In what ways do the tool's dimensions affect its performance?
❷ How could this invention have helped save labor in Hellenistic Greece?
❸ What does the use of the Archimedes screw in Europe in the 1500s tell us about the geographic distribution of Greek ideas?
❹ Archimedes also invented the compound pulley, often called a block and tackle. Design a scale model of a compound pulley. What would the dimensions of the actual pulley be? How could such a pulley save labor?

REVIEW

Have students complete the Section 4 Review on p. 145.

ASSESS

Have students complete Daily Quiz 6.4. As Alternative Assessment, you may want to use the homework assignment or graphic organizer in this section's lessons.

RETEACH

Have students complete Main Idea Activity for English Language Learners and Special-Needs Students 6.4. Then have them create flash cards with terms from Section 4 on one side with an appropriate explanation on the other. Let pairs of students use their flash cards to reinforce section concepts.
ENGLISH LANGUAGE LEARNERS, COOPERATIVE LEARNING

EXTEND

Organize students into groups to create maps of the Hellenistic world. Each group should draw its map and add illustrations of sculptures, buildings, reliefs of rulers, and other period art and artifacts at appropriate locations. Each image should include a descriptive caption.
BLOCK SCHEDULING, COOPERATIVE LEARNING

Medicine. Hellenistic scientists added greatly to the ancient world's medical knowledge. Alexandria, Egypt was the center of medical science. As Greek and Egyptian traditions came together, Hellenistic doctors learned from the Egyptian art of embalming to examine and catalog the parts of the human body.

To learn more about anatomy, Alexandrian doctors studied the bodies of executed criminals. They learned much about the human body; for example, Herophilus (huh·RAHF·uh·luhs) concluded that the brain is the center of the nervous system. This and other medical advances allowed Hellenistic doctors to perform delicate surgery.

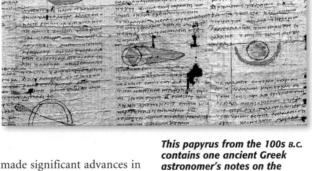

This papyrus from the 100s B.C. contains one ancient Greek astronomer's notes on the cosmos.

Astronomy and geography. Hellenistic scientists made significant advances in astronomy as they came into contact with the knowledge of the Egyptians and Babylonians. They used principles of geometry to track the movements of stars and planets. **Aristarchus** (ar·uh·STAHR·kuhs) correctly believed that the earth and other planets moved around the sun, but he failed to convince others. Hipparchus (hi·PAHR·kuhs) used trigonometry to predict eclipses. He used the sun and the moon to calculate the length of the year.

Hellenistic geographers knew that Earth was round. At Alexandria, **Eratosthenes** (er·uh·TAHS·thuh·neez) calculated the distance around the earth with amazing accuracy. He did so by finding the angle of the sun's rays from different points on the globe. Eratosthenes was considered one of the most brilliant mathematicians and astronomers of his time. He was honored by the Hellenistic ruler of Egypt to head the great Library of Alexandria.

✔ **READING CHECK: Supporting a Point of View** Why is it important today to study Hellenistic achievements in science? Many scientific fields of today draw basic understanding from Hellenistic discoveries.

Holt Researcher
go.hrw.com
KEYWORD: Holt Researcher
FreeFind: Eratosthenes
After reading more about Eratosthenes on the Holt Researcher, assess his significance to science.

SECTION 4 REVIEW

1. **Identify** and explain the significance:
   Zeno
   Epicurus
   Euclid
   Archimedes
   Aristarchus
   Eratosthenes

2. **Categorizing** Copy the table below. Each column lists a field of study in which Hellenistic thinkers were active. List the major Hellenistic accomplishments in each subject area. Give the names of any scientists or philosophers identified with the work.

	Philosophy	Math, Physics	Medical Science	Astronomy, Geography
Hellenistic Achievements				

3. **Finding the Main Idea**
   a. In what way did new understanding of the term "Greek" help to unify the Hellenistic world?
   b. How did the primary ideas of the four major Hellenistic philosophies differ from each other? How were they similar?

4. **Writing and Critical Thinking**
   Making Predictions Describe the possible outcomes that might have been achieved had more Hellenistic scientists put their discoveries to work.
   Consider:
   • the achievements of Greek scientists
   • the practical uses their achievements could have had
   • how these discoveries would have changed Greek life

Homework Practice Online
keyword: SP3 HP6

❶ Identify
• Zeno, p. 143
• Epicurus, p. 143
• Euclid, p. 143
• Archimedes, p. 143
• Aristarchus, p. 145
• Eratosthenes, p. 145

❷ Philosophy: Stoicism (Zeno), Epicureanism (Epicurus), Cynicism (Diogenes), Skepticism (Pyrrho); Math, Physics: *Elements* (Euclid), *pi* and lever (Archimedes); Medical Science: anatomy, surgery; Astronomy, Geography: circumference of Earth (Eratosthenes), Earth moves around sun (Aristarchus), length of year (Hipparchus)

❸ a. promoted a shared sense of cultural and social unity

b. similar: focused on ethics; different: Cynics—simple, natural lifestyles; Skeptics—knowledge is uncertain, peace comes from acceptance of change; Stoics—people must accept their fate without complaint; Epicureans—self-control and moderation

❹ Predictions should mention saving labor and making the economy more efficient. Practical devices could have led to less need and support for slavery.

GREECE'S GOLDEN AND HELLENISTIC AGES **145**

REVIEW AND ASSESSMENT RESOURCES

REPRODUCIBLE RESOURCES

▸ Vocabulary Activity 6

TECHNOLOGY RESOURCES

▸ Chapter 6 Test Generator (on the One-Stop Planner)
▸ Global Skill Builder CD–ROM
▸ HRW Web Site

REINFORCEMENT, REVIEW, and ASSESSMENT

▸ Chapter 6 Review, pp. 146–147
▸ Chapter 6 Tutorial for Students, Parents, Mentors, and Peers
▸ Chapter 6 Test (Form A or B)
▸ Alternative Assessment Handbook
▸ Chapter 6 Test for English Language Learners and Special-Needs Students

REVIEW

Have students complete the Chapter 6 Review on pages 146–147.

ASSESS

Use one of the chapter tests to assess students' understanding of the content. For Alternative Assessment, see the Portfolio Activities and Alternative Assessment Handbook.

CHAPTER 6 REVIEW ANSWERS

Understanding Main Ideas

1. balanced proportions; scenes from everyday life; admiration for human form

2. glorified humans; showed harmony, balance, order, and moderation; combined beauty and usefulness

3. believed in natural laws that could be discovered

4. histories became more accurate, objective; dramas reflected belief in gods; comedies questioned beliefs, poked fun

5. expanded conquest from Greece into Africa and Asia, including Persia

6. spread Greek culture; combined Macedonians and Persians; encouraged marriage between Macedonians and Persians; actions showed he wanted a united empire

7. Women appeared in public more often and won property rights. All Greeks benefited from more widespread education.

8. trade increased; small middle class thrived

Reviewing Themes

1. brought city-states under rule of one leader

2. Anyone who adopted the Hellenistic culture would be considered Greek.

3. Increased trade and the growth of cities helped many prosper.

CHAPTER 6 Review

Creating a Time Line

Copy the time line below onto a sheet of paper. Complete the time line by filling in the events, individuals, and dates from the chapter that you think were significant. Pick three events and explain why you think they were significant.

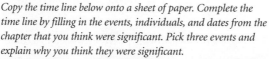

| 500 B.C. | 350 B.C. | 200 B.C. |

Writing a Summary

Using standard grammar, spelling, sentence structure, and punctuation, write an overview of the events in the chapter.

Identifying People and Ideas

Identify the following terms or individuals and explain their significance:

1. Parthenon
2. Socrates
3. Plato
4. Aristotle
5. Pythagoras
6. aristocracy
7. dramas
8. Philip II of Macedon
9. Alexander the Great
10. Hellenistic culture

Understanding Main Ideas

SECTION 1 *(pp. 130–132)*

Greek Art of the Golden Age

1. What were the main features of Greek arts of the golden age?
2. How did the Greeks of the golden age use art to express their values and ideals?

SECTION 2 *(pp. 133–137)*

Philosophers and Writers of the Golden Age

3. What basic approach to knowledge did philosophers and scientists of the golden age share?
4. How did Greeks of the golden age comment on their society through literature and comedy and drama?

SECTION 3 *(pp. 138–141)*

Alexander the Great

5. In what ways did Alexander the Great build on the accomplishments of Philip II of Macedon?
6. What specific actions did Alexander take to unify the Hellenistic world, and what do these actions tell us about his view of rule and leadership?

SECTION 4 *(pp. 142–145)*

The Spread of Hellenistic Culture

7. How did the social and economic changes of the Hellenistic Age work to improve the status of women and ordinary Greeks?
8. What major economic developments took place during the Hellenistic Age?

Reviewing Themes

1. Government In what way did the rise of Macedon under Philip II influence unity among the Greek city-states?
2. Culture How did new ideas of what it meant to be Greek influence the growth of Hellenistic culture?
3. Economics Why was the Hellenistic Age a time of economic prosperity for many?

Thinking Critically

1. Finding the Main Idea Why are the 400s B.C. generally known as the golden age of Greece?
2. Problem Solving How did Aristotle propose to deal with the problem of corruption in government?
3. Supporting a Point of View Provide evidence to support the claim that the approach to history used by Herodotus and Thucydides was a good system.
4. Drawing Conclusions How did the cities founded by Alexander the Great influence the spread of Greek culture?

Writing About History

Analyzing Information Using a major Greek or Hellenistic figure from the 400s B.C. or 300s B.C. as a main character, create an outline for a short story. Use the graphic organizer below to help you organize your story.

Setting:	
Main Character:	
Secondary Character:	
Conflict:	
Plot:	
Resolution:	

CLOSE

Have students compare and contrast the ideas of philosophers and scientists in the golden age and in Hellenistic times.

RETEACH

Have students rewrite each question they missed on the test and then use their textbooks and notes to answer the question in a complete sentence. Then have students take the Form B Test to assess their mastery of the material. **ENGLISH LANGUAGE LEARNERS**

Portfolio Extensions

Link to TODAY

1. Ask students to write an essay comparing and contrasting the Hellenistic world with the modern-day United States.
2. Have students create philosophy brochures with a page each devoted to the three great philosophers of the golden age—Socrates, Plato, and Aristotle—and the four main schools of Hellenistic times—Cynicism, Skepticism, Stoicism, and Epicureanism. Students might use computer software to illustrate and print their brochures.
3. Ask students to imagine they are critical reviewers. Have them select one particular field—architecture, sculpture, drama, history—and create a short guide to major Greek works in that field. The guide may contain illustrations and captions.

Building Social Studies Skills

Interpreting a Time Line

Study the time line below. Then answer the questions that follow.

338 B.C.	146 B.C.
Philip II becomes ruler of all Greece.	Romans complete conquest of Greece.

336 B.C.
Philip II is assassinated; Alexander becomes king of Macedon.

1. Which statement correctly describes the span of the time line?
   a. It spans from the beginning of Philip's rule in Greece until the end of Alexander's rule in Greece.
   b. It spans from the unification of Greece under one king until the conquest of Greece by Rome.
   c. It spans events during Philip's reign through events during Alexander's reign.
   d. It spans Alexander's reign and the Roman conquest of Greece.

2. What are some other events that belong on this time line? Give specific dates for the events.

Drawing Inferences

Read the following passage from *The Republic* by Plato. Then answer the questions.

> "And so we may venture to assert that anyone who can produce the best blend of the physical and intellectual sides of education and apply them to the training of character is producing harmony in a far more important sense than any mere musician."

3. Which of the following is the best statement of what this passage implies?
   a. Physical training is more important than intellectual training.
   b. A teacher's goal should be to help a student develop character.
   c. Musical training is more important than both physical and intellectual training.
   d. A teacher's goal should be to give students more physical education than intellectual education.
   e. Harmony and character are best developed when a teacher emphasizes intellectual education.

4. What would your school day be like if it were based on the statement you chose in question 3 above? Give specific examples.

Alternative Assessment

Link to TODAY

Building Your Portfolio

Culture

The Hellenistic empire united people from different ethnic and religious groups into one common culture, much like the United States today. Compile a list of the ways in which different regions and groups of people contribute to the economy and culture of the United States. Then use the list to create a chart that summarizes your findings.

---

internet connect

go.hrw.com

Internet Activity: go.hrw.com
KEYWORD: SP3 WH6

Ancient Athens

Choose a topic on Greece's Golden and Hellenistic Ages to:
- research Athens's golden age and create a newspaper article describing a representative political development.
- identify currents of Greek thought in art from different time periods.
- report on the scientific contributions of the ancient Greeks.

Thinking Critically

1. arts and sciences and philosophy flourished

2. combine the best of monarchy, aristocracy, and democracy to create a limited democracy

3. Herodotus based his writing on actual travels and noted whether observations were his own or others'. Thucydides based his writing on his personal experience. Both led to more accurate history writing.

4. Cities were centers of trade and learning, both of which help spread culture.

Writing About History

Stories will vary but should include accurate facts about the figure chosen.

Building Social Studies Skills

1. b

2. Answers will vary but might include 331 B.C.–Persia is destroyed; 323 B.C.–Alexander the Great dies; 301 B.C.–Alexander's empire is split by generals.

3. b

4. Answers will vary.

Building Your Portfolio

Answers should include the contributions of various groups and regions to U.S. economy and culture.

The Roman World

CHAPTER RESOURCE MANAGER

	Objectives	Pacing Guide	Reproducible Resources
SECTION 1 **Founding the Roman Republic** (pp. 150–154)	• Identify the role geography played in Italy's and Rome's development. • Explain the form of government in the Roman Republic. • Examine the Conflict of the Orders and how it changed the early Roman Republic. • Compare and contrast the roles of citizens and noncitizens as Rome expanded its power.	**Regular** 1.5 day / **Block Scheduling** 1 day *Block Scheduling Handbook with Team Teaching Strategies, 7.1*	**RS** Guided Reading Strategy 7.1 **RS** Graphic Organizer Activity 7 **E** Hands-on History Activity 7
SECTION 2 **Rome Expands Its Borders** (pp. 155–157)	• Discuss the Punic Wars and how Rome gained control over Carthage. • Identify political, economic, and social changes caused by Roman expansion.	**Regular** 1 day / **Block Scheduling** .5 day *Block Scheduling Handbook with Team Teaching Strategies, 7.2*	**RS** Guided Reading Strategy 7.2 **PS** Readings in World History 25: Rome's Perfect Location
SECTION 3 **The Birth of the Roman Empire** (pp. 158–161)	• Identify the political events in Rome that helped weaken the Roman Republic. • Explain how the reign of Julius Caesar served as a transition between the Roman Republic and the Roman Empire. • Describe the events and conditions that marked the first two centuries of the Roman Empire.	**Regular** 1.5 day / **Block Scheduling** 1 day *Block Scheduling Handbook with Team Teaching Strategies, 7.3*	**RS** Guided Reading Strategy 7.3 **SM** Geography Activity 7 **PS** Readings in World History 26
SECTION 4 **Roman Society and Culture** (pp. 162–167)	• Explain how the Romans built a strong and unified empire. • Describe how Roman citizens made a living and led their daily lives. • Discuss the role played by science and the arts in the empire.	**Regular** 1.5 day / **Block Scheduling** .5 day *Block Scheduling Handbook with Team Teaching Strategies, 7.4*	**RS** Guided Reading Strategy 7.4
SECTION 5 **The Rise of Christianity** (pp. 168–171)	• Describe how the conditions Jews faced in Judaea contributed to the rise of Christianity. • Identify the difficulties early Christians experienced while under the influence of the Roman Empire. • Discuss the changes that occurred during the late Roman Empire that helped establish Christianity and stabilize the church.	**Regular** 1 day / **Block Scheduling** .5 day *Block Scheduling Handbook with Team Teaching Strategies, 7.5*	**RS** Guided Reading Strategy 7.5 **PS** Readings in World History 27: Christians in the Roman Empire
SECTION 6 **The Fall of the Western Empire** (pp. 172–177)	• Identify the problems the Roman Empire had to deal with during the A.D. 200s. • Describe how the reigns of Diocletian and Constantine slowed the decline of the empire. • List the factors that led to the final decline of the Roman Empire in the West.	**Regular** 1 day / **Block Scheduling** .5 day *Block Scheduling Handbook with Team Teaching Strategies, 7.6*	**RS** Guided Reading Strategy 7.6 **PS** Readings in World History 28 **E** Creative Teaching Strategy 7

Chapter Resource Key

PS	Primary Sources	**A**	Assessment	🎵	Music
RS	Reading Support	**REV**	Review	📼	Video
IC	Interdisciplinary Connections	**ELL**	Reinforcement and English Language Learners	🌐	Internet
E	Enrichment	💻	Transparencies	🖥	Holt Presentation Maker Using Microsoft® PowerPoint®
SM	Skills Mastery	💿	CD-ROM		

One-Stop Planner CD-ROM

See the **One-Stop Planner** for a complete list of additional resources for students and teachers.

One-Stop Planner CD-ROM

It's easy to plan lessons, select resources, and print out materials for your students when you use the **One-Stop Planner** CD–ROM with **Test Generator.**

Technology Resources

One-Stop Planner 7.1

World History Teaching Transparency: Geography and History 4; Everyday Life 4

Homework Practice Online

One-Stop Planner 7.2

CNN. Presents World Cultures: Yesterday and Today Segment 7: In the Shadow of Mt. Vesuvius

Homework Practice Online

One-Stop Planner 7.3

Holt Researcher: World History: Caesar, Augustus

Homework Practice Online

One-Stop Planner 7.4

World History and Cultures Video Program 5: What Made Rome Great?

Homework Practice Online

Online Maps, Charts, and Graphs: Roman Roads in A.D. 14

One-Stop Planner 7.5

Holt Researcher: World History: Jesus

Religions of the World Video Series: Christianity

Homework Practice Online

One-Stop Planner 7.6

Homework Practice Online

Online Maps, Charts, and Graphs: Division of the Roman Empire

Reinforcement, Review, and Assessment

Daily Quiz 7.1

Main Idea Activity 7.1

English Audio Summary 7.1

Spanish Audio Summary 7.1

REV Section 1 Review, p. 154

Daily Quiz 7.2

Main Idea Activity 7.2

English Audio Summary 7.2

Spanish Audio Summary 7.2

REV Section 2 Review, p. 157

Daily Quiz 7.3

Main Idea Activity 7.3

English Audio Summary 7.3

Spanish Audio Summary 7.3

REV Section 3 Review, p. 161

Daily Quiz 7.4

Main Idea Activity 7.4

English Audio Summary 7.4

Spanish Audio Summary 7.4

REV Section 4 Review, p. 167

Daily Quiz 7.5

Main Idea Activity 7.5

English Audio Summary 7.5

Spanish Audio Summary 7.5

REV Section 5 Review, p. 171

Daily Quiz 7.6

Main Idea Activity 7.6

English Audio Summary 7.6

Spanish Audio Summary 7.6

REV Section 6 Review, p. 177

internet connect

HRW ONLINE RESOURCES
GO TO: go.hrw.com
Then type in a keyword.

TEACHER HOME PAGE
KEYWORD: SP3 Teacher

CHAPTER INTERNET ACTIVITIES
KEYWORD: SP3 WH7
Choose an activity to:
• analyze the *Aeneid* to learn the connection between ancient Troy and Roman culture.
• create a model or structure that employs Roman architectural, artistic, or decorative styles.
• research the destruction of Pompeii and review the tectonic causes of volcanoes.

CHAPTER ENRICHMENT LINKS
KEYWORD: SP3 CH7

ONLINE ASSESSMENT
Homework Practice
KEYWORD: SP3 HP7

Standardized Test Prep
KEYWORD: SP3 STP7

Rubrics
KEYWORD: SS Rubrics

ONLINE MAPS, CHARTS, AND GRAPHS
KEYWORD: SP3 MCG

CONTENT UPDATES
KEYWORD: SS Content Updates

HOLT PRESENTATION MAKER
KEYWORD: SP3 PPT7

ONLINE READING SUPPORT
KEYWORD: SS Strategies

CURRENT EVENTS
KEYWORD: S3 Current Events

Meeting Individual Needs

Ability Levels

Level 1 Basic level activities designed for all students encountering new material

Level 2 Intermediate level activities designed for average students

Level 3 Challenging activities designed for honors and gifted and talented students

English Language Learners These activities address the needs of students with Limited English Proficiency.

Chapter Review and Assessment

IC Vocabulary Activity 7

Global Skill Builder CD–ROM

HRW Web Site

REV Chapter 7 Tutorial for Students, Parents, Mentors, and Peers

REV Chapter 7 Review, pp. 178–179

A Chapter 7 Test Generator (on the One-Stop Planner)

A Chapter 7 Test (Form A or B)

A Alternative Assessment Handbook

A Chapter 7 Test for English Language Learners and Special-Needs Students

CHAPTER 7

Section 1 — Founding the Roman Republic

Section 2 — Rome Expands Its Borders

Section 3 — The Birth of the Roman Empire

Section 4 — Roman Society and Culture

Section 5 — The Rise of Christianity

Section 6 — The Fall of the Western Empire

Build on What You Know

Ask students to answer the following questions:

How might Greek achievements have spread throughout the ancient world?

Consider:

- the effects of trade and travel
- the establishment of Greek colonies throughout the Mediterranean
- the conquests of Alexander the Great

How might Greek culture have influenced the Romans?

Consider:

- the influence of Greek culture on other societies
- Greek achievements in the arts and sciences
- Greek ideas on government, law, and citizenship

EXPLORING THE TIME LINE

GLOBAL EVENTS

internet connect

TOPIC: Ovid
GO TO: go.hrw.com
KEYWORD: SP3 WH7

Have students access the Internet through the HRW Go site to conduct research on Ovid, one of the great Roman poets. Then have students create a detailed time line of Ovid's life, including the publication of his greatest works. At the bottom of the time line, students should write a brief paragraph describing one of Ovid's works and explaining what it tells us about the Roman Empire.

CHAPTER 7

1000 B.C.–A.D. 476

The Roman World

Mosaic of a theater scene from Pompeii

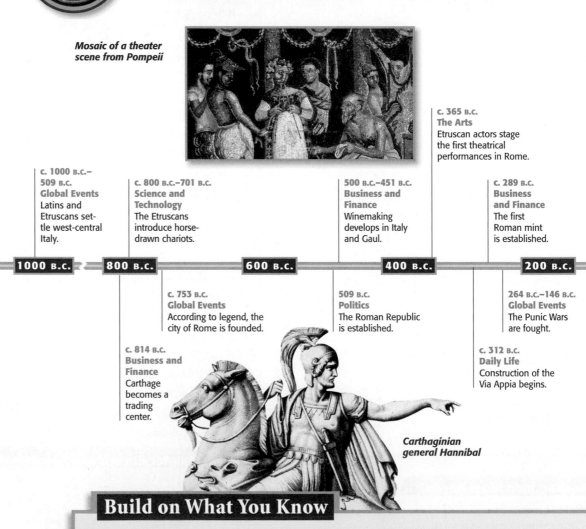

Carthaginian general Hannibal

c. 1000 B.C.–509 B.C.
Global Events
Latins and Etruscans settle west-central Italy.

c. 800 B.C.–701 B.C.
Science and Technology
The Etruscans introduce horse-drawn chariots.

500 B.C.–451 B.C.
Business and Finance
Winemaking develops in Italy and Gaul.

c. 365 B.C.
The Arts
Etruscan actors stage the first theatrical performances in Rome.

c. 289 B.C.
Business and Finance
The first Roman mint is established.

1000 B.C. — **800 B.C.** — **600 B.C.** — **400 B.C.** — **200 B.C.**

c. 814 B.C.
Business and Finance
Carthage becomes a trading center.

c. 753 B.C.
Global Events
According to legend, the city of Rome is founded.

509 B.C.
Politics
The Roman Republic is established.

c. 312 B.C.
Daily Life
Construction of the Via Appia begins.

264 B.C.–146 B.C.
Global Events
The Punic Wars are fought.

Build on What You Know

After the Persian wars, Athens became the center of Greece's golden age. The Greek contributions during this period in science, mathematics, art, and philosophy still influence civilizations today. They also had an effect on the cultures of the ancient world, especially that of Rome. Although the Hellenistic Age came to an end as the Romans conquered much of the Mediterranean, the influence of the Greeks lived on in Roman culture. In this chapter, you will learn about Roman society and how Rome's location and its policies contributed to the expansion of Roman power.

To help students create their Themes Journal entries, provide the following examples of appropriate **agree/disagree** *statements.*

Government

Agree A strong army and government help ensure order and peace among diverse peoples.

Disagree Cooperation among different groups and a sense of unity are more important to an empire than a strong army and government.

Culture

Agree The contributions of earlier cultures provide a foundation for a later culture's progress.

Disagree A culture that depends upon another's contributions will not be innovative and unique, characteristics that are key to greatness.

Global Relations

Agree An empire that enslaves conquered people creates hatred and resistance toward its rule.

Disagree By enslaving conquered peoples, an empire ensures control over those who might threaten its rule.

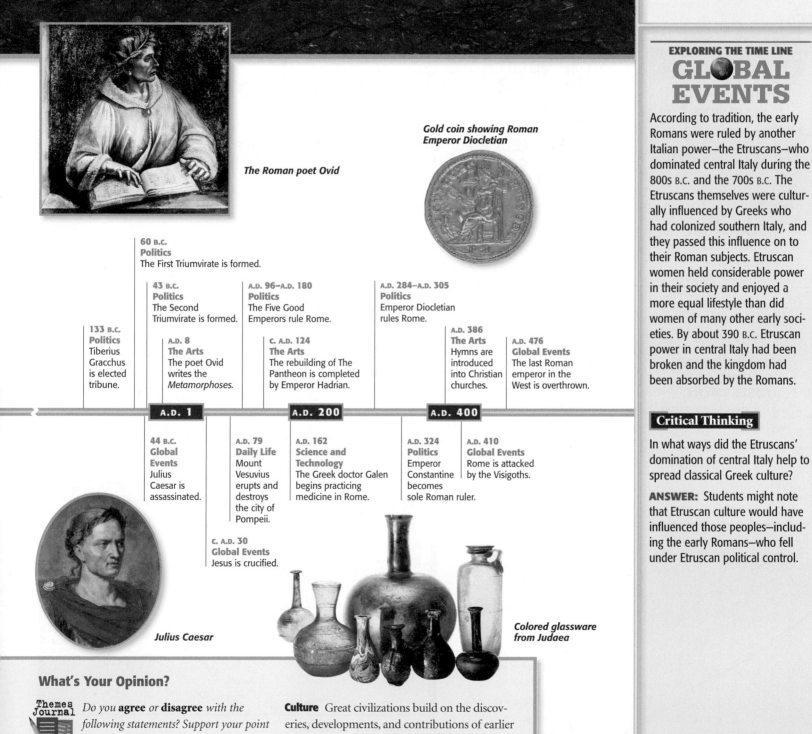

The Roman poet Ovid

Gold coin showing Roman Emperor Diocletian

133 B.C.
Politics
Tiberius Gracchus is elected tribune.

60 B.C.
Politics
The First Triumvirate is formed.

43 B.C.
Politics
The Second Triumvirate is formed.

A.D. 8
The Arts
The poet Ovid writes the *Metamorphoses.*

A.D. 96–A.D. 180
Politics
The Five Good Emperors rule Rome.

C. A.D. 124
The Arts
The rebuilding of The Pantheon is completed by Emperor Hadrian.

A.D. 284–A.D. 305
Politics
Emperor Diocletian rules Rome.

A.D. 386
The Arts
Hymns are introduced into Christian churches.

A.D. 476
Global Events
The last Roman emperor in the West is overthrown.

A.D. 1   **A.D. 200**   **A.D. 400**

44 B.C.
Global Events
Julius Caesar is assassinated.

A.D. 79
Daily Life
Mount Vesuvius erupts and destroys the city of Pompeii.

C. A.D. 30
Global Events
Jesus is crucified.

A.D. 162
Science and Technology
The Greek doctor Galen begins practicing medicine in Rome.

A.D. 324
Politics
Emperor Constantine becomes sole Roman ruler.

A.D. 410
Global Events
Rome is attacked by the Visigoths.

Julius Caesar

Colored glassware from Judaea

EXPLORING THE TIME LINE
GLOBAL EVENTS

According to tradition, the early Romans were ruled by another Italian power—the Etruscans—who dominated central Italy during the 800s B.C. and the 700s B.C. The Etruscans themselves were culturally influenced by Greeks who had colonized southern Italy, and they passed this influence on to their Roman subjects. Etruscan women held considerable power in their society and enjoyed a more equal lifestyle than did women of many other early societies. By about 390 B.C. Etruscan power in central Italy had been broken and the kingdom had been absorbed by the Romans.

Critical Thinking

In what ways did the Etruscans' domination of central Italy help to spread classical Greek culture?

ANSWER: Students might note that Etruscan culture would have influenced those peoples—including the early Romans—who fell under Etruscan political control.

What's Your Opinion?

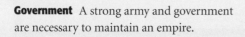 *Do you* **agree** *or* **disagree** *with the following statements? Support your point of view in your journal.*

Government A strong army and government are necessary to maintain an empire.

Culture Great civilizations build on the discoveries, developments, and contributions of earlier cultures.

Global Relations An empire that enslaves conquered peoples is destined to fall.

OBJECTIVES

1 **Identify the role geography played in Italy's and Rome's development.**

2 **Describe the form of government of the Roman Republic.**

3 **Explain the Conflict of the Orders and how it changed the early Roman Republic.**

4 **Compare and contrast the roles of citizens and noncitizens as Rome expanded its power.**

📶 LET'S GET STARTED!

As students enter the classroom, ask them to write down Greek advances in the arts, architecture, medicine, mathematics, and the sciences during the Classical and Hellenistic periods. Students should write a brief description of each advance and explain how it contributed to the civilization. Have volunteers share their responses with the class. Tell students that in Section 1 they will learn how contact with these ideas helped the culture of Rome to grow.

REPRODUCIBLE RESOURCES

▸ Guided Reading Strategy 7.1
▸ Graphic Organizer Activity 7
▸ Hands-on History Activity 7

TECHNOLOGY RESOURCES

▸ One-Stop Planner 7.1
▸ World History Teaching Transparency: Geography and History 4; Everyday Life 4
▸ Homework Practice Online

REINFORCEMENT, REVIEW, AND ASSESSMENT

▸ Section 1 Review, p. 154
▸ Daily Quiz 7.1
▸ Main Idea Activity 7.1
▸ English Audio Summary 7.1
▸ Spanish Audio Summary 7.1

MAP ANSWER
Sicily

SECTION 1

READ TO DISCOVER

❶ What role did geography play in Italy's and Rome's development?
❷ How was the government of the Roman Republic set up?
❸ What was the Conflict of the Orders, and how did it change the early Roman Republic?
❹ How were the roles of citizens and noncitizens under Roman rule different?

DEFINE

republic
dictator
consuls
veto
checks and balances
praetors
censors
tribunes
patricians
plebeians

▶ WHY IT MATTERS TODAY

The United States and other democracies are in debt to the Roman Republic for controls on government power. Use **CNNfyi.com** or other **current event** sources to explore how the United States protects its people against abuses of government power. Record your findings in your journal.

CNNfyi.com

Founding the Roman Republic

The Main Idea
The early Romans established a powerful and well-organized republic that grew and changed over time.

The Story Continues *Although the power of the Greeks waned, their culture would live on in a new civilization that grew out of western Italy. In about 750 B.C. a group of villages along the Tiber River formed what would become the center of Roman civilization.*

The Land: Its Geography and Importance

The geography of Italy had a great deal to do with the rise of Roman power. Italy looks like a giant boot. Its top is sheltered by the Alps to the north. Its toe and heel slice into the Mediterranean Sea to the south. To the east lies the Adriatic Sea. This location made it an excellent base from which to control both the eastern and the western halves of the region. The Apennine Mountains, which run the full length of the boot, are not very rugged. This made early trade and travel relatively easy.

Not everything about Italy's geography worked to its advantage, however. The Alps in the north separate Italy from the rest of Europe. Several pathways cut through the mountains, creating avenues for the movement of peoples. Over the centuries, enemy armies have streamed into Italy through these passages. Italy's long coastline has also made it open to attack from the sea.

✔ **READING CHECK: Identifying Cause and Effect** How was Italy helped and hurt by its geography? protected by mountains, helped to control Mediterranean, overland travel made easy; separated from rest of Europe; vulnerable to enemy attacks

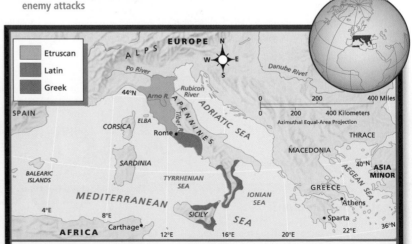

Ancient Italy, c. 600 B.C.
Interpreting Maps Rome's location on the Italian Peninsula protected the city from sea invasions and encouraged trade in all directions.
■ **Skills Assessment: Locate** On what island did the Greeks establish colonies?

TEACH OBJECTIVE 1

LEVEL 1: Ask students to list geographical advantages of the Italian peninsula. *(center of the Mediterranean region; low mountains do not hinder inland trade; access by land and sea)* Have students locate Rome on the map on page 150. Ask them to use this map and the information on page 150 to list advantages of Rome's location. *(on the Tiber, so water and transportation available; not on coast, so protected from sea invasion; near easy crossing on Tiber, so Rome became a major trading center)*

ENGLISH LANGUAGE LEARNERS

Rome and the Beginning of an Empire

People lived in Italy as early as the Paleolithic period. But it was not until after 2000 B.C. that waves of invaders swept through the mountain passes and overran the peninsula. As in Greece, these invaders came from north of the Black and Caspian Seas.

The founding of Rome. Sometime before the mid-700s B.C., a group of people called the Latins moved into west-central Italy. This plains region was called Latium (LAY-shee-uhm). Some of the Latin settlers built villages along the Tiber River. In time, these villages united to form Rome.

In the late 600s B.C., Rome came under the rule of Etruscan kings from northern Italy. The Etruscans had a written language, which the Romans adapted. The Etruscans crafted jewelry, made fine clothing, and worked skillfully in metal, pottery, and wood. These city dwellers also knew how to pave roads, drain marshes, and construct sewers. Under the Etruscans, Rome grew into a large and prosperous city. Over time the Etruscans blended into the general Roman population. Their culture, however, continued to influence the Romans.

Some Greeks also settled in ancient Italy. Greek colonies in southern Italy and on the island of Sicily became city-states. These city-states were as disunited and quarrelsome as those of Greece. Nonetheless, the Greek culture of these colonies strongly influenced the Romans. For instance, although they went by different names, many Roman gods mirrored Greek gods. Jupiter, for example, had the same traits as the Greek god Zeus. Roman myths were also similar to Greek myths.

A strategic location. Rome was built on seven hills along the Tiber River, about 15 miles inland from the coast. This location protected the city from invasion by sea. Rome's location gave its people economic advantages as well. The city lay along a shallow part of the Tiber, making it one of the easiest places for miles to cross the river. This put Rome at the center of trade routes that spread out across the land in all directions.

✔ **READING CHECK: Finding the Main Idea** How was Rome helped by its location? Its location provided defense from sea invasions. Also, Rome lay at a natural river crossing, helping to promote the city as a hub of overland trade and transportation.

The Early Roman Republic

In 509 B.C. wealthy Roman landowners overthrew the Etruscan king and vowed never again to be ruled by a monarch. In place of the monarchy, the Romans established a republic. A **republic** is a form of government in which voters elect officials to run the state. In the Roman Republic, only adult male citizens were entitled to vote and to take part in government. Three important groups of citizens helped govern the republic: the Senate, the magistrates, and a variety of popular assemblies.

Senate. The Senate was the most influential and powerful of the three governing bodies because it controlled public funds and decided foreign policy. Sometimes the Senate also acted as a court. In times of emergency, the senators could propose that a citizen be named **dictator,** or absolute ruler. A dictator could rule for up to six months. During that period, he had complete command over the army and the courts. Over time, the size of the Senate changed dramatically.

Primary Source ◆ EYEWITNESS ◆

Romulus and Remus: The Legend

According to legend, Rome was founded by twin brothers, Romulus and Remus. Livy, a Roman historian, retold the legend in his *A History of Rome.*

"Romulus and Remus . . . were suddenly seized by an urge to found a new settlement on the spot. . . . they determined to ask the [guardian] gods . . . to declare . . . which of them should govern the new town once it was founded, and give his name to it. . . . The followers of each promptly saluted their masters as king. . . . Angry words ensued, followed all too soon by blows, and . . . Remus was killed. . . . This, then, was how Romulus obtained sole power. The newly built city was called by its founder's name." **How does Livy imply that the gods participated in the founding of Rome?**

Geography

Rome's location on the Italian peninsula, slightly inland on a shallow part of the Tiber River, protected Rome from invasion from the sea, yet encouraged trade.

Critical Thinking

Look at the map on page 150. Why do you think the Greeks decided to establish colonies on the island of Sicily?

ANSWER: Answers will vary. Students might suggest that the mountains in the north protected the peninsula, its location promoted control of the Mediterranean, and its terrain made overland travel relatively easy.

The Etruscans worshiped a great variety of gods, and their religion was very important to them. The priests believed that they could discover the future by studying and interpreting natural phenomena or animal entrails.

PRIMARY SOURCE EYEWITNESS ANSWER
The gods influenced the outcome of the brothers' fight so that Romulus won.

ALL LEVELS: Have students work in pairs to create an organizational chart of the Roman Republic government. Instruct them to include all governing bodies *(Senate, popular assemblies, magistrates)* and officials. *(consuls, praetors, censors, dictator, tribunes)* ENGLISH LANGUAGE LEARNERS, COOPERATIVE LEARNING

 HOMEWORK List duties of the assemblies. Write an explanation of how the tribunes influenced assembly decisions.

Teacher to Teacher

Paul Horne of Columbia, South Carolina, suggested the following activity: Have the class list direct Roman contributions to the U.S. form of government, such as the veto. Then ask the class to think of indirect contributions, such as the president's status as commander-in-chief of the armed forces. Have students discuss which contribution is most important.

Linking Past to Present

Coins can be useful in linking together a civilization's political history. Many coins used by both ancient civilizations and those today have images and/or inscriptions engraved on their surface. Such images frequently show powerful leaders. The inscription often states the leader's motto. Also, coins can shed light on a society by their relative abundance and distribution. For example, large hoards of coins might suggest political or economic instability.

Critical Thinking

Ask students what they might deduce about U.S. society based on an examination of coins used today.

ANSWER: Answers will vary, but students might suggest that former presidents are revered by our society; liberty and religious principles are held in high regard; historic government buildings indicate the stability and importance of our government.

The Forum, which was made up of many important and beautiful buildings, served as the center of all government business. Today, its ruins stand as monuments to the grand style of Roman architecture with its towering columns and graceful arches.

Magistrates. The magistrates who made up the second group of Roman leaders were elected officials. The magistrates included consuls, praetors, and censors. After the monarchy ended in 509 B.C., two individuals were elected to one-year terms to serve as **consuls,** or chief executives. The consuls ran the government, commanded the army, and could appoint dictators. Although powerful, consuls governed with the advice of the Senate. In addition, each consul could **veto,** or refuse to approve, the acts of the other consul. (The Latin word *veto* means "I forbid.") This division of power was an example of the principle of **checks and balances,** which prevents any one part of the government from becoming too powerful. The United States and many other nations of the modern world later adopted the veto and the principle of checks and balances as safeguards in their own governments.

The Romans elected the **praetors** (PREE·tuhrz) to help the consuls. In times of war, praetors commanded armies. In times of peace, they oversaw the Roman legal system. The number of praetors varied over time, but they continued to head specific Roman courts. The interpretations of legal questions made by praetors formed much of the civil law in Rome.

Censors registered citizens according to their wealth, appointed candidates to the Senate, and oversaw the moral conduct of all citizens. Censors became very powerful magistrates in the Roman Republic.

Assemblies. Several assemblies existed in the Roman Republic. Citizens in these assemblies voted on laws and elected officials, including the consuls. Some assemblies voted to make war or peace, while others served as courts. The assemblies elected 10 officials called **tribunes,** who had some power over actions by the Senate and other public officials. If the tribunes believed actions were not in the public interest, they could refuse to approve them.

✔ **READING CHECK: Analyzing Information** How did the Romans organize the government of their republic? The government was based on a system of checks and balances. Citizens elected senators and magistrates to make and execute laws and served on representative assemblies that oversaw defense and that acted as courts.

TEACH OBJECTIVE 3

ALL LEVELS: Copy the following graphic organizer on the board, omitting the italicized answers. Call on students to identify characteristics of these two groups of Romans before the Conflict of the Orders. Discuss what rights the plebeians gained over time. (*join army, hold office, form assembly, elect tribunes, Twelve Tables*)

ENGLISH LANGUAGE LEARNERS, COOPERATIVE LEARNING

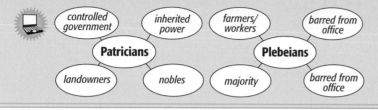

TEACH OBJECTIVE 4

LEVEL 3: Have students write an essay comparing and contrasting the roles and rights of citizens and noncitizens under Roman rule and evaluating the consequences of Roman policy in this regard. Tell students to use standard grammar, spelling, sentence structure, and punctuation.

The Conflict of the Orders

The types of people who served as officials in the Roman government changed over time. These changes stemmed from the attempts of common people to win more rights. The struggles became known as the Conflict of the Orders.

In the early republic, Romans were divided into two classes of people: patricians and plebeians. **Patricians** were powerful landowners who controlled the government. As nobles, they inherited their power. **Plebeians,** who made up most of the population, were mainly farmers and workers. For many years, plebeians had few rights. They could vote, but they were barred from holding most public offices. Plebeians could not even know Roman laws because the laws were not written down. In court, a judge stated and applied the law, but only patricians served as judges.

Over time, plebeians increased their power through demands and strikes. They gained the right to join the army, hold government office, form their own assembly, and elect tribunes. In one of their greatest victories, they forced the government to write down the laws of the Roman Republic. In about 450 B.C. the Romans engraved their laws on tablets called the Twelve Tables. The laws were placed in the Forum, the chief public square, for all to view.

The first plebeians were appointed to the government in the late 400s B.C. After 342 B.C. a plebeian always held one of the consul positions. By about 300 B.C. many plebeians had become so powerful and wealthy themselves that they joined with patricians to form the Roman nobility. From that time on, the distinction between patricians and plebeians was not as important. Membership in the nobility was still very important, however. Since government officials were not paid a salary, only wealthy nobles could afford to hold office. Thus, the nobles still controlled the republic.

✔ **READING CHECK: Drawing Conclusions** What effect did the Conflict of the Orders have on the early Roman Republic? helped plebeians to gain more rights, resulted in a written code of law, weakened political distinctions between patricians and plebeians

The Republic Grows

The years of the Roman Republic were not a time of peace. For more than 200 years after the republic was founded, the Romans fought many wars against neighboring peoples. By 265 B.C. they controlled all of Italy south of the Rubicon, a river on Italy's northeast coast. The Romans extended their republic with both a well-organized, impressive army and wise political policies.

The role of the Roman army. Every adult male citizen who owned land was required by law to serve in the Roman army. In general the soldiers themselves enforced army discipline, which tended to be very strict. The major unit of the army was the legion, consisting of from 4,500 to 6,000 citizens called *legionnaires*. The Romans also later established the *auxilia*, which were units made up of noncitizens. In general during this time, Roman army units were well trained, and morale among the troops was usually high.

INTERPRETING THE VISUAL RECORD

Legionnaires Roman soldiers' helmets were made of either bronze or iron. Their body armor was first made of hardened leather. Later, overlapping bronze sections were sewn together. *What does the carved relief sculpture below reveal about the protection that a Roman soldier's uniform gave him?*

Culture

The Roman army was more than a match against most of its opponents. Legionnaires were known for their high standards of training, fighting ability, discipline, and stamina. They routinely marched 20 miles a day and were skilled bridge and road builders. Their abilities often allowed them to surprise their enemies by arriving on the battlefield with unexpected speed, strength, and organization.

Critical Thinking

What advantages did legionnaires have over enemy armies that typically maneuvered and fought as individuals?

ANSWER: The disciplined, well-trained, and cohesive Roman legions fought as a powerful unit and could concentrate their strength with overwhelming force against disorganized, poorly disciplined forces.

VISUAL RECORD ANSWER

Students should note that legionnaires' armor combined protection and mobility, and that the most vulnerable parts of the soldier's body were also the most heavily armored.

VISUAL RECORD ANSWER

(page 154)
Students should suggest that Rome, like the United States, took a periodic census, and that Roman census workers personally visited people's homes to make sure they were counted.

Discuss how the Roman republican form of government is reflected in U.S. state and national governments.

REVIEW

Have students complete the Section 1 Review on p. 154.

ASSESS

Have students complete Daily Quiz 7.1. As Alternative Assessment, you may want to use the Roman government chart or the essay exercise in this section's lessons.

RETEACH

Have students complete Main Idea Activity for English Language Learners and Special-Needs Students 7.1. Then have students write the section's headings and subheadings on paper and list the main ideas of the section in the appropriate spaces.
ENGLISH LANGUAGE LEARNERS

EXTEND

Invite students to create a family scrapbook from the days of the Roman Republic. Have them use their textbooks, the library, the Internet, and other resources to find out about daily life.
BLOCK SCHEDULING

SECTION 1 REVIEW ANSWERS

❶ Define
- republic, p. 151
- dictator, p. 151
- consuls, p. 152
- veto, p. 152
- checks and balances, p. 152
- praetors, p. 152
- censors, p. 152
- tribunes, p. 152
- patricians, p. 153
- plebeians, p. 153

❷ Senate: controlled public funds, decided foreign policy; Magistrates: consuls ran government, commanded army, could appoint dictators; Assemblies: voted on laws, elected officials

❸ a. Rome lay inland, protected from sea invasion, and along an easy river crossing.

b. All adult male citizens were entitled to vote and participate in government; government was divided into branches; each consul could veto acts of the other consul.

c. strong, well-trained army projected Roman power and culture; full or partial citizenship was granted to inhabitants of other Italian cities; allies were allowed to remain independent; land policies enabled them to control conquered areas and to spread their culture

❹ Students might mention that granting citizenship encouraged loyalty to Rome, although partial citizens could not vote.

INTERPRETING THE VISUAL RECORD

The census The Romans periodically took a census—an official count of their population. Today the U.S. government takes a census by mail every 10 years. Government workers personally visit those who do not mail in forms to make sure they are counted. *What does this relief show about the ways Romans conducted their census?*

Link to Today **How is the U.S. census today similar to the Roman census?**

The role of wise policies. The Romans had a talent for ruling other people. Because they wanted the people they conquered to be loyal to Rome, the Romans granted full citizenship to the inhabitants of nearby Italian cities. They granted partial citizenship to the people of more-distant cities, including the Greek city-states in Italy. Although partial citizens could own property and marry, under Roman law they could not vote. As the Romans made allies in more distant areas, they allowed the allies to remain independent, but these areas had to provide soldiers for the Roman army.

The Romans also expected conquered peoples to provide land for Roman farmers. This land policy helped the Romans to maintain control over conquered areas. It also led to the spread of the Latin language, Roman law, and other aspects of Roman culture throughout Italy.

✔ **READING CHECK: Contrasting** What specific right enjoyed by full citizens was denied to partial citizens as Rome expanded? the right to vote

---

SECTION 1 REVIEW

1. Define and explain the significance:
republic
dictator
consuls
veto
checks and balances
praetors
censors
tribunes
patricians
plebeians

2. Categorizing Copy the chart below. Use it to organize the three main parts of the government of the Roman Republic.

Government Group	Functions

3. **Finding the Main Idea**

a. How did the location of Rome help it become a seat of trade and power?

b. How was the government of the Roman Republic an example of checks and balances?

c. How did the military organization of the Roman army and the republic's wise policies work together to help Rome extend its power?

4. **Writing and Critical Thinking**

Drawing Conclusions How might the granting of the rights of citizenship have affected Rome's ability to rule conquered peoples?
Consider:
- the rights and roles of citizens
- the rights and roles of noncitizens

go. hrw .com **Homework Practice Online**
keyword: SP3 HP7

OBJECTIVES

1 **Discuss the Punic Wars and how Rome gained control over Carthage.**

2 **Explain how expansion changed the Roman Republic.**

SECTION 2

Rome Expands Its Borders

READ TO DISCOVER

❶ How did Rome gain control over Carthage?

❷ How did expansion change the Roman Republic?

DEFINE

equites

IDENTIFY

Punic Wars
Hannibal
Scipio
Spartacus

WHY IT MATTERS TODAY

Economic factors often play an important role in conflicts between countries. Use **CNNfyi.com** or other **current event** sources to find a current conflict in which economics plays a role. Record your findings in your journal.

CNNfyi.com

The Main Idea
Through warfare and alliances, the Romans greatly expanded the lands under their control.

The Story Continues *"Our republic was not made by the genius of one man, but of many, nor in the life of one, but through many centuries and generations." This statesman's words reflected the Romans' pride in their civilization. As generations passed, the power and influence of the republic grew even more.*

Rome Fights Carthage

By the middle 200s B.C., the Roman Republic controlled all of the Italian Peninsula south of the Rubicon. Rome soon came into conflict with Carthage, a powerful city on the coast of North Africa that had once been a Phoenician colony. Carthage was now a great commercial power whose empire spanned the western Mediterranean. Carthage had colonies and markets on Sicily, an island off the southern coast of Italy. After the Romans moved into southern Italy, Carthage feared that they would also try to take Sicily. The Romans feared that the Carthaginian navy would control the Mediterranean and prevent Roman expansion overseas. These fears sparked three costly conflicts that we call the **Punic Wars** because the Latin adjective for *Phoenician* is *punicus*.

The First Punic War. The First Punic War began in 264 B.C. At first Rome had no navy, but it quickly built one. Rome used a Carthaginian ship it had captured as a model. The Romans employed land warfare tactics at sea. By equipping their ships with "boarding bridges," they could ram their vessel into a Carthaginian ship and then let down the bridge. Heavily armed soldiers then stampeded across the bridge and took the enemy. In 241 B.C., after 23 years of war, Carthage asked for peace. The Romans made Carthage pay a large sum of money for the damages it had caused and forced it to give up Sicily. Rome now had a major territory outside Italy.

The Second Punic War. The Second Punic War began in 218 B.C. In Spain, **Hannibal,** one of the greatest generals of all time, assembled a huge Carthaginian army that included foot soldiers, horse soldiers, and elephants. The army marched across the Alps into Italy. The crossing was difficult, and many in Hannibal's force died.

Despite the losses, the Romans were no match for Hannibal's army. Hannibal won several victories, causing the Romans to retreat before him. Because Hannibal

INTERPRETING THE VISUAL RECORD

Rome's navy During the First Punic War, Rome became a naval force equal to the Carthaginian fleet. *What does this relief imply about the size and strength of Roman ships?*

TEACH OBJECTIVE 1

ALL LEVELS: Discuss the Punic Wars as a class. Then have students work with a partner to complete the chart showing the causes and outcomes of each war.

ENGLISH LANGUAGE LEARNERS

TEACH OBJECTIVE 2

LEVEL 1: Have students list changes that resulted from Roman expansion. **ENGLISH LANGUAGE LEARNERS**

LEVEL 3: Ask students to identify major challenges posed to Rome by its expansion and to suggest possible solutions.

HOMEWORK Have students write a summary of how the Roman Republic acquired the territory shown on the map on page 156. Use standard grammar, spelling, sentence structure, and punctuation.

Punic Wars		
	Causes	**Results**
First Punic War	Carthage was afraid Rome would take Sicily; Rome was afraid Carthage would close the Adriatic Sea and the Strait of Messina.	Carthage asked for peace; had to pay indemnity and give up control of Sicily.
Second Punic War	Hannibal invaded Italy.	Carthage asked for peace; paid an indemnity and lost the Spanish colonies.
Third Punic War	Some Romans passionately hated Carthage; Rome declared war.	Carthage was destroyed.

MAP ANSWERS

1. Pyrenees, Alps, Apennines

2. advantages: surprise, maneuverability, allowed interior attack of Italy; disadvantages: difficult terrain, bad weather, created supply problems

Global Relations

Hannibal successfully regained several territories for Carthage in the Second Punic War, including much of what is now Spain, before his army was weakened while crossing the Alps. In Italy, Hannibal's position was further weakened when his plans to ally with free Italians, Macedonians, Spaniards, and Gauls failed. Hannibal never received reinforcements from Carthage, leaving him too weak to mount a powerful attack against Rome. His allies lost interest as victory began to fade and as the Romans became more aggressive. Although Hannibal's tactics and skills far surpassed those of most Roman generals, Rome ultimately claimed victory in the Second Punic War.

Critical Thinking

Ask students what factors cost Hannibal an early victory.

ANSWER: Students might mention Hannibal's dependence on foreign allies, distance from Carthage and reinforcements, and loss of soldiers and elephants while crossing the Alps.

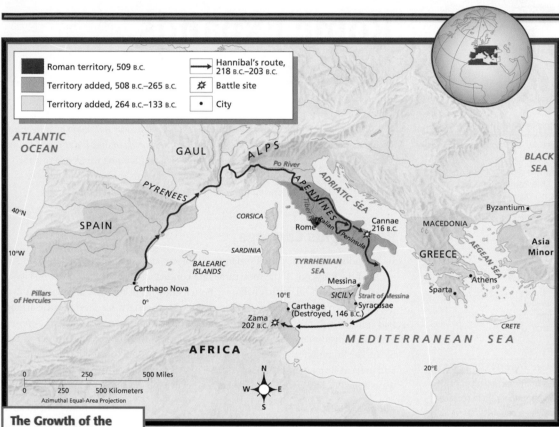

The Growth of the Roman Republic, 509 B.C.–133 B.C.

Interpreting Maps Rome and Carthage fought three Punic Wars between 264 B.C. and 146 B.C.

■ **Skills Assessment:** Trace Hannibal's route from Spain to Carthage. **1. Places and Regions** Across which mountain ranges did his army advance during the journey? **2. Comparing and Contrasting** What advantages and disadvantages did this route provide?

did not have the equipment to attack the cities, he spent years laying waste to the countryside, raiding farms and taking crops and livestock. He also tried to win away Rome's allies. The Roman policy of sharing citizenship and political power proved its value, however, as most of the republic's allies remained loyal. The historian Polybius wrote that after their defeat at Cannae in 216 B.C., the Romans vowed to conquer the enemy or die on the field of battle.

 "Hannibal's joy in his victory over the Romans was exceeded by his frustration, as he saw with astonishment the endurance and greatness of the Romans when they deliberated on national policy."

Polybius, *The Histories*, Vol. VI

Finally, Rome turned the tables by invading Africa and threatening Carthage. Hannibal's government ordered him home to defend the city. In Africa he met his match—the Roman general **Scipio** (SIP·ee·oh). In 202 B.C. at the battle of Zama, near Carthage, Scipio and the Romans defeated Hannibal and his army. Once more Carthage had to pay a huge sum of money. It also had to give up most of its navy and its colonies in Spain. Carthage remained independent, but it had lost all its power. Rome was now the most powerful force in the western Mediterranean.

The Third Punic War. Although Carthage was no longer a threat, some Romans still hated the city. Thus, the Roman Senate decided to crush Carthage. In 149 B.C. Rome again declared war on its old enemy. After a bitter siege, Carthage was destroyed in 146 B.C.

During the Second Punic War, Macedonia had been allied with Carthage. To get revenge, Rome started a war against Macedonia and defeated it in 197 B.C. The Greek cities came under Roman "protection." By 133 B.C. Rome had extended its control over the entire region. It was now the supreme power in the Mediterranean.

✔ **READING CHECK: Sequencing** How did Rome gain control over the Mediterranean? defeated Carthage in a series of three wars

The Problems of Expansion

Because Rome now controlled a vast area, the republic and its government had to change. It remained a republic, but the Senate gained almost complete control over the army and foreign policy. The nobles gained even more power.

The Romans governed the new territories, called provinces, loosely. They did not allow the people of the provinces to become citizens, nor did they make them allies. Instead, the Romans simply made the people of each province subjects of Rome. Each province was administered by a governor who was backed by the power of the Roman army. Some provincial governors took bribes and paid little, if any, attention to the needs of the people. In addition, tax collectors tried to squeeze as much money as they could from the provinces.

The Romans also had problems at home. The Roman farmer-soldiers who returned from the Punic Wars were sickened to find their livestock killed, their homes in ruins, and their olive groves or vineyards uprooted. The farmers did not have enough money to restore their farms and thus had little choice but to sell the land. As time passed, Rome became dependent on the provinces for grain, its chief food.

Many of the farmers who lost their land moved to the cities. Not all of them could find jobs there, however, and they depended on the government for food. In contrast, trade within Rome's vast empire had created a class of business people and landowners called **equites** (EK·wuh·teez). They had great wealth and political influence. Within the republic, the gap between rich and poor, powerful and powerless, continued to grow.

✔ **READING CHECK: Identifying Cause and Effect** What changes occurred in the Roman Republic as a result of Roman expansion? Senate gained almost complete control over the army and foreign policy; nobles gained more power

HISTORY MAKER

Spartacus (unknown–71 B.C.)

Romans often enslaved conquered peoples. Some slaves enjoyed fairly good treatment. For example, some slaves could buy their freedom. By Roman law, a freed slave became a citizen.

Other slaves led such horrible lives that they revolted. The most brutal revolt, led by a slave named **Spartacus,** began in 73 B.C. More than 70,000 slaves took part. By 71 B.C. the Roman army had crushed the uprising. Spartacus died in battle. Some 6,000 rebels were crucified—nailed or tied to crosses and left to die. **Why do you think Spartacus and his followers revolted?**

SECTION 2 REVIEW

1. **Define** and explain the significance:
   equites

2. **Identify** and explain the significance:
   Punic Wars
   Hannibal
   Scipio
   Spartacus

3. **Comparing** Copy the chart below. Use it to detail the changes in the Roman Republic that resulted from Rome's expansion.

Changes in the Roman Republic		
Government	Agriculture	Society

4. **Finding the Main Idea**
   a. In what ways were Rome and Carthage different?
   b. What were the final results of the Punic Wars?

5. **Writing and Critical Thinking**
   Making Generalizations Write a character sketch describing what an average Roman citizen-soldier might have been like.
   Consider:
   - soldiers' actions during and after the Punic Wars
   - the changing society

Homework Practice Online

keyword: SP3 HP7

OBJECTIVES

1 Identify the political events in Rome during the first century B.C. that helped weaken the Roman Republic.

2 Explain how the reign of Julius Caesar served as a transition between the Roman Republic and the Roman Empire.

3 Describe the events and conditions that marked the first two centuries of the Roman Empire.

🔊 *LET'S GET STARTED!*

As students enter the classroom, ask them to write a list of the challenges that faced Rome as it expanded after the Punic Wars. *(government corruption, changes in agriculture, loss of discipline and devotion to the state)* Ask students how they think these problems might have weakened the Roman Republic. Tell students that in Section 3 they will learn that these challenges ultimately brought about the end of the Roman Republic and the rise of the Roman Empire.

SECTION **3**

READ TO DISCOVER

❶ What political events during the first century B.C. helped weaken the Roman Republic?

❷ How did the reign of Caesar serve as a transition between the Roman Republic and the Roman Empire?

❸ What events and conditions marked the first two centuries of the Roman Empire?

DEFINE

triumvirate

IDENTIFY

the Gracchi
Gaius Marius
Lucius Cornelius Sulla
Julius Caesar
Gnaeus Pompey
Cleopatra
Marc Antony
Augustus (Octavian)
Pax Romana
Julio-Claudian Emperors
Five Good Emperors

WHY IT MATTERS TODAY

The actions of political leaders can have a strong effect on a country. Use CNNfyi.com or other **current event** sources to find a current country in which a leader is abusing power. Record your findings in your journal.

CNN**fyi**.com

The Birth of the Roman Empire

The Main Idea
Bitter political power struggles within the Roman Republic led to the creation of the Roman Empire.

The Story Continues *As the Roman Republic expanded its borders, its problems increased. One Roman official noted the corruption of the government in a letter to his brother. "Remember that this is Rome," he wrote, "a city made up of many people, in which plots, lies, and all kinds of vices abound."*

A Weakening Republic

By 133 B.C. the Roman Republic faced many problems. Brave leaders attempted reform, but the days of the republic were numbered.

Two brothers, Tiberius and Gaius (GAY·uhs) Gracchus (GRAK·uhs), saw the need for reform. Together the brothers were known as **the Gracchi.** Tiberius was elected tribune in 133 B.C. He was deeply troubled by the fate of the farmer-soldier. Although his suggested land reforms made him popular with the common people, they angered and frightened many senators. A mob of senators and their supporters clubbed Tiberius and hundreds of his followers to death.

Gaius was elected tribune in 123 B.C. and again in 122 B.C. He used public funds to buy grain, which was then sold to the poor at low prices. This and other acts outraged the senators, who sought to cancel some of the laws Gaius had passed. Gaius and many of his supporters were eventually killed in a riot. The deaths of the Gracchi marked a turning point in Roman history. From this point on, violence replaced respect for the law as the primary tool of politics.

The Social War. During this period, Rome's relationship with its allies throughout the Italian Peninsula entered a crisis. Citizens of the Italian cities had served in the Roman army and had endured much hardship in defense of Rome during the Punic Wars. The ruling groups of these cities wanted to share in the benefits of Rome's growing power. Above all, they wanted the right to hold public offices in the Roman government, and they called for Roman citizenship. The Senate, however, sought to maintain its hold on power and stubbornly resisted the allies' demands.

Finally, in 91 B.C., the allies rebelled. The war that followed was called the Social War, from the Latin word *socius,* meaning "ally." Many of the allied cities' troops had served with the legions and were as well trained and disciplined as the Romans themselves. Thus, the war that followed was one of the bloodiest in Rome's history. Ultimately, Rome won. The Senate, however, finally agreed to the allies' calls for citizenship and political participation. With this decision, people throughout Italy began to view themselves as Romans, and the Roman state grew to include all of the peninsula.

Gaius Marius, a Roman general who was elected consul in 107 B.C., brought major changes to the Roman political scene. He created an army of volunteers who were well rewarded with money, newly conquered land, and war loot. As more generals followed suit, troops became more loyal to them than to the government.

TEACH OBJECTIVE 1

LEVEL 1: Copy the following cause-and-effect flow-chart on the board, omitting the italicized answers, and have students complete it after reading Section 3.

ENGLISH LANGUAGE LEARNERS

Gracchus brothers introduce reforms	→	*angry senators kill both Gracchus brothers*
violence = primary tool of Roman politics	→	*leaders recruit personal armies*
Sulla marches on Rome; civil war	→	*Sulla establishes dictatorship*

In 88 B.C. **Lucius Cornelius Sulla** was elected consul. After his term expired, he wanted to take a military command that promised to gain him great fame and fortune. His enemies in Rome, led by Marius, tried to prevent him from doing so. Sulla responded by marching on Rome, an action that led to civil war. Sulla triumphed, and from 82 B.C. to 79 B.C. he ruled as dictator. Sulla tried to restore power to the Senate, enlarging it by 300 members and giving it complete control over the government. More and more, however, an army commander with loyal troops could force the Senate to do his bidding.

✔ **READING CHECK: Identifying Cause and Effect** In what ways did political events help weaken the Roman Republic? The republic was weakened by civil violence, loss of respect for law, civil war, and the rise of private armies.

Caesar in Power

Julius Caesar, a nephew of Marius, was becoming a popular general during this time. Caesar was a powerful public speaker who spent a great deal of money to win support. As a result, Caesar built a huge following among Rome's poor.

The First Triumvirate. In 60 B.C. Caesar joined with two other popular generals, **Gnaeus Pompey** (PAHM·pee) and Licinius Crassus. The three formed a political alliance called the First Triumvirate. **Triumvirate** means "rule of three." With the support of Pompey and Crassus, Caesar became consul in 59 B.C.

Caesar knew he could not win power without a loyal army, so he obtained a special command in Gaul, a region that is now France. During the next 10 years, Caesar brought all of Gaul under Roman rule. Meanwhile, Crassus died in battle in 53 B.C. Pompey was made sole consul in 52 B.C. Jealous of Caesar's rising fame, he ordered Caesar home without his army. Caesar refused to give up his military command and take second place to Pompey. Instead, he marched his army toward Rome in 49 B.C.

On January 10 Caesar led his troops across the Rubicon into Italy. With this act, he declared war on the republic. Pompey and his followers fled to Greece, where Caesar defeated him and then marched into Egypt. He put **Cleopatra,** a daughter of the ruling Ptolemy family, on the throne as a Roman ally. In 46 B.C. Caesar returned triumphant to Rome. Two years later, the Senate declared him dictator for life.

The rule of Caesar. Caesar increased the Senate to 900 members but reduced its power. Many senators, fearing Caesar's ambition and popularity, formed a conspiracy against him. Two were men Caesar considered friends: Gaius Cassius and Marcus Brutus. On March 15—the Ides of March—44 B.C., the conspirators killed Caesar in the Senate. Suetonius, a Roman historian, described the scene.

> *History Makers Speak*
> **❝As soon as Caesar took his seat the conspirators crowded around him. . . . Tillius Cimber came up close, pretending to ask a question. . . . Cimber caught hold of his shoulders. 'This is violence!' Caesar cried, and at that moment . . . one of the Casca brothers with a sweep of his dagger stabbed him just below the throat. . . . Confronted by a ring of drawn daggers, he drew the top of his gown over his face and did not utter a sound . . . though some say that when he saw Marcus Brutus . . . he reproached him in Greek with: 'You, too, my child?'❞**
>
> Gaius Suetonius Tranquillus, *The Twelve Caesars*

✔ **READING CHECK: Sequencing** What steps did Julius Caesar take to gain and keep power over the Roman Republic? reduced power of the Senate; assumed role of dictator

HISTORY MAKER

Julius Caesar
(100 B.C.–44 B.C.)

One of Caesar's greatest qualities was his willingness to show mercy toward his defeated enemies. True to form, once in power, Caesar forgave Pompey's supporters in the Senate. These men were among those who murdered Caesar.

What If? How might the history of the Roman Republic have been different if Caesar had shown less mercy?

History Maker

JULIUS CAESAR. Caesar's shrewdly calculated rise to power echoed his boldness on the battlefield. His brilliant conquest of Gaul made him extremely popular. Pompey, fearing Caesar's popularity, persuaded the Senate to order Caesar to disband his army and return to Rome. Caesar disobeyed and led his army toward Rome, which resulted in civil war across the Roman world. When Caesar crossed the Rubicon River–the border between Gaul and Italy south of which no Roman general could lead an army–he said "the die is cast," meaning that there was no turning back from rebellion. Today, people use the phrase "crossing the Rubicon" to describe a momentous and irreversible decision.

Critical Thinking

How might Rome's history have differed had Caesar balked at crossing the Rubicon with his army?

ANSWER: The Roman Republic may have continued, and Rome's drive toward empire may have faltered.

HISTORY MAKER ANSWER

Students might suggest that if Caesar had not shown mercy toward his defeated enemies and freed them, he might not have been murdered.

TEACH OBJECTIVE 2

ALL LEVELS: As students read the section "Caesar in Power" on page 159, have them complete a web diagram that includes characteristics and events related to Caesar. Then draw a web on the board and fill it in with students' responses.
ENGLISH LANGUAGE LEARNERS

HOMEWORK Write an essay explaining how Julius Caesar's reign was a transition between the Roman Republic and the Roman Empire. Use standard grammar, spelling, sentence structure, and punctuation.

TEACH OBJECTIVE 3

LEVEL 3: Assign pairs of students to study a Roman leader of this time and to write a profile that explains the leader's significance. Encourage students to use their textbooks, the library, the Internet, and other sources. Invite students to read their profiles aloud.

CLOSE

List characteristics of Roman politics before, during, and after the rule of Julius Caesar.

Interdisciplinary Connection

LANGUAGE. Forms of Julius Caesar's name–the Russian word *czar* and the German word *kaiser*–have been adapted by later cultures to express imperial power and supreme rule.

Critical Thinking

How have Roman names influenced calendars used today?

ANSWER: Students might suggest the months of July (named for Julius Caesar) and August (Augustus Caesar).

Linking Past to Present

Emperor Hadrian was famous for his military defenses. He had great walls built in many places across the empire to protect its borders. Parts of his walls still exist today.

Critical Thinking

Why do you think Hadrian spent so much money and effort on the defense of Rome's borders?

ANSWER: Students should note that Rome's borders were extensive and required continuous patrolling to maintain.

HISTORY MAKER ANSWER

Students might point out that Augustus is shown in towering proportions, indicating his greatness and supremacy.

HISTORY MAKER

Augustus
(63 B.C.–A.D. 14)

Augustus's funeral followed Roman tradition. His body was burned on a funeral pyre and his ashes were buried with great ceremony. After a senator reported seeing Augustus's spirit rise through the flames, the Senate declared that the Divine Augustus should be made a god of the state. **How does this sculpture demonstrate a new Roman view of a divine ruler?**

Holt Researcher go.hrw.com
go.hrw.com
KEYWORD: Holt Researcher
FreeFind: Caesar
Augustus
After reading more about Caesar and Augustus on the CD–ROM, create political campaign posters comparing the qualities of each man.

The Roman Empire

Caesar had chosen his grandnephew, Octavian, as his heir. A struggle for power, however, broke out after Caesar's death.

The Second Triumvirate. Octavian was 19 years old when Caesar was murdered. **Marc Antony,** a general and an ally of Caesar's, drove out the conspirators and took control in Rome. Then Octavian and Antony—along with Lepidus, Caesar's second-in-command—formed the Second Triumvirate. Marc Antony led an army east, reconquering Syria and Asia Minor from the armies of Brutus and Cassius. Then he joined his ally Cleopatra in Egypt. Meanwhile, Octavian forced Lepidus to retire and built his own power in Italy.

Antony and Octavian divided the Roman world. Antony took the east, and Octavian the west. In time, however, Octavian persuaded the Senate to declare war on Antony and Cleopatra. In 31 B.C., in a naval battle at Actium in Greece, Octavian defeated their fleet. Within a year, Octavian captured Alexandria. Seeing that they could not escape, Antony and Cleopatra committed suicide.

Octavian: the first Augustus. Octavian was determined to avoid Julius Caesar's fate. When the Senate appointed him consul, Octavian did not present himself as king or emperor. Instead, he called himself *princeps,* or "first citizen." In 27 B.C. the Senate gave Octavian the title *Augustus,* or "the revered one." He has been known ever since as Augustus Caesar, or simply **Augustus.**

Although Augustus never used the title *emperor,* historians generally refer to him as the first Roman emperor. This is because beginning with the reign of Augustus, the Roman Republic became the Roman Empire. Augustus began a series of military conquests that greatly expanded the empire's frontiers. Under his rule, the empire stretched from Spain in the west to Syria in the east, and from Egypt and the Sahara in the south to the Rhine and Danube Rivers in the north. Augustus hoped to push the borders of Rome even further. He ordered his legions to drive north of the Rhine River. Roman forces moved into Germany as far as the Elbe River. In A.D. 9, however, German tribes defeated the invaders. The Germans' victory forced Rome to accept the Rhine River as the boundary of its northern frontier.

The reign of Augustus began a period known as the **Pax Romana,** or "Roman Peace." This period of peace would last for more than 200 years. Peace came at a price, however. The political system that Augustus created greatly reduced the traditional powers of the Senate, assemblies, and magistrates. Thus, there was always a threat that an emperor would abuse his power. Over the years, some did.

The Pax Romana emperors. Augustus died in A.D. 14. For the next 54 years, relatives of Julius Caesar, called the **Julio-Claudian Emperors,** ruled the empire. Tiberius, who reigned from A.D. 14 to A.D. 37, was the adopted son of Augustus. Tiberius proved to be an adequate, but disliked, ruler. Caligula, his brutal and insane successor, was murdered in A.D. 41. Claudius, an intelligent man who administered the empire wisely, followed Caligula. During his rule the Roman legions conquered Britain. But even Claudius could not escape the violence that often ended an emperor's reign. It is believed that his wife, Agrippina, poisoned him in A.D. 54. Nero, the last of the Julio-Claudians, also came to an untimely end. Blamed for a disastrous fire that swept Rome, Nero killed himself rather than face certain assassination.

REVIEW

Have students complete the Section 3 Review on p. 161.

ASSESS

Have students complete Daily Quiz 7.3. As Alternative Assessment, have students complete the cause-and-effect chart or Caesar web diagram in this section's lessons.

RETEACH

Have students complete Main Idea Activity for English Language Learners and Special-Needs Students 7.3. Have students identify

three events during the time the republic fell that changed the course of Roman history. **ENGLISH LANGUAGE LEARNERS**

EXTEND

Have students write a brief script and stage a mock trial of Caesar's assassins. Students should take the roles of judge, prosecutor, defense attorney, and conspirators.
COOPERATIVE LEARNING, BLOCK SCHEDULING

Emperors of the Pax Romana 27 B.C.–A.D. 180				
27 B.C.–A.D. 14* Augustus	**A.D. 14–A.D. 68** **Julio-Claudian Emperors** Tiberius (14–37) Caligula (37–41) Claudius (41–54) Nero (54–68)	**A.D. 68–A.D. 69** **Army Emperors** Galba, Otho, Vitellius (Chosen by various legions during a succession crisis)	**A.D. 69–A.D. 96** **Flavian Emperors** Vespasian (69–79) Titus (79–81) Domitian (81–96)	**A.D. 96–A.D. 180** **The Five Good Emperors** Nerva (96–98) Trajan (98–117) Hadrian (117–138) Antoninus Pius (138–161) Marcus Aurelius (161–180)

*Dates of reign

Because the Romans never developed a rule for selecting a new emperor, many emperors named their successors. The Roman army, however, often refused to accept the new emperors. In A.D. 69 alone, four different emperors ruled Rome.

Vespasian, the last emperor to come to power in A.D. 69, was the first of the Flavian emperors. The Flavians ruled the empire until A.D. 96, when Emperor Nerva came to power. He was the first of a series of rulers known as the **Five Good Emperors.** Together, they ruled Rome for almost 100 years. Hadrian and Marcus Aurelius were among this notable group of Roman emperors. Hadrian, who ruled from A.D. 117 to A.D. 138, was born in Spain. Thus, he understood the provinces and spent a great deal of time trying to Romanize them. To help protect the boundaries of the empire, Hadrian built fortifications along the frontier. In northern Britain, for example, he built Hadrian's Wall, which stretched from sea to sea. Marcus Aurelius, the last of the Good Emperors, began his reign in A.D. 161. He was a well-educated man who preferred studying Stoic philosophy to fighting wars. Nevertheless, he had to defend the empire against invaders from the north and the east. These invaders would play a key role in the future of Rome.

Marcus Aurelius was forced to begin military activity on the frontiers almost immediately after he came to power.

✔ **READING CHECK: Finding the Main Idea** What characterized the first two centuries of the Roman Empire? territorial expansion, loss of senatorial power, decline of representative government, the Pax Romana

SECTION 3 REVIEW

1. **Define** and explain the significance:
   triumvirate

2. **Identify** and explain the significance:
   the Gracchi
   Gaius Marius
   Lucius Cornelius Sulla
   Julius Caesar
   Gnaeus Pompey
   Cleopatra
   Marc Antony
   Augustus (Octavian)
   Pax Romana
   Julio-Claudian Emperors
   Five Good Emperors

3. **Sequencing** Make a time line like the one below. Complete it by showing the main events in Julius Caesar's rise to power.

   ┤ 78 B.C. ├   ┤ 44 B.C. ├

   returns to Rome   made dictator; murdered

Finding the Main Idea

4.
   a. What political changes during the first century B.C. helped lead to the end of the Roman Republic?
   b. In what ways did Julius Caesar's rule mark a shift from a republic to an empire?
   c. Contrast the rule of the Julio-Claudians with the rule of the Five Good Emperors.

Writing and Critical Thinking

5. **Identifying a Point of View** Explain how the Roman view of power and authority changed from the first century B.C. through the first two centuries of the Roman Empire.
   Consider:
   • the earlier vow by Romans never to be ruled by a king
   • Rome's republican government, with its checks and balances
   • the murder of Julius Caesar
   • the establishment of the empire

go. **Homework Practice Online**
hrw.com
   keyword: SP3 HP7

SECTION 3 REVIEW ANSWERS

❶ **Define**
• triumvirate, p. 159

❷ **Identify**
• the Gracchi, p. 158
• Gaius Marius, p. 158
• Lucius Cornelius Sulla, p. 159
• Julius Caesar, p. 159
• Gnaeus Pompey, p. 159
• Cleopatra, p. 159
• Marc Antony, p. 160
• Augustus (Octavian), p. 160
• Pax Romana, p. 160
• Julio-Claudian Emperors, p. 160
• Five Good Emperors, p. 161

❸ First Triumvirate, 60 B.C.; elected consul, 59 B.C.; Crassus dies, 53 B.C.; Pompey sole consul, 52 B.C.; marches on Rome, 49 B.C.; named dictator for life, 44 B.C.; assassinated, 44 B.C.

❹ a. death of the Gracchi, leaders buying loyalty of soldiers, generals using their armies to control the Senate

b. established First Triumvirate, seized sole power, weakened Senate, used army to enforce his personal will, expanded boundaries of the republic

c. Julio-Claudian: rule inconsistent; Five Good Emperors: wise policies and effective measures to defend the empire

❺ Students should mention that Romans of the Republic held that political power should be shared among citizens. This view gradually changed as Romans came to accept a more autocratic, centralized, and exclusive form of government in return for peace and stability.

OBJECTIVES

1 Explain how the Romans built a strong and unified empire.

2 Describe the daily lives and occupations of Roman citizens.

3 Explain the role of science and the arts in the Roman Empire.

SECTION 4

READ TO DISCOVER

❶ How did the Romans build a strong and unified empire?

❷ How did citizens of the Roman Empire make a living and lead their daily lives?

❸ What part did science and the arts play in the empire?

DEFINE

gladiators
aqueducts

IDENTIFY

Galen
Ptolemy
Virgil
Horace
Ovid
Tacitus
Plutarch

WHY IT MATTERS TODAY

European and American cultures have borrowed heavily from the culture of the early Romans. Use CNNfyi.com or other **current event** sources to find a current example of an idea or object that is based on Roman culture. Record your findings in your journal.

CNNfyi.com

Roman Society and Culture

The Main Idea
Over the course of centuries, the Romans built a cultural heritage that continues to influence us today.

The Story Continues *The Pax Romana was one of the longest periods of peace and stability the world has ever known. As a result, the Romans made great advances, many of which affect people even today. If you were to travel to Europe today, for example, you could find your way by using the same road system built by the Romans two thousand years ago.*

Building a Strong Empire

Several factors helped the Romans build their empire and maintain order. First, the Romans organized a strong government and revised their laws. Second, widespread trade and good transportation strengthened the economy and unified the empire. Finally, a strong army defended the frontiers and controlled the provinces.

Government and law. The Roman government was the strongest unifying force in the empire. It helped keep order and enforce the laws. The emperor ran the government, made all policy decisions, and appointed officials of the provinces, including the provincial governors. These officials were responsible to the government in Rome for the effective, peaceful, and profitable administration of the provinces.

Roman law also helped unify the empire. To fit the needs of their huge empire, the Romans changed the laws—the code of the Twelve Tables—in two important ways. First, the government passed new laws as needed. Second, judges interpreted the old laws to fit new circumstances. Roman judges helped develop the belief that certain basic legal principles should apply to all humans. This idea came from the Greek view that law was dictated by nature and therefore common to all people.

Trade and transportation. Widespread trade of farm goods and other products also helped unify the empire. The Roman government developed policies that were designed to encourage trade and commerce. Throughout the time of the Pax Romana, agriculture was the most important occupation in the empire. In Italy many farmers worked on large estates. In the provinces, small farms were fairly common.

Most trade within the empire centered around grain, wine, oil, other food items, and everyday items such as cloth, pottery, and glassware. Foreign trade often included luxury goods such as African ivory, Chinese silk, and Indian pepper. Most of these goods ended up in Rome. From there, they could be carried to wealthy customers throughout the sprawling empire along its overland and seagoing trade routes.

During the Pax Romana, the Romans imported silk, linen, glassware, jewelry, and furniture from East Asia. From India came spices, cotton, and many luxuries new to the Romans.

LEVEL 1: Discuss ways the Romans built a strong empire. Then copy the following graphic organizer on the board, omitting the italicized answers. Have students complete it to understand why the Roman Empire was strong.

ENGLISH LANGUAGE LEARNERS

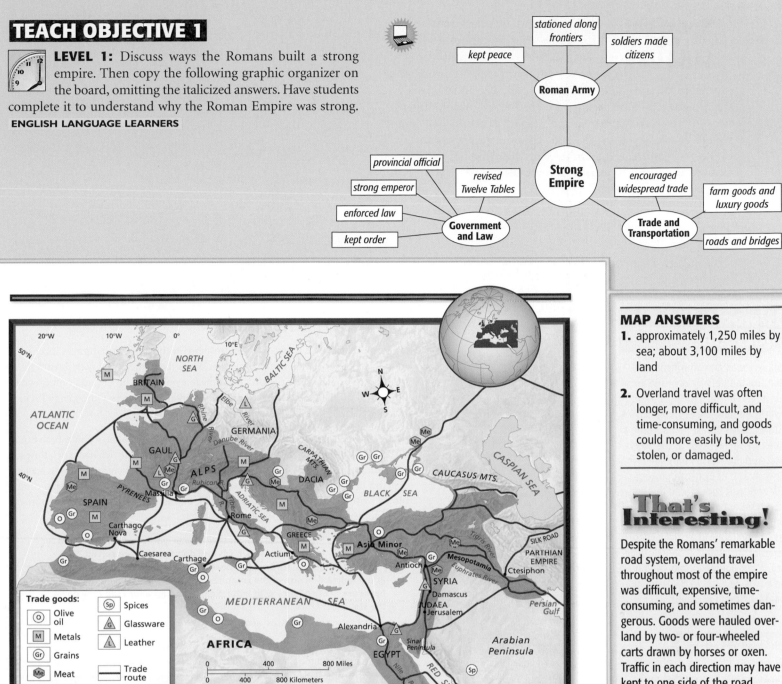

Roman Army
- *kept peace*
- *stationed along frontiers*
- *soldiers made citizens*

Strong Empire

Government and Law
- *provincial official*
- *strong emperor*
- *revised Twelve Tables*
- *enforced law*
- *kept order*

Trade and Transportation
- *encouraged widespread trade*
- *farm goods and luxury goods*
- *roads and bridges*

Trade in the Roman Empire, A.D. 117

Interpreting Maps Although an improved system of roads made it easier to transport goods across land, most goods still traveled by sea or river in the A.D. 100s. Historians estimate that it was 28 times more expensive to move goods by land than by sea.

■ **Skills Assessment:**
1. The World in Spatial Terms How far would it have been to move goods from Rome to Alexandria by sea? By land? **2. Drawing Conclusions** Why might the land route have been more expensive?

MAP ANSWERS

1. approximately 1,250 miles by sea; about 3,100 miles by land

2. Overland travel was often longer, more difficult, and time-consuming, and goods could more easily be lost, stolen, or damaged.

That's Interesting!

Despite the Romans' remarkable road system, overland travel throughout most of the empire was difficult, expensive, time-consuming, and sometimes dangerous. Goods were hauled overland by two- or four-wheeled carts drawn by horses or oxen. Traffic in each direction may have kept to one side of the road, although historians are uncertain which side was held. An edict from the reign of Emperor Diocletian in A.D. 301 indicates that bulk shipments of grain could be carried by sea from Spain to Syria at less than the cost of moving the same cargo overland a distance of 75 miles.

Nearly everywhere it went during the Pax Romana, the Roman army built roads and bridges. These well-constructed road systems served to move reinforcements and supplies quickly. They also promoted trade, travel, and communication throughout the empire. About 60,000 miles of paved highways extended to army outposts. Bridges spanned rivers, and highways linked all provincial cities to Rome. These roads were built to last. The top pavement rested on several layers of broken stone and crushed chalk. The good surfaces made travel fast. This was especially true of Rome's major road systems, which were designed to carry heavy military and trade traffic.

The Roman army. The Roman army, too, helped strengthen the empire by keeping peace. Citizen soldiers served for 16 to 20 years in the Roman legions. They were stationed in large fortified camps along the frontiers. People often settled around these camps, which eventually grew into cities. Often men from the provinces or from border areas enlisted in the Roman army. In return they were promised Roman citizenship at the end of their enlistment. Thus a vast army of veterans guarded the frontiers.

If necessary, the army used force to maintain peace in the provinces. In A.D. 60, for example, an uprising in Britain left some 70,000 Romans and their allies dead. The army soon crushed the rebels and destroyed their lands. More often, however, provincial governors aligned themselves with local leaders. This helped ensure that the locals would work to keep the peace.

✔ **READING CHECK: Summarizing** What aspects of Roman rule helped unify and strengthen the Roman Empire? *growing trade, good transportation, strong government, revised laws, and strong army*

Point out to the class that some practices that we abhor today—such as slavery and forced labor—were common and considered normal in the time of the Roman Empire. Ask students to use various sources—their textbooks, the library, and the Internet—to research slavery in the ancient world. Their aim should be to assess the social and economic impact of slavery on Roman culture. Ask them to share their findings and conclusions with the class. **BLOCK SCHEDULING, COOPERATIVE LEARNING**

Historical Sidelight

Slavery was an enduring institution on the Italian peninsula and throughout much of the ancient world. Among the Etruscan city-states, slave unrest had become a major issue as early as the 300s B.C. and may have contributed to the decline of Etruscan power. Slavery was widespread throughout the Roman Empire and was relied upon to provide essential skills and labor in virtually every area of social and economic activity. A considerable body of Roman law was devoted to the regulation and treatment of slaves.

Critical Thinking

How would the Romans benefit by passing laws to protect slaves?

ANSWER: Students might suggest a well-treated slave would be less rebellious, and slave owners would be protecting their own investment.

A ROMAN BANQUET MENU

Appetizers
✦ Jellyfish and eggs
✦ Sow's udders stuffed with salted sea urchins
✦ Broiled tree fungi with peppered fish-fat sauce
✦ Sea urchins with spices, honey, oil and egg sauce

Main Course
✦ Fallowed deer roasted with onion sauce, rue, Jericho dates, raisins, oil and honey
✦ Boiled ostrich with sweet sauce
✦ Turtle dove boiled in its feathers
✦ Roasted parrot
✦ Dormice stuffed with pork and pine kernels
✦ Ham boiled with figs and bay leaves, rubbed with honey, baked in pastry crust
✦ Flamingo boiled with dates

Dessert
✦ Stewed roses with pastry
✦ Stoned dates stuffed with nuts and pine kernels, fried in honey
✦ Hot African sweet-wine cakes with honey

Bowl with remains of eggs recovered from a Roman site

Life in the Empire

The Pax Romana was a time of great prosperity throughout the empire. Citizens did not share equally in this wealth, however. While the rich enjoyed great luxuries, the majority of Romans were poor. Many of the free poor lived on the land. Some owned their own small plots, but many were laborers or tenant farmers. Others crowded into the cities. Slavery was also widespread in the empire.

Daily life. Rich citizens usually had both a city home and a country home. Each home had many conveniences, such as running water and baths. The rich had much time for recreation and leisure. They attended huge banquets, at which exotic foods, such as jellyfish or boiled ostrich, were often served. The historian Ammianus Marcellinus noted with contempt that the rich held dinner parties primarily to impress one another.

History Makers Speak
❝Sometimes too at their dinner-parties scales are called for to weigh the fish, birds and dormice that are served. The guests are bored to death by repeated expressions of wonder at the unheard-of size of the creatures, especially when some thirty secretaries are in attendance with writing-cases and notebooks to take down the statistics.❞

Ammianus Marcellinus, quoted in *Readings in the Classical Historians* by Michael Grant

In contrast, many of Rome's residents lived in crowded multistory apartment houses made of wood. The average Roman home was sparsely furnished with simple, very basic furniture made of wood. These pieces offered little style or comfort. Rome's working people could barely make a living. The government provided free grain to city residents, but food was still scarce. Most Romans ate simple meals that included bread, cheese, and fruit.

Slaves and slavery. Slaves were among the least fortunate of the empire's population. Historians estimate that by the time Augustus took power, there were several million slaves in Italy representing a large fraction of the entire population. Slavery was also common in the eastern empire, where it had existed for centuries. It was much less common in Britain and other parts of the western empire. Life could be cruel for slaves. Until the mid-second century A.D., there was nothing to stop masters from treating slaves in any way they wished. Records indicate that slaves who worked the mines or large farms were often treated with extreme harshness and brutality. Life was probably better for household slaves. Often, skilled slaves held positions of trust, serving as doctors, teachers, or secretaries. Unlike slaves in Greece, Roman slaves could buy their freedom or be freed by order of their masters. Nevertheless, Roman slaves enjoyed few legal rights or protections and were dependent on the good will of their masters.

Historians do not believe that slavery was essential to the Roman economy. With so many poor workers available, the labor of a free worker would have been as cheap as—or cheaper than—slave labor. A person gained status, as well as an easier lifestyle, by owning slaves.

ALL LEVELS: Group students and inform them that they are creative consultants for a movie to be set in the Roman Empire during the Pax Romana. Tell them that creative consultants advise filmmakers on the historical aspects of a movie. Their job is to check for historical accuracy and to offer plot advice. Each group is to work together on one aspect of daily life or contribution to the arts and sciences in the Roman Empire. Groups should put together a portfolio of images, diagrams, and narrative descriptions. Encourage students to be creative by building models or developing illustrative materials and costume designs. Detailed information should be included to help the prop and set builders, make-up artists, wardrobe specialists, and others working on the film. **COOPERATIVE LEARNING**

The roles of men, women, and children. The family was at the heart of Roman society. The father held most of the power. He made all important decisions, controlled family property, and conducted religious ceremonies. Women were not without power, however. The mother managed the household, did the buying of food and household needs, and helped her husband entertain guests. Evidence indicates that women also participated in family decision-making. By the end of the republic, moreover, women—especially among the patrician class—had political influence. Women could also own property and accept inheritances.

Early education took place at home. Fathers taught their sons the duties of citizenship, while mothers taught their daughters to manage a household. Children from the richest families continued their formal education at home. Other children attended schools throughout the empire. Boys and girls entered elementary school at a relatively early age to study reading, writing, arithmetic, and music. If their families could afford it, boys went on to secondary school, where they studied grammar, Greek, literature, composition, and expressive speech. In most cases, girls did not receive as lengthy an education as did boys.

Religion. The early Romans sought to achieve harmony with their gods. These included the *lares* (LAIR·eez), who were ancestral spirits. Family worship focused on Vesta, the spirit who guarded fire and hearth. Over time, Roman religious beliefs were increasingly influenced by Greek thought.

By the time of the empire, a state religion had evolved. Based on the old family religion, this state religion had its own temples, ceremonies, and processions. Its purpose was to promote patriotism and loyalty to the state. In 12 B.C. Augustus became its chief priest. Since the Romans believed that gods and spirits were everywhere, it was necessary to please them through rituals and sacrifice. Thus, religious ritual was a part of daily and state life.

Fun and games. The Romans enjoyed many types of amusements and entertainment. They liked the theater, particularly comedies and satires. Mimes, jugglers, dancers, acrobats, and clowns were all popular. Romans also enjoyed brutal sports. Many spectators watched chariot racing in the huge Circus Maximus of Rome, a racetrack that could hold thousands of spectators. Romans also flocked to the Colosseum, the great arena in Rome. Wild beasts, made more fierce by hunger, fought humans or other animals in the arena. Combat between **gladiators**—trained fighters who were usually slaves—drew the largest crowds. A gladiator fight most often ended in death for one or both men. Public executions of criminals also drew large crowds and served as a warning to would-be lawbreakers. Sometimes these executions took the form of public combat between two or more condemned criminals. The Roman senator Seneca described one such public execution.

 66 The combatants have absolutely no protection. Their whole bodies are exposed to one another's blows and thus each never fails to injure his opponent. . . . The spectators demand that combatants who have killed their opponents be thrown to combatants who will in turn kill them. . . . For every combatant, therefore, the outcome is certain death. **99**

Seneca, quoted in *Egypt, Greece and Rome* by Charles Freeman

✔ **READING CHECK: Summarizing** What was daily life like for the Romans? growing contrast between rich and poor; family-centered society; daily religious practice; varied forms of entertainment

DAILY LIFE

Baths

The Romans were fond of bathing, and they built baths wherever they settled. The baths were often filled with water of different temperatures. Bathers would go from one pool to another. They combined the dips with exercises followed by massages with fine oils. Romans used public baths as social gathering places. Here people could meet, gossip, and even carry on business.

Today public baths are popular gathering places throughout Japan and other countries. In the United States, public swimming pools serve the same purpose as the Roman baths.

What role did public baths serve in Rome?

Daily Life

All classes of people in the Roman Empire loved spectacular entertainment. Rome's largest race course, the Circus Maximus, hosted chariot races. The chariots thundered around an oval track, making dangerously tight turns at either end. Fans loved to bet on their favorite teams, and successful charioteers were considered heroes.

Gladiator contests were even more popular. Many of the gladiators were slaves who had been trained to fight. In the arena, they battled singly or in groups. A skilled gladiator might even win his freedom.

The emperors paid for these amusements with taxes collected from the empire. In much the same spirit, emperors also provided free grain to feed the poor. Critics warned against this "bread and circuses" policy, but were largely ignored.

ACTIVITY: Have students create a political cartoon about daily life in Rome during the Pax Romana. Encourage them to use their cartoons to point out subtle signs of decay and decline of Roman culture.

DAILY LIFE ANSWER
social gathering places

TEACH OBJECTIVE 3

LEVEL 2: Have students discuss how life in the Roman Empire presented a complex picture of great progress and achievement contrasted against corruption, injustice, and violence. Be sure they support their views with specific examples.

LEVEL 3: Tell students that the Romans renamed the Greek gods but changed the myths themselves very little. Encourage students to read a Roman myth and summarize it for the class, comparing it with the Greek counterpart.

HOMEWORK Make a two-column chart to identify positive and negative aspects of life during the Roman Empire.

CLOSE

Write a short summary of life during the Pax Romana.

REVIEW

Have students complete the Section 4 Review on p. 167.

CONNECTING TO SCIENCE AND TECHNOLOGY ANSWER
system was sloped from mountain areas down to cities

Science, Technology & Society

The finest surviving example of a Roman aqueduct is the Pont du Gard in Nimes, France. It is 885 feet long and 185 feet high. It has three tiers of arches that are constructed of stone blocks. It was built about A.D. 14 to bring water to Nimes from higher ground north of the city. Surviving aqueducts and roads demonstrate the enduring nature of Roman engineering and construction.

🎮 internet connect

TOPIC: Roman Art
GO TO: go.hrw.com
KEYWORD: SP3 WH7

Have students access the Internet through the HRW Go site to conduct research on how the art and architecture of Rome reflected the empire's power and glory. Then ask students to create a model of a structure that employs Roman architectural, artistic, or decorative styles.

Science and the Arts

The Romans were a practical people who were not much interested in learning just to learn. Rather, they wanted to collect and organize information and put it to use.

Science, engineering, and architecture. During the A.D. 100s, the physician **Galen** wrote several volumes that summarized all the medical knowledge of his day. For centuries people thought he was the greatest authority on medicine. People also accepted **Ptolemy**'s theories of astronomy for almost 1,500 years. Ptolemy, a scientist and scholar from the great Egyptian city of Alexandria, developed a system of astronomy and geography—the Ptolemaic system—based on the belief that the sun, the planets, and the stars revolved around the earth. Ptolemy's studies in geography contributed to the classical world's understanding of the earth's physical features.

The Romans used scientific knowledge from the Greeks to plan cities, build water and sewage systems, and improve farming and livestock breeding. Roman engineers were masters at building roads, bridges, arenas, and public buildings. In most cities, the Romans built **aqueducts.** These bridgelike structures carried water from the mountains.

The Romans, unlike the Greeks, knew how to build the arch and the vaulted dome. The most important contribution of Roman architects, however, was the use of concrete, which made large buildings possible. Roman architects designed great public buildings—courthouses, palaces, temples, arenas, and triumphal arches—for the emperor and the government. Their buildings were large as well as pleasing to the eye.

CONNECTING TO
Science and Technology

The Roman Aqueducts

The Roman aqueduct system carried water from the mountains to the city, often by aboveground channels. These channels occasionally ran over valleys on stone arches. Other parts of the aqueduct system were made of underground stone or terra-cotta pipes. Waterproof cement lined the pipes to stop leaks. The Romans carefully sloped the aqueduct system to allow gravity to move water along its path. An aqueduct not only carried water, it also purified it. Reservoirs were constructed along the aqueduct course. Sediment carried in the water was deposited in these reservoirs.

> **Understanding Science and Technology**
>
> **How does the structure of the aqueduct system enable gravity to cause water to flow?**

Many Roman aqueducts contained filtering systems. Water flowed through the filter's upper chambers. Dirt and sediment dropped into lower chambers, which were periodically cleaned.

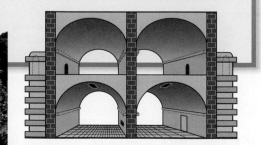

ASSESS

Have students complete Daily Quiz 7.4. As Alternative Assessment, you may want to use the graphic organizer or homework exercise in this section's lessons.

RETEACH

Have students complete Main Idea Activity for English Language Learners and Special-Needs Students 7.4. Have partners make cards labeled *Strong Empire, Daily Life,* and *Achievements.* Tell them to write supporting details of each concept on each card.

EXTEND

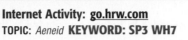

internet connect

Internet Activity: go.hrw.com
TOPIC: *Aeneid* **KEYWORD: SP3 WH7**

Have students access the Internet through the HRW Go site to conduct research on Virgil's *Aeneid.* Ask students to select certain passages of the *Aeneid* and draw connections between Virgil's work and ancient Troy and Roman culture. Then ask students to summarize their findings in a one-page essay.

Literature. Augustus and several of the Good Emperors encouraged the development of art and literature. **Virgil,** who lived during Augustus's reign, was the greatest of the Roman poets. His epic poem, the *Aeneid,* tells the story of Aeneas, a prince of Troy. Another Roman poet, **Horace,** wrote of human emotions in odes, satires, and epistles (letters). A third poet, **Ovid,** wrote love lyrics and the *Metamorphoses,* a collection of myths written in verse. The great Roman historian **Tacitus** wrote *Annals,* a history of Rome under the Julio-Claudian emperors. In this work, Tacitus expresses his criticism of the government set up by Augustus. Tacitus was especially concerned with the growing gap between rich and poor and with the decline of Roman moral standards. He strongly criticized the pampered and luxurious lifestyles of the wealthy and the loss of public virtue and respect for the rule of law. Tacitus called for a return to the simpler, more straightforward and traditional behavior that he believed had characterized the republic. **Plutarch,** a Greek, wrote *Parallel Lives,* a collection of Greek and Roman biographies. Each description of a famous Greek is followed by a description of a Roman whose life is similar to the Greek's life in some important way.

Language. Romans learned the alphabet from the Etruscans, who had adapted the Greeks' alphabet. Later they changed some of the letters. Today we use the Roman, or Latin, alphabet of 23 letters, plus *J, Y,* and *W,* which the English added after Roman times.

Long after the end of the Roman Empire, the Latin language continued to be used in most of Europe. The Roman Catholic Church held services in Latin until the A.D. 1960s. Latin is the parent of the modern Romance (from the word *Roman*) languages. These include Italian, French, Spanish, Portuguese, and Romanian. Many of the scientific terms we use today have either Greek or Latin origins. In fact, a large fraction of all English words have Latin origins.

✔ **READING CHECK: Analyzing Information** In what ways did the Romans contribute to science, architecture, literature, and language? They collected and organized knowledge in these fields and applied it to practical situations.

INTERPRETING THE VISUAL RECORD

Latin Nearly all medieval European universities used Latin in their classes. *What does this page tell us about the impact of the Latin language over time?*

SECTION 4 REVIEW

1. Define and explain the significance:
gladiators
aqueducts

2. Identify and explain the significance:
Galen
Ptolemy
Virgil
Horace
Ovid
Tacitus
Plutarch

3. Summarizing Make a chart like this to summarize the lives of the Romans.

	Description
Daily Life	
Slavery	
Roles of men and women	
Religion	
Entertainment	

4. **Finding the Main Idea**

a. What factors contributed to the strength of the Roman Empire? How?

b. What do you think are the five most important contributions the Romans made to law and government, engineering and architecture, and literature and language? Explain your answers.

5. **Writing and Critical Thinking**

Making Generalizations Imagine that you are a teenager belonging to the upper class and living in the Roman Empire during the Pax Romana. Write a short diary entry recounting the events of a typical day.

Consider:
• the importance of your family
• the kind of schooling and education you receive
• how being a boy or a girl influences your life

Homework Practice Online

keyword: SP3 HP7

VISUAL RECORD ANSWER

Latin was used in written texts for centuries.

SECTION 4 REVIEW ANSWERS

❶ **Define**
• gladiators, p. 165
• aqueducts, p. 166

❷ **Identify**
• Galen, p. 166
• Ptolemy, p. 166
• Virgil, p. 167
• Horace, p. 167
• Ovid, p. 167
• Tacitus, p. 167
• Plutarch, p. 167

❸ **Daily Life:** homes varied for rich and poor; **Slavery:** widespread; **Roles:** men made important decisions, controlled property; women managed households; **Religion:** numerous gods and goddesses; **Entertainment:** theater, chariot racing, gladiatorial contests, athletic events

❹ **a.** government unified empire and helped enforce the law; widespread trade; army kept peace

b. law and government: laws, role of judges, belief that certain basic legal principles apply to all humans, role of emperor, rights of citizens to appeal decisions of leaders; engineering and architecture: plan cities, water and sewage systems, arch and vaulted dome, use of concrete; literature and language: poetry, history, biographies, alphabet

❺ Students might want to include a description of family or daily events.

SECTION 5

OBJECTIVES

1 **Describe how the conditions Jews faced in Judaea contributed to the rise of Christianity.**

2 **Identify the difficulties early Christians experienced in the Roman Empire.**

3 **Explain the changes that helped establish Christianity and stabilize the church during the late Roman Empire.**

SECTION 5

READ TO DISCOVER

❶ How did the conditions Jews faced in Judaea contribute to the rise of Christianity?

❷ What difficulties did early Christians experience while under the influence of the Roman Empire?

❸ What changes occurred during the late Roman Empire that helped establish Christianity and stabilize the church?

DEFINE

rabbis
martyrs
bishops
patriarchs
pope

IDENTIFY

Jesus

WHY IT MATTERS TODAY

The Roman government at first tried to stop the spread of Christianity. Use **CNNfyi.com** or other **current event** sources to find examples of religious groups around the world that currently face government opposition. Record your findings in your journal.

CNNfyi.com

The Rise of Christianity

The Main Idea
The rise of Christianity and its gradual spread across the empire changed the culture of the Romans.

The Story Continues *Although the Pax Romana was marked by a lack of military conflicts, the Romans still faced challenges. Unifying a vast empire that included many different peoples with varying cultures and beliefs was often difficult. Most Roman officials considered their culture and beliefs superior to all others. One of their greatest challenges would come from a group of people whose ideals and values soon threatened those of the empire.*

The Beginning of Christianity

To keep peace, the Romans allowed people in the provinces to practice their different religions, as long as the people honored the gods of Rome and the "divine spirit" of the emperor. Since most people of the time were polytheistic, worshipping more gods did not present a great problem.

Jews and the Roman Empire. In Roman times most Jews lived in Judaea, which became a Roman province in A.D. 6. At first, Jews were not required to honor Roman gods or the "divine spirit" of the emperor because the Romans did not want to violate the Jewish belief in one God. Still, some Jews, known as the Zealots, feared Judaism would be weakened by outside influences and therefore supported rebellion against Rome to establish their own independent state. Other Jews believed that God would soon send a Messiah, or savior, to lead the Jews to freedom.

In A.D. 66 to A.D. 70 the Jews revolted against Rome. Afterward, the Romans sacked the Jewish holy city of Jerusalem and destroyed all but the western wall of the Second Temple. The Jewish historian Josephus recounted the attack on the temple:

> **History Makers Speak** ❝As the flames shot into the air the Jews sent up a cry that matched the calamity and dashed to the rescue, with no thought now of saving their lives or husbanding their strength; for that which hitherto they had guarded so devotedly was disappearing before their eyes.❞
>
> Josephus, quoted in *Readings in the Classical Historians* by Michael Grant

Today the western wall is known as the Wailing Wall. Jews consider it a sacred site of their faith. The destruction of the Second Temple marked a major turning point in Jewish history. With the temple gone, the priests' role weakened. **Rabbis**—Jewish scholars who interpreted scripture and were learned in Jewish law—became the leaders of Jewish congregations.

In A.D. 70 Roman soldiers destroyed the Second Temple and removed many of its sacred objects as spoils of war.

TEACH OBJECTIVE 1

LEVEL 1: Have students draw time lines and enter the events that signaled increasing problems between the Roman government and the Jews of Judaea. *(Jews excused from honoring Roman gods; Jews revolted; Jerusalem sacked by Romans; Second Temple destroyed; rabbis became religious leaders; Jews revolted again; Hadrian suppresses revolt; Jews banned from Jerusalem.)* **ENGLISH LANGUAGE LEARNERS**

TEACH OBJECTIVES 1 and 2

LEVEL 3: Have students write an analysis of the message of Christianity and relate it to the spread of the religion. Remind them to use standard grammar, spelling, sentence structure, and punctuation.

In A.D. 135 the Roman army, under the emperor Hadrian, brutally put down the last Jewish revolt. Afterward, Hadrian banned all Jews from the holy city of Jerusalem. Jews built communities outside Jerusalem, however. Here they carried on their Jewish faith and culture. In this setting, Christianity arose. This new religion was founded by the followers of the Jewish teacher **Jesus** of Nazareth.

The teachings of Jesus. Jesus had begun teaching around A.D. 27. He wandered the countryside with his disciples, or followers. According to the Gospels, Jesus created great excitement wherever he went. He performed miracles of healing and defended the poor. The teachings of Jesus as he traveled through the Judaean countryside have become one of the greatest influences on the Western world. His life and teachings are recorded in the Gospels of Matthew, Mark, Luke, and John. The Gospels make up the first four books of the New Testament of the Christian Bible.

Jesus's teachings were grounded in Jewish traditions. He emphasized that people must love God above all else, and they must love others as they love themselves. Jesus taught that there is only one true God. He also taught that God cares more for people, especially those who are suffering, than he does for laws and rituals. Jesus explained these views in the Sermon on the Mount.

> **Primary Source**
>
> **❝Blessed are you who are poor, for yours is the kingdom of God.**
> **Blessed are you who hunger now, for you will be satisfied.**
> **Blessed are you who weep now, for you will laugh.**
> **Blessed are you when men hate you, when they exclude you and insult you.❞**
>
> Luke 6:20–22, N.I.V.

Jesus's teachings were for all people. They promised forgiveness and eternal life for those who accepted by faith what God had already done for them.

The death of Jesus. The Romans feared that Jesus would lead an uprising. To them, he was an enemy of the state. Jesus was arrested and put on trial before Pontius Pilate, the Roman governor. Soon afterward, Jesus was crucified.

According to the Gospels, Jesus arose from the dead after his crucifixion. He remained on Earth for 40 more days. Then he ascended into heaven. His followers believed that the resurrection and the ascension proved that Jesus was the Messiah. They called him Jesus Christ, after the Greek word for Messiah—*Christos*. They believed Christ had died for the sins of human beings. Through his death, all people could be redeemed, or saved, from God's final judgment. The resurrection became the central event of a new religion—Christianity.

✔ **READING CHECK: Identifying Cause and Effect** What factors and events in Judaea contributed to the rise of Christianity? *Jesus's teachings grounded in Jewish traditions; teachings were for all people; Jewish revolts against Roman rule led to their expulsion from Jerusalem*

The Spread of Christianity

Jesus's disciples believed that the day of God's final judgment was coming soon. They set out to spread this message, working mainly in the Jewish communities of Palestine. At first Christianity spread slowly. Its appeal increased, however, as life in the empire became more difficult. Christianity accepted everyone, poor and rich alike. It promised hope and freedom from the penalties of sin and death.

Holt Researcher

go.hrw.com

KEYWORD: Holt Researcher

FreeFind: Jesus

After reading more about Jesus on the CD-ROM create an illustration or collage that describes something about his life or teachings.

INTERPRETING THE VISUAL RECORD

Jesus and children Jesus often used children as examples in his teachings. According to the Gospel of Matthew, Jesus once said, "Unless you change and become like children, you will never enter the kingdom of heaven." *Why do you think Jesus suggested his followers become like children?*

Culture

During Roman times, many Jews left their homeland of Judaea and settled around the Mediterranean region. Many of those who migrated began to speak Greek instead of Hebrew. Two Greek words became an important part of Jewish history and tradition.

The Greek word *diaspora*, which means "scattering," refers to the fact that some Jews migrated and settled in other parts of the world. The Greek word *synagogue*, or "a bringing together," was used for the places where Jews gathered to read the sacred Torah. By meeting in synagogues, Jews were able to share ideas, hold their communities together, and preserve their ancient traditions. Today, synagogues can be found in most major cities of the world.

Critical Thinking

How did synagogues help Jewish culture to survive the diaspora?

ANSWER: Synagogues helped Jews come together to share ideas, develop communities, and preserve traditions.

VISUAL RECORD ANSWER

Students might suggest that Jesus was referring to children's faithfulness, trust, innocence, and lack of worldly skepticism.

ALL LEVELS: Copy the following flowchart on the board, omitting the italicized answers. Have students enter the major events in the development of Christianity.
ENGLISH LANGUAGE LEARNERS

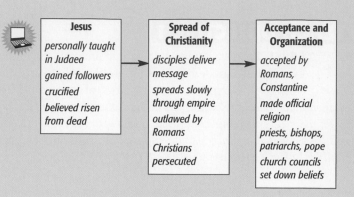

Jesus	→	Spread of Christianity	→	Acceptance and Organization
personally taught in Judaea *gained followers* *crucified* *believed risen from dead*		*disciples deliver message* *spreads slowly through empire* *outlawed by Romans* *Christians persecuted*		*accepted by Romans, Constantine* *made official religion* *priests, bishops, patriarchs, pope* *church councils set down beliefs*

HOMEWORK Use the graphic organizer to write a paragraph about the development of Christianity. Remember to use standard grammar, spelling, sentence structure, and punctuation.

Linking Past to Present

Religious persecution has occurred throughout history and still continues today. In the 1990s, religious differences and intolerance ignited conflicts around the world. In the Balkan states of southeastern Europe, for example, various religious groups were embroiled in civil wars based on centuries-old animosities. In Israel, conflict between Jews and Palestinian Arabs continued. After the Persian Gulf war of 1991, thousands of Shiite Muslims fled Iraq to escape the army of Iraq's Sunni government. In Tibet, Buddhists were persecuted by the Chinese government, which continued to be intolerant of Tibetan religious beliefs.

ACTIVITY: Assign students to research these or other examples of modern religious conflict, using primary and secondary sources such as media and news services.

MAP ANSWERS

1. Mediterranean Sea

2. Students should note that it allowed easy travel between the cities.

One person who did much to spread Christianity was the martyr Paul, who founded churches throughout the eastern Mediterranean.

At first the Roman government viewed Christians as a Jewish sect and thus freed them from the obligation to worship the emperor. By the A.D. 100s, however, Rome recognized that Christians were different. Christians often spoke out against the idea of worshiping more than one god. They also tried to convert others to their point of view. The Romans came to view these actions as an attack on Roman religion and law and soon outlawed Christianity. The Romans occasionally seized Christian property and executed Christians. Many Christians became **martyrs,** meaning they were put to death for their beliefs. These Roman efforts, however, failed to stop the spread of Christianity.

In the A.D. 200s, after the era of the Five Good Emperors, violence and unrest again shook the Roman Empire. Many people turned to Christianity for hope. By the A.D. 300s, the Christian church had become so large that the government could not punish all its members. In response, Roman law accepted Christianity as a religion.

✔ **READING CHECK: Analyzing Information** What difficulties did Christians experience under Roman rule? persecution, property seizures, execution

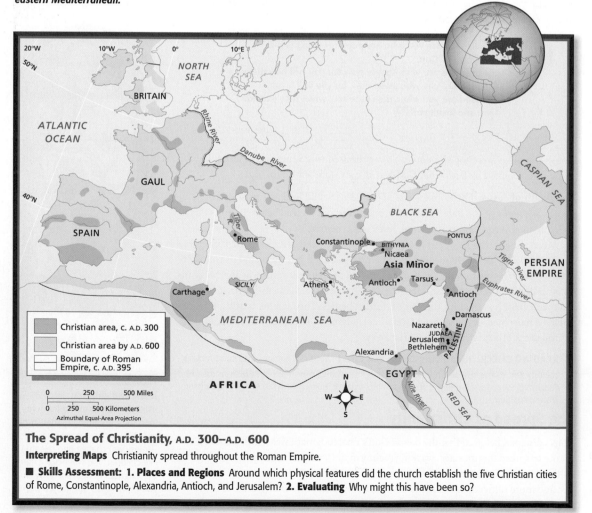

The Spread of Christianity, A.D. 300–A.D. 600
Interpreting Maps Christianity spread throughout the Roman Empire.
■ **Skills Assessment: 1. Places and Regions** Around which physical features did the church establish the five Christian cities of Rome, Constantinople, Alexandria, Antioch, and Jerusalem? **2. Evaluating** Why might this have been so?

CLOSE
Discuss the influence of Jesus Christ on history.

REVIEW
Have students complete the Section 5 Review on p. 171.

ASSESS
Have students complete Daily Quiz 7.5. As Alternative Assessment, use the time line exercise or the development of Christianity graphic organizer in this section's lessons.

RETEACH
Have students complete Main Idea Activity for English Language Learners and Special-Needs Students 7.5. Ask students to explain how the structure of the Roman Empire helped spread Christianity. **ENGLISH LANGUAGE LEARNERS**

EXTEND
Assign various groups of students to one major religion studied so far to review its historical origins, central ideas, and how it spread. Have each group represent its religion during a panel discussion to compare those three factors. **COOPERATIVE LEARNING, BLOCK SCHEDULING**

The Romans Adopt Christianity

The situation of Christians improved greatly in A.D. 312. In that year, the Roman emperor Constantine declared his support for Christianity. Constantine promoted Christianity throughout the empire and was baptized on his deathbed in A.D. 337. In A.D. 391 the emperor Theodosius made Christianity the official religion of the empire. Within 400 years Christianity had spread across the Roman Empire.

During the later years of the Roman Empire, the Christian church became well organized. Priests conducted local services and ceremonies. Above the priests were **bishops,** who headed the church in each city. Rome, Constantinople, Alexandria, Antioch, and Jerusalem became centers of the church. The bishops of these empire cities were called **patriarchs.** Over time the patriarch of Rome took the title of **pope** (from a Latin word meaning "father"). The pope claimed to be supreme over the other patriarchs. The bishops traced their authority from Jesus's disciples, mainly Peter, who was considered the first pope. Any decisions made by the bishops and the pope were equivalent to those coming directly from the disciples, who had received their authority straight from Jesus.

Church councils also helped strengthen the Christian church. In A.D. 325 the council at Nicaea (ny·SEE·uh) wrote down the main beliefs of the church. It claimed the existence of the Trinity—three persons, or forms, in one God (Father, Son, and Holy Spirit). Today the Trinity is a central belief of Christians.

✔ **READING CHECK: Sequencing** What changes and events occurred during the late Roman Empire that helped establish Christianity and stabilize the church? Christianity became empire's official religion; church became better organized; church councils collected and spread main beliefs

INTERPRETING THE VISUAL RECORD **The Trinity** This stained glass window from a modern Christian church in Chicago, Illinois, portrays the idea of the Trinity.

Link to Today What does this window tell us about the strength of the Christian church over time?

SECTION 5 REVIEW

1. **Define** and explain the significance:
rabbis
martyrs
bishops
patriarchs
pope

2. **Identify** and explain the significance:
Jesus

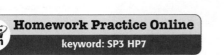
Homework Practice Online
keyword: SP3 HP7

3. **Sequencing** Make a flow chart like the one below to sequence the main events that led to the rise of Christianity in the Roman Empire.

Second Temple destroyed

4. **Finding the Main Idea**
a. Review the information about Judaism in Chapter 2. In what ways was Christianity the same as Judaism? In what ways was it different?
b. What caused the church to become stronger and more established during the later years of the Roman Empire?

5. **Writing and Critical Thinking**
Identifying a Point of View Write a paragraph explaining why the Romans feared Jesus and considered Christianity a threat.
Consider:
• what Jesus said and taught
• how people responded to Jesus and his teachings

SECTION 5 REVIEW ANSWERS

❶ **Define**
• rabbis, p. 168
• martyrs, p. 170
• bishops, p. 171
• patriarchs, p. 171
• pope, p. 171

❷ **Identify**
• Jesus, p. 169

❸ Suggestions: Jews expelled from Judaea, teachings and execution of Jesus, Christian persecution, internal strife, legal acceptance of Christianity, conversion of Constantine, Rome's official religion

❹ **a.** similarities: roots in the Old Testament (the Torah), similar ethical codes and belief in one God, persecuted by the Romans; differences: Christians believe that Jesus was the Messiah, followers redeemed by Jesus's resurrection

b. unrest throughout the Roman Empire; Emperor Constantine supported Christianity; Theodosius made it the official religion of the empire; church structure; church councils recorded Christian belief

❺ Students may note that the Romans considered him an enemy of the state and feared he would lead an uprising.

OBJECTIVES

1 Identify the problems the Roman Empire had to deal with during the A.D. 200s.

2 Explain how the reigns of Diocletian and Constantine slowed the decline of the empire.

3 List the factors that led to the final decline of the Roman Empire in the West.

READ TO DISCOVER

❶ What problems did the Roman Empire have to deal with during the A.D. 200s?

❷ How did the reigns of Diocletian and Constantine slow the decline of the empire?

❸ What factors led to the final decline of the Roman Empire in the West?

DEFINE

inflation

IDENTIFY

Diocletian
Constantine
Goths
Vandals
Huns
Attila

WHY IT MATTERS TODAY

In many countries today, governments depend upon military power to control their citizens. Use **CNNfyi.com** or other **current event** sources to identify modern governments that use armed force to maintain political power. Record your findings in your journal.

CNNfyi.com

The Fall of the Western Empire

The Main Idea
Internal conflicts and invading forces weakened the Roman Empire and led to its decline.

The Story Continues *One Roman leader who strongly supported Christianity was Empress Galla Placidia (c. A.D. 390–A.D. 450). The era in which she lived was not a good one for the Romans, however. Years of poor leadership and conflicts with other peoples began to take their toll. Eventually such problems would result in the collapse of the Roman Empire.*

Troubled Times Arise

The last of the Good Emperors, Marcus Aurelius, died in A.D. 180. His son, Commodus, proved to be an unpopular emperor who was killed in his bed on the last day of A.D. 192. Within a few years the empire began to slide into crisis. Between A.D. 235 and A.D. 284, many ambitious men competed for the title of emperor. Throughout this period invaders threatened the borders and civil war tore at the empire.

Rising inflation. In an effort to collect more taxes, the government had granted citizenship to all free people of the empire in A.D. 212. But defense of the frontiers and civil wars were costly, and the end of expansion meant wealth was no longer pouring into the empire. The result was a shortage of silver for coins—the main form of official currency. Emperors responded by decreasing the amount of silver in each coin so that they could mint more money. By A.D. 270 a silver coin contained little actual silver. To receive the same amount of silver as before, merchants raised prices. A rise in prices caused by a decrease in the value of money is called **inflation.**

Increasing insecurity. As the economic crisis deepened and attacks on the borders continued, daily life became harder for many people. Many small farmers were forced to sell their farms to land speculators and large landowners. During the A.D. 250s and 260s, Athens and Antioch were both sacked by invaders. The rich were able to escape the cities for the countryside, but city workers were not so lucky. They were unable to leave their jobs and, in any case, they had no other place to go.

✔ **READING CHECK: Identifying Cause and Effect** How did events and government policies contribute to the empire's economic problems in the A.D. 200s? policies led to inflation, growing insecurity

Inflation became so severe that some people stopped using money and traded goods and services with others.

LEVEL 1: Draw a chart on the board titled *Problems in Roman Empire* and have students complete it as they read "Troubled Times Arise" on page 172. Then ask students to use a problem-solving process to determine whether they think these problems were insurmountable.
ENGLISH LANGUAGE LEARNERS

HOMEWORK Ask students to imagine the Western Roman Empire during its last days and to describe this image in words or pictures, using computer software as appropriate.

Two Able Emperors Attempt Reform

By A.D. 284 the Romans had made some progress in pushing back the invaders. Things were far from secure, however, and the economy was still shaky. It would take the efforts of two emperors—**Diocletian** and **Constantine**—to slow the empire's decline.

Diocletian. Diocletian (dy·uh·KLEE·shuhn), a general in the Roman army, was made emperor in A.D. 284. An able administrator, he realized that the empire had grown too large for one person to manage. He appointed a co-emperor and two assistants, or caesars. Diocletian ruled in the East, his co-emperor in the West. Under Diocletian the government controlled almost every aspect of life. Defense and security of the empire came first. Individual freedom was second. Diocletian ended lawlessness within the empire by driving out the invading barbarian tribes. He also tried, although unsuccessfully, to improve the economy by controlling prices and wages.

Diocletian and his co-emperor retired in A.D. 305. Their caesars now became co-emperors, with their sons as caesars. When Constantius, the new emperor in the West, died suddenly in A.D. 306, his son Constantine took his place as emperor. The emperor in the East, however, refused to recognize Constantine as co-emperor. The divided rule Diocletian had created quickly broke down. Civil war once again racked the empire.

Constantine. In the end Constantine won out and became sole emperor in A.D. 324. Constantine is remembered for many things, including supporting Christianity throughout the empire. According to the historian Eusebius, Constantine began supporting Christianity after receiving a vision the day before his victory over his rival for emperor:

> *History Makers Speak*
>
> **❝Around noontime, when the day was already beginning to decline, he saw before him in the sky the sign of a cross of light. He said it was above the sun and it bore the inscription, 'Conquer with this.' The vision astounded him, as it astounded the whole army that was with him. ❞**
>
> Eusebius, quoted in *Readings in the Classical Historians* by Michael Grant

Constantine is also remembered for creating a new capital city in the East called Constantinople. The new capital served as a base from which to defend the eastern empire.

After Constantine died in A.D. 337, the empire was stable for about 50 more years. The government, however, was inefficient and corrupt. By A.D. 400, two empires existed, one in the West and one in the East. As the western empire grew weaker and weaker, the eastern empire became the center of power and wealth.

✔ **READING CHECK: Analyzing Information** What reforms and other actions did Diocletian and Constantine introduce that helped delay the decline of the Roman Empire? divided rule; imposed strong government controls; drove out barbarian invaders

---

Diocletian's Wage and Price Controls

Wages per day
Farm laborer . . . . 24 denarii
Sewer cleaner . . . 25 denarii
Carpenter . . . . . . 50 denarii
Wall painter . . . . . 75 denarii
Picture
  painter . . . . 150 denarii
Baker . . . . 50 denarii

Prices per pound
Pork . . . . 12 denarii
Beef . . . . 8 denarii
Sea fish . . . . 24 denarii
Second-
  quality fish . . . . 15 denarii

Interpreting the Chart
Diocletian passed wage and price controls in an attempt to curb inflation. The move did not work. People hoarded goods and prices soared. *What can you tell about Roman society from the amounts set for various jobs and goods?*

Constantinople, the empire's new capital city, was built on the site of the former Greek city of Byzantium. Today it is the Turkish city of Istanbul.

Economics

During the A.D. 200s and 300s large landowners on the Roman frontiers began to hire their own armies and build fortifications to protect their holdings.

Landowners took displaced farmers, craftspeople, and entire villages under their protection in exchange for servitude, leading to the development of the "villa economy." Some historians contend that the feudal system that dominated much of Western Europe for the next 1,000 years had its roots in the villa economy of the late Western Roman Empire.

Critical Thinking

Ask students why people were willing to surrender their freedom to serve landowners.

ANSWER: Students might point out that the growing instability and insecurity that characterized the late empire frightened the people.

INTERPRETING THE CHART ANSWER
Students might suggest that Roman society valued artists and skilled workers over general laborers. They might also note that many Romans could barely afford food prices.

LEVEL 2: Have students list the accomplishments and policies of Diocletian and Constantine. Then compare and contrast the lists in a group discussion.
ENGLISH LANGUAGE LEARNERS

LEVEL 3: Discuss using a problem-solving process. Then have students write edicts for both Diocletian and Constantine to deliver to the Roman people announcing new policies and reforms that the emperor hopes will solve the problems facing the Roman Empire. If time permits, have some of the students give their speeches to the class.

ALL LEVELS: Discuss the role that the barbarian invasions played in the fall of Rome. Have students compare the map on page 174 with the map on page 170. *(Much of the spread of Christianity coincided with the barbarian invasions.)* Ask students for the results of the invasions. *(separate tribal kingdoms rather than one united empire, people left cities, farm fields destroyed, learning declined)* **ENGLISH LANGUAGE LEARNERS**

Global Relations

In the A.D. 500s a Goth named Jordanes wrote *On the Origins and History of the Goths,* in which he claimed that the Amazons, a group of female warriors from Roman myths, were in fact Goths. According to Jordanes, when the men of the Gothic army were away, "a neighboring tribe attempted to carry off women of the Goths as prizes. But they made a brave resistance, . . . and routed in disgrace the enemy who had come upon them." Inspired by this victory, the Goths chose two women to lead them in the conquest of new territories.

Critical Thinking

Why would this tale be considered inspirational to the Goths?

ANSWER: The women are shown as brave warriors, capable of defeating the enemy and bringing glory to the Goths.

MAP ANSWERS

1. Adrianople, A.D. 378

2. The Roman Army was no longer assured of defeating its barbarian opponents.

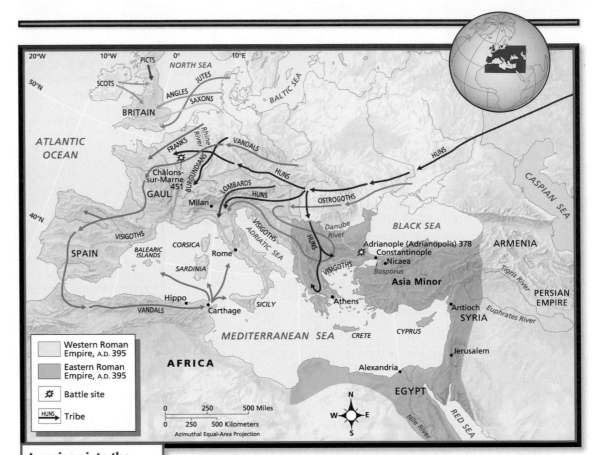

Western Roman Empire, A.D. 395
Eastern Roman Empire, A.D. 395
☼ **Battle site**
HUNS→ **Tribe**

Invasions into the Roman Empire, A.D. 340–A.D. 481

Interpreting Maps By the A.D. 300s, invading tribes were attacking the Roman Empire on most of its frontiers. This contributed greatly to the collapse of the Western Roman Empire.

■ **Skills Assessment:**
1. Locate Locate the place and date of the major battle that took place in the Eastern Roman Empire. **2. Analyzing Information** How did this attack reflect the weakening of Roman forces?

The Final Invasions

Diocletian and Constantine were able to hold the empire together through their efforts and reforms. The threat of invasion from the north and east never disappeared, however. The most troublesome of the invaders were the Germans. These tribes—the **Goths** (made up of the western Visigoths and eastern Ostrogoths), **Vandals,** Franks, and others—lived north of the Rhine and Danube Rivers.

The Goths and the Vandals. By the late A.D. 300s large numbers of Goths were flooding into the empire in an attempt to escape invaders from the east. The Romans treated them badly. In response, the Goths revolted in A.D. 378. The heavily armed Goths quickly crushed the large Roman army when they met in battle at Adrianople. Among the dead was the eastern emperor Valens. The Romans no longer had the upper hand against the invaders. In the wake of the defeat, the Romans allowed the Goths to settle in the empire under their own leaders. In return, the Goths agreed to join the Roman army. The peace this brought was short-lived. In A.D. 410 the Visigoth king Alaric and his troops sacked Rome. It was the first time Rome had been sacked in 800 years.

While the Romans were busy defending themselves against the Visigoths, the Vandals crossed the border with little opposition. They proved to be a serious threat to the empire. In A.D. 429 the Vandals invaded North Africa, quickly conquering the area. In A.D. 455 they returned to Europe to sack Rome. Today's use of the word "vandal" suggests the terror and destruction that accompanied these continuing invasions.

Decline of the Roman Empire		
Political/Military	**Economic**	**Social**
• *inadequate government for size of empire* • *competition for power* • *army interference made government unstable* • *dependence on German troops*	• *expense of defending and maintaining empire* • *heavy taxes* • *loss of income* • *decline of manufacturing and agriculture*	• *too many poor* • *loss of patriotism, interest in government, and political honesty*

The Huns. The Goths had moved into the empire to escape the advancing Huns. The **Huns** were nomadic peoples from Asia who lived by raiding and plundering. The Greek historian Ammianus Marcellinus described the Huns in vivid detail:

> *History Makers Speak*
> **"They have squat bodies, strong limbs, and thick necks.... They wear garments of linen or of the skins of fieldmice stitched together, and there is no difference between their clothing whether they are at home or abroad.**
> **Once they have put their necks into some dingy shirt they never take it off or change it until it rots and falls to pieces from incessant [constant] wear.... Buying or selling, eating or drinking, are all done by day or night by horseback, and they even bow forward over their beasts' narrow necks to enjoy a deep and dreamy sleep."**

Ammianus Marcellinus, quoted in *Readings in the Classical Historians* by Michael Grant

By the mid-400s the Huns were led by the fierce **Attila.** In A.D. 451 Attila launched an attack on Gaul. His troops were defeated by an army of Romans and Visigoths in a great battle near Châlons-sur-Marne. Attila's army quickly broke up, but it was too late to save the Western Roman Empire. In A.D. 476 a barbarian commander overthrew Romulus Augustulus, the last Roman emperor in the West.

Results of the invasions. The Germans who invaded the West were made up of many different tribes. Thus, they set up separate tribal kingdoms once they were in power. This made it impossible for them to rule a united empire. In many areas, people left the cities in search of food and greater safety. In the country, soldiers often trampled crops during battles, and weeds choked the fields. Learning declined as schools and libraries were destroyed. Over time, knowledge of the world and the past declined.

✔ **READING CHECK: Drawing Inferences** What roles did the Goths, Vandals, and Huns play in the decline of the Roman Empire in the West? invasions displaced people, caused instability and destruction

Causes of the Decline

People sometimes refer to the overthrow of Romulus Augustulus as the "fall" of the Roman Empire. Actually, no such thing as a single fall occurred. Instead, the empire in the West gradually declined. The empire in the East would remain until A.D. 1453.

For centuries historians have debated how this mighty empire could disappear. The most obvious cause of the final collapse is the mass of German invasions triggered by the Huns pushing westward from Asia. This put a terrible strain on Roman resources, already spread too thin. Overwhelmed and short on Roman recruits, the army became dependent on German troops, who gained more and more power and freedom. But this was simply the last blow. It took centuries to set the stage for the final outcome. Between the A.D. 200s and the A.D. 400s almost no part of Roman life—political, military, economic, or social—escaped decay.

Political and military weaknesses. In an age of slow transportation, the Roman Empire grew too fast and too large. Rome tried to control this vast empire with a government designed for a small city-state. Faced with governing the entire Mediterranean world, the system failed. Competition for power, oppressive public service, and corrupt courts added to the problems. The army also contributed to the decline by interfering with the choice of emperor and making the government unstable.

Analyzing Primary Sources

Identifying Bias What evidence of bias is there in Ammianus Marcellinus's description of the Huns? Ammianus shows bias by using disparaging language to describe the Huns' appearance, dress, and habits.

Continuous conflict with nomadic peoples from central and southwestern Asia posed an ever-growing threat to Rome during the late empire.

History Maker

ATTILA. Attila was notorious for his ruthlessness. In about A.D. 445 he murdered his brother to become sole ruler of the Huns. Attila invaded Italy, sacked several cities, and may have taken the entire peninsula had his army not been decimated by the plague.

ACTIVITY: Have students use the library or other resources to write a short research report on Attila the Hun and present their findings to the class.

Government

One of Rome's legacies came from the empire's policy of recognizing the legal rights of noncitizens and foreigners. The Romans developed the *ius gentium*, a body of international law, to help them deal with people from beyond the empire. They also understood that circumstances were constantly changing, so they left the law open to interpretation by jurisprudents, or judges.

Critical Thinking

In what way might the establishment of noncitizens' rights have affected their role in the empire?

ANSWER: Students might suggest that by having certain rights protected, noncitizens might be more willing to share in the support of the empire.

The costs of defending Rome's borders against invaders such as the Huns and the Goths had a severe and escalating impact on the Roman economy. Funds used in the empire's defense could no longer be dedicated to meeting internal needs, and the imperial infrastructure in the West—roads, ports, communication networks, and essentials such as public water supplies—could no longer be maintained. Ask pairs of students to use their texts, the library, and the Internet to search for information on Rome's economic decline during the fourth and fifth centuries. They should aim to identify links between growing defense costs and declining living standards in the West. Ask them to share their findings and conclusions with the class.

BLOCK SCHEDULING, COOPERATIVE LEARNING

Linking Past to Present

Edward Gibbon was one of the first historians to study the past with the aim of linking historical events and developments to the present. His six-volume *History of the Decline and Fall of the Roman Empire* presents a model of exceptional scholarship, wide-ranging analysis, and relevance that continues to influence today's writers and students. In addition, Gibbon was an outstanding stylist whose work reflects literary mastery, as well as profound knowledge and insight. In many ways his work is as applicable today as it was when first published in 1788.

Critical Thinking

Why might Gibbon's approach to the writing of history be considered as important as the knowledge he contributed?

ANSWER: Students might suggest that Gibbon's pioneering approach—a conscious effort to link and relate the past and the present—greatly enhanced the meaning and importance of historical study.

SKILLS PRACTICE ANSWERS

1. combined economic, social, political, and military causes

2. Essays will vary, but points of view should be supported.

SKILL-BUILDING STRATEGIES — Making Generalizations and Predictions

Why the Western Empire Fell

Many factors contributed to the fall of the Western Roman Empire. It is possible to make generalizations about the causes of the fall by analyzing information about these factors. It is also possible to use the same information to make predictions about how the Romans might have prevented the decline. Examine the information below, then complete the Skills Practice.

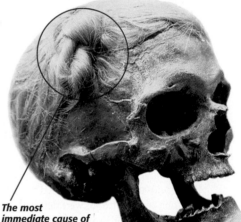

The most immediate cause of the fall of the Western Roman Empire was the series of invasions by Germanic groups. This skull shows the topknot that Germanic soldiers wore to identify themselves.

A Historian's View:
Historian Edward Gibbon summed up his view of the causes of the fall of Rome.

"This long peace, and the uniform government of the Romans, introduced a slow and secret poison into the vitals of the empire. The minds of men were gradually reduced to the same level, the fire of genius was extinguished, and even the military spirit evaporated."

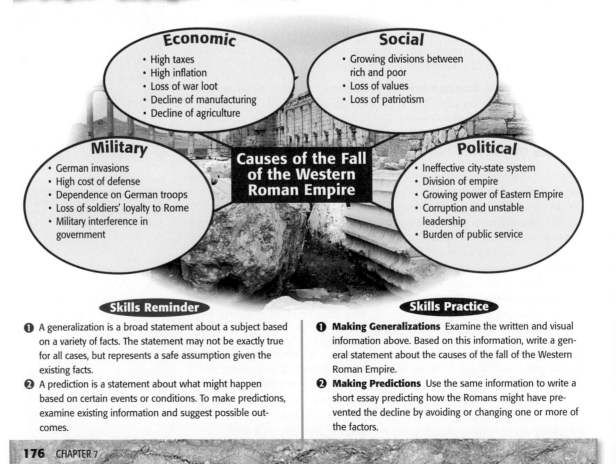

Economic
- High taxes
- High inflation
- Loss of war loot
- Decline of manufacturing
- Decline of agriculture

Social
- Growing divisions between rich and poor
- Loss of values
- Loss of patriotism

Military
- German invasions
- High cost of defense
- Dependence on German troops
- Loss of soldiers' loyalty to Rome
- Military interference in government

Causes of the Fall of the Western Roman Empire

Political
- Ineffective city-state system
- Division of empire
- Growing power of Eastern Empire
- Corruption and unstable leadership
- Burden of public service

Skills Reminder

❶ A generalization is a broad statement about a subject based on a variety of facts. The statement may not be exactly true for all cases, but represents a safe assumption given the existing facts.

❷ A prediction is a statement about what might happen based on certain events or conditions. To make predictions, examine existing information and suggest possible outcomes.

Skills Practice

❶ **Making Generalizations** Examine the written and visual information above. Based on this information, write a general statement about the causes of the fall of the Western Roman Empire.

❷ **Making Predictions** Use the same information to write a short essay predicting how the Romans might have prevented the decline by avoiding or changing one or more of the factors.

CLOSE

Debate whether the fall of the Western Roman Empire was inevitable or whether it could have been prevented.

REVIEW

Have students complete the Section 6 Review on p. 177.

ASSESS

Have students complete Daily Quiz 7.6. As Alternative Assessment, you may want to use the graphic organizer exercise in this section's lessons.

RETEACH

Have students complete Main Idea Activity for English Language Learners and Special-Needs Students 7.6. Then ask each student to create an annotated time line of the fall of the western empire.
ENGLISH LANGUAGE LEARNERS

EXTEND

Have students create collages that highlight Roman legacies in the modern world, including contributions to the arts and sciences.
BLOCK SCHEDULING

Ambitious generals often seized control, assassinated the emperor, and took the throne. The soldiers lost their loyalty to Rome. Instead, they served anyone who could pay them more. Faced with poor leadership, discipline crumbled. Also, some Roman leaders recruited whole tribes of German troops, granting them money and goods in return for their service. As a result, the Romans became too dependent upon German troops for defense.

Economic decline. Strains on the economy were possibly even more damaging. The defense and maintenance of the empire was expensive. Heavy taxes crushed the people. But even heavy taxes could not provide enough money. The problem was compounded once the empire stopped expanding. The government could no longer depend upon the gold and goods it plundered during foreign wars. As manufacturing and agriculture declined, the Roman economy grew increasingly weaker and more fragmented.

Social change. Roman wealth had always been in the hands of a small part of the population. As the empire grew, the number of poor citizens increased. The division between the rich and the poor contributed to social decay. Most early Romans were stern, honest, hard-working, and patriotic people who believed it was their duty to serve the government. Romans of the later empire lost this patriotism. Most took little interest in the government and lacked political honesty.

✔ **READING CHECK Analyzing Information** What long-term factors contributed to the decline of the Roman Empire in the West? *political and military weakness; economic decline; social change*

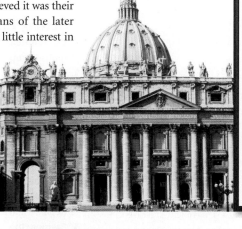

St. Peter's Basilica is an enduring example of Roman architecture.

Rome: An Enduring Legacy
The Roman Empire collapsed more than 1,500 years ago. Even so, the Roman influence still survives. The letters you see on this page are a gift from the Romans. Roman numerals are still used. Also, our calendar is based on the one developed by Julius Caesar in A.D. 46.

Roman influence is also evident throughout the world. Two key influences are Roman law and Christianity. In addition, Roman bridges and Roman roads remain today. The ruins of many Roman buildings continue to inspire people. In these and many more ways, Rome lives on. **Can you identify evidence of Roman influence in the photograph of St. Peter's Basilica?**

THEN AND NOW ANSWER
Students should note the dome, the use of columns, and the massive architectural style.

SECTION 6 REVIEW ANSWERS

❶ **Define**
• inflation, p. 172

❷ **Identify**
• Diocletian, p. 173
• Constantine, p. 173
• Goths, p. 174
• Vandals, p. 174
• Huns, p. 175
• Attila, p. 175

❸ Rise: military power and conquest, the Republic's growing political disorder, Caesar's dictatorship and the reduction of the Senate, the birth of the Pax Romana; Fall: economic and political decline, division of the empire, growing division between rich and poor, growing military weakness, continuing German invasions

❹ **a.** population decline, civil unrest, barbarian invasions, inflation and economic decline, inefficiency and corruption in government

b. disunity of separate tribal kingdoms, people left the cities, armies destroyed crops, learning declined as schools and libraries were destroyed

❺ Students might suggest that a better system of succession could have been developed, taxes lowered, and expansion continued.

SECTION 6 REVIEW

1. **Define** and explain the significance: inflation

2. **Identify** and explain the significance:
Diocletian
Constantine
Goths
Vandals
Huns
Attila

3. **Evaluating** Use the following graphic organizer to outline the factors that led to the rise and fall of the Western Roman Empire.

4. **Finding the Main Idea**
a. What problems faced the Roman Empire during the A.D. 200s?
b. How did invasions by the Visigoths, Huns, and others contribute to the problems in the Roman Empire?

5. **Writing and Critical Thinking**
Problem Solving Write a brief newspaper editorial expressing your opinion about what Rome might have done differently to solve some of its problems and lessen its decline.
Consider:
• problems within the empire
• solutions tried by Diocletian
• forces outside the empire

Homework Practice Online
keyword: SP3 HP7

REVIEW AND ASSESSMENT RESOURCES

REPRODUCIBLE RESOURCES
▶ Vocabulary Activity 7

TECHNOLOGY RESOURCES
▶ Chapter 7 Test Generator (on the One-Stop Planner)
▶ Global Skill Builder CD–ROM
▶ HRW Web Site

REINFORCEMENT, REVIEW, and ASSESSMENT
▶ Chapter 7 Review, pp. 178–179
▶ Chapter 7 Tutorial for Students, Parents, Mentors, and Peers
▶ Chapter 7 Test (Form A or B)
▶ Alternative Assessment Handbook
▶ Chapter 7 Test for English Language Learners and Special-Needs Students

REVIEW
Have students complete the Chapter 7 Review on pages 178–179.

ASSESS
Use one of the chapter tests to assess students' understanding of the content. For Alternative Assessment, see the Portfolio Activities and Alternative Assessment Handbook.

Understanding Main Ideas

1. senate, magistrates, assemblies

2. Plebeians increased power

3. Rome became supreme in Mediterranean.

4. new territories governed loosely, farmer-soldiers forced to sell lands and move to cities

5. formed the First Triumvirate and conquered new territory

6. Augustus expanded frontiers; emperor became supreme

7. widespread trade of farm goods

8. government systems, laws

9. founded on teachings of Jesus, belief in redemption due to Jesus's resurrection

10. conversion of Constantine, structure, church councils clarified Christian belief

11. Diocletian appointed a co-emperor and caesars. Constantine supported Christianity.

12. population decline, civil unrest, barbarian invasions

Reviewing Themes

1. government and legal system, powerful Roman army

2. scientific and medical knowledge, Roman alphabet

3. became rigid

CHAPTER 7 Review

Creating a Time Line

Copy the time line below onto a sheet of paper. Complete the time line by filling in the events, individuals, and dates from the chapter that you think were significant. Pick three events and explain why you think they were significant.

| 1000 B.C. | 500 B.C. | A.D. 1 | A.D. 500 |

Writing a Summary

Using standard grammar, spelling, sentence structure, and punctuation, write an overview of the events in the chapter.

Identifying People and Ideas

Identify the following terms or individuals and explain their significance:

1. republic
2. checks and balances
3. dictator
4. Punic Wars
5. Pax Romana
6. Julius Caesar
7. Augustus (Octavian)
8. aqueducts
9. Jesus
10. Constantine

Understanding Main Ideas

SECTION 1 *(pp. 150–154)*
Founding the Roman Republic
1. How was the Roman Republic's government organized?
2. How did the Conflict of the Orders change how the Roman Republic was governed?

SECTION 2 *(pp. 155–157)*
Rome Expands Its Borders
3. What was the outcome of the Punic Wars?
4. What problems occurred as a result of Rome's expansion?

SECTION 3 *(pp. 158–161)*
The Birth of the Roman Empire
5. How did Julius Caesar rise to power?
6. How did the republic become the Roman Empire?

SECTION 4 *(pp. 162–167)*
Roman Society and Culture
7. What was the economy of the Roman Empire like?
8. In what areas did Rome make great contributions to the world? Give examples to support your answers.

SECTION 5 *(pp. 168–171)*
The Rise of Christianity
9. How did Christianity begin and what was unique about it?
10. What factors helped Christianity gain acceptance in the Roman Empire?

SECTION 6 *(pp. 172–177)*
The Fall of the Western Empire
11. How did Diocletian and Constantine try to strengthen the Roman Empire?
12. What were some causes of Rome's decline?

Reviewing Themes

1. **Government** What two major factors helped Rome unify its empire and maintain peace?
2. **Culture** What ideas and inventions did the Romans borrow and adapt from the Greeks?
3. **Global Relations** How did Rome's relationship with the people it conquered change over time?

Thinking Critically

1. **Comparing** Compare the role of citizens in Athenian democracy with that of citizens in Rome's republic.
2. **Contrasting** How did the governments of the Roman Republic and the Roman Empire differ?
3. **Sequencing** Trace the spread of Christianity in the Roman world.
4. **Identifying Cause and Effect** How did the use of written law strengthen Rome's government?

Writing About History

Analyzing Information Romans were skilled builders who developed many new ideas. Write a description of how Roman engineering ideas are used today. Use the following chart to organize your thoughts before you begin writing.

	Roman Examples	Examples Today
Ideas and Innovations in Architecture and Engineering		

Building Social Studies Skills

Interpreting Maps

Study the map below. Then use the information on the map to help you answer the questions that follow.

Ancient Italy, c. 600 B.C.

1. Which of the following statements correctly describes how geographic factors influenced Rome's rise to power?

   a. The Alps protected Italy from invasion from the north.

   b. The rugged Apennine Mountains made it difficult to unify Italy.

   c. Italy's location helped Rome control the eastern and western Mediterranean.

   d. Italy's rugged coast discouraged sea trade.

2. Using information from the map, support your choice of statements in question 1.

Analyzing Primary Sources

Read the following quote by the historian Polybius, who lived in Rome during the 100s B.C., then answer the questions.

"Having then got rid of these rulers by assassination or exile, they do not venture to set up a king again, being still in terror of the injustice to which this led before; nor dare they intrust the common interests again to more than one, considering the recent example of their misconduct: and therefore, as the only sound hope left them is that which depends upon themselves, they are driven to take refuge in that; and so changed the constitution from an oligarchy to a *democracy*."

3. Which of the following statements best describes the author's point of view?

   a. People cannot pick good leaders.

   b. People have no control over their leaders.

   c. Power should be limited to a few people.

   d. Democracy is a response to past abuses.

4. When interpreting a primary source, historians examine the historical context in which the source was written. What events in Rome's history might have influenced Polybius's point of view? Give specific examples.

Alternative Assessment

Building Your Portfolio

Link to TODAY

Government

America's views on the rights and responsibilities of its citizens, including the notion of equality before the law, owe much to ancient Rome and to Jewish and Christian beliefs. Compile a list of the ways in which these legal and moral traditions have influenced American practices. Then use the list to create a chart that summarizes your findings.

internet connect

Internet Activity: go.hrw.com
KEYWORD: SP3 WH7

Choose a topic on the Roman World to:

• analyze the *Aeneid* to learn the connection between ancient Troy and Roman culture.

• create a model or structure that employs Roman architectural, artistic, or decorative styles.

• research the destruction of Pompeii and review the tectonic causes of volcanoes.

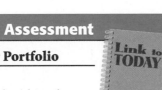

CHAPTER 8

Africa

CHAPTER RESOURCE MANAGER

Objectives	Pacing Guide	Reproducible Resources
SECTION 1 **Africa's Early History** (pp. 182–186) • Identify what geographic features of Africa affected human cultures. • Describe how historians have learned about the migrations of early African peoples. • Explain the predominant patterns of life in early African societies.	**Regular** 1.5 day / **Block Scheduling** 1 day *Block Scheduling Handbook with Team Teaching Strategies, 8.1*	**RS** Guided Reading Strategy 8.1 **E** Hands-on History Activity 8: African Festivals **E** Creative Teaching Strategy 8: Museum of Early African History
SECTION 2 **The Kingdoms of Kush and Aksum** (pp. 187–190) • Explain how Kush developed as an independent kingdom. • Analyze the factors that helped Aksum develop as an independent kingdom.	**Regular** 1.5 day / **Block Scheduling** 1 day *Block Scheduling Handbook with Team Teaching Strategies, 8.2*	**RS** Guided Reading Strategy 8.2 **RS** Graphic Organizer Activity 8: African Kingdoms
SECTION 3 **Trading States of Africa** (pp. 191–195) • Discuss how trade developed along the East African coast. • Explain how the kingdoms of West Africa became rich and powerful.	**Regular** 1.5 day / **Block Scheduling** 1 day *Block Scheduling Handbook with Team Teaching Strategies, 8.3*	**RS** Guided Reading Strategy 8.3 **SM** Geography Activity 8: The Spread of Ironworking **PS** Readings in World History 49: Blind Man and Lame Man **PS** Readings in World History 50: Mansa Musa's Pilgrimage

Chapter Resource Key

PS	Primary Sources	**A**	Assessment	🎵	Music
RS	Reading Support	**REV**	Review	📼	Video
IC	Interdisciplinary Connections	**ELL**	Reinforcement and English Language Learners	🌐	Internet
E	Enrichment	✋	Transparencies	💻	Holt Presentation Maker Using Microsoft® PowerPoint®
SM	Skills Mastery	💿	CD–ROM		

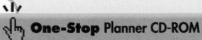

One-Stop Planner CD-ROM

See the **One-Stop Planner** for a complete list of additional resources for students and teachers.

One-Stop Planner CD-ROM

It's easy to plan lessons, select resources, and print out materials for your students when you use the **One-Stop Planner** CD–ROM with **Test Generator**.

Technology Resources

- One-Stop Planner 8.1
- World History and Cultures Video Program 7: Early African Traditions
- Regions of the World Music Audio CD Program 16: Southern Africa: Bantu Choral Folk Songs: Pete Seeger with the Song Swappers
- World History Teaching Transparency: Geography and History 7: North Africa and the Sahara
- World History Teaching Transparency: Regional and World Map 36: Africa
- Homework Practice Online

- One-Stop Planner 8.2
- Regions of the World Music Audio CD Program 13: North Africa: Arabic songs of Lebanon and Egypt
- Homework Practice Online

- One-Stop Planner 8.3
- Holt researcher: World History: Sonni 'Ali, Askia the Great
- CNN. Presents World Cultures: Yesterday and Today Segment 24: The Farms of Zimbabwe
- CNN. Presents World Cultures: Yesterday and Today Segment 32: A Kenyan Reggae Festival
- World History Teaching Transparency: Geography and History 13: African Trading Kingdoms
- World History Teaching Transparency: Everyday Life 13: Great Zimbabwe
- Homework Practice Online
- Online Maps: Cities of Africa, A.D. 1200
- Online Maps, Charts, and Graphs: African Trade, c. 1450–1600
- Online Maps: African Caravan Routes

Reinforcement, Review, and Assessment

Daily Quiz 8.1
Main Idea Activity 2.1
English Audio Summary 8.1
Spanish Audio Summary 8.1
REV Section 1 Review, p. 186

Daily Quiz 8.2
Main Idea Activity 8.2
English Audio Summary 8.2
Spanish Audio Summary 8.2
REV Section 2 Review, p. 190

Daily Quiz 8.3
Main Idea Activity 8.3
English Audio Summary 8.3
Spanish Audio Summary 8.3
REV Section 3 Review, p. 195

internet connect

HRW ONLINE RESOURCES
GO TO: go.hrw.com
Then type in a keyword.

TEACHER HOME PAGE
KEYWORD: SP3 Teacher

CHAPTER INTERNET ACTIVITIES
KEYWORD: SP3 WH8
Choose an activity to:
- research threats to the Congo Basin's ecosystem.
- explore the ancient kingdom of Nubia.
- analyze language development in Africa.

CHAPTER ENRICHMENT LINKS
KEYWORD: SP3 CH8

ONLINE ASSESSMENT
Homework Practice
KEYWORD: SP3 HP8
Standardized Test Prep
KEYWORD: SP3 STP8
Rubrics
KEYWORD: SS Rubrics

ONLINE MAPS, CHARTS, AND GRAPHS
KEYWORD: SP3 MCG

CONTENT UPDATES
KEYWORD: SS Content Updates

HOLT PRESENTATION MAKER
KEYWORD: SP3 PPT8

ONLINE READING SUPPORT
KEYWORD: SS Strategies

CURRENT EVENTS
KEYWORD: S3 Current Events

Meeting Individual Needs

Ability Levels

Level 1 Basic level activities designed for all students encountering new material

Level 2 Intermediate level activities designed for average students

Level 3 Challenging activities designed for honors and gifted and talented students

English Language Learners These activities address the needs of students with l imited English Proficiency.

Chapter Review and Assessment

IC Vocabulary Activity 8
Global Skill Builder CD–ROM
HRW Web Site
REV Chapter 8 Tutorial for Students, Parents, Mentors, and Peers
REV Chapter 8 Review, pp. 196–197
A Chapter 8 Test Generator (on the One-Stop Planner)
A Chapter 8 Test (Form A or B)
A Alternative Assessment Handbook
A Chapter 8 Test for English Language Learners and Special-Needs Students

Build on What You Know

Ask students to answer the following questions:

How might scientists have learned about early human life in Africa?

Consider:

- the work of archaeologists
- the kinds of artifacts found at archaeological digs
- the study of languages and of stories passed on through storytellers

Based on your knowledge of early civilizations, how might early African civilizations have passed cultural elements on to succeeding cultures?

Consider:

- the migration of early peoples and the spread of language
- the impact of trade, travel, and conquests
- the spread of religion

EXPLORING THE TIME LINE

GL🌐BAL EVENTS

▣ **internet** connect

go hrw .com

TOPIC: Conquest and Diffusion

GO TO: go.hrw.com

KEYWORD: SP3 WH8

Have students access the Internet through the HRW Go site to conduct research on the conquest and cultural diffusion among the early African civilizations of Egypt, Kush, and Aksum. Then ask students to create a chart that shows the cultural effects of conquest on each of these groups of peoples. Students' charts should include appropriate examples and evidence drawn from their research.

◆ **CHAPTER** ◆
8

1800 B.C.–A.D. 1500

Africa

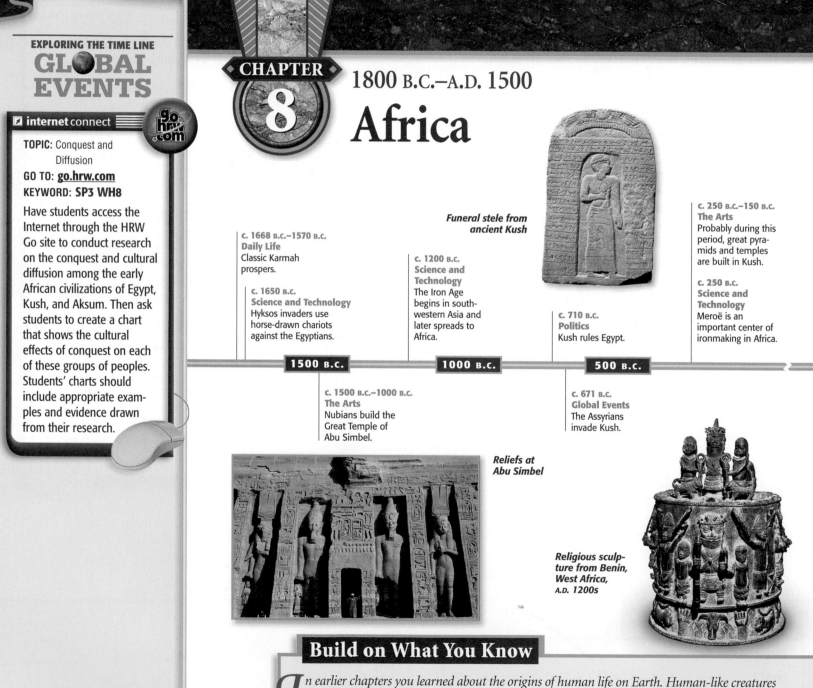

Funeral stele from ancient Kush

c. 1668 B.C.–1570 B.C.
Daily Life
Classic Karmah prospers.

c. 1650 B.C.
Science and Technology
Hyksos invaders use horse-drawn chariots against the Egyptians.

c. 1200 B.C.
Science and Technology
The Iron Age begins in southwestern Asia and later spreads to Africa.

c. 710 B.C.
Politics
Kush rules Egypt.

c. 250 B.C.–150 B.C.
The Arts
Probably during this period, great pyramids and temples are built in Kush.

c. 250 B.C.
Science and Technology
Meroë is an important center of ironmaking in Africa.

1500 B.C.   **1000 B.C.**   **500 B.C.**

c. 1500 B.C.–1000 B.C.
The Arts
Nubians build the Great Temple of Abu Simbel.

c. 671 B.C.
Global Events
The Assyrians invade Kush.

Reliefs at Abu Simbel

Religious sculpture from Benin, West Africa, A.D. 1200s

Build on What You Know

*I*n earlier chapters you learned about the origins of human life on Earth. Human-like creatures lived and developed in the rugged highlands of East Africa almost 4 million years ago. In fact, many scientists are convinced that the continent of Africa may very well have been where our species began. You also learned that the continent gave birth to one of the world's earliest civilizations, the remarkable culture of Egypt, in North Africa. In this chapter, you will learn about early civilizations that emerged, flourished, and then gave way to succeeding cultures in other parts of the African continent.

What's Your Opinion?

Economics

Agree People always trade for goods that they cannot grow or produce themselves but that are needed as basic necessities of life.

Disagree Important trade goods are often luxuries that only the rich can afford.

Geography

Agree A region's physical environment influences the kinds of economic activities that people can successfully undertake in that region.

Disagree A region's physical environment has little effect on the development of trade and commerce.

Global Relations

Agree People who lack natural resources to meet their needs often conquer others to gain those resources.

Disagree People can get what they need through trade and hard work.

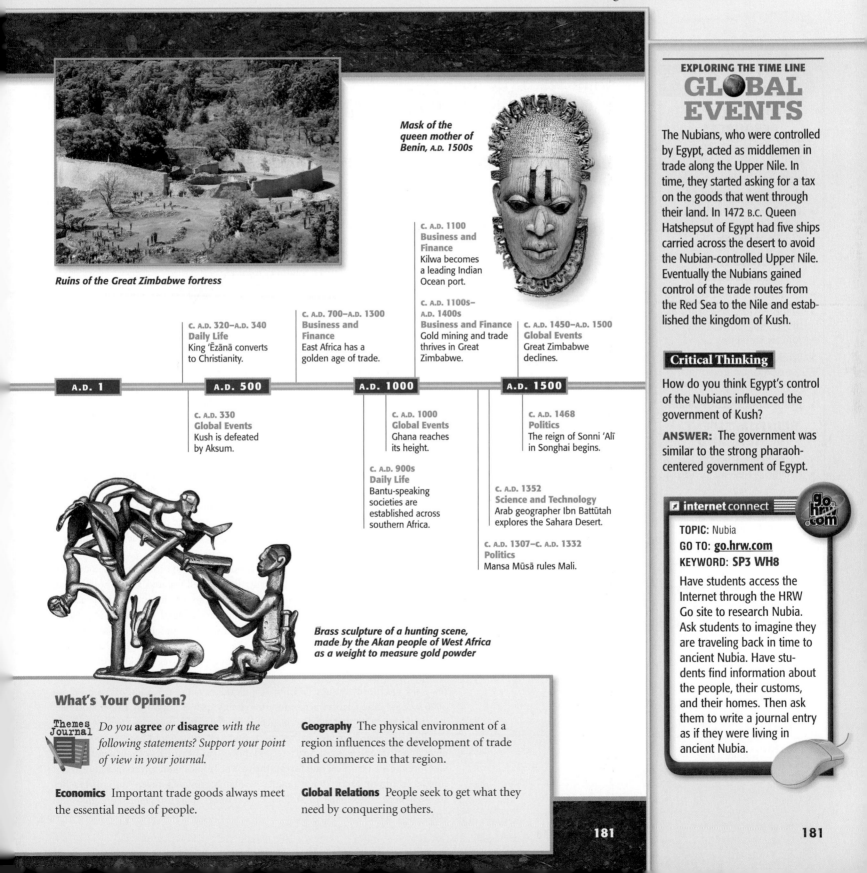

Ruins of the Great Zimbabwe fortress

Mask of the queen mother of Benin, A.D. 1500s

c. A.D. 1100 Business and Finance Kilwa becomes a leading Indian Ocean port.

c. A.D. 320–A.D. 340 Daily Life King 'Ēzānā converts to Christianity.

c. A.D. 700–A.D. 1300 Business and Finance East Africa has a golden age of trade.

c. A.D. 1100s– A.D. 1400s Business and Finance Gold mining and trade thrives in Great Zimbabwe.

c. A.D. 1450–A.D. 1500 Global Events Great Zimbabwe declines.

A.D. 1 **A.D. 500** **A.D. 1000** **A.D. 1500**

c. A.D. 330 Global Events Kush is defeated by Aksum.

c. A.D. 1000 Global Events Ghana reaches its height.

c. A.D. 1468 Politics The reign of Sonni 'Alī in Songhai begins.

c. A.D. 900s Daily Life Bantu-speaking societies are established across southern Africa.

c. A.D. 1352 Science and Technology Arab geographer Ibn Battūtah explores the Sahara Desert.

c. A.D. 1307–c. A.D. 1332 Politics Mansa Mūsā rules Mali.

Brass sculpture of a hunting scene, made by the Akan people of West Africa as a weight to measure gold powder

What's Your Opinion?

 Themes Journal *Do you* **agree** *or* **disagree** *with the following statements? Support your point of view in your journal.*

Economics Important trade goods always meet the essential needs of people.

Geography The physical environment of a region influences the development of trade and commerce in that region.

Global Relations People seek to get what they need by conquering others.

EXPLORING THE TIME LINE
GLOBAL EVENTS

The Nubians, who were controlled by Egypt, acted as middlemen in trade along the Upper Nile. In time, they started asking for a tax on the goods that went through their land. In 1472 B.C. Queen Hatshepsut of Egypt had five ships carried across the desert to avoid the Nubian-controlled Upper Nile. Eventually the Nubians gained control of the trade routes from the Red Sea to the Nile and established the kingdom of Kush.

Critical Thinking

How do you think Egypt's control of the Nubians influenced the government of Kush?

ANSWER: The government was similar to the strong pharaoh-centered government of Egypt.

internet connect

TOPIC: Nubia
GO TO: go.hrw.com
KEYWORD: SP3 WH8

Have students access the Internet through the HRW Go site to research Nubia. Ask students to imagine they are traveling back in time to ancient Nubia. Have students find information about the people, their customs, and their homes. Then ask them to write a journal entry as if they were living in ancient Nubia.

OBJECTIVES

1 Identify what geographic features of Africa affected human cultures.

2 Describe how historians have learned about the migrations of early African peoples.

3 Explain the predominant patterns of life in early African societies.

SECTION 1

READ TO DISCOVER

❶ What geographic features of Africa affected human cultures?

❷ How did historians learn about the migrations of early peoples?

❸ What were the predominant patterns of life in many early African societies?

DEFINE

savannas
tropical rain forests
jungle
linguists
oral traditions
matrilineal

IDENTIFY

Bantu

WHY IT MATTERS TODAY

Many African Americans look to Sub-Saharan Africa as the homeland of their ancestors. Use **CNNfyi.com** or other **current event** sources to find out how African Americans view and celebrate their ancestry. Record your findings in your journal.

CNNfyi.com

Africa's Early History

The Main Idea
Although the geography of Africa varies, many early societies there shared common cultural traits.

The Story Continues *The African American poet Countee Cullen once asked, "What is Africa to me?" He was writing about his lost African heritage, but the question could be asked by anyone practically anywhere in the world today. Most scientists believe that human life began in Africa. Yet much about the early civilizations of Africa remains a mystery to most modern people. Within its history is the story of a great continent that housed a wealth of cultures.*

The Physical Setting

In the northeast corner of Africa, the Neolithic people of ancient Egypt had begun to move toward civilization by about 3800 B.C. Other great civilizations also thrived on the African continent. Written records, still-standing monuments, and ruins are evidence of early North African civilizations. They arose on the narrow slice of land between the Mediterranean Sea and the great Sahara. Equally important cultures developed south of the desert. This vast portion of the continent is called Sub-Saharan Africa. The physical geography of Sub-Saharan Africa strongly influenced the growth of human societies there.

The plateau. Much of Sub-Saharan Africa is a plateau. This highland is dimpled by river basins and valleys. Like a great upside-down bowl, it drops sharply to a coastal plain. The steep shoreline has few natural harbors. Most rivers—like the Congo, Niger, and Zambezi—are blocked by rapids. Therefore boats could not go far upstream from the ocean. This protected the interior from invasion, but it also made trade and communication among Africans harder.

The enormous Sahara Desert covers about one-fourth of the African continent. Thousands of years ago, the Sahara was fertile and well watered. Over the course of centuries, however, changing wind and weather patterns have caused the area to become increasingly dry and barren. The southern edge of the desert is a region known as the Sahel, from the Arabic word for "shore." Rainfall in the Sahel is both sparse and uncertain, and the area is often the scene of harsh droughts that may last for years. For this reason farming is difficult throughout the region. South of the Sahel are vast stretches of dry grasslands called **savannas.** The savannas are dotted with a few trees and thorny bushes. Farming techniques began to spread in Africa by about 3000 B.C. Savanna farmers began to grow grains such as sorghum, millet, and rice. Where the savannas met the deserts, people herded cattle.

Rainfall is much greater farther south. So too is the amount of vegetation. Some areas in central and western Africa receive more than 100 inches of rain a year. There, vast forests called **tropical rain forests** thrive. The tropical rain forests include areas of jungle. In **jungle** areas, dense tangles of plants grow wherever sunlight reaches through the tall trees to the forest floor. Early farmers in the forested regions grew root crops such as yams.

TEACH OBJECTIVE 1

ALL LEVELS: Draw a large outline map of Africa. Divide the class into three groups and assign one of the following regions to each: desert, savanna, and tropical rain forest. Have each group choose a color to code its region on the map and design symbols to represent the natural vegetation, crops, and livestock suited to the region *(Rain forest—green/ trees and yams; savanna—brown/ grasses, sorghum, millet, rice; desert—yellow/ cattle.)* Have each group complete its part of the map.

ENGLISH LANGUAGE LEARNERS, COOPERATIVE LEARNING

LEVEL 3: Have students read pages 182–183 and locate the Congo Basin on the map on page 183. Prompt them to discuss how natural barriers such as a river that is hard to navigate, a rain forest, mountains, and deadly insects might affect the culture of a region. *(Rain forests, insects, mountains, and rapids-filled rivers can hinder trade, travel, and invasions; a farming culture could develop in the river valley.)*

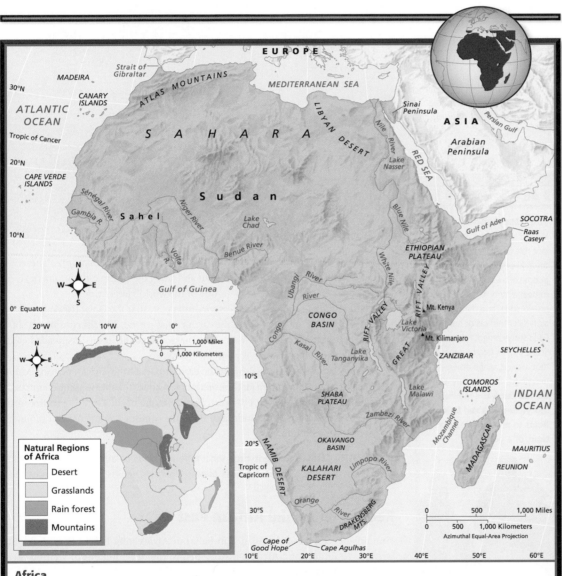

Africa

Interpreting Maps The major natural regions of Africa have climates that affect how people can live and what they can grow.

■ **Skills Assessment: 1. The World in Spatial Terms** Where does Africa lie in relation to the equator? **2. Drawing Conclusions** How might its position relative to the equator affect Africa's climate?

Geography

Sub-Saharan Africa's main rivers are long but are blocked by rapids. This protected African peoples from invaders but also made it hard for Africans to carry on trade among themselves.

Critical Thinking

Look at the map on page 183. What other geographic factors kept early African peoples apart?

ANSWER: Students might suggest that mountains and rain forests acted as natural barriers between groups of African peoples.

That's Interesting!

The tsetse fly infects cattle and horses, as well as people, with sleeping sickness. In animals, sleeping sickness is called *nagana*. Because of *nagana*, African farmers have not been able to depend on livestock for plowing fields or providing fertilizer.

The hot, wet climate of the rain forests provides breeding grounds for insects. Some of them carry deadly diseases. Among the diseases are malaria and yellow fever, carried by mosquitoes, and sleeping sickness, carried by tsetse flies. Although modern medicine can treat these diseases, many Africans perished from them in earlier centuries.

Farther south of the rain forests are more dry grasslands. These are broken in the south by yet more stretches of harsh desert. The Kalahari Desert and the Namib Desert range from the center of southern Africa westward to the Atlantic coast and, like the Sahara to the north, are largely barren and desolate.

Technology Resources

World History Teaching Transparency: Geography and History 7: North Africa and the Sahara

Methods to Discover the Past

Language — spread of languages, oral tradition (stories, songs, poems), new words

Cultural Exchange — music, styles of art

Other — spread in cultivated plants, changes in climate, excavation of artifacts

ENGLISH LANGUAGE LEARNERS, COOPERATIVE LEARNING

VISUAL RECORD ANSWER

shows mountains, plateau, and savanna

Interdisciplinary Connection

LANGUAGE. Some Bantu languages spoken today are Zulu in South Africa, Makua in Mozambique, Shona in Zimbabwe, Bemba in Zambia, Swahili in Tanzania, Ganda in Uganda, Kongo in Congo, and Fang in Cameroon.

Critical Thinking

Have students turn to the political map of Africa in the Atlas. Ask how they can determine in which directions early Bantu speakers migrated if they started in West Africa.

ANSWER: Bantu speakers migrated east and south.

DAILY LIFE ANSWER
The storyteller preserves traditions by telling stories of important events and people in a village's history.

LINK TO TODAY ANSWER
By studying modern African languages, people can learn about the migration of early groups of people who lived in Africa.

Technology Resources
Regions of the World
Music Audio CD Program
16

INTERPRETING THE VISUAL RECORD

Mount Kilimanjaro Mount Kilimanjaro, in Tanzania, is a dormant volcano and the tallest mountain in Africa. *How does this image reflect Africa's great geographic variety?*

DAILY LIFE

The Storytellers
Storytellers played an important role in African society. At the end of the workday, the people of a village gathered to hear a story. Using words, music, song, and dance, the storyteller told his or her tale. Each story carried a message. Some stories taught important lessons, while others described village history. **How do you think the modern storyteller pictured below helps to preserve the traditions of a people?**

Link to Today How does the study of modern languages help us understand African history?

Other natural features. The African plateau has six large depressions. These vast drainage basins formed around Lake Chad and along the continent's five major rivers. Lake Victoria, in east central Africa, is one of the world's largest lakes.

Perhaps the most remarkable feature of the plateau is the Great Rift Valley. It was formed millions of years ago when the earth's crust parted. The rift runs north-south near the plateau's eastern edge. Many long, narrow lakes lie in this steep-sided crack. Among them are Lake Tanganyika and Lake Malawi.

Isolated mountain peaks also dot the eastern part of the African plateau. Mount Kenya and Mount Kilimanjaro jut thousands of feet above the surrounding countryside. A main highland region is the Ethiopian Plateau in the northeast. It is a source of the Nile River. The Drakensberg Mountains lie in the southeast. Some African mountain ranges have active volcanoes.

✔ **READING CHECK: Categorizing** What different kinds of landforms, climates, and features are in Sub-Saharan Africa? plateau highlands, deserts, dry savanna grasslands, tropical rain forests, and jungles

Rediscovering the African Past

Humans developed societies in Sub-Saharan Africa long before they developed writing. To understand African history before the development of writing there, scholars use many methods to analyze limited evidence.

Language. For example, **linguists**—scientists who study languages—have used computers to compare modern African words. Linguists have shown how **Bantu,** a family of closely related African languages, spread. Their study suggests to anthropologists and historians that for centuries people have migrated throughout Sub-Saharan Africa.

The "cradle land" of Bantu lies in west central Africa. This area is along the present border of Nigeria and Cameroon. From there, perhaps 2,000 years ago or earlier, Bantu-speaking people began migrating east and south into what is now Gabon. These migrations continued for about 1,000 years, possibly longer. Over time the Bantu language group became one of Africa's largest.

Information about the history and the cultural development of Africa also comes from the study of **oral traditions.** These are poems, songs, and stories passed by word of mouth from one generation to another. Often these tales hold some moral lesson or tell of the deeds of past kings and heroes. Africans have always had a strong sense

TEACH OBJECTIVE 3

LEVEL 2: Have students discuss the patterns of life in early Africa. Discussions should include the village as the basic unit of society, the role of women as farmers, matrilineal inheritance of property, religions with gods linked to nature and human activities, and the role of the village elders. **COOPERATIVE LEARNING**

HOMEWORK Have students find examples of women's roles in present-day African societies. Ask them to identify those societies in which matrilineal inheritance is still practiced.

CLOSE

Have students summarize how geography influenced ways of life in early African societies.

REVIEW

Have students complete the Section 1 Review on p. 186.

---

of their own history. Some societies had oral historians, like the griots (GREE·ohz) of West Africa. Griots were highly trained speakers and entertainers who memorized the oral tradition of their village. Through their performances they amused and also taught their audiences. Kings and noble families often hired griots to keep a record of their achievements. Today individual families and villages in Africa still remember important events by telling about them in poetry and song. As stories are passed along, each generation adds events from its own time. Historians and anthropologists have now written down much of this oral African tradition.

Cultural exchange. Other scholars have also helped discover Africa's past. Among them are those who study music. They have found, for example, that the design and tuning of xylophones in East Africa are like those in Indonesia, in Southeast Asia. This similarity suggests that at an early date there was cultural exchange between Africa and Asia.

Certain languages also show that there was early contact between Africa and Asia. Malagasy is an example. This language is spoken on the Indian Ocean island of Madagascar, off eastern Africa. It has many words spoken by people in Indonesia. In addition, scholars have noted the prevalence of the banana in Africa. This crop is native to Asia.

Through such study of musical instruments, language, and plants, scholars have determined that cultural exchange between parts of Africa and Asia probably took place over thousands of years.

Other evidence. Scholars have discovered that the people of Sub-Saharan Africa were able to deal with their often harsh environment. For example, wheat and barley did not grow well south of the Sahara near sea level. Crops such as millet and sorghum did, however. The early people of the Sahel domesticated these grains. In later centuries, they became staple crops throughout Sub-Saharan Africa. Over the years, the climate in the Sahel became increasingly drier. People either migrated south or shifted more to herding.

Archaeologists have carefully excavated sites throughout Africa. Their work has added much to our understanding of African history and our knowledge of early lifestyles and social patterns. Archaeologists working today in Africa use scientific methods and tools, up-to-date technology, and detailed analysis to study the evidence they unearth. They also use knowledge drawn from many different fields of learning, such as history and other social sciences, earth sciences, and mathematics. Archaeological evidence shows that many early Sub-Saharan cultures were complex, well organized, and wealthy. We know, too, that many had contact with early cultures from other parts of the ancient world.

✔ **READING CHECK: Summarizing** What methods have been used by scholars to learn about the history of Sub-Saharan Africa? linguistic study, oral traditions, musical studies, and archaeological methods

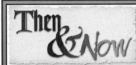

Trumpets
Trumpet music conveys universal themes that have been sounded around the world for centuries. People used trumpets to mourn at funerals. Early Africans also used horns to send messages over long distances. Today, in Nigeria, horns are still sounded at celebrations.

How did early Africans use trumpet music?

Bronze horn player from Benin

Link to Today

What does the use of trumpets in ancient Africa and modern America reflect about the universality of such music?

The great American trumpeter, Wynton Marsalis, is famed for his powerful music.

AFRICA **185**

THEN AND NOW ANSWER
Students should list the following uses of early trumpets: to mourn at funerals; to send messages long distances.

LINK TO TODAY ANSWER
Students might suggest that musical instruments such as trumpets have been used for centuries and throughout all parts of the world.

Linking Past to Present

Today in many parts of Africa, women still do most of the work raising crops. They farm mainly by hand, bending over the fields all day with their babies on heir backs. Men usually look after the livestock, though in some communities they farm for prospective in-laws as part of a marriage agreement.

Critical Thinking

Why do you think African men sometimes farm for their prospective bride's family?

ANSWER: Students might note that families in Africa still pass property through the female line of the family.

ASSESS

Have students complete Daily Quiz 8.1. As Alternative Assessment, you many want to use the hand-drawn maps or the graphic organizer.

RETEACH

Have students complete Main Idea Activity for English Language Learners and Special-Needs Students 8.1. Then have them write a diary entry describing a day in the life of an early African teenager. **ENGLISH LANGUAGE LEARNERS**

EXTEND

internet connect

Internet Activity: go.hrw.com
TOPIC: African Languages **KEYWORD: SP3 WH8**

Have students access the Internet through the HRW Go site to conduct research on African languages. Ask students to summarize one language or language group. They should include information about where the language is spoken, the current number of speakers, and information about the roots of the language.

VISUAL RECORD ANSWER

Students should note that Africans traditionally build their homes using materials that are easily available.

SECTION 1 REVIEW ANSWERS

❶ **Define**
- savannas, p. 182
- tropical rain forests, p. 182
- jungle, p. 182
- linguists, p. 184
- oral traditions, p. 184
- matrilineal, p. 186

❷ **Identify**
- Bantu, p. 184

❸ Mountains—north, south, east; Desert—north, south; Grasslands—west, east, central; Tropical Rain Forest—west, central

❹ **a.** The natural environment determined what crops people in early African cultures grew. Grains grew best on the savannas; yams in tropical rain forests; cattle herding took place in areas between deserts and savannas.

b. Xylophones used in traditional music of East Africa are similar to such instruments in Indonesia; the Malagasy language spoken in Madagascar contains words spoken in Indonesia; and the banana plant grown in Africa is native to Asia.

c. very important because it survived even when kingdoms rose and fell

❺ Students' poems will vary.

INTERPRETING THE VISUAL RECORD

African houses This Bantu house illustrates a traditional style of building. Houses are constructed of thatch and dried mud, sometimes reinforced with woven strips of wood. *Based on this picture, what can you infer about traditional Africans' relationship with their natural environment?*

Patterns of Life

Based on their studies of limited evidence, experts have drawn conclusions about patterns of life in early Africa. Many believe that most early Africans lived in small, independent farming, herding, or fishing villages. Ties of kinship and age bound each society together.

Women in particular played a crucial role in both the African family and economy. Unlike Europe and Asia, in Africa women were the primary farmers. Historians believe that societies in many parts of Sub-Saharan Africa were **matrilineal.** In other words, people traced their ancestors and inherited property through their mothers rather than fathers.

Religion was important in many African cultures, and many shared similar religious ideas. In most African societies, people believed that spirits populated the world. These included the spirits of ancestors, who remained an important part of the ongoing life of the clan. Most religions included a supreme creator god. They linked other gods to certain aspects of nature or to human activities, such as farming.

The pace of life and the calendar of daily activity in most early African villages were set by the seasonal cycles of planting and harvesting crops. Village elders, the traditional leaders of community life in many parts of Africa, usually had authority over daily life and work. Their position in village society was respected and unquestioned. The village-centered society of traditional Africa flourished through the rise and fall of kingdoms. Over centuries, this timeless lifestyle survived as the basic unit of African social, political, and economic development. Today it remains a vital part of the African heritage.

✔ **READING CHECK: Making Generalizations** What do scholars believe about the role of women in many early African societies? *played crucial roles in social and economic life as primary farmers*

SECTION 1 REVIEW

1. **Define** and explain the significance:
   savannas
   tropical rain forests
   jungle
   linguists
   oral traditions
   matrilineal

2. **Identify** and explain the significance:
   Bantu

3. **Analyzing Information** Copy the chart below. Use it to place check marks to show the main natural regions in various parts of Africa.

Main Natural Region	Part of Africa				
	North	West	South	East	Central
Mountains					
Desert					
Grasslands					
Tropical Rain Forest					

4. **Finding the Main Idea**
   a. How did people decide what crops to grow in early African cultures?
   b. What evidence is there of cultural exchange between early Africa and Asia?
   c. How important was the village in early African societies?

5. **Writing and Critical Thinking**
   Making Generalizations Write a short poem about a day in an early African village.
   Consider:
   - the importance of family relationships and events, such as marriage or birth
   - the importance of planting and harvesting crops
   - the role of religion in early African cultures

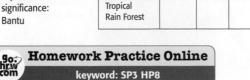
Homework Practice Online
keyword: SP3 HP8

SECTION 2

OBJECTIVES

1 Explain how Kush developed as an independent kingdom.
2 Analyze the factors that helped Aksum develop as an independent kingdom.

📻 *LET'S GET STARTED!*

As students enter the classroom, ask them to think about political units other than villages that might have developed in Sub-Saharan Africa. Have them write down some ideas and give a brief description of each political unit. *(Answers might include city-states, kingdoms, and empires.)* Tell students that in Section 2 they will learn how the independent kingdoms of Kush and Aksum developed.

SECTION 2

READ TO DISCOVER

❶ How did Kush develop as an independent kingdom?

❷ How did Aksum develop as an independent kingdom?

IDENTIFY

King 'Ēzānā

▶ WHY IT MATTERS TODAY

Trade is an important economic activity, in early Africa and in today's world. Use **CNNfyi.com** or other **current event** sources to find out about goods traded to and from Africa today. Record your findings in your journal.

CNNfyi.com

The Kingdoms of Kush and Aksum

The Main Idea
The kingdoms of Kush and Aksum dominated much of Sub-Saharan Africa.

The Story Continues *Some Sub-Saharan African peoples continued to live in small, independent villages. Others, however, established small city-states, kingdoms, and even empires. One of these was the kingdom of Kush. Kush arose along the upper Nile River in an Egyptian area known as Nubia. Because of its close connection with Egypt, Kush's culture resembled that of the Egyptians in many ways.*

Kush Arises

Kush thrived as an important corridor of trade. Gold, ivory, ebony, and ostrich feathers were transported through Nubia. Here caravans hauled goods from the Red Sea to barges on the Nile. In about 1600 B.C. a Nubian trading center on the Nile called Karmah emerged. Recent archaeological discoveries reveal a rich cultural exchange between Karmah and Egypt. Kush may have traced its roots to the city of Karmah.

Over the next few centuries, Kush became a distinct kingdom. The capital of its ruling dynasty was located at Napata, a city that lay upstream along the Nile from Karmah. At first Kush maintained close economic and cultural ties with Egypt. In about 1520 B.C., however, the rulers of Egypt's New Kingdom brought Nubia and Kush under their control. For the next 500 years, Kush was governed by the pharaohs. During this time, however, the Nubian kingdom appears to have grown increasingly isolated from Egyptian rule. Many historians believe that in the years between about 1100 B.C. and about 1000 B.C., communication and cultural exchange between Kush and Egypt diminished. Some 300 years later, in about 710 B.C., Kush conquered Upper Egypt, and a Kush dynasty ruled a unified Egypt for about 50 years.

The Lion Temple of ancient Kush reflects the kingdom's power and glory.

SECTION 2 RESOURCES

REPRODUCIBLE RESOURCES

▶ Guided Reading Strategy 8.2

▶ Graphic Organizer Activity 8: African Kingdoms

TECHNOLOGY RESOURCES

▶ One-Stop Planner 8.2

▶ Regions of the World Music Audio CD Program 13: North Africa: Arabic songs of Lebanon and Egypt

▶ Homework Practice Online

REINFORCEMENT, REVIEW, AND ASSESSMENT

▶ Section 2 Review, p. 190

▶ Daily Quiz 8.2

▶ Main Idea Activity 8.2

▶ English Audio Summary 8.2

▶ Spanish Audio Summary 8.2

ALL LEVELS: Have students read the material titled "Kush Arises" on pages 187–188 of the text. Then have them construct a chart that lists the geographic, economic, political, and cultural factors that led to Kush's development and fall.

KUSH		
Factors	Development of	Fall of
Geographic	*Nile River, Red Sea; fertile soil near Meroë*	*Infertile soil*
Economic	*Control of trade routes to Egypt between Nile River and Red Sea*	*Lost control of trade routes*
Political	*Controlled Egypt; survived Assyrians*	*Taken over by Aksum*
Cultural	*Use of iron, pottery; built pyramids and temples; written language*	

ENGLISH LANGUAGE LEARNERS, COOPERATIVE LEARNING

Geography

Today the temple and pyramid ruins of Kush stand in desert lands. Long ago, however, huge herds of cattle grazed in the area.

Critical Thinking

Ask students what cattle grazing near Kush 2,500 years ago tells about the climate at that time.

ANSWER: A much wetter climate existed for grass to grow and to provide drinking water for cattle.

Interdisciplinary Connection

ART. The artisans of Aksum were known for their work with stone. They are perhaps best known for making massive stone obelisks called stelae. Some of these monumental pillars nearly reached 100 feet or more in height and were carved from single blocks of stone.

Critical Thinking

Ask students to speculate about the purposes Aksumite stelae might have served.

ANSWER: Stelae might have commemorated events in the lives of rulers or the community.

MAP ANSWER

cities in Kush: Karmah, Napata, Meroë; seaport in Aksum: Adulis

In 671 B.C. the Assyrians, armed with iron weapons, invaded Kush, greatly weakening the kingdom. Evidence suggests that about 80 years later, Napata was captured by an Egyptian force. The kingdom of Kush reorganized, however, and a new period of growth and cultural achievement began. The new capital city of Meroë may have been an early center of ironworking in Africa. The region's fertile soil made Meroë an ideal location for agriculture.

Kush was located across trade routes between the Red Sea and the Nile. Caravans brought cultural influences as well as goods from other peoples. The people of Meroë adapted these to their own culture. The Greek historian Herodotus wrote this description of Meroë, based on travelers' accounts:

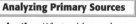
Analyzing Primary Sources

Evaluating What evidence does Herodotus provide to suggest that the people of Meroë had contact with other peoples and cultures? mention of Greek gods and practices

Primary Source

"In twelve days [one] reaches a big city named Meroë, said to be the capital city of the Ethiopians [the inhabitants of the kingdom of Kush]. The inhabitants worship Zeus and Dionysus alone of the gods, holding them in great honor. There is an oracle of Zeus there, and they make war according to its pronouncements [declarations]."

Herodotus, quoted in *African Civilization Revisited,* by Basil Davidson

Some historians believe that Kush's civilization reached its height between about 250 B.C. and about A.D. 150. The people of Meroë built impressive pyramids and temples and crafted beautiful pottery and metal ornaments. They developed a written form of their language. A period of decline set in, however. Some historians believe the decline occurred because the land lost its fertility. Kush may also have lost control of trade routes as they were taken over by a rival state, Aksum.

✔ **READING CHECK: Drawing Inferences** What led to the growth of the kingdom of Kush? its location as a corridor of trade

Aksum

Aksum lay in the rugged Ethiopian Highlands south of Kush. The kingdom straddled the important trade routes that stretched from the Red Sea into Egypt and the interior of Africa. By about the A.D. 100s, the people of Aksum had developed an independent kingdom that boasted a thriving ivory trade. As Kush declined, Aksum increasingly competed with it for control of trade in eastern Africa. Aksum sent gold, rhinoceros horns, ivory, incense, and decorative obsidian stone to Mediterranean countries by way of Egypt. The Aksumites imported glass, metal ornaments, and pottery, as well as wine and olive oil. Aksum also minted its own coins.

By about A.D. 300 Aksum was a military power. In about A.D. 350 **King 'Ēzānā** of Aksum conquered Kush. He set up a thriving kingdom. Like other kings of Aksum, 'Ēzānā held power over surrounding chiefdoms.

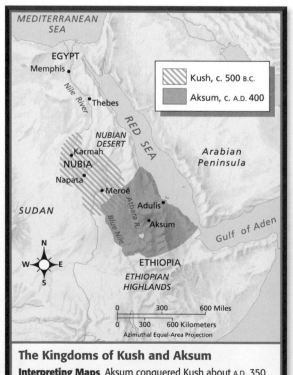

The Kingdoms of Kush and Aksum

Interpreting Maps Aksum conquered Kush about A.D. 350.

■ **Skills Assessment: Human Systems** Through what river cities in Kush would goods be transported? Through what seaport in Aksum would goods be transported?

LEVEL 1: Make a chart titled *Aksum*, similar to the one for Kush, on the chalkboard. Have students read "Aksum" on pages 188 and 190 and study the map on page 188. Then ask students to complete the chart by working alone or in pairs to identify geographic, economic, political, and cultural factors in the development of the independent kingdom of Aksum.
ENGLISH LANGUAGE LEARNERS, COOPERATIVE LEARNING

LEVEL 3: Ask students what geographic factors are important for the growth of trade. *(location on a river, seaports, clear routes for trade)* Have students look at the map on page 188 and make a list of ways Aksum's location helped it become a trading kingdom. Have students discuss how Aksum's power increased by conquering Kush.

HOMEWORK Have students write a brief summary of the importance of King 'Ēzānā's conversion to Christianity.

SKILL-BUILDING STRATEGIES — Using Artifacts as Historical Evidence

The Kingdom of Kush

Scientists have learned much about Kush by studying artifacts that they have found. Artifacts include everything from pottery and tools to coins and buildings. Artifacts are an important part of historical research because they allow historians to gain a more complete understanding of the past. Much like photographs, artifacts offer valuable clues about customs, beliefs, and details of daily life. In order to gain the historical insight that artifacts offer, however, historians must know how to examine them properly.

Shown here are a relief plaque of a winged, lion-headed goddess found at Meroë (left); a decorated gold cylinder, possibly used for holding papyrus, from the tomb of a Kushite king near Napata (center); and a gold plaque depicting a king of Meroë honoring the Egyptian god Horus (right).

Skills Reminder

To evaluate an artifact as historical evidence, determine what the artifact is and what purpose it might have served. If possible, find out who created it and when. Examine the artifact carefully. Study the artifact's construction and design. Note such things as what material the artifact is made from as well as what tools might have been used to create it. Consider also how the artifact might have been used. Use what you have learned from written sources about the particular people and time period surrounding the artifact to gain a better understanding of the object. Based on your examination of the artifact, as well as other information you have gathered, draw conclusions about the people who created the object or the time period in which it existed.

Skills Practice

❶ What do the artifacts show?
❷ Based on these artifacts, do you think that religion was important in Kush? Why or why not?
❸ What other conclusions might you draw about the people of Kush from these artifacts?
❹ Based on your analysis of the artifacts, their materials, and their construction, what conclusions can you draw concerning the level of Kushite technology and craftsmanship?
❺ Choose a group from this chapter and find an artifact from its culture in a book or on the Internet. Write a paragraph describing the artifact and explaining what you think that artifact says about the group.

SKILLS PRACTICE ANSWERS

1. human figures, animals, symbols

2. Answers will vary. Students might say yes because gods and goddesses appear on many artifacts.

3. People used symbols in their writing; animals were important.

4. The Kushites had a high level of craftsmanship and technology.

5. Answers should include what the construction, design, and materials tell about the level of craftsmanship and technology.

Science, Technology & Society

The Great Enclosure of Musawwarat is a Kush ruin in modern Sudan. It consists of sandstone structures surrounding a temple. The temple is on a raised platform and can be entered only by climbing a ramp. Recent work by archaeologists shows that underground pipes for irrigation supplied water to gardens within the enclosure.

Critical Thinking

Ask students what the Great Enclosure shows about the level of Kush technology.

ANSWER: suggests a high level of technology

CLOSE

Have students create a Venn diagram to compare Kush and Aksum.

ASSESS

Have students complete Daily Quiz 8.2. As Alternative Assessment, you may want to use the graphic organizers and lists of factors that led to the development of Kush and Aksum.

RETEACH

Have students complete Main Idea Activity for English Language Learners and Special-Needs Students 8.2. Then ask them to apply absolute chronology by making a time line of major events in the development of Kush and Aksum.
ENGLISH LANGUAGE LEARNERS

EXTEND

Have students work in small groups to use the process of historical inquiry to conduct research on the ivory trade in Africa in about A.D. 100. **COOPERATIVE LEARNING, BLOCK SCHEDULING**

HISTORY MAKER ANSWER
Aksum became a Christian kingdom in Africa.

SECTION 2 REVIEW ANSWERS

❶ **Identify**
• King 'Ēzānā, p. 188

❷ Kush: Nile River, Nubia, iron-working, pyramids, cities of Karmah, Napata, and Meroë, conquest of Egypt; Aksum: Ethiopian Highlands, city of Adulis, Christianity; Overlapping characteristics: kingdoms, trade routes between Red Sea and Nile River, ties with Egypt, written languages, lost control of trade routes, land less productive

❸ **a.** Both arose as trading kingdoms and retained their power as long as they controlled important trade routes.

b. Kush conquered Egypt and later was attacked by the Assyrians. This event forced the Kushites to set up a new capital in Meroë. Aksum conquered Kush and later lost control of political and economic power to Arab forces.

❹ Descriptions of Meroë will vary but should include its location on the Nile River on fertile land; its pyramids and temples; and farming, ironworking, and trade as ways of making a living.

190

He collected tribute from neighboring rulers. At the port city of Adulis his officials collected taxes on trade goods. During his reign 'Ēzānā converted to Christianity. He made it the official religion of Aksum. 'Ēzānā's religious beliefs were reflected in his rule. He declared:

> **History Makers Speak**
>
> **❝I will rule the people with righteousness and justice, and will not oppress them, and may they preserve this Throne which I have set up for the Lord of Heaven.❞**
>
> King 'Ēzānā, quoted in *African Civilizations* by Graham Connah

King 'Ēzānā's conversion to Christianity was a key event in the history of eastern Africa. The form of Christianity that grew throughout the region incorporated many of the people's traditional beliefs and customs. Thus its appeal was strong and widespread. 'Ēzānā's conversion, moreover, had an impact on Christianity in eastern Africa that was similar to the effect that Constantine's conversion had on Christianity in the Roman Empire. Christianity became a powerful influence throughout the region. This development laid the foundations of the Ethiopian Church that continues to thrive today and that forms an important element of the area's cultural tradition.

Aksum became a major center of long-distance trade throughout coastal East Africa. Between the A.D. 300s and 600s, for example, it dominated the African side of the Red Sea trade. Its location and dominance brought great wealth to Aksum. The kingdom's power and prosperity began to decline, however, in the A.D. 600s. This was caused by several factors. Environmental problems such as erosion—caused by excessive land use and the destruction of forests—made the land less productive. The Persians, a trade rival, had gained control over much of the Red Sea trade. Beginning in the early A.D. 700s, moreover, the rise of Islamic Arab power led to new economic and political competition with Aksum. Arab forces won control of both the Arabian and the African sides of the Red Sea. As a result Aksum gradually lost control over most of its external trade and steadily declined as a commercial and political power.

✔ **READING CHECK: Drawing Conclusions** How would Aksum's location on the Red Sea and the Ethiopian Highlands have helped it conquer Kush? *straddled trade routes from Red Sea to Egypt and African interior*

Analyzing Primary Sources

Identifying a Point of View What does this excerpt tell us about King 'Ēzānā's approach to rule? *He believed in a just and moral approach to rule.*

HISTORY MAKER

King 'Ēzānā (unknown–c. A.D. 360)

King 'Ēzānā of Aksum was known as the "king of kings." Late in life he became a Christian and declared Christianity the official religion of his kingdom. Aksum thus became the first Christian kingdom in Africa. **How did Aksum differ from other African kingdoms?**

SECTION 2 REVIEW

1. **Identify** and explain the significance: King 'Ēzānā

2. **Categorizing** Copy the Venn diagram below. Use the diagram to organize characteristics of Kush and Aksum. In the far left circle, list characteristics of Kush alone. In the far right circle, list characteristics of Aksum alone. In the overlapping area, list characteristics that both Kush and Aksum shared.

Kush   Aksum

3. **Finding the Main Idea**
   a. How did trade affect the development of both Kush and Aksum?
   b. What role did conquest play in the histories of Kush and Aksum?

4. **Writing and Critical Thinking**
   Summarizing Write a description of social and economic activities in Meroë, the capital city of Kush.
   Consider:
   • its location
   • the structures built there
   • the livelihoods of the people there
   • the area's geographic advantages

Homework Practice Online
keyword: SP3 HP8

LET'S GET STARTED!

As students enter the classroom, have them look at the map on page 192. Ask them to write the location of the areas highlighted on the map in relation to the kingdoms of Kush and Aksum. *(southeast and west)* Tell students that in Section 3 they will learn about trading kingdoms that developed along the East Coast of Africa and in West Africa.

SECTION 3

READ TO DISCOVER

❶ How did trade develop along the East African coast?

❷ How did kingdoms of West Africa become prosperous and powerful?

IDENTIFY

Swahili
Shona
Tunka Manin
Mansa Mūsā
Sonni 'Alī
Mohammed I Askia

WHY IT MATTERS TODAY

The Swahili language is still used in East Africa. It is the official language of Tanzania and Kenya. Use CNNfyi.com or other **current event** sources to learn about the Swahili language. Record your findings in your journal.

CNNfyi.com

Trading States of Africa

The Main Idea
Trade strongly influenced cultures on the east and west coasts of Africa.

The Story Continues *Trade kept Africa well connected to the rest of the world. Ancient Greek traders were familiar with parts of East Africa, which they called "Azania." One sailor's handbook written by an Egyptian-Greek merchant described several trading villages along the "Azanian" coast. Traders there would swap African items such as ivory, rhinoceros horns, coconut oil, and tortoise shells for iron tools, weapons, and cotton cloth.*

East Africa and Great Zimbabwe

No kingdoms as large as Kush and Aksum emerged on the coast of East Africa. Instead, several city-states dominated coastal trade in the Indian Ocean. Sailing ships were powered by the seasonal monsoon winds. Trade routes linked all shores of the Indian Ocean. Africans exported gold, ivory, hides, and tortoise shells. They imported porcelain and weapons. They also sold slaves.

The spread of the Islamic religion from Arabia to northeastern Africa spurred trade. In fact, strong trade activity began in the A.D. 700s and lasted through the A.D. 1300s and possibly later. The opportunity to make money attracted merchant families and adventurers to Africa. Groups of Muslim settlers from Arabia and Persia began to move onto the East African coast. At the same time, people from Indonesia settled on the island of Madagascar, off the coast of East Africa. These groups, strongly influenced by the ideals of Islam, formed a new, trade-based society in coastal East Africa that combined elements of African, Asian, and Islamic cultures.

Swahili states. Over several generations a unique African culture, **Swahili,** developed in East Africa. The people of this culture spoke Swahili, a Bantu language with Arabic and Persian influences. Swahili speakers were not a single ethnic group. They were bound together by both language and their association with trade.

Among the earliest of the trading city-states along the Indian Ocean coast were Mogadishu (moh·guh·DEE·shoo), Pate, and Mombasa. These centers were in the north, but commerce gradually shifted southward. By the late A.D. 1200s the city-state of Kilwa had become a leading port.

INTERPRETING THE VISUAL RECORD

Dhow These Tanzanians are sailing a boat, called a "dhow" (DOW), similar to those that Arab traders used to visit the East African coast centuries ago. *In what way does this picture demonstrate the fact that different cultures influence and borrow from one another?*

SECTION 3 RESOURCES

REPRODUCIBLE RESOURCES

▸ Guided Reading Strategy 8.3

▸ Geography Activity 8

TECHNOLOGY RESOURCES

▸ One-Stop Planner 8.3

▸ Holt researcher: World History: Sonni 'Ali, Askia the Great

▸ CNN Presents World Cultures: Yesterday and Today Segments 24, 32

▸ Homework Practice Online

REINFORCEMENT, REVIEW, AND ASSESSMENT

▸ Section 3 Review, p. 195

▸ Daily Quiz 8.3

▸ Main Idea Activity 8.3

▸ English Audio Summary 8.3

▸ Spanish Audio Summary 8.3

VISUAL RECORD ANSWER

East Africans still use boats similar to those introduced by Arab traders.

Under Kilwa's leadership the East African coast flourished. Ibn Battūtah, a famous Islamic traveler of the A.D. 1300s, praised Kilwa. He called it one of the most beautiful, well-built cities in the world. Modern archaeological digs have uncovered a massive trade center and a large mosque. They reveal Kilwa's great wealth and achievements.

Great Zimbabwe. Kilwa grew as a trade port. Gold was shipped from mines along the Zambezi River in southcentral Africa. No later than A.D. 947, gold and other goods had moved from inland to the coast. They were exchanged for such needed goods as salt, tools, and cloth.

When Indian Ocean trade grew after the A.D. 900s, the demand for gold greatly increased. Kingdoms competed for control over both mining and shipping gold. The **Shona** were a people who had migrated onto the plateau of what is today Zimbabwe. Over centuries the Shona gained control over local peoples and, with it, over the gold that they mined and traded.

Historians believe that the Shona probably attained great wealth and power. They built fortified enclosures. Great Zimbabwe was probably the largest and most important of these fortresses. It became the center of the Shona state. Excavations have been made on its 60-acre site that reveal a hilltop fortification with many rooms and mazelike passageways. Below the hill was a thick stone-block wall, stone buildings, and a tower. The building stones were cut so finely that they stayed in place without mortar.

For unknown reasons Great Zimbabwe declined in the A.D. 1400s. One explanation is that the population grew too fast. It may have outpaced dwindling supplies of food and water.

✔**READING CHECK: Identifying Cause and Effect** What factors helped make East Africa a center for trade? location, weather and wind patterns, resources

Camel caravans crossed the Sahara with salt to trade with West African kingdoms. For centuries camels were the main form of transportation across the desert.

Trading States of Africa, c. A.D. 1230–1591

Interpreting Maps Prosperous kingdoms and city-states developed across Sub-Saharan Africa hundreds of years ago.

■ **Skills Assessment: Places and Regions** Compare this map with the map on page 183. In what type of region or regions did these cultures arise?

Legend:
- Great Zimbabwe, c. 1300s–1400s
- Mali, c. 1230s–1400s
- Swahili States, 1400s
- Songhay, 1468–1591

Map labels: MOROCCO, BARBARY STATES, MEDITERRANEAN SEA, Cairo, EGYPT, Persian Gulf, SAHARA, 20°N, Timbuktu, Tondibi, Gao, Kangaba, Niani, GHANA, HAUSA, Lake Chad, Niger R., Nile River, RED SEA, 0° Equator, Congo River, Mogadishu, Mombasa, Kilwa, ATLANTIC OCEAN, 20°S, Zambezi R., KALAHARI DESERT, Limpopo R., Sofala, MADAGASCAR, INDIAN OCEAN, 20°W, 0°, 20°E, 40°E

0 500 1,000 Miles
0 500 1,000 Kilometers
Azimuthal Equal-Area Projection

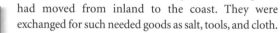

192

TEACH OBJECTIVE 2

ALL LEVELS: Ask students to read the material entitled "West Africa." Divide the class into four groups. Assign the introductory paragraphs to one group; assign "Ghana," "Mali," and "Songhai" each to the other groups. Ask each group to compile a summary that includes geographic area covered; goods traded; important events in sequence; rulers; cities; cultural accomplishments. Have a representative from each group present the summary to the class. **ENGLISH LANGUAGE LEARNERS, COOPERATIVE LEARNING**

LEVEL 3: Have students discuss the role of Islamic traders in the development of trade in Ghana, Mali, and Songhai. Then assign groups of students to conduct research on trade routes, goods traded, and impact of Islam on one of the West African trading kingdoms. Have students present their research as the class takes notes. **COOPERATIVE LEARNING**

West Africa

Several important societies flourished in West Africa. They lay between Lake Chad and the Atlantic Ocean and included the kingdoms of Ghana, Mali, and Songhai. Knowledge of them comes from oral accounts and the writings of African scholars and Islamic traders.

The wealth and strength of these kingdoms depended on control of the trade routes across the Sahara. At the desert's southern edge, commerce developed. There, gold mined south of the Sahel was traded for salt mined in the desert. This trade was mutually important. The people of the Sahel needed salt to flavor and preserve their food, while the gold that they traded for salt had obvious value. Traders from the north wanted gold for coins and for buying goods from Europe. Where this gold-for-salt exchange took place, cities grew and flourished. Thus areas of West Africa became major centers of commerce.

The gold-for-salt exchange was an important part of the region's trade. Indeed, West Africa produced large amounts of gold until about A.D. 1500. In time the traders also exchanged ivory and even slaves for textiles, jewels, and copper.

Monarchs ruled the West African kingdoms. Often adorned in gold, these monarchs oversaw elaborate ceremonies. They also administered justice. One way of conducting a trial was recounted by Islamic historian al-Bakri, who traveled throughout the area and who left accurate eyewitness accounts.

> **Primary Source**
> **❝**When a man is accused of denying a debt or having shed blood or some other crime, a headman takes a thin piece of wood, which is sour and bitter to taste, and pours upon it some water which he then gives to the defendant to drink. If the man vomits, his innocence is recognized and he is congratulated. If he does not vomit and the drink remains in his stomach, the accusation is accepted as justified.**❞**
>
> Al-Bakri, quoted in *The Horizon History of Africa,* edited by Alvin Josephy, Jr.

Below the royal family on the social scale were government officials. Then came merchants, farmers, fishers, and cattle breeders. Slaves ranked among the last.

Ghana. The earliest of the West African kingdoms was Ghana, where long-range trade networks encouraged higher levels of political organization. The kingdom of Ghana was established by the Soninke people sometime after the A.D. 300s. The Soninke lived in the western Sahel, northwest of the present-day nation of Ghana. Their kingdom began around the old trading village of Kumbi, or Kumbi Saleh, in what is now Mauritania. There the Soninke participated in and profited from the gold-for-salt exchange between North and West Africa. They used iron tools to farm and to clear more land for farming and grazing. They also probably developed agriculture along the upper Niger River.

CONNECTING TO Art

Sculpture: Royal Figure from West Africa

The Yoruba people, in what is now Nigeria, began sculpting life-sized, naturalistic heads more than 700 years ago. The heads were made in bronze, which is difficult to cast. The Yoruba, however, achieved artistic and technical excellence.

The casting shown here is of a Yoruba king. The beaded crown may have symbolized his importance. The vertical lines may represent ritual scarring.

Understanding the Arts

What do you think the artist wanted to reveal about this ruler?

Analyzing Primary Sources

Contrasting In what basic way did the West African system of justice described by al-Bakri differ from our American system of justice today? It depended upon physical demonstration rather than written law.

CONNECTING TO ART ANSWER

Students might say that the crown shows how powerful the ruler is and the scars indicate that this king took part in rituals.

Linking Past to Present

During the 1500s the gold trade shifted to the southern coast of West Africa, where Africans traded gold with Europeans for weapons. Called the Gold Coast, this part of West Africa eventually became a colony of Britain. Today the Gold Coast is the nation of Ghana. Kwame Nkrumah, the first president of Ghana, named the new nation after the ancient West African kingdom. In 1957 Ghana was the first British colony in Sub-Saharan Africa to gain independence from European control.

Critical Thinking

Ask students why Nkrumah might have chosen the name Ghana for the new country in West Africa.

ANSWER: Students might point out that he named the first independent nation after the first kingdom in West Africa as a reminder of a time when the region was not ruled by others.

Technology Resources

go.hrw.com Online Maps, Charts, and Graphs: African Trade, c. 1450–1600

HISTORY MAKER
Mansa Mūsā
(unknown–c. A.D. 1332)

In A.D. 1324 Mansa Mūsā, the king of Mali, traveled to Mecca, in what is today the country of Saudi Arabia. This trip was no ordinary journey. Mansa Mūsā traveled with a party of as many as 80,000 other people.

The group included hundreds of slaves, each carrying four-pound bars of gold. In fact, Mansa Mūsā brought a huge treasury on his journey. His entire party was richly dressed, many wearing expensive silks and gold ornaments.

The king's great display of wealth showed people the vast riches and power of Mali. It was said that Mansa Mūsā spent so much gold during his trip that the value of the precious metal fell in areas through which he passed. **Why do you think Mansa Mūsā wanted to demonstrate his great wealth?**

INTERPRETING THE VISUAL RECORD

Malian mosque As a devout Muslim, Mansa Mūsā encouraged the building of mosques. This one in Dejenné, Mali, dates from the A.D. 1300s. *What does the size of this mosque say about the influence of Islam in West Africa?*

As the Soninke settled in larger communities, kings arose to act as war leaders and to negotiate with foreign merchants. Ghanaian kings were powerful and wealthy from the gold trade. They were able to build large armies to conquer new territory. The kingdom of Ghana reached its peak around A.D. 1050. One of the most powerful Ghanaian rulers was **Tunka Manin,** who ruled in about A.D. 1067. Tunka Manin commanded an army of 200,000 warriors, well equipped with bows, arrows, and iron-pointed spears. In the late A.D. 1000s, however, Ghana began to decline. In A.D. 1076 the Berbers—who had once controlled the salt trade—invaded from the north, destroying Kumbi Saleh. The Soninke began to lose control of the salt trade to neighboring peoples. Finally, probably in about A.D. 1235, the neighboring Malinke people overthrew Ghana and established the empire of Mali.

Mali. The rise of a successor kingdom—Mali—followed the fall of Ghana. The kingdom of Mali came to power in the area that had been Ghana. It also spread over large areas to the north and west along the upper Niger River.

Mali's power reached its peak under its great ruler **Mansa Mūsā.** Mūsā reigned in the early A.D. 1300s. He was a supporter of education, the arts, and public building. Under his rule, the city of Timbuktu became a leading center of learning. Its large university attracted scholars from Egypt and Arabia.

Mūsā is famous for his historic pilgrimage to Mecca, an Islamic holy place in Arabia. He was accompanied by thousands of other pilgrims. Most notably he brought large amounts of gold with him in a great display of West African power and wealth. The Islamic traveler Ibn Battūtah visited Mali and noted:

History Makers Speak

❝[The people of Mali] are seldom unjust and have a greater abhorrence [hatred] of injustice than any other people. Their Sultan [leader] shows no mercy to any one guilty of the least act of it. There is complete security in their country. Neither traveler nor inhabitant in it has anything to fear from robbers or men of violence.❞

Ibn Battūtah, quoted in *The Horizon History of Africa,* edited by Alvin Josephy, Jr.

Disputes over Mansa Mūsā's successor weakened Mali. Rival members of the royal court fought for leadership of the empire. This conflict greatly weakened central authority within Mali. The kingdom kept control of the desert trade routes until the A.D. 1400s. Then in A.D. 1468 rebel leader **Sonni 'Alī** captured Timbuktu and built up the kingdom of Songhai. During the Songhai period the city of Gao (GAH·oh) became one of West Africa's busiest commercial centers.

CLOSE

Have students imagine they are traders in East Africa or West Africa during the time period covered in this section. Have them write an advertisement for their goods.

REVIEW

Have students complete the Section 3 Review on p. 195.

ASSESS

Have students complete Daily Quiz 8.3. As Alternative Assessment, you may want to use the graphic organizer from this section's lessons.

RETEACH

Have students complete Main Idea Activity for English Language Learners and Special-Needs Students 8.3. Then have them write the main idea for each of the section's headings.

ENGLISH LANGUAGE LEARNERS, COOPERATIVE LEARNING

EXTEND

Have students work in small groups to conduct research on the gold trade in Africa in the A.D. 900s and present the information in a written or visual form.

Songhai. The kingdom of Songhai was centered on the important trading city of Gao, on the Niger River. The new kingdom stretched from the Atlantic Ocean almost to Lake Chad. It covered an area even larger than Mali. Sonni 'Alī was both a skilled soldier and an able administrator. He kept tight control over the kingdom, dividing it into several provinces. Each province had a governor and officials who reported directly to him.

'Ali built a fleet of warships to patrol the Niger River, which had become a major shipping route. Sonni 'Alī and his successor, **Mohammed I Askia,** built Songhai into a strong kingdom. Under Askia's rule Timbuktu became a great commercial center. Goods came from Europe, India, and China. The growing number of merchants included Arabs, Jews, Italians, and many others. Timbuktu was also a thriving cultural center. As Mansa Mūsā had done, Askia supported a revival of Islamic scholarship based around the university there. Travelers reported that books and manuscripts imported to the markets of Timbuktu were sold for higher prices than any other merchandise.

Despite this prosperity, however, problems arose. The Songhai Empire began to experience a steady decline after the reign of Mohammed I Askia. For one thing, the Tuareg, Fulani, Malinke, and other subject peoples fought among themselves. The empire also had many powerful neighbors. In 1591 a Moroccan army equipped with firearms defeated Songhai troops, spelling the end of the empire.

✔ **READING CHECK: Evaluating** How important was trade in West Africa? Why? key to rise of powerful, trade-based kingdoms and to West African economy

The great cultural and commercial city of Timbuktu was a center of trade in the Songhai Empire.

Holt Researcher

go.hrw.com
KEYWORD: Holt Researcher
FreeFind: Sonni 'Ali
   Mohammed I Askia
After reading more about Sonnī 'Alī and Mohammed I Askia on the Holt Researcher, create a time line of the major events of their reigns.

SECTION 3 REVIEW

1. **Identify** and explain the significance:
   Swahili
   Shona
   Tunka Manin
   Mansa Mūsā
   Sonni 'Alī
   Mohammed I Askia

2. **Comparing** Copy the chart below. Use it to compare the various political states in Sub-Saharan Africa.

State	Location in Africa	Important Features
Swahili States		
Great Zimbabwe		
Ghana		
Mali		
Songhai		

3. **Finding the Main Idea**
   a. How did the Swahili culture develop in East Africa?
   b. How could the people of Great Zimbabwe have preserved their kingdom?
   c. How did Mansa Mūsā influence Mali?

4. **Writing and Critical Thinking**
   Analyzing Information Write a travelogue describing Mali when Mansa Mūsā ruled.
   Consider:
   • the importance of trade
   • the public buildings, art, and university Mūsā supported
   • Ibn Battūtah's account of the people of Mali

Homework Practice Online
keyword: SP3 HP8

SECTION 3 REVIEW ANSWERS

❶ **Identify**
• Swahili, p. 191
• Shona, p. 192
• Tunka Manin, p. 194
• Mansa Mūsā, p. 194
• Sonni 'Alī, p. 194
• Mohammed I Askia, p. 195

❷ Swahili States: eastern Africa; Swahili culture, trading ports, Muslim settlers. Great Zimbabwe: eastern Africa; Shona people, hilltop fortifications. Ghana: western Africa; trading center. Mali: western Africa; rule by Mansa Mūsā, university at Timbuktu, Islam. Songhai: western Africa; Gao, kingdom divided into provinces, Niger River shipping route

❸ **a.** from the Swahili language, a combination of Bantu with Arabic and Persian influences, and the activities of Swahili speakers, especially in trade

b. could have found new sources of food and water or relocated part of the population

c. made Timbuktu a center of learning; supported the arts, education, and public building; made Islam an important aspect of the culture

❹ Travelogues should mention the importance of trade, public buildings, art, the university, and people's hatred of injustice.

AFRICA **195**

195

REVIEW AND ASSESSMENT RESOURCES

REPRODUCIBLE RESOURCES

▸ Vocabulary Activity 8

TECHNOLOGY RESOURCES

▸ Chapter 8 Test Generator (on the One-Stop Planner)
▸ Global Skill Builder CD–ROM
▸ HRW Web Site

REINFORCEMENT, REVIEW, and ASSESSMENT

▸ Chapter 8 Review, pp. 196–197
▸ Chapter 8 Tutorial for Students, Parents, Mentors, and Peers
▸ Chapter 8 Test (Form A or B)
▸ Alternative Assessment Handbook
▸ Chapter 8 Test for English Language Learners and Special-Needs Students

REVIEW

Have students complete the Chapter 8 Review on pages 196–197.

ASSESS

Use one of the chapter tests to assess students' understanding of the content. For Alternative Assessment, see the Portfolio Activities and Alternative Assessment Handbook.

CHAPTER 8 REVIEW ANSWERS

Understanding Main Ideas

1. a vast plateau

2. the Sahara

3. languages, oral traditions, musical instruments, crops, excavations

4. matrilineal societies

5. At first Kush engaged in trade and cultural exchanges with Egypt. About 1520 B.C. Kush came under Egypt's control. About 710 B.C. Kush conquered Upper Egypt and ruled all of Egypt for 50 years.

6. Control of trade routes brought control of wealth, culture, and political power.

7. Land lost fertility; Kush lost control of trade routes.

8. It incorporated many traditional beliefs and customs.

9. Muslims

10. Swahili; language and trade

11. led to power and wealth

12. the gold-for-salt trade

Reviewing Themes

1. Gold, ivory, and ebony were traded for goods people needed.

2. The land and climate limited where people could live and what crops they could grow. Access to rivers and the sea provided opportunities for trade.

3. by trade and conquest

Review

Creating a Time Line

Copy the time line below onto a sheet of paper. Complete the time line by filling in the events, individuals, and dates from the chapter that you think were significant. Pick three events and explain why you think they were significant.

1800 B.C.	1000 B.C.	A.D. 500

Writing a Summary

Using standard grammar, spelling, sentence structure, and punctuation, write an overview of the events in the chapter.

Identifying People and Ideas

Identify the following terms or individuals and explain their significance.

1. linguists
2. Bantu
3. oral traditions
4. matrilineal
5. King 'Ēzānā
6. Swahili
7. Shona
8. Mansa Mūsā
9. Sonni 'Alī
10. Mohammed I Askia

Understanding Main Ideas

SECTION 1 *(pp. 182–186)*

Africa's Early History

1. What is the main natural landform of Sub-Saharan Africa?
2. What geographical feature made trade and communication difficult in many parts of Africa?
3. What are some of the tools that scholars have used to uncover the history of Africa?
4. How was early African society organized?

SECTION 2 *(pp. 187–190)*

The Kingdoms of Kush and Aksum

5. What was the relationship of the kingdom of Kush to Egypt?
6. Why was control of trade routes important in the growth of Kush and Aksum?
7. What factors may have explained the decline of the kingdom of Kush?
8. How did Christianity become important in the kingdom of Aksum?

SECTION 3 *(pp. 191–195)*

Trading States of Africa

9. Who established trading centers along the East African coast?
10. What unique culture developed in coastal East Africa, and what factors bound the different peoples of this culture together?
11. Why was control of gold mining important in East Africa?
12. What general factors helped to promote the rise of West African kingdoms?

Reviewing Themes

1. **Economics** What types of goods were traded in Africa and how did they meet people's needs?
2. **Geography** How did the natural environment affect the people of Africa?
3. **Global Relations** How did the rulers of African kingdoms get what they wanted from others?

Thinking Critically

1. **Contrasting** How did early East African societies differ from the early African societies of Kush, Aksum, and West Africa?
2. **Identifying Bias** Why is it helpful to have observations of African societies from Arab travelers and historians who lived during the historical period?
3. **Making Generalizations** How were the people of Africa able to build complex civilizations and share cultural ideas with one another and with people from other lands?

Writing About History

Evaluating Write an evaluation in which you describe the major similarities and differences in the development of the kingdoms of Kush and Mali. Use the Venn diagram below to organize your thoughts before writing.

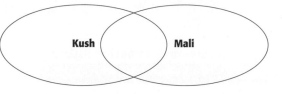

Kush   Mali

CLOSE

Divide students into three groups and assign one section from this chapter to each group. Have students create a summary of the main ideas in their section.

COOPERATIVE LEARNING

RETEACH

Have students who had trouble with the test use their textbooks to correct their tests. Then when they are ready, have them take the Form B Test to assess their mastery of the material. **ENGLISH LANGUAGE LEARNERS, COOPERATIVE LEARNING**

Portfolio Extensions

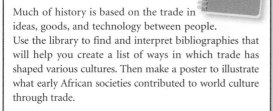

1. Ask students to imagine that they are living in a tropical rain forest about 3000 B.C. Tell them to write a letter to a friend who lives on a savanna. Have them compare the environment, foods, and diseases of their two regions.

2. Divide the class into small groups. Ask each group to select one of the early African kingdoms (Kush, Aksum, Ghana, Mali, or Songhai), the Swahili states, or Great Zimbabwe and write a television script for a documentary that describes the importance of trade to the people of their kingdom or state.

3. Have students write a story about the history of their family, school, or town that could be told orally in the manner of the African storytellers. Allow students to tell their stories to the class.

Building Social Studies Skills

Interpreting a Graph

Study the graph below. Then use the information on the graph to help you answer the questions that follow.

Average Maximum Temperatures in African Cities (in Fahrenheit)

Cairo, Egypt; Capetown, South Africa; Lagos, Nigeria; Nairobi, Kenya
January, July

1. Which of the following is a correct general statement about temperatures in African cities?
   a. Lagos has a greater year-round temperature change than Cairo does.
   b. There is less than a 4°F difference between July temperatures in Capetown and Lagos.
   c. The average maximum temperature in Cairo is 93.9°F.
   d. The temperature in Nigeria and Kenya does not change significantly during the year.

2. Why are the temperatures in Capetown highest in January, while in Cairo they are lowest in January?

Identifying Values and Opinions

Read the following excerpt from the Greek historian Herodotus, who wrote during the 400s B.C. Then answer the questions.

"As for Libya [Africa], we know that it is washed on all sides by the sea except where it joins Asia, as was first demonstrated, so far as our knowledge goes . . . by a Phoenician crew with orders to sail west-about and return to Egypt and the Mediterranean by way of the Straits of Gibraltar. These men made a statement which I do not myself believe . . . to the effect that as they sailed on a westerly course round the southern end of Libya, they had the [morning] sun on their right . . . ."

3. Which of the following from the excerpt expresses values or opinions held by the author?
   a. "so far as our knowledge goes" and "which I do not myself believe"
   b. "we know that it is washed on all sides by the sea"
   c. "these men made a statement"
   d. "to the effect that as they sailed on a westerly course"

4. Which of the statements in the excerpt are factual? Give reasons for your choices.

Alternative Assessment

Building Your Portfolio

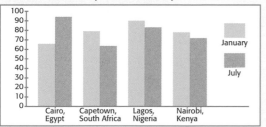

Economics

Much of history is based on the trade in ideas, goods, and technology between people. Use the library to find and interpret bibliographies that will help you create a list of ways in which trade has shaped various cultures. Then make a poster to illustrate what early African societies contributed to world culture through trade.

internet connect

Internet Activity: go.hrw.com
KEYWORD: SP3 WH8

Choose a topic on Africa to:
• research threats to the Congo Basin's ecosystem.
• explore the ancient kingdom of Nubia.
• analyze language development in Africa.

Thinking Critically

1. Early East African societies: based on the village; Kush, Aksum, and West Africa: based on trading centers that grew into kingdoms

2. provide eyewitness accounts of someone who was not part of the societies

3. through the development of technology and trade

Writing About History

Similarities: trading kingdoms; had large public buildings; Differences; location and time periods

Building Social Studies Skills

1. d

2. They are on opposite sides of the equator.

3. a

4. First sentence can be verified.

Building Your Portfolio

Trade influences languages, foods, and ways of making things. Posters should include Christianity and Islam.

AFRICA **197**

197

The Americas

CHAPTER RESOURCE MANAGER

	Objectives	Pacing Guide	Reproducible Resources
SECTION 1 **The Earliest Americans** (pp. 200–202)	• Explain how people first arrived in the Americas. • Describe changes that the development of agriculture brought to the Americas.	**Regular** 1.5 day / **Block Scheduling** 1 day *Block Scheduling Handbook with Team Teaching Strategies, 9.1*	**RS** Guided Reading Strategy 9.1 **E** Hands-on History Activity 9: Touring Native American Cities
SECTION 2 **Cultures of North America** (pp. 203–207)	• Explain how geography and climate affected life in different regions of North America. • Distinguish between the early American cultures in the Pacific Northwest, the Southwest, the Great Plains, and the Eastern Woodlands.	**Regular** 1.5 day / **Block Scheduling** 1 day *Block Scheduling Handbook with Team Teaching Strategies, 9.2*	**RS** Guided Reading Strategy 9.2 **PS** Readings in World History 51: Women Leaders in North American Indian Societies
SECTION 3 **Mesoamerica and Andean South America** (pp. 208–211)	• Identify the characteristics of the Olmec, Toltec, and Maya cultures. • Explain how the Aztec and Inca built and strengthened their empires.	**Regular** 1.5 day / **Block Scheduling** 1 day *Block Scheduling Handbook with Team Teaching Strategies, 9.3*	**RS** Guided Reading Strategy 9.3 **RS** Graphic Organizer Activity 9: Mesoamerican Empires **SM** Geography Activity 9: The Maya Empire **PS** Readings in World History 52: The Incas: Worshippers of the Sun **E** Creative Teaching Strategy 9: A Food Fair of the Americas

Chapter Resource Key

- **PS** Primary Sources
- **RS** Reading Support
- **IC** Interdisciplinary Connections
- **E** Enrichment
- **SM** Skills Mastery
- **A** Assessment
- **REV** Review
- **ELL** Reinforcement and English Language Learners
- Transparencies
- CD–ROM
- Music
- Video
- Internet
- Holt Presentation Maker Using Microsoft® PowerPoint®

One-Stop Planner CD-ROM

See the **One-Stop Planner** for a complete list of additional resources for students and teachers.

One-Stop Planner CD-ROM

It's easy to plan lessons, select resources, and print out materials for your students when you use the **One-Stop Planner** CD–ROM with **Test Generator.**

Technology Resources

- One-Stop Planner 9.1
- World History and Cultures Video Program 8: Tools and Transformations
- Homework Practice Online
- Online Maps, Charts, and Graphs: Bering Land Bridge
- Online Maps, Charts, and Graphs: Methods of Subsistence in Early Americas

- One-Stop Planner 9.2
- World History Teaching Transparency: Geography and History 8: Native American Culture Areas
- World History Teaching Transparency: Regional and World Maps 31: The United States and Canada
- Homework Practice Online

- One-Stop Planner 9.3
- Holt Researcher: World History: Moctezuma II
- Regions of the World Music Audio CD Program 5: South America: Traditional Music of Peru I: Festivals of Cuzco
- CNN. Presents World Cultures: Yesterday and Today Segment 13: Inca's Frozen Past
- World History Teaching Transparency: Everyday Life 8: The Maya Number System
- Homework Practice Online
- Online Maps, Charts, and Graphs: The Aztec and Inca, c. 1500

Reinforcement, Review, and Assessment

- Daily Quiz 9.1
- Main Idea Activity 9.1
- English Audio Summary 9.1
- Spanish Audio Summary 9.1
- REV Section 1 Review, p. 202

- Daily Quiz 9.2
- Main Idea Activity 9.2
- English Audio Summary 9.2
- Spanish Audio Summary 9.2
- REV Section 2 Review, p. 207

- Daily Quiz 9.3
- Main Idea Activity 9.3
- English Audio Summary 9.3
- Spanish Audio Summary 9.3
- REV Section 3 Review, p. 211

internet connect

HRW ONLINE RESOURCES
GO TO: go.hrw.com
Then type in a keyword.

TEACHER HOME PAGE
KEYWORD: SP3 Teacher

CHAPTER INTERNET ACTIVITIES
KEYWORD: SP3 WH9
Choose an activity to:
- research Inca history and take a virtual hike to Machu Picchu.
- learn Maya number glyphs and calculate your birthday.
- explore Olmec art, architecture, and culture.

CHAPTER ENRICHMENT LINKS
KEYWORD: SP3 CH9

ONLINE ASSESSMENT
Homework Practice
KEYWORD: SP3 HP9
Standardized Test Prep
KEYWORD: SP3 STP9
Rubrics
KEYWORD: SS Rubrics

ONLINE MAPS, CHARTS, AND GRAPHS
KEYWORD: SP3 MCG

CONTENT UPDATES
KEYWORD: SS Content Updates

HOLT PRESENTATION MAKER
KEYWORD: SP3 PPT9

ONLINE READING SUPPORT
KEYWORD: SS Strategies

CURRENT EVENTS
KEYWORD: S3 Current Events

Meeting Individual Needs

Ability Levels

Level 1 Basic level activities designed for all students encountering new material

Level 2 Intermediate level activities designed for average students

Level 3 Challenging activities designed for honors and gifted and talented students

English Language Learners These activities address the needs of students with Limited English Proficiency.

Chapter Review and Assessment

- IC Vocabulary Activity 9
- Global Skill Builder CD–ROM
- HRW Web Site
- REV Chapter 9 Tutorial for Students, Parents, Mentors, and Peers
- REV Chapter 9 Review, pp. 212–213

- A Chapter 9 Test Generator (on the One-Stop Planner)
- A Chapter 9 Test (Form A or B)
- A Alternative Assessment Handbook
- A Chapter 9 Test for English Language Learners and Special-Needs Students

Build on What You Know

Ask students to answer the following questions:

Why might the study of Asian, African, and Mediterranean civilizations be important to the study of early civilizations in the Americas?

Consider:

- the geographic origins of the first Americans
- the eventual connections between the different continents

Why might hunters from Asia have moved into the Americas during the Ice Age?

Consider:

- the effect of climatic changes on geographic features
- the availability of natural resources

EXPLORING THE TIME LINE

GLOBAL EVENTS

📶 **internet** connect

TOPIC: Mayan Architecture
GO TO: go.hrw.com
KEYWORD: SP3 WH9

Have students access the Internet through the HRW Go site to conduct research on Mayan architecture. Then have students build a model of a Mayan home, temple, palace, or city. Finally, ask students to write a brief paragraph about the Mayan culture and explain any distinctively Mayan feature on their model.

CHAPTER 9

1800 B.C.–A.D. 1500

The Americas

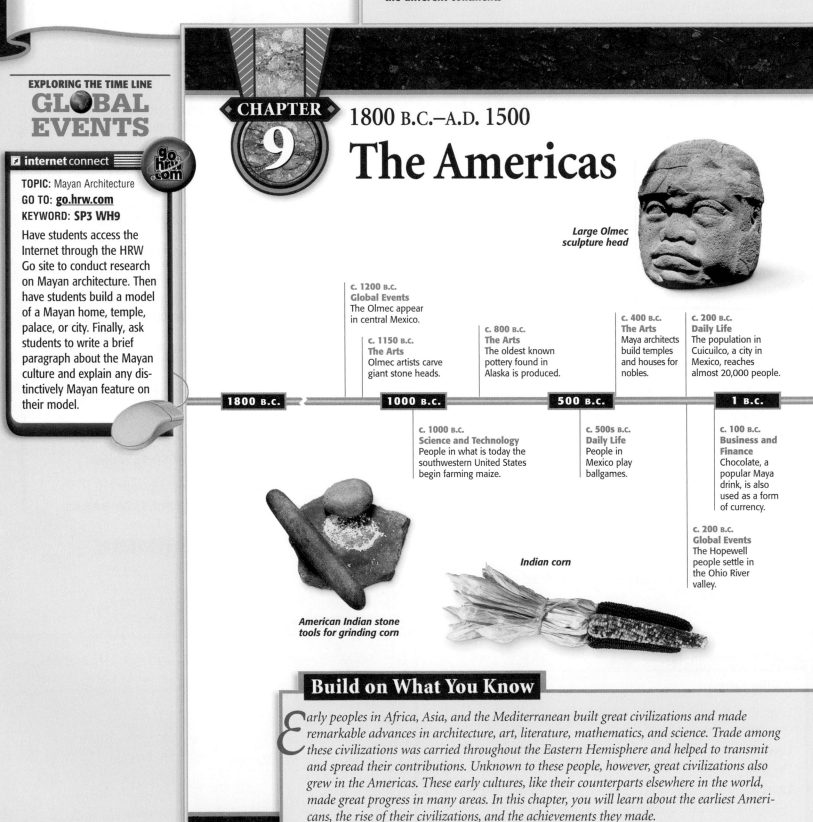

Large Olmec sculpture head

c. 1200 B.C.
Global Events
The Olmec appear in central Mexico.

c. 1150 B.C.
The Arts
Olmec artists carve giant stone heads.

c. 800 B.C.
The Arts
The oldest known pottery found in Alaska is produced.

c. 400 B.C.
The Arts
Maya architects build temples and houses for nobles.

c. 200 B.C.
Daily Life
The population in Cuicuilco, a city in Mexico, reaches almost 20,000 people.

1800 B.C.   1000 B.C.   500 B.C.   1 B.C.

c. 1000 B.C.
Science and Technology
People in what is today the southwestern United States begin farming maize.

c. 500s B.C.
Daily Life
People in Mexico play ballgames.

c. 100 B.C.
Business and Finance
Chocolate, a popular Maya drink, is also used as a form of currency.

c. 200 B.C.
Global Events
The Hopewell people settle in the Ohio River valley.

Indian corn

American Indian stone tools for grinding corn

Build on What You Know

Early peoples in Africa, Asia, and the Mediterranean built great civilizations and made remarkable advances in architecture, art, literature, mathematics, and science. Trade among these civilizations was carried throughout the Eastern Hemisphere and helped to transmit and spread their contributions. Unknown to these people, however, great civilizations also grew in the Americas. These early cultures, like their counterparts elsewhere in the world, made great progress in many areas. In this chapter, you will learn about the earliest Americans, the rise of their civilizations, and the achievements they made.

What's Your Opinion?

To help students create their Themes Journal entries, provide the following examples of appropriate **agree**/**disagree** *statements.*

Geography

Agree Changes in the weather or the climate have no effect on geographical features.

Disagree Changes in the weather or the climate can create or destroy geographical features.

Science, Technology & Society

Agree Civilizations in different parts of the world create similar technologies.

Disagree Civilizations in different parts of the world develop unique technologies.

Government

Agree A conquering nation can keep peace by permitting regional diversity.

Disagree Regional diversity promotes new ideas that can undermine the efforts of a conquering nation to keep peace.

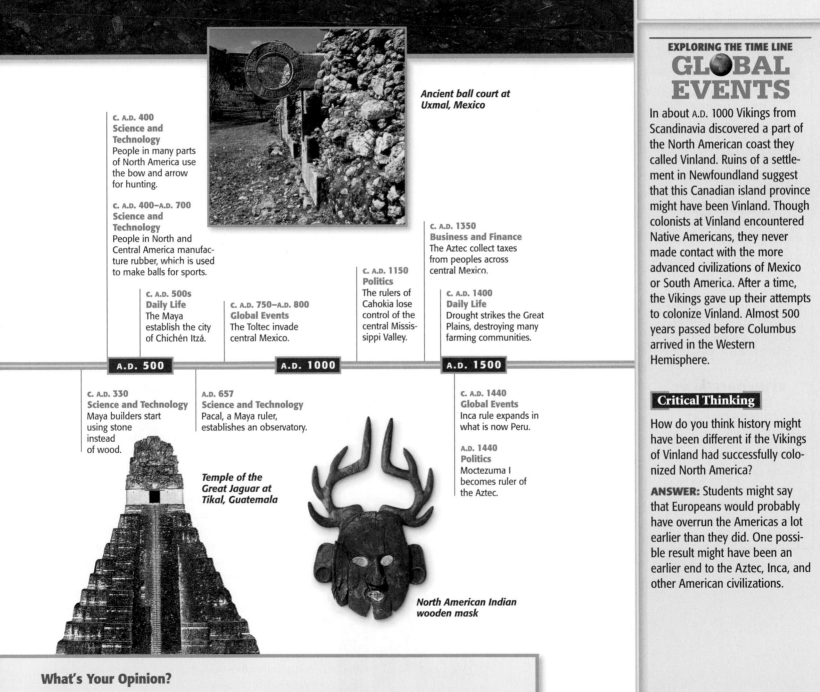

Ancient ball court at Uxmal, Mexico

c. A.D. 400
Science and Technology
People in many parts of North America use the bow and arrow for hunting.

c. A.D. 400–A.D. 700
Science and Technology
People in North and Central America manufacture rubber, which is used to make balls for sports.

c. A.D. 500s
Daily Life
The Maya establish the city of Chichén Itzá.

c. A.D. 750–A.D. 800
Global Events
The Toltec invade central Mexico.

c. A.D. 1150
Politics
The rulers of Cahokia lose control of the central Mississippi Valley.

c. A.D. 1350
Business and Finance
The Aztec collect taxes from peoples across central Mexico.

c. A.D. 1400
Daily Life
Drought strikes the Great Plains, destroying many farming communities.

A.D. 500 **A.D. 1000** **A.D. 1500**

c. A.D. 330
Science and Technology
Maya builders start using stone instead of wood.

A.D. 657
Science and Technology
Pacal, a Maya ruler, establishes an observatory.

Temple of the Great Jaguar at Tikal, Guatemala

c. A.D. 1440
Global Events
Inca rule expands in what is now Peru.

A.D. 1440
Politics
Moctezuma I becomes ruler of the Aztec.

North American Indian wooden mask

EXPLORING THE TIME LINE
GLOBAL EVENTS

In about A.D. 1000 Vikings from Scandinavia discovered a part of the North American coast they called Vinland. Ruins of a settlement in Newfoundland suggest that this Canadian island province might have been Vinland. Though colonists at Vinland encountered Native Americans, they never made contact with the more advanced civilizations of Mexico or South America. After a time, the Vikings gave up their attempts to colonize Vinland. Almost 500 years passed before Columbus arrived in the Western Hemisphere.

Critical Thinking

How do you think history might have been different if the Vikings of Vinland had successfully colonized North America?

ANSWER: Students might say that Europeans would probably have overrun the Americas a lot earlier than they did. One possible result might have been an earlier end to the Aztec, Inca, and other American civilizations.

What's Your Opinion?

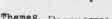

Do you **agree** *or* **disagree** *with the following statements? Support your point of view in your journal.*

Geography Changes in the weather or the climate do not affect geographical features.

Science, Technology & Society Civilizations throughout the world create similar technologies independent of one another.

Government Permitting regional diversity is one way a conquering nation can keep peace.

SECTION 1 RESOURCES

REPRODUCIBLE RESOURCES

▸ Guided Reading Strategy 9.1

▸ Hands-on History Activity 9: Touring Native American Cities

TECHNOLOGY RESOURCES

▸ One-Stop Planner 9.1

▸ World History and Cultures Video Program 8: Tools and Transformations

▸ Homework Practice Online

▸ Online Maps, Charts, and Graphs: Methods of Subsistence in Early Americas

REINFORCEMENT, REVIEW, AND ASSESSMENT

▸ Section 1 Review, p. 202

▸ Daily Quiz 9.1

▸ Main Idea Activity 9.1

▸ English Audio Summary 9.1

▸ Spanish Audio Summary 9.1

SECTION 1

READ TO DISCOVER

❶ How did people arrive in the Americas?

❷ What changes did the development of agriculture bring to the Americas?

DEFINE

strait

IDENTIFY

Beringia

▶ WHY IT MATTERS TODAY

Changes in climate affect the way that people live in the world today. Use CNNfyi.com or other **current event** sources to explore how climate change can lead to changes in lifestyles. Record your findings in your journal.

The Earliest Americans

The Main Idea
The earliest Americans came from Asia and migrated throughout the continent over several thousand years.

The Story Continues *According to one Native American myth, people once lived on a floating island. One day their ruler said to them, "We will make a new place where another people may grow." The story goes on to describe events that led to the creation of Earth. The population of the Americas may have begun in a similar way. When people from another land decided to move eastward, they launched a migration that developed into Native American cultures.*

The Land and the People

The Americas stretch more than 9,000 miles from Greenland in the north to Cape Horn at the southern tip of South America. Almost every type of climate and terrain can be found somewhere on the continents.

The physical setting. Jagged mountains curve like a backbone near the western coast of the Americas. Known as the Rocky Mountains in North America, they extend through Mexico into South America, where they are called the Andes. To the east are flatter lands dotted here and there by mountains.

The Americas include two of the world's great river systems. The Mississippi River flows through much of North America and serves as a major transportation route. In South America, the Amazon River flows through dense rain forests before emptying into the Atlantic Ocean. At some 4,000 miles, the Amazon is the second-longest river in the world. Only the Nile in Africa is longer.

In the north, off the coast of present-day Alaska, the Americas are separated from Asia by a narrow strip of water called a **strait.** Known now as the Bering Strait, this body of water is fairly shallow. Today it averages between about 100 feet and about 160 feet in depth. During the Ice Age, much of the world's water was trapped in glaciers. Thus the bottom of the Bering Strait became a land "bridge." This land bridge, today called **Beringia,** provided a means for Asians to move into the Americas.

First arrivals. Many historians think that early peoples migrated from Asia to the Americas between 35,000 or more years ago and about 8,000 years ago. These earliest

Early American peoples hunted large animals such as the American mastodon—a relative of the woolly mammoth—whose skeleton is shown here.

TEACH OBJECTIVE 1

LEVEL 1: Discuss why the land bridge may have encouraged people from Asia to move into North America.
ENGLISH LANGUAGE LEARNERS

TEACH OBJECTIVE 2

LEVEL 3: Have students use page 202 to write a two- or three-paragraph essay describing how agriculture changed the lives of early Americans.

TEACH OBJECTIVE 2

ALL LEVELS: Have students complete the following chart comparing farming to hunting.

	Communities	Food Sources
Hunting	nomadic groups on the move	constantly changing
Farming	settled towns	stable and reliable

HOMEWORK Have students use an atlas or encyclopedia to find out the distance across the Bering Strait at its narrowest point. *(50 miles)*

Americans may have followed animal herds across the land bridge in a series of waves of different peoples. Changes in Asia's climate, too, may have forced people northward and across the land bridge. From there they drifted toward warmer climates. Many of these people may have been hunter-gatherers who depended on hunting, fishing, and collecting plants to live.

Some people moved into the eastern and central areas of North America. Others migrated farther south, through Mexico and Central America, an area called Mesoamerica. From there the South American continent spread out before them. Evidence suggests that humans entered South America as early as 10,500 B.C.

Creation myths. Many Native American peoples use creation myths to explain their origins. These traditional stories, which are found in many civilizations around the world and vary from place to place, explain how the world was formed and how people came into being. Many creation myths include information about a creator or supreme being and about a people's duties in relation to their creator. These myths may be passed down orally, through the act of storytelling, or recorded in written form. Historians often examine creation myths for evidence of a people's customs and values. Some Native American creation myths are long and detailed, and many tell a story of people emerging from an underground world.

The Jicarilla Apache, who live in modern-day New Mexico, believe that animals and people once lived in the underworld. The people discovered a hole that led to Earth. The story ends with the Jicarilla Apache arriving in their homeland.

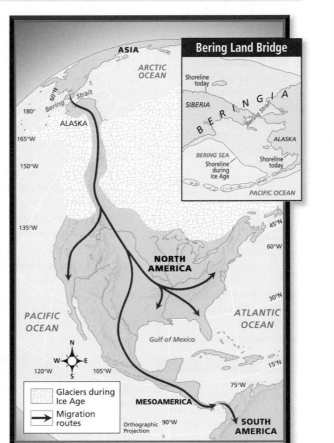

Bering Land Bridge

Migration to America

Interpreting Maps Early nomadic peoples from Asia spread throughout the Americas.

■ **Skills Assessment: Environment and Society** What geographic feature enabled nomads to travel to the Americas?

"All the people came up. They traveled east until they arrived at the ocean; then they turned south until they came again to the ocean; then they went west to the ocean, and then they turned north. And as they went, each tribe stopped where it wanted to. But the Jicarillas continued to circle around the hole where they had come up from the underworld. Three times they went around it, when the Ruler became displeased and asked them where they wished to stop. They said, 'In the middle of the earth.' So he led them to a place very near Taos and left them, and there near the Taos Indians, the Jicarillas made their home."

Jicarilla Apache tale, quoted in *American Indian Myths and Legends*

✔ **READING CHECK: Identifying Cause and Effect** How did climate change affect the geography of the Americas? created a land bridge between the Americas and Asia

MAP ANSWER
Bering land bridge

Culture

The Jicarilla Apache tribe belong to a larger native group called the Apache. These people live in the American Southwest, including parts of Arizona, New Mexico, Colorado, and Texas, as well as Chihuahua and Sonora, which are states in northern Mexico. Today the Jicarilla Apache number several thousand, although there are about 2.5 million American Indians and Alaskan natives in the United States.

ACTIVITY: Have students identify some of the major Native American groups living in the United States today and plot their traditional homelands on a map. Tell students that many, but not all, Native Americans live on reservations.

Technology Resources

go. hrw .com Online Maps, Charts, and Graphs: Bering Land Bridge

CLOSE

Have students compare the American mastodon on page 200 with the Clovis points on page 202. What can they conclude about the skills of early American hunters?

REVIEW

Have students complete the Section 1 Review on p. 202.

ASSESS

Have students complete Daily Quiz 9.1. As Alternative Assessment, you may want to use the chart exercise.

RETEACH

Have students complete Main Idea Activity for English Language Learners and Special-Needs Students 9.1. Then have students write brief summaries for the sections' headings.
ENGLISH LANGUAGE LEARNERS

EXTEND

Have students use sources to find out what farming was like in the Americas before A.D. 1500. **BLOCK SCHEDULING**

DAILY LIFE ANSWER
probably tools or weapons and possibly a small amount of food

VISUAL RECORD ANSWER

Spear points were used to pierce the hides of large animals. These well-made stone tools suggest that the early hunter-gatherers had other useful stone tools.

SECTION 1 REVIEW ANSWERS

❶ **Define**
• strait, p. 200

❷ **Identify**
• Beringia, p. 200

❸ Because much of the world's water was trapped in glaciers, people migrated from Asia to North America across a land bridge called Beringia.

❹ **a.** Scientific theories use climate and geography to explain how people migrated to North America; Native American myths are traditional stories.

b. During the Ice Age, the world's water was trapped in glaciers. The bottom of the Bering Strait became a land bridge called Beringia, which permitted people to cross from Asia to North America.

❺ Students might mention how having a reliable food source affected their activities.

DAILY LIFE

Hunter-Gatherers

In most American hunter-gatherer societies, the men hunted and fished, while the women gathered plants, berries, and nuts to eat. These nomadic groups needed large areas of land to search for food. When the food supply in an area was gone, the group moved on.

Because of this constant movement, few lasting settlements existed. People had few possessions, taking only what they could carry with them. **What items might hunter-gatherers carry with them?**

INTERPRETING THE VISUAL RECORD

Clovis points Early Americans hunted with spears tied to stone tips like the ones pictured here. These tips are called Clovis points because they were first found in Clovis, New Mexico. *What do these spear points tell us about the tools early hunter-gatherers had?*

The Development of American Agriculture

The first people who arrived in the Americas were nomads who lived by hunting wild animals and gathering plants. Among the many animals they hunted were mammoths and mastodons, creatures the size of modern elephants. Camels and horses also populated the Western Hemisphere. Early nomadic peoples may have been following movements of these large game animals in their migrations.

About 11,000 years ago, many scholars believe, massive climate changes may have taken place in the Americas. Glaciers melted and water covered the land bridge. In the new climate, many large animals became extinct. The hunter-gatherers increasingly relied on plants as a food source. Gradually, a new way of life emerged—farming. The earliest known farming in the Americas began in Mexico, then spread north and south. The first farmers raised crops such as beans, corn, and squash. In South America and the Caribbean, farmers also raised avocados and sweet potatoes. In the highlands of Peru, the potato was the most important food.

Farming began in the Americas within a few thousand years of its start in other parts of the world. However, it developed more slowly here than in other areas. Apparently, early Native American farmers never invented the plow, partly because they did not have large animals such as the horse to pull it. For this same reason, early Native American farmers did not have wheeled farming vehicles, even though they knew about the wheel. Many farmers used simple digging sticks to plant rows of seeds.

Many people throughout the Americas depended on farming for their food supply. The rise of agriculture ensured a food supply that was relatively stable and reliable. This led, in turn, to the growth of populations and to the development of villages and towns that were surrounded by farmlands. At first, most of these early farmers practiced subsistence farming—raising just enough food crops for survival. Over time, however, farming techniques improved and increased crop production provided food surpluses that supported ever-larger populations and settlements. Having a reliable food source also allowed some people in early societies to make advances in activities other than farming.

✔ **READING CHECK: Drawing Conclusions** Why did early Americans turn from hunting and gathering to agriculture? large prehistoric animals became extinct

SECTION 1 REVIEW

1. **Define** and explain the significance:
   strait

2. **Identify** and explain the significance:
   Beringia

3. **Identifying Cause and Effect** Copy the graphic organizer below. Use it to explain the arrival of people in the Americas.

   Asia → North America
   Beringia

4. **Finding the Main Idea**
   a. How do scientific theories of the arrivals of people in the Americas differ from Native American creation myths?
   b. How did climate change create opportunities for early peoples?

5. **Writing and Critical Thinking**
   Evaluating Write a myth that reflects the changes that the development of agriculture brought to the earliest Americans.
   Consider:
   • life before the development of agriculture
   • life after the development of agriculture

Homework Practice Online
keyword: SP3 HP9

SECTION 2

OBJECTIVES

1 Explain how geography and climate affected life in different regions of North America.

2 Distinguish between the early American cultures in the Pacific Northwest, the Southwest, the Great Plains, and the Eastern Woodlands.

🔊 LET'S GET STARTED!

As students enter the classroom, prompt them to look at the picture of the Anasazi cliff dwelling on page 203. Then ask them to speculate about the people who built the cliff dwelling. (*Students might speculate that the cliff-builders were settled farmers, fairly numerous, and skilled at building with brick or stone.*) Explain that cultures adapt to their environment by using local resources for shelter, food, and other needs. Tell students that in Section 2 they will learn about the different cultures that developed in North America.

SECTION 2

READ TO DISCOVER

❶ How did geography and climate affect life in different regions of North America?

❷ What distinguished the early American cultures in the Pacific Northwest, the Southwest, the Great Plains, and the Eastern Woodlands?

DEFINE

potlatches
adobe
buffalo
tepees

IDENTIFY

Hohokam
Pueblo
Hopewell
Mississippians

WHY IT MATTERS TODAY

Ancient sites such as mounds or communal houses are popular tourist sites in America today. Use CNNfyi.com or other **current event** sources to explore how the people of the United States learn from these sites. Record your findings in your journal.

CNNfyi.com

Cultures of North America

The Main Idea
The culture of North American peoples varied greatly on the basis of geographic differences.

The Story Continues *Although the first Americans came from Asia, they eventually formed many new cultures throughout the Americas. One Native American myth recounts this distribution. "For a long time everyone spoke the same language, but suddenly people began to speak in different tongues. Kulsu [the Creator] . . . sent each tribe to a different place to live."*

Western North America

The greatest diversity of early American groups could be found in what is now the United States and Canada. In many cases, the geography of a region shaped the culture that developed there. For example, the peoples of western North America faced a common problem of how to find resources. In large areas of the western desert, water was hard to find. People there sometimes had to live off of insects, small plants, and small game.

The Northwest. The people along the northwest coast of North America probably fared the best of any western groups. Many northwestern groups relied on fishing. These people were also expert weavers and woodworkers. They are remembered today in part because of their totem poles—great wooden carvings of people and beasts that represented the community's history. Some peoples in the Pacific Northwest held festive gatherings called **potlatches.** At a potlatch a chief or clan leader would display the clan's material goods, such as canoes or blankets. The leader would then give most of them away to guests, enhancing the host family's social status.

The Southwest. The **Hohokam** people lived in what is today the southwestern United States. Archaeologists are uncertain when the Hohokam peoples first settled in the Southwest. One of their major communities, located along the banks of the now dry Gila River in present-day southern Arizona, has been dated to anywhere from 300 B.C. to A.D. 500. Hohokam farmers flourished in this arid region by building extensive irrigation networks. They used these networks to water fields and grow crops such as beans, corn, and cotton. During the A.D. 1300s and 1400s, however, climate changes led the Hohokam to abandon their communities.

SECTION 2 RESOURCES

REPRODUCIBLE RESOURCES

▶ Guided Reading Strategy 9.2

▶ Readings in World History 51: Women Leaders in North American Indian Societies

TECHNOLOGY RESOURCES

▶ One-Stop Planner 9.2

▶ World History Teaching Transparency: Geography and History 8: Native American Culture Areas

▶ World History Teaching Transparency: Regional and World Maps 31: The United States and Canada

▶ Homework Practice Online

REINFORCEMENT, REVIEW, AND ASSESSMENT

▶ Section 2 Review, p. 207

▶ Daily Quiz 9.2

▶ Main Idea Activity 9.2

▶ English Audio Summary 9.2

▶ Spanish Audio Summary 9.2

The ancient Anasazi civilization flourished in southwestern North America. The Anasazi built cliff dwellings like this one in what is now Colorado.

TEACH OBJECTIVE 1

LEVEL 1: Have students match each region's geography and climate with a way of life by filling in the flowchart graphic. Then discuss in class how each example demonstrates the influence of geography or climate on way of life.

COOPERATIVE LEARNING, ENGLISH LANGUAGE LEARNERS

Region		Way of Life
seacoast	→	fishing
desert	→	irrigated farming
high plains	→	hunting buffalo
forest region	→	hunting, fishing, farming

TEACH OBJECTIVE 1

ALL LEVELS: Have students identify the culture areas of North America on the flowchart graphic. *(seacoast: Northwest; desert: Southwest, Great Basin, or Great Plains; high plains: Great Plains; forest region: Eastern Woodlands or Southeast)* Discuss in greater detail how climate and geography affected the cultures of these regions. *(These factors helped determine types of food and clothing, art, and religious beliefs in cultures of the regions.)*

Interdisciplinary Connection

LINGUISTICS. Scientists who study languages are known as linguists and their field of study as linguistics. These scientists examine the origins of human languages and how they are interrelated. Linguists often work closely with anthropologists to trace the origins of modern people. Before the arrival of large numbers of Europeans in the New World, about 300 Indian languages were spoken in North America. Though most of these languages were not written and some have been lost, the diversity that linguists find among the surviving languages is far greater than exists among modern European languages.

Critical Thinking

Why do you think that studying languages of various peoples helps linguists learn about their history and origins?

ANSWER: If two modern languages are closely related, the cultures to which they correspond probably had close contacts down through history. On the other hand, languages showing no similarities indicate widely separated development of cultures through history.

MAP ANSWER
Great Plains, Plateau, Great Basin

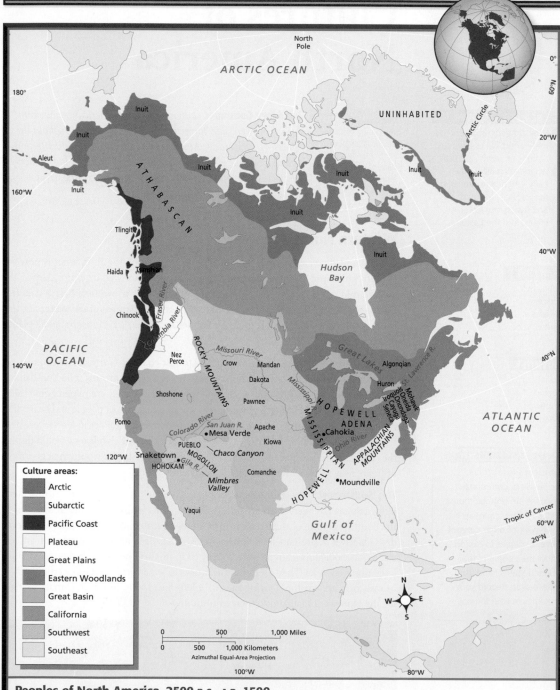

Peoples of North America, 2500 B.C.–A.D. 1500

Interpreting Maps Various groups of people settled across the North American continent, adapting to geographic conditions from the Arctic to the Southwest.

■ **Skills Assessment: Places and Regions** Which native North American cultural groups are enclosed on all sides by land?

TEACH OBJECTIVE 2

LEVEL 2: Tell students to imagine they are magazine editors working on an issue entitled "Cultures of North America." Assign one of the culture areas from the map on page 204 to students working in groups. Have each group develop a detailed outline and a magazine story on its assigned culture area.
COOPERATIVE LEARNING

 HOMEWORK Have students write a short summary explaining how geography influenced the development of cultures in North America.

TEACH OBJECTIVE 2

LEVEL 3: Have students compare the map of North America on page 204 with a map of present-day North America. Prompt them to name states or provinces that correspond approximately with native culture areas. Have students pose questions about the geographic distribution of culture areas shown on the map.

Another southwestern group, the **Pueblo,** built permanent houses with **adobe,** or sun-dried brick, and raised corn. This Zuni Pueblo tale explains how corn got its taste.

> **Primary Source**
>
> **❝**The Ashiwi [first people] tasted the food, but it was hot, like chili pepper, and they did not like it. 'It isn't fit to eat,' they said to the witches. So one at a time the witches called the crow, the owl, and the coyote, and those three tasted the crops. As the birds and the coyote ate, the food became milder and mellower, so that at last it was just right.... But from that time forth the people had to watch their fields, for the crow and the owl and the coyote like the food so much that they will steal it from the farmers if they can.**❞**
>
> Zuni tale, quoted in *American Indian Mythology*

The Great Plains. The area between the Rocky Mountains and the Mississippi River is known today as the Great Plains. The people in this region hunted the huge herds of wild **buffalo** that roamed the land. Because there were no horses in North America at the time, the Plains peoples had to hunt on foot. At times they used the jump-kill method, scaring a herd of buffalo into stampeding over a cliff. At other times the Plains peoples built corrals into which they drove the buffalo.

The Plains peoples used the buffalo for many purposes. They ate its meat. They used its hide to make clothing and to build cone-shaped tents called **tepees.** The buffalo became sacred in the religion of the Plains peoples. They held ceremonies before a hunt and gave thanks afterward.

The Plains peoples used dogs to help them carry goods such as buffalo meat. Their tools were made from bone, stone, and wood. They also made pottery. Some groups on the Plains also farmed, growing crops like beans, corn, and squash. These people lived in square or rectangular houses built in a small pit.

In about A.D. 1400 life on the Great Plains grew increasingly difficult. New peoples arrived on the plains from the north. They pushed many Plains peoples out of their homelands. In addition, a series of droughts struck the region. In some areas farming became impossible, and many people had to abandon their villages and move in order to survive.

✔ **READING CHECK: Analyzing Information** In what ways did the early peoples of western North America adapt their societies to the environment and resources available to them? food supply, housing, and materials were all taken from immediate environment

Until modern times, great herds of buffalo roamed the American plains.

Analyzing Primary Sources

Drawing Inferences In what way could this tale have been used to teach ancient farmers about good farming methods? teaches that farmers must guard against animals

YOUNG PEOPLE IN HISTORY

Young Native Americans

Even very young Native American children participated in the daily life of their tribes. Playtime usually consisted of games that imitated the roles boys and girls would have as adults. Girls played with deerskin dolls, built small tepees, and learned to sew and weave. Boys learned to hunt with small bows and arrows. Children also spent many hours with the elders of the tribe, learning the history of their people. **How did the activities of Native American children teach them to become adults?**

YOUNG PEOPLE IN HISTORY ANSWER
Native American children prepared for adult roles by playing games that imitated adult roles.

 **That's Interesting!**

The buffalo that roamed the American Great Plains probably once numbered as many as 50 million. Most were rapidly killed off after the coming of railroads to the West. By 1889, less than 1,000 buffalo were left in the entire United States. Today there are several hundred thousand. Many live on government preserves. Others are raised by ranchers.

Cahokia was the largest ceremonial center in North America. Have students imagine that they are residents of Cahokia during the city's period of greatest prosperity. Have them work in groups to create a model of the city. Ask volunteers to explain their models to the class.

COOPERATIVE LEARNING, BLOCK SCHEDULING

CLOSE

Have students identify ways archaeologists and anthropologists analyze limited evidence to determine that the chiefs of Cahokia carried on a far-flung trade. (*They might determine that goods and materials found at Cahokia came from far away.*)

SKILLS PRACTICE ANSWERS

1. People fished, hunted, or gathered food, depending on where they lived.

2. Early North American cultures relied on their environment to meet their needs.

3. Students should use information from the chapter and the chart to support their thesis statements.

VISUAL RECORD ANSWER

(from page 207)
Students might note engineering, surveying, building, and mathematical skills.

SKILL-BUILDING STRATEGIES — Formulating a Thesis Statement

Early North American Cultures

If you were going to write an essay about early North American cultures, you would start by determining what you wish to describe, explain, or prove. The information or the data you have gathered and your stated purpose help you formulate your thesis statement. A thesis statement expresses the main idea of your essay. It usually follows these criteria: 1) It is a generalization, 2) It uses significant data to express a point of view, and 3) It measures how the various parts of the data interact with or relate to each other.

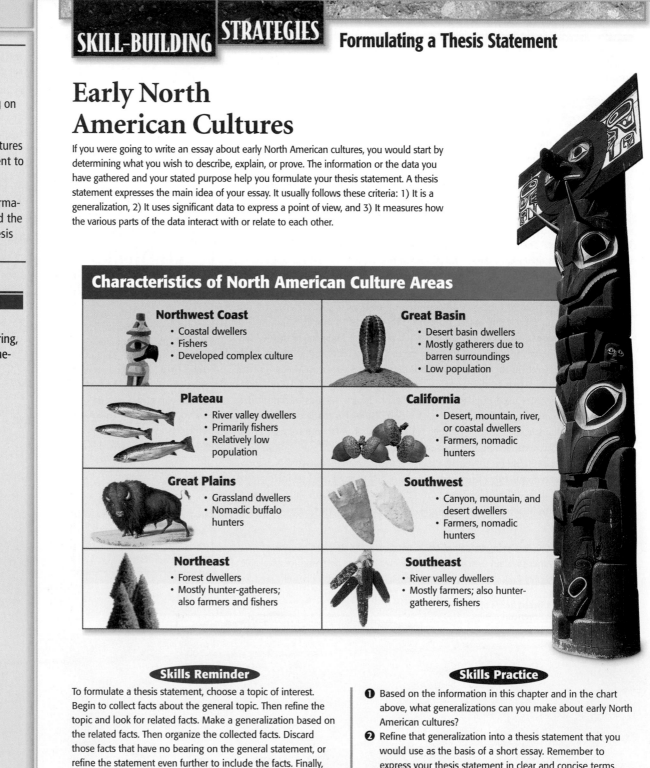

Characteristics of North American Culture Areas

Northwest Coast
- Coastal dwellers
- Fishers
- Developed complex culture

Great Basin
- Desert basin dwellers
- Mostly gatherers due to barren surroundings
- Low population

Plateau
- River valley dwellers
- Primarily fishers
- Relatively low population

California
- Desert, mountain, river, or coastal dwellers
- Farmers, nomadic hunters

Great Plains
- Grassland dwellers
- Nomadic buffalo hunters

Southwest
- Canyon, mountain, and desert dwellers
- Farmers, nomadic hunters

Northeast
- Forest dwellers
- Mostly hunter-gatherers; also farmers and fishers

Southeast
- River valley dwellers
- Mostly farmers; also hunter-gatherers, fishers

Skills Reminder

To formulate a thesis statement, choose a topic of interest. Begin to collect facts about the general topic. Then refine the topic and look for related facts. Make a generalization based on the related facts. Then organize the collected facts. Discard those facts that have no bearing on the general statement, or refine the statement even further to include the facts. Finally, refine the generalization, turning it into a thesis statement that can be proved.

Skills Practice

❶ Based on the information in this chapter and in the chart above, what generalizations can you make about early North American cultures?

❷ Refine that generalization into a thesis statement that you would use as the basis of a short essay. Remember to express your thesis statement in clear and concise terms.

❸ Using your thesis statement, write a short essay about early North American cultures.

REVIEW

Have students complete the Section 2 Review on p. 207.

ASSESS

Have students complete Daily Quiz 9.2. As Alternative Assessment, you may want to use the Characteristics of North American Culture Areas chart on p. 206.

RETEACH

Have students complete Main Idea Activity for English Language Learners and Special Needs Students 9.2. Then ask students to make flashcards with key terms from the section. Pair students and have them quiz each other using their flashcards. **COOPERATIVE LEARNING, ENGLISH LANGUAGE LEARNERS**

EXTEND

Have students research a particular Native American culture to find out what daily life was like for a young person living in that culture. Have students write and illustrate a journal entry based on their research. **COOPERATIVE LEARNING, BLOCK SCHEDULING**

The Eastern Woodlands

The Eastern Woodlands stretch from what is now Canada to the Gulf of Mexico and from the Atlantic Ocean to the Mississippi River. Some of North America's most sophisticated cultures developed in this region.

One such group, the **Hopewell,** settled in the Ohio Valley region sometime from about 300 B.C. to 200 B.C. The Hopewell left behind many earthen mounds, perhaps used for burial. Some of the mounds are in the shapes of animals. The jewelry, tools, and weapons found in the burial mounds reveal that the Hopewell were skilled artists. Objects such as grizzly bear teeth from the Rocky Mountains and shark teeth from the Gulf Coast have also been found in mounds. These objects show that trade connected diverse peoples across North America.

The **Mississippians** were another group that lived in the Eastern Woodlands region. Their culture flourished from about A.D. 700 to A.D. 1550. They lived along the Mississippi River and as far east as present-day South Carolina. Corn was their most important crop, and their successful farming methods allowed the Mississippians to develop a complex and extensive culture. Like the Hopewell before them, the Mississippians were great mound builders. Many large settlements centered around ceremonial mound constructions. In these settlements, mounds usually marked a central plaza, in the middle of which stood a temple built on a much larger mound. Outside the ceremonial centers were villages where people farmed, hunted, and fished. The city of Cahokia, located near the present-day city of East St. Louis, was the largest of the ceremonial centers of North America. Between A.D. 1050 and A.D. 1250 Cahokia was home to perhaps 30,000 people. The chiefs of Cahokia carried on a far-flung trade for copper, shells, and mica.

INTERPRETING THE VISUAL RECORD

Serpent mound This serpent-shaped mound in present-day Ohio is more than 400 yards long. It was probably built by the Adena or Hopewell people. *What skills would the builders of this mound have needed?*

✔ **READING CHECK: Evaluating** What evidence is there that Eastern Woodlands societies were advanced cultures? They established cities, conducted trade over long distances, and built earthen mounds.

SECTION 2 REVIEW

1. Define and explain the significance:
potlatches
adobe
buffalo
tepees

2. Identify and explain the significance:
Hohokam
Pueblo
Hopewell
Mississippians

3. Comparing and Contrasting Copy the chart below. Use it to compare and contrast the lives of peoples in the Pacific Northwest, the Southwest, the Great Plains, and the Eastern Woodlands.

	Achievements	Group Organization
Pacific Northwest		
Southwest		
Great Plains		
Eastern Woodlands		

4. Finding the Main Idea

a. What role did long-distance trade play in the Native American cultures of the Eastern Woodlands?

b. How was life for early Americans in the Pacific Northwest different from life in the Southwest?

5. Writing and Critical Thinking

Making Generalizations Describe the life of peoples on the Great Plains.
Consider:
• the importance of the buffalo
• problems that the Native American peoples of the Great Plains faced
• resources available in the Plains environment

Homework Practice Online
keyword: SP3 HP9

SECTION 2 REVIEW ANSWERS

❶ **Define**
• potlatches, p. 203
• adobe, p. 205
• buffalo, p. 205
• tepees, p. 205

❷ **Identify**
• Hohokam, p. 203
• Pueblo, p. 205
• Hopewell, p. 207
• Mississippians, p. 207

❸ Pacific Northwest: Achievements—fishing, weaving, woodworking, potlatches; Organization—clan or family. Southwest: Achievements—irrigation networks, cliff dwellings; Organization—pueblos. Great Plains: Achievements—hunted buffalo, made tools, made pottery, farmed; Organization—villages. Eastern Woodlands: Achievements—mound builders, skilled artists, farmers; Organization—ceremonial centers or villages

❹ **a.** Trade connected diverse peoples across North America.

b. Pacific Northwest: had abundant fish to eat, became skilled weavers and woodworkers; Southwest: lived near the Gila River, built irrigation networks

❺ Students should include the many uses of buffalo and the problems caused by droughts.

THE AMERICAS **207**

OBJECTIVES

1 Identify the characteristics of the Olmec, Toltec, and Maya cultures.

2 Explain how the Aztec and Inca built and strengthened their empires.

MAP ANSWER

Inca

READ TO DISCOVER

❶ What were the characteristics of the Olmec, Toltec, and Maya cultures?

❷ How did the Aztec and Inca build and strengthen their empires?

DEFINE

chinampas
quipu

IDENTIFY

Olmec
Chavín
Maya
Toltec
Aztec
Inca
Quechua

WHY IT MATTERS TODAY

The descendants of the earliest Americans remain active in Mexico and Peru today. Use **CNNfyi.com** or other **current event** sources to explore the lives of these people. Record your findings in your journal.

CNNfyi.com

Mesoamerica and Andean South America

The Main Idea
Mesoamerica and Peru were home to large Native American empires that made many advances.

The Story Continues *During the 1500s people from Spain came into contact with the Inca Empire in Andean South America. One Spanish priest described the idol the Inca had made to represent their sun god: "It was an impressive image . . . all worked in finest gold with a wealth of precious stones, in the likeness of a human face . . . the [sun's] rays were reflected from it so brightly that it actually seemed to be the sun." The Inca were just one of the early South American peoples to create advanced civilizations.*

Early Civilizations

By about 1500 B.C. the peoples of Mesoamerica and Andean South America lived in villages. In another 500 years, food surpluses allowed the growth of ceremonial and trading centers. Priests and high officials lived in the centers of these new cities. The common people lived in nearby farming villages.

Civilizations in Central and South America, c. 200 B.C.– A.D. 1535

Interpreting Maps
Many cultures throughout Central and South America made contributions in the areas of art, science, and religion.

■ **Skills Assessment: Places and Regions**
What civilization controlled the western coast of South America?

Olmec, c. 200 B.C.
Maya, c. A.D. 600
Toltec, c. A.D. 1100
Aztec, c. A.D. 1478
Inca, c. A.D. 1500

NORTH AMERICA
Gulf of Mexico
Tula
Teotihuacan
Chichén Itzá
Yucatán Peninsula
Tenochtitlán
15°N
Tikal
CARIBBEAN SEA
Central America
PACIFIC OCEAN
Chan Chan
MOCHE
CHAVÍN
Amazon River
SOUTH AMERICA
Machu Picchu
Cuzco
Titicaca
ANDES MOUNTAINS
0°
15°S
30°S
0   500   1,000 Miles
0   500   1,000 Kilometers
Miller Cylindrical Projection
105°W   90°W   75°W

LEVEL 1: Draw three triangles on the board and label them Olmec, Maya, and Toltec. Ask students to identify the earliest and latest civilizations. *(Olmec; Toltec)* Have students write details about each culture in the blanks at the bottom of the triangles.
COOPERATIVE LEARNING, ENGLISH LANGUAGE LEARNERS

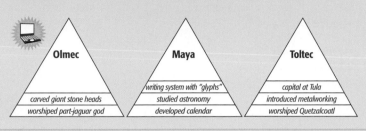

Olmec	Maya	Toltec
carved giant stone heads	writing system with "glyphs"	capital at Tula
worshiped part-jaguar god	studied astronomy	introduced metalworking
	developed calendar	worshiped Quetzalcoatl

The Olmec and Chavín. The **Olmec** civilization was the earliest of these cultures in Mexico. The Olmec flourished for about 800 years, starting in 1200 B.C. Olmec society seems to have had a large class of farmers and a small elite. This elite held military, political, and religious power. Their art suggests that the Olmec worshiped a god that was part jaguar and part human. The Olmec left behind at least 15 giant stone heads. They were carved from a stone called basalt that came from 50 miles away. The heads weigh up to 40 tons each. Only an advanced society could have developed the technology to move these stones.

About the same time that the Olmec lived in Mexico, a culture called **Chavín** developed in Andean South America. Chavín artists created ceramic religious vessels and decorated seashells with images of cats. The Olmec and Chavín cultures mysteriously disappeared between 400 B.C. and 200 B.C.

The Maya. Perhaps the most advanced people in the Americas were the **Maya.** They occupied most of the Yucatán peninsula and lands as far south as present-day El Salvador. The Maya were skilled architects and engineers. They built many steep, pyramid-shaped temples several stories tall. They also developed the only complete writing system constructed by early cultures in the Americas. The Maya writing system was based on pictographic characters called hieroglyphs, or "glyphs."

Religion lay at the heart of Maya society. Maya religion was complex and involved the worship of many gods. It was also closely tied to agriculture. One of the most important gods was the rain god. In times of drought, Maya priests might offer human sacrifices to the gods, hoping for rain.

The Maya also studied astronomy. They learned to predict solar eclipses and devised an accurate agricultural calendar. The Maya developed a counting system that included the number zero.

This Maya observatory is located in Chichén Itzá on the Yucatán Peninsula.

CONNECTING TO Science and Technology

Ancient Maya Astronomers

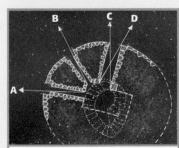

A. Due south.
B. Moon sets in south here.
C. Due west; sun sets here on the vernal equinox.
D. Moon sets in north here.

The ancient Maya considered stars and planets to be gods. They watched them to predict events on Earth that the gods controlled. As a result, the Maya made many accurate observations of the skies. They developed a 365-day calendar. They correctly figured out that the moon operates on a 29- or 30-day cycle. The planet Venus was one of the Maya's most important "stars." They determined that Venus took 584 days to reappear at the same given point on the horizon.

None of these measurements were exact, but they were all very accurate. All of this was accomplished without

sophisticated instruments. In most cases Maya temples were high enough to give observers a clear view of the horizon. Maya observatories were carefully designed and positioned. Windows were lined up with various astronomical reference and measuring points, as shown in the diagram at the left.

Understanding Science and Technology

How would the alignment of the windows in the Maya temple aid astronomers?

CONNECTING TO SCIENCE AND TECHNOLOGY ANSWER
The alignment of the windows helped the Maya observe the movement of the astronomical points.

Technology Resources
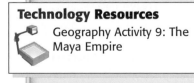
Geography Activity 9: The Maya Empire

Technology Resources
World History Teaching Transparency: Everyday Life 8

ALL LEVELS: Have small groups list characteristics of Inca and Aztec civilizations. Suggest that students consider government, social organization, religion, communications, and military organization. Then compile class lists from the group lists. **COOPERATIVE LEARNING**

LEVEL 3: Have students write short essay comparing and contrasting the Aztec and Inca civilizations.

HOMEWORK Have students list the major achievements of the Olmec, Toltec, Maya, Aztec, and Inca civilizations.

CLOSE

Have students choose one of the illustrations of art or architecture in this section and explain how it reflects the culture that produced it.

REVIEW

Have students complete the Section 3 Review on p. 211.

History Maker

TOPILTZIN. In the A.D. 900s the king of the Toltecs, Topiltzin, began building an empire in central Mexico. He introduced the cult (religion) of Quetzalcoatl and added the god's name to his own. Unfortunately, Topiltzin became involved in a civil war, and he and his followers lost. In A.D. 987, Topiltzin was forced out of Tula, the Toltec capital. According to legend, he went to Mexico's gulf coast, embarked on a raft made of snakes, and promised to return one day to save his people.

Critical Thinking

Ask students how this legend reflects the culture that produced it.

ANSWER: The legend suggests that people of later times were hoping for salvation from hardship or cruel rulers. It may also indicate that many supporters of Topiltzin remained after he was forced out of Tula.

Technology Resources

CNN Presents World Cultures: Yesterday and Today Segment 13: Inca's Frozen Past

Technology Resources

Online Maps, Charts, and Graphs: The Aztec and Inca, c. 1500

Holt Researcher

go.hrw.com
KEYWORD: Holt Researcher
FreeFind: Moctezuma II

After reading more about Moctezuma II on the Holt Researcher, assess how his religious beliefs affected his rule over the Aztec.

The Aztec Calendar Stone was used in ceremonies honoring the sun god Tonatiuh, whose face is in the center. The statue of the feathered serpent represents the god Quetzalcoatl.

In about A.D. 900 a series of catastrophes struck the Maya civilization. The population declined sharply, and people fled from the cities. Scholars believe that a variety of reasons caused this decline. Maya farming methods may have worn out the soil. Warfare between Maya city-states may have worsened. Possibly the peasants revolted and overthrew the nobles and priests.

The Toltec. In about A.D. 800 a people called the **Toltec** invaded central Mexico from the north. The Toltec were ruled by a military class. Their capital city was Tula. Their empire spread as far south as the Yucatán Peninsula. There they encountered the crumbling Maya Empire. The influence of Toltec religion and designs can be seen in the ruins of Chichén Itzá (chee·CHEN eet·sah), the chief Maya city of this era.

Like the Maya, the Toltec erected pyramid-shaped buildings. They introduced metalworking into the region. The Toltec spread the worship of their god, Quetzalcoatl (kwet·suhl·koh·AH·tl), represented by a feathered serpent. Quetzalcoatl became one of the chief gods of ancient Mexico and northern Central America. The Toltec also practiced human sacrifice. In the late A.D. 1100s Tula was destroyed, ending Toltec power.

✔ **READING CHECK: Identifying Cause and Effect** In what ways did surplus food produced by farming help civilizations grow in Mexico and Peru? allowed classes of nobles and priests to develop

The Aztec and Inca Empires

In about A.D. 1200 peoples from the north invaded central Mexico. A number of the invaders fought one another in central Mexico. Out of these struggles emerged the strongest group—the Aztec.

The Aztec. The **Aztec** had been wandering warriors. They settled on an island in Lake Texcoco and built their city, Tenochtitlán (tay·NAWCH·teht·LAHN). The Aztec gradually came to rule central Mexico. Conquered peoples paid tribute or taxes to Aztec rulers. Tenochtitlán grew to include pyramid-temples, marketplaces, and palaces for nobles and wealthy families. In the A.D. 1400s Tenochtitlán may have held up to 200,000 people or even more.

The Aztec borrowed from the cultures of the people they conquered or met. Aztec artisans learned metalworking, pottery making, and weaving. They produced fine art. The Aztec also learned to use calendars and mathematics. Like other peoples of the region they worshiped Quetzalcoatl.

Many Aztec farmed on **chinampas**—raised fields made with mud taken from the bottoms of lakes. This method increased the amount of food farmers could grow. Chinampas remain in use today.

The military dominated Aztec society. Warriors earned prestige, wealth, and power. The Aztec believed that the sun god was in a constant struggle with the forces of darkness. They wanted the sun god to stay strong so that he could bring a new day each morning. Thus the Aztec "fed" the sun god with human sacrifices. Warfare gave the Aztec a means of capturing victims to be sacrificed.

The Aztec empire had grown rapidly. However, it also declined in a short time. In the late A.D. 1400s unrest grew among surrounding peoples who had been forced to pay oppressive tribute to the Aztec, greatly weakening the empire.

ASSESS

Have students complete Daily Quiz 9.3. As Alternative Assessment, have students make fact charts for the cultures presented in the section.

RETEACH

Have students complete Main Idea Activity for English Language Learners and Special-Needs Students 9.3. Then have pairs of students prepare notes for an oral summary of Section 3.

COOPERATIVE LEARNING, ENGLISH LANGUAGE LEARNERS

EXTEND

▸ internet connect

Internet Activity: go.hrw.com
TOPIC: Machu Picchu **KEYWORD:** SP3 WH9

Have students access the Internet through the HRW Go site to research Machu Picchu. Ask students to take notes on the Inca trail, Inca history, and on the culture of Peru today. Then ask them to use the interactive template provided to create a brochure on Machu Picchu.

The Inca. During the height of Aztec power in Mexico, another civilization was growing in the Andes Mountains of South America. These people, the **Inca,** worshipped the sun and moon. Their name meant "children of the sun."

The Inca Empire expanded steadily. By the end of the A.D. 1400s, it stretched along most of the west coast of South America and far into the Andes Mountains. Inca lands included much of what is now Peru, Ecuador, Bolivia, and Chile. The empire's capital was Cuzco. The Inca emperor had absolute power but used it to improve the empire. The Inca built fortresses and irrigation systems. They laid roads, many of which were paved. Pack animals called llamas carried goods across the empire's mountainous terrain. Swift runners brought news from outlying areas to the Inca capital. Groups of relay runners could carry messages over long distances in a single day. Inca rulers constructed storehouses throughout the empire and stored surplus food to distribute when crops failed.

The Inca ruled a vast empire made up of hundreds of groups who spoke different languages. In an effort to unify these people, Inca rulers tried to eliminate regional differences. They sometimes moved entire villages to colonize new lands. The Inca established an educational system, particularly for the children of nobles. Students from all over the empire learned the imperial language and laws as well as Inca religion and history. Even today millions of people in South America speak **Quechua** (KE·chuh·wuh), once the official language of the Inca Empire. The excellent system of roads and communication also helped to unify the empire.

The Inca never developed a system of writing. Instead, they kept records by means of **quipu,** a series of knots on parallel strings. On these quipus officials stored information such as records of harvests, population numbers, and important dates. Inca technology included the capacity to produce ceramics, textiles, and metals. The Inca also became advanced in the practice of medicine. Inca surgeons used anesthetics and could even perform operations on the brain.

✔ **READING CHECK: Identifying Points of View** How did the Inca and the Aztec differ in their views of how to rule? Inca: brought conquered peoples into one imperial culture; Aztec: dominated conquered peoples militarily

HISTORY MAKER

Juanita
(c. A.D. 1400)

In 1995, scientists found a young girl's frozen body in the mountains of Peru. The young girl, whom they named Juanita, was well preserved. Her body tells us many things about Inca culture.

Juanita may have died in an Inca religious ceremony. The Inca often sacrificed children to honor the gods. There is evidence that the Inca may have put Juanita to death to stop a nearby volcano from erupting. **What does the discovery of Juanita tell us about Inca religion?**

SECTION 3 REVIEW

1. Define and explain the significance:
chinampas
quipu

2. Identify and explain the significance:
Olmec
Chavín
Maya
Toltec
Aztec
Inca
Quechua

3. Sequencing Copy the time line below. Use it to show the development of civilizations in Peru and Mexico.

1800 B.C.   Peru   A.D. 1500

1800 B.C.   Mexico   A.D. 1500

4. **Finding the Main Idea**
   a. Why did the Aztec treatment of conquered peoples differ from how the Inca treated conquered peoples?
   b. What do the giant stone heads left behind by the Olmec tell us about their society?
   c. What were the architectural and artistic achievements of the Olmec, Chavín, Maya, and Toltec civilizations?
   d. Why might the Maya culture be viewed as possibly the most advanced of the early American civilizations?
   e. What steps did the Inca take to unify their empire?

5. **Writing and Critical Thinking**
   Evaluating Assess the importance of developments in astronomy, mathematics, and architecture that developed in Mesoamerica and Andean South America.
   Consider:
   • what the major developments were
   • how they affected early Native American societies

go.hrw.com
Homework Practice Online
keyword: SP3 HP9

HISTORY MAKER ANSWER
The Inca sacrificed children in religious ceremonies.

SECTION 3 REVIEW ANSWERS

❶ Define
• chinampas, p. 210
• quipu, p. 211

❷ Identify
• Olmec, p. 209
• Chavín, p. 209
• Maya, p. 209
• Toltec, p. 210
• Aztec, p. 210
• Inca, p. 211
• Quechua, p. 211

❸ Peru: include Chavín's disappearance, Incan expansion; Mexico: include Olmec culture, decline of Mayan culture

❹ a. Aztec used power to dominate. Inca used power to unify.

b. discovered way to move the stones

c. Olmec: giant stone heads; Chavín: ceramic religious vessels; Maya: pyramid-shaped temples; Toltec: pyramid-shaped temples

d. skilled architects and engineers; developed a writing system, agricultural calendar, and a counting system

e. tried to eliminate regional differences; urged villages to colonize new lands; organized an educational system

❺ Students' answers should include major developments and their significance.

CHAPTER 9

REVIEW AND ASSESSMENT RESOURCES

REPRODUCIBLE RESOURCES

▶ Vocabulary Activity 9

TECHNOLOGY RESOURCES

▶ Chapter 9 Test Generator (on the One-Stop Planner)
▶ Global Skill Builder CD–ROM
▶ HRW Web Site

REINFORCEMENT, REVIEW, and ASSESSMENT

▶ Chapter 9 Review, pp. 212–213
▶ Chapter 9 Tutorial for Students, Parents, Mentors, and Peers
▶ Chapter 9 Test (Form A or B)
▶ Alternative Assessment Handbook
▶ Chapter 9 Test for English Language Learners and Special-Needs Students

REVIEW

Have students complete the Chapter 9 Review on pages 212–213.

ASSESS

Use one of the chapter tests to assess students' understanding of the content. For Alternative Assessment, see the Portfolio Activities and Alternative Assessment Handbook.

CHAPTER 9 REVIEW ANSWERS

Understanding Main Ideas

1. Water trapped in glaciers during the Ice Age created a land bridge that Asians used to migrate to North America.

2. Agriculture ensured a stable and reliable food supply that allowed population growth.

3. Native Americans never invented the plow, lacked domesticated animals to pull farming vehicles, and used simple digging sticks to plant seeds.

4. extensive irrigation networks

5. New peoples arrived from the north, pushing many Plains peoples out of their homelands. Droughts made farming impossible in some places.

6. perhaps to use for burial

7. worshiped many gods, closely tied to agriculture, included human sacrifices

8. They wanted the sun to stay strong so that it could bring a new day each morning.

9. built fortresses, irrigation systems, paved roads, and storehouses to store surplus food

Reviewing Themes

1. The Bering Strait became a land bridge called Beringia.

2. prediction of solar eclipses, accurate calendar, counting system that included zero, irrigation systems, paved roads

3. They forced oppressive tributes.

212

CHAPTER 9 Review

Creating a Time Line

Copy the time line below onto a sheet of paper. Complete the time line by filling in the events, individuals, and dates from the chapter that you think were significant. Pick three events and explain why you think they were significant.

| 1800 B.C. | A.D. 1 | A.D. 1500 |

Writing a Summary

Using standard grammar, spelling, sentence structure, and punctuation, write an overview of the events in the chapter.

Identifying People and Ideas

Identify the following terms or individuals and explain their significance:

1. strait
2. Beringia
3. potlatches
4. adobe
5. Hohokam
6. Pueblo
7. Hopewell
8. Mississippians
9. Olmec
10. Chavín
11. Toltec
12. chinampas
13. Quechua
14. quipu

Understanding Main Ideas

Section 1 *(pp. 200–202)*

The Earliest Americans

1. How do scholars explain the arrival of people in the Americas, and what role did climate changes play in allowing migrations to the Americas?
2. In what ways did the development of farming allow people to form towns and cities?
3. In what ways did farming in the Americas differ from farming in other parts of the world?

Section 2 *(pp. 203–207)*

Cultures of North America

4. What methods did the Hohokam use to enable their farming communities to flourish in a dry climate?
5. Why were the A.D. 1400s difficult years on the Great Plains?
6. Why did the Hopewell and Mississippian peoples build mounds?

Section 3 *(pp. 208–211)*

Mesoamerica and Andean South America

7. What were the religious beliefs of the Maya?
8. Why did the Aztec sacrifice human beings?
9. How did Inca rulers work to improve their empire?

Reviewing Themes

1. **Geography** How did climate changes allow for migration into the Western Hemisphere?
2. **Science, Technology & Society** What ideas in astronomy, mathematics, and architectural engineering developed in Mesoamerica and Peru?
3. **Government** Why did the Aztec face revolts from the people they had conquered?

Thinking Critically

1. **Evaluating** Why do scholars know less about American civilizations than about those that developed in Asia or Europe at the same time?
2. **Contrasting** How did civilizations in North America differ from those in Mexico and in Peru?
3. **Supporting a Point of View** Which civilization was more effective in dealing with conquered people, the Inca or the Aztec? Explain.
4. **Identifying Cause and Effect** What role did military force and invasion play in shaping civilizations in the Western Hemisphere?

Writing About History

Comparing Write a report describing the similarities and differences between the Great Plains peoples and the Aztec. Use the chart below to organize your thoughts before writing.

	Great Plains	Aztec
Food resources		
Buildings		
Religious beliefs		

CLOSE

Have each student prepare an answer to the following question: What do you consider the most significant achievement of early cultures in the Americas?

RETEACH

Have students who had difficulty with the test rewrite each question that they missed and use their textbooks to answer the questions in complete sentences. When students are ready, have them take the Form B Test to assess their mastery of the material.

ENGLISH LANGUAGE LEARNERS

Portfolio Extensions

Link to TODAY

1. Have students work in groups to write a proposal for a new business in their community. Have them use a decision-making process to determine whether the business is suited to the geography of their region. Students should gather information, identify options, and predict the consequences of starting their proposed business.

2. Ask students to choose a Native American culture of North America and list its characteristics. Then have them indicate how each characteristic is related to the geographic region in which the culture lived.

3. Have students create a chart summarizing the ideas in astronomy, mathematics, and architectural engineering that developed in Mesoamerica and Andean South America.

Building Social Studies Skills

Using Artifacts as Historical Evidence

Study the image of Aztec artifacts below. Then answer the questions that follow.

Aztec plates, platter, and water pitcher from the late 1400s

1. Which of the following statements best summarizes the historical evidence these artifacts give?
   a. The Aztec preferred red pottery.
   b. Many Aztec had sets of dinnerware for formal occasions.
   c. The Aztec had high-quality pottery that was sometimes made for serving food.
   d. The Aztec used plates but not cups.

2. What clues do the objects in the photograph give about the lifestyle of the Aztec? Give reasons for your answer.

Categorizing Information

Read the paragraph below. Then answer the questions that follow.

Archaeologists and historians have learned much from the main cities of the Maya, Aztec, and Inca cultures. Teotihuacán, the Maya city, is located about 25 miles northeast of Mexico City. Artifacts show that the Maya had a writing system, studied astronomy, and had an accurate calendar. The Aztec city of Tenochtitlán was located on the site of present-day Mexico City. The city had a system of canals and aqueducts to bring water. Metalwork and pottery have also been found. Cuzco in southern Peru was the main city of the Inca. Artifacts show that the Inca were master builders with stone, did fine metalwork, and were advanced in the medical arts.

3. Which of the following gives the best categories for organizing the information in the paragraph?
   a. Culture, Government, City, Achievements
   b. Culture, City, Location, Achievements
   c. City, Location, Religion, Artifacts
   d. City, Location, Achievements

4. Use the information you have gained from Chapter 9 to identify other information about these three cultures that would fit in the categories you have chosen. Give specific examples.

Alternative Assessment

Building Your Portfolio

Link to TODAY

Geography

Just as with early American societies, the cultures of people in the world today vary based on geography. Choose one African country, one Asian country, and one northern European country. Create a list of ways in which people in these different places have adapted their economies and lifestyles to the geographic region in which they live. Create a chart to summarize your findings.

internet connect

Internet Activity: go.hrw.com
KEYWORD: SP3 WH9

Choose a topic on the Americas to:
- research Inca history and take a virtual hike to Machu Picchu.
- learn Maya number glyphs and calculate your birthday.
- explore Olmec art, architecture, and culture.

go.hrw.com

Thinking Critically

1. Many American civilizations did not have written languages.

2. Mexico and Peru: built large pyramid-temples, devised accurate calendars and counting systems, had more complex civilizations

3. Answers will vary. The Inca tried to eliminate regional differences.

4. Invaders pushed the Great Plains people off their land; Toltec invaded central Mexico; Aztec were warriors; Inca conquered and built an empire.

Writing About History

Great Plains: food—buffalo, beans, corn, and squash; buildings—tepees; religion—the buffalo

Aztec: food—crops; buildings—pyramid-temples, palaces, marketplaces; religion—worshiped sun god, practiced human sacrifice

Building Social Studies Skills

1. c

2. possible answers: advanced technology, appreciation for art, and social customs

3. d

4. Students should include additional information about Maya, Aztec, and Inca cultures.

Building Your Portfolio

Students' charts may include economy, government, religion, daily life, climate, and geography.

CROSS-CULTURAL CONNECTIONS *Literature*

Spotlight on LITERATURE

Morality plays and tales involve a direct conflict between good and evil and teach a moral lesson. These stories, which were popular in Europe during the 1400s and 1500s, focus on a hero who faces diabolic forces. Have students research morality plays, such as *Everyman*, or morality tales, such as *Pilgrim's Progress*. Ask them to identify the plot and the universal theme of the story. (*Our journey through life involves many struggles.*)

Spotlight on LITERATURE

In 1952 Pierre-François-Marie-Louis Boulle wrote *The Bridge on the River Kwai*, a tale of morality among British troops in a Japanese prison camp. In 1957 the story was adapted to an award-winning movie. Have students research *The Bridge on the River Kwai* and tell how it depicts the triumph of human spirit in times of war. (*Captured prisoners of war refuse to give in to the demands of their enemies to build a bridge. Later they build the bridge for the Japanese, only to eventually destroy it.*)

Culture

Every culture reflects prevailing attitudes toward life through myths, fables, morality tales, or other literary means. Fables are brief narratives about wise or foolish actions that teach a moral lesson. Aesop, credited with some of the most well-known fables, is believed to have lived in Greece between 620 and 560 B.C. The *Panchatantra,* composed in about 200 B.C., is the oldest known collection of Indian fables. These tales are described as a textbook on the wise conduct of life and are much lengthier than Aesop's fables. Jean de La Fontaine was a seventeenth-century French poet who wrote fables in verse form. Each fable, drawn largely from Aesop, is a short tale of beasts behaving like humans. Each fable comments on human behavior.

ACTIVITY: Have students find examples of fables from ancient cultures. Then have students compare the content, the moral lesson, and the way the story is presented.

UNDERSTANDING LITERATURE ANSWER

Both men showed a curiosity about nature. Neither Icarus nor the man who loved frog songs showed self-restraint. Icarus didn't listen to the advice of his father. The man was too curious about the frog songs. Both stories had tragic endings.

CROSS-CULTURAL CONNECTIONS *Literature*

Morality Tales

Stories that answer the question "How should we behave?" are called morality tales. These teaching tales pass down a culture's ideas about avoiding foolish mistakes and making good choices. Different cultures often expressed similar values in their morality tales. Metamorphoses, written by the Roman poet Ovid (43 B.C.–A.D. 17), retells the ancient Greek myth of Icarus and his father, Daedalus, who attempt to escape from captivity by fashioning birds' wings with which to fly. Ovid's telling of the Icarus myth reflects the Greek belief in the dangers of hubris, or excessive pride that causes individuals to reach beyond their limits. American Indian tales had similar themes. A story from the Menominee, who lived in the Great Lakes region, tells of a man who loved frog songs and lay down on the ground to better hear them. "The Man Who Loved the Frog Songs" teaches self-restraint and respect for nature by describing the consequences of failing to honor these values.

Scene depicting Icarus's fall

Metamorphoses *by Ovid*

[Daedalus] schemed and planned, made small drawings, and . . . started to build an object of feathers and wax by means of which he might perhaps take wing, leap up in the air, and glide through it to swoop and swim in the sky like a gull. . . . At last, with two pairs of wings completed, [Daedalus] told the boy how he had planned their escape and what to do and what to avoid. "Do not fly too low, where the sea spray can soak your wings and make the feathers soggy and heavy. But don't go too high, where the heat of the Sun's fire can melt the wax. Keep to a middle range if you can, and don't try

to show off—it isn't a game but a matter of life and death." . . . [Icarus] flaps his wings and rises higher—but nothing bad happens. He figures he still has plenty of margin and rises higher still. It's exciting, wonderful fun, as he soars and wheels, but he doesn't notice the wax on his wings is melting and feathers are falling out. . . . He is falling. He cries out. His father hears him, and watches in horror the plummeting body splash into the sea that takes its name from its victim.

"The Man Who Loved the Frog Songs" by the Menominee

In the morning, when he woke up, the frogs spoke to him, saying, "We are not happy, but in a very deep sadness. You seem to like our crying, but our reason for weeping is this: in early spring, when we first thaw out and revive, we wail for our dead, because many of us do not wake up from our winter sleep. Now you will cry in your turn as we did!" True enough, the next spring the man's wife and children all died, and the man himself died too, in payment for his having been too curious to hear the frogs.

Early Native American carving of a frog

| **Understanding Literature** | What similar themes do you see between the stories of Icarus and the man who loved frog songs? |

Government

Write the following chart on the board and ask students to describe the role of each group in the government of Greek city-states. Challenge students to compare these roles with those of government leaders and citizens today.

Kings	Aristocrats	Tyrants	Citizens
depended on landowners, who gained more power and eventually overcame kings	nobles controlled military, economy, laws; hoplites defended cities; tyrants took power	fair tyrants promoted trade; unjust tyrants were overthrown by citizens	male citizens took part in government; women and slaves not citizens

Global Relations

Have students work with partners to list the various causes that led to the decline of the Western Empire and ways some emperors attempted reform. Then have them work together to use a problem-solving process to identify a problem, list options, consider advantages and disadvantages, and choose a solution. Have them write a newspaper article describing the problem and suggesting a solution.

BUILDING YOUR Portfolio

Government

Studying the governments of earlier civilizations helps historians to understand how and why these governments succeeded or failed. Imagine that you are a writer living in the city-state of Athens. Your task is to write a history of the Athenian government from its origins to the rise of democracy, and to explain the role of the Athenian citizen in government. How might this information help modern governments? How would you organize your history, and what information would you include?

Relief of a Roman legionnaire and an attacking barbarian

Temple of Athena Nike on the Acropolis of Athens

Global Relations

There was no single cause for the decline of the Roman Empire; instead a number of events and circumstances helped bring about the demise of Rome. Imagine that you are an envoy of the Emperor of Rome during the last years of Roman dominance. You have been sent on a mission to document the condition of the empire. Prepare a journal that will be used in writing a detailed report on the problems the empire faces. Your journal should include information that explains how and why Rome has failed to manage its empire.

Further Reading

Adkins, Lesley and Roy A. Adkins. *Handbook to Life in Ancient Rome.* New York: Facts on File, 1994. An overview of different aspects of life in Rome.

Connoly, Peter and Hazel Dodge. *The Ancient City: Life in Classical Athens and Rome.* New York: Oxford University Press, 1998. Everyday life in ancient Greece and Rome is the subject of this book.

Fagan, Mark. *Kingdoms of Gold, Kingdoms of Jade: The Americas Before Columbus.* London: Thames and Hudson, 1991. A history of the Americas before 1492.

Koslow, Philip. *Centuries of Greatness: The West African Kingdoms 750-1900.* A vast and comprehensive survey that looks at the politics, military, and culture of West African kingdoms.

Martin, Thomas R. *Ancient Greece from Prehistoric to Hellenistic Times.* New Haven: Yale University Press, 1996. An overview of life and culture in Ancient Greece.

internet connect

Internet Activity
KEYWORD: SP3 U2

In assigned groups, develop a multimedia presentation about civilizations in Greece, Rome, Africa, and the Americas. Choose information from the chapter Internet Connect activities and the Holt Researcher that best reflects the major topics of the period. Write an outline and a script for your presentation, which may be shown to the class.

go.hrw.com

Interdisciplinary Connection

LITERATURE. An allusion is a brief reference to a person, event, or thing in history or from a previous work of literature. It is used to suggest far more than what it actually says. Several references often used as allusions come from the era of the Roman Empire. Julius Caesar described his campaign and eventual defeat of Pompey with the words *Veni, vidi, vici,* which means "I came, I saw, I conquered." Caesar was assassinated on March 15 (the Ides of March). When he saw that he had been stabbed by Marcus Brutus, a man he had trusted, Caesar said *"Et tu, Brute"* ("You too, Brutus"). William Shakespeare made some of these phrases famous in his play *Julius Caesar.*

Critical Thinking

Ask students to suggest times when they or classmates may use some of the sentences listed above as allusions and why. Then ask them to explain what the reference "Nero fiddled while Rome burned" alludes to.

ANSWER: Answers will vary but may include that *"Veni, vidi, vici"* is used at athletic events to show pride in winning. "Beware the Ides of March" may be used to refer to an upcoming event that may have ominous outcomes. Nero is blamed for a fire that swept Rome. The allusion might refer to someone who does nothing about a catastrophic situation.

EXAMINING THE VISUAL RECORD

❶ What cultural clues about the Sung dynasty are evident in this painting?

ANSWER: Students may mention clothing, hairstyles, and the importance of cultural pursuits.

The Sung dynasty was a period of remarkable cultural achievement in Chinese history. Artists excelled in literature, music, the decorative arts, and architecture. For example, Sung architects were particularly noted for their creation of tall pagodas. These six- or eight-sided structures, reaching as high as 360 feet (110m), have roofs that curve upward at the corners. Some Sung pagodas have survived to the present day.

❷ What does this painting suggest about the importance of literature in Chinese society?

ANSWER: It was highly valued.

The improvement of printing methods and the creation of public schools throughout China led to a significant increase in literary output during the Sung dynasty. In particular, many short tales called *ku-wen* were written. Sung poets created a new type of poetry called *tz'u*, which were sung poems that expressed both joy and despair. They became the distinctive literary form of the Sung dynasty.

ACTIVITY: Ask students to use primary and secondary sources to research cultural achievements during the Sung dynasty that express universal themes.

UNIT 3 The World in Transition

395–1589

the 1200s the nomadic Mongols invaded China and brought economic growth, governmental reorganization, and more contact with Europeans. The Japanese developed a feudal political system and distinctive forms of literature and art. Chinese culture and religion influenced Japan, as well as Korea and Southeast Asia.

◆CHAPTER◆ **13** The Rise of the Middle Ages

The period after the collapse of the Roman Empire—about 500 to 1500—is called the Middle Ages. During this period, barbarian tribes created small, weak kingdoms in Europe. Under Charlemagne, the Franks emerged as the most powerful of these kingdoms. Medieval life was organized around a political system called feudalism and an economic system known as the manorial system. The Catholic Church had great influence and power in both spiritual and secular matters.

◆CHAPTER◆ **14** The High Middle Ages

During the late Middle Ages, western Europe underwent a number of significant changes. The Crusades brought new ideas and goods to the continent. This helped increase trade, which led to the development of a new economic system and encouraged the growth of towns and cities. Medieval culture flourished despite the fact that Europeans engaged in almost continuous warfare. Strong monarchies developed in England, France, and Spain, while the Holy Roman Empire remained disunited.

Main Events
- The rise of the Byzantine Empire
- The development of Islamic religion and culture
- The development of Asian civilizations
- The beginning of the Middle Ages
- The cultural conflict of the Crusades

Main Ideas
- What was the Byzantine Empire?
- What were some of the characteristics of the Islamic world?
- What effect did the Mongol Empire have on the civilizations of Eastern Asia?
- What was life like in the Middle Ages? How did the Crusades change medieval culture?

Islamic engraved globe, c. 1067

Main Events
Ask students to select two Main Events and list questions they would like to have answered about the topics. Later, when you have completed Unit 3, ask students to return to their original questions and write an answer using the information they learned in the unit.

Main Ideas
Ask each student to read the Main Ideas and write brief answers to the questions. Share the *Consider* points with students as necessary. Later, when you have completed Unit 3, ask students to analyze their original answers by comparing them to information they learned in the unit. Tell them to revise or expand their answers as necessary.

Characteristics of the Byzantine Empire and the Islamic World
Consider:
- the religious and cultural influence of the Byzantine Empire
- Muslim achievements in science, art, and literature

The Effects of Mongol Invasions and the Crusades
Consider:
- the changes Mongol rule brought to China
- political and economic changes in Europe

This painting from the period of China's Sung dynasty (c. 1000) shows scholars organizing literature. **217**

CROSS-CULTURAL CONNECTIONS

Focus On: Culture

📢 LET'S GET STARTED!

As students enter the classroom, ask them to make a list of the defining characteristics of their culture. Have students keep their lists to compare with cultural characteristics of other societies that they will read about in Cross-Cultural Connections. Tell students that in this unit they will learn about unique elements of culture in the Byzantine Empire, the Islamic Empire, Japan, and medieval Europe.

ALL LEVELS: Have students read the Cross-Cultural Connections text and fill out the graphic organizer below with cultural examples and religious sources. Tell students that religion is an important and common source of cultural expression in many societies.

ENGLISH LANGUAGE LEARNERS

Byzantine Empire	Islamic Empire	Japan	Medieval Europe
icons	calligraphy	tea ceremony	cathedrals
Eastern Orthodox	Islam	Zen Buddhism	Catholicism

Interdisciplinary Connection

BYZANTINE ART. Religion was the central focus of art in the Byzantine Empire. The Byzantine style of architecture and painting remained remarkably consistent from the 500s to the 1400s. Architectural and pictorial expression became inseparable, as frescoes and mosaics decorated the interior walls and ceilings of churches. The iconographic style of these art forms is defined by the use of lines and flat areas of color, rather than realistic form. Instead of a three-dimensional human figure, the viewer confronts a spiritual force expressed through energetic lines and vibrant color.

Critical Thinking

Compare Byzantine art with classical Greek art. How are the styles different and how do they reflect different purposes?

ANSWER: Byzantine art is flat and uses dynamic lines and color; Greek art is representational of the human figure. The Byzantine style evokes a spiritual presence; the Greek style celebrates the beauty of the human form.

CROSS-CULTURAL CONNECTIONS

Focus On: Culture

Main Idea What is culture? Many different elements make up a society's culture including art, music, literature, religious beliefs, and institutions of government and education. No two cultures are exactly alike—each develops unique traditions and beliefs. The societies in this unit all developed unique cultural traits that still define many groups descended from them today.

Japan

Byzantine Empire and Russia

Islamic Empire

Medieval Europe

395   432   552   570   1250   1573   1500   1589

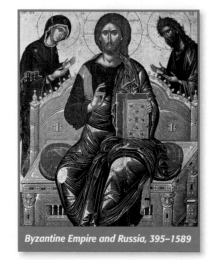

Byzantine Empire and Russia, 395–1589

Icons Beginning in the 500s, icons, or holy images, played an important role in public and private religious life in the Byzantine Empire. Enemies saw icons as a form of idol worship. For believers, however, these images were a way to get close to God. Most icons were painted on wood, but some were also made of gold or ivory. Icons came in all sizes, from large screens that decorated churches to small images that could be carried in a pocket. Most homes had at least one icon, and they were displayed during important public ceremonies. In 726 Emperor Leo III outlawed the use of icons. However, they remained an important part of Byzantine culture. This icon showing Jesus gazing at the viewer reflects the typical Byzantine style of iconographic religious art.

Calligraphers often kept their valuable pens and inks in special boxes. In some instances, scribes even had their pens and inks buried with them.

Calligraphy In Islamic culture, calligraphy is considered a great art form. This style of fine handwriting first developed in Arabic culture in the 500s, before the rise of Islam. Later, Islamic scribes, or writers, made copies of the Qur'an with calligraphy. Scribes also used calligraphy in government documents, books, and inscriptions for buildings, palaces, and tombs. Calligraphers studied with a master for many years to learn their skill, usually specializing in two or three of the six classic styles. One style included beautiful floral designs and geometric patterns. In another technique, scribes worked words into the shapes of animals or objects. Whatever the form, calligraphy was the most highly valued art form in the Islamic world. The document pictured here is a copy of the Qur'an created in the 1300s.

Islamic Empire, 570–1250

REVIEW

Have students review the information about cultural expression in various societies. Ask them to use standard grammar, spelling, sentence structure, and punctuation to answer the question in "Why It Matters Today" and to share their answers with the class.

ASSESS

Have students complete their answer to the question in "Why It Matters Today" and add it to their portfolio. As Alternative Assessment, use the graphic organizer in this lesson.

EXTEND

Have students work in groups to prepare a cultural review of one of the societies discussed in Unit 3. Tell students to use information from their textbooks, the library, computer software, and any other available resources to research their society's culture. Groups should make a visual presentation that includes tangible items such as food, photographs, and/or illustrations of the cultural characteristics of their chosen society. **BLOCK SCHEDULING, COOPERATIVE LEARNING**

Tea Ceremonies Tea began its important role in Japanese culture in the 1100s, when Buddhist priests brought back tea leaves from China. During the Kamakura period (1192–1600), monks first practiced tea drinking as a way to stay awake during long meditations. Later, other members of society, such as shoguns, samurai, and merchants, began drinking tea. In the late 1500s a formal tea tradition developed in Japan. During these tea ceremonies, people gathered in a special room isolated from the rest of the house. Sometimes while drinking their tea, they would listen to poetry or quietly think about a piece of art. Tea ceremonies offered the Japanese a means of spiritual reflection and a way to leave behind the world's worries.

Japan, 552–1573

Medieval Europe, 432–1500

◀ **Cathedrals** During the Middle Ages cathedrals were the ultimate architectural expression of Christian faith in Europe. Between the 1100s and 1500s, this new church architecture created high ceilings and beautiful stained glass windows that provided more space and light than older churches. Intricate carvings inside and outside the cathedrals completed these inspiring works of art. Building cathedrals required the help of the entire community. Wealthy community members donated money. Artisans created intricate carvings and sculpture, and peasants and laborers provided the backbreaking work to build the structure. Cathedrals often took more than a century to complete. Inside the great cathedrals, such as the one shown here, the faithful could not help but feel they were closer to heaven.

Sculptors often carved horrible-looking creatures known as gargoyles on cathedrals with the belief that they would help scare away demons.

Why It Matters Today

Cultural differences often led to conflict during the Middle Ages. Yet contact between cultures also increased knowledge and led to new developments. Cultural exchange continues to take place today. **What examples of beneficial cultural exchanges do you see in the world today? What are some examples of cultural conflict?**

History Maker

SEN RIKYU. During the 1500s Sen Rikyu created a formal tea ceremony that became a national art form in Japan. The ceremony is based on the principles of Zen Buddhism. While Sen attended the court of military dictator Toyotomi Hideyoshi, he developed a style known as *wabi*. Still popular in Japan today, *wabi* emphasizes four qualities—harmony, respect, cleanliness, and tranquility. Using simplicity as the ceremony's fundamental concept, Sen defined the rules of procedure, the utensils to be used, the teahouse architecture, and the tea garden landscaping. For his contributions, Sen Rikyu is regarded as one of the greatest figures in Japanese cultural history.

Critical Thinking

Why do you think the concept of simplicity is the basis of the tea ceremony?

ANSWER: Answers will vary, but students may suggest that simplicity allows for better focus or meditation during the ceremony.

WHY IT MATTERS TODAY ANSWER

Answers will vary, but examples include benefits—international organizations addressing global issues, exchange of knowledge, increased tolerance for other cultures; conflicts—Middle East, Balkans, terrorist attacks on September 11, 2001.

The Byzantine Empire and Russia

CHAPTER RESOURCE MANAGER

Objectives	Pacing Guide	Reproducible Resources
SECTION 1 **The Byzantine Empire** (pp. 222–228) • Identify the factors that contributed to the growth and strength of the Byzantine Empire. • Explain how the Christian church came to be divided. • Analyze the cultural contributions made by the Byzantines. • Explain the factors that contributed to the downfall of the Byzantine Empire.	**Regular** 1.5 day **Block Scheduling** 1 day *Block Scheduling Handbook with Team Teaching Strategies, 10.1*	**RS** Guided Reading Strategy 10.1 **RS** Graphic Organizer Activity 10: The Byzantines **SM** Geography Activity 10: Constantinople–Crossroads of Europe and Asia **PS** Readings in World History 29: Justinian's Code **PS** Readings in World History 30: Justinian Puts Down a Rebellion
SECTION 2 **The Rise of Russia** (pp. 229–232) • Explain why different peoples settled in eastern Europe. • Describe how Kievan Russia differed from the Byzantine Empire.	**Regular** 1.5 day **Block Scheduling** 1 day *Block Scheduling Handbook with Team Teaching Strategies, 10.2*	**RS** Guided Reading Strategy 10.2 **PS** Readings in World History 31: The *Pravda Russkaia* **E** Hands-on History Activity 10: Food and Fashion in Byzantium and Early Russia
SECTION 3 **Russia and the Mongols** (pp. 233–235) • Identify the ways in which Mongol rule affected Kievan Russia. • Describe the effects of Moscow's growing power and independence.	**Regular** 1 day **Block Scheduling** .5 day *Block Scheduling Handbook with Team Teaching Strategies, 10.3*	**RS** Guided Reading Strategy 10.3 **PS** Readings in World History 32: Ivan the Terrible's Punishment of Novgorod **E** Creative Teaching Strategy 10: Barbarian Information Agency

Chapter Resource Key

PS Primary Sources	**REV** Review	Video	**One-Stop** Planner CD-ROM
RS Reading Support	**ELL** Reinforcement and English Language Learners	Internet	See the *One-Stop Planner*
IC Interdisciplinary Connections		Holt Presentation Maker Using Microsoft® PowerPoint®	for a complete list of additional resources for students and teachers.
E Enrichment	Transparencies		
SM Skills Mastery	CD-ROM		
A Assessment	Music		

One-Stop Planner CD-ROM

It's easy to plan lessons, select resources, and print out materials for your students when you use the **One-Stop Planner** CD–ROM with **Test Generator.**

Technology Resources

- One-Stop Planner 10.1
- Holt Researcher: World History: Justinian, Theodora
- World History and Cultures Video Program 9: The Russian Orthodox Church
- World History Teaching Transparency: Geography and History 9: Roman Catholicism and Orthodoxy
- World History Teaching Transparency: Everyday Life 9: The Role of the Byzantine Emperor
- World History Teaching Transparency: Art and History 9: Sant' Apollinare in Classe, Apse Mosaic
- Homework Practice Online
- Online Maps, Charts, and Graphs: Growth of the Byzantine Empire, 1050

- One-Stop Planner 10.2
- Holt Researcher: World History: Rurik
- Regions of the World Music Audio CD Program 9: Russia, Ukraine, and Belarus: Russian Choral Music
- Homework Practice Online
- Online Maps, Charts, and Graphs: Kiev as a Strategic City, 1000s

- One-Stop Planner 10.3
- Homework Practice Online
- Online Maps, Charts, and Graphs: Russian Expansion, 1533

Reinforcement, Review, and Assessment

Daily Quiz 10.1
Main Idea Activity 10.1
English Audio Summary 10.1
Spanish Audio Summary 10.1
REV Section 1 Review, p. 228

Daily Quiz 10.2
Main Idea Activity 10.2
English Audio Summary 10.2
Spanish Audio Summary 10.2
REV Section 2 Review, p. 232

Daily Quiz 10.3
Main Idea Activity 10.3
English Audio Summary 10.3
Spanish Audio Summary 10.3
REV Section 3 Review, p. 235

internet connect

HRW ONLINE RESOURCES
GO TO: go.hrw.com
Then type in a keyword.

TEACHER HOME PAGE
KEYWORD: SP3 Teacher

CHAPTER INTERNET ACTIVITIES
KEYWORD: SP3 WH10
Choose an activity to:
- summarize the global influence of the Roman ideas in the Justinian Code upon contemporary political issues such as individual rights and responsibilities.
- research Ivan IV and find out why he was called "Ivan the Terrible."
- create a piece of art or design a building or church in the Byzantine style.

CHAPTER ENRICHMENT LINKS
KEYWORD: SP3 CH10

ONLINE ASSESSMENT
Homework Practice
KEYWORD: SP3 HP10
Standardized Test Prep
KEYWORD: SP3 STP10
Rubrics
KEYWORD: SS Rubrics

ONLINE MAPS, CHARTS, AND GRAPHS
KEYWORD: SP3 MCG

CONTENT UPDATES
KEYWORD: SS Content Updates

HOLT PRESENTATION MAKER
KEYWORD: SP3 PPT10

ONLINE READING SUPPORT
KEYWORD: SS Strategies

CURRENT EVENTS
KEYWORD: S3 Current Events

Meeting Individual Needs

Ability Levels

Level 1 Basic level activities designed for all students encountering new material

Level 2 Intermediate level activities designed for average students

Level 3 Challenging activities designed for honors and gifted and talented students

English Language Learners These activities address the needs of students with Limited English Proficiency.

Chapter Review and Assessment

- IC Vocabulary Activity 10
- Global Skill Builder CD–ROM
- HRW Web Site
- REV Chapter 10 Tutorial for Students, Parents, Mentors, and Peers
- REV Chapter 10 Review, pp. 236–237

- A Chapter 10 Test Generator (on the One-Stop Planner)
- A Chapter 10 Test (Form A or B)
- A Alternative Assessment Handbook
- A Chapter 10 Test for English Language Learners and Special-Needs Students

Build on What You Know

Ask students to answer the following questions:

What were some of the achievements of the Roman Empire?

Consider:

- science and engineering
- literature
- language

What factors led to the decline of the Roman Empire?

Consider:

- invaders
- the economy
- social change

EXPLORING THE TIME LINE
GLOBAL EVENTS

▣ **internet** connect ≣

TOPIC: First Russian Czar

GO TO: go.hrw.com

KEYWORD: SP3 WH10

Have students access the Internet through the HRW Go site to conduct research on Yaroslav I, one of the great leaders of Russia and remembered as Yaroslav the Wise. Yaroslav the Wise introduced Russia's first law code, the *Pravda Russkia*. Have students write a biography of Yaroslav the Wise. The biography should include some facts about the country Yaroslav ruled, his greatest accomplishments, and why he is remembered today.

CHAPTER 10

A.D. 395–A.D. 1589

The Byzantine Empire and Russia

A.D. 395
Global Events
The Roman Empire splits into the Eastern Roman Empire and the Western Roman Empire.

A.D. 535
Politics
Belisarius occupies the Ostrogoth kingdom in Italy.

A.D. 600
The Arts
Coptic art—a combination of Byzantine, Egyptian, Arab, and Greek styles—has developed.

A.D. 900
Science and Technology
Vikings have highly developed shipbuilding.

C. A.D. 900s
Business and Finance
The Italian cities of Venice and Genoa begin to develop as maritime trading powers.

A.D. 300 ———————— **A.D. 550** ———————— **A.D. 800**

A.D. 425
Politics
Germanic tribes settle in western Roman provinces.

A.D. 553 Business and Finance
The Byzantine Empire attempts to monopolize the silk industry.

A.D. 542
Daily Life
Rats from Egypt bring the plague to Constantinople.

Early Christian/Byzantine wall mosaic

Constantinople, C. A.D. 950

Build on What You Know

Native peoples in the Americas lived successfully off the land by hunting, gathering, and farming. Their cultures thrived for hundreds of years. Eventually some of these cultures became civilizations, some of which made great advances. Some civilizations acquired more land and wealth, often by invading neighboring peoples. In Europe the Roman Empire had suffered from invasions by Germanic peoples. Part of the empire remained intact, however, and began to grow again. In this chapter, you will learn about Byzantine and Russian civilizations and how they gained their power.

What's Your Opinion?

 To help students create their Themes Journal entries, provide the following examples of appropriate **agree/disagree** *statements.*

Government

Agree A powerful leader is the most important factor in a strong government.

Disagree A successful government depends upon a strong military.

Geography

Agree In order to survive, a civilization must develop near bodies of water.

Disagree Civilizations most likely to survive develop in geographic isolation and face few threats from invaders.

Global Relations

Agree Citizens should think and act as their rulers do in order to gain their favor.

Disagree Good rulers tolerate differences in opinion and beliefs from the people they govern.

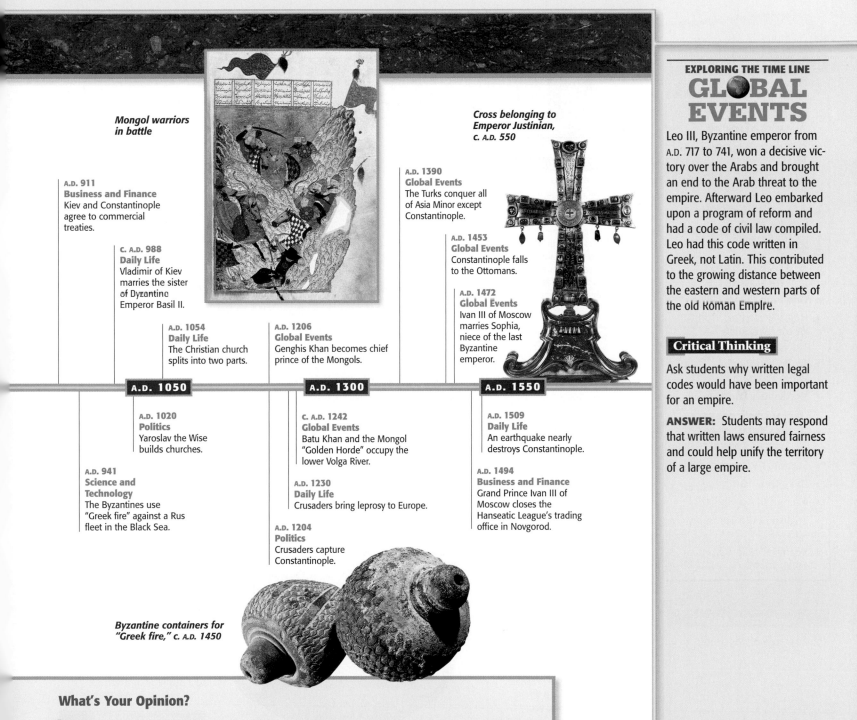

Mongol warriors in battle

Cross belonging to Emperor Justinian, c. A.D. 550

A.D. 911
Business and Finance
Kiev and Constantinople agree to commercial treaties.

C. A.D. 988
Daily Life
Vladimir of Kiev marries the sister of Byzantine Emperor Basil II.

A.D. 1054
Daily Life
The Christian church splits into two parts.

A.D. 1206
Global Events
Genghis Khan becomes chief prince of the Mongols.

A.D. 1390
Global Events
The Turks conquer all of Asia Minor except Constantinople.

A.D. 1453
Global Events
Constantinople falls to the Ottomans.

A.D. 1472
Global Events
Ivan III of Moscow marries Sophia, niece of the last Byzantine emperor.

A.D. 1050	A.D. 1300	A.D. 1550

A.D. 1020
Politics
Yaroslav the Wise builds churches.

A.D. 941
Science and Technology
The Byzantines use "Greek fire" against a Rus fleet in the Black Sea.

C. A.D. 1242
Global Events
Batu Khan and the Mongol "Golden Horde" occupy the lower Volga River.

A.D. 1230
Daily Life
Crusaders bring leprosy to Europe.

A.D. 1204
Politics
Crusaders capture Constantinople.

A.D. 1509
Daily Life
An earthquake nearly destroys Constantinople.

A.D. 1494
Business and Finance
Grand Prince Ivan III of Moscow closes the Hanseatic League's trading office in Novgorod.

Byzantine containers for "Greek fire," c. A.D. 1450

EXPLORING THE TIME LINE
GLOBAL EVENTS

Leo III, Byzantine emperor from A.D. 717 to 741, won a decisive victory over the Arabs and brought an end to the Arab threat to the empire. Afterward Leo embarked upon a program of reform and had a code of civil law compiled. Leo had this code written in Greek, not Latin. This contributed to the growing distance between the eastern and western parts of the old Roman Empire.

Critical Thinking

Ask students why written legal codes would have been important for an empire.

ANSWER: Students may respond that written laws ensured fairness and could help unify the territory of a large empire.

What's Your Opinion?

 Do you **agree** *or* **disagree** *with the following statements? Support your point of view in your journal.*

Government Governments are most successful when they have a powerful leader.

Geography Civilizations develop successfully only if the patterns of their historic settlement follow bodies of water.

Global Relations Rulers expect the people they govern to always think and act as they do.

OBJECTIVES

1 Identify the factors that contributed to the growth and strength of the Byzantine Empire.

2 Explain how the Christian church came to be divided.

3 Analyze the cultural contributions made by the Byzantines.

4 Explain the factors that contributed to the downfall of the Byzantine Empire.

READ TO DISCOVER

❶ What factors contributed to the growth and strength of the Byzantine Empire?

❷ How did the Christian church come to be divided?

❸ What cultural contributions did the Byzantines make?

❹ What factors contributed to the downfall of the Byzantine Empire?

DEFINE

dowry
icon
iconoclasts
heresy
excommunication
mosaic

IDENTIFY

Justinian
Justinian Code
Theodora
Belisarius
"Greek fire"
Iconoclastic Controversy
Cyril and Methodius
Hagia Sophia
Ottoman Turks

▶ WHY IT MATTERS TODAY

The city of Istanbul in Turkey was once the ancient city of Constantinople. Use **CNNfyi.com** or other **current event** sources to explore what life today is like in Istanbul. Record your findings in your journal.

CNNfyi.com

The Byzantine Empire

The Main Idea
The Eastern Roman Empire lived on in the Byzantine Empire, which was centered around Constantinople.

The Story Continues *The "fall" of the Roman Empire was really only half a fall. Although Germanic tribes defeated the Western Roman Empire in the A.D. 400s and 500s, the Eastern Roman Empire successfully fought off the invaders. Also called the Byzantine Empire, it included Greece, Asia Minor, Syria, Egypt, and other areas. Through the Byzantines the glory of the Roman Empire lived on.*

The Growth of the Byzantine Empire

Many leaders of the Byzantine Empire hoped to revive the glory and power of the Roman Empire. The emperor **Justinian,** who ruled from A.D. 527 to A.D. 565, led the Byzantines in this revival. Justinian's accomplishments made this one of the greatest periods in Byzantine history.

The Justinian Code. One of the Byzantines' greatest contributions to civilization was the preservation of Roman law. In about A.D. 528 Justinian ordered his scholars to collect the laws of the Roman Empire. This collection, known as the **Justinian Code,** was organized into four parts. The first part, the *Code,* contained useful Roman laws. The second part, the *Digest,* summarized Roman legal opinions. The *Institutes* was a guide for law students. The last part was the *Novellae,* which contained laws passed after A.D. 534.

The Justinian Code formed the basis of Byzantine law. It covered such areas as crime, marriage, property, and slavery. By the A.D. 1100s, the Justinian Code was also being used in western Europe. It provided a framework for many European legal systems. The Code preserved the Roman idea that people should be ruled by laws rather than by the whims of leaders. This is the basis of English civil law, one of the major legal systems in the world today.

Able advisers. Justinian chose the people around him wisely. One of his advisers was his wife, **Theodora.** With Theodora's urging, Justinian changed Byzantine law to affect the status of women. He altered divorce laws to give greater benefit to women. He also allowed Christian women to own property equal to the value of their dowry. A **dowry** meant the money or goods a wife brought to a husband at marriage.

INTERPRETING THE VISUAL RECORD

Byzantine goldwork This golden Byzantine goblet from the A.D. 700s is decorated with Roman figures. *What do the relief figures that adorn this goblet suggest about the strength of the Roman tradition in the Byzantine Empire?*

TEACH OBJECTIVE 1

ALL LEVELS: Have students create a chart titled *Strengths of the Byzantine Empire* with the following headings: *Political Strengths, Military Strengths, Economic Strengths.* Tell students to fill in their charts as they read their textbook. After students have completed their charts, have them discuss which of the strengths they have listed might be important in making a nation strong today. Students should also analyze which of these strengths are comparable to those of the United States today. **ENGLISH LANGUAGE LEARNERS**

TEACH OBJECTIVE 1

ALL LEVELS: Have students use their textbooks to make a list of the political, military, and economic strengths of the Byzantine Empire in one column of a two-column chart. In the other column, tell students to write why this strength was important to the empire. For example:

Strength	Importance
Byzantine princes married princesses from other countries.	These marriages brought the empire into alliances with other countries.

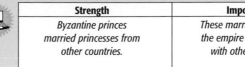

The Byzantine Empire, A.D. 526–A.D. 565

Interpreting Maps As a result of Emperor Justinian's victories over Germanic invaders, he recaptured many of the lands around the Mediterranean coast.

■ **Skills Assessment: Human Systems** What city in northern Africa did Justinian regain?

In A.D. 532 a rebellion called the Nika Revolt threatened to overthrow Justinian. During the attack Justinian wanted to flee Constantinople. Theodora talked him into staying and fighting. In a fierce battle Justinian's troops defeated the rebels.

Justinian wisely made **Belisarius** (bel·uh·SAR·ee·uhs) general of the army. An experienced commander, Belisarius also led the troops that crushed the Nika Revolt. He won former Roman lands back from the Germanic tribes. Thus during Justinian's reign the Byzantine Empire reached its greatest size.

✔ **READING CHECK: Identifying Cause and Effect** What effects did the political and legal ideas in Justinian's Code have on Byzantine and other societies?
reinforced rule of law, formed basis of legal systems

Strengths of the Empire

An all-powerful emperor and a strong central government ruled the empire. Government officials made sure the empire ran smoothly. These officials were skilled, efficient, and well paid. The Byzantines were clever diplomats. For example, emperors created alliances through marriage with foreign powers.

Holt Researcher

go.hrw.com
KEYWORD: Holt Researcher
FreeFind: Justinian
Theodora
After reading more about Justinian and Theodora on the Holt Researcher, create a chart listing the ways in which they affected future generations of people.

TEACH OBJECTIVE 2

LEVEL 1: Ask students to explain the Iconoclastic Controversy. *(It was the debate between the opponents and defenders of icons.)* How were the Byzantines different from the Western church? *(They did not recognize the pope's authority; some of them venerated icons.)* What caused the Christian church to split? *(The pope's council threatened to excommunicate iconoclasts.)*
ENGLISH LANGUAGE LEARNERS

TEACH OBJECTIVE 3

LEVEL 3: Have students read the paragraphs under the "Byzantine Culture" heading on pages 226 and 227. Then ask them what seems to be the unifying theme among these different elements of the Byzantine culture. *(importance of religion)* Organize the class into three groups: creators of the Cyrillic alphabet, Byzantine artists, and architects who built the Hagia Sophia. Tell each group to prepare a debate speech in which students will explain why their group has made the most important contribution to Byzantine culture. Members of the opposing groups should ask questions from the floor. **COOPERATIVE LEARNING**

Interdisciplinary Connection

LANGUAGE ARTS. The word *icon* also has come to mean an emblem or a symbol. People function as icons. For instance, Michael Jordan may be considered an icon representing athletic excellence. An icon is also the graphic symbol on a computer display screen that suggests the purpose of an available function.

Critical Thinking

Ask students to suggest other icons, both people and things.

ANSWER: Answers will vary, but students might suggest John F. Kennedy, Marilyn Monroe, traffic signs, or flags.

MAP ANSWER
forums

HISTORY MAKER ANSWER
She influenced Justinian to improve the status of women and worked to change laws to protect women.

Constantinople, C. A.D. 600

Interpreting Maps Constantinople's location on vital trade routes made it a great commercial center.

■ **Skills Assessment: Human Systems** What types of public buildings flourished in Constantinople?

Key to Historic Places

■ Structure   ▭ Wall   ▬ Major road

1 – Acropolis
2 – Church of the Apostles (Holy Apostles)
3 – Church of SS Serglus and Bacchus
4 – Forum of St. John of Studius
5 – Forum of Arcadius
6 – Column of Constantine
7 – Forum of Theodosios
8 – Forum of Bovis
9 – Forum of Constantine
10 – Golden Gate
11 – Hagia Sophia (St. Sophia)
12 – Hippodrome
13 – Imperial Hormisdas Palace
14 – Palace of Blachernae
15 – St. Irene

The Byzantine Empire had effective forces to protect its frontiers. Military forces were well trained, and weapons and armor were well designed.

During the A.D. 500s the Byzantines built a strong navy, in which ships were equipped with a chemical weapon known as **"Greek fire."** When sprayed or thrown onto enemy ships, the liquid burst into flames, setting them on fire.

The East had always been the richest part of the Roman Empire. At the heart of this wealth lay Constantinople. This grand city was strategically located where Europe meets Asia. Constantinople looked over the Bosporus Strait. This allowed the Byzantines to control the sea trade routes between Asia and Europe.

Goods from as far away as Scandinavia and China came into Constantinople. Imperial tax policies raised huge government revenues. The government used this income to pay soldiers and government officials. The emperor also paid for large, magnificent public buildings with these taxes.

✔ **READING CHECK: Making Generalizations** What kind of government did the Byzantine Empire have? **strong, centralized government**

HISTORY MAKER

Empress Theodora (C. A.D. 500–A.D. 548)

Theodora influenced Justinian to improve the status of women in society. She worked to change many laws so as to protect women. She donated money to churches and orphanages. **How did Theodora try to improve the lives of women?**

The Christian Church

The Christian church was an important part of life in the Byzantine Empire. However, church leaders in the West and East had different ideas about church practices. These differences led to a final division in the Christian church.

The pope was the most powerful leader of the Christian church in the West. The Byzantines, however, did not recognize the pope's authority. In the East the patriarch of Constantinople was the most powerful church leader.

Byzantines differed from the Western church on many issues. They also disagreed among themselves on issues of religious practice and belief within the Byzantine Church. One important debate concerned the role of icons. An **icon** is a holy picture of Jesus, the Virgin Mary, or the saints. Many Byzantines kept icons in their homes and venerated, or honored, them in churches. However, some Byzantines were iconoclasts. **Iconoclasts** believed that having icons in church was the same as worshipping idols. They felt this was wrong.

ALL LEVELS: Ask students to name social improvements benefiting women that occurred during Justinian's reign. (*Women gained greater benefit from divorce laws and could own property.*) Ask students to keep in mind other empires they have studied while generating a short written response to the following statement: *Women were better off in Justinian's time than any previous time in history.* Remind students that their responses should include details and facts. After students have completed their responses, discuss their ideas as a class.

ENGLISH LANGUAGE LEARNERS

Spotlight on CITIZENSHIP

Have students write a short story, from the perspective of a woman, that incorporates one or more of the changes Justinian made to improve the status of women. Tell students they may conduct additional research or review Chapter 5, about the Greek city-states, or Chapter 7, about the Roman Empire, to find out more about the daily life of women before Justinian's reforms. **BLOCK SCHEDULING**

SKILL-BUILDING STRATEGIES — Identifying Bias

Views of Justinian and Theodora

Justinian and Theodora did many great things for the Byzantine Empire. Yet at times they could be harsh with their enemies. Their supporters viewed them as wise rulers protecting the empire. Their enemies viewed them as tyrants who forced their beliefs on others. Interpreting different aspects of rulers can be difficult for historians. In judging the usefulness of sources, historians must recognize the biases held by the author of the source. In the simplest sense, bias means the prejudice, or slanted viewpoint, a speaker or writer holds. Pre-existing biases often shape the ways observers describe historical events, causing them to leave out important facts or make statements without much supporting evidence. Historians themselves can even present a biased view of events.

Justinian (fifth from right) and his attendants

A Historian's View:

Procopius (pruh·KOH·pee·uhs) was a Byzantine historian who lived during the reign of Justinian. In *The Secret History* he described the rule of Justinian and Theodora.

"... **they were a pair of blood-thirsty demons.** ... **For they plotted together to find the easiest and swiftest means of destroying all races of men and all their works** ... **[Justinian] would order tens of thousands of quite innocent persons to be put to death, cities to be razed to the ground, and all their possessions to be confiscated for the Treasury.** ... **His ambition being to force everybody into one form of Christian belief he wantonly destroyed everyone who would not conform, and that while keeping up a pretense of piety. For he did not regard it as murder, so long as those who died did not happen to share his beliefs.**"

Theodora (third from right) and her attendants

Skills Reminder

Bias in historical sources may be either positive or negative. In either case, bias results in distortions that may mislead observers who do not carefully evaluate the source. Bias may cause observers to draw inaccurate conclusions or to misunderstand descriptions and outcomes of historical events. To identify bias, look for clues. What words or phrases convey a positive or negative meaning? Look at the evidence. Decide whether you agree or disagree with the attitude, based on the evidence presented. Analyze what information has been left out by the author. Assess how this changes the conclusions that may be drawn based on the source's description or analysis.

Skills Practice

❶ How did Procopius feel about the rule of Justinian and Theodora? What words and phrases indicate this?
❷ How does Procopius's description of Justinian's behavior support the same outlook?
❸ What information about Justinian and Theodora does Procopius leave out? How might this change the conclusions the reader draws about their reign?
❹ Read an article from a newspaper, magazine, or the Internet about a recent event and try to identify the author's bias. If possible, read another source's coverage of the same event. Do both authors have a similar or different bias?

That's Interesting!

After Justinian's death, the Muslims made inroads in the present-day Middle East and North Africa, and many of the people in these lands welcomed their conquerors as liberators. Some of these people shared religious beliefs more in common with those of Islam than with those of Orthodox Christianity. People in Egypt, Syria, and Palestine all found their new rulers a welcome change from the Byzantines.

SKILLS PRACTICE ANSWERS

1. He felt their rule was unjust and ruthless, as indicated by phrases such as "blood-thirsty demons," and "he wantonly destroyed everyone who would not conform."

2. He described him carrying out very ruthless acts.

3. He leaves out the positive things they accomplished, leading the reader to draw a very negative conclusion about their reign.

4. Students' answers will vary.

Technology Resources

World History Teaching Transparency: Everyday Life 9: The Role of the Byzantine Emperor

LEVEL 2: Have students create a time line extending from A.D. 1000 to A.D. 1500, labeled with events that contributed to the decline of the Byzantine Empire. Under each event, have students write a statement that explains its significance. (*Possible answers: early A.D. 1000s—Saljuq Turks capture most of Asia Minor. The loss of territory weakened the empire; A.D. 1096–A.D. 1099—Western European armies recaptured western Asia Minor for the Byzantines. This action restored and ensured the stability of Constantinople; A.D. 1204—Western Europeans captured Constantinople for themselves. The empire lost its most* important city; A.D. 1261—the Byzantines recaptured Constantinople. This action ensured the existence of the empire; A.D. 1453—Ottoman Turks captured Constantinople. The Byzantine Empire came to an end.)

 HOMEWORK Remind students that most people in the Byzantine Empire could not read. Have students use computer software or other means to create visual images that would help nonreaders understand important aspects of the Byzantine Empire.

Culture

In A.D. 787 the Second Council of Nicaea, called by the Byzantine empress Irene, met in an attempt to resolve the issue of iconoclasm. The council decided that icons should be revered but not worshiped and that they could remain in churches. This council—attended mostly by Byzantine delegates, although some papal legates from Rome did attend—was the last council accepted by both the Roman Catholic Church and the Orthodox Church.

Critical Thinking

Ask students if they think this compromise was a good way to deal with the conflict over icons. Have them support their point of view.

ANSWER: Some students might suggest that the compromise seemed to address the concerns of both sides. Other students might argue that the compromise happened too late, seems to have been mostly a Byzantine decision, and failed to prevent the division of the churches.

Technology Resources

World History Teaching Transparency: Geography and History 9: Roman Catholicism and Orthodoxy

Major Disagreements Between the Roman Catholic and Eastern Orthodox Churches		
	Roman Catholic	**Eastern Orthodox**
Clergy	No married priests allowed	Married priests allowed
Icons	Veneration accepted	Veneration initially rejected, later accepted
Leadership	Roman pope was supreme church authority	Rejected supremacy of Roman pope over local leaders
Trinity	Accepted the view that the Holy Spirit combines both Father and Son	Maintained supremacy of the Father in the Trinity

This debate between the opponents and defenders of icons is called the **Iconoclastic Controversy.** In A.D. 726 Emperor Leo III, an iconoclast, ordered the destruction of icons. However, many people refused to give up their icons. In the West, church leaders also condemned the use of icons. Many people in western Europe, however, could not read or write. Icons portrayed images and symbols that helped them to learn about Christianity.

In A.D. 787 the pope in Rome called bishops together to discuss the Iconoclastic Controversy. This council decided that it was a heresy *not* to allow the veneration of icons. A **heresy** is an opinion that conflicts with official church beliefs. The council threatened iconoclasts with **excommunication.** An excommunicated person cannot be a member of the church anymore.

The council's decision caused friction between the pope in Rome and the patriarch in Constantinople. Finally the Christian church split into two churches in 1054. The church in the West became the Roman Catholic Church, with the pope at its head. In the East it became the Eastern Orthodox Church, with the patriarch of Constantinople as leader. The two churches aré still separate today. Ironically, the Eastern Church eventually came to accept icons, and they are now recognized as an important part of Eastern Orthodox tradition.

✔ **READING CHECK: Drawing Inferences** How did the council of bishops in Rome feel about Byzantine views of Christianity?
that they were heretical

Byzantine Culture

While western Europe struggled to find a new way of life, Constantinople was the center of a great civilization. The Byzantine Empire provided a great service for cultures that followed it. Byzantine scholars produced many original works. In addition, they passed on to future generations the learnings of ancient Greece, Rome, and the East.

The Byzantine Empire also brought Mediterranean culture to lands beyond its borders. For example, the brothers **Cyril** (SIR·uhl) **and Methodius** (muh·THOH·dee·uhs) were Christian missionaries. They tried to teach the Bible to Slavs in central and eastern Europe. The Slavs had no written language, so Cyril and Methodius created an alphabet for them. This alphabet came to be known as Cyrillic (suh·RIL·ik). Many Slavic peoples today use Cyrillic or an alphabet derived from it.

The missionary brothers Cyril and Methodius present a scroll showing the Cyrillic alphabet.

LEVEL 3: Ask students what other systems of law had been developed by early civilizations. *(Babylonians and the Code of Hammurabi, Hittites, Greece and Draco's code of laws, and Solon's reforms)* Ask students in what way each of the four parts of the Justinian Code would have contributed to the overall system of laws in the Byzantine Empire. *(The* Code *reorganized Roman law; the* Digest *could be used when a law was not fully understood; the* Institutes *could be used for making new laws; the* Novellae *contained the updated laws.)* Close by asking students how we know that the Justinian Code was successful and efficient. *(It was the basis of many European legal systems.)*

Teacher to Teacher

Scott Whitlow of Round Rock, Texas, suggested the following activity: Have students research and write reports or create presentations on some aspect of Byzantine architecture, icons, art, or symbols. These studies should explain how these items reflect Byzantine history.

Link to Today Although the Hagia Sophia was built in the A.D. 500s as a Christian church, it was used after 1453 as an Islamic mosque. How does the Hagia Sophia today reflect the history of the Byzantine Empire?

The interior of the Hagia Sophia was dramatically illuminated with natural lighting.

Government

Over time Byzantine emperors eliminated paganism from the Byzantine Empire. Emperors closed pagan temples and dismantled pagan shrines.

Critical Thinking

Ask students why Byzantine emperors might have wanted to destroy paganism.

ANSWER: Students' responses will vary, but they might answer that the Byzantine emperors wanted to be more revered than the pagan gods.

LINK TO TODAY ANSWER

It reflects the Byzantines' Christian beliefs and the importance of religion in their art.

Technology Resources

 World History Teaching Transparency: Art and History 9: Sant' Apollinare in Classe, Apse Mosaic

Art. Religion was the main subject of Byzantine art. Murals and icons covered the walls, floors, and ceilings of churches. Floors, walls, and arches glowed with mosaics. A **mosaic** is a picture or design made from small pieces of enamel, glass, or stone. The location of an image indicated its importance. For example, an image of the Father was always found in the dome of the church. To modern eyes Byzantine art may appear stiff or artificial. Byzantine artists did not try to imitate reality. They tried to inspire adoration of the religious figures and help people look toward an afterlife.

Architecture. The Byzantines created great religious architecture. One of the world's great buildings is the church of **Hagia Sophia** (meaning "holy wisdom") in Constantinople. Justinian ordered the building of the Hagia Sophia in A.D. 532. The Hagia Sophia is a huge building, considered by many to be an architectural and engineering wonder. Justinian devoted a great deal of money and energy to its completion, one reason that it was completed in the amazingly short time of about six years.

A huge dome sits on top of the church. The dome is 180 feet high and 108 feet wide. Romans and other peoples had built domes before. However, Byzantine architects were the first to solve the problem of placing a round dome over a rectangular building. The Hagia Sophia was completed in A.D. 537. The Byzantine historian Procopius described what he saw when entering the church:

> **History Makers Speak**
>
> **❝**The entire ceiling is covered with pure gold, which adds to its beauty. . . . who could tell of the beauty of the columns and marbles with which the church is adorned? One would think that one had come upon a meadow full of flowers in bloom. Whoever enters there to worship perceives at once that it is not by any human strength or skill, but by the favour of God that this work has been perfected; his mind rises sublime to commune with God, feeling that He cannot be far off. . . . **❞**
>
> Procopius, *The Secret History,* translated by G. A. Williamson

Analyzing Primary Sources

Identifying a Point of View
According to Procopius, how would citizens feel upon entering the Hagia Sophia? awed, closer to God

✔ **READING CHECK: Supporting a Point of View** What evidence would you give to show that the Byzantines built upon previous cultures and contributed to future cultures? retained and passed on Roman legal system, Greek and Roman scholarship

THE BYZANTINE EMPIRE AND RUSSIA **227**

The Decline of the Empire

After Justinian died in A.D. 565, the Byzantine Empire suffered from many wars and conflicts with outside powers. To the east there was war with the Persians. The Lombards, a Germanic tribe, settled in Italy. The Avars and Slavs invaded the Balkan Peninsula. The Muslim Empire conquered Syria, Palestine, and much of North Africa. By A.D. 650 the Byzantines had lost many lands.

This painting by an Italian artist dramatizes the Ottoman Turks' conquest of Constantinople in 1453.

During the A.D. 1000s the Seljuq Turks, a nomadic people from central Asia, captured much of Asia Minor. This region was an important source of food and soldiers for the empire. Next the Turks prepared to attack Constantinople. The Byzantine emperor asked the West to help defend Constantinople. From A.D. 1096 to A.D. 1099 a western European army seized and eventually returned western Asia Minor to the Byzantines. In A.D. 1204, however, Western forces turned against the Byzantine Empire and captured Constantinople.

In A.D. 1261 the Byzantines recaptured Constantinople. The Byzantine Empire lasted for almost 200 more years. However, it never regained its former strength. In the A.D. 1300s a rising Asian power, the **Ottoman Turks,** began to threaten Byzantine territory. By the mid-1300s the Ottomans had begun to move into the Balkans. In A.D. 1361 they took Adrianople, one of the empire's leading cities. With the Ottoman capture of Constantinople in A.D. 1453, the Byzantine Empire finally came to an end.

✔ **READING CHECK: Identifying Cause and Effect** Why was the Seljuq Turks' invasion of Asia Minor so harmful to the Byzantine Empire? Asia Minor was main source of food supply and soldiers

---

SECTION 1 REVIEW

1. Define and explain the significance:
   dowry
   icon
   iconoclasts
   heresy
   excommunication
   mosaic

2. Identify and explain the significance:
   Justinian
   Justinian Code
   Theodora
   Belisarius
   "Greek fire"
   Iconoclastic Controversy
   Cyril and Methodius
   Hagia Sophia
   Ottoman Turks

3. Comparing and Contrasting Copy the Venn diagram below. Use it to organize the similarities and differences between the Eastern and Western Christian churches.

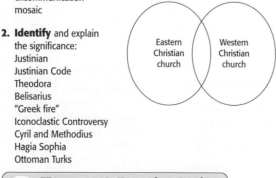

Eastern Christian church   Western Christian church

4. **Finding the Main Idea**

a. What might have happened if Justinian had not survived the Nika Revolt?

b. How might the Byzantine military have been affected by a bad economy?

c. What factors contributed to the division of the Christian church?

d. How did Justinian's interest in Roman law affect European legal systems for years to come?

e. What events and developments led to the gradual decline of the Byzantine Empire?

5. **Writing and Critical Thinking**

Categorizing Develop a table in which you classify the advantages and disadvantages of having an all-powerful emperor and a strong, centralized government in the Byzantine Empire.

Consider:
- how the Byzantine Empire grew
- the results of collecting large tax revenues
- the role of the emperor and the government in the development of the empire's code of law
- the actions of the emperor and the government to manage the empire and to ensure its security from outside attack

go. hrw .com **Homework Practice Online**
keyword: SP3 HP10

OBJECTIVES

1 Explain why different peoples settled in eastern Europe.
2 Describe how Kievan Russia differed from the Byzantine Empire.

SECTION 2

The Rise of Russia

READ TO DISCOVER

❶ Why did different peoples settle in eastern Europe?
❷ How did Kievan Russia differ from the Byzantine Empire?

DEFINE

steppe
boyars
taiga

IDENTIFY

Rurik
Rus
Yaroslav the Wise
Pravda Russkia
Vladimir I

WHY IT MATTERS TODAY

The economy in Kievan Russia depended largely on agriculture. Use CNNfyi.com or other **current event** sources to explore the Russian economy today. Record your findings in your journal.

CNNfyi.com

The Main Idea
Kievan Russia established many practices and traditions that defined Russian culture.

The Story Continues *The people who came to rule Russia were first mentioned in historical records in A.D. 860. In that year they launched a fierce surprise attack against the city of Constantinople. "The unexpectedness of the incursion [attack] and its extraordinary speed . . . ," recalled one Byzantine leader, "prove that this blow has been sent from heaven like a thunderbolt." Although the attack was unsuccessful, the Byzantines would not soon forget this fighting force.*

The Setting and People

A large plain stretches across eastern Europe and central Asia. It extends eastward from the Carpathian (kahr•PAY•thee•uhn) Mountains in Europe to the Ural (YOOR•uhl) Mountains at the western edge of Asia. In the south this plain is grassy and mostly treeless and is called the **steppe.** The steppe has black, fertile soil that is ideal for agriculture, particularly in the area that is now Ukraine.

The Ural Mountains run north and south at the eastern edge of the plain. These mountains are often considered the boundary between the continents of Europe and Asia. Europe and Asia actually form a huge landmass that is called Eurasia. Many rivers crisscross the plain and provide a network of transportation within the region. The Dniester, Dnieper, and Don Rivers are ideal for trade because they flow into the Black Sea and give access to the Mediterranean. Other major rivers, such as the Vistula, Neman, and Dvina, do not flow into the Black Sea and thus have somewhat less impact on trade. They provide important regional transportation links, however.

The southern part of eastern Europe has been inhabited since Neolithic times. Probably beginning during the very late 1500s B.C., several groups from this region invaded southwest Asia. These invasions took place over the course of centuries. After about the A.D. 400s, Slavs settled in much of eastern Europe. Other peoples, including the Avars, Huns, and Magyars, invaded the region at different times. These invaders frequently made the Slavs their subjects. From their servitude comes the word "slave."

During the A.D. 800s Vikings from Scandinavia drove into eastern Europe. Trade was the primary interest of the Vikings as they moved into the area.

INTERPRETING THE VISUAL RECORD

Viking ships Vikings from Scandinavia used longboats to conduct trade. *What design characteristics of this Viking longboat made it an excellent craft for navigating the shallow waters of coastal and inland rivers, as well as the open sea?*

LEVEL 3: Have students look at the map on page 230. Ask them what is the most outstanding feature of Kievan Russia. (*Many Viking trade routes cut through the territory.*) Ask them what benefit this might have had for the people who lived in this region. (*It gave them access to other goods as well as an outlet for trading their own goods.*) Ask students why they think Kiev and not Novgorod became the most important city. (*Answers will vary, but students might suggest that because Kiev was closer to southern Europe and Asia Minor its inhabitants were more easily able to trade goods and learn about new ideas.*)

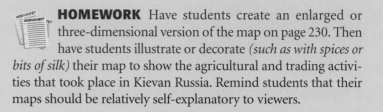

HOMEWORK Have students create an enlarged or three-dimensional version of the map on page 230. Then have students illustrate or decorate (*such as with spices or bits of silk*) their map to show the agricultural and trading activities that took place in Kievan Russia. Remind students that their maps should be relatively self-explanatory to viewers.

Economics

The corridor from the Baltic Sea to the Black Sea, inhabited by the Eastern Slavs, was an important trade route for furs, amber, wax, metal, slaves, and various foodstuffs. The trade route was an unsettled and often dangerous area. A Persian geographer once reported that one town along the trade route produced excellent swords, but "strangers are killed whenever they visit it."

Critical Thinking

Ask students what effect the danger of the routes might have had on trade.

ANSWER: Students might answer that the dangerous trade routes would have either prevented trade or raised the prices of goods from that area so that traders would be repaid for their risks.

MAP ANSWER

rivers

Technology Resources

Online Maps, Charts, and Graphs: Kiev as a Strategic City, 1000s

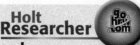

Holt Researcher

go.hrw.com
KEYWORD: Holt Researcher
FreeFind: Rurik
After reading more about Rurik on the Holt Researcher, create a travel log about the journeys of the Rus under Rurik, including why they chose to take over certain places.

The numerous large and small rivers of eastern Europe enabled them to build far-flung water-going trade routes.

✔ **READING CHECK: Categorizing** What groups of people lived in eastern and southeastern Europe between the late 1500s B.C. and the A.D. 800s? *Slavs, Avars, Huns, Magyars, and Vikings*

Kievan Russia

Cities such as Novgorod and Kiev lay along the Viking trade routes. **Rurik,** the leader of a people called the **Rus,** took control of Novgorod in A.D. 862. Rurik and his successors soon came to rule over Kiev as well as over Slavic tribes along the Dnieper River. The region under their control came to be called the Rus. The word *Russia* probably comes from this name. Kiev prospered because of its location along the rich trade route between Constantinople and the Baltic Sea. Kiev became the most important principality in Kievan Russia and served as the capital for nearly 300 years after about A.D. 879. As early as A.D. 911, Kiev was powerful enough to win a favorable trade treaty with the Byzantine Empire. Other principalities paid tribute to Kiev. Some towns, however, remained more independent.

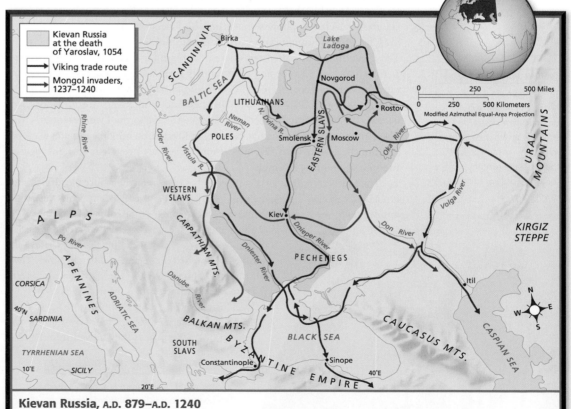

Kievan Russia, A.D. 879–A.D. 1240

Interpreting Maps A network of rivers crosses the plain between the Carpathian and Ural Mountains.

■ **Skills Assessment: Environment and Society** What common geographic feature did the Kievan trade routes follow?

TEACH OBJECTIVE 1

ALL LEVELS: Have students read the paragraphs under the "Religion" heading on page 231. Then have students create a cause-and-effect chart and fill it in with facts about Kievan Russia and Christianity. For example:

Cause	Effect
Religious themes dominated Kievan culture.	*The majority of Kievan literature was written to serve religious purposes.*

Ask students how Kievan Russia's religion differed from that of the Byzantine Empire. (*Kievan religion was both Christian and pagan.*) **ENGLISH LANGUAGE LEARNERS**

TEACH OBJECTIVE 2

LEVEL 1: Ask students to describe the Pravda Russkia. (*It was the legal code written by Yaroslav I. It combined elements of Slavic tribal customs with older laws and traditions and outlined lawful responses in cases of violence and other harmful activity.*) How was the Pravda Russkia similar to the Justinian Code? (*They both contained elements of older laws.*) How was it different? (*It also included elements of Slavic tribal customs.*) **ENGLISH LANGUAGE LEARNERS**

Government. Many areas in Kievan Russia were led by princes who governed with the advice of councils made up of **boyars,** or nobles. Another institution in Kievan Russia was the *veche,* or town meeting. When the prince requested it, all heads of households would meet in the public marketplace. They discussed important matters like wars, disputes between princes, or emergencies.

Yaroslav I ruled from A.D. 1019 to A.D. 1054, a great period in Russian history. He came to be known as **Yaroslav the Wise.** He built many churches and introduced Russia's first law code, the **Pravda Russkia** (the "Russian Justice"). Yaroslav's code seems to have combined elements of tribal customs and older laws and traditions. It outlined lawful responses in cases of violence and other harmful activity.

> **History Makers Speak**
>
> **"If a man kills a man: the brother is to avenge his brother; the son, his father; or the father, his son. . . . If there is no avenger, [the murderer pays compensation of] 40 *grivna*. . . . If a slave runs away . . . and [if a freeman who conceals that slave] does not declare him for three days. and [the owner of the slave] discovers him on the third day, he [the owner] receives his slave back and 3 *grivna* for the offense . . . if a slave strikes a freeman and hides in [his master's] house, and his master is not willing to give him up, the master has to pay 12 *grivna*, and the offended freeman beats the slave whenever he finds him. . . ."**

"The Pravda Russkia," from *Medieval Russian Laws,* translated by George Vernadsky

Religion. Traders and Greek missionaries brought Christianity to Kievan Russia in the A.D. 800s. However, little Christian activity took place until the mid-900s. In the A.D. 980s the ruler **Vladimir I** sent observers to Christian church services in several places. His officials were impressed with what they saw at the Hagia Sophia in Constantinople. They admired the services and rituals of Orthodox Christianity. Moreover, Vladimir wanted to marry Anna, the sister of the Byzantine emperor. In A.D. 988 he converted to Christianity. After converting he ordered all Kievans to become Christians. He also had all pagan statues destroyed.

Many Kievans still worshiped the spirits of their ancestors or gods of nature. However, the Byzantine church became a more and more important force in Kievan Russia. The patriarch in Constantinople chose the bishop of the Kievan church. Monasteries became centers of religious thought, social service, and the arts. This further strengthened the church. When the Christian church split in A.D. 1054, the Kievans followed the Eastern Orthodox Church.

Religious themes dominated Kievan culture during this period. Most writing focused on religion, in the form of hymns and sermons. Icon painting became the most distinctive Kievan art form. Artists also created mosaics and frescoes. Much of the decorative painting created by Kievan artists was designed to illustrate religious ideas and figures. The visual quality of these works was often powerful and stylized. Many Kievan mosaics, frescoes, and icons portrayed a deep and thoughtful spirituality. These art forms helped viewers to reflect on the meaning of religious ideas and values.

Economy. Kievan Russia included two major agricultural regions. North of the steppe lies the **taiga** (TY·guh). The taiga has great forests and receives much rainfall. However, winters are long and cold, and the growing season on the taiga is short. Therefore, everyone in a farm family worked long hours to grow and harvest crops. The steppe gets less rain than the taiga. However, the steppe has a milder climate and a longer growing season. People there had more time to plant and harvest crops.

HISTORY MAKER

Yaroslav the Wise
(A.D. 980–A.D. 1054)

Yaroslav's Pravda Russkia was in use until the A.D. 1550s in some parts of Russia. Before his death he divided his kingdom among his sons with instructions on how to rule. They ignored these instructions and civil war soon broke out. **How did Yaroslav continue to affect Russia after his death?**

Town Meetings

All free men in Kievan Russia had the right to speak at the *veche*—a village or town meeting. Town meetings like these continue today. They have become popular in the United States, where they are used to address many issues. Citizens sometimes discuss safety concerns or hear ideas for improving neighborhoods. The U.S. government has organized town meetings to share information with communities. Presidential candidates often hold town meetings to allow voters to ask questions and state their opinions. **What situations might make a town decide to hold a meeting?**

That's Interesting!

Historians have never successfully determined the origin of the Slavs. One of the problems with tracing their ancestry is that the name Slav was not used until about A.D. 530; before that time the people who became known as the Slavs were most often referred to as the Venedi and the Antes.

HISTORY MAKER ANSWER
His Pravda Russkia was still in use well after his death.

THEN & NOW ANSWER
safety concerns; ideas for improving neighborhoods; share information; question political candidates

Technology Resources
Regions of the World Music Audio CD Program 9: Russia, Ukraine, and Belarus: Russian Choral Music

CLOSE

Have each student write a paragraph that describes the political, economic, and social life of Kievan Russia.

REVIEW

Have students complete the Section 2 Review on p. 232.

ASSESS

Have students complete Daily Quiz 10.2. As Alternative Assessment, you may want to use the map or chart exercises in this section's lessons.

RETEACH

Have students complete Main Idea Activity for English Language Learners and Special-Needs Students 10.2. Then ask them to use correct social studies terminology to write a question that covers the main idea for each subsection in the section.
ENGLISH LANGUAGE LEARNERS

EXTEND

Have interested students use computer software to acquire information and prepare a class report on the Pravda Russkia. Students might also report on its similarities to and differences from the Justinian Code. **BLOCK SCHEDULING**

VISUAL RECORD ANSWER

The rivers were very important to economic activity.

SECTION 2 REVIEW ANSWERS

❶ Define
- steppe, p. 229
- boyars, p. 231
- taiga, p. 231

❷ Identify
- Rurik, p. 230
- Rus, p. 230
- Yaroslav the Wise, p. 231
- Pravda Russkia, p. 231
- Vladimir I, p. 231

❸ Students' charts should include the following from top to bottom: Political System—prince, council, *veches*; Social Classes—local princes and their families, boyars, artisans and merchants, peasants

❹ a. The flat terrain allowed for invasion; the numerous rivers provided a network of transportation and enabled trade. The fertile soil was ideal for farming.

b. Kiev prospered and gained power because of its location along the rich trade route between Constantinople and the Baltic Sea.

c. They traded with each other.

❺ Students' paragraphs will vary but should include how Vladimir's religion affected his policies and how the people reacted to these changes.

INTERPRETING THE VISUAL RECORD

Kievan trade This modern painting shows one Russian artist's idea of what trade on the rivers of Kievan Russia may have looked like. ***Based on this image, what was the impact of geography on economic activity in Kievan Russia?***

Kievan Russia traded agricultural goods and other products with the Byzantines. These products included wood, iron, salt, furs, and honey. Kievan Russia also provided slaves for the Byzantines. In return, the Kievans received goods such as wine, silk, spices, and fruit. From western Europe they received jewelry, silver, and textiles. By the early A.D. 1000s, trade had helped Kievan Russia become a strong, wealthy power.

Several social classes emerged in Kievan Russia. At the top were the local princes and their families, followed by the boyars. Next were the town artisans and merchants, who devoted themselves to trade. The largest and lowest class, however, were the peasants. Peasants lived in small villages in the country and produced the crops that fed Kievan Russia. The clergy formed another important group. They were not directly involved in the government or economic activities. Some clergy, however, enjoyed considerable influence over daily life in Kievan Russia. Clergy performed religious ceremonies and ran hospitals and charities.

✔ **READING CHECK: Contrasting** How did Kievan Russia's government and religion differ from the Byzantine Empire's? Kievan government was based on Slavic custom and law, and followed the Orthodox Church.

SECTION 2 REVIEW

1. Define and explain the significance:
steppe
boyars
taiga

2. Identify and explain the significance:
Rurik
Rus
Yaroslav the Wise
Pravda Russkia
Vladimir I

3. Summarizing Copy the charts below. Use them to show the organization of the Kievan political system and the Kievan social classes.

Kievan political system   Kievan social classes

4. **Finding the Main Idea**

a. What geographic features characterize the plain of eastern Europe and central Asia, and why did these features attract human settlement?

b. What importance did geography have in the development of Kiev as a powerful city?

c. How did Kievan Russia and the Byzantine Empire similarly increase their wealth?

5. **Writing and Critical Thinking**

Identifying Cause and Effect Write a paragraph explaining how Vladimir I's conversion to Christianity affected Russia.
Consider:
- how his religion affected Vladimir's policies
- how the people reacted to these changes

Homework Practice Online

keyword: SP3 HP10

SECTION 3

OBJECTIVES

1 Identify the ways in which Mongol rule affected Kievan Russia.

2 Describe the effects of Moscow's growing power and independence.

LET'S GET STARTED!

As students enter the classroom, ask them to write changes that occur in people's lives when outside invaders seize control of their region. *(Students might list changes such as a new form of government, a different dominant religion, and changes in the economic system.)* Tell students that in Section 3 they will learn about how Mongol rule affected Kievan Russia.

SECTION 3

READ TO DISCOVER

❶ In what ways did Mongol rule affect Kievan Russia?

❷ What were the effects of Moscow's growing power and independence?

DEFINE

czar

"third Rome"

IDENTIFY

Vladimir Monomakh
Polovtsy
Ivan III
Ivan the Terrible

WHY IT MATTERS TODAY

Eastern Europe has suffered from civil wars and internal conflicts for many years. Use **CNNfyi.com** or other **current event** sources to explore a current conflict or political unrest in an Eastern European country. Record your findings in your journal.

CNNfyi.com

Russia and the Mongols

The Main Idea
Under Mongol rule the power of Kiev weakened while Moscow became stronger.

The Story Continues *When Yaroslav the Wise's rule ended in A.D. 1054, Kiev declined in power. During the first quarter of the A.D. 1100s, however, the city enjoyed a brief revival under the leadership of* **Vladimir Monomakh,** *who ruled from A.D. 1113 to A.D. 1125. In protecting the Kievan state, Vladimir was merciless against his enemies. As a result, Kiev was often at war during his reign.*

Attacks on Kiev

Kiev had declined because Kievan rulers gave the outlying towns to their sons to rule independently. Eventually these princes fought among themselves—and with Kiev itself—to expand their territory. At the same time the **Polovtsy** interfered with Kiev's trade. The Polovtsy were a Turkish people who after A.D. 1055 controlled the area south of Kiev. Vladimir Monomakh made his reputation by leading military campaigns against the Polovtsy. At one point he ordered the deaths of some 200 of their princes. Kievan trade may also have suffered from competition with Italian city-states that had developed new trade routes.

In A.D. 1169 and A.D. 1203, groups of princes sacked Kiev, ruining the city's prosperity. New invaders, the Mongols, took advantage of Kiev's weakness. The Mongols came from the Asian steppe east of the Ural Mountains. By A.D. 1240 they had conquered or destroyed almost every city in Kievan Russia. The Mongols continued across the Carpathian Mountains into Hungary and Poland. In A.D. 1242 they defeated the Hungarian and Polish armies. However, the Mongol leader Batu called off his attack to return to Russia. He wanted to influence the choice of the next Mongol leader. Thus Hungary and Poland escaped long-term Mongol rule.

Kievan Russia under the Mongols. Mongols controlled Kievan Russia until the late A.D. 1400s. This long Mongol presence had a strong influence on the Slavic way of life. The Mongols sought to gain wealth from the region. They taxed the people heavily. As long as the Slavs paid, they could keep their own government and customs. Russian peasants in the conquered lands probably paid taxes in several ways. They may have paid in money or in goods, or they may have paid their Mongol overlords with labor.

Although the Mongols formed only a small ruling class, they influenced Slavic society in several ways. They built important roads and improved methods of taxation and communication. Some Mongol words entered the language that came to be called Russian, as did some Mongol customs, traditions, and patterns of behavior.

Skilled cavalry archers like the warrior pictured here helped the Mongols seize Kievan Russia.

SECTION 3 RESOURCES

REPRODUCIBLE RESOURCES

▶ Guided Reading Strategy 10.3

▶ Readings in World History 32: Ivan the Terrible's Punishment of Novgorod

▶ Creative Teaching Strategy 10: Barbarian Information Agency

TECHNOLOGY RESOURCES

▶ One-Stop Planner 10.3

▶ Homework Practice Online

▶ Online Maps, Charts, and Graphs: Russian Expansion, 1533

REINFORCEMENT, REVIEW, AND ASSESSMENT

▶ Section 3 Review, p. 235

▶ Daily Quiz 10.3

▶ Main Idea Activity 10.3

▶ English Audio Summary 10.3

▶ Spanish Audio Summary 10.3

TEACH OBJECTIVE 1

ALL LEVELS: Ask students how the Mongols influenced Russian culture. *(Mongols' words became part of the Russian language; Mongols built roads and improved methods of taxation and communication.)* Then ask how these influences make sense in terms of the Mongols' goal in Russia. *(Mongols would want to have good roads, communication, and systems of taxation to ensure that the Russians delivered taxes to the Mongols.)*

TEACH OBJECTIVE 2

LEVEL 1: Have students create a chart with the following headings: *Ivan I, Ivan III, Ivan IV.* Tell students to fill in their charts with characteristics and accomplishments of each leader. After students have completed their charts, have them discuss who was the best ruler. **ENGLISH LANGUAGE LEARNERS**

HOMEWORK Have students use at least one primary or secondary source, such as computer software, to write a short report about one of the early rulers of Moscow.

That's Interesting!

Some historians have estimated that the Mongol domination of Kievan Russia slowed the development of that region by some 150 to 200 years. Records from the period show a decline from the Kievan style of life and high cultural standards. Although the Mongol invasion left Kiev in ruins, some cities, such as Moscow and Tver, grew and prospered.

HISTORY MAKER ANSWER

He was ruthless, yet Russia prospered under his rule.

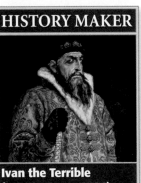

HISTORY MAKER

Ivan the Terrible
(A.D. 1530–A.D. 1584)

Ivan IV had a violent and unpredictable temper. Some people trace his violent nature to tragedies in his life. When he was very young, for example, Ivan's mother was murdered by nobles. As a ruler, he gained a reputation for cruelty toward his enemies.

Following the death of his wife in A.D. 1560, Ivan felt deep despair and became more ruthless than ever. Accusing the boyars of murdering his wife, Ivan ordered the execution of many nobles. Despite his violent behavior, Russia prospered under Ivan. In Russian, his nickname means "awe-inspiring." **How can Ivan IV's nickname be interpreted in different ways?**

Kievan Russia and its neighbors. During Mongol rule the Slavs of eastern Europe had some contact with central and western Europe. In the A.D. 1300s Lithuania and Poland took territory away from Kievan Russia. They formed a kingdom that was hostile to the eastern Slavs. There were also religious conflicts. The Poles had been converted to western Christianity, while the Slavs kept their Eastern Orthodox faith. This set the Slavs apart from both the Poles and the Mongols. To some degree, moreover, the Slavs became suspicious of western Europeans and their influence. Even today, this suspicion has not completely disappeared.

✔ **READING CHECK: Summarizing** How did society in Kievan Russia change under Mongol rule? transportation and communication improved; Mongol words entered language

The Rise of Moscow

In time Mongol rule grew weaker. The princes of the region became more independent. During the early A.D. 1300s Moscow, or Muscovy, became a major Russian principality. Moscow's leader, Prince Ivan I, achieved this by cooperating with the Mongols. In return the Mongols awarded him with the title of Great Prince in A.D. 1328. Around the same time, the leader of the Orthodox Church moved to Moscow. This increased the city's power even more.

From A.D. 1462 to A.D. 1505 **Ivan III,** also called Ivan the Great, ruled as Great Prince. By this time Moscow had begun to assert its independence from the Mongols. By A.D. 1480 Ivan III no longer acknowledged the Mongol khan as Moscow's supreme ruler. He united many principalities. Ivan III became the first ruler of the independent state called Russia. He gained more territory through military conquest. His rule began a long tradition of absolute monarchy in Russia.

Ivan the Terrible. In A.D. 1533 the three-year-old Ivan IV became ruler of Russia. Because of his youth, for many years the boyars were actually in control. In A.D. 1547 Ivan IV finally took power for himself. He considered himself to be the true heir of the Roman and Byzantine Empires. Thus he took the title of **czar,** or caesar. Ivan was an able administrator who sponsored the development of a modernized legal code. He renewed trade with western Europe and opened the vast territory of Siberia to Russian settlement. During his reign, Ivan built the power and authority of the Russian monarchy.

Ivan formed a personal group of civil servants called the *oprichniki* (aw·PREECH·nee·kee). The *oprichniki* arrested boyars and gave their land to Ivan's supporters. He also led his army in an attack on Novgorod, destroying the city. Sometimes Ivan's actions were puzzling and cruel. In A.D. 1581 he even murdered his oldest son. These acts earned him the nickname **Ivan the Terrible.** However, Ivan did lay the foundations for a new Russian state. This state included old Kievan Russia and stretched from Siberia to the Caspian Sea. The czar had absolute power.

The growth of the church. The Orthodox Church in Russia grew more powerful by acquiring land. Much land was acquired by the church through donations from the faithful. By about A.D. 1500 the church was a major Russian landowner.

During Mongol rule, the Russian Orthodox Church had become more and more independent of Constantinople. In A.D. 1448 Russian bishops chose their own leader for the Orthodox Church in Moscow. In A.D. 1589 Moscow's church leader was named patriarch. This helped to make Moscow the center of the Russian church.

CLOSE

Ask students to imagine they are teenagers living in Kievan Russia under Mongol rule. Have students write a short journal entry that describes their daily lives.

REVIEW

Have students complete the Section 3 Review on p. 235.

ASSESS

Have students complete Daily Quiz 10.3. As Alternative Assessment, you may want to use the chart exercise in this section's lessons.

RETEACH

Have students complete Main Idea Activity for English Language Learners and Special-Needs Students 10.3. Then have them write three statements about each subsection.
ENGLISH LANGUAGE LEARNERS , COOPERATIVE LEARNING

EXTEND

Have students study illustrations or slides of Russian art of the period to look for examples of Byzantine influence. Students should make a chart of elements that are common to both artistic traditions. **BLOCK SCHEDULING , COOPERATIVE LEARNING**

A turning point in the development of the Russian church took place in A.D. 1453 with the fall of Constantinople to the powerful army of the Ottoman sultan, Mehmed II. The Turks' victory over the proud and ancient city of the Byzantine emperors removed a major source of competition for church leadership in the Orthodox Christian world.

With the fall of once-mighty Constantinople, Russians proclaimed Moscow to be the **"third Rome."** A Russian churchman explained this phrase by stating that the first Rome had fallen because of heresy. The second Rome, Constantinople, had been conquered by non-Christians. The churchman then claimed that Moscow—the third Rome—would bring the spiritual light of Christian orthodoxy to the whole world.

The new sense of Russian confidence reflected in the churchman's statements is seen in the art and architecture of this period. Domed churches were built and filled with beautiful artwork. Sparkling chandeliers and candles lit every space. These churches were meant to inspire awe, religious wonder, and a mystical feeling of spirituality among the people who worshiped there.

✔ **READING CHECK: Analyzing Information** In what ways did the Russian Orthodox Church gain from Moscow's growing power? prospered financially, became politically independent of Constantinople

INTERPRETING THE VISUAL RECORD

St. Basil In keeping with the Russian Orthodox Church's growth in power, magnificent new churches were built. This photo shows the Cathedral of St. Basil the Blessed, built in Moscow between A.D. 1554 and A.D. 1560. *How does this church reflect a new Russian sense of power and confidence?*

SECTION 3 REVIEW

1. **Define** and explain the significance:
   czar
   "third Rome"

2. **Identify** and explain the significance:
   Vladimir Monomakh
   Polovtsy
   Ivan III
   Ivan the Terrible

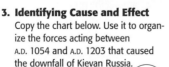
Homework Practice Online
keyword: SP3 HP10

3. **Identifying Cause and Effect**
   Copy the chart below. Use it to organize the forces acting between A.D. 1054 and A.D. 1203 that caused the downfall of Kievan Russia.

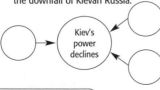
Kiev's power declines

4. **Finding the Main Idea**
   a. How did the distribution of land among Kievan princes help the Mongols to invade?
   b. How was Ivan IV's use of absolute rule different than Ivan III's?

5. **Writing and Critical Thinking**
   Contrasting Create a dialogue between a peasant and a prince discussing the differences in their lives and their ancestors' lives under the Mongols and Kievan Russia.
   Consider:
   • what life may have been like for a peasant during both eras
   • what life may have been like for landowners during both eras

THE BYZANTINE EMPIRE AND RUSSIA **235**

VISUAL RECORD ANSWER
The church is very grand.

internet connect
TOPIC: Byzantine Art
GO TO: go.hrw.com
KEYWORD: SP3 WH10
Have students access the Internet through the HRW Go site to conduct research on Byzantine Art. Then ask them to create a piece of art or design a building or church in Byzantine style. Have students display their creation to the class.

SECTION 3 REVIEW ANSWERS

❶ **Define**
• czar, p. 234
• "third Rome," p. 235

❷ **Identify**
• Vladimir Monomakh, p. 233
• Polovtsy, p. 233
• Ivan III, p. 234
• Ivan the Terrible, p. 234

❸ Students' charts should include civil war; invasion by Polovtsians; Mongol invasion

❹ a. Towns were weakened when Kievan princes began to fight among themselves.

b. He was cruel and ruthless.

❺ Students' dialogues will vary but should consider the relationship between peasants and landowners, especially regarding taxation.

CHAPTER 10

REVIEW AND ASSESSMENT RESOURCES

REPRODUCIBLE RESOURCES

▶ Vocabulary Activity 10

TECHNOLOGY RESOURCES

▶ Chapter 10 Test Generator (on the One-Stop Planner)
▶ Global Skill Builder CD–ROM
▶ HRW Web Site

REINFORCEMENT, REVIEW, and ASSESSMENT

▶ Chapter 10 Review, pp. 236–237
▶ Chapter 10 Tutorial for Students, Parents, Mentors, and Peers
▶ Chapter 10 Test (Form A or B)
▶ Alternative Assessment Handbook
▶ Chapter 10 Test for English Language Learners and Special-Needs Students

REVIEW

Have students complete the Chapter 10 Review on pages 236–237.

ASSESS

Use one of the chapter tests to assess students' understanding of the content. For Alternative Assessment, see the Portfolio Activities and Alternative Assessment Handbook.

CHAPTER 10 REVIEW ANSWERS

Understanding Main Ideas

1. It provided the basis for many European legal systems and for English civil law.

2. strong centralized government and strong military

3. The Christian church split into two churches, the Eastern and Western.

4. passed on learnings of ancient Greece, Rome, and the East; Cyrillic alphabet; murals; icons; mosaics; Hagia Sophia

5. civil wars, conflicts with outside powers, Turkish capture of Asia Minor, Ottoman capture of Constantinople

6. They benefited from Viking trade.

7. Individual households had the least power, while princes had the most power.

8. taxes

9. Ivan I, Ivan III, Ivan the Terrible

10. They believed Moscow would bring spiritual light to the whole world.

Reviewing Themes

1. Yes, they participated in town meetings.

2. It allowed them both to engage in profitable trade.

3. Byzantine Empire, because of its strong central government; Mongol princes became independent, weaker.

236

CHAPTER 10

Creating a Time Line

Copy the time line below onto a sheet of paper. Complete the time line by filling in the events, individuals, and dates from the chapter that you think were significant. Pick three events and explain why you think they were significant.

A.D. 527   **1019**   **1480**

Writing a Summary

Using standard grammar, spelling, sentence structure, and punctuation, write an overview of the events in the chapter.

Identifying People and Ideas

Identify the following terms or individuals and explain their significance:
  1. Justinian
  2. Iconoclastic Controversy
  3. excommunication
  4. Hagia Sophia
  5. Rurik
  6. Pravda Russkia
  7. Polovtsy
  8. Ivan the Terrible
  9. czar
  10. "third Rome"

Understanding Main Ideas

Section 1 *(pp. 222–228)*
The Byzantine Empire
  1. Why was Justinian's Code important?
  2. How was the Byzantine Empire able to last for 1,000 years?
  3. What was the result of the Iconoclastic Controversy?
  4. What are some cultural highlights of the Byzantine Empire?
  5. What led to the decline of the Byzantine Empire?

Section 2 *(pp. 229–232)*
The Rise of Russia
  6. How did Slavs benefit from the Vikings' travels in the southern part of eastern Europe?
  7. Who had the least and most power in Kievan Russia?

Section 3 *(pp. 233–235)*
Russia and the Mongols
  8. What demands did the Mongols make on the Kievan Russians?
  9. Which rulers helped the rise of Moscow?
  10. Why did the Russian Orthodox Church call Moscow the "third Rome"?

Reviewing Themes

  1. Government Did Kievan Russia have a form of government in which citizens had a voice? Explain.
  2. Geography What effects did access to bodies of water have on the Byzantine Empire and Kievan Russia?
  3. Global Relations Which lasted longer, Mongol rule in Russia or the Byzantine Empire? How did the way in which these two powers ruled make a difference?

Thinking Critically

  1. Comparing What similar factors contributed to the wealth of the Byzantine Empire and Kievan Russia?
  2. Analyzing Information The Mongols in Russia were concerned with increasing their wealth through collecting taxes. Why did they bother improving the roads?
  3. Making Predictions What might have happened to Kievan Russia if the Mongols had not invaded?

Writing About History

Making Predictions Write a newspaper editorial about the struggle for power following Yaroslav's death. Using the chart below, make a list of what might happen if the land is divided among the princes. Incorporate the list into an editorial. Discuss what might happen to the council of boyars, *veches*, and Russia's trade business.

If the land is divided up . . .
1.
2.
3.
4.

Have students draw a time line covering the time period from A.D. 300 to A.D. 1500 and add events from this chapter.

RETEACH

Have students who had difficulty with the test outline the chapter and compile a chapter glossary. When they are ready, have students take the Form B Test to assess their mastery of the material.

ENGLISH LANGUAGE LEARNERS, COOPERATIVE LEARNING

Portfolio Extensions

Link to TODAY

1. Have students locate primary and secondary sources, such as computer software, about the Byzantine Empire and Kievan Russia to prepare a written report about the development of trade.

2. Using pictures in encyclopedias as models, have students draw a building plan of the church of Hagia Sophia. Discuss how this

building demonstrates an artistic ideal from Byzantine culture.

3. Have students imagine that they are traders in the Byzantine Empire or Kievan Russia. Have them write journal entries describing their experiences.

Building Social Studies Skills

Building and Using Chronology

Order the statements below in their correct chronological sequence. Then use the information to answer the questions that follow.

Selected Events in the History of Kievan Russia, c. A.D. 500–A.D. 1300

1. Kiev becomes the capital of Kievan Russia, **c. A.D. 882.**
2. Beginning of Kievan economic and political decline, **c. A.D. 1170.**
3. Kiev is destroyed by Mongols under Batu Khan, **A.D. 1240.**
4. Christianity is introduced to Kiev, **c. A.D. 988.**
5. Kiev is incorporated into the Kingdom of Poland, **A.D. 1569.**
6. Kiev is founded, **c. A.D. 550.**

1. Which of the following best represents the actual chronological order of events shown above?
   a. 1, 6, 4, 5, 2, 3
   b. 6, 1, 4, 2, 3, 5
   c. 5, 6, 1, 3, 4, 2
   d. 6, 1, 4, 2, 5, 3

2. According to the chronology you have constructed, why might the Mongols have found Kiev a relatively easy target for destruction?

Identifying a Point of View

Read the following quote. It is from the preface to the book of laws compiled by the Byzantine emperor Justinian. Then answer the questions.

> "The maintenance of . . . government depends upon two things, namely, the force of arms and the observance of the laws: and, for this reason, the fortunate race of the Romans obtained power and precedence over all other nations in former times, and will do so forever, if God should be propitious [kind] . . ."

3. Which of the following statements best describes Justinian's point of view?
   a. The Romans will continue to have power over other nations for all time.
   b. A government succeeds only if it has a strong military to maintain order.
   c. The Romans succeeded because they enforced their laws and had a strong military.
   d. Laws must be obeyed for a government to gain power.

4. An individual's background and experience often influence that person's point of view. What personal experiences might have influenced Justinian's point of view? Give specific examples.

Thinking Critically

1. their location along waterways and ability to engage in profitable trade

2. Better transportation would have ensured that the Russian taxes were paid and delivered to the Mongols.

3. Moscow might not have gained strength and the Russian Orthodox Church might not have become independent of Constantinople.

Writing About History

Students' editorials will vary, but lists might include: the council of boyars would be disassembled; the *veches* would end; and trade would suffer.

Building Social Studies Skills

1. b

2. Kiev was in a period of economic and political decline.

3. c

4. Justinian was successful in reviving the glory and power of the Roman Empire by using Roman laws as the basis for the Justinian Code.

Building Your Portfolio

Students should locate and trace the Black Sea, Baltic Sea, Mediterranean Sea, Bosporus, Nile River, and Volga River. Remind them to identify cities and the goods that were traded.

Alternative Assessment

Building Your Portfolio

Link to TODAY

Geography

Trace a physical map of Eurasia. Locate and highlight the rivers, straits, seas, and oceans that contributed to the growth of the Byzantine Empire and Kievan Russia. You may also want to include what goods were being traded and where. Identify cities, such as Constantinople and Kiev, as well as dates when trade was occurring in these cities. Create a key to help others interpret your map.

☑ internet connect

go.hrw.com

Internet Activity: go.hrw.com
KEYWORD: SP3 WH10

Choose a topic on the Byzantine Empire and Russia to:

- summarize the global influence of the Roman ideas in the Justinian Code upon contemporary political issues such as individual rights and responsibilities.
- research Ivan IV and find out why he was called "Ivan the Terrible."
- create a piece of art or design a building or church in the Byzantine style.

CHAPTER 11

The Islamic World

CHAPTER RESOURCE MANAGER

	Objectives	Pacing Guide	Reproducible Resources
SECTION 1 **The Rise of Islam** (pp. 240–242)	• Describe how geography affected the people of the Arabian Peninsula. • Explain how Islam began. • Identify the main beliefs of Islam.	**Regular** 1 day **Block Scheduling** .5 day *Block Scheduling Handbook with Team Teaching Strategies, 11.1*	**RS** Guided Reading Strategy 11.1 **E** Hands-on History Activity 11: Muhammad's World
SECTION 2 **The Spread of Islam** (pp. 243–247)	• Explore how the Muslims expanded their empire. • Explain why the Islamic community divided.	**Regular** 1.5 day **Block Scheduling** 1 day *Block Scheduling Handbook with Team Teaching Strategies, 11.2*	**RS** Guided Reading Strategy 11.2 **SM** Geography Activity 11: The Spread of Islam **PS** Readings in World History 33: The Muslim Conquest of Spain
SECTION 3 **Islamic Civilization** (pp. 248–253)	• Describe how the location of Arabia affected trade in the Muslim Empire. • Explain what Muslim society and family life were like. • Identify Muslim achievements in science. • Explore how Islam influenced Arab art and literature.	**Regular** 1.5 day **Block Scheduling** 1 day *Block Scheduling Handbook with Team Teaching Strategies, 11.3*	**RS** Guided Reading Strategy 11.3 **RS** Graphic Organizer Activity 11: Science and Islam **PS** Readings in World History 34, 35: Muslim Towns and Trade in North Africa; Social Classes in Muslim India **E** Creative Teaching Strategy 11: The Islamic Heritage Museum

Chapter Resource Key

PS	Primary Sources	**A**	Assessment	🎵	Music
RS	Reading Support	**REV**	Review	📼	Video
IC	Interdisciplinary Connections	**ELL**	Reinforcement and English Language Learners	🌐	Internet
E	Enrichment			💻	Holt Presentation Maker Using Microsoft® PowerPoint®
SM	Skills Mastery	💾	Transparencies		
		💿	CD-ROM		

One-Stop Planner CD-ROM

See the **One-Stop Planner** for a complete list of additional resources for students and teachers.

One-Stop Planner CD-ROM

It's easy to plan lessons, select resources, and print out materials for your students when you use the **One-Stop Planner** CD–ROM with *Test Generator.*

Technology Resources

- One-Stop Planner 11.1
- Holt Researcher: World History: Muhammad
- World History and Cultures Video Program 10: At the Crossroads
- Regions of the World Music Audio CD Program 11: The Persian Gulf and Interior: Classical
- CNN. Presents World Cultures: Yesterday and Today Segment 9: Pilgrimage to Mecca
- Homework Practice Online

- One-Stop Planner 11.2
- World History and Cultures Video Program 10: At the Crossroads
- World History Teaching Transparency: Geography and History 10: Islam in Spain
- Religions of the World Video Series: Islam
- Homework Practice Online
- Online Maps, Charts, and Graphs: Muslim Lands in the 1100s

- One-Stop Planner 11.3
- Holt Researcher: World History: Scheherazade
- World History Teaching Transparency: Art and History 10: Stoneware Bowl
- Religions of the World Video Series: Islam
- Homework Practice Online
- Online Maps, Charts, and Graphs: Muslim Trade Routes

Reinforcement, Review, and Assessment

- Daily Quiz 11.1
- Main Idea Activity 11.1
- English Audio Summary 11.1
- Spanish Audio Summary 11.1
- REV Section 1 Review, p. 242

- Daily Quiz 11.2
- Main Idea Activity 11.2
- English Audio Summary 11.2
- Spanish Audio Summary 11.2
- REV Section 2 Review, p. 247

- Daily Quiz 11.3
- Main Idea Activity 11.3
- English Audio Summary 11.3
- Spanish Audio Summary 11.3
- REV Section 3 Review, p. 253

internet connect

HRW ONLINE RESOURCES
GO TO: go.hrw.com
Then type in a keyword.

TEACHER HOME PAGE
KEYWORD: SP3 TEACHER

CHAPTER INTERNET ACTIVITIES
KEYWORD: SP3 WH11
Choose an activity to:
- research Muslim contributions to medicine and science.
- research and report on Islamic culture.
- create a chart of Islamic calligraphy designs.

CHAPTER ENRICHMENT LINKS
KEYWORD: SP3 CH11

ONLINE ASSESSMENT
Homework Practice
KEYWORD: SP3 HP11
Standardized Test Prep
KEYWORD: SP3 STP11
Rubrics
KEYWORD: SS Rubrics

ONLINE MAPS, CHARTS, AND GRAPHS
KEYWORD: SP3 MCG

CONTENT UPDATES
KEYWORD: SS Content Updates

HOLT PRESENTATION MAKER
KEYWORD: SP3 PPT11

ONLINE READING SUPPORT
KEYWORD: SS Strategies

CURRENT EVENTS
KEYWORD: S3 Current Events

Meeting Individual Needs

Ability Levels

Level 1 Basic level activities designed for all students encountering new material

Level 2 Intermediate level activities designed for average students

Level 3 Challenging activities designed for honors and gifted and talented students

English Language Learners These activities address the needs of students with Limited English Proficiency.

Chapter Review and Assessment

- IC Vocabulary Activity 11
- Global Skill Builder CD–ROM
- HRW Web Site
- REV Chapter 11 Tutorial for Students, Parents, Mentors, and Peers
- REV Chapter 11 Review, pp. 254–255

- A Chapter 11 Test Generator (on the One-Stop Planner)
- A Chapter 11 Test (Form A or B)
- A Alternative Assessment Handbook
- A Chapter 11 Test for English Language Learners and Special-Needs Students

237b

Build on What You Know

Ask students to answer the following questions:

What are some ways religion is spread?

Consider:

- **Buddhism**
- **Christianity**

What were some contributions made by the Byzantine Empire?

Consider:

- the Justinian Code
- changes in the Christian church
- art and architecture

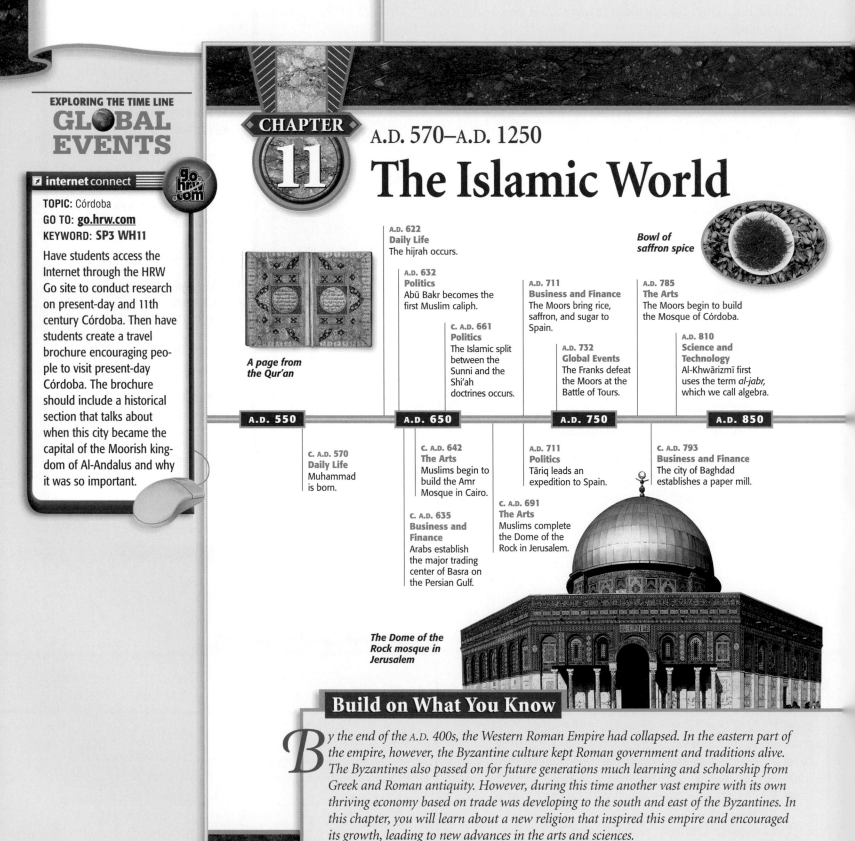

CHAPTER 11

A.D. 570–A.D. 1250

The Islamic World

A page from the Qur'an

A.D. 622
Daily Life
The hijrah occurs.

A.D. 632
Politics
Abū Bakr becomes the first Muslim caliph.

C. A.D. 661
Politics
The Islamic split between the Sunni and the Shi'ah doctrines occurs.

A.D. 711
Business and Finance
The Moors bring rice, saffron, and sugar to Spain.

A.D. 732
Global Events
The Franks defeat the Moors at the Battle of Tours.

Bowl of saffron spice

A.D. 785
The Arts
The Moors begin to build the Mosque of Córdoba.

A.D. 810
Science and Technology
Al-Khwārizmī first uses the term *al-jabr*, which we call algebra.

| A.D. 550 | A.D. 650 | A.D. 750 | A.D. 850 |

C. A.D. 570
Daily Life
Muhammad is born.

C. A.D. 642
The Arts
Muslims begin to build the Amr Mosque in Cairo.

C. A.D. 635
Business and Finance
Arabs establish the major trading center of Basra on the Persian Gulf.

A.D. 711
Politics
Tāriq leads an expedition to Spain.

C. A.D. 691
The Arts
Muslims complete the Dome of the Rock in Jerusalem.

C. A.D. 793
Business and Finance
The city of Baghdad establishes a paper mill.

The Dome of the Rock mosque in Jerusalem

Build on What You Know

By the end of the A.D. 400s, the Western Roman Empire had collapsed. In the eastern part of the empire, however, the Byzantine culture kept Roman government and traditions alive. The Byzantines also passed on for future generations much learning and scholarship from Greek and Roman antiquity. However, during this time another vast empire with its own thriving economy based on trade was developing to the south and east of the Byzantines. In this chapter, you will learn about a new religion that inspired this empire and encouraged its growth, leading to new advances in the arts and sciences.

Themes Journal *To help students create their Themes Journal entries, provide the following examples of appropriate* **agree**/**disagree** *statements.*

Science, Technology & Society

Agree Scientists can achieve great advances when they build on the knowledge of other cultures.

Disagree Scientific achievements are likely to occur in a culturally isolated society.

Global Relations

Agree When one nation conquers another, both can engage in a mutually beneficial exchange of knowledge.

Disagree The ideas of a conquered people are not likely to blend well with the ideas of their conquerors.

Culture

Agree Religious beliefs have no influence on a society's government, art, or science.

Disagree A society's religion and culture are heavily dependent upon one another.

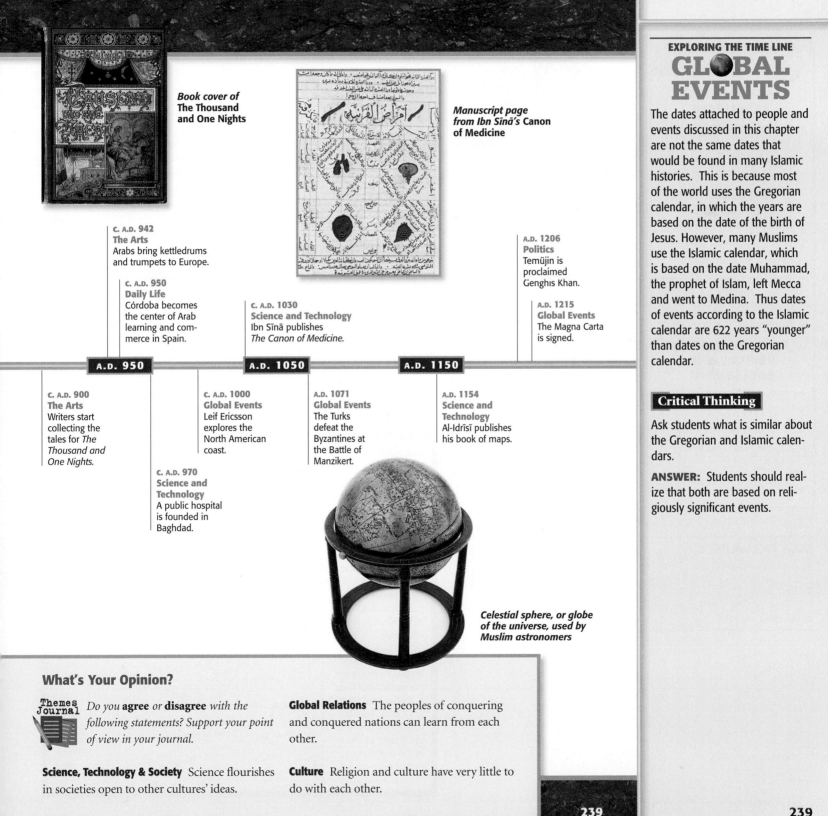

Book cover of The Thousand and One Nights

Manuscript page from Ibn Sīnā's Canon of Medicine

C. A.D. 942
The Arts
Arabs bring kettledrums and trumpets to Europe.

C. A.D. 950
Daily Life
Córdoba becomes the center of Arab learning and commerce in Spain.

C. A.D. 1030
Science and Technology
Ibn Sīnā publishes *The Canon of Medicine.*

A.D. 1206
Politics
Temüjin is proclaimed Genghıs Khan.

A.D. 1215
Global Events
The Magna Carta is signed.

A.D. 950   **A.D. 1050**   **A.D. 1150**

C. A.D. 900
The Arts
Writers start collecting the tales for *The Thousand and One Nights.*

C. A.D. 1000
Global Events
Leif Ericsson explores the North American coast.

A.D. 1071
Global Events
The Turks defeat the Byzantines at the Battle of Manzikert.

A.D. 1154
Science and Technology
Al-Idrīsī publishes his book of maps.

C. A.D. 970
Science and Technology
A public hospital is founded in Baghdad.

Celestial sphere, or globe of the universe, used by Muslim astronomers

EXPLORING THE TIME LINE
GLOBAL EVENTS

The dates attached to people and events discussed in this chapter are not the same dates that would be found in many Islamic histories. This is because most of the world uses the Gregorian calendar, in which the years are based on the date of the birth of Jesus. However, many Muslims use the Islamic calendar, which is based on the date Muhammad, the prophet of Islam, left Mecca and went to Medina. Thus dates of events according to the Islamic calendar are 622 years "younger" than dates on the Gregorian calendar.

Critical Thinking

Ask students what is similar about the Gregorian and Islamic calendars.

ANSWER: Students should realize that both are based on religiously significant events.

What's Your Opinion?

Themes Journal *Do you* **agree** *or* **disagree** *with the following statements? Support your point of view in your journal.*

Science, Technology & Society Science flourishes in societies open to other cultures' ideas.

Global Relations The peoples of conquering and conquered nations can learn from each other.

Culture Religion and culture have very little to do with each other.

OBJECTIVES

1 **Describe how geography affected the people of the Arabian Peninsula.**

2 **Explain how Islam began.**

3 **Identify the main beliefs of Islam.**

MAP ANSWERS

1. many waterways

2. Red Sea

3. Arabian Desert

SECTION 1

READ TO DISCOVER

❶ How did geography affect the people of the Arabian Peninsula?

❷ How did Islam begin?

❸ What were the main beliefs of Islam?

DEFINE

bedouins
hijrah
jihad
mosques

IDENTIFY

Muhammad
Islam
Muslims
Qur'an

WHY IT MATTERS TODAY

The largest country of the Arabian Peninsula is Saudi Arabia. Use CNNfyi.com or other **current event** sources to explore the culture of Arabia today and its relationship with the United States. Record your findings in your journal.

CNNfyi.com

The Rise of Islam

The Main Idea
The founding of the Islamic religion in the Arabian Peninsula changed and unified the Arab world.

The Story Continues *As the Byzantines were struggling to carry on the traditions of the Roman Empire, another empire was developing on the Arabian Peninsula based on a new religion. This faith would affect cultures and civilizations in a large part of the world. It is still one of the strongest spiritual movements in the world of today.*

Arabia: Its Geography and People

The Arabian Peninsula is bordered on the south by the Arabian Sea, on the east by the Persian Gulf, on the west by the Red Sea, and to the north by the Syrian Desert. Except for narrow strips along the coasts, most of the Arabian Peninsula is desert. Because the desert dwellers could not grow crops, many herded sheep and camels. These Arab herders, called **bedouins** (BEH·duh·wuhnz), were nomads. Whole bedouin families moved with their flocks from one grazing area to another. The bedouins were organized into tribes. The leader of a tribe was called a sheikh (SHAYK). This title was a sign of respect that was given to a man because of his knowledge or position.

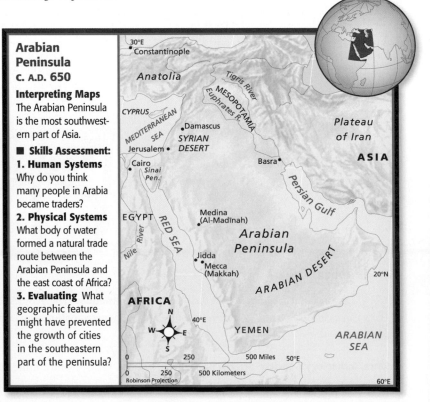

Arabian Peninsula
C. A.D. 650

Interpreting Maps
The Arabian Peninsula is the most southwestern part of Asia.

■ **Skills Assessment:**
1. Human Systems
Why do you think many people in Arabia became traders?

2. Physical Systems
What body of water formed a natural trade route between the Arabian Peninsula and the east coast of Africa?

3. Evaluating What geographic feature might have prevented the growth of cities in the southeastern part of the peninsula?

TEACH OBJECTIVE 1

LEVEL 1: As a class, discuss the geography of the Arabian Peninsula. Then draw a two-column chart on the board or overhead projector. Label one column *Desert Arabs* and the other *Coastal Arabs*. Have students complete the chart by listing the differences in geography and lifestyle of each.
ENGLISH LANGUAGE LEARNERS

HOMEWORK Have each student use standard grammar, spelling, sentence structure, and punctuation to write a paragraph explaining why some non-Muslim peoples might readily have accepted Islam. Select students to read their paragraphs to the class.

TEACH OBJECTIVE 2

LEVEL 3: Ask students to create an annotated time line of the development of Islam. Have volunteers use their time lines to explain how Islam began.

TEACH OBJECTIVE 3

ALL LEVELS: Ask students to describe the major beliefs of Islam. Have them list the five chief obligations of a Muslim.
ENGLISH LANGUAGE LEARNERS

The areas along the coasts generally had milder climates that could support greater numbers of people. Towns grew up in these areas, and the townspeople became traders. For example, goods from Asia and Africa entered the port of Jidda on the Red Sea. From there they were transported inland to the city of Mecca (Makkah). Mecca was on a caravan route running north across the desert to Syria. Through trade, Arabs in the towns met and were influenced by people from many different cultures.

✔ **READING CHECK: Contrasting** How did the lifestyle of the desert Arabs differ from the lifestyle of the Arabs who lived along the coasts? nomadic herders instead of traders

The Prophet Muhammad

In Mecca in about A.D. 570, a man named **Muhammad** was born into a poor clan of Mecca's ruling tribe. Like many Arabs in Mecca, Muhammad made a living as a caravan trader. As a trader, he came in contact with a variety of people. Some, such as Christians and Jews, were monotheists. They believed in a single god. Many of them, particularly the Arabs, were polytheists who worshiped many gods.

When he was about 40 years old, Muhammad reported that the angel Jibreel (Gabriel, in English) told him that he was called to be a prophet of God (in Arabic, Allah) and revealed verses that Muhammad was to recite. A little later, he was instructed to teach others. Over the next several years Muhammad reported receiving many more revelations.

The merchant rulers at Mecca were very much against Muhammad's teaching. They thought his ideas criticized their conduct and attitudes and threatened their authority. Every year Arab pilgrims came to Mecca to worship at the Kaaba (KAH·buh). The Kaaba was a stone building filled with idols that some people worshiped. The merchant rulers may have feared that Muhammad's teachings about one god might stop such pilgrimages. Before long, they began to harass Muhammad and his followers. Eventually Muhammad looked for a more accepting place.

In A.D. 622 Muhammad and his followers settled in the town of Yathrib. This journey from Mecca to Yathrib is known as the **hijrah** (hi·JY·ruh). Hijrah means "flight" or "migration." Later, Yathrib became known as Medina, or Al-Madinah, the "City of the Prophet." Eventually the year of the hijrah became the first year of the Muslim calendar.

After the move to Yathrib, Muhammad gained followers in greater numbers. Desert tribes began to accept his ideas, increasing tensions between Mecca and Medina. Several years of war followed. Finally, Mecca submitted. Muhammad went back to Mecca in A.D. 630. The idols in the Kaaba were destroyed, and it then became a holy place for Muhammad's followers. Muhammad rededicated the Kaaba to the worship of the One God, Allah.

Soon Arabs everywhere began to accept Muhammad's ideas. Through a combination of wise policies, tolerance, and force, Muhammad converted many of the bedouin tribes to his new religion, called **Islam.** By A.D. 632, when he died, many Arab tribes had become followers of Muhammad. Within a very few years, Islam had spread across Arabia and the Middle East and into North Africa.

✔ **READING CHECK: Sequencing** What were the important events in the development of Islam? vision of Muhammad; hijrah; conquered Mecca and destroyed idols

Today the Kaaba in the Great Mosque at Mecca serves as a spiritual sanctuary for Muslims.

Link to Today Why might modern followers of Islam consider the Kaaba a special place?

Holt Researcher

go.hrw.com
KEYWORD: Holt Researcher
FreeFind: Muhammad
After reading more about Muhammad on the Holt Researcher, write a short essay explaining how he changed life on the Arabian Peninsula and beyond.

Daily Life

Bedouins camped in tents in groups of related families. The scarcity of rainfall in the desert prevented the nomadic bedouins from staying in one place for more than a few days. By that time, the animals had exhausted the grass supply in the area. In years when rainfall was scarce, tribes often had to travel hundreds of miles to find water and grazing land. Incursions on another tribe's land inevitably led to clashes, which normally took the form of raiding the rival's herds.

Critical Thinking

Ask students to suggest how this lifestyle of scarce resources and frequent conflict might affect a culture.

ANSWER: Students might suggest that a culture would probably come to emphasize virtues such as bravery and skill in battle.

LINK TO TODAY ANSWER
It's an important part of the history of Islam.

Technology Resources

CNN Presents World Cultures: Yesterday and Today Segment 9: Pilgrimage to Mecca

THE ISLAMIC WORLD **241**

CLOSE

Discuss with students what the origins and teachings of Islam have in common with other major world religions.

REVIEW

Have students complete the Section 1 Review on p. 242.

ASSESS

Have students complete Daily Quiz 11.1. As Alternative Assessment, you may want to use the chart or time line exercises in this section's lessons.

RETEACH

Have students complete Main Idea Activity for English Language Learners and Special-Needs Students 11.1. Then ask each student to write a paragraph about the development of Islam. **ENGLISH LANGUAGE LEARNERS**

EXTEND

Have students develop a list of questions they would ask Muhammad in a half-hour interview if they were either a bedouin or a Meccan. **BLOCK SCHEDULING**

SECTION 1 REVIEW ANSWERS

❶ Define
- bedouins, p. 240
- hijrah, p. 241
- jihad, p. 242
- mosques, p. 242

❷ Identify
- Muhammad, p. 241
- Islam, p. 241
- Muslims, p. 242
- Qur'an, p. 242

❸ Students' time lines should include the vision of Muhammad, the hijrah, and the conquest of Mecca and destruction of idols.

❹ a. Mecca was near waterways and on a caravan route, which allowed merchants to engage in profitable trade.

b. It led Muhammad to teach about a single God, Allah.

c. Followers settled in Medina and their numbers grew. Nomadic tribes began to accept Muhammed's ideas and helped spread Islam.

❺ Students' dialogues will vary but should consider the beliefs of polytheists and Muslims.

Technology Resources

Regions of the World Music Audio CD Program 11: The Persian Gulf and Interior: Classical Music of Iran

---

THE FIVE PILLARS OF ISLAM

1. The profession of faith.
This includes acknowledging that there is no god but God (Allah) and that Muhammad is the messenger of God. It implies belief in earlier messengers.

2. The five daily prayers.
This includes following a ritual of washing and prescribed movements and facing the direction of Mecca.

3. Paying zakat.
This is an annual tax used to help the poor and others in need.

4. Fasting during the holy month of Ramadan. (RAH·muh·dahn)
Muslims eat and drink nothing from dawn to sunset. This reminds them of the importance of self-discipline, dependence on the Creator, and the feelings of the poor.

5. Making a pilgrimage to Mecca at least once, if possible.
During the pilgrimage, which takes place during a certain time of the year, Muslims meet to pray and perform rituals to remind them of the faith of Abraham, and the unity and equality of Muslims all over the world.

The Faith of Islam

Islam is based on the central beliefs that there is only one God, and that each believer must obey God's will. In fact, in Arabic the word *Islam* means "submission to [the will of] God." Followers of Islam are called **Muslims.** Today millions of people throughout the world are Muslims. The largest Muslim communities are in Asia, North Africa, and parts of eastern Europe.

The holy book of Islam is the **Qur'an** (kuh·RAN). According to Muslims, the Qur'an is the word of God as revealed to Muhammad. This includes rules and instructions for right living. There are five basic acts of worship, called the Five Pillars of Islam, required of all Muslims. There are other rules for Muslims to follow as well, such as living humble lives, being tolerant and generous, and not eating pork or drinking alcoholic beverages. Islam also emphasizes the importance of the **jihad** (ji·HAHD), which means "the struggle to defend the faith." Some Muslims believed that anyone who died in this struggle would be rewarded in heaven.

Muhammad taught that God had revealed the Qur'an as a sacred guide for all people. First written in Arabic, the Qur'an was not rapidly translated into other languages because Muslims believed that God's revelations might be lost or changed. As a result, Arabic became the common language of Muslims in religion, law, and literature. Muslims memorize and recite the Qur'an in Arabic.

Muslims worship in **mosques.** Mosques have no furnishings, only mats or rugs on which to kneel, and they never contain images of people or even animals. There is no official clergy in Islam. Men who are trained in the Qur'an and Islamic law guide the people in worship. On Friday at noon, Muslims gather together for congregational prayer and sermons. In most Islamic cultures, women say the same prayers at home or in a section of the mosque set aside for them.

✔ **READING CHECK: Finding the Main Idea** What are the central beliefs of Islam? one God; obey God's will

---

SECTION 1 REVIEW

1. Define and explain the significance:
bedouins
hijrah
jihad
mosques

2. Identify and explain the significance:
Muhammad
Islam
Muslims
Qur'an

3. Sequencing Copy the time line below. Use it to organize and identify events in the rise of Islam.

C. A.D. 610 — A.D. 632

Muhammad reports receiving a revelation from God.

Muhammad dies.

4. Finding the Main Idea

a. In what way did the geographic location of Mecca help its early merchant rulers establish their base of power there?

b. How did belief in Muhammad's prophethood lead to the religion of Islam?

c. What role did settled and nomadic Arabs play in the spread of Islam throughout the Arabian Peninsula?

5. Writing and Critical Thinking

Comparing Imagine a meeting between a polytheist of Mecca and a convert to Islam. Write a dialogue between them comparing their faiths.
Consider:
• the beliefs of the polytheists
• the beliefs of Muslims

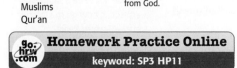 **Homework Practice Online**
keyword: SP3 HP11

SECTION 2

The Spread of Islam

READ TO DISCOVER

❶ How did the Muslims expand their empire?
❷ Why did the Islamic community divide?

DEFINE

caliph
imams
sultan

IDENTIFY

Abū Bakr
'Umar
Sunni
Shi'ah
Sufi
Rābi'ah al-'Adawīyah
Tāriq
Moors

▶ WHY IT MATTERS TODAY

Several million Muslims live in North America. Use **CNNfyi.com** or other **current event** sources to find out where the largest Islamic communities in North America are located. Record your findings in your journal.

CNNfyi.com

The Main Idea
After the death of Muhammad, the Islamic world greatly expanded, but soon split into two factions.

The Story Continues *According to the Qur'an and the Hadith, or sayings of the prophet, during a journey to Jerusalem, Muhammad traveled through seven heavens to visit the throne of God. Although some followers refused to believe the story at first, one faithful convert named Abū Bakr accepted it immediately. For his faithfulness he was called "The Upright."*

Expansion Under Abū Bakr and 'Umar

When Muhammad died in A.D. 632, his followers chose **Abū Bakr** (uh·BOO BAK·uhr) as his successor. Abū Bakr was Muhammad's oldest friend and one of his early converts. He was given the title **caliph** (KAY·luhf), meaning "successor to the Prophet." During his rule, Abū Bakr helped to bring the Arabic tribes together. He also began to expand Islam's influence northward.

In A.D. 634 **'Umar** (OO·mahr) succeeded Abū Bakr as caliph. 'Umar was a strong leader with a well-run government. Under 'Umar, Muslim expansion continued and people began to share in the empire's wealth. He continued conquering neighboring territories of non-Muslims. In about A.D. 640, for example, the growing armies of Islam under 'Umar's leadership won much of the once-mighty Persian Empire and took control of Iraq. Every victory further encouraged people from across the region to accept Islam. Within 25 years of Muhammad's death, the Muslim Empire included parts of Syria, Persia, and North Africa.

The Arab policy toward conquered people made expansion easier. Fierce and fearless in war, Arabs also entered into many treaties without battle. They were often more tolerant than other conquerors. They did not demand that all conquered people convert to Islam. In the early years, Arabs were particularly tolerant of Christians and Jews.

Muslims called Christians and Jews "People of the Book." Muhammad had accepted the Torah and the Christian Bible as part of God's teachings. Christians, Jews, and some other groups could choose to accept Islam or to pay extra taxes. Some people who refused both options were killed. Many conquered people, however, either paid or converted to Islam.

The caliphs who came after 'Umar expanded Muslim influence even more as the power of other empires, such as the Byzantines, was weakening. Within about 100 years after Muhammad's death, Muslims had swept eastward through part of India and moved westward to conquer much of North Africa. During this time of expansion, the Muslims also conquered islands in the Mediterranean Sea. These gave them control of important trade routes. In A.D. 711 a powerful Muslim force invaded Spain and thus brought Islam to Europe. Muslim troops also tried to conquer Constantinople, but their attempt failed when Byzantine armies successfully defended the city.

✔ **READING CHECK: Sequencing** What steps did Abū Bakr and 'Umar take to spread Islam? unified Arabic tribes; conquered neighboring non-Muslim lands

SECTION 2 RESOURCES

REPRODUCIBLE RESOURCES

▶ Guided Reading Strategy 11.2
▶ Geography Activity 11: The Spread of Islam
▶ Readings in World History 33: The Muslim Conquest of Spain

TECHNOLOGY RESOURCES

▶ One-Stop Planner 11.2
▶ World History and Cultures Video Program 10: At the Crossroads
▶ World History Teaching Transparency: Geography and History 10: Islam in Spain
▶ Religions of the World Video Series: Islam
▶ Homework Practice Online

REINFORCEMENT, REVIEW, AND ASSESSMENT

▶ Section 2 Review, p. 247
▶ Daily Quiz 11.2
▶ Main Idea Activity 11.2
▶ English Audio Summary 11.2
▶ Spanish Audio Summary 11.2

LEVEL 1: Refer students to the map on page 244 of their textbook and ask how far Islam spread under Muhammad. *(through much of the Arabian Peninsula)* Ask how much farther it spread under Abū Bakr and 'Umar. *(throughout the Arabian Peninsula and well into North Africa and Persia)* Ask how much farther it spread in the approximate 100 years after Muhammad's death. *(throughout Persia and North Africa and into India and Europe)* Have students identify two activities that contributed to the rapid spread of Islam. *(war and trade)* **ENGLISH LANGUAGE LEARNERS**

Teacher to Teacher

Mary Catherine Rahman of Chicago, Illinois, suggested the following activity: Have students trace a political map of the present-day Middle East and North Africa. Students should then add information about the spread of Islam from page 244 of their textbook. Have students list the modern countries that were wholly or partly included in the Islamic Empire by 750. Students should then research and list the major religion of each country today.

MAP ANSWERS

1. A.D. 633–A.D. 661

2. It may have caused some people in North Africa and China to convert to Islam.

Global Relations

The period of expansion that began under Abū Bakr and continued under 'Umar was not originally intended as an organized series of military campaigns designed to create an empire. The conflicts did not become strategically organized campaigns until the first battles had been successful.

Critical Thinking

Ask students what the goals of the early fighting might have been.

ANSWER: Students might answer that the goals of the early battles might have been to obtain wealth.

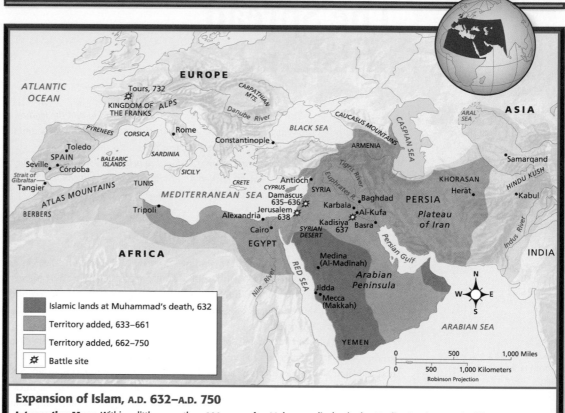

Expansion of Islam, A.D. 632–A.D. 750

Interpreting Maps Within a little more than 100 years after Muhammad's death, the Muslim Empire stretched from western Europe eastward to the border of China.

■ **Skills Assessment: 1. The World in Spatial Terms** What years saw the greatest expansion of the Muslim Empire? **2. Making Predictions** How might the expansion of Islam have affected the history of areas such as North Africa and China?

The Islamic Community Divides

The system of Islamic government allowed the caliphs to exercise great authority. From the beginning, however, people could not agree about who should be caliph. Eventually these disagreements split the Muslim community. The split began when 'Umar's successor, 'Uthmān (ooth·MAHN), was murdered. 'Uthmān was killed because rebels believed he favored his own clan. 'Alī was chosen to succeed 'Uthmān as caliph. 'Uthmān's relative Mu'awiyah (mooh·AH·wee·ya) protested. He accused 'Alī of helping the killers. War broke out between the two sides. In A.D. 661 'Alī was assassinated, and Mu'awiyah became caliph.

Most Muslims agreed to accept Mu'awiyah as caliph. These Muslims eventually became known as the **Sunni** (SOOH·nee). They were followers of the Sunna, meaning "way of the Prophet" or "habitual practice." The Sunni believed that agreement among the Muslim people should settle religious matters.

'Alī's followers insisted that only his descendants should be caliphs. This group later became known as the **Shi'ah** (SHEE·ah). The Shi'ah believed that 'Alī's descendants, called **imams** (i·MAHMZ), should decide religious and worldly matters.

TEACH OBJECTIVE 2

LEVEL 3: Form students into triads to decide whether the death of Muhammad, Abū Bakr, or 'Umar was a more critical event for Muslims. *(Students should recognize that while Islam survived after Muhammad's death, his successors were faced with maintaining Muslims' political unity.)* Use the responses to launch a discussion of the divisions that arose among Muslims after 'Umar's death. Ask whether these disputes were about power or Islamic principles. *(power)* **COOPERATIVE LEARNING**

The split between the two groups continued. The rift deepened when Mu'awiyah's descendants killed 'Alī's son Husayn. According to the Shi'ah, on a day of reckoning, Husayn's mother, Fātimah, will take her son's blood-stained shirt to God and say:

Primary Source

“**Oh God, you have given me and my son a promise. For the sake of his sacrifice, have mercy upon the people of the Last Prophet!**”

Fātimah, from *Islam in Practice: Religious Beliefs in a Persian Village,* by Reinhold Loeffler

Then, in memory of Husayn's death, God will forgive the sins of the Shi'ah and there will be peace. Today the division between the Shi'ah and the Sunni still exists. Less than 10 percent of the world's Muslims are Shi'ah.

Later another group within Islam developed. Muslim mystics known as **Sufi,** such as **Rābi'ah al-'Adawīyah,** tried to live simple lives centered on God. They turned away from worldly possessions and success. The Sufi believed that faith in God was the only mark of a person's worth.

✔ **READING CHECK: Comparing and Contrasting** What are the similarities and differences between the Sunni and the Shi'ah? both follow teachings of Muhammad, but disagree about who should be caliphs

The Empire Continues to Spread

Despite this split, the Muslim Empire continued to spread. Soon a North African people called the Berbers converted to Islam. In A.D. 711 a Berber general named **Tāriq** led a Muslim army to Spain. They crossed the Mediterranean at the great rock that guards the strait between Africa and Europe. The rock became known as *Jabal Tāriq,* or "Mount Tāriq." In English it is called the Rock of Gibraltar.

The Moors. Tāriq's Muslim army conquered Spain quickly. Those Muslims who made Spain their home were called **Moors.** Within a few years, the Moors crossed over the Pyrenees to raid central France. In A.D. 732 the Franks defeated the Moors at the Battle of Tours and the Moors eventually withdrew from France. They continued to rule parts of Spain, however, for more than 700 years.

Suleymaniye Mosque in Istanbul, Turkey

Analyzing Primary Sources

Identifying a Point of View Why might the Shi'ah consider Husayn's death a special sacrifice? died for his faith

HISTORY MAKER

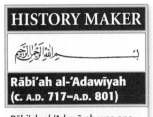

Rābi'ah al-'Adawīyah
(C. A.D. 717–A.D. 801)

Rābi'ah al-'Adawīyah was one of the greatest Sufi mystics. Abandoned at a young age, she was later sold into slavery. While she filled her days with hard work, Rābi'ah spent her nights praying to Allah for help, guidance, and deliverance.

One night, a great light appeared above her head. Her master, recognizing her devotion to Allah, set her free. Rābi'ah went on to become one of the first female Sufi mystics. Her religious poetry and other writings still inspire Muslims today.

Because no known images of Rābi'ah al-'Adawīyah exist, the calligraphy above is used to symbolize her. It translates as: "In the name of Allah Most Gracious, Most Merciful." **How is Rābi'ah al-'Adawīyah important to Islam?**

Government

While 'Uthmān was thought by many to be a well-meaning man, he enraged many Arabs by appointing his relatives to important positions. In addition, 'Uthmān accepted gifts sent by his governors and their representatives. The rebellion against 'Uthmān began in al-Kufah among 'Ali's followers and grew in strength in Egypt. Five hundred rebels went to Medina in A.D. 656. They stormed 'Uthmān's home. Muhammad, son of Abū Bakr, was the first to break into the residence and attack 'Uthmān. 'Uthmān was killed by the rebels.

Critical Thinking

Ask students what factor might have compounded the tension caused by 'Uthmān appointing his relatives to power.

ANSWER: Students might answer that there was disagreement over who should be caliph.

HISTORY MAKER ANSWER
She was one of the first female Sufi mystics.

ALL LEVELS: Have students work in pairs to create two diagrams that illustrate how Sunni and Shi'ah Muslims differed over where religious and secular authority originate and the proper relationship between the two types of authority. Select volunteer pairs to duplicate their diagrams on the chalkboard or overhead projector and explain them to the class.

ENGLISH LANGUAGE LEARNERS , COOPERATIVE LEARNING

HOMEWORK Using the textbook discussion as a reference, have each student outline the issues and events that led to the split between Sunnis and Shi'ahs.

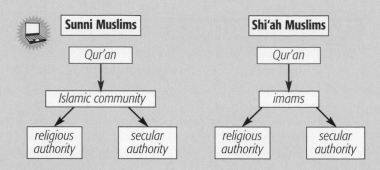

Sunni Muslims

Qur'an → Islamic community → religious authority / secular authority

Shi'ah Muslims

Qur'an → imams → religious authority / secular authority

CLOSE

Organize a class discussion about the causes and effects of the dispute between the Sunni and Shi'ah Muslims.

History Maker

MUHAMMAD. According to Islamic tradition, after Muhammad was approached by the angel Jibreel, he was afraid and confused, and he considered ending his life. He changed his mind, however, when he heard a voice telling him he was "the Messenger of God." Muhammad told Khadijah, his wife, that he was afraid he had been possessed by an evil spirit. According to tradition, Khadijah told him that she would go to the home of her cousin, who was a Christian, and ask his opinion. Khadijah's cousin said that if what she told him was true, then she and Muhammad should not worry, because Muhammad was the Prophet of his people.

Critical Thinking

Ask students why the fact that Khadijah's cousin was a Christian might have been significant.

ANSWER: This endorsement from a Christian might have made it easier to convert Christians to Islam.

SKILLS PRACTICE ANSWERS

1. Students should use dates to arrange events in order.

2. Sequence shows cause-and-effect relationships.

Technology Resources

go.hrw.com Online Maps, Charts, and Graphs: Muslim Lands in the 1100s

---

SKILL-BUILDING STRATEGIES   **Understanding Sequence**

The Expansion of Islam

Certain events happened in a certain way to help Islam succeed. Understanding the sequence in which events happened can help us understand why some events occurred as they did.

In A.D. 711, less than a century after Muhammad's death, a Muslim army led by the Berber general Tāriq invaded Spain.

Abū Bakr followed Muhammad as the leader of Islam and became the faith's first caliph in A.D. 632.

This Persian image shows Muhammad, his face covered, entering a town (possibly Medina or Mecca), probably at some point between A.D. 622 and A.D. 632.

A troop of Muslim Turkish cavalry is shown in battle formation in this image, c. A.D. 1050–c. A.D. 1100.

Skills Reminder

A sequence is an arrangement of things or events in a logical order. Creating a sequence helps you understand information. From the pattern you create, you can decide how events or things are related to each other. To help sequence information, look for calendar references; time periods; and clue words, such as *first, second, after, before, meanwhile,* or *later*. If there are no calendar references or clue words, look for an implied sequence. For example, could one event have happened without another taking place first?

Skills Practice

❶ Study the images and captions above. They show and describe historical events that occurred during the early history of Islam. These events helped lead to the rise and spread of Islam. The events described have been placed in random order. Reorganize the events to place them in their proper sequence.

❷ How does understanding the sequence in which these historical events occurred help to explain how Islam succeeded?

The great era of Arab Muslim expansion lasted until the 1100s. After that, the Turks became the ruling force in Islam. The Islamic empire, though, continued to expand under the Turks.

The Turks and Islam. Turkish-speaking groups from the steppes of central Asia began to move west and south. These tough, nomadic people lived as much by fighting and raiding as by herding. They developed a warlike culture that encouraged expansion and conquest. The conquests brought these Turkish peoples into contact with Arab and Persian Muslims of the Middle East. By the late A.D. 900s, large numbers of Turks had converted to Islam. Many of these people settled around the great Muslim city of Baghdad, in what is now Iraq, where they served the caliph as troops. The Turks supported Islamic law, but their growing power caused political authority to gradually shift away from the caliph. A **sultan** ruled the Turks and claimed to serve the caliph, who still played an important symbolic role. By the mid-1000s the Turks had won control of Baghdad. During the next century, they became the dominant ruling force throughout much of the Islamic world.

During the A.D. 1000s, Turkish Muslims seized Syria, Mesopotamia, and much of Asia Minor. The Turks were skillful warriors. They won a major victory against the Byzantines at the Battle of Manzikert in A.D. 1071. Meanwhile, Turkish Muslims began raiding northern India. The Indians fought fiercely. The Turks, however, fought on horseback. They used their horses cleverly and succeeded. By the early A.D. 1200s they controlled most of northern India.

In the A.D. 1250s outside forces slowed Turkish Muslim expansion. Christians from the West captured cities in a series of wars. Meanwhile, Mongols from the East destroyed Baghdad.

✔ **READING CHECK: Supporting a Point of View** What evidence would you give that the Muslims had a large and well-trained army? conquered parts of Spain, Syria, Mesopotamia, and Asia Minor

INTERPRETING THE VISUAL RECORD

Flag bearers This artwork from A.D. 1237 shows the flag bearers of an Islamic caliph. *How do the flag bearers indicate the importance of the caliph, even during the reign of the Turks?*

SECTION 2 REVIEW ANSWERS

❶ **Define**
- caliph, p. 243
- imams, p. 244
- sultan, p. 247

❷ **Identify**
- Abū Bakr, p. 243
- 'Umar, p. 243
- Sunni, p. 244
- Shi'ah, p. 244
- Sufi, p. 245
- Rābi' ah al-'Adawīyah, p. 245
- Tāriq, p. 245
- Moors, p. 245

❸ Arabs: A.D. 637–1100s; Iraq, parts of Syria, Persia, and North Africa, Spain; Turks: A.D. 900s–1250; Baghdad, Syria, Mesopotamia, much of Asia Minor, northern India

❹ **a.** It borders many bodies of water, but is also connected by land to parts of Asia and Africa.

b. It may have slowed expansion.

❺ Students should consider the organization of the government and military, policies toward conquered people, and how conquered people reacted to Islam.

SECTION 2 REVIEW

1. **Define** and explain the significance:
   caliph
   imams
   sultan

2. **Identify** and explain the significance:
   Abū Bakr   Sufi
   'Umar   Rābi'ah al-'Adawīyah
   Sunni   Tāriq
   Shi'ah   Moors

3. **Categorizing** Copy the chart below. Use it to organize the areas that the Muslims conquered during the expansion of the Muslim Empire.

	Arabs	Turks
Years		
Areas		

4. **Finding the Main Idea**
   a. In what ways did the geography of the Arabian Peninsula contribute to the spread of Islam?
   b. What effect might the split in the Islamic community have had on the expansion of the Muslim Empire?

5. **Writing and Critical Thinking**
   Evaluating Explain why the Muslims were able to expand their empire so rapidly.
   Consider:
   • how the Muslim government and military were organized
   • what the Muslim policies were toward conquered people
   • how conquered people reacted to Islam

Homework Practice Online
keyword: SP3 HP11

THE ISLAMIC WORLD **247**

OBJECTIVES

1 Describe how the location of Arabia affected trade in the Muslim Empire.

2 Explain what Muslim society and family life were like.

3 Identify Muslim achievements in science.

4 Explore how Islam influenced Arab art and literature.

SECTION 3

READ TO DISCOVER

❶ How did the location of Arabia affect trade in the Muslim Empire?

❷ What were Muslim society and family life like?

❸ What Muslim achievements were made in science?

❹ How did Islam influence Arab art and literature?

DEFINE

astrolabe
minaret

IDENTIFY

al-Rāzī
Ibn Sīnā
al-Idrīsī
The Thousand and One Nights

▶ WHY IT MATTERS TODAY

The role of women in Muslim society has changed throughout the years. Use **CNNfyi**.com or other **current event** sources to explore the role of women in Muslim societies today. Record your findings in your journal.

CNNfyi.com

Islamic Civilization

The Main Idea
Muslims made many advances in economics, government, education, science, and the arts.

The Story Continues *Islam became more than just a religion. It was also a great cultural movement that affected virtually every aspect of life within the Islamic Empire. As one Muslim saying expressed: "Islam, the government, and the people are like the tent, the pole, the ropes, and the pegs. The tent is Islam; the pole is the government; the ropes and pegs are the people. None will do without the others."*

A Culture of Traders

The Arabs had been traders for centuries before their empire developed. Muhammad himself had been a trader. It is not surprising, then, that trade was important to Muslim culture. The empire was at the center of a world trade network that linked Europe, Asia, and Africa. India and China sent goods to ports in Syria and Egypt.

As trade grew, other cultures increasingly demanded the quality goods that Muslims produced, such as textiles manufactured from silk, cotton, and wool, as well as beautiful woven tapestries and carpets. Muslims also made metal products from gold and silver. Steel swords from Damascus and from the Spanish city of Toledo became world famous. Luxuries such as jewelry, perfumes, and spices were in great demand. Muslim artisans produced pottery and glassware. Artisans in North Africa and Spain made fine leather goods. All this trade made the Islamic Empire wealthy.

Muslims exchanged ideas with other cultures as well. Both Córdoba and Toledo in Spain were famous centers of learning. Christian and Jewish scholars carried Muslim ideas from Spain into western Europe. Sicily under the Muslims was known for its astronomers and geographers. They, too, influenced Europeans. Many Europeans, in fact, viewed the Muslim world as a source of advanced knowledge in many scientific areas and in banking and commerce.

✔ **READING CHECK:**
Evaluating How important was the location of the Arabian Peninsula to trade in the Muslim Empire? enabled them to trade with Europe, Asia and Africa

Muslim merchants carried goods across a far-flung network of trade routes.

LEVEL 1: Have students list some items that Muslims produced and traded. *(silk, cotton, and wool textiles, woven tapestries, carpets, metal products, jewelry, perfumes, leather goods)* In addition to goods, ask students what else Muslims exchanged with other cultures. *(ideas)*

ENGLISH LANGUAGE LEARNERS

HOMEWORK Assign each student to create a three- or four-panel cartoon strip showing how Muslim culture was spread by Muslims' interaction with other peoples.

Government and Society

Under Arab rule, the Muslim Empire was organized into provinces. At first one caliph headed the government. Disagreement over succession to the position developed, however. In time, these disputes led to the breakup of the empire into three areas, or caliphates. The caliphates were ruled by caliphs in Baghdad, Cairo, and Córdoba.

Muslims throughout the Islamic Empire lived according to the Qur'an. It guided both their religious life and daily life—there was no separation. The Qur'an gave detailed instructions about how society should be organized and how people should live. All Muslims were expected to follow the Islamic laws in public and private life.

Slavery was common in Arabia. The Qur'an urged Muslims to free their slaves. Those who chose to keep slaves were required to treat them humanely. No free Muslim could be enslaved, and the children of a female slave and her master were free.

The family was the core of Muslim daily life. Muslims showed concern for all members of their family—parents, children, grandparents, aunts, uncles, and cousins. They particularly respected the elderly. In Islamic families everyone had specific roles and duties. Men were responsible for the family's needs. Women had the right to just treatment, and they could control property, but they were not required to contribute to the family's needs. As the Qur'an stated:

This illustration from an Arabic book shows the great detail used in Islamic art.

Primary Source

❝Women have such [as many] honourable rights as obligations, but their men have a degree [of rights and obligations] above them.❞

The Qur'an

Parents usually arranged marriages for their children. However, the Qur'an gave a woman the right to refuse the arrangement. The groom was required to give his bride a marriage gift of property or money.

It was common in Arabia for a man to have several wives. The Qur'an restricted a Muslim man to four wives, and he had to treat them equally. In fact, the Qur'an gave women more rights than they had received under traditional Arab law. For example, if a woman got divorced, she kept her own money and was free to remarry. She could also inherit money and own property. Muslim women enjoyed more freedom than most women at the time. Later, however, women began to be secluded and lost some rights.

The government supported schools and libraries. The family and the mosque also took responsibility for education. A person who could speak and write well was thought to be educated. Students attended religious study groups at the mosque. Advanced students could attend schools established for the study of science, mathematics, or law.

✔ **READING CHECK: Identifying Bias** How did old Arab customs and Islamic law affect Muslim family life? *established custom of polygamy*

Analyzing Primary Sources

Drawing Inferences How does this passage show that the Qur'an guided more than just religious beliefs? *defines social roles of men and women*

internet connect

TOPIC: Muslim Science
GO TO: go.hrw.com
KEYWORD: SP3 WH11

Have students access the Internet through the HRW Go site and research Muslim contributions to medicine and science. Have students prepare multimedia presentations of their findings or oral reports with visual aids.

Reproducible Resources

PS   Readings in World History 35: Social Classes in Muslim India

TEACH

Point out that Hinduism began to develop about 4,000 years ago in the Indian subcontinent. Today Hinduism is the main religion of India and is closely tied to India's history and culture. Unlike most other major world religions, Hinduism has no founder, no clear beginning, and no central authority, hierarchy, or organization. Hinduism includes the worship of many different gods that range from local deities to pan-Indian gods or even a single high God. There is no single belief that unites all followers of the religion. There are, however, several widely held beliefs that are common among Hindus. Most believe in the sanctity of the ancient religious writings known as the Vedas and in an eternal and infinite source of reality called *brahman*. Other common beliefs include *ahimsa*—noninjury to living things—and *samsara*—a continuous cycle of rebirth.

Have students work in groups to find answers to the following questions: How many people in the world are followers of Hinduism? In which countries other than India is Hinduism practiced? What are some common beliefs and practices of Hinduism?

Culture

One of the most important concepts in the study of geography and religion is the idea of sacred space. Followers of nearly all religions perceive certain places as holy or sacred. These places are visited, venerated, and respected by the religion's followers. Sacred places are usually clearly marked, and important ritual behaviors, ceremonies, and activities take place there. In fact, certain behaviors such as taking off one's shoes or not taking photographs may be required of all visitors.

Hindus believe the waters of the Ganges River have the power to cleanse sin, and hundreds of temples line the river's banks. In addition to the Ganges, other sacred rivers in India include the Indus, Narmada, and Yamuna.

ACTIVITY: Have students create a map of sacred places in India using the library and other resources. Then have them analyze the distribution of India's sacred sites.

HISTORY MAKER ANSWER

He taught that the key to enlightenment was to live apart from the material world.

HINDUISM

HISTORY MAKER

Mahavira
(c. 599 B.C.–527 B.C.)

Over the years many religious leaders added to and expanded Hindu thought. One such person was Mahavira, also known as Vardhamana. He was born into a warrior clan in northeastern India. At the age of 30 he left his home and entered the forest to find spiritual fulfillment. He got rid of all his personal possessions, then spent more than 12 years wandering the countryside with nothing to his name and little contact with other people.

After he felt he had gained the answers to his questions about life, Mahavira began teaching others. He believed the key to enlightenment was to live apart from the material world as much as possible. Many early Hindus were influenced by his ideas. Eventually his beliefs became the basis of Jainism, a new religion. **How did Mahavira influence Hindus?**

▲ **Sacred Texts:**
The Vedas, Bhagavad Gita

Festival of Holi

Hindus consider it a sacred duty to bathe in the holy waters of the Ganges River. This ritual cleanses the bather's mind and spirit.

▲ **Sacred Sites:**
Ganges River, city of Varanas

Sacred Creature:
The cow

The cow is a particularly sacred animal in the Hindu faith in part because of the important role it has played in sustaining life.

SPECIAL DAYS

Festival of Holi, in spring; Diwali, or Deepavali (Festival of Lights) in autumn

TEACH

Explain that Buddhism originated about 2,500 years ago in the foothills of the Himalayas in what is now India as an offshoot of Hinduism. The Buddha sent monks to preach the faith to others. During the Buddha's lifetime, the new religion spread throughout northern India. In the 200s B.C. missionaries introduced Buddhism to Sri Lanka. Missionaries and traders later introduced Buddhism to China (c. 100 B.C.–A.D. 200), Korea and Japan (c. A.D. 300–500), Southeast Asia (c. A.D. 400–600), Tibet (c. A.D. 700), and Mongolia (c. A.D. 1500). Buddhism developed many regional forms such as Mahayana in China, Korea, and Japan; Theravada in Sri Lanka and mainland Southeast Asia; and Lamaism in Tibet and Mongolia. While Buddhism diffused throughout much of Asia, it declined in India.

Using the information above, have students create a map showing the origin and diffusion of Buddhism in Asia. The maps should show the direction of the religion's spread and dates when it reached certain areas.

BUDDHISM

Buddha Day festival

Bodhi tree

▲ **Sacred Site:**
Bodhgaya

◄ **Sacred Text:**
The Pali Canon

Sacred Objects:
Statues of the Buddha

HISTORY MAKER

Siddhartha Gautama
(c. 563 B.C.–483 B.C.)

Siddhartha Gautama was born the son of an Indian prince. At the age of 29, he left his palace and was shocked by the suffering he saw. As a result, he wondered about the great problems of life.

Gautama decided to spend the rest of his life seeking answers to his questions. In what is now called the Great Renunciation, he put aside all his possessions, left his family, and set out to search for truth. One day, while meditating under a bodhi tree near the town of Bodhgaya, Gautama realized the key to ending suffering. This led to the development of the Four Noble Truths and the Eightfold Path, which all Buddhists follow. After his experience under the bodhi tree, Gautama became known as the Buddha, or "enlightened one." **How did Siddhartha Gautama reject his old life?**

SPECIAL DAY

Buddha Day, celebrated at the full moon in May

Tell students that Confucius was China's most famous and influential teacher and philosopher. His ideas and personal views on how to live a moral and proper life have influenced Chinese culture for more than 2,000 years. In addition, Confucian ideas diffused to other countries, particularly Japan, the Koreas, and Vietnam. One of the fundamental beliefs of followers of Confucianism is that all people have the ability to learn and improve themselves. Confucius spent many years studying Chinese rituals, history, music, poetry, arithmetic, archery, and charioteering. In his 30s, Confucius began teaching. He wanted to make education widely available. As his fame spread, many people came to listen to his teachings. Confucius lectured on topics such as the ancient classics and self-improvement. He helped to establish teaching as a profession and way of life.

Have students research the life, philosophy, teachings, and influence of Confucius. Then ask them to discuss which educational philosophies of Confucius are still important concepts today.

Culture

In ancient Chinese thought there are two complementary forces contained in all things—yin and yang. Yin is thought of as Earth, female, dark, passive, and yielding. It is associated with the Moon, winter, even numbers, and valleys and streams. Yang is conceived of as heaven, male, light, active, and forceful. It is associated with the Sun, summer, odd numbers, and mountains.

According to belief, a balance of yin-yang forces is essential to universal harmony. As one of the forces increases, the other decreases. When the two forces are in balance, they are represented as the light and dark halves of a circle.

ACTIVITY: Have students draw a circle with light and dark halves representing a balance of yin-yang forces. Then have them list the ideas and symbols associated with each half of the circle.

HISTORY MAKER ANSWER

because Confucius had little to say about gods, the meaning of death, or life after death

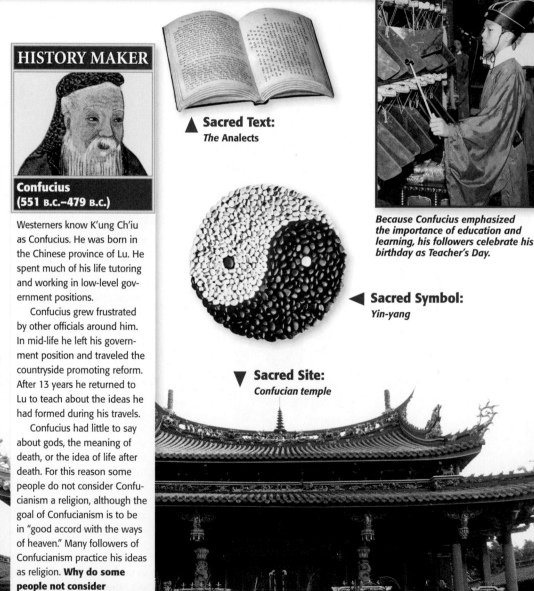

CONFUCIANISM

HISTORY MAKER

Confucius
(551 B.C.–479 B.C.)

Westerners know K'ung Ch'iu as Confucius. He was born in the Chinese province of Lu. He spent much of his life tutoring and working in low-level government positions.

Confucius grew frustrated by other officials around him. In mid-life he left his government position and traveled the countryside promoting reform. After 13 years he returned to Lu to teach about the ideas he had formed during his travels.

Confucius had little to say about gods, the meaning of death, or the idea of life after death. For this reason some people do not consider Confucianism a religion, although the goal of Confucianism is to be in "good accord with the ways of heaven." Many followers of Confucianism practice his ideas as religion. **Why do some people not consider Confucianism a religion?**

▲ **Sacred Text:**
The Analects

Because Confucius emphasized the importance of education and learning, his followers celebrate his birthday as Teacher's Day.

◄ **Sacred Symbol:**
Yin-yang

▼ **Sacred Site:**
Confucian temple

SPECIAL DAY

Teacher's Day, in August or September

Point out that Christianity is the world's largest religion, both in number of followers and by area. More than 1.8 billion people are Christian—roughly one third of the world's population. Christianity is the dominant religion in most of North and South America, Europe and Russia, Australia, New Zealand, the Philippines, and many parts of sub-Saharan Africa. Despite Christianity's widespread distribution, it is fragmented into many separate denominations with different religious hierarchies and practices. In the United States, there are hundreds of different Christian groups. Some major regional patterns include an area of Baptist and other conservative denominations in the South; Lutherans in Wisconsin, Minnesota, and the Dakotas; Mormons in Utah; and Roman Catholics in southern Louisiana, the Southwest, and Northeast.

Have students create a map showing major regional patterns of Christian groups in the United States. Then ask them to identify historical and cultural factors that might explain these patterns.

CHRISTIANITY

▲ **Sacred Text:**
The Bible

▲ **Sacred Sites:**
*Bethlehem,
Jerusalem*

*A Christmas
candlelight service*

◄ **Sacred Symbol:**
Cross

HISTORY MAKER

Jesus
(c. 6 B.C.–C. A.D. 30)

According to the Gospels, Jesus was born in Bethlehem, near Jerusalem, but grew up in Nazareth. He was a Jewish carpenter. In time he began preaching. As he traveled through the villages of Judaea, he assembled 12 disciples to help him preach. Jesus often taught using parables, or stories intended to teach a moral lesson. His followers believe that Jesus was the Son of God and that he was resurrected after his death. **Why do you think Jesus taught using parables?**

Daily Life

Buildings such as churches can reflect the history, culture, beliefs, and regional geography of the places where they are found.

Christian churches vary greatly in architectural style, size, ornateness, building materials, and other factors. For example, Europe's gothic cathedrals are typically huge stone structures with vaulted ceilings, stained glass windows, flying buttresses, gargoyles, and other decorations. In contrast, many Protestant churches in the United States are very simple in design and decoration.

Critical Thinking

Ask students how geographers use church architecture to learn about the history, culture, and physical geography of different regions.

ANSWER: They study the distribution of such factors as the age of churches, building materials used, and cultural characteristics.

**HISTORY MAKER
ANSWER**
to teach moral lessons to ordinary people in simple terms

SPECIAL DAYS

Christmas, on December 25th (January 6th for some Orthodox churches); Easter, in the spring

Tell students that the Five Pillars of Islam provide Muslims with the basis for living a proper and moral life. The Five Pillars are 1) a profession of faith demonstrated by the statement "There is no god but Allah, and Muhammad is His messenger"; 2) daily prayer; 3) giving charity to the poor; 4) fasting from dawn to sunset during the holy month of Ramadan; and 5) making a pilgrimage to the holy city of Mecca once in a lifetime. The Five Pillars are important symbolic acts of faith. For example, fasting during the month of Ramadan is a demanding physical exercise. This practice binds members of the Muslim community together and symbolizes the importance of spiritual matters over the phys-

ical demands of the body. Every evening after dark, families and friends congregate to break their fast and celebrate their faith.

Have students research the Five Pillars of Islam. Then lead a discussion on the importance of these symbolic acts of faith in Muslim communities.

Daily Life

The use of prayer rugs developed many years after the death of Muhammad, but some Muslims use them to cover the ground on which they worship. Prayer rugs are usually 2–4 feet wide and 4–8 feet long. They are often decorated with special religious designs or prayers.

Islamic art generally does not include images of humans or animals. Therefore, prayer rugs are characterized by rich colors and detailed geometric patterns. These decorations always include the arched mihrab, or prayer place, that is pointed toward Mecca when the rug is used in prayer.

Critical Thinking

Ask students why prayer rugs are special objects for Muslims.

ANSWER: used during worship; decorated with religious designs or prayers

HISTORY MAKER ANSWER

Islam prohibits the use of images for Muhammad.

ISLAM

HISTORY MAKER

Muhammad
(C. A.D. 570—A.D. 632)

In Islam, Muhammad is a messenger or prophet of God. Muhammad was born in Mecca (Makkah) and orphaned at an early age. He was from a respected but poor family. They belonged to a leading tribe of caravan merchants and keepers of Abraham's shrine and pilgrimage site, the Kaaba.

Islam prohibits the use of images for Muhammad. The symbol above, which means "Muhammad is the Prophet of God," is often used in place of his picture. **Why is a symbol used in place of Muhammad's image?**

▲ **Sacred Text:**
Qur'an

▲ **Special Objects:**
Prayer rugs

Muslim woman praying during Ramadan

Thousands of Muslim pilgrims gather around the Kaaba in Mecca.

Sacred Sites:
Mecca (Makkah), Al-Madīnah, Jerusalem

SPECIAL DAYS

Fast of Ramadan, during the entire ninth month of the Islamic year; 'Id al-Fitr, at the end of Ramadan; and 'Id al-Adha, at the end of the hajj in the twelfth lunar month

Portfolio Extensions

1. Have students work in groups to create a collage for each of the major religions covered in this feature. Collages may include photocopies or drawings of buildings or other sacred places, symbols or sacred objects, and founders or other leaders. Have groups display and discuss their collages, noting similarities among the religions.

2. Have each student research one of the special days listed for a religion covered in this feature. Students should create presentations that include traditions, songs, and/or foods associated with each special day. Then have students create a class calendar showing when these special days are celebrated.

3. Discuss the information provided in the bibliography for this feature (Further Reading). Then divide students into groups and assign each group one of the religions covered in this feature. Have each group create a bibliography for its assigned religion.

BUILDING YOUR Portfolio

World Religions Review

Culture

The major religions of the world share many common ideas and histories. Using what you have read in this feature and in previous chapters, create a chart comparing the historical origins, central ideas, and spread of Judaism, Hinduism, Buddhism, Confucianism, Christianity, and Islam.

Global Relations

Religion has played an important role in many historical events and continues to shape events even today. Using what you have read in this book, as well as other sources, pick one of the religions covered in this feature and create a booklet identifying examples of its influence on both historic and modern world events.

A Roman Catholic patriarch and a Jewish rabbi shake hands. Christianity and Judaism, like other major religions, share many traditions and beliefs.

Further Reading

Breuilly, Elizabeth, et al. *Religions of the World: The Illustrated Guide to Origins, Beliefs, Traditions, and Festivals.* Checkmark Books, 1997.

Crim, Keith, general editor. *The Perennial Dictionary of World Religions.* Harper San Francisco, 1989.

Smith, Huston. *The Illustrated World's Religions: A Guide to Our Wisdom Traditions.* Harper San Francisco, 1995.

Sullivan, Lawrence E. *Enchanting Powers: Music in the World's Religions.* Harvard University Press, 1997.

Wilson, Andrew, editor. *World Scripture: A Comparative Anthology of Sacred Texts.* Paragon House, 1995.

🖅 internet connect

Internet Activity: go.hrw.com
KEYWORD: SP3 Religions
KEYWORD: Holt Researcher

In assigned groups, develop a multimedia presentation about one of the world religions in this feature. Choose information from the HRW Go site and from the Holt Researcher that best reflects the major historical events, ideas, and traditions of that religion.

go.
hrw
.com

The Civilizations of East Asia

CHAPTER RESOURCE MANAGER

Objectives	Pacing Guide	Reproducible Resources
SECTION 1 **China under the Sui, Tang, and Sung Dynasties** (pp. 266–271)	• Explain how Chinese civilization advanced during the Sui and Tang dynasties. • Describe what daily life was like for the Chinese people during the Sung dynasty.	**Regular** 1.5 day / **Block Scheduling** 1 day *Block Scheduling Handbook with Team Teaching Strategies, 12.1*	**RS** Guided Reading Strategy 12.1 **RS** Graphic Organizer Activity 12: The Dynasties **PS** Readings in World History 45: A Woman's Hundred Years **E** Hands-on History Activity 12: Warriors, Writers, and Inventors
SECTION 2 **The Mongol Empire** (pp. 272–275)	• Explore how the Mongol invaders were able to conquer and rule so much of Asia. • Examine the effect Mongol rule had on China.	**Regular** 1.5 day / **Block Scheduling** 1 day *Block Scheduling Handbook with Team Teaching Strategies, 12.2*	**RS** Guided Reading Strategy 12.2 **PS** Readings in World History 46: Kublai Khan's Great Park at Shangdu
SECTION 3 **Japan, Korea, and Southeast Asia** (pp. 276–283)	• Investigate how the geography of Japan influenced its development. • Analyze how China influenced the early development of Japan. • Describe how changes in government influenced society in feudal Japan. • Examine how Southeast Asia was influenced by China and India.	**Regular** 1.5 day / **Block Scheduling** 1 day *Block Scheduling Handbook with Team Teaching Strategies, 12.3*	**RS** Guided Reading Strategy 12.3 **SM** Geography Activity 12: The Wind That Saved Japan **PS** Readings in World History 47: Drinking Tea for a Long Life **PS** Readings in World History 48: Actors and Entertainers in Feudal Japan **E** Creative Teaching Strategy 12: Asian Travelogues

Chapter Resource Key

PS Primary Sources
RS Reading Support
IC Interdisciplinary Connections
E Enrichment
SM Skills Mastery
A Assessment

REV Review
ELL Reinforcement and English Language Learners
Transparencies
CD-ROM
Music

Video
Internet
Holt Presentation Maker Using Microsoft® PowerPoint®

One-Stop Planner CD-ROM

See the **One–Stop Planner** for a complete list of additional resources for students and teachers.

One-Stop Planner CD-ROM

It's easy to plan lessons, select resources, and print out materials for your students when you use the **One-Stop Planner** CD–ROM with **Test Generator**.

Technology Resources

- One-Stop Planner 12.1
- Holt Researcher: World History: Empress Wu
- World History and Cultures Video Program 12: The Golden Age of Asian Civilization
- World History Teaching Transparency: Art and History 13: Landscape on a Fan
- World History Teaching Transparency: Everyday Life 12: Chinese Tea Processing
- Homework Practice Online
- Online Maps, Charts, and Graphs: Changan, 750
- Online Maps, Charts, and Graphs: Population Shifts in China, 750–1250

- One-Stop Planner 12.2
- Holt Researcher: World History: Genghis Khan
- Homework Practice Online
- Online Maps, Charts, and Graphs: Mongol Empire, 1200s

- One-Stop Planner 12.3
- Holt Researcher: World History: Sejong
- Regions of the World Music Audio CD Program 20: Japan and the Koreas: Music of the One-String Ichigenkin
- CNN. Presents World Cultures: Yesterday and Today Segment 12: Buddhism in Mongolia
- World History Teaching Transparency: Geography and History 12: New Cultures in Asia, c. 670–1392
- Homework Practice Online

Reinforcement, Review, and Assessment

Daily Quiz 12.1

Main Idea Activity 12.1

English Audio Summary 12.1

Spanish Audio Summary 12.1

REV Section 1 Review, p. 271

Daily Quiz 12.2

Main Idea Activity 12.2

English Audio Summary 12.2

Spanish Audio Summary 12.2

REV Section 2 Review, p. 275

Daily Quiz 12.3

Main Idea Activity 12.3

English Audio Summary 12.3

Spanish Audio Summary 12.3

REV Section 3 Review, p. 283

internet connect

HRW ONLINE RESOURCES
GO TO: go.hrw.com
Then type in a keyword.

TEACHER HOME PAGE
KEYWORD: SP3 Teacher

CHAPTER INTERNET ACTIVITIES
KEYWORD: SP3 WH12
Choose an activity to:
- understand similarities and differences of Chinese, Japanese, and Korean art.
- research the early development of Korea, Vietnam, and the Khmer Empire of Southeast Asia.
- learn more about Genghis Khan.

CHAPTER ENRICHMENT LINKS
KEYWORD: SP3 CH12

ONLINE ASSESSMENT
Homework Practice
KEYWORD: SP3 HP12
Standardized Test Prep
KEYWORD: SP3 STP12
Rubrics
KEYWORD: SS Rubrics

ONLINE MAPS, CHARTS, AND GRAPHS
KEYWORD: SP3 MCG

CONTENT UPDATES
KEYWORD: SS Content Updates

HOLT PRESENTATION MAKER
KEYWORD: SP3 PPT12

ONLINE READING SUPPORT
KEYWORD: SS Strategies

CURRENT EVENTS
KEYWORD: S3 Current Events

Meeting Individual Needs

Ability Levels

Level 1 Basic level activities designed for all students encountering new material

Level 2 Intermediate level activities designed for average students

Level 3 Challenging activities designed for honors and gifted and talented students

English Language Learners These activities address the needs of students with Limited English Proficiency.

Chapter Review and Assessment

- IC Vocabulary Activity 12
- Global Skill Builder CD–ROM
- HRW Web Site
- REV Chapter 12 Tutorial for Students, Parents, Mentors, and Peers
- REV Chapter 12 Review, pp. 284–285

- A Chapter 12 Test Generator (on the One-Stop Planner)
- A Chapter 12 Test (Form A or B)
- A Alternative Assessment Handbook
- A Chapter 12 Test for English Language Learners and Special-Needs Students

Build on What You Know

Ask students to answer the following questions:

What advances were made in China under the Han dynasty?

Consider:

- the government
- trade
- the arts and sciences

How did the philosophies of ancient China influence its development?

Consider:

- Confucianism
- Daoism
- Legalism

EXPLORING THE TIME LINE
GLOBAL EVENTS

internet connect

TOPIC: Marco Polo
GO TO: go.hrw.com
KEYWORD: SP3 WH12

Have students access the Internet through the HRW Go site to conduct research on Marco Polo. In about 1275, Marco Polo visited the court of Kublai Khan. Have students pretend to be Marco Polo and compose a journal entry for one of the days Polo visited Khan's court.

CHAPTER 12

A.D. 552–A.D. 1573

The Civilizations of East Asia

C. A.D. 584
Science and Technology
Work begins on the Grand Canal.

A.D. 589
Politics
The Sui dynasty reunites China.

A.D. 618
Politics
The Tang dynasty begins in China.

A ceramic Chinese vase, from between A.D. 960 and A.D. 1127

C. A.D. 750
Daily Life
About 70 million people live in China.

C. A.D. 950
Science and Technology
The Chinese first use gunpowder in warfare.

C. A.D. 960
Business and Finance
Foreign trade begins to expand in China.

C. A.D. 960
The Arts
Chinese artisans perfect the craft of porcelain making.

A.D. 550   **A.D. 750**   **A.D. 950**

C. A.D. 700
Global Events
Buddhism is flourishing in Korea.

A.D. 700s
Daily Life
Zen Buddhism becomes the dominant form of Buddhism in Korea.

C. A.D. 670
Politics
The Kingdom of Silla unifies Korea.

A.D. 868
The Arts
The Chinese produce the world's first known printed book, the *Diamond Sutra*.

A.D. 960–A.D. 1279
Politics
The Sung dynasty exists in China.

A figure of a Bactrian camel from the Tang dynasty

An illustration of the Buddha preaching, from the Diamond Sutra

Build on What You Know

The people of the Islamic world fashioned a unique society based on a powerful religious ideal. Their culture lay at the crossroads of many civilizations and spread with the movement of people and with trade. In little more than a century after the death of Muhammad in A.D. 632, Islamic culture and beliefs had been carried throughout much of the Middle East, through large parts of Africa, Asia, and the Mediterranean, and even into Europe. In this chapter, you will learn about the unique cultures of East Asia that, like Islamic civilization, reflected a strong spiritual influence.

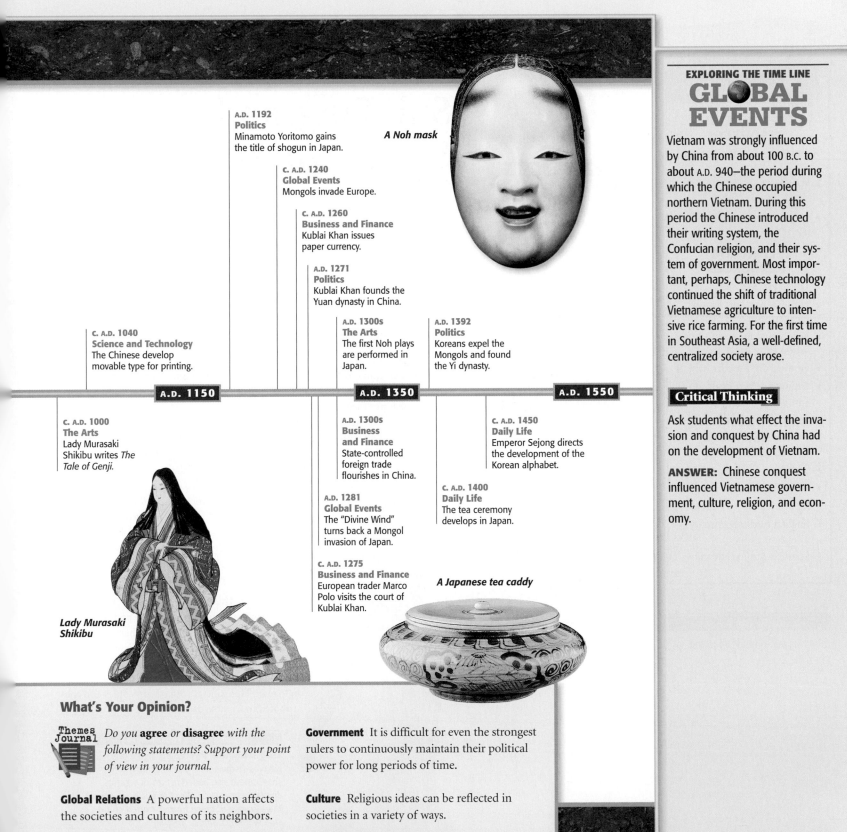

A.D. 1192
Politics
Minamoto Yoritomo gains the title of shogun in Japan.

A Noh mask

C. A.D. 1240
Global Events
Mongols invade Europe.

C. A.D. 1260
Business and Finance
Kublai Khan issues paper currency.

A.D. 1271
Politics
Kublai Khan founds the Yuan dynasty in China.

C. A.D. 1040
Science and Technology
The Chinese develop movable type for printing.

A.D. 1300s
The Arts
The first Noh plays are performed in Japan.

A.D. 1392
Politics
Koreans expel the Mongols and found the Yi dynasty.

A.D. 1150

A.D. 1350

A.D. 1550

C. A.D. 1000
The Arts
Lady Murasaki Shikibu writes *The Tale of Genji.*

A.D. 1300s
Business and Finance
State-controlled foreign trade flourishes in China.

C. A.D. 1450
Daily Life
Emperor Sejong directs the development of the Korean alphabet.

A.D. 1281
Global Events
The "Divine Wind" turns back a Mongol invasion of Japan.

C. A.D. 1400
Daily Life
The tea ceremony develops in Japan.

C. A.D. 1275
Business and Finance
European trader Marco Polo visits the court of Kublai Khan.

A Japanese tea caddy

Lady Murasaki Shikibu

What's Your Opinion?

 Do you **agree** *or* **disagree** *with the following statements? Support your point of view in your journal.*

Global Relations A powerful nation affects the societies and cultures of its neighbors.

Government It is difficult for even the strongest rulers to continuously maintain their political power for long periods of time.

Culture Religious ideas can be reflected in societies in a variety of ways.

OBJECTIVES

1 Explain how Chinese civilization advanced during the Sui and Tang dynasties.

2 Describe what daily life was like for the Chinese people during the Sung dynasty.

SECTION 1

READ TO DISCOVER

❶ How did Chinese civilization advance during the Sui and Tang dynasties?
❷ What was daily life like for the Chinese people during the Sung dynasty?

IDENTIFY

Grand Canal
Li Bo
Du Fu
Empress Wu
Zen
Diamond Sutra

WHY IT MATTERS TODAY

The differences between city and rural life are as real today in China as they were over 1000 years ago. Use **CNNfyi.com** or other **current event** sources to explore differences in the daily lives of people your age living in the cities or in the country. Record your findings in your journal.

China under the Sui, Tang, and Sung Dynasties

The Main Idea
The Sui, Tang, and Sung dynasties shaped China but could not maintain control over it.

The Story Continues *The fall of the Han dynasty in the 200s led to a long era of instability and decline in China. Hordes of invaders swept in and destroyed Han cities. An observer described visiting one such city in the 300s. "At this time in the city . . . there were not more than 100 families," he wrote. "Weeds and thorns grew thickly as if in a forest."*

The Sui and Tang Dynasties

The collapse of the Han dynasty in 220 signaled a long era of social and political disruption in China. Wave after wave of invaders swept into China from beyond its borders. Over time, these peoples settled in China, set up kingdoms, and adopted Chinese customs. In the late 500s one of these groups succeeded in reuniting China under its rule. The new dynasty, known as the Sui, came into power in 589. During their brief rule, the Sui emperors began construction of the **Grand Canal.** They connected existing and newly dug waterways, linking northern and southern China for the first time. The canal was one of the engineering marvels of the ancient world.

Despite their accomplishments, however, the Sui dynasty did not last. The rulers tried to do too much at once. They tried unsuccessfully to conquer southern Manchuria and northern Korea. In 615 invading Turks defeated them. An uprising in 618 ended the Sui dynasty and brought the Tang dynasty to power.

Expansion under the Tang. The early Tang rulers defeated the invading Turks to the north and west. They extended China's frontiers farther west than ever before. The Tang rulers made contact with India and with the Muslim Empire to the south and the west. To the east, Chinese ideas greatly influenced the people of Korea and Japan. This contact with other peoples also contributed to Chinese culture.

INTERPRETING THE VISUAL RECORD

Tang sculpture This ceramic figure of a girl was discovered in a Tang dynasty tomb. The Chinese also buried figures of servants, animals, and guards. *What might have been the purpose of these figures buried alongside wealthy Chinese people?*

TEACH OBJECTIVE 1

LEVEL 1: Remind students that many cultural, political, and economic changes occurred in China under the Sui and Tang dynasties. Have students make web diagrams of these changes, filling in circles for *Arts, Economy, Government, Society,* and *Technology.* Organize students into pairs or triads to compare and discuss differences in their web diagrams and to revise their entries if necessary.

ENGLISH LANGUAGE LEARNERS, COOPERATIVE LEARNING

The Tang made Xi'an their capital. During the 700s and 800s, about 2 million people lived there. This made Xi'an the largest city in the world at that time. Xi'an was both the center of government and a center of culture. People from many parts of the world settled there. Arabs, Persians, Jews, Greeks, and native Chinese lived side by side.

China flourished under the Tang dynasty. The Tang only ruled until 907, but they began what would be another golden age in China. For many years China was the most powerful and wealthy country in the world.

Literature under the Tang. The Tang dynasty marked a high point in the development of Chinese literature. Some 2,300 known poets lived and worked during the era of the Tang dynasty. Together, these poets wrote nearly 49,000 known works. Among the best of these poets were **Li Bo** (Li Po) and **Du Fu.** They both wrote during the 700s.

Li Bo, a Daoist, spent much of his life seeking pleasure. His poems describe life's delights in light, happy, elegant terms. His love of life, however, may have caused his death. According to legend, Li Bo became tipsy after drinking too much and drowned while reaching from a boat for the moon's reflection in the water.

Du Fu, on the other hand, wrote about serious subjects. He was a devout follower of the teachings of Confucius. Du Fu's carefully written verses showed his deep concern for the suffering and tragedy of human life. Du Fu used his poet's gift to

CONNECTING TO
Science and Technology

The Grand Canal

The Grand Canal is the world's oldest and longest canal system. It connects the Chinese cities of Hangzhou and Beijing, and is almost 1,000 miles long. Before the development of railroads, the canal was a convenient way to travel and transport goods between the northern and southern parts of China.

The canal was created over many hundreds of years. It was made by digging trenches to link lakes, rivers, and other canals. Dams were built to equalize water levels.

As railroads developed, the Grand Canal's importance faded, and it fell into a state of disrepair. By 1949 only small boats were able to use it. China repaired and modernized the canal system between 1958 and 1964. Today the Grand Canal again serves as a way for boats to transport goods and passengers.

> **Understanding Science and Technology**
>
> **Why would floods be harmful to the Grand Canal?**

The Grand Canal is still an important waterway today, as this photo indicates.

Linking Past to Present

Sui emperors established a system of government departments and ministries to rule more effectively. They increased the size of the state education system, reformed the civil service system, and built upon the efforts of the Han emperors to control the independence of local officials. One result of Sui reforms was more efficient collection of taxes. The royal coffers swelled, allowing vast public works projects like the Grand Canal and extensive repairs of the Great Wall.

Critical Thinking

Limiting the terms of government officials is a historical method of reform that some states and localities have adopted today. What arguments might be advanced for and against this idea?

ANSWER: Term limits might be seen as restricting voters' freedom of choice and forcing the removal of officials who are doing a good job. On the other hand, they also keep officials from becoming entrenched and self-serving.

SCIENCE AND TECHNOLOGY ANSWER

Flooding would cause erosion of the canal walls.

LEVEL 3: Ask students to recall how Buddhism arrived in China. *(by missionaries from India)* Ask students why it flourished in Tang China. *(supported by Empress Wu and wealthy believers; similar to Daoism)* Have students explain how Buddhism's popularity caused problems for its followers. *(The government feared the growing wealth of the Buddhist monasteries.)* Ask what other religions were popular at the time. *(Daoism, Neo-Confucianism)* Have students speculate whether the government would have reacted against Buddhism if it had been a "native" religion like Daoism or Neo-Confucianism. *(Answers will vary but students should note that many Buddhist sects in China were uniquely Chinese.)*

Global Relations

During the Tang dynasty Chinese inventions flourished and spread to the outside world through China's increased contact with other peoples. The Chinese improved the manufacture of paper and porcelain, invented the wheelbarrow, and used gunpowder during this period. In addition, the use of coal as a fuel originated in northern China sometime in the 300s.

Critical Thinking

Ask students what they can conclude about how Chinese inventions reached foreign countries.

ANSWER: Trade spread new Chinese inventions throughout the world.

MAP ANSWER
the Grand Canal

---

call for an end to the frontier wars and destructive uprisings that tore at Tang China. One of Du Fu's greatest works was entitled "A Song of War Chariots." This poem, a classic example of descriptive poetry, creates a mood of great sadness. It tells of the sorrow of parting as a young soldier goes off to fight. The poem also suggests that the life of a Tang soldier could be brutal and harsh.

Analyzing Primary Sources

Drawing Inferences How does Du Fu's poem reflect Chinese history? reflects experiences of Chinese soldiers in battle

 Primary Source

>**The war-chariots rattle,
>The war-horses whinny,
>Each man of you has a bow and a quiver at his belt.
>Father, mother, son, wife, stare at you going,
>Till dust shall have buried the bridge beyond Xi'an,
>They run with you, crying, they tug at your sleeves,
>And the sound of their sorrow goes up to the clouds . . .
>Men of China are able to face the stiffest battle,
>But their officers drive them like chickens and dogs.
>Whatever is asked of them,
>Dare they complain?**

Du Fu, from Cyril Birch, ed., *Anthology of Chinese Literature*

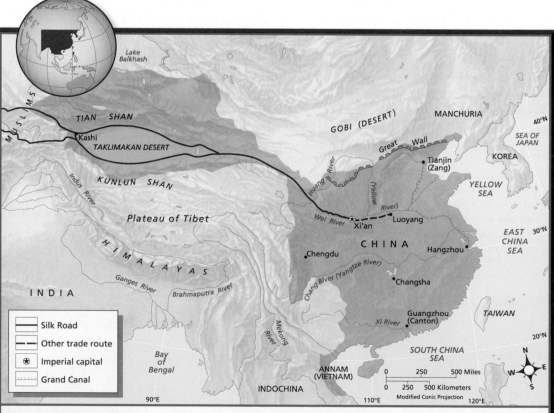

Tang Dynasty, A.D. 814

Interpreting Maps The Tang rulers extended their empire westward into Central Asia and southward into Indochina.

■ **Skills Assessment: Physical Systems** Along what waterway could Tang people travel between the cities of Tianjin and Hangzhou?

TEACH OBJECTIVE 2

ALL LEVELS: Have students work in pairs to complete four-cell charts that list how urban life and rural life in Sung China was similar to urban and rural life in the United States today. Charts should be headed as follows:

	Urban Life in China	Rural Life in China
Similar in USA		
Different from USA		

ENGLISH LANGUAGE LEARNERS, COOPERATIVE LEARNING

Religion in Tang China. Missionaries from India brought Buddhism to China during the Han dynasty. Buddhism reached its peak under the Tang. **Empress Wu,** who ruled from 690 to 705, was an outspoken supporter of Buddhism. She was a strong leader and an able administrator. Empress Wu was also the only woman to hold the Chinese throne in her own name.

Wealthy Buddhists donated land for monasteries. Many different forms, or sects, of Buddhism appeared. The most famous sect is best known by its later Japanese name, **Zen.** Zen Buddhism stressed meditation as a means to enlightenment. It was similar in many ways to Daoism. Following the Buddhists' example, Daoists formed sects that appealed to the masses of peasants. In later years many Chinese adopted a mix of Buddhist and Daoist teachings.

In time the growing wealth of the Buddhist monasteries alarmed government officials. They seized the monasteries' lands and took art objects for the emperor's treasury. In the last century of the Tang dynasty, government officials persecuted Buddhists. They destroyed thousands of shrines and monasteries. They forced more than 250,000 monks and nuns to give up their duties and return to ordinary life. Buddhism continued to exist in China. However, it was never again so important a force in Chinese life.

The Tang rulers brought back Confucianism, especially its emphasis on ethics. This movement, called Neo-Confucianism, or "new Confucianism," remained the main religion of China's ruling classes until the early 1900s. Tang rulers built temples to Confucius and required government officials to study Confucian classics.

The decline of the Tang dynasty. The Tang dynasty reached its height in about 750. It then gradually declined under the rule of weak emperors. By 900 nomads had begun to invade China. In 907 a warlord who had murdered the emperor years earlier seized the throne for himself. The Tang dynasty ended.

✔ **READING CHECK: Finding the Main Idea** What were the main accomplishments in Chinese culture during the Sui and Tang dynasties? development of powerful literature, Buddhism and Confucianism

China under the Sung Dynasty

In 960 Zhao Kuangyin (JOW KWAHNG·yin) established the Sung dynasty. China continued to flourish under Sung leadership. The emperors, however, never succeeded in winning control of all China. Rulers from Tibet held a kingdom in the northwest. A powerful Mongol tribe that held Manchuria increasingly threatened northeastern China. Like the Tang rulers before them, moreover, the Sung emperors faced constant pressure from foreign invasions and civil wars. Nevertheless, China under the Sung was a land of cultural and artistic progress.

By the mid-900s the main foreign danger to China came from the north. Mongols called the Qidan (CHI·DAHN) had taken Chinese territory in southern Manchuria. In time they invaded as far south as the Huang River. Finally the Sung agreed to a treaty with the Qidan. The Sung emperors had to pay a huge tribute to the Mongol invaders to avoid war. By 1042 the Sung were paying more than 200,000 ounces of silver to the Qidan every year. This was a great economic hardship.

Another Central Asian people, the Juchen, also moved into Manchuria. They took over northern China in 1126. The Juchen established the Jin dynasty in the north. Their capital was located at what is now Beijing. Hangzhou (HANG·CHOW) in the south became the new capital of the Sung dynasty.

HISTORY MAKER

Empress Wu
(c. 625–705)

Wu Hou first entered royal life at a young age as a member of the Tang emperor's household. She eliminated her female rivals within the palace and in A.D. 655 was made empress.

Wu Hou had her political opponents exiled or even executed. The emperor was often ill and relied on Wu Hou to manage state affairs. In 690 Wu Hou took power in her own name. Although ruthless against her opponents, Empress Wu ruled with great efficiency and she brought about needed social changes. **What did Empress Wu do once she gained power?**

Holt Researcher

go.hrw.com
KEYWORD: Holt Researcher
FreeFind: Empress Wu
After reading more about Empress Wu on the Holt Researcher, write a newspaper article describing her political, economic, and social influence on China.

Government

The most compelling problem that Zhao Kuangyin faced was the almost absolute power held by local military leaders. In order to assert his authority, Zhao Kuangyin—himself a former general—transferred generals to other posts, coaxed them into retirement, and limited their scope of operations. As these military leaders retired or died, he replaced them with civilian administrators from the central government.

Though successful in consolidating power, Zhao Kuangyin's military reform weakened the competence and effectiveness of the fighting forces. The Sung were never able to reconquer Vietnam, any of central Asia, or the northern steppe.

Critical Thinking

Ask students what factors in Zhao Kuangyin's background might have led him to consider military leaders a threat to his rule.

ANSWER: Zhao Kuangyin had been a general and had seized power to establish the Sung dynasty.

HISTORY MAKER ANSWER
She had her political opponents exiled or executed.

Reproducible Resources
PS Readings in World History 45: A Woman's Hundred Years

HOMEWORK Ask students to imagine that they are either rural or city teenagers in Sung China. Have students write diary entries in their chosen roles for a typical day in their family lives. Read selected diary entries aloud and have the class critique how accurately they represent family life in rural or urban China.

CLOSE

Ask students to list some important changes that occurred in government and society during the Tang and Sung dynasties. Write students' responses on the chalkboard.

Economics

Under Sung government policies, China underwent a period of major economic change. International trade with Japan and Southeast Asia grew. Trade between regions remained limited to valuable commodities like porcelain and silk. The overall increase in trade created new opportunities for rural peasants, many of whom became entrepreneurs engaged in timber-growing, papermaking, weaving, and a variety of other new occupations. Villagers imported any raw materials they lacked. A cash economy also replaced the barter system during the Sung period. When copper, the common medium of exchange, was in short supply, the world's first paper money was printed in 1024.

Critical Thinking

Ask students how the introduction of paper money would affect the growth of a nation's economy.

ANSWER: Economic expansion would no longer be limited by the need to barter goods.

MAP ANSWER
about 700 miles

Technology Resources

World History Teaching Transparency: Art and History 13: Landscape on a Fan; Everyday Life 12: Chinese Tea Processing

The Sung and Jin Empires, A.D. 1141

Interpreting Maps After capturing the Sung capital city, the Jin's Juchen warriors expanded southward beyond the Huang River.

■ **Skills Assessment: Using Geography** About how far apart were the Sung and Jin capitals?

Trade and arts. Despite their troubles, the Sung emperors kept Chinese civilization at a high level. Foreign trade expanded. Hangzhou and Guangzhou became key port cities. Caravans brought in goods from Central Asia and India.

Exports included gold, silver, and copper. One of China's most valuable exports was porcelain, a fine, translucent pottery. Sung artisans perfected the art of making porcelain. They created delicate vases with colorful and complex designs. Sung artists also produced beautiful landscape paintings, inspired by the Daoist love of nature.

The civil service system. The Chinese further improved their civil service system during the Sung dynasty. Examinations took place in the capital every three years. To qualify, an individual first had to pass an examination at the local level. The Sung ended the need for sponsorship. This practice had allowed only those from important families to take the examinations.

Because some people tried cheating to pass the civil service exams, a system was developed to stop corruption. Applicants were assigned numbers and did not use their names on the exams. Guards probably watched over them as they took the exams. Clerks copied their answers so that their handwriting could not be recognized. Finally, three judges read each paper.

Great inventions. The Chinese invented gunpowder during the Han dynasty. At that time it was used only for fireworks and signals. Gunpowder was first used for warfare during the 900s. Printing was another important Chinese invention. The Chinese had learned very early how to make ink and paper. By 500 artisans were making seals of metal or wood that had inscriptions carved in reverse. The images they created resembled today's block prints. The world's first known printed book was the *Diamond Sutra,* a Buddhist religious text produced in China in 868. Movable type was developed in the 1040s. However, it was not as practical to use as carved blocks.

Peasant life. By about 1050 China's population was about 100 million people. Most were peasants who lived and worked in the countryside. Two important changes took place in peasant life during the Tang and Sung dynasties.

One change was an improvement in farming methods. Water-control projects allowed farmers to irrigate more fields so that they could grow more rice. A new type of quick-ripening rice from Southeast Asia let farmers grow two crops each year instead of one. Peasants could sell surplus food in the many small market towns. Another important crop during those years was tea, which was made into a drink that was popular throughout China.

The second major change made life harder for the peasants. New taxes levied by the Tang rulers fell particularly hard on them. Peasants who could not pay their taxes had to sell their farms. They became tenant farmers, paying high rents to landlords.

CHAPTER 12

REVIEW

Have students complete the Section 1 Review on p. 271.

ASSESS

Have students complete Daily Quiz 12.1. As Alternative Assessment, you may want to use the web diagram or chart exercises in this section's lessons.

RETEACH

Have students complete Main Idea Activity for English Language Learners and Special-Needs Students 12.1. Then have students who are having difficulty work in pairs to ask each other questions based on the section subheads.
ENGLISH LANGUAGE LEARNERS

EXTEND

Have groups of students create pamphlets on various aspects of the Tang and Sung dynasties. Pamphlets might focus on politics; famous artists or writers; scientific, mathematical, and technological advances; agriculture, industry, foreign trade, or religious developments. Suggest that groups include appropriate images to illustrate their pamphlets and use correct social studies terminology. **BLOCK SCHEDULING**

Photograph © 1978 The Metropolitan Museum of Art

This image is taken from a Chinese scroll of the 1100s. Entitled "Spring Festival on the River," the image portrays a prosperous and orderly society.

City life. During the Sung dynasty, more Chinese than ever before lived in cities and towns. Hangzhou was said to have had a population of about 2 million, with perhaps as many as 2 million more living near the city. The cities of Sung China bustled with activity. Shipments of farm produce arrived daily in the marketplaces. Shopkeepers sold embroidered silks, printed books, and handicrafts. Shoppers watched puppet shows, plays, dancers, and acrobats in the streets.

Wealthy Chinese probably lived in fine homes surrounded by gardens and artificial lakes. Ordinary people, on the other hand, probably lived in crowded apartments, often in extended families of several generations. Some people had no homes at all and had to beg for food. The Sung government set up hospitals and orphanages to help the poor, but poverty and overcrowding remained a serious problem.

During this period the status of women in Chinese society began to change. There was less work for them to do in the cities than on the farms. The custom of footbinding spread among the wealthy classes. Girls' feet would be tied tightly with strips of linen, with their toes tucked underneath. Their feet would not be allowed to grow. The result was crippling. The custom was meant to show that a man was successful. His wife did not have to do housework because he could afford servants. Eventually, small feet became viewed as a sign of feminine beauty.

The custom of footbinding survived in China for centuries, as this photograph of a Chinese woman from the 1900s reveals.

✔ **READING CHECK: Categorizing** What developments during the Sung dynasty improved life for the Chinese people? Which made life worse? development of trade and arts, civil service improvements, inventions, improved farming methods; heavy taxation

SECTION 1 REVIEW ANSWERS

❶ Identify
- Grand Canal, p. 266
- Li Bo, p. 267
- Du Fu, p. 267
- Empress Wu, p. 269
- Zen, p. 269
- *Diamond Sutra*, p. 270

❷ Sui: Grand Canal; Tang: expanded frontiers; Sung: foreign trade expanded, civil service and tax systems revised

❸ a. Literature flourished; Buddhism reached its peak; Neo-Confucianism began; porcelain making and landscape painting became important.

b. Farming methods improved. New taxes forced some peasants to become tenant farmers. Many people lived in cities. Status of women improved.

❹ Students' poems and lyrics will vary but should reflect information about daily life and culture in Hangzhou.

Technology Resources

go. hrw .com Online Maps, Charts, and Graphs: Population Shifts in China, 750–1250

SECTION 1 REVIEW

1. **Identify** and explain the significance:
   Grand Canal
   Li Bo
   Du Fu
   Empress Wu
   Zen
   Diamond Sutra

2. **Categorizing** Copy the chart below. Use it to identify the principal accomplishments of the Sui, the Tang, and the Sung dynasties.

Sui dynasty		
Tang dynasty		
Sung dynasty		

3. **Finding the Main Idea**
   a. What were the most noteworthy advances in Chinese culture during the Sui, Tang, and Sung dynasties?
   b. How did life improve for ordinary people during the Sung dynasty?

4. **Writing and Critical Thinking**
   Evaluating Imagine yourself visiting Hangzhou. Write a poem or a song lyric about your impressions of the Sung capital.
   Consider:
   • what daily life was like for individuals living in the city
   • what items you might want to trade for to take back home with you

go. hrw .com **Homework Practice Online**
keyword: SP3 HP12

OBJECTIVES

1 **Explore how the Mongol invaders were able to conquer and rule so much of Asia.**

2 **Examine the effect Mongol rule had on China.**

READ TO DISCOVER

❶ How were the Mongol invaders able to conquer and rule so much of Asia?

❷ What effect did Mongol rule have on China?

IDENTIFY

Genghis Khan
Kublai Khan
Batu
Golden Horde
Marco Polo

WHY IT MATTERS TODAY

Changing political boundaries can have important consequences for people. Use CNNfyi.com or other **current event** sources to locate a place in the world where changing boundaries have changed peoples' lives. Record your findings in your journal.

CNNfyi.com

The Mongol Empire

The Main Idea
The powerful Mongol people established a large and strong empire in China and other areas.

The Story Continues *"The Tartars—that is, the Mongols—are the most obedient people in the world in regard to their leaders,"* noted a European traveler in the 1240s. *"They hold them [their leaders] in the greatest reverence and never tell them a lie."* The Chinese learned about Mongol leaders firsthand, as the invaders came to control the entire land.

Genghis Khan and the Mongols

The Mongols lived north of China in the rugged steppe region now called Mongolia. Although they were never a numerous people, the Mongols' culture encouraged the skills of battle. Mongol leaders could mobilize much of the population to engage in conquest. At its height, the Mongol army had about 100,000 cavalry. Mounted warriors enjoyed a great advantage over foot soldiers. Mongol cavalry could cover up to 100 miles in a day. Special saddles and iron stirrups allowed them to fire arrows accurately while riding at top speed. They made good use of their speed and mobility on horseback. In battle Mongol riders would surround their enemy like hunters surrounding wild game.

The Mongol armies were highly skilled in the use of massed firepower, rapid movement, and maneuvers. They would wear down an enemy through constant attack or threat of attack. They also used powerful weapons, possibly including catapults and

INTERPRETING THE VISUAL RECORD

Mongols This manuscript from the 1200s illustrates a battle between Mongol tribes. *What does this picture tell us about Mongol armor and weapons?*

TEACH OBJECTIVE 1

LEVEL 2: Have students compare the map on page 273 with maps in the Reference Section to list modern nations that were once part of the Mongol Empire. *(China, Mongolia, Russia, North and South Korea, Pakistan [part], Afghanistan, Iran, Iraq, Azerbaijan, Turkey [part], Armenia, Georgia, Turkmenistan, Uzbekistan, Kazakhstan, Ukraine, Poland, Hungary)* Ask how the Mongols were able to establish and govern so vast an empire. *(well-organized armies and superior troops, military technology, and tactics; divided empire into four parts)*

TEACH OBJECTIVE 1

LEVEL 1: Have students create a flowchart that shows important events in the Mongol conquest of Asia.
ENGLISH LANGUAGE LEARNERS

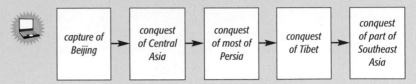

capture of Beijing → conquest of Central Asia → conquest of most of Persia → conquest of Tibet → conquest of part of Southeast Asia

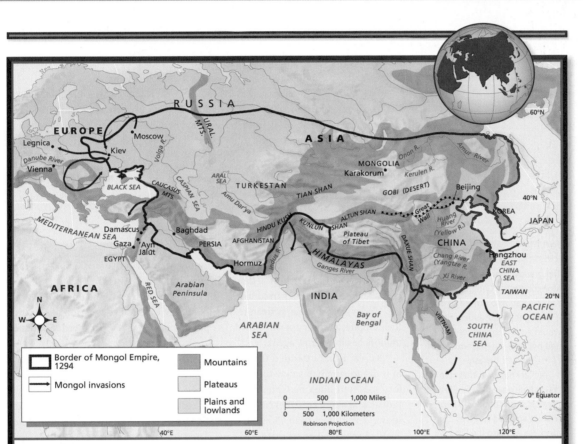

Mongol Empire, A.D. 1294

Interpreting Maps Under the leadership of Genghis Khan and his grandson Kublai Khan, Mongol soldiers captured much of Asia. **Skills Assessment: Places and Regions** What country did the Mongols unsuccessfully try to invade across the East China Sea?

---

giant crossbows mounted on stands. Battle provided a way for individual soldiers to acquire riches, honor, and personal power. The evidence suggests, too, that many of the Mongol generals were extremely capable.

The fiercest Mongol leader of all time was **Genghis Khan,** who lived from about 1162 to 1227. Originally named Temujin, he took the title Genghis Khan, meaning "Universal Ruler," in 1206. He went on to create an immense empire.

Mongol conquests. In the early 1200s, Mongols under Genghis Khan swept down from Karakorum, their capital. They captured the city now called Beijing and named it Khanbalik (kahn·buh·LEEK). They then turned westward, conquering Central Asia and most of Persia. Led by **Kublai** (KOO·bluh) **Khan,** a grandson of Genghis Khan, they conquered the rest of China. They also conquered the area now called Tibet and part of Southeast Asia. They tried but failed to capture Japan.

Another grandson of Genghis Khan, **Batu,** invaded Europe around 1240. His troops swept across Russia, Poland, and Hungary to the outskirts of Vienna. They plundered city after city, either killing the inhabitants or taking them as slaves. Frightened Europeans called the Mongolian invaders the **Golden Horde.** This name referred to the gold color of the Mongol tents in the sun. The Mongols soon left Poland and Hungary. They controlled Russia, however, for almost 200 years.

Holt Researcher

go.hrw.com
KEYWORD: Holt Researcher
FreeFind: Genghis Khan
After reading more about Genghis Khan on the Holt Researcher, create a collage that shows the changes his invasions brought to other parts of the world.

Science, Technology & Society

Mongol soldiers spent their lives in the saddle. During long marches they could even sleep while on their horses. At one time in Hungary, the cavalry traveled 270 miles in three days. The Mongols also used an iron stirrup and a powerful bow that could be used effectively from the saddle.

Critical Thinking

Ask students what advantages horsemanship gave the Mongols.

ANSWER: It gave them better mobility and versatility.

internet connect

TOPIC: Genghis Khan
GO TO: go.hrw.com
KEYWORD: SP3 WH12

Have students access the Internet through the HRW Go site to conduct research on Genghis Khan. Remind students that Genghis Khan ruled the largest empire in history, reaching from Korea and China to Russia and Iraq. Ask students to write a biography of Genghis Khan. Students may wish to use the interactive template to write their biographies.

MAP ANSWER

Japan

TEACH OBJECTIVE 2

ALL LEVELS: Have students suggest headlines for a news story on the political, economic, or cultural consequences of the Mongols' rule of China. List responses on the board. *(Examples: Mongols Restore Peace and Prosperity; Khan Extends Grand Canal; New Roads Improve Trade; Heavy Taxes Burden Nation)* Then have students choose one of the headlines and write a short news article to accompany it.

 HOMEWORK Have students create editorial cartoons supporting a point of view on Mongol discrimination against the Chinese.

TEACH OBJECTIVE 2

LEVEL 3: Have students prepare to hold a mock trial of Kublai Khan for alleged crimes against the Chinese people. Pairs of students should serve as prosecution and defense teams. Other students should be witnesses for the prosecution and the defense. Remaining class members should serve as jurors, evaluating Khan's political choices and decisions and voting on the defendant's guilt or innocence. To actively involve jurors during the trial, require each to write an explanation of his or her vote, citing the testimony that influenced it. **COOPERATIVE LEARNING**

Daily Life

In spite of Kublai Khan's use of the Chinese way of governing, the Mongols did not wish to become Chinese. They kept their own values and ways of life. Mongol women did not adopt the Chinese custom of foot binding, and they continued to dress in their own styles of clothing.

Critical Thinking

Ask students to suggest reasons why the Mongols relied on Chinese administrative structures to rule.

ANSWER: Students might answer that the Mongols had no existing bureaucratic and governmental structures of their own that could control such a huge empire.

HISTORY MAKER ANSWER

conquered China; first emperor of the Mongol dynasty; use of paper money; extended Grand Canal; improved trade; improved communication system

Reproducible Resources

PS Readings in World History 46: Kublai Khan's Great Park at Shangdu

HISTORY MAKER

Kublai Khan (1215–1294)

The grandson of the great Mongol warrior Genghis Khan, Kublai Khan also proved to be a great general and ruler. He would go on to conquer China and become the first emperor of the Mongol dynasty.

Kublai Khan was known for his capable governing and his mercy toward conquered peoples. He stressed religious toleration. He was also the first ruler to use only paper money. **What were some of Kublai Khan's achievements?**

Mongol rule. The Mongol Empire was divided into four parts. These four parts remained united until the 1300s, then slowly began to drift apart.

In 1260 Kublai Khan was given the title of Great Khan. He was recognized as the head of the whole Mongol Empire. He adopted many Chinese ways and introduced Chinese ceremonies to his court. He also relied on Chinese officials in the lower and middle ranks of the government. Kublai Khan built two palaces, one in Mongolia and one near Beijing.

✔ **READING CHECK: Identifying Cause and Effect** How were the Mongol nomads able to conquer so much of Asia? powerful, well-organized army of skilled cavalry

China under the Mongols

In 1271 Kublai Khan announced the beginning of his own dynasty. Called the Yuan dynasty, it covered northern China, with its capital at Beijing. In 1279 Yuan forces defeated the Sung dynasty in southern China. The Yuan ruled China until 1368.

Under Mongol rule, China prospered in many ways. Once the Mongols secured their empire, a century of war ended. The population, which had dropped to about 60 million, began to grow again.

Kublai Khan extended the length of the Grand Canal by hundreds of miles in order to supply his new capital with food from the southern farmlands. He also fostered routes linking China with India and Persia. This greatly improved trade. Probably as many as 10,000 courier stations, each stabling hundreds of horses used by relay riders, dotted Yuan China. These stations, set about 25 miles from one another, enabled mounted couriers to carry news and imperial messages throughout the empire. The efficient Yuan system of communications connected to virtually every corner of the empire and helped to maintain unity and order. Improved trade and communication encouraged China's economic growth. At the same time, however, heavy taxes enforced by the Yuan emperors may have weakened the economy and created many hardships for farmers and merchants. Over time, the emperors' harsh taxes and frequent demands for tribute helped to undermine Yuan authority and to promote growing resentment toward Mongol rule.

Contact with Europeans. During Mongol rule, contact between China and the rest of the world increased. King Louis IX of France and the pope in Rome both sent ambassadors to China. Christian missionaries also traveled there, as did travelers from other non-European nations.

It was during the reign of Kublai Khan that the Italian **Marco Polo** traveled to China. Marco Polo was a famous merchant and explorer. At about the age of seventeen

Marco Polo, pictured here in Mongol dress, brought news of Kublai Khan's empire back to Europeans.

CLOSE

Organize a class debate in which students argue that Mongol rule was either positive or negative overall.

REVIEW

Have students complete the Section 2 Review on p. 275.

ASSESS

Have students complete Daily Quiz 12.2. As Alternative Assessment, you may want to use the map or flowchart exercises in this section's lessons.

RETEACH

Have students complete Main Idea Activity for English Language Learners and Special-Needs Students 12.2. Then have students write a paragraph that summarizes what they have learned in Section 1. **ENGLISH LANGUAGE LEARNERS**

EXTEND

Have students work together to create a comic book, storyboard, or multimedia presentation about the Mongols' conquest or rule of China, using computer software, biographies, and artifacts to acquire information. **BLOCK SCHEDULING**

he left Venice with his father and uncle. After three years of difficult travel they arrived in China. Kublai Khan was impressed with the young Marco Polo. He employed Polo as his special representative. Polo traveled around China for 17 years and became famous. In his book *The Travels of Marco Polo*, he described Kublai Khan's court to his fellow Europeans:

> **History Makers Speak**
> **❝When the Great Khan is holding court, the seating at banquets is arranged as follows. He himself sits at a much higher table than the rest . . . His principal wife sits next to him on the left. On the right, at a somewhat lower level, sit his sons in order of age . . . . They are placed so that their heads are on a level with the Great Khan's feet. Next to them are seated the other noblemen at other tables lower down again. . . . All the wives of the Khan's sons and grandsons and kinsmen are seated on his left at a lower level, and next to them the wives of his nobles and knights lower down still.❞**
>
> Marco Polo, *The Travels of Marco Polo,* trans. by R.E. Latham

Analyzing Primary Sources

Drawing Inferences What can you infer about the society of the Yuan dynasty from the way that people were seated at Kublai Khan's banquet? organized by hierarchy, social and political status

Chinese-Mongol relations. The Yuan dynasty did much that was good for China. However, there were still tensions between the Mongols and the Chinese. For one thing, they spoke different languages. More importantly, the Mongols did not treat the Chinese as equals. Only Mongols or other non-Chinese people could hold important positions in the government. Mongol law punished Chinese criminals more harshly than non-Chinese ones. Moreover, the Mongols did not allow marriage between different groups of people.

Kublai Khan died in 1294, leaving China to weak successors. During the period after his death, the country experienced many problems. The Huang River flooded, destroying crops and causing famine. Rebellions sprang up. Finally, in 1368, the Yuan dynasty was overthrown.

The Mongols influenced China in several ways. They brought greater contact with Europe. They made local governments more responsible to the central government in Beijing. Later Chinese dynasties built on these political reforms by giving more powers to the emperor.

✔ **READING CHECK: Making Generalizations** What were the good and bad effects of Mongol rule in China? improved communication, transportation, and trade; unequal treatment, harsh taxes and laws

Paper money, as well as coins like those shown here, served as currency during the reign of Kublai Khan. Eventually only paper money was used.

SECTION 2 REVIEW ANSWERS

❶ **Identify**
• Genghis Khan, p. 273
• Kublai Khan, p. 273
• Batu, p. 273
• Golden Horde, p. 273
• Marco Polo, p. 274

❷ Students should include the capture of Beijing, the conquest of Tibet, and the conquest of part of Southeast Asia.

❸ **a.** Their culture encouraged battle skills. Their leaders wanted to create an empire.

b. Students might answer that Mongol rule was good because of improved communication, transportation, and trade. Students might answer that Mongol rule was bad because of unequal treatment and harsh taxes and laws.

❹ Students' letters will vary but should consider the impact of Mongol rule on the Chinese people and should address Kublai Khan formally.

SECTION 2 REVIEW

1. **Identify** and explain the significance:
   Genghis Khan
   Kublai Khan
   Batu
   Golden Horde
   Marco Polo

2. **Sequencing** Copy the graphic organizer below. Use it to illustrate the events that led the Mongol nomads from the plains of Central Asia to become rulers of China.

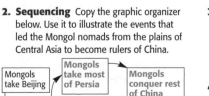

Mongols take Beijing → Mongols take most of Persia → Mongols conquer rest of China

Mongols in Central Asia

Mongols take Tibet, SE Asia

3. **Finding the Main Idea**
   a. Why did the Mongol invaders want to conquer so much land in Asia?
   b. Overall, was Mongol rule good or bad for the average Chinese person? Explain your answer.

4. **Writing and Critical Thinking**
   Supporting a Point of View Write a letter to Kublai Khan requesting that he change some policy of his government with which you disagree.
   Consider:
   • the impact of Mongol rule on the Chinese people
   • the way you think the Great Khan might expect to be addressed

Homework Practice Online
go.hrw.com
keyword: SP3 HP12

OBJECTIVES

1 Investigate how the geography of Japan influenced its development.

2 Analyze how China influenced the early development of Japan.

3 Describe how changes in government influenced society in feudal Japan.

4 Examine how Southeast Asia was influenced by China and India.

SECTION 3

READ TO DISCOVER

❶ How did the geography of Japan influence its development?

❷ How did China influence the early development of Japan?

❸ How did changes in government influence society in feudal Japan?

❹ How was Southeast Asia influenced by China and India?

DEFINE

kami
shogun
samurai
seppuku
daimyo

IDENTIFY

Shinto
The Tale of Genji
Fujiwara
Minamoto
Ashikaga
Bushido
Yi
Sejong

▸ WHY IT MATTERS TODAY

Powerful nations can have enormous influence on their smaller neighbors. Use CNNfyi.com or other **current event** sources to locate a place in the world where a large nation is changing the lives of people in a smaller nation. Record your findings in your journal.

CNNfyi.com

Japan, Korea, and Southeast Asia

The Main Idea
China's culture strongly influenced other countries in eastern and southeastern Asia.

The Story Continues *Japan is a chain of islands in the western Pacific Ocean off the east coast of Asia. A Chinese observer once wrote about Japan, "The land of [Japan] is warm and mild. In winter as in summer, the people live on raw vegetables and go about barefoot." Although Japan is a country of great scenic beauty, its environment has often turned against its people.*

The Physical Setting

The modern nation of Japan consists of a string of thousands of islands in the western Pacific Ocean off the east coast of Asia. This island chain stretches over a distance of nearly 1,400 miles. The great majority of present-day Japan's large population lives on the country's four largest islands. These include Honshu (HAWN·shoo), Hokkaido (hoh·KY·doh), Kyushu (KYOO·shoo), and Shikoku (shee·KOH·koo). No place in Japan is more than about 100 miles from the ocean.

Japan is very mountainous. As a result, only a relatively small part of its land can be used for farming. Hard-working Japanese farmers still are able to produce a great deal of food. They are aided by plentiful rainfall, sunny days, and long growing seasons in some areas. Many rivers provide easy irrigation. Nature is not always kind to Japan, however. Earthquakes, tidal waves, and typhoons often strike the islands.

Until modern times, the seas surrounding Japan protected the islands from foreign influences. The Japanese people could choose whether or not they wanted to have contact with other peoples. At times in their history, they have showed interest in the outside world. At other times they have preferred to live in isolation.

The Mongols under Kublai Khan tried twice to conquer Japan without success. In 1281, a Mongol fleet carrying more than about 140,000 soldiers assembled to invade Japan. A powerful typhoon wrecked the fleet. The grateful Japanese called the storm *kamikaze*, or "Divine Wind."

✔ **READING CHECK: Finding the Main Idea** How did the geography of Japan affect Japanese contact with other peoples? isolated Japan, limited contact

This detail from a Japanese painting is meant to depict the "Divine Wind."

Japan's Beginnings

In prehistoric times migrants from the Asian mainland settled the Japanese islands. By the first centuries A.D. these migrants had organized themselves into clans.

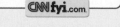

TEACH OBJECTIVE 1

LEVEL 1: Write the following questions on the board: *What geographic similarities do Korea and Japan share? How are Korea and Japan different geographically? How did those similarities and differences influence the development of each?* Pair students and ask them to prepare an answer to each question. Have pairs share their answers with the class.
ENGLISH LANGUAGE LEARNERS, COOPERATIVE LEARNING

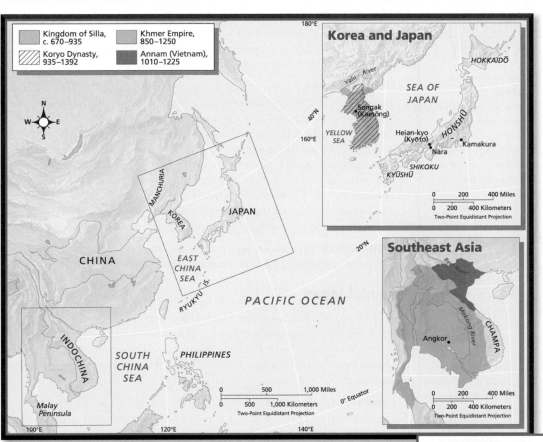

The most powerful clans lived on the island of Honshu. Since then the Japanese people have come together to form a strong, unified society.

Early history. Religion played an important role in helping Japanese culture form. From earliest times, the Japanese believed in gods or nature spirits called **kami.** They believed that these spirits lived in natural objects. For example, kami could be in sand, waterfalls, or trees. Many Japanese clans trace their origins to a particular kami. This religion is now called **Shinto,** meaning "way of the kami." Shinto has no established scripture or doctrine. Shinto worship involves prayers and rituals to please the kami. People might ask for many children or bountiful crops. Shinto is also concerned with ritual cleanliness.

Shinto helped unify Japan under imperial rule. Early emperors seem to have acted as Shinto priests. For all of Japan's history, probably only one imperial family has reigned—the Yamato clan. The first Yamato emperor probably came to power during the early 300s.

Few records of early Japanese history exist. The Chinese, however, knew about Japan before 100. The Japanese adapted Chinese writing by at least the early 700s, and possibly much earlier. Another Chinese influence was Buddhism, introduced in 552. At first the emperor's advisers disliked the new religion. Eventually, the rulers allowed Buddhist temples to be built. Many people in the Japanese court became Buddhists.

Japan, Korea, and Southeast Asia, c. A.D. 670–1392

Interpreting Maps Japan is a long, narrow country made up of four main islands. The Korean peninsula gave birth to the country of Korea.

■ **Skills Assessment:**
1. Using Geography At the narrowest point, approximately how much distance separates Korea from Japan?
2. Drawing Inferences How might this affect the relationship between the two countries?

Government

In A.D. 702 the Taiho Code, based on the Chinese bureaucratic model, divided Japan into three levels of governmental administration: provinces, districts, and villages. Taxes were collected in goods, such as grain or cloth, or in labor. Furthermore, all males were liable for conscription into the military. However, a Chinese-style civil service examination system was not retained by the Japanese. Thus despite much borrowing from the mainland—religion, written language, government, laws, tax systems, and land reform—the aristocratic families retained ultimate authority.

Critical Thinking

Ask students to suggest how government positions were probably obtained in Japan in the absence of civil service examinations.

ANSWER: Students should suggest that such positions were obtained by birth into one of the powerful families or clans.

MAP ANSWERS
1. approximately 125 miles

2. They probably interact frequently and influence each other's culture.

Spotlight on CULTURE

The Japanese writing system combines Chinese characters, called *kanji*, with two syllabic or phonetic systems called *kana*. In Chinese each character represents one sound. In Japanese a character can have different pronunciations. *Kana*, believed to have been influenced by India's Sanskrit, adds inflectional endings to Chinese characters. This allows the use of Japanese words that cannot be written in Chinese alone. Today, students of Japanese must learn and memorize 1,945 *kanji* characters and the 48 *kana* modifiers. The *kana* characters distinguish words containing the same *kanji*. Have students study some examples of Japanese characters and practice writing some of them.

History Maker

LADY MURASAKI SHIKIBU.
Today every Japanese student studies passages from *The Tale of Genji*, written by Lady Murasaki Shikibu. Parts of the book's 54 chapters have been adapted for traditional Noh and Kabuki plays as well as for movies and television dramas. The book has been translated into English several times. The most exact translation was published in 1976.

ACTIVITY: Have students read parts of *The Tale of Genji* in English translation. Assign each student a passage from the book to read for the class.

YOUNG PEOPLE IN HISTORY ANSWER
They were taught martial arts skills as well as social skills.

YOUNG PEOPLE IN HISTORY

Training to Become a Samurai

Young men and even some young women trained to become samurai warriors in feudal Japan. Their training included learning the art of warfare and, later, the ways of peace.

To become a samurai demanded strict training in the martial arts. Many samurai developed great skill handling a sword. But a samurai also learned other lessons, such as the proper way to conduct a tea ceremony and how to write poetry. Above all, a samurai trained to overcome his or her fear of death. **In what ways was a samurai's training a balance between the martial arts and proper social conduct?**

Samurai suit of armor

Analyzing Primary Sources

Identifying Cause and Effect In what ways did Bushido, the "way of the warrior," help to support and strengthen the militaristic society of feudal Japan? encouraged loyalty, devotion to duty

In later centuries, Buddhism spread among the common people and became an important part of Japanese life. It did not replace Shinto, however. Most Japanese believed in both religions. For example, they may have celebrated births and marriages according to Shinto rituals and may have held funerals according to Buddhist rituals.

Chinese influence. Chinese art, science, government, and fashion influenced Japanese society. In 702 the Japanese emperor issued a new law code modeled on Tang dynasty laws. It centralized the government and gave the emperor more power over the lives of his people. In 794 the Japanese built a capital named Heian-kyo (HAY·ahn kyoh), which became the modern city of Kyoto (KYOH·toh). At the capital, the ruling class began to turn away from Chinese influence. Japanese culture became less dependent on Chinese models. For example, poets began to write in Japanese. Female writers were particularly important at Heian. Lady Murasaki Shikibu wrote **The Tale of Genji** in about 1000. It told the story of Prince Genji, the perfect courtier, and was the world's first novel. It is considered a literary masterpiece.

✔ **READING CHECK: Summarizing** What changes helped Japan develop its own culture?
rise of Shinto, spread of Buddhism, movement away from Chinese influence

Feudal Japan

After the 800s, the political system adapted from China began to decline. In its place, Japan developed a system of local power. In Japan the feudal system contained two general sources of power. One was the central government, where important families influenced the emperor. The other was a group of powerful local landowners who had their own warriors.

Government in feudal Japan. The first family to gain control over the central government was the **Fujiwara**. The Fujiwara had power from the mid-800s to the mid-1100s. In 1185 the **Minamoto** clan gained power. The reign of this clan marked a change in the way the government was run. In 1192 the emperor granted Minamoto Yoritomo the title of **shogun**, or general. The emperor kept his throne, but the shogun had control of the military, finances, and laws. In 1331, the Emperor Go-Daigo tried to regain power but failed. One of his generals, Ashikaga Takauji (ah·shee·KAH·gah tah·KOW·jee) claimed the shogunate for his own clan. The **Ashikaga** shoguns ruled for nearly 250 years.

At the local level, however, wealthy landlords held power. They hired warriors called **samurai** for protection. In some ways, the samurai were similar to European knights. A samurai was fiercely loyal to his lord and clan. His power rested on his skill with the sword. The samurai followed a code of behavior called **Bushido**. This means the "way of the warrior." Bushido stressed bravery, loyalty, and honor. Samurai would accept physical hardship without complaint and did not fear death. As one samurai scholar wrote,

History Makers Speak

❝The business of the samurai consists in reflecting on his own station in life, in discharging loyal service to his master . . . and with due consideration of his own position, in devoting himself to duty above all.❞

Yamaga Soko, quoted in Conrad Totman, *A History of Japan*

If samurai displeased their masters or were defeated in battle, they might practice seppuku. **Seppuku** was ceremonial suicide, also known in the West as hara-kiri. It was a way to avoid the dishonor that accompanied defeat or disobedience.

LEVEL 2: Ask students to summarize various ways in which China influenced the development of Japanese society. List responses on the board. *(artistic designs, Buddhism, fashion, government methods, writing)* Then hold a class debate over which item on the list was the most important influence. *(Positions will vary, but students should support their point of view. Buddhism was very influential, but Shinto remained popular. Chinese writing allowed literature to develop, but Japan eventually adopted its own writing system.)*

SKILL-BUILDING STRATEGIES Reading a Chart

Japan's Feudal System

In Japan's feudal system some groups at lower levels of power actually had more influence than those at higher levels. For example, although the emperor and the shoguns held the top positions, they were often just figureheads. The daimyo had the most real power and were the most responsible for running the business of daily life for most of Japanese society. Reading an organization chart can help to show relationships within this system, using connecting lines to show who has authority over whom.

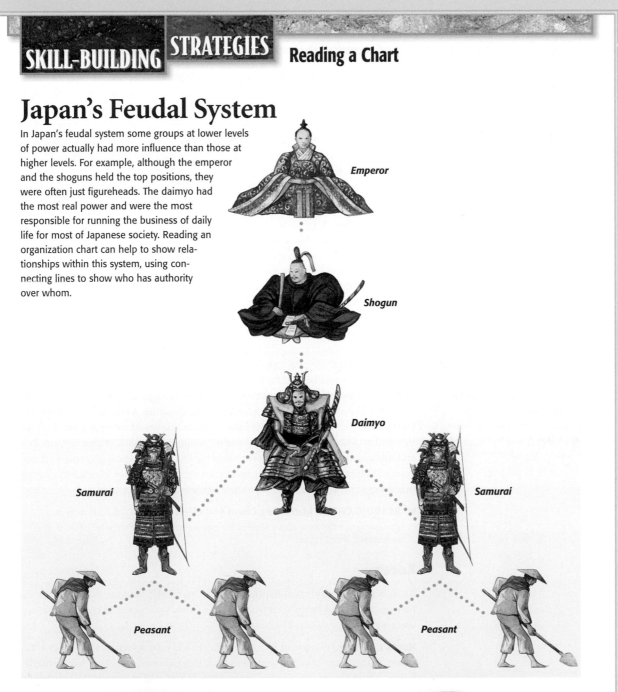

Emperor

Shogun

Daimyo

Samurai

Samurai

Peasant

Peasant

Skills Reminder

Charts are an effective way of visually organizing and communicating information to show relationships, comparisons, and contrasts. To read a chart, identify the type of chart and its purpose. Then identify the details given by the chart, such as labels and leader lines. Assess how the details relate to each other and what information this provides about a subject.

Skills Practice

❶ What can you determine about Japan's feudal system from the chart above?

❷ Using what you know about charts, draw an organization chart like the one above that shows the structure of the United States government. You may need to use an American government textbook to find the information necessary to practice this skill.

Citizenship

Samurai warriors originally fought on horseback and were trained in sword fighting, archery, and martial arts. The position of samurai officially ended in the 1870s when the government forbade them to wear their swords in public. Today samurai occupy a place in Japanese culture much like that held by the cowboys of the old West in America. Samurai movies are the "westerns" of Japanese entertainment.

Critical Thinking

Ask students how a samurai's life and duties compare to those of the American cowboy of a later era.

ANSWER: Both worked for large landowners and lived physically demanding lives.

SKILLS PRACTICE ANSWERS

1. that it was based upon a hierarchical organization

2. Student charts should show the equality of the executive branch, the legislative branch, and the judicial branch. Cabinet posts and the federal court system should be included under the executive branch and judicial branch, respectively.

LEVEL 3: Have five students take the roles of emperor, shogun, daimyo, samurai, and peasant. Have each class member, in turn, direct a "yes" or "no" question to one of the five students. Do not allow direct questions about a student's identity, such as "Are you the peasant?" When all class members have had a chance to ask their question, have each write out his or her prediction of the identity of each role player. See how many students can correctly identify all five. Conclude the activity by discussing what each role player's answers reveal about power in feudal Japan.

That's Interesting!

Many of Japan's gardens were attached to Buddhist temples and were designed by the monks. The aesthetics of their design link them with meditation and landscape painting, both important activities of the monks. Some of these gardens are monochromatic and quite abstract, containing only rocks and raked white gravel.

VISUAL RECORD ANSWER

tranquility

Reproducible Resources

PS Readings in World History 47: Drinking Tea for a Long Life

---

INTERPRETING THE VISUAL RECORD

Zen garden Shown above is a Zen garden in contemporary Japan. The sand has been raked into spare, clean lines to represent the Zen Buddhist values of simplicity and appreciation of nature. ***What mood is suggested by the design of the landscape?***

The daimyo. In time local lords known as **daimyo** (DY·mee·oh), or "great names," gained great power. These lords and their samurai became the most powerful people in Japan during the Ashikaga shogunate. For a century, Japan had no effective central government and warfare was common. Despite this situation, Japan continued to grow economically and socially. Peasants produced greater crop yields, which meant more tax money for the daimyo. The daimyo promoted trade, which they also taxed. The taxes were very likely used to pay for the wars. Wars could offer people of lower status a chance to rise in society. Any man who could use a sword or lance could possibly join a daimyo's army. Those who fought well could be promoted to a higher rank.

Zen Buddhism. A religious awakening occurred in feudal Japan as Buddhists established new sects. Some taught that salvation could come through faith alone. Older sects asked people to give money to monasteries or study Buddhist scriptures. Therefore, the new sects appealed to ordinary people.

Zen Buddhism was introduced from China in the 1100s. It particularly interested warriors. Zen taught salvation through enlightenment, not faith. This perspective was very similar to the views embodied in Daoism. Zen Buddhism also taught that the life of the body was not important. Zen Buddhists developed self-discipline through long hours of meditation. These skills helped warriors in battle.

The Ashikaga shoguns supported Zen Buddhism. They encouraged the artistic efforts of Zen monks. New art forms inspired by Zen appeared in the late 1300s and early 1400s. One was landscape architecture, or the art of gardens. By arranging rocks, trees, and water, Zen artists tried to represent the beauty of nature. A related art form was the tea ceremony, designed to produce spiritual calm. People would gather in a simple room by a garden to quietly drink tea and admire the beauty of nature. Another important Zen art form was the Noh play. First performed in the 1300s, these were highly stylized dance dramas. Noh plays drew on religious, historical, or romantic themes. Male actors wearing masks would perform on a bare stage while a chorus chanted the story.

✔ **READING CHECK: Identifying Cause and Effect** How did the confusion in government offer new opportunities for people in Japanese society? offered ways to improve social status

Korea

Korea is a rugged, mountainous peninsula that juts south from Manchuria into the sea between China and Japan. As is true of Japan, Korea's political and cultural development was strongly shaped by China.

Korea's history. Because of its location, Korea has long served as a bridge that has allowed the passage of people and ideas from the mainland of eastern Asia to neighboring island chains. The Korean Peninsula was first settled in prehistoric times by nomadic peoples from northeastern Asia. These people enjoyed abundant sources of food, including wild deer, fish and other seafoods, and certain plant foods. Agriculture—especially rice farming—reached Korea from China, perhaps as early as about 1500 B.C. Metalworking techniques also spread from China to early Korea.

As early as 300 B.C., migrants from China began to arrive in Korea, bringing with them knowledge of metalworking and agriculture. Not long afterward, the first strong Korean kingdom, Chosŏn, emerged in the northern part of the peninsula. By the early 100s B.C. Chosŏn was strong enough to hold some control over much of the Korean Peninsula.

ALL LEVELS: Have students think about Chinese influences on the development of Japanese and Korean civilizations. Ask them to list the similarities that Vietnam's development shares with either of these countries. *(Japan and Vietnam: Buddhism, Chinese writing system, Chinese influences on government; Korea and Vietnam: conquest by China, Buddhism, Confucianism, Chinese influences on government)* **ENGLISH LANGUAGE LEARNERS**

HOMEWORK Have each student develop a diagram or chart that shows the similarities and differences in China's influence on the development of Japanese, Korean, and Vietnamese culture. Select students to copy their diagram or chart on the chalkboard and explain it.

Chinese Influences in Asia			
Influence	**Japan**	**Korea**	**Vietnam**
Religion	✔	✔	✔
Writing System	✔		✔
Government/Political Structure	✔	✔	✔
Technology	✔	✔	
Fashion	✔		
Literature	✔	✔	

In about 108 B.C. troops from Han China invaded Korea, conquered the kingdom of Chosŏn, and turned it into a Han colony. For the next 400 years the Chinese maintained tight control over northwestern Korea, allowing native Koreans little or no voice in their government. Elsewhere on the peninsula, however, three Korean kingdoms—Koguryo, Paekche, and Silla—arose in opposition to Chinese rule. Because these native kingdoms also fought amongst themselves, they were unable to challenge China's dominance in Korea. With the fall of the Han dynasty, Koguryo invaded the north and took over the one-time Chinese colony.

Unification under the Silla. Korea's three kingdoms continued to fight one another for the next several centuries. During the early A.D. 600s China's Sui dynasty attempted to conquer Korea but failed. Later, however, the rulers of Silla formed a strategic alliance with the Tang emperor of China. Working together, the armies of Silla and China conquered Paekche and Koguryo. Silla then turned on the Tang forces and drove them from Korea. By about 670 the kingdom of Silla had united Korea for the first time. Over time, Silla was weakened by internal rebellions and the loss of leadership. During the early 900s a new kingdom, Koryo (from which comes the name Korea), grew to challenge Silla's rule. By 935 Koryo had overthrown Silla and had taken control of the peninsula.

Korea remained independent throughout the era of the Tang dynasty. But in the mid-1200s the peninsula once again fell under the control of its powerful neighbor to the west, and Korea became part of the Mongol Empire. It was not until 1392 that Koreans regained their independence by driving out the Mongols. The **Yi** dynasty arose to rule the peninsula, lasting for centuries until Japan annexed Korea in 1910.

The growth of Korean culture. The culture and civilization of China has had a strong and lasting influence on Korea. Chosŏn, the first true kingdom in Korea, was founded in part by immigrants from China and clearly reflected many elements of Chinese culture. Korean rulers adopted Chinese as their written language, and they embraced China's Confucian traditions and ideas. They also followed the Chinese model of government. Korean rulers built dynasties controlled by hereditary kings. The rulers of Koryo used an examination process to select and train their government administrators. This process was based in large part on China's Confucian civil service system. The kings of Koryo, moreover, built Kaesong, a great capital city much like Xi'an, the imperial city of China's Tang dynasty.

During the 300s the ideals of Chinese Buddhism were brought to Korea. Many Koreans accepted the Buddhist philosophy and built magnificent temples that became major centers of learning. Buddhist teachings became part of Korean culture, philosophy, and morality. During the period of the three kingdoms, Buddhism became Korea's state religion. In the 700s Zen was introduced. It became the dominant form of Buddhism throughout the peninsula. Later, Korean scholars also studied the philosophy of Confucius and the Korean government adopted the Chinese civil service system.

INTERPRETING THE VISUAL RECORD

Dragon's head This gold and bronze dragon's head was fashioned in Korea to decorate the top of a flagstaff. *What does this metalwork suggest about Korean artistic and technological skills during the Silla and Koryo periods?*

Global Relations

As the ancient tribal systems broke down, Silla's government and culture were heavily influenced by China. Silla regularly sent tribute missions to the Tang capital. In addition, many students and monks from Silla pursued their education and training in China. Thus a flow of new ideas and philosophies arose. Eventually the people of Silla embraced Buddhism and duplicated the Tang political system.

Critical Thinking

Ask students why they think Silla accepted Tang systems.

ANSWER: Students might suggest that Silla wanted to replace older tribal customs.

VISUAL RECORD ANSWER

They were very advanced.

THE CIVILIZATIONS OF EAST ASIA **281**

CLOSE

Ask students to describe the influence of China and India on the countries of mainland Southeast Asia.

REVIEW

Have students complete the Section 3 Review on p. 283.

Culture

The kingdom of Silla lacked its own writing system in which the people could transcribe their native language. Therefore they used the Chinese writing system.

This fact probably affected the degree of Chinese influence in Korea that exists even today. The most visible form of this influence may be seen in Korea's place-names and personal names. Because they were written in Chinese, original Korean names were replaced with their Chinese equivalents.

Despite the difficulty of fitting the polysyllabic Korean language into the Chinese format, there was a great deal of literary activity in Silla. Histories, poetry, and Buddhist writings were published along with Korean translations of Chinese texts, though few exist today.

Critical Thinking

Ask students how the adoption of Chinese characters to transcribe the Korean language would have encouraged the Chinese cultural influence.

ANSWER: Students might answer that the use of Chinese characters would have made it easier for Koreans to learn to read Chinese and would have introduced Chinese sounds and patterns into the Korean language.

Technology Resources

Regions of the World Music Audio CD Program 20: Japan and the Koreas

Holt Researcher

go.hrw.com
KEYWORD: Holt Researcher
FreeFind: Sejong
After reading more about Sejong on the Holt Researcher, use a problem-solving process to evaluate how his administration improved upon Chinese traditions.

Koreans learned to use movable type from the Chinese. They advanced this technology by casting type blocks in metal.

Despite the strength of China's influence, however, Korea did not become an identical copy of its huge neighbor to the west. Instead, Koreans worked to maintain the strength and identity of their culture and traditions. As one ruler of Koryo insisted in 982, "Let us follow China in poetry, history, music, ceremony, and the [principles of Confucius], but in riding and dressing let us be Koreans." Thus, the people of ancient Korea built a civilization that was, in many important ways, unique and distinct from that of China. Korean Buddhism, for example, included many elements of traditional Korean beliefs.

Another important difference between Korean and Chinese cultures was the presence of a powerful nobility in Korea. Korean aristocrats, unlike Chinese nobles, had great influence on the country's political development. As a result, the power of Korea's Confucian-style government administration was limited. Korean society differed from that of China, too, because it never developed a large, well-educated social class of merchants, government administrators, and scholars. In China, this group formed a kind of middle class between the traditional nobles and the peasant farmers. Korean society, however, was more sharply divided between its small upper class and its very large lower class.

During the 1400s the emperor **Sejong** ordered the development of a Korean alphabet. The Koreans borrowed the Chinese invention of movable wood type and then improved upon it. They designed movable type blocks made of metal, which was far more durable and produced sharper images.

✔ **READING CHECK: Contrasting** How did Korean aristocrats differ from Chinese nobles? had great influence on Korea's political development

Civilization in Southeast Asia

The mainland of Southeast Asia (also known as Indochina) is made up of the modern nations of Cambodia, Laos, Malaysia, Myanmar, Thailand (formerly Siam), and Vietnam. Like Japan and Korea, the kingdoms and peoples of ancient Southeast Asia were strongly and continuously influenced by China, which borders Southeast Asia to the north. The civilization of India, which lies to the region's northwest, also helped to shape Southeast Asian lifestyles, traditions, and beliefs. In a broader sense, however, the cultures that developed in Southeast Asia have their own distinct identities.

Northern Vietnam—known as Annam—was controlled by China throughout much of its history. By the 900s the Vietnamese had made several attempts to throw off Chinese dominance. It was not until 939, however, that the people of northern Vietnam won their independence from China. Soon after, Vietnam fell into widespread disorder and political violence. Finally, the emergence of several dynasties led to growing stability and the first steps toward the unification of the country.

The Vietnamese civilization that developed during these years was heavily influenced by contact with China. For example, Vietnam adopted Mahayana Buddhism from the Chinese. Over time, this form of Buddhism became the guiding philosophy of the Vietnamese culture. Daoism and Confucianism also contributed to the development of Vietnam's culture and society. In addition, Vietnam used the writing system and political organization of the Chinese.

Much of the rest of mainland Southeast Asia was shaped by Indian culture and tradition. Early in the history of Southeast Asia, people from India began to settle in the region, many of them perhaps Hindu and Buddhist missionaries.

The Sanskrit language came into use, helping to spread Indian literature and thought. In present-day Cambodia, ruins of the city of Angkor Thom and the huge temple of Angkor Wat offer reminders of Indian influence. Reliefs with scenes from the Hindu epics adorn Angkor Wat, one of the architectural wonders of the Far East.

Centered in modern-day Cambodia, the Khmer Empire grew to control much of Southeast Asia in the years between about 850 and about 1250. Khmer rulers, strongly influenced by Indian culture, adopted many Hindu and Buddhist beliefs. For many years, Khmer society embraced the Indian principle of a god-king. The rulers probably used forced labor and income from taxes to build elaborate cities, government centers, and magnificent temple complexes. At the same time, Khmer leaders undertook major construction projects for the public good. These included hospitals, travelers' rest-houses, and canal and water-control systems designed to encourage rice farming throughout the region.

The Khmer kings' abuse of their royal powers eventually led to social discontent and rebellion. The ideas of Theravada Buddhism became increasingly widespread throughout much of Southeast Asia. This Buddhist philosophy had no place for splendid ceremonies, elaborate temples such as Angkor Wat, or the concept of a god-king. Over time, the all-powerful Khmer kings were overthrown and Theravada Buddhism became the predominant form of Buddhism in Southeast Asia.

✔ **READING CHECK: Categorizing** In what ways did Korea and Southeast Asia develop their own cultures despite the influences of China and India? worked to maintain their own cultures and traditions, rejected many Chinese and Indian influences over time

INTERPRETING THE VISUAL RECORD

Angkor Wat The temple of Angkor Wat in Cambodia is one of the architectural wonders of the Far East. It is decorated with scenes from Hindu epics.

Link to Today How does this temple show evidence of Indian influence on Southeast Asian art and beliefs?

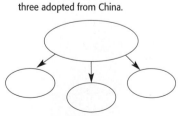

SECTION 3 REVIEW

1. **Define** and explain the significance:
   kami   seppuku
   shogun   daimyo
   samurai

2. **Identify** and explain the significance:
   Shinto   Ashikaga
   The Tale of Genji Bushido
   Fujiwara   Yi
   Minamoto   Sejong

3. **Summarizing** Copy the graphic organizer below. Label the largest oval China and the others Japan, Korea, and Southeast Asia. Use it to identify the institutions and customs that the latter three adopted from China.

4. **Finding the Main Idea**

   a. How did the breakup of the central government in Japan lead to changes in feudal Japanese society?

   b. How did China influence the societies of Japan, Korea, and Southeast Asia?

5. **Writing and Critical Thinking**

   Supporting a Point of View What are the advantages and disadvantages of Bushido—the "way of the warrior"—as a code of behavior in feudal Japan?
   Consider:
   • the nature of society in feudal Japan and the values that it emphasized
   • the skills and behaviors that could help a person to advance in feudal Japan
   • the ways a person could express bravery, loyalty, and honor in daily life

Homework Practice Online
keyword: SP3 HP12

THE CIVILIZATIONS OF EAST ASIA **283**

REVIEW AND ASSESSMENT RESOURCES

REPRODUCIBLE RESOURCES

▸ Vocabulary Activity 12

TECHNOLOGY RESOURCES

▸ Chapter 12 Test Generator (on the One-Stop Planner)
▸ Global Skill Builder CD–ROM
▸ HRW Web Site

REINFORCEMENT, REVIEW, and ASSESSMENT

▸ Chapter 12 Review, pp. 284–285
▸ Chapter 12 Tutorial for Students, Parents, Mentors, and Peers
▸ Chapter 12 Test (Form A or B)
▸ Alternative Assessment Handbook
▸ Chapter 12 Test for English Language Learners and Special-Needs Students

REVIEW

Have students complete the Chapter 12 Review on pages 284–285.

ASSESS

Use one of the chapter tests to assess students' understanding of the content. For Alternative Assessment, see the Portfolio Activities and Alternative Assessment Handbook.

CHAPTER 12 REVIEW ANSWERS

Understanding Main Ideas

1. literature flourished; Zen, Confucianism revived

2. Farming methods improved, but taxes forced some peasants to become tenant farmers. Poverty and overcrowding remained problems in cities.

3. skillful warriors with powerful weapons

4. Communication, transportation, and trade improved, but citizens were subject to unequal treatment and harsh taxes and laws.

5. It was isolated and had little contact with other peoples.

6. Buddhism, writing, law code, governmental methods, artistic designs, medical knowledge, fashion

7. People had opportunities to improve their social status.

8. Chinese philosophies, writing system, political structure, Buddhism, Hinduism

Reviewing Themes

1. heavily influenced by Chinese society and culture

2. could not defend themselves against Mongol invasions

3. Buddhism, and later Zen Buddhism, became a part of Japanese culture. Korea accepted the Buddhist philosophy. Vietnam adopted Mahayana Buddhism from China.

284

CHAPTER 12 Review

Creating a Time Line

Copy the time line below onto a sheet of paper. Complete the time line by filling in the events, individuals, and dates from the chapter that you think were significant. Pick three events and explain why you think they were significant.

A.D. 552   A.D. 1000   A.D. 1573

Writing a Summary

Using standard grammar, spelling, sentence structure, and punctuation, write an overview of the events in the chapter.

Identifying People and Ideas

Identify the following terms or individuals and explain their significance:

1. Grand Canal
2. Empress Wu
3. Zen
4. *Diamond Sutra*
5. Genghis Khan
6. Kublai Khan
7. Golden Horde
8. Shinto
9. shogun
10. samurai

Understanding Main Ideas

Section 1 *(pp. 266–271)*

China under the Sui, Tang, and Sung Dynasties

1. What were the most important developments in Chinese culture during the Sui, Tang, and Sung dynasties?
2. Did life improve for ordinary people during the Sung dynasty? Explain.

Section 2 *(pp. 272–275)*

The Mongol Empire

3. How were the Mongol nomads able to gain power in China?
4. How did China change under Mongol rule?

Section 3 *(pp. 276–283)*

Japan, Korea, and Southeast Asia

5. How did Japan's geography affect its relations with its neighbors?
6. How did China influence Japanese society and culture?

7. What unique features of society in feudal Japan were the result of political confusion?
8. What were the influences of China and India on societies in Korea and Southeast Asia?

Reviewing Themes

1. **Global Relations** How did proximity to China affect the rest of Asian civilization?
2. **Government** Why were the rulers of the several Chinese dynasties unable to retain their hold on power?
3. **Culture** How were the various forms of Buddhism reflected in east Asian cultures?

Thinking Critically

1. **Drawing Inferences** How did the Sung and Yuan dynasties change China?
2. **Identifying Bias** Would Marco Polo have said that Kublai Khan's rule was good for China? Why or why not?
3. **Contrasting** How did the culture of feudal Japan differ from earlier Japanese culture?

Writing About History

Categorizing Write a report explaining the impact of Chinese culture on life in Mongol society and on Japan. Use the chart below to organize your thoughts before writing.

	Mongol society	Japanese society
Government		
Religion		
Art & literature		
Daily life		

CLOSE

Ask students to describe how the role of emperor in Japan was different from the role of emperor in China.

RETEACH

Have students who had difficulty with the test work in small groups to develop several questions about the information in the chapter. Then have each group use its questions to quiz the other groups. When they are ready, have groups take the Form B Test to assess their mastery of the material.

ENGLISH LANGUAGE LEARNERS

Portfolio Extensions

1. Have students research American products that are marketed in other nations. Have them transfer the information into a visual medium, using computer software as appropriate, to advertise one of the products.

2. Have students choose an example of American literature, drama, or music and write a paragraph or two about how it reflects the history of American culture.

3. Assign students to find out about fashions in other parts of the world. Have them determine which styles reflect the influence of American culture.

Building Social Studies Skills

Drawing Inferences

Study the chart below. Then use the information from the chart to answer the questions that follow.

The Sui Dynasty—Successes versus Problems	
Some Sui Successes	**Some Sui Problems**
• Reunited China	• Suffered defeats in Korea
• Rebuilt the Great Wall	• Constant demands for labor
• Constructed canals	• Heavy spending
• Built strong central government	• Excesses at court

1. Which statement below most accurately describes an inference that may be drawn from the chart?
   a. The Sui rulers were generally popular among the people they ruled.
   b. Military defeats in Korea probably had little effect on Sui rule at home.
   c. The people were probably willing to support heavy imperial spending, since it benefited them.
   d. Military defeats in foreign lands may have caused the Sui rulers to lose prestige among their people.

2. The Sui dynasty ruled for a relatively brief period of time. Write a short paragraph in which you analyze some of the factors in the dynasty's history that might explain why it could not maintain its rule.

Analyzing a Primary Source

Read the following quote from Ibn Battūtah, a Moroccan Muslim who traveled in China during the 1300s. Then answer the questions.

> "In regard to portraiture there is none . . . who can match . . . [the Chinese] in precision, for in this art they show a marvellous talent. This is a custom of theirs, making portraits of all who pass through their country. In fact they have brought this to such perfection that if a stranger commits any offence that obliges him to flee from China, they send his portrait far and wide. A search is then made for him and wherever the person bearing a resemblance to that portrait is found, he is arrested."

3. Which statement best describes what you can infer about the Chinese attitude toward foreigners?
   a. They wanted to impress them with their artistic ability.
   b. They respected their privacy.
   c. They disliked them.
   d. They did not completely trust them.

4. What is your opinion of how the Chinese kept track of strangers? Give reasons for your point of view.

Alternative Assessment

Building Your Portfolio

Culture

Historical China had a powerful influence on the cultures of other nations. Using your textbook and other sources, make a list of ideas, institutions, and advances in mathematics, science, and technology that originated in China. Use a poster board to prepare a map of the world or a collage to trace the spread of these ideas to other civilizations.

▸ internet connect

Internet Activity: go.hrw.com
KEYWORD: SP3 WH12

Choose a topic on the Civilizations of East Asia to:

• understand similarities and differences of Chinese, Japanese, and Korean art.

• research the early development of Korea, Vietnam, and the Khmer Empire of Southeast Asia.

• learn more about Genghis Khan.

Thinking Critically

1. The Chinese civil service system was perfected; important innovations in the use of gunpowder and printing were made; farming methods were improved; heavy taxation was implemented.

2. Yes, because Marco Polo was a merchant and trade improved under Kublai Khan's rule.

3. A system of local power emerged.

Writing About History

Students should include: Mongol—administrative organization, ceremonies; Japan—Buddhism, writing, law code, governmental methods, artistic designs, roads, medical knowledge, fashion

Building Social Studies Skills

1. d

2. Factors include trying to do too much at once, unsuccessful attempts to conquer southern Manchuria and northern Korea, invasion by Turks, and uprising.

3. d

4. Answers will vary but students should support their point of view.

Building Your Portfolio

Students' lists may include the civil service system, gunpowder, and printing.

The Rise of the Middle Ages

CHAPTER RESOURCE MANAGER

	Objectives	Pacing Guide	Reproducible Resources
SECTION 1 **The Rise of the Franks** (pp. 288–293)	• Describe how Frankish rulers gained control of Europe. • Explain what caused the decline of Charlemagne's empire.	**Regular** 1.5 day / **Block Scheduling** 1 day *Block Scheduling Handbook with Team Teaching Strategies, 13.1*	**RS** Guided Reading Strategy 13.1 **PS** Readings in World History 37: Peasant Life During the Time of Charlemagne
SECTION 2 **Feudalism and the Manorial System** (pp. 294–299)	• Explore how feudalism helped shape political and social development in Europe during the Middle Ages. • Identify the ways in which the manorial system influenced economic growth in Europe during the Middle Ages.	**Regular** 1.5 day / **Block Scheduling** 1 day *Block Scheduling Handbook with Team Teaching Strategies, 13.2*	**RS** Guided Reading Strategy 13.2 **PS** Readings in World History 38: The Table of a Thirteenth-Century English Lord
SECTION 3 **The Church** (pp. 300–303)	• Describe how the church hierarchy fit into society. • Explain how the practices of monasticism changed. • Explore how the church influenced life in medieval Europe.	**Regular** 1 day / **Block Scheduling** .5 day *Block Scheduling Handbook with Team Teaching Strategies, 13.3*	**RS** Guided Reading Strategy 13.3 **SM** Geography Activity 14: The Structure of the Church
SECTION 4 **The Struggle for Power in England and France** (pp. 304–309)	• Explain how the kingdom of England was formed. • Identify the achievements of William the Conqueror and his successors. • Describe how Parliament and common law affected political developments in England. • Explore how the French kings gained power over their nobles.	**Regular** 1.5 day / **Block Scheduling** 1 day *Block Scheduling Handbook with Team Teaching Strategies, 13.4*	**RS** Guided Reading Strategy 13.4 **SM** Geography Activity 13: England Under the Normans **PS** Readings in World History 39
SECTION 5 **The Clash over Germany and Italy** (pp. 310–313)	• Describe how the Holy Roman emperors used their power. • Explain how the struggle between the popes and emperors developed.	**Regular** 1 day / **Block Scheduling** .5 day *Block Scheduling Handbook with Team Teaching Strategies, 13.5*	**RS** Guided Reading Strategy 13.5 **PS** Readings in World History 40 **E** Creative Teaching Strategy 13

Chapter Resource Key

PS Primary Sources
RS Reading Support
IC Interdisciplinary Connections
E Enrichment
SM Skills Mastery
A Assessment

REV Review
ELL Reinforcement and English Language Learners
   Transparencies
   CD-ROM
   Music

   Video
   Internet
   Holt Presentation Maker Using Microsoft® PowerPoint®

One-Stop Planner CD-ROM

See the *One-Stop Planner* for a complete list of additional resources for students and teachers.

One-Stop Planner CD-ROM

It's easy to plan lessons, select resources, and print out materials for your students when you use the **One-Stop Planner** CD–ROM with **Test Generator**.

Technology Resources	Reinforcement, Review, and Assessment
One-Stop Planner 13.1 Homework Practice Online	Daily Quiz 13.1 Main Idea Activity 13.1 English Audio Summary 13.1 Spanish Audio Summary 13.1 REV Section 1 Review, p. 293
One-Stop Planner 13.2 Homework Practice Online Online Maps, Charts, and Graphs: A Medieval Manor	Daily Quiz 13.2 Main Idea Activity 13.2 English Audio Summary 13.2 Spanish Audio Summary 13.2 REV Section 2 Review, p. 299
One-Stop Planner 13.3 Holt Researcher: World History: Benedict, Hildegard of Bingen Homework Practice Online Online Maps, Charts, and Graphs: A Monk's Day	Daily Quiz 13.3 Main Idea Activity 13.3 English Audio Summary 13.3 Spanish Audio Summary 13.3 REV Section 3 Review, p. 303
One-Stop Planner 13.4 Holt Researcher: World History: William the Conqueror World History Teaching Transparency: Art and History 11: Bayeux Tapestry Homework Practice Online	Daily Quiz 13.4 Main Idea Activity 13.4 English Audio Summary 13.4 Spanish Audio Summary 13.4 REV Section 4 Review, p. 309
One-Stop Planner 13.5 Holt Researcher: World History: Innocent III, John Paul II Homework Practice Online Online Maps, Charts, and Graphs: Holy Roman Empire at the Death of Otto I	Daily Quiz 13.5 Main Idea Activity 13.5 English Audio Summary 13.5 Spanish Audio Summary 13.5 REV Section 5 Review, p. 313

internet connect

HRW ONLINE RESOURCES
GO TO: go.hrw.com
Then type in a keyword.

TEACHER HOME PAGE
KEYWORD: SP3 Teacher

CHAPTER INTERNET ACTIVITIES
KEYWORD: SP3 WH13
Choose an activity to:
- evaluate primary and secondary sources about Charlemagne.
- create a poster on medieval art and architecture.
- write a report on daily life in the Middle Ages.

CHAPTER ENRICHMENT LINKS
KEYWORD: SP3 CH13

ONLINE ASSESSMENT
Homework Practice
KEYWORD: SP3 HP13
Standardized Test Prep
KEYWORD: SP3 STP13
Rubrics
KEYWORD: SS Rubrics

ONLINE MAPS, CHARTS, AND GRAPHS
KEYWORD: SP13 MCG

CONTENT UPDATES
KEYWORD: SS Content Updates

HOLT PRESENTATION MAKER
KEYWORD: SP3 PPT13

ONLINE READING SUPPORT
KEYWORD: SS Strategies

CURRENT EVENTS
KEYWORD: S3 Current Events

Meeting Individual Needs

Ability Levels

Level 1 Basic level activities designed for all students encountering new material

Level 2 Intermediate level activities designed for average students

Level 3 Challenging activities designed for honors and gifted and talented students

English Language Learners These activities address the needs of students with Limited English Proficiency.

Chapter Review and Assessment

IC Vocabulary Activity 13 Global Skill Builder CD-ROM HRW Web Site REV Chapter 13 Tutorial for Students, Parents, Mentors, and Peers REV Chapter 13 Review, pp. 314–315	A Chapter 13 Test Generator (on the One-Stop Planner) A Chapter 13 Test (Form A or B) A Alternative Assessment Handbook A Chapter 13 Test for English Language Learners and Special-Needs Students

Build on What You Know

Ask students to answer the following questions:

What were some of the cultural achievements of Asia?

Consider:

- China
- Japan
- Korea

What were some of the reasons for the collapse of the Roman Empire?

Consider:

- the economy
- social change
- invaders

EXPLORING THE TIME LINE
GL🌐BAL EVENTS

🌐 internet connect

TOPIC: Troubadours
GO TO: go.hrw.com
KEYWORD: SP3 WH13

Have students access the Internet through the HRW Go site to conduct research on troubadours. Then ask them to pretend they are modern-day troubadours. Have students write a song in one of the troubadour genres: *canso* (courtly love-song), *dansa* (mock-popular song based on a dance form), *escondig* (a lover's apologia), *gap* (a challenge), *pastorela* (an encounter between a knight and a shepherdess), *planh* (a lament), and *joc partit* (songs of debate). Have students read or sing their song to the class.

CHAPTER 13

A.D. 432–A.D. 1328
The Rise of the Middle Ages

A medieval crossbow

C. A.D. 476
Global Events
The last Western Roman emperor is deposed.

C. A.D. 542
Daily Life
A devastating plague begins to move across Europe, resulting in a decades-long population decline.

A.D. 782
Politics
Charlemagne executes Saxon hostages.

C. A.D. 797
Daily Life
French kings establish a royal messenger service.

| A.D. 425 | A.D. 525 | A.D. 725 | A.D. 825 |

A.D. 455
Global Events
Vandals attack Rome.

C. A.D. 500
Science and Technology
Architects develop the first plans for the Vatican in Rome.

C. A.D. 750
Daily Life
Beds become popular in France and Germany.

C. A.D. 787
Global Events
The first Viking raids into Britain occur.

Viking carving of a lion's head, A.D. 800s

Illustration of the invasion of England by Danish Vikings

Build on What You Know

Great civilizations flourished in East and Southeast Asia in the thousand years after about the A.D. 500s. The cultures that emerged in China, Korea, Japan, and Southeast Asia reached new heights of achievement. Change and growth also characterized the civilizations that emerged in Europe during these same years. The barbarian peoples who overran much of the Roman Empire brought with them behaviors and traditions that gradually developed into a new and distinct European civilization. In this chapter, you will learn how new European societies and cultures arose from the ashes of Rome's collapse.

What's Your Opinion?

Government

Agree Political leaders should deal only with matters of the state, and religious leaders should concern themselves only with church matters.

Disagree It is important for issues of church and state to be considered in relation to each other.

Constitutional Heritage

Agree It is not important to list and define individual rights in a constitution.

Disagree Citizens may be subject to the whims of their leaders if individual rights are not included and defined in a constitution.

Economics

Agree An agricultural economy is more stable and desirable than an industrial economy.

Disagree Both farming societies and industrial societies have advantages and disadvantages.

Detail from the Bayeux Tapestry depicting a battle scene between the English and the Normans

C. A.D. 900
Daily Life
European nobles begin to build fortified castles.

C. A.D. 1110
The Arts
The earliest recorded miracle play is performed in England.

C. A.D. 1125
The Arts
The "troubadour" tradition of wandering musicians begins in France.

C. A.D. 1190s
Science and Technology
The magnetic compass is used by mariners in Western Europe.

C. A.D. 1253
Business and Finance
Linen is made in England.

C. A.D. 1269
Business and Finance
The first English toll roads are built.

C. A.D. 1314
Politics
Scotland becomes independent under Robert I, the Bruce.

C. A.D. 1317
Politics
French law excludes women from inheriting the throne.

A.D. 925   **A.D. 1125**   **A.D. 1225**   **A.D. 1325**

C. A.D. 900s
Science and Technology
The crossbow is used in Europe.

C. A.D. 1124
Business and Finance
Coins are first minted in Scotland.

C. A.D. 1170
The Arts
Chrétien de Troyes writes the courtly love story "Lancelot."

A.D. 1215
Politics
King John I signs Magna Carta.

C. A.D. 1305
Business and Finance
Edward I standardizes measures, including the yard and the acre.

EXPLORING THE TIME LINE
GLOBAL EVENTS

The development of local trade contributed to the growth of towns and cities in the 1000s. Rural peasants provided the towns with food and livestock, and in exchange they bought the manufactured goods produced in the towns. As peasants began to focus their economic activity on the towns, the power of feudal lords began to decrease.

Critical Thinking

Ask students what peasants may have found in the city that they found appealing.

ANSWER: Students may answer that peasants found freedom and consumer goods in the towns.

An idealized illustration of medieval knights

The castle of the Counts of Flanders

What's Your Opinion?

 *Do you **agree** or **disagree** with the following statements? Support your point of view in your journal.*

Government Successful governments should establish a firm separation between the powers of church and state.

Constitutional Heritage Individual rights do not need to be included and defined in a constitution.

Economics Farming societies promote more secure and peaceful lifestyles than do societies that are centered upon industrial growth.

SECTION 1

READ TO DISCOVER

❶ How did Frankish rulers gain control of Europe?

❷ What caused the decline of Charlemagne's empire?

DEFINE

medieval

IDENTIFY

Middle Ages
Clovis
Merovingians
Charles Martel
Carolingians
Charlemagne
Louis the Pious
Magyars
Vikings

WHY IT MATTERS TODAY

The Vikings were known for their shipbuilding ability. Use CNNfyi.com or other **current event** sources to discover how ships are part of peoples' lives in Scandinavia today. Record your findings in your journal.

CNNfyi.com

The Rise of the Franks

The Main Idea
A new European civilization arose based on Roman and Germanic values and traditions.

The Story Continues *"Charles was large and strong, and of lofty stature. . . . his appearance was always stately and dignified . . . His gait [stride] was firm, his whole carriage manly, and his voice clear."* This is how one observer described Charlemagne, one of the strong rulers who helped bring order to Europe in the Middle Ages.

The Frankish Rulers

For hundreds of years following the breakup of the Western Roman Empire, Europe was the scene of widespread disorder and change. Waves of barbarian invasion and settlement brought new customs and lifestyles to many parts of western Europe. Over time the social and political patterns typical of life in the empire merged with new patterns brought by barbarian peoples who settled in the West.

An age of transition. Gradually Europeans began to restore order in their lives. Many historians see the years between the 400s and about 1500 as a transition in the development of Western culture. Thus this period is generally known as the **Middle Ages,** or the **medieval** period of European development. It is the time in history between the end of the classical age and the beginnings of the modern world.

Many Germanic tribes plundered Europe and established small kingdoms. One tribe proved to have a lasting impact on European history. This group of loosely organized Germanic peoples, known as the Franks, did much to shape the new culture of post-Roman Europe.

Clovis and the Merovingians. The Franks first came into contact with the Roman Empire during the 200s, when they began moving into the lower Rhine River valley. In 481 a ruler named **Clovis** became king of one of the Frankish tribes. Clovis and his successors were called **Merovingians** because Clovis traced his family back to an ancestor named Merovech. Clovis was an able military leader. He and his troops conquered and absorbed other Frankish tribes. Soon they controlled all of northern Gaul.

Because Clovis had by this time become a Christian, the Franks received the support of the Christian church. The Franks soon seized and began to rule southwestern Gaul. This is the area that today is occupied by France, which is named for the Franks. When Clovis died, his sons divided the kingdom, as was often the Frankish custom.

INTERPRETING THE VISUAL RECORD

Frankish warrior This medallion depicts a mounted Frankish warrior with his lance at the ready. Note the lack of a stirrup, which was a later development. *Why did the Frankish artist who crafted this object show the warrior on horseback?*

The Merovingian kings who ruled after Clovis were generally weak. Eventually the chief of the royal household, known as the "mayor of the palace," became the real ruler of each kingdom. One of these mayors was Pépin II, who ruled from 687 to 714. Pépin and his successors united the Frankish kingdoms.

Charles Martel and Pépin the Short. After Pépin II died, his son, **Charles Martel,** known as Charles the Hammer, became mayor of the palace. Charles Martel's cavalry defeated the Spanish Moors in 732 when they invaded France. This halted the Muslim advance in western Europe, although Muslim raids continued.

Charles Martel died in 741. His son, Pépin III, called "the Short," became the Merovingian kingdom's joint mayor of the palace with his brother, Carloman. Pépin, already king in all but name, overthrew Childeric III, the last Merovingian ruler, and claimed the Frankish throne for his own. In 751 Pépin was anointed king of the Franks. Pépin III's coronation established the **Carolingians,** a new line of Frankish rulers. The pope's confirmation of Pépin's rule, moreover, strengthened the legitimacy of the new Carolingian dynasty. This was because European Christians believed that the pope's blessing came directly from God. Over time monarchs throughout western Europe sought the church's blessing in order to support their rule.

The pope sought Pépin's help against the Lombards, a Germanic tribe that was attacking central Italy and threatening Rome. Pépin led a Frankish army into Italy and defeated the Lombards. The Franks won control of the territory around Rome and gave it to the pope. This gift of land is called the Donation of Pépin. It created the Papal States, which for centuries remained the stronghold of the church. The alliance that grew between the Franks and the church as a result of these actions made each side stronger. It also paved the way for the rise of **Charlemagne,** Pépin's son and the greatest of all Frankish kings.

Charlemagne's empire. Charlemagne inherited the Frankish throne in 768 and ruled until 814. During the 46 years of his reign, Charlemagne worked to build a "new Rome" centered in what is now France and Germany. As a devout Christian he helped to spread church teachings and Christian beliefs. His rule did much to bring civilization, order, and learning to barbarian Europe during the 800s.

Charlemagne spent much of his life at war. He defeated the Lombards in Italy, the Saxons in northern Germany, and the Avars in central Europe. He tried to conquer all of Muslim Spain, but failed. He was able, however, to drive the Moors back across the Pyrenees, a mountain range that separates Spain and France. Charlemagne's victory over the Moors added a small strip of Spanish land, called the "Spanish March," to his large empire. It also created a "buffer zone"—a kind of frontier—between Christian and Muslim Europe.

On Christmas Day of the year 800, Charlemagne was in Rome to worship at Saint Peter's Basilica. As Charlemagne knelt in prayer, Pope Leo III placed a crown on his head and declared him "Emperor of the Romans." Although the Roman Empire was long gone, the title indicates Charlemagne's importance to western Europe. He had united much of western Europe for the first time in

The simple, unadorned throne of Charlemagne, or "Charles the Great," did not reveal his power and importance.

HISTORY MAKER

**Charlemagne
(c. 742–814)**

As emperor, Charlemagne united most of the Christian lands in western Europe. During his reign, Charlemagne strengthened the political power of the Franks. He also set into motion a cultural rebirth throughout Europe by supporting education, creating libraries, and sponsoring the collection and copying of ancient Roman manuscripts. Charlemagne's rule became a model for later kings in medieval Europe. **What were some of Charlemagne's accomplishments as a ruler?**

LEVEL 1: Have students draw time lines that trace the Frankish rulers' involvement in the Christian faith from Clovis to Charlemagne. *(The following events should be included: Clovis converts to Christianity after victory; the pope crowns Pepin III "king by the grace of God;" Pepin aids the pope in defending Rome; Pope Leo III crowns Charlemagne "Emperor of the Romans.")* Ask students why they think this friendly relationship between church and state developed. *(Students may note that the relationship was of mutual benefit.)* **ENGLISH LANGUAGE LEARNERS**

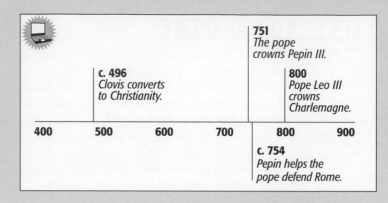

c. 496
Clovis converts to Christianity.

751
The pope crowns Pepin III.

800
Pope Leo III crowns Charlemagne.

400   500   600   700   800   900

c. 754
Pepin helps the pope defend Rome.

Government

Until Clovis united the Frankish tribes under his leadership, the Franks were divided into two major groups, the Salians and the Ripuarians. The Salian Franks lived along the northern Rhine River, while the Ripuarian Franks lived along the southern Rhine. In the 300s the Salian Franks became allies of the Romans, and in the next century, migrated into Gaul.

After Clovis became the leader of the Salian Franks—reputedly by murdering many of his own relatives—he overthrew the Romans in Gaul in 486. After converting to Christianity and gaining the support of the church, Clovis expanded his empire to include most of Gaul.

Critical Thinking

Ask students to explain the importance of Clovis's empire, though it did not outlast his death.

ANSWER: Students might suggest that Clovis's empire established the idea of a French monarchy. Students might also suggest that it foreshadowed the creation of Charlemagne's empire 400 years later.

INTERPRETING THE VISUAL RECORD

The crowning of Charlemagne
Pope Leo III crowns Charlemagne Emperor of the Romans. *Which figure—Charlemagne or Pope Leo—is depicted as more powerful in this French illustration from the 1300s? Why might that be so?*

400 years. Because of this, Europe regarded Charlemagne as the successor to the Roman emperors. The pope's coronation of Charlemagne was also significant because it showed the close ties that existed between the Franks and the Christian church.

Charlemagne was very conscious of his unique position as leader of a new western order. He saw himself, moreover, as the inheritor of Roman authority. He aimed to live up to the image of a Roman emperor in his actions, his policies, and the glory of his empire. He was greatly admired for his skills as a warrior as well as for his devotion to Christianity.

Government. Charlemagne's empire was divided into regions, each governed on the emperor's behalf by an official known as a count. Charlemagne established his capital at the northern Frankish city of Aix-la-Chapelle (EKS·LAH·shah·PEL), today the bustling German city of Aachen (AH·kuhn). The emperor used oaths of fidelity to ensure that the counts and other Carolingian officials ruled effectively under his command. Appointed officials helped Charlemagne run his empire. These officials were called *missi dominici* or "the lord's messengers." They would travel through the empire to hear complaints, investigate official misconduct, and determine the effectiveness of laws. The *missi dominici* ensured that the counts were serving the emperor and not themselves. Charlemagne viewed the *missi dominici* as his direct representatives and gave them a great deal of authority to make decisions in his name.

History Makers Speak ❝Let the *missi* themselves make a diligent investigation whenever any man claims that an injustice has been done to him by any one . . . and they shall administer the law fully and justly in the case of the holy churches of God and of the poor, of wards [orphans] and widows, and of the whole people.❞

Charlemagne, quoted in D.C. Munro, ed., *Translations and Reprints from the Original Sources of European History*, Vol. IV, *Laws of Charles the Great*

Education and learning. Although Charlemagne himself was not formally educated, he placed great value on education. He started schools at his palace for his own children and other young nobles. Scholars—usually monks—were invited from all over western Europe to teach at the school. Charlemagne appointed one of Europe's most respected thinkers, Alcuin (AL·kwihn) of York, to head the school and establish its course of learning. Alcuin developed a curriculum based on the Roman model, emphasizing grammar, rhetoric, logic, mathematics, music, and astronomy. Charlemagne also brought together scholars to produce a readable Bible. They used a new script called Caroline minuscule. The new Bible was used throughout Charlemagne's empire. Charlemagne also ordered the empire's bishops to create libraries.

Although some scholars claim Charlemagne never learned to write, he could read. Saint Augustine's *City of God* was one of his favorite books. Throughout his rule Charlemagne encouraged—sometimes forced—the empire's people to convert to Christianity.

✔ **READING CHECK: Summarizing** What steps did Charlemagne take to help assure that his officials ruled effectively and honestly? frequent personal inspections; appointed *missi dominici* to investigate complaints

Spotlight on DAILY LIFE Help students find excerpts from primary sources such as *The History of the Franks* written by Gregory of Tours or an early biography of Charlemagne. You may need to help students interpret the archaic language of such sources. When students have read an excerpt or two, have them summarize what they learned about daily life in the Middle Ages. Then discuss how these excerpts differ from the way that modern historians record events. **BLOCK SCHEDULING**

The Decline of the Frankish Empire

The proud empire that Charlemagne had built and governed so well did not long survive his death in 814. His descendants did not inherit Charlemagne's energy, his ability, or his long-range point of view. As a result, the empire's strength declined rapidly. By the mid-800s the once mighty Carolingian state had begun to divide and collapse.

The empire after Charlemagne's death. Charlemagne's only surviving son, **Louis the Pious,** proved to be a well-educated and religious king but a weak and shortsighted ruler. When Louis died in 840, his sons Lothair, Charles the Bald, and Louis the German agreed to divide the empire among themselves after much dispute. This agreement, signed in 843, became known as the Treaty of Verdun.

Instead of uniting to overcome enemies from within and beyond the splintered empire, Charlemagne's grandsons and their successors fought among themselves. By

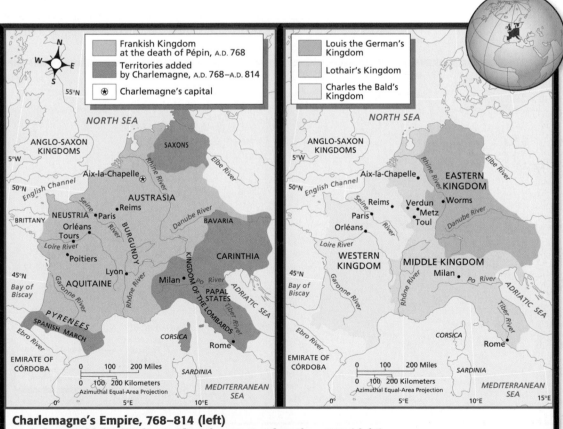

**Charlemagne's Empire, 768–814 (left)
and The Frankish Kingdoms After the Treaty of Verdun, 843 (right)**

Interpreting Maps The Carolingian Empire, begun under Pépin III and expanded by Charlemagne, brought much of western Europe under Frankish rule. Charlemagne's grandsons divided the empire into three separate kingdoms.

■ **Skills Assessment: 1. Human Systems** Identify the Germanic tribes that Charlemagne incorporated into his empire.
2. Analyzing Information Whose kingdom after 843 claimed the most major cities?

Culture

Charlemagne's interest in education extended foremost to his children. When his sons and daughters were young, Charlemagne educated them in math, science, and other subjects. As the boys grew up, he taught them horsemanship and war skills, while the girls learned how to spin thread and make cloth.

Critical Thinking

Ask students what political reasons Charlemagne might have had for spending so much time on his children's education.

ANSWER: Students might suggest that Charlemagne hoped to leave the empire in capable hands.

MAP ANSWERS
1. Saxons

2. Lothair's

TEACH OBJECTIVE 2

LEVEL 3: Ask students why Charlemagne's vast empire did not last long after his death. *(Frankish practice of dividing the kingdom among the king's sons, numerous invasions)* Have students use their textbooks to list the most prominent invading peoples. *(Muslims, Magyars, Vikings)* Have students use computer software to learn more about Vikings, the most feared invaders. Have students write short stories about Viking characters in the 800s. Stories should be creative, but settings and characters should be based on historical facts. **BLOCK SCHEDULING**

 HOMEWORK Ask students to explain how the history of the Western world might have been different if Charlemagne's descendants had been able to hold his empire together.

CLOSE

Organize the class into three groups. Have each group evaluate the accomplishments of Clovis, Charles Martel, or Charlemagne by listing the political choices and decisions they made.

The Franks were famous for their swords, which were in great demand across Europe. These swords were known for their balance and strength. Frankish foot soldiers used short swords and carried spears, bows and arrows, and shields. The cavalry carried both long and short swords, spears, and round shields. In addition, Charlemagne's mounted soldiers wore rudimentary armor and helmets, possibly the early stages of the armored knight of later centuries.

MAP ANSWERS

1. Muslim

2. Students might guess that it was because of Constantinople's favorable location.

870 the middle kingdom had been divided between the rulers of the eastern and western kingdoms. To make matters worse, powerful lords in these two kingdoms became increasingly independent of the Carolingian monarchs. These lords thought they could best serve their own interests by defying the weakening rule of the central monarchs.

Charlemagne's empire was further undermined by invasions of different peoples from beyond the empire's frontiers. Muslims from Africa invaded the Mediterranean coast. Slavs from the east raided central Europe. Another group from the east, the nomadic **Magyars** who settled in what is now Hungary, terrorized Europe for about 50 years before they were finally defeated.

The Vikings. The most feared invaders of western Europe during the 800s and the 900s were the **Vikings** from Scandinavia in the north. Vikings, or "Norsemen," were Germanic peoples from what are now the countries of Norway, Sweden, and Denmark. The Vikings' customs and myths centered on pagan gods. Archaeologists have excavated Viking burial mounds that include boats and tools for use in the afterlife. The Vikings would sometimes place a dead person in a boat and burn it. In about 930 an Arab, Ibn Fadlan, witnessed the funeral of a Viking chieftain. The chieftain's ship was hauled onto the land, and his body

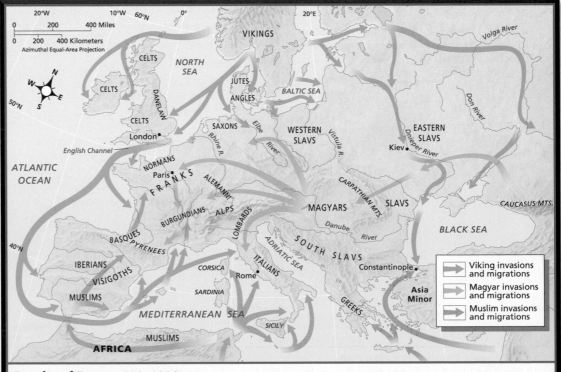

Peoples of Europe, 600–1000

Interpreting Maps Beginning in the early Middle Ages, new waves of invasions by Muslim, Germanic, and Slavic peoples swept across western Europe.

■ **Skills Assessment: 1. Human Systems** What major group of invaders was most concentrated in the Mediterranean Basin?
2. Drawing Inferences Why might both the Vikings and the Muslims have been drawn to Constantinople?

was placed on the ship along with rich grave goods. A historian, using Ibn Fadlan's account, described the Arab observer's experience:

Primary Source **“**On the day of the burial, . . . the slave girl said, 'Lo, I see my lord and master he calls to me. Let me go to him.' Aboard the ship waited the old woman called the Angel of Death, who would kill her. The girl drank from a cup . . . and sang a long song. She grew fearful and hesitant. At once the old woman grasped her head and led her into the tent.
Inside the tent the girl died beside her master by stabbing and strangling. Then the ship was fired.**”**

Ibn Fadlan, quoted in Robert Paul Jordan, "Viking Trail East," *National Geographic Magazine,* March 1985

Although the Vikings were ruled by kings and nobles, their government was surprisingly democratic for its time. Assemblies of landowners made the laws. The Vikings were primarily farmers but also gathered, fished, and hunted. In the spring and summer the Vikings would travel south and west along the coasts of mainland Europe and the British Isles. They sailed rivers into Germany, France, and the Baltic area. The Vikings would raid and loot settlements and bring captives back to work as slaves on their farms in Scandinavia. Their way of capturing towns was often savage and cruel. Their use of axes and large dogs struck terror into people. The Vikings were also skilled in siege operations and could capture even strongly fortified towns.

Their sturdy ships carried the Vikings across the Atlantic Ocean to what is now Iceland, Greenland, and North America. In time they settled in England, Ireland, and parts of continental Europe. A large Viking settlement in northwestern France gave that region its name—Normandy, from the French word for "Northmen."

✔ **READING CHECK: Finding the Main Idea** Why were groups such as the Magyars and Vikings able to invade the Frankish Empire successfully? Charlemagne's successors fought among themselves instead of uniting to overcome invaders.

Figure of the head of a Viking from about 850

SECTION 1 REVIEW

1. **Define** and explain the significance:
   medieval

2. **Identify** and explain the significance:
   Middle Ages
   Clovis
   Merovingians
   Charles Martel
   Carolingians
   Charlemagne
   Louis the Pious
   Magyars
   Vikings

3. **Categorizing** Copy the diagram and use it to show how Charlemagne organized his government and what responsibilities were held by the various officials.

   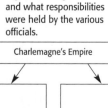

   Charlemagne's Empire

4. **Finding the Main Idea**
   a. What actions helped Charlemagne to unify his empire?
   b. In what ways did the actions of Charlemagne's grandsons cause the Carolingian Empire to become vulnerable to invaders from the north, south, and east?

5. **Writing and Critical Thinking**
   Comparing and Contrasting Imagine that you are living in Paris at the end of the 800s. Write a journal entry in which you compare daily life in the western kingdom to stories that you have heard of life in the Carolingian Empire during Charlemagne's reign.
   Consider:
   • the actions that Charlemagne took to centralize and expand the empire
   • the effects of the Treaty of Verdun on the unity and security of the empire

go.hrw.com **Homework Practice Online**
keyword: SP3 HP13

THE RISE OF THE MIDDLE AGES **293**

SECTION 2

OBJECTIVES

1 Explore how feudalism helped shape political and social development in Europe during the Middle Ages.

2 Identify the ways in which the manorial system influenced economic growth in Europe during the Middle Ages.

🎙 *LET'S GET STARTED!*

As students enter the classroom, have them think about the importance of land ownership throughout history and in the United States today. Ask them if one must own land to prosper economically. *(no)* Have them explain how land ownership today is usually transferred between individuals. *(It is usually bought, sold, or inherited.)* Tell students that in Section 2 they will learn about land ownership in the Middle Ages.

SECTION 2 RESOURCES

REPRODUCIBLE RESOURCES

▸ Guided Reading Strategy 13.2

▸ Readings in World History 38: The Table of a Thirteenth-Century English Lord

TECHNOLOGY RESOURCES

▸ One-Stop Planner 13.2

▸ Homework Practice Online

REINFORCEMENT, REVIEW, AND ASSESSMENT

▸ Section 2 Review, p. 299

▸ Daily Quiz 13.2

▸ Main Idea Activity 13.2

▸ English Audio Summary 13.2

▸ Spanish Audio Summary 13.2

VISUAL RECORD ANSWER

Lord is seated on a throne, wearing a crown; vassals are showing respect

---

SECTION 2

READ TO DISCOVER

❶ How did feudalism help to shape political and social development in Europe during the Middle Ages?

❷ In what ways did manorialism influence economic growth in Europe during the Middle Ages?

DEFINE

feudalism
fief
vassal
primogeniture
manorialism
serfs
chivalry

WHY IT MATTERS TODAY

Feudal Europe was the scene of frequent local wars and conflicts. Use **CNNfyi.com** or other **current event** sources to investigate how continual conflict affects the people of a region and the lifestyles they follow. Record your findings in your journal.

CNNfyi.com

Feudalism and the Manorial System

The Main Idea
Feudalism and manorialism structured and organized European society in the Middle Ages.

The Story Continues *Society in the Middle Ages was strongly shaped by relationships of loyalty and service between higher and lower nobles. "I urge you . . . to maintain towards [your overlord] . . . a devoted and certain fealty [loyalty] both of body and soul," one mother advised her son. For centuries the nature of this binding relationship organized medieval society on the basis of military service and land ownership.*

Feudalism

Within 100 years of Charlemagne's death, organized, large-scale government in Europe all but disappeared. By the 900s most Europeans were governed by small, local, independent leaders, most often by local lords. The political organization these leaders represented is known as **feudalism.**

The system. Within the feudal system a powerful noble granted land to a lesser noble. Actual ownership of the land remained with the noble who made the grant. The noble who received the grant was entitled to use of the land and its products, but could not "own" the land. This grant of land allowed the lesser noble to "maintain" himself and his household. In return for maintenance, the lesser noble promised loyalty, military assistance, and other services to the lord who granted the land. The person who granted land was a lord and the grant of land was called a **fief.** The person who received the fief was a **vassal.** The transaction of a noble granting land and a vassal receiving land created a contract between the two. A vassal could further divide the land he had been granted and grant it to others, such as knights. Thus, a vassal could also be a lord.

Eventually the fief became hereditary, as legal possession of the land passed from a vassal to his son. By about 1100 it had become customary for the eldest son of a lord or vassal to inherit ownership or possession of the land. This system of inheritance from father to eldest son is called **primogeniture** (pry·moh·JE·nuh·choohr). Women's rights regarding legal property were limited. A woman might have had fiefs in her dowry. However, when she married, her husband gained control over her dowry. In most cases a woman regained control of the property in her dowry if her husband died.

INTERPRETING THE VISUAL RECORD

Lord and vassal This stained-glass window depicts the relationship between a lord and his vassals. *How can you tell that the lord is more powerful than the vassals in this picture?*

TEACH OBJECTIVES 1 and 2

LEVEL 2: Tell students to imagine that they work for a time travel agency. They need to develop a brochure explaining feudalism and the manorial system to travelers who wish to visit medieval Europe. Students' brochures should include the following: definitions of terms such as *vassal, fief,* and *lord*; information about the roles various individuals play within the system; information about feudal justice and warfare; and a brief note about chivalry. Encourage students to include illustrations and graphic organizers to help clarify the system of feudalism—a graphic representation of the feudal hierarchy would be particularly helpful. Tell students to remember that the purpose of their brochure is to prepare travelers to exist within the political system they will encounter during their expedition.

Throughout the Middle Ages local lords held many of the powers associated with government. Kings were also bound by the customs and obligations of feudalism. In theory every landholder was a vassal to the king. In practice, however, the king controlled only those who lived on his feudal lands. Even the church was part of the feudal system. The medieval church owned vast amounts of land and had many vassals who were granted fiefs in return for military protection and service.

Warfare. Wars were common during the Middle Ages. Many wars grew out of private fights between feudal lords, or lords and vassals, and were local conflicts that involved only a handful of nobles and their knights. In other cases, wars could be large-scale events that involved whole regions and that could be immensely destructive.

Knights in the Middle Ages wore armor in battle and were heavily armed. In the early Middle Ages, armor was made of chain mail—small, interlocking metal links stitched to a knee-length leather shirt. The knight would also wear an iron helmet and carry a sword, a large shield, and a lance. With the introduction of gunpowder during the late Middle Ages, overlapping metal plates replaced chain mail. Often, plate armor was so heavy that knights had to be hauled onto their horses with cranes. Battle horses were much larger than today's saddle horses. The warhorses of the Middle Ages probably resembled today's Clydesdales and Percherons in size, weight, and power.

In medieval times wars had different effects on society. For nobles, wars were an opportunity for glory and wealth. For most people of the Middle Ages, however, war was a major cause of suffering and hardship. The church tried to limit the general suffering caused by war by issuing several decrees that prohibited acts of violence and private warfare near churches and other holy buildings. If the decrees were not obeyed, the church threatened punishment. The church also forbade violence against cattle and agricultural equipment as well as certain types of persons, including clergy, women, merchants, and pilgrims. The church tried to get all lords to accept another decree that forbade fighting on certain days, such as weekends and holy days. However, restrictions on fighting could almost never be enforced strictly. Private wars continued until kings became strong enough to stop them.

Feudal justice. Feudal justice differed greatly from Roman justice. A feudal trial was decided in one of three ways: trial by battle; compurgation, or oath taking; and trial by ordeal. A trial could be a duel between accuser and accused—or their representatives—in which the outcome determined innocence or guilt.

The drawbridge, arched entrance, stone walls, and notched battlements of Manorbier Castle in Wales are typical of the medieval style.

Citizenship

As early as the 1000s, knights carried personal symbols mounted on banners or shields into battle. In the 1100s it became customary for sons to inherit their fathers' banners and shields. Later, three-dimensional crests, mostly of animals, were added to helmets. In time these crests became badges of nobility. By the 1200s the crest, helmet, and shield had been incorporated into a family coat of arms.

Critical Thinking

Ask students why they think knights first wore such symbols.

ANSWER: Students might suggest that knights needed something to identify them when their faces were covered with helmets.

VISUAL RECORD ANSWER

They would make it easier to stay on the horse.

LEVEL 3: Have students use their textbooks to create mock contracts that represent the relationship between a medieval noble and a peasant who worked his land. These contracts, which should resemble modern legal agreements, must include a list of each party's obligations to the other.

HOMEWORK Ask students to imagine that they are the teenage sons or daughters of an English lord and have them write a journal entry from this point of view. Then have students write another journal entry from the point of view of a peasant teenager.

Economics

The most important nobles held large fiefs received directly from the king, and they in turn divided their land and granted fiefs to lesser nobles. This division continued down to the level of the lowest noble, who held a single manor. Originally the granting of fiefs was repeated whenever a lord or vassal died, but eventually control of the fief became hereditary.

Critical Thinking

Ask students what advantages hereditary control of fiefs would have held compared to redistributing the fiefs whenever a lord or vassal died.

ANSWER Students might suggest that hereditary control gave nobles further incentives to take care of their lands and protect them so their children could inherit them.

SKILLS PRACTICE ANSWERS

1. second sentence of first paragraph

2. first sentence of first paragraph, both sentences of second paragraph

3. Students' answers will vary.

SKILL-BUILDING STRATEGIES Establishing a Fact from a Values Statement

The Rise of Feudalism

When reading sources on the rise of feudalism, readers should be careful to distinguish between facts and values statements. A fact can be proven true or false. A values statement is an opinion that represents a particular point of view. For example, a writer can state that Charlemagne was a successful ruler. That is a values statement because it is based on the writer's idea of success. Sometimes a fact and a values statement can be included in the same sentence. For example, a writer may state that Charlemagne spoke Greek and Latin so beautifully he could have taught both languages. Charlemagne's ability to speak the languages can be proven true or false. However, whether he spoke them beautifully is a matter of opinion.

A Historian's View

The statement below discusses one historian's view of the best way to define feudalism.

"The simplest way will be to begin by saying what feudal society was not. Although obligations arising from blood-relationship played a very active part in it, it did not rely on kinship alone...feudal ties...developed when those of kinship proved inadequate...

European feudalism should therefore be seen as the outcome of the violent dissolution of older societies. It would in fact be unintelligible without the great upheaval of the Germanic invasions which, by forcibly uniting the two societies originally at very different stages of development, disrupted both of them and brought to the surface a great many...social practices of an extremely primitive nature."

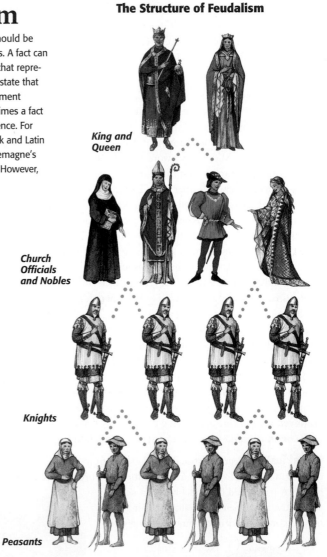

The Structure of Feudalism

King and Queen

Church Officials and Nobles

Knights

Peasants

Skills Reminder

To distinguish a fact from a values statement, review the difference between a fact and a values statement. Then identify words that suggest a value or opinion. For example, adjectives such as *great, wonderful, horrible* are words that express feelings. "I" statements can also help determine whether a statement is a point of view. *In my opinion* or *I think* express a point of view. Finally, ask questions about the sentence. Can "That meal I had was really awful" mean more than one thing? What is the fact in the statement and what is the opinion?

Skills Practice

❶ Which sentences in the historian's statement contain facts?

❷ Which sentences in the historian's statement contain values statements?

❸ While listening to a radio or TV news report, identify the factual information provided by the report. Then identify statements of opinion and values statements, and analyze how those statements are used to influence the listener's/viewer's conclusions.

LEVEL 1: Have students create a graphic organizer like the one shown. Have students, either independently or with guidance, find at least three details from the text that describe peasant life. Examples are listed in italics on the chart. Then, in small groups, have students fill in the other side of the chart, comparing poverty in feudal Europe to poverty in the United States today. Discuss and debate conclusions. **ENGLISH LANGUAGE LEARNERS**

Poverty in Feudal Europe	Poverty in the Modern U.S.
"fear of my master"	
did not own their own land	
opportunity for protection from lord	
couldn't leave manor without permission ("not a free man")	

In compurgation, the accuser and the accused were supported by people who swore that the person they represented was telling the truth. The oath takers were probably similar to character witnesses in today's trials. The outcome of a trial by ordeal was determined by how the accused survived a particular ordeal. The accused had to carry a piece of hot iron, plunge his hand in a pot of boiling water, or survive extended immersion in cold water. If the accused person's wounds healed quickly and well, he was innocent; if not, he was guilty.

✔ **READING CHECK: Analyzing Information** What were some aspects of feudalism? grant of land in exchange for loyalty, military service; localized government

The Manorial System

Feudalism provided social and political structure to the culture of the Middle Ages. Similarly, **manorialism** shaped the economy of much of Europe during these years. The system took its name from the manors of the Middle Ages. Manors were large farming estates that included manor houses, cultivated lands, woodlands, pastures, fields, and villages.

Central authority and organized trade—key parts of most modern economies—were almost nonexistent during the Middle Ages. Thus people who lived on manors needed to be self-sufficient. They sought to produce everything they needed, including food, clothing, and shelter. Some items, however, such as iron, salt, wool, wine, and certain manufactured goods, were purchased.

A lord and several peasant families shared the land of the manor. Generally the lord kept about one third of the manor's lands, called the domain, for himself. The manor's peasants farmed the remaining two-thirds of the land for themselves. In return for being able to work the land, the peasants gave the lord some of their crops and helped to farm his land. The peasants also provided other services on the manor and paid many kinds of taxes.

Ideally a manor village was located along a stream or river, which provided waterpower for the village mill. For safety a small group of houses were clustered near the manor house or castle. The land surrounding the manor house included the village, vegetable plots, cultivated fields, pastures, and forests. Cultivated land was often divided into three large fields for growing grain. Only two of the three fields were planted at one time. The third field could lie fallow, or unplanted, for a season to regain its fertility. The three fields were divided into small strips distributed among the peasants. If the lord's domain was divided, he too had strips of land in each field.

Peasant life. Peasants' lives were difficult in medieval times because they spent long hours at backbreaking work in the fields. A text written during the Middle Ages described a typical workday from a peasant's point of view.

 Primary Source **❝**. . . I work very hard. I go out at dawn, driving the oxen to the field, and I yoke them to the plough; however hard the winter I dare not stay at home for fear of my master; but, having yoked the oxen and made the plough-share . . . fast to the plough, every day I have to plough a whole acre or more. . . . It is hard work, because I am not a free man.**❞**

Aelfric, *Colloquy,* translated by G.G. Coulton in *The Medieval Village*

INTERPRETING THE VISUAL RECORD

Peasant farmers This stylized image from the 1400s illustrates the work of medieval peasants during harvest time. *What evidence does this illustration provide of tools and techniques used by farm workers during the Middle Ages?*

Analyzing Primary Sources

Summarizing According to this account, why did the peasant find his work to be especially hard? He was not a free man.

VISUAL RECORD ANSWER

Farmers are using handheld tools to harvest crops.

Technology Resources

go.hrw.com Online Maps, Charts, and Graphs: A Medieval Manor

TEACH OBJECTIVES 1 and 2

ALL LEVELS: Have students read the subsection entitled "Chivalry" on pages 298 to 299. Discuss the characteristics of the code of chivalry. (*Knights had to be brave, fight fairly, be loyal, keep their word, treat conquered foes gallantly, be courteous to women.*) Show students sample images of medieval or modern coats of arms and point out the unique symbolism of each. Then have students create coats of arms for themselves, considering events, people, places, or animals that were or are significant in their lives or represent themselves. Encourage students to use images in their coat of arms that represent the characteristics of the code of chivalry that they feel they possess. Their family might also suggest a symbol. **ENGLISH LANGUAGE LEARNERS**

CLOSE

Have each student list three aspects of the feudal system and three aspects of the manorial system. Then lead a class discussion on how the two systems worked together.

Science, Technology & Society

Although castles were the homes of the aristocracy, their main purpose was to defend against attack. The strongest part of the castle was the keep, where the lord and his family lived. The keep was surrounded by a wall or a series of walls, which were flanked by towers. The outermost walls were often protected by moats or by the sheer drop of cliffs. Castles proved to be effective defensive fortifications until the use of gunpowder allowed artillery to penetrate castle walls.

Critical Thinking

Ask students to speculate on how the invention of gunpowder might have affected the manorial system.

ANSWER: Students might suggest that when castles no longer provided protection for the lord, his authority was weakened.

YOUNG PEOPLE IN HISTORY ANSWER

so that they might improve their status by learning the skills and responsibilities that were expected of high-ranking noblewomen

YOUNG PEOPLE IN HISTORY

Preparing for Life as a Noblewoman

Young girls from the families of lesser nobles often went to live in the households of higher-ranking noblewomen. There they would be trained in the skills and responsibilities that were expected of women in their rank.

Generally the young noblewoman was taught to sew, to weave, to cook, to play musical instruments, and to sing. She learned, as well, the social conduct that was proper for women of the nobility. In some cases girls and young women were also instructed in the skills of household supervision. **Why might noble parents send their daughters to train in the households of higher-ranking nobles?**

Young women of the nobility serve a noblewoman.

Most peasants—called **serfs**—could not leave the land without the lord's permission. Their meals consisted mainly of black bread, lentils, some vegetables, and ale. Because livestock helped work the fields, and because peasants were generally forbidden to hunt on the lord's land, they could rarely afford to eat meat. Compared to life expectancies today, average life spans in the Middle Ages were very short. Among the factors that severely limited the life expectancies of most Europeans were disease, starvation, and frequent warfare. Very likely, peasants lived, worked, and died in the village in which they had been born.

Nobles' lifestyles. Frequently people think of the Middle Ages as a time when lords and knights lived in elegant castles. The upper classes of the Middle Ages, however, generally did not live in luxury or even in comfort by today's standards.

A castle was a fortified base from which the lord enforced his authority and protected the surrounding countryside. In the early Middle Ages, castles were simple structures made from earth and wood. Later they were made from stone.

Castles were usually built on hills or other landforms that would prevent easy attack. If a castle was on flat land that was difficult to defend, a ditch called a moat was built around it and sometimes flooded with water. A drawbridge extended across the moat to allow entry to the castle's courtyard. If the castle was attacked, the drawbridge could be raised.

A building called the "keep" was the main part of the castle. The keep was a strong tower that usually contained storerooms, workshops, and perhaps barracks and the lord's living quarters. In the great hall the lord received visitors. The castle's rooms had thick walls and small windows with no glass. As a result the rooms were usually dark and chilly. The lord spent most of his day looking after his land and dispensing justice among his vassals and serfs.

A lord or the head of a peasant family depended on his wife and children for help. Marriage was viewed as a way to advance one's fortune. Through marriage a man might acquire land. While marriage might bring a man land, it usually produced children who had to be cared for. A lord would often provide dowries for any daughters. Among peasants, children were often welcomed as a source of farm labor.

Chivalry. By the late 1100s a code of conduct known as **chivalry** had begun to bring major changes to feudal society. Chivalry was a system of rules that dictated knights' behavior towards others. The word chivalry comes from the French word *cheval*, meaning "horse," and refers to the fact that knights were mounted soldiers.

To become a knight, a boy had to belong to the noble class and had to pass through two stages of training. The first stage began at about the age of seven, when a boy would serve as a knight's page, or attendant. The page would learn knightly manners and begin to learn how to use and care for weapons. As a teenager the page would

REVIEW

Have students complete Section 2 Review on p. 299.

ASSESS

Have students complete Daily Quiz 13.2. As Alternative Assessment, you may want to use the time travel or contract exercises in this section's lessons.

RETEACH

Have students complete Main Idea Activity for English Language Learners and Special-Needs Students 13.2. Then ask them to

write a question and answer that covers the main idea for each subsection. **ENGLISH LANGUAGE LEARNERS**

EXTEND

The mutual-dependency relationships basic to manorialism may remind students of a term from science class: *symbiosis*. Ask a group of students to research symbiotic relationships in nature and report on some of these to the class. Have them point out parallels with feudal-manorial society. **BLOCK SCHEDULING, COOPERATIVE LEARNING**

become a knight's assistant, called a squire. The squire would take care of the knight's horse, armor, and weapons. Then, probably when the knight thought that the squire was ready, the squire would accompany the knight into battle. If the squire proved himself to be a skilled and courageous fighter, he would be knighted in an elaborate religious ceremony.

A knight in full armor, wearing a closed helmet, often could be distinguished from other knights only by his coat of arms. The knight's coat of arms was a graphic symbol that identified him and that represented his personal characteristics. The coat of arms was painted or stitched onto the knight's shield or outer coat, his flag, or possibly his horse's trappings. Generally the coat of arms was passed along from one generation to the next.

According to the code of chivalry, knights were expected to be courageous in battle and to fight fairly. If a knight used tricks and strategy to overcome an opponent, he was considered a coward. A knight was expected to be loyal to his friends and to keep his word. He was required to treat his conquered foes gallantly. A knight was also expected to be courteous to women and the less powerful.

Chivalry did much to improve the rough and crude manners of early feudal lords. Behavior, however, did not become perfect by any modern standard. A knight was required to extend courtesy only to people of his own class. Toward others his attitude and actions could be coarse, bullying, and arrogant.

✔ **READING CHECK: Drawing Inferences** How did manorialism complement feudalism?
feudalism provided social and political structure; manorialism provided economic structure

INTERPRETING THE VISUAL RECORD

Coats of arms The knights shown battling in this image bear coats of arms on their clothing and shields. A knight's coat of arms helped to identify him when he was fully armored. *What might the characters and symbols shown on each coat of arms represent?*

SECTION 2 REVIEW

1. **Define** and explain the significance:
feudalism
fief
vassal
primogeniture
manorialism
serfs
chivalry

2. **Making Generalizations** Copy the graphic organizer below to demonstrate the responsibilities of lords and peasants on a manor.

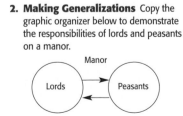

3. **Finding the Main Idea**
a. How was medieval Europe different from previous civilizations?
b. What were the chief political and economic characteristics of feudalism and manorialism?

4. **Writing and Critical Thinking**
Summarizing Imagine that you are a squire in service to a knight, or a young noblewoman in service to a lady. Compose a journal entry that describes your duties and goals.
Consider:
• the relationship between the squire and knight or the young noblewoman and the lady
• the responsibilities of the servant

Homework Practice Online
keyword: SP3 HP13

VISUAL RECORD ANSWER
personal characteristics

SECTION 2 REVIEW ANSWERS

❶ **Define**
• feudalism, p. 294
• fief, p. 294
• vassal, p. 294
• primogeniture, p. 294
• manorialism, p. 297
• serfs, p. 298
• chivalry, p. 298

❷ Peasants: farmed the land, gave some crops to the lord, paid taxes; Lords: managed land, kept domain

❸ **a.** Organized, large scale government was replaced by small, local, independent leaders.

b. feudalism: powerful nobles granted land to lesser nobles in exchange for loyalty and military assistance; system of primogeniture manorialism: a lord and several peasant families shared the land of the manor; peasants farmed two thirds of the land, provided services, and paid taxes

❹ Students' journal entries will vary but should incorporate what students have read about the relationship between squires and knights or ladies and ladies-in-waiting and the responsibilities of the servant.

THE RISE OF THE MIDDLE AGES **299**

299

SECTION 3

▸ READ TO DISCOVER

❶ How did the church hierarchy fit into society?

❷ How did the practices of monasticism change?

❸ How did the church influence life in medieval Europe?

▸ DEFINE

sacraments
curia
cardinals
monasticism
abbot
abbess
canon law
interdict
heretics
tithe
simony

▸ IDENTIFY

Saint Benedict
Hildegard of Bingen
Saint Patrick
Saint Augustine
Inquisition

▸ WHY IT MATTERS TODAY

Papal powers and influence today differ greatly from the powers of the medieval popes. Use **CNNfyi.com** or other **current event** sources to find examples of papal authority in today's world. Record your findings in your journal.

CNNfyi.com

The Church

The Main Idea
The Roman Catholic Church was a central part of daily life in Europe during the Middle Ages.

The Story Continues *Throughout the Middle Ages the church was one of the few sources of leadership and stability that people could rely upon. One historian has noted that "The continuity and the authority of the Church of Rome stood out in marked contrast against . . . the short-lived kingdoms which rose and fell in [the early Middle Ages]." As a result, the Catholic church became one of medieval Europe's most powerful and enduring institutions.*

The Church Hierarchy

The medieval church had broad political powers, probably because Europe's central governments were weak if they existed at all. The church filled the need for leadership by performing many of the functions that modern governments provide today. Throughout most of the Middle Ages, the church was one of the only institutions whose presence was felt throughout Europe. Its powers extended across kingdoms and through every social and political level. The church was also a great economic force during the Middle Ages. By the 1100s the medieval church was one of Europe's leading landowners, and many of its leaders were powerful feudal overlords.

The parish priest. Within the church, members of the clergy were organized according to a strict hierarchy of rank. Each rank within the clergy had different responsibilities and powers. The parish priest held the lowest rank in the church hierarchy. The parish itself was the smallest division in the church, and the priest directly served the people in his parish. He was responsible for their religious instruction and for the moral and spiritual life of the community as a whole. In some remote parishes, however, people might still have mixed pagan beliefs and superstitions with elements of Christianity.

Although he held the lowest rank in the church, the parish priest was one of its most important officers. He could administer five of the seven **sacraments.** The sacraments were ceremonies at which participants received God's direct favor, or grace, to help ward off the consequences of sin. By the 1100s the church recognized seven sacraments that are still practiced today. Parish priests could perform baptism, Holy Communion, penance, matrimony, and the anointing of the sick and dying. Bishops performed the sacraments of confirmation and the taking of holy orders.

The bishop. The bishop managed a group of parishes called a diocese. The cathedral, the bishop's official church, was usually located in the principal city of the diocese. *Cathedra* is the Latin word for the bishop's throne, or chair. The king or powerful nobles usually controlled the selection of bishops on

This jeweled silver cup was made in Germany in the 1200s for use during the sacrament of Holy Communion.

HOMEWORK Ask each student to write a paragraph explaining the relationship between the church and the nobility. Have volunteers read their paragraph aloud. Encourage the class to respond to and discuss each response.

pope

cardinals/curia: advisers to the pope

archbishop: had some authority over bishops and other dioceses in the province

bishop: managed a diocese, administered confirmation and holy orders, appointed parish priests, managed church property

parish priest: conducted church services, supervised moral and religious instruction, administered five of the seven sacraments

the basis of family connections and political power. Many bishops were feudal lords or vassals in their own right and had vassals themselves.

Church leadership. A group of several dioceses, called an archdiocese, was managed by an archbishop. An archbishop had all the powers and responsibilities of a bishop and also had authority over the bishops of the archdiocese.

The pope held supreme authority in the church. The pope was advised by the **curia,** a group of counselors drawn from the highest ranks of the clergy. The curia's most important and powerful members were **cardinals,** the "princes of the church," who advised the pope on legal and spiritual matters. From the late 1100s on, only cardinals could elect the pope. With very few exceptions, a commoner could move up in the medieval world only by being a member of the church hierarchy. A man of great ability, regardless of birth, could rise to great heights within the church, although this did not happen often.

✔ **READING CHECK: Drawing Inferences** Why was the role of the parish priest among the most important within the hierarchy of the church? directly served the people of a parish; responsible for community's moral and spiritual life; administered five of the seven sacraments

Monasticism

The medieval church was made up of two types of clergy. Priests, bishops, and the pope were secular clergy. The word *secular* comes from the Latin word *saeculum,* which means "the present world." Secular clergy gave sacraments and preached the gospel among people in the everyday world. The second group of clergy was called regular clergy. The word *regular* comes from the Latin word *regula,* which means "rule." Male monks made up the regular clergy because they had to live in accordance with strict rules. Female nuns also lived in accordance with strict rules, but they were not considered clergy because only men could fulfill that role in the church.

Monastic lifestyles. Monks and nuns believed that they had to withdraw from the world and its temptations to live a Christian life. They chose to serve God through fasting, prayer, and self-denial. During the early centuries of Christianity, monks lived alone and practiced their devotion to God in many ways. They sometimes inflicted extreme physical suffering on themselves to prove their dedication. Eventually most monks and nuns gave up the hermit's lifestyle and formed religious communities. Monks lived in communities called monasteries, while nuns lived in convents. **Monasticism** refers to the way of life in convents and monasteries.

The Benedictine Rule. In some places efforts were made to organize the monastic communities before the 500s. Around that time a young Roman named Benedict became disgusted with the worldly corruption he witnessed. He left Rome to worship God as a hermit. Benedict's reputation for holiness spread and he attracted many followers. To accommodate his growing following, Benedict established a monastery at Monte Cassino, in the mountains of central Italy. Benedict—later **Saint Benedict**—created rules to govern monks' lives. Monasteries and convents all over Europe adopted these standards, called the Benedictine Rule.

CONNECTING TO Art

Print Design: The Lindisfarne Gospels
As part of their monastic duties, monks copied important books, including the Bible, by hand. When they copied the Bible—considered God's sacred word—the monks sought to create particularly beautiful manuscripts. They illustrated, or *illuminated,* pages with gold leaf, colors, and detailed designs. This page from the Lindisfarne Gospels was produced in about 700 at the monastery of Lindisfarne, one of England's earliest centers of monastic learning.

Understanding the Arts

What does this print demonstrate about the monks' view of their work?

Culture

Among the most lasting and impressive architectural sites from the Middle Ages are monasteries and abbeys.

ACTIVITY: Have students use computer software to acquire images of monasteries. Have them work in groups to create a floor plan for a monastery, using information from the text and images they find.

CONNECTING TO ART ANSWER
The print demonstrates that the monks took great care to create beautiful work because they considered the Bible to be God's sacred word.

🖉 internet connect

TOPIC: Medieval Art
GO TO: **go.hrw.com**
KEYWORD: **SP3 WH13**

Have students access the Internet through the HRW Go site to conduct research on early medieval art and architecture. Have students find elements of medieval art and architecture that interests them and create an illustrated poster. Students may wish to use the interactive templates provided.

TEACH OBJECTIVE 2

LEVEL 3: Ask students why they think monastic life appealed to so many people during the Middle Ages. *(Monasteries and convents offered a feeling of stability.)* Have students use their textbooks to summarize the Benedictine Rule as a bulleted list in their notes.

The Benedictine Rule

• *A monk can own absolutely nothing.*
• *Everything a monk uses or wears belongs to the monastery.*
• *The abbot controls and distributes property.*

TEACH OBJECTIVE 3

LEVEL 1: Ask students to put themselves in the shoes of a medieval European. Whom might they fear more, church or king? Have students compare powers of church and king. Guide them to the idea that the powers of excommunication and interdict often seemed more mighty and frightening than the powers of the monarch. True, a king might imprison or even execute, but if the church excommunicated a person, he would not only be shunned in life but doomed for eternity.
ENGLISH LANGUAGE LEARNERS

Linking Past to Present

Among medieval nobility, marriages were usually arranged for political advantage; love was of little importance. Young people could not choose their partner. Instead, parents often betrothed their children at a young age. The bride's dowry, or inheritance, became the husband's property. It was not unusual in such arranged marriages for men to take concubines. Wives, however, were expected to remain true to their husbands, and could be put aside by their husbands if unable to bear children.

Critical Thinking

Ask students how the lot of medieval noblewomen compares to that of modern American women.

ANSWER: Some students might say that modern American women have many more freedoms, which include the right to own property, the freedom to marry, and the right to vote. Others might say that American women still suffer under the control of men.

HISTORY MAKER ANSWER
wrote religious music, founded a convent, criticized corrupt church practices

HISTORY MAKER

Hildegard of Bingen (1098–1179)

Nuns played an important role in the medieval church. The German nun **Hildegard of Bingen,** for example, wrote religious music and a medical text. She also founded the convent at Rubertsberg and served as its first abbess. Hildegard was a vocal critic of corrupt church practices. She was later named a saint of the church. **How did Hildegard of Bingen contribute to the church?**

Holt Researcher

go.hrw.com
KEYWORD: Holt Researcher
FreeFind: Benedict
         Hildegard of Bingen
After reading more about Benedict and Hildegard of Bingen on the Holt Researcher, draw a sketch of a stained-glass window that reflects their influence on monastic life.

The Benedictine Rule was fairly strict. Everything a monk or nun used or wore belonged to their community. Even the monk's time and labor belonged to his monastery. An **abbot** was the elected head of the community and controlled and distributed all property. An **abbess** served a similar role for women in convents. Monks and nuns spent many hours of each day in prayer. The rest of their days were taken up with tasks that the abbot or abbess assigned them.

The spread of monastic influence. Monks and nuns often took care of the needy in medieval society. In time many monasteries became rich as pious nobles gave money or land to monasteries in return for spiritual favor. Convents also received some gifts, but they generally did not become as wealthy as many monasteries.

Some monks left their monasteries to become missionaries. For example, **Saint Patrick** is credited with bringing Christianity to Ireland in 432. Monastic schools in Ireland were the basis of an advanced culture that lasted from about 500 to about 800. **Saint Augustine** led a group of monks to England. Eventually all of England accepted Christianity. Augustine became the Archbishop of Canterbury, and Canterbury became the center of the Christian church in England.

✔ **READING CHECK: Identifying Cause and Effect** How did Saint Benedict change monasticism? created rules to organize and govern monks' lives

The Church and Medieval Life

The Christian clergy—secular and regular alike—played a major role in medieval institutions and everyday life. Throughout the Middle Ages the church enjoyed great political, economic, and social influence across most of Europe.

Political role. In the Papal States the pope was both political and religious leader. Many popes claimed that the church held political as well as spiritual power over all monarchs. Church leaders also held positions of power as feudal lords and as advisors to kings and nobles.

The church had its own code of law, called **canon law,** and its own courts. Members of the clergy could be tried in this court and the court would rule accordingly, perhaps excommunicating them. An excommunicated person was cut off from the church and could not receive the sacraments or be buried in sacred ground. Excommunication was greatly feared by Christians because it effectively removed an individual from society.

The court could also issue an **interdict** against an entire region. All churches in that region would be closed, and clergy would be forbidden to perform marriages, burials, or other sacraments. People in an interdicted area could be at risk of eternal punishment. In many cases the church used its power of interdiction to turn a region's people against rulers who opposed church powers and policies. The church did not allow anyone to question the basic principles of the Christian religion. People who denied the truth of the church's principles or who preached beliefs not approved by the church were considered **heretics.** They were viewed as unbelievers whose sinful beliefs attacked the church and who thus deserved eternal damnation. In a sense, heresy was a threat to the church in the way that treason is a threat to a government.

The medieval church also had the power to tax. The parish priest collected a **tithe,** or one-tenth of a Christian person's income. The church also received a large income from its own lands. By the early 1200s, when the church was at the height of its power, it was perhaps the wealthiest single institution in Europe.

CLOSE

Have students write a paragraph that explains the hierarchy of the church.

REVIEW

Have students complete Section 3 Review on p. 303.

ASSESS

Have students complete Daily Quiz 13.3. As Alternative Assessment, you may want to use the chart exercise in this section's lessons.

RETEACH

Have students complete Main Idea Activity for English Language Learners and Special-Needs Students 13.3. Then have students decide on the best and worst characteristic of the medieval church. **ENGLISH LANGUAGE LEARNERS**

EXTEND

Have each student conduct library research to write a report about Saint Benedict. Their reports should consider his important contributions to monasticism. **BLOCK SCHEDULING**

Economic and social role. The spiritual teachings of the church did much to shape the European economy of the Middle Ages. For example, the church generally did not approve of people gaining wealth at the expense of others. Instead it taught that people who labored should be regarded with the dignity of free people. Monks participated in agriculture and some monasteries were involved in large-scale trade.

The church considered the family a sacred institution. It did not allow divorce and said special prayers for family members. The clergy was involved with social work and took care of the poor and needy. Some religious orders even established hospitals.

Problems of the church. The church's great wealth and influence led to many problems. One major problem concerned lay investiture—the practice of a noble, such as a king, appointing a friend or relative to be a bishop or abbot. Church leaders held that only a member of the clergy could grant spiritual authority to another member. During the Middle Ages, moreover, people could buy high positions within the church hierarchy. This practice was called **simony.** The purchaser might have expected to gain wealth through his position, either from church income or by charging high fees for performing religious services. As time went on the practice of simony came under growing criticism from inside and outside the church.

Many church leaders and lay rulers attempted to bring about church reform. Two religious groups dedicated themselves to this goal. Saint Francis of Assisi founded the order of Franciscans in 1209. Saint Dominic founded the order of the Dominicans in 1216. Members of these orders, called friars, lived and preached among the people.

In the mid-1200s the church attempted to reform itself with the help of the Dominicans. The church ordered the Dominicans to seek out heretics and to stamp out teachings that opposed church doctrines. This search for heretics is known as the **Inquisition.** Heretics who confessed to sinful teachings or practices were forced to perform penance, a ritual designed to bring forgiveness. Those who did not confess were turned over to the government for punishment or execution, which sometimes involved burning at the stake. The church believed that these severe actions were needed to stop the spread of heresy in the Christian world.

✔ **READING CHECK: Summarizing** How was the church involved in the political and economic life of the Middle Ages? enjoyed broad political power across Europe; teachings helped to shape economic activity

DAILY LIFE

The Parish Church
The parish church was an important part of a medieval town. Houses in towns and villages were sometimes little more than small wood huts. Some parish churches, however, were built of stone and were among the largest buildings in the town. **Why was a church often among the most important buildings in a medieval town or village?**

DAILY LIFE ANSWER
The church was typically the center of medieval life.

SECTION 3 REVIEW ANSWERS

❶ Define
- sacraments, p. 300
- curia, p. 301
- cardinals, p. 301
- monasticism, p. 301
- abbot and abbess, p. 302
- canon law, p. 302
- interdict, p. 302
- heretics, p. 302
- tithe, p. 302
- simony, p. 303

❷ Identify
- Saint Benedict, p. 301
- Hildegard of Bingen, p. 302
- Saint Patrick, p. 302
- Saint Augustine, p. 302
- Inquisition, p. 303

❸ from bottom to top: parish priest, bishop, archbishop, curia and cardinals, pope

❹ a. conducted services in village church, supervised moral and religious instruction

b. monks and nuns withdrew from world to practice devotion to God, church developed communities for them

c. forced heretics to perform penance, punished or executed them

❺ Students' dialogues will vary but should consider facts about monasticism.

SECTION 3 REVIEW

1. Define and explain the significance:
sacraments
curia
cardinals
monasticism
abbot
abbess
canon law
interdict
heretics
tithe
simony

2. Identify and explain the significance:
Saint Benedict
Hildegard of Bingen
Saint Patrick
Saint Augustine
Inquisition

Homework Practice Online
go.hrw.com
keyword: SP3 HP13

3 Categorizing Construct a chart like the one below to show the organization of church hierarchy during the Middle Ages.

Church Hierarchy

4.
Finding the Main Idea
a. Why was the role of the parish priest important to the church?
b. Describe how monasticism developed during the Middle Ages.
c. How did the church attempt to reform itself?

5.
Writing and Critical Thinking
Supporting Points of View Write a dialogue between two peasants who are debating whether or not to join a monastic order or convent.
Consider:
- the lifestyles of monks, nuns, and peasants
- the advantages and disadvantages of monasticism
- the purpose of monasticism

THE RISE OF THE MIDDLE AGES **303**

OBJECTIVES

1 **Explain how the kingdom of England was formed.**

2 **Identify the achievements of William the Conqueror and his successors.**

3 **Describe how Parliament and common law affected political developments in England.**

4 **Explore how the French kings gained power over their nobles.**

SECTION 4

READ TO DISCOVER

❶ How was the kingdom of England formed?

❷ What were the achievements of William the Conqueror and his successors?

❸ How did the parliamentary system and common law affect political developments in England?

❹ How did the French kings gain power over their nobles?

DEFINE

shires
common law

IDENTIFY

Alfred the Great
Edward the Confessor
William the Conqueror
Henry II
Thomas Becket
Eleanor of Aquitaine
Magna Carta
Simon de Montfort

▶ WHY IT MATTERS TODAY

Some challenges facing governments today are very similar to those that confronted the monarchies of the Middle Ages. Use CNNfyi.com or other **current event** sources to find examples of issues that representative governments, such as the U.S. Congress or the British Parliament, are currently discussing. Record your findings in your journal.

CNNfyi.com

The Struggle for Power in England and France

The Main Idea
Royal power gained supremacy over the power of the nobles in England and France during the Middle Ages.

The Story Continues *Kings, nobles, and church leaders sought to gain power over one another throughout the Middle Ages. King Philip II of France, for example, sought to control the election of bishops in the French church. "We warn the canons and monks," Philip ordered, "to elect someone who will be pleasing to God and useful to the realm." The struggle for power among these groups was a continuing theme in the development of medieval Europe.*

Anglo-Saxon and Norman England

In Europe before the 1000s, kings and lords often struggled for power. Some lords were as powerful as kings and served the kings when they wished. Some kings, however, tried to control the nobles. From this continual struggle for power the kingdoms of England and France emerged. Over time the power of the monarchs in these kingdoms became supreme.

Anglo-Saxon England. By about 450 Roman rule in Britain ended. Following the legions' withdrawal, Germanic tribes moved into the island, first as raiders, then as settlers. The culture that emerged from this Germanic settlement was named "Anglo-Saxon" after two of these tribes, the Angles and the Saxons. England, the "land of the Angles," refers to the eastern island of the British Isles, except for Scotland in the north and Wales in the west.

Over time the Anglo-Saxons formed several independent kingdoms in England. These kingdoms became known as Northumbria, in northern England and what is now southern Scotland; Mercia, in central England; and Wessex, in southern England. Eventually the Anglo-Saxons divided these kingdoms into governmental districts called **shires.** A shire was governed by a shire-reeve, which became the word *sheriff.*

Alfred the Great. By the early 800s the kings of Wessex controlled almost all of England. Viking raiders from the north, however (called "Danes" by the English), challenged the rule of Wessex and overran much of England. In 871 **Alfred the Great** came to the throne of Wessex determined to drive the Danes from the island. Alfred made a temporary peace after being defeated by the Danes. He spent the next five years building a powerful army and a fleet of fighting ships. In 876 Alfred attacked the Danes. By 886 the exhausted and weakened Danes had sued for peace.

Statue of Alfred the Great

ALL LEVELS: Ask students to look at the series of maps on page 308, which represent the growth of France. In their textbooks, students should read about the shifting of power in England between the 400s and the 1100s. Then have students create a map progression for England. Students should create three to five rough maps appropriately colored and keyed to show major shifts in boundaries and power between the Anglo-Saxons, the Danes, and the Normans. Encourage students to consult additional sources in order to complete their maps as accurately as possible. **ENGLISH LANGUAGE LEARNERS**

The treaty that resulted allowed the Danes to live in parts of Mercia and Northumbria, where they were allowed to govern themselves.

Danish rule. During the 900s Alfred's successors were able to win more land back from the Danes. At the same time they unified the country, strengthened its government, and spread Christianity throughout the land. However, the Danes began to attack again at the end of the century. By 1013 the Danes once again controlled the entire country.

In 1016 King Canute of Denmark took the throne of England and most of Scandinavia in a combined kingdom. Canute was a wise ruler and spent much of his time in England. His sons, however, were weak rulers. By 1042 the Danish line had died out and the Anglo-Saxon nobles chose **Edward the Confessor** as their new king.

The Norman Conquest. Edward the Confessor was part Anglo-Saxon and part Norman. The powerful Duchy of Normandy was located in northwestern France. When Edward died without leaving an heir in 1066, a distant relative—Duke William of Normandy—claimed the English throne. The Anglo-Saxons refused to recognize his claim. Instead they selected Edward's brother-in-law, Harold of Wessex, to be king. William, determined to win the throne of England, crossed the English Channel with a powerful force of Norman knights. In a decisive battle William defeated Harold's Anglo-Saxon army at Hastings in October 1066. In December of that year, he was crowned King William I of England.

William, known today as **William the Conqueror,** soon overcame armed Anglo-Saxon resistance to his rule. In the years after the conquest, the Normans' laws, customs, and language were introduced in England. However, the Anglo-Saxons did not quickly accept them. Anglo-Saxon was a Germanic language. Norman French, in contrast, was based on Latin. As a result, the language of the Norman-English nobility continued to be French, while the language of most people in England continued to be Anglo-Saxon. Slowly, however, the lifestyles, laws, and customs of England grew to combine elements of both Anglo-Saxon and Norman cultures.

✔ **READING CHECK: Summarizing** Why is the year 1066 significant in English history?
It is the year of the Norman invasion of England.

The Conqueror and His Successors

William ruled England from 1066 to 1087. He brought feudalism from France to the newly conquered England. William shaped England's new feudal system, however, so that the king, not the nobles, held supreme authority. He required each feudal lord to swear personal loyalty directly to him. This meant that all English lords were vassals of the king. William also stopped the lords from uniting against him by scattering their fiefs throughout England. The new king's actions laid a strong foundation for centralized government and a strong monarchy in England.

The king also worked to determine the population, wealth, and ways that land was divided and used in his new kingdom. William sent royal commissioners to every English shire. Their task was to count each shire's people, assess landholdings, and measure type and value of property. The results of this great survey helped the king to set up an accurate, central tax system. The records that were gathered became known as the Domesday, or Doomsday, Book.

Holt Researcher go.hrw.com

KEYWORD: Holt Researcher

FreeFind:

William the Conqueror

After reading more about William the Conqueror on the Holt Researcher, evaluate his decision to take the throne by force, taking into account historical context. Then analyze how such a tactic would be viewed in the world today.

INTERPRETING THE VISUAL RECORD

Domesday Book This page from the Domesday Book is a record of property holdings in Bedfordshire and of boundary settlements among small tenants. *In what way was the Domesday Book evidence of the strength of William the Conqueror's monarchy?*

Economics

Besides the nobility and the peasants, another segment of feudal society began to emerge during the Middle Ages: the *burgher*, or free townsman. Burghers were merchants, craftsmen, and day laborers. In addition, runaway serfs frequently went to towns to find work. As trade between nations began to increase, the burghers started to gain some wealth and power. They built defenses for their towns and sometimes paid feudal lords for military protection.

Critical Thinking

Ask students to describe how burghers differed from peasants.

ANSWER: Students should recognize that they were not bound to the land as peasants were.

VISUAL RECORD ANSWER

It measured the monarchy's wealth and allowed the king to collect taxes centrally.

TEACH OBJECTIVE 2

LEVEL 2: Have students read about the Norman Conquest and the policies of William the Conqueror and his successors. Then have them write letters to the editorial section of a fictional medieval newspaper evaluating the changes brought about by William and his successors. The letters should be written from the perspective of commoners who have lived under the rule of one or more of these Norman kings.

Economics

The laws put forward by Henry II to try clergy members in secular courts were called the Constitutions of Clarendon. Thomas Becket opposed the church's approval of these laws for two years before Henry ordered him arrested. Becket fled to France. With the pope's intervention, Becket returned to England. He excommunicated the bishops who had signed the Constitutions of Clarendon. Outraged, Henry was rumored to have said, "Will no one here rid me of this meddlesome priest?" Four knights consequently murdered the archbishop while he prayed at Canterbury. The Christian world was horrified. Rumors of miracles at Canterbury began to circulate. Becket was soon canonized. Henry ultimately rescinded part of the Constitutions.

Critical Thinking

What were the results of Henry II's attempt to eliminate Becket's popular influence and his opposition to Henry's wishes?

ANSWER: The murders helped martyr and immortalize Becket and caused part of the Constitutions of Clarendon to be rescinded.

HISTORY MAKER ANSWER

created a center of medieval culture, helped build a strong nation

HISTORY MAKER

Eleanor of Aquitaine (c. 1122–1204)

Eleanor of Aquitaine was wife to two kings: first to Louis VII of France, and later to Henry II of England. She was also one of the most powerful women in medieval Europe.

As queen, Eleanor played an active role in the leadership of both France and England. In France, she created a center of medieval culture at the court of Poitiers. And although Eleanor's marriage to Henry II of England was often troubled, she and the king built a strong partnership and a strong kingdom.

How did Eleanor of Aquitaine use her position as queen?

Analyzing Primary Sources

Analyzing Information What evidence does Roger of Wendover cite to show that England's nobles were prepared to support their demands with armed rebellion? arrived in "military array"; spoke in "bold tones" that threatened John

Reforms under William's successors. Henry I, one of William the Conqueror's sons, ruled from 1100 to 1135. Henry was an able ruler and administrator who set up a new department, the exchequer, to handle the kingdom's finances. This made the central government more efficient. He also made an important contribution to England's legal system. Henry sent traveling judges throughout the country to try cases. This action weakened the feudal lords because the king's royal court, not the lords' feudal courts, dispensed justice.

Henry II, who ruled from 1154 to 1189, also made decisions that increased royal authority. Instead of performing feudal military service for the king, his vassals—the nobles—could pay him a fee. He would use the money to hire mercenaries, or soldiers from different places. In this way Henry II would have an army made up of soldiers who were loyal to him because he was paying them. An army made up of nobles might not have been as loyal.

England's legal system grew under Henry II's direction. Traveling judges established routes, or circuits, and further strengthened royal law throughout England. During the late 1100s the 12-member jury developed in the court system. Juries decided civil as well as criminal cases. Trial by jury to determine guilt or innocence replaced the feudal trial by ordeal and combat.

Henry aimed to increase the authority of his royal courts at the expense of the church. Thus he sought to try certain members of the clergy who had already been judged in church courts. **Thomas Becket,** the Archbishop of Canterbury, refused to allow his clergy to be tried in royal courts. Becket and Henry, who had once been good friends, became bitter enemies over the issue. Four of the king's knights, believing that they were helping Henry, murdered the archbishop in his cathedral.

Even though Henry II denied any part in the murder, he did penance to appease the church. Henry had to abandon his attempts to reduce the power of the English church. Becket was named a saint, and his shrine in Canterbury became a popular destination for pilgrims.

The last years of Henry II's reign were troubled. His sons plotted against him and his marriage to **Eleanor of Aquitaine** was stormy. The French lands that Eleanor had brought to Henry when they married, moreover, involved England in new conflicts with the French. Nevertheless, the years of Henry's rule had strengthened the English monarchy at the feudal lords' expense. Later kings were able to build upon Henry's work.

King John and Magna Carta. One of Henry II's sons, King John, is known for his actions that led to a revolt among England's nobles. John demanded that the nobles pay more taxes to support his wars in France. In 1215 a powerful group of high nobles—barons of the kingdom—joined together against the king and his demands. Their threats of an armed uprising against the throne forced John to accept a document known as **Magna Carta** (Latin for "Great Charter"). One eyewitness described the confrontation between John and the nobles who opposed his harsh and high-handed rule:

History Makers Speak

❝[The] nobles came to [King John] in gay military array, and demanded the confirmation of the liberties and laws of King Edward, with other liberties granted to them and to the kingdom and Church of England . . . The King, hearing the bold tones of the barons in making this demand, much feared an attack from them . . .❞

Roger of Wendover, "An Account of Magna Carta," quoted in *Problems in Western Civilization: The Challenge of History,* Vol. I, L. F. Schaefer, D. H. Fowler, and J. E. Cooke, eds.

TEACH OBJECTIVES 3 and 4

LEVEL 3: Organize students into four groups. Assign two groups to study English politics and the other two to study French politics between 1000 and 1350. Each group will prepare a multi-media presentation outlining the evolution of royal power in their assigned kingdom. Presentations on England should include information about rulers and their policies, Magna Carta and its impact on English society, Parliament, and common law. Presentations on France should include information about rulers and their policies, the growth of royal territory, the central government, and taxation policies. Encourage students to include maps, charts, illustrations, excerpts from documents, and any other interesting items they find. **COOPERATIVE LEARNING**

TEACH OBJECTIVES 3 and 4

LEVEL 1: Ask students to list the goals of William the Conqueror and successors and the Capetian kings. Ask them to support their point of view on how well these rulers accomplished their goals.
ENGLISH LANGUAGE LEARNERS

Magna Carta protected the liberties of the nobles. It also provided a limited outline of rights for England's ordinary people. King John agreed not to collect any new or special taxes without the consent of the Great Council, a body of important nobles and church leaders who advised the king. John also promised not to take property without paying for it. He promised not to sell, refuse, or delay justice. The king also agreed to let any accused person be judged by a jury of his or her peers. John's acceptance of Magna Carta meant that the king—like his subjects—had to obey the law or face revolt and overthrow. Magna Carta made the law the supreme power in England.

✔ **READING CHECK: Summarizing** What contributions did William the Conqueror and his successors make to England? built strong, efficient, well-financed government and monarchy; improved legal system

Parliament and Common Law

Two other major developments took place in England in the years following Magna Carta. The first was the growth of Parliament and the beginnings of representative government. The second was the growth of **common law**—law based upon customs and judges' decisions, rather than upon written codes.

Parliament. A widespread revolt of nobles against King Henry III in the 1260s rocked England and again threatened the monarchy. **Simon de Montfort,** a powerful lord who led the revolt, aimed to build middle-class support for the nobles' cause. In this way, de Montfort reasoned, both the middle class and the nobility could combine forces against the king. In 1265 de Montfort asked representatives of the middle class to meet with the nobles and clergy who made up the Great Council. The middle-class representatives included four knights from each shire and two burgesses—leading citizens—from each of several major towns.

The practice of having members of the middle class meet with the clergy and the nobles in the Great Council remained. This representative body eventually became the English Parliament. Over time Parliament was divided into two parts, called "houses." Nobles and the clergy made up the House of Lords, and knights and burgesses made up the House of Commons.

The early Parliament mainly served to advise the king, but it also had the right to refuse new taxes sought by the king. As England's centralized government grew, taxes were needed to help meet its ever-increasing costs. Parliament's power to accept or reject new taxes became more and more important.

Common law. Edward I ruled England from 1272 to 1307. Edward, one of England's greatest monarchs, divided the king's court into three branches. The Court of the Exchequer kept track of the kingdom's financial accounts and tried tax cases. The Court of Common Pleas heard cases between ordinary citizens. The Court of the King's Bench conducted trials that concerned the king or the government.

The decisions made by the new royal courts were collected and used as the basis for future court verdicts. This collection of decisions became known as common law because it was applied equally and in common to all English people. Common law differed greatly from law that was based on statutes, such as Roman law. It was a "living law" in the sense that it changed to meet changing conditions.

✔ **READING CHECK: Comparing** How are the parliamentary system and common law similar to the government and laws practiced in the United States? used as basis for future court verdicts; applied equally and in common to all

CONNECTING TO
Civics

Magna Carta
Magna Carta became a cornerstone of constitutional government and rule by law. Its original purpose was to limit the king's powers and protect the nobles' feudal rights. It included such concepts as church freedom, trial by jury, freedom from taxation without cause and consent, and due process of law. The document's final article empowered a group of barons to take up arms against the king if he violated its conditions.

Over time the freedoms guaranteed by Magna Carta spread to all citizens. Today the Charter forms part of the British Constitution, and its ideas can be found in our own United States Constitution.

Understanding Civics

What are some of the liberties ensured by Magna Carta that are also guaranteed in our United States Constitution?

Interdisciplinary Connection

LITERATURE. The murder of Thomas Becket heavily influenced literature. Throughout the Middle Ages pilgrims flocked to Becket's tomb at Canterbury. They inspired Geoffrey Chaucer to write his masterpiece, *The Canterbury Tales*. Becket's murder also inspired the English writer T.S. Eliot to dramatize Becket's last hours in his 1935 play *Murder in the Cathedral*. Similarly the playwright Jean Anouilh [ah-nwee-yuh] immortalized the archbishop's career in his 1959 play *Becket; or, The Honour of God*.

Critical Thinking

Ask students what elements of Becket's life or death might have inspired so many literary interpretations.

ANSWER: Students might answer that Becket's willingness to choose principles over politics is a virtue many cultures find important.

UNDERSTANDING CIVICS ANSWER
freedom of religion, right to a jury trial, due process, right to bear arms

THE RISE OF THE MIDDLE AGES **307**

Magna Carta	U.S. Bill of Rights
"Scutage [a tax]…shall be levied in our kingdom only by the common counsel of our kingdom…."	
"No freeman shall be… imprisoned…except by lawful judgment of his peers or by the law of the land."	
"To no one will we sell, to no one will we deny or delay right of justice."	

CLOSE

Ask students how the rise of the Capetian kings in France illustrates the feudal struggle for power. How did the Capetians add to their power?

Constitutional Heritage

In June of 1215, King John rode to meet his angry nobles at Runnymede, a wide meadow on the banks of the Thames River. No one present on that day could have guessed that the nobles' demands, written in the form of the document we now call Magna Carta, would later become the cornerstone of constitutional government and representative democracy.

ACTIVITY: Organize the class into groups of four students and pass out copies of Magna Carta and the U.S. Constitution. Ask students to compare and contrast the two documents. Have each group list elements of the U.S. Constitution that were clearly influenced by Magna Carta.

MAP ANSWERS
1. Paris

2. Kings married women who owned lands or took control of lands of noble families that died out

Rise of the Capetian Kings in France

The last Carolingian king died in 987. In the same year a group of nobles chose Hugh Capet to be King of France. Capet and his descendants, a line known as the Capetians, ruled for more than 300 years.

Hugh Capet ruled only a small area called the Île-de-France (eel·duh·FRAHNS). Feudal lords ruled the rest of France, holding areas known as duchies. The Capetians aimed to develop a strong central government and to unite the duchies of France under the rule of the monarchy.

The growth of royal territory. The Capetians sought to increase the lands under their control in several ways. For example, some Capetian kings married noblewomen whose dowries included great fiefs. They also took control of the lands of noble families that had died out. The Capetians looked, as well, to conquer French lands held by the English kings since the days of William the Conqueror. Philip II, known as Philip Augustus, particularly favored this policy of taking English holdings in France. King Philip, who ruled from 1180 to 1223, greatly increased royal landholdings by taking large provinces, such as Normandy and Maine, from the English.

Strengthening the central government. The Capetian kings appointed well-trained officials to run the government. They also extended the jurisdiction of the royal courts. The Parliament of Paris, the highest of the royal courts, eventually became a kind of supreme court, hearing appeals from all parts of the kingdom.

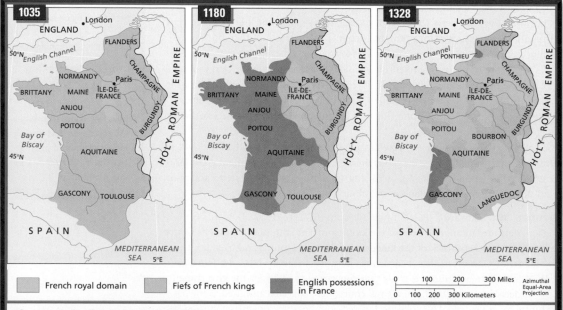

The Growth of France, 1035–1328

Interpreting Maps In 1035 the French royal domain—land that was personally owned by the French monarch—was limited to the Île-de-France. Within 300 years, the royal domain had grown many times over, and the king controlled most of France.

■ **Skills Assessment: 1. Locate** Identify the principal city of the Île-de-France. **2. Making Generalizations** How did the king control those parts of France that were not part of the royal domain?

REVIEW

Have students complete Section 4 Review on p. 309.

ASSESS

Have students complete Daily Quiz 13.4. As Alternative Assessment, use map or presentation exercises in this section's lessons.

RETEACH

Have students complete Main Idea Activity for English Language Learners and Special-Needs Students 13.4. Have partners outline the section and compile a chapter glossary, using outline and glossary to create flashcards to quiz each other on correct social studies terminology. **ENGLISH LANGUAGE LEARNERS**

EXTEND

Have each student choose and read a tale from Chaucer's *The Canterbury Tales* and prepare a shortened, modernized version for dramatic reading, using standard grammar, spelling, sentence structure, and punctuation. Encourage audience questions. **BLOCK SCHEDULING**

The Capetians' struggle for power continued under Philip IV (Philip the Fair), who ruled France from 1285 to 1314. Philip was able to increase royal power over the French church by taxing the clergy. When Pope Boniface VII opposed Philip, the king had him arrested. Following Boniface's death in 1303, Philip influenced the election of the next pope, Clement V. The shrewd king also moved to build his popularity among the French people. Philip convened the Estates General, a representative body made up of the three major social classes in France. The Estates General included commoners as well as nobles and members of the clergy. By involving the Estates General in his government, Philip secured widespread support in his struggle against the church.

Royal power in France was greatly strengthened under Philip IV and the earlier Capetian rulers. Despite the centralizing reforms they achieved, however, France remained largely feudal in its political organization. The Capetian kings had a vision of France as a united country, but the idea of unification under the monarchy had little appeal at the local level. Thus the Capetians failed to achieve their great aim. By the 1300s, moreover, the dynasty itself had reached an end, for although Philip IV had three sons, none produced an heir to the throne. In 1328 the last of the Capetian rulers, Charles IV, died. A new line of French kings—the Valois—came into power.

Philip IV was one of France's mightiest rulers during the Middle Ages. In this 15th-century illustration, Philip is shown giving an audience to a French noble.

✔ **READING CHECK: Comparing** How was the Estates General of France similar to England's Parliament? Both were representative bodies composed of the society's major classes.

SECTION 4 REVIEW

1. **Define** and explain the significance:
   shires
   common law

2. **Identify** and explain the significance:
   Alfred the Great
   Edward the Confessor
   William the Conqueror
   Henry II
   Thomas Becket
   Eleanor of Aquitaine
   Magna Carta
   Simon de Montfort

3. **Sequencing** Create a time line like the one below. Complete it to show the major events in the early development of representative government in medieval England.

   1215   late 1200s

   1265

4. **Finding the Main Idea**
   a. How did William the Conqueror's actions in 1066 change England?
   b. In what ways did Magna Carta support the rise of representative government in England?
   c. What role did Simon de Montfort play in the development of Parliament?
   d. Why did the kings of France seek to weaken church power in their lands?

5. **Writing and Critical Thinking**
   Supporting a Point of View Write a paragraph that supports the following statement: "Americans today are governed by a constitution that traces its origins back to events in England in the 1200s."
   Consider:
   • the struggle for power between England's kings and nobles during the Middle Ages
   • the rights and freedoms that are guaranteed by our Constitution and Bill of Rights

Homework Practice Online
keyword: SP3 HP13

SECTION 4 REVIEW ANSWERS

❶ **Define**
• shires, p. 304
• common law, p. 307

❷ **Identify**
• Alfred the Great, p. 304
• Edward the Confessor, p. 305
• William the Conqueror, p. 305
• Henry II, p. 306
• Thomas Becket, p. 306
• Eleanor of Aquitaine, p. 306
• Magna Carta, p. 306
• Simon de Montfort, p. 307

❸ Possible answers—1265: Simon de Montfort asks representatives of middle class to meet with nobles and clergy; 1272–1307: reign of Edward I, who divided kings' court into three branches

❹ **a.** led to a combination of Anglo-Saxon and Norman culture in England

b. forced the king to seek the advice of the Great Council

c. led the revolt of nobles, sought support of middle class

d. to increase royal power

❺ Students' paragraphs should support the statement with evidence from the chapter.

OBJECTIVES

1 **Describe how the Holy Roman emperors used their power.**

2 **Explain how the struggle between the popes and emperors developed.**

VISUAL RECORD ANSWER

It incorporates Christian symbols.

READ TO DISCOVER

❶ How did the Holy Roman emperors use their power?

❷ How did the struggle between the popes and emperors develop?

IDENTIFY

Otto I
Henry III
Henry IV
Pope Gregory VII
Frederick Barbarossa
Innocent III

WHY IT MATTERS TODAY

The Italian cities of Milan, Bologna, and Padua were great commercial centers during the Middle Ages. Use CNNfyi.com or other **current event** sources to investigate the role of these cities in Italian and world commerce today. Record your findings in your journal.

CNNfyi.com

The Clash over Germany and Italy

The Main Idea
Political conflict between the medieval popes and the German emperors weakened both sides.

The Story Continues *The struggle between church and state was particularly bitter in the Holy Roman Empire. Both the emperor and the pope held that their authority came from God. Pope Innocent III, who led the medieval church to its greatest power, claimed divine supremacy over all worldly rulers. According to Innocent, ". . . our power is not from man but from God." Ultimately the conflict between church and state weakened both.*

The Holy Roman Empire

While Charlemagne was still alive, Italy was part of his empire. However, his death in 814 caused Italy to fall into a state of disorder. Several of Charlemagne's descendants inherited the title of Holy Roman Emperor. However, they did not really rule Italy. In the years around 900, the Byzantine Empire held parts of Italy. The pope ruled the Papal States, while Arab Muslims ruled Sicily and frequently attacked the Italian mainland.

In Germany the great feudal lords elected **Otto I** their king in 936. Otto, a powerful and forceful ruler, became known as Otto the Great. Otto worked to develop a strong kingdom in Germany like that of the Capetians in France. However, the German king was also interested in Italy. In 951 Otto moved to seize territory in northern Italy. When Pope John XII struggled with Roman nobles, he begged Otto for help. The pope rewarded Otto's support by crowning him Emperor of the Romans in 962.

Otto's title was the same as that granted to Charlemagne 162 years earlier. Otto ruled Germany and northern Italy, however—a much smaller area than Charlemagne had held. Nevertheless, the empire stood as a major power in Europe for hundreds of years after Otto's crowning. It endured—in name, at least—until the early 1800s. Over time, however, the Holy Roman Empire was weakened by internal divisions, the rise of other European powers, and the ambitions of local nobles who sought to break from imperial control. Imperial power gradually declined until the emperor became little more than a figurehead. But the once mighty empire did leave an enduring legacy: a close and lasting tie between Germany and Italy.

INTERPRETING THE VISUAL RECORD

The coronation of Otto I Pope John XII placed this crown on the head of Otto I in 962, naming Otto "Emperor of the Romans." *In what way does the emperor's crown symbolize the relationship between church and state in the Holy Roman Empire of the Middle Ages?*

ALL LEVELS: Assign *An Exchange Between Pope Gregory VII and Emperor Henry IV* from **Readings in World History.** Use the Reading Review questions to launch an opening discussion about the relationship of the popes to the Holy Roman emperors. Point out the ongoing animosity between the two powerful men. Ask students what they think this escalating power struggle indicated. *(need for separation of church and state, that each leader wanted to establish the supremacy of their type of power)* **ENGLISH LANGUAGE LEARNERS**

LEVEL 1: Have students use graphic organizers to illustrate how the Concordat of Worms would divide power between popes and emperors. Discuss the division that existed between popes and emperors.

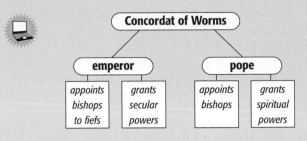

Concordat of Worms

emperor		pope	
appoints bishops to fiefs	grants secular powers	appoints bishops	grants spiritual powers

---

The reign of Emperor **Henry III** between 1046 and 1056 represented the height of imperial power. Henry, like Charlemagne, viewed the church as a branch of the imperial government. He expected the church to actively support the empire and its ruler. During Henry's reign, three different men claimed the papacy. Henry removed these men from office and elected a German as pope. He also chose the next three popes.

✔ **READING CHECK: Comparing** In what major way was Henry III's view of the church similar to the view of Charlemagne? Henry, like Charlemagne, viewed the church as a branch of the imperial government.

Struggles between the Papacy and European Rulers

Henry III's death in 1056 brought his five-year-old son, **Henry IV,** to the imperial throne. Powerful German nobles saw Henry's youth as an opportunity to regain their independence and feudal powers. The church, too, moved to restore the power it had lost during Henry III's reign. At the age of about 15, Henry moved to strengthen his imperial rule. Eventually Henry's actions brought him into conflict with one of the great leaders of the medieval church, **Pope Gregory VII.** The struggle between Henry and Gregory reflected the clash between church and state that was a continuing issue in the Middle Ages.

Gregory and Henry IV. Pope Gregory was both devout and able. He worked to bring spiritual reform to the church by increasing the power and authority of the papacy. Gregory believed that the church was the supreme spiritual and temporal power on the earth. He felt that rulers and ordinary people alike were subject to the will of the church and its pope. Gregory did not hesitate to use the terrible punishment of excommunication as a way to resolve conflicts of church and state.

The conflict between Henry IV and Gregory VII concerned the old issue of lay investiture—the appointment of bishops by temporal rulers. Henry believed that he had the right to appoint bishops of the German church. Gregory angrily opposed lay investiture and responded to the emperor's attempt to name bishops by excommunicating Henry. In addition, Gregory released the emperor's subjects from their vows of loyalty to their ruler and urged the nobles to elect another emperor.

Imperial submission. Fearing rebellion, Henry sought the pope's mercy. During the harsh winter of 1077, Henry traveled to meet the pope. They met at Canossa, in the mountains of northern Italy. Henry and his attendants had to make their way through treacherous, ice-covered peaks. When he finally reached Canossa, the humiliated Henry waited in the bitter cold for three days to be admitted to the pope's presence. When they finally met, Henry pleaded for the pope's mercy. As a result, the pope revoked Henry's excommunication.

The struggle over lay investiture continued, however. Finally, in 1122, representatives of both sides met in the German city of Worms to settle the conflict. The agreement they reached, known as the Concordat of Worms, limited imperial power over the German church. The emperor could appoint bishops to fiefs. Only the pope, however, had the power to name bishops, whose spiritual authority came directly from the church.

INTERPRETING THE VISUAL RECORD

Meeting at Canossa In 1077 Pope Gregory VII (left) and Emperor Henry IV (center) settled some of their differences at Canossa. Countess Matilda of Tuscany (right) helped arrange the meeting. *What visual clues does the artist provide to indicate the dominant figure in this painting?*

Interdisciplinary Connection

ART. The illustration of Charlemagne's coronation on page 290 comes from the *Grandes Chroniques de France*, a French chronicle from the 1300s. The artist shows Pope Leo III wielding supreme power over Charlemagne by bestowing on him a measure of civil power. Earlier the coronation was portrayed differently. The earliest representation, a mosaic from the 800s, shows Saint Peter bestowing equal power upon Leo and Charlemagne, with Leo in charge of spiritual and Charlemagne in charge of civil matters.

Critical Thinking

Ask students to compare effects of the representations. What may have happened between the 800s and 1300s that would cause this shift in representation?

ANSWER: Students may suggest that the shift was caused by the struggle between monarchs and the church.

VISUAL RECORD ANSWER

Henry IV is shown kneeling, while the pope, shown very large, is above him.

Reproducible Resources

PS Readings in World History 40: An Exchange Between Pope Gregory VII and Emperor Henry IV

TEACH OBJECTIVES 1 and 2

LEVEL 3: Have pairs of students prepare a staged interview of Pope Innocent III, taking on the roles of the pope and an interviewer. Together students should generate at least five intelligent questions and research the answers. Questions might deal with Innocent's background, policies concerning both the church and secular politics, and his more notable actions as pope. Questions and answers should give the audience a well-rounded picture of Innocent III and highlight his importance in the history of the church. Have students take turns staging their interview for the class. **COOPERATIVE LEARNING**

HOMEWORK Have students select one of the following topics to study in more detail: Otto I, Pope John XII, Henry III, the Concordat of Worms, Frederick Barbarossa, or the Lombard League. Then have students write two or three paragraphs about their topics, using correct social studies terminology. Call on volunteers to share their findings with the class.

CLOSE

Lead a class discussion about the conflict between Pope Gregory VII and Henry IV. Ask students to summarize how the conflict developed and how it was resolved.

Culture

During the Inquisition, inquisitors initially allowed the accused a month's grace period to renounce their heresy. If they did, they received a light penance. After the grace period, the inquisitors put all other accused heretics on trial. The inquisitors commonly tortured the accused to elicit information. Most of the accused were found guilty. While some were burned at the stake, the most common punishments were fines, penance, imprisonment, and confiscation of property.

Critical Thinking

Ask students what might be the consequences of enforcing religious doctrine in this way.

ANSWER: Students might answer that the Inquisition could have unified medieval society by forcing people into similar behavior or beliefs. However, it stifled free thought.

THEN AND NOW ANSWER

John Paul II uses the power of persuasion to influence political affairs, while Innocent III was more directly involved.

Then & Now

The Pope

The popes of the Middle Ages had great political power. In 1075 Pope Gregory VII said that the pope had power over all Christians and could get rid of church and political leaders. Pope Innocent III was involved in many of Europe's political affairs. He even overthrew two of Germany's kings.

Over time the papacy turned its attention to making the pope the spiritual leader of all Roman Catholics. Today the pope works to create and uphold the laws, traditions, and spiritual beliefs of the church. Officially the pope has less political power, although recent popes like John Paul II have tried to influence nations and their leaders through the power of persuasion. **How did Pope Innocent III's involvement in world political affairs differ from the approach of John Paul II?**

Holt Researcher

go.hrw.com
KEYWORD: Holt Researcher
FreeFind: Innocent III
          John Paul II
After reading more about Innocent III and John Paul II on the Holt Researcher, analyze how they each influenced the eras in which they lived.

The Concordat of Worms recognized the spiritual leadership of the popes. Conflict between popes and emperors did not end in 1122, however. The German emperors continued to interfere in Italian politics and to threaten the popes' rule in the Papal States. The popes, in turn, opposed all attempts by the emperors to gain control in Italy.

Frederick Barbarossa. Frederick I, also known as **Frederick Barbarossa** (Frederick of the Red Beard), ruled Germany from 1152 to 1190. Frederick, like other emperors before him, sought to gain control of Italy.

In the northern Italian region known as Lombardy, the great trading centers of Bologna, Padua, Verona, and Milan had grown increasingly independent of imperial control. Each of these city-states had a wealthy merchant class. Frederick, seeking to strengthen his rule by gaining wealth, set out to capture the Lombard cities. Frederick sent imperial representatives to take control of the cities' governments. When Milan resisted, Frederick captured and destroyed the city and drove out the people.

The other city-states refused Frederick's demands. With the help of the pope, they united to form the Lombard League. They raised a powerful army that defeated Frederick in 1176. In the peace settlement that followed, the cities of the League recognized Frederick as overlord. In return, Frederick let the cities govern themselves. The Lombard League's success showed the growing political power of cities in medieval Europe.

Innocent III. Between 1198 and 1216, the strongest of the medieval popes—**Innocent III**—greatly strengthened the church and increased its worldly power. Innocent was a skillful political leader who, like Gregory VII before him, believed in the supreme earthly power of the papacy. To Innocent, emperors and kings were no more than servants of the church. Because of this belief Innocent felt that he had the authority to settle all political, as well as spiritual, problems. Temporal rulers and nobles could advise the pope, but they could not control him.

 History Makers Speak
❝Just as the founder of the universe [God] established two great lights in the firmament of heaven, a greater one to preside over the day and a lesser to preside over the night, so too . . . he instituted two great dignities [pope and monarch], a greater one [the pope] to preside over souls . . . and a lesser one [the monarch] to preside over bodies . . . These are the pontifical authority and the royal power.❞

Innocent III, quoted in *The Crisis of Church & State: 1050–1300*, by Brian Tierney

Fresco portrait of Pope Innocent III

REVIEW

Have students complete Section 5 Review on p. 313.

ASSESS

Have students complete Daily Quiz 13.5. As Alternative Assessment, you may want to use the graphic organizer or interview exercises in this section's lessons.

RETEACH

Have students complete Main Idea Activity for English Language Learners and Special-Needs Students 13.5. Then direct each student to write a question about the material under each heading or subheading. **ENGLISH LANGUAGE LEARNERS**

EXTEND

Have interested students conduct further research, using primary and secondary sources including biographies, on the power struggle between Henry IV and Gregory VII. Ask them to prepare and present to the class an oral report that details their findings. **BLOCK SCHEDULING**

Innocent III involved himself in disputes all over Europe. He freely used his powers of excommunication and interdiction to settle conflicts. When he quarreled with King John of England, Innocent placed the entire realm under interdict. To have the interdict lifted, John was forced to become the pope's vassal and to pay an annual tithe to Rome. Innocent also used the interdict against the king of France, Philip Augustus, after Philip tried to have his marriage annulled. Innocent forced Philip to take his wife back and to restore her to her place as queen of France. Innocent also dominated nearly all of Italy. In Germany he overthrew two kings and put rulers of his choice on the throne.

Innocent was able to greatly increase papal authority and prestige in medieval Europe. Conditions in Europe, as well as Innocent's personal skill, helped him to build church power. Later popes, however, lacked both Innocent's abilities and the favorable conditions that had helped him to become supreme. As a result, papal power slowly declined after Innocent's death in 1216.

The great goal of uniting Germany and Italy was never achieved. During the early 1200s Emperor Frederick II tried to bring the two regions together under imperial rule. Like earlier emperors, however, Frederick failed.

Not only did imperial attempts to unify Italy and Germany fail, but each country also remained divided into small, independent cities and feudal states. The emperor had little real control over the fragmented kingdom. Italy remained divided into three regions. Northern Italy was controlled by the Lombard cities. The Papal States held power in Italy's center, and the kingdom of Sicily controlled the south. Neither Italy nor Germany were unified until the 1800s.

✔ **READING CHECK: Comparing** How were the aims of Gregory VII and Innocent III similar? Both sought to make church power superior to temporal authority.

A bitter quarrel between Pope Innocent III and King John of England, shown hunting in this image, caused England to be placed under the Church's dreaded interdict.

SECTION 5 REVIEW ANSWERS

❶ **Identify**
- Otto I, p. 310
- Henry III, p. 311
- Henry IV, p. 311
- Pope Gregory VII, p. 311
- Frederick Barbarossa, p. 312
- Pope Innocent III, p. 312

❷ Frederick seized control of the city-states' governments; Frederick destroyed Milan; the city-states formed the Lombard League and defeated Frederick.

❸ **a.** It represented a conflict over power and authority of spiritual and temporal rulers.

b. Students may suggest that each wanted supreme power.

❹ Students' letters should use information from the chapter to support their arguments.

SECTION 5 REVIEW

1. **Identify** and explain the significance:
   Otto I
   Henry III
   Henry IV
   Pope Gregory VII
   Frederick Barbarossa
   Pope Innocent III

2. **Summarizing** Copy the graphic organizer shown below. Use it to summarize the actions and events that led to Frederick Barbarossa's defeat by the Lombard League.

3. **Finding the Main Idea**
   a. Why was the issue of lay investiture considered so important by both German emperors and popes?
   b. Why do you think emperors and popes were unable to cooperate or to build alliances that would have strengthened both?

4. **Writing and Critical Thinking**
   Supporting a Point of View Imagine yourself as a literate citizen of the Holy Roman Empire during the late 1100s. Write a letter to Frederick Barbarossa with the aim of convincing him that the powers of church and state should be separate.
   Consider:
   - the extensive powers of the Holy Roman emperors
   - how Otto's empire might have benefited from a separation of church and state
   - why both the pope and the emperor might have gained by resolving their conflict for power

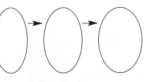

Homework Practice Online
keyword: SP3 HP13

THE RISE OF THE MIDDLE AGES **313**

REVIEW AND ASSESSMENT RESOURCES

REPRODUCIBLE RESOURCES
▶ Vocabulary Activity 13

TECHNOLOGY RESOURCES
▶ Chapter 13 Test Generator (on the One-Stop Planner)
▶ Global Skill Builder CD–ROM
▶ HRW Go Site

REINFORCEMENT, REVIEW, and ASSESSMENT
▶ Chapter 13 Review, pp. 314–315
▶ Chapter 13 Tutorial for Students, Parents, Mentors, and Peers
▶ Chapter 13 Test (Form A or B)
▶ Alternative Assessment Handbook
▶ Chapter 13 Test for English Language Learners and Special-Needs Students

REVIEW

Have students complete Chapter 13 Review on pages 314–315.

ASSESS

Use one of the chapter tests to assess students' understanding of the content. For Alternative Assessment, see the Portfolio Activities and Alternative Assessment Handbook.

CHAPTER 13 REVIEW ANSWERS

Understanding Main Ideas

1. shows the king's closeness to the church and might lead to the belief that God favors the king

2. established constitutional government, rule by law; limited power of monarchies

3. Land was inherited by the eldest son of a lord or vassal.

4. The manners of feudal lords were improved, but knights were courteous only to their own class.

5. It was organized into a hierarchy with the most powerful leader at the top.

6. He organized a monastic movement and created rules to govern monks' lives.

7. lay investiture, simony

8. 1066: Norman conquest; 1215: Magna Carta

9. through the verdicts of judges in the royal courts

10. English kings were made subject to the law.

11. He was more interested both in seizing control of Italy and building a strong kingdom in Germany.

12. Henry II tried to transfer trials of the clergy from church to royal courts. Becket refused to allow this. Henry IV insisted on the right to lay investiture, but Gregory VII disagreed.

314

Creating a Time Line

Copy the time line below onto a sheet of paper. Complete the time line by filling in the events, individuals, and dates from the chapter you think were significant. Pick three events and explain why you think they were significant.

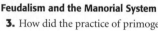

| 455 | 768 | 1066 | 1215 |

Writing a Summary

Using standard grammar, spelling, sentence structure, and punctuation, write an overview of the events in the chapter.

Identifying People and Ideas

Identify the following terms or individuals and explain their significance:

1. Middle Ages
2. Charlemagne
3. feudalism
4. primogeniture
5. manorialism
6. Saint Benedict
7. Inquisition
8. Thomas Becket
9. Magna Carta
10. Eleanor of Aquitaine

Understanding Main Ideas

SECTION 1 (pp. 288–293)
The Rise of the Franks
1. Why would the pope's blessing strengthen a king's rule?
2. How did Magna Carta and the type of government that it fostered affect events in Europe?

SECTION 2 (pp. 294–299)
Feudalism and the Manorial System
3. How did the practice of primogeniture exclude women or peasants from controlling land?
4. How were feudal lords and peasants affected by the principles of chivalry?

SECTION 3 (pp. 300–303)
The Church
5. How was the church's organization similar to that of a centralized government?
6. What overall effect did Benedict have on the development of monasticism?
7. What were some of the problems the church faced in the Middle Ages?

SECTION 4 (pp. 304–309)
The Struggle for Power in England and France
8. Why are the years 1066 and 1215 significant to English history?
9. Describe how common law developed in England.
10. How did royal power in France and England differ?

SECTION 5 (pp. 310–313)
The Clash over Germany and Italy
11. Why was Otto's rule different than the Capetians' in France?
12. Contrast the conflicts between Henry II and Thomas Becket and Henry IV and Pope Gregory VII.

Reviewing Themes

1. **Government** How could religious leaders and kings have avoided many wars in the Middle Ages?
2. **Constitutional Heritage** How did Magna Carta and the type of government it fostered affect events in Europe?
3. **Economics** When would working the land for the lord of a manor not have provided a living for a peasant?

Thinking Critically

1. **Drawing Inferences** Why was it so important for kings, emperors, the church, and nobles to possess land?
2. **Analyzing Information** Why did the Concordat of Worms not end the struggles between popes and emperors?
3. **Identifying Cause and Effect** How did church officials, such as bishops, become involved in feudalism?

Writing About History

Comparing Write a report comparing the life of a present-day teenager to that of a squire or a young noblewoman in service to a higher-ranking noblewoman. Use the chart below to help you organize your thoughts.

	Squire or young noblewoman	Present-day teenager
Food		
Clothes		
Education		
Duties		
Chances for movement in society		

Ask students how the church became part of the feudal system in Europe. Then have them explain in what ways the church was independent of the feudal system.

RETEACH

Pair students who had difficulty with the test. Have pairs compile a chapter list of important places, people, and concepts.

Have students take the Form B Test to assess their mastery of the material.

ENGLISH LANGUAGE LEARNERS, COOPERATIVE LEARNING

Portfolio Extensions

1. Have students conduct research on agricultural economies in Europe today. Have them find out about major crops and modern technology. Have them compare current methods and products with those in medieval Europe. Then ask them to create graphs, charts, maps, or other visuals to illustrate their findings.

2. Have students use computer software to find information about Alfred the Great and present the information in the form of a time line.

3. Have students further research medieval manors and construct a scale model of a typical manor, labeling all structures and areas on their model.

Building Social Studies Skills

Interpreting Maps

Study the map below. Then use the information on the map to answer the questions that follow.

The Vikings in Britain, 700s–1100s

1. Based on the map, which of the following statements best describes how geographic factors influenced Viking settlement in England and Ireland?
   a. Britain is an island.
   b. The Vikings were in search of croplands.
   c. The Vikings settled along rivers and coastal areas.
   d. Open land for settlement was plentiful in Britain.

2. How successful do you think the Vikings were at expanding their settlements in England and Ireland? Explain your answer.

Decision Making

Read the quote below about London in the 1200s. Then answer the questions that follow.

> "In the thirteenth century, London succeeded in piping water from springs at Tyburn to a fountain in West Cheap, but there was neither pressure nor abundant quantity of water. The authorities intended the fountain to provide drinking water for the poor, and household water for the neighborhood. . . . but the chief sources of water . . . remained the wells, streams, . . . and the River Thames—the ultimate destination of most of London's garbage and sewage."

3. Which of the following statements best expresses what you think about an issue described in the quote?
   a. Piping water to a fountain was not a good idea because people would have fought over the water.
   b. The poor people in London did not have enough water and the authorities should have drilled wells for them.
   c. Dumping garbage and sewage into the Thames polluted it and the water would have been harmful to drink.
   d. The authorities should not have piped water from Tyburn because that left the people of Tyburn without water.

4. Why did you choose the statement you did in question 3? Use a decision-making process to explain your answer.

Alternative Assessment

Building Your Portfolio

Economics

The economies of modern, industrialized nations differ greatly from those of medieval societies. Research ways in which the high-technology economy of the United States functions differently than the agricultural economies of medieval Europe. Use a decision-making process to decide if you would rather live in the United States today or in medieval Europe. Write a summary of the steps you took to reach your decision.

---

internet connect

Internet Activity: go.hrw.com
KEYWORD: SP3 WH13

Choose a topic on the Rise of the Middle Ages to:
- evaluate primary and secondary sources about Charlemagne.
- create a poster on medieval art and architecture.
- write a report on daily life in the Middle Ages.

Reviewing Themes

1. by agreeing to separate matters of church and state

2. King John demanded that the nobles pay more taxes. The threat of an armed uprising forced the king to sign Magna Carta.

3. if the lord demanded all the crops that the peasant produced

Thinking Critically

1. Land ownership created power and authority.

2. The emperors continued to threaten the popes' rule. The popes firmly opposed emperors' attempts to seize power in Italy.

3. The church granted some of its lands as fiefs. Bishops served as feudal lords and vassals.

Writing About History

Reports should compare the food, clothes, education, duties, and social mobility of each.

Building Social Studies Skills

1. c

2. Viking settlements were scattered throughout England and Ireland, but many areas had few Viking settlements.

3. Answers will vary.

4. Students should support their answers.

Building Your Portfolio

Summaries might include the importance of land ownership and education.

The High Middle Ages

CHAPTER RESOURCE MANAGER

Objectives	Pacing Guide	Reproducible Resources
SECTION 1 **The Crusades** (pp. 318–322) • Identify the main causes of the Crusades. • Describe the outcome of the First Crusade. • Describe the outcomes of the other major crusades. • Explain how the Crusades affected Europe.	**Regular** 1.5 day / **Block Scheduling** 1 day *Block Scheduling Handbook with Team Teaching Strategies, 14.1*	**RS** Guided Reading Strategy 14.1 **PS** Readings in World History 41: Salasin's Courage and Steadfastness **E** Hands-on Activity 14: The Crusaders
SECTION 2 **The Revival of Trade** (pp. 323–326) • Explain factors that led to the revival of trade in Europe. • Describe goods traded in Europe and explain why fairs began. • Identify important business developments that resulted from the growth of trade.	**Regular** 1.5 day / **Block Scheduling** 1 day *Block Scheduling Handbook with Team Teaching Strategies, 14.2*	**RS** Guided Reading Strategy 14.2
SECTION 3 **The Growth of Towns** (pp. 327–330) • Identify rights townspeople gained during the late Middle Ages. • Explain how merchant and craft guilds contributed to their communities. • Describe how the growth of cities helped lead to the decline of serfdom.	**Regular** 1.5 day / **Block Scheduling** 1 day *Block Scheduling Handbook with Team Teaching Strategies, 14.3*	**RS** Guided Reading Strategy 14.3 **RS** Graphic Organizer Activity 13: The Growth of Towns **SM** Geography Activity 14
SECTION 4 **Life and Culture in the Middle Ages** (pp. 331–335) • Analyze changes in language and literature during the Middle Ages. • Examine changes in education during the Middle Ages. • Identify developments made in philosophy and science. • Describe the characteristic architecture of the later Middle Ages.	**Regular** 1.5 day / **Block Scheduling** 1 day *Block Scheduling Handbook with Team Teaching Strategies, 14.4*	**RS** Guided Reading Strategy 14.4 **E** Creative Teaching Strategy 14: Power and the Pope
SECTION 5 **Wars and the Growth of Nations** (pp. 336–340) • Identify how the Hundred Years' War affected England and France. • Analyze how Spain's rulers both strengthened and weakened their nation. • Explain why the Holy Roman Empire remained weak throughout the later Middle Ages.	**Regular** 1.5 day / **Block Scheduling** 1 day *Block Scheduling Handbook with Team Teaching Strategies, 14.5*	**RS** Guided Reading Strategy 14.5
SECTION 6 **Challenges to Church Power** (pp. 341–343) • Identify the factors that led to the decline of the Catholic Church in the later Middle Ages. • Describe how the Babylonian Captivity and the Great Schism affected the church. • Explain why teachers and priests challenged the church during the later Middle Ages.	**Regular** 1.5 day / **Block Scheduling** 1 day *Block Scheduling Handbook with Team Teaching Strategies, 14.6*	**RS** Guided Reading Strategy 14.6 **PS** Readings in World History 44: The Papal Court at Avignon

Chapter Resource Key

PS Primary Sources
RS Reading Support
IC Interdisciplinary Connections
E Enrichment
SM Skills Mastery

A Assessment
REV Review
ELL Reinforcement and English Language Learners
Transparencies
CD-ROM

Music
Video
Internet
Holt Presentation Maker Using Microsoft® PowerPoint®

One-Stop Planner CD-ROM

See the **One-Stop Planner** for a complete list of additional resources for students and teachers.

One-Stop Planner CD-ROM

It's easy to plan lessons, select resources, and print out materials for your students when you use the **One-Stop Planner** CD-ROM with **Test Generator.**

Technology Resources

- One-Stop Planner 14.1
- World History Teaching Transparency: Geography and History 11: Trade Routes in the Middle Ages
- Religions of the World Video Series: Islam
- Religions of the World Video Series: Christianity
- Homework Practice Online

- One-Stop Planner 14.2
- Homework Practice Online
- Online Maps, Charts, and Graphs: European Trade in the 1200s

- One-Stop Planner 14.3
- World History Teaching Transparency: Everyday Life 14: The Triumph of Death
- Homework Practice Online
- Online Graphs: Largest Cities in Africa, Asia, Europe, c. 1200

- One-Stop Planner 14.4
- Holt Researcher: World History: Geoffrey Chaucer
- World History and Cultures Video Program 11: Cathedrals and Castles
- Homework Practice Online

- One-Stop Planner 14.5
- Holt Researcher: World History: Joan of Arc
- Homework Practice Online
- Online Maps: England and France on the Eve of the Hundred Years' War; The Hundred Years' War by 1453

- One-Stop Planner 14.6
- World History Teaching Transparency: Geography and History 14: The Great Schism
- Religions of the World Video Series: Christianity
- Homework Practice Online

Reinforcement, Review, and Assessment

Daily Quiz 14.1
Main Idea Activity 14.1
English Audio Summary 14.1
Spanish Audio Summary 14.1
REV Section 1 Review, p. 322

Daily Quiz 14.2
Main Idea Activity 14.2
English Audio Summary 14.2
Spanish Audio Summary 14.2
REV Section 2 Review, p. 326

Daily Quiz 14.3
Main Idea Activity 14.3
English Audio Summary 14.3
Spanish Audio Summary 14.3
REV Section 3 Review, p. 330

Daily Quiz 14.4
Main Idea Activity 14.4
English Audio Summary 14.4
Spanish Audio Summary 14.4
REV Section 4 Review, p. 335

Daily Quiz 14.5
Main Idea Activity 14.5
English Audio Summary 14.5
Spanish Audio Summary 14.5
REV Section 5 Review, p. 340

Daily Quiz 14.6
Main Idea Activity 14.6
English Audio Summary 14.6
Spanish Audio Summary 14.6
REV Section 6 Review, p. 343

internet connect

HRW ONLINE RESOURCES
GO TO: go.hrw.com
Then type in a keyword.

TEACHER HOME PAGE
KEYWORD: SP3 Teacher

CHAPTER INTERNET ACTIVITIES
KEYWORD: SP3 WH14
Choose an activity to:
- create a propaganda poster about the Crusades.
- learn more about the monarchies of Henry VII, Louis IX, and Ferdinand and Isabella of Spain.
- explore the effects of the Black Death on Europe in the 1300s.

CHAPTER ENRICHMENT LINKS
KEYWORD: SP3 CH14

ONLINE ASSESSMENT
Homework Practice
KEYWORD: SP3 HP14
Standardized Test Prep
KEYWORD: SP3 STP14
Rubrics
KEYWORD: SS Rubrics

ONLINE MAPS, CHARTS, AND GRAPHS
KEYWORD: SP3 MCG

CONTENT UPDATES
KEYWORD: SS Content Updates

HOLT PRESENTATION MAKER
KEYWORD: SP3 PPT14

ONLINE READING SUPPORT
KEYWORD: SS Strategies

CURRENT EVENTS
KEYWORD: S3 Current Events

Meeting Individual Needs

Ability Levels

Level 1 Basic level activities designed for all students encountering new material

Level 2 Intermediate level activities designed for average students

Level 3 Challenging activities designed for honors and gifted and talented students

English Language Learners These activities address the needs of students with Limited English Proficiency.

Chapter Review and Assessment

IC Vocabulary Activity 14
    Global Skill Builder CD-ROM
    HRW Web Site
REV Chapter 14 Tutorial for Students, Parents, Mentors, and Peers
REV Chapter 14 Review, pp. 344–345
A Chapter 14 Test Generator (on the One-Stop Planner)
A Chapter 14 Test (Form A or B)
A Alternative Assessment Handbook
A Chapter 14 Test for English Language Learners and Special-Needs Students

Build on What You Know

Ask students to answer the following questions:

How did feudalism and manorialism shape civilization in the Middle Ages?

Consider:

• **the relationship between lords and peasants**

• **the relationship between kings and lords**

• **the self-sufficiency of a manor village**

How might the Christian church have influenced the politics and economy of Europe in the later Middle Ages?

Consider:

• **the church's role in education**

• **the church's power of taxation**

• **the struggles between popes and kings**

EXPLORING THE TIME LINE
GLOBAL EVENTS

◩ internet connect ▤

TOPIC: Joan of Arc
GO TO: go.hrw.com
KEYWORD: SP3 WH14

Have students access the Internet through the HRW Go site to conduct research on Joan of Arc. Students should take notes on her life, accomplishments, and significance to history. Then have them write a biography of this French heroine. Students should use standard grammar, punctuation, and sentence structure.

◆ **CHAPTER**
14

1000–1500
The High Middle Ages

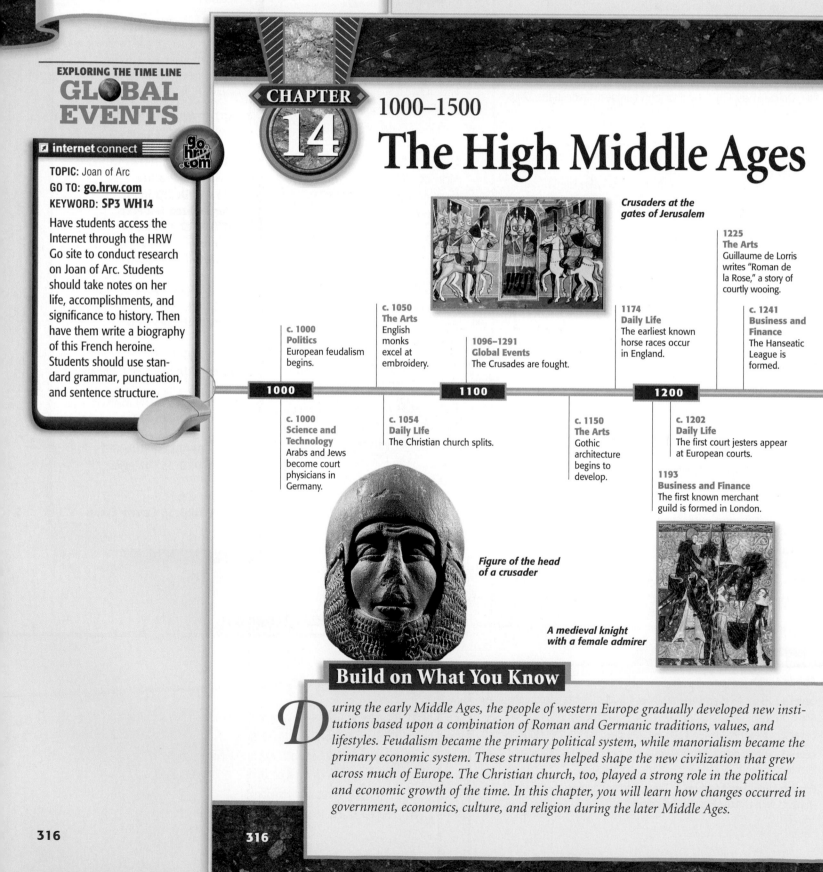

Crusaders at the gates of Jerusalem

c. 1000
Politics
European feudalism begins.

c. 1050
The Arts
English monks excel at embroidery.

1096–1291
Global Events
The Crusades are fought.

1174
Daily Life
The earliest known horse races occur in England.

1225
The Arts
Guillaume de Lorris writes "Roman de la Rose," a story of courtly wooing.

c. 1241
Business and Finance
The Hanseatic League is formed.

1000   **1100**   **1200**

c. 1000
Science and Technology
Arabs and Jews become court physicians in Germany.

c. 1054
Daily Life
The Christian church splits.

c. 1150
The Arts
Gothic architecture begins to develop.

1193
Business and Finance
The first known merchant guild is formed in London.

c. 1202
Daily Life
The first court jesters appear at European courts.

Figure of the head of a crusader

A medieval knight with a female admirer

Build on What You Know

During the early Middle Ages, the people of western Europe gradually developed new institutions based upon a combination of Roman and Germanic traditions, values, and lifestyles. Feudalism became the primary political system, while manorialism became the primary economic system. These structures helped shape the new civilization that grew across much of Europe. The Christian church, too, played a strong role in the political and economic growth of the time. In this chapter, you will learn how changes occurred in government, economics, culture, and religion during the later Middle Ages.

What's Your Opinion?

 To help students create their Themes Journal entries, provide the following examples of appropriate **agree/disagree** *statements.*

Global Relations

Agree Enemies focus on destroying one another's way of life rather than learning about it.

Disagree Learning an enemy's strengths and weaknesses is a major focus during wartime.

Economics

Agree Towns serve as centers for trade, and trade generates new businesses that help towns grow.

Disagree Self-sufficiency contributes more than trade to a town's growth, and trade depends more on itinerant merchants than on populous centers.

Government

Agree The development of a new nation requires groups to relinquish power to a central government.

Disagree The development of new nations simply legitimizes leaders who are already the most powerful.

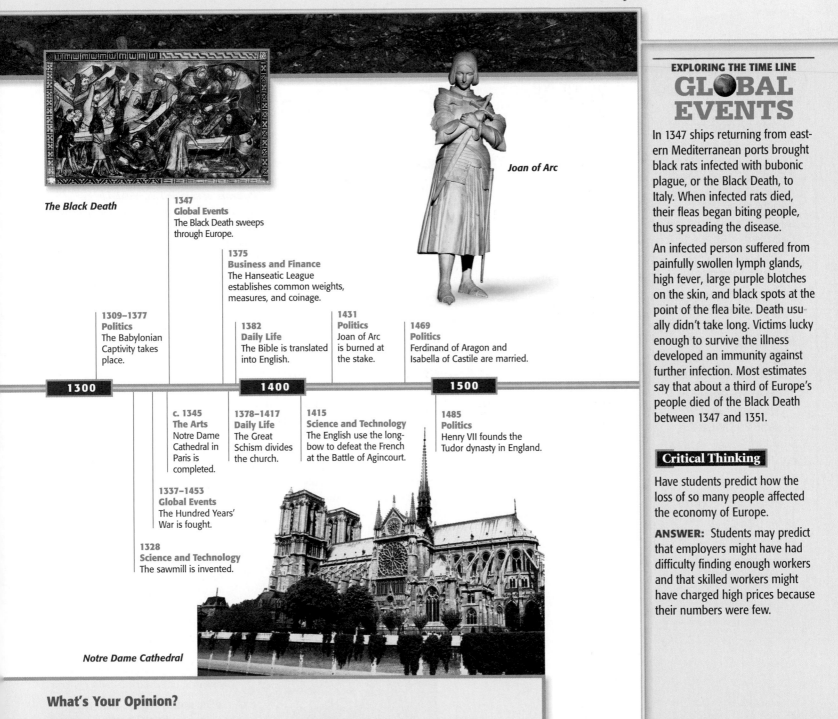

The Black Death

Joan of Arc

1347
Global Events
The Black Death sweeps through Europe.

1375
Business and Finance
The Hanseatic League establishes common weights, measures, and coinage.

1309–1377
Politics
The Babylonian Captivity takes place.

1382
Daily Life
The Bible is translated into English.

1431
Politics
Joan of Arc is burned at the stake.

1469
Politics
Ferdinand of Aragon and Isabella of Castile are married.

1300

1400

1500

c. 1345
The Arts
Notre Dame Cathedral in Paris is completed.

1378–1417
Daily Life
The Great Schism divides the church.

1415
Science and Technology
The English use the long-bow to defeat the French at the Battle of Agincourt.

1485
Politics
Henry VII founds the Tudor dynasty in England.

1337–1453
Global Events
The Hundred Years' War is fought.

1328
Science and Technology
The sawmill is invented.

Notre Dame Cathedral

EXPLORING THE TIME LINE
GLOBAL EVENTS

In 1347 ships returning from eastern Mediterranean ports brought black rats infected with bubonic plague, or the Black Death, to Italy. When infected rats died, their fleas began biting people, thus spreading the disease.

An infected person suffered from painfully swollen lymph glands, high fever, large purple blotches on the skin, and black spots at the point of the flea bite. Death usually didn't take long. Victims lucky enough to survive the illness developed an immunity against further infection. Most estimates say that about a third of Europe's people died of the Black Death between 1347 and 1351.

Critical Thinking

Have students predict how the loss of so many people affected the economy of Europe.

ANSWER: Students may predict that employers might have had difficulty finding enough workers and that skilled workers might have charged high prices because their numbers were few.

What's Your Opinion?

 Do you **agree** *or* **disagree** *with the following statements? Support your point of view in your journal.*

Global Relations Two groups of people cannot learn from each other when they are at war because of religion.

Economics The growth of trade and the growth of towns are related and dependent upon one another.

Government Shifts in the balance of political power almost always take place as new nations develop.

OBJECTIVES

1 Identify the main causes of the Crusades.

2 Describe the outcome of the First Crusade.

3 Describe the outcomes of the other major crusades.

4 Explain how the Crusades affected Europe.

SECTION 1

READ TO DISCOVER

❶ What were the main causes of the Crusades?

❷ What was the outcome of the First Crusade?

❸ What were the outcomes of the other major crusades?

❹ How did the Crusades affect Europe?

IDENTIFY

Seljuq Turks
Urban II
Crusades
Saladin
Children's Crusade

▸ WHY IT MATTERS TODAY

Conflicts continue today in the Holy Land. Use **CNNfyi.com** or other **current event** sources to find information on recent conflicts between the Israelis and the Palestinians. Record your findings in your journal.

CNNfyi.com

The Crusades

The Main Idea
European Christians tried to end Islamic rule of Palestine in a series of wars called the Crusades.

The Story Continues *To Christians, as well as to Jews and Muslims, Palestine was a holy land. Jerusalem, said one pope, was "the land which the Redeemer of mankind illuminated by his coming," the land where Jesus had lived, preached, and died. In the 600s Muslim Arabs took control of Palestine. They generally let Christians and Jews there practice their religions, travel freely, and trade. During the Middle Ages, however, this situation changed.*

Causes of the Crusades

During the late 1000s, the **Seljuq Turks,** a Muslim people from Central Asia, gained control of Palestine—known among Christians as "the Holy Land." The Turks went on to attack Asia Minor, part of the Byzantine Empire. When they threatened the capital city of Constantinople, the Byzantine emperor called on Pope **Urban II** in Rome for help. Because Christian pilgrims to Palestine reported that they had been persecuted by the Turks, the Byzantine emperor's appeal met with a warm reception.

Urban was eager to regain the Holy Land from the Turks. In 1095 he called a meeting of church leaders and feudal lords. They met in Clermont, France. Urban asked the lords to stop fighting among themselves and join in a great war to win back the Holy Land. They would "wear the cross of Christ on their right shoulder or back, and with one voice . . . cry out: 'God wills it, God wills it, God wills it!'"

Thus began the **Crusades,** a series of military expeditions to regain the Holy Land. At least 10,000 Europeans took up the cause. They sewed a cross of cloth on their clothes and were called crusaders. (The Latin word *cruciata* means "marked with a cross.")

Crusaders joined the cause for different reasons. Some went to save their souls. They believed that if they died on crusade they would go straight to heaven. Some knights hoped to gain land and wealth in Palestine and southwest Asia. Some merchants saw a chance to make money. Thus the Crusades appealed to a love of adventure and the promise of rewards, both spiritual and material.

✔ **READING CHECK: Identifying Cause and Effect** Why did Pope Urban II call for a crusade? to free the Holy Land from Seljuq control

Pope Urban II called upon the nobles of western Europe to free the Holy Land from Seljuq rule.

TEACH OBJECTIVE 1

LEVEL 1: Copy the graphic organizer on the chalk-board, omitting the italicized answers. Then work with the students to complete a chain of causes and effects that led to the First Crusade. **ENGLISH LANGUAGE LEARNERS**

HOMEWORK Have students make a chart with two columns entitled *Upside* and *Downside*. Then have them categorize what they consider the positive and negative aspects of the Crusades in the appropriate columns.

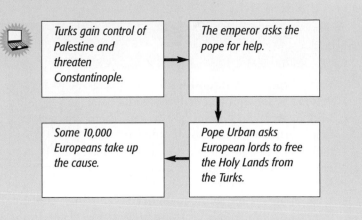

Turks gain control of Palestine and threaten Constantinople. → The emperor asks the pope for help.

Some 10,000 Europeans take up the cause. ← Pope Urban asks European lords to free the Holy Lands from the Turks.

The First Crusade

The First Crusade lasted from 1096 to 1099. French and Italian lords led several armies of crusaders from Europe to Constantinople. The Byzantine emperor, glad for help from the West against the Turks, was nonetheless suspicious of the crusaders. Seeing the crusader armies approach his city, the emperor feared they might capture and plunder the capital. After much discussion the emperor allowed the crusaders to pass through Constantinople.

Across Asia Minor the crusaders continued their long, hot march toward Palestine. In their wool and leather garments and heavy armor, the armies suffered severely from the heat. They lacked enough food and water because they had few pack animals to carry supplies. Despite such difficulties, the crusaders forged on to capture the city of Antioch.

The crusaders then marched down the coast toward Palestine and their main target—the holy city of Jerusalem. Fleets of ships from Italy brought supplies. The Turks, quarreling among themselves, were disunited and therefore unable to prevent the crusaders from surrounding the city. After a series of vicious battles, the crusaders captured Jerusalem. In a terrible massacre, they slaughtered its Muslim and Jewish inhabitants.

What If? The Byzantine emperor called for help from the pope in Rome to control the Turks in the Holy Land. **How might the history of European trade have been different if the Byzantine Christians had gained control of the Holy Land from the Turks and had not needed western Europeans' help?**

🖥 **internet connect** go.hrw.com

TOPIC: Crusades
GO TO: go.hrw.com
KEYWORD: SP3 WH14

Have students access the Internet through the HRW Go site to find information on the genesis of the Crusades and the rationalizations that Europeans posed at the time for undertaking the Crusades. After researching students should draw their own opinions on whether or not Europeans were justified in their actions. Then have students create propaganda posters that could have been used during the Middle Ages to persuade people to their opinion.

WHAT IF? ANSWER
Students' answers might include that Europeans would have taken longer to forge national identities because fellow countrymen would not have fought side by side in the Crusades.

MAP ANSWERS
1. Constantinople
2. the Third Crusade

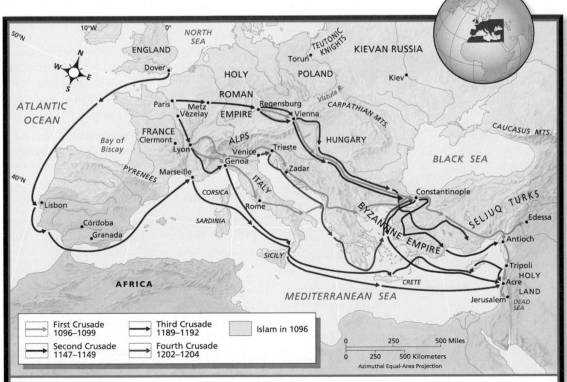

The Major Crusades, 1096–1204

Interpreting Maps The crusaders set out from many European cities to free the Holy Land from the Turks.

■ **Skills Assessment: 1. Places and Regions** Near what city did the routes of the four crusades cross? **2. Comparing** Which crusade brought armies from the farthest distance to the Holy Land?

Teacher to Teacher

Scott Whitlow of Round Rock, Texas, suggested the following activity: Introduce the Middle Ages to students by having them brainstorm images they usually think of when they hear the term *Middle Ages*. Refer to this list as you go through the main ideas and Read to Discover questions in the chapter. Point out how these images relate to the main historical themes students should learn. You might also have students speculate why the era is called the Middle Ages.

TEACH OBJECTIVE 2

ALL LEVELS: Have students work in pairs to create a chart of the political, economic, and cultural effects of the First Crusade. (*political: Europeans control Holy Land, European institutions spread, crusaders set up small states; economic: feudalism spread, trade between Europe and the Holy Land, Italian shipping business grew; cultural: Europeans wore Eastern clothes and ate Eastern foods, Christians grew to respect Muslims*)
ENGLISH LANGUAGE LEARNERS, COOPERATIVE LEARNING

That's Interesting!

In the crusader states, a new type of knight developed—the monk-knight. The most famous of these orders were the Templars and the Hospitallers. The Hospitallers were founded to care for sick pilgrims in Jerusalem and the Templars to protect Christian pilgrims traveling to the Holy Land.

Both of these religious groups, however, developed into fighting forces dedicated to the defense of Christendom. They also grew wealthy from bequests, and the monk-knights lived in a world of plenty with the best horses, armor, and weapons.

Analyzing Primary Sources

Identifying Bias How might a crusader's description of the attack and capture of Jerusalem differ from those of the Muslim writers Ibn al-Athīr and Ibn al-Qalanisi? might emphasize that Jerusalem was restored to Christian control, avoid description of the inhabitants' slaughter

The Arab historians Ibn al-Athīr and Ibn al-Qalanisi described the crusaders' actions after their conquest of Jerusalem. According to them,

 History Makers Speak
❝The population was put to the sword by the Franks [crusaders], who pillaged for a week. . . . the Franks slaughtered more than 70,000 people, among them a large number of Imams and Muslim scholars who had left their homelands to live in the pious seclusion of the Holy Place.❞

Ibn al-Athīr, quoted in Michael Foss, *People of the First Crusade*

❝The Jews [who lived in Jerusalem and who had been trapped by the crusaders' siege of the city] had gathered in their synagogue and the Franks burnt them alive. They also destroyed monuments of saints and the tomb of Abraham, may peace be upon him.❞

Ibn al-Qalanisi, quoted in Michael Foss, *People of the First Crusade*

The crusaders' capture of Jerusalem brought much of the Holy Land under European control. As a result, European customs and institutions were put into place in parts of southwest Asia and the Holy Land. The crusaders set up four small states. They introduced the idea of European feudalism and subdivided the land into fiefs, with lords and vassals. Trade between Europe and the Holy Land sprang up. Italian ships carried most of the trade goods.

Changes happened to the European occupiers during this time as well. The Christians and Muslims lived alongside each other and grew to respect each other. Many Europeans adopted Eastern customs and began to wear Eastern clothes and eat Eastern foods.

✔ **READING CHECK: Analyzing Information** What did the crusaders achieve as a result of the First Crusade? brought much of the Holy Land under European control

Other Major Crusades

For almost 100 years, European Christians held onto Palestine. Little by little, however, the Turks won back their lost lands. Popes and European rulers tried to stop them during three more major crusades.

The crusaders attack Jerusalem.

The Second Crusade. By 1146 the Turks had united their forces. They started taking back cities that the crusaders had captured. In 1147 the Second Crusade began. King Louis VII of France and German king Conrad III led separate armies across Europe. At the city of Damascus, the two armies joined forces. The combined forces failed to recapture the city, however. The Turks held. In 1149 the crusaders returned to Europe in disgrace.

The Third Crusade. In 1187 the Muslim leader **Saladin** gained control of Jerusalem. Three European rulers—Holy Roman Emperor Frederick Barbarossa, King Philip II of France, and King Richard I of England—then led separate armies in the Third Crusade. The crusade lasted from 1189 to 1192. It, too, failed. When Barbarossa drowned on the way to the Holy Land, his army turned back. Philip and Richard quarreled, and Philip

TEACH OBJECTIVE 3

LEVEL 2: Have students write five false statements about the outcomes of the other major crusades on a sheet of paper. Ask them to skip spaces between each statement. Then tell students to exchange papers with a partner and correct the partner's false statements in the spaces provided. **COOPERATIVE LEARNING**

TEACH OBJECTIVE 4

LEVEL 3: Ask students to imagine a reunion of elderly crusaders. Then have them write speeches that the attendees might give about their lives since the Crusades. Tell students to use information under "Results of the Crusades."

CLOSE

Ask students to write a short paragraph in which they make predictions about which changes brought about by the Crusades were most important to Europe's development. Have students share their predictions with the class.

took his army back home to seize English lands in France. Richard and the forces under his command remained in the Holy Land, but they could not recapture Jerusalem. Richard settled for a truce with Saladin. Through the truce, the crusaders received control of some towns along the Palestinian coast. The truce also allowed Christians to enter Jerusalem freely.

The Fourth Crusade. Pope Innocent III gathered a group of French knights for the Fourth Crusade. In 1202 they left on ships provided by the Italian city-state of Venice. The Venetians persuaded the crusaders to attack Zadar—a trade rival to Venice—as they moved down the Adriatic coast. Because Zadar was a Christian city, however, the crusaders who attacked it were later excommunicated by Innocent III.

Then in 1204, the crusaders attacked and looted Constantinople, another Christian city. They stole many things that were holy to the Byzantine Christians. The Venetians gained control of Byzantine trade. Constantinople remained under western European control for about 60 years. The Byzantines eventually regained the city, but they never regained their strength. The once-mighty empire collapsed when the Turks seized Constantinople in 1453.

Other crusades. In 1212 the short-lived and unfortunate **Children's Crusade** took place. Young people from across Europe decided to march to the Holy Land and regain it for Christian Europe. The young crusaders lacked adequate training, equipment, and supplies. By the time they reached the Mediterranean coast, the army of children was little more than a hungry and disorganized mob. The pope sent some of them back home. Others reached southern France, where they were tricked into boarding ships that carried them off into slavery instead of to the Holy Land. Several thousand children, most from Germany and France, were lost in the course of this tragedy.

For many years, European crusaders tried to recapture the Holy Land. The Crusades continued until 1291, when the Muslims captured the city of Acre (AH·kruh). Acre was the last Christian stronghold in the Holy Land and, with its fall, the Crusades ended.

✔ **READING CHECK: Supporting a Point of View** What evidence would you give to show that from 1147 the Crusades were a failure? Crusades in 1147 and after failed to regain European control of the Holy Land

Results of the Crusades

The goal of the Crusades was to take the Holy Land from the Turks. All the Crusades except the first failed to reach that goal. By the end of the Crusades, the Muslims again controlled Palestine. In Europe, however, the Crusades helped bring about many changes.

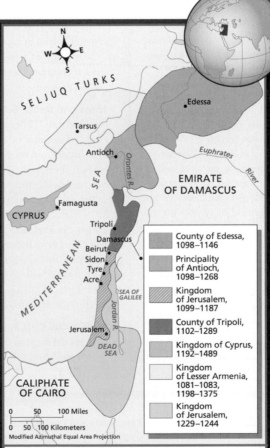

Crusader States from 1098

Interpreting Maps During and after the First Crusade, crusaders set up small states in the Middle East.

■ **Skills Assessment: 1. Places and Regions** Name the four states set up by crusaders between 1098 and 1102. How long did each state stay under the crusaders' control?
2. Drawing Conclusions Compare this map with the map on page 319. Why might it have been difficult for the crusaders to maintain control of these states?

Map legend:
- County of Edessa, 1098–1146
- Principality of Antioch, 1098–1268
- Kingdom of Jerusalem, 1099–1187
- County of Tripoli, 1102–1289
- Kingdom of Cyprus, 1192–1489
- Kingdom of Lesser Armenia, 1081–1083, 1198–1375
- Kingdom of Jerusalem, 1229–1244

Interdisciplinary Connection

LITERATURE. Since the 1800s the medieval folk hero Robin Hood has been linked with Richard the Lion-Hearted.

However, in the original tales from the 1300s, Robin treats women and the poor kindly but rebels against all authority. These early versions make no mention of Richard and were probably set in the England of the late 1300s, long after the Crusades were over.

Critical Thinking

Ask students to give reasons why the story of Robin Hood changed over the years.

ANSWER: A possible response is that different generations reshaped the story to fit their idea of heroic.

Technology Resources

World History Teaching Transparency: Geography and History 11: Trade Routes in the Middle Ages

CONNECTING TO GEOGRAPHY

The World of Arab Geographers

In Chapter 11 you read how Europeans learned about the geographical achievements of the Muslims. Arab geographers had published the world's first climatic atlas in the 900s. One Arab geographer, al-Muqaddasī, wrote a geographic encyclopedia in which he discussed not only physical systems such as climate and land but also human systems such as religion, society, commerce, and agriculture.

During the 1100s the great geographer al-Idrīsī completed his *Amusement for Him Who Desires to Travel Around the World.* He is also credited with creating the world's first globe.

Understanding Geography

What effect might such new geographical knowledge have had on Europeans?

Weapons and warfare. During the Crusades, the weapon of choice for many European soldiers was the crossbow. This weapon was a powerful bow that was held horizontally. It fired a short, heavy arrow called a bolt with the pull of a trigger. The crossbow required far less skill to use than did the traditional bow. Yet it was a deadly weapon that was capable of penetrating chain mail and plate armor. From the Byzantines and Muslims, Europeans also discovered new ways to wage war. For example, they learned how to undermine walls and use catapults to throw rocks. From the Muslims, they may have learned about gunpowder.

Political changes. To raise money to go on crusade, some lords had sold their land. Without land, they had no power in the feudal system. Many nobles also died fighting in the Crusades. With fewer lords, the power of European kings grew stronger. The kings placed new taxes and led armies drawn from their entire country. All these changes helped bring an end to feudalism.

During the Crusades, the Christian church became more powerful also. As organizers of crusades, the popes took on more importance. This was particularly true after the First Crusade.

Ideas and trade. Between 1096 and 1291, thousands of crusaders traveled through the Holy Land. They exchanged ideas with crusaders from other parts of Europe. They also gained knowledge from the Byzantines and Muslims whom they met. When the crusaders returned home, these new ideas helped to enrich European culture.

Changes in trade also took place. Italian cities became major trading centers. Ships from Italian cities carried crusaders to the Holy Land. The ships came back loaded with foods from southwest Asia. Europeans began buying such goods as apricots, lemons, melons, rice, and sugar.

✔ **READING CHECK: Summarizing** In what ways did the Crusades change Europe? new methods and weapons of war; strengthened monarchies; new ideas and trade patterns

Map drawn by Arab geographer al-Idrīsī

SECTION 1 REVIEW

1. **Identify** and explain the significance:
   Seljuq Turks
   Urban II
   Crusades
   Saladin
   Children's Crusade

2. **Comparing and Contrasting** Copy the web diagram below. Use it to compare and contrast the outcomes of the first four Crusades.

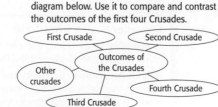

First Crusade — Second Crusade — Outcomes of the Crusades — Other crusades — Fourth Crusade — Third Crusade

3. **Finding the Main Idea**
   a. What issues led to the Crusades?
   b. What long-term importance did the Crusades have for Europe?

4. **Writing and Critical Thinking**
   Identifying Cause and Effect Imagine you are a soldier during the Crusades. Write a field report identifying how new technology is changing the way you fight.
   Consider:
   - new forms of technology used by Muslims and Europeans during the Crusades
   - how this technology affected warfare

Homework Practice Online
keyword: SP3 HP14

OBJECTIVES

1 Explain factors that led to the revival of trade in Europe.

2 Describe goods traded in Europe and explain why fairs began.

3 Identify important business developments that resulted from the growth of trade.

LET'S GET STARTED!

As students enter the classroom, have them study the picture of the annual fair at Lendit on page 325. Ask them to find the similarities between the fair and a modern department store. (*A variety of goods are sold, the sellers advertise their wares—with flags at the fair and signs at the stores.*) Tell students that in Section 2 they will learn more about shopping in the High Middle Ages.

SECTION 2

READ TO DISCOVER

❶ What factors led to the revival of trade in Europe?

❷ What kinds of goods were traded, and why did fairs begin?

❸ What important business developments resulted from the growth of trade?

DEFINE

barter economy
domestic system
usury
capital
market economy

WHY IT MATTERS TODAY

Many nations have entered trade agreements with rules about prices and taxes, somewhat like the Hanseatic League. Use **CNNfyi.com** or other **current event** sources to find examples of trade agreements among nations today. Record your findings in your journal.

CNNfyi.com

The Revival of Trade

The Main Idea
The Crusades spurred a revival of trade and led to economic growth throughout western Europe.

The Story Continues *It is fair day in a medieval town. Merchants from throughout Europe and even Asia and Africa hoist colorful tents and stalls and display their wares: spices from the East, silk from China, woolens from Flanders, cheese, leather goods, jewelry. Entertainers arrive as well—jugglers, acrobats, and musicians. Such a fair would not have been found 200 years earlier. After the Crusades, however, a fair was held somewhere on almost any given day of the year.*

Trade Routes

After the collapse of the Roman Empire in the 400s, trade almost died out in western Europe. With the rise of the Middle Ages, manors grew or made nearly everything they needed. Towns and cities, which depended on trade and manufacturing, shrank in population.

Because of the Crusades, trade began to grow again in Europe. Italy was the earliest site of this trade revival. Towns and trade had declined less there. Lying between northern Europe and southwest Asia, Italy's location also favored trade.

Trade in Italy. Northern Europeans wanted Asian goods, and those goods could be bought in southwest Asia. The Italian city-states of Genoa, Pisa, and Venice became important trading centers, acting as go-betweens for traders from Asia and northern Europe. The Crusades increased this trade. Ships from Italian city-states carried crusaders to Palestine. On their return trips, they brought back goods from Asia. These goods then traveled overland from Italy into central and northern Europe. This overland trade route led to the growth and increasing wealth of cities along its path.

Trade in northern Europe. Trade also began to grow again in northern Europe. Kiev, in what is now Ukraine, became a trading center. Before the year 1000, Viking traders from Kiev traveled to Constantinople. There they collected goods from Asia to bring back to cities in northern Europe.

Flanders became another important northern trading center. Now a part of Belgium, France, and the Netherlands, Flanders in the 1100s was the meeting point of several trade routes. Many traders came to Flanders from England, France, Germany, or countries along the Baltic Sea. They were eager to buy the fine woolen cloth made there. Flemish cities such as Bruges and Ghent grew in population and wealth.

The Hanseatic League. German cities on the Baltic and North Seas also became important trading centers. The most important were Bremen, Hamburg, and Lübeck. Germany's weak central government could not control trade. For that reason, the German trading cities joined together to form the Hanseatic League. In time, about 100 cities were members of the league. They set up trading posts in England, Flanders, Russia, and Scandinavia. During the 1300s and 1400s, the Hanseatic League increased trade in northwestern Europe.

SECTION 2 RESOURCES

REPRODUCIBLE RESOURCES
▸ Guided Reading Strategy 14.2

TECHNOLOGY RESOURCES
▸ One-Stop Planner 14.2
▸ Homework Practice Online
▸ Online Maps, Charts, and Graphs: European Trade in the 1200s

REINFORCEMENT, REVIEW, AND ASSESSMENT
▸ Section 2 Review, p. 326
▸ Daily Quiz 14.2
▸ Main Idea Activity 14.2
▸ English Audio Summary 14.2
▸ Spanish Audio Summary 14.2

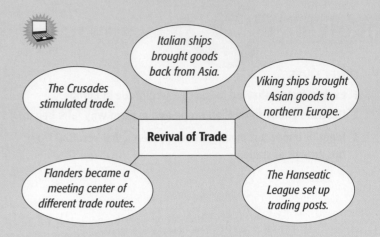

LEVEL 1: On the chalkboard, draw the web to the right, omitting the italicized words. Tell students to fill the ovals with reasons for the revival of trade in Europe.

ENGLISH LANGUAGE LEARNERS

Italian ships brought goods back from Asia.

The Crusades stimulated trade.

Viking ships brought Asian goods to northern Europe.

Revival of Trade

Flanders became a meeting center of different trade routes.

The Hanseatic League set up trading posts.

MAP ANSWERS

1. Italian city-states

2. The Hanseatic League controlled trading in those areas.

Culture

A noble household in the Middle Ages spent more than one-tenth its total income on clothing. Luxurious fabrics, such as some imported silk, signified the wearer's wealth and high rank.

Camlet was an especially magnificent fabric of silk and wool probably imported from the Middle East and was closely associated with nobility. In fact, the court of the legendary King Arthur was called Camelot, a name derived from camlet.

Critical Thinking

Ask students whether clothing is still a good indicator of wealth.

ANSWER: Students may think clothing is a good indicator of wealth because only wealthy people can afford high-quality fabrics. Or, they may think that clothing is no longer a good indicator of wealth because mass-produced clothing offers similar-looking styles and fabrics at a wide range of prices.

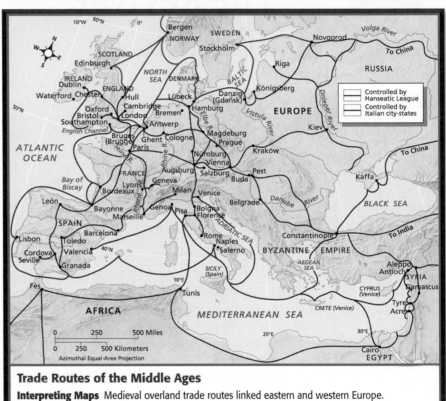

Trade Routes of the Middle Ages

Interpreting Maps Medieval overland trade routes linked eastern and western Europe.

■ **Skills Assessment: 1. Human Systems** Who controlled most of the trade routes in Europe?

2. Evaluating Why did they not control trade in the North Sea and Baltic Sea?

The rules of the Hanseatic League were strict. Any member city that did not follow the league's rules lost its trading rights. Sometimes a country's ruler took away the rights of a Hanseatic trader. When that happened, the league stopped shipping goods to that country. This placed great pressure on the ruler to restore the trader's rights. League members also waged wars to win back trading rights.

✔ **READING CHECK: Making Generalizations** How did the geographic locations of Italy, Kiev, and Flanders and the power of the Hanseatic League revive trade in Europe? locations along major sea and overland trade routes promoted trade and manufacturing

Trade Goods and Markets

The Crusades had increased Europeans' demand for goods from Asia, especially those goods considered "exotic" or new. European merchants in the Middle Ages made their highest profits trading in luxury goods, including dyes, medicines, silks, and spices. Europeans also wanted manufactured goods such as cotton cloth, linen, and art objects. Moreover, Asia supplied Europe with fruit, grain, and rugs. In exchange Europe offered its own goods and products. Baltic countries traded fish, fur, and timber. Leather, oil, and soap came from Spain, and France produced wine. Venice exported glassware, and England and Flanders traded fine woolen cloth.

TEACH OBJECTIVE 2

ALL LEVELS: Organize the class into groups of four. Assign each group the role of either medieval merchants or rulers. Have the merchants plan how to attract more buyers for their goods. Have the rulers plan how to profit from the increased trade in their kingdoms. Have each group present its plan to the class.
ENGLISH LANGUAGE LEARNERS, COOPERATIVE LEARNING

TEACH OBJECTIVE 3

LEVEL 3: Give students this analogy: Homes were to manufacturing in the Middle Ages as factories are to manufacturing today. Have pairs of students use the example as a model to create ten

analogies that compare manufacturing, banking, and investing in the Middle Ages to today. **COOPERATIVE LEARNING**

 HOMEWORK Have students use information in the section to create a chart comparing the characteristics of a barter economy with those of a market economy.

As trade grew, merchants needed places where they could exchange goods. Many villages held weekly market days. These local markets, however, did not attract large crowds. Then some merchants started selling goods during church festivals. Some local rulers also allowed fairs for the sale of imported goods. They placed a tax on each item that was sold. In return for the taxes, local rulers arranged special services for merchants. Armed guards protected merchants from robbery. They also kept the fairgrounds safe for everyone.

The most important and best-known fairs were held in Champagne. This section of northeastern France was on the trade route from Italy. At different times each year, four towns in Champagne held six fairs. Each fair lasted 49 days.

At first, business at fairs was done through a simple **barter economy.** Goods and services were exchanged for other goods and services without using money. As the fairs grew larger, a fixed value was placed on goods. This value could be in terms of goods, services, or money. However, local rulers each issued their own coins. Money changers placed a value on currencies from one region in relation to currencies from another region. Based on their value, money changers then exchanged coins from one region for coins of another. Little money ever changed hands at fairs. Buyers and sellers, however, started thinking of the value of a good in terms of money.

Although the major purpose of fairs was the buying and selling of goods, they became important social events as well. Fairs provided entertainment with clowns, jugglers, and musicians. People traveled from great distances to attend the large fairs. They met other travelers and shared news and ideas. In that way, fairs helped people broaden their outlook on the world.

✔ **READING CHECK: Finding the Main Idea** Why were fairs important during the Middle Ages? promoted economic growth and social activity and communication

Manufacturing, Banking, and Investment

The revival of trade in Europe during the Middle Ages led to three important business developments, each of which greatly affected economic life and progress down to the present day. During these years a new system of manufacturing began, a banking system developed, and the practice of investing wealth started.

Manufacturing. The system of manufacturing that developed during the Middle Ages was called the **domestic system.** Manufacturing took place in workers' homes rather than in a shop or factory. A good example of the domestic system was the woolen industry. An individual would buy wool and then hand it out to several workers. Each worker completed a different task, such as spinning, weaving, or dyeing. Then the owner of the wool collected the spun wool or finished cloth and sold it at the highest possible price. The domestic system began in towns but gradually spread to the countryside.

The annual fair at Lendit, France

CONNECTING TO
Economics

Trade Fairs of the Middle Ages

Fairs in the Middle Ages were colorful events. They were also the main method of carrying out trade. Because of the fairs, easier ways to trade developed.

For example, some goods were sold by length or weight. Because people came from all over Europe to trade fairs, a standard system of weights and measures was needed. The troy weight was set to weigh gold and silver. This weight, named for the town of Troyes, France, is still used today.

Trade fairs also helped develop the bill of exchange. This note was a written promise to pay a sum of money at a later time.

Understanding Economics

Why did new ways of carrying on trade develop from fairs?

CONNECTING TO ECONOMICS ANSWER
Standards were needed that people all over Europe would accept and use.

Economics

In the 1200s Italian traders regularly made the overland journey north to attend the international fairs at Champagne. Italian traders were thus able to sell their goods to the many inhabitants of the lands bordering the eastern part of France.

A century later, however, Italian merchants often traveled by ship instead. Ships sailed from Venice and Genoa to northern ports. This shift in travel routes made Flanders the most important location for merchants to do business.

Critical Thinking

Ask students how they think this shift in trade affected the people of Champagne.

ANSWER: Students will probably conclude that the people of Champagne suffered economically when the Italian merchants shifted their business to Flanders. Point out that regions which suffer economic setbacks often cultivate new businesses and that Champagne is now known for champagne rather than for fairs.

CLOSE

Help the class develop a flowchart that shows the chain of causes and effects that connected the revival of trade in Europe and the development of a market economy.

REVIEW

Have students complete the Section 2 Review on p. 326.

ASSESS

Have students complete Daily Quiz 14.2. As Alternative Assessment, you may want to use the revival of trade graphic organizer or the comparison activity in this section's lessons.

RETEACH

Have students complete Main Idea Activity for English Language Learners and Special-Needs Students 14.2. Then have them rewrite the section's headings as questions and answer the questions with main ideas from the section.
ENGLISH LANGUAGE LEARNERS

EXTEND

Have students use the medieval illustration on page 326 as a model to create their own illustrations of another aspect of business in the Middle Ages. **BLOCK SCHEDULING**

SECTION 2 REVIEW ANSWERS

❶ Define
• barter economy, p. 325
• domestic system, p. 325
• usury, p. 326
• capital, p. 326
• market economy, p. 326

❷ Italy: Genoa, Pisa, and Venice were go-betweens for traders from Asia and northern Europe. Northern Europe: Kiev was a city to which Vikings brought goods back from Constantinople. Bruges and Ghent were meeting points of several trade routes. Hanseatic League: Bremen, Hamburg, Lübeck, and other cities on the Baltic and North Seas joined together to control trade.

❸ a. Buyers and sellers started thinking of value in terms of money. Travelers exchanged ideas and broadened people's outlooks.

b. helped spread the domestic system of manufacturing from towns to the countryside; increased borrowing and created a demand for bills of exchange; encouraged investment in new businesses

❹ Students' advertisements will vary but should include material from the section.

Banking. Another new business system of the later Middle Ages was banking. The word *bank* comes from the old Italian word *banca*, meaning "money changer's bench." Money changers were the first bankers. Besides exchanging currencies at fairs, money changers began to provide other services. Lending money was the most important service early bankers offered. Rulers, nobles, and merchants often borrowed money to pay for their activities. During the early Middle Ages, Jews, who were not allowed to own land or join most groups for skilled workers, became the main moneylenders. The Christian church did not allow **usury** (YOO-zhuh-ree), or charging interest on loans. By the late Middle Ages, however, some Christians had also become moneylenders. Most law codes by then allowed the collection of interest on loans for business matters.

Bankers also made it easier to move money from one place to another. They developed special notes called bills of exchange. These notes were used in place of money. For example, a merchant might deposit money with a banker in Ghent in return for a bill of exchange in the amount of the deposit. The merchant could then cash the bill of exchange with a banker in Venice. This system was somewhat like present-day checking accounts.

Investing. In the later Middle Ages, Europeans began investing capital. **Capital** is wealth that is earned, saved, and invested to make profits. Sometimes, several people called investors formed a partnership. They put together their capital to pay for a new business. In that way, each partner shared in the cost. If the business made money, each partner would receive part of the profits.

Manufacturing, banking, and investing capital were the first steps toward the creation of a **market economy.** In a market economy, land, labor, and capital are controlled by individual persons. The medieval market economy formed the basis for our modern capitalist system.

This medieval illustration portrays aspects of banking and finance.

✔ **READING CHECK: Summarizing** What new business systems developed because of the revival of trade in Europe? manufacturing, banking, and investment

SECTION 2 REVIEW

1. **Define** and explain the significance:
   barter economy
   domestic system
   usury
   capital
   market economy

2. **Identifying Cause and Effect** Copy the chart below. Use it to show which cities in Italy, northern Europe, and the Hanseatic League became important trading centers and explain why each did.

Italy	Northern Europe	Hanseatic League

3. **Finding the Main Idea**

   a. What economic and social changes did fairs bring about in the Middle Ages?

   b. How did the revival of trade lead to the domestic system, a banking system, and the investing of capital?

4. **Writing and Critical Thinking**

   Analyzing Information Choose a town in Europe during the Middle Ages, and write an advertisement to attract people to its fair.
   Consider:
   • the location of the town
   • goods that will be for sale and where they are from
   • entertainment that will be provided

go. hrw .com **Homework Practice Online**
keyword: SP3 HP14

OBJECTIVES

1 **Identify** rights townspeople gained during the late Middle Ages.

2 **Explain** how merchant and craft guilds contributed to their communities.

3 **Describe** how the growth of cities helped lead to the decline of serfdom.

SECTION 3

The Growth of Towns

READ TO DISCOVER

❶ What rights did townspeople gain during the later Middle Ages?

❷ How did merchant and craft guilds contribute to their communities?

❸ How did the growth of cities help lead to the decline of serfdom?

DEFINE

merchant guild
craft guilds
apprentice
journeyman
middle class

IDENTIFY

Black Death

► WHY IT MATTERS TODAY

Today different groups of workers organize into unions for many of the same reasons that medieval workers formed craft guilds. Use **CNNfyi.com** or other **current event** sources to find information about current union activities. Record your findings in your journal.

CNNfyi.com

The Main Idea
The growth of European towns accompanied the revival of trade during the Middle Ages.

The Story Continues *As trade increased in the late 900s, European towns grew larger and new towns sprang up. In the 1300s, however, the populations of both town and countryside throughout Europe would be devastated by, as the Welsh called it, "death coming into our midst like black smoke."*

The Rights of Townspeople

Trade and cities generally grow together. As towns grew in the Middle Ages, townspeople saw that they did not fit into the manorial system. They played little part in the farming economy of villages. Instead, townspeople made their living by making and trading goods.

Manor lords, however, still controlled the towns. They would give up control only if given something in return. In some towns the people won self-government by peaceful means. In others, they resorted to violence. Some lords granted their towns charters of liberties. A charter was a written statement of the town's rights. In time, townspeople throughout Europe gained four basic rights.

1. **Freedom.** Anyone who lived in a town for a year and a day became free. This included serfs who escaped from a manor to a town.

2. **Exemption.** Townspeople won the right of being exempt, or free, from ever having to work on the manor.

3. **Town justice.** Towns had their own courts. Leading citizens tried cases that involved townspeople.

4. **Commercial privileges.** Townspeople could sell goods freely in the town market. They could also charge tolls to outsiders who wanted to trade there.

✔ **READING CHECK: Summarizing** What rights did townspeople gain? freedom, exemption from manor work, town justice, and commercial privileges

Guilds

As trade increased, towns grew larger and richer. Merchants and workers began to unite in associations called guilds.

Merchants. In each town, a **merchant guild** had the sole right to trade there. Merchants from other towns or nations could trade there only if they paid a fee. Merchant guilds also helped their members and members' families. For example, guilds looked after members who were in trouble and made loans to members. When guild members died, the guild aided the widow and children.

TEACH OBJECTIVE 1

LEVEL 1: On the chalkboard, write the four basic rights of medieval townspeople. *(freedom, exemption, town justice, and commercial privileges)* Then tell students to use the reading to explain each one. Ask students to compare these rights with those of American citizens.
ENGLISH LANGUAGE LEARNERS

TEACH OBJECTIVE 2

LEVEL 3: Have students compose letters that members of a merchant or craft guild might write to townspeople who question the worth of guilds. Tell students to explain how the existence of guilds helps the entire community. Letters should contain standard grammar, spelling, sentence structure, and punctuation. Ask volunteers to share their letter with the class.

That's Interesting!

People in the Middle Ages made no distinction between fine artists and craft workers. Master painters often went from creating portraits to painting banners or designing clothes. During the late 1300s the court painter to the Duke of Burgundy also decorated chairs and did mechanical repairs.

Citizenship

The growth of towns led to the rise of the merchant class. The degree of freedom in European towns and cities varied. The lords sought the support of towns against kings, while kings sought the support of townsmen against subjects perceived as too powerful. They gave towns charters and privileges. Wealthy merchants typically became the dominant figures of the new town life and fought for their corporate privileges.

Critical Thinking

Ask students to use a problem-solving process to evaluate the merchants' solution to the problem of control by feudal lords.

ANSWER: Students might say that merchants traded control by the lords for control by a king; or, the king profited from the merchants' prosperity and so allowed them much freedom.

This illustration from about 1480 depicts medieval craft workers at their trades: an apprentice grinding colors (bottom left), a fresco painter (top), and a chest painter (bottom right).

Workers. In time, skilled workers came together in **craft guilds.** Each guild had members from a single craft, such as shoemaking or weaving. The craft guilds set rules for wages, hours, and working conditions. They also set standards for the quality of work. The guilds looked after ill members and those who could no longer work. Perhaps most important, the craft guilds controlled the training of skilled workers.

The master workers of each guild trained boys and men who wanted to join their guild. First, a boy served as an **apprentice.** His parents paid a master worker to house, feed, clothe, and train the boy. Apprentice training could take five to nine years. Next, the young man became a **journeyman,** a skilled worker who was paid wages by a master. After some time, a journeyman could become a master himself by making a masterpiece—a piece of work worthy of a master. If masters of the journeyman's guild approved his masterpiece, the journeyman could open his own shop. He was then a guild member. Some girls also served as apprentices.

The rise of the middle class. In time, towns' guild members—merchants and master workers—became the **middle class.** They were between the class of nobles and that of peasants and unskilled workers. The middle class favored kings over nobles because kings could provide stable governments that would protect trade, business, and property. In turn, kings looked to the middle class for advice. They also gave members of the middle class jobs in government. In these ways, during the later Middle Ages the middle class started to gain power.

✔ **READING CHECK: Problem Solving** If you were a young person in the Middle Ages who wanted work, how might a guild help you? under the guild's guidance a young person could become an apprentice, a journeyman, and finally a master worker and member of the guild

Medieval Towns

In the Middle Ages, most northern and western European cities had fewer than 2,000 people. A few cities were larger. By the 1200s, for example, about 150,000 people lived in Paris. Growing commercial cities like London, Ghent, and Bruges had about 40,000 residents each.

Town life. Towns offered serfs a chance to improve their lives. Some serfs escaped to towns to gain freedom. Others were pushed off the land as farming methods changed. They moved to cities to find jobs. Serfs who stayed on the manors sold their crops in town markets. They paid the manor lord with money rather than with their labor.

In the Middle Ages, cities often stood on hilltops or lay along river bends. Such locations made cities easier to defend. Most cities had little land, so houses were built several stories high. Each story extended a little beyond the one below it. At their tops, the houses almost touched over the middle of the street, darkening the narrow roadway below. Cities also had large public buildings, including churches or cathedrals, town halls, and guild halls.

ALL LEVELS: Copy the following chart on the chalkboard, omitting the italicized words.

The Decline of Serfdom	
Serfs could leave for towns.	
Serfs could earn money by selling crops to townspeople.	
Changing agricultural methods pushed them off the land.	
The Black Death killed many people in Europe so the demand for workers increased.	

Have students list factors that contributed to the decline of serfdom in the left column. Then ask the class rank the importance of each factor and write the result in the right column.
ENGLISH LANGUAGE LEARNERS, COOPERATIVE LEARNING

HOMEWORK Tell students to make a Venn diagram showing the similarities and differences between merchant and craft guilds.

CLOSE

Have students write diary entries like those survivors of the Black Death might write about their experiences during the plague.

SKILL-BUILDING STRATEGIES
Using Maps to Analyze Historical Patterns

The Spread of the Black Death

Between 1347 and 1351, Europe and the Mediterranean world were devastated by the "Black Death"—a deadly plague. Carried from China along sea and overland trade routes, the Black Death quickly swept through Europe's population. By studying a map that illustrates the spread of the plague, we can develop conclusions regarding its effect on the civilization of the late Middle Ages.

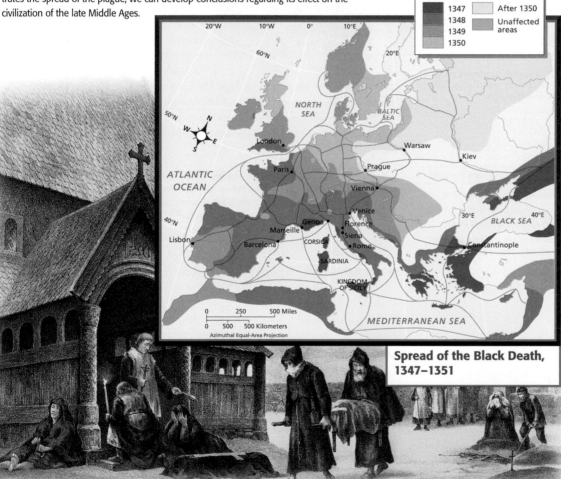

Spread of the Black Death, 1347–1351

Geography

Plagues are not a thing of the past. An outbreak of pneumonic plague—a more serious and almost always fatal form of the Black Death—hit western India in 1994, killing scores of people. Agencies such as the Centers for Disease Control track current outbreaks of such highly infectious diseases.

ACTIVITY: Have students search the library or computer software for more information on current outbreaks of infectious diseases. Then have them use the information to create maps that show the geographic distribution of plagues. Good sources of information include the World Health Organization and the Centers for Disease Control.

SKILLS PRACTICE ANSWERS

1. carried along shipping trade routes; carried on overland trade routes

2. The plague traveled west from China.

3. Ships traveled to more places than overland traders.

Skills Reminder

To use a map to analyze historical patterns, define the map's overall topic. Then identify the historical context of the map and the events or changes it is designed to illustrate. Connect the information on the map to the historical context of the subject. Analyze the change, trend, or pattern that is illustrated by the map and build a hypothesis to explain why it took place. Finally, determine how the map helps to show the change, pattern, or trend that came to represent a new historical reality.

Skills Practice

Study the map above and answer the following questions:
1. How was the plague carried from Marseille to North Africa? From Marseille to Paris?
2. Why might Paris have been stricken by the plague earlier than London but later than Constantinople?
3. Why might the plague have been slower to reach eastern Europe than it was to reach western and northern Europe?

REVIEW

Have students complete the Section 3 Review on p. 330.

ASSESS

Have students complete Daily Quiz 14.3. As Alternative Assessment, you might have students make an outline of the section or use the serfdom chart in this lesson.

RETEACH

Have students complete Main Idea Activity for English Language Learners and Special-Needs Students 14.3. Then have students

review the section by stating the main idea of each paragraph in a sentence. **ENGLISH LANGUAGE LEARNERS**

EXTEND

Have students write short skits depicting a serf's first day in a city such as Paris or London. Suggest students research first-person accounts as well as use information from the section.
BLOCK SCHEDULING

SECTION 3 REVIEW ANSWERS

❶ **Define**
- merchant guild, p. 327
- craft guilds, p. 328
- apprentice, p. 328
- journeyman, p. 328
- middle class, p. 328

❷ **Identify**
- Black Death, p. 330

❸ Apprentice: trains five to ten years; Journeyman: paid wages, creates masterpiece; Master Worker: opens own shop, joins guild

❹ **a.** Serfs and townspeople exempted from working on manors.

b. gave loans to members, aided widows and children, trained workers, cared for ill and elderly members

c. Serfs escaped to towns. Demand for workers grew as a result of the Black Death.

❺ Reports should include: rights of townspeople, opportunities for serfs, easily defended locations, dark streets, wastes in gutters, fear of robbers, and the spread of disease.

The devastating plague of 1347 through 1351 was carried by flea-infested rats.

Analyzing Primary Sources

Drawing Conclusions What effect would such circumstances have on people's beliefs and morale? weaken faith, promote insecurity, and reduce morale

The Black Death. The growing cities of the Middle Ages could be exciting places. However, many were also dark, unsafe, dirty, and unhealthy. There were no streetlights or police. People did not go out alone at night for fear of robbers. Waste was dumped into open gutters. For that reason, diseases spread quickly through the crowded cities.

Beginning in 1347, one such disease, a terrible plague called the **Black Death,** swept through Europe. The plague began in Asia and spread along busy trade routes. It entered ports by way of trading ships. Black rats on the ships carried the disease. The plague was spread to people by bites from fleas on the rats.

No one knows the exact number of plague deaths in Europe. They happened so rapidly and in such great numbers that often survivors could not keep up with burying the dead.

 History Makers Speak
❝They died by the hundreds, both day and night, and all were thrown in . . . ditches and covered with earth. And as soon as those ditches were filled, more were dug. And I buried my five children with my own hands.❞

Angolo di Tura, quoted in *The Black Death,* by Robert S. Gottfried

Some entire villages and towns were wiped out. By some estimates, about 25 million people died in Europe from 1347 to 1351—about one-third of the entire population.

The Black Death caused many changes in Europe. People's faith in God was shaken. The church lost some of its power and importance. Relations between the upper classes and lower classes changed. Workers, now in short supply, demanded higher wages. In several European countries, peasants staged uprisings.

✔ **READING CHECK: Analyzing Information** What role did towns and cities begin to play in the lives of serfs? offered serfs a chance to improve their lives

---

SECTION 3 REVIEW

1. **Define** and explain the significance:
   merchant guild
   craft guilds
   apprentice
   journeyman
   middle class

2. **Identify** and explain the significance:
   Black Death

3. **Sequencing** Copy the flowchart below. Use it to show the sequence of steps required to become a guild member.

   Apprentice → Journeyman → Master Worker

4. **Finding the Main Idea**
   a. How would the rights won by townspeople help break down manorialism?
   b. How did merchant and craft guilds help their members?
   c. How did the growth of towns and the Black Death lead to the decline of serfdom?

5. **Writing and Critical Thinking**
   Categorizing Write a short report that gives the advantages and disadvantages of living in a medieval city.
   Consider:
   - the rights of townspeople
   - health and safety factors
   - opportunities for work

 **Homework Practice Online**
keyword: SP3 HP14

OBJECTIVES

1 Analyze changes in language and literature during the Middle Ages.

2 Examine changes in education during the Middle Ages.

3 Identify developments made in philosophy and science.

4 Describe the characteristic architecture of the later Middle Ages.

🔊 *LET'S GET STARTED!*

As students enter the classroom, write these words on the chalkboard: *culture, educate, language, literature,* and *romance.* Tell students to find each word's origin in the dictionary. *(All originated with Latin words.)* Explain that Latin was the language of educated people during the early Middle Ages. Tell students that in Section 4 they will learn how spoken languages such as Middle English became part of European literature.

Life and Culture in the Middle Ages

READ TO DISCOVER

❶ How did languages and literature change during the Middle Ages?

❷ In what ways did education change?

❸ What developments were made in philosophy and science?

❹ What kind of architecture characterized the later Middle Ages?

DEFINE

vernacular languages
troubadours
scholasticism

IDENTIFY

Dante Alighieri
Geoffrey Chaucer
Peter Abelard
Thomas Aquinas
Gothic

▶WHY IT MATTERS TODAY

Styles of architecture continue to change today, just as they did during the Middle Ages. Use CNNfyi.com or other **current event** sources to find examples of recent buildings designed in new styles. Record your findings in your journal.

CNNfyi.com

The Main Idea
Much of medieval European life and culture centered on the Christian church and faith.

The Story Continues *"There was a knight, a most distinguished man, / Who from the day on which he first began / To ride abroad had followed chivalry, / Truth, honour, generousnous, and courtesy."* Early civilizations arose only after humans had settled in towns and cities. In much the same way, medieval culture—as shown in the lines of poetry above—could flourish once city life regained importance.

Language and Literature

Throughout the Middle Ages, European culture underwent many changes. Some of these changes took place in language and literature. Since the collapse of the Roman Empire, Latin had remained the written and spoken language of educated people in western Europe. However, people with little education spoke **vernacular languages.** These languages were everyday speech that varied from place to place. Present-day French, Italian, and Spanish came from early vernacular languages that were related to Latin. Present-day English and German came from other vernacular languages.

This manuscript from the 1200s shows a traveling singer performing.

SECTION 4 RESOURCES

REPRODUCIBLE RESOURCES
▶ Guided Reading Strategy 14.4
▶ Creative Teaching Strategy 14

TECHNOLOGY RESOURCES
▶ One-Stop Planner 14.4
▶ Holt Researcher: World History: Geoffrey Chaucer
▶ World History and Cultures Video Program 11
▶ Homework Practice Online

REINFORCEMENT, REVIEW, AND ASSESSMENT
▶ Section 4 Review, p. 335
▶ Daily Quiz 14.4
▶ Main Idea Activity 14.4
▶ English Audio Summary 14.4
▶ Spanish Audio Summary 14.4

THE HIGH MIDDLE AGES **331**

LEVEL 1: On the chalkboard, copy the following chart, omitting the italicized words. Help students identify the kinds of literature described in the middle column of the chart and give an example from the text.

ENGLISH LANGUAGE LEARNERS

Vernacular Literature in the Middle Ages		
Kind of Literature	**Characteristics**	**Example**
troubadour songs	**poems about love and chivalry**	*love songs*
romances	**fictional stories, sometimes of heroes**	*King Arthur and his Knights of the Round Table*
fabliaux	**short comic stories written in rhymed verse**	*"Reynard the Fox"*
national epic	**long poem about a hero**	*The Song of Roland*
miracle, morality, and mystery plays	**short dramas with religious or Biblical themes**	*"Noah's Flood"*

History Maker

DANTE ALIGHIERI. Dante first saw Beatrice when they were both nine years old. His love for her was the purely spiritual *amor amicitiae,* defined by St. Thomas Aquinas as a love in which the beloved "is loved in love of friendship . . . simply and for its own sake." Beatrice was most likely Beatrice Portinari, who wed Simone de' Bardi at age 22 and died in 1290.

Dante later married another woman but never stopped loving Beatrice. After Dante's enemies exiled him from Florence in 1302, he wrote of Beatrice as his guide through Paradise in *The Divine Comedy.*

ACTIVITY: Have students find a translation of *The Divine Comedy* at the library and look for passages about Beatrice. Ask them to note what attributes the ideal woman had in the Middle Ages.

Holt Researcher

go.hrw.com
KEYWORD: Holt Researcher
FreeFind: Geoffrey Chaucer
After reading more about Geoffrey Chaucer on the Holt Researcher, identify some of the universal themes in his works that still make them relevant today.

Analyzing Primary Sources

Identifying a Point of View How does the author of the epic poem portray Roland? heroic, heedless of pain, courageous

*Dante's **The Divine Comedy** masterpiece describes an imaginary journey in which he is guided through heaven by Beatrice, a woman he loves in a spiritual way.*

Early vernacular literature. During the Middle Ages writers began to use vernacular languages in their works. Troubadours' songs were one of the first forms of vernacular literature. **Troubadours** were traveling singers who wrote poems about love and chivalry. They sang their love poems in castles and in towns.

Romances, or fictional stories, written in vernacular were popular with medieval audiences. The best-known English romances were the adventures of King Arthur and his Knights of the Round Table.

Also popular were the French *fabliaux* (FA·blee·oh). These were short comic stories written in rhymed verse. The *fabliaux* laughed at the high ideals of chivalry, human foolishness, and the clergy. Animal stories, or fables, such as "Reynard the Fox," delighted medieval audiences too.

Another kind of vernacular literature was the national epic—a long poem about a hero. France's national epic was *The Song of Roland,* written in about 1100. The poem is set during the period of Charlemagne's wars with the Moors. It describes the death of Roland, one of Charlemagne's brave, loyal knights.

> **66Roland with pain and anguish winds
> His Olifant [horn], and blows with all his might.
> Blood from his mouth comes spurting scarlet-bright.
> He's burst the veins of his temples outright.
> From hand and horn the call goes shrilling high:
> King Carlon [Charlemagne] hears it who through the passes rides . . .
> Quoth Charles: 'I hear the horn of Roland cry!
> He'd never sound it but in the thick of fight.'99**

From The Song of Roland

Drama written in vernacular languages also developed during the Middle Ages. Miracle plays, morality plays, and mystery plays were short dramas with religious or biblical themes. At Christmas and Easter, the plays were sometimes part of church services. Later, as towns grew, they were also presented in town marketplaces. A favorite play was *Noye's Fludde,* "Noah's Flood."

The flowering of vernacular literature. During the Middle Ages vernacular literature reached its height in the works of two great medieval writers, **Dante Alighieri** and **Geoffrey Chaucer.** Dante Alighieri, commonly known simply as Dante, was born in the region of Tuscany, Italy, in 1265. He wrote his poems using the Tuscan form of Italian. People throughout Italy read Dante's works. In that way, the Tuscan dialect became Italy's written language. Today Dante is thought of by many historians and other scholars as the father of the Italian language.

Many readers consider *The Divine Comedy* to be Dante's greatest work of literature. In the course of this remarkable creative piece, Dante takes an imaginary journey through the three realms where a Christian soul might go after death. The three scenes of Dante's narrative include hell, purgatory, and heaven. The author placed his friends and supporters in heaven and his political enemies in hell. Dante used his descriptive narrative to point out the faults that he saw in Italian society.

TEACH OBJECTIVE 2

LEVEL 3: Have students write a short paper in which they describe whether or not they think a university such as those in Paris or Oxford in the 1300s would provide an education appropriate for today's students. Have them give reasons for their answers.

TEACH OBJECTIVE 3

ALL LEVELS: Write the following on the chalkboard: *Thomas Aquinas argued that science and reason were in conflict with faith.* Organize students in groups and tell the groups to decide whether they agree or disagree with Thomas Aquinas. Have each group explain its decision. **ENGLISH LANGUAGE LEARNERS, COOPERATIVE LEARNING**

HOMEWORK Have students find illustrations of two technical improvements or innovations of the Middle Ages. *(winches, pulleys, oxen plows, oxen yokes, windmills, waterwheels)* Tell them to write a paragraph explaining how these advances made life easier.

Geoffrey Chaucer's writing and imagination had a great influence on literary styles and approaches. Chaucer was born in England about 1340 and spent much of his life in service to the English crown. He fought in France and, for about 10 years, served as a diplomat throughout western Europe. He was elected to the English Parliament in 1386.

Chaucer's most famous work is *The Canterbury Tales,* a group of stories told from the point of view of about 30 pilgrims traveling to the shrine of Saint Thomas à Becket at Canterbury. Chaucer's pilgrims poke fun at English society, especially at the clergy. Many church people, Chaucer believed, had made service to the church a profitable occupation rather than a spiritual calling.

Chaucer wrote numerous works in addition to *The Canterbury Tales.* Like Dante before him, Chaucer wrote in the vernacular, in the dialect known as Middle English, a forerunner to the modern English of today. Chaucer's use of the dialect and the popularity of his works gave Middle English great literary prestige. Later writers and poets followed his example by crafting their works in the vernacular.

Pilgrims in a scene from The Canterbury Tales

✔ **READING CHECK: Summarizing** What important changes took place in language and literature in the Middle Ages? Why? The more widely spoken and written vernacular languages began to replace Latin.

Education

During the early Middle Ages, few people received an education. Those who did were mainly nobles and the clergy. Schooling was carried out at monasteries and in churches. As towns grew larger, however, other schools opened. These schools were somewhat like the schools in Athens under Plato and Aristotle. A teacher would set up a school and try to attract students. He admitted any males who wanted to study and could pay a fee.

In time, teachers and students united to form guilds to protect and gain rights for themselves. Such a guild was called a *universitas,* Latin for "association of people." Later, the word *university* came into use.

Between the late 1000s and the late 1200s, four great universities developed. The universities in Paris and at Oxford in England were best known for teaching theology, the study of religious beliefs, as well as the liberal arts—Latin, logic, rhetoric, mathematics, astronomy, and music. Students at the University of Bologna in Italy studied civil law and church law. The University at Salerno taught medicine.

A lecturer teaches at a medieval university.

By the end of the 1400s, many more universities had opened throughout Europe. By that time, all universities had the same programs. Students had to pass certain stages of study before receiving their degrees. The first degree was the bachelor of arts, which was similar to finishing an apprenticeship in a craft guild. After more studying and tests, students could receive the master of arts degree. At that point, students were admitted to the guild of teaching. Some students then went on to study law, medicine, or theology.

✔ **READING CHECK: Comparing** How were medieval universities like guilds? organized like guilds to protect and gain rights for themselves, trained people

In the 1200s the English monk Roger Bacon used detailed observation and controlled experiments to understand the natural world. He also predicted technological innovations in the future: "Machines may be made by which the largest ships, with only one man steering them, will move faster than if they were filled with rowers; wagons may be built which will move with unbelievable speed and without the aid of beasts." Have students research Roger Bacon's experiments and compare his methods to the scientific method used today.

TEACH OBJECTIVE 4

LEVEL 2: Show students exterior pictures of a Romanesque church (Pisa Cathedral) and a Gothic church (Notre Dame in Paris). Have them point out the Gothic church and list the features that identify it as Gothic architecture.

CLOSE

Have students either praise or criticize Gothic architecture in letters to the pastor of a medieval parish.

HISTORY MAKER ANSWER

wrote great work of scholasticism, became official philosopher of medieval church

Daily Life

Philosophers were not the only ones reading during the Middle Ages. Many noble households had collections of books, although the typical library was small.

The small number is understandable since ordering books was an expensive process. A new prayer book, for example, required purchasing more than 200 sheets of vellum—paper made from lambskin—and hiring a scribe at a university to copy the text. In addition to religious works, noble families owned romances and cookbooks.

ACTIVITY: Have students copy a paragraph from their textbook in neat print. Then ask them to discuss the drawbacks of having to write each copy of a book by hand and to reflect on changes after the introduction of the printing press.

HISTORY MAKER
Thomas Aquinas (c. 1224–1274)

Thomas Aquinas was one of the greatest scholars of the Middle Ages. His *Summa Theologiae* is among the most important works of the medieval religious philosophy known as scholasticism.

Aquinas, a Dominican friar, became the official philosopher of the medieval church. He argued that science and reason were in conflict with faith. One of his most famous arguments was his rational proof of the existence of God. Aquinas's approach to logic was based in part upon the ideas of Aristotle and of several Arab thinkers. **How did Thomas Aquinas's faith affect his scholarly work?**

Philosophy and Science

Muslim scholars had kept the works of Greek and Roman philosophers and scientists alive. During the Middle Ages, this knowledge was passed on to Europeans.

Philosophy. Medieval European philosophers tried to make Aristotle's ideas work with those of early church writers. Aristotle placed the most importance on human reason. For the church writers, however, faith was most important. This attempt to bring together faith and reason is called **scholasticism.**

Peter Abelard, an important philosopher of scholasticism, taught in Paris in the 1100s. Abelard wrote a book called *Sic et Non* ("Yes and No"), which raised many questions about the church's teachings. In it he included quotations from the Bible, statements from popes, and writings of church philosophers. Abelard showed that many of them conflicted with one another.

Probably the greatest medieval philosopher was **Thomas Aquinas,** a monk of the Dominican order. His principal work, *Summa Theologiae,* summarized medieval Christian thought.

Science. Few advances were made in science during the Middle Ages. The Bible and the church were the main sources for information about the world. Only two subjects received serious attention: mathematics and optics, the study of light. Europeans did make some technical advances that helped with everyday life, however. They designed better winches and pulleys to make lifting and pulling heavy objects easier. They made iron plows and better oxen yokes to make farming easier. Europeans also began to use windmills and waterwheels, inventions for drawing water that had been invented in Asia.

✔ **READING CHECK: Making Generalizations** How did religion affect philosophy and science during the Middle Ages? Philosophy and science were studied in the context of religious faith.

Architecture

During the Middle Ages, church architecture was the main art form. Between about 1000 and about 1150, most architects followed the Romanesque style of architecture. They used arches, domes, vaults, and low horizontal lines in their churches. This style was like that used in the Roman Empire. A Romanesque church had a heavy domed stone roof. To support the roof, the walls were low with few windows. As a result, these churches were very dark inside.

During the mid-1100s, master builders developed a different style of church architecture. Many people did not like the new style and called it **Gothic** after the barbarian Goths. Gothic churches had tall spires. On the outside walls, builders placed rows of supporting structures called flying buttresses. The flying buttresses were connected to the church's walls with arches and carried part of the roof's weight. The church's walls could therefore be high and thin. Everything in Gothic churches—pointed arches, tall spires, and high walls—reached toward heaven.

Large stained-glass windows were set in the high walls. They filled the inside of the churches with light. Statues of the holy family, saints, and rulers lined the inside of Gothic churches, and relief sculptures adorned the walls.

The Gothic church was an example of how life had changed in the later Middle Ages. This tall building towered above the growing town around it. Traders did business in the marketplace near its walls. Religious plays were presented within and

REVIEW

Have students complete the Section 4 Review on p. 335.

ASSESS

Have students complete Daily Quiz 14.4. As Alternative Assessment, you may want to use the summarizing graphic organizer or the point of view exercise at the end of this section.

RETEACH

Have students complete Main Idea Activity for English Language Learners and Special-Needs Students 14.4. Then have students

EXTEND

Tell students to imagine they are troubadours who will perform a poem in the court of an important noble. Have them research one of the medieval ideals of chivalry or courtly love and write the poem. **COOPERATIVE LEARNING, BLOCK SCHEDULING**

INTERPRETING THE VISUAL RECORD

Cathedral of Notre Dame in Paris The Cathedral of Notre Dame is a good example of Gothic architecture. Its high walls hold large stained-glass windows. Flying buttresses support the walls. *When looking at this cathedral, in what direction are the viewer's eyes pulled—up, down, or sideways? Why is this so?*

VISUAL RECORD ANSWER

up; height of the walls, narrow arches and windows

SECTION 4 REVIEW ANSWERS

1 Define
- vernacular languages, p. 331
- troubadours, p. 332
- scholasticism, p. 334

2 Identify
- Dante Alighieri, p. 332
- Geoffrey Chaucer, p. 332
- Peter Abelard, p. 334
- Thomas Aquinas, p. 334
- Gothic, p. 334

3 Language and Literature: literature in vernacular languages; Education: great universities; Architecture: style changed to Gothic

4 a. Dante wrote in Tuscan, which became the dominant Italian language; Chaucer wrote in Middle English, was emulated by later writers

b. philosophers tried to bring faith and reason together in scholasticism; the Bible and church were sources of scientific information; church architecture main art form

5 Students' outlines should reflect medieval culture and use of the vernacular.

outside it. The highest artistic skills of the medieval world went into the building of this monument to God.

Gothic cathedrals were constructed in many parts of Europe, including France, England, and Germany. One of the earliest of these magnificent structures, begun in about 1140, was the abbey of Saint-Denis in Paris. Construction of the towering cathedral of Notre Dame, also in Paris, began in the early 1160s and continued in stages for about a century thereafter.

✔ **READING CHECK: Contrasting** How did the Romanesque and Gothic styles of church architecture differ from each other? dark, low walls, heavy domes versus towering, light, spacious

These gargoyles are found on the exterior of the Cathedral of Notre Dame.

SECTION 4 REVIEW

1. **Define** and explain the significance:
   vernacular languages
   troubadours
   scholasticism

2. **Identify** and explain the significance:
   Dante Alighieri
   Geoffrey Chaucer
   Peter Abelard
   Thomas Aquinas
   Gothic

Homework Practice Online
keyword: SP3 HP14

3. **Summarizing** Copy the web diagram below. Use it to list ways in which language and literature, education, and architecture changed during the Middle Ages.

   Language and Literature

   Changes in Late Middle Ages

   Architecture   Education

4. **Finding the Main Idea**
   a. How did the writings of Dante and Chaucer reflect the history of the cultures in which they were produced?
   b. How did the church and religion influence medieval philosophy, science, and architecture?

5. **Writing and Critical Thinking**
   Making Generalizations Write an outline for a drama that might have been performed during the Middle Ages.
   Consider:
   - how medieval dramas reflected the culture of the times
   - how vernacular language influenced them

THE HIGH MIDDLE AGES **335**

OBJECTIVES

1 Identify how the Hundred Years' War affected England and France.

2 Analyze how Spain's rulers both strengthened and weakened their nation.

3 Explain why the Holy Roman Empire remained weak throughout the later Middle Ages.

🎧 LET'S GET STARTED!

As students enter the classroom, tell them to scan the section for dates. Have them arrange the dates on a time line leaving space beside each year. Tell students that in Section 5 they will learn about events that united nations during the period on their time line.

VISUAL RECORD ANSWER

could be used to shoot foot soldiers from a distance

SECTION 5

READ TO DISCOVER

❶ How did the Hundred Years' War affect England and France?

❷ How did Spain's rulers both strengthen and weaken their nation?

❸ Why did the Holy Roman Empire remain weak throughout the later Middle Ages?

IDENTIFY

Hundred Years' War
War of the Roses
Henry Tudor
Joan of Arc
Louis XI
Ferdinand
Isabella
Habsburg

▸ WHY IT MATTERS TODAY

England and France have continued to be rivals at certain times but allies at others. Use **CNNfyi.com** or other **current event** sources to find out how these two nations, along with other western European countries, have attempted to work together economically in recent years. Record your findings in your journal.

CNNfyi.com

Wars and the Growth of Nations

The Main Idea
The late Middle Ages saw the development of individual nations united under strong monarchs.

The Story Continues *Americans today fly the American flag and sing the national anthem to show their patriotism, or feeling of loyalty to their country. Under feudalism in the early Middle Ages, people of a country did not feel any such loyalty. This would change during the later Middle Ages, however, as states began to form and kings began to build their kingdoms as organized nations.*

England

By the late Middle Ages, England's feudal lords had lost much of their power to its king. The new class of townspeople supported a strong king. A single system of law and courts and a larger army of soldiers helped strengthen the king. In addition, as the country prospered, more taxes were paid to the king.

In the early 1300s the English king Edward III also held land in France. This made him a vassal of the French king. This fact helped lead to a series of conflicts between England and France called the **Hundred Years' War** (1337–1453).

The Hundred Years' War. In 1328 the last male member of France's Capetian dynasty died. Edward III claimed the French throne. The French assembly chose Philip VI, the Count of Flanders, as king instead. In 1337 Edward brought an army to Flanders, hoping to gain control of this rich trading area.

Thus the Hundred Years' War began. It continued for 116 years as a series of raids and battles. Sometimes there were long periods of uneasy peace. England won many battles but lost the war. By 1453 France controlled all of England's French lands except Calais.

The Hundred Years' War saw the use of new weapons in Europe. At the Battle of Agincourt (AJ·uhn·kohrt) in 1415, English foot soldiers used longbows. With these bows they could fire arrows quickly, hitting targets up to 200 yards away. French knights on horseback were no match for the English and their

INTERPRETING THE VISUAL RECORD

The longbow The six-foot longbow and its three-foot arrows, accurate over a range of 200 yards, helped the English defeat the French at Agincourt. ***How does this illustration suggest that longbows were important in battle?***

TEACH OBJECTIVE 1

LEVEL 1: Make a chart on the board titled *Effects of the Hundred Years' War* and work with students to list its effects on England and on France. *(England lost all its French lands except Calais; knightly warfare was weakened by the use of longbows, cannons, and gunpowder; Parliament gained more power over the king. France: English soldiers robbed the French people and destroyed their property; the French starved even during peacetime; the French king became more powerful.)*
ENGLISH LANGUAGE LEARNERS

longbows. Both the English and the French used gunpowder and cannons in battle. Castles no longer provided protection for a feudal lord because one powerful cannon blast could break through a castle's wall. Longbows, gunpowder, and cannons further weakened knightly warfare.

Besides loss of life and land, the Hundred Years' War had another important effect on England. Parliament, particularly the House of Commons, gained more power over the king. Members of the House of Commons were angry about the way the war was going. They won the right of a special council to advise the king and the right to consider new taxes before they were discussed by the House of Lords. By the late 1300s, the king needed Parliament's consent on all special taxes.

The War of the Roses. Shortly after the Hundred Years' War ended, a war for England's throne began. In 1455 the York and Lancaster families started the **War of the Roses.** The white rose was the badge of the House of York. The red rose was used by the House of Lancaster. In 1485 **Henry Tudor** of the House of Lancaster won the war. He defeated King Richard III of York. However, Henry married a daughter from the House of York. As King Henry VII, he set up a strong monarchy in England once again.

✔ **READING CHECK: Identifying Cause and Effect** Why did the Hundred Years' War begin and what were its results? English claims to the French throne; France won all English lands in France except Calais

France

During the Hundred Years' War, France suffered more than England because the war took place on French soil. Bands of English soldiers robbed the people and destroyed their property. Even during times of peace, the French people starved.

> *History Makers Speak*
>
> **And in truth when good weather came, in April, those who in the winter had made their beverages from apples and sloe plums emptied the residue of their apples and their plums into the street with the intention that the pigs of St. Antoine would eat them. But the pigs did not get to them in time, for as soon as they were thrown out, they were seized by poor folk, women and children, who ate them with great relish, . . . for they ate what the pigs scorned to eat, they ate the cores of cabbages without bread or without cooking, grasses of the fields without bread or salt.**
>
> Quoted in J.B. Ross and M.M. McLaughlin, eds., *The Portable Medieval Reader*

A fight for the throne. During the Hundred Years' War, a fight for power broke out within the royal family. The House of Burgundy sided with the English against the House of Orléans, preventing France from uniting against the English. Finally in 1429, with the help of a young girl named **Joan of Arc,** Charles VII of Orléans was crowned king of France. The French backed their king and drove the English out.

Territory held in 1430 by:

☐ France	✷ French victory
☐ England	✷ English victory
☐ Burgundy	

France and the Hundred Years' War, 1337–1453

Interpreting Maps Until 1429 the English had won the major battles of the Hundred Years' War.

■ **Skills Assessment:**
1. Places and Regions Which of the three powers represented by the map held the least amount of physical territory?
2. Finding the Main Idea What battle marked the end of the Hundred Years' War, and who was the victor?

Government

In 1381 English peasants staged a revolt. Sir John Froissart, a French historian, reported:

"Many in the city of London envious of the rich and noble . . . said among themselves that the country was badly governed, and that the nobility had seized upon all the gold and silver. These wicked Londoners, therefore, began to . . . show signs of rebellion; they also invited all those who held like opinions in the adjoining counties to come to London; . . . in number about 60,000, were brought to London, under command of Wat Tyler . . . a bad man and a great enemy to the nobility."

Critical Thinking

Ask students to identify the bias of Froissart and to support their answer with examples.

ANSWER: Froissart is biased in favor of the nobility. He shows little sympathy for the rebels by calling them "wicked" and their leader "a bad man."

Technology Resources

go.hrw.com Online Maps, Charts, and Graphs: The Hundred Years' War by 1453

ALL LEVELS: Organize the class into two groups and plan a panel discussion. Have the members of one group defend the actions of Isabella and Ferdinand from 1479 to 1515. Ask the students in the other group to criticize the rulers' policies.
ENGLISH LANGUAGE LEARNERS, COOPERATIVE LEARNING

HOMEWORK Assign each student one of the following people: Edward III, Philip VI, Richard III, Henry VII, Joan of Arc, Charles VII, Louis XI, Ferdinand II, or Maximilian I. Have students research their assigned person to find answers to these questions: What did the person try to accomplish? How did the person influence his or her nation? Then ask students to share their information with the class.

HISTORY MAKER ANSWER

led French troops to victory at Orléans, became symbol of French patriotism

MAP ANSWERS

1. Castile, Aragon
2. Spain and Portugal

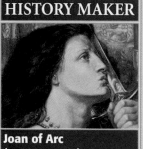

internet connect

TOPIC: Rulers
GO TO: go.hrw.com
KEYWORD: SP3 WH14

Have students access the Internet through the HRW Go site to find information about the monarchies of Henry VII, Louis XI, and Ferdinand and Isabella of Spain. Ask students to decide in their opinion which of these rulers developed the strongest monarchy. Then have them create a chart of that monarch's accomplishments. Ask volunteers to present their charts to the class and explain why they chose the ruler they did.

HISTORY MAKER

Joan of Arc (c. 1412–1431)

Joan of Arc, the "Maid of Orléans," is a revered figure in French history. Believing that God spoke to her through visions, Joan left home to aid the French king, Charles VII, in his struggle against the English. Her strong faith persuaded thousands to follow her into battle. Her most crucial test came when the teenage Joan led French troops to victory against the English at Orléans.

A short time later, Joan was captured by English troops. She was accused of heresy, tortured, and burned at the stake. Today Joan of Arc is a Catholic saint and a symbol of French patriotism. **What was Joan of Arc's role in building the nation of France?**

Holt Researcher

go.hrw.com
KEYWORD: Holt Researcher
FreeFind: Joan of Arc
After reading more about Joan of Arc on the Holt Researcher, create a cause-and-effect chart showing how her religious faith influenced her actions, which ultimately affected political events in France.

A return of strong kings. During the Hundred Years' War, the French Estates General controlled finances and passed laws. This representative assembly was similar to the English Parliament. It took its name from the groups that assembled for its meetings: clergy (First Estate), nobles (Second Estate), and common people (Third Estate). After the war, however, the Estates General lost some of its power.

In 1461 **Louis XI** followed Charles VII as king of France. Louis made the French monarchy even stronger. He set up a harsh but efficient government with high taxes. Through diplomacy and scheming, he seized the lands of the House of Burgundy. Under Louis, France became a united country. As in England, French feudal lords lost much power to their king. They kept many rights, however, and remained wealthy and important until the mid-1700s. French peasants, unlike those in England, gained little freedom. They still owed services to the manor and its lord.

✔ **READING CHECK: Supporting a Point of View** How would you support the view that France grew as a nation after the Hundred Years' War? Feudal lords lost power to the king, who unified France under royal control

Spain

Spain became a united nation in 1479 under **Ferdinand** of Aragon and **Isabella** of Castile. In 1492 the Spanish army captured Granada, the last stronghold of the Moors, or Muslims, in Spain. In 1515 Ferdinand and Isabella added the kingdom of Navarre to their territory. Ferdinand and Isabella took powers away from church courts and from the nobles. Fervent Catholics, they did not look kindly on non-Christians in Spain. In 1492 they ordered all Jews to become Christians or leave Spain. Later, they gave the Moors the same choice. Most Jews and Moors did leave the country. As a result, Spain was robbed of many of its leaders in industry and trade.

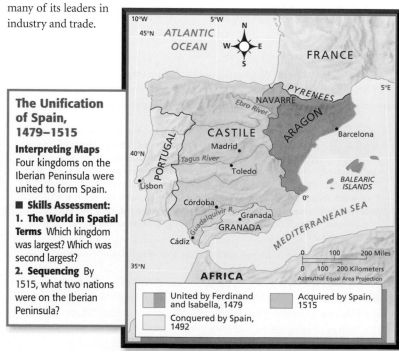

The Unification of Spain, 1479–1515

Interpreting Maps Four kingdoms on the Iberian Peninsula were united to form Spain.

■ **Skills Assessment:**
1. The World in Spatial Terms Which kingdom was largest? Which was second largest?
2. Sequencing By 1515, what two nations were on the Iberian Peninsula?

United by Ferdinand and Isabella, 1479
Conquered by Spain, 1492
Acquired by Spain, 1515

LEVEL 3: Have students create a flowchart showing the rise of the Habsburgs. Refer them to material under "The Holy Roman Empire" for steps in the chart.

| A Habsburg was elected emperor in 1273. | → | The Habsburgs used their position to arrange marriages with powerful families. |

| Through marriage the Habsburg family gained control of Austria and nearby lands. | → | More well-planned marriages gave the Habsburgs control of much of the empire's territory. |

The Habsburgs became the most powerful family in Europe.

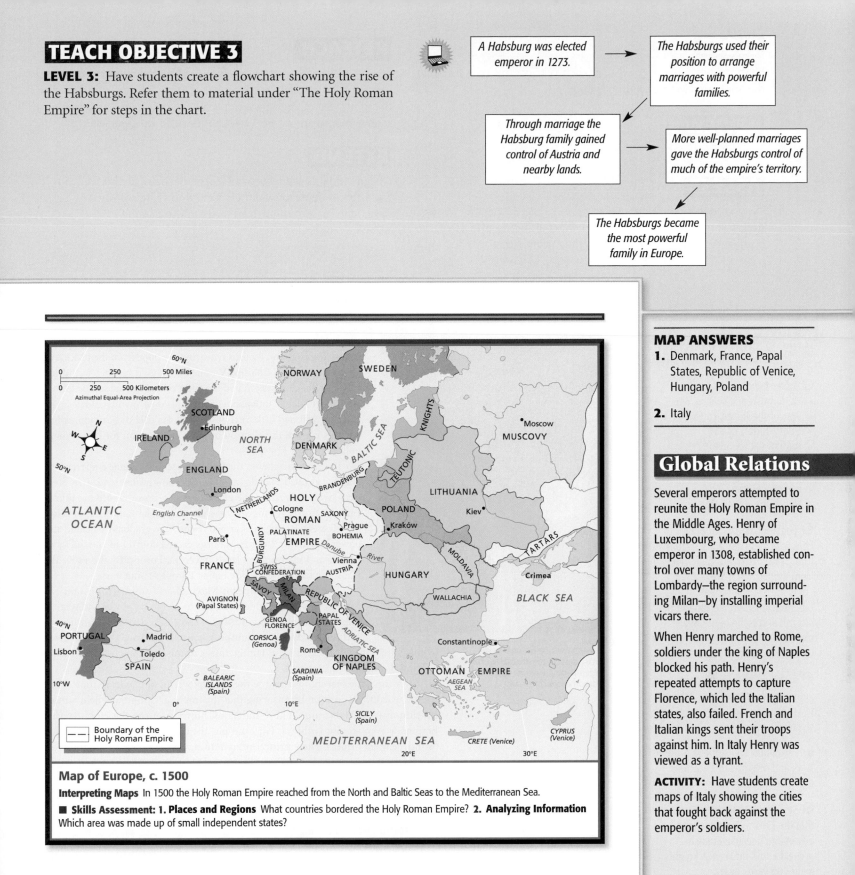

Map of Europe, c. 1500

Interpreting Maps In 1500 the Holy Roman Empire reached from the North and Baltic Seas to the Mediterranean Sea.

■ **Skills Assessment: 1. Places and Regions** What countries bordered the Holy Roman Empire? **2. Analyzing Information** Which area was made up of small independent states?

MAP ANSWERS

1. Denmark, France, Papal States, Republic of Venice, Hungary, Poland

2. Italy

Global Relations

Several emperors attempted to reunite the Holy Roman Empire in the Middle Ages. Henry of Luxembourg, who became emperor in 1308, established control over many towns of Lombardy—the region surrounding Milan—by installing imperial vicars there.

When Henry marched to Rome, soldiers under the king of Naples blocked his path. Henry's repeated attempts to capture Florence, which led the Italian states, also failed. French and Italian kings sent their troops against him. In Italy Henry was viewed as a tyrant.

ACTIVITY: Have students create maps of Italy showing the cities that fought back against the emperor's soldiers.

✔ **READING CHECK: Comparing and Contrasting** How did Ferdinand and Isabella's policies both help and hurt Spain? gave Spain a strong monarchy but weakened business and trade through discrimination

The Holy Roman Empire

By the 1500s England, France, and Spain had each formed powerful nations. Germany and Italy, which made up the Holy Roman Empire, remained divided into states and regions ruled by princes and knights. Over time, the Holy Roman emperors had given up much of their power to these nobles in return for military support. Therefore the emperors lacked the power needed to exercise complete control.

In the early days the rulers of many German states, along with the pope, elected the Holy Roman emperor. Gradually the number who could vote for emperor decreased. Finally, by a decree issued in 1356, Emperor Charles IV ruled that only

CLOSE

Help students add an event for each year on the time line that they prepared before reading Section 5.

REVIEW

Have students complete the Section 5 Review on p. 340.

ASSESS

Have students complete Daily Quiz 14.5. As Alternative Assessment, you may want to use the chart showing effects of the Hundred Years' War or the flowchart exercise in this section's lesson.

RETEACH

Have students complete Main Idea Activity for English Language Learners and Special-Needs Students 14.5. Tell students to write the main idea of each paragraph in a sentence and organize the sentences into an outline. **ENGLISH LANGUAGE LEARNERS**

EXTEND

Assign students scenes from George Bernard Shaw's play *Saint Joan*. Tell students to read their scene and write a summary. Then have them present their summaries to the class. **BLOCK SCHEDULING**

SECTION 5 REVIEW ANSWERS

❶ Identify
- Hundred Years' War, p. 336
- War of the Roses, p. 337
- Henry Tudor, p. 337
- Joan of Arc, p. 337
- Louis XI, p. 338
- Ferdinand, p. 338
- Isabella, p. 338
- Habsburg, p. 340

❷ England: Henry Tudor of Lancaster defeated King Richard III of York, married a daughter from the House of York; France: Louis the XI used scheming and diplomacy; Spain: Ferdinand of Aragon and Isabella of Castille united their two territories, captured Granada and Navarre

❸ a. In England, Parliament gained more power over the king. In France, the king became stronger.

b. Ferdinand and Isabella ordered Jews and Muslims to become Christian or leave Spain.

❹ Students should emphasize that the English longbow was an advantage because English archers could hit French knights from 200 yards away.

This portrait by an unknown artist depicts the Habsburg ruler Maximilian I, who became Holy Roman emperor in 1493.

seven electors—three archbishops and four German princes—would choose the emperor. By thus removing the pope from the process of electing emperors, Charles IV hoped to rebuild his own authority. However, the new system had the effect of making the seven electors almost completely independent rulers in their own territories. The emperor still had little real power, but the title did carry prestige. For this reason, the election became an occasion for bribery and political favors.

In 1273 a member of the **Habsburg** family became emperor. The Habsburgs ruled a small state in what is now Switzerland. They were weak, with little land. The Habsburgs did, however, use the title of emperor to arrange marriages with powerful families. They also followed careful strategies of armed conquest to gradually win land and power. In this way, the Habsburgs gained control of the duchy of Austria and surrounding lands in central Europe. By the 1400s the Habsburg family was clearly one of Europe's rising stars.

The Habsburg emperor Maximilian I followed his family's strategy of marriage and conquest to add to its power and wealth. Maximilian's marriage brought The Netherlands, Luxembourg, and Burgundy under Habsburg control. His son, Philip, followed by marrying into the Spanish royal family, thus gaining large Spanish and Italian holdings for the Habsburgs.

Over time, the Habsburgs became the most powerful family in Europe. They strengthened their position by ensuring that the imperial throne was held almost continuously by Habsburgs. They could not, however, unite the Holy Roman Empire or even regions within it. For example, the German states were still ruled by independent princes. These princes refused to surrender power to the emperor. Nor could Italy be united. The Papal States, ruled by the pope, stretched across the middle of the Italian Peninsula. The geographic location of the Papal States effectively blocked efforts to bring all of Italy under centralized imperial control.

✔ **READING CHECK: Drawing Inferences** Why were emperors unable to unite the Holy Roman Empire? **Independent princes in Germany and the pope in Italy refused to surrender power to the emperors.**

SECTION 5 REVIEW

1. **Identify** and explain the significance:
   Hundred Years' War
   War of the Roses
   Henry Tudor
   Joan of Arc
   Louis XI
   Ferdinand
   Isabella
   Habsburg

2. **Summarizing** Copy the chart below. Use it to name important rulers in England, France, and Spain and to show how they united their nations.

England	France	Spain

   Ways Ruler United the Country

3. **Finding the Main Idea**

   a. In what ways did the Hundred Years' War affect England and France differently?

   b. What happened in Spain in 1492 that changed the country's population?

4. **Writing and Critical Thinking**

   Analyzing Information Write a script for a newscast that describes the Battle of Agincourt and analyzes its importance.
   Consider:
   - the English use of the longbow
   - the French use of horses
   - the outcome of the battle

Homework Practice Online
keyword: SP3 HP14

OBJECTIVES

1 Identify the factors that led to the decline of the Catholic Church in the later Middle Ages.

2 Describe how the Babylonian Captivity and the Great Schism affected the church.

3 Explain why great teachers and priests challenged the church during the later Middle Ages.

SECTION 6

READ TO DISCOVER

❶ What factors led to the decline of Catholic Church power during the late Middle Ages?

❷ How did the Babylonian Captivity and the Great Schism affect the church?

❸ Why did growing numbers of teachers and priests challenge the church during the later Middle Ages?

IDENTIFY

Babylonian Captivity
Great Schism
John Wycliffe
Jan Hus

▶ WHY IT MATTERS TODAY

Today the pope often tries to work with government leaders to improve the lives of their people. Use CNNfyi.com or other **current event** sources to find information about recent visits of the pope with world leaders. Record your findings in your journal.

CNNfyi.com

Challenges to Church Power

The Main Idea
During the late Middle Ages the Catholic Church lost some of its political power in many parts of Europe.

The Story Continues *A papal palace in France? Three men claiming to be pope? Europe was indeed changing. Kings were developing strong national governments with rich treasuries. Townspeople were increasing in number and importance. Such changes had to affect the one power that had unified medieval Europe—the church.*

Church Power Weakens

Innocent III was pope from 1198 to 1216. Under him the medieval papacy reached the height of its power. After Innocent, however, the worldly power of the church began to weaken. This happened for several reasons.

First, power was shifting. The kings of England, France, and Spain were forming strong governments. The increased number of townspeople gave them added importance too. Many felt that church laws limited their trade and industry. Also, people began to question some church practices. For example, they found fault with its great wealth, its method of raising money, and the worldly lives of some clergy members.

In 1294 a conflict arose between the pope and a monarch. After this conflict, King Philip IV of France ordered the clergy in France to pay taxes. This angered Pope Boniface VIII. In 1302 Boniface decreed that popes had power over worldly rulers.

Philip responded by calling the first-ever meeting of the Estates General. He wanted support against Boniface. Philip charged the pope with heresy and of selling jobs in the church. He also wanted a church council to put Boniface on trial. Philip then had his envoys in Rome take the pope prisoner. Although Boniface was quickly let go, he died soon after. For the next 100 years, the church continued to lose power.

✔ **READING CHECK: Analyzing Information** How did changes that were taking place in Europe help lead to the struggle between Philip IV and Boniface VIII? Power began shifting from the church to monarchs; people began to question church practices

SECTION 6 RESOURCES

REPRODUCIBLE RESOURCES
▶ Guided Reading Strategy 14.6
▶ Readings in World History 44: The Papal Court at Avignon

TECHNOLOGY RESOURCES
▶ One-Stop Planner 14.6
▶ World History Teaching Transparency: Geography and History 14: The Great Schism
▶ Religions of the World Video Series: Christianity
▶ Homework Practice Online

REINFORCEMENT, REVIEW, AND ASSESSMENT
▶ Section 6 Review, p. 343
▶ Daily Quiz 14.6
▶ Main Idea Activity 14.6
▶ English Audio Summary 14.6
▶ Spanish Audio Summary 14.6

This portrait shows Philip IV, sometimes called "Philip the Fair," and his family.

THE HIGH MIDDLE AGES **341**

TEACH OBJECTIVE 1

ALL LEVELS: Organize students into two groups to present arguments why the French clergy in 1300 should or should not pay taxes. **ENGLISH LANGUAGE LEARNERS, COOPERATIVE LEARNING**

TEACH OBJECTIVE 2

LEVEL 3: Have students write four cause-and-effect relationships about the Babylonian Captivity and the Great Schism. (*Example: cause—popes living in Avignon; effect—people thought French kings controlled the popes.*)

HOMEWORK Have students demonstrate how problem-solving techniques were used to end the Great Schism.

TEACH OBJECTIVE 3

LEVEL 1: Help the class complete the Venn diagram showing how John Wycliffe and Jan Hus were alike and different.

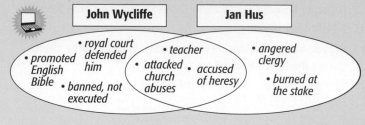

John Wycliffe

Jan Hus

- promoted English Bible
- royal court defended him
- banned, not executed
- teacher
- attacked church abuses
- accused of heresy
- angered clergy
- burned at the stake

Linking Past to Present

Perhaps no pope has more involved himself with bringing greater freedoms throughout the world than Pope John Paul II. His calls for peace and freedom have contributed to great political reform. He is considered an instrumental figure in the democratic changes in Poland and in the collapse of the Soviet Union.

More recently the pope visited Beirut, where he called for peaceful coexistence between Muslims and Christians, and Cuba, where he preached his message of love and solidarity.

ACTIVITY: Tell students to compare the role of the popes discussed in the section with that of John Paul II. Have students discuss the popes' effectiveness in promoting peace, freedom, and political reform.

The Babylonian Captivity and the Great Schism

After Boniface died, Philip had a French bishop elected pope. The new pope took the name Clement V. In 1309 Clement moved the headquarters of the church to Avignon, France. Until then, Rome had been the center of the church for 1,000 years. After Clement, the next six popes were French and lived in Avignon also.

The years that the popes lived in Avignon are called the **Babylonian Captivity** (1309–1377). The period was named for the time the ancient Hebrews were forced to live in Babylon, more than 1,800 years earlier. During the Babylonian Captivity, people in other countries lost respect for the church. They felt that the popes were being controlled by French kings.

In 1377 the French pope Gregory XI returned to Rome. A year later he died. Meeting in Rome, the cardinals elected an Italian pope to please local mobs, but later elected a French pope, who took up residence at Avignon. Until 1417 the church had two and sometimes three popes. This period of church history is called the **Great Schism** (SI·zuhm). The church was divided into opposing groups. For political reasons, each pope had the support of certain national rulers and their people and clergy.

Finally a church council met in Constance in 1414. Three years later, the Council of Constance ended the Great Schism. It removed the Italian and French popes; a third pope resigned. The council then elected a new Italian pope. It also suggested that other councils be held to correct church problems.

✔ **READING CHECK: Drawing Conclusions** How did the church become weaker during the Babylonian Captivity and the Great Schism? People lost respect for the church, and competition among opposing popes weakened papal and church authority.

More Problems for the Church

The Babylonian Captivity and Great Schism not only weakened the authority of the pope but they also increased criticism of the church. Some of this criticism came from within the church itself.

In 1324 two teachers at the University of Paris wrote *Defender of the Faith*. It claimed that the pope was the elected head of the church alone. He had no power over worldly rulers. It also stated that the church's power belonged with a council of clergy

INTERPRETING THE VISUAL RECORD

The Babylonian Captivity The popes had many enemies during the era known as the "Babylonian Captivity." The papal palace in Avignon was, in reality, a highly defensible fortress. It was built on land 190 feet above the town and surrounded by three miles of high, thick walls.

Link to Today Judging from this modern-day photograph, why might popes in Avignon have felt safe?

and lay people. *Defender of the Faith* directly opposed the ideas in Pope Boniface's *Unam Sanctum*.

In the late 1300s **John Wycliffe** was a priest and teacher at Oxford University. Wycliffe attacked the wealth of the church and the immorality of some of its clergy. He also did not believe in the absolute power of the pope. Wycliffe wanted to replace the authority of the church, which he believed had been undermined, with that of the Bible. He held that individuals should be allowed to read and interpret scripture for themselves, without church intervention. This idea had great appeal among many Europeans who felt that the church and its clergy had surrendered spiritual authority. Wycliffe promoted the first translation of the Bible into English from Latin. English people could then read the Bible and decide for themselves what it meant. The church accused Wycliffe of being a heretic. The English royal court defended him. Because of this political support, unlike some other prominent heretics, Wycliffe was not executed. Instead he was banned from teaching and forced to retire. Wycliffe wrote to one duke: "I believe that in the end the truth will conquer."

Like many others in England and the rest of Europe, Jan Hus read Wycliffe's works. Hus was a religious reformer and teacher at the University of Prague. He also criticized abuses in the church. His attacks angered the clergy. Hus was excommunicated. In 1414 the Council of Constance declared him a heretic and ordered his death. He was burned at the stake the following year.

Despite the church's reaction to their ideas, Wycliffe and Hus would have a profound impact on many people. Their questioning of church authority set the stage for later reformers who would radically alter the history of the Christian church.

✔ **READING CHECK: Summarizing** Who was finding fault with the church in the 1300s and 1400s, and what changes did they suggest? reformers from within the church, such as John Wycliffe and Jan Hus; suggested translating Bible and eliminating church abuses

On July 6, 1415, Jan Hus was led to his death. He was burned alive at the stake for heresy.

SECTION 6 REVIEW

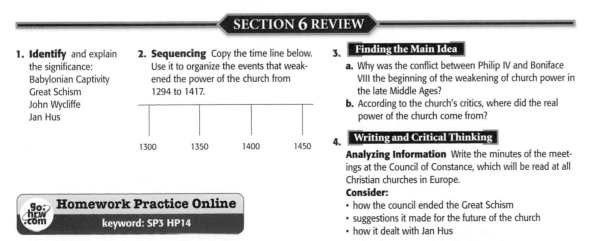

1. **Identify** and explain the significance:
   Babylonian Captivity
   Great Schism
   John Wycliffe
   Jan Hus

2. **Sequencing** Copy the time line below. Use it to organize the events that weakened the power of the church from 1294 to 1417.

   |1300|1350|1400|1450|

3. **Finding the Main Idea**

   a. Why was the conflict between Philip IV and Boniface VIII the beginning of the weakening of church power in the late Middle Ages?

   b. According to the church's critics, where did the real power of the church come from?

4. **Writing and Critical Thinking**

   Analyzing Information Write the minutes of the meetings at the Council of Constance, which will be read at all Christian churches in Europe.

   Consider:
   - how the council ended the Great Schism
   - suggestions it made for the future of the church
   - how it dealt with Jan Hus

Homework Practice Online
keyword: SP3 HP14

REVIEW AND ASSESSMENT RESOURCES

REPRODUCIBLE RESOURCES
▸ Vocabulary Activity 14

TECHNOLOGY RESOURCES
▸ Chapter 14 Test Generator (on the One-Stop Planner)
▸ Global Skill Builder CD–ROM
▸ HRW Web Site

REINFORCEMENT, REVIEW, and ASSESSMENT
▸ Chapter 14 Review, pp. 344–345

▸ Chapter 14 Tutorial for Students, Parents, Mentors, and Peers
▸ Chapter 14 Test (Form A or B)
▸ Alternative Assessment Handbook
▸ Chapter 14 Test for English Language Learners and Special-Needs Students

REVIEW

Have students complete the Chapter 14 Review on pages 344–345.

ASSESS

Use one of the chapter tests to assess students' understanding of the content. For Alternative Assessment, see the Portfolio Activities and Alternative Assessment Handbook.

CHAPTER 14 REVIEW ANSWERS

Understanding Main Ideas

1. to recapture Holy Lands from the Turks

2. Kings grew stronger; new ideas changed culture; Italian cities became trading centers.

3. Europeans wanted Asian goods because of exposure during Crusades.

4. The domestic system developed to meet demand for goods; banks lent money and provided bills of exchange; investors wanted profits from increased trade.

5. Merchant and craft guilds formed and many serfs moved to towns.

6. Universities developed; scholars tried to bring together faith and logic in scholasticism; Romanesque church architecture gave way to Gothic.

7. Parliament gained more power over the king in England while the French king became stronger.

8. Ferdinand and Isabella united Spain, but the Holy Roman Empire remained divided in small states.

9. the conflict between the French king and the pope, the Babylonian Captivity, the Great Schism, and criticism from scholars

Reviewing Themes

1. Europeans were introduced to new ideas and goods when they traveled to the Middle East.

CHAPTER 14 Review

Creating a Time Line
Copy the time line below onto a sheet of paper. Complete the time line by filling in the events, individuals, and dates from the chapter that you think were significant. Pick three events and explain why you think they were significant.

| 1100 | 1200 | 1300 | 1400 | 1500 |

Writing a Summary
Using standard grammar, spelling, sentence structure, and punctuation, write an overview of the events in the chapter.

Identifying People and Ideas
Identify the following terms or individuals and explain their significance:

1. Urban II
2. Crusades
3. domestic system
4. craft guilds
5. vernacular languages
6. Dante Alighieri
7. scholasticism
8. Joan of Arc
9. Great Schism
10. John Wycliffe

Understanding Main Ideas

SECTION 1 *(pp. 318–322)*
The Crusades
1. Why did Europeans fight in the Crusades?
2. How did the Crusades affect the government, economy, and culture of Europe?

SECTION 2 *(pp. 323–326)*
The Revival of Trade
3. Why did trade begin again in Europe during the late Middle Ages?
4. How did the revival of trade help in the development of manufacturing, banking, and investing?

SECTION 3 *(pp. 327–330)*
The Growth of Towns
5. How did life for people in towns change in the late Middle Ages?

SECTION 4 *(pp. 331–335)*
Life and Culture in the Middle Ages
6. How did education, philosophy, and architecture change in the later Middle Ages?

SECTION 5 *(pp. 336–340)*
Wars and the Growth of Nations
7. How did the Hundred Years' War affect the governments of England and France?
8. Why did Spain become a strong nation and the Holy Roman Empire become weaker?

SECTION 6 *(pp. 341–343)*
Challenges to Church Power
9. What events led to the weakening of the church during the later Middle Ages?

Reviewing Themes
1. **Global Relations** How did the Crusades promote an exchange of ideas and goods?
2. **Economics** How did the growth of trade and towns bring changes to the feudal and manorial systems?
3. **Government** What groups lost power as Europe's kings established strong nations?

Thinking Critically
1. **Making Generalizations** How did the church influence life during the Middle Ages?
2. **Analyzing Information** How did trade, universities, and large churches help medieval towns grow?
3. **Comparing and Contrasting** In what ways were the development of strong central governments in England, France, and Spain alike and different?
4. **Summarizing** What were the main advances in literature during the later Middle Ages?

Writing About History
Comparing and Contrasting Medieval Europe evolved over centuries from the ruins of the Roman Empire. Compare and contrast the institutions of medieval Europe with the Roman Empire at its height. Use the compare-contrast diagram below to organize your thoughts before writing.

Roman Empire		Medieval Europe
	Government	
	Economy	
	Religion	
	Culture	
	Thought	

CLOSE

Have students choose a work of literature about or from the High Middle Ages. Ask them to select passages that describe an aspect of daily life and read those passages to the class.

RETEACH

Have students who had trouble with the test work in pairs. Ask them to outline the chapter. From the outline have the pair create flashcards and quiz each other on the chapter content. Then have students take the Form B test to assess their mastery of the material.

ENGLISH LANGUAGE LEARNERS, COOPERATIVE LEARNING

Portfolio Extensions

1. Have students collect additional information on one of the Crusades. Then tell them to write a diary entry like one a crusader might write about experiences on the journey to the Holy Land.

2. Have students find one or more sources on medieval knighthood, read about the values of chivalry and the love of battle, and compare them to the values of earlier eras. Then have them present oral reports about their findings to the class.

3. Have students research and analyze the effects that the longbow and cannon had on warfare in the Middle Ages. Then ask them to write an explanation of the effects.

Building Social Studies Skills

Reading a Chart

Study the chart below. Then answer the questions that follow.

The Hundred Years' War in France

Date	BattleSite	What Happened
1346	Crécy	English king claimed French throne. English army invaded France and defeated French army.
1356	Poitiers	English won great victory over French. French king captured.
1415	Agincourt	After intervals of peace, English renewed claim to French throne. English army defeated French army.
1429	Orléans	Joan of Arc led French army. French defeated English.
1453	Castillon	French defeated English. Only Calais on English Channel remained in English hands.

1. Which statement correctly describes what you can infer from the chart?

  a. The year 1429 was a turning point in the Hundred Years' War.

  b. The Battle of Poitiers lasted for many days.

  c. In 1346 the French army was massed along the English Channel.

  d. The city of Calais is an English colony.

2. What effect did Joan of Arc have on the Hundred Years' War? Give specific examples.

Understanding Frames of Reference

Read this quote from *Sir Gawain and the Green Knight*, a romance from the 1300s about King Arthur's court. Then answer the questions.

> "'Good sir,' said Gawain, 'Will you give my message to the high lord of this house, that I ask for lodging?' . . . 'Yes, by Saint Peter,' replied the porter, 'and I think you may lodge here as long as you like, sir knight.' . . . Then the prince . . . appeared from his chamber to meet in mannerly style the man in his hall. 'You are welcome to dwell here as you wish,' he said, 'treat everything as your own, and have what you please in this place.'"

3. Which of the statements below best describes how the author of *Sir Gawain and the Green Knight* might react to a short story that displayed a mocking attitude toward the manners of chivalry?

  a. He would not understand it.

  b. He would probably find it amusing.

  c. He would probably be offended by it.

  d. He would think that the story was similar to what he wrote.

4. How did the Crusades contribute to the decline of the lifestyle of chivalry portrayed in the quote? Give specific examples.

Alternative Assessment

Building Your Portfolio

Economics

Before and since the Middle Ages and even today, the shift of people from the country to towns affects not only the economy but also the government and culture of a region. Using your textbook and other sources, compile a list of previous and modern-day areas of the world where such a population shift has occurred or is occurring. Use the list to create a cause-effect chart of this shift from country to town.

internet connect

Internet Activity: go.hrw.com
KEYWORD: SP3 WH14

Choose a topic on the High Middle Ages to:

• create a propaganda poster about the Crusades.

• learn more about the monarchies of Henry VII, Louis XI, and Ferdinand and Isabella of Spain.

• explore the effects of the Black Death on Europe in the 1300s.

---

2. Manors were no longer self-sufficient and power shifted from feudal lords to merchants and kings.

3. the nobles and the church

Thinking Critically

1. unified Europe and was the main source of information

2. attracted new residents and supplied jobs

3. Leaders in England and Spain brought unity through war and marriage. Louis XI united France through diplomacy and scheming.

4. vernacular literature such as poems by troubadours, romances, *fabliaux,* epics, and drama

Writing About History
Answers will vary, but might include differences in architecture, rulers, lifestyles, and religious beliefs.

Building Social Studies Skills
1. a

2. inspired French patriotism, led French to victory at Orléans

3. c

4. introduced Europeans to new ideas, revived trade, led to the growth of towns and the decline of the manorial system

Building Your Portfolio
Students should focus on the urbanization of developing nations in Latin America, Africa, and Asia.

CROSS-CULTURAL CONNECTIONS *Literature*

Spotlight on LITERATURE

Epic poetry is also known as heroic poetry—literature created to celebrate acts of skill and courage by a people's warriors and rulers. For example, during the Middle Ages, the French wrote *chansons de geste* (songs of heroic deeds) that celebrated the age of Charlemagne and other legendary French figures. Have students write a poem or song that reflects heroic deeds in their country. The deeds may be historic or contemporary. *(Answers will vary.)*

Spotlight on LITERATURE

Many cultures have a tradition of epic poetry. Like cultural epics, heroic epics began as stories passed down through generations in an oral form. Heroic epics were often sung by bards, such as the *mabo* of the Fulani people in Africa's Sudan. A *mabo* would travel with a nobleman setting out on a quest for adventure. After witnessing his lord's heroic deeds, the *mabo* then composed an epic poem called *baudi*. Ask students to research epic poetry and identify a translated epic poem that conveys the universal theme of heroism. Have students recite an excerpt from their chosen epic to the class.

Linking Past to Present

In most cultures, the spread of literacy brings an end to the composition of oral epic poetry. Today, some groups still compose oral heroic poetry. Scholars have collected examples of oral epic poetry from illiterate or semiliterate peoples in Russia, Central Asia, and Greece. Scholars argue that these examples prove ancient poets like Homer also could have composed very long oral epic poems. The lengthy poems are possible because a bard blends well-known scenes with new details each time he sings a poem. In 1934 one scholar wrote down an epic poem of 12,000 lines, sung by an illiterate bard from southern Serbia.

Critical Thinking

Why do you think some cultural groups continue a tradition of oral poetry?

ANSWER: For illiterate groups, oral poetry continues to provide an effective way to preserve their history and culture.

UNDERSTANDING LITERATURE ANSWER

similarities—dying heroes killed in battle, killed by people whom they know, make speeches on their deathbeds; differences—different reactions to death, different attitudes: Siegfried expresses anger and resentment; Arcita expresses love, regret, and forgiveness

CROSS-CULTURAL CONNECTIONS *Literature*

Epic Poetry

Epics are dramatic poems that often glorify a nation's history and its heroes. Literary epics can express and even define a nation's sense of its history and destiny. The German national epic, the Nibelungenlied *(nee·buh·LOONG·uhn·LEET), was first written down in the 1100s. It was one of the first European epics to be written in the language that ordinary people spoke. In the following excerpt from the* Nibelungenlied, *the hero Siegfried (ZEEG·freed) is killed by his brother-in-law King Gunther (GOON·tuhr). Geoffrey Chaucer wrote* The Canterbury Tales *during the 1300s, when an English national identity was first forming. Chaucer's tales are told by a group of pilgrims on their way to a holy shrine at Canterbury. The following passage from the Knight's tale in* The Canterbury Tales *reflects the English ideal of chivalry. Arcita has been fatally wounded in a battle with Palamon over Emily, whom they both love. Here he bids both his foe and his lover goodbye.*

The Nibelungenlied

When lord Siegfried felt the great wound, maddened with rage he bounded back from the stream with the long shaft jutting from his heart.

The hero's face had lost its color and he was no longer able to stand. His strength had ebbed away, for in the field of his bright countenance he now displayed Death's token. Soon many fair ladies would be weeping for him. . . . "You vile cowards," he said as he lay dying. ". . . I was always loyal to you, but now I have paid for it. Alas, you have wronged your kinsmen so that all who are born in days to come will be dishonored by your deed. . . . You will be held in contempt and stand apart from all good warriors." The knights all ran to where he lay wounded to death. It was a sad day for many of them. Those who were at all loyal-hearted mourned for him, and this, as a gay and valiant knight, he had well deserved.

The Canterbury Tales *by Geoffrey Chaucer*

Farewell my sweet foe! O my Emily!
Oh take me in your gentle arms I pray,
For love of God, and hear what I will say.
"I have here with my cousin Palamon,
Had strife [conflict] and rancour [ill will] many a day that's gone,
For love of you and for my jealousy.
May Jove [the Greek god Jupiter] so surely guide my soul for me,
To speak about a lover properly,
With all the circumstances, faithfully—
That is to say, truth, honour, and knighthood,
Wisdom, humility and kinship good,
And generous soul and all the lover's art—
So now may Jove have in my soul his part
As in this world, right now, I know of none
So worthy to be loved as Palamon,
Who serves you and will do so all his life.
And if you ever should become a wife,
Forget not Palamon, the noble man."

Understanding Literature

What similarities exist in these German and English epics? How do they differ? What attitudes are expressed in the dying words of the two soldiers?

Culture

Have students choose a non-European country and research its architecture within the period 395–1589. Students should use magazine pictures or their own drawings to create an illustrated report of their findings.

Geography

Have students study a physical map of Asia. Then ask students to map a route for traveling between east and west Asia during the 800s. Draw the following graphic organizer on the board and have students copy it as a guide. After students have completed their plans, have them work in small groups to discuss and evaluate the effectiveness of their routes.

Problem-Solving Process

↓

Identify the problem—What are you trying to do?

↓

Gather information—What are the geographic obstacles? Where could you find supplies such as water and food?

↓

List and consider options—What routes are possible?

↓

Consider advantages and disadvantages—What are the good and bad points of various routes?

↓

Choose and implement a solution

BUILDING YOUR Portfolio

Bronze and enamel dish crafted by an Islamic artist in the 1100s

Culture

Architecture is an important expression of culture in all societies. Imagine you are an art historian preparing a lecture on church architecture during the Middle Ages in Europe. Write an outline for a lecture describing the importance of church architecture during this period and the building techniques and materials used. Explain what the churches and cathedrals of the Middle Ages reveal about religious life in medieval society. Use the bibliography below to help you in your research. When your outline is done, prepare a bibliography of the sources you used.

Further Reading

Browning, Robert. *The Byzantine Empire.* Washington, D.C.: Catholic University of America, 1992. A general overview of the Byzantine Empire.

Cantor, Norman F., ed. *The Encyclopedia of the Middle Ages.* New York: Viking, 1999. A reference work covering politics, culture, daily life, religion, and important figures of the Middle Ages.

Dersin, Denise, ed. *What Life Was Like: In the Lands of the Prophet, Islamic World A.D. 570–1405.* Alexandria, Virginia: Time-Life Books, 1999. An overview of the history and culture of the Islamic world.

Hanawalt, Barbara. *The Middle Ages: An Illustrated History.* New York: Oxford University Press, 1999. A sweeping survey of the Middle Ages from 400–1500.

Ross, Frank and Michael Goodman. *Oracle Bones, Stars, and Wheelbarrows: Ancient Chinese Science and Technology.* New York: Houghton-Mifflin, 1990. An overview of early Chinese contributions to science and technology.

Geography

Geography significantly influences historical development. Imagine you are an Arab trader living in Morocco during the mid-1100s. You have just returned from a profitable trip to Constantinople. Your task is to create a map showing your journey and a chart of the types of goods you took with you and the types of goods you brought back. Be specific about the geographic obstacles you encountered, the places you stopped, and how the items you bought and sold reflected people's needs during this time.

Examples of medieval architecture: Chartres Cathedral in France (right) and the Monastery of St. Mary the Victorious in Portugal (below).

internet connect

go.hrw.com

Internet Activity
KEYWORD: SP3 U3

In assigned groups, develop a multimedia presentation about early East Asia, the Byzantine Empire, the Islamic Empire, or medieval Europe. Choose information from the chapter Internet Connect activities and the Holt Researcher that best reflects the major topics of the period. Write an outline and a script for your presentation, which may be shown to the class.

Culture

In South India, between the 600s and 1700s, Hindu temples were built in a distinctive style. The pyramid shape of the temples' towers sets this style apart. Outer temple walls are covered with bands of floral and animal carvings as well as ornately carved sculptures. The pyramid tower is made up of layers, each holding miniature shrines. Finally, the tower is topped by a dome-shaped cupola and finial. The earliest examples of Dravida temples were cut out of rock in the 600s. However, the style is best shown in the extraordinary Brhadisvara temple at Thanjavur which was built in about 1003–10 by Rajaraja the Great. Enormous labor and skill were required to complete temples built in the South Indian style.

Critical Thinking

How is the architecture of Hindu temples similar to European cathedral architecture?

ANSWER: Both are ornately carved and required a great deal of skill and labor to produce.

UNIT 4 — The Age of Exploration

EXAMINING THE VISUAL RECORD

❶ Why do you think the sun is included in this painting?

ANSWER: It is important in navigation.

The earliest sailors used the sun, stars, and coastal landmarks to guide their vessels. In the early 1400s Prince Henry the Navigator created nautical charts and tables of the declinations of the sun (angular distance from the celestial equator). Scholars believe Columbus probably carried a compass, a cross-staff, and a table of the sun's declination to navigate his journey across the Atlantic in 1492.

❷ How does the artist portray Columbus's ship?

ANSWER: fast, majestic, strong

During the 1400s the Spanish and Portuguese used caravels for voyages of exploration. Caravels were relatively small, light, and agile ships that usually carried three to four masts with lateen (triangular) sails. These features allowed caravels to sail against the wind, have incredible speed, and navigate well on the open sea as well as coastal waters. In Columbus's 1492 voyage, both the *Niña* and the *Pinta* were caravels. Columbus put square sails on the *Niña* to increase the ship's ability to run before the wind.

ACTIVITY: Ask students to research shipbuilding during the 1400s and 1500s. Students should present their findings in an illustrated report that focuses on one type of ship from this period.

UNIT 4 — The Age of Exploration and Expansion

1300–1868

CHAPTER 17 **Asia in Transition**

Two powerful dynasties, the Ming and the Qing, ruled China as a self-sufficient state for more than 500 years. During this time, internal trade increased, population grew, and popular culture developed. However, growing contact with Europeans weakened the Qing dynasty and gradually undermined China's sovereignty. Despite its rulers' desire to prevent foreign contact and trade, European influence also began to be felt in Japan.

CHAPTER 18 **Islamic Empires in Asia**

During the 1300s and 1400s the Ottomans built a strong empire in the area of present-day Turkey.

Meanwhile, Safavid rulers created a powerful Shi'ite Muslim empire in what is today Iran. In the 1500s Mongols attacked Turkish Muslim rulers in India and established the Mughal Empire. During the following two centuries, the Mughals unified a vast and diverse Muslim empire.

CHAPTER 15

The Renaissance and Reformation

1350–1700

CHAPTER 16

Exploration and Expansion

1400–1800

CHAPTER 17

Asia in Transition

1368–1868

CHAPTER 18

Islamic Empires in Asia

1300–1700

Main Events

- The significance of the Renaissance and the Reformation
- The impact of European exploration, expansion, and colonization
- The effects of the West on China and Japan
- The growth of Islamic empires

Main Ideas

- What was the Renaissance?
- Why did the Reformation happen and what effect did it have on Europe?
- What accounted for the interest in exploration? Why was it important?
- How did China and Japan deal with the increased interest of the West?
- Where were the Ottoman, Safavid, and Mughal Empires?

Sextant used by sailors in the 1700s to navigate

This painting shows one artist's conception of Columbus crossing the Atlantic. 349

CROSS-CULTURAL CONNECTIONS

🔊 LET'S GET STARTED!

Ask students to describe the ingredients in spaghetti. *(at least noodles and tomato sauce)* Then ask them to identify the ethnic origin of the dish. *(Italian)* Explain to students that many foods that we identify with European countries actually contain ingredients that were not native to those nations. For example, both tomatoes and cocoa are native to the Americas and were introduced to Europe through the Columbian Exchange. Tell students to read page 394 for more information about the Columbian Exchange.

TEACH

ALL LEVELS: Ask students to give examples of the exchanges between different world regions and help them fill out the graphic organizer below with the information shown in italics.
ENGLISH LANGUAGE LEARNERS

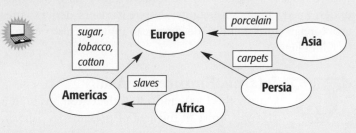

Daily Life

During the Renaissance the dramatic growth of European cities reflected the continent's economic resurgence. Several cities became important centers for economic activity. Lisbon was the base of the Portuguese seafaring empire. Seville became the Spanish gateway to the New World. England's cloth-making and banking activities were centered in London. Lyons, France, became an important market center and capital of the silk industry. In Belgium, Antwerp developed as a center for international banking and the primary European market for German copper and silver, Portuguese spices, and Italian alum. Antwerp more than doubled its population in the late 1400s and doubled it again by 1560.

Critical Thinking

How are economic growth and population growth related?

ANSWER: Growing populations create increased demand for goods and services. Economic growth provides the food and other services necessary for the survival of a larger population.

CROSS-CULTURAL CONNECTIONS

Focus on: Economics

Main Idea **What events changed the economies of nations throughout the world?** A changing economy set in motion a number of dramatic events during the Renaissance. Cities became vital centers of economic activity. Rich merchants and bankers used their wealth to support the arts. Hoping to gain access to the treasures of the East, European monarchs became interested in overseas exploration. Exploration brought Europeans into contact with other peoples, which at times led to conflict.

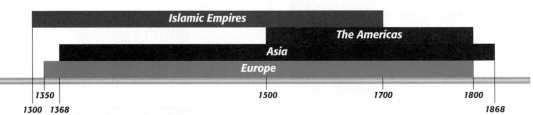

Europe, 1350–1800

During the Renaissance, monarchs and other wealthy Europeans began acquiring Eastern luxury items, such as this beautiful Persian carpet woven by highly skilled craftspeople in the late 1500s.

◀ **The European Marketplace** The Renaissance was not simply a period of artistic rebirth, it was also a time of significant economic growth. Between the 1300s and 1600s, several factors changed the European economy. New and more efficient methods of bookkeeping improved business practices. An increase in population, the rise of cities, a greater supply of money, and advances in transportation and communication meant that more people could buy a wider variety of goods. The center of business activity was the local marketplace, such as the Naples market pictured here. People came to markets to buy and sell food, household items, livestock, and tools. Merchants offered goods made by local artisans alongside exotic items from faraway lands.

The Slave Trade in the Americas Overseas exploration led to increased trade between European and African countries. The Portuguese, British, and French were among the first to participate in the Atlantic slave trade. In this exchange, Europeans captured or bought enslaved Africans in West Africa and transported them to the New World. Here they were sold to planters in North and South America or the Caribbean to fill a growing need for plantation labor. As European demand for plantation products such as sugar, tobacco, and cotton increased, the demand for slaves also rose. During the 1500s and 1600s, the Atlantic slave trade became centrally important to the economies of the colonial powers. This illustration shows slaves working on a Brazilian plantation in 1662.

The Americas, 1500–1800

REVIEW

Tell students to imagine that they are traveling around the world sampling cuisine and other products from each continent that was involved in the Columbian Exchange. Have students create postcards to send back to the United States from each continent. Each postcard should identify the continent that the student is visiting and contain a brief message identifying foods he or she ate that were introduced to the continent during the Columbian Exchange. Have volunteers explain their postcards to the class.

ASSESS

Have students complete their answer to the question in "Why It

Matters Today" and add it to their portfolio. As Alternative Assessment, use the graphic organizer in this lesson.

EXTEND

Have students research the economic relationship between Europe and Asia between 1350 and 1800. Tell students to address the following questions in a research paper using standard grammar, spelling, sentence structure, and punctuation: How were economic ties created between the continents? What goods were exchanged? Did one continent benefit from the exchanges more than the other? **BLOCK SCHEDULING**

Economic Growth Under the Ming China's economy grew strong during the Ming dynasty (1368-1644). Despite an official effort to discourage foreign trade, the European and Japanese demand for Chinese goods flourished. Europeans particularly prized the fine pottery Marco Polo had described as *porcellana* during his visit to China in the late 1200s. During the Ming period, Chinese artists created porcelain masterpieces with government support. Bright patterns—such as the one on this porcelain jar—became the dominant style in the late Ming period.

Asia, 1368–1868

Islamic Empires, 1300–1700

Safavid Prosperity Under the rule of Shah 'Abbās the Great in the late 1500s and early 1600s, the Safavid Empire in Persia reached new economic and cultural heights. 'Abbās encouraged manufacturing and trade, and Persian artisans produced carpets, fabrics, and ceramics that were prized around the world. This prosperity also helped Safavid arts and culture flourish, especially in the capital city of Eṣfahān. Carefully planned and filled with major works of art and architecture, Eṣfahān became known as one of the most beautiful cities of its day. In Eṣfahān Shah 'Abbās built the Palace of Chihil Soutoun, which is where the fresco at left can be seen. In the fresco, a Persian princess writes a letter in a park while a kneeling attendant offers her a drink.

This handle in the form of a horse's head was made in the Mughal Empire sometime between about 1658 and 1710.

Why It Matters Today

Economic growth and foreign trade between the 1400s and 1800s led to a level of cultural contact most of the world had never before experienced. Today, economic factors such as trade, marketing, and advertising lead to cultural contact and cultural change. **What examples of economic influence on culture can you find today?**

Global Relations

Ming rulers worked hard to prevent Chinese contact with people from other countries. They prohibited private dealings with foreigners and did not let their subjects travel abroad. However, these restrictions were unpopular and not enforceable. As a result, widespread smuggling took place. When Europeans first visited China's coast in 1514, Ming rulers did not welcome them. As a result, Portuguese traders became involved in what the Ming called piracy and smuggling. The Spaniards soon developed an active illegal trade with China as well.

Critical Thinking

Why do you think Ming rulers prohibited foreign contact?

ANSWER: Answers may vary, but students may suggest that the Ming believed interactions with foreigners would weaken their empire.

WHY IT MATTERS TODAY ANSWER

Answers will vary but specific examples should be from the factors listed—trade, marketing, and advertising.

The Renaissance and Reformation

CHAPTER RESOURCE MANAGER

Objectives	Pacing Guide	Reproducible Resources
SECTION 1 **The Italian Renaissance** (pp. 354–358) • Identify the factors that led to the Italian Renaissance and describe the characteristics of Renaissance thought. • Explain how Renaissance writers combined classical teachings and Christian doctrine. • Describe how Renaissance art differed from art of the Middle Ages.	**Regular** 1.5 day / **Block Scheduling** 1 day *Block Scheduling Handbook with Team Teaching Strategies, 15.1*	**RS** Guided Reading Strategy 15.1 **RS** Graphic Organizer Activity 15: Renaissance Accomplishments **PS** Readings in World History 53: Advice to Princes
SECTION 2 **The Northern Renaissance** (pp. 359–362) • Explain how the ideas of the Italian Renaissance spread to other parts of Europe. • Describe how northern Renaissance writers differed from Italian Humanists. • List the principal characteristics of northern Renaissance art.	**Regular** 1.5 day / **Block Scheduling** 1 day *Block Scheduling Handbook with Team Teaching Strategies, 15.2*	**RS** Guided Reading Strategy 15.2 **SM** Geography Activity 15: The Spread of the Renaissance
SECTION 3 **The Protestant Reformation** (pp. 363–367) • Discuss the developments that led to the Reformation. • Describe how Martin Luther protested against the Roman Catholic Church and began a new church. • Identify the factors that caused the spread of Protestantism. • Explain the role that Calvinism played in the Reformation.	**Regular** 1.5 day / **Block Scheduling** 1 day *Block Scheduling Handbook with Team Teaching Strategies, 15.3*	**RS** Guided Reading Strategy 15.3 **PS** Readings in World History 54: Luther's Refusal at the Diet of Worms
SECTION 4 **The Catholic Reformation** (pp. 368–371) • Describe how the Catholic Church responded to the Reformation. • Discuss the results of the Reformation and the Counter-Reformation.	**Regular** 1.5 day / **Block Scheduling** 1 day *Block Scheduling Handbook with Team Teaching Strategies, 15.4*	**RS** Guided Reading Strategy 15.4 **E** Creative Teaching Strategy 15: TV Documentary on the Renaissance and Reformation
SECTION 5 **Culture and Daily Life** (pp. 372–377) • Explain why Europeans believed in superstitions. • Describe the characteristics of daily life that were typical in Europe during the Reformation. • Explain how knowledge spread to European villages. • Identify the factors that caused changes in the daily lives of Europeans.	**Regular** 1.5 day / **Block Scheduling** 1 day *Block Scheduling Handbook with Team Teaching Strategies, 15.5*	**RS** Guided Reading Strategy 15.5 **PS** Readings in World History 55: Sports in England **E** Hands-on History Activity 15: Renaissance Dining

Chapter Resource Key

PS	Primary Sources	**A**	Assessment	♫ Music
RS	Reading Support	**REV**	Review	📼 Video
IC	Interdisciplinary Connections	**ELL**	Reinforcement and English Language Learners	🖥 Internet
E	Enrichment		Transparencies	Holt Presentation Maker Using Microsoft® PowerPoint®
SM	Skills Mastery		CD-ROM	

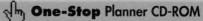

One-Stop Planner CD-ROM

See the **One-Stop Planner** for a complete list of additional resources for students and teachers.

One-Stop Planner CD-ROM

It's easy to plan lessons, select resources, and print out materials for your students when you use the **One-Stop Planner** CD–ROM with **Test Generator.**

<table>
<tr><th colspan="2">Technology Resources</th><th colspan="2">Reinforcement, Review, and Assessment</th></tr>
<tr>
<td>

One-Stop Planner, Lesson 15.1

Holt Researcher: World History: Petrarch

Holt Researcher: World History: Leonardo da Vinci & Michelangelo

CNN. Presents World Cultures: Yesterday and Today Segment 14: Divinci for Sale

Homework Practice Online

</td>
<td>

Daily Quiz 15.1

Main Idea Activity 15.1

English Audio Summary 15.1

Spanish Audio Summary 15.1

REV Section 1 Review, p. 358

</td>
</tr>
<tr>
<td>

One-Stop Planner, Lesson 15.2

World History and Cultures Video Program 14: The Renaissance Perspective

Homework Practice Online

</td>
<td>

Daily Quiz 15.2

Main Idea Activity 15.2

English Audio Summary 15.2

Spanish Audio Summary 15.2

REV Section 2 Review, p. 362

</td>
</tr>
<tr>
<td>

One-Stop Planner, Lesson 15.3

Holt Researcher: World History: John Calvin

Religions of the World Video Series: Christianity

Homework Practice Online

</td>
<td>

Daily Quiz 15.3

Main Idea Activity 15.3

English Audio Summary 15.3

Spanish Audio Summary 15.3

REV Section 3 Review, p. 367

</td>
</tr>
<tr>
<td>

One-Stop Planner, Lesson 15.4

World History teaching Transparency: Everyday Life 11: A University Classroom in the Middle Ages

Religions of the World Video Series: Christianity

Homework Practice Online

Online Maps, Charts, and Graphs: European Religions, 1600

</td>
<td>

Daily Quiz 15.4

Main Idea Activity 15.4

English Audio Summary 15.4

Spanish Audio Summary 15.4

REV Section 4 Review, p. 371

</td>
</tr>
<tr>
<td>

One-Stop Planner, Lesson 15.5

World History and Cultures Video Program 15: A Different Way of Thinking

Homework Practice Online

Online Maps, Charts, and Graphs: Printing Centers in Europe Before 1500

</td>
<td>

Daily Quiz 15.5

Main Idea Activity 15.5

English Audio Summary 15.5

Spanish Audio Summary 15.5

REV Section 5 Review, p. 377

</td>
</tr>
</table>

⊿ internet connect

HRW ONLINE RESOURCES
GO TO: go.hrw.com
Then type in a keyword.

TEACHER HOME PAGE
KEYWORD: SP3 Teacher

CHAPTER INTERNET ACTIVITIES
KEYWORD: SP3 WH15

Choose an activity to:
- create a pamphlet on the Reformation and its leaders.
- report on the economic, social, and technological influences of Johannes Gutenberg's printing press.
- create a biography on one of the Renaissance writers in this chapter.

CHAPTER ENRICHMENT LINKS
KEYWORD: SP3 CH15

ONLINE ASSESSMENT
Homework Practice
KEYWORD: SP3 HP15
Standardized Test Prep
KEYWORD: SP3 STP15
Rubrics
KEYWORD: SS Rubrics

ONLINE MAPS, CHARTS, AND GRAPHS
KEYWORD: SP3 MCG

CONTENT UPDATES
KEYWORD: SS Content Updates

HOLT PRESENTATION MAKER
KEYWORD: SP3 PPT15

ONLINE READING SUPPORT
KEYWORD: SS Strategies

CURRENT EVENTS
KEYWORD: S3 Current Events

Meeting Individual Needs

Ability Levels

Level 1 Basic level activities designed for all students encountering new material

Level 2 Intermediate level activities designed for average students

Level 3 Challenging activities designed for honors and gifted and talented students

English Language Learners These activities address the needs of students with Limited English Proficiency.

Chapter Review and Assessment

IC Vocabulary Activity 15

Global Skill Builder CD–ROM

HRW Web Site

REV Chapter 15 Tutorial for Students, Parents, Mentors, and Peers

REV Chapter 15 Review, pp. 378–379

A Chapter 15 Test Generator (on the One-Stop Planner)

A Chapter 15 Test (Form A or B)

A Alternative Assessment Handbook

A Chapter 15 Test for English Language Learners and Special-Needs Students

Build on What You Know

Ask students to answer the following questions:

How do the art and literature of a society reflect its culture?

Consider:

- the epic poetry of Greece's Homeric Age
- the art and literature of Greece's Golden and Hellenistic Ages
- the glorification of God reflected in churches

What factors led to earlier shifts in religious thought and practice?

Consider:

- the origination of Christianity during Roman times
- the splitting of the Christian church into the Roman Catholic Church and the Eastern Orthodox Church
- the Babylonian Captivity and the Great Schism

CHAPTER 15

1350–1700

The Renaissance and Reformation

Renaissance banker Cosimo de Medici

1351–1353 Global Events
Florence successfully defends itself against a Milanese invasion.

1375 Politics
Florence organizes a league that rebels against Pope Gregory XI.

1434 Politics
Banker Cosimo de Medici gains control of Florence.

1463 Daily Life
English law forbids common folk from wearing gold or purple, which are reserved for royalty.

1350

1400

1450

1378 Business and Finance
Cloth workers in Florence revolt to reform the city's guild system.

1408 Business and Finance
St. George's Bank is founded in Genoa.

1427 Business and Finance
The ruler of Florence introduces an income tax.

c. 1450 Science and Technology
Johannes Gutenberg develops a printing press with movable type.

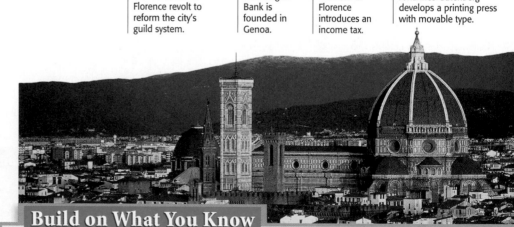

The city of Florence and its cathedral, the Duomo

Build on What You Know

During the Middle Ages, religion wielded great influence over art, government, and literature. The Catholic Church was the leading religious institution in western Europe. Also during the Middle Ages, the Crusades spurred a revival of trade in western Europe. Towns and cities began to grow again. Nations formed strong governments and began to challenge church laws that limited trade and industry. In this chapter, you will learn about the changes in art, literature, and thought that marked this new era in European life. You will also learn about new ideas in religion that challenged the moral authority of the Catholic Church.

What's Your Opinion?

Global Relations

Agree Religious practices and beliefs serve as common, unifying factors for people of different regions.

Disagree Differing opinions regarding religious practices and beliefs drive people of different regions apart.

Science, Technology & Society

Agree New technologies allow for ideas to spread more easily, leading eventually to changes in cultural values.

Disagree New technologies allow those in power to increase the flow of propaganda, thus supporting the cultural status quo.

Culture

Agree Ideas and works from ancient cultures are either lost over time or so outdated that they do not affect other cultures.

Disagree Ideas and works from ancient cultures are often revisited and reinterpreted by other cultures, providing building blocks for new thoughts and accomplishments.

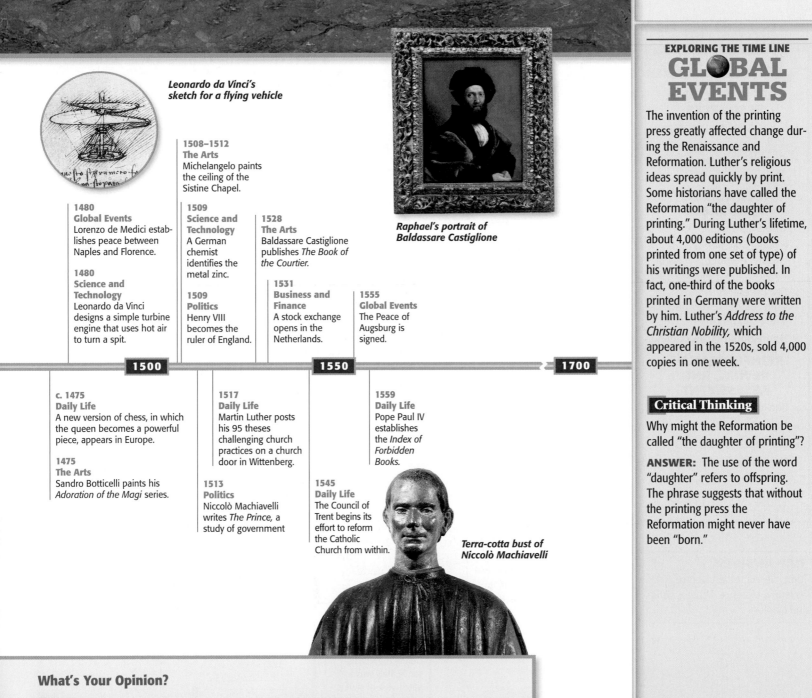

Leonardo da Vinci's sketch for a flying vehicle

Raphael's portrait of Baldassare Castiglione

1508–1512
The Arts
Michelangelo paints the ceiling of the Sistine Chapel.

1480
Global Events
Lorenzo de Medici establishes peace between Naples and Florence.

1480
Science and Technology
Leonardo da Vinci designs a simple turbine engine that uses hot air to turn a spit.

1509
Science and Technology
A German chemist identifies the metal zinc.

1509
Politics
Henry VIII becomes the ruler of England.

1528
The Arts
Baldassare Castiglione publishes *The Book of the Courtier.*

1531
Business and Finance
A stock exchange opens in the Netherlands.

1555
Global Events
The Peace of Augsburg is signed.

1500 — **1550** — **1700**

c. 1475
Daily Life
A new version of chess, in which the queen becomes a powerful piece, appears in Europe.

1475
The Arts
Sandro Botticelli paints his *Adoration of the Magi* series.

1517
Daily Life
Martin Luther posts his 95 theses challenging church practices on a church door in Wittenberg.

1513
Politics
Niccolò Machiavelli writes *The Prince,* a study of government

1545
Daily Life
The Council of Trent begins its effort to reform the Catholic Church from within.

1559
Daily Life
Pope Paul IV establishes the *Index of Forbidden Books.*

Terra-cotta bust of Niccolò Machiavelli

EXPLORING THE TIME LINE
GLOBAL EVENTS

The invention of the printing press greatly affected change during the Renaissance and Reformation. Luther's religious ideas spread quickly by print. Some historians have called the Reformation "the daughter of printing." During Luther's lifetime, about 4,000 editions (books printed from one set of type) of his writings were published. In fact, one-third of the books printed in Germany were written by him. Luther's *Address to the Christian Nobility,* which appeared in the 1520s, sold 4,000 copies in one week.

Critical Thinking

Why might the Reformation be called "the daughter of printing"?

ANSWER: The use of the word "daughter" refers to offspring. The phrase suggests that without the printing press the Reformation might never have been "born."

What's Your Opinion?

Global Relations Religion brings people of different regions together.

Science, Technology & Society New technologies can advance the spread of ideas that change cultural values.

Culture Ideas and works from ancient times do not affect other cultures.

OBJECTIVES

1 **Identify** the factors that led to the Italian Renaissance and describe the characteristics of Renaissance thought.

2 **Explain** how Renaissance writers combined classical teachings and Christian doctrine.

3 **Describe** how Renaissance art differed from art of the Middle Ages.

🎙️ *LET'S GET STARTED!*

Display examples of medieval and Renaissance art, such as Pietro Cavallini's *Birth of the Virgin* for medieval and Raphael's *School of Athens* for Renaissance. Have volunteers compare these works. *(Medieval art portrays ideal type, hides human form; Renaissance art focuses on human form and individuality.)* Explain that in Section 1, students will learn more about the ideals and values of the Renaissance.

MAP ANSWER

Turin, Genoa, Milan, Venice, Ravenna, Florence, Urbino, Rome, and Naples

---

READ TO DISCOVER

1 How did the Renaissance begin, and what characterized the thought of this era?

2 How were Renaissance writers able to bring classical teachings and Christian doctrine together?

3 How did Renaissance art differ from art of the Middle Ages?

DEFINE

humanists
perspective

IDENTIFY

Renaissance
Isabella d'Este
Francesco Petrarch
Niccolò Machiavelli
Leonardo da Vinci
Michelangelo

▶ WHY IT MATTERS TODAY

Works of Renaissance art remain popular throughout the world today. Use **CNNfyi.com** or other **current event** sources to learn more about Renaissance art on display in museums. Record your findings in your journal.

CNNfyi.com

The Italian Renaissance

The Main Idea
The Renaissance brought a renewed interest in Greek and Roman culture and a new way of thinking.

The Story Continues *On November 4, 1966, the Arno River in northern Italy flooded its banks and sent a torrent of water into the museums, cathedrals, and libraries of the city of Florence. News of the flood damage alarmed the world. Why? Because Florence contained the world's greatest store of Renaissance art and literature. This outpouring of creativity that began in the 1300s changed the course of Western civilization.*

An Era of Awakening

In the early 1300s, a movement began in Italy that would alter how Europeans viewed themselves and their world. The **Renaissance**—or "rebirth"—was both a philosophical and artistic movement and the era when that movement flourished. It was marked by a renewed interest in ancient Greek and Roman literature and life. Medieval scholars had studied ancient history and tried to bring everything they learned into harmony with Christian teachings.

By contrast, Italian Renaissance scholars studied the ancient world to explore its great achievements. A new emphasis on the power of human reason developed, and many advances were made in the arts and sciences.

Renaissance Italy, c. 1500

Interpreting Maps During the Renaissance, Italy was a patchwork of states.

■ **Skills Assessment: Human Systems** What commercial cities became the centers of city-states?

ALL LEVELS: Have students work in pairs to create a list of factors that led to the Renaissance (*ruins of the Roman Empire a reminder of Roman glory; contact with Byzantine civilization through Crusades and trade; knowledge of Arab and African achievements in science and medicine; an artistic awakening; the study of classical Greek and Roman literature and life; scholars' search for new knowledge*) Then ask students to copy the graphic organizer as shown, omitting the italicized answers. Work with students to fill in the ovals. Use the completed graphic organizer to discuss the nature of thought during the Renaissance. **ENGLISH LANGUAGE LEARNERS, COOPERATIVE LEARNING**

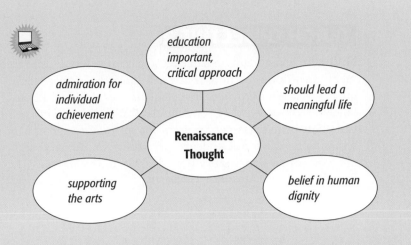

admiration for individual achievement

education important, critical approach

should lead a meaningful life

Renaissance Thought

supporting the arts

belief in human dignity

Causes. In many ways it was natural that the Renaissance would begin in Italy. Ruins of the Roman Empire reminded Italians of Roman glory. The Crusades and trade had brought them into contact with the Byzantine civilization, whose scholars had preserved Greek and Roman learning. In addition, trade with southwestern Asia and Africa helped Italians learn of Arab and African achievements in science and medicine. Over time, these and other factors helped to encourage curiosity and the search for new knowledge among some Italian thinkers.

Italian cities such as Florence, Milan, Naples, Rome, and Venice had grown rich through trade and industry. Their citizens included educated, wealthy merchants and bankers. In Florence, for example, the Medici (MED·ee·chee) family grew rich, first as bankers and then as rulers of that city-state. As leader of Florence, Lorenzo de Medici used his wealth to become a great patron of the arts. In Mantua, **Isabella d'Este** filled her palace with paintings and sculptures by the finest Renaissance artists.

The humanities. In the early Renaissance of the 1300s, Italian scholars turned to classical Greek and Roman literature to study grammar, history, poetry, and rhetoric. These studies are called the humanities, and people who specialized in them were **humanists.** Renaissance humanists searched out manuscripts written in Greek and Latin. Often, they found more than one copy of a work. If the copies differed, the humanists compared them to determine which was the most authentic. In doing so, they displayed a critical approach to learning and scholarship. That is, they sought to verify through investigation. Some Christian scholars also turned to Jewish teachers to learn Hebrew, a language of the Bible. While there were still laws that restricted Jewish life, many Jewish humanists continued to strive for knowledge and to develop new ideas.

As humanists studied classical manuscripts, they came to believe that it was important to understand how things worked. This belief led humanists to emphasize education. They also maintained that a person should lead a meaningful life. People should also become actively involved in practical affairs, such as supporting the arts.

Although fascinated by the classics, most humanists were Catholics who remained committed to Christian teachings. For that reason, they sometimes felt a tension between their studies and their religion. Humanists viewed life not only as preparation for the afterlife, but also as a joy in itself. Along with a belief in human dignity came an admiration for individual achievement. Many individuals of this period displayed a variety of talents by being, for example, both poets and scientists.

✔ **READING CHECK: Summarizing** What were the main features of Renaissance humanist thought? critical approach, studied classics, admired human achievement

Italian Renaissance Writers

One of the first humanists was **Francesco Petrarch** (PEE·trahrk), who lived from 1304 to 1374. Like many humanists, Petrarch became famous as a scholar and a teacher. He also wrote poetry. His sonnets to Laura, an imaginary ideal woman, are considered some of the greatest love poems in literature.

Petrarch's main influence grew out of his desire to continue the work of the classical writers. Petrarch believed that the classical writers were committed to virtue in public and private life. He thought these writers could best be imitated by studying their writings. The study of ancient Greek and Roman literature came to be called classical education. Knowledge of classical Greek and Latin became the mark of an

HISTORY MAKER

Isabella d'Este (1474–1539)

The court of Isabella d'Este was one of the most brilliant of the Italian Renaissance. Educated in languages and poetry, Isabella was a woman of keen intelligence and power.

Isabella used her wealth to support artists and scholars. She housed many writers, sculptors, and painters in her own court and hired famous architects to design parts of her palace. She was the subject of several paintings, including the portrait shown above. **How did Isabella d'Este support the arts?**

Holt Researcher

go.hrw.com
KEYWORD: Holt Researcher
FreeFind: Francesco Petrarch
After reading more about Francesco Petrarch on the Holt Researcher, write a sonnet that reflects the ideals of the humanists.

Interdisciplinary Connection

HUMANITIES. Today many college students specialize in the humanities. They major in such fields as philosophy, foreign language, literature, history, or religion. Students whose major is in the humanities receive what is called a liberal arts degree.

ACTIVITY: Look through college catalogs for a list of humanities classes. Have students choose one that interests them and explain why they would like to study that subject.

internet connect

TOPIC: Renaissance men
GO TO: go.hrw.com
KEYWORD: SP3 WH15

Have students access the Internet through the HRW Go site to find more information on one of the Renaissance men in this chapter. Have students write a biography about that person. Remind students to include information about the person's life, major accomplishments, and historical significance in the biography.

Culture

This excerpt from Baldassare Castiglione's *The Book of the Courtier* describes the proper role of the gentleman: "I would have him speak not always of serious subjects but also of amusing things, such as games and jests and jokes, according to the occasion. He should always, of course, speak out fully and frankly, and avoid talking nonsense." Of gentlewomen, Castiglione wrote: "She should know how to choose topics suitable for the kind of person she is addressing.... She should not introduce… jests and jokes into a discussion about serious things. She should not… [pretend] to know what she does not know, but she should seek modestly to win credit for knowing what she does."

Critical Thinking

Ask students to compare Castiglione's ideas about gentlemen and gentlewomen.

ANSWER: Students should note that both gentlemen and gentlewomen should know how to speak appropriately for the occasion.

VISUAL RECORD ANSWER

Relations were very formal and polite as indicated by the distance between the two central figures.

Reproducible Resources

PS   Readings in World History 53: Advice to Princes

educated person. Petrarch thought it important to lead a full and active life here on earth. He also worried that his desire for fame, a relatively common ambition, might hurt his chances for salvation.

Other writers displayed less tension between spiritual and earthly quests. **Niccolò Machiavelli** (mahk·yah·VEL·lee), a Florentine diplomat and historian, lived from 1469 to 1527. In 1513 he wrote the essay *The Prince*. Machiavelli sought to describe government not in terms of lofty ideals but in the way it actually worked. He argued that a ruler should be concerned only with power and political success. Today some people refer to ruthless behavior to get ahead as "Machiavellian."

Analyzing Primary Sources

Analyzing Information Why does Machiavelli argue that fear is a more effective tool for ruling than love is? love will not overcome people's self-interest

History Makers Speak

❝A controversy has arisen about this: whether it is better to be loved than feared, or vice versa. My view is that it is desirable to be both loved and feared; but it is difficult to achieve both and, if one of them has to be lacking, it is much safer to be feared than loved.... Men are less hesitant about offending or harming a ruler who makes himself less loved than one who inspires fear. For love is sustained by a bond of gratitude, which because men are excessively self-interested, is broken whenever they see a chance to benefit themselves. But fear is sustained by a dread of punishment that is always effective.❞

Niccolò Machiavelli, *The Prince*

Machiavelli can be considered a humanist because he looked to the ancient Romans as models. The lack of concern for conventional morality in *The Prince*, however, sets him apart from other humanists of the time.

Baldassare Castiglione (kahs·teel·YOH·nay), an Italian diplomat, lived from 1478 to 1529. In 1528 he published what was probably the most famous book of the Renaissance, *The Book of the Courtier*. The setting for the book is the court at Urbino, an Italian city-state where Castiglione lived for many years. In his book, Castiglione used real people engaged in fictional conversations to explain how gentlemen and gentlewomen should act in polite society.

✔ **READING CHECK: Contrasting** In what way does Machiavelli's work differ from that of other humanists? lack of concern for morality

INTERPRETING THE VISUAL RECORD

Renaissance relationships The Italian writer Baldassare Castiglione wrote *The Book of the Courtier* to contrast the coarse knight of the Middle Ages with the refined courtier of the Renaissance. *How does the artist depict relations between ladies and gentlemen at the court?*

Italian Renaissance Artists

Like literature, art flourished during the Italian Renaissance. During this era Italian artists produced some of the world's greatest masterpieces.

Medieval paintings had stressed the world beyond everyday life. They used formal figures to express religious concerns. Renaissance artists, in contrast, created realistic scenes and images. They depicted lifelike human figures in their paintings. Even the backgrounds of Renaissance paintings differed from those of medieval paintings. Earlier artists had often portrayed the Holy Land. Renaissance painters showed the rugged Italian countryside they knew so well.

Renaissance painters used a technique called **perspective** to make their paintings more lifelike. They made distant objects smaller than those in the foreground of the painting. This technique created the illusion of depth on the flat canvas.

TEACH OBJECTIVE 3

LEVEL 2: Have students list features of medieval art. Then have them list features of Renaissance art. Have them work in groups to make a comparison chart on posterboard. *(for example, Medieval Art: stressed religion and the world beyond everyday life, depicted formal and stylized figures, depicted the Holy Land; Renaissance Art: depicted religious and non-religious subjects, depicted realistic and lifelike human figures, depicted the rugged Italian countryside)* **COOPERATIVE LEARNING**

TEACH OBJECTIVES 1, 2, and 3

LEVEL 3: Ask students to write an essay describing how Italian Renaissance art, literature, and thought were reflective of the period. *(Students' essays should include a discussion of the combination of religious themes with the humanistic values of the era, and site specific examples.)*

CLOSE

Ask students to write a journal entry on the following question: Why was the Renaissance considered a time of rebirth? Encourage students to consider the rediscovery of ancient achievements, human reason, and the many advances in the arts and sciences.

SKILL-BUILDING STRATEGIES   Using Art to Understand Values

Renaissance Art

Studying works of art produced during a specific period in history can teach us a great deal about the values of the people who created the art. For example, much of the art of the Middle Ages reflects religious values. In general, medieval art developed themes of faith and religious spirituality, rather than of human individuality. In contrast, Renaissance art combined such religious themes with the humanistic values of the era. As humanity became the center of life on earth, artists placed realistic human beings at the center of their works.

Shown above is a detail from Michelangelo's **Creation of Adam**, *part of the fresco on the ceiling of the Sistine Chapel in Rome. It portrays God touching the hand of Adam, who, according to the Bible, was the first man on Earth.*

The **Pietà**, *by Michelangelo, is both detailed and lifelike. It shows the Virgin Mary mourning over the body of her son, Jesus, after his crucifixion.*

SKILLS PRACTICE ANSWERS

1. realistic and dignified depiction of the figures

2. religious themes and humanistic values

3. Answers will vary.

Skills Reminder

To understand the values reflected by a piece of art, identify when the artwork was produced and what historical period it represents. Identify the theme—is it taken from religion, mythology, or daily life? Note the subject of the work of art and the details. Then use the theme and its treatment to infer the values of the historical period in which the artist created the work.

Skills Practice

❶ What artistic ideals and visual principles are reflected in Michelangelo's works?

❷ What Renaissance values are reflected in Michelangelo's fresco and in his *Pietà*?

❸ Find and study a modern work of art. Explain how this artwork reflects the values of modern society.

The works of Titian, like the Assumption of the Virgin shown here, are masterworks of Renaissance art.

Giotto (JAWT·oh), who lived from about 1276 to 1337, was a magnificent early realist painter. According to legend, a fly in one of Giotto's works looked so real that an observer tried to brush it off the painting. Another important early realist was Masaccio (mah·ZAHT·choh), who lived from 1401 to 1428. Masaccio used light and shadows to create a powerful sense of depth in his paintings.

Scholars often call the late 1400s and early 1500s the High Renaissance. There were many great painters during this period. Four made particularly outstanding contributions to the arts.

Leonardo da Vinci (dah·VEEN·chee), who lived from 1452 to 1519, was a man of many talents. He was an architect, engineer, painter, sculptor, and scientist. He made sketches of plants and animals, as well as detailed drawings of a flying machine and a submarine. Da Vinci's science improved the quality of his paintings. His studies in anatomy helped him draw realistic human figures. He used mathematics to organize the space in his paintings. People throughout the world still marvel at his mural *The Last Supper*. Perhaps his most famous painting is the portrait called the *Mona Lisa*.

Another master of Renaissance art, **Michelangelo** (mee·kay·LAHN·jay·loh), lived from 1475 to 1564. Michelangelo was a brilliant painter. Millions of people have visited the Sistine Chapel of the Vatican, the residence of the pope in Rome, to view the frescoes Michelangelo painted on the chapel ceiling. His sculptures of biblical figures such as David also continue to be admired. In addition to his art, Michelangelo wrote poetry and helped to design St. Peter's Basilica in Rome.

Rafael (RAF·ee·el), who lived from 1483 to 1520, became so popular in Florence that the pope hired him to help beautify the Vatican. Rafael painted frescoes in the papal chambers. He is also known for his madonnas, paintings of the Virgin Mary.

Titian (TISH·uhn), who lived from about 1488 to 1576, spent most of his life in Venice. His works, such as *The Assumption of the Virgin,* are known for their sense of drama and rich colors. The Holy Roman emperor was a patron of Titian. In fact, Titian was one of the first painters to become wealthy from his work.

✔ **READING CHECK: Contrasting** How did Renaissance and medieval art differ from each other? Renaissance art more realistic, showed scenes from real world

Holt Researcher go.hrw.com
KEYWORD: Holt Researcher
FreeFind: Leonardo da Vinci Michelangelo
After reading more about Leonardo da Vinci and Michelangelo on the Holt Researcher, draw a sketch or write a description of an art piece that reflects their style.

SECTION 1 REVIEW

1. **Define** and explain the significance:
   humanists
   perspective

2. **Identify** and explain the significance:
   Renaissance
   Isabella d'Este
   Francesco Petrarch
   Niccolò Machiavelli
   Leonardo da Vinci
   Michelangelo

3. **Analyzing Information** Copy the graphic organizer below. Use it to explain the characteristics of Renaissance thought, literature, and art.

   Thought
   Literature | Art

4. **Finding the Main Idea**
   a. What were the events that led to the Renaissance in Italy?
   b. How did religion influence Renaissance art and thought?
   c. What ethical issues did humanists struggle with during the Italian Renaissance?

5. **Writing and Critical Thinking**
   Evaluating Choose one of the Renaissance artworks pictured in this section or one in an art book or encyclopedia. Describe both the work and your impressions of it.
   Consider:
   • the technique of perspective
   • the mixture of religious and humanist values
   • what thoughts and feelings the work of art brings about

Homework Practice Online
keyword: SP3 HP15

OBJECTIVES

1 Explain how the ideas of the Italian Renaissance spread to other parts of Europe.

2 Describe how northern Renaissance writers differed from Italian humanists.

3 List the principal characteristics of northern Renaissance art.

🔊 LET'S GET STARTED!

As students enter the classroom, tell them that they are going to start class by playing a game. Select a volunteer to receive a whispered message. Have that person whisper it to another, and so on, down the line. The last person in the chain will say the received message aloud. Use the game as a springboard for discussion about how ideas travel to new places, changing along the way. Explain that in Section 2 students will learn how ideas traveled from Italy to the rest of Europe during the Renaissance.

SECTION 2

READ TO DISCOVER

❶ How were the ideas of the Italian Renaissance spread to other parts of Europe?

❷ In what ways did northern Renaissance writers differ from Italian humanists?

❸ What were the principal characteristics of northern Renaissance art?

IDENTIFY

Johannes Gutenberg
Desiderius Erasmus
Thomas More
William Shakespeare
Flemish school

WHY IT MATTERS TODAY

William Shakespeare remains perhaps the most popular playwright in the world. Use CNNfyi.com or other current event sources to learn about modern plays or movies based on Shakespeare's work. Record your findings in your journal.

CNNfyi.com

The Northern Renaissance

The Main Idea
Art and literature in northern Europe also began to reflect Renaissance thought, styles, and values.

The Story Continues *"What a piece of work is a man! How noble in reason! How infinite in faculty!" Those powerful lines from Shakespeare's* Hamlet *celebrate the human potential and reflect how Renaissance humanist thought spread from Italy into northern Europe.*

The Spread of Ideas

Numerous mountain passes pierced the rugged Alps in northern Italy. These passageways allowed people and ideas to pass from Italy to northern Europe. The Danube, Rhine, and Rhone Rivers provided even easier routes. Renaissance ideas, often carried by northern European students who had studied in Italy, soon traveled to Germany, the Netherlands, France, and England. As increased commerce created new wealth and more people could afford higher education, many new universities were established in these countries.

A remarkable new process—printing—also helped spread Renaissance ideas. Hundreds of years earlier, the Chinese had learned how to etch writing or pictures onto wooden blocks. Printers put ink on the blocks and then pressed them onto paper. More ink was placed on the block, and the process was repeated. In this way writing or pictures could be reproduced many times. The Chinese also had learned how to assemble blocks from many separate pieces, or type, that could be used repeatedly. This was the beginning of movable type.

The European invention of printing appears to have been independent of the Chinese process. Scholars believe that in about 1450, **Johannes Gutenberg** of Mainz, Germany, became the first European to use movable type to print books. Gutenberg used his printing press to print copies of the Bible.

Not all Europeans were enthusiastic about Gutenberg's invention. Some complained that books printed on paper would not last long. Others noted that hand-copied manuscripts were far more beautiful than printed books. Scribes, who made a living by hand-copying manuscripts, realized that the printing press threatened their profession. The impact of Gutenberg's work was economic as well as social and technological.

This Latin version of the Gutenberg Bible was printed in Mainz in 1456.

SECTION 2 **RESOURCES**

REPRODUCIBLE RESOURCES

▸ Guided Reading Strategy 15.2

▸ Geography Activity 15: The Spread of the Renaissance

TECHNOLOGY RESOURCES

▸ One-Stop Planner 15.2

▸ World History and Cultures Video Program 14: The Renaissance Perspective

▸ Homework Practice Online

REINFORCEMENT, REVIEW, AND ASSESSMENT

▸ Section 2 Review, p. 362

▸ Daily Quiz 15.2

▸ Main Idea Activity 15.2

▸ English Audio Summary 15.2

▸ Spanish Audio Summary 15.2

TEACH OBJECTIVE 1

LEVEL 1: Have students imagine that no method of printing has ever been invented and that all written material must be copied by hand. Ask students how their lives might be different in this scenario. *(Getting an education would be difficult; fewer people would read; people would know less about distant places.)* Discuss how the invention of the printing press affected learning, culture, and the spread of ideas in Europe.

ENGLISH LANGUAGE LEARNERS

TEACH OBJECTIVE 2

ALL LEVELS: Help students complete a chart similar to the one shown. Tell them to include general descriptions as well as specific

Italian humanist	Characteristics in common	Northern humanist
interested in human achievement	interested in early Greek and Roman culture (classics)	interested in early Christian period
Petrarch (Sonnets to Laura), Machiavelli (The Prince), Castiglione (The Book of the Courtier)	used critical method of study	Erasmus (The Praise of Folly), More (Utopia), Shakespeare (Hamlet, Romeo and Juliet, Macbeth)

Interdisciplinary Connection

LITERATURE. In *Utopia*, Sir Thomas More called for rulers to tend to the affairs of their own nations rather than make war against other Europeans. However, More did not hold out much hope that things would change. His imaginary traveler from *Utopia* explains: "Suppose I were at the court of the French king [and I could prove] that all this warmongering [would] ... end in naught ... what reception from my listeners ... do you think this speech of mine would find?" More's reply was, "Not a very favorable one."

Critical Thinking

Ask students why More might have been interested in promoting peace.

ANSWER: Students may answer that after so much war in Europe, More, like many others, hoped for some stability.

Gutenberg's printing press with movable metal type allowed books to be printed quickly and economically.

Analyzing Primary Sources

Problem Solving How does More propose to solve the problem of poverty? Do you think it would be effective? total employment; probably not

---

Such obstacles did not slow the spread of the printing press. Other European publishers quickly adopted the new technology. By 1475 printing presses operated in England, France, Germany, Italy, and several other European nations. The books that these printing presses produced helped spread new humanist ideas to a large audience.

✔ **READING CHECK: Identifying Cause and Effect** How did the printing press affect life in Europe? spread Renaissance ideas

Northern Renaissance Writers

The most influential humanist of northern Europe was **Desiderius Erasmus** (i·RAZ·muhs), a Dutch scholar who lived from about 1466 to 1536. As a young man, Erasmus entered a monastery. He later left the monastery so he could pursue his studies of the classics. Erasmus learned about the ideas of the Italian humanists from printed books.

Unlike the Italian humanists, Erasmus and other northern humanists were interested in the early Christian period as well as early Greek and Roman culture. Erasmus believed that the ideas of Christianity and of classical civilization could be harmonized. He used the critical method of the Italian humanists to study the Bible. Erasmus and other northern humanists criticized the church's lack of spirituality. They believed that medieval scholars had made Christian faith less spiritual and more complicated and ceremonial. Erasmus argued for a return to the original, simple message of Jesus.

Erasmus's most famous book was entitled *The Praise of Folly*. In this book he ridiculed ignorance, superstition, and vice among Christians. He criticized fasting, pilgrimages to religious shrines, and even the church's interpretation of the Bible.

Thomas More, an English humanist and friend of Erasmus, took a similar view. Early in life More showed an interest in the classics, and in 1516 he published *Utopia*. In this work, More condemned governments as corrupt and argued that private ownership of property causes unnecessary conflicts between people. He contrasted life in Europe with his description of an imaginary, ideal society. The word *utopia* has come to mean "an ideal place or society." In More's imaginary world, all male citizens were equal. Everyone worked to support the society.

> *History Makers Speak*
>
> **"... wherever you are, you always have to work. There's never any excuse for idleness.... Everyone has his eye on you, so you're practically forced to get on with your job, and make some proper use of your spare time. Under such a system, there's bound to be plenty of everything, and, as everything is divided equally among the entire population, there obviously can't be any poor people or beggars."**
>
> Thomas More, *Utopia*

More's *Utopia* became popular in Europe, where it was translated into German, Italian, French, English, Dutch, and Spanish. Thomas More wrote widely in both prose and verse. His work was read and generally acclaimed by humanist thinkers throughout much of Europe. Later in life More served King Henry VIII of England. Because More refused to agree that the king was the supreme head of the church in England, Henry had him executed. Some 400 years later, the Catholic Church made More a saint for his faith and service to the church.

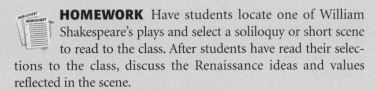

HOMEWORK Have students locate one of William Shakespeare's plays and select a soliloquy or short scene to read to the class. After students have read their selections to the class, discuss the Renaissance ideas and values reflected in the scene.

TEACH OBJECTIVE 3

LEVEL 3: Ask students to describe characteristics that differentiate northern Renaissance art from that of Italy. (*Students should mention northern art's more realistic depiction of figures and everyday subject matter.*) Draw attention to Holbein's *The French Ambassadors.* Have volunteers identify objects in the painting that make the ambassadors seem down-to-earth. (*the guitarlike instrument, the open book, etc.*) Now have students write a paragraph describing how they would set up a studio shot to depict a classmate or friend. Encourage them to pay attention to props they might use to make the subjects seem easy to know.

CLOSE

Ask students to list the factors that helped spread Renaissance ideas to other parts of Europe. (*travel to and from Italy, the invention of the printing press*) Then lead a class discussion on the aspects of the Renaissance that were unique to northern Europe. (*humanists' interest in early Christian culture, more realistic human figures and subject matter in artwork*)

English literature during the Renaissance reached its peak in the late 1500s and early 1600s. In classical dramas, angry gods punished humans. In English Renaissance drama, playwrights such as Christopher Marlowe wrote plays that tended to focus on human, rather than godly, actions. Marlowe used powerful language and imagery to convey his thoughts. Some of his work was composed in verse form.

William Shakespeare stands out as the leading literary figure of the time. Shakespeare built on the traditions established by Marlowe and other playwrights. Shakespeare's great strength lay in his ability to transform well-known stories into dramatic masterpieces. He portrayed personality and human emotions with a skill that few writers have matched. The moody *Hamlet*, the young lovers *Romeo and Juliet*, and the tragic *Macbeth* seem as real today as when Shakespeare created them.

✔ **READING CHECK: Contrasting** How did Erasmus and More differ from Italian humanists in their outlooks on life? interested in early Christian as well as classical culture

Northern Renaissance Artists

Northern European merchants carried Italian paintings home. Painters from northern Europe studied with Italian masters. In these ways, the dynamic new painting techniques of Italian artists inspired other artists.

In Flanders a group of painters developed their own distinct style. Known among some historians and critics as the **Flemish school,** these painters are credited with perfecting certain techniques of painting in oil on canvas.

The Flemish brothers Jan and Hubert van Eyck paid great attention to detail. Their work reveals a strong interest in facial expressions. In their masterpiece, the altar-piece they painted for a church in the city of Ghent, the faces of Adam and Eve look realistic. They are markedly different from the symbolic depictions of the Middle Ages.

William Shakespeare is probably the most widely known author in all of English literature. His insight into human nature and use of the English language mark his many plays and his poetry.

This detail from the center panel of the Ghent Altar-piece, called the Adoration of the Lamb, reveals the van Eycks' attention to detail. The face of Eve (above) is from one of the wings of the altar-piece.

Geography

Ghent is one of Belgium's oldest cities and the historic capital of Flanders. The city has retained more traces of its past than any other Belgian town. One historical highlight is a bell tower called the Belfry, crowned by a gilded (gold-covered) copper dragon forged in 1377. The feudal castle of the counts of Flanders, one of the most spectacular moated castles still standing, dates from 1180. The Cathedral of St. Bavon, which dates from the 1100s, houses Hubert and Jan van Eyck's altar-piece The Adoration of the Lamb.

Critical Thinking

What is the historical significance of Ghent?

ANSWER: It has retained many traces of its past. Some of its architecture dates from the 1100s.

ASSESS

Have students complete Daily Quiz 15.2. As Alternative Assessment, you may want to use the chart on Renaissance humanists or art in this section's lessons.

RETEACH

Have students complete Main Idea Activity for English Language Learners and Special-Needs Students 15.2. Then write the main idea of each heading in this section. **ENGLISH LANGUAGE LEARNERS**

EXTEND

Have students imagine that they are living in northern Europe after studying in Florence. Ask them to write a letter to a friend back in Italy describing the Renaissance as it exists in the North. Encourage students to include their own thoughts and preferences. Remind them to use standard grammar, spelling, sentence structure, and punctuation. **BLOCK SCHEDULING**

VISUAL RECORD ANSWER

The subject matter and the human figures are realistic. By comparison, Italian Renaissance art depicted human figures as looking more like Greek gods.

SECTION 2 REVIEW ANSWERS

❶ Identify
- Johannes Gutenberg, p. 359
- Desiderius Erasmus, p. 360
- Thomas More, p. 360
- William Shakespeare, p. 361
- Flemish school, p. 361

❷ Italian: interested in human achievement, figures in artwork looked like Greek gods; Both: interested in early Greek and Roman culture (classics), use of perspective in painting, reflected ideas of Christian humanism; Northern: interested in early Christian period, more realistic figures and subject matter in artwork

❸ a. Books could be printed quickly and economically.

b. interested in early Christian culture as well as the classics, valued spirituality in the church

❹ Student responses will vary but should reflect the characteristics and use of utopian literature.

INTERPRETING THE VISUAL RECORD

Northern Renaissance art This painting by Holbein, *The French Ambassadors,* is an example of the artist's style of total control of surface and design. *In what way is this painting more realistic than an Italian Renaissance painting?*

One of the most famous Flemish artists, Pieter Brueghel (BROO·guhl) the Elder, painted in the mid-1500s. Brueghel loved the countryside and the peasants of his native Flanders. He painted lively scenes of village festivals and dances. On the other hand, Brueghel also used his paintings to criticize the intolerance and cruelty he saw around him.

The German artist Albrecht Dürer (DYUR·uhr), who lived from 1471 to 1528, was famous for his copper engravings and woodcuts. Dürer studied in Germany and Venice. He also studied the classics and humanism. Dürer became one of the first artists to see the possibilities of printed illustrations in books.

Another German artist, Hans Holbein the Younger, who lived in the early 1500s, was influenced by Italian and Flemish styles of painting. Holbein traveled through Europe painting portraits of famous people. His work includes portraits of Erasmus, Thomas More, and King Henry VIII of England. This emphasis on portrait painting reflected the Renaissance interest in the individual.

Northern European artists of the Renaissance were certainly inspired by the techniques of Italian artists, such as the use of perspective. Thus, some of the characteristics of Renaissance painting in northern Europe resemble elements of Italian painting. However, the two styles also illustrate the differences between northern and southern European artists and their societies. Many Italian paintings by artists such as Michelangelo depict human figures based on the models of Greek and Roman art. Athletic figures with rippling muscles demonstrate the artist's admiration of the human form. In the work of many northern artists, however, the figures seem more like Europeans of the 1500s—bald, frail, and imperfect—than like Greek gods. However, some northern artists did often depict the early fathers of the Christian church, emphasizing the importance of the Bible as the basis for Christianity. In this way the work of the northern European artists continued to reflect the ideas of Christian humanism.

✔ **READING CHECK: Supporting a Point of View** What evidence would you give that realism was important in northern Renaissance art? more realistic human figures, subject matter

---

SECTION 2 REVIEW

1. **Identify** and explain the significance:
   Johannes Gutenberg
   Desiderius Erasmus
   Thomas More
   William Shakespeare
   Flemish school

2. **Comparing and Contrasting** Copy the Venn diagram below. Use it to show which characteristics the Italian Renaissance and the northern Renaissance shared and which were unique to each.

   Italian Northern

3. **Finding the Main Idea**
   a. Why did the printing press spread so quickly throughout Europe?
   b. What were the main ideas and values of the northern Renaissance?

4. **Writing and Critical Thinking**
   Analyzing Information Write a short story about a utopian society.
   Consider:
   - the elements of utopian literature, including its imaginary nature
   - the use of utopias to analyze governmental and social systems

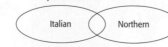

Homework Practice Online

keyword: SP3 HP15

OBJECTIVES

1 **Discuss the developments that led to the Reformation.**

2 **Describe how Martin Luther protested against the Roman Catholic Church and began a new church.**

3 **Identify the factors that caused the spread of Protestantism.**

4 **Explain the role that Calvinism played in the Reformation.**

As students enter the classroom, ask them how they would feel if they had worked hard for a good grade, and then were told that they could get that grade only if they paid for it. Have students relate this system to the church's selling of indulgences in the 1500s, the practice of selling pardons for sin. Prompt students to speculate what might happen if many people became outraged about indulgences. *(They might revolt.)* Explain that in Section 3 students will learn about a religious revolution called the Reformation.

SECTION 3

READ TO DISCOVER

1 What developments led to the Reformation?

2 How did Martin Luther protest against the Roman Catholic Church and begin a new church?

3 What factors caused the spread of Protestantism?

4 What role did Calvinism play in the Reformation?

DEFINE

indulgences
sects
predestination
theocracy

IDENTIFY

Reformation
Martin Luther
Henry VIII
John Calvin
Huguenots

WHY IT MATTERS TODAY

Different Christian denominations continue today in the United States and throughout the world. Use CNNfyi.com or other **current event** sources to determine the doctrines and beliefs of some of the main denominations. Record your findings in your journal.

CNNfyi.com

The Protestant Reformation

The Main Idea
The Protestant Reformation split the Catholic Church and created several new churches.

The Story Continues *In the early 1500s a young German law student was returning to school from a visit home when he got caught in a violent thunderstorm. A blinding bolt of lightning struck nearby. The young man shouted, "Saint Anne, help! I will become a monk!" Not only did he enter a monastery, but the young Martin Luther also went on to create a religious revolution.*

An Era of Reform

The humanist Erasmus was not alone in his criticism of the church and some Christian practices. In about 1500 several northern humanists argued that the Roman Catholic Church had lost sight of its spiritual mission. Their claims would lead to a reform movement that would split the church in western Europe. This religious revolution is called the **Reformation.**

Causes. Some northern humanists maintained that the church seemed more interested in its income than in saving souls. They claimed that the popes acted as political leaders and warriors instead of setting an example of moral leadership. Some priests engaged in vice and misconduct instead of encouraging spiritual and moral behavior. These northern humanists sought a new emphasis on personal faith and spirituality.

The Catholic Church, however, ignored their concerns. The humanists then urged believers who were unhappy with traditional religion to withdraw from the church and meet with like-minded people.

The beginning. The first break with the Roman Catholic Church took place in what is now Germany. The political situation there helped lay the foundation for the Reformation. Unlike some countries during the 1500s, "Germany" was not a unified nation. Although it formed the core of the Holy Roman Empire, "Germany" was made up of about 300 independent states. Weak rulers could not control independent ideas about religion, nor could they prevent abuses of power by the pope.

In Rome, as Pope Leo X was continuing the rebuilding of St. Peter's Basilica, the Vatican sent a monk named Johann Tetzel to raise funds in the northern German states. Tetzel asked people to buy **indulgences,** or pardons from punishment for sin.

This German woodcut criticizes the pope himself, showing him as a moneychanger at the sale of indulgences.

SECTION 3 RESOURCES

REPRODUCIBLE RESOURCES

▶ Guided Reading Strategy 15.3

▶ Readings in World History 54: Luther's Refusal at the Diet of Worms

TECHNOLOGY RESOURCES

▶ One-Stop Planner 15.3

▶ Holt Researcher: World History: John Calvin

▶ Religions of the World Video Series: Christianity

▶ Homework Practice Online

REINFORCEMENT, REVIEW, AND ASSESSMENT

▶ Section 3 Review, p. 367

▶ Daily Quiz 15.3

▶ Main Idea Activity 15.3

▶ English Audio Summary 15.3

▶ Spanish Audio Summary 15.3

ALL LEVELS: Have students work in pairs or groups to complete the graphic organizer as shown. Explain to them that Luther's excommunication is at the top of the triangle in order to represent a turning point. Events leading up to his expulsion should be written on the left side of the organizer, and events that occurred afterward, up until the formation of the Lutheran Church, belong on the right side. **ENGLISH LANGUAGE LEARNERS, COOPERATIVE LEARNING**

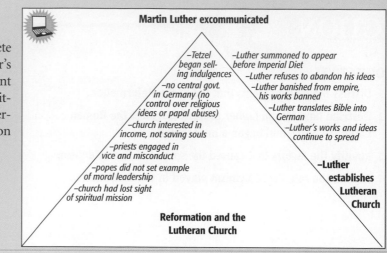

Martin Luther excommunicated

–Tetzel began selling indulgences

–no central govt. in Germany (no control over religious ideas or papal abuses)

–church interested in income, not saving souls

–priests engaged in vice and misconduct

–popes did not set example of moral leadership

–church had lost sight of spiritual mission

–Luther summoned to appear before Imperial Diet

–Luther refuses to abandon his ideas

–Luther banished from empire, his works banned

–Luther translates Bible into German

–Luther's works and ideas continue to spread

–Luther establishes Lutheran Church

Reformation and the Lutheran Church

HISTORY MAKER ANSWER

Luther disagreed with church practices such as the sale of indulgences. He claimed that the Bible was the sole religious authority and argued that salvation could not come through ceremonies or priests. Instead, he believed that God viewed all people of faith equally.

The general belief held by those Germans who bought Tetzel's indulgences was that the money raised would go to the construction of St. Peter's Basilica. What the public did not know, however, was that some of the money was going to a noble from the Hohenzollern family named Albert of Brandenburg. Albert had purchased the position of archbishop of Mainz, but because he was too young his appointment violated church law. Pope Leo decided that Albert could take the office provided he pay the church a large sum of money, which he did by borrowing. The church also authorized the sale of indulgences—with half of the money raised going to Albert to help him pay off his debt. Like the rest of the public, Luther knew nothing about this arrangement.

HISTORY MAKER

Martin Luther (1483–1546)

Martin Luther never wanted to leave the Roman Catholic Church. As a priest and teacher, he was strongly committed to his religious beliefs. He felt it necessary, however, to challenge certain church practices that he believed were unnecessary or wrong.

The church responded by throwing Luther out. As a result, Luther founded the Lutheran Church. **Why did Luther challenge the Catholic Church?**

Analyzing Primary Sources

Making Generalizations What behavior did Luther hope that Christians would engage in? charity

---

Indulgences had originally been a reward for pious deeds, such as helping a poor person go on a crusade. Renaissance popes, in contrast, sold indulgences simply to raise money. This misuse of indulgences outraged northern humanists, who wanted the church to become more spiritual. The concern became particularly widespread in the German states, where rulers allowed sellers of indulgences to move freely about.

✔ **READING CHECK: Drawing Inferences** How did the sale of indulgences play a role in the beginning of the Reformation? created opposition in northern Europe

Martin Luther

One critic of Tetzel's behavior was a monk named **Martin Luther.** Luther had quit law school and entered a monastery to spend his life in search of salvation. But Luther found that the church's methods for overcoming sin gave him no comfort. He did all the things required of him. Nothing, however, relieved his feeling of inadequacy.

Through his biblical studies, Luther received a revelation. On the basis of this new insight, Luther developed beliefs that later became known as Lutheranism. Luther taught that ceremonies and good deeds made no difference in saving a sinner. The only thing that counted, Luther decided, was an inner faith in God. People could receive salvation only through the grace of God, not through their own actions. According to Luther, simple faith could lead everyone to salvation. This idea was called "justification by grace through faith."

Luther's protest. Luther claimed that Tetzel committed a grave error by asking people to give up money for false promises of forgiveness. In 1517 Luther challenged Tetzel. He posted his 95 theses, or statements, about indulgences on a church door.

(32) **"Those who believe that they can be certain of their salvation because they have indulgence letters will be eternally [cursed], together with their teachers." (43) "Christians are to be taught that he who gives to the poor or lends to the needy does a better deed than he who buys indulgences."**

Martin Luther, *Luther's Works*

News rapidly spread across Europe that a monk had publicly challenged the selling of indulgences. Luther clearly considered himself a reformer who was working from within the main tradition of the church. Initially, he probably did not intend to break with Rome and the Catholic Church. Because he challenged church practices, however, church leaders denounced him.

Break with the church. By 1520 Luther openly disagreed with many church doctrines. He claimed that the Bible was the sole religious authority. Popes and bishops could not tell a person what to believe. Luther argued that ceremonies could not make up for sins and that priests had no special role in helping people to salvation. He believed that God viewed all people of faith equally. Luther considered his church "a priesthood of all believers."

Luther took advantage of the printing press to spread his ideas. In his writings, Luther continued to attack certain church practices and approaches. In 1521 Pope Leo X declared Luther a heretic. He excommunicated, or expelled, Luther from the Roman Catholic Church.

LEVEL 1: Work with students to create a list of factors that led to the spread of Protestantism. *(many Europeans' desire for a simpler, more direct religion; German rulers' establishment of Lutheran Church within their states; Charles V's inability to defeat Protestant princes; Peace of Augsburg; Henry VIII's desire for a divorce and subsequent creation of Anglican Church)* Then discuss how these events, though they took place at different times in various parts of Europe, all contributed to what has become known as the Protestant Reformation. **ENGLISH LANGUAGE LEARNERS**

 HOMEWORK Have students prepare a time line of the events discussed in this section. Students may illustrate their time lines.

Holy Roman Emperor Charles V then summoned Luther to appear before the Imperial Diet, a special meeting of the empire's rulers, at the city of Worms (VOHRMZ). There Luther was commanded to abandon his ideas. He refused. After the Diet of Worms the emperor declared Luther an outlaw and banned the printing and sale of his works. However, he lacked the power to enforce this ruling. Frederick the Wise, the Elector of Saxony (Luther's home state), whisked Luther away to hide until the uproar over the confrontation at the Diet of Worms died down. While under the protection of Frederick, Luther translated the Bible into German. Now all literate Christians in the German states could read the Bible themselves.

Protestantism. Emperor Charles V continued to oppose Luther's teachings. He did what he could to keep Lutheranism from spreading. The princes who supported Luther protested the emperor's treatment of Lutheranism. Because of the protest, Luther's followers and later reformers came to be called "Protestants."

Luther's works and ideas continued to spread. In time he established a new church, the Lutheran Church. He kept the organization of the new church very simple. Based on Luther's belief in the "priesthood of all believers," Lutheran ministers were less important than Catholic priests were. According to Luther, Christians were fully capable of interpreting and understanding scripture for themselves.

✔ **READING CHECK: Sequencing** What events led to the development of Protestantism?
Luther's protest, Diet of Worms, spread of Luther's ideas

The Spread of Protestantism

Luther had touched a very deep desire among many people in Europe for a simpler, more direct religious faith. Within a short time, many German rulers established the Lutheran Church within their states. In addition, dozens of reformers appeared who criticized both the Roman Catholic Church and the Lutheran Church.

Charles V tried to stop the spread of Protestantism. At first his attention was focused on fighting the Ottoman Turks and the French. Finally, in 1546, he sent his armies against the Protestant princes in Germany. Although his armies won most of the battles, the emperor could not defeat the princes or the Lutheran Church. Charles finally reached a compromise with the princes in 1555. The Peace of Augsburg stated that each German ruler had the right to choose the religion for his state. His subjects had to either accept the ruler's decision or move away. Almost all the princes of the northern German states chose Luther's faith in opposition to Rome.

The rise of sects. During the 1520s and 1530s, hundreds of new religious groups appeared in Germany and Switzerland. These groups, known as **sects**, did not form organized churches. Many did not have clear-cut authority, discipline, membership, or rules. The sects were societies of a few people gathered together, usually with a preacher as their leader. Most of the sects later died out.

The Anglican Church. In England the Protestant Reformation came about in an entirely different way than in Germany. It was the king, **Henry VIII**, who caused the break between England and the Roman Catholic Church. The break was a political move that had

This portrait depicts Emperor Charles V on horseback at the Battle of Muhlberg in 1546.

🔲 **internet** connect

TOPIC: Reformation and its Leaders
GO TO: go.hrw.com
KEYWORD: SP3 WH15
Have students access the Internet through the HRW Go site to find information on the Reformation and its leaders. Ask them to create an illustrated pamphlet about some of the most prominent leaders and the roles they played in the Reformation. Students may wish to use the interactive template provided.

History Maker

ANGELA DE MERICI. Angela de Merici was at the center of the group of women who founded the Ursuline order in the Catholic Church. Merici's interest in educating women in the Christian faith began when she was about 20. In Brescia Merici recruited other women to help with her work, and in 1535 the group formed the Ursulines.

Critical Thinking

Ask students why religious reformers focused on education.

ANSWER: It might be easier to train a new generation than to change people's minds.

TEACH OBJECTIVE 4

LEVEL 3: Ask students to write an essay describing Calvinism and its role in the Reformation. Remind them to use standard grammar, spelling, sentence structure, and punctuation.

CLOSE

Ask students to respond to the following question: In what way was the sale of indulgences an important catalyst in the early stages of the Reformation? Encourage students to consider how certain events or actions can energize a particular cause.

Teacher to Teacher

Laura Watkins of Acton, Massachusetts, suggested the following activity: Using a modern Atlas or Internet sources, find a current map of religious distribution in Europe. Have students compare that map with the one of European Religions in 1600 on page 370. Have students suggest what the maps reflect about the long-term impact of the Protestant Reformation on Europe.

Linking Past to Present

Today, the population of Switzerland is approximately half Catholic and half Protestant. The country has a tiny Jewish community as well.

Critical Thinking

How does the religious makeup of Switzerland today compare to the time of the Reformation?

ANSWER: Students should recognize that Calvinism dominated Switzerland during the Reformation.

This famous portrait of Henry VIII was painted by Hans Holbein the Younger.

little to do with religious beliefs. In fact, before 1529, Henry VIII had defended the church against Luther's teachings. The pope had even granted Henry the title "Defender of the Faith."

England's break with Rome took place because Henry VIII wanted to divorce his wife, Catherine of Aragon. Henry was unhappy because Catherine had not had a son who could succeed him. The royal couple did have a daughter, Mary. However, England had no tradition of a ruling queen. Henry also wanted a divorce because he hoped to marry Anne Boleyn, a lady-in-waiting at the court.

The Catholic Church did not usually permit divorces. Although the pope was allowed to make exceptions to this general rule, Pope Clement VII refused to meet Henry's demand. This angered Henry. The king withdrew England from the Catholic Church and began a new church. Parliament passed a series of laws that created the Church of England, with the king as its head. Also known as the Anglican Church, the Church of England kept the organization and ceremonies of the Catholic Church. Over time, it also adopted some Protestant doctrines.

The Anglican Church granted Henry VIII a divorce. The king eventually married six times in all. He finally fathered a son, the future Edward VI. Of greater importance, Henry VIII's creation of the Anglican Church paved the way for the Protestant Reformation in England.

✔ **READING CHECK: Contrasting** How did the spread of Protestantism in England differ from that in the rest of Europe? resulted from the king's desire for a divorce

Calvinism

Huldrych Zwingli (TSVING·lee) was the vicar at the cathedral in Zurich, Switzerland, in the early 1500s. He was greatly influenced by the humanist writings of Erasmus. In fact, Zwingli was already calling for religious reform in Switzerland when he heard about Luther's 95 theses. Zwingli and Luther met and discovered they shared many ideas about church doctrine. They disagreed, however, about forms of worship and the use of religious images. For example, Zwingli's followers covered up wall decorations in churches. In 1531 Zwingli died in a battle between Catholics and Protestants. His work was carried on by a French Protestant named **John Calvin.**

Holt Researcher

go.hrw.com
KEYWORD: Holt Researcher
FreeFind: John Calvin
After reading more about John Calvin on the Holt Researcher, write an outline for a sermon he might have given explaining his views.

Calvin's church. In Switzerland John Calvin founded a Protestant church that had a strong following. Then in 1536 he formulated and published a complete and clear set of religious beliefs, *The Institutes of the Christian Religion.* This work explained exactly what the faithful should believe on every major religious question. Calvin's followers—called Calvinists—now had a code that united and strengthened them against opposition and persecution.

Like Luther, Calvin relied on faith and on the Bible. Calvin also emphasized **predestination,** the idea that at the beginning of time God had decided who would be saved. Predestination was a common belief among Protestant thinkers in the 1500s. Calvin explained the logic of predestination. Those who were predestined—or chosen beforehand—for salvation were called "the elect." They formed a special community of people who were expected to follow the highest moral standards. These standards placed great emphasis on self-discipline. The individual was expected to be completely dedicated to God's wishes.

REVIEW

Have students complete the Section 3 Review on p. 367.

ASSESS

Have students complete Daily Quiz 15.3. As Alternative Assessment, you may want to use the graphic organizer on the Reformation or the essay exercise in this section's lessons.

RETEACH

Have students complete Main Idea Activity for English Language Learners and Special-Needs Students 15.3. Then ask students to write a question and answer that covers the main idea for each heading and subheading in the section. Have volunteers read their questions to the class. Have the class try to answer each question. **ENGLISH LANGUAGE LEARNERS**

EXTEND

Prompt students to imagine they are John Calvin during the Reformation. Have them create pamphlets, similar to travel brochures, that encourage people to move to Geneva. Pamphlets should highlight the key characteristics of Calvinism and life in Geneva. *(predestination or "elect" status, dedication to God's wishes, strict laws governing behavior, righteous living)* **BLOCK SCHEDULING**

In 1536 Calvin moved to the city of Geneva, where his doctrine of Calvinism became the official religion. In fact, Geneva became a **theocracy,** a government ruled by religious leaders who claimed God's authority. Calvinists attached great importance to righteous living. Thus citizens' lives were strongly regulated. Laws prohibited card playing, dancing, profane language, and showy dress. Breaking these laws resulted in severe punishment. Rather than being seen as a burden, however, this strictness was the heart of Calvinism's appeal. It gave its followers a sense of mission and discipline. Calvinists felt that they were setting an example and making the world fit for "the elect."

Calvinism spreads. In France many people, including high-ranking nobles, converted to Calvinism. These people were called **Huguenots** (HYOO·guh·nahts). Although France remained primarily Catholic, at one point about one third of the French nobility had become Calvinists. The Catholic French monarchs considered the Huguenots a threat to national unity. Beginning in 1562, the Huguenots defended themselves in a series of bloody civil wars with the Catholics. In 1598 King Henry IV issued the Edict of Nantes (NANTS). This proclamation gave the Huguenots freedom of worship and some political rights.

Calvinist minorities also existed in Poland and Hungary in eastern Europe. Large Calvinist populations were found in Scotland, in the northern Netherlands, and in some parts of the German states. In these areas the strength of the Calvinists among the nobility persuaded the rulers to change their views. In a form called Puritanism, Calvinism would play a vital role in England and in its North American colonies. By 1600 Calvinist churches were well established in parts of Europe.

✔ **READING CHECK: Finding the Main Idea** What role did John Calvin and Calvinism play in the Reformation? established theocracy in Geneva, led to wars in France

This German woodcut depicts the Saint Bartholomew's Day Massacre in 1572. Pro-Catholic forces in France murdered thousands of Huguenots in the massacre.

SECTION 3 REVIEW

1. **Define** and explain the significance:
   indulgences
   sects
   predestination
   theocracy

2. **Identify** and explain the significance:
   Reformation
   Martin Luther
   Henry VIII
   John Calvin
   Huguenots

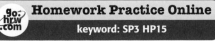
Homework Practice Online
keyword: SP3 HP15

3. **Sequencing** Copy the flow chart below. Use it to illustrate the chain of events that led up to and occurred during the Reformation.

   ☐ → ☐ → ☐

4. **Finding the Main Idea**
   a. What did Luther hope to achieve by posting the 95 theses?
   b. Would life in England have been different if the pope had granted Henry VIII a divorce?
   c. How did the views of John Calvin differ from those of the Catholic Church?

5. **Writing and Critical Thinking**
   Supporting a Point of View Imagine that you are calling for reform of the Catholic Church during the 1500s. Write several theses to persuade people that the sale of indulgences is wrong.
   Consider:
   • what indulgences were and why they were sold
   • Luther's objections to indulgences

THE RENAISSANCE AND REFORMATION **367**

SECTION 3 REVIEW ANSWERS

❶ Define
• indulgences, p. 363
• sects, p. 365
• predestination, p. 366
• theocracy, p. 367

❷ Identify
• Reformation, p. 363
• Martin Luther, p. 364
• Henry VIII, p. 365
• John Calvin, p. 366
• Huguenots, p. 367

❸ northern humanists express concerns about the church—church ignores concerns—humanists urge people to withdraw—Tetzel begins selling indulgences—humanists outraged by sales—Martin Luther criticizes church—Luther excommunicated—Luther establishes Lutheran Church—Henry VIII breaks with Catholic Church—Church of England created—John Calvin founds Protestant Church in Switzerland (Calvinism)—French Huguenots given freedom of worship after bloody civil wars

❹ a. Luther hoped to stop a practice he felt corrupted the church and misled the people.

b. Answers will vary; England might have remained Roman Catholic.

c. Calvin believed in predestination of the elect; the Catholic Church held that salvation was open to all through its ceremonies.

❺ Responses will vary. Remind students to use standard grammar, spelling, sentence structure, and punctuation in their writing.

SECTION 4

OBJECTIVES

1 Describe how the Catholic Church responded to the Reformation.

2 Discuss the results of the Reformation and the Counter-Reformation.

LET'S GET STARTED!

As students enter the classroom, remind them that the Catholic Church ignored early criticism from humanists. Ask them to predict whether the church would continue to ignore threats to its dominance or respond in some manner. Have them explain the reasoning behind their predictions. Tell students that in Section 4 they will learn about the Catholic Reformation, also known as the Counter-Reformation.

SECTION 4 RESOURCES

REPRODUCIBLE RESOURCES

▶ Guided Reading Strategy 15.4

▶ Creative Teaching Strategy 15

TECHNOLOGY RESOURCES

▶ One-Stop Planner 15.4

▶ World History teaching Transparency: Everyday Life 11

▶ Religions of the World Video Series: Christianity

▶ Homework Practice Online

▶ Online Maps: European Religions, 1600

REINFORCEMENT, REVIEW, AND ASSESSMENT

▶ Section 4 Review, p. 371

▶ Daily Quiz 15.4

▶ Main Idea Activity 15.4

▶ English Audio Summary 15.4

▶ Spanish Audio Summary 15.4

SECTION 4

READ TO DISCOVER

1 How did the Catholic Church respond to the Reformation?

2 What were the results of the Reformation and the Counter-Reformation?

IDENTIFY

Counter-Reformation
Council of Trent
Jesuits
Ignatius de Loyola

WHY IT MATTERS TODAY

Catholic and Protestant churches have made great strides toward acceptance and toleration of each other. Yet in some places, conflict still exists. Use CNNfyi.com or other current event sources to learn more about theological conflicts that continue today between Christian groups. Record your findings in your journal.

CNNfyi.com

The Catholic Reformation

The Main Idea
The Catholic Church countered the Protestant Reformation by making its own reforms.

The Story Continues *Ignatius de Loyola was a Spanish soldier whose leg had been shattered fighting for Charles V. Loyola's long period of recovery gave him time to reflect. Like Martin Luther, Loyola wondered how he could attain salvation for his sins. Unlike Luther, Loyola came to believe that one could be saved by doing good deeds. He put this belief to work in one of the many steps the Catholic Church took to combat the Reformation.*

The Counter-Reformation

It took some time for the Catholic Church to recognize that Protestantism posed a serious threat. At first the pope dismissed Luther's criticisms. A number of people within the Catholic Church, including Erasmus, had called for reform even before Luther appeared. They too had been ignored. As the Protestants gained ground, reformers finally convinced the pope of the drastic need for change.

In the 1530s the Catholic Church started a major reform effort known as the **Counter-Reformation.** It is sometimes called the Catholic Reformation. The Counter-Reformation began as an attempt to return the church to an emphasis on spiritual matters. It also allowed the church to make its doctrines more clear. In addition, it was a campaign to stop the spread of Protestantism.

Counter-Reformation tactics. Pope Paul III, who reigned as pope from 1534 to 1549, worked to revive a spiritual outlook in the Catholic Church. He appointed devout and learned men as bishops and cardinals.

Pope Paul III also brought the Inquisition to Rome. Since 1478 Spanish authorities had been putting accused heretics on trial. Punishments included extreme cruelties such as burning at the stake. In the past, governments had sometimes used extreme punishments against criminals and traitors. Now the church also used them. The leaders of the Inquisition did not focus on punishing Protestants. Instead, they regarded it as their responsibility to keep Catholics within the church.

In 1559 another method of combating heresy was introduced by Pope Paul IV. He established the *Index of Forbidden Books.* Catholics were banned from reading the listed books, which were considered harmful

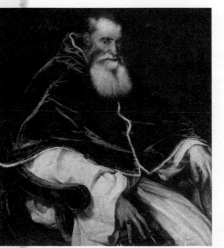

Pope Paul III worked to reform the Catholic Church against the threat of the Protestant Reformation.

Goal	Methods used
revive spirituality	*ended abuses surrounding sale of indulgences, tightened discipline within clergy*
combat heresy	*brought the Inquisition to Rome, established Index of Forbidden Books*
define Catholic doctrine	*supported dependence on priests, salvation through ceremonial actions and individual faith, notion of free will in every person*
slow the spread of Protestantism	*better-educated priests worked more forcefully for the church, old and new religious orders such as Jesuits spread Catholicism*

to faith or morals. The index revealed the role of the printing press in spreading the Reformation. Before printed books, the church could easily find and burn manuscripts it regarded as dangerous. Once books could be printed, it was easier simply to forbid people to read them.

The Council of Trent. Pope Paul III knew that attacks on Protestantism would fail unless Catholic doctrines were clearly defined. However, church authorities often disagreed about complicated matters. In 1545 Paul summoned church leaders to the Italian city of Trent. The **Council of Trent** met during three different periods between 1545 and 1563. It defined the official church position on matters of doctrine.

The Council of Trent acted to end the abuses that surrounded the sale of indulgences and to tighten discipline within the clergy. In most cases the council supported the Catholic beliefs that Protestants had rejected. It emphasized the need for ceremonies, arguing that God should be worshiped with splendor. It noted that people must depend on priests because God granted forgiveness only through the church. Unlike Luther, the council claimed that salvation came from ceremonial church actions as well as from individual faith. The council also stressed that every person had free will.

The decisions made at the Council of Trent were effective for many within the Catholic Church. While some people found the simplicity of Protestantism appealing, others found the Catholic ceremonies comforting. They were moved by the beautiful churches, respected the authority of the priests, and wanted to believe that a person could gain salvation through good works.

Soldiers of the Counter-Reformation. To further strengthen support for the church, existing Catholic religious orders reformed their rules, and new religious orders formed. One such order was the Society of Jesus, known as the **Jesuits.**

Ignatius de Loyola founded the Jesuits in 1534. In 1540 Pope Paul III recognized the Jesuits as an official order of the Catholic Church. Loyola believed that salvation could be achieved, in part, by doing good deeds. His followers took vows of chastity, poverty, and obedience to the pope.

History Makers Speak

❝Putting aside all private judgement, we should keep our minds prepared and ready to obey promptly and in all things the true spouse of Christ our Lord, our Holy Mother, the hierarchical church [represented by the pope].❞

Ignatius de Loyola, *The Spiritual Exercises of St. Ignatius,* translated by Anthony Mottola

---

DAILY LIFE

Effects of the Inquisition

The Inquisition punished people who questioned the teachings of the Catholic Church. This soon came to affect the growing publishing industry that arose out of the Renaissance. In 1559 the Catholic Church published a list of books that were banned because they criticized the church. This list also identified the printers who had published these books. Catholics who possessed or helped to distribute these books could be called before the Inquisition and severely punished or excommunicated. **How did the Inquisition attempt to restrict the spread of information?**

Analyzing Primary Sources

Identifying Bias What in Loyola's statement would particularly please the pope? calls for complete obedience to pope

---

INTERPRETING THE VISUAL RECORD

Council of Trent Pope Paul III commissioned the Venetian painter Titian to record the Council of Trent in session. *How does this picture reflect the Catholic Church at this time?*

DAILY LIFE ANSWER
The Inquisition severely punished or excommunicated Catholics who possessed or distributed books criticizing the church.

VISUAL RECORD ANSWER

The formal setting and the ceremonial dress reflect the hierarchical (multi-level and unequal) nature of the church of that time.

That's Interesting!

The *Index of Forbidden Books* was first declared in A.D. 405, but it was under Pope Paul IV in the 1500s that it took the form in which it would remain for over 400 years. Over the years, the works of such great thinkers as Erasmus, David Hume, Thomas Hobbes, and Voltaire appeared on the list. The works of Bellarmine, a Jesuit cardinal, were even included! The *Index's* influence could be felt throughout Europe, sometimes in surprising ways. For instance, when the Bodleian library was founded at the University of Oxford in the early 1600s, its list of purchases was based on the *Index*.

LEVEL 1: Have students list long-term results of the Reformation and Counter-Reformation. *(many different churches in Europe, strong interest in education, growth in university enrollment, reading more important, remaining lack of tolerance for new ideas, increased power for national governments, decreased power for the pope)* **ENGLISH LANGUAGE LEARNERS**

HOMEWORK Have students create recruiting posters for the Jesuit order during the Reformation. Students can use their textbook, the library, and computer software to supplement information in their textbooks about the Jesuit order. Have students share their posters with the class.

LEVEL 3: Have students write essays comparing Protestant and Catholic churches and their respective actions throughout the Reformation and Counter-Reformation. Remind students to use standard grammar, spelling, sentence structure, and punctuation.

CLOSE

Ask students to write a journal entry on why the Catholic Reformation was also known as the Counter-Reformation. Encourage students to consider the reactionary aspect of the Catholic Reformation and the lasting effects of this era on organized religion throughout Europe.

Linking Past to Present

Today, Catholics throughout the world are launching efforts to reform the church. Some Catholics in Europe and in the United States are signing petitions calling for reforms such as the appointment of female priests and the right of a priest to marry. These Catholics also want the church to concern itself with non-religious issues, such as social justice and preservation of the environment.

ACTIVITY: Have students write an opinion paper explaining whether greater attention should be paid to social issues in the Catholic Church.

MAP ANSWERS

1. England: Anglican; Ireland: Roman Catholic; Spain: Roman Catholic; Sweden: Lutheran

2. Answers will vary. Conflict or even religious wars might occur.

Loyola organized the Jesuits like a military body, with discipline and strict obedience. The Jesuits quickly became the most effective agents in spreading Catholicism. By 1556 the order had about 1,000 members. Their missions took them as far away as China and Japan. In Europe their preaching slowed the spread of Protestantism in France, Germany, and Poland. The Jesuits stressed education, and founded some of the best colleges in Europe. They combined humanist values with Catholic doctrine to produce educated, dedicated supporters of the church.

✔ **READING CHECK: Summarizing** What reforms did the Catholic Church institute during the Counter-Reformation? clarified doctrines, established order of Jesuits

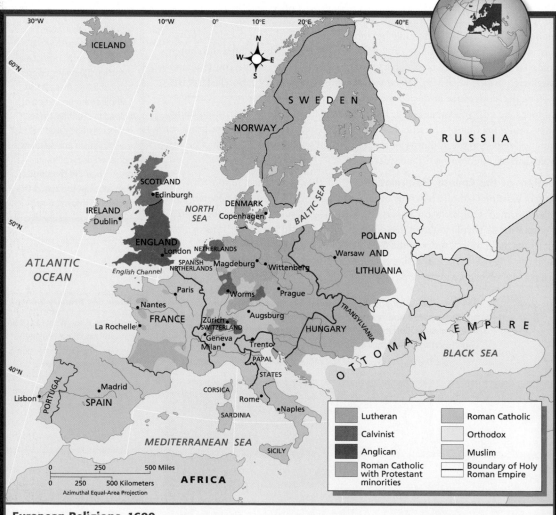

European Religions, 1600

Interpreting Maps The Reformation gained many converts in northern Europe, but southern Europe remained largely Catholic.

■ **Skills Assessment: 1. Places and Regions** What religion was dominant in England? Ireland? Spain? Sweden? **2. Making Predictions** What might result when such various religious groups come into contact?

REVIEW

Have students complete the Section 4 Review on p. 371.

ASSESS

Have students complete Daily Quiz 15.4. As Alternative Assessment, you may want to use the graphic organizer on the Counter-Reformation or the essay exercise from this section's lessons.

RETEACH

Have students complete Main Idea Activity for English Language Learners and Special-Needs Students 15.4. Then ask each student to create an annotated time line of the Catholic Reformation. Ask volunteers to present their time lines to the class. **ENGLISH LANGUAGE LEARNERS**

EXTEND

Have students research the Inquisition and present their findings to the class. Encourage them to use their textbooks, the library, computer software, and other sources of information on the subject. **BLOCK SCHEDULING**

Results of the Religious Upheaval

Some people hoped that the era of religious reformation would bring about tolerance. It did not. The period from the 1530s through the mid-1600s was a time of devastating religious wars in France, Germany, the Netherlands, and Switzerland. Not until the mid-1600s, when the wars ended, could the results of the Reformation and Counter-Reformation be seen.

The most striking result of the religious struggle was the appearance of many different churches in Europe. In Italy, where Protestantism was never a powerful force, interest in Catholic Church reform remained strong. In fact, most people in southern and eastern Europe and the native population of Ireland remained Catholic. However, France and the Netherlands had large numbers of Protestants. In England and northern Europe, including Scandinavia, various Protestant faiths became established with the backing of the central government.

Another far-reaching result of the Reformation and the Counter-Reformation was a strong interest in education. During the 1400s and 1500s, many new universities had appeared because of humanist interest in learning. After the 1500s, enrollment in these universities grew dramatically. Religious reformers supported education. Jesuits and other religious orders worked to strengthen the faith of Catholics in their schools. Protestants believed that people could find their way to Christian faith by studying the Bible. As a result, reading became increasingly important. But education did not bring greater tolerance for new ideas. Both Catholic and Protestant authorities opposed views that differed from their own.

Finally, the Reformation led to an increase in the power of national governments and a decrease in the power of the pope. In Protestant regions such as England, each government took responsibility for the leadership of the official church. In some Catholic areas such as France, rulers loyal to the pope managed to gain some degree of control over their churches.

Many schools, including the Dutch University of Leiden shown here, were established during the Reformation.

✔ **READING CHECK: Identifying Cause and Effect** How did the religious conflicts of the 1500s change life in Europe? diversity of churches appeared, education grew, national governments gained more power

---

SECTION 4 REVIEW

1. **Identify** and explain the significance:
   Counter-Reformation
   Council of Trent
   Jesuits
   Ignatius de Loyola

2. **Summarizing** Copy the graphic organizer below. Use it to record ways in which the Catholic Church made reforms in response to the Protestant Reformation.

   ```
   Reformation  ──→  [ Counter-Reformation ]
                ──→  [                      ]
                ──→  [                      ]
   ```

3. **Finding the Main Idea**
   a. Why did Catholic leaders feel the need to launch the Counter-Reformation?
   b. Were the results of the Counter-Reformation era largely positive or negative? Support your view.

4. **Writing and Critical Thinking**
   Identifying Cause and Effect Imagine that you have lived through the religious turmoil of the 1500s. Write a journal entry about the changes you have seen in Europe.
   Consider:
   • the spread of Protestantism
   • the growth of universities
   • the growing power of national governments

Homework Practice Online
keyword: SP3 HP15

SECTION 4 REVIEW ANSWERS

❶ **Identify**
• Counter-Reformation, p. 368
• Council of Trent, p. 369
• Jesuits, p. 369
• Ignatius de Loyola, p. 369

❷ ended abuses surrounding sale of indulgences; tightened discipline within clergy; brought Inquisition to Rome; established *Index of Forbidden Books*; reaffirmed Catholic doctrine; old and new religious orders (e.g., Jesuits) spread Catholicism

❸ **a.** They finally realized that Protestantism posed a threat to the Catholic Church.

b. Answers will vary. As a positive result, the Counter-Reformation solidified and improved the Catholic Church. As a negative result, it helped cause religious wars.

❹ Responses should include the spread of Protestantism, the growth of universities, and the growing power of national governments.

THE RENAISSANCE AND REFORMATION **371**

OBJECTIVES

1 Explain why Europeans believed in superstitions.

2 Describe the characteristics of daily life that were typical in Europe during the Reformation.

3 Explain how knowledge spread to European villages.

4 Identify the factors that caused changes in the daily lives of Europeans.

SECTION 5

READ TO DISCOVER

❶ Why did Europeans believe in superstitions?

❷ What characteristics were typical of daily life in Europe during the Reformation?

❸ How did knowledge spread to European villages?

❹ What factors caused changes in the daily lives of Europeans?

DEFINE

broadsides
almanacs
standard of living

WHY IT MATTERS TODAY

Almanacs were a popular source of information in Europe during the 1500s. Today people still use almanacs. Use **CNNfyi.com** or other **current event** sources to find and scan different almanacs to see the kinds of information they contain. Record your findings in your journal.

CNNfyi.com

Culture and Daily Life

The Main Idea
As the ideas of the Reformation took hold, daily life throughout Europe began to change.

The Story Continues *The ideas that marked European lifestyles during the Renaissance, the Reformation, and the Counter-Reformation involved relatively few, and mostly upper-class, people. Ordinary people had their own views about themselves and the world around them—ideas that included witches flying at night and other superstitions, and village processions that mocked the powerful and the foolish.*

Superstitions

Although towns had grown in number and population, most Europeans still lived in or near small villages. They spent their entire lives struggling with nature in order to raise food. People close to the land never knew what life might bring next. A cow might fall ill, or lightning might burn down a cottage. Moreover, during the 1500s the population of Europe was increasing at a time of social and political upheaval. War, famine, and plague continued to affect people. At any time, life could take an unexpected turn for the worse. Many people looked to superstitions to explain and control their lives.

The world of spirits. Although most Europeans were Christians, they considered God to be a distant, unknowable force. They explained many of the events that took place around them as the doings of spirits. Because of this belief in spirits, most Europeans believed that nothing was an accident. Bad spirits—demons—made life difficult. If lightning struck a house, a demon had caused it. If a pitcher of milk spilled, a demon was the reason. In fact, many superstitions that may seem strange or difficult to explain today began during this period.

Village priests usually accepted these beliefs, or they ignored them. The ordinary villager was not very satisfied with the priests' explanation that misfortune was God's will, or perhaps God's punishment for sin. Villagers still, however, believed

that a priest's actions could have positive effects. For example, every spring a priest would go out into the fields, bless the earth, and pray for good crops. His blessing of a husband and wife at a wedding supposedly gave the new couple a good start in life. Baptism was thought to protect a newborn child.

Belief in fortune telling was common during the 1400s and the 1500s.

LEVEL 1: Have students share some common superstitions. *(Students might mention bad luck from breaking a mirror, for example.)* Ask them why they think some people believe in such things. *(Superstitions help people believe they can control fate.)* Discuss the superstitious nature of European villagers during the Renaissance and Reformation. Ask why superstitions were so widespread during this era. *(Most people were very poor and uneducated and had little control over their destinies; because science was primitive, people understood little about the natural world.)* **ENGLISH LANGUAGE LEARNERS**

HOMEWORK Have students write magazine articles about the "witch hunts" of Europe during the 1500s and 1600s. The articles should include historical data as well as students' own opinions about why the wave of witch hunting occurred. Students can use their textbooks, the library, and computer software. Remind them to use correct grammar, spelling, sentence structure, and punctuation.

The priest was not the only person to whom the villagers turned in times of trouble. They also looked to a man or woman who was considered "wise" or "cunning." This person, usually an older village member, was thought to have a special understanding of how the world worked.

Ordinary people would explain their problem—a lost ring, a cruel husband, a sick pig—to the "wise" folk. People would also report anything unusual, even something simple like a frog jumping into a boat. Such events were taken as a warning. The wise man or woman would explain what the warning meant. Sometimes wise folk recommended a remedy for warding off evil. Remedies included chanting a spell, drinking a special potion, or wearing a good-luck charm.

Belief in witchcraft. Wise people were part of a traditional belief in witchcraft. Wise people were often called "good witches." If their relationship with their neighbors turned sour, or if misfortunes began to occur, they might be accused of being "bad witches." It was believed that bad witches had made a pact with the devil. In many cases, a person accused of witchcraft was an elderly widow. Without a husband or family, she would be the most defenseless person in the community. Such a woman was an easy target to attack.

Stories about witches became more sensational as they spread through the countryside. Outrageous accusations were made. A person might be accused of flying on a broomstick, sticking pins into dolls, or dancing with the devil in the woods at night. In some of these cases, a priest might be asked to hold a ceremony to exorcise, or drive out, a demon that was thought to have taken over the witch's body. In other cases, the accused person might be dragged to a bonfire, tied to a stake, and burned, perhaps with the approval of the local lord.

An enormous outburst of "witch hunting" occurred in Europe in the mid-1500s and lasted for more than one hundred years. Those accused of being witches were put on trial. The punishment was death. Both religious and secular leaders accepted witches as an explanation for problems in the world around them. The example of Jean Bodin, a French scholar, shows that even learned people believed in witches.

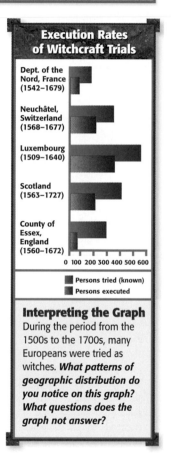

Execution Rates of Witchcraft Trials

Dept. of the Nord, France (1542–1679)

Neuchâtel, Switzerland (1568–1677)

Luxembourg (1509–1640)

Scotland (1563–1727)

County of Essex, England (1560–1672)

0 100 200 300 400 500 600

■ Persons tried (known)
■ Persons executed

Interpreting the Graph
During the period from the 1500s to the 1700s, many Europeans were tried as witches. *What patterns of geographic distribution do you notice on this graph? What questions does the graph not answer?*

> **History Makers Speak**
> **"**Now, if there is any means to appease the wrath of God, to gain his blessing, to strike awe into some by the punishment of others, to preserve some from being infected by others, to diminish the number of evil-doers . . . and to punish the most detestable crimes of which the human mind can conceive, it is to punish with the utmost rigor the witches. . . . Now it is not in the power of princes to pardon a crime which the law of God punishes with the penalty of death—such are the crimes of witches.**"**

Jean Bodin, *Witchcraft in Europe*

Eventually fewer cases of witchcraft were reported. As the religious wars came to an end, people experienced greater security in their lives. They were less likely to worry about the influence of witches in everyday life.

✔ READING CHECK: Identifying Cause and Effect How did concerns about events in daily life lead to a belief in superstitions? people looked for explanations/control

Analyzing Primary Sources

Identifying a Point of View
What is Bodin's opinion of the belief in witches? supports belief in witches

This English engraving shows a suspected witch being "swum" at a 1612 witchcraft trial.

Global Relations

The witch hunts of the 1500s and 1600s carried over to the English colonies in North America. In May 1692 a series of trials began in Salem in the Massachusetts Bay Colony. Government officials, encouraged by religious leaders, set up a special court to try women accused of practicing witchcraft. As many as 150 people were imprisoned. Suspicions fell even on the governor's wife. In all, 19 convicted "witches" were hanged. By September 1692, however, public hysteria died down, the trials were stopped, and the prisoners released. The Massachusetts legislature eventually overturned the convictions and granted payments to families of the victims.

Critical Thinking

What effect might the accusation of the governor's wife have had on the witch trials?

ANSWER: Accusations against the governor's wife probably accelerated opposition to the witch trials.

INTERPRETING THE GRAPH ANSWERS
Luxembourg tried and executed the most persons. Questions will vary but may include why different countries had various execution rates.

TEACH OBJECTIVE 2

LEVEL 2: Have students examine the painting by Pieter Brueghel the Younger on page 376. Ask them to write down what they can conclude about peasant life as they observe how the people are dressed, their facial expressions, and the activities in which they are involved. Have volunteers read their observations to the class. Then discuss characteristics of daily life during the Renaissance and Reformation era.

TEACH OBJECTIVE 3

ALL LEVELS: Ask students to identify and describe the main ways in which village people learned about the world outside of their villages. *(printed works such as broadsides, books, almanacs, and Bible translations; traveling preachers; primary schools)* Divide the class into small groups. Have each group create either a broadside, an almanac page, or the message brought by a traveling preacher. Then have the groups share their work with the class.

ENGLISH LANGUAGE LEARNERS, COOPERATIVE LEARNING

THEN AND NOW ANSWER

Answers may include tug-of-war, leap frog, and walking on stilts.

Culture

Guilds flourished in Europe between the 1000s and 1500s. They were an important part of the economic and social fabric of that time. A guild was generally one of two types: merchant guild or craft guild. Merchant guilds were associations of the merchants in a town or city. Craft guilds were associations of the artisans and craftsmen in an industry (such as weavers, masons, painters, or blacksmiths). Guilds performed a variety of important functions in the local economy, such as maintaining standards of quality and trying to bring about stable prices.

Critical Thinking

Why might a person join a merchant or craft guild?

ANSWER: Students may suggest that guilds could provide aid and protection for members and further their professional interests.

Daily Life

For most Europeans in the 1500s and 1600s, daylight meant work and night meant sleep. Because farming was so time-consuming, people needed all the daylight hours to raise food. By evening most farmers were exhausted from working all day. Few could afford the candles needed for light. Still, people did find time for relaxation.

Forms of recreation. Every village had a gathering place where people came together to drink, sew, do simple chores, or tell stories. Some played games such as skittles, a form of bowling. Occasionally traveling companies of actors passed through and put on shows. The people also enjoyed special holidays during the year. Some were church holidays, while others honored a local saint or tradition. During some holidays, the villagers donned costumes and would often put on their own ceremonies.

One favorite holiday ceremony poked fun at village life. This ceremony went by different names in different parts of Europe. Whether it was called "rough music," "charivari," or "abbeys of misrule," the basic ceremony was much the same. The young men of the village formed a procession. They made fun of people who had behaved in unusual ways or had violated local custom.

Sometimes the marchers had more serious targets. They might want to show how things would be if the poor or the weak had power. They would dress someone like a bishop or put the poorest man in the village on a throne. At this point the jokes were no longer lighthearted. They revealed the resentment villagers felt about the privileges their rulers possessed.

Violence and protest in the village. People of this time identified closely with those of their own kind. In large towns, members of the same profession joined together in guilds and other groups. In small villages, which contained perhaps a few dozen families, whole communities tended to work and make decisions together.

Because villagers lived in close-knit communities, anyone who upset village traditions or behaved oddly was treated harshly. Quarrels between neighbors were common, and the bonds of mutual reliance that held the community together could loosen in times of stress. The strain of hardship or famine could cause villagers to respond violently. For example, if a local baker was suspected of hoarding bread or sending it elsewhere to make higher profits, villagers might band together to ransack the baker's shop.

Games

People throughout the ages have played games for fun. In some cultures, games are a way for children to learn useful skills. Games provide relaxation and recreation.

Dice have been found in Egyptian tombs. The earliest form of the modern game of backgammon may date from about 3000 B.C. In recent years, people of all ages have been fascinated by the new games and twists on old games made possible by electronics and the computer.

Can you identify some games in the painting by Pieter Brueghel that people still play today?

Children's games in the 1500s

✔ **READING CHECK: Making Generalizations** What were the main features of daily life in Europe during this period? hard work, holiday ceremonies, close-knit communities

LEVEL 3: Have students create detailed before-and-after charts comparing Europe in about 1400 and Europe in about 1600. Remind students to list the differences as well as explain the reasons for them. Their graphic organizer can take the form as shown. Close by asking students what remained the same. (*Nobles and other privileged people still lived better than most peasants and the urban poor; peasants generally ate the same meals they'd been eating for centuries; peasants continued to live in thatched-roof cottages.*)

Europe c. 1400	Europe c. 1600
population decreased by Black Death, so labor in great demand resulting in higher wages	population growing rapidly, which led to inflation
diet consisted mainly of cheese and eggs, people rarely ate meat or fish	new vegetables, coffee, tea, spices, and chocolate introduced
people ate mostly with fingers	forks and spoons came into use
people lived in thatched-roof cottages	in cities, houses were built with brick and stone
peasants trapped in rural poverty	many people moved to cities

The Spread of Knowledge

In the 1500s the world beyond the village began to affect village life. Printed works, and in some areas traveling preachers, inspired these changes.

Books for the masses. Few ordinary villagers could read. In some cases even the village priest could not read. Nevertheless, soon after the invention of movable type, publishers started selling popular works. Single printed sheets known as **broadsides** began to appear. A broadside might include a royal decree or news of some sensational crime or other event. Books and broadsides arrived in the village, carried by peddlers who brought goods from the outside world. When the villagers gathered together, they might enjoy listening to someone read the latest broadside.

Romances and epics of the classical era appealed to nobility. Publishers also found subjects that appealed to country folk and produced cheap books for this new market. The most common books were **almanacs,** which published predictions about the weather and prospects for growing crops. Almanacs also contained calendars, maps, and medical advice. The books were best-sellers because they spoke to the beliefs and concerns of ordinary people.

Religious ideas and education. Soon after Luther's break with the church in 1521, new religious ideas began to spread beyond urban areas. Sometimes preachers came to visit. Peddlers might sell books on religious themes. Perhaps people heard stories that attacked the church. The messages of Luther and Calvin traveled in this manner, as did translations of the Bible.

As Protestants and Catholics battled for the loyalties of ordinary people, leaders of both sides encouraged the founding of primary schools in the villages and towns. Both Protestant and Catholic leaders believed that knowledge would lead a person to support the faith. In spite of this common

CONNECTING TO
Science and Technology

The Printing Press

During the Middle Ages books were written and copied by hand. The work was usually done by Christian monks, and it took a long time to produce a book. A German, Johannes Gutenberg, developed a faster way to print things by inventing the printing press in about 1450. Gutenberg developed the use of movable type. He then modified a wine press to push the paper onto the inked type, which made an impression on the paper. With the new press he could print ten sheets of paper per hour. The printing press allowed ideas and knowledge to be spread faster and farther than

ever before. Many of today's presses are computerized and can print pages at high speeds. Daily life today is filled with printed materials, from books and magazines to posters and leaflets.

screw

type form

platen (flat plate)

bed

Understanding Science and Technology

How was the Gutenberg printing technique an improvement over older techniques?

SCIENCE, TECHNOLOGY & SOCIETY ANSWER
Copying by hand took a long time and made books expensive. Printing was much quicker and reduced the costs of books.

History Maker

JOHANNES GUTENBERG. Johannes Gutenberg, the man credited with inventing the printing press, was the son of an upper-class citizen of Mainz, a German town. A skilled metalworker, Gutenberg moved to the nearby town of Strassburg between 1428 and 1430. In 1438 acquaintances of Gutenberg learned that he was working on a new invention–the printing press–which he was trying to keep secret. Gutenberg borrowed money from Johann Fust, a wealthy businessman, to finish work on his printing press. However, the two men had a falling out. Fust went to court and won a lawsuit against Gutenberg. Afterward, Gutenberg probably operated a printing shop during the 1450s and 1460s, though no one knows for sure.

Critical Thinking

Why did Johannes Gutenberg want to keep his work on the printing press a secret?

ANSWER: Students might suggest that if others learned of Gutenberg's work, they may have tried to profit by taking his idea and producing their own printing press.

The printing press, invented by Johannes Gutenberg, was a revolutionary technological advance. As the use of Gutenberg's technology spread throughout Europe, so too did new ideas and knowledge. Similarly, the Internet today can be viewed as a revolutionary technological advance. Organize the class into small groups and have each group brainstorm ideas for their own inventions that would profoundly impact our world today. Have them select one of their ideas to develop further. Each group should write a brief description of what their proposed invention would do and what long-term effects it might have on society. **BLOCK SCHEDULING, COOPERATIVE LEARNING**

Interdisciplinary Connection

SCIENCE. The depopulation caused by the Black Death had environmental as well as economic consequences. The shortage of agricultural workers meant that many marginal lands could not be farmed. As a result land that had been almost completely deforested and converted to farmland was allowed to return to its natural state.

Critical Thinking

Ask students to suggest how this reforestation might have been beneficial to Europeans.

ANSWER: These forests would have been a useful source of wood for building and heating.

concern for education, the followers of the differing religions struggled to coexist peacefully. However, because education became part of the struggle for followers, neither side included tolerance in its teachings.

✔ **READING CHECK: Summarizing** In what ways did knowledge spread to European villages? printed books became available; primary schools were founded

Changes in Daily Life

In addition to undergoing religious and political change during the Renaissance and Reformation eras, Europeans experienced other changes.

The economy. The measure of the quality of life—the **standard of living**—is affected by many factors, including environment, health, home life, income, and working conditions. During the Renaissance peasants made up as much as 85 to 90 percent of the total European population, except in the highly urbanized areas of northern Italy and Flanders. As the manorial system continued to decline, so too did medieval concepts and practices of serfdom. Increasingly, the labor dues owed by a peasant to his lord were converted into rents paid in money. By the end of the 1400s, especially in western Europe, more and more peasants were becoming legally free. Furthermore, the Black Death of the 1300s had reduced the population by at least one third. This meant that there were now fewer people to work the land. Some peasants prospered, therefore, because their labor was in demand, which often resulted in higher wages.

By 1550, when the religious wars were ravaging Europe, conditions changed again. The population was growing rapidly. With population growth came inflation, a rise in prices for goods. After 1550 wages could not keep up with the rise in prices, especially of farm goods.

Diet. During this period, white bread made from wheat was rare. Meat was scarce and expensive, and fish only a little less so. Salt had long been an important trade item because it was needed to preserve foods, but it, too, was expensive. Cheese and eggs—cheap sources of protein—were an important part of the diet everywhere in Europe. Butter was not widely used outside northern Europe until the 1700s.

The image above shows some of the foods typical of European diets in the 1500s and 1600s. In the painting below, by Pieter Brueghel the Younger, peasants of the era share a meal as they rest from their work.

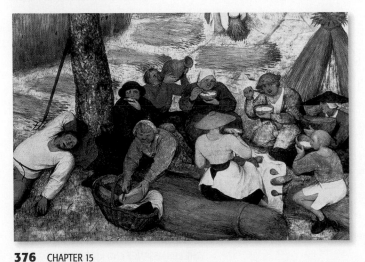

Most spices introduced into Europe from the East had been considered luxury items. By the 1500s and 1600s, the importation of spices had become very competitive. Increased competition often meant a drop in prices.

In the 1500s traders introduced new vegetables to Europe. Europeans had the opportunity to try asparagus, green beans, lettuce, melons, spinach, and tomatoes. Traders also brought new luxury items such as coffee and tea. Not everyone had access to the new and varied diets, however. Wealthy people still lived better than most people did. Peasants and the urban poor usually ate the same simple meals they had eaten for centuries.

CLOSE

Have students work in pairs to summarize the main ideas presented in Section 5. Each partner should take two of the questions in "Read to Discover" and share the answer with their partner.

REVIEW

Have students complete the Section 5 Review on p. 377.

ASSESS

Have students complete Daily Quiz 15.5. As Alternative Assessment, you may want to use the before-and-after chart or magazine article exercise in this section's lessons.

RETEACH

Have students complete Main Idea Activity for English Language Learners and Special-Needs Students 15.5. Then have each student write a few questions based on Section 5 content. Ask students to take turns answering their classmates' questions.
ENGLISH LANGUAGE LEARNERS

EXTEND

Organize students into groups. Have each group create a skit depicting the life and culture of ordinary people during the Renaissance and Reformation. Encourage students to use props and costumes. **BLOCK SCHEDULING, COOPERATIVE LEARNING**

Customs and table settings that we know today were not common in the early Renaissance period. People usually ate with their fingers. They picked what they wanted to eat from a common dish. In some areas people ate from wooden plates. Guests brought their own knives. Forks did not come into use until the 1500s, and spoons were not common until the 1600s.

Housing. After the 1500s brick and stone became more common construction materials in the growing cities of Europe. In the countryside housing remained much as it had during the Middle Ages. Peasants lived in small, thatch-roofed houses. Glass was expensive and often difficult to obtain, even for the wealthy. The scarcity of glass meant that most houses had shutters instead of glass windows. Peasant houses usually contained only the necessities of rural life—a large cooking pot, a bench, a table, and some tools. The lucky few had a bed. Most people slept on sacks filled with straw.

Decline of traditional culture. Many peasants were trapped in poverty. Hoping to escape their fate, some migrated to the cities. The movement of people from countryside to city during the Renaissance and Reformation eras further changed traditional popular culture. In the city, food came from a shop rather than directly from the fields. Local governments helped out when disasters occurred. If famine struck, authorities passed out bread. If plagues broke out, the government set up hospitals and quarantined sick people.

Gradually, the residents of cities and towns became more sophisticated in their attitudes. In particular, people's understanding of how things happen in the world began to change. Superstition no longer played an important role in people's views of daily life. Instead, people sought rational explanations for day-to-day events. They had less need for magic and "wise" folk. Some scholars have called this very important development the "disenchantment" of the world—the removal of "enchantment," or magic, from nature.

✔ **READING CHECK: Contrasting** In what ways did life in Europe change during the early Renaissance? *standard of living rose for some, people moved from country to cities, better diet, rational thinking more widespread*

INTERPRETING THE VISUAL RECORD

Daily work This sophisticated urban couple of the 1500s are working together in their banking business. *Compare this picture with the picture of peasants on the previous page. What role did women play in the world of work?*

VISUAL RECORD ANSWER
Women did many of the same jobs as men.

SECTION

5 REVIEW ANSWERS

❶ Define
• broadsides, p. 375
• almanacs, p. 375
• standard of living, p. 376

❷ long, hard days of work; holiday ceremonies; close-knit communities; odd behavior treated harshly; widespread belief in superstition and witchcraft

❸ a. broadsides and books, founding of new schools

b. Townspeople and city folk became more sophisticated; people sought rational explanations for everyday events.

c. Answers will vary. Factors suggesting a better life include: increase in education, movement from country to city, and better diet. Students may note that most peasants' lives remained unchanged.

❹ Responses will vary but should incorporate a mindset typical of villagers at the time.

SECTION 5 REVIEW

1. Define and explain the significance:
broadsides
almanacs
standard of living

2. Summarizing Copy the concept map below. Use it to explain features of daily life in Europe during the 1500s.

Daily Life—1500s

Homework Practice Online
keyword: SP3 HP15

3. **Finding the Main Idea**
a. What evidence would you give that the printing press had significant influence during the Renaissance?
b. Why did urban life lead to the growing "disenchantment" of the world?
c. Did life improve for most Europeans during the 1500s?

4. **Writing and Critical Thinking**
Analyzing Information Imagine that you are a European villager. Prepare a broadside that explains why people believe in superstitions.
Consider:
• attitudes toward God and nature
• the role of "wise" folk in village life

THE RENAISSANCE AND REFORMATION **377**

CHAPTER 15

REVIEW AND ASSESSMENT RESOURCES

REPRODUCIBLE RESOURCES

▶ Vocabulary Activity 15

TECHNOLOGY RESOURCES

▶ Chapter 15 Test Generator (on the One-Stop Planner)
▶ Global Skill Builder CD–ROM
▶ HRW Web Site

REINFORCEMENT, REVIEW, and ASSESSMENT

▶ Chapter 15 Review, pp. 378–379
▶ Chapter 15 Tutorial for Students, Parents, Mentors, and Peers
▶ Chapter 15 Test (Form A or B)
▶ Alternative Assessment Handbook
▶ Chapter 15 Test for English Language Learners and Special-Needs Students

REVIEW

Have students complete the Chapter 15 Review on pages 378–379.

ASSESS

Use one of the chapter tests to assess students' understanding of the content. For Alternative Assessment, see the Portfolio Activities and Alternative Assessment Handbook.

CHAPTER 15 REVIEW ANSWERS

Understanding Main Ideas

1. critical approach, studied classics, admired human achievement

2. use of perspective, more realistic portrayals

3. travelers to and from Italy, printing press

4. interested in early Christian as well as classical culture

5. created opposition in northern Europe

6. Peace of Augsburg, rise of sects, creation of Anglican Church, Calvinism

7. clarified doctrines, brought Inquisition to Rome, established order of Jesuits

8. education and reading became more important, more universities

9. People looked for explanations for everyday occurrences.

10. The world beyond the village became known through the availability of printed works.

Reviewing Themes

1. They led to conflict.

2. It increased the spread of new ideas.

3. They provided one of the main features of Renaissance humanist thought.

CHAPTER 15 Review

Creating a Time Line

Copy the time line below onto a sheet of paper. Complete the time line by filling in the events, individuals, and dates from the chapter that you think were significant. Pick three events and explain why you think they were significant.

1400   1500   1600

Writing a Summary

Using standard grammar, spelling, sentence structure, and punctuation, write an overview of the events in the chapter.

Identifying People and Ideas

Identify the following terms or individuals and explain their significance:

1. Renaissance
2. humanists
3. Niccolò Machiavelli
4. Leonardo da Vinci
5. Johannes Gutenberg
6. Reformation
7. Martin Luther
8. Counter-Reformation
9. broadsides
10. standard of living

Understanding Main Ideas

SECTION 1 *(pp. 354–358)*
The Italian Renaissance

1. What were the main values that generally characterized the Italian humanists?
2. What new painting styles and techniques developed during the Italian Renaissance?

SECTION 2 *(pp. 359–362)*
The Northern Renaissance

3. How did northern Europeans learn about the Italian Renaissance?
4. How did northern Renaissance writers differ from the writers of the Italian Renaissance?

SECTION 3 *(pp. 363–367)*
The Protestant Reformation

5. What role did the sale of indulgences by the church play in the Reformation?
6. In what ways did Protestantism spread?

SECTION 4 *(pp. 368–371)*
The Catholic Reformation

7. What actions did the Catholic Church take during the Counter-Reformation?
8. How did the Reformation and Counter-Reformation affect education?

SECTION 5 *(pp. 372–377)*
Culture and Daily Life

9. Why did Europeans believe in superstitions?
10. What factor was mainly responsible for the decline of traditional culture?

Reviewing Themes

1. **Global Relations** What effect did the ideas of Luther and other religious reformers have on the relations between different groups in Europe?
2. **Science, Technology & Society** What effect did the printing press have on the ways that Europeans understood their world?
3. **Culture** How did the classical literature of Greece and Rome influence the development of humanism?

Thinking Critically

1. **Identifying Cause and Effect** What events contributed to the beginning of the Renaissance?
2. **Contrasting** How did Renaissance humanist thought differ from medieval thought?
3. **Sequencing** What were the main events of the Reformation and the Counter-Reformation?
4. **Evaluating** How effective were the reforms of the Counter-Reformation?

Writing About History

Contrasting Write a report explaining the differences between Calvinism, Catholicism, and Lutheranism. Use the chart below to organize your thoughts before writing.

	Calvinism	Catholicism	Lutheranism
Path to salvation			
Church organization			

Arrange a panel discussion on the following topic: The Reformation and Counter-Reformation would not have occurred if not for the invention of the printing press.

RETEACH

Group students who had trouble with the test into pairs. Have them use their textbooks to correct their tests. Ask them to create questions and answers covering chapter content. Then have students take the Form B test to assess their mastery of the material.

**ENGLISH LANGUAGE LEARNERS ,
COOPERATIVE LEARNING**

Portfolio Extension

1. During the Reformation, religious leaders created posters, called "broadsides," to persuade people to embrace their religion. The posters were composed mostly of images, because most people could not read. Have students create a broadside for either the Protestant or Catholic cause in the 1500s. Posters should include positive images and slogans to attract people to the cause.

2. Have students imagine that they are Renaissance authors or artists. Have them write a poem or short play reflecting the ideas of humanism or create an original painting, drawing, or sculpture based on Renaissance ideas. Ask them to write a short presentation for their work, explaining how it reflects the ideas of the Renaissance.

Building Social Studies Skills

Using Artifacts as Historical Evidence

Study the photograph below. Then answer the questions that follow.

Italian Renaissance bookbinding with velvet and silverwork

1. Which of the following best describes the historical evidence this artifact provides?
   a. Many people had books during the Renaissance.
   b. Italian bookbinding reached its height during the Renaissance.
   c. All Renaissance books were bound with velvet and silver.
   d. During the Renaissance, some Italians had books with fancy bindings.

2. What clues does this bookbinding give about life during the Italian Renaissance? Give your reasons.

Identifying Cause and Effect

Read the following excerpt by an art historian about the Italian artist Michelangelo. Then answer the questions.

> "Michelangelo's life story is a series of quarrels, disappointments, and interruptions. If we except the Sistine Ceiling, he was forced to leave undone more work than he was allowed to finish, largely because of . . . his patron Pope Julius II . . . . Some twenty-four years after the completion of the ceiling Michelangelo was called upon to do another stupendous fresco, this time for the end wall of the same chapel. *The Last Judgment* . . . reflects the bitterness of the aging genius."

3. Which of the following correctly states the reason the author gives for Michelangelo's bitterness?
   a. His whole life he had been forced to do what his patron required.
   b. He did not want to leave the chapel ceiling unfinished.
   c. He felt he was too old to do another fresco.
   d. He thought his patron would interrupt him once again.

4. Most artists of the Italian Renaissance supported themselves by working for patrons. Do you think this system was successful? Give your reasons.

Alternative Assessment

Building Your Portfolio

Science, Technology & Society

The printing press helped spread new ideas down through the centuries. With computers, current printing technology has changed, and the Internet spreads information almost instantly around the world. Using your textbook and other sources, create a bibliography of the important printed works that have had a great influence on people and events.

⚿ internet connect

Internet Activity: go.hrw.com
KEYWORD: SP3 WH15

Choose a topic on the Renaissance and Reformation to:
- create a pamphlet on the Reformation and its leaders.
- report on the economic, social, and technological influences of Johannes Gutenberg's printing press.
- create a biography on one of the Renaissance writers in this chapter.

Exploration and Expansion

CHAPTER RESOURCE MANAGER

	Objectives	Pacing Guide		Reproducible Resources
SECTION 1 **The Scientific Revolution** (pp. 382–387)	• Identify the factors that contributed to the Scientific Revolution. • Explain how Copernicus, Kepler, and Galileo challenged traditional thought. • Describe some of the important scientific discoveries of this period.	**Regular** 1.5 day *Block Scheduling Handbook with Team Teaching Strategies, 16.1*	**Block Scheduling** 1 day	**RS** Guided Reading Strategy 16.1 **PS** Readings in World History 56: On the Motion of the Heart and Blood
SECTION 2 **The Foundations of European Exploration** (pp. 388–391)	• Identify technological advances that made European exploration possible. • Describe the effect of the Commercial Revolution. • Explain the role mercantilism played in the colonies.	**Regular** 1.5 day *Block Scheduling Handbook with Team Teaching Strategies, 16.2*	**Block Scheduling** 1 day	**RS** Guided Reading Strategy 16.2 **E** Hands-on History Activity 16: A Sailor's Life **E** Creative Teaching Strategy 16: Talk Show: Changing Europe's Worldview
SECTION 3 **Voyages of Portugal and Spain** (pp. 392–399)	• Describe what the early Portuguese explorers accomplished. • Discuss how the voyages of Christopher Columbus influenced the world. • Explain why the Atlantic slave trade prospered.	**Regular** 1.5 day *Block Scheduling Handbook with Team Teaching Strategies, 16.3*	**Block Scheduling** 1 day	**RS** Guided Reading Strategy 16.3 **RS** Graphic Organizer Activity 16: Explorers and Explorations **SM** Geography Activity 16: Crossing the Atlantic **PS** Readings in World History 57: First Impressions of the New World
SECTION 4 **The Spanish and Dutch Empires** (pp. 400–407)	• Describe how Spain extended its power abroad and at home. • Explain why the Dutch were successful in the 1600s. • Analyze why the Spanish Empire declined.	**Regular** 1.5 day *Block Scheduling Handbook with Team Teaching Strategies, 16.4*	**Block Scheduling** 1 day	**RS** Guided Reading Strategy 16.4

Chapter Resource Key

PS	Primary Sources	**A**	Assessment	🎵	Music
RS	Reading Support	**REV**	Review	📼	Video
IC	Interdisciplinary Connections	**ELL**	Reinforcement and English Language Learners	🌐	Internet
E	Enrichment	✏️	Transparencies	💻	Holt Presentation Maker Using Microsoft® PowerPoint®
SM	Skills Mastery	💿	CD-ROM		

One-Stop Planner CD-ROM

See the *One-Stop Planner* for a complete list of additional resources for students and teachers.

One-Stop Planner CD-ROM

It's easy to plan lessons, select resources, and print out materials for your students when you use the **One-Stop Planner** CD–ROM with **Test Generator**.

Technology Resources

- One-Stop Planner 16.1
- Holt Researcher: World History: Nicolaus Copernicus, Galileo Galilei
- Holt Researcher: World History: Robert Boyle
- Homework Practice Online

- One-Stop Planner 16.2
- Homework Practice Online
- Online Maps: Major European Trading Areas, c. 1500
- Online Maps: European Trade Goods, c. 1500
- Online Maps: European Finance and Trade, c. 1500

- One-Stop Planner 16.3
- Holt Researcher: World History: Isabella, Christopher Columbus
- World History and Cultures Video Program 16
- CNN. Presents Geography: Yesterday and Today Segment 15: Worlds Meet in the Americas
- Homework Practice Online
- Online Maps: European Idea of the Atlantic Before Columbus
- Online Maps: Treaty of Tordesillas, 1494

- One-Stop Planner 16.4
- Homework Practice Online
- Online Maps: French and Dutch Imports, 1770s
- Online Maps: Portuguese Imports, 1770s
- Online Maps: Spanish Imports, 1770s
- Online Maps: British Imports, 1770s
- Online Maps: Empires in the Americas, 1700
- Online Maps: Africa in 1750

Reinforcement, Review, and Assessment

- Daily Quiz 16.1
- Main Idea Activity 16.1
- English Audio Summary 16.1
- Spanish Audio Summary 16.1
- REV Section 1 Review, p. 387

- Daily Quiz 16.2
- Main Idea Activity 16.2
- English Audio Summary 16.2
- Spanish Audio Summary 16.2
- REV Section 1 Review, p. 391

- Daily Quiz 16.3
- Main Idea Activity 16.3
- English Audio Summary 16.3
- Spanish Audio Summary 16.3
- REV Section 3 Review, p. 399

- Daily Quiz 16.4
- Main Idea Activity 16.4
- English Audio Summary 16.4
- Spanish Audio Summary 16.4
- REV Section 4 Review, p. 407

internet connect

HRW ONLINE RESOURCES
GO TO: go.hrw.com
Then type in a keyword.

TEACHER HOME PAGE
KEYWORD: SP3 Teacher

CHAPTER INTERNET ACTIVITIES
KEYWORD: SP3 WH16
Choose an activity to:
- research the Scientific Revolution and create a database of scientists, dates, and contributions.
- learn more about an explorer described in this chapter.
- explain the political, economic, and cultural impact of Spanish expansion in Mesoamerica and Andean South America.

CHAPTER ENRICHMENT LINKS
KEYWORD: SP3 CH16

ONLINE ASSESSMENT
Homework Practice
KEYWORD: SP3 HP16
Standardized Test Prep
KEYWORD: SP3 STP16
Rubrics
KEYWORD: SS Rubrics

ONLINE MAPS, CHARTS, AND GRAPHS
KEYWORD: SP3 MCG

CONTENT UPDATES
KEYWORD: SS Content Updates

HOLT PRESENTATION MAKER
KEYWORD: SP3 PPT16

ONLINE READING SUPPORT
KEYWORD: SS Strategies

CURRENT EVENTS
KEYWORD: S3 Current Events

Meeting Individual Needs

Ability Levels

Level 1 Basic level activities designed for all students encountering new material

Level 2 Intermediate level activities designed for average students

Level 3 Challenging activities designed for honors and gifted and talented students

English Language Learners These activities address the needs of students with Limited English Proficiency.

Chapter Review and Assessment

- IC   Vocabulary Activity 16
- Global Skill Builder CD-ROM
- HRW Web Site
- REV   Chapter 16 Tutorial for Students, Parents, Mentors, and Peers
- REV   Chapter 16 Review, pp. 408–409
- A   Chapter 16 Test Generator (on the One-Stop Planner)
- A   Chapter 16 Test (Form A or B)
- A   Alternative Assessment Handbook
- A   Chapter 16 Test for English Language Learners and Special-Needs Students

Build on What You Know

Ask students to answer the following questions:

How might the Italian Renaissance and the Protestant Reformation have affected how people thought about the natural world?

Consider:

- challenges to traditional authority
- study of newly-discovered ancient manuscripts
- curiosity about ideas

What changes in technology and society might have encouraged the quest for new knowledge?

Consider:

- the influence of the printing press
- the role of stronger monarchies as patrons of learning and exploration

---

EXPLORING THE TIME LINE
GLOBAL EVENTS

internet connect

go.hrw.com

TOPIC: Mercator projection map and other technological advances

GO TO: go.hrw.com

KEYWORD: SP3 WH16

Have students access the Internet through the HRW Go site to conduct research on the first Mercator projection map and other technological inventions that helped foster exploration and expansion in the 1500s and 1600s. Then have students create a museum display highlighting two or three of these inventions (for example, maps, navigation tools, and ships). Their display should include pictures, drawings, or models of the inventions along with text that explains how the invention aided explorers in reaching their goals.

1400–1800

Exploration and Expansion

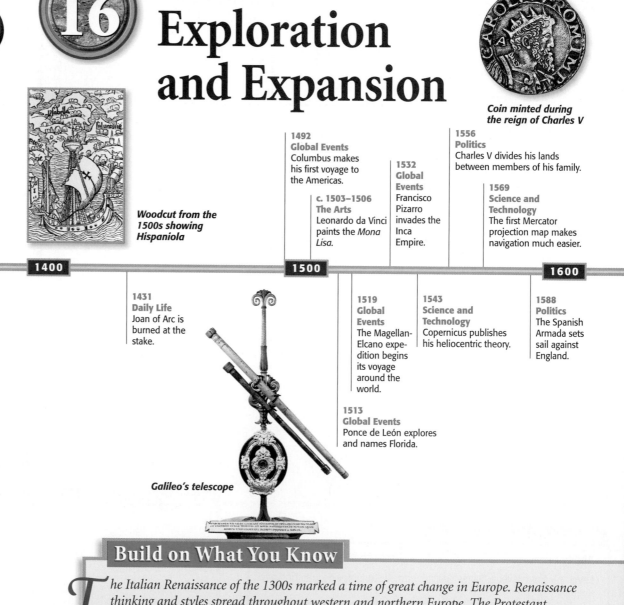

Coin minted during the reign of Charles V

Woodcut from the 1500s showing Hispaniola

1492
Global Events
Columbus makes his first voyage to the Americas.

c. 1503–1506
The Arts
Leonardo da Vinci paints the *Mona Lisa.*

1532
Global Events
Francisco Pizarro invades the Inca Empire.

1556
Politics
Charles V divides his lands between members of his family.

1569
Science and Technology
The first Mercator projection map makes navigation much easier.

1400

1431
Daily Life
Joan of Arc is burned at the stake.

1519
Global Events
The Magellan-Elcano expedition begins its voyage around the world.

1513
Global Events
Ponce de León explores and names Florida.

1500

1543
Science and Technology
Copernicus publishes his heliocentric theory.

1588
Politics
The Spanish Armada sets sail against England.

1600

Galileo's telescope

Build on What You Know

The Italian Renaissance of the 1300s marked a time of great change in Europe. Renaissance thinking and styles spread throughout western and northern Europe. The Protestant Reformation of the 1500s led to new social, political, and economic patterns across Europe. The Reformation challenged traditional approaches to religious thought and the individual's role in society. During this same era, new ways of studying and understanding the natural world brought about a scientific revolution. In this chapter, you will learn about the causes and effects of this revolution in thought.

What's Your Opinion?

Science, Technology & Society

Agree Scientists are an educated elite who rarely discuss their ideas with ordinary people.

Disagree Most gains in standards of living result from advances in science and technology.

Economics

Agree The need for natural resources motivates governments to look for new sources.

Disagree Cultures develop around available resources; they just decide they "need" other resources they find through exploration.

Global Relations

Agree Conquering powers pursue their own interests, not those of the people they conquer.

Disagree Exploration is a quest for knowledge; conquest has different motives, such as power.

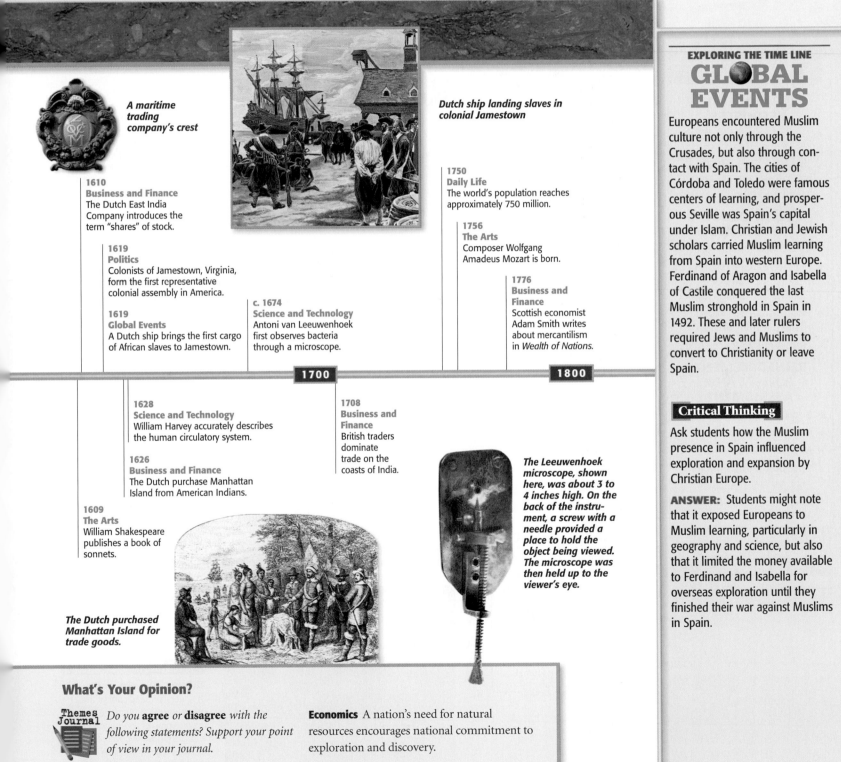

A maritime trading company's crest

Dutch ship landing slaves in colonial Jamestown

1610
Business and Finance
The Dutch East India Company introduces the term "shares" of stock.

1619
Politics
Colonists of Jamestown, Virginia, form the first representative colonial assembly in America.

1619
Global Events
A Dutch ship brings the first cargo of African slaves to Jamestown.

c. 1674
Science and Technology
Antoni van Leeuwenhoek first observes bacteria through a microscope.

1750
Daily Life
The world's population reaches approximately 750 million.

1756
The Arts
Composer Wolfgang Amadeus Mozart is born.

1776
Business and Finance
Scottish economist Adam Smith writes about mercantilism in *Wealth of Nations*.

1700

1800

1628
Science and Technology
William Harvey accurately describes the human circulatory system.

1626
Business and Finance
The Dutch purchase Manhattan Island from American Indians.

1609
The Arts
William Shakespeare publishes a book of sonnets.

1708
Business and Finance
British traders dominate trade on the coasts of India.

The Leeuwenhoek microscope, shown here, was about 3 to 4 inches high. On the back of the instrument, a screw with a needle provided a place to hold the object being viewed. The microscope was then held up to the viewer's eye.

The Dutch purchased Manhattan Island for trade goods.

What's Your Opinion?

 *Do you **agree** or **disagree** with the following statements? Support your point of view in your journal.*

Science, Technology & Society A society's approach to scientific study has little impact upon daily lifestyles and standards of living.

Economics A nation's need for natural resources encourages national commitment to exploration and discovery.

Global Relations Exploration can lead to confrontations and mistreatment of conquered peoples.

Europeans encountered Muslim culture not only through the Crusades, but also through contact with Spain. The cities of Córdoba and Toledo were famous centers of learning, and prosperous Seville was Spain's capital under Islam. Christian and Jewish scholars carried Muslim learning from Spain into western Europe. Ferdinand of Aragon and Isabella of Castile conquered the last Muslim stronghold in Spain in 1492. These and later rulers required Jews and Muslims to convert to Christianity or leave Spain.

Critical Thinking

Ask students how the Muslim presence in Spain influenced exploration and expansion by Christian Europe.

ANSWER: Students might note that it exposed Europeans to Muslim learning, particularly in geography and science, but also that it limited the money available to Ferdinand and Isabella for overseas exploration until they finished their war against Muslims in Spain.

OBJECTIVES

1 **Identify the factors that contributed to the Scientific Revolution.**

2 **Explain how Copernicus, Kepler, and Galileo challenged traditional thought.**

3 **Describe some of the important scientific discoveries of this period.**

VISUAL RECORD ANSWER

through observation and experimentation

SECTION 1

READ TO DISCOVER

1 What factors contributed to the Scientific Revolution?
2 How did Copernicus, Kepler, and Galileo challenge traditional thought?
3 What were some of the important scientific discoveries of this period?

DEFINE

scientific method
geocentric theory
heliocentric theory

IDENTIFY

Roger Bacon
Scientific Revolution
Nicolaus Copernicus
Johannes Kepler
Galileo Galilei
Isaac Newton
Andreas Vesalius
René Descartes
Francis Bacon
Robert Boyle

▸ WHY IT MATTERS TODAY

Scientific discoveries can have both positive and negative effects on society. Use **CNNfyi.com** or other **current event** sources to find several social issues that involve science or technology. Record your findings in your journal.

CNNfyi.com

The Scientific Revolution

The Main Idea
The Scientific Revolution challenged and changed the way people thought about the world.

The Story Continues *In the early 1600s Spanish writer Miguel de Cervantes published a novel called* Don Quixote de la Mancha. *It told the story of an aging man stuck in the myths of the past. Cervantes's humorous tale reflected a new world that was rejecting the legends of old for a reality based on science.*

From Magic to Science

Until well into the 1500s, most Europeans saw little difference between science and magic. Alchemists used spells and magic formulas to try to change one substance to another—for example, lead into gold. Astrologers believed that the position of the stars in the sky influenced human life. People still believed many explanations of natural events proposed by Aristotle almost 2,000 years earlier. These people were called natural philosophers. They relied on religious teachings and the works of classical Greek and Roman thinkers to explain the mysteries of nature. Many scientists before the Renaissance were like **Roger Bacon,** an English philosopher and scientist of the 1200s. Bacon, a Franciscan monk who had studied at Oxford and Paris, was viewed as a leading scholar of his time. He was one of the earliest to favor a system of scientific experimentation, rather than faithful acceptance of religious ideas and ancient beliefs, as a means of finding truth. Nevertheless, he was shaped by the thinking of the time and mainly practiced alchemy. Famed for his teaching, Bacon became known as Doctor Mirabilis—wonderful teacher.

The spirit of the Renaissance encouraged curiosity, investigation, discovery, and the practical application of the knowledge of nature to everyday life. Some people felt freer to question old ideas and beliefs. They were more willing to use new approaches to answering questions about the natural world. During the era of the **Scientific Revolution,** people began using experiments and mathematics to understand these mysteries. The study of nature became more organized. They were no longer content to explain the world in terms of religious thought, magic, or the ideas of ancient writers.

INTERPRETING THE VISUAL RECORD

Alchemy Alchemists sought to understand and control the natural world through the use of magic. Some of their procedures and tools, however, were similar to those of early and later scientists. *Based on the picture, how might alchemists have contributed to the development of early scientific procedures?*

TEACH OBJECTIVE 1

LEVEL 1: Ask students to name causes of the Scientific Revolution. Write the answers in a web diagram on the board. Ask students how each cause contributed to the Scientific Revolution. **ENGLISH LANGUAGE LEARNERS**

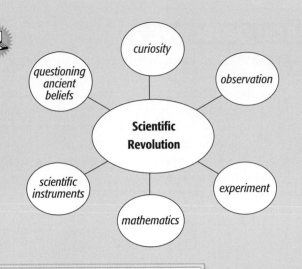

This new approach produced answers to many questions in physics, astronomy, and anatomy. It formed the basis for what we know today as science. Before the 1600s the word science meant "to know." After the 1600s the sense of the word changed into the narrower meaning it has today.

✔ **READING CHECK: Drawing Inferences** What role did the Renaissance play in the development of science? *encouraged curiosity, investigation, and discovery*

The New Study of Nature

As scientists spent more time examining the world around them, they observed things that did not agree with traditional explanations. For this reason, early scientists of the 1500s began to question ancient beliefs. They learned to form conclusions based on what they could observe with their own senses. They also used three new tools—scientific instruments, mathematics, and experiments. This new approach to study and knowledge marked the beginnings of the Scientific Revolution. It was a turning point in thinking that led to a rapid increase in people's understanding of the world.

The ability to conduct experiments was key to this new approach to learning. Scientists used newly invented instruments such as the barometer, the microscope, the telescope, the air pump, and the thermometer. These tools greatly improved their ability to observe and measure. Scientists used mathematics to check and apply those measurements. Also, they repeated their experiments to make sure they got the same results. Then they drew conclusions about what they observed. This manner of study is called the **scientific method.**

✔ **READING CHECK: Drawing Conclusions** Why did the study of nature change during the 1500s and the 1600s? *Scientists formed conclusions based on observation and made use of new tools and instruments to observe and measure.*

Astronomy, Physics, and Anatomy

Three areas of study were especially interesting to some of the strongest thinkers of the times. Astronomy was the study of stars, planets, and other bodies in the sky. Another area, physics, focused on changes and properties of matter and energy. Scientists in the field of anatomy studied the structure of the human body, mainly by examining dead bodies. Several European scientists helped to shape the modern study of these important sciences.

Copernicus. In the A.D. 100s, the astronomer Ptolemy stated that Earth was the center of the universe. The sun and the planets, according to Ptolemy, moved around Earth. Ptolemy's theory is called the **geocentric,** or "Earth-centered," **theory.** The Greek word for Earth is *geo.* People believed this theory for many centuries.

During the early 1500s, Polish scientist **Nicolaus Copernicus** began to abandon Ptolemy's geocentric theory. Instead, he argued that the sun was the center of the universe. Copernicus developed the **heliocentric,** or "sun-centered," **theory.** *Helio* is the Greek word meaning "sun." Copernicus realized that his theory explained many of the then-known facts about astronomy.

When Copernicus's theory was published in 1543, people paid little attention. The theory seemed to deny what people's senses told them. Anyone could "see" that the sun and planets moved around Earth. Anyone could "feel" that solid Earth did not move.

HISTORY MAKER

Nicolaus Copernicus (1473–1543)

Nicolaus Copernicus, the great Polish scientist, is viewed today as the founder of modern astronomy. His heliocentric theory demonstrated that the earth is a moving planet and that it revolves around the sun. Copernicus became a symbol of the new ideas and approaches that brought about the Scientific Revolution. **How did Copernicus change our understanding of the universe?**

Model of Copernicus's theory of planetary revolutions

ALL LEVELS: Explain the difference between the geocentric theory *(sun, planets, and stars revolve around Earth)* and the heliocentric theory. *(Earth and other planets revolve around sun)* Then divide students into groups of three to six. Have each group plan and perform a short role-play about Copernicus, Kepler, or Galileo. Tell students their skit should explain the scientist's ideas in simple words and show how those ideas challenged traditional thought.
ENGLISH LANGUAGE LEARNERS, COOPERATIVE LEARNING

LEVEL 3: Have students write an essay about how changing from a geocentric to a heliocentric view of the universe might affect people's attitudes about other aspects of life. *(Essays will vary but might mention the idea that nature does not revolve around people, creation is like an impersonal machine, and what seems obvious is not necessarily true.)* Discuss the essays in class. Ask students if any modern scientific discoveries affect the ways people think about their lives. *(relativity, quantum theory, space exploration)*

CONNECTING TO MATH ANSWER
geometry of circles and ellipses; formulas about speed of objects in motion

Interdisciplinary Connection

MATH. Kepler acknowledged the difficulties that others would have understanding his work. He wrote: "It is extremely difficult nowadays to write mathematical books, especially astronomical ones. For unless use is made of an exact precision in the proportions, explanations, demonstrations and conclusion the book will not be mathematical; if such use is made, then the reading of it becomes very difficult . . . That is why nowadays there are few suitable readers; the majority generally despise and reject such works . . . . I myself, who pass for a mathematician, tire my brain in reading my own work . . . ."

Critical Thinking

Ask students to write a sentence summarizing Kepler's dilemma in their own words. Then ask them to try to suggest a way Kepler could communicate his ideas more effectively.

ANSWER: Suggestions may include making drawings or models of planetary orbits.

CONNECTING TO Math

Kepler's Laws of Planetary Motion

Johannes Kepler tried to use mathematics to prove that the planets orbit around the sun. Kepler discovered three "laws" about how planets move in space. These laws are referred to as Kepler's laws of planetary motion.

Using the observations made by his employer, Tycho Brahe, Kepler found that planets travel around the sun in oval-shaped orbits called ellipses. Kepler's second discovery was that planets move faster when they are closer to the sun. Kepler's third law relates to the time it takes for a planet to complete an orbit around the sun.

Understanding Math

How would math help Kepler prove that his discoveries were true?

Kepler and Galileo. Copernicus had neither the instruments nor the mathematics to prove his theory. Proof came later with the work of two other scientists. **Johannes Kepler,** a German astronomer, and **Galileo Galilei,** an Italian scientist, each helped to confirm Copernicus's new understanding of the universe.

Johannes Kepler was a brilliant mathematician who used models, observation, and mathematics to test Copernicus's heliocentric theory. Some of the ideas on which Copernicus had based his theory were wrong. That slowed Kepler down, but he eventually proved the heliocentric theory correct. He published his laws of planetary motion in 1609. It took the work of an Italian scientist, however, to produce clear evidence that the earth moves around the sun.

Galileo Galilei had read of a Dutch device that made distant objects appear larger. Galileo built his own device—a telescope—and began studying the heavens. His telescope was very simple compared to those made today. However, Galileo was able to see things that no one had ever seen. He saw the mountains and valleys of the moon. He observed the rings around Saturn and spots on the sun. Galileo also observed the moons circling Jupiter. He used these observations to argue that not every heavenly body revolves around Earth. Galileo drew sketches of the things he observed through his telescope.

When Galileo published his findings in 1632, the work caused an uproar. Many scholars who still believed in Ptolemy's old geocentric theory refused to accept Galileo's findings. Church scholars disapproved because Galileo's theory seemed to contradict the Bible. Some said that the telescope was an invention of the devil.

In the central panel of this ceiling fresco, Galileo Galilei is shown demonstrating the use of his telescope. Later, Galileo was called before the Inquisition and forced to renounce his discoveries. He spent the rest of his life under house arrest.

HOMEWORK Have students choose a scientific instrument mentioned in the chapter and explain why it was important in the Scientific Revolution.

Spotlight on CULTURE

Tell students that most scientific writing was in Latin, but Galileo chose to write in Italian. Ask the class how the Scientific Revolution might have been different if scientists like Copernicus (Polish) and Kepler (German) had written just in their own languages. *(They might have had less communication with scientists in other countries but more readers in their own countries.)* Ask how the growing use of national languages in place of Latin might affect society and culture. *(nationalism, less dependence on authority for information)*

BLOCK SCHEDULING

Traditional scholars in physics were also displeased with Galileo. They believed, as Aristotle had said, that heavier objects fell faster than lighter ones. Using experiments and mathematics, Galileo proved this false. If there is no friction from air, all objects fall at the same rate. Galileo's discoveries formed the basis for the modern science of mechanics—the study of objects in motion.

Newton. In 1687 English scientist **Isaac Newton** published a book building on the work of Copernicus, Kepler, and Galileo. They had shown that the planets, including Earth, revolve around the sun. They had not, however, been able to explain why these bodies moved as they did.

After many experiments and measurements, Newton realized that the force that holds the planets in their orbits and the force that causes objects to fall to Earth are one and the same. He proposed the law of universal gravitation, which states that all bodies attract each other. Moreover, the force of this attraction can be measured. Both Kepler's Proof and Galileo's discoveries about falling objects were really examples of the law of universal gravitation. Newton also explained the laws of motion and developed the mathematical means of measuring motion. In one sweeping system, Newton tied together the movement of all things in the heavens and on Earth.

Newton's work had a huge impact on the science of his time. Even today, his laws of motion and gravitation are applied in the development of everything from automobile seatbelts to space travel. Furthermore, Newton's work changed the way people viewed the world. No longer would most well-educated Europeans see the universe as a place in which everything moved according to the constant attention of God and His angels. Most Europeans still accepted God as creator of the universe. However, they now began to think of that creation as a kind of giant mechanical clock. Once wound up by the divine clockmaker, it moved according to natural and universal laws of motion. So great was Newton's influence that the English poet Alexander Pope wrote:

 《Nature and nature's laws lay hid in night;
God said, 'Let Newton be!' and all was light. **》**

Alexander Pope, epitaph intended for Sir Isaac Newton

Vesalius and Harvey. The great Renaissance artist Leonardo da Vinci was a student of the human body. To those who tried to describe the body, he once said, "I advise you not to trouble with words unless you are speaking to blind men." **Andreas Vesalius,** a Flemish scientist, heeded da Vinci's words and pioneered the study of anatomy. Vesalius refused to accept descriptions of human muscles and tissues written by Galen 1,400 years earlier. He did his own studies to see how the human body was constructed. In 1543, Vesalius published a seven-volume book called *On the Fabric of the Human Body.* The illustrations of the human body that Vesalius included in his work were amazingly detailed for the time. They helped readers to gain a visual understanding of the many complicated components of the body and of how they work together.

English physician William Harvey made equally important contributions. Using laboratory experiments, Harvey studied the circulation of blood. He described how blood moved through the veins and arteries. He also observed the working of the body's most important muscle—the heart.

✔ **READING CHECK: Making Generalizations** How did the work of early scientists during the Scientific Revolution lay the foundation for modern science? introduced new approaches to knowledge and new methods and instruments

HISTORY MAKER

Galileo Galilei (1564–1642)

Galileo believed that scientific study would change the way people understood themselves and their world. Science, he felt, would lead to higher standards of living at every level of society. He believed, too, that science would weaken the social and economic barriers that separated people.

Because Galileo's findings challenged the traditional beliefs of the Catholic Church, church leaders kept him from teaching or writing about his ideas. **According to Galileo, in what ways would scientific progress affect society as a whole?**

Holt Researcher

go.hrw.com
KEYWORD: Holt Researcher
FreeFind:
   Nicolaus Copernicus
   Galileo Galilei
After reading more about Copernicus and Galileo on the Holt Researcher, write an imaginary dialogue between the two discussing their ideas about the universe.

HISTORY MAKER ANSWER
Galileo thought science would lead to higher standards of living and would weaken the social and economic barriers that separated people.

History Maker

SIR ISAAC NEWTON. The new ideas of Copernicus, Kepler, and Galileo met with either indifference or criticism. For Sir Isaac Newton, however, publishing *The Mathematical Principles of Natural Philosophy* in 1687 led to a seat in Parliament, knighthood, directorship of the royal mint, and the presidency of the Royal Society.

Critical Thinking

Ask students why the reaction to Newton's ideas was so different from the reaction to the ideas of Copernicus, Kepler, or Galileo.

ANSWER: Students may answer that by the late 1600s, people were more open to new ideas because the earlier scientists had paved the way.

That's Interesting!

Harvey explained his theories about blood circulation in a 72-page book in 1628. Many physicians accepted his argument immediately, but Harvey believed that many would not understand his work. By the time of his death in 1657, however, most people had come to believe his theories.

LEVEL 2: Ask students to create a chart of discoveries made during the Scientific Revolution. Have them organize their ideas under the headings *Astronomy, Physics, Anatomy, Chemistry,* and *Mathematics. (heliocentric theory; all objects fall at the same speed, laws of motion and universal gravitation; construction of human body, circulation of blood; oxygen, conservation of matter; calculus)* Then have students describe the significance of as many of these discoveries as they can. *(heliocentric theory—changed basic view of the universe; objects fall at the same speed—laid the foundation for modern science of mechanics; construction of human body and circulation of blood—laid basis for modern medicine)*

CLOSE

Ask students which they think had greater influence, specific advances in technology or a change in the way people think about science. Have students support their arguments with specific examples of scientists, discoveries, inventions, or ways of thought.

HISTORY MAKER ANSWER

It became the basis of our view of the universe and its physical properties.

Culture

Although Descartes worked to develop a scientific worldview that would not conflict with his Christianity, the Catholic Church did not share his assessment. Descartes's works were placed on the church's *Index,* a list of prohibited books. Louis XIV refused to allow Descartes to be buried in France with a religious ceremony because he perceived the skepticism Descartes advocated as dangerous.

Critical Thinking

Why would the church object to Descartes's ideas even though he believed that the existence of God was an incontrovertible fact?

ANSWER: Students may answer that the church feared that by claiming all ideas could be doubted, Descartes might encourage others to doubt ideas he himself believed.

HISTORY MAKER

René Descartes (1596–1650)

René Descartes explained that the universe operates in a machine-like way according to the basic laws of physics. His philosophy became the basis of our modern Western view of the universe and its physical properties. **How did Descartes's view of the universe influence today's science?**

Analyzing Primary Sources

Identifying a Point of View How would Descartes view information that was assumed to be true or that was accepted as true on the basis of faith or tradition? He would doubt or reject it.

The Triumph of the New Science

The effects of discoveries made during the Scientific Revolution were felt throughout Europe. So much had been learned that scientists believed that the scientific method offered a map that could easily be followed in the search for knowledge.

During the Counter-Reformation, religious orders had helped to revive faith in church teachings. New scientific "orders" spread knowledge of the developments of the Scientific Revolution. Schools and societies devoted to science appeared in Rome, England, and France. The printing press helped scientists as it had helped religious reformers. Most of the new scientific societies published journals. Scientists everywhere could now read about scientific studies being done in Europe.

Descartes. French philosopher and mathematician **René Descartes** (day·KAHRT) was a leader of the Scientific Revolution. His ideas led to great advances in mathematics, the sciences, and philosophy.

Descartes felt that no assumptions should be accepted without question. He developed a philosophy based on his own reason. In *Discourse on Method* (1637), Descartes stated that all assumptions had to be proven on the basis of known facts. Only ideas that were true beyond all doubt could be accepted without risk. He believed, for example, that his own existence was proven by the fact that he could think. Descartes wrote, "I think, therefore I am." From this basic truth, he built a method of questioning that followed a clear, orderly progression of logical reasoning.

 History Makers Speak **❝[I] was never to accept anything as true that I did not know to be evidently so: that is to say carefully to avoid precipitancy [hasty conclusions based upon assumptions, rather than observed facts] and prejudice, and to include in my judgements nothing more than what presented itself so clearly and so distinctly to my mind that I might have no occasion to place it in doubt.❞**

René Descartes, *Discourse on Method*

In Descartes's view, all fields of scientific knowledge were connected, thus they should be studied together. Descartes's interests ranged across many fields. His work included studies in geometry and algebra, the scientific method, astronomy, and the physical sciences. He created a mathematical description of the way that light reflects from a smooth surface. This explanation led to the law of refraction, a basic principle in the study of optics. Much of Descartes's work challenged traditional church teachings. He was forced to live in the Protestant kingdom of Sweden, where he died in 1650.

Francis Bacon. English philosopher and scientist **Francis Bacon** lived around the same time as Descartes. Bacon believed that scientific theories could be developed only through observation. He said that no assumption could be trusted unless it could be proven by repeatable experiments. Bacon relied on truths that could be demonstrated physically, rather than through deductive thinking or reasoning. In 1620 he published *Novum Organum,* a book that outlined this new system of knowledge.

Other scientific discoveries. During the 1500s and the 1600s, scientific discoveries were made throughout Europe. German Gottfried Liebnitz (LIP·nits) and the English thinker Isaac Newton developed calculus, a new branch of mathematics. The two did not work together. They developed their mathematical ideas independent of one another.

Dutch scientist Antoni van Leeuwenhoek (LAY·ven·hook) used the microscope, invented in the late 1500s, to discover bacteria. He called them animalcules. He studied

REVIEW

Have students complete the Section 1 Review on p. 387.

ASSESS

Have students complete Daily Quiz 16.1. As Alternative Assessment, you may want to use the chart of scientific discoveries exercise in this section's lessons.

RETEACH

Have students complete Main Idea Activity for English Language Learners and Special-Needs Students 16.1. Then have students

work in pairs to design flash cards with main ideas on one side and their meaning on the other. Have one student read the definition aloud and ask the other to name the idea.
ENGLISH LANGUAGE LEARNERS , COOPERATIVE LEARNING

EXTEND

Have students learn more about Robert Boyle and his significance. Have them write a dialogue between Boyle and a traditional alchemist, showing how Boyle's innovations pioneered the modern science of chemistry. **BLOCK SCHEDULING**

and wrote about a whole range of tiny life forms never before seen by the human eye.

An English-Irish scientist, **Robert Boyle,** helped to pioneer the modern science of chemistry. Chemistry studies the composition of matter and how it changes. In 1662, Boyle showed that temperature and pressure affect the space that a gas occupies. An English chemist, Joseph Priestley, discovered the element oxygen in 1774. Antoine Lavoisier (luhv·WAHZ·ee·ay), a French scientist, later named it.

Before Lavoisier, people believed that fire was an element. He showed that fire resulted when a substance rapidly combined with oxygen. Lavoisier also showed that steam mixes with the air and becomes invisible. In this way, Lavoisier proved that matter can change form, but that it can neither be destroyed nor created. This idea is known as the law of conservation of matter. It is one of the most important principles in the study of chemistry.

Priestley and Lavoisier made their discoveries in the late 1700s. By this time, the scientific approach had spread across Europe. The store of human knowledge and understanding had increased beyond measure and in a very brief span of time. In fact, speed of discovery and rapid spread and exchange of knowledge were important characteristics of the Scientific Revolution. These resulted, in part, from the printing press, the rise of scientific societies, and other communications improvements.

The French Academy of Sciences was founded in 1666.

Holt Researcher

go.hrw.com
KEYWORD: Holt Researcher
FreeFind: Robert Boyle
After reading more about Robert Boyle on the Holt Researcher, write a short essay describing his contributions to science.

✔ **READING CHECK: Drawing Inferences** Why did so many important scientific advances take place in so brief a period of time? In part, because new developments in communication helped to speed discovery, the spread of knowledge, and the exchange of ideas.

SECTION 1 REVIEW

1. **Define** and explain the significance:
   scientific method
   geocentric theory
   heliocentric theory

2. **Identify** and explain the significance:
   Roger Bacon
   Scientific Revolution
   Nicolaus Copernicus
   Johannes Kepler
   Galileo Galilei
   Isaac Newton
   Andreas Vesalius
   René Descartes
   Francis Bacon
   Robert Boyle

3. **Identifying Cause and Effect** Copy the web diagram below. Use it to show what factors led to the Scientific Revolution and what contribution each of the major scientists made.

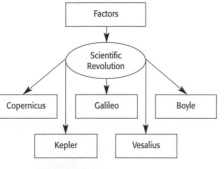

4. **Finding the Main Idea**
   a. Why were the scientific developments of the 1500s and the 1600s later called the Scientific Revolution?
   b. What did the work of Galileo, Newton, Vesalius, van Leeuwenhoek, and Lavoisier have in common?
   c. How did communications advances contribute to learning, discovery, and new scientific methods in Europe?

5. **Writing and Critical Thinking**
   Evaluating Write a short article for a science magazine describing the importance of the 1500s and the 1600s in the history of science.
   Consider:
   • how the study of science changed during this period
   • what discoveries were made that led to today's scientific and technical knowledge

Homework Practice Online
keyword: SP3 HP16

SECTION 2

OBJECTIVES

1 **Identify technological advances that made European exploration possible.**

2 **Describe the effect of the Commercial Revolution.**

3 **Explain the role mercantilism played in the colonies.**

LET'S GET STARTED!

As students enter the classroom, ask them to think about explorers they have studied and the resources those people needed for their journeys. Then ask students to think about space exploration today and write down things a country needs in order to explore space. *(technology, money, government commitment)* Have volunteers share their responses with the class. Tell students that in Section 2 they will learn how Europeans got the technology and other resources they needed for long sea voyages of exploration in the 1400s and 1500s.

SECTION 2 RESOURCES

REPRODUCIBLE RESOURCES

▶ Guided Reading Strategy 16.2

TECHNOLOGY RESOURCES

▶ One-Stop Planner 16.2
▶ Homework Practice Online
▶ Online Maps: Major European Trading Areas, c.1500
▶ Online Maps: European Trade Goods, c. 1500
▶ Online Maps: European Finance and Trade, c. 1500

REINFORCEMENT, REVIEW, AND ASSESSMENT

▶ Section 2 Review, p. 391
▶ Daily Quiz 16.2
▶ Main Idea Activity 16.2
▶ English Audio Summary 16.2
▶ Spanish Audio Summary 16.2

VISUAL RECORD ANSWER

globe, books, wall chart

SECTION 2

READ TO DISCOVER

1 What technological advances made European exploration possible?
2 What effect did the Commercial Revolution have?
3 What role did mercantilism play in the colonies?

DEFINE

compass
joint-stock company
mercantilism
favorable balance of trade
tariffs
subsidies

IDENTIFY

Commercial Revolution

▶ WHY IT MATTERS TODAY

Social changes in one region of the world often cause people to move to other countries. Use CNNfyi.com or other **current event** sources to find out what recent social changes have caused people to leave their native countries. Record your findings in your journal.

The Foundations of European Exploration

The Main Idea
Technological improvements led to exploration and fostered the growth of a new economy.

The Story Continues *Scientific advances would soon affect trade and the balance of political power in Europe. Rewards were offered to anyone who could invent a device for measuring longitude, since that would help ships sail more accurately and help nations compete for supremacy. It took over 100 years for someone to succeed. During that time, however, many other devices were invented that changed the global economy forever.*

Improvements in Technology

Since the time of the Crusades, Europeans had known about the riches of the East. Spices, silks, and jewels were prized as objects of trade because of their value. They came from the distant lands of India, China, and the islands of Southeast Asia. Traveling to and from these distant lands safely was essential if Europeans wished to compete with other traders. They began to focus on finding new sea routes to the East. To do this, Europeans needed better maps, navigation instruments, and ships. In short, they needed more advanced technology.

Mapmaking. Mapmaking improved during the Renaissance because of Europeans' growing interest in ancient geographers. Most scholars knew—as Ptolemy's maps had shown—that the world was round. During the Renaissance, information about Africa and Asia, unknown by Ptolemy, was added to his maps. The Americas, of course, were not yet known. Explorers believed that they could reach Asia more easily by sailing west across the Atlantic Ocean. Daring sea captains soon set out to find new trade routes to the East. Their discoveries opened whole new worlds to trade and settlement.

Navigation. Improved navigation instruments were just as important during this Age of Exploration as were more accurate maps. New navigation technology enabled ships to sail beyond sight of land without getting lost. One of the most important instruments to be developed during this time was the **compass.** In the 1100s, European navigators had learned that they could magnetize an iron needle. They rubbed the needle on a piece of lodestone—a kind of magnetic rock. When they floated the needle on water, it would point

INTERPRETING THE VISUAL RECORD

The Astronomer The Dutch artist Jan Vermeer, who worked during the 1600s, often showed his subjects in the midst of work activities. Vermeer's *The Astronomer* shows research and work connected to mapmaking. ***What tools are being used by the astronomer to study the earth's surface?***

ALL LEVELS: Have students create four-column charts about technology that aided overseas exploration in the 1400s. The first column should identify the technological advances. *(maps, compass, astrolabe; changes in ships, rudder, sails)* The second column should describe each advance and the third column should explain how it aided exploration. In the fourth column, students should rank the advances by their importance to exploration, from "1" (most important) to "5" (least important). Select students to explain their rankings.

ENGLISH LANGUAGE LEARNERS

HOMEWORK Have students imagine they are European sailors in the late 1400s. Have them write a letter to a friend explaining how new technology will make their voyage of exploration less dangerous.

TEACH OBJECTIVE 2

LEVEL 3: Ask volunteers to name ways expeditions were financed. *(bank loan, joint-stock company, monarch)* Have each student write and present a speech to persuade a banker, individual investor, or monarch to fund an expedition.

to the north. At some point during the 1200s or the 1300s, navigators created a true compass by fixing a magnetized needle to a card marked with directions.

New ships. If Europeans were to safely sail to the East, they needed better ships. Until well into the 1400s, long ships sometimes known as galleys were used by European sailors. These clumsy ships could sail using wind power only in the direction in which the wind blew. They sailed mostly along the coastlines. Sailors had to use long, heavy wooden oars to drive a galley against the prevailing winds.

In the late 1400s Spanish and Portuguese designers made important advances in ship-building technology. They built ships that were longer and larger than galleys. They also changed the size and shape of the sails. They moved the rudder—a steering device—from the side of the ship to its rear. These changes allowed ships to sail against the wind. Ships traveled more quickly and could be steered more easily. They could make way more reliably in different types of weather conditions, as well.

✔ **READING CHECK: Analyzing Information** Why did technological advances make sailors more able to explore distant lands? Mariners were better able to navigate, and ships could travel farther, faster, and under a greater variety of conditions.

Economic Changes

Improved ways of doing business also played an important part in new exploration. In some cases, banks added services to meet the needs of exploration. In other cases, Europeans changed basic economic practices. The changes were so great that many historians refer to the period between the late 1400s and the 1700s as the **Commercial Revolution.**

In many places in Europe before the 1300s and the 1400s, the value of coins could change depending on the amount of precious metal they contained. This changing value restricted European trade. Merchants and tradespeople needed a standard system of money.

As early as the mid to late 1200s, Italian cities were producing coins with fixed values. The gold florin of Florence and the ducat (DUHK·uht) of Venice were very dependable. This encouraged international trade and banking. In turn, banks could store large sums of money that they could lend governments or businesses wanting to explore overseas.

During the Commercial Revolution, individual merchants joined together into a new kind of business organization called a **joint-stock company.** Owners raised money by selling shares, or stock, in the company. Investors who bought the stock became co-owners and shared in the profits. The more shares they owned, the more of the profits they would receive. Joint-stock companies raised large sums of money from investors to finance exploration.

During the 1400s and 1500s, European monarchs supported exploration and colonization. Gaining riches through conquest and discovery would make them more powerful than rival countries. Although Italy had led the way in the Commercial Revolution, the Italians did not colonize. Instead, Portugal, Spain, and France built overseas empires. Trade shifted to these Atlantic nations.

✔ **READING CHECK: Identifying Cause and Effect** What effect did the standardization of money have on the ability of countries to trade? it encouraged international trade and banking

CONNECTING TO Science and Technology

The Astrolabe—An Early Guidance System

Sailors of the 1500s had only a few simple tools—such as the astrolabe—to guide them. Using the position of the sun and stars, these explorers sailed the oceans of the world. They could plot and hold a course and measure their progress. Of equal importance, they could estimate where they were with respect to land.

Astrolabes were usually made of brass or iron. A sailor would sight a star along the bar shown in the picture. By lining up the bar with markings on the disk, he could figure out the latitude of his ship's position. Astrolabes were used until the invention of more accurate instruments in the 1500s and 1600s.

Understanding Science and Technology

In addition to knowing distance north or south of the equator, what other information would a sailor need to know his exact position?

Interdisciplinary Connection

LANGUAGE ARTS. The use of *port* and *starboard* to designate the sides of a ship originates from the placement of the rudder on early vessels. The long oar that served as the rudder was always on the helmsman's right side as he faced forward. Because the rudder steered the vessel, the right side became known as the "steer-board"—now starboard—side of the ship. The rudder's location also kept the right side of the ship from being brought against the dock. Thus, the left side was always the one to be tied up when the ship was in port—making it the "port" side of the vessel.

ACTIVITY: Have students identify other words related to ships and use a dictionary to learn their origins. (Words will vary but might include *gunwale, rudder, stern, tack,* and *tiller.*) Have students report to the class any word origins they find particularly interesting.

CONNECTING TO SCIENCE AND TECHNOLOGY ANSWER
where he was with respect to land

Alfred J. Hamel of Worcester, Massachusetts, suggested the following activity: Have students use newspapers and other media sources to find modern references to mercantilism, such as tariff bills, balance of trade, free trade, etc. Have students discuss the positive and negative consequences of mercantilist policies in the modern economy.

TEACH OBJECTIVE 3

LEVEL 1: Have students draw a web diagram showing the reasons why Europeans established colonies.
ENGLISH LANGUAGE LEARNERS

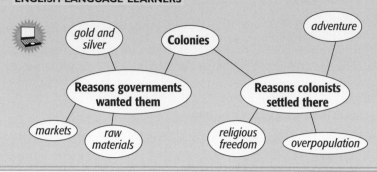

VISUAL RECORD ANSWER

large port, many ships, many trade goods, much business activity

Linking Past to Present

The world's nations in 1948 launched a major effort to reduce international tensions resulting from the remnants of mercantilism. A multinational treaty called the General Agreement on Tariffs and Trade (GATT) created a mechanism to reduce tariffs and other economic barriers between nations. Average tariffs on manufactured goods fell from about 40 percent to less than 5 percent by the 1980s, and regions adopted duty-free trade arrangements like the European Union and the North American Free Trade Agreement (NAFTA). However, some nations have introduced new subsidies or import quotas for certain industries or products, in a movement called neomercantilism.

Critical Thinking

What might rulers in the 1500s have said about GATT or NAFTA?

ANSWER: Students may answer that rulers would have disapproved because free trade agreements keep nations from protecting and accumulating wealth.

INTERPRETING THE VISUAL RECORD

Lisbon Lisbon, capital of Portugal, was one of Europe's busiest seaports during the Age of Exploration. *How does this picture reflect Lisbon's role as a leading European trade center and sea power?*

Mercantilism

Economic and political changes linked to overseas expansion contributed to a new economic theory. **Mercantilism** stated that a country's government should do all it could to increase the country's wealth, which was measured by the amount of gold and silver the country possessed. According to this belief, the world contained a fixed amount of wealth. To increase its own wealth, one country had to take wealth from another country.

Balance of trade. According to mercantilists, a country could build wealth in two ways. It could mine gold and silver either at home or in its colonies. Or it could sell more goods than it bought from foreign countries, thus creating a favorable balance of trade. With a **favorable balance of trade,** a country received more gold and silver from other nations than it paid to them. This situation both strengthened the country and weakened its foreign rivals.

A favorable balance of trade was, therefore, the aim of many mercantilist countries. To achieve a favorable balance of trade, a country could do several things. First, it could reduce the amount of goods coming into it from other countries by placing **tariffs,** or import taxes, on these goods. The importer of a particular good paid the tariff and added that cost to the price of the good. The higher price discouraged people from buying it.

Second, a country could encourage exports. Manufactured goods, such as woolen cloth, were more valuable than raw materials, such as wool. Countries therefore encouraged manufacturing and the export of manufactured goods. They provided government **subsidies,** or grants of money, to help businesspeople start new industries and build ships.

Third, a country could work to gain and control overseas sources of raw materials and precious metals. A nation that controlled overseas sources of these goods would not need to import them from competing nations. Foreign countries were always considered rivals and might at any time become active enemies. The goal of winning overseas sources of materials helped fuel the race to gain colonies.

The role of colonies. Colonies played a major role in mercantilism. During the 1500s and after, European powers aimed to colonize overseas lands that were rich in gold, silver, and raw materials that could not be produced at home. A powerful nation sought to buy raw materials from its own colonies. That way, the country's wealth would remain with its own people. Most European colonial powers, moreover, forbid their colonies to sell raw materials to other countries. According to mercantilism, control of colonial markets and raw materials was key to a nation's success.

People in the home country's colonies provided strong markets for its manufactured goods. Governments passed strict laws that forbade colonies from buying foreign goods. In many cases, moreover, colonies were not allowed to manufacture goods. This forced colonies to buy manufactured goods only from their home country. Mercantilists argued that such laws were justified because colonies existed to benefit the home country.

✔ **READING CHECK: Finding the Main Idea** What was the overall aim of mercantilism?
to increase a country's wealth

CLOSE

Ask students which factor influenced European expansion most—technology, the Commercial Revolution, or mercantilism. Have them support their answers.

REVIEW

Have students complete the Section 2 Review on p. 391.

ASSESS

Have students complete Daily Quiz 16.2. As Alternative Assessment, you may want to use the persuasive speech or web diagram exercise in this section's lessons.

RETEACH

Have students complete Main Idea Activity for English Language Learners and Special-Needs Students 16.2. Then have them write brief definitions of "commercial revolution" and "mercantilism."

ENGLISH LANGUAGE LEARNERS

EXTEND

Have students draw political cartoons that illustrate one of the effects of mercantilism—such as accumulation of gold and silver, national self-sufficiency, or establishing an empire.

BLOCK SCHEDULING

Social Change

Advances in navigation and government economic policies by themselves did not lead to European exploration and overseas colonization. Certain social changes also helped create in people the desire to explore and resettle.

For one thing, the Renaissance and the Scientific Revolution had created a desire among many Europeans to learn more about the world and had added to the general store of geographic knowledge. Thus, simple curiosity and a spirit of discovery moved many people to explore the world outside Europe.

After the year 1500, moreover, the population of Europe increased. Some urban areas became very crowded. Adventurous people knew that overseas colonies might offer harsh living conditions. Some people were willing to accept these hardships, however, in return for the opportunity to gain land and possible wealth by settling in overseas colonies.

Other people went overseas hoping to reap quick profits. Tales of gold and silver and precious jewels—as well as fertile soil—persuaded thousands that easy wealth lay overseas. A few even went in search of fabulous cities with enormous riches, such as the legendary El Dorado (which means "the gilded one" in Spanish) in South America.

Finally, the Reformation and Counter-Reformation had led to the religious and political persecution of many. French Huguenots and others went overseas to seek religious freedom for themselves and to escape persecution at home. Some Christians went to spread their religion to non-Europeans.

In many cases, there was no single reason that motivated a person or group of people to explore or colonize. Rather, a combination of these hopes and aims led Europeans to leave their old lives for new and, to them, unknown lands.

✔ **READING CHECK: Summarizing** Why were some Europeans willing to explore and colonize distant lands? curiosity and spirit of discovery; hope of wealth or better way of life; escape religious persecution or spread religion

Gold and cinnamon were highly sought-after trade goods.

DAILY LIFE

The New Commercial Economy

World exploration led to a new kind of economy in Europe. Goods brought from Africa, Asia, and the New World made many countries in Europe rich. Spices, silks, gold, silver, and precious stones were some of the most sought-after items.

The Portuguese, Spanish, and Dutch were the first European powers to build trading empires. Trade and commerce eventually replaced farming as the leading economic activity in Europe. Over time, the new commercial economy generally helped to spread wealth and improve living standards.

How did European countries benefit from the changes of the Commercial Revolution?

DAILY LIFE ANSWER
Increased trade made them wealthy.

SECTION 2 REVIEW ANSWERS

❶ Define
- compass, p. 388
- joint-stock company, p. 389
- mercantilism, p. 390
- favorable balance of trade, p. 390
- tariffs, p. 390
- subsidies, p. 390

❷ Identify
- Commercial Revolution, p. 389

❸ Technological Advances: compass, astrolabe, better ships made long sea voyages safer; Economic Changes: banks and joint-stock companies funded exploration; Mercantilism: made nations want colonies for gold, silver, raw materials; Social Changes: crowding and persecution gave people reasons to settle in colonies

❹ a. Ships had to be able to sail out of sight of land without getting lost.

b. They kept colonial wealth for the home country and made colonies buy manufactured goods from the home country.

❺ Students' letters might mention overcrowding and persecution at home, dangers of sea travel, hopes for wealth, or escape from persecution.

SECTION 2 REVIEW

1. Define and explain the significance:
compass
joint-stock company
mercantilism
favorable balance of trade
tariffs
subsidies

2. Identify and explain the significance:
Commercial Revolution

3. Summarizing Copy the table below. Fill in the ways in which each factor influenced exploration and colonization.

Factors	Influence on Exploration and Colonization
Technological Advances	
Economic Changes	
Mercantilism	
Social Changes	

4. **Finding the Main Idea**

a. Why were technological developments necessary before nations could begin exploration and colonization?

b. How did trade laws that limited colonies' economic freedom support the idea of mercantilism?

5. **Writing and Critical Thinking**

Supporting a Point of View Imagine you are living in the 1500s. Write a letter to a relative explaining why you will or will not leave Europe to settle in a colony.

Consider:

- what conditions are like in your home country
- what you might gain or lose by traveling to a distant land

go. Homework Practice Online
hrw .com
keyword: SP3 HP16

Reproducible Resources

E Creative Teaching Strategy 16: Talk Show: Changing Europe's Worldview

EXPLORATION AND EXPANSION **391**

OBJECTIVES

1 Describe what the early Portuguese explorers accomplished.

2 Discuss how the voyages of Christopher Columbus influenced the world.

3 Explain why the Atlantic slave trade prospered.

SECTION 3

READ TO DISCOVER

1 What did early Portuguese explorers accomplish?

2 How did the voyages of Christopher Columbus influence the world?

3 Why did the Atlantic slave trade prosper?

DEFINE

triangular trade

IDENTIFY

Prince Henry
Bartolomeu Dias
Vasco da Gama
Christopher Columbus
Columbian Exchange
Treaty of Tordesillas
Amerigo Vespucci
Ferdinand Magellan
Middle Passage

▶ WHY IT MATTERS TODAY

People have always been interested in exploring what is beyond their present environment. Use **CNNfyi.com** or other **current event** sources to discover what kind of exploration is going on today. Record your findings in your journal.

CNNfyi.com

Voyages of Portugal and Spain

The Main Idea
Voyages sponsored by the Portuguese and Spanish led to new colonies and to the Atlantic slave trade.

The Story Continues *Life aboard a trading ship could be very difficult. "[Four galleys] were away three years, but only one galley returned and even on that galley most of the crew had died," one eyewitness recalled. "And those which survived could hardly be recognized as human." Despite such experiences, numerous sailors made voyages in search of riches for themselves and their countries.*

Portugal's First Explorers

Portuguese and Spanish explorers made the first European voyages into unknown waters. Curiosity, religion, and economic goals drove these courageous men forward. Their voyages resulted in great advances for the sponsoring governments and served as the foundation for future empires.

One man largely responsible for Portugal's interest in exploration was **Prince Henry** of the Portuguese royal family. Also known as "The Navigator," Prince Henry's first goal was to find gold for Portugal. The Portuguese also hoped to find a way to the rich spice trade of the Indies and to spread the Christian faith.

Henry gathered many of Europe's best geographers and navigators to plan expeditions. By about 1420 or earlier his navigators were exploring westward into the Atlantic, and by the 1430s they were moving southward along the west coast of Africa. These explorations taught navigators about currents, wind patterns, and climates, knowledge they needed as they ventured farther from home. Henry's explorers claimed the Azores for Portugal. In Africa, they began to trade for slaves, gold, and ivory.

The success of these early voyages of discovery and exploration created great excitement throughout Europe. Success encouraged more voyages. In 1488 **Bartolomeu Dias** sailed around the Cape of Good Hope at the southern tip of Africa. Although Dias had to turn back, he had found the route to the Indian Ocean.

Using this knowledge, **Vasco da Gama** sailed eastward across the Indian Ocean. He landed in India in 1498. Several years later, da Gama made a second voyage to India. He returned to Portugal, his ships full of valuable goods.

Thanks to Dias and da Gama, an overseas trade route from Europe to India and the East Indies was now available. Rich cargoes of spices and jewels arrived in Portugal. This direct ocean route saved the Portuguese from having to deal with middlemen traders. Now, the Portuguese could journey directly to the sources of the trade goods they sought. In many cases, too, ships could carry goods more cheaply than could overland caravans. Nor could Portuguese merchants be blocked or charged high tolls by competing powers that controlled overland routes. Overseas trade promised wealth for merchants and sailors and goods for Europe's markets.

✔ **READING CHECK: Summarizing** What did the Portuguese gain from the voyages of their early explorers? wealth and overseas trade routes

LEVEL 1: To help students understand the economic motivations for the early voyages of exploration, lead a discussion using the following questions as a guide: What was the traditional way Asian goods moved west before the voyages of exploration? *(by various land and sea routes to the Middle East)* Why did Europeans begin to desire Asian goods? *(result of Crusades)* Before the voyages of exploration, what groups controlled the trade of these goods with Europe? *(Arab and Italian merchants)* Why did this trade process make Asian goods so expensive in Europe? *(high overland transportation costs, payments to Arab or Italian middlemen)* Have students refer to the map on pages 396–397 to answer the following questions: How did Dias and da Gama enable Portugal to trade directly with Asia? *(Dias found route to Indian Ocean; da Gama built on Dias's exploration and sailed to India.)* Why did Portugal take the lead in finding a sea route? *(location on the Atlantic; Prince Henry)* How did these explorations give Portugal a trade advantage over other European nations? *(allowed Portuguese to establish direct trade with Asian markets)* **ENGLISH LANGUAGE LEARNERS**

An idealized portrait of Vasco da Gama meeting Indian royalty.

Christopher Columbus

Spain, too, became interested in the search for new trade routes. A Genoan navigator named **Christopher Columbus** had studied the writings of Marco Polo and Ptolemy's description of a round Earth. Columbus believed that a shorter route to Asia could be found by sailing westward instead of sailing around the tip of Africa. King Ferdinand and Queen Isabella of Spain agreed to finance Columbus's voyage of exploration.

In August 1492, Columbus set sail from Palos, Spain. His three small ships— the *Niña*, the *Pinta*, and the *Santa Maria*—sailed westward across the Atlantic. On October 12, 1492, the small fleet landed at a tiny island that Columbus named San Salvador. It was a historic moment when Columbus and his captains planted the Spanish flag. Columbus claimed the land that he had reached for Spain. Later, in reporting his discovery, Columbus wrote:

❝It appears to me that the people [the Native Americans who met Columbus] are ingenious [clever], and would be good servants and I am of the opinion that they would very readily become Christians, as they appear to have no religion. They very quickly learn such words as are spoken to them.❞

Christopher Columbus, extracts from journal, quoted in *Internet Medieval Source Book*, by Paul Halsall

After exploring other islands in the area Columbus returned triumphantly to Spain in 1493. Columbus believed the islands he had found lay off the east coast of India. Thus, he called them the Indies and their inhabitants Indians. However, Columbus had actually discovered islands in the Americas. They later became known as the West Indies. Between 1493 and 1504, Columbus made three more voyages to the "Indies." For the rest of his life, he believed that he had landed off the coast of Asia.

There was a major difference between the Portuguese explorers and Columbus. The Portuguese already knew that the lands they sailed to existed. Earlier people had written of their journeys between Europe and Asia and Europe and Africa. Columbus believed he was traveling to one of these lands by a different route. Earlier Viking voyages to the Americas were unknown. When Columbus stepped ashore in what is now the Bahamas, he stepped on land that was altogether new and unknown to Europeans.

✔ **READING CHECK: Finding the Main Idea** What significant event happened in 1492?

Columbus landed at San Salvador

HISTORY MAKER

Queen Isabella (1451–1504)

Queen Isabella was one of Spain's greatest rulers. Her court was a center of learning and culture. With her husband, Ferdinand, she also helped to unify Spain.

Isabella approved the voyage of Christopher Columbus to India. Columbus found the New World and the great Spanish empire in the Americas was born. **What important events took place during Isabella's rule?**

Holt Researcher

go.hrw.com
KEYWORD: Holt Researcher
FreeFind:
    Isabella
    Christopher Columbus
After reading more about Isabella and Columbus on the Holt Researcher, create a Venn diagram that shows the similarities and differences in their beliefs about the lands and people Columbus encountered.

HISTORY MAKER ANSWER
Columbus sailed west across the Atlantic Ocean and discovered islands in the Americas; Spain was unified.

Global Relations

Even before the Europeans, the Chinese sought to establish maritime trade routes. Between 1405 and 1433 the Chinese Muslim navigator Zheng He led seven naval expeditions in Chinese ships that visited Southeast Asia, India, East Africa, and Arabia to secure trade with these regions. A change in the Chinese government's foreign policies, however, prohibited additional expeditions. China returned to using other nations' commercial fleets to carry its goods.

Critical Thinking

Ask students how European exploration and expansion might have been affected if the Chinese had continued to expand their maritime trade routes.

ANSWER: Students might suggest that Europeans would have had less access to Asian ports, so they might have concentrated even more on transatlantic exploration.

Technology Resources
Online Maps: European Idea of the Atlantic Before Columbus

EXPLORATION AND EXPANSION **393**

LEVEL 3: Have students imagine they are European cartographers (mapmakers) around 1500 who have been hired by the rulers of Spain or Portugal to make a map of newly-discovered territories. The rulers have asked them to illustrate the map with pictures of trade goods, scenery, or people from the regions shown. Invite students to present their maps to the class.

Interdisciplinary Connection

HEALTH. Although few European explorers had active diseases, they still carried many germs that were highly contagious to American Indians. Passing these germs to just a few Indians could rapidly infect large areas. Large, prosperous towns found by Spanish explorers in what is now the southeastern United States in the early 1540s no longer existed in 1560, when Spanish colonists in Florida tried to find them to acquire food. Diseases brought by the explorers had destroyed the towns. It is estimated that by the early 1600s, the Mesoamerican Indian population was 90 to 95 percent smaller than it had been a hundred years before.

Critical Thinking

Ask students why they think European diseases were so devastating to American Indians.

ANSWER: Students should mention that people who have never been exposed to a disease lack resistance to it.

CONNECTING TO GEOGRAPHY ANSWER
Students' answers will vary.

Technology Resources
**go.
hrw
.com** Online Maps: Treaty of Tordesillas, 1494

CONNECTING TO GEOGRAPHY

The Columbian Exchange

The effects of the Columbian Exchange are still felt today. For example, diet on both sides of the Atlantic changed. Potatoes from the Andes now feed millions of people in Europe. Corn, first grown by Native Americans, is a staple around the world today. Wheat was not grown in the Americas until it was brought there by Europeans. The tomato first grew not in Italy, but in the Americas.

Horses, cattle, goats, sheep, and other animals crossed the Atlantic with Europeans. North America, in exchange, gave Europe and Asia the turkey, the gray squirrel, and the muskrat.

Understanding Geography

What elements of the Columbian Exchange can you identify in your area?

The Impact of Columbus's Voyages

In the years following Columbus's voyages, a massive exchange took place between the so-called New World and the Old World of Europe. This interaction is often called the **Columbian Exchange.** Products, plants, animals, and even diseases traveled between the Western and Eastern Hemispheres. For example, gold and silver mined in South America were shipped eastward to Spain. This helped Spain become a major world power.

The exchange affected the way people in both worlds lived. American foods such as potatoes, tomatoes, beans, and corn were introduced in Europe. The Spanish brought horses to the Americas, thus changing the lifestyles of many Native American groups forever. This was especially true in areas such as the Great Plains.

Not everything the Columbian Exchange brought to the New World was helpful. European sailors carried smallpox and other diseases westward. The native population of Spanish America had no immunity to these diseases and millions died.

✔ **READING CHECK: Drawing Conclusions** Who benefited most—Europeans or Native Americans—from the Columbian Exchange? Why? Europeans, because they gained riches, resources and new foods and exported diseases

Dividing the New Lands

During the late 1400s Spain and Portugal—Europe's most active seagoing explorers—often claimed the same newly discovered lands. To settle these conflicts, Pope Alexander VI issued an edict in 1493. The Pope's edict drew an imaginary line from north to south through the middle of the Atlantic Ocean. Alexander gave Spain the rights to all newly discovered lands west of the line. Portugal could claim discoveries east of the line. Neither country, however, could take lands already held or claimed by another Christian ruler.

A year later, the **Treaty of Tordesillas** between Spain and Portugal moved the line farther west. This soon had an important impact. In 1500 the Portuguese navigator Pedro Cabral set sail westward for India. Cabral's tiny fleet of 13 ships was blown off course, and the Portuguese made landfall on the coast of what is now Brazil. Under the Treaty of Tordesillas, Cabral was able to claim this incredibly rich land for Portugal.

Over time, Spain took control of most of Central and South America. The Spanish also claimed the Philippines. In addition to the Brazilian coast, Portugal claimed lands on the eastern and western coasts of Africa. The Portuguese also claimed lands in Asia and the East Indies.

✔ **READING CHECK: Identifying a Point of View** How might the right of Spain and Portugal to claim lands not already occupied by Christians have been viewed by the people of those lands? as arrogant and hostile

Vespucci, Balboa, and Magellan

Other European explorers followed Columbus westward. **Amerigo Vespucci** was an Italian navigator. Between 1497 and 1504, he crossed the Atlantic several times as part of Spanish and Portuguese expeditions. Unlike others, Vespucci did not think the land he saw was part of Asia. He called it a New World. A German mapmaker, impressed with Amerigo's argument, called the land America after Vespucci.

In 1513 Vasco Núñez de Balboa of Spain made an overland crossing of the Isthmus of Panama. Reaching a vast ocean, he named it the South Sea and claimed it for Spain. Balboa's discovery made it clear that the New World was not part of Asia.

HOMEWORK Have students list all the explorers mentioned in Section 3. Have them use standard grammar, spelling, sentence structure, and punctuation to write one sentence explaining why each explorer was important.

TEACH OBJECTIVE 3

LEVEL 2: Working individually or in pairs, have students create a chain-of-events chart of the origins of the transatlantic slave trade. **ENGLISH LANGUAGE LEARNERS, COOPERATIVE LEARNING**

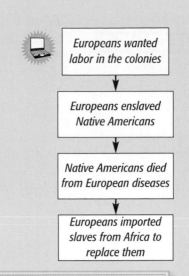

> Europeans wanted labor in the colonies
> ↓
> Europeans enslaved Native Americans
> ↓
> Native Americans died from European diseases
> ↓
> Europeans imported slaves from Africa to replace them

Ferdinand Magellan, a Portuguese navigator sailing for Spain, proved Balboa was correct. In 1519 he set out from Spain with five ships to cross the Atlantic to South America. The ships sailed along its eastern shore until they reached the southernmost tip. After passing through the strait now named for him, Magellan found himself in a great ocean. He named it the Pacific Ocean because it was so calm. In Latin the word *pacificus* means "peaceful." This was Balboa's "South Sea."

Magellan sailed westward across the Pacific. He reached the Philippine Islands and died there in 1521 in a fight with the islanders. His crew, led by one of his officers, sailed on. In 1522 one ship and 18 crew members returned to Spain. They had made the first round-the-world voyage.

✔ **READING CHECK: Making Generalizations** What did Vespucci, Balboa, and Magellan contribute to Europeans' knowledge of the world? *knowledge that the western lands were a New World, not a part of Asia*

Portuguese Expansion

After the voyages of Dias and da Gama, the Portuguese dreamed of controlling trade with Asia. In about 1510 they conquered part of the southwest coast of India. The port of Goa (GOH·uh) became their administrative center. From India they moved on to the East Indies. They conquered Malacca (muh·LAK·uh) on the southwest coast of the Malay Peninsula and the Moluccas (muh·LUHK·uhz), a group of islands. Europeans called them the Spice Islands because of their large crops of valuable spices.

Next, the Portuguese added the island of Ceylon—now Sri Lanka—to their chain of trading bases. Ceylon was in a key location between Goa and Malacca. With its tea and spices, Ceylon helped the Portuguese control trade with the East Indies. The Portuguese also gained footholds in China and Japan. Finally, they established several armed trading posts on the East African coast. The Portuguese also established a colony in Brazil where they built huge agriculture estates.

✔ **READING CHECK: Drawing Inferences** Why did the trading posts set up by the Portuguese allow them to control trade with the East? *allowed them to block others' routes to the East and gave them uncontested access to Asian goods and markets*

The Slave Trade

As they did in Asia, the Portuguese went to Africa to trade. At first, they maintained friendly relations with the Africans. Christian missionaries wanted to convert the continent's residents. Friendly relations soon collapsed, however, as the economic interests of the Portuguese—in gold and, over time, in slaves—became obvious.

Despite the fact that Europeans themselves had been slaves in the Byzantine, Arab, and Turkish empires, during the 1500s they began to use slave labor in their own overseas empires. Europeans tried enslaving Native Americans, but the system did not work well due to the devastation of the Native American population caused by disease and the difficulties of enslaving people in their own land. Instead, the Europeans began to rely more heavily on enslaved Africans.

The slave trade grew quickly when the Portuguese set up sugar plantations on islands off the coast of Africa. To make a profit, large numbers of slaves were required. Plantation owners got these slaves from the African mainland. Later, the Dutch, English, and French also became active in the slave trade. By the early 1600s the slave trade was the chief focus of European relations with Africa.

HISTORY MAKER

Ferdinand Magellan (c. 1480–1521)

Ferdinand Magellan became a page in the Portuguese court at a youthful age. Over time, he grew to become an experienced navigator and sailor.

Magellan became convinced that he could reach the Spice Islands in East Asia by sailing west. The circumnavigation of the globe by his fleet was not only a great achievement of navigation and courage; it was also the first proof that the world was round. **What was the outcome of Magellan's voyage?**

HISTORY MAKER ANSWER
Magellan died, but his crew completed the journey around the world, proving it was round.

Geography

Portugal's Atlantic seacoast was not its only reason for exploring Atlantic trade routes. Economic activities between Spain and Portugal had declined. Traditional maritime routes in the Mediterranean were dominated by ships from Italian city-states.

Critical Thinking

Ask students how these other factors might have driven the Portuguese to explore the Atlantic.

ANSWER: Students may answer that the Atlantic was the only trade route open to the Portuguese.

Reproducible Resources

PS Readings in World History 57: First Impressions of the New World

ALL LEVELS: Divide students into small groups. Have each group discuss any advantages and disadvantages of the slave trade from the point of view of one of the following individuals: a plantation owner in the Americas, a slave, the owner of a slave ship, or the ruler of an African kingdom. Have each group prepare a skit or drawing about the slave trade from the character's point of view and present it to the class.

ENGLISH LANGUAGE LEARNERS, COOPERATIVE LEARNING

Geography

Because of their focus on trade with Asia, the nations that sponsored early European explorers were as interested in finding a way around or through the Americas as they were in claiming and colonizing new lands. Magellan's last voyage was intended to find a water route through South America to the ocean that Balboa had discovered six years earlier.

Later, Jacques Cartier and Henry Hudson explored the St. Lawrence and Hudson Rivers, respectively, looking for a passage to Asia. Hudson also sailed far to the north in this quest, exploring what came to be known as Hudson Bay. When he found no passage to the Pacific, his crew mutinied and left him there to die. The Northwest Passage was not successfully navigated until 1906, when the Norwegian Roald Amundsen finally accomplished the feat.

internet connect

TOPIC: Explorers
GO TO: go.hrw.com
KEYWORD: SP3 WH16

Have students access the Internet through the HRW Go site to learn more about the explorer of their choice and his voyages. Have students write a biography of the explorer they choose.

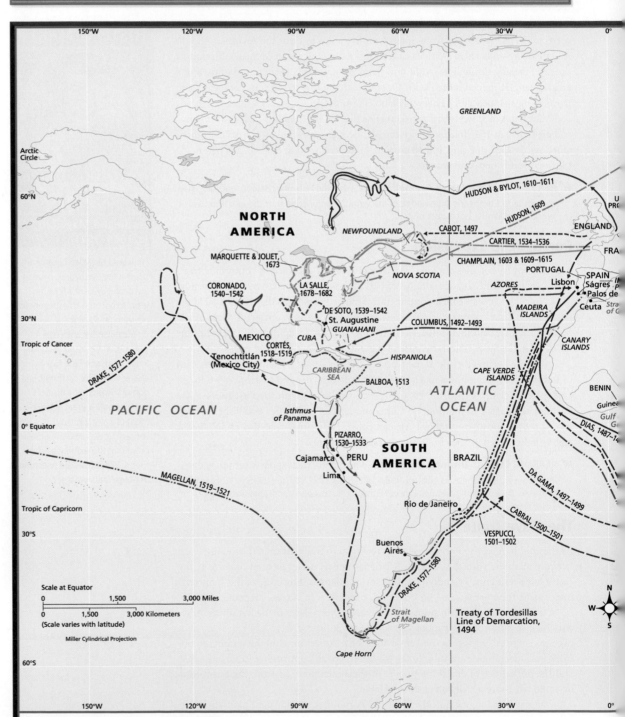

European Explorations, 1487–1682

Interpreting Maps The map shows the routes taken by Portuguese, Spanish, French, English, and Dutch explorers. They sailed both east and west to discover new lands.

LEVEL 2: Ask students to name the kinds of people who might be on a ship crossing the Atlantic Ocean in the 1500s. *(Answers will vary but might include explorers, mapmakers, sailors, slaves, slave merchants, settlers.)* Then have students imagine they are on a ship crossing the Atlantic. Have them write a diary of the voyage. The first entry should explain who they are and why they are on the ship.

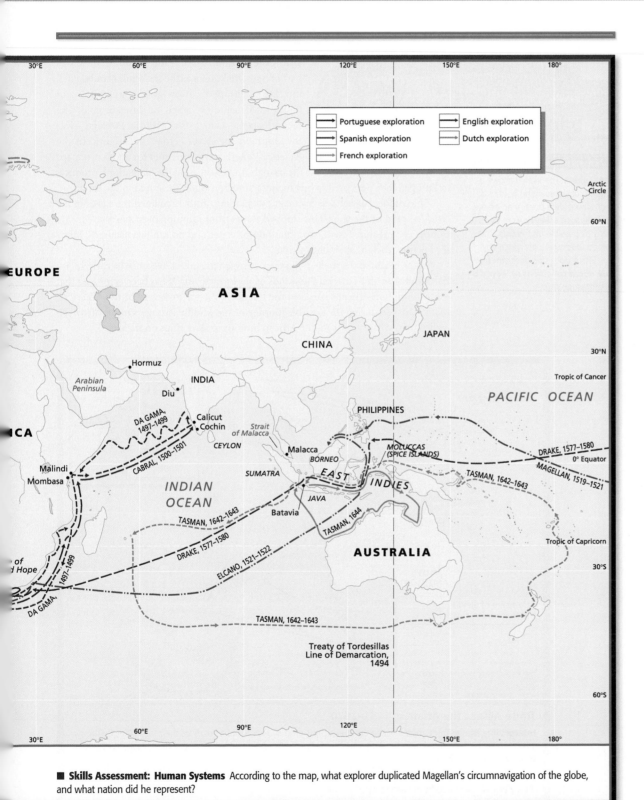

Global Relations

The second Portuguese mission to India was led by Pedro Cabral. After his accidental visit to Brazil when he was blown off course, he eventually reached Calicut. There he and his crew encountered problems with the Arab merchants controlling the port. The Arabs attacked the Portuguese trading booths, killing some of the sailors. Cabral bombarded the city and then sailed south to the rival city of Cochin to trade.

Critical Thinking

Ask student why the Arab merchants were hostile to the Portuguese.

ANSWER: Students might suggest that the merchants realized the Portuguese threatened their monopoly on trade between Asia and Europe.

MAP ANSWER
Drake; England

■ **Skills Assessment: Human Systems** According to the map, what explorer duplicated Magellan's circumnavigation of the globe, and what nation did he represent?

Divide the class into three groups representing Asia, Africa, and America. Ask each group to discuss how Europe's interactions with its assigned region changed because of the voyages of exploration. *(Asia—established direct contact by ship; Africa—developed large-scale slave trade; America—learned it existed, gold and silver)* Have each group appoint one student to report to the class.

Economics

One cause of Portugal's decline as a trading empire was the system it set up for controlling trade. The rulers of Portugal tried to establish a monopoly over all trade within their trading sphere. Anyone trading at Asian ports was required to buy a license from Portugal and to pay duties to Portuguese officials.

Eventually this system broke down because Portugal did not have the strength to enforce it. Portugal could not prevent rivals from trading in the area, and local Asian merchants began to avoid paying for licenses.

Critical Thinking

Ask students why Portugal established such a system and why the system failed.

ANSWER: Students may suggest that Portugal wanted to control Asian trade because of mercantilist ideas, and that the system failed because Portugal was not strong enough to prevent rivals from trading in the area or to enforce the licensing requirement.

MAP ANSWER
About 7,000 miles

INTERPRETING THE VISUAL RECORD

Slave ships This sketch shows a diagram of slaves in the hold of a ship. Slaves were positioned below decks in such a way as to fit as many as possible on the ship. This helped to ensure a profitable voyage. *What does this diagram indicate about conditions on board a typical slave ship?*

Triangular trade. Slave trade in the Atlantic was part of a system known as the **triangular trade.** First, merchants shipped cotton goods, weapons, and liquor to Africa in exchange for slaves or gold. The second stage—called the **Middle Passage**—was the shipment of slaves across the Atlantic to the Americas. There, slaves were sold for goods produced on the plantations. To complete the triangle, merchants sent the plantations' products to Europe. They were used to buy manufactured products to be sold in the Americas.

The Middle Passage was brutal and degrading. Traders chained the slaves in the crowded hold of the ship. This stopped slaves from jumping overboard or causing trouble aboard ship. Slaves had little food or water and no sanitary facilities. Many died before reaching their destination.

At the height of the trade in the years between the mid-1700s and the early 1800s, European slave ships carried thousands of slaves each year. It has been estimated that some 10 million Africans survived the horrible journey to slavery in the Americas. Many perished during the horrible journey of the Middle Passage. Others died even earlier, on the hard trip from the African interior to slave ships on the coast.

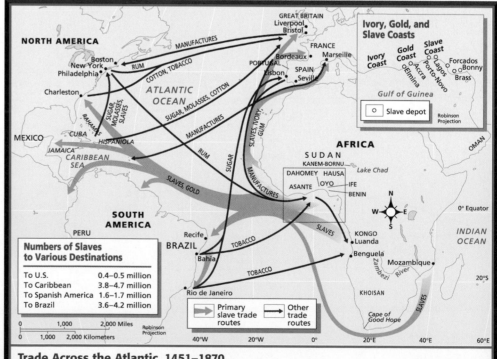

Trade Across the Atlantic, 1451–1870

Interpreting Maps Trade routes linked European ports with coastal Africa as early as the mid-1400s. By the 1700s, these routes extended to the Americas in a distinctly triangular pattern. Over the years, millions of slaves were carried along these routes.

■ **Skills Assessment: The World in Spatial Terms** Approximately how far would a trip for slaves have been if they were transported from Luanda to Charleston?

REVIEW
Have students complete the Section 3 Review on p. 399.

ASSESS
Have students complete Daily Quiz 16.3. As Alternative Assessment, you may want to use the chain-of-events activity in this section's lessons.

RETEACH
Have students complete Main Idea Activity for English Language Learners and Special-Needs Students 16.3. Then have students write one sentence summarizing the main idea for each section in the chapter. **ENGLISH LANGUAGE LEARNERS**

EXTEND
Have students imagine they are Africans recently sold to European slave traders and put on a ship with no explanation. Have them write about their thoughts and expectations. **BLOCK SCHEDULING**

African kingdoms and slavery. During the 1400s and the 1500s, strong states began to rise in West Africa. Some of these kingdoms profited from the slave trade. Not all African states participated in the slave trade with Europeans. Many African societies, however, had practiced slavery well before the Europeans' arrival. Slaves were sometimes taken in war or during raids on neighboring groups. In some traditional African societies, slaves might be allowed to gain their freedom. Generally, they played a distinct role in society. Europeans, on the other hand, considered slaves as property to be bought and sold for profit.

Some Africans who lived in the interior helped the Europeans capture and move slaves. In return they received European-made arms and other goods. Neighboring groups either had to participate or be taken as slaves. During the years of the slave trade, native populations in some parts of Africa were greatly reduced. As demands for slaves increased, population losses had disastrous effects on Africa's development and progress.

✔ **READING CHECK: Supporting a Point of View** In what ways can you support the view that the slave trade slowed the development of the African continent? Talent and labor were drained and traditional lifestyles were disrupted.

The Portuguese Empire Weakens

The great Portuguese empire declined almost as rapidly as it had grown. The Portuguese government did not have the financial wealth to support so large an empire. Thousands of soldiers and sailors were needed to maintain and expand the empire, but many never returned from overseas. Shipwrecks and battles with enemies cost both money and lives. With its small population, Portugal could not replace the losses it suffered as a result of exploration and colonization.

Finally in 1580 Spain annexed Portugal. Portugal did not regain its independence until 1640. Under Spanish control, Portugal's trade was greatly restricted and its overseas colonies were neglected. Only Brazil and Angola survived as major Portuguese colonies.

✔ **READING CHECK: Drawing Conclusions** How did the relative size of Portugal and Spain influence their success in expansion and colonization? Portugal, unlike Spain, lacked the wealth and the population needed to sustain expansion and colonization.

Primary Source
◆ EYEWITNESS ◆

Olaudah Equiano was a native African who was captured and enslaved by other Africans. Eventually he was bound over to European slave traders. Years later he published an account of his experiences, which included his first impressions of the white slave traders and their ship.

"When I looked round the ship too and saw a large furnace of copper boiling and a multitude of black people of every description chained together . . . I no longer doubted my fate. . . . When I recovered a little I found some black people about me. . . . I asked them if we were not to be eaten by those white men with horrible looks, red faces, and loose hair. . . I now saw myself deprived of all chance of returning to my native country." **What did Equiano think that the slave traders were going to do to him?**

SECTION 3 REVIEW ANSWERS

❶ **Define**
- triangular trade, p. 398

❷ **Identify**
- Prince Henry, p. 392
- Bartolomeu Dias, p. 392
- Vasco da Gama, p. 392
- Christopher Columbus, p. 393
- Columbian Exchange, p. 394
- Treaty of Tordesillas, p. 394
- Amerigo Vespucci, p. 394
- Ferdinand Magellan, p. 395
- Middle Passage, p. 398

❸ Europe to Africa: cotton goods, weapons, liquor; Africa to Americas: slaves, gold; Americas to Europe and Africa: sugar, cotton, tobacco, rum

❹ **a.** Dias found route to Indian Ocean, 1488; da Gama reached India, 1498; Columbus reached the Americas, 1492; Magellan sailed west across the Pacific, 1521

b. There may have been more development and progress.

❺ Students might suggest that Spain and Portugal gained wealth temporarily but lost in the long run because they did not develop industry or agriculture at home. They should note extreme negative effects for people in the Americas who died of European diseases and people from Africa who were enslaved.

SECTION 3 REVIEW

1. **Define** and explain the significance:
   triangular trade

2. **Identify** and explain the significance:
   Prince Henry
   Bartolomeu Dias
   Vasco da Gama
   Christopher Columbus
   Columbian Exchange
   Treaty of Tordesillas
   Amerigo Vespucci
   Ferdinand Magellan
   Middle Passage

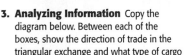
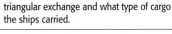

Homework Practice Online
keyword: SP3 HP16

3. **Analyzing Information** Copy the diagram below. Between each of the boxes, show the direction of trade in the triangular exchange and what type of cargo the ships carried.

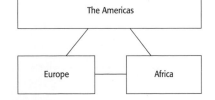

The Americas

Europe   Africa

4. **Finding the Main Idea**
   a. Sequence the important discoveries of the explorers listed in question 2.
   b. What do you think might have happened on the African continent if the European slave trade had not taken place?

5. **Writing and Critical Thinking**
   Comparing and Contrasting Write a paragraph pointing out the positive and negative effects of the explorations of the Spanish and Portuguese.
   Consider:
   • the economic benefits to both countries
   • the effects on human life and populations

OBJECTIVES

1 Describe how Spain extended its power abroad and at home.

2 Explain why the Dutch were successful in the 1600s.

3 Analyze why the Spanish Empire declined.

LET'S GET STARTED!

As students enter the classroom, ask them to write a list of examples of conquest or colonization, based on previous chapters or their knowledge of current events. Ask students why nations conquer places and establish colonies. *(Answers will vary but may include natural resources, wealth, power, control of strategic sites.)* Tell students that in Section 4 they will learn how the Spanish and Dutch built empires through conquest and colonization in other parts of the world.

SECTION 4 RESOURCES

REPRODUCIBLE RESOURCES

▶ Guided Reading Strategy 16.4

TECHNOLOGY RESOURCES

▶ One-Stop Planner 16.4
▶ Homework Practice Online
▶ Online Maps: French and Dutch Imports, 1770s
▶ Online Maps: Portuguese Imports, 1770s
▶ Online Maps: Spanish Imports, 1770s
▶ Online Maps: British Imports, 1770s

REINFORCEMENT, REVIEW, AND ASSESSMENT

▶ Section 4 Review, p. 407
▶ Daily Quiz 16.4
▶ Main Idea Activity 16.4
▶ English Audio Summary 16.4
▶ Spanish Audio Summary 16.4

VISUAL RECORD ANSWER

strong metal armor

SECTION 4

READ TO DISCOVER

1 How did Spain extend its power abroad and at home?
2 Why were the Dutch successful in the 1600s?
3 Why did the Spanish Empire decline?

DEFINE

viceroys
guerrilla warfare

IDENTIFY

Ponce de León
Hernán Cortés
Moctezuma II
Francisco Pizarro
Charles V
Philip II
William of Orange

▶ WHY IT MATTERS TODAY

Two ways that nations increase their land are conquest and colonization. Use **CNNfyi.com** or other **current event** sources to find examples of both processes going on today. Record your findings in your journal.

CNNfyi.com

The Spanish and Dutch Empires

The Main Idea
Spain created an empire in the Americas, while the Dutch set up trading colonies in Asia and the Americas.

The Story Continues *As Spanish explorers spread into the Americas, they came ready to conquer. "Some of them were dressed in glistening iron from head to foot," wrote one observer. "They terrified everyone who saw them." Their tactics established a powerful empire for Spain.*

Spain's Colonial Empire

Throughout the 1500s Spain was the most powerful nation in Europe, with the largest overseas empire. While Portugal focused mainly on Africa and Asia, Spain turned to the Americas. Beginning with Columbus, Spaniards explored the West Indies, Central America, and parts of North and South America. At first, they believed these lands were in the East Indies. However, the natural resources of the Americas provided riches other than spices and jewels.

Spanish explorers sailed outward from the Caribbean to the North American mainland. In 1513 **Ponce de León** sailed northward to what is now Florida. A later voyage to Florida in 1528, led by Pánfilo de Narváez, ended in disaster and shipwreck. A handful of survivors from this tragic voyage traveled overland across what is now the southwestern United States and Mexico. Their travels opened even more land to Spanish claims and settlement.

Conquests. Other Spanish explorers went to the Yucatán in Mexico. There they learned of the great Maya and Aztec civilizations. In 1519, with 11 ships and about 600 men, **Hernán Cortés** invaded Mexico. He seized the Aztec ruler **Moctezuma II**, also known as Montezuma. Cortés captured and destroyed the great Aztec city of Tenochtitlán. The Spanish later built Mexico City on its ruins. Spanish horses and guns, unknown in the Americas, helped the Spanish defeat the great Aztec armies, as did a smallpox epidemic that swept through the Aztecs.

INTERPRETING THE VISUAL RECORD

Cortés Hernán Cortés, at the head of about 600 Spanish soldiers, carved out a huge empire in Mexico and plundered the mighty Aztec civilization. Cortés is pictured here capturing the Aztec ruler Moctezuma II. *According to this picture, what advantages did the Spanish have over the Aztec?*

TEACH OBJECTIVE 1

LEVEL 1: Have students draw and color a map showing Spanish conquests in the 1500s. Then have them create a diagram showing how Spain directed colonial government. **ENGLISH LANGUAGE LEARNERS**

The Spanish also found rich civilizations in South America. In 1530 **Francisco Pizarro** led 180 men and 37 horses on an expedition. They traveled from the Isthmus of Panama to the capital of the Inca Empire in what is now Peru. In 1533 Pizarro claimed the land from present-day Ecuador to Chile for Spain.

Cortés and Pizarro destroyed many Aztec and Inca statues and temples. The gold and silver from these religious objects and buildings made the explorers and the Spanish treasury wealthy.

In time Spain controlled the West Indies, southern and western North America, Central America, and much of South America. Unlike Europeans in Africa and Asia, the Spanish established settlements throughout their vast empire.

Colonial government and society. Spain directed the colonial government. Officials called **viceroys** represented the monarchy in the colonies and reported to the Council of the Indies in Spain. The council planned and directed the empire's growth on behalf of the Spanish crown.

For a time, the colonies produced enormous wealth for Spain. There were rich silver mines in the regions that are now Peru and northern Mexico. Agriculture and trade remained important, but mineral resources were the main assets of Spain's colonies.

European diseases such as smallpox, typhus, and measles weakened the Native American societies conquered by Cortés and Pizarro. From what is now the southwestern United States through Mexico and much of Central America, millions of Native Americans died. Whole cultures that had lived and thrived for centuries were wiped out or broken up in a matter of a relatively few years. Exact losses cannot be accurately determined, but many historians believe that the numbers were enormous. This tragic outcome of expansion and colonization also promoted the growth of slavery. The Spaniards needed workers for mines and farms in the New World. To make up for the loss of native labor, they imported slaves from Africa.

✔ **READING CHECK: Analyzing Information** What were some of the factors that allowed so few Europeans to conquer large numbers of peoples in the Americas? European horses and guns, and European diseases that weakened native populations

Spain's Colonial Rivals

The Spanish government wanted to keep the wealth of the Americas to themselves. They made laws keeping foreigners out of the Spanish colonies. Only Spanish ships could carry gold and silver out of the Americas.

Making laws, however, was easier than enforcing them. The French, Dutch, and English envied Spain's American wealth. They tried various methods to capture a share of it. They traded in Spanish American ports, their monarchs encouraged pirates to attack Spanish ships, and pirates raided Spanish towns.

Spain's rivals also tried to establish colonies in the Americas, ignoring Pope Alexander's line down the middle of the ocean. Despite their efforts, these rival countries had only limited success before 1600.

✔ **READING CHECK: Making Predictions** What did Spain's rivals hope to gain by having pirates attack Spanish ships and colonial towns? a share of America's great wealth

INTERPRETING THE VISUAL RECORD

Pizarro Francisco Pizarro and a handful of Spanish conquistadores overthrew the mighty Inca Empire of Peru. Here, Pizarro is shown refusing mercy to Atahualpa, the last emperor of the Inca. *What visual technique has the artist used to depict Pizarro's dominance in this scene?*

Culture

In his letters, Hernán Cortés described Tenochtitlán: "This city has many squares where trading is done and markets are held continuously. There is also one square...where every kind of merchandise produced in these lands is found.... There are shops like apothecaries', where they sell ready-made medicines as well as liquid ointments and plasters. There are shops like barbers' where they have their hair washed and shaved, and shops where they sell food and drink."

✏ internet connect

TOPIC: Mesoamericans
GO TO: go.hrw.com
KEYWORD: SP3 WH16

Have students access the Internet through the HRW Go site to learn more about the Aztec and Inca civilizations. Ask students to write an informative report on the political, economic, and cultural impact of Spanish expansion.

VISUAL RECORD ANSWER

Pizarro appears taller than the Inca. The Inca are shown in submissive poses with crossed arms and bent knees.

TEACH OBJECTIVE 1

LEVEL 3: Ask students to imagine they are advisers to King Philip II of Spain. Have them write the advice they would give the king about how to improve the economy of Spain. As examples, suggest they consider possible changes in foreign policy, religious policy, or ways to become less dependent on imports. Have volunteers present their advice to the class, pretending that they are speaking to the king.

Government

A series of family accidents brought Charles V to the Spanish throne. He was the grandson of King Ferdinand of Aragon and Queen Isabella of Castile, who had sponsored Columbus's voyages. Isabella outlived her only son, her eldest daughter, and her first grandchild; so her second daughter, Joan, inherited her throne. Joan's husband, Philip I of the Netherlands, died when their son Charles was six years old.

Because Joan was mentally ill, her father Ferdinand ruled on her behalf. Ferdinand's death made Charles king of Spain in addition to the Netherlands. After becoming Holy Roman Emperor, Charles controlled more of Europe than any ruler since Charlemagne in the early 800s. Although Philip II received just part of that empire, he also ruled England because he was married to Queen Mary of England. The English pushed him aside after Mary's death.

ACTIVITY: Have students make a family tree from Isabella to Philip II. Lead a class discussion about the advantages and disadvantages of a system of choosing rulers based on marriage and inheritance.

Charles V

While their explorers were expanding the empire abroad, Spanish kings expanded their authority in Spain itself. One of the greatest of these kings was **Charles V.** Charles was a member of the Habsburgs, an old German family. Charles took the Spanish throne in 1516. Three years later he was elected Holy Roman Emperor.

With Charles's titles and power, he was torn between conflicting demands. As king of Spain, he had to adopt a Spanish viewpoint. As Holy Roman Emperor, he was expected to support German aims. Finally, as the political leader of Christian Europe, Charles had to defend Europe against the Ottoman Turks.

The nearly continuous religious wars during Charles's reign drained Spain's human resources and treasury. Spain lacked industries and the government did little to promote them. So much of Spain's land was devoted to raising sheep for wool that the country could not produce enough food to feed its people. Food prices increased many times over between 1500 and 1650.

Charles realized that the Spanish and Holy Roman empires had become too large for one man to rule. In 1556 he gave up his throne and divided the vast lands among members of his family. Charles's son **Philip II** received Spain and its possessions. His branch of the family became known as the Spanish Habsburgs. Charles's brother Ferdinand I was already king of Hungary and Bohemia. Now he became Holy Roman Emperor and head of the Austrian Habsburgs.

✔**READING CHECK: Finding the Main Idea** What were some of the factors that led Charles to split up his lands? realized that the Spanish and Holy Roman empires had become too large for one ruler to govern; was exhausted by continuing religious warfare

King Philip II of Spain personally managed the daily operations of the royal government.

Philip II

Unlike his father, Philip II was born and educated in Spain. He ruled from 1556 until his death in 1598. Philip was a dedicated monarch who worked long hours at being king. His goal was to strengthen Spain's hold as Europe's leading power. Philip built a new royal residence, El Escorial, 25 miles from Madrid. From there he took control of every facet of government. This nearly paralyzed his administration. Philip also saw himself as the leader of the Counter-Reformation. A very devout Catholic, he ordered the Spanish Inquisition to stamp out heresy at home. Abroad, Philip involved Spain in wars to defend Catholicism and bring glory to Spain. These efforts were so costly that taxes could never keep up with expenses. As bankers charged more and more interest on loans to Spain, the country's financial woes increased.

Although Philip was unable to defeat all the enemies of Spain and Catholicism, he did manage to defeat the Ottoman Empire in the Mediterranean. His attempted invasion of Protestant England by the huge Spanish Armada in 1588, however, ended in disaster. An attempt to invade France to prevent a Protestant from becoming king was also an expensive failure. Yet these setbacks were not the costliest errors in Philip's policy making.

✔ **READING CHECK: Drawing Inferences** Why might the kind of control that Philip exerted over his government paralyze his administration? slowed decision-making and the flow of government business

TEACH OBJECTIVE 2

LEVEL 2: Have students work in small groups to make a web diagram, like the one shown, of the reasons for Dutch success in the 1600s. Ask them to extend the web diagram with ways these traits helped the Dutch succeed. *(answers may include banking, the Dutch East India Company, didn't attempt religious conversions, good sailors, good ships)* **COOPERATIVE LEARNING**

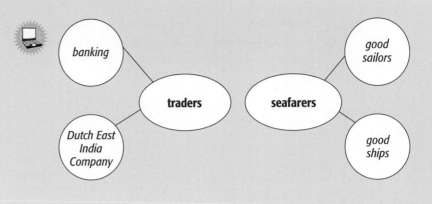

The Rise of the Dutch

Philip II's most costly policies were those toward the Netherlands, one of Europe's great trading centers since the Middle Ages. Philip had inherited the Netherlands. Because Calvinism was becoming popular in the area, Philip treated his Dutch subjects harshly. First, he ignored the Netherlands' long tradition of self-rule. He insisted that he, rather than the local nobles, held all authority. Second, he taxed Dutch trade heavily to pay for Spanish wars. Third, he persecuted the Calvinists. These actions turned the people's distrust of Philip to outright rebellion.

The Netherlands break from Spain. In 1568 **William of Orange** led a revolt against Philip. The people of the Calvinist northern provinces lived on land below sea level. Large dikes protected the land. The people opened the dikes, flooding the countryside and leaving Philip's army helpless. William sent small bands of soldiers on quick raids to keep the Spanish army confused. Today this military technique is called **guerrilla warfare.**

In 1579 under William's leadership, the northern provinces declared their independence from Spain. William was killed in 1584, but his descendants continued the war with Spain on and off until 1648. The southern provinces were heavily Catholic and remained under Spanish control as the Spanish Netherlands.

Dutch society. Because the Netherlands lay on the North Sea, the Dutch were a seafaring people. They built very efficient ships and were expert sailors. For these reasons, they ruled European commerce throughout the 1600s. Their ships carried most of Europe's trade and the city of Amsterdam became a world financial center. All segments of Dutch business stood as models of efficiency.

Calvinists became the dominant religious group in the Netherlands. Generally, however, the Dutch followed policies of religious tolerance. Amsterdam became a lively cultural center. Scholars such as René Descartes and artists such as Rembrandt and Vermeer thrived in this comfortable setting.

The Dutch colonial empire. In 1602 the Dutch East India Company was founded. It had total control over trading between the Netherlands and the East Indies. The first Dutch overseas colony was founded on the island of Java in 1619. The Dutch took over the entire island, with its valuable crops of sugar, tea, coffee, and spices. From Java, they expanded westward to Sumatra and eastward to the Spice Islands. Their colony at the Cape of Good Hope allowed them to supply and protect their trade routes to Asia.

The Dutch also gained a foothold in Japan. Because the Dutch did not come as missionaries, the Japanese allowed them to open a trading center in Nagasaki. In the Western Hemisphere the Dutch established colonies in the West Indies, South America, and North America. In 1626 they purchased Manhattan Island from the Native Americans and built the city of New Amsterdam there.

The Dutch colonial empire was much different from that of the Spanish. The Dutch never tried to convert conquered peoples to Christianity. They did not force them to speak Dutch or live under the laws of the Netherlands. The Dutch came as traders, with the sole intention of making money. This goal reflected their businesslike society.

✔ **READING CHECK: Drawing Inferences** In what ways did the Dutch gain access to trading opportunities that other countries had missed? They made no attempt to force their culture or religious beliefs on other societies.

CONNECTING TO
Art

Painting:
Young Woman with Water Jug
In the 1600s the economy of the Netherlands prospered. Dutch merchants grew rich enough to buy handsome silks and linens for their wives. Some commissioned artists to paint for them. Dutch artists such as Rembrandt and Vermeer flourished. This painting, one of Vermeer's finest works, gives us a close look at Dutch daily life.

Understanding the Arts

What does this painting tell us about life in the Netherlands in the 1600s?

CONNECTING TO ART ANSWER
Students' answers will vary but may include luxury, fine fabrics, goods from Asia such as the tablecloth, or international interests as shown in the wall map.

Geography

The Dutch entered the Asian trade in part due to a work by a Dutch writer, Jan Huyghen van Linschoten. From 1583 to 1589 Linschoten worked for the Portuguese archbishop in Goa, on the coast of India. After his return to the Netherlands, Linschoten published his *Itinerario*, which gave a geographical description of the world, sailing directions for reaching India and America, and his own observations of Asia. Up to that time the Dutch had sailed on Portuguese ships but Dutch ships had not gone to Asia. The first Dutch fleet to use Linschoten's directions sailed in 1595. Others followed, and competition between the Dutch and Portuguese grew fierce. Formation of the Dutch East India Company consolidated competing Dutch companies.

Critical Thinking

Ask students why Linschoten was particularly qualified to write the *Itinerario*.

ANSWER: Students should mention his experience in Goa.

HOMEWORK Have students study the map on pages 404–405 and identify and describe at least three patterns of distribution of European colonies in 1700.

 Have students identify Dutch colonies on the map on pages 404–405, then look at a modern map to identify the countries in those locations today. Ask students to use computer software to identify ways the heritage of Dutch rule influences the culture of those countries today.

Culture

In the Spanish colonies, the agricultural estate, or hacienda, was almost entirely self-contained. It was not just a source of income for its owner but also a source of pride, as status was often based on the size of the hacienda and the number of cattle or peasants on it. The owner of the hacienda had absolute control over his subjects. The peasants who lived on the hacienda existed on what they could plant on their small plots, and the rest of the hacienda was used for its main agricultural product, such as cattle, tobacco, coffee, or sugar.

Critical Thinking

Ask students how the structure of the hacienda reflects Spanish culture and political or economic thought.

ANSWER: Students may compare the power of the hacienda owner to the power of kings in Spain. In addition, they may say that mercantilist ideas encouraged colonial production of raw materials like sugar to send to the home country.

Technology Resources

go. hrw .com Online Maps: Empires in the Americas, 1700

Technology Resources

go. hrw .com Online Maps: Africa in 1750

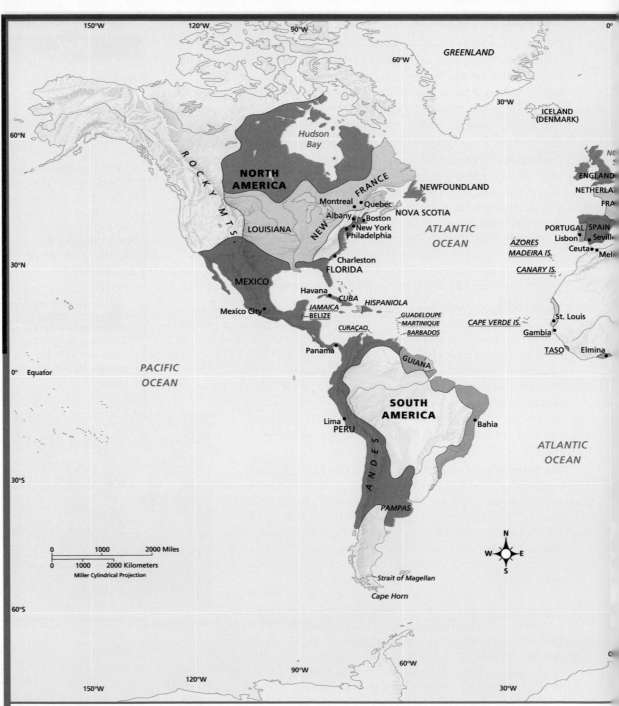

European Overseas Empires, 1700

Interpreting Maps The map shows the territories around the globe that were held by European countries in 1700.

TEACH OBJECTIVES 1 and 2

ALL LEVELS: Organize students into small groups to present skits about life in the colonies of Spain and the Netherlands. Each group should script a scene that would have been typical in the lives and interactions of the native people and the Spanish or Dutch colonists. Suggest that groups decide on their basic story line and assign characters before developing their script. After the groups complete their scripts, have them present their skits to the class. **ENGLISH LANGUAGE LEARNERS, COOPERATIVE LEARNING**

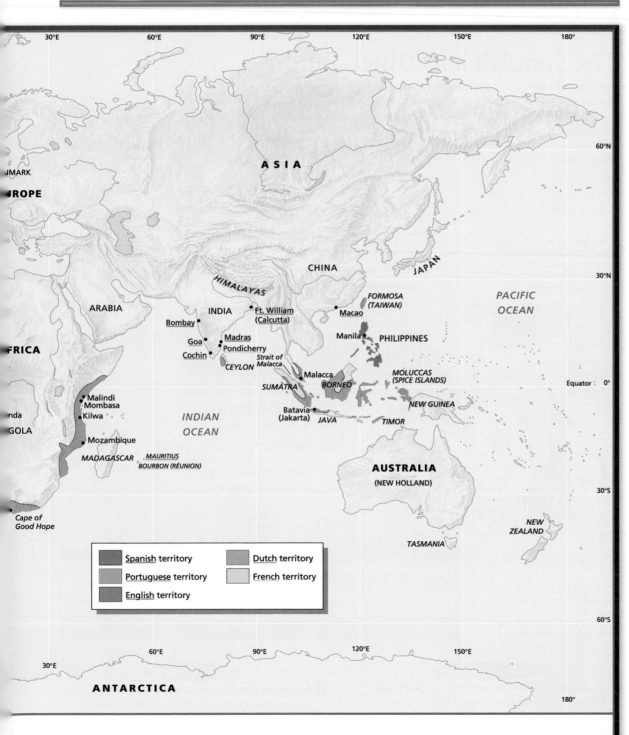

Geography

Australia was the last continent to be colonized by Europeans. Medieval European mythology tells of a Great Southland, or *Terra Australis*, but its existence and location remained a mystery. It was not near the established trade routes, and prevailing winds carried ships away from it.

A Dutch East India Company trader, Abel Tasman, finally reached Australia in 1642. For the next 100 years ships sailing to Indonesia sometimes stopped on Australia's coast. However, no European colonies were established there until the late 1700s.

Critical Thinking

Ask students why it took so long for European explorers to find Australia.

ANSWER: Students should answer that it was off the main trade routes and protected by prevailing winds.

MAP ANSWER

Spanish colonies were in North and South America and the Philippines; English and French colonies were primarily in North America; most other colonies were in coastal areas; Portuguese were primarily on east coasts of Africa and South America; Dutch were in islands of Southeast Asia, with smaller holdings in South Africa and northern South America.

■ **Skills Assessment: The World in Spatial Terms** What patterns can you identify regarding the distribution of European colonies in 1700?

ALL LEVELS: Pair students and have them develop a "Top Ten" list of reasons for Spain's decline as a world power. Select pairs to present their lists to the class, working up from the tenth reason to the number one reason. *(Lists might include ineffective rulers, Dutch revolt, defeat of Armada, expulsion of Jews and Moriscos, lack of industrial development, inflation resulting from colonial gold and silver, and so on.)* Record each pair's number one reason on the board for comparison.
ENGLISH LANGUAGE LEARNERS, COOPERATIVE LEARNING

Ask students to explain whether they would rather have lived in the Spanish Empire or the Dutch Empire. Ask them how their lives might differ if they were conquered people in the Spanish Empire or the Dutch Empire. Then ask how their lives might differ if they were Europeans in each empire.

Historical Sidelight

Unrest in the Aztec and Inca Empires contributed to their defeat by the Spanish. Both groups had built their empires in the 1400s, often through the conquest of their neighbors, and both had to put down frequent rebellions in the decades that followed. The Inca were in the midst of a civil war when the Spanish arrived in 1530. Cortés and Pizarro exploited such tensions among native peoples to gain control of both empires.

Critical Thinking

Ask students how conditions within the Aztec and Inca Empires affected Spanish conquest.

ANSWER: Both empires were weakened by internal struggles, which aided Spanish efforts to conquer them.

SKILLS PRACTICE ANSWERS

1. Long term causes: Philip II's treatment of Dutch subjects, war with Spain; Immediate causes: founding of Dutch East India Company in 1602, colony in Java in 1619, purchase of Manhattan Island in 1626; Effects: established trade throughout the world, developed businesslike society

2. Spanish tried to convert conquered peoples to Christianity; Dutch came as traders to make money. What were the long-term effects of these empires?

SKILL-BUILDING STRATEGIES Making Charts

The Spanish and Dutch Empires

The stories of the Spanish and Dutch empires can be complicated. Sometimes in order to understand complex material it helps to organize information in the form of a chart. Charts can include such formats as time lines and family trees, as well as classification charts, organization charts, and flowcharts. In making charts, readers are able to organize, simplify, and summarize information in a way that often makes it easier to understand and remember.

Some Spanish missionaries hoped colonization would lead to the conversion of Native Americans to Catholicism.

The Dutch colony of New Amsterdam controlled a strategic position on the east coast of North America.

Causes and Effects of Spain's Age of Empire

LONG-TERM CAUSES
Columbus's landing in the Caribbean
Spanish exploration and conquest
Founding of colonies in North and South America

IMMEDIATE CAUSES
Conquest of the Aztec by Cortés, 1521
Conquest of the Inca by Pizarro, 1533
Spanish treasure fleets from the Americas

Spain's Golden Age 1492 to mid-1600s

EFFECTS
Rise in Spanish wealth and influence
Increase in the prices of Spanish goods because of high inflation caused by American silver and gold
Spain's dependency upon goods from other countries

Skills Reminder

To create a chart from written text, it helps to follow headings and word cues to identify appropriate details and determine what facts support the chart. Make sure you present the information in a clear and easy-to-follow manner using such visual aids as heading, lines, or arrows. The final product should help to visually summarize and order information.

Skills Practice

❶ Examine the flowchart above. Using the information in your textbook, create a similar chart showing the causes and effects of the Dutch Empire.
❷ What were some of the differences in the Spanish and Dutch empires? What other questions do the charts raise?

REVIEW

Have students complete the Section 4 Review on p. 407.

ASSESS

Have students complete Daily Quiz 16.4. As Alternative Assessment, you may want to use the "Top Ten" exercise in this section's lessons.

RETEACH

Have students complete Main Idea Activity for English Language Learners and Special-Needs Students 16.4. Then have students study the "Causes and Effects of Spain's Age of Empire" chart on page 406 and restate each part of the chart in their own words.

ENGLISH LANGUAGE LEARNERS

EXTEND

Have students make time lines that illustrate how events in Spain's European empire relate chronologically to the growth of the Spanish and Dutch Empires overseas. Suggest they plot European developments on one side of the time line and colonial developments on the other. Suggest they color-code their time lines to distinguish Dutch from Spanish events.

BLOCK SCHEDULING

The Spanish Empire Declines

Many factors played a part in the decline of the Spanish Empire. A growing population meant that more people needed to be fed, clothed, and housed. At the same time, gold and silver flowed into Spain from the colonies. Shortages and this increase in the amount of money drove prices up in Spain. Because it cost more to produce goods in Spain than in any other country, demand for Spanish-made products declined. This loss of markets, in turn, led to a general decline in Spain's industry and commercial activity.

A capable middle class might have helped Spanish industries to develop. Many Spanish nobles, however, preferred military service. Others chose careers in the church rather than in secular life. In addition, the Spanish crown expelled first the Jews and then the Moriscos—Moorish converts to Christianity—from Spain. Unfortunately for the Spanish economy, many of those expelled were skilled bankers, businesspeople and commercial leaders, and artisans. The persecution of the Jews and the Moriscos conducted by the Spanish crown and the church further weakened Spain's economy and drained talent and capability from the country.

Much of the empire's wealth simply passed through Spain and was used to buy goods from other countries. With the gold and silver they received for goods sold in Spain, countries such as France, England, and the Netherlands grew strong. They developed their own industries at Spain's expense.

At home, people became discontented with high taxes and inflation. Along with agricultural failures, this discontent drove many people from their homes. Eventually, many people emigrated from Spain.

Moorish rulers of Granada pay tribute to the Spanish royal couple.

✔ **READING CHECK: Categorizing** What were the major problems that led to the decline of the Spanish Empire? *growing population, shortages and increased costs, expulsion of Jews and Moriscos, flow of money out of Spain*

❶ Define
• viceroys, p. 401
• guerrilla warfare, p. 403

❷ Identify
• Ponce de León, p. 400
• Hernán Cortés, p. 400
• Moctezuma II, p. 400
• Francisco Pizarro, p. 401
• Charles V, p. 402
• Philip II, p. 402
• William of Orange, p. 403

❸ Economics in Spain: inflation, high taxes, unfavorable balance of trade; Actions of Colonies: piracy, trade in Spanish ports, establish colonies in Americas; Actions of Charles V: wars, financial problems; Actions of Philip II: expensive wars, loss of Netherlands

❹ a. They conquered the Aztec and Inca and established settlements.

b. The Dutch emphasized trade and did not try to convert local people to Christianity.

c. Increases in the amount of gold and silver drove up prices. The demand for Spanish-made goods declined.

❺ Students' diaries will vary.

SECTION 4 REVIEW

1. Define and explain the significance:
viceroys
guerrilla warfare

2. Identify and explain the significance:
Ponce de León
Hernán Cortés
Moctezuma II
Francisco Pizarro
Charles V
Philip II
William of Orange

3. Identifying Cause and Effect
Copy the web diagram below. Fill in each box to show how it contributed to the decline of the Spanish Empire.

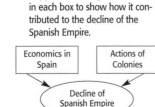

4. **Finding the Main Idea**
a. How did the Spanish expand their colonial empire?
b. How did the Dutch colonial empire differ from the Spanish colonial empire?
c. What developments limited the ability of the Spanish to fully benefit from their vast and rich overseas empire?

5. **Writing and Critical Thinking**
Making Generalizations In a diary entry, describe a day in the life of a Spanish colonist in the Americas.
Consider:
• ways in which things would have been better or worse than in Spain
• what was involved in meeting and dealing with native peoples

Homework Practice Online
keyword: SP3 HP16

REVIEW AND ASSESSMENT RESOURCES

REPRODUCIBLE RESOURCES

▸ Vocabulary Activity 16

TECHNOLOGY RESOURCES

▸ Chapter 16 Test Generator (on the One-Stop Planner)
▸ Global Skill Builder CD–ROM
▸ HRW Web Site

REINFORCEMENT, REVIEW, and ASSESSMENT

▸ Chapter 16 Review, pp. 408–409
▸ Chapter 16 Tutorial for Students, Parents, Mentors, and Peers
▸ Chapter 16 Test (Form A or B)
▸ Alternative Assessment Handbook
▸ Chapter 16 Test for English Language Learners and Special-Needs Students

REVIEW

Have students complete the Chapter 16 Review on pages 408–409.

ASSESS

Use one of the chapter tests to assess students' understanding of the content. For Alternative Assessment, see the Portfolio Activities and Alternative Assessment Handbook.

CHAPTER 16 REVIEW ANSWERS

Understanding Main Ideas

1. observation, experiments, mathematics, questioning old beliefs

2. Earth moves around sun; laws of planetary motion, universal gravitation, conservation of matter; circulation of blood; calculus; bacteria; oxygen

3. compass, astrolabe, standardization of money, joint-stock companies

4. led to use of colonies for gold, silver, raw materials, letting colonies trade just with home country

5. Asia accessible by sea around southern tip of Africa

6. began contact between Europeans and people of Americas, Columbian Exchange

7. European demand for labor in colonies, devastation of American Indian population by European diseases

8. good ships and sailors, focus on trade, Dutch East India Company

9. inflation caused by influx of gold and silver, industrial decline, lack of middle class, expulsion of Jews and Moriscos

Reviewing Themes

1. new ways of thinking about the world, less acceptance of old beliefs, technology for maritime exploration

---

CHAPTER 16 Review

Creating a Time Line

Copy the time line below onto a sheet of paper. Complete the time line by filling in the events, individuals, and dates from the chapter that you think were significant. Pick three events and explain why you think they were significant.

| 1400 | 1600 | 1800 |

Writing a Summary

Using standard grammar, spelling, sentence structure, and punctuation, write an overview of the events in the chapter.

Identifying People and Ideas

Identify the following terms or individuals and explain their significance:

1. heliocentric theory
2. Galileo Galilei
3. mercantilism
4. Vasco da Gama
5. tariffs
6. Christopher Columbus
7. triangular trade
8. Middle Passage
9. Hernán Cortés
10. Philip II

Understanding Main Ideas

SECTION 1 (pp. 382–387)

The Scientific Revolution

1. How did the study of nature change during the Scientific Revolution?
2. What were some of the important scientific discoveries made during this period?

SECTION 2 (pp. 388–391)

The Foundations of European Exploration

3. What kinds of changes in science and economics made European exploration possible?
4. What role did mercantilism play in the way European countries dealt with their colonies?

SECTION 3 (pp. 392–399)

Voyages of Portugal and Spain

5. What new knowledge did early Portuguese explorers provide that increased successful exploration?
6. How did the voyages of Christopher Columbus influence the world?
7. What were some of the factors leading to the Atlantic slave trade?

SECTION 4 (pp. 400–407)

The Spanish and Dutch Empires

8. What led to the successful rise of Dutch exploration in the 1600s?
9. What factors led to the decline of the Spanish Empire?

Reviewing Themes

1. **Science, Technology & Society** How did the era known as the Scientific Revolution lead to developments in other areas of society?
2. **Economics** How did the theory of mercantilism influence nations' decisions to explore and colonize?
3. **Global Relations** What determined the kinds of relationships that European explorers formed with conquered peoples?

Thinking Critically

1. **Comparing and Contrasting** Compare and contrast the ways in which the Portuguese, Spanish, and Dutch went about exploration and colonization.
2. **Supporting a Point of View** Which European nation engaged in exploration, trade, and colonization during the age of exploration had the greatest effect on other peoples? Explain your answer.
3. **Sequencing** Trace the events leading to the rise and decline of the Spanish Empire.

Writing About History

Categorizing Many factors influenced European exploration. In turn, exploration had many effects on both Europeans and non-Europeans. Fill in the following chart, listing the political, economic, cultural, and technological influences of European expansion on both Europeans and non-Europeans.

Effects of European Conquest		
	Europeans	**Non-Europeans**
Political		
Economic		
Cultural		
Technological		

CLOSE

Have the class debate the statement: "European exploration and expansion between 1400 and 1700 lay the foundations of the modern world."

RETEACH

Have students write one or more phrases that summarize the main ideas of each heading or subheading. **ENGLISH LANGUAGE LEARNERS**

Portfolio Extensions

1. Have students make a "What If?" poster with at least five different scenes about the era of exploration and expansion. Each scene should show the short-term and long-term results if one event of the period had been different in some way. Remind them to consider what might realistically have been different in technology, exploration, politics, weather, battles, etc.

2. Organize students into groups of four or five. Have the groups locate and use biographies to research the life of one scientist, explorer, or other person in the chapter and prepare a short play to perform for the class. Plays should illustrate personality and feelings as well as why the person is important.

3. Have students imagine they are a newspaper reporter writing a feature story on an important event of exploration or expansion. Encourage them to be creative and dramatic in their writing while using correct social studies terminology.

Building Social Studies Skills

Interpreting Maps

Study the map below. Then use the information to answer the questions that follow.

Cabral's Route, April 1500

1. Which of the following correctly describes Cabral's course from Lisbon to the Cape of Good Hope?

   a. First south, then west

   b. First southwest, then southeast

   c. First northwest, then northeast

   d. First southeast, then southwest

2. Cabral did not intend to follow the course he did. He was blown off course. Why was this course change significant? Give specific reasons.

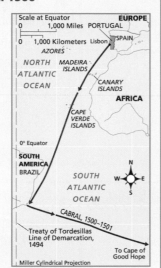

Scale at Equator
0   1,000 Miles
0   1,000 Kilometers
EUROPE
PORTUGAL
SPAIN
Lisbon
AZORES
NORTH ATLANTIC OCEAN
MADEIRA ISLANDS
CANARY ISLANDS
CAPE VERDE ISLANDS
AFRICA
0° Equator
SOUTH AMERICA
BRAZIL
SOUTH ATLANTIC OCEAN
CABRAL, 1500–1501
Treaty of Tordesillas Line of Demarcation, 1494
To Cape of Good Hope
Miller Cylindrical Projection

Problem Solving

Read the following quote written in 1517 by a Spanish priest in Mexico. Then answer the questions.

> "As the Indians saw that the Spaniards did not attack them . . . they came . . . unarmed with kindly faces. . . . They asked the captain by signs what he wanted to which he replied 'water to drink.' The Indians showed him a round walled-up well of good water . . . where [the Spaniards] took all the water needful for the ships. . . . When day broke, all the Indians came out of their town armed with bows and arrows, shields and lances . . . to tell [the Spaniards] to go to their ships. The Spaniards obeyed their order. . . ."

3. Which of the following is the best explanation of why the Indians changed their behavior toward the Spanish?

   a. The Indians thought the Spanish had stayed too long.

   b. The Indians had only pretended to be kind.

   c. Water was scarce and the Spanish had taken too much.

   d. The Indians realized the Spanish were after their gold.

4. Why did you choose the statement you did in question 3? Explain your reasoning, using a problem-solving process.

Alternative Assessment

Building Your Portfolio

Economics

The idea of a favorable balance of trade developed during the 1500s and the 1600s. Today, most nations still take steps to keep their imports and exports balanced. Using your textbook and other sources, find statistics and other information about economic processes that countries such as the United States, Great Britain, and Japan use to maintain favorable trade balances. Summarize your findings in a poster.

internet connect
go.hrw.com

Internet Activity: go.hrw.com
KEYWORD: SP3 WH16

Choose a topic on Exploration and Expansion to:

- research the Scientific Revolution and create a database of scientists, dates, and contributions.
- learn more about an explorer described in this chapter.
- explain the political, economic, and cultural impact of Spanish expansion in Mesoamerica and Andean South America.

---

2. desire for gold and silver, use of colonies as source of raw materials and market for manufacturers

3. whether colonists tried to enslave conquered peoples

Thinking Critically

1. Portuguese: focus on routes around Africa to Asia for spices; Spanish: focus on Americas for gold, silver, plantation products; Dutch: emphasis on Asian spice trade

2. Spain: devastation of the Americas by diseases; Portugal: leadership in the African slave trade

3. Isabella and Ferdinand unite Spain; and sponsor Columbus; expulsion of Jews and Moriscos; Cortés conquers Aztecs; Pizarro conquers Incas; Spanish settlements established in Americas; Philip II loses Netherlands

Writing About History

Europeans: empires, trade, spread culture; non-Europeans: conquered, provided labor, changed lifestyles, new weapons

Building Social Studies Skills

1. b

2. He landed in Brazil and claimed it for Portugal.

3. Answers will vary.

4. Answers will vary.

Building Your Portfolio

Students' posters will vary.

CHAPTER RESOURCE MANAGER

	Objectives	Pacing Guide	Reproducible Resources
SECTION 1 **The Ming and Qing Dynasties** (pp. 412–416)	• Explain why the Chinese showed little interest in overseas trade during the Ming dynasty. • Describe how the Qing dynasty came to rule China. • Discuss changes that occurred in the Chinese economy under Qing rule. • Analyze reasons for the decline of the Qing dynasty.	**Regular** 1.5 day **Block Scheduling** 1 day *Block Scheduling Handbook with Team Teaching Strategies, 17.1*	**RS** Guided Reading Strategy 17.1 **E** Hands-on History Activity 17: Asian Empires
SECTION 2 **China and Europeans** (pp. 417–421)	• Characterize early contact between Portugal and China. • Explain why China and Great Britain went to war in the mid-1800s. • Describe how internal rebellions contributed to the decline of the Qing dynasty.	**Regular** 1.5 day **Block Scheduling** 1 day *Block Scheduling Handbook with Team Teaching Strategies, 17.2*	**RS** Guided Reading Strategy 17.2 **RS** Graphic Organizer Activity 17: Asia and the West **PS** Readings in World History 69: The Treaty of Nanjing, 1842
SECTION 3 **The Tokugawa Shoguns in Japan** (pp. 422–427)	• Explain how the Tokugawa shogunate came to power. • Discuss why Japan's rulers sought to isolate their nation from foreign influence. • Identify characteristics of society and culture under the Tokugawa shogunate. • Describe how Japanese isolation was brought to an end.	**Regular** 1.5 day **Block Scheduling** 1 day *Block Scheduling Handbook with Team Teaching Strategies, 17.3*	**RS** Guided Reading Strategy 17.3 **SM** Geography Activity 17: The Struggle for Korea **PS** Readings in World History 70: Yoshida Shoin: Philosopher of the Meiji Restoration **E** Creative Teaching Strategy 17: The Way of the Shogun

Chapter Resource Key

PS Primary Sources	**REV** Review	Video	**One-Stop** Planner CD-ROM	
RS Reading Support	**ELL** Reinforcement and English Language Learners	Internet	See the *One-Stop Planner* for a complete list of additional resources for students and teachers.	
IC Interdisciplinary Connections		Holt Presentation Maker Using Microsoft® PowerPoint®		
E Enrichment	Transparencies			
SM Skills Mastery	CD-ROM			
A Assessment	Music			

One-Stop Planner CD-ROM

It's easy to plan lessons, select resources, and print out materials for your students when you use the **One-Stop Planner** CD–ROM with *Test Generator.*

Technology Resources

- One-Stop Planner 17.1
- Regions of the World Music Audio CD Program 19: China, Mongolia, and Taiwan: Beating the Dragon Robe: A Traditional Chinese Opera
- World History Teaching Transparency: Regional and World Map 37: East and Southeast Asia
- World History Teaching Transparency: Art and History 16: Cicada on a Palm Leaf
- Homework Practice Online
- Online Maps, Charts, and Graphs: Expansion of the Manchu by 1643

- One-Stop Planner 17.2
- CNN Presents World Cultures: Yesterday and Today Segment 19: Hong Kong: Past and Present
- Religions of the World Video Series: Christianity
- Homework Practice Online

- One-Stop Planner 17.3
- Holt Researcher: World History: Oda Nobunaga
- Holt Researcher: World History: Toyotomi Hideyoshi
- Holt Researcher: World History: Tokugawa Ieyasu
- Regions of the World Music Audio CD Program 20: Japan and the Koreas: Music of the One-String Ichigenkin
- Religions of the World Video Series: Christianity
- Homework Practice Online

Reinforcement, Review, and Assessment

- Daily Quiz 17.1
- Main Idea Activity 17.1
- English Audio Summary 17.1
- Spanish Audio Summary 17.1
- REV Section 1 Review, p. 416

- Daily Quiz 17.2
- Main Idea Activity 17.2
- English Audio Summary 17.2
- Spanish Audio Summary 17.2
- REV Section 2 Review, p. 421

- Daily Quiz 17.3
- Main Idea Activity 17.3
- English Audio Summary 17.3
- Spanish Audio Summary 17.3
- REV Section 3 Review, p. 427

internet connect

HRW ONLINE RESOURCES
  GO TO: go.hrw.com
  Then type in a keyword.

TEACHER HOME PAGE
  KEYWORD: SP3 Teacher

CHAPTER INTERNET ACTIVITIES
  KEYWORD: SP3 WH17
Choose an activity to:
- analyze art of the Ming and Qing dynasties and explain how they reflect the cultures in which they were produced.
- learn more about Kabuki theater and *Bunraku,* Japanese puppet theater.
- examine an issue from the point of view of a Japanese samurai warrior.

CHAPTER ENRICHMENT LINKS
  KEYWORD: SP3 CH17

ONLINE ASSESSMENT
  Homework Practice
  KEYWORD: SP3 HP17
  Standardized Test Prep
  KEYWORD: SP3 STP17
  Rubrics
  KEYWORD: SS Rubrics

ONLINE MAPS, CHARTS, AND GRAPHS
  KEYWORD: SP3 MCG

CONTENT UPDATES
  KEYWORD: SS Content Updates

HOLT PRESENTATION MAKER
  KEYWORD: SP3 PPT17

ONLINE READING SUPPORT
  KEYWORD: SS Strategies

CURRENT EVENTS
  KEYWORD: S3 Current Events

Meeting Individual Needs

Ability Levels

Level 1   Basic level activities designed for all students encountering new material

Level 2   Intermediate level activities designed for average students

Level 3   Challenging activities designed for honors and gifted and talented students

English Language Learners   These activities address the needs of students with Limited English Proficiency.

Chapter Review and Assessment

- IC Vocabulary Activity 17
- Global Skill Builder CD–ROM
- HRW Web Site
- REV Chapter 17 Tutorial for Students, Parents, Mentors, and Peers
- REV Chapter 17 Review, pp. 428–429

- A Chapter 17 Test Generator (on the One-Stop Planner)
- A Chapter 17 Test (Form A or B)
- A Alternative Assessment Handbook
- A Chapter 17 Test for English Language Learners and Special-Needs Students

Section 1 *The Ming and Qing Dynasties*

Section 2 *China and Europeans*

Section 3 *The Tokugawa Shoguns in Japan*

Build on What You Know

Ask students to answer the following questions:

How might changes during the Tang and Sung dynasties have affected dynasties that followed?

Consider:

- **the influence of Buddhism**
- **the structure of Chinese society**

In what ways did Chinese culture influence early Japan?

Consider:

- **forms of government**
- **language and literature**

EXPLORING THE TIME LINE
GLOBAL EVENTS

internet connect

TOPIC: Chinese Opium Wars
GO TO: **go.hrw.com**
KEYWORD: SP3 WH17

Have students access the Internet through the HRW Go site to research the Chinese Opium Wars. Ask students to write a letter of response from Queen Victoria to Lin Tse-Hsu's plea for England to cease its shipments of opium into China. Explain your (her) refusal to intervene on behalf of the Chinese people, and the justification for importing opium in trade for tea.

CHAPTER

17

1368–1868

Asia in Transition

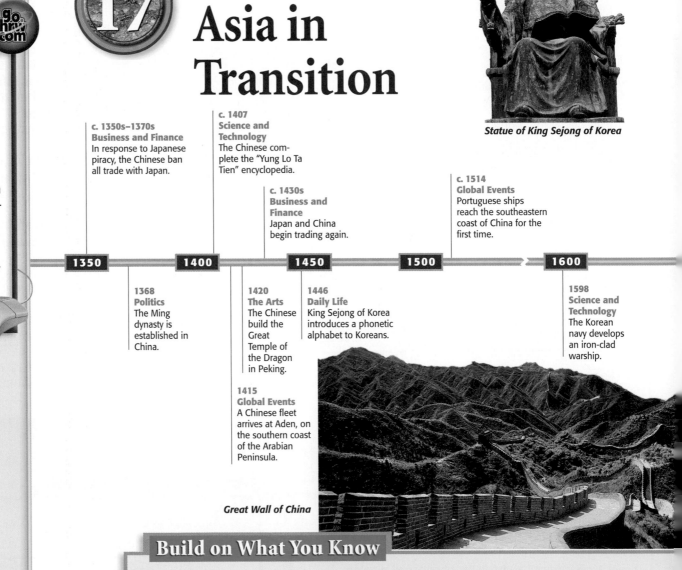

Statue of King Sejong of Korea

c. 1350s–1370s
Business and Finance
In response to Japanese piracy, the Chinese ban all trade with Japan.

c. 1407
Science and Technology
The Chinese complete the "Yung Lo Ta Tien" encyclopedia.

c. 1430s
Business and Finance
Japan and China begin trading again.

c. 1514
Global Events
Portuguese ships reach the southeastern coast of China for the first time.

| 1350 | 1400 | 1450 | 1500 | 1600 |

1368
Politics
The Ming dynasty is established in China.

1420
The Arts
The Chinese build the Great Temple of the Dragon in Peking.

1446
Daily Life
King Sejong of Korea introduces a phonetic alphabet to Koreans.

1598
Science and Technology
The Korean navy develops an iron-clad warship.

1415
Global Events
A Chinese fleet arrives at Aden, on the southern coast of the Arabian Peninsula.

Great Wall of China

Build on What You Know

East Asia was one of the great cradles of early civilization. Over many centuries and through the course of many dynasties, China had expanded and its distinct culture had spread throughout much of Asia. Then China was conquered by the Mongols, who established the Yuan dynasty. Meanwhile, the people of Japan had developed a feudal society of their own, with a rich culture and a heritage of unique traditions and values. In this chapter, you will learn how both Chinese and Japanese rulers became increasingly concerned and threatened by the growing activity of foreigners, especially Europeans, in and around their lands.

What's Your Opinion?

To help students create their Themes Journal entries, provide the following examples of appropriate agree/disagree statements.

Global Relations

Agree Avoiding outside influence helps nations maintain their own cultural identity.

Disagree Isolation prevents nations from sharing and therefore benefiting from new ideas and developments.

Economics

Agree Economic growth does not depend on cultural attitudes.

Disagree Economic growth is stimulated by interaction with other peoples.

Government

Agree A strong central government can keep a nation and its culture unified.

Disagree A strong central government prevents growth and change.

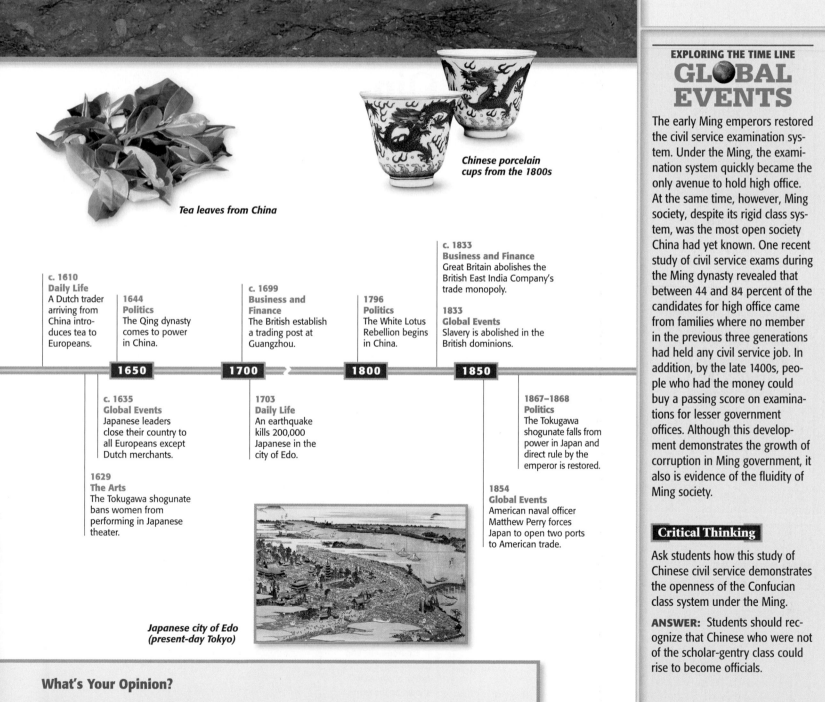

Tea leaves from China

Chinese porcelain cups from the 1800s

c. 1610
Daily Life
A Dutch trader arriving from China introduces tea to Europeans.

1644
Politics
The Qing dynasty comes to power in China.

c. 1699
Business and Finance
The British establish a trading post at Guangzhou.

1796
Politics
The White Lotus Rebellion begins in China.

c. 1833
Business and Finance
Great Britain abolishes the British East India Company's trade monopoly.

1833
Global Events
Slavery is abolished in the British dominions.

| 1650 | 1700 | 1800 | 1850 |

c. 1635
Global Events
Japanese leaders close their country to all Europeans except Dutch merchants.

1629
The Arts
The Tokugawa shogunate bans women from performing in Japanese theater.

1703
Daily Life
An earthquake kills 200,000 Japanese in the city of Edo.

1867–1868
Politics
The Tokugawa shogunate falls from power in Japan and direct rule by the emperor is restored.

1854
Global Events
American naval officer Matthew Perry forces Japan to open two ports to American trade.

Japanese city of Edo (present-day Tokyo)

EXPLORING THE TIME LINE
GLOBAL EVENTS

The early Ming emperors restored the civil service examination system. Under the Ming, the examination system quickly became the only avenue to hold high office. At the same time, however, Ming society, despite its rigid class system, was the most open society China had yet known. One recent study of civil service exams during the Ming dynasty revealed that between 44 and 84 percent of the candidates for high office came from families where no member in the previous three generations had held any civil service job. In addition, by the late 1400s, people who had the money could buy a passing score on examinations for lesser government offices. Although this development demonstrates the growth of corruption in Ming government, it also is evidence of the fluidity of Ming society.

Critical Thinking

Ask students how this study of Chinese civil service demonstrates the openness of the Confucian class system under the Ming.

ANSWER: Students should recognize that Chinese who were not of the scholar-gentry class could rise to become officials.

What's Your Opinion?

*Do you **agree** or **disagree** with the following statements? Support your point of view in your journal.*

Global Relations Nations can protect themselves by isolating their people and cultures from other nations.

Economics Cultural attitudes toward trade, commerce, and interaction with other peoples do not affect a country's economic growth.

Government A country requires a strong central government to provide certain services for its citizens and to protect its culture.

OBJECTIVES

1 **Explain why the Chinese showed little interest in overseas trade during the Ming dynasty.**

2 **Describe how the Qing dynasty came to rule China.**

3 **Discuss changes that occurred in the Chinese economy under Qing rule.**

4 **Analyze reasons for the decline of the Qing dynasty.**

LET'S GET STARTED!

As students enter the classroom, ask them to write a paragraph discussing whether they think the United States would be better-off or worse-off if the government prohibited all immigration and world trade. *(Most students will suggest that the nation would be worse-off.)* Have volunteers share their responses with the class. Tell students that in Section 1 they will learn how a policy of isolation affected the Ming and Qing dynasties in China.

MAP ANSWERS

1. the Great Wall

2. the Grand Canal

READ TO DISCOVER

❶ Why did the Chinese show little interest in overseas trade during the Ming dynasty?

❷ How did the Qing dynasty come to rule China?

❸ What changes occurred in the Chinese economy under Qing rule?

❹ Why did the Qing dynasty decline?

DEFINE

junks
queue
philology

IDENTIFY

Hsüan-yeh
White Lotus Rebellion

WHY IT MATTERS TODAY

China remains an important trading country in the world today. Use CNNfyi.com or other **current event** sources to learn more about China and international trade. Record your findings in your journal.

The Ming and Qing Dynasties

The Main Idea
Two powerful dynasties, the Ming and the Qing, ruled China as a self-sufficient state for more than 500 years.

The Story Continues *The Mongol Yuan dynasty borrowed many ideas from the Chinese in order to establish an effective imperial government. They wisely followed the advice of a Chinese-trained official who said: "The [Mongol] empire was created on horseback, but it cannot be governed on horseback." In 1368, however, a former Buddhist monk named Zhu Yuanzhang (JOO YOO-en-JAHNG) overthrew the Yuan and established the Ming, or "Brilliant," dynasty. The Ming would remain in power in China for almost 300 years.*

Ming Foreign Policy

During the early period of the Ming dynasty—the late 1300s and early 1400s—the Chinese were probably the most skilled sailors in the world. For example, they built large, sturdy ships that Europeans called **junks.** Some junks were more than 400 feet long. The Chinese had been navigating their ships with the compass, which they probably invented, since the early 1100s. In 1405 the Ming emperor financed a fleet that sailed around Southeast Asia to India. Another Chinese fleet sailed across the Indian Ocean. This fleet reached the southern coast of the Arabian Peninsula in 1415.

These and other voyages of trade and discovery took place almost 100 years

The Ming Empire, 1424

Interpreting Maps During the Ming dynasty, the imperial capital was moved back from Nanjing to Beijing.

■ **Skills Assessment:**
1. Environment and Society What Chinese feat of engineering shown on the map would block movement from one place to another? **2. Drawing Conclusions** What feat of engineering would help movement?

⊛ Capital city

0   250   500 Miles
0   250   500 Kilometers
Modified Conic Projection

GOBI (DESERT) MANCHURIA
Great Wall Beijing
Wei River Huang R. (Yellow R.) Grand Canal
CHINA Nanjing
Chang River (Yangtze R.) Hangzhou
Chongqing
Guangzhou (Canton) Xi River
ANNAM (VIETNAM) Mekong R.

SEA OF JAPAN
CHOSŎN (KOREA)
YELLOW SEA
EAST CHINA SEA
TAIWAN
SOUTH CHINA SEA

40°N
130°E
30°N
20°N
110°E   120°E

LEVEL 1: Organize the class into groups. Within each group, designate a student to be the emperor and divide the remainder of the group into two factions during the Ming dynasty—one representing court officials who favor continued trade with the outside world and the other representing court officials who wish to end that trade. Each faction should present arguments in support of its position to the emperor. After hearing the arguments, the emperor must decide on a course of action regarding international trade and report his or her decision to the class. Discuss with the class the consequences each decision might have for China. **ENGLISH LANGUAGE LEARNERS, COOPERATIVE LEARNING**

before Vasco da Gama sailed from Portugal to India by going around the tip of Africa. The Chinese clearly had the ability to become a great seafaring power. However, the naval expeditions of the early Ming period did not continue for very long. Later Ming emperors had little interest in sea power or in foreign trade. They stopped financing naval expeditions. For a time they even outlawed overseas trade.

Attitudes toward trade. After defeating the Mongols in 1368, the Ming emperors tried to rid China of all Mongol influences. They wanted China to be as great as it had been during the Han, Tang, and Sung dynasties. As part of that effort, the Ming emperors restored Confucianism as the official philosophy of the government. Confucian philosophy divided society into four classes.

The Four Classes under Confucianism			
Scholar-gentry	**Farmers**	**Artisans**	**Merchants**
This landed, highly literate class helped staff the royal bureaucracy.	They produced food and paid the taxes that supported the empire.	They made beautiful and useful objects.	At the bottom of the social order, they made their living by selling objects that peasants and artisans had produced.

The Ming emperors wanted China to be self-sufficient. They refused to rely upon foreign trade as a source of government revenue. In the minds of the emperors, foreign trade did not bring enough benefits to China to make it a worthwhile endeavor. This view differed from that of European monarchs, who were strongly influenced by the ideas of mercantilism.

The northern frontier. The Ming emperors also wanted to make sure that no Central Asian people ever conquered China again. They focused their efforts on the long northern land frontier. To protect that frontier, the Ming strengthened the Great Wall of China. They encouraged soldiers to move with their families into the frontier zone by offering them free land. The Ming also encouraged peasants and city dwellers to move there. When the Ming emperors first came to power, Nanjing, in central China, was their capital. In 1421, however, the imperial capital was relocated to Beijing in the north.

The Ming emperors also tried to prevent nomadic tribes in the north from uniting into a powerful fighting force. Tribes that submitted to the Ming sent tribute to Beijing. In return, the Ming gave nomadic leaders honors, gifts, and titles.

Defending the frontier required constant attention and a great deal of money. The overseas expeditions were also extremely expensive. The Ming did not have enough revenue to do both. They chose frontier defense over trade and sea travel.

✔ **READING CHECK: Identifying Cause and Effect**
Why did the Ming emperors abandon overseas expeditions? little interest in sea power or foreign trade

What If? The Chinese had the means to become a great sea power. **What might have happened if they had used this ability as the Spanish and English did later?**

This busy festival scene provides a view of life in China during the Ming dynasty.

WHAT IF? ANSWER
Answers will vary, but students may suggest that China would not have been isolated and may have made voyages of exploration and established colonies like the Western nations.

Government

Tell students that in 1402 the Ming emperor decided to build a new capital on the site of the Mongol Yuan dynasty's capital city, now called Beijing. During most of the Ming and Qing dynasties, access to the palace was limited only to employees and a few very high officials. For this reason it became known as the Forbidden City.

Critical Thinking

Ask students how the isolation of the Ming emperors inside the walls of the Forbidden City might have affected the way in which they governed.

ANSWER: Answers will vary, but students should recognize the potential problems that arise when rulers are out of touch with the people they govern.

TEACH OBJECTIVE 2

ALL LEVELS: Review with students how earlier Chinese dynasties fell. Then discuss with the class if the fall of the Ming dynasty and the rise of the Qing dynasty fit the pattern of Chinese political history. **ENGLISH LANGUAGE LEARNERS**

HOMEWORK Have students write letters to the editor of a Ming-era newspaper about the government's trade policy. Select students to read their letters to the class.

Teacher to Teacher

David Olson of Angola, Indiana, suggested the following activity: Have students create compare-and-contrast charts that examine how China and Japan responded to European and American encroachment into their territories and then create a time line of crucial events.

History Maker

MATTEO RICCI. Jesuit Matteo Ricci was an early Christian missionary in China. Ricci arrived in Macao in 1582. For nearly two decades he unsuccessfully sought the emperor's support for his work. In 1601 he finally was allowed to settle in the capital. He remained there until his death in 1610. During his life in China, Ricci developed a system for spelling Chinese words using the Western alphabet and devised Chinese terms for Christian ideas.

Critical Thinking

Ask students why the emperor was reluctant to allow missionary work.

ANSWER: He wanted to maintain traditional ideas and values.

HISTORY MAKER ANSWER

He encouraged the integration of Western ideas.

internet connect

TOPIC: Ming/Qing Art
GO TO: go.hrw.com
KEYWORD: SP3 WH17

Have students access the Internet through the HRW Go site to research the art of the Ming and Qing dynasties. Ask students to create a museum exhibit to display for the class.

HISTORY MAKER

Hsüan-yeh (1654–1722)

Hsüan-yeh was a remarkable and energetic ruler. He increased the size of the Chinese empire, presided over the civil service examination system and flood control efforts, and constructed grain storehouses in case of famine. He also sponsored literary and educational projects.

Hsüan-yeh wanted to learn more about Western ways. He opened Chinese ports to foreign trade and strongly encouraged the introduction of Western education and arts. **How did Hsüan-yeh extend Western influences in China?**

Analyzing Primary Sources

Drawing Conclusions Why was canal travel dangerous at times? overcrowding; the lock system

Founding the Qing Dynasty

In the early 1600s a new and serious threat to the Ming dynasty emerged. In Manchuria, to the northeast of China, a chieftain named Nurhachi unified many tribes into a single people, the Manchu. Nurhachi's son captured eastern Mongolia and Korea. He then declared the beginning of a new dynasty, the Qing.

In 1644 the Manchu captured Beijing with the help of a Chinese general. The Qing dynasty ruled China from this time until 1912. Once again, despite the efforts of the Ming, outsiders had conquered China and established their own dynasty.

The Qing emperors were not Chinese, but they adopted Chinese culture and ruled the country with traditional Chinese techniques. One such Qing ruler was the emperor **Hsüan-yeh** (shoo·AHN·yeh).

At the same time, Qing emperors tried to keep the Manchu people, a minority in the empire, separate and distinct from the far more numerous Chinese. All Manchu had to study the Manchu language and cultural traditions. The Qing emperors could marry only Manchu women. They banned further emigration of Chinese to Manchuria, which was set apart as a tribal homeland for the Manchu. Finally, the Qing required all Chinese men to wear their hair tied in a **queue** (tail), a style that was common among the Manchu. The queue symbolized Chinese submission to Manchu rule.

✔ **READING CHECK: Drawing Inferences** Why did Qing rulers strive to keep the Chinese and Manchu people separate? as a means of keeping the Manchu minority distinct from the more numerous Chinese

Economy, Culture, and Society

Generally life under the Ming and Qing dynasties was similar. Both Ming and Qing emperors kept traditional political institutions. Both supported traditional ideas and values. However, changes soon occurred to alter some of their traditions.

Economy. China's economy continued to grow during the Qing dynasty. Some regions of Qing China began to specialize in the manufacture or production of certain goods. The Lower Yangtze region, inland from present-day Shanghai, for example, became a center for the weaving of cotton cloth. Traders transported such goods along canals, coastal waterways, and rivers. Father Matteo Ricci, an Italian missionary to China in the late 1500s and early 1600s, described this canal traffic.

History Makers Speak

❝So great is the number of boats that frequently many days are lost in transit by crowding each other, particularly when water is low in the canals. To prevent this, the water is held back at stated places by wooden locks, which also serve as bridges. . . . At times . . . the rush of water is so high and strong, at the exit from one lock or the entrance to another, that the boats are capsized and the whole crew is drowned.❞

Matteo Ricci, from *China in the Sixteenth Century*

The Chinese also sent goods such as tea and silk by caravan to Central Asia and Russia. Despite government disapproval, some ships continued to sail to Southeast Asia and India to trade.

As they had during the Sung dynasty, Chinese cities continued to grow. Peace and urban growth contributed to the increase of trade within China's borders. In theory, the Chinese and their Qing rulers still looked down on merchants.

TEACH OBJECTIVE 3

LEVEL 2: Have the class act as an advisory council to the Qing emperor and debate the following issue: Should Chinese merchants continue trading with peoples of Central and Southeast Asia, Russia, and India? How might such trade affect Chinese society? **COOPERATIVE LEARNING**

TEACH OBJECTIVE 4

LEVEL 3: Copy the accompanying graphic organizer on the chalkboard, omitting the italicized answers. Have each student complete the diagram by filling in the effect for each cause listed.

Decline of Qing Dynasty	
Cause	**Effect**
overpopulation	*lack of food for peasants*
government inefficiency	*political unrest*
natural disasters	*social turmoil*

CLOSE

Have interested students research in greater depth the Manchu conquest of the Ming dynasty. Have them report their findings to the class.

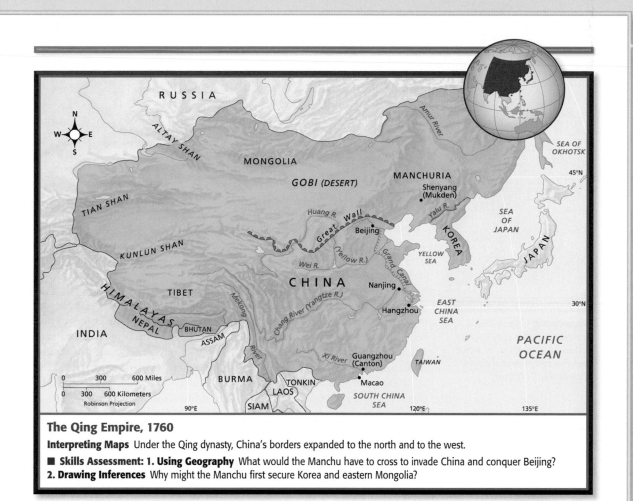

The Qing Empire, 1760

Interpreting Maps Under the Qing dynasty, China's borders expanded to the north and to the west.

■ **Skills Assessment: 1. Using Geography** What would the Manchu have to cross to invade China and conquer Beijing?

2. Drawing Inferences Why might the Manchu first secure Korea and eastern Mongolia?

Culture

Although the Qing are remembered for their patronage of the arts and learning, in 1772 they began a campaign to eliminate writings the emperor's advisers thought objectionable on political or moral grounds. Especially targeted were works considered to be anti-Manchu in tone and those that dealt with security matters such as border defenses. In all, more than 2,000 works were ordered destroyed.

Critical Thinking

Have students draw conclusions about the wisdom of the Qing efforts at censorship. Would such a campaign, had it succeeded, make the nation more secure, or would it limit the growth of Chinese arts and culture?

ANSWER: Answers will vary but should demonstrate understanding that any political benefits of such censorship would be offset by cultural drawbacks.

MAP ANSWERS

1. the Great Wall

2. They could secure it without having to cross the Great Wall.

In reality, however, they needed merchants to supply city-dwellers with clothing, food, and other essential goods.

Although cities grew, most of China's people still lived in the countryside. They increased the amount of land used for farming. In addition to rice, wheat, and tea, the rural Chinese planted new crops such as peanuts, sweet potatoes, and tobacco, which had been introduced from the Americas. The sweet potato became known as "the poor man's food" in southern China because it grew well in soil unsuited for the growing of rice. It also had more nutritional value than most other food crops.

Popular culture and society. As in Europe, the growth of cities and the increasing wealth of urban people led to the growth of popular culture in China. As early as the 1300s city people read novels and plays in the common everyday language. During the Ming and Qing dynasties, these popular novels and plays increased in number. Old tales about bandits and corrupt officials, once recited by street storytellers, now appeared in novels by professional authors. The writings of this period realistically portrayed Chinese society and family life.

Scholarship also flourished under both the Ming and the Qing. Scholars wrote detailed histories of earlier dynasties and essays on Confucian ethics. They studied ancient writings, much like the Renaissance humanists in Europe had. Qing scholars studied **philology,** the history of literature and language. In the 1700s Chinese scholars began to organize a manuscript library of rare works from the past.

Ivory figurine depicting a Daoist, c. 1500s–1600s

REVIEW

Have students complete the Section 1 Review on p. 416.

ASSESS

Have students complete Daily Quiz 17.1. As Alternative Assessment, you may want to use the graphic organizer or the homework exercise in this section's lessons.

RETEACH

Have students complete Main Idea Activity for English Language Learners and Special-Needs Students 17.1. Then organize the class into two groups: the Ming dynasty and the Qing dynasty. Ask students in each group to prepare outlines that summarize the history of each dynasty.
ENGLISH LANGUAGE LEARNERS, COOPERATIVE LEARNING

EXTEND

Have students imagine that they are soldiers on guard at the Great Wall of China. Ask them to write diary entries describing such a life. Encourage them to think about reasons for volunteering to go to the frontier, their daily routine, and what they might do in case of an invasion. Encourage students to be as creative as possible, but to use standard grammar, spelling, sentence structure, and punctuation. **BLOCK SCHEDULING**

VISUAL RECORD ANSWER

It was done on a small scale and by hand.

SECTION 1 REVIEW ANSWERS

1 Define
- junks, p. 412
- queue, p. 414
- philology, p. 415

2 Identify
- Hsüan-yeh, p. 414
- White Lotus Rebellion, p. 416

3 Stable: class structure, attitudes toward foreign trade, political institutions, ideas and values; Changed: growth of cities, growth of population, popular culture, scholarship, government inefficiency and corruption

4 a. increased trade, increased population, growth of popular culture and scholarship

b. suspicion and distrust

5 Answers will vary but should demonstrate understanding that governmental inefficiency and corruption would have a negative impact on the nation.

Technology Resources
Regions of the World Music Audio CD Program 19

Technology Resources
World History Teaching Transparency: Art and History 16

416

INTERPRETING THE VISUAL RECORD

Silk weaving Chinese silk weavers during the Qing dynasty worked on manual looms. *What does this image reveal about silk weaving in China?*

China's society continued to be based on the family. The family, like the state, reflected the Confucian belief that each person had a role in life. The male head of the family directed the activities of family members for the good of the family as a whole. When a daughter married, she went to live with the family of her new husband.

✔ **READING CHECK: Summarizing** How did the Chinese economy change during the eras of Ming and Qing rule? Trade and manufacturing specialization grew.

Decline of the Qing Dynasty

Under Qing rule China's population grew rapidly. Chinese farmers raised more crops, making it possible to feed more people. Peace also contributed to China's population growth. From about 1750 to the mid-1800s, China's population grew to more than 400 million people.

Qing China's rapidly growing population placed increasing pressure on the government. The Qing, however, found it increasingly difficult to meet the challenges posed by change and growth. Corruption at court and government inefficiency became more widespread. Growing numbers of bureaucrats demanded bribes in return for government services. During these years, China's enormous class of peasant farmers found it more and more difficult to hold their small farms and to support themselves and their families. Unrest spread throughout many parts of China. Disastrous floods and famine in various parts of China made the situation worse, as did growing pressure by the Western powers to gain economic control in China.

In 1796 discontent over increased taxes and growing government inefficiency led to a peasant rebellion. Members of a Buddhist cult called the White Lotus Society led the revolt, which was called the **White Lotus Rebellion.** After a difficult struggle, the government restored order in the early 1800s. Although it survived the rebellion, the Qing dynasty was seriously weakened. In addition, the basic causes of civil discontent remained. Rebellions occurred frequently after about 1850. The Qing dynasty was clearly in decline.

✔ **READING CHECK: Problem Solving** How might the Qing dynasty have brought peace to China? by maintaining higher standards of government service

---

SECTION 1 REVIEW

1. **Define** and explain the significance:
   junks
   queue
   philology

2. **Identify** and explain the significance:
   Hsüan-yeh
   White Lotus Rebellion

3. **Comparing and Contrasting** Copy the graphic organizer below. Use it to describe what remained stable and what changed during the Ming and Qing dynasties.

   Ming and Qing Dynasties
   Stable   Changed

4. **Finding the Main Idea**
   a. What changes did the growth of cities bring to China?
   b. What attitudes might Chinese rulers have had toward foreigners during the period of the Ming and Qing dynasties?

5. **Writing and Critical Thinking**
   Supporting a Point of View Imagine that you are involved in a rebellion against the Qing dynasty. Write a pamphlet that explains why you oppose Qing rule.
   Consider:
   • the spread of government inefficiency
   • the growth of corruption among officials

Homework Practice Online
keyword: SP3 HP17

416 CHAPTER 17

OBJECTIVES

1 Characterize early contact between Portugal and China.

2 Explain why China and Great Britain went to war in the mid-1800s.

3 Describe how internal rebellions contributed to the decline of the Qing dynasty.

SECTION 2

China and Europeans

READ TO DISCOVER

❶ What characterized early contact between Portugal and China?

❷ Why did China and Great Britain go to war in the mid-1800s?

❸ How did internal rebellions contribute to the Qing dynasty's decline?

DEFINE

free trade
extraterritoriality
"unequal" treaties

IDENTIFY

Opium War
Treaty of Nanjing
Taiping Rebellion

WHY IT MATTERS TODAY

Free trade remains an important economic concept and practice in the world today. Use CNNfyi.com or other **current event** sources to learn more about free trade in the modern world economy. Record your findings in your journal.

CNNfyi.com

The Main Idea
Growing contact with Europeans weakened the Qing dynasty and gradually undermined China's sovereignty.

The Story Continues *For more than 300 years after the first European trading stations were opened in China, European merchants and diplomats confronted a culture that viewed outsiders as inferior barbarians. In the early 1790s, for example, a British ambassador to the imperial Qing court offered gifts to the emperor. In turn, the emperor stated to the ambassador that ". . . we possess all things. I set no value on [foreign-made] objects strange or ingenious, and have no use for your country's manufactures."*

The Portuguese

In about 1514 Portuguese ships reached the southeastern coast of China. Over time the Portuguese were able to build trade ties with China. Finally, in 1557, the Chinese allowed the Portuguese to establish a trading station at Macao.

Portugal's influence, however, was not limited to trade. Jesuit missionaries also arrived on Portuguese ships. They used their knowledge of astronomy to gain admission to the emperor's inner circle. The emperor, who oversaw the prediction of eclipses and the timing of the seasons, appreciated the Jesuits' help in revising the Chinese calendar. He appointed Jesuit missionaries to official positions in his palace. He also gave them the opportunity to convert a number of high-ranking Chinese officials to Christianity. Gradually the Jesuits gained great power—economic and political, as well as spiritual—within the imperial court. Some even served as trusted advisers to the throne, quietly helping to shape imperial policies.

The Jesuits' power aroused jealousy and concern among some Chinese leaders. As a result, Qing rulers became suspicious of Christians and began to turn against them. The emperors realized that Chinese Catholics were expected to promise faith and allegiance to the pope. The Qing rulers feared that this would undermine the people's loyalty to the imperial throne and might bring about rebellion and overthrow. The emperors denounced Christianity as anti-Confucian, and the number of converts dwindled. China also deported European missionaries to Macao for a time.

✔ **READING CHECK: Summarizing** What was the initial Chinese attitude toward the Jesuits, and why did it change over time? initially positive, appreciative of their knowledge; later became suspicious, fearful of Jesuits' intentions

INTERPRETING THE VISUAL RECORD

Jesuits in China This early map of Nanjing, China, indicates the location of the Jesuit missions there. *Who do you think produced this map—European or Chinese mapmakers? Why?*

SECTION 2 RESOURCES

REPRODUCIBLE RESOURCES

▶ Guided Reading Strategy 17.2

▶ Graphic Organizer Activity 17: Asia and the West

TECHNOLOGY RESOURCES

▶ One-Stop Planner 17.2

▶ Religions of the World Video Series: Christianity

▶ Homework Practice Online

REINFORCEMENT, REVIEW, AND ASSESSMENT

▶ Section 2 Review, p. 421

▶ Daily Quiz 17.2

▶ Main Idea Activity 17.2

▶ English Audio Summary 17.2

▶ Spanish Audio Summary 17.2

VISUAL RECORD ANSWER

Europeans—the emphasis on Jesuit missions, the European spellings, and the overall style

ASIA IN TRANSITION **417**

TEACH OBJECTIVE 1

![clock icon] **ALL LEVELS:** Have students write essays summarizing the establishment of Portuguese trade in China and events that followed. (*Students' essays should mention the trading station at Macao established in 1557, the presence of Jesuit missionaries on Portuguese ships, the ways Jesuits gained power in the imperial court, and that Qing leaders came to fear the Jesuits' power.*) Then ask students to share and discuss their essays. **ENGLISH LANGUAGE LEARNERS**

TEACH OBJECTIVE 2

LEVEL 1: Copy the following graphic organizer on the chalkboard, omitting the italicized answers. Have students indicate above the arrows products traded between the countries. Use completed diagrams to discuss the trade imbalance between China and Great Britain. **ENGLISH LANGUAGE LEARNERS, COOPERATIVE LEARNING**

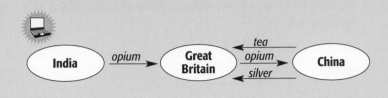

Culture

Deterioration of relations between Rome and Beijing resulted from a disagreement that developed among rival Catholic missionaries in the late 1600s over whether Chinese Christians should be allowed to continue their practice of honoring Confucius and their own ancestors. The Jesuits, who ministered mainly to the sophisticated upper classes, said yes on the grounds that such rites were not religious in nature. The Dominicans and Franciscans, who worked among the poorer and more superstitious people, strongly disagreed and appealed to the pope for a ruling in the matter. In 1704 the Vatican ruled in their favor, much to the displeasure of the emperor, who had backed the Jesuits in the dispute. When the Vatican tried to enforce its decision, relations between the missionaries and the Qing quickly deteriorated.

Critical Thinking

Ask students how a different ruling might have changed the course of relations between the Qing dynasty and Western nations.

ANSWER: Answers will vary but should show understanding that tolerance of long-standing Chinese cultural traditions on the part of the missionaries might have led to better relations.

The British were not the only admirers of Chinese tea, as the German advertisement at the top shows. Another Chinese product prized by Europeans was porcelain, like the decorative plate below it.

Analyzing Primary Sources

Identifying a Point of View
What argument did Lin make to try to persuade Britain to stop importing opium into China? asked Queen Victoria to do for China what she would want done for Britain

The British

During the late 1600s the British established a trading post at Guangzhou. By the early 1700s British ships regularly visited the port. The British came to China to buy silk and tea, which the Dutch had introduced to Europe in the 1600s. Great Britain had become a land of tea drinkers who regarded Chinese tea as the best in the world.

The British East India Company monopolized the new trade in Chinese teas. To get adequate supplies of tea, the company agreed to Chinese restrictions. Company ships could dock only at Guangzhou, and company representatives were required to stay in Guangzhou, where they lived in a special foreign settlement outside the city walls. Chinese regulations, moreover, demanded that the British trade only with a small number of officially approved Chinese merchants.

For a time, the Chinese policy worked. Contact between the British and Chinese people was kept to a minimum. In the late 1700s, however, two new developments—new ideas about trade and the sale of opium—damaged relations between the two nations.

Free trade ideas. The concept of **free trade** had developed in the West as a reaction to mercantilism. Supporters of free trade argued that governments should not restrict or interfere with international trade. British traders who did not work for the British East India Company resented the company's monopoly on the tea trade.

The British government became involved in the free trade debate. In part it did so because it hoped to gain additional overseas markets for British goods. In 1793 and again in 1816, British officials asked the Chinese government to open several more ports to British ships. Their efforts failed. In 1833 Great Britain abolished the British East India Company's monopoly on trade with China. Within a year the once-powerful company was little more than a managing agency for the British government in India.

The opium trade. The second development that came between the two countries involved the expansion of the tea trade. The British East India Company had paid for its tea purchases with cotton from India. There was a limit to Chinese demand for cotton, yet the British demand for tea kept growing. The company had to find a new product to exchange for tea. The product it chose was an addictive drug, opium.

From the late 1700s onward, British India produced opium and exported it to China. Opium addiction spread among the Chinese people. The Chinese government became alarmed, especially since China's silver supply was being used to pay for the opium. During these years, a huge trade imbalance grew, with far more silver flowing out of China than was being brought in. Chinese officials, fearing that China's economy was being undermined by the British, demanded that opium sales stop and that all opium cargoes be turned over to them. One Chinese official even pleaded with Queen Victoria of England to stop the opium trade.

 "Let us suppose that foreigners came from another country, and brought opium into England, and seduced the people of your country to smoke it. Would not you . . . look upon such a procedure with anger . . . ? Now we have always heard that your Highness possesses a most kind and benevolent [good] heart. Surely then you are incapable of doing or causing to be done unto another that which you would not wish another to do to you."

Lin Tse-hsü, from *Commissioner Lin and the Opium War*

TEACH OBJECTIVE 3

LEVEL 3: Have students imagine they are participants in the Taiping Rebellion. As a class, have them discuss the problems they see in Chinese society under the Qing dynasty and possible courses of action to take. On the board, list the problems and courses of action that are discussed. Then have the class vote on the best course of action to take. **COOPERATIVE LEARNING**

HOMEWORK Have students write three short editorial articles about the advantages or disadvantages of opening China to Western trade. One editorial should be from a perspective of a Western government, another from the Qing government's viewpoint, and the third from the point of view of a Chinese merchant. Select students to share their editorials with the class.

The Opium War. The British government did not respond to China's demands. When the Chinese tried to forcibly stop the opium trade, war broke out. The conflict between China and Britain, known as the **Opium War,** lasted from 1839 to 1842. Chinese army and naval forces were no match for the better-armed and better-trained British. A small British naval force that included iron-hulled steamships easily defeated Chinese forces as it sailed up the coast from Guangzhou. In 1842 the British gained control of the region near Nanjing. At that point, Qing officials agreed to negotiate on British terms.

Under the terms of the 1842 **Treaty of Nanjing,** China gave the island of Hong Kong to the British. It also opened five ports to British trade. British goods entering China through these ports were subject to a fixed, low tariff. In addition, British subjects in the ports would be governed by British, not Chinese, laws and would be tried in British courts. This requirement that foreigners must follow the laws of their home country instead of the laws of the country in which they live is called **extraterritoriality.**

More concessions. Great Britain did not keep its trade monopoly in China for long. Other Western powers, including France and the United States, also demanded trade treaties with China. Because the Chinese signed the treaties under the pressure of defeat and fear of further invasion, they called them **"unequal" treaties.** Most of the benefits of these treaties went to foreign powers. The Chinese gained little from them.

In 1856 China again went to war with Great Britain over a trade dispute. British forces, with French aid, again defeated the Chinese. The Chinese were forced to sign another "unequal" treaty. This treaty opened additional ports on the coast and along the Yangtze River. The Chinese had to allow the British to open an embassy in Beijing. Great Britain also took out a long-term lease on a small section of the Chinese mainland located opposite of Hong Kong. Finally the Chinese government had to agree to protect Christian missionaries and their converts in China.

Other foreign powers followed Britain and opened their own embassies in Beijing. In separate treaties, Russia also gained trade privileges and extraterritoriality. It received land bordering the Sea of Japan, or East Sea. The Russians established the port of Vladivostok in the southern part of this territory.

✔ **READING CHECK: Drawing Inferences** What was the British attitude toward the Chinese people and Chinese values? viewed Chinese interests, values as subordinate to British needs

Global Relations

Western trade with China from 1760 to 1842 was considered by the Chinese to be a gracious grant by the Son of Heaven to barbarians from distant lands. However, the Chinese government would not directly involve itself in dealings with Western traders. Instead, this task was assigned to special Chinese merchants known as the *Cohong*. Foreigners were allowed to live in specified areas in the port of Canton only while engaged in trade, were not allowed the company of their wives, and were discouraged from learning Chinese. Foreign merchants could only communicate with government officials through *Cohong* intermediaries. Western traders endured these cumbersome regulations and restrictions. The end of the *Cohong* system was a major British goal in negotiating the Treaty of Nanjing.

Critical Thinking

Why did Western traders resent the Chinese trade regulations?

ANSWER: To the Westerners, the system seemed needlessly complicated and unwelcoming.

VISUAL RECORD ANSWER

British naval superiority over the Chinese

Reproducible Resources

PS   Readings in World History 69: The Treaty of Nanjing, 1842

INTERPRETING THE VISUAL RECORD

The Opium War This painting from Britain's National Maritime Museum illustrates the British merchant steamer *Nemesis* attacking and destroying Chinese junks at Chuenpez, Canton. *What do you think viewers in the 1800s were supposed to learn from examining this image?*

The Chinese island of Hong Kong was ceded to Great Britain after the first Opium War in 1842. Hong Kong and the peninsula of Kowloon were leased to Great Britain for 99 years. The lease expired in 1997, and the area reverted to Chinese control. Have students research the history and development of this economic powerhouse.

CLOSE

Ask students to summarize ways that contact with Europeans affected China. Then have them debate whether China should have remained isolated from Europeans.

The Taiping rebel force at its greatest consisted of about one million people. They captured the city of Nanjing in 1853 and made it the capital of their kingdom. They were not driven out of Nanjing until 1864.

SKILLS PRACTICE ANSWERS

1. Reports will vary but should include a bibliography, the reasons for choosing the Web sites used, and a research outline.

2. Charts or tables will vary.

Technology Resources

CNN. Presents World Cultures: Yesterday and Today Segment 19: Hong Kong: Past and Present

---

SKILL-BUILDING STRATEGIES — Using the Internet in Historical Research

The History of China

There are a wealth of sources that can be used to learn about the history of China. Thanks to computers, that information is easier than ever to find. While the computer has revolutionized many aspects of society, it also has made a significant contribution to the field of historical research. The Internet, for example, contains numerous databases, or information organized in a way that allows you to retrieve it quickly and easily with a few strokes of the keyboard. While it is an extremely valuable research tool, not all of the information on the Internet is accurate. In using the Internet for historical research, it is important that you evaluate the quality of its content.

Navigate to a Web page that contains information that is relevant to your research topic or that can help you to find such information. Type the address of the Web page—its URL—here and press ENTER or RETURN to reach the page of your choice.

Carefully review the Web page to determine its content or whether it can direct you via links to other relevant pages. Click on links that may be of interest or that may help you to extend your research.

The home page of a Web site may contain useful navigational links that describe other pages within the site and that will take you to selected pages. Click on these links to move forward or backward through the site, to learn more about its content, and to evaluate the scope of its coverage. The page may also contain links to other related Web sites that may provide valuable information.

This Web page contains links and shortcuts to a broad number of other pages and activities on the Web. Explore these to determine if they will be useful as you conduct your research project. Such shortcuts may help you to sharpen the focus of your search.

HISTORY OF CHINA

Back Forward Reload Home Search Print Stop

Location: http://go.hrw.com/hrw.nd/gohrw_rls1/pKeywordResults?keyword=history%20of%20china

HOLT, RINEHART AND WINSTON   SOCIAL STUDIES

HISTORY OF CHINA

History

HOME I ENRICHMENT LINKS I MAPS AND CHARTS I HELP

The History of China

Use the links below to research the history of China.

Jesuit Translations
Browse some of the documents Jesuit missionaries translated at this Web site.

Chinese Cultural Studies
A brief political history of China.

China During the Ming and Qing Dynasties
A timeline of events from the fifteenth century to nineteenth century.

The Opium War
Learn more about the causes and outcomes of China's Opium War.

Women in Chinese History
A detailed bibliography of women in Chinese History

Return to Top I HISTORY OF CHINA
Copyright © by Holt, Rinehart and Winston. All rights reserved.
Terms of Use

Skills Reminder

To evaluate historical information on the Internet, determine if the site is published by a reputable authority or agency. In the case of individual Web publishers, try to find out if the author has credentials in the field or has a list of printed publications to his or her credit. Determine the objectivity of the site. Many Web sites are designed to sell products or to promote causes. The site's facts may be correct, but you should assess the author's point of view before deciding whether to use the information. Then evaluate the accuracy of the information. On the Internet, where anyone can be a publisher, there is a great deal of inaccurate information. Avoid sites with spelling or grammatical errors. Sites that attempt to dazzle the reader with eye-catching graphics and dramatic colors at the expense of content and substance should not be used. Also avoid sites filled with unsupported claims and undocumented arguments. Remember: a Web site's information should be as well documented as a printed page in a bound book.

Skills Practice

❶ Use the computer system at your school or library to locate one or more Web sites on one of the following:
  • the history of the Jesuits in China.
  • the geographic patterns and distribution of goods between the West and China during the 1700s and 1800s.
  • the Opium War.
  Use information from the Web sites to write a one-page report on the topic you chose. Include a bibliography of the Web sites you used and who produced them. Include also a brief explanation of why you chose these sites, including questions you asked and your research outline.

❷ Working with a partner, research the Internet and create a database in the form of a chart or table about a topic in this chapter. If you have it available, use a database management system (DBMS) to add, delete, change, or update information on the chart or table.

REVIEW

Have students complete the Section 2 Review on p. 421.

ASSESS

Have students complete Daily Quiz 17.2. As Alternative Assessment, you may want to use the graphic organizer exercise in this section's lessons.

RETEACH

Have students complete Main Idea Activity for English Language Learners and Special-Needs Students 17.2. Then have them list the steps leading to the decline of the Qing dynasty. **ENGLISH LANGUAGE LEARNERS**

EXTEND

Assign students specific time periods within the Ming or Qing dynasties. Have students research and record events in China above the time line and important world events below the time line. **BLOCK SCHEDULING**

Rebellions

An event that occurred within China made the intrusion of the Western powers even easier. In the mid-1800s southern and central China were torn by a great rebellion. The leader of this revolt was Hong Xiuquan (hoohng shee·oo·choo·ahn), who had been influenced by Christian teachings. Saying that he was the younger brother of Jesus, Hong declared that his mission was to establish a new dynasty. It was to be called Taiping, meaning "Heavenly Kingdom of Great Peace." Hong's ideas attracted many followers.

The **Taiping Rebellion** lasted from 1850 to 1864. It caused terrible destruction in southern China and the Yangtze valley. Millions of people were killed. Cities and farmlands were destroyed. To make matters more difficult for Qing rulers, Muslims in central and western China launched their own rebellions at the same time. After a long struggle, the Qing finally put down these rebellions in the late 1870s.

The Taiping Rebellion and the other revolts seriously weakened both the Qing dynasty and the nation as a whole. At the same time, foreign powers in China, seeking to take advantage of the nation's internal turmoil, demanded further concessions and the opening of more treaty ports. Continuing foreign interference in China's political and economic affairs was a serious problem for the nation and its Qing rulers. It weakened China's sovereignty and undermined the emperor's prestige. It also reduced the country's control over its own economy. Increasingly, the independence of China and its rulers was viewed by the Western powers as a sham.

In this painting, soldiers in the Taiping Rebellion attack a Chinese town.

✔ **READING CHECK: Analyzing Information** What role did religion play in rebellions against the Qing?
Rebellions were motivated, in part, by Christian and Muslim teachings

---

SECTION 2 REVIEW

1. **Define** and explain the significance:
   free trade
   extraterritoriality
   "unequal" treaties

2. **Identify** and explain the significance:
   Opium War
   Treaty of Nanjing
   Taiping Rebellion

3. **Sequencing** Copy the flowchart below. Use it to sequence the events that occurred between China and Britain between the 1600s and late 1800s. You may want to add more boxes.

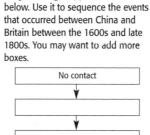

No contact

↓

↓

↓

Trade with British in control

4. **Finding the Main Idea**
   a. In what two ways did the Portuguese influence the Chinese?
   b. In what ways did unsuccessful rebellions succeed in weakening China?
   c. Why was the collection of China's customs duties by foreigners seen as a blow to Chinese sovereignty?

5. **Writing and Critical Thinking**
   Identifying Cause and Effect Imagine that you are a Chinese person who has witnessed the Opium War. Write a letter to a friend that explains the causes of the war and its effect on the Chinese.
   Consider:
   • the conflicts over free trade and the importation of opium
   • the terms of the "unequal" treaty

Homework Practice Online
keyword: SP3 HP17

SECTION 2 REVIEW ANSWERS

❶ **Define**
• free trade, p. 418
• extraterritoriality, p. 419
• "unequal" treaties, p. 419

❷ **Identify**
• Opium War, p. 419
• Treaty of Nanjing, p. 419
• Taiping Rebellion, p. 421

❸ no contact, limited contact, conflict, Opium War, Treaty of Nanjing, trade with British in control

❹ a. opened up trade, introduced Christianity

b. They caused destruction and death; they forced the government to spend money and time in quelling them; they distracted the government from tending to other matters.

c. It reduced China's control over its own economy.

❺ Answers will vary but should include mention of British resentment of Chinese trade restrictions, Chinese anger at the opium trade, and the terms of the Treaty of Nanjing.

SECTION 3

OBJECTIVES

1 **Explain how the Tokugawa shogunate came to power.**

2 **Discuss why Japan's rulers sought to isolate their nation from foreign influence.**

3 **Identify characteristics of society and culture under the Tokugawa shogunate.**

4 **Describe how Japanese isolation was brought to an end.**

LET'S GET STARTED!

As students enter the classroom, ask them to write a brief paragraph telling what they know about the nation of Japan. Have students share their knowledge of Japan in a class discussion as you write key facts on the chalkboard. Tell students that in Section 3 they will learn about the history of Japan during the time of the Tokugawa shoguns.

SECTION 3 RESOURCES

REPRODUCIBLE RESOURCES

▶ Guided Reading Strategy 17.3

TECHNOLOGY RESOURCES

▶ One-Stop Planner 17.3
▶ Holt Researcher: World History: Oda Nobunaga
▶ Holt Researcher: World History: Toyotomi Hideyoshi
▶ Holt Researcher: World History: Tokugawa Ieyasu
▶ Homework Practice Online

REINFORCEMENT, REVIEW, AND ASSESSMENT

▶ Section 3 Review, p. 427
▶ Daily Quiz 17.3
▶ Main Idea Activity 17.3
▶ English Audio Summary 17.3
▶ Spanish Audio Summary 17.3

MAP ANSWER

good harbor, centrally located, little threat of attack from Asian mainland

---

SECTION 3

READ TO DISCOVER

1 How did the Tokugawa shogunate come to power?
2 Why did Japan's rulers seek to isolate their nation from foreign influence?
3 What were society and culture like under the Tokugawa shogunate?
4 How was Japanese isolation brought to an end?

DEFINE

consulates

IDENTIFY

Oda Nobunaga
Toyotomi Hideyoshi
Tokugawa Ieyasu
Matthew Perry
Treaty of Kanagawa

▶ WHY IT MATTERS TODAY

Japan has one of the world's leading economies today. Use **CNNfyi.com** or other **current event** sources to learn about the Japanese economy and international trade. Record your findings in your journal.

CNNfyi.com

The Tokugawa Shoguns in Japan

The Main Idea
Despite their desire for isolation, Japan's rulers were unable to prevent foreign contact and trade.

The Story Continues *China's culture influenced that of early Japan. Over time the Japanese became increasingly isolated, especially from the rising nations of the West. By the 1850s, however, many Japanese were calling for an end to isolationism. For example, philosopher Yoshida Shoin believed that Japan would advance only if it blended Eastern thought with Western technology. Shoin urged the Japanese people to take action if their leaders failed to, arguing that "if it is true loyalty and service you seek, then you must abandon this fief and plan a grassroots uprising."*

Founding the Tokugawa Shogunate

In 1467 rival branches of the Ashikaga family in Japan became involved in a dispute over the selection of the next shogun. This conflict marked the beginning of 100 years of bitter, widespread, and almost constant warfare in Japan. Sensing the weakness and deep divisions within the Ashikaga family, local daimyo fought for control of the country. In the late 1500s a series of three daimyo emerged victorious from this long and destructive struggle. These powerful daimyo established themselves as overlords of the other daimyo and built a centralized feudal system in Japan.

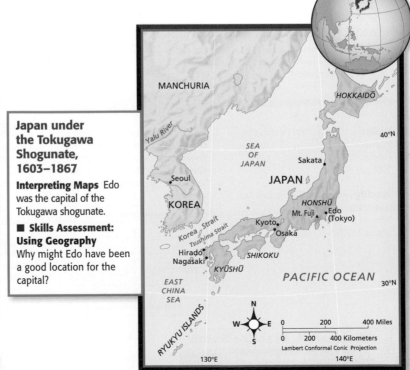

Japan under the Tokugawa Shogunate, 1603–1867

Interpreting Maps Edo was the capital of the Tokugawa shogunate.

■ **Skills Assessment: Using Geography** Why might Edo have been a good location for the capital?

422

422 CHAPTER 17

TEACH OBJECTIVE 1

ALL LEVELS: Pair students to develop a diagram of the power structure of Japan under the Tokugawa shoguns. Select pairs to copy their diagrams on the chalkboard and explain them to the class. Ask the class how the size of the Tokugawa landholdings increased the family's political power. *(Taxes from their lands would sustain a large army of samurai.)* Then have students make changes in the chalkboard diagrams to illustrate what could have happened if the Tokugawa shoguns had permitted daimyo alliances. *(Changes could create blocks of daimyo and their samurai that could have been used against the shogun.)* Ask how the Tokugawa discouraged any such opposition.

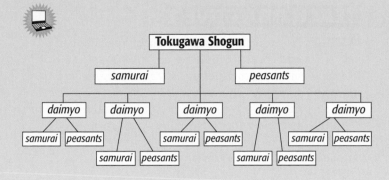

```
                    Tokugawa Shogun
              ┌───────────┴───────────┐
           samurai                 peasants
     ┌────────┼──────────┬──────────┼────────┐
  daimyo   daimyo     daimyo     daimyo    daimyo
  ┌──┴──┐  │    │    ┌──┴──┐   │    │    ┌──┴──┐
samurai peasants   samurai peasants    samurai peasants
        samurai peasants        samurai peasants
```

Oda Nobunaga. The first of these overlords, **Oda Nobunaga** (ohd·ah noh·boo·NAH·gah), began his rise to power as a minor daimyo. Through conquests and alliances, Nobunaga captured the city of Kyoto in 1568. He ended the Ashikaga shogunate in 1573 and then started to strengthen his power in central Japan. Before Nobunaga could defeat his rivals, however, one of his own vassals attacked him in 1582. Wounded, Nobunaga committed suicide.

Toyotomi Hideyoshi. The second of the overlords, **Toyotomi Hideyoshi** (toh·yoh·TOH·mee HEE·day·yoh·shee), had led Nobunaga's army. After Nobunaga's death, Hideyoshi succeeded him. During the 1580s Hideyoshi defeated several powerful daimyo in battle. He forced other daimyo to pledge their loyalty to him. Hideyoshi did not totally defeat other daimyo. Instead he weakened them by reducing the size of their territories so that they could not threaten him again. He also carried out a "sword hunt" to disarm the peasants. Thereafter peasants could no longer become warriors. Only men born into warrior families could become warriors.

In 1592 and again in 1597, Hideyoshi sent his army to invade Korea. He wanted to build an empire and give Japanese warriors the chance to fight. At first the Japanese invasion of Korea succeeded. As the battles continued, however, a Chinese army that was aiding the Koreans pushed Hideyoshi's warriors back to the coast. When Hideyoshi died in 1598, the Japanese left Korea and returned home.

Tokugawa Ieyasu. Hideyoshi's most powerful vassal, **Tokugawa Ieyasu** (toh·kuh·GAH·wah ee·YAH·soo) succeeded him as overlord. Ieyasu established his capital at Edo (AY·doh), the city that is now Tokyo. Other daimyo resisted Ieyasu, but he defeated them in 1600. In 1603 Ieyasu became shogun.

Tokugawa Ieyasu crushed his defeated rivals. He did allow some 250 to 260 daimyo to keep possession of their private lands. However, Ieyasu's actions clearly demonstrated that he was prepared to expand or reduce the size of their territories in the future. The Tokugawa family would keep the title of shogun for more than 250 years. They established a government known as the Tokugawa shogunate.

Tokugawa rule. The political system established by the Tokugawa shogunate was a cross between feudalism and a central monarchy. Within his domain, each daimyo governed as an almost absolute ruler. Local peasants paid taxes to support the daimyo and those who

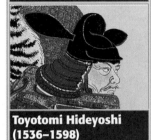

HISTORY MAKER

Toyotomi Hideyoshi (1536–1598)

Born to a peasant family and poorly educated, Toyotomi Hideyoshi worked hard to make up for his humble beginnings. He rose from warrior to one of the greatest generals in Oda Nobunaga's army. When he succeeded Nobunaga, Hideyoshi continued the unification of Japan. **How did Hideyoshi make up for his humble beginnings?**

Holt Researcher

go.hrw.com
KEYWORD: Holt Researcher
FreeFind: Oda Nobunaga
   Toyotomi Hideyoshi
   Tokugawa Ieyasu
After reading more about the overlords on the Holt Researcher, create a time line of the major events during their reigns.

That's Interesting!

Early Portuguese traders introduced playing cards to Japan in the late 1500s. Card playing quickly became popular throughout Japan. In response to this "barbarian" activity, a new daimyo warrior code was adopted that prohibited samurai from "gambling, cards, and other games of chance."

HISTORY MAKER ANSWER

He defeated other powerful daimyos in battle and forced them to pledge loyalty to him.

Reproducible Resources

SM Geography Activity 17: The Struggle for Korea

Reproducible Resources

PS Readings in World History 70: Yoshida Shoin: Philosopher of the Meiji Restoration

Reproducible Resources

E Creative Teaching Strategy 17: The Way of the Shogun

VISUAL RECORD ANSWER

He is wearing a sword.

INTERPRETING THE VISUAL RECORD

Preparing for war Japanese warriors regularly exercised and meditated to keep fit for battle. *What evidence suggests that at least one man who is meditating is a warrior?*

LEVEL 1: Ask students why a government might limit its people's trade and contact with other nations. *(Responses should include to maximize government's power and control, to protect the nation's domestic businesses, and to protect the nation's culture.)* List responses on the chalkboard as you discuss them. Tell students to refer to the chalkboard list as they study the foreign policies of Japan's Tokugawa shoguns.

ENGLISH LANGUAGE LEARNERS

Government

One of the consequences of Tokugawa Ieyasu's defeat of his rivals and confiscation of their lands was the creation of a large number of masterless samurai, called *ronin*. Some of these samurai became retainers of other daimyo, some moved into cities, and others became teachers, physicians, and Confucian scholars. However, it is estimated that during the first 50 years of the shogunate, as many as 200,000 impoverished and dissatisfied armed warriors roamed Japan. Finding a way to deal with this potentially disruptive force was a major problem for the early Tokugawa shoguns.

Critical Thinking

How might the Tokugawa shoguns have successfully solved the problem posed by the ronin?

ANSWER: The shoguns could have added ronin warriors to their own armies, encouraged ronin to follow new vocations, or disarmed the ronin by force.

Technology Resources

Religions of the World Video Series: Christianity

This mounted Japanese warrior and his horse display traditional weapons and military dress.

served him, such as the samurai. The Tokugawa family had its own private domain, which included roughly one fourth of the nation's resources. Thus the Tokugawa did not rule the entire country directly. Nor did they personally tax the entire population. In this way Japan remained politically and economically decentralized to some degree.

Because of their wealth and military power, however, the Tokugawa had considerable influence over the daimyo. Some historians believe that the Tokugawa shoguns prohibited the daimyo from making alliances with one another. Most daimyo had to spend every other year in Edo, the shogun's capital. When they returned to their own domains, the daimyo left their families in Edo as hostages. Maintaining two residences—one in Edo and one in the provinces—proved very expensive for the daimyo. Traveling to and from Edo in a grand procession also drained their financial resources. In addition, living in Edo transformed many daimyo from warriors to courtiers. In this manner the Tokugawa shoguns maintained control over the daimyo.

The Tokugawa shogunate shaped Japanese life in several ways. Its strong central government brought more than two centuries of stability to Japan. Tokugawa control of the daimyo helped to keep peace in the countryside. In addition, the Tokugawa set trade restrictions and limited contact with foreigners. By doing so, they achieved almost complete isolation from Europe by 1650. Their desire for isolation was in response to contact with foreigners that had occurred beginning in the 1500s.

✔ **READING CHECK: Sequencing** What events led to the establishment of the Tokugawa shogunate? century of warfare among competing daimyo, overthrow of Ashikaga shogun

Foreign Contact

Japanese soldiers and sailors had traveled overseas since the 1000s. In the early 1400s, during the Ashikaga shogunate, Japan's ships had sailed to China and Korea seeking trade. At times the Japanese acted as pirates, taking whatever they could from local peoples.

The Portuguese in Japan. In the mid-1500s the daimyo began to trade with the Portuguese, whose ships appeared in Japanese waters. Portuguese traders brought two items new to the Japanese: muskets and Christianity.

Apparently Oda Nobunaga had used troops armed with muskets in his battles against rival daimyo. However, some samurai did not approve of the musket. It violated the traditional samurai fighting ethic, which was based on skill. Anyone armed with a musket could overcome years of samurai training with a single shot.

In the wake of the Portuguese traders came Christian missionaries. Among the missionaries were the Jesuits, who achieved notable success during the Counter-Reformation in Europe. The Jesuits concentrated on converting the daimyo to Christianity. After a daimyo converted to Christianity, the Jesuits would seek converts in the daimyo's domain. It has been estimated that by the early 1600s the missionaries had converted as many as 300,000 Japanese to Christianity.

Closing the country. The Tokugawa shoguns concluded that Christianity was an undesirable threat to their rule. The shoguns saw Christianity as a force that might weaken their authority because it taught loyalty to a power other than the Tokugawa shogun. The shoguns also feared that Christianity would be a divisive belief in their tradition-based society. Early in the 1600s the shoguns acted on their concerns by forcing Portuguese traders and missionaries to leave the country.

LEVEL 2: Call on students to identify changes that the Tokugawa shoguns made in Japan and list responses on the chalkboard. *(expelled Portuguese, limited Dutch traders, banned shipbuilding and overseas travel, adopted Confucian ideal of social classes, educated warriors to be government officials, paid warriors' salaries, required each daimyo to live in his castle town)* Next, organize the class into small groups and assign each group one of the chalkboard changes. Have each group discuss how its assigned change would help bring stability to Japan and report its conclusions to the class. Then ask the class why cities and the arts would be more likely to grow in a stable society. *(Lack of unrest would promote commerce and culture.)* **COOPERATIVE LEARNING**

HOMEWORK Have students write an essay expressing whether they would like to live in a society where one's status is determined by heredity. Tell students to consider the advantages and disadvantages of Japan's social system under the Tokugawa shoguns. Remind students to use standard grammar, spelling, sentence structure, and punctuation.

By this time the Portuguese faced stiff competition in East Asia from Dutch traders. The Dutch had accepted a strictly controlled trading relationship with the Tokugawa shogunate. The shoguns themselves controlled the small amount of trade Japan conducted with the Dutch. In addition, a few Dutch merchants were allowed to live near Nagasaki. These Dutch merchants were the only Europeans allowed to trade in Japan after the 1630s.

The Tokugawa enforced other strict rules in order to keep Japan isolated from foreign influences. They banned most overseas trade. The Japanese people were prohibited from traveling abroad. Like China, Japan concentrated on domestic affairs and tried to ignore the outside world. Because Japan is an island nation, and because its leaders could take active steps to secure its coasts, the country was able to achieve a high degree of isolation.

✔ **READING CHECK: Decision Making** Why did the Tokugawa shogunate want to keep Japan isolated? saw Christianity and Western technology as threats to Tokugawa rule and to Japanese traditions, values

Life in Tokugawa Japan

The Tokugawa shoguns, like most emperors in neighboring China, did not promote change. The concept of stability was more important to the Japanese. The Confucian ideas, which the Japanese borrowed from the Chinese, supported this ideal.

Social classes. The Tokugawa shoguns adopted—with some changes—the Confucian ideal of social classes. The warrior class in Japan filled roughly the same role as the scholar-gentry in China. Therefore the samurai stood at the top of the Japanese social order. Peasants, artisans, and merchants followed in descending order of importance.

A person's social class was determined by birth. Sons followed the occupations of their fathers. For example, a person born into an artisan family in Osaka remained a member of the artisan class in Osaka for life.

The Tokugawa shoguns encouraged members of the samurai to study the Confucian classics. The shoguns established schools in the various domains to prepare young samurai for their peacetime roles as government officials. The shoguns, however, did not adopt the Chinese civil service examination system. In Japan, samurai became officials by heredity alone. Males born into low-ranking samurai families worked as low-ranking officials in their domain. Those born into high-ranking families served as high-ranking officials.

Kabuki theater is a purely Japanese art form. Often much interaction between actors and spectators takes place.

Theater: Kabuki
Kabuki, the most popular form of Japanese theater, began during the Tokugawa period. Based on street dances, Kabuki grew into a colorful art form with detailed costumes and makeup. The makeup is designed to show a character's emotions, such as anger or bravery. A Kabuki play includes song and dance. Older Kabuki plays had little speaking, but more modern ones have more. Actors use dramatic gestures to tell the story.

In 1629 women were banned from performing Kabuki. Since then, men and boys have played both male and female roles. Kabuki actors usually spend years learning the Kabuki style before being allowed to perform.

Understanding the Arts

Why do you think the Tokugawa might have banned women from Kabuki?

Interdisciplinary Connection

LANGUAGE ARTS. Tell students to imagine that they are Portuguese traders in Japan. Have them write letters home describing their life in Japan and what they have observed about its government and society.

CONNECTING TO ART ANSWER
Tokugawa codes of social conduct limited the role of women in society. Performing on stage was not considered an appropriate activity for women.

🖥 **internet connect**

TOPIC: Japanese Theater
GO TO: go.hrw.com
KEYWORD: SP3 WH17

Have students access the Internet through the HRW Go site to gather examples of Kabuki theater or to learn about *Bunraku,* Japanese puppet theater, which also flowered during the Tokugawa period. Have students present illustrated reports to the class.

Technology Resources
Regions of the World Music Audio CD Program 20: Japan and the Koreas: Music of the One-String Ichigenkin

LEVEL 3: Invite the class to imagine that they are daimyo in the shogun's court at Edo. Assume the role of the shogun and ask students for their advice as daimyo on how to respond to Perry's demand for U.S. trading privileges in Japan. Have the daimyo debate whether opening trade with the United States is in Japan's best interests. Have the daimyo propose courses of action that might satisfy the United States but still preserve Japan's culture and isolation. (*offer only emergency shelter, rest stop, or better treatment of shipwrecked sailors; limit the ports where trade can occur*) Then ask them to weigh all this information and suggest a response to Perry. Conclude the activity by comparing the class's proposed response to the course the shogun actually took.
BLOCK SCHEDULING

CLOSE

Have interested students locate and use biographies to find out more about Matthew Perry or one of the other people mentioned in the section. Have them report their findings to the class.

Government

The dominance of the warrior class during the Tokugawa period hurt Japan in a number of ways. Edict and Confucian prejudice forbid samurai from engaging in trade. This left them unprepared to deal with Japan's spreading commercial economy. The samurai refused to tax merchants. By the 1700s, however, government income rarely kept up with expenses. Deficits, forced loans, and currency devaluation resulted. Ironically, although they refused to tax merchants, the Tokugawa shoguns came to rely heavily on them for loans and provisions to keep their government afloat.

Critical Thinking

How did the Tokugawa refusal to tax merchants affect the development of Japanese society?

ANSWER: Growing debt may have influenced the decision to open Japan to foreign trade.

VISUAL RECORD ANSWER

The instruments and music played are probably traditional. The musicians are women; they are probably affluent; they are performing outdoors; they are reading words and/or musical notation.

The shoguns usually required a samurai to live in the castle town of his daimyo. Instead of living on income from country estates, samurai now received salaries. This policy gave the shoguns greater control over the samurai, who could not develop wealth independently. It also eliminated any opportunity for the samurai to revolt against their lords.

Change and culture. As in China, the rulers of Japan could not prevent economic, political, and social change within their country. Much of the change that took place in Japan resembled that which occurred in China. Internal trade expanded. Various regions of the country began to specialize in certain crops and handicrafts. Cities grew in size. Many artisans and merchants became well-off.

These changes did not please everyone. One writer claimed that corruption had taken root in the government and that the common people were not prospering.

Analyzing Primary Sources

Identifying a Point of View Why did Yamagata Daini criticize merchants and trading? felt that merchants took advantage of farmers, that trade drew people away from the land

INTERPRETING THE VISUAL RECORD

Popular music This musical trio from the Tokugawa period includes a singer, a lute player, and a flutist. *What information can be gathered about the music and musicians in this image?*

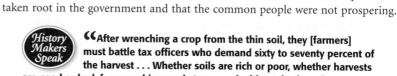

> **History Makers Speak** "After wrenching a crop from the thin soil, they [farmers] must battle tax officers who demand sixty to seventy percent of the harvest . . . Whether soils are rich or poor, whether harvests are good or bad, farmers shiver and starve; and, ultimately, they give up farming. . . . Tillers become scarce and fields turn to wasteland . . . Those good at selling grow rich; those good at farming go hungry."

Yamagata Daini, from *A History of Japan*

There were some positive changes in Japanese life, however. As in both Europe and China, urban growth and increased wealth led to the rise of a popular culture. By the early 1700s new forms of art, literature, and theater had taken root. Many of these new forms appealed to the tastes of ordinary city residents.

✔ **READING CHECK: Categorizing** How would you classify the view of the Tokugawa shoguns and the Chinese emperors toward change—as supportive of or as resistant to change? Both were resistant to change.

The End of Japan's Isolation

As part of the Tokugawa plan to keep Japan isolated, the government refused to give shelter to ships from other nations during storms. This policy angered many Westerners. Western nations that sought commercial expansion wanted Japan to follow China's lead and end its isolation.

In 1853 President Millard Fillmore of the United States sent Commodore **Matthew Perry** and a powerful naval force to Japan. Perry had orders to negotiate a treaty that would guarantee the safety of U.S. sailors and open Japanese ports to American trade. Perry's squadron of heavily armed, steam-powered warships sailed into Tokyo Bay on July 8, 1853. In a show of force and dignity, Perry ceremoniously presented a letter from President Fillmore that urged the Japanese to accept the American treaty. Perry promised to return for an answer the following year.

REVIEW

Have students complete the Section 3 Review on p. 427.

ASSESS

Have students complete Daily Quiz 17.3. As Alternative Assessment, have students complete the diagram exercise in this section's lessons.

RETEACH

Have students complete Main Idea Activity for English Language Learners and Special-Needs Students 17.3. Have students discuss whether the Tokugawa shoguns' foreign policies benefited the Japanese people. **ENGLISH LANGUAGE LEARNERS, COOPERATIVE LEARNING**

EXTEND

Have students create a letter to the editor or a political cartoon about Commodore Perry's arrival in Japan. Tell students that the letter or cartoon can express the point of view of their choice, such as an American trader. **BLOCK SCHEDULING**

The American visit sparked controversy within Japan. Some powerful leaders favored military resistance and continued isolation. Others, however, believed that Japan could not hold out against the United States. The shogun, worried about the threat of a naval attack by the Americans, reluctantly agreed to negotiate when Perry returned in 1854.

The negotiations between the shogun and Perry led to the **Treaty of Kanagawa** (kah·NAH·gah·wah) in 1854. Under the treaty the Japanese opened two ports to let Americans obtain fuel, shelter, and supplies. The opening of the ports permitted trade to begin between the two nations. Within two years, Japan signed similar treaties with Great Britain, the Netherlands, and Russia. As part of the agreements, foreign nations were allowed to establish **consulates**—diplomatic offices headed by consuls.

In 1858 the governments of Japan and the United States signed a new treaty. The two countries agreed to exchange ministers. In addition, the treaty allowed foreign residence in Edo and Osaka, extraterritorial privileges, and international trade. The Japanese also opened more treaty ports to the United States. Similar agreements between Japan and other nations soon followed.

Japanese opponents of the Tokugawa shogunate criticized the government for signing treaties with foreign powers. To many samurai, the government's inability to resist Western demands cast doubt on its right to rule Japan. Many Japanese began to complain about the weakness of the government abroad and its strict rule at home. In the 1860s civil war broke out in Japan. Supporters of the Tokugawa shogunate battled its opponents. Calling for major reforms, the anti-Tokugawa forces overthrew the shogunate in 1867. They restored the power of the emperor, moving Japan toward a more centralized government. The new emperor, a teenager, named his reign Meiji, meaning "Enlightened Rule."

✔ **READING CHECK: Problem Solving** Could the Tokugawa have resisted Western demands and retained control of Japan? Students should note that Western technology and military power might have been used to overthrow the Tokugawa.

In this woodblock print, a Japanese artist recorded Commodore Perry's arrival in Edo Bay in 1853.

SECTION 3 REVIEW

1. **Define** and explain the significance:
   consulates

2. **Identify** and explain the significance:
   Oda Nobunaga
   Toyotomi Hideyoshi
   Tokugawa Ieyasu
   Matthew Perry
   Treaty of Kanagawa

3. **Categorizing** Copy the diagram. Use it to show the levels of government and classes in Japan during the era of Tokugawa rule.

4. **Finding the Main Idea**
   a. Was the policy of isolation good for Japan and the Japanese people? Why or why not?
   b. What changes in Japanese society occurred under the Tokugawa shogunate?

5. **Writing and Critical Thinking**
   Decision Making Imagine that you are the shogun considering Matthew Perry's request for a treaty. Should you support such a treaty?
   Consider:
   • why the Americans wanted a treaty
   • how a treaty might benefit Japan
   • how a treaty might harm Japan
   • what actions a refusal might bring

go.hrw.com Homework Practice Online
keyword: SP3 HP17

SECTION 3 REVIEW ANSWERS

❶ **Define**
• consulates, p. 427

❷ **Identify**
• Oda Nobunaga, p. 423
• Toyotomi Hideyoshi, p. 423
• Tokugawa Ieyasu, p. 423
• Matthew Perry, p. 426
• Treaty of Kanagawa, p. 427

❸ From top: shogun, daimyo, samurai, peasant, artisan, merchant

❹ **a.** Answers will vary but should reflect understanding that, as in China, isolationist policies had both positive and negative effects.

b. Internal trade expanded, cities grew, regions specialized in certain crops and crafts, artisans and merchants prospered, popular culture developed.

❺ Answers will vary. Students should recognize that opening trade might lead to economic growth but would also allow unwanted cultural changes. Students should also understand that Japanese refusal to sign the treaty would probably lead to a powerful U.S. military response.

ASIA IN TRANSITION **427**

REVIEW AND ASSESSMENT RESOURCES

REPRODUCIBLE RESOURCES
▸ Vocabulary Activity 17

TECHNOLOGY RESOURCES
▸ Chapter 17 Test Generator (on the One-Stop Planner)
▸ Global Skill Builder CD–ROM
▸ HRW Web Site

REINFORCEMENT, REVIEW, and ASSESSMENT
▸ Chapter 17 Review, pp. 428–429
▸ Chapter 17 Tutorial for Students, Parents, Mentors, and Peers
▸ Chapter 17 Test (Form A or B)
▸ Alternative Assessment Handbook
▸ Chapter 17 Test for English Language Learners and Special-Needs Students

REVIEW
Have students complete the Chapter 17 Review on pages 428–429.

ASSESS
Use one of the chapter tests to assess students' understanding of the content. For Alternative Assessment, see the Portfolio Activities and Alternative Assessment Handbook.

CHAPTER 17 REVIEW ANSWERS

Understanding Main Ideas
1. to concentrate resources on defending borders

2. The economy grew.

3. created unrest that weakened the dynasty

4. China resented importation of opium by Great Britain.

5. China defeated, forced to allow more foreign trade

6. China had to open additional ports, allow British embassy, lease Hong Kong to Great Britain, protect Christians.

7. prohibited daimyo alliances, forced all daimyo to spend every other year at Edo, and kept daimyo family members as hostages

8. thought Christianity might weaken their authority

9. under threat of military response if they did not

Reviewing Themes
1. Western nations insisted on establishing open trade.

2. limited and regulated trade until China's defeat in the Opium Wars

3. internal rebellion and weakening of the dynasty

428

CHAPTER 17 Review

Creating a Time Line
Copy the time line below on a sheet of paper. Complete the time line by filling in the events, individuals, and dates from the chapter that you think were significant. Pick three events and explain why you think they were significant.

1400   1500   1600

Writing a Summary
Using standard grammar, spelling, sentence structure, and punctuation, write an overview of the events in the chapter.

Identifying People and Ideas
Identify the following terms or individuals and explain their significance:
1. Hsüan-yeh
2. free trade
3. Treaty of Nanjing
4. extraterritoriality
5. "unequal" treaties
6. Taiping Rebellion
7. Tokugawa Ieyasu
8. Matthew Perry
9. Treaty of Kanagawa
10. consulates

Understanding Main Ideas

Section 1 (pp. 412–416)
The Ming and Qing Dynasties
1. Why did the Chinese abandon overseas exploration?
2. How did the Chinese economy change under the Ming and Qing emperors?
3. How did government corruption affect the Qing dynasty?

Section 2 (pp. 417–421)
China and Europeans
4. Why did the Chinese resist free trade with Great Britain?
5. What were the effects of the Opium War on China?
6. What generally were the terms of the "unequal" treaties?

Section 3 (pp. 422–427)
The Tokugawa Shoguns in Japan
7. How did the Tokugawa shogunate weaken daimyo power?
8. Why did the Japanese rulers see the Jesuits as a threat?
9. Why did Japan open ports to American ships?

Reviewing Themes
1. **Global Relations** Why did Chinese and Japanese efforts to maintain isolation fail in the 1800s?
2. **Economics** How did attitudes about foreigners affect trade in China?
3. **Government** What was the result of the Qing dynasty's inability to provide services and loss of control over bureaucratic corruption?

Thinking Critically
1. **Identifying Cause and Effect** How did urban growth promote economic change in Asia?
2. **Comparing** Why did the Qing dynasty and the Tokugawa shogunate both collapse?
3. **Identifying Bias** Did British treatment of the Chinese reflect a concern for foreign peoples? Explain.
4. **Evaluating** What were the main difficulties that Asian societies faced during this period in history?
5. **Making Predictions** What might have happened if the Qing dynasty had improved tax reform and increased government services?

Writing About History
Comparing Write a report comparing China under the Qing dynasty with Japan under the Tokugawa shogunate. Use the chart below to organize your thoughts before writing.

Factors	China	Japan
Economy		
Government rule		
Popular culture		
Relations with foreign powers		

CLOSE

Have interested students research the presence and influence of American culture in China and Japan today. Have them report their findings to the class.
BLOCK SCHEDULING

RETEACH

Organize students into three groups, with each group responsible for one of the chapter's sections. Have members of each group create maps or diagrams illustrating the main events and including any relevant dates and captions. Have each group present its work to the class. **ENGLISH LANGUAGE LEARNERS, COOPERATIVE LEARNING**

Portfolio Extensions

Link to TODAY

1. Ask students to imagine that they are living during the early days of the Ming dynasty. Have them write editorials expressing the opinion that more resources should be devoted to seagoing exploration and foreign trade.
BLOCK SCHEDULING

2. Organize the class into small groups. Ask each group to select one aspect of Chinese government or culture during the Ming and Qing dynasties to define and describe.
BLOCK SCHEDULING

3. Have students create posters or collages in which they illustrate historical highlights of the Ming and Qing dynasties.
BLOCK SCHEDULING

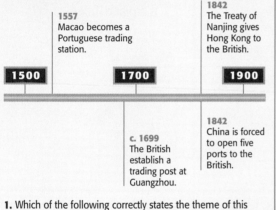

Building Social Studies Skills

Interpreting a Time Line
Study the time line below. Then answer the questions that follow.

1557
Macao becomes a Portuguese trading station.

1842
The Treaty of Nanjing gives Hong Kong to the British.

1500 **1700** **1900**

c. 1699
The British establish a trading post at Guangzhou.

1842
China is forced to open five ports to the British.

1. Which of the following correctly states the theme of this time line?
 a. The British and Portuguese traded with China for hundreds of years.
 b. European pressure slowly changed China's trade policies.
 c. Chinese ports were closed to the British until 1842.
 d. European pressure quickly changed China's trade policies.

2. What was the reason for the Treaty of Nanjing and what effect did it have on China? Support your answer with specific examples.

Identifying Bias
Read the following quote by Francis Xavier, a Jesuit missionary who went to Japan in 1549. Then answer the questions.

> "The people whom we have met so far are the best who have as yet been discovered, and it seems to me that we shall never find among heathens another race to equal the Japanese. They are a people of very good manners, good in general, and not malicious [mean]; they are men of honor to a marvel, and prize honor above all else in the world. . . . They have one quality which I cannot recall in any people of Christendom; this is that [they] . . . render as much honor to a poor gentleman as if he were passing rich."

3. Which of the following best describes how the author's experience influenced his viewpoint?
 a. Based on his experience, he was amazed the Japanese were so honorable.
 b. His experiences led him to believe manners were important.
 c. Since he was a poor missionary, he was surprised to be treated as if he were rich.
 d. He was surprised the Japanese were good people, because he had heard they were warriors.

4. How did the Tokugawa shoguns react to the Jesuit missionaries? Give specific examples.

Alternative Assessment

Building Your Portfolio
Link to TODAY

Economics

Opening new trade markets among nations is as topical an issue today as it was during the Qing dynasty and the Tokugawa shogunate. Using your textbook and other sources, compile a list of important trade treaties, both historical and modern day. Use the list to write a short summary of world trade.

internet connect

Internet Activity: go.hrw.com
KEYWORD: SP3 WH17

Choose a topic on Asia in Transition to:
- analyze art of the Ming and Qing dynasties.
- learn more about Kabuki theater and *Bunraku*, Japanese puppet theater.
- examine an issue from the point of view of a Japanese samurai warrior.

go. hrw .com

Thinking Critically
1. contributed to growth of internal trade and merchant class

2. government corruption and inefficiency, political unrest, Western intrusion

3. may suggest that the British were more concerned with gaining trade advantages

4. Western culture, isolationism, overpopulation, inability to adapt and change

5. might have retained power

Writing About History
Reports should show many similarities.

Building Social Studies Skills
1. b

2. China was defeated in Opium War, forced China to open foreign trade; examples will vary

3. a

4. The Tokugawa felt threatened by the Jesuits and eventually ejected them from Japan.

Building Your Portfolio
Lists will vary. Students should conclude that, over time, world trade continues to grow and expand.

Islamic Empires in Asia

CHAPTER RESOURCE MANAGER

	Objectives	Pacing Guide	Reproducible Resources
SECTION 1 **The Ottoman Empire** (pp. 432–435)	• Explain how the Ottomans built and expanded their empire. • Describe how the Ottomans organized their government and society.	**Regular** 1.5 day / **Block Scheduling** 1 day *Block Scheduling Handbook with Team Teaching Strategies, 18.1*	**RS** Guided Reading Strategy 18.1 **RS** Graphic Organizer Activity 18: Change in the Islamic Empire **PS** Readings in World History 71: Süleyman the Magnificent Captures Belgrade **E** Hands-on History Activity 18: The Ottoman World
SECTION 2 **The Safavid Empire** (pp. 436–438)	• Discuss the role of religion in the development of the Safavid Empire. • Explain how 'Abbās the Great brought the empire to its height.	**Regular** 1.5 day / **Block Scheduling** 1 day *Block Scheduling Handbook with Team Teaching Strategies, 18.2*	**RS** Guided Reading Strategy 18.2 **SM** Geography Activity 18: Islam and Trade
SECTION 3 **The Mughal Empire in India** (439–443)	• Explain the events that led to the beginning of the Mughal Empire. • Identify the policies that allowed for the expansion of the Mughal Empire. • Describe the Mughal Empire at its height.	**Regular** 1.5 day / **Block Scheduling** 1 day *Block Scheduling Handbook with Team Teaching Strategies, 18.3*	**RS** Guided Reading Strategy 18.3 **E** Creative Teaching Strategy 18: Training Seminar: How to Run an Empire

Chapter Resource Key

PS Primary Sources
RS Reading Support
IC Interdisciplinary Connections
E Enrichment
SM Skills Mastery
A Assessment

REV Review
ELL Reinforcement and English Language Learners
Transparencies
CD-ROM
Music

Video
Internet
Holt Presentation Maker Using Microsoft® PowerPoint®

One-Stop Planner CD-ROM

See the *One-Stop Planner* for a complete list of additional resources for students and teachers.

It's easy to plan lessons, select resources, and print out materials for your students when you use the **One-Stop Planner** CD–ROM with **Test Generator.**

Technology Resources	Reinforcement, Review, and Assessment
One-Stop Planner 18.1 Homework Practice Online	Daily Quiz 18.1 Main Idea Activity 18.1 English Audio Summary 18.1 Spanish Audio Summary 18.1 REV Section 1 Review, p. 435
One-Stop Planner 18.2 Holt Researcher: World History: 'Abbās Homework Practice Online	Daily Quiz 18.2 Main Idea Activity 18.2 English Audio Summary 18.2 Spanish Audio Summary 18.2 REV Section 2 Review, p. 438
One-Stop Planner 18.3 World History and Cultures Video Program 13: The Mughals in India World History Teaching Transparency: Everyday Life 10: Nomadic Encampment Homework Practice Online	Daily Quiz 18.3 Main Idea Activity 18.3 English Audio Summary 18.3 Spanish Audio Summary 18.3 REV Section 3 Review, p. 443

🖥 **internet** connect ≡

HRW ONLINE RESOURCES
  GO TO: go.hrw.com
  Then type in a keyword.
TEACHER HOME PAGE
  KEYWORD: SP3 Teacher

CHAPTER INTERNET ACTIVITIES
  KEYWORD: SP3 WH18
Choose an activity to:
• create an illustrated time line of the major events in the history of the Ottoman Empire.
• research life and society in the Safavid Empire.
• create a newspaper on the impact of the siege of Vienna in 1683.

CHAPTER ENRICHMENT LINKS
  KEYWORD: SP3 CH18

ONLINE ASSESSMENT
  Homework Practice
  KEYWORD: SP3 HP18
  Standardized Test Prep
  KEYWORD: SP3 STP18
  Rubrics
  KEYWORD: SS Rubrics

ONLINE MAPS, CHARTS, AND GRAPHS
  KEYWORD: SP3 MCG

CONTENT UPDATES
  KEYWORD: SS Content Updates

HOLT PRESENTATION MAKER
  KEYWORD: SP3 PPT18

ONLINE READING SUPPORT
  KEYWORD: SS Strategies

CURRENT EVENTS
  KEYWORD: S3 Current Events

Meeting Individual Needs

Ability Levels

Level 1   Basic level activities designed for all students encountering new material

Level 2   Intermediate level activities designed for average students

Level 3   Challenging activities designed for honors and gifted and talented students

English Language Learners   These activities address the needs of students with Limited English Proficiency.

Chapter Review and Assessment

IC   Vocabulary Activity 18
  Global Skill Builder CD–ROM
  HRW Web Site
REV   Chapter 18 Tutorial for Students, Parents, Mentors, and Peers
REV   Chapter 18 Review, pp. 444–445

A   Chapter 18 Test Generator (on the One-Stop Planner)
A   Chapter 18 Test (Form A or B)
A   Alternative Assessment Handbook
A   Chapter 18 Test for English Language Learners and Special-Needs Students

Build on What You Know

Ask students to answer the following questions:

How might the rulers of an empire or dynasty control their subjects?

Consider:

- military threats
- religious persecution
- rigid class system
- limited contact with outsiders and foreign books

Why might the rulers of China and Japan have wanted to avoid change while Islamic rulers were trying to expand?

Consider:

- security of power vs. growth of power and glory
- cultural stability vs. spread of new ideas
- continued economic control vs. greater wealth

EXPLORING THE TIME LINE
GLOBAL EVENTS

internet connect

go.hrw.com

TOPIC: Islamic Art

GO TO: go.hrw.com

KEYWORD: SP3 WH18

Ask students to access the Internet through the HRW Go site to conduct research on Islamic art. Have students list five key points that differentiate Islamic art from other cultures' art movements. Ask students to expand on the representation of humans and animals in Islamic art.

CHAPTER 18

1300–1700

Islamic Empires in Asia

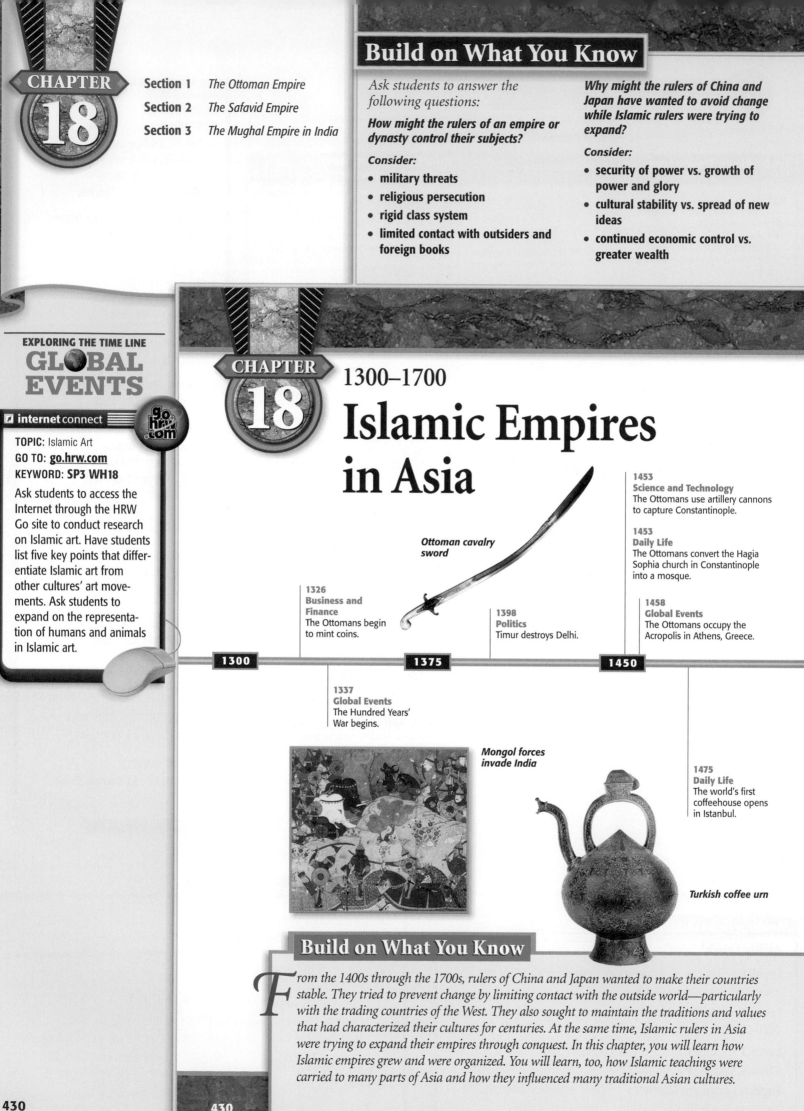

Ottoman cavalry sword

1326
Business and Finance
The Ottomans begin to mint coins.

1398
Politics
Timur destroys Delhi.

1453
Science and Technology
The Ottomans use artillery cannons to capture Constantinople.

1453
Daily Life
The Ottomans convert the Hagia Sophia church in Constantinople into a mosque.

1458
Global Events
The Ottomans occupy the Acropolis in Athens, Greece.

1300   **1375**   **1450**

1337
Global Events
The Hundred Years' War begins.

Mongol forces invade India

1475
Daily Life
The world's first coffeehouse opens in Istanbul.

Turkish coffee urn

Build on What You Know

From the 1400s through the 1700s, rulers of China and Japan wanted to make their countries stable. They tried to prevent change by limiting contact with the outside world—particularly with the trading countries of the West. They also sought to maintain the traditions and values that had characterized their cultures for centuries. At the same time, Islamic rulers in Asia were trying to expand their empires through conquest. In this chapter, you will learn how Islamic empires grew and were organized. You will learn, too, how Islamic teachings were carried to many parts of Asia and how they influenced many traditional Asian cultures.

What's Your Opinion?

*To help students create their Themes Journal entries, provide the following examples of appropriate **agree**/**disagree** statements.*

Global Relations

Agree A civilization that expands by conquest needs a large, strong military to subdue and control new lands.

Disagree A civilization that expands by conquest can maintain power through loyal citizens who can spread their culture and belief systems.

Culture

Agree The religious policies followed by a culture's leader can either unify or divide the culture.

Disagree The religious policies followed by a culture's leader will have little effect on the strength of the culture.

Government

Agree The effectiveness of a government depends upon its rulers' moral and ethical strength.

Disagree The effectiveness of a government depends upon the loyalty of its subjects.

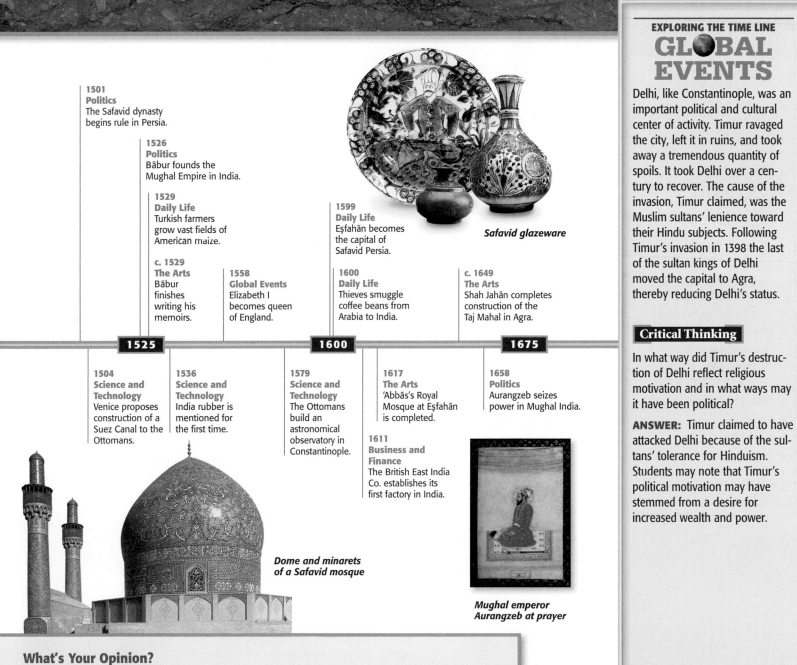

1501
Politics
The Safavid dynasty begins rule in Persia.

1526
Politics
Bābur founds the Mughal Empire in India.

1529
Daily Life
Turkish farmers grow vast fields of American maize.

c. 1529
The Arts
Bābur finishes writing his memoirs.

1558
Global Events
Elizabeth I becomes queen of England.

1599
Daily Life
Eşfahān becomes the capital of Safavid Persia.

1600
Daily Life
Thieves smuggle coffee beans from Arabia to India.

c. 1649
The Arts
Shah Jahān completes construction of the Taj Mahal in Agra.

Safavid glazeware

1525

1600

1675

1504
Science and Technology
Venice proposes construction of a Suez Canal to the Ottomans.

1536
Science and Technology
India rubber is mentioned for the first time.

1579
Science and Technology
The Ottomans build an astronomical observatory in Constantinople.

1617
The Arts
'Abbās's Royal Mosque at Eşfahān is completed.

1611
Business and Finance
The British East India Co. establishes its first factory in India.

1658
Politics
Aurangzeb seizes power in Mughal India.

Dome and minarets of a Safavid mosque

Mughal emperor Aurangzeb at prayer

EXPLORING THE TIME LINE
GLOBAL EVENTS

Delhi, like Constantinople, was an important political and cultural center of activity. Timur ravaged the city, left it in ruins, and took away a tremendous quantity of spoils. It took Delhi over a century to recover. The cause of the invasion, Timur claimed, was the Muslim sultans' lenience toward their Hindu subjects. Following Timur's invasion in 1398 the last of the sultan kings of Delhi moved the capital to Agra, thereby reducing Delhi's status.

Critical Thinking

In what way did Timur's destruction of Delhi reflect religious motivation and in what ways may it have been political?

ANSWER: Timur claimed to have attacked Delhi because of the sultans' tolerance for Hinduism. Students may note that Timur's political motivation may have stemmed from a desire for increased wealth and power.

What's Your Opinion?

*Do you **agree** or **disagree** with the following statements? Support your point of view in your journal.*

Global Relations A civilization that expands by conquest must support a large, strong military.

Culture The religious policies followed by a culture's leadership can help to unify or divide that culture.

Government The character of its rulers determines the effectiveness of a government.

431

OBJECTIVES

1 **Explain how the Ottomans built and expanded their empire.**

2 **Describe how the Ottomans organized their government and society.**

As students enter the classroom, ask them to write down what they recall about the Ottomans. *(Muslim Turks who created an empire in Asia Minor and Europe)* Tell students that in Section 1 they will learn about the Ottoman Empire's expansion, its government, and its society.

SECTION 1

READ TO DISCOVER

1 How did the Ottomans build and expand their empire?

2 How did the Ottomans organize their government and society?

DEFINE

ghazis
reaya
millets

IDENTIFY

Osman
Janissaries
Timur
Mehmed II
Süleyman

WHY IT MATTERS TODAY

The present-day country of Turkey was once the center of the Ottoman Empire. Use **CNNfyi**.com or other **current event** sources to find out what kind of government Turkey has today. Record your findings in your journal.

CNNfyi.com

The Ottoman Empire

The Main Idea
With their tough, disciplined army and strong rulers, the Ottomans built a powerful empire.

The Story Continues *During the 1300s and 1400s the Ottoman Empire built and expanded its power. Ottoman leaders such as Mehmed the Conqueror sought to capture the city of Constantinople. An observer described Mehmed's goals: "The empire of the world . . . must be one, one faith and one kingdom. To make this unity there is no place in the world more worthy than Constantinople."*

The Rise of the Ottomans

The first Ottomans were Turkish soldiers known as **ghazis,** or warriors for Islam. They had come to Anatolia (formerly called Asia Minor) with other Turks to escape the Mongols. In the late 1200s a ghazi leader named **Osman** had great success fighting the Byzantines. His tribe members became known as Ottomans.

During the 1300s the Ottomans took over a large part of Anatolia. Eventually Ottoman forces went to Europe. They tried to capture Constantinople but failed. In 1361 the Ottomans captured Adrianopolis, the second most important Byzantine city. They made the city their capital and renamed it Edirne. By 1396 the first Ottoman sultan had been appointed.

The elite Ottoman army. The Ottoman sultans created a highly trained troop of slave soldiers called **Janissaries.** Janissaries were young war captives and Christian slaves from Europe. First they were schooled in Islamic laws and converted to Islam, then trained as special soldiers. Janissaries belonged to the sultan, serving him for life. Eventually the Janissaries gained power and influence. They became an important political group in the Ottoman Empire.

Timur challenges the Ottomans. The Turko-Mongol leader **Timur** interrupted the Ottoman expansion. Timur was born in 1336 in what is now Uzbekistan. He claimed he was descended from the great Mongol leader Genghis Khan. Timur created an army and built his power in central Asia. Then he began a career of conquest.

By the end of the 1300s, Timur's forces were close to Ottoman territory. Several ghazi rulers fled to his court when the Ottomans conquered their states. They asked Timur to help them get their land back. In 1402 Timur invaded Anatolia. His forces defeated the Ottomans at the Battle of Ankara and captured the sultan. Timur made the Ottomans return the territory they had taken from the other ghazi rulers.

This richly decorated illustration from about 1500 shows an Ottoman sultan dining.

TEACH OBJECTIVE 1

LEVEL 1: Ask students to refer to the map on page 433 and describe how the Ottoman Empire grew from its original boundaries. *(expanded into eastern Europe, western Asia, and northern Africa)* Ask students which time period on the map was the period of greatest growth for the empire. *(1454–1519)* **ENGLISH LANGUAGE LEARNERS**

TEACH OBJECTIVE 1

ALL LEVELS: Copy the following graphic organizer on the chalkboard, omitting the italicized answers. Use it to help students organize the people responsible for the growth of the Ottoman Empire. **ENGLISH LANGUAGE LEARNERS**

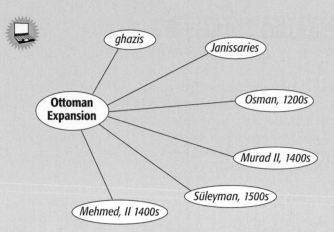

Recovery and expansion. Timur's victory over the Ottomans caused a crisis in the Ottoman Empire. A civil war broke out over who should be the next sultan. Finally Murad II took power and began a new period of expansion. In 1444 Murad's army defeated the last European crusaders at the Battle of Varna. After Murad's rule, **Mehmed II** became sultan. Mehmed conquered Constantinople in 1453, renamed the city Istanbul, and made it the Ottoman capital.

The greatest Ottoman sultan was **Süleyman,** who ruled from 1520 to 1566. He brought the Ottoman Empire to its height. Known as "the Magnificent" in Europe, Süleyman was called "the Lawgiver" by his own people.

Süleyman expanded the Ottoman Empire, conquering Hungary in 1526. Three years later the Ottomans nearly captured the city of Vienna. Vienna marked the limit of Ottoman expansion in Europe. By this time, however, the Ottomans ruled most of eastern Europe, western Asia, and northern Africa.

✔ **READING CHECK: Summarizing** What important military conquests led to the expansion of the Ottoman Empire? *conquests of Constantinople, Hungary*

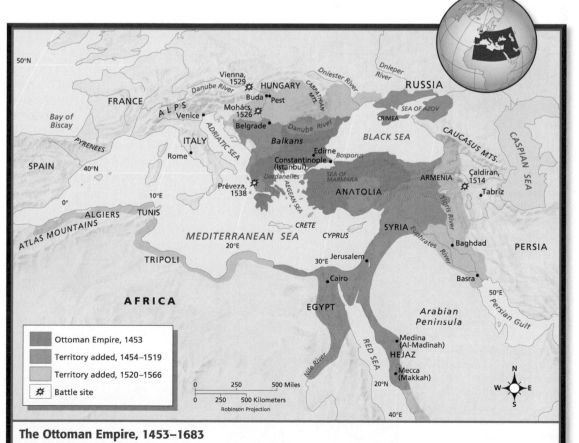

The Ottoman Empire, 1453–1683

Interpreting Maps At its height under Süleyman, the Ottoman Empire included parts of eastern Europe, western Asia, and northern Africa.

■ **Skills Assessment: The World in Spatial Terms** Which two battle sites are found at about the 40° N parallel?

Geography

Constantinople's position between eastern Europe and Asia at the point that connects the Black Sea with the Mediterranean Sea has made it useful as both a barrier and as a bridge. It was an important center for religion, culture, and power for centuries.

Critical Thinking

Ask students why Constantinople was such an important conquest for the Ottomans.

ANSWER: The city's position gave the Ottomans a foothold in Europe and a seaport.

⊞ internet connect

TOPIC: Ottoman Empire
GO TO: go.hrw.com
KEYWORD: SP3 WH18

Have students access the Internet through the HRW Go site to conduct research on the Ottoman Empire. Then ask them to create an illustrated time line of the major events in the history of the Ottoman Empire. Students should briefly state some of the far-reaching and long-lasting effects this Empire has had on the continents of Africa, Asia, and Europe.

MAP ANSWER

Préveza, Çaldiran

LEVEL 3: Draw two columns on the chalkboard. Entitle one *Ottoman Society* and the other *U.S. Society*. Ask students to list details about Ottoman society and record those under the appropriate title. *(Ideas may include ruling class, reaya, personal ability, millets, and religious freedom.)* Then have students compare their list to aspects of U.S. society. *(Ideas may include the U.S. government, common citizens, citizens elected into office, state governments, and religious freedom.)*

HOMEWORK List the governmental responsibilities of the millet. Describe how the system may have engendered loyalty among different religious groups.

Spotlight on CULTURE

The basic purpose of the millet system was to solve a problem of discord within the subject class. The Ottomans attempted to preserve peace among the subject class by keeping them separated from each other. However, Christians such as the Greeks and Armenians hated Jews and Muslims and engaged in violent conflicts with them. The sultan's efforts to protect his subjects proved difficult. Ask pairs of students to research the conflicts between Christians, Muslims, and Jews. Then have each pair define the specific problems and develop a method for solving those problems. Have them share their solutions with the rest of the class. **COOPERATIVE LEARNING, BLOCK SCHEDULING**

Government

The three requirements for becoming members of the Ottoman ruling class were: proclaiming loyalty to the sultan and his state; adhering to the practice of Islam; and knowing and practicing specific customs, behavior, and language known as the Ottoman Way. The members of the ruling class were considered slaves to the sultan, who had ultimate control over their possessions and their lives.

Critical Thinking

Ask students why the Ottoman people had to follow the three criteria for becoming part of the ruling class.

ANSWER: Students may suggest that giving power to people who did not support the sultan would ultimately weaken the empire. Adhering to the requirements made the government's participants culturally similar and more likely to carry out their duties as rulers and defenders of the empire.

HISTORY MAKER ANSWER

He built fortresses, roads, bridges, and mosques, supported the arts, and made Constantinople the cultural and commercial center of his empire.

Ottoman Government and Society

The sultans were the supreme rulers of Ottoman society. Those second in command to the sultan were called grand viziers (vuh-ZIRZ). Ottoman society was divided into two major groups. One group was the small ruling class of Ottomans. The other included the masses of ordinary subjects, called **reaya** or the "protected flock." People did not have to remain in one of these groups for life. Reaya with ability could become part of the ruling class. Ottomans who lacked ability became reaya.

Europeans who observed Turkish society were impressed. One observer was Ogier Ghiselin de Busbecq, the Holy Roman Emperor's ambassador to Süleyman's court. He described his view of how the system worked.

> **History Makers Speak**
>
> **❝No distinction is attached to birth among the Turks; the deference to be paid to a man is measured by the position he holds in the public service. . . . it is by merit that men rise in the service, a system which ensures that posts should only be assigned to the competent. Each man in Turkey carries in his own hand his ancestry and his position in life, which he may make or mar as he will.❞**
>
> Ogier Ghiselin de Busbecq, *The Life and Letters of Ogier Ghiselin de Busbecq*

The millet system. Different groups of people made up the reaya. Muslim Turks lived in the heart of the empire in Anatolia. Christians and Jews of various ethnic groups lived in the Balkans. Muslim Arabs lived in the Fertile Crescent and along the shore of northern Africa. Religious differences caused tension among these groups.

The sultans allowed the different groups to practice their own religions. They were organized into separate religious communities called **millets.** The millets were under the general control of the sultan, but they governed themselves. Each millet operated under its own laws and customs. It had its own courts and collected taxes. It also was responsible for the education, health, and safety of its members.

Slow decline begins. Süleyman the Magnificent died in 1566. His death marked the start of a slow decline of Ottoman power and influence as European states such as France, Spain, and Poland became stronger. Although the Ottoman army and navy

Analyzing Primary Sources

Drawing Inferences What does it mean to say, "Each man in Turkey carries in his own hand his ancestry and his position in life"? One's position in society was based on merit, not on birth.

HISTORY MAKER

Süleyman the Magnificent (c. 1495–1566)

As sultan of the Ottoman Empire, Süleyman was a brave and daring warrior. He is most remembered, however, for his accomplishments at home.

Süleyman surrounded himself with a group of able advisers. He built strong fortresses for defense as well as numerous roads, bridges, and mosques. He supported the arts and helped to make Constantinople the cultural and commercial center of his empire. **How did Süleyman improve the Ottoman Empire?**

This Ottoman image of the 1500s shows the Turks blockading the French port of Marseille.

CLOSE

Have students write a summary of the decline of the Ottoman Empire.

REVIEW

Have students complete the Section 1 Review on p. 435.

ASSESS

Have students complete Daily Quiz 18.1. As Alternative Assessment, you may want to use the conquests graphic organizer exercise in this section's lessons.

RETEACH

Have students complete the Main Idea Activity for English Language Learners and Special-Needs Students 18.1. Then have each student create a detailed outline covering the origin and expansion of the Ottoman empire. **ENGLISH LANGUAGE LEARNERS**

EXTEND

Have students write a dialogue with opposing opinions about the benefits of Ottoman government and social structure.

were generally strong, they suffered some defeats. In 1571, for example, Philip II of Spain led a European navy against the Ottomans. The Europeans defeated the Turks at the Battle of Lepanto, near Greece. In 1683 troops led by the Polish king John III Sobieski again stopped the Turks outside Vienna.

By the 1600s the Ottoman government and economy faced real problems as well. During these years, the empire lost control of the highly profitable silk and spice trades between Europe and Asia. European naval powers opened new sea routes to Asia that bypassed the Turks and destroyed their trade monopoly. At the same time, the power and prestige of the Ottoman sultans weakened. The government became increasingly corrupt due to internal power struggles within its growing bureaucracy. Rebellions among the Janissaries, the Ottomans' elite slave troops, added to the empire's troubles. During the late 1700s the Ottomans lost the Crimean Peninsula and lands around the Black Sea and the Sea of Azov to the Russians. The French invaded Egypt, an Ottoman possession, in 1798. Ottoman lands in the Balkans were also lost. Some sultans attempted to reform Ottoman government and military structures but had limited success. The Ottoman Empire struggled to survive, finally ending in 1923 when Turkey established itself as a republic.

✔ **READING CHECK: Analyzing Information** What problems did the Ottoman Empire face? economic problems, competition with Europe, corruption, and rebellions

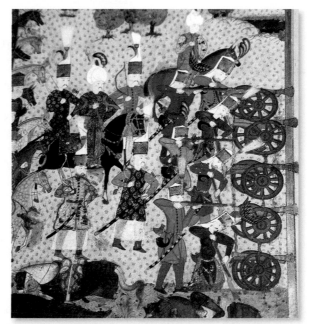

INTERPRETING THE VISUAL RECORD

Ottomans in battle This painting shows Süleyman the Magnificent at the Battle of Mohács in Hungary. *What does this picture tell us about Ottoman military technology?*

SECTION 1 REVIEW

1. **Define** and explain the significance:
   ghazis
   reaya
   millets

2. **Identify** and explain the significance:
   Osman
   Janissaries
   Timur
   Mehmed II
   Süleyman

3. **Sequencing** Copy the chart below. Use it to organize the major conquests and defeats that the Ottomans experienced between 1300 and 1700.

Conquests

Defeats

4. **Finding the Main Idea**
   a. What role did the Janissaries play in the success of the Ottoman Empire?
   b. How important do you think the Ottoman social system was to the success of the empire?

5. **Writing and Critical Thinking**
   Evaluating Explain your view of the Ottoman Empire's focus on military conquest.
   Consider:
   • how the people conquered were affected
   • how the Ottoman people were affected
   • the cost in both money and lives

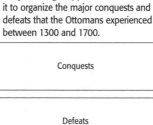
Homework Practice Online
keyword: SP3 HP18

Students should note that the Ottomans had cannons, guns, and gunpowder.

SECTION 1 REVIEW ANSWERS

❶ **Define**
• ghazis, 432
• reaya, p. 434
• millets, p. 434

❷ **Identify**
• Osman, p. 432
• Janissaries, p. 432
• Timur, p. 432
• Mehmed II, p. 433
• Süleyman, p. 433

❸ Conquests: Anatolia in the 1300s, Adrianopolis in 1361, Constantinople in 1453, Hungary in 1526, Vienna in 1529; Defeats: Battle of Ankara in 1402, Battle of Lepanto in 1571, Vienna in 1683

❹ a. Janissaries served as highly trained slave soldiers who fought to expand the empire.

b. Religious tolerance and social mobility may have kept large numbers loyal to the empire.

❺ Answers will vary.

OBJECTIVES

1 **Discuss the role of religion in the development of the Safavid Empire.**

2 **Explain how 'Abbās the Great brought the empire to its height.**

VISUAL RECORD ANSWER

Horses provided an advantage in battle.

▸ READ TO DISCOVER

1 How was religion responsible for the development of the Safavid Empire?

2 How did 'Abbās the Great bring the Safavid Empire to its height?

▸ DEFINE

kizilbash

▸ IDENTIFY

Safī od-Dīn
Esmā'īl
Tahmāsp
'Abbās

▸ WHY IT MATTERS TODAY

The Iranian (Persian) government has kept Shi'ah Islam as the state religion from the time of the Safavids up to the present day. Use **CNNfyi.com** or other **current event** sources to explore how religious differences affect Iran's relationship with other countries. Record your findings in your journal.

CNNfyi.com

The Safavid Empire

The Main Idea
The Safavid rulers created a powerful Shi'ah Muslim empire with a prospering economy and culture.

The Story Continues *While the Ottomans were building their empire, the Safavid dynasty was gaining power in Persia. Shah Esmā'īl, the founder of this new empire, was driven by religious zeal. "I am committed to this action," he said. "God and the Immaculate [pure] Imams are with me, and I fear no one."*

The Rise of the Safavids

The Safavid (sah·FAH·vid) Empire was bounded on the west by the Ottoman Empire and on the east by the Mughal Empire of India. Today, much of what was the Safavid Empire is the country of Iran.

The Safavids were descended from **Safī od-Dīn,** head of the family in the 1200s. Like most Persians, the Safavids were Muslims. They belonged to the Sunni branch of Islam. In about 1399, however, the Safavids shifted from Sunni to the Shi'ah sect. As Shi'ah, they were persecuted by the Sunni.

Toward the end of the 1400s, the Safavids developed a military group to fight for political power. This army was called the **kizilbash,** meaning "Red Heads," for the red hats they wore. Other Persians killed or imprisoned many Safavids, but one of the youngest, **Esmā'īl** (is·mah·EEL), escaped into hiding. In about 1500 Esmā'īl became head of the kizilbash. In a series of victories, he brought all of modern Iran and part of present-day Iraq under his rule. In 1501 he captured the city of Tabrīz and made it the Safavid capital. Esmā'īl took the ancient Persian title of shah, or "king of kings," and reigned until 1524.

✔ **READING CHECK: Summarizing** What problems did the Safavids face during the 1400s? Sunni persecution, including murder and imprisonment

Esmā'īl's religious policy. As soon as Esmā'īl became shah, he proclaimed that Shi'ah would be the religion of the Safavid Empire. Most Persians were Sunni, but Esmā'īl forced them to convert. Many people considered Esmā'īl a Muslim saint as well as shah, which helped in the process of conversion. Shi'ah gave the Persians an identity distinct from the great number of Sunni—Turks and Arabs—

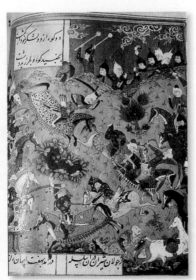

INTERPRETING THE VISUAL RECORD

Continuing conflict Until the late 1580s the Safavids were often outmatched by the stronger Ottoman army. *What generalizations can be drawn from this image?*

ALL LEVELS: Copy the following chart on the chalk-board, omitting the italicized answers. Use it to help students understand the role of religion in the development of the Safavid Empire. **ENGLISH LANGUAGE LEARNERS**

Cause		Effect
Esmā'īl's religious enthusiasm	→	*fought to control Persia*
Safavids became Shi'ah in 1399	→	*persecuted by Sunni*
forced conversion to Shi'ah	→	*gained distinction and national unity*

HOMEWORK Write a short paragraph summarizing the role of religion in the rise of the Safavid Empire.

LEVEL 1: Have students list reasons why they think Shah 'Abbās was called "the Great." *(military reforms, territory recovery, improvements to Eşfahān, economic prosperity)* Then ask students to write a paragraph telling whether they think 'Abbās's activities qualify him for his nickname. **ENGLISH LANGUAGE LEARNERS**

LEVEL 3: Ask students to write a fictional interview with Shah 'Abbās. Tell them to include questions that pertain to the Shah's improvements to the Safavid Empire. Have students make their interviews interesting and creative by describing the setting of the interview, how he looks, and his personality.

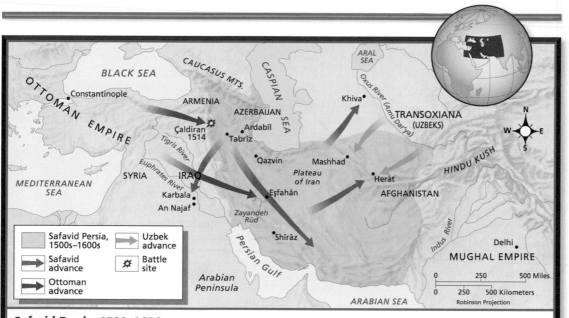

Safavid Persia, 1500–1636

Interpreting Maps As Safavid rulers expanded their empire, they clashed with the Ottomans and the Uzbeks for control of key territory.

■ **Skills Assessment: Human Systems** The Safavids relocated their capital from Tabrīz to Qazvīn and later to Eşfahān. What do you think motivated the first move?

who lived around them. The Persian language and history also contributed to a strong sense of identity, which continues in modern Iran.

Esmā'īl's support of Shi'ah threatened Persia's neighbors—the Sunni Ottomans and Uzbek tribes to the northeast. In 1514 the Ottomans invaded northwestern Persia. They defeated the Safavids at the Battle of Çaldiran. The struggle continued through the mid-1500s. After Esmā'īl died, his son **Tahmāsp** tried to carry on the fight. However, by the 1570s the Safavids had lost territory to both the Ottomans and the Uzbeks.

✔**READING CHECK: Finding the Main Idea** Why did Esmā'īl make Shi'ah the religion of the empire? to develop distinct Persian identity, unify the nation

Shah 'Abbās the Great

When Tahmāsp died in 1576, the Safavid Empire was unstable. The kizilbash were no longer loyal to the shah. The struggles against the Ottomans and Uzbeks were going badly. Then in 1587 'Abbās, called "the Great," became shah.

Military reforms. 'Abbās realized he needed troops that would be loyal to him. He reformed the military, using the Ottoman army as a model. He created troops of foreign slaves who had been prisoners of war. After they were converted to Islam, they were trained for army service. These slave-soldiers belonged to the shah and were loyal only to him.

Eventually 'Abbās was ready to take on the Ottomans and Uzbeks. In 1598 his improved army defeated the Uzbeks and regained control of northeastern Persia. In a few years 'Abbās recovered all the territory the Safavids had lost.

Holt Researcher
go.hrw.com
KEYWORD: Holt Researcher
FreeFind: Abbas
After reading more about 'Abbās on the Holt Researcher, write a list of questions you would ask him if you had a chance to interview him. Then write his possible responses.

Linking Past to Present

With a population of more than a million, Eşfahān today is the third-largest city in Iran. Located about 200 miles south of Tehran, Eşfahān is a major transportation center. It is also noted for its gardens and squares and its medieval mosques and ancient palaces. Eşfahān is famous for its traditional handicrafts, such as lacework, metalwork, carpets, and hand-printed textiles. The old art of tile making also has been revived for use in restoring its many historical monuments.

Critical Thinking

Ask students what they might conclude about a society that works to restore its historical monuments.

ANSWER: Students might suggest that the society holds the monuments in high regard, has sufficient wealth to maintain its historical structures, and wishes to remember its history.

MAP ANSWER
Tabriz was too close to the Ottoman Empire and therefore vulnerable.

The height of the empire. In about 1599 'Abbās moved the Safavid capital to Eṣfahān on the Plateau of Iran. Eṣfahān soon became one of the most beautiful cities in the world. 'Abbās planned his new capital city carefully. It had wide streets and a huge central square. It had splendid mosques and monuments, as well as public baths and open markets. The center of Eṣfahān was an enormous rectangular park that was large enough for polo games and that was surrounded by an arcade of shops. Large inns scattered throughout the city had central courtyards where camel caravans could be housed and rested. Eṣfahān became known throughout Europe and the Middle East as a political, spiritual, and commercial center of the first order.

Even 'Abbās liked to walk around his city. Christian monks who had a mission in Eṣfahān kept a record of what they observed.

Analyzing Primary Sources

Drawing Inferences How do you think the shopkeepers probably reacted to 'Abbās's behavior? probably complimented by his visit, awed by his presence

Primary Source

❝He ['Abbās] will come to the greengrocers, fruiterers, and those who sell preserves and sweetmeats. Here he will take a mouthful of this, there another of that . . . . Or he will enter the shop of a shoemaker, pick up a pair of shoes that takes his fancy, put them on at the door and then continue on his way.**❞**

From Clive Irving, *Crossroads of Civilization: 3000 Years of Persian History*

'Abbās's reign was also a time of economic development. The shah encouraged manufacturing and foreign trade. Carpet weaving became a major industry. Fine Persian rugs began to appear in the homes of wealthy Europeans. Persian merchants exported rich fabrics such as brocade, damask, and silk. The Safavids produced beautiful tiles and ceramics for their own use as well as for trade.

'Abbās died in 1629. For a while after his death, the Safavids continued to rule. However, rulers after 'Abbās proved increasingly inept. The empire began to decline and had ended by 1736. Eventually Persia split into a number of small states.

This glazeware from about 1625 shows typical Safavid artistry.

✔ **READING CHECK: Supporting a Point of View** What evidence would you give that 'Abbās was an especially capable ruler? successful military reforms, recapture of lost territory, policies of economic growth

SECTION 2 REVIEW

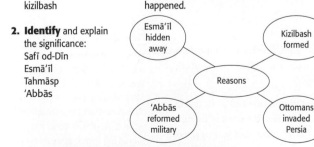

1. **Define** and explain the significance:
   kizilbash

2. **Identify** and explain the significance:
   Safī od-Dīn
   Esmā'īl
   Tahmāsp
   'Abbās

3. **Identifying Cause and Effect** Copy the model below. Give the reasons why each event happened.

   Esmā'īl hidden away

   Kizilbash formed

   Reasons

   'Abbās reformed military

   Ottomans invaded Persia

4. **Finding the Main Idea**

   a. What effect did the Safavid religious policy have on Persia?

   b. What were the results of the military reforms carried out under 'Abbās?

   c. What might a visitor to Eṣfahān in the early 1600s conclude about the Safavid Empire?

5. **Writing and Critical Thinking**

   Summarizing Imagine you are a visitor to Eṣfahān during Abbās's time. Write a description of your experience.
   Consider:
   • what the city looks like
   • what the people are doing in their everyday lives
   • what products and industries you see
   • in what ways the city of Eṣfahān symbolizes Safavid strength and prosperity

Homework Practice Online
keyword: SP3 HP18

OBJECTIVES

1 **Explain** the events that led to the beginning of the Mughal Empire.

2 **Identify** the policies that allowed for the expansion of the Mughal Empire.

3 **Describe** the Mughal Empire at its height.

📢 LET'S GET STARTED!

As students enter the classroom, ask them to list the ways in which the policies of rulers like Süleyman and Shah ʿAbbās affected their empires. *(Süleyman's aggression helped expand the Ottoman empire; he tolerated others' religions and allowed various groups to govern themselves; he supported the arts and improvements such as roads, bridges, and mosques. Shah ʿAbbās expanded his empire with a slave military force and improved the empire's capital and its economy.)* Tell students that in Section 3 they will learn how the policies of rulers in India affected the success of the Mughal Empire.

SECTION 3

READ TO DISCOVER

❶ How did the Mughal Empire begin?

❷ How did the Mughal Empire expand?

❸ What was the Mughal Empire like at its height?

IDENTIFY

Rajputs
Bābur
Akbar
Shah Jahān
Taj Mahal
Sikh
Aurangzeb

WHY IT MATTERS TODAY

The Taj Mahal in Agra, India, was built by a Mughal emperor. Thousands of tourists visit it each year. Use **CNNfyi.com** or other **current event** sources to find out more about this architectural masterpiece. Record your findings in your journal.

CNNfyi.com

The Mughal Empire in India

The Main Idea
The Mughal rulers of India worked to unify and improve their vast, diverse Muslim empire.

The Story Continues *In 1605 the Mughal Empire was at the height of its glory. When Jahāngīr, son of Akbar, inherited his father's empire, his coronation ceremony reflected this splendor: "For forty days and forty nights I caused the ... great imperial state drum, to strike up, without ceasing, the strains of joy and triumph;" he wrote, "... around my throne, the ground was spread by my directions with the most costly brocades [silks] and embroidered carpets.... Emirs of the empire, covered from head to foot in gold and jewels ... stood round in brilliant array."*

The Origin of the Mughal Empire

During the 1300s Turkish Muslims controlled India, with Delhi as the capital of their sultanate. By the 1500s the power of the Delhi sultans had been greatly weakened. Indian warrior princes called **Rajputs** (RAHJ·poots) began to challenge them. The internal weakness of the sultanate drew the attention of India's powerful neighbors, as it had during Timur's time, and left India open to Mongol attack.

The attack came from a young leader known as "Bābur the Tiger." **Bābur** (also, Zahīr-ud-Dīn Muhammad) was a descendant of the Mongol leader Timur. He had tried to build an empire in central Asia, but the Uzbek people had driven him out. Bābur then focused on India. In 1526 he attacked the Sultanate of Delhi. A major battle took place at Panipat, a town north of Delhi. Bābur was greatly outnumbered, but he won the battle, as he described in his autobiography.

History Makers Speak

❝The kingdom of Hindustan [India] ... was under the control of ... [the sultan at Delhi] ... His standing army was estimated at one hundred thousand. He and his commanders were said to have one thousand elephants. In such a state of affairs and with such strength, we put our trust in God ... and faced a ruler with a huge army and vast realm. ... God did not let our pains and difficulties go for naught and defeated such a powerful opponent and conquered a vast kingdom like Hindustan.❞

from The Baburnama: Memoirs of Babur, Prince and Emperor

This painting from about 1590 shows the richness and ease of life at the Mughal court.

SECTION 3 RESOURCES

REPRODUCIBLE RESOURCES

▶ Guided Reading Strategy 18.3

▶ Creative Teaching Strategy 18: Training Seminar: How to Run an Empire

TECHNOLOGY RESOURCES

▶ One-Stop Planner 18.3

▶ World History and Cultures Video Program 13: The Mughals in India

▶ World History Teaching Transparency: Everyday Life 10: Nomadic Encampment

▶ Homework Practice Online

REINFORCEMENT, REVIEW, AND ASSESSMENT

▶ Section 3 Review, p. 443

▶ Daily Quiz 18.3

▶ Main Idea Activity 18.3

▶ English Audio Summary 18.3

▶ Spanish Audio Summary 18.3

Mughal Origins		
	Rajputs	**Babur**
who	*Indian warrior princes*	*Mongol leader, descendant of Timur*
what	*weakened power of sultans*	*attacked Sultanate of Delhi*
when	*1500s*	*1526*
where	*Delhi*	*Panipat*
why	*gain power*	*build an empire*
how	*challenged Delhi sultans*	*defeated sultan in battle*

History Maker

AKBAR. Unlike Bābur, Akbar was a native of India. Indians, whatever their religion, were his countrymen. Though he could have remained at a distance from his subjects, the young Akbar would sometimes visit anonymously with villagers to gather information about their lives. He learned about the diversity among his subjects and how different they were from their foreign rulers.

Critical Thinking

For what reasons might Akbar have instituted his tolerant religious policies?

ANSWER: His political intelligence may have prompted him to satisfy people of various religions, or he may have had respect for his subjects' beliefs.

MAP ANSWER
Goa, Calicut

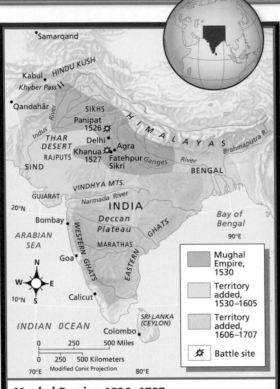

Mughal Empire, 1526–1707

Interpreting Maps Many generations of Mughal emperors supported the arts and united most of India.

■ **Skills Assessment: Human Systems** What two cities on the west coast of the Indian subcontinent remained independent during Mughal rule?

After the victory at Panipat, Bābur occupied Delhi and the surrounding region. This territory became the core of the Mughal Empire.

✔ **READING CHECK: Summarizing** What role did Bābur play in establishing the Mughal Empire? founded the empire

The Growth of Mughal Power

Bābur's grandson, **Akbar,** was the greatest Mughal emperor. He took the throne at the age of 13 and reigned from 1556 to 1605. Akbar gained support for his government in various ways. He married a Rajput princess and gave other Rajputs government positions. At times he used force to maintain power. By 1605 Akbar controlled all of northern and much of central India.

Akbar introduced an improved tax system that helped him control his empire. Taxes were based on an average of what a village might produce over a 10-year period. When the harvest was poor, the tax did not have to be paid. In a good harvest, the villagers could keep anything above the tax level.

Akbar was a great supporter of the arts. He encouraged Hindu as well as Muslim artists. Mughal artists, influenced by the Persian style, created delicate, colorful miniature paintings. Akbar also encouraged the development of literature in the Hindi and Urdu languages. The Mughals made great achievements in architecture, blending Persian, Islamic, and Hindu styles.

Religious policy. Perhaps most importantly, Akbar was tolerant of all religions. He repealed the special tax that non-Muslims had been forced to pay. Over time, however, he began to think of himself as a divine ruler. In the late 1500s he established a creed called the Divine Faith. The motto for the creed was *Allahu Akbar,* meaning either "God is great" or "Akbar is God." The creed blended elements of Islam, Hinduism, Jainism, Christianity, and other religions. It attracted few followers beyond Akbar's court because Muslims strongly opposed it.

Economy and trade. During Akbar's reign the economy improved. The empire's wealth and resources, and its location along the sea routes to Asia, attracted European traders. India had impressive quantities of jewels and gold. The climate allowed the peasants to grow a variety of crops and allowed more than one harvest a year. European travelers thought India's rulers lived in greater luxury than their European kings. India's cities, such as Agra and Delhi, were filled with beautiful buildings and monuments. The Mughal cities seemed much larger than any in Europe.

✔ **READING CHECK: Making Generalizations** What role did Akbar play in the growth of the Mughal Empire? won control of all northern India, much of central India; created policies that helped to maintain Mughal strength

The Height of the Mughal Empire

The Mughal Empire was at its height during the reign of **Shah Jahān.** He ruled from 1628 to 1658. By this time the empire had expanded to reach its greatest extent of territory, including both northern and southern India.

Shah Jahān is best known for the two famous buildings that were constructed during his reign. The magnificent **Taj Mahal** at Agra remains one of the architectural wonders of the world. Shah Jahān had the Taj Mahal built as a tomb for his beloved wife, Mumtāz Mahal. It is made of marble inlaid with semiprecious gems. The other building, the Hall of Private Audience, is in the Red Fort at Delhi. This was Shah Jahān's palace. In the Hall of Private Audience are carved these famous lines: "If there be Paradise on Earth, It is Here, It is Here, It is Here!" These great buildings were enormously expensive to build.

At the same time, the Mughals were engaged in military campaigns against Persia. Their huge armies were very expensive to maintain. They believed these armies were necessary to hold their empire together. To meet his expenses, Shah Jahān increased taxes. His subjects had to pay him half of the crops they raised. Many people suffered under this terrible burden.

A new religion. Under the Mughals, a blending of Hindu and Muslim cultures occurred. In the 1500s an Indian mystic named Nānak tried to unite the Hindu and Muslim religions. Out of Nānak's teaching arose a new religion—the **Sikh** (SEEK) faith. This faith called for devotion to one God, a lack of idols, and a less rigid social system. These ideas conflicted with Hindu beliefs. Nānak became the first guru (leader or teacher) of the Sikhs. By the late 1600s the Sikhs had become militant. They became fierce enemies of the Mughal Empire and the Muslims.

INTERPRETING THE VISUAL RECORD

The Taj Mahal Shah Jahān brought workers and materials from all over India and central Asia to build the Taj Mahal. It took more than 20,000 workers and over 20 years to finish the job. *What statement does this building make about the power of the Mughals?*

HOMEWORK Tell students to imagine they are foreign ambassadors to India during the height of the Mughal Empire. Have them write a letter to an associate in their home country describing what they have seen and what is happening in the empire.

TEACH OBJECTIVE 2

LEVEL 3: Ask students to write an essay that compares and contrasts the reigns of two of the Mughal rulers in this section. Have them write their essays using a particular frame of reference. They should decide which ruler had the strongest character and how his character affected the empire. (*Students should use similar details from Section 3, though their decisions about character will vary.*)

CLOSE

Have students give their opinions about the policies of each ruler discussed in Section 3. Ask students to evaluate the success of each ruler and whether their character played a part in that success.

internet connect

go.hrw.com

TOPIC: The Safavid Empire
GO TO: go.hrw.com
KEYWORD: SP3 WH18

Have students access the Internet through the HRW Go site to research life and society in the Safavid Empire. Ask students to write a report on the Empire. They may wish to use the interactive template provided.

SKILLS PRACTICE ANSWERS

1. political, religious, social

2. Though viewed by some to be a politically effective rule, it strikes others as cruelly intolerant and inconstant.

3. Summaries will vary greatly, but students may wish to focus on religious zeal, government corruption, or economic prosperity or decline.

SKILL-BUILDING STRATEGIES — Understanding Frames of Reference

The Reign of Aurangzeb

A frame of reference is a set of ideas, conditions, or beliefs. Historians use different frames of reference to analyze a person, an event, or an era. For example, a historian may examine a subject from a social, economic, legal, or political frame of reference. As a result, different scholars may tell a very different story about the same historical subject. They can come to different conclusions based on their frame of reference. Knowing a historian's frame of reference helps you to understand what you read. Understanding different interpretations about Aurangzeb's rule requires analysis of the frames of reference used by the historians.

Historians' Views

"The predominant trait of the Mughal rulers of India was their political instinct. . . . Aurangzeb displayed this character to an eminent [outstanding] degree."

Mughal Empire in India

"[The] intolerance of Aurangzeb . . . hastened the ruin of the dynasty . . . his bigotry and persecutions rendered him hateful to his Hindu subjects."

A History of the Sikhs

"Aurangzeb's government made itself ridiculous by violently enforcing for a time, then relaxing, and finally abandoning a code of puritanical morals opposed to the feelings of the entire population . . ."

The Cambridge History of India

Skills Reminder

To understand frames of reference, first identify what factors the author emphasizes, such as economics, politics, or social outcomes. Also, identify the context in which the information is given. For example, is an analysis of a leader's rule being offered in the history of a people whom he conquered? Assess how this frame of reference might influence the information. Finally, compare how authors using different frames of reference might come to different conclusions about an event.

Skills Practice

❶ Study the passages above about the reign of the Mughal ruler Aurangzeb. What frame of reference is each historian using?
❷ What conclusions can you draw about Aurangzeb's rule from these passages?
❸ Write a brief summary of the rise and fall of either the Ottoman or Safavid empires using a particular frame of reference.

Despite his abuses Shah Jahān was an extremely vigorous ruler. During the 30 years of his rule, he put down several rebellions, built a magnificent new capital at Delhi, and conquered new territories in the Deccan. He also launched an unsuccessful attempt to recapture the old Mughal homeland in central Asia. The shah's Peacock Throne, designed to inspire awe, was the greatest symbol of Mughal splendor. The throne was encrusted with gold and the largest diamonds, emeralds, and other precious gems. Shah Jahān also sought to make Delhi the world's most beautiful capital as a means of reflecting his power.

Aurangzeb. In 1657 Shah Jahān became ill. His son Muhī-ud-Dīn Muhammad, known by his princely title of **Aurangzeb** (AWR·uhng·zeb), killed his older brother, imprisoned Shah Jahān, and declared himself emperor.

A devout Sunni Muslim, Aurangzeb followed strict Islamic law in his personal life. He dressed simply and expected his courtiers to follow his example. He ended government spending on buildings and monuments. He banned most celebrations, particularly those that included wine and music.

Aurangzeb persecuted all other faiths in the Mughal Empire. He insisted on strict observance of Islamic holy laws. He restored the hated tax on Hindus and destroyed thousands of Hindu temples. He also oppressed the Shi'ah and Sufi Muslims. When crowds gathered outside the Red Fort to protest, Aurangzeb used elephants to crush them. Religious groups rioted throughout the empire.

Under Aurangzeb the Mughal Empire was the largest it would ever be. Unfortunately, the widespread revolts and economic problems weakened the empire. Aurangzeb may have regretted the bloodshed of his reign. When he died in 1707, he wondered aloud whether his actions would please his God.

This image dating from the mid-1600s portrays Shah Jahān at the height of his power.

✔ **READING CHECK: Contrasting** How was the reign of Aurangzeb different from the reign of Shah Jahān? imposed strict Islamic law; ended government spending on buildings and monuments; persecuted other religions

SECTION 3 REVIEW

1. **Identify** and explain the significance:
   Rajputs
   Bābur
   Akbar
   Shah Jahān
   Taj Mahal
   Sikh
   Aurangzeb

2. **Sequencing** Copy the chart below. Use it to organize important events in the history of the Mughal Empire.

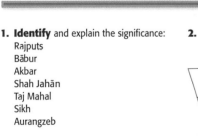

   1. Bābur wins battle at Paniput.
   2.
   3.
   4.
   5.
   6. Aurangzeb dies.

3. **Finding the Main Idea**
   a. What evidence shows that Akbar tried to unify his empire?
   b. How did Shah Jahān improve the empire?
   c. How did Shah Jahān raise funds for his ambitious building programs and his military policies?
   d. In what ways did the strict policies of Aurangzeb represent a return to intolerance in Mughal India?

4. **Writing and Critical Thinking**
   Drawing Conclusions Explain how Aurangzeb harmed the Mughal Empire.
   Consider:
   • his policies toward other religions
   • his response to protests
   • his strict observance of Islamic laws

Homework Practice Online

keyword: SP3 HP18

REVIEW AND ASSESSMENT RESOURCES

REPRODUCIBLE RESOURCES

▶ Vocabulary Activity 18

TECHNOLOGY RESOURCES

▶ Chapter 18 Test Generator (on the One-Stop Planner)
▶ Global Skill Builder CD–ROM
▶ HRW Web Site

REINFORCEMENT, REVIEW, and ASSESSMENT

▶ Chapter 18 Review, pp. 444–445
▶ Chapter 18 Tutorial for Students, Parents, Mentors, and Peers
▶ Chapter 18 Test (Form A or B)
▶ Alternative Assessment Handbook
▶ Chapter 18 Test for English Language Learners and Special-Needs Students

REVIEW

Have students complete the Chapter 18 Review on pages 444–445.

ASSESS

Use one of the chapter tests to assess students' understanding of the content. For Alternative Assessment, see the Portfolio Activities and Alternative Assessment Handbook.

CHAPTER 18 REVIEW ANSWERS

Understanding Main Ideas

1. parts of eastern Europe, western Asia, and northern Africa

2. They fought for the expansion of the empire.

3. allowed the various groups to govern themselves

4. unified Persians; threatened Persia's neighbors

5. Shi'ah gave Persians an identity and helped unify them.

6. 'Abbās regained control of lands lost to the Ottomans and Uzbeks and led his people into a time of prosperity.

7. Bābur conquered the town of Panipat and then took Delhi and the surrounding region.

8. gained Rajput support, improved the tax system and the empire's economy

9. Shah Jahan spent heavily while Aurangzeb halted government spending.

Reviewing Themes

1. the histories of the Janissaries and the kizilbash

2. Tolerant policies benefited the Ottomans. Forcing subjects to accept the Shi'ah faith strengthened the Safavid Empire. In Mughal India, persecution and oppression weakened governmental control.

3. People with ability could become part of the ruling class.

444

CHAPTER 18 Review

Creating a Time Line

Copy the time line below onto a sheet of paper. Complete the time line by filling in the events, individuals, and dates from the chapter that you think were significant. Pick three events and explain why you think they were significant.

| 1300 | 1400 | 1500 | 1600 | 1700 |

Writing a Summary

Using standard grammar, spelling, sentence structure, and punctuation, write an overview of the events in the chapter.

Identifying People and Ideas

Identify the following terms or individuals and explain their significance:

1. millets
2. Janissaries
3. Süleyman
4. kizilbash
5. Esmā'īl

6. 'Abbās
7. Bābur
8. Akbar
9. Shah Jahān
10. Aurangzeb

Understanding Main Ideas

Section 1 *(pp. 432–435)*

The Ottoman Empire

1. What territory was included in the Ottoman Empire at its height?
2. Why were the Janissaries important to the Ottoman sultans?
3. How did the Ottoman Turks maintain peace among the various ethnic groups within their widespread empire?

Section 2 *(pp. 436–438)*

The Safavid Empire

4. What role did the Shi'ah religion play in the strengthening of the Safavid Empire and in the empire's relations with its neighbors?
5. How did Shi'ah affect the Persians' ideas about themselves?
6. Why did the Persians of the Safavid Empire call 'Abbās "the Great"?

Section 3 *(pp. 439–443)*

The Mughal Empire in India

7. What event marks the beginning of the Mughal Empire?
8. What were Akbar's most important accomplishments?
9. How did Aurangzeb's approach to government spending differ from Shah Jahān's?

Reviewing Themes

1. **Global Relations** What evidence is there that the Islamic empires supported large, strong militaries?
2. **Culture** How did religious policies affect the Islamic empires?
3. **Government** What effect did the character of individual rulers have on the Islamic empires?

Thinking Critically

1. **Drawing Inferences** In what way did the building of the Taj Mahal contribute to the decline of the Mughal Empire?
2. **Comparing** Compare the policy toward Sunni Muslims in the Ottoman Empire to the policy in the Safavid Empire.
3. **Supporting a Point of View** What evidence would you give that in the Ottoman Empire ordinary people had an equal chance for success?

Writing About History

Comparing and Contrasting Write a report describing the similarities and differences among the Ottoman, Safavid, and Mughal empires. Use the chart below to organize your thoughts before you write.

	Ottoman	Safavid	Mughal
Title used by ruler			
Most successful ruler			
Official branch of Islam			
Policy toward other religions			
Present name of country			

CLOSE

Ask students the following question: Is the life of an empire most affected by the size and strength of its military, its leader's religious policies, or the personal character of its rulers? Divide students into groups of similar opinion and allow each group to define its position with details and examples from the text as support. **COOPERATIVE LEARNING**

RETEACH

Have students who had trouble with the test use their textbooks to correct their tests. Then have them take the Form B test to assess their mastery of the material. **ENGLISH LANGUAGE LEARNERS , COOPERATIVE LEARNING**

Portfolio Extensions

1. Ask students to summarize the effects of religion on their own community. Have them consider the divisions between doctrines, prejudice, wealth, social status, etc.

2. Put students into pairs. Ask them to select one ruler discussed in Chapter 18 and describe his religious policies.

3. Have students imagine they are living during the height of the Mughal Empire. Tell them to write a letter in which they express their opinion about the Shah's military campaigns or about the building of the Taj Mahal.

Building Social Studies Skills

Interpreting Maps

Study the map below. Then answer the questions that follow.

The Ottomans in Hungary, c. 1520–c. 1565

1. Which of the following statements best describes the Ottoman expansion into Hungary during the 1500s?

   a. The Ottomans' victory at Mohács had little impact on their movement into Hungary.

   b. The Ottomans' victory at Mohács allowed them to expand north, east, and west.

   c. Within ten years of their victory at Mohács, the Ottomans had taken control of all Hungary.

   d. Their victory at Mohács enabled the Ottomans to win control of the entire Mediterranean basin.

2. Why do you think the location of Mohács was important to Ottoman plans to conquer Hungary?

Sequencing

Read the sentences below about the Mughal rulers. Then answer the question that follows.

A. Shah Jahān (ruled 1628–1658) built the Taj Mahal.

B. The greatest Mughal emperor was Akbar. By the end of his reign in the early 1600s, Akbar controlled much of northern and central India.

C. Bābur occupied Delhi in 1526 and founded the Mughal Empire.

D. Economic problems had weakened the government by the time Aurangzeb died in 1707.

E. By the early years of the 1500s, the Muslim Sultanate of Delhi was suffering from internal weakness and was being increasingly challenged by the Rajput princes and their armies.

3. Which of the following shows the events listed in the order in which they occurred?

   a. B, C, A, D, E

   b. C, A, D, E, B

   c. D, E, A, B, C

   d. E, C, B, A, D

4. What were the main differences between the way Akbar and Aurangzeb ruled the Mughal Empire? Give specific examples.

Alternative Assessment

Building Your Portfolio

Culture

In the world today, religious policies still unify or divide cultures. Use your textbook and other sources to find examples of cultures that have been either unified or divided by the religious policies of governments. Then prepare a script about your findings that a television reporter could read on the evening news.

internet connect

Internet Activity: go.hrw.com
KEYWORD: SP3 WH18

Choose a topic on Islamic Empires in Asia to:

- create an illustrated time line of the major events in the history of the Ottoman Empire.
- research life and society in the Safavid Empire.
- create a newspaper article on the impact of the siege of Vienna in 1683.

Thinking Critically

1. The expensive building put a burden on the taxpayers and was one cause of economic problems in the Mughal empire.

2. The leaders of the Ottoman Empire encouraged the Sunni Muslim religion while the Safavid ruler, Esmā'īl, forced his people to convert to Shi'ah.

3. Students might suggest that the class system of rulers and reayas allowed people of any birth to find a place in the ruling class if they showed the proper ability.

Writing About History

Answers might include details about military, political, cultural, economic successes/failures of each empire.

Building Social Studies Skills

1. b

2. located in central Hungary and allowed Ottomans to expand in all directions

3. d

4. Akbar supported religious tolerance and the arts and improved the economy; Aurangzeb persecuted non-Sunni religions, crushed dissent, and created civil unrest.

Building Your Portfolio

Students' answers will vary but should include current cultures of places such as Israel, Bosnia, Ireland, or England and may include examples of government policies.

CROSS-CULTURAL CONNECTIONS *Literature*

Spotlight on LITERATURE

The exact nature of poetry can be difficult to define, partly because it is written in so many different forms. *Encyclopaedia Britannica* defines poetry as "literature that evokes a concentrated imaginative awareness of experience or a specific emotional response through language chosen and arranged for its meaning, sound, and rhythm." Have students study the forms of poetic verse shown below—rhyming couplets, sonnet, and haiku—and then write a

poem in one of these forms. Students may write about a subject of their choice.

Spotlight on LITERATURE

The poems below express feelings about death—a universal theme in poetry. Have students use primary and secondary sources, including computer software, to find several contemporary poems about death. Then have students use standard grammar, spelling, sentence structure, and punctuation to write a brief essay comparing the forms of their chosen poems with the ones in this feature. Which form best expresses feelings about death? Which is their favorite? Why?

Culture

Some scholars believe poetry may have been the first way people used language. Poetry probably began in rituals reciting magical spells to bring a good harvest. Humans now use poetry to affect the human spirit rather than the natural world. While poetic form is different in various cultures, the language usually follows a definite and predictable pattern. In ancient Greek poetry, the rhythm of syllables created a pattern. Rhyming patterns were first used in the poetry of the Romance languages, particularly French. The ballad, the sonnet, and blank verse all developed later in English poetry. While it is difficult to define, most people recognize poetry by the fact that it is written in lines and therefore looks different from prose on a printed page.

ACTIVITY: Ask students to research the history of poetry in a particular culture. Then have students create a time line that notes the important developments and works of poetry in that culture's history.

UNDERSTANDING LITERATURE ANSWER

similarities in purpose: all three authors talk about death and their legacies; differences in style: Shah-nameh is very long and rhymes, haiku is very short, sonnet is medium in length and has a strict pattern of rhyme and rhythm; similarities in tone: all are nostalgic

CROSS-CULTURAL CONNECTIONS *Literature*

Styles of Verse

Throughout the world's diverse societies, many forms of poetry have developed. Each culture's poetry has distinctive sounds and styles. The Persian poet Firdawsi (c. 935–1020) told the story of his nation's kings in an epic named Shah-nameh. *This massive work contains 60,000 rhyming couplets. In the excerpt below the hero Sekander promises to care for King Dara as the king dies. William Shakespeare (1564–1616), an English writer, also wrote about death, but in a very different style. His sonnets are 14-line poems with a strict pattern of rhythm and rhyme. Japanese poet Banzan's haiku poem—written on his deathbed in 1730—follows the typical haiku form. In the original Japanese it contains five syllables in the first line, seven in the second, and five in the third.*

Shah-nameh *by Firdawsi*

"I will have physicians brought for you from India and Rum [Rome] and I will cause tears of blood to flow for the pain you have suffered. . . . My heart bled and a cry issued from my lips when yesterday I heard from my elders that we two are of one stock and share a single shirt. Why should we extirpate [wipe out] our seed in rivalry?"

On hearing this, Dara said in a strong voice, ". . . Marry my pure-bodied daughter and maintain her in security in your palace. . . . It may be that by her you will have a noble son who will restore the name of Esfandiyar [an ancestor] to glory."

Shown here is the manuscript of a poem by the Japanese haiku master Bashō.

Haiku by Banzan

Mame de iyo
mi wa narawashi no
kusa no tsuyu.

(Translation:)
Farewell
I pass as all things do
dew on the grass.

"Sonnet 19" by William Shakespeare

Devouring time,
　blunt thou the lion's
　paws,
And make the earth
　devour her own
　sweet brood;
Pluck the keen teeth
　from the fierce
　tiger's jaws,
And burn the long-lived
　phoenix in her blood.
Make glad and sorry seasons as
　thou fleet'st,
And do whate'er thou wilt, swift-footed time,
To the wide world and all her fading sweets.
But I forbid thee one most heinous crime:
O, carve not with thy hours my love's fair brow,
Nor draw no lines there with thine antique pen.
Him in thy course untainted do allow
For beauty's pattern to succeeding men.
Yet do thy worst, old time; despite thy wrong
My love shall in my verse ever live young.

Understanding Literature

What similarities and differences do you find among these poems in their purpose, style, and tone?

Economics

During the 1500s and 1600s the Mughal Empire dominated the Indian subcontinent. Much of the empire's growth came as a result of increasing contact and trade with foreign countries. Have students research the economic history of the Mughal Empire. Then ask students to copy the graphic organizer below and complete it with their findings.

```
          ┌─────────────────────┐
          │   Mughal economy    │
          └─────────────────────┘
   ┌───────────┬───────────┬───────────┐
┌─────────┐ ┌─────────┐ ┌─────────┐
│ primary │ │ primary │ │ major   │
│ exports │ │ imports │ │ trading │
│         │ │         │ │ partners│
└─────────┘ └─────────┘ └─────────┘
```

Global Relations

Using the map on page 433 as a guide, have students create their own map of the Ottoman Empire. Encourage students to be creative in their presentation of the map's information. Remind them to include labels for important cities, bodies of water, and neighboring countries. Students should also use a key to identify relevant information. Then have students write five questions to accompany their map.

UNIT 4 — BUILDING YOUR Portfolio

Economics

A search for wealth motivated European exploration of the New World. Imagine that you are an English adventurer who wishes to undertake a voyage to America in the 1500s. You will need the financial support of the Queen to make the journey. Your task is to write a proposal showing why your trip to the New World would be economically beneficial to England. What types of evidence would you use to show the importance of exploration for the economic welfare of the kingdom?

Ottoman ceramic pitcher and plate

Ferdinand Magellan and his fleet setting sail from Spain in 1519

Global Relations

During the 1400s and 1500s, the Ottoman Turks expanded the boundaries of their empire, conquering much of eastern Europe. Imagine that you are a soldier advancing with the Ottoman armies through eastern Europe in the 1520s. Create a diary in which you recount your experiences, including your impressions of European society, government, and religion. Based on your observations, discuss your view of the relations between the Ottoman Empire and the various kingdoms of eastern Europe.

Further Reading

Dersin, Denise, ed. *What Life Was Like: At The Rebirth Of Genius, Renaissance Italy 1400-1550.* Alexandria, Virginia: Time-Life Books, 1999. A survey of daily life and culture in Renaissance Italy.

Goodwin, Jason. *Lords of the Horizons: A History of the Ottoman Empire.* New York: Owl Books, 2000. A thorough survey of the Ottoman Empire from its beginnings to its collapse.

Hale, J. R., ed. *The Thames and Hudson Encyclopedia of the Italian Renaissance.* London: Thames and Hudson, 1988. A reference work on the history, politics, culture, and society of the Italian Renaissance.

Meltzer, Milton. *Columbus and the World Around Him.* New York: Watts Franklin, 1990. A history of Christopher Columbus and his four voyages.

Pilbeam, Mavis. *Japan Under The Shoguns, 1185-1868.* New York: Raintree/Steck-Vaughn, 1999. A history of the shogunates, and a look at everyday life in Japan and the role of the samurai.

internet connect — go.hrw.com

Internet Activity
KEYWORD: SP3 U4

In assigned groups, develop a multimedia presentation about the Age of Exploration and Expansion. Choose information from the chapter Internet Connect activities and the Holt Researcher that best reflects the major topics of the period. Write an outline and a script for your presentation, which may be shown to the class.

History Maker

ZHENG HE. Nearly a century before the European era of exploration, the Chinese undertook extensive seafaring voyages. In the early 1400s the Chinese emperor appointed Zheng He to lead the Ming dynasty's mission to restore control over South and Southeast Asia. The Chinese had already developed an extensive maritime trade to acquire spices and raw industrial materials. Technological developments in shipbuilding and navigation allowed the Chinese to extend their influence in the region. In 1405 Zheng He set sail on his first voyage, commanding 62 ships and 27,800 men and traveling to many countries. When Zheng returned to China in 1415, he brought representatives from more than 30 states of South and Southeast Asia to pay homage to the Chinese emperor. Although Zheng He's seven expeditions did not establish the trading empires created by European explorers, his voyages did extend China's political control over maritime Asia.

Critical Thinking

How did Chinese seafaring expeditions differ from European voyages?

ANSWER: Chinese expeditions occurred a century earlier and did not establish trading empires like the European expeditions did.

CHAPTER

The Modern World

CHAPTER RESOURCE MANAGER

Objectives	Pacing Guide	Reproducible Resources

SECTION 1
Revolution to Imperialism
(pp. 450–457)

- Explain how European monarchies changed from the 1500s to the 1800s.
- Describe new ideas about government that occurred in Britain and the United States.
- Explain how the French Revolution differed from the American Revolution.
- Describe how life changed during the Industrial Revolution.
- Describe how nationalist movements and imperialism affected the world.

Regular	Block Scheduling
1 day	.5 day

Block Scheduling Handbook with Team Teaching Strategies, Epilogue 1

RS Guided Reading Strategy Epilogue 1
PS Readings in World History 59: A Day in the Life of Louis XIV

SECTION 2
World War in the Twentieth Century
(pp. 458–463)

- Describe the causes of World War I.
- Explain how the Great Depression affected governments.
- Explain how Africa, Asia, and Latin America changed during the 1930s.
- Describe the events that led to World War II.

Regular	Block Scheduling
1 day	.5 day

Block Scheduling Handbook with Team Teaching Strategies, Epilogue 2

RS Guided Reading Strategy Epilogue 2
PS Readings in World History 108: The Morning of the 500-ton Bomb

---

SECTION 3
Europe and the Americas Since 1945
(pp. 464–467)

- Explain how the Allied powers dealt with Germany after the war.
- Describe the causes of the Cold War.
- Analyze how European nations fared after the war.
- Explain how political unrest affected life in Latin American nations.

Regular	Block Scheduling
1 day	.5 day

Block Scheduling Handbook with Team Teaching Strategies, Epilogue 3

RS Guided Reading Strategy Epilogue 3

SECTION 4
Asia, Africa, and the Middle East Since 1945
(pp. 468–473)

- Describe how Japan recovered from the devastation of World War II.
- Explain why communism led to greater tensions and conflict in Asia.
- Describe how African nations dealt with independence.
- Explain why violence marred life in the Middle East.

Regular	Block Scheduling
1 day	.5 day

Block Scheduling Handbook with Team Teaching Strategies, Epilogue 4

RS Guided Reading Strategy Epilogue 4
PS Readings in World History 118: Nelson Mandela Explains Why There Is a South African Resistance Movement

---

SECTION 5
The Modern Era and Beyond
(pp. 474–477)

- Describe how the superpowers dealt with a changing world.
- Explain how technological developments affected health, the environment, and entertainment.

Regular	Block Scheduling
1 day	.5 day

Block Scheduling Handbook with Team Teaching Strategies, Epilogue 5

RS Guided Reading Strategy Epilogue 5
RS Graphic Organizer Activity Epilogue: Technological Innovations and Challenges
SM Geography Activity Epilogue: After the Cold War

SECTION 6
A Day That Changed the World
(pp. 478–483)

- Describe how the United States was attacked on September 11, 2001, and how people responded.
- Explain how the events of September 11, 2001, affected the U.S. economy.
- Identify the immediate steps U.S. leaders and their allies took to find those responsible for the attacks and bring them to justice.

Regular	Block Scheduling
1 day	.5 day

Block Scheduling Handbook with Team Teaching Strategies, Epilogue 6

RS Guided Reading Strategy Epilogue 6
E Creative Teaching Strategy Epilogue: Emergency Response Team

---

Chapter Resource Key

PS Primary Sources
RS Reading Support
IC Interdisciplinary Connections
E Enrichment
SM Skills Mastery

A Assessment
REV Review
ELL Reinforcement and English Language Learners
 Transparencies
 CD-ROM

 Music
 Video
 Internet
 Holt Presentation Maker Using Microsoft® PowerPoint®

One-Stop Planner CD-ROM

See the *One-Stop Planner* for a complete list of additional resources for students and teachers.

One-Stop Planner CD-ROM

It's easy to plan lessons, select resources, and print out materials for your students when you use the **One-Stop Planner** CD–ROM with *Test Generator.*

Technology Resources

One-Stop Planner Epilogue 1
Holt Researcher: World History: Mary I, Elizabeth I
Holt Researcher: World History: Napoleon Bonaparte, Josephine de Beauharnais
World History Teaching Transparency: Geography and History 17: The Fight for Independence, 1776–1781
Homework Practice Online
Online Maps, Charts, and Graphs: European Industrialization, Mid-1800s

One-Stop Planner Epilogue 2
Holt Researcher: World History: Benito Mussolini, Adolf Hitler
Holt Researcher: World History: Mohandas Gandhi
CNN. Presents World Cultures: Yesterday and Today Segment 27: The Great Depression
Homework Practice Online
Online Maps, Charts, and Graphs: The New Imperialism, 1900

One-Stop Planner Epilogue 3
World History and Cultures Video Program 26: Television and the Cold War
World History Teaching Transparency: Geography and History 29: The Economy of Latin America
Homework Practice Online
Online Maps, Charts, and Graphs: Communist Europe in 1949

One-Stop Planner Epilogue 4
World History Teaching Transparency: Regional and World Map 37: East and Southeast Asia
Homework Practice Online
Online Maps, Charts, and Graphs: Iran-Iraq War, 1980–1988

One-Stop Planner Epilogue 5
Homework Practice Online
Online Maps, Charts, and Graphs: Breakup of the Soviet Union, 1991

One-Stop Planner Epilogue 6
Homework Practice Online
Online Maps, Charts, and Graphs: Southwest Asia

Reinforcement, Review, and Assessment

Daily Quiz Epilogue 1
Main Idea Activity Epilogue 1
English Audio Summary Epilogue 1
Spanish Audio Summary Epilogue 1
REV Section 1 Review, p. 457

Daily Quiz Epilogue 2
Main Idea Activity Epilogue 2
English Audio Summary Epilogue 2
Spanish Audio Summary Epilogue 2
REV Section 2 Review, p. 463

Daily Quiz Epilogue 3
Main Idea Activity Epilogue 3
English Audio Summary Epilogue 3
Spanish Audio Summary Epilogue 3
REV Section 3 Review, p. 467

Daily Quiz Epilogue 4
Main Idea Activity Epilogue 4
English Audio Summary Epilogue 4
Spanish Audio Summary Epilogue 4
REV Section 4 Review, p. 473

Daily Quiz Epilogue 5
Main Idea Activity Epilogue 5
English Audio Summary Epilogue 5
Spanish Audio Summary Epilogue 5
REV Section 5 Review, p. 477

Daily Quiz Epilogue 6
Main Idea Activity Epilogue 6
English Audio Summary Epilogue 6
Spanish Audio Summary Epilogue 6
REV Section 6 Review, p. 483

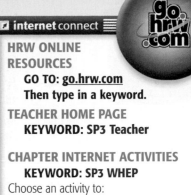

internet connect

HRW ONLINE RESOURCES
GO TO: go.hrw.com
Then type in a keyword.

TEACHER HOME PAGE
KEYWORD: SP3 Teacher

CHAPTER INTERNET ACTIVITIES
KEYWORD: SP3 WHEP
Choose an activity to:
• write a biography of Louis XIV, the "Sun King."
• research the Cold War and look for elements of popular culture that reflect Cold War anxieties.
• create a time line sequencing the major events of apartheid in South Africa.

CHAPTER ENRICHMENT LINKS
KEYWORD: SP3 CHEP

ONLINE ASSESSMENT
Homework Practice
KEYWORD: SP3 HPEP
Standardized Test Prep
KEYWORD: SP3 STPEP
Rubrics
KEYWORD: SS Rubrics

ONLINE MAPS, CHARTS, AND GRAPHS
KEYWORD: SP3 MCG

CONTENT UPDATES
KEYWORD: SS Content Updates

HOLT PRESENTATION MAKER
KEYWORD: SP3 PPTEP

ONLINE READING SUPPORT
KEYWORD: SS Strategies

CURRENT EVENTS
KEYWORD: S3 Current Events

Meeting Individual Needs

Ability Levels

Level 1 Basic level activities designed for all students encountering new material

Level 2 Intermediate level activities designed for average students

Level 3 Challenging activities designed for honors and gifted and talented students

English Language Learners These activities address the needs of students with Limited English Proficiency.

Chapter Review and Assessment

IC Vocabulary Activity Epilogue
Global Skill Builder CD–ROM
HRW Web Site
REV Epilogue Tutorial for Students, Parents, Mentors, and Peers
REV Epilogue Review, pp. 484–485
A Epilogue Test Generator (on the One-Stop Planner)
A Epilogue Test (Form A or B)
A Alternative Assessment Handbook
A Epilogue Test for English Language Learners and Special-Needs Students

CHAPTER

Build on What You Know

Ask students to answer the following questions:

What are some factors that might help a nation develop and become strong?

Consider:

• the system of government
• the land and resources
• the economy

What are some reasons nations come into conflict with one another?

Consider:

• political systems
• religion
• expansion policies
• ethnic differences

EXPLORING THE TIME LINE

GL⊙BAL EVENTS

internet connect

TOPIC: The Sun King
GO TO: go.hrw.com
KEYWORD: SP3 WHEP

Have students access the Internet through the HRW Go site to conduct research on Louis XIV, the Sun King. Have them write a biography of Louis XIV that includes facts about his life, his reign, and the luxury of his court. Have students explain why Louis XIV was called the Sun King and how his behavior and policies affected France.

CHAPTER

1500 to the Present

The Modern World

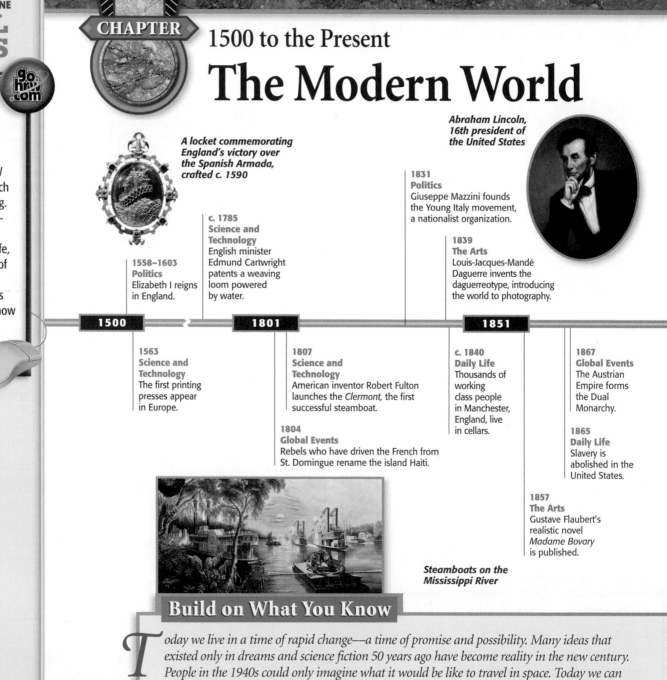

A locket commemorating England's victory over the Spanish Armada, crafted c. 1590

1558–1603
Politics
Elizabeth I reigns in England.

c. 1785
Science and Technology
English minister Edmund Cartwright patents a weaving loom powered by water.

Abraham Lincoln, 16th president of the United States

1831
Politics
Giuseppe Mazzini founds the Young Italy movement, a nationalist organization.

1839
The Arts
Louis-Jacques-Mandé Daguerre invents the daguerreotype, introducing the world to photography.

1500	1801	1851

1563
Science and Technology
The first printing presses appear in Europe.

1807
Science and Technology
American inventor Robert Fulton launches the *Clermont,* the first successful steamboat.

1804
Global Events
Rebels who have driven the French from St. Domingue rename the island Haiti.

c. 1840
Daily Life
Thousands of working class people in Manchester, England, live in cellars.

1867
Global Events
The Austrian Empire forms the Dual Monarchy.

1865
Daily Life
Slavery is abolished in the United States.

1857
The Arts
Gustave Flaubert's realistic novel *Madame Bovary* is published.

Steamboats on the Mississippi River

Build on What You Know

Today we live in a time of rapid change—a time of promise and possibility. Many ideas that existed only in dreams and science fiction 50 years ago have become reality in the new century. People in the 1940s could only imagine what it would be like to travel in space. Today we can watch the massive space shuttle slice through the clouds on its way to dock with an orbiting space station. Other frontiers remain on Earth—in science labs, in industry and business, in the oceans, and in classrooms. A new generation is now being prepared to meet today's challenges, explore tomorrow's frontiers, and strive to enhance the quality of human life.

What's Your Opinion?

Economics

Agree Jobs and goods are plentiful when an economy is growing.

Disagree Only those with money and freedom can benefit from a growing economy.

Culture

Agree Conflict occurs when one group tries to impose its religion on another group.

Disagree Religious differences enrich a society.

Science, Technology & Society

Agree Technology gives a small percentage of people a high standard of living at the expense of the world's environment.

Disagree Advances in technology benefit all people.

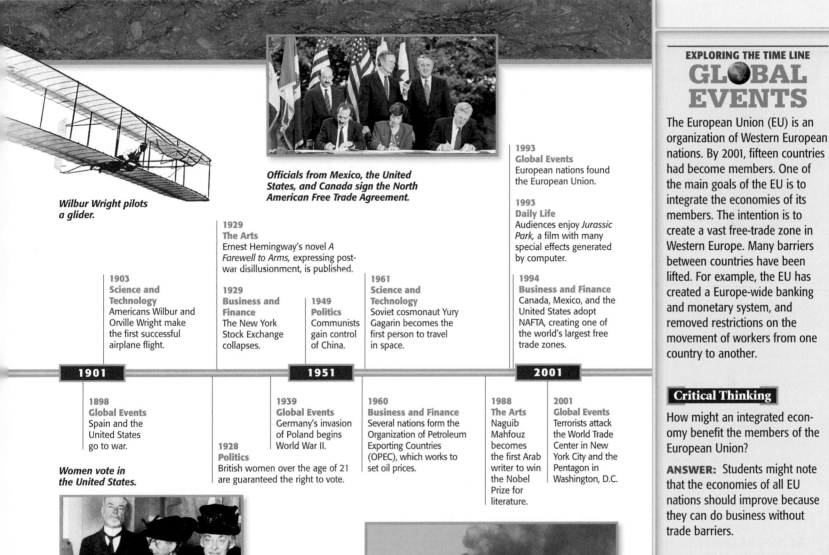

Wilbur Wright pilots a glider.

Officials from Mexico, the United States, and Canada sign the North American Free Trade Agreement.

**1903
Science and Technology**
Americans Wilbur and Orville Wright make the first successful airplane flight.

**1929
The Arts**
Ernest Hemingway's novel *A Farewell to Arms,* expressing post-war disillusionment, is published.

**1929
Business and Finance**
The New York Stock Exchange collapses.

**1949
Politics**
Communists gain control of China.

**1961
Science and Technology**
Soviet cosmonaut Yury Gagarin becomes the first person to travel in space.

**1993
Global Events**
European nations found the European Union.

**1993
Daily Life**
Audiences enjoy *Jurassic Park,* a film with many special effects generated by computer.

**1994
Business and Finance**
Canada, Mexico, and the United States adopt NAFTA, creating one of the world's largest free trade zones.

1901

1951

2001

**1898
Global Events**
Spain and the United States go to war.

Women vote in the United States.

**1928
Politics**
British women over the age of 21 are guaranteed the right to vote.

**1939
Global Events**
Germany's invasion of Poland begins World War II.

**1960
Business and Finance**
Several nations form the Organization of Petroleum Exporting Countries (OPEC), which works to set oil prices.

**1988
The Arts**
Naguib Mahfouz becomes the first Arab writer to win the Nobel Prize for literature.

**2001
Global Events**
Terrorists attack the World Trade Center in New York City and the Pentagon in Washington, D.C.

New York City's Manhattan Island following the terrorist attack on September 11, 2001

EXPLORING THE TIME LINE
GLOBAL EVENTS

The European Union (EU) is an organization of Western European nations. By 2001, fifteen countries had become members. One of the main goals of the EU is to integrate the economies of its members. The intention is to create a vast free-trade zone in Western Europe. Many barriers between countries have been lifted. For example, the EU has created a Europe-wide banking and monetary system, and removed restrictions on the movement of workers from one country to another.

Critical Thinking

How might an integrated economy benefit the members of the European Union?

ANSWER: Students might note that the economies of all EU nations should improve because they can do business without trade barriers.

What's Your Opinion?

 *Do you **agree** or **disagree** with the following statements? Support your point of view in your journal.*

Economics A growing economy benefits all people.

Culture Religious differences lead to conflict and bloodshed.

Science, Technology & Society Technology that improves the quality of life for individuals can prove harmful to society as a whole.

OBJECTIVES

1 Explain how European monarchies changed from the 1500s to the 1800s.

2 Describe new ideas about government that occurred in Britain and the United States.

3 Explain how the French Revolution differed from the American Revolution.

4 Describe how life changed during the Industrial Revolution.

5 Describe how nationalist movements and imperialism affected the world.

SECTION 1

READ TO DISCOVER

❶ How did European monarchies change from the 1500s to the 1800s?

❷ What new ideas about government occurred in Britain and the United States?

❸ How did the French Revolution differ from the American Revolution?

❹ How did life change during the Industrial Revolution?

❺ How did nationalist movements and imperialism affect the world?

DEFINE

federal system of government
capitalism
socialism
communism
imperialism

IDENTIFY

Louis XIV
Peter the Great
Catherine the Great
Elizabeth I
English Bill of Rights
Enlightenment
Industrial Revolution
Napoléon Bonaparte
Otto von Bismarck

▶ WHY IT MATTERS TODAY

Constitutional changes made in Europe years ago still affect our government today. Use **CNNfyi.com** or other **current event** sources to learn more about the systems of government we share with European countries today. Report your findings in your journal.

CNNfyi.com

Revolution to Imperialism

The Main Idea
European nations strengthened their governments and economies and built colonial empires.

The Story Continues *"I am your anointed Queen. I will never be by violence constrained to do anything." So goes a famous statement by England's Queen Elizabeth I, one of England's strongest monarchs. Yet in England, unlike countries on the continent, the absolute monarchy would never quite take hold. Eventually some of England's colonies would launch a revolution that would change not only politics, but also the entire fabric of Western society.*

Monarchs in Europe

The years after about 1500 saw the rise of powerful European monarchs. As rulers strengthened their power, they often came into conflict with other countries. Many nations experienced internal conflicts as well.

France. In 1589 Henry IV became the first French monarch of a new royal house—the Bourbons. Henry had been a Huguenot, a member of a Protestant minority group. However, he converted to Catholicism to help bring peace and unity to France. In 1618, eight years after his death, the Thirty Years' War began in Prague as a Protestant rebellion against the Holy Roman Empire. The war eventually weakened the Holy Roman Empire and the Habsburg family that controlled it.

In 1643 **Louis XIV** became the king of France. He ruled for 72 years, the longest reign in French history. He believed in the divine right of kings—that God had chosen him to rule the nation. Louis XIV's court became the ideal for European royalty. Louis also wanted to extend France's territory east to the Rhine River. To accomplish this, he fought four wars between 1667 and 1713. These wars put a great financial strain on France.

Russia. In 1613 the Russian national assembly elected Michael Romanov to be czar. The Romanov dynasty ruled Russia for the next 300 years. In 1682 Peter I—known to history as **Peter the Great**—became czar. Peter ruled Russia until 1725. He believed that Russia had to become more like the rest of Europe. Peter reorganized Russia along western European lines. Peter was succeeded by his second wife, Catherine I.

Peter's grandson, Peter III, married Catherine II, a German princess. Peter III was unpopular and in 1762 was murdered by nobles who supported Catherine II. Known as **Catherine the Great,** she ruled from 1762 to 1796. Catherine's greatness lay mainly in her foreign policy. She continued land expansion begun by Peter the Great. In a successful war against the Turks, Catherine gained control of most of the northern shore of the Black Sea and the region of the Crimea. She also helped Russia acquire much of Poland.

Catherine the Great, empress of Russia, 1762–1796

TEACH OBJECTIVE 1

LEVEL 1: Review the meaning of the phrases "divine right of kings" and "absolute monarchy" with students. Then help students fill in the graphic organizer that follows to summarize how European monarchies changed. Ask students to identify the monarch who made each change.
ENGLISH LANGUAGE LEARNERS

France
changed religion to unify country fought wars to extend territory

European Monarchies

Russia
reorganized to make country more European fought wars to extend territory

England
made country stable and prosperous prevented conflict and strengthened Protestantism

England. In the late 1400s a new royal family, the Tudors, became England's rulers. The first Tudor king was Henry VII, who made England stable and prosperous. His son, Henry VIII, established a new official church for England, the Anglican Church. Mary I, the oldest daughter of Henry VIII, took the throne in 1553 to become the first reigning queen of England. Mary, a devoted Catholic, was determined to make England a Catholic nation again. When Mary I died in 1558, her Protestant half-sister **Elizabeth I** became queen. Elizabeth was an able politician who used the monarchy and Parliament to prevent conflict and to strengthen Protestantism. Although Elizabeth managed Parliament skillfully, she could not prevent some members, particularly Puritans, from questioning her policies. Puritans were people who felt the Anglican Church was still too much like the Catholic Church.

Elizabeth died in 1603 without an heir to succeed her. King James VI of Scotland, the son of Mary Queen of Scots, became King James I of England in 1603. King James was a strong supporter of the Anglican Church and had no tolerance for the Puritans. The main opposition to James I came from Parliament, where the Puritans had a strong voice.

✔ **READING CHECK: Categorizing** How did the monarchies of Europe change from the 1500s to the 1700s? **Some European monarchies grew in power.**

Revolution in England and America

Like his father, James I, Charles I believed in the divine right of kings. This put him in conflict with Parliament. Many members of Parliament felt that Charles was a tyrant.

Civil War. In 1640 the Puritan-controlled House of Commons ended the king's power to dissolve Parliament. It passed a law stating that Parliament must meet at least once every three years and kept the king from raising taxes on his own. Meanwhile, a rebellion broke out in Ireland. Parliament needed a big army to put down the Irish rebellion. Not trusting the king, they proposed that Parliament be in command of the army, but Charles refused. He led troops to the House of Commons to arrest some of his opponents. With neither side compromising, a civil war began in 1642.

Oliver Cromwell, a rising Puritan leader, organized his troops into a powerful army that defeated Charles in 1645. The Cromwell-controlled Parliament abolished the monarchy and the House of Lords. It proclaimed England a commonwealth, or republic. A special court tried Charles for treason. He was beheaded in front of the palace at Whitehall in 1649. His son fled to France, and Oliver Cromwell took control of England.

Cromwell tried to establish a republican government ruled by Parliament. However, Cromwell often quarreled with Parliament, which resented his power. He eventually dissolved Parliament and ruled alone until his death in 1658. Soon the English people began turning against republican government. In 1660 Parliament invited Charles II, the son of Charles I, to return to England. The reign of Charles II is called the Restoration.

It appeared that Charles's younger brother James, a Roman Catholic, would succeed him. Two political parties developing in Parliament at this time had opposing ideas about this royal succession. The two parties, the Tories and the Whigs, were about equal in strength. Tories usually supported the Anglican Church. As believers in a hereditary monarchy, however, they would be willing to accept a Roman Catholic king. The Whigs wanted a strong Parliament and opposed having a Catholic ruler.

Holt Researcher

go.hrw.com
KEYWORD: Holt Researcher
FreeFind: Mary I
         Elizabeth I
After reading more about Mary I and Elizabeth I on the Holt Researcher, create a compare-and-contrast chart listing the political, economic, and cultural influence each had on England.

Charles I opens a session of Parliament.

History Maker

OLIVER CROMWELL. Oliver Cromwell was a contradictory figure. He was a deeply religious man who believed he was only an instrument of God's purpose. He supported representative government and wanted to create a constitutional base for his power. On the other hand, Cromwell was a gifted general who suppressed uprisings in Ireland and Scotland. He led an infamous Irish campaign in which thousands of Irish soldiers and hundreds of civilians were killed.

Critical Thinking

Ask students to describe how present-day views of Cromwell might differ depending on a person's background and experience.

ANSWER: Students should recognize that Cromwell might be hated in Ireland but respected in England.

LEVEL 2: Have students work in pairs to create a two-column chart comparing the new systems of government in Britain and the United States. *(Student charts should include the following ideas: Britain–English bill of rights, gave Parliament power over ruler, constitution limited ruler's power; United States—Declaration of Independence, recognized equality of all people, Constitution created a central government with specific powers and gave all other powers to the states and to the people)* **COOPERATIVE LEARNING**

Economics

The American colonies were a rich source of products for Britain. Before the Revolutionary War, Britain was the largest market for American tobacco, indigo, and rice. Britain also imported other products from the colonies, such as furs, fish, and hemp.

America's pine forests were particularly important to Britain. The timbers needed to build ships—especially tall timbers for masts—were almost depleted in England. Along with timber, Britain's merchant ships and navy needed pitch, tar, turpentine, and resin. These, too, came from American pine forests.

Critical Thinking

What was the relationship between America's natural resources and the start of the Revolutionary War?

ANSWER: Britain claimed ownership of the colonies' resources. Colonists thought this was repressive.

VISUAL RECORD ANSWER

Seated in a semicircle, everyone is equal and can speak directly face-to-face.

INTERPRETING THE VISUAL RECORD

Enlightenment salons Marie-Thérèse Geoffrin's salon in the Hotel Rambouillet provided a weekly opportunity for European artists and writers to meet with one another and to discuss the ideas of the Enlightenment. *How might the salon pictured below encourage the free exchange of ideas?*

When Charles II died in 1685, his Catholic brother came to the throne. James's belief in absolute royal rule antagonized both Whigs and Tories. Leaders in Parliament invited James's daughter, Mary, and her Dutch husband, William of Orange, to replace James on the throne. When William landed in England with an army in 1688, James fled to France. Parliament gave the crown to William and Mary as the joint rulers William III and Mary II. The opponents of James II had combined to bring about what is known as the Glorious Revolution, a bloodless transfer of power in the monarchy.

Parliament soon passed laws attempting to safeguard against arbitrary rule. In 1689 Parliament formalized the **English Bill of Rights,** which established the power of Parliament over the ruler. By 1700 England was still a monarchy, but Parliament held most of the power. Great Britain had become a limited constitutional monarchy. The monarch remained the head of state. With powers limited by the British constitution, however, the king or queen was required to consult Parliament. This system has changed very little since the 1700s.

English colonial expansion. England was slow to establish colonies in North America. Private companies or individuals founded the first British colonial settlements. In 1607 they established Jamestown, in what is now Virginia. It was the first permanent English settlement in North America. In 1620 settlers founded Plymouth, in what is now Massachusetts.

The British policy of mercantilism held that the colonies existed for the economic benefit of the home country. The colonies would supply raw materials and then provide a market for Britain's manufactured goods. Parliament passed laws to enforce this policy beginning in the 1650s. The colonists had to sell certain products only to Britain—even if better prices were available in another country. They also were discouraged from manufacturing their own goods. For example, woolen cloth they had made could not be shipped outside their own colony.

The American Revolution. The ideas of a new philosophical movement soon came to influence the British colonies in North America. The 1700s have been called the Age of **Enlightenment.** Some people believed that reason and the scientific method could logically explain human nature. Thinkers of the Enlightenment were not only philosophers but also critics of society. For example, Jean-Jacques Rousseau (roo·SOH) wrote that good government must be based on popular sovereignty. By this he meant that government must be created and controlled by the people.

Some people in the British colonies took these words to heart. In 1763 after a Native American uprising, the British barred colonists from settling west of the Appalachians. The government also began imposing new taxes on the colonies. With each new tax law, colonial resistance increased. Some laws were repealed, but others were not. With no representatives in the British Parliament, the colonists argued against this "taxation without representation." They called it tyranny. Relations between Britain and the colonies grew steadily worse. As the colonists hardened their resistance to British policies, King George III was determined to force their obedience.

In April 1775, British troops in Boston tried to seize colonial guns and gunpowder stored nearby. At the towns of Lexington and Concord, the British fought with groups of armed colonists. The American Revolution had begun. On July 4, 1776, the Continental

Spotlight on CULTURE

The French national flag is called the Tricolor. It has three vertical stripes of blue, white, and red. Blue and red represent the city of Paris, and white is the color of the Bourbon rulers. General Lafayette, the French general who also served in the American Revolution, invented the Tricolor. Ask students to compare the American flag to the French flag. *(The American flag has thirteen red and white stripes symbolizing the original thirteen states. White stars on a blue field represent the states.)*

Congress adopted the Declaration of Independence, establishing the United States of America as an independent nation. The Declaration of Independence showed the influence of Enlightenment philosophers. It declared that all men are created equal and have the right to "life, liberty, and the pursuit of happiness." Although women and slaves were not included, the demand for broader equality and justice was a great step forward.

By 1781 the Americans had won the Revolutionary War. The first American government, established by the Articles of Confederation, was very weak. In May 1787 delegates from the states met in Philadelphia to revise the Articles. The Constitution they adopted provided for a **federal system of government.** The central, or federal, government was given many important powers. It could declare war, raise armies, and make treaties. It could coin money and regulate trade with foreign countries. The states and the people retained all other powers.

✔ **READING CHECK: Sequencing** How did ideas about government among British subjects gradually lead from absolute monarchy to the federalism of the United States?
Subjects demanded a stronger voice in government and more direct representation.

The French Revolution and Napoléon

For more than 100 years, France had been the largest and most powerful nation in Europe, ruled by a monarch who claimed absolute power. When the French Revolution began in 1789, however, the king lost all power within months.

The French Revolution. In the mid-1700s discontent in France began to grow due to economic crisis. In this situation, the people demanded more say in government. In 1789 a group representing the majority of the people declared itself to be the National Assembly. This act marked the beginning of the French Revolution.

By August 4, 1789, the National Assembly had formally done away with feudalism in France. The assembly then adopted the Declaration of the Rights of Man and of the Citizen. This document dealt with basic human rights and political powers. It stated that men are born equal and remain equal before the law. It granted freedom of speech, of the press, and of religion. It guaranteed the right to take part in government, declaring that all citizens had an equal right to hold public office. The document also guaranteed the right to a fair trial. The Declaration defined the principles that became the slogan of the French Revolution: "liberty, equality, fraternity." In 1791 the National Assembly finished writing a constitution for France. This constitution limited the authority of the king and divided the government into three branches—executive, legislative, and judicial.

King Louis XVI agreed to his new limited powers, but secretly plotted to restore the Old Regime. When Louis and his family tried to escape France in 1791, they were arrested and sent back to Paris.

The French Republic. A new body, the National Convention, governed France for three years. Its first act was to declare the end of the monarchy and the beginning of a republic. The National Convention brought Louis XVI to trial and found him guilty of plotting against the security of the nation. On January 21, 1793, Louis XVI was beheaded by the guillotine. The rest of Europe found this execution shocking. Even in the United States, people were disturbed by the National Convention's radical methods.

A group called the Jacobins, which controlled the National Convention, arrested many other delegates who opposed their policies. The Jacobins worked to suppress all opposition and revolts within France. The Reign of Terror, as it became known, lasted from September 1793 to July 1794.

This illustration, possibly from an early printing of the Declaration of the Rights of Man and of the Citizen, dramatically portrays a symbol of one of the Declaration's key ideas—equality.

That's Interesting!

The Bastille in Paris was a notorious fortress and state prison. Its most famous prisoner, "The Man in the Iron Mask," died there in 1703.

On July 14, 1789 the people of Paris attacked the Bastille, captured the gunpowder stored there, and released the prisoners. Within days, they had torn the fortress down. The fall of the Bastille became the symbol of revolutionary spirit. July 14, Bastille Day, is celebrated as a national holiday in France.

ALL LEVELS: Remind students that industrialization changed the way people lived. There were technological advances, changes in economic systems, and changes in culture. Help students list examples of each. *(technological advances: electricity as a source of power and light, telephone, internal combustion engine; economic system changes: capitalism—individuals control production, socialism—government controls production, communism—government controls production; cultural changes: new forms of entertainment— sports, concerts, plays, shows; new artistic movements— romanticism, realism, impressionism, abstraction)*

ENGLISH LANGUAGE LEARNERS

Interdisciplinary Connection

MUSIC. Russian composer Pyotr Ilich Tchaikovsky wrote romantic works that were often built around stories and events. In 1880 he composed the *1812 Overture* to commemorate Napoléon's defeat in Russia. The original idea was for it to be performed with a large orchestra, a military band, cathedral bells, and cannon fire. Today, it is sometimes still performed with a cannon.

ACTIVITY: Have students listen to a recording of the *1812 Overture*. Encourage them to listen for the church bells and cannonlike sounds.

VISUAL RECORD ANSWER

Napoléon is the central figure holding the crown, while the pope and clergy watch.

INTERPRETING THE VISUAL RECORD

The coronation This painting shows Napoléon crowning his wife Joséphine empress after crowning himself emperor, while behind him the pope and clergy look on. The coronation ceremony took place in Notre Dame Cathedral, Paris. *How does the artist suggest that power rested with Napoléon and not with the church?*

Holt Researcher

go.hrw.com
KEYWORD: Holt Researcher
FreeFind:
　　Napoleon Bonaparte
　　Josephine de
　　　Beauharnais
After reading more about Napoléon and Joséphine on the Holt Researcher, describe how their coronation marked the end of the French Revolution.

In 1795 the National Convention completed another constitution. The new constitution created an executive branch made up of five directors. This gave the new government its name—the Directory. The Directory governed France for four years. However, no one was pleased with it. Prices rose out of control, and peasants, workers, and poor people suffered. The Directory was soon as unpopular as the Old Regime had been. Like the Old Regime, it went bankrupt.

The Napoléonic Era. Under the Directory, ongoing wars with Great Britain, Austria, and Sardinia offered opportunities for able military leaders. Between 1795 and 1799, a young general named **Napoléon Bonaparte** came to the public's attention. Napoléon's supporters believed that only he could win victories abroad and restore order at home.

In 1799 the legislature did away with four of the five directors. Armed troops surrounded the legislature and forced most of its members to leave. Those who stayed turned the government over to Napoléon. Seizing power by force like this is referred to as a coup d'état, French for a "stroke of state." Although Napoléon's government kept the form of a republic, the coup d'état of 1799 made him dictator of France. In 1804 the people voted to declare France an empire, with Napoléon as emperor. By 1809 Napoléon dominated Europe. Over time, however, the armies of Napoléon's opponents' grew stronger. By March 1814 Napoléon was defeated and went into exile. Louis XVIII, the brother of Louis XVI, came to the throne. France had a king again.

However, the restored king and his family made many enemies among the French people. Learning of this discontent, Napoléon led the army into Paris. As the king fled, Napoléon once again ruled France. In response, Prussia, Great Britain, and the Netherlands sent armies toward France. On June 18, 1815, the allied and the French armies met at Waterloo, where the British and their Prussian allies dealt Napoléon his final defeat. Napoléon gave up the throne, and the Bourbon monarchs once again took power.

The major European powers wanted to restore order, keep the peace, and suppress the ideas of the Revolution. Hundreds of delegates met at the Congress of Vienna, in Austria, to reshuffle countries and gain back losses. In the end, France was surrounded by a ring of strong states so that it could not again threaten the peace of Europe. After 1815 European rulers emphasized this conservative view in politics. Many monarchs moved to strengthen their own power. European governments took special steps to prevent revolution. A number of countries formed alliances to avoid war.

✔ **READING CHECK: Finding the Main Idea** How did the French Revolution fail to obtain its main goals? It failed to provide broad economic opportunity and true representative government.

The Industrial Revolution and Age of Reform

During the 1700s an intense phase of technological development known as the **Industrial Revolution** began in Great Britain. Industrialization spread from Britain to the United States in the late 1700s and early 1800s. By the end of the 1800s, other European nations such as France and Germany had also begun to industrialize. The Industrial Revolution was part of the economic system known as **capitalism,** in which individuals control the factors of production. The development of capitalism

LEVEL 1: Ask students to define nationalism and imperialism. *(Nationalism: interest in traditions and culture of a nation and in unification. Imperialism: ambition to dominate, expand territory, and acquire colonies.)* Then have students give examples of nationalism *(Garibaldi in Italy, Bismarck in Germany, Nicholas I in Russia)* and imperialism *(European colonies in Africa, Britain in India, Europeans in Southeast Asia, United States in Pacific, Cuba, Puerto Rico.)* **ENGLISH LANGUAGE LEARNERS**

led to the creation of new economic theories. Scottish economist Adam Smith argued that governments should not be involved in business decisions. Smith believed that supply and demand and competition would regulate business activities. Some people disagreed with Smith, claiming that business owners mistreated their employees. These people demanded reform.

Some reformers advocated a system called **socialism,** in which government owns the means of production and operates them for the welfare of the people. Other reformers thought that the entire capitalist system should be changed. Karl Marx, a German journalist, believed that all wealth is created by labor. Marx advocated a system called **communism,** in which labor controlled production and profits. In the *Communist Manifesto*, Marx and Friedrich Engels called for a revolution of the proletariat, or working class.

> **❝The Communists . . . declare that their ends can be attained only by the forcible overthrow of all existing social conditions. Let the ruling classes tremble at a Communistic revolution. The proletarians have nothing to lose but their chains. They have a world to win.❞**
>
> Karl Marx and Friedrich Engels, from the *Communist Manifesto*

The Industrial Revolution changed more than ways of organizing work and businesses. New inventions improved the quality of life. During the 1870s inventors learned how to use electricity as a power source. Other new inventions included the electric light, the telephone, and the internal combustion engine, which made the automobile possible. Scientific advancements improved the quality of life.

People in the 1800s enjoyed many new forms of entertainment. Sports became more organized, with official rules and national competitions. Cultural activities such as concerts, plays, and vaudeville shows became widely available. New artistic movements also developed. The romanticism of the early 1800s appealed to sentiment and imagination. During the mid-1800s realists sought to portray living conditions and social settings as they really were. Impressionist painters tried to capture images of objects at a particular moment and in a particular light. A growing interest in abstract forms pointed the way toward new artistic interests in the 1900s.

As the Industrial Revolution brought new problems and opportunities, many people introduced reforms to improve the quality of life. In Britain reformers worked to expand voting rights. In France a revolution in 1848 led to the creation of a new republican government. The Second Republic lasted until 1871, when France lost the Franco-Prussian War. In 1875 a new constitution established the Third Republic.

Slavery was a major political issue in the United States during the early 1800s. By 1860 the conflict over slavery led southern states to break with the Union, forming the Confederate States of America. Civil war raged until 1865, when the Confederacy surrendered. Congress amended the Constitution to abolish slavery, grant citizenship to former slaves, and extend the vote to all men regardless of "race, color, or previous condition of servitude." Women, however, did not receive their voting rights until 1920.

The struggle for independence was an important feature of life in Latin America. In 1791 slaves in the French colony of Saint Domingue rebelled. In 1804 another rebel army won independence for the colony, which was renamed Haiti. Important Latin American revolutionaries included South

---

Analyzing Primary Sources

Drawing Conclusions Why might capitalists view Marx's vision as a threat? Marx called for the violent overthrow of existing social and economic conditions.

This painting of a factory shows one artist's view of the Industrial Revolution.

Science, Technology & Society

Scientific advances in medicine helped improve the quality of life during the Industrial Revolution. Joseph Lister's work to prevent the spread of bacteria was one of the most important innovations in the history of medicine.

Lister was a surgeon. In 1861, he was in charge of a surgical block in Glasgow's Royal Infirmary. There he developed a technique for preventing contact between contaminated surfaces and open wounds. He was able to keep wounds free of harmful bacteria. Lister, as a recent biographer put it, "made surgery safe."

Critical Thinking

What was the medical problem that Joseph Lister solved?

ANSWER prevented wounds from becoming contaminated with harmful bacteria

CLOSE

Ask students to give examples of European nations that strengthened their governments and built empires between 1600 and 1900.

REVIEW

Have students complete the Section 1 Review on p. 457.

Culture

Vienna was the capital of Austria-Hungary. Vienna had been known for centuries as one of Europe's foremost cultural centers. It was best known for the many world-famous composers who had lived and worked there.

During the last half of the 1800s Vienna grew rapidly, and music continued to flourish. The composers Brahms, Bruckner, and Mahler were living there. Vienna was also the home of composer Johann Strauss, who helped establish the operetta and the Viennese waltz as distinctive art forms.

Critical Thinking

Ask students why they think so many composers lived and worked in Vienna.

ANSWER The people of Vienna must have been very interested in music.

CONNECTING TO CIVICS ANSWER

Some equated nationalism with liberalism and individual freedom. Bismarck's government used nationalism to unite separate states into the German nation.

CONNECTING TO
Civics

Nationalism
In the early 1800s Germans began to take a new interest in their national traditions, language, and customs. This spirit expressed itself in art, literature, and music, and helped inspire political steps toward unification.

Many Germans associated nationalism with liberalism. They believed that representative government and individual freedoms would advance along with nationalistic principles. However, Otto von Bismarck used nationalism mainly as a tool to help Prussia gain control over the rest of Germany.

Understanding Civics

How did different people view the connection between nationalism and government rule in Germany?

King William I of Prussia (right) helped Bismarck create a form of nationalism that suppressed liberal activities.

The Prussian Army was a powerful force in European affairs during the mid-1800s and after.

America's Simón Bolívar, Mexico's Miguel Hidalgo y Costilla, and Brazil's Dom Pedro. By 1825 most of Latin America had won independence.

✔ **READING CHECK: Evaluating** How did the Industrial Revolution influence political reforms? promoted demands for improved quality of life, greater social and economic equality

Nationalism in Europe

Latin America was not the only region to experience turmoil during the 1800s. A number of nationalist movements arose in Europe, as kingdoms unified into larger, more powerful nations. In Italy, the Young Italy movement spread the ideals of liberation and unification. In 1860 Giuseppe Garibaldi led an army that gained control of Sicily and Naples. Additional wars added territory to the new state. A lack of political experience, however, led to scandals, and economic tensions increased between the regions of the country.

During the mid-1800s the region known today as Germany remained a patchwork of independent states. In Prussia, King William I chose **Otto von Bismarck** to lead the cabinet. Bismarck built up industry and the army to lessen Austria's power. In 1871 representatives formed the German Empire, which included all the German states except Austria. King William I was named kaiser, or emperor.

Bismarck initially opposed German socialists, but he eventually endorsed reforms including insurance against sickness paid for by employers. Some Prussians, however, grew dissatisfied with the rigid control of the federal government. They formed parties opposed to Bismarck's rule. William II, who came to the throne in 1888, believed that Bismarck had become too powerful. He forced Bismarck to resign.

Czar Nicholas I introduced the nationalist movement in Russia in the 1830s. Nicholas began a program of "Russification" to force non-Russian people to adopt Russian culture. Czar Alexander II began a cautious reform program that included freedom for serfs. Radical groups demanded faster change, however, and in 1881 extremists killed the czar. In response, the next two czars worked to end liberalism. To avoid losing his throne in the Revolution of 1905, Czar Nicholas II agreed to a few limited reforms.

In 1866 Prussia defeated Austria. As a result, Hungary demanded more freedom. In response, in 1867 Austria formed the Dual Monarchy, also called Austria-Hungary. Although there was only one ruler, Austria and Hungary each had its own parliament. Economic differences and ethnic tensions led to additional division between Austria and Hungary.

✔ **READING CHECK: Finding the Main Idea** How did nationalist movements influence governments in Europe and Latin America? In some cases, nationalism led to civil and political turmoil, national unification, or reforms.

The Age of Imperialism

During the 1800s many European nations sought to expand their rule by taking control of colonies around the world. A number of factors contributed to the spread of **imperialism**—the ambition of a powerful nation to dominate another nation or region.

ASSESS

Have students complete Daily Quiz Epilogue 1. As Alternative Assessment, you may want to use the graphic organizer in this section's lessons.

RETEACH

Have students complete Main Idea Activity for English Language Learners and Special-Needs Students Epilogue 1. Then have students summarize the main ideas of each heading and subheading in the section. **ENGLISH LANGUAGE LEARNERS**

EXTEND

Organize students into small groups. Assign each group one of the following nations: Britain, France, or Russia. Each group should choose a historical figure from the section to represent their country. Have them prepare a biographical sketch of that person. Then have each group report its findings to the class. **BLOCK SCHEDULING, COOPERATIVE LEARNING**

Industrialization increased the demand for raw materials and for new markets for finished goods. In addition, nationalists believed that having colonies increased their nation's prestige. Finally, some Europeans hoped to share cultural advantages with people whom they regarded as "less fortunate."

Europeans scrambled to gain colonies in Africa. The Ottoman Empire, which controlled most of North Africa in the 1800s, was weak. As a result, France, Great Britain, and Italy were able to acquire colonies in North Africa. In central Africa, Europeans created colonies regardless of traditional territories or ethnic loyalties. British, Dutch, and German settlers clashed in South and Southwest Africa.

Imperialism took a different course in Japan, however. The Meiji emperor regained control of Japan and ended the rule of the Tokugawa shogunate. The new government encouraged modernization. By the end of the 1800s, Japan had the foundations of an industrial economy. After war broke out in 1894, Japan gained control of some Chinese territory. As the European presence in China increased, Japan lost control of some of the territory it had won during the war.

Resistance to British rule in India led Britain to tighten its control over that country. Britain, France, and the Netherlands established colonies in Southeast Asia and on Pacific islands. The United States gained control of parts of Samoa, Hawaii, and Wake Island. These islands provided locations for naval bases and fueling stations across the Pacific.

During the Industrial Revolution, Latin America supplied much of the world's agricultural products and raw materials. Industrialized nations gained economic power in Latin America. After winning the Spanish-American War in 1898, the United States gained control of Cuba, the Philippines, Puerto Rico, and Guam. The United States also established military governments in several countries during the early 1900s. In 1914 American troops entered Mexico in response to American fears of violence in the Mexican civil war.

✔ **READING CHECK: Contrasting** How did imperialism affect Africa? Japan? Africa was divided among colonial powers; Japan was forced to modernize.

HISTORY MAKER

Queen Liliuokalani (1838–1917)

Queen Liliuokalani was the first woman ever to become ruler of the Hawaiian Islands. She was also the last.

As queen, Liliuokalani faced increasing pressure from American businessmen who wanted the islands to be a part of the United States. In order to avoid bloodshed, she agreed to step down from the throne. In so doing, she opened the way for the United States to annex Hawaii, a move she bitterly opposed. After leaving the throne, she withdrew from public life. **Why did Liliuokalani give up control of Hawaii?**

HISTORY MAKER ANSWER
to avoid bloodshed

◆SECTION◆
1 REVIEW ANSWERS

❶ **Define**
• federal system of government, p. 453
• capitalism, p. 454
• socialism, p. 455
• communism, p. 455
• imperialism, p. 456

❷ **Identify**
• Louis XIV, p. 450
• Peter the Great, p. 450
• Catherine the Great, p. 450
• Elizabeth I, p. 451
• English Bill of Rights, p. 452
• Enlightenment, p. 452
• Industrial Revolution, p. 454
• Napoléon Bonaparte, p. 454
• Otto von Bismarck, p. 456

❸ Global relations: revolutions; Reforms: improved quality of life; Culture: new forms of entertainment; Economics: socialism, communism

❹ a. positive: nationalism and reform; negative: imperialism and war

b. Europeans created colonies and exported resources regardless of the wishes of the native inhabitants.

❺ Students' paragraphs should include the goals, methods, and outcomes of the revolutions.

SECTION 1 REVIEW

1. **Define** and explain the significance:
   federal system of government
   capitalism
   socialism
   communism
   imperialism

2. **Identify** and explain the significance:
   Louis XIV
   Peter the Great
   Catherine the Great
   Elizabeth I
   English Bill of Rights
   Enlightenment
   Industrial Revolution
   Napoléon Bonaparte
   Otto von Bismarck

3. **Identifying Cause and Effect**
   Copy the chart below. Use it to explain the effects of industrialization.

Global relations	
Reforms	
Culture	
Economics	

4. **Finding the Main Idea**
   a. Was the strengthening of monarchies after about 1500 a positive development or a negative development for European countries? Explain your answer.
   b. How did the colonial ambitions of imperialistic European countries affect nations and peoples in other parts of the world?

5. **Writing and Critical Thinking**
   Comparing and Contrasting
   Imagine you are a political journalist of the late 1700s. Write a paragraph comparing and contrasting the French and American revolutions.
   Consider:
   • the goals of the revolutions
   • the methods of the revolutions
   • the outcomes of the revolutions

Homework Practice Online
go.hrw.com
keyword: SP3 HPEP

OBJECTIVES

1 **Describe the causes of World War I.**

2 **Explain how the Great Depression affected governments.**

3 **Explain how Africa, Asia, and Latin America changed during the 1930s.**

4 **Describe the events that led to World War II.**

LET'S GET STARTED!

As students enter the classroom, ask them to list factors or conditions that might turn a limited, local conflict into a world war. *(Students might mention fighting between distant colonies or alliances that drag other nations into war.)* Tell students that in Section 2 they will learn how wars affected the lives of millions of people around the world during the first half of the 1900s.

SECTION 2

READ TO DISCOVER

① What caused World War I?

② How did the Great Depression affect governments?

③ How did Africa, Asia, and Latin America change during the 1930s?

④ What events led to World War II?

DEFINE

fascism

IDENTIFY

Bolsheviks
League of Nations
New Deal
Benito Mussolini
Adolf Hitler
Joseph Stalin
Mohandas Gandhi
Mao Zedong
D-Day

▶ WHY IT MATTERS TODAY

Conflicts in the Balkans still command the attention of the world today. Use **CNNfyi.com** or other **current event** sources to learn more about current Balkan conflicts. Record your findings in your journal.

CNNfyi.com

World War in the Twentieth Century

The Main Idea
War and economic depression marred the lives of many people during the first half of the 1900s.

The Story Continues *German chancellor Theobald von Bethmann Hollweg was convinced that the war that began in 1914 would be brief. "This may be a violent storm, but short—very short. I count on a war of not more that three, or perhaps at the very most, four months. . . ." World War I, however, lasted four years and took millions of lives.*

World War I and the Russian Revolution

The growth of nationalism and imperialism increased the national pride and power of many European countries. Some of these nations glorified armed strength. This militaristic attitude encouraged the use of force to solve problems. As these European nations grew more powerful and extended their reach around the globe, conflicts and rivalries developed. To maintain their newfound strength, nations formed alliances. In 1882 Austria-Hungary, Germany, and Italy formed the Triple Alliance. France, Great Britain, and Russia formed the Triple Entente in 1907.

War and revolution. Nationalism was a powerful force in Serbia, a Balkan state that had once been part of the Ottoman Empire. Serbian nationalists hoped to make their country the center of a large Slavic state. Nationalists particularly wanted to gain the provinces of Bosnia and Herzegovina, which would provide landlocked Serbia with an outlet on the Adriatic Sea. In 1878, however, Bosnia and Herzegovina became protectorates of Austria-Hungary, which annexed the two provinces in 1908. Serbian nationalists were infuriated. In June 1914 a Serbian terrorist assassinated Archduke Francis Ferdinand, heir to the Austro-Hungarian throne.

In response to the assassination, Austria-Hungary declared war on Serbia. Other declarations of war soon followed. Germany declared war on Russia in August 1914 and on France a few days later. With the outbreak of war, new alliances quickly formed. Austria-Hungary, Bulgaria, Germany, and the Ottoman Empire formed a new alliance called the Central Powers. France, Great Britain, and Russia formed the Allied Powers, also called the Allies. By the end of the war, 32 countries were members of the Allied Powers.

The armies fighting in World War I made use of a number of new and vastly more destructive weapons. The machine gun

In 1914 this illustration of the assassination of Archduke Ferdinand and his wife appeared in French newspapers.

TEACH OBJECTIVE 1

LEVEL 1: Tell students that as European nations became more powerful and extended their influence around the world, conflicts and rivalries developed. In 1914 these rivalries erupted into war. Then help students create a chart like the one on the right to discuss as a class.
ENGLISH LANGUAGE LEARNERS

World War I	
Causes	**Examples**
growth of nationalism and imperialism	*nationalism in Serbia, imperialism in Austria-Hungary*
new weapons and military strength encouraged use of force	*machine guns, tanks, airplanes, submarines, poison gas*
formation of alliances	*Triple Alliance, Triple Entente, Central Powers, Allied Powers*
assassination	*Archduke Ferdinand and his wife*

made infantry attacks difficult and often deadly for soldiers. In response, soldiers dug systems of trenches. The British introduced armored vehicles called tanks. The airplane allowed soldiers the opportunity to observe enemy positions and troop movements. At times the pilots engaged in air battles called dogfights. Germany made effective use of submarines, known as U-boats, to attack enemy shipping. The Germany army also used poison gas, which proved particularly deadly in the trenches.

Revolution. As the war began, Russia faced severe economic problems. As a result, Russian soldiers were poorly equipped and had few supplies. The Russian army suffered huge casualty rates, with 1.7 million soldiers dead, nearly 5 million wounded or disabled, and more than 2 million taken prisoner. These hardships increased discontent on the home front. In 1917 Czar Nicholas II, who could not control his subjects or the army, abdicated his throne. Aleksandr Kerensky established a provisional Russian government. Radical socialists called **Bolsheviks** overthrew the Kerensky government in November 1917. The Bolsheviks renamed themselves the Communist Party and signed a peace agreement with the Central Powers in March 1918. By 1921 they had defeated their main opposition within Russia. One year later they named their land the Union of Soviet Socialist Republics, or the Soviet Union.

Peace and a "new Europe." In January 1918 U.S. president Woodrow Wilson set forth the Fourteen Points, his plan for the postwar world. The Fourteen Points were designed to end military aggression and increase economic stability around the world. In November 1918, German leaders signed an armistice, or agreement to stop fighting. Delegates of the victorious nations held a peace conference in Paris in January 1919. Delegates considered reparations, or payment for war damages, and the creation of a **League of Nations**—a world organization that would maintain peace.

Delegates at the Paris Peace Conference produced the Treaty of Versailles, which spelled out the terms of peace between Germany and the Allied Powers. Germany had to accept full blame for starting the war and pay $33 billion in reparations. It lost large amounts of land along its northern western, and eastern borders, as well as its overseas colonies. Germany also had to agree not to fortify the Rhineland—territory located on the west bank of the Rhine River in Germany.

The treaty restored Poland as an independent nation. Austria-Hungary became two separate nations. The treaty created several new European nations, including Czechoslovakia, Estonia, Finland, Latvia, Lithuania, and Yugoslavia. The former Ottoman Empire was divided into the nations of Iraq, Palestine, Syria, and Transjordan. Finally, the treaty created a League of Nations. Although 59 nations eventually joined the League, the United States refused to become a member.

✔ **READING CHECK: Finding the Main Idea** How did World War I contribute to the Russian Revolution? created new hardships and increased discontent

The Great Depression and the Rise of Totalitarianism

The loss of life during World War I caused many people to rethink their views on life, politics, and society. Following the war, many people rejected the belief in continual human progress first expressed

More than 2 million American soldiers served in France in World War I. Some are seen here marching through the Arc de Triomphe in Paris, where today an eternal flame burns to honor French war dead.

ALL LEVELS: Tell students that the Great Depression affected economies around the world and contributed to political unrest in Europe. Then have students work in groups to report on the effects of the Great Depression in the following countries: France and Great Britain, Italy and Germany, the Soviet Union, and the United States. *(France and Great Britain: Political problems, high prices, and high unemployment lead to labor unrest; Italy and Germany: Economic and political problems lead to the formation of Fascist party in Italy and Nazi party in Germany; Soviet Union: Economic problems lead to the dictatorship of Joseph Stalin; United*

States: Government programs of relief and reform help ease economic problems and unemployment.)

ENGLISH LANGUAGE LEARNERS, COOPERATIVE LEARNING

Government

Several of Roosevelt's New Deal programs provided immediate relief. The Works Progress Administration (WPA) gave unemployed people temporary jobs in public works and artistic projects. The Civilian Conservation Corps (CCC) employed young men on projects in national forests. Probably the most far-reaching New Deal program was the Social Security Act. It provided unemployment benefits, pensions for the elderly, and disability insurance. It also set maximum work hours and minimum wages in some industries.

ACTIVITY: Have students work together to create a display about New Deal programs. The display should include the name of each program, its abbreviation, and its purpose.

VISUAL RECORD ANSWER

It affected banks, and people were worried about their savings.

INTERPRETING THE VISUAL RECORD

The crash Crowds gather along Wall Street during the stock market crash. *What does this gathering reflect about the crash?*

Holt Researcher

go.hrw.com
KEYWORD: Holt Researcher
FreeFind: Benito Mussolini
Adolf Hitler
After reading more about Benito Mussolini and Adolf Hitler on the Holt Researcher, create a Venn diagram comparing the ideology and actions of the two leaders.

---

during the Enlightenment. Writers, musicians, and painters abandoned traditional forms and used new ideas and techniques. Motion pictures became popular in the postwar era, as many people sought escape and entertainment from their daily lives.

Economic crisis. World War I also changed the world economy. The United States emerged from war stronger than its allies. Its financial status reflected its potential as a world leader. Economic problems, however, soon appeared. Many Americans invested heavily in the stock market in the hope of earning quick profits. When the New York Stock Exchange collapsed in 1929, Americans lost millions of dollars. The stock market crash marked the beginning of the Great Depression, a long period of economic struggle, widespread unemployment, and financial instability that quickly became global in scope.

The U.S. government became involved in reviving the American economy. Franklin D. Roosevelt, who was elected president in 1932, introduced a program of relief and reform called the **New Deal.** The New Deal did not end the Great Depression, but its broad-based social and economic programs eased the poverty of many citizens.

Political tensions. Economic problems and political conflicts affected life in several European nations after World War I. In France, government scandals led to a general workers' strike. A new government introduced reforms, but prices continued to rise. In Britain, high unemployment led to widespread labor unrest. While Britain and France were able to remain democracies, some postwar European governments grew more authoritarian. Unrest in Austria, for example, led to a shift away from democracy. Hungary and Poland became military dictatorships.

Italy, Germany, and the Soviet Union also became dictatorships after the war. When economic turmoil weakened the Italian government, **Benito Mussolini** organized the Fascist Party. The party was based on **fascism,** a political philosophy that places the needs of the state above the needs of the individual. After becoming premier in 1922, Mussolini set up a dictatorship and established a police state. In Germany, revolutions, a troubled economy, and new political parties threatened the stability of the government. One such party was the National Socialist German Workers Party, or Nazis. **Adolf Hitler,** leader of the Nazis, was profoundly anti-Jewish. In 1933 the German president appointed Hitler chancellor. Hitler then took the title *der Führer,* or "the leader," and named his regime the Third Reich.

The Soviet Union suffered economic troubles after World War I. In response, Soviet leader Vladimir Ilyich Lenin announced the New Economic Policy (NEP) in 1922. The NEP allowed some free enterprise in industry. After Lenin's death, new leader **Joseph Stalin** ended the NEP and created the Five-Year Plan. This plan included expansion of heavy industry and collective farming, on which people could share resources. Many who opposed Stalin's policies were executed, imprisoned, or exiled. Scholars estimate that by 1939 more than 5 million people had been arrested, deported, sent to forced labor camps, or executed.

✔ **READING CHECK: Summarizing** How did economic problems affect the governments of the United States, Germany, and Italy? The U.S. government became more directly involved in its economy, while Germany and Italy became dictatorships.

LEVEL 3: Ask students to list reasons why a nationalist movement might grow in a country. (*Students might mention colonial rule, foreign invasion, or economic hardship.*) Then have students discuss causes and effects of nationalist movements in the 1930s in Turkey, India, China, Japan, and Latin America. (*Turkey: cause—Greek occupation, effect—new government formed; India: cause—British colony, effect—independence; China: cause—foreign economic influence, effects—Nationalist party formed, emperor abdicated, Communist party formed; Japan: causes—economic depression, western influences, effects—militarism, imperialism; Latin America: causes—economic depression, repression, effect—military dictatorships*)

Nationalist Movements Around the World

As new leaders took power in Europe, similar changes occurred in other parts of the world. The British Empire grew weaker in the years after World War I. Although Britain maintained its right to defend Egypt and the Suez Canal, Egypt grew increasingly independent. Zionism, a nationalist movement that called for a Palestinian homeland for Jews, created tensions in the eastern Mediterranean. Britain focused its attention, however, on India, its largest colony. **Mohandas Gandhi** led the growing Indian nationalist movement. While Indians struggled for independence, a 1931 act of Parliament recognized Australia, Canada, New Zealand, and South Africa as independent nations. These four countries joined with Great Britain in an organization called the British Commonwealth of Nations.

Turkey, Persia, and Africa. After World War I, Greek troops occupied Turkey. Nationalists opposed the Greek troops, and in 1923 a new Turkish government was formed, with Mustafa Kemal as president. Kemal worked to modernize and westernize Turkey, banning traditional clothing and introducing the use of family surnames. Kemal took the name Atatürk, meaning "father of the Turks."

Nationalists also took control of Persia. In 1921 Reza Khan took control of the country, calling himself Reza Shah Pahlavi. Like Atatürk, Reza Shah wanted to modernize his country. He strengthened the army, built roads and hospitals, and gave women more rights. Reza Shah also strictly controlled the press and suppressed political parties. In 1935 he changed the name of the country to Iran.

During the 1930s many Africans called for independence. The leaders of African independence movements were typically young, Western-educated men, such as Nnamdi Azikiwe of Nigeria and Jomo Kenyatta of Kenya.

Asia and Latin America. European and American influence in China led to tensions even before World War I. By the end of the 1800s, foreign interests dominated the Chinese economy and government. A popular uprising known in English as the Boxer Rebellion attempted to restore Chinese sovereignty. The Boxers destroyed churches, railways, mines, and other evidence of foreign encroachment in traditional Chinese life. In response, the imperialist powers sent an army to Beijing and crushed the rebellion. The foreign powers then imposed heavy penalties on the Chinese, including fines for destroyed property and additional trade concessions. As China declined, a new political party, the Kuomintang, or Chinese Nationalist Party, pushed for reforms. In 1912 the Kuomintang forced the last Chinese emperor to abdicate. The Nationalists' reforms, however, did not ease the suffering of China's huge peasant population. As a result, many people turned to the Chinese Communist Party. The Nationalists forced the Communists, led by **Mao Zedong,** to flee in a year-long retreat called the Long March.

Japan's postwar problems also had originated before World War I. A series of wars led to economic pressures even as Japan's military grew stronger. Population growth forced many Japanese to move to other countries, and a lack of raw materials led to high import costs. By the beginning of the Great Depression, many people believed that Japan's hardships were the result of the country's increasing move toward westernization. Military leaders began to assert more control over the government and to look for areas that would enable Japan to expand. Manchuria was one of the most promising areas.

Holt Researcher
go.hrw.com
KEYWORD: Holt Researcher
FreeFind: Mohandas Gandhi
After reading more about Mohandas Gandhi on the Holt Researcher, write an analysis of his influence on events of the 20th century.

Cartoon depicting European countries dividing China

Linking Past to Present

Iran has changed dramatically since 1935. Both the first Shah and his son, Mohammad Reza Pahlavi, were committed to reforming and modernizing Iran. By the 1960s, Iran had close relations with the West, particularly the United States.

These policies were opposed by many Islamic clerics. They viewed the influx of Westerners as a threat to the traditional values of Shi'ah Islam. In 1980, a revolution led by the Ayatollah Khomeini replaced the Shah with an Islamic republic. Efforts were made to suppress Western influence. Anti-American sentiment was strong. When Khomeini died in 1989, more moderate clerical leaders gained control of the government. By 2001 Iran's relations with the United States had improved.

Critical Thinking

Why was anti-American sentiment so strong among Iran's fundamentalist clerics?

ANSWER They felt that Western values were luring Iranians away from traditional Islamic values.

TEACH OBJECTIVE 4

LEVEL 1: Ask students what invasions Japan, Italy, and Germany made between 1931 and 1938. (*1931: Japan into Manchuria; 1935: Italy into Ethiopia; 1938: Germany into Austria and the Sudetenland [Czechoslovakia]*) Then ask what invasion started World War II. (*Germany invaded Poland. To support Poland, Great Britain and France declared war on Germany.*)
ENGLISH LANGUAGE LEARNERS

HOMEWORK Have students use library resources and the Internet to research one of the regions discussed in Section 2. They should find out what political and social changes took place in the region between World War I and World War II.

CLOSE

Ask students to give examples of the causes and effects of nationalist movements around the world in the first half of the 1900s.

VISUAL RECORD ANSWER

It was an act of war, and the country would fight back.

Economic developments also spurred change in Latin America. Industrialization led to urban growth and provided more jobs. Labor union activity increased, and the middle class grew in size. Political parties formed, but Latin American governments did not shift toward democracy. Instead the economic hardships of the Great Depression led many people to support military dictatorships that took control of governments in several countries.

✔ **READING CHECK: Making Generalizations** What factors contributed to political changes in Africa, Asia, and Latin America after World War I? the rise of nationalism and independence movements

World War II

Economic hardships and political conflicts resulting from the Great Depression led to increased international tensions. In the early 1930s militarists came to power in Japan. In 1931 Japanese forces invaded and occupied Manchuria. By 1939 Japan controlled about one fourth of China. Like Japan, Italy sought additional territory. Italian forces invaded Ethiopia in 1935. No other nation was willing to use military force to oppose the invasion.

During the 1930s Germany formed alliances with Italy and Japan. Together they became known as the Axis Powers. In 1938 German troops invaded Austria. Shortly thereafter Adolf Hitler declared that the Sudetenland, a part of Czechoslovakia, rightfully belonged to Germany. Britain and France accepted this demand in the hope that Hitler's aggression would end. In September 1939, however, German troops invaded Poland, sparking World War II.

German forces invaded western European nations in 1940. German air raids, however, failed to force a British surrender. By 1941 German troops controlled Greece and the Baltic Peninsula and had entered Libya in North Africa. Although Soviet and German leaders had signed a non-aggression pact, the German army invaded the Soviet Union in June 1941.

The United States initially refused to enter the war, choosing instead to provide aid to Britain by supplying war materials on credit. By the fall of 1940, U.S. warships escorted British ships across the Atlantic. On December 7, 1941, Japanese planes bombed the U.S. naval base at Pearl Harbor, Hawaii. The U.S. Congress declared war on Japan the next day. In response, Germany declared war on the United States.

Hitler wanted to impose one government on all Europe. He also wanted to eliminate all but the "Aryan race," which he considered to be superior. To achieve this goal, Hitler ordered the extermination of Europe's Jewish population. Jews who were not shot or murdered by poison gas suffered in concentration camps in Germany and Poland. More than 6 million Jews, as well as millions of Slavs, Gypsies, and others, were killed in the Holocaust.

In November 1942 U.S. and British troops landed in North Africa. The Axis forces there surrendered in May 1943. That July Allied troops invaded Sicily and prepared to invade Italy. On June 6, 1944—also called **D-Day**—the Allies invaded northwest France. Allied troops arrived at the German border in September. Hitler committed suicide in April 1945, and German leaders surrendered that May.

INTERPRETING THE VISUAL RECORD

Pearl Harbor Americans were shocked and outraged by the Japanese attack on Pearl Harbor. *What do these headlines suggest about public concern over the bombing?*

To defeat Japan, the Allies relied on a strategy of island hopping, capturing strate- gically important Japanese-held islands while bypassing others. The Allies also carried out air attacks against the Japanese homeland. On August 6, 1945, a U.S. bomber dropped a deadly weapon on the Japanese city of Hiroshima. President Harry Truman announced the use of the atomic bomb.

> *History Makers Speak*
>
> **"Sixteen hours ago an American airplane dropped a bomb on Hiroshima . . . With this bomb we have now added a new and revolutionary increase in destruction to supplement the grow- ing power of our armed forces. . . . It is an atomic bomb. It is a harnessing of the basic power of the universe. The force from which the sun draws its power has been loosed against those who brought war to the Far East."**
>
> Harry S Truman, from *Public Papers of the Presidents*

At least 80,000 people were killed at Hiroshima, with many more wounded. The United States dropped a sec- ond bomb on August 9, on the industrial city of Nagasaki, and the Japanese surrendered on August 14.

✔ **READING CHECK: Sequencing** What events led to the outbreak of World War II?

INTERPRETING THE VISUAL RECORD

Midway The U.S. victory in the Bat- tle of Midway crippled the Japanese navy. *From the painting, what can you determine about the type of fighting that took place during the Battle of Midway?*

Analyzing Primary Sources

Supporting a Point of View
How did Truman justify the use of the new weapon against the Japanese?

VISUAL RECORD ANSWER

intense air and sea fighting

‹SECTION›
2 REVIEW ANSWERS

❶ Define
• fascism, p. 460

❷ Identify
• Bolsheviks, p. 459
• League of Nations, p. 459
• New Deal, p. 460
• Benito Mussolini, p. 460
• Adolf Hitler, p. 460
• Joseph Stalin, p. 460
• Mohandas Gandhi, p. 461
• Mao Zedong, p. 461
• D-Day, p. 462

❸ 1917: Russian Revolution takes place; 1918: World War I ends; 1929: Great Depression begins; 1939: World War II begins; 1941: Japan bombs Pearl Harbor

❹ a. imperialist expansion sparked conflicts

b. United States: social and eco- nomic programs; Latin America: military dictatorships; Europe: fas- cism, nazism, dictatorships; Asia: nationalism, communism, mili- tarism; Africa: independence movements

c. faced revolts, revolutions, loss of colonies

d. Japanese attack on Pearl Harbor

❺ Paragraphs should include the League's mandate to maintain peace and the lack of power to carry it out.

SECTION 2 REVIEW

1. **Define** and explain the significance: fascism

2. **Identify** and explain the significance:
Bolsheviks
League of Nations
New Deal
Benito Mussolini
Adolf Hitler
Joseph Stalin
Mohandas Gandhi
Mao Zedong
D-Day

3. **Summarizing** Copy the time line below. Use it to summarize the major global events from 1914 to 1945.

1914				1945
	1918		1939	
	1917	1929		1941

4. **Finding the Main Idea**

a. How did imperialism contribute to the coming of World War I?

b. What were some of the economic and political effects of the Great Depression on the United States and the nations of Latin America, Europe, Asia, and Africa?

c. In what ways did the rise of nationalist movements in Latin America, Asia, Africa, and the Middle East affect European imperialist nations?

d. Why did the United States enter World War II?

5. **Writing and Critical Thinking**

Evaluating Imagine you are a political scientist at work during the postwar years. Write a one-paragraph report in which you evaluate the effectiveness of the League of Nations.
Consider:
• why the League of Nations was created
• how European powers responded to the invasion of Ethiopia and to Hitler's demand for the Sudentenland

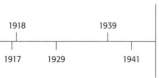

Homework Practice Online
keyword: SP3 HPEP

OBJECTIVES

1 Explain how the Allied powers dealt with Germany after the war.

2 Describe the causes of the Cold War.

3 Analyze how European nations fared after the war.

4 Explain how political unrest affected life in Latin American nations.

REPRODUCIBLE RESOURCES

▶ Guided Reading Strategy Epilogue 3

TECHNOLOGY RESOURCES

▶ One-Stop Planner Epilogue 3

▶ World History and Cultures Video Program 26: Television and the Cold War

▶ World History Teaching Transparency: Geography and History 29: The Economy of Latin America

▶ Homework Practice Online

▶ Online Maps, Charts, and Graphs: Communist Europe in 1949

REINFORCEMENT, REVIEW, AND ASSESSMENT

▶ Section 3 Review, p. 467

▶ Daily Quiz Epilogue 3

▶ Main Idea Activity

▶ English Audio Summary Epilogue 3

▶ Spanish Audio Summary Epilogue 3

SECTION 3

READ TO DISCOVER

1 How did the Allied powers deal with the Germany after the war?

2 What caused the Cold War?

3 How did European nations fare after the war?

4 How did political unrest affect life in Latin American nations?

DEFINE

market economy
command economy

IDENTIFY

United Nations
Truman Doctrine
Marshall Plan
NATO
Warsaw Pact
Nikita Khrushchev
Martin Luther King Jr.
John F. Kennedy
Cuban missile crisis
NAFTA

▶ WHY IT MATTERS TODAY

The United Nations remains an important force in international affairs today. Use **CNNfyi.com** or other **current event** sources to learn about the United Nations. Record your findings in your journal.

CNNfyi.com

Europe and the Americas Since 1945

The Main Idea
A conflict known as the Cold War dominated world affairs in the post–World War II era.

The Story Continues *Former British Prime Minister Winston Churchill spoke to an American audience in 1946. Churchill warned, "From Stettin in the Baltic to Trieste in the Adriatic, an iron curtain has descended across the Continent." His remarks reflected increasing concerns over the growing influence of the Soviet Union in Europe after World War II.*

Aftermath of the War in Europe

Many changes faced Europe and the Americas at the end of World War II. The first challenge was to end Nazi control and prevent future wars. Allied leaders had held meetings at Yalta and Potsdam in 1945 to discuss the division of Germany into four zones. Each major Allied power was to control one zone. After the war in Europe ended, all German air, land, and sea forces were dismantled. The Allies completed the occupation of their respective zones. When the horrors of the Holocaust became public knowledge, a special international court met at Nürnberg, Germany. The court charged 22 Nazi leaders with crimes against peace and crimes against humanity. Of the defendants, 12 were sentenced to death, 7 were sentenced to life imprisonment, and 3 were found not guilty. The court also declared the Nazi Party a criminal organization.

In April 1945, representatives from 51 nations met in San Francisco to form an international organization to replace the League of Nations. The **United Nations** (UN) was established to maintain international peace and security, to deter aggressors, and promote international cooperation. The two most important bodies of the UN are the Security Council and the General Assembly. The Security Council helps to resolve international disputes. Britain, China, France, the Soviet Union, and the United States were the original permanent members of the Council. Ten other members are elected for two-year rotating terms. The General Assembly draws up the UN budget and elects the organization's secretary-general.

✔ **READING CHECK: Finding the Main Idea** Why did nations come together to form the United Nations after World War II? to restore and maintain global peace, security, and cooperation

Origins of the Cold War

The alliance between the Soviet Union and the Western Allies did not last long after the end of the war. The Soviet Union followed a plan for European reconstruction very different from the plan of the United States. The conflict between the two nations became known as the Cold War. Fighting broke out at times, but the Cold War was largely a battle of ideas rather than of troops.

After the war Joseph Stalin imposed a communist-led government in Poland and tried to maintain troops on the Soviet border with Turkey. The Soviet Union expanded its influence throughout Eastern Europe. In response, the United States

TEACH OBJECTIVES 1 and 2

ALL LEVELS: Organize students into small groups. Have each group create a chart similar to the one on the right to show the steps that were taken in Europe after World War II and at the beginning of the Cold War.

ENGLISH LANGUAGE LEARNERS, COOPERATIVE LEARNING

After World War II

Action	Reason	Description
Germany occupied by major Allies	prevent rearmament	four zones: United States, Britain, France, Soviet Union
Truman Doctrine	contain communism	U.S. pledge to help resist Communism
Marshall Plan	to help rebuild Europe	financial aid from U.S.
United Nations	maintain peace	international organization
North Atlantic Treaty Organization (NATO)	security alliance for mutual defense	United States and non-communist European nations
Warsaw Pact	security alliance for mutual defense	Soviet Union and communist European nations

developed a policy of **containment,** or restricting the spread of communism wherever possible. In March 1947 U.S. president Harry Truman announced what became known as the **Truman Doctrine,** in which the United States pledged its support to free peoples who resisted a communist takeover.

In addition to the Truman Doctrine, the United States supported other nations through the European Recovery Plan. Also known as the **Marshall Plan,** this program assisted European nations in rebuilding their economies. The plan provided more than $13 billion in aid to 17 European nations between 1948 and 1952. The Soviet Union and its allies refused to accept Marshall Plan assistance.

The future of Germany was another source of Cold War tension. By 1948 the Western Allies had begun the process of forming a unified German government. The Soviet Union opposed this plan and blockaded the East German border. In response, the United States and Britain organized an airlift of goods to West Berlin. The airlift lasted until May 1949. That same month, the Federal Republic of Germany, also known as West Germany, was established from the U.S., British, and French occupation zones. In October the Soviet Union established the German Democratic Republic, or East Germany, in the zone that it controlled.

In 1949 the United States and 11 European nations formed the North Atlantic Treaty Organization (**NATO**). Greece and Turkey joined NATO in 1952. West Germany joined in 1955. Member nations agreed that if one member was attacked, all members would unite in defense against the aggressor.

The Soviet Union also created an alliance system. European communist nations adopted a 20-year, mutual defense agreement called the **Warsaw Pact.** The combined troop strength contributed by member countries meant that the Warsaw Pact greatly outnumbered NATO in terms of ground troops. This difference in ground troop strength reinforced the Western reliance on using the threat of nuclear war to deter aggression.

✔ **READING CHECK: Making Predictions** How might the Soviets have perceived the U.S. policy of containment? as an attack on Soviet growth and as support for enemies of the Soviet Union

Reconstruction, Reform, and Reaction in Europe

Postwar Europe experienced a remarkable economic and political recovery. The Western Allies remained committed to democracy and the principles of majority rule and capitalism. Most followed the ideal of the **market economy,** in which competition among private businesses and individuals determines what goods and services will be produced. In contrast, the communist bloc practiced a **command economy,** in which the government makes all economic decisions.

Many Western nations experienced great levels of economic growth. West Germany rebuilt its economy so quickly that many East Germans escaped to the West to find jobs and economic security. In response, the Soviet Union built a wall capped with barbed wall to prevent people from fleeing from East Berlin to West Berlin. The Berlin Wall became a powerful symbol of the Cold War.

During the 1950s several European nations sought to unify sectors of their economies. The European Coal and Steel Community (ECSC) was formed in 1952 to unite the facilities of the nations that produced Western Europe's steel and coal. In 1957 Belgium, France, Italy, Luxembourg, the Netherlands, and West Germany formed the European Economic Community (EEC), or Common Market. The ECSC, EEC, and the Atomic Energy Community merged in 1967 to form the European Community.

Shown here is a Soviet propaganda poster from the mid-1940s. The theme of this poster reflects the military and industrial buildup that would continue throughout the Cold War.

Daily Life

After World War II the people of Europe were left with unimaginable destruction. Much of the land was like a moonscape. Cities had been flattened by bombs or consumed by fire. The countryside was blackened and useless. Roads were scarred with shell holes and bomb craters. Railways and bridges had been destroyed, and harbors filled with sunken ships.

In the midst of this destruction were millions of displaced people. Between 1939 and 1945, at least 60 million European civilians had been uprooted from their homes. Twenty-seven million had left their own countries or been driven out by force. When the war ended, Europe was a land of refugees.

🔲 **internet** connect

TOPIC: Cold War
GO TO: go.hrw.com
KEYWORD: SP3 WHEP

Have students access the Internet through the HRW Go site to learn more about the Cold War. Tell them to look for elements of popular culture that reflect Cold War anxieties and attitudes and to collect three to five examples. For each example, have students write a paragraph that explains how it reflects a Cold War attitude.

LEVEL 1: Write the headings "Western Europe" and "Eastern Europe" on the chalkboard. Then help students generate a list of characteristics under each heading that describes how each region fared after World War II. (*West: remarkable recovery, market economy, economic growth, European Economic Community; East: command economy, failed economic policies, power struggles, revolts against control*) **ENGLISH LANGUAGE LEARNERS**

LEVEL 3: Have students create a cause-and-effect chart that shows how political unrest has affected life in Central America and South America since 1945. (*Central America: causes—civil wars, conflicts between communism and democracy; effects—deaths, U.S. involvement; South America: cause—military governments; effects—suppression, war, drug-related violence*)

HOMEWORK Have students research and prepare a brief oral presentation about the Cuban missile crisis.

Global Relations

In 1959 U.S. vice president Richard Nixon flew to Moscow to open the first U.S. exhibition ever held in the Soviet Union. Nikita Khrushchev was his host. Nixon had been warned that Khrushchev was a blunt man who liked to argue. Nixon was ready. Nixon and Khrushchev toured the exhibition together. In front of a model kitchen they began to argue over who could afford such a kitchen. Soon, the men were standing nose-to-nose, jabbing fingers at each other. It was not really the kitchen they were arguing about. It was the difference between two ways of life–the Soviet way versus the American way. Their famous argument has come to be known as the Kitchen Debate.

Critical Thinking

In what way was the kitchen a symbol of two different ways of life?

ANSWER: In a market economy, such a kitchen would be available to many people. In a command economy it would not.

In the Soviet Union, a power struggle took place after the death of Joseph Stalin. Eventually **Nikita Khrushchev** emerged as Stalin's successor. In February 1956 Khrushchev shocked the Soviet leadership when he denounced Stalin's policies. Khrushchev lifted restrictions on intellectuals and artists, and loosened the central government's tight control of the economy. In 1964, after his economic policies failed, Khrushchev was forced to resign. Leonid Brezhnev became the leader of the Soviet Union.

During the 1950s and 1960s several Eastern European nations tried to gain their independence from the Soviet Union. In 1953 Soviet tanks and troops put down an East German revolt. Poland gained some limited freedoms after threatening a revolt in 1956. That same year, the Soviets violently suppressed a rebellion in Hungary. An effort to introduce reforms in Czechoslovakia in 1968 also led to an invasion by Warsaw Pact troops.

✔ **READING CHECK: Contrasting** How does a market economy differ from a command economy? In a market economy competition determines what goods and services will be offered. In a command economy the government makes all economic decisions.

The United States and Canada

The United States and Canada both enjoyed growing economies and powerful roles in international affairs after World War II. Each nation, however, also faced problems. In the United States, members of several minority groups increasingly demanded equal rights. In the 1960s Congress passed legislation that promised political equality to African Americans and other minorities.

Civil rights leader **Martin Luther King Jr.** advocated the use of nonviolent protest methods, such as boycotts, marches, and sit-ins, to win equality. King received the Nobel Peace Prize in 1964. Although he rejected violence, some of his opponents were willing to use force. In 1968 King was murdered.

The Cold War also led to crises in the United States. In 1959 the Cuban government fell to Marxist rebels. President **John F. Kennedy** authorized an invasion of Cuba in 1961, but the operation failed. In 1962 a U.S. spy plane discovered Soviet nuclear missile sites in Cuba. Kennedy demanded that the Soviet Union remove the missiles and ordered a blockade to prevent more weapons from entering the island. For 13 days during the **Cuban missile crisis** the world stood on the brink of war. Finally the Soviet Union agreed to remove the missiles. In return, the United States pledged not to invade Cuba in the future.

In Canada agricultural and industrial production increased dramatically after World War II. Much of the capital necessary for industrial production came from the United States. The two nations also worked together to build the St. Lawrence Seaway, a major waterway linking the Great Lakes with the Atlantic Ocean. The two nations also maintained a close relationship on military defense and international issues.

Dr. Martin Luther King Jr. delivered his "I Have a Dream" speech at the Lincoln Memorial in Washington, D.C.

✔ **READING CHECK: Summarizing** How were the economies of Canada and the United States linked? through investment, industrial partnership, and joint projects such as the St. Lawrence Seaway

Latin America Since 1945

A growing population, petroleum deposits, and rapid industrialization increased Latin America's influence after 1945. Changes brought new challenges.

CLOSE
Discuss the economic role the United States has played in Europe and North America since 1945.

REVIEW
Have students complete the Section 3 Review on p. 467.

ASSESS
Have students complete Daily Quiz Epilogue 3. As Alternative Assessment, you may want to use the charts in this section's lessons.

RETEACH
Have students complete Main Idea Activity for English Language Learners and Special-Needs Students Epilogue 3. Then have them write a main idea question and answer for each subsection.
ENGLISH LANGUAGE LEARNERS

EXTEND
Ask students to research the impact of Martin Luther King Jr. on the African American civil rights movement and write a brief report of their findings. **BLOCK SCHEDULING**

Mexico. In 1945 Mexico appeared to be one of the most stable countries in Latin America. The Institutional Revolutionary Party (PRI), which controlled the country, suppressed opposition and resisted demands for political reform. The economy improved in the 1970s but declined again in the 1980s. In 1994 Canada, Mexico, and the United States negotiated the North American Free Trade Agreement (**NAFTA**). This agreement eliminated trade barriers between the three nations, promoting the development of the Mexican economy. Economic relations between the two nations increased further after reform candidate Vicente Fox won the presidency in 2000.

Central America. In Nicaragua and El Salvador, civil wars led to thousands of deaths. Conflict between communism and democracy led to U.S. involvement in Nicaragua during the 1980s. By the 1990s leaders in Nicaragua and El Salvador were working toward peace and democracy. The United States also became involved in Panama. General Manuel Noriega, the Panamanian dictator, was accused of helping narcotics dealers smuggle illegal drugs into the United States. In 1989 President George Bush sent troops to Panama to capture Noriega and restore order.

South America. Many South American nations suffered political turmoil in the postwar era. In Argentina a series of military and civilian governments failed to bring economic and political stability to the nation. During the 1970s and 1980s the military harshly suppressed dissent and opposition. Military leaders lost power only after Britain defeated Argentina in a conflict over the Falkland Islands. Brazil also experienced political unrest and economic chaos until the early 1990s.

In Chile the military overthrew a Marxist government in 1973. The new military government executed some who had opposed it. In 1989 free elections ended the military regime and spurred economic growth. During this same period Colombia became a major source for illegal drugs. Colombian authorities and U.S. law officers worked together to end the power of the drug organizations, but drug-related violence continued into the 2000s.

✔ **READING CHECK: Evaluating** How did the United States influence economic and political development in Latin America? through trade alliances such as NAFTA, commerce, and military assistance or intervention

CONNECTING TO Economics

NAFTA
The North American Free Trade Agreement was designed to promote free trade between the United States, Canada, and Mexico. NAFTA officially went into effect on January 1, 1994. By dropping trade barriers such as tariffs, the agreement makes it easier for the three nations to buy and sell their products to each other. For example, Mexico now purchases 75 percent of its agricultural products from the United States. Special NAFTA rules promote the purchase and use of home-grown North American products.

Understanding Economics
What might be the advantages and disadvantages of NAFTA?

A migrant worker from Mexico harvests apples on a farm in the United States.

CONNECTING TO ECONOMICS ANSWER
helps Mexican economy; possible negative effect on imports from other continents

SECTION 3 REVIEW ANSWERS

❶ Define
- market economy, p. 465
- command economy, p. 465

❷ Identify
- United Nations, p. 464
- Truman Doctrine, p. 465
- Marshall Plan, p. 465
- NATO, p. 465
- Warsaw Pact, p. 465
- Nikita Khrushchev, p. 466
- Martin Luther King Jr., p. 466
- John F. Kennedy, p. 466
- Cuban missile crisis, p. 466
- NAFTA, p. 467

❸ United States: civil rights—boycotts, marches, sit-ins; cold war—Cuban missile crisis; Canada: international issues—St. Lawrence Seaway, military defense; economic growth—U.S. capital for industrialization

❹ a. with repression and invasion

b. growing population, political turmoil, stagnant economies

❺ Students should consider Stalin's expansionist policies and the German border blockade

---

SECTION 3 REVIEW

1. **Define** and explain the significance:
   market economy
   command economy

2. **Identify** and explain the significance:
   United Nations
   Truman Doctrine
   Marshall Plan
   NATO
   Warsaw Pact
   Nikita Khrushchev
   Martin Luther King Jr.
   John F. Kennedy
   Cuban missile crisis
   NAFTA

3. **Summarizing** Copy the web diagram below. Use it to explain events in the United States and Canada during the postwar era.

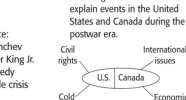

4. **Finding the Main Idea**
   a. How did the Soviet Union respond to demands for independence from Eastern European nations?
   b. What common concerns affected Latin American nations after 1945?

5. **Writing and Critical Thinking**
   Supporting a Point of View Why did U.S. leaders believe they had to contain communism?
   Consider:
   • the collapse of the Allied alliance at the end of the war
   • Soviet actions in Eastern Europe

go.hrw.com
Homework Practice Online
keyword: SP3 HPEP

SECTION 4

OBJECTIVES

1 **Describe how Japan recovered from the devastation of World War II.**

2 **Explain why communism led to greater tensions and conflict in Asia.**

3 **Describe how African nations dealt with independence.**

4 **Explain why violence marred life in the Middle East.**

🔊 LET'S GET STARTED!

As students enter the classroom, ask them to list characteristics of current living conditions in Asia, Africa, and the Middle East. *(Students may include overcrowding in Asia, famine in Africa, or armed conflict in the Middle East.)* Tell students that in Section 4 they will learn what has happened in Asia, Africa, and the Middle East since the end of World War II.

SECTION 4 RESOURCES

REPRODUCIBLE RESOURCES

▸ Guided Reading Strategy Epilogue 4

▸ Readings in World History 118: Nelson Mandela Explains Why There Is a South African Resistance Movement

TECHNOLOGY RESOURCES

▸ One-Stop Planner Epilogue 4

▸ World History Teaching Transparency: Regional and World Map 37: East and Southeast Asia

▸ Homework Practice Online

▸ Online Maps, Charts, and Graphs: Iran-Iraq War, 1980–1988

REINFORCEMENT, REVIEW, AND ASSESSMENT

▸ Section 4 Review, p. 473

▸ Daily Quiz Epilogue 4

▸ Main Idea Activity Epilogue 4

▸ English Audio Summary Epilogue 4

▸ Spanish Audio Summary Epilogue 4

SECTION 4

READ TO DISCOVER

1 How did Japan recover from the devastation of World War II?

2 Why did communism lead to greater tensions and conflict in Asia?

3 How did African nations deal with independence?

4 Why did violence mar life in the Middle East?

DEFINE

apartheid

IDENTIFY

Great Leap Forward
Deng Xiaoping
Corazon Aquino
Ho Chi Minh
Jawaharlal Nehru
Indira Gandhi
Benazir Bhutto
Nelson Mandela
Camp David Accords
OPEC

WHY IT MATTERS TODAY

The Japanese economy remains one of the most influential in the world today. Use CNNfyi.com or other **current event** sources to learn about the modern economy in Japan. Record your findings in your journal.

CNNfyi.com

Asia, Africa, and the Middle East Since 1945

The Main Idea
The postwar era brought opportunities and conflicts to the nations of Asia, Africa, and the Middle East.

The Story Continues *Writer Sakaguchi Ango described Japanese attitudes toward the United States after World War II. "Yesterday's enemy is today's friend . . . To cooperate with yesterday's enemy— no, to become bosom friends—is an everyday occurrence, and the more bitter the enemy, the more intimate we become." This attitude set the stage for Japan's revival during the postwar era.*

The Japanese Miracle

Like Latin America, the nations of Africa, Asia, and the Middle East experienced economic, political, and social change after World War II. At the end of the war, Japan lost all the territory it had gained during its period of expansion. Its population faced severe shortages of food and other necessities. The Japanese economy was in ruins. United States troops occupied the island nation. General Douglas MacArthur became the country's virtual ruler. He demilitarized Japan, oversaw war-crimes trials, and supervised the creation of a new constitution. Japan became a parliamentary democracy, with the emperor serving as a symbolic ruler.

The Japanese economy recovered quickly, and Japan became Asia's leading economic power. For many years, the United States was Japan's best customer and its leading supplier of raw materials and agricultural products. As a result, Japan bought more from the United States than the United States bought from Japan. In the late 1960s, however, this trade imbalance shifted to Japan's benefit. Some American politicians pressured their government to limit Japanese imports such as automobiles. The trade imbalance improved in the 1990s, when Japan loosened restrictions on foreign imports. During the 1990s, however, a recession weakened the Japanese economy. Economic growth declined, and unemployment rose. The Japanese economy remained troubled in the early 2000s.

Postwar economic growth brought great changes to Japan. Prosperity allowed families to buy consumer goods such as automobiles. However, the Japanese worked longer hours and encountered higher costs of living than did many Western workers. As women entered the workforce in increasing numbers, they gained greater freedom. Changing roles led to a decline in the importance of the family. As a result, young people began to make decisions regarding marriage partners and careers that their parents would have made for them in the past.

✔ **READING CHECK: Finding the Main Idea** What changes did postwar economic growth bring to the Japanese people? Changes included greater consumption of goods, longer work hours, higher costs of living, more freedom for women, and reduced importance of the family.

The Influence of Communist China

After the end of World War II, the Chinese Communist Party controlled much of northern China. In 1949 they drove the Nationalists from power. The Communists faced difficult challenges. Years of war had devastated China. In 1953 the

Communists issued their first Five-Year Plan for economic growth. The plan stressed the rapid buildup of heavy industry. The Communists redistributed farmland to peasants, brutally destroying the traditional landlord class in the process. Peasants organized their lands into collective farms. In 1958 the government announced a second Five-Year Plan, known as the **Great Leap Forward.** China encouraged families to make their own iron and steel in small backyard furnaces. Industrial output decreased, however, and food shortages led to famine that took the lives of some 20 million people.

China after Mao. In 1966 Chinese leader Mao Zedong launched the Cultural Revolution, a violent attempt at social change. Radical students called the Red Guards destroyed property and beat, tortured, or killed some of their opponents. After Mao's death in 1976, moderates and radicals struggled for power. The moderates won control, with **Deng Xiaoping** as their leader. Deng introduced economic reforms, but some Chinese called for a more democratic government. In the spring of 1989, hundreds of thousands of pro-democracy activists occupied Tiananmen Square in Beijing. Shen Tong described the activists' goals.

Mao Zedong's ideas were collected in "the little red book."

> *History Makers Speak*
>
> **❝We see the movement in three stages. The first is to gain attention so that the people of China will understand our concerns. The second is to make our [university] campuses democratic castles and strengthen our own commitment to democratic reform, while giving students in other cities and those in other sectors of society—workers, peasants, and journalists—the time to gain their own political awareness. And third . . . we will probably hold a nationwide pro-democracy movement . . . to educate people as to what democratic reform is all about.❞**
>
> Shen Tong, from *Neither Gods nor Emperors*

After protesters began a hunger strike, the government sent in the army to end the demonstrations. For two days troops shot at people they saw on the streets. The democracy movement was crushed. In response, many countries imposed economic sanctions on China. Tourism dwindled, and the Chinese economy grew weaker. Economic reforms encouraged a rebound during the 1990s, but unemployment, labor unrest, and poverty remained widespread in the early 2000s.

Analyzing Primary Sources

How did Shen Tong hope to build greater support for China's pro-democracy movement? gain public attention, strengthen democracy on university campuses, and hold a nationwide pro-democracy campaign

That's Interesting!

In 1990 Avon Products Inc., the American cosmetics company, was allowed to expand into China. Women in China had long been employed in jobs for which they were overqualified or received low wages. Selling Avon products increased finances, job satisfaction, and self-esteem. In 1998, however, direct selling was made illegal in China. The crackdown was intended to eliminate unscrupulous pyramid schemes, but there were reports that the large and enthusiastic sales meetings had made Chinese officials nervous. China's Avon representatives were out of business.

Chinese human-rights demonstrators and uniformed soldiers mingle during a 1989 protest in Beijing's Tiananmen Square.

ALL LEVELS: Have students complete a time line that shows dates and events related to communism in Asia. *(Time lines should list events related to Communist China, Korea, and Southeast Asia. Events include driving Nationalists out of China, 1949; killing demonstrators in Tiananmen Square, 1989; conflict between North and South Korea, 1950; war in Vietnam, 1950s–1970s; conflict in Cambodia, 1970s–1980s)* **ENGLISH LANGUAGE LEARNERS**

HOMEWORK Have students research and write a paragraph describing the events of the 1989 Tiananmen Square protests in Beijing.

Daily Life

Taiwan's culture is a colorful mix of modern Chinese and Western influences. Chinese music and dance are popular, but performances by foreign artists are frequent. Both traditional Chinese exercises and modern Western sports are popular. Baseball is a favorite.

The latest international trends in clothing are picked up quickly because Taiwan makes Western-style fashion for export. Taiwan's television stations have carried many foreign programs for years. And, since the 1980s, there has been an influx of Western commercial items such as fast food and cosmetics.

Critical Thinking

Ask students whether they think the Western influence in Taiwan is positive or negative.

ANSWER: positive: cosmopolitan influence, spread of ideas; negative: loss of traditional culture

---

HISTORY MAKER ANSWER

restored democracy and encouraged free enterprise

Taiwan and Korea. When the Communists gained control of China in 1949, the Nationalists fled to the island of Taiwan, about 100 miles off the coast of China. In Taiwan they set up a separate government called the Republic of China. Although the island lacked raw materials, Taiwan became a major producer and exporter of manufactured goods. Tensions between China and Taiwan persisted, however. In 1995 and 1996 China carried out military exercises off the coast of Taiwan. The United States sent aircraft carriers to the area to show its support for Taiwan.

At the end of World War II, Korea was divided into two separate nations. With Chinese assistance, communist North Korea attempted to conquer South Korea in 1950. Under the leadership of the United States, the United Nations sent troops to Korea to stop the takeover. Tensions between the two Koreas continued, but showed signs of easing in the early 2000s.

✔ **READING CHECK: Identifying Cause and Effect** How did communism lead to heightened tensions and warfare in Asia? through conflict between communist and noncommunist nations in the region

Independence Struggles in Southeast Asia

Southeast Asia consists of 10 countries: Brunei, Myanmar (formerly Burma), Cambodia, Indonesia, Laos, Malaysia, the Philippines, Singapore, Thailand, and Vietnam. All except Thailand were once colonies. The United States controlled the Philippines after the Spanish-American War until its independence in 1946. Under the leadership of Ferdinand Marcos, the Philippines endured martial law and a sinking economy. In 1986 **Corazon Aquino** ran against Marcos in a special election. Marcos fled the country when it became apparent that he had rigged the election. Aquino restored constitutional democracy and encouraged free enterprise. Aquino and her successors, however, proved unable to end poverty and corruption in the Philippines.

After the French were forced out of Vietnam, that country spent some 20 years at war. **Ho Chi Minh,** head of the communist guerrilla movement and leader of North Vietnam, encouraged rebellion in the south. The United States assisted the South Vietnamese, but the Communists succeeded and unified the country in 1976. Years of war drained the nation's resources, forcing communist leaders to adopt elements of the free enterprise system. United States president Bill Clinton visited Vietnam in 2000 in an effort to improve relations with Vietnam.

Vietnamese Communists encouraged rebels called the Khmer Rouge in neighboring Cambodia. In 1975 the Khmer Rouge established a brutal Marxist regime. Between 1975 and 1977, more than 1 million Cambodians starved to death or were executed. Vietnam invaded Cambodia in 1978, and conflict between the Khmer Rouge and Vietnam continued through the 1980s. Vietnam withdrew its troops in the late 1980s.

Indonesia gained independence from the Netherlands in 1949. Sukarno, the nation's leader, enacted many reforms, but his rule became increasingly authoritarian. In 1968 Sukarno was driven from office. General Suharto, the new leader, introduced some economic reforms. Western leaders, however, criticized Suharto for human rights abuses, and he resigned from office in 1998. Indonesia experienced economic difficulties and ethnic violence into the early 2000s.

During the 1950s a pro-Western military dictatorship ruled Thailand. Since the Vietnam War, control has shifted between civilian and military governments. Thailand has also had varied success economically. The economy expanded during the late 1980s and early 1990s, but weakened in a regional recession in 1996.

HISTORY MAKER

Corazon Aquino (1933–   )

When political enemies killed her husband, Corazon Aquino stepped into the political arena herself as a candidate for president. Although well-educated, Corazon Aquino had little political experience. Until her husband's death, she had been a full-time homemaker.

The election was close. At first it looked as if Aquino had lost. But when her supporters uncovered voter fraud, they challenged the results. Even after taking office, Aquino faced challenges from people who wanted to destroy democracy. She survived no fewer than six coup attempts. **How did Corazon Aquino affect politics in the Philippines?**

TEACH OBJECTIVE 3

LEVEL 3: Have students create charts similar to the one on the right to show what challenges African countries faced after independence. Discuss their charts in class.

Challenges African Countries Faced	
Challenges	**Examples**
Economic	*needed assistance from United States or Soviet Union during Cold War; superpowers involved in political conflicts*
Political	*conflicts in South Africa over apartheid; civil war in Angola; conflicts in Ethiopia and Somalia; ethnic violence in Rwanda*
Environmental	*land overuse, drought, desertification*
Health	*population growth, disease, AIDS, Ebola virus*

In 1963 Malaya (now West Malaysia), Singapore, Sarawak, and Sabah (now North Borneo) united to form the Federation of Malaysia. Challenges including ethnic conflict, pollution, and overpopulation faced the federation. Singapore left the group in 1965. Since that time, Lee Kwan Yew and his People's Action Party have dominated Singapore. Lee placed strict controls on unions, political activity, and the media. He stepped down in 1990, but the party remained in control. Singapore remains one of the world's most prosperous countries.

After gaining independence from Britain in 1948, Burma established a coalition government. In 1962, however, the army took over the government. Burma was renamed Myanmar in 1989. Although an opposition party won the elections held in 1990, the military refused to give up power.

✔ **READING CHECK: Contrasting** In what way were the development of Burma, Cambodia, Indonesia, and the Philippines similar after World War II? All gained independence from Western nations in the immediate postwar years.

South Asia After Empire

In the years after World War II, the peoples of South Asia moved from colonial rule to independence. Indian nationalists had called for independence from Britain before World War II ended. Indian leader Mohandas Gandhi insisted upon Britain's complete separation from India.

Led by Muhammad Ali Jinnah, the Muslim League called for Britain to create separate Hindu and Muslim states. In spite of many efforts, the Muslim League and the Indian National Congress proved unable to resolve their differences, and the British agreed to divide India. Areas with a Muslim majority became known as East and West Pakistan. These areas were separated geographically by India, a primarily Hindu nation. As religious groups relocated across new borders, violent clashes broke out that claimed some 1 million lives. Six months after the partition, a Hindu fanatic assassinated Gandhi.

Jawaharlal Nehru, first prime minister of India, hoped to create a democratic nation with a socialist economy. Nehru chose a policy of nonalignment, refusing to ally with either the United States or the Soviet Union during the Cold War. Two years after Nehru's death, his daughter, **Indira Gandhi,** was elected prime minister. Her terms in office were very controversial, and she was assassinated in 1984. India's development was hampered by social and religious tensions and a population that grew faster than the economy.

East Pakistan and West Pakistan were separated by some 1,000 miles of Indian territory. In 1971 East Pakistan gained independence and became Bangladesh. Both nations faced many challenges, including rapid population growth, poverty, illiteracy, and a lack of natural resources. They also experienced political instability. For the first half of the 1970s, a civilian government ruled Pakistan. In 1977, however, a military government imposed martial law and tried to return the country to traditional Muslim ways. Free elections were not held until 1988, when **Benazir Bhutto** became the first woman to head a Muslim nation. The government of Bangladesh was also overthrown by a military coup in the mid-1970s. In 1991 civilian government returned with the election of Khalida Zia, Bangladesh's first female prime minister.

✔ **READING CHECK: Analyzing Information** What role did religion play in the South Asian independence movements? sometimes acted to unite nationalist movements; sometimes divided them and created conflict

India's first prime minister, Jawaharlal Nehru, and his daughter, Indira Gandhi, made a state visit to the United States in December, 1956.

Geography

The climate and landscape of Bangladesh are characterized by one thing—water. There are five main river systems in Bangladesh. Each year between June and October the rivers overflow and cover the countryside. Severe floods regularly damage crops, ruin villages, and take a heavy toll on human and animal life.

During the monsoon season, heavy rain and intense storms occur. The winds cause the waters of the Bay of Bengal to inundate coastal areas, often causing heavy losses. Since the early 1700s more than 1 million people have been killed in such storms.

Critical Thinking

Ask students how the climate and landscape of Bangladesh may have molded ways of life.

ANSWER: Students may mention moving to high ground every year, not building permanent dwellings, expecting high death tolls.

LEVEL 2: Write the following list of countries and dates on the board, omitting the information in parentheses:

Egypt, 1952 *(republic established)*; Palestine, 1947 *(divided into Jewish and Arab states)*; Israel, 1967 *(fights Six-Day War with Palestine)*; Iran, 1979 *(Islamic republic established)*; Iraq, 1990 *(attacks Kuwait, provokes Persian Gulf War)*

Have students work in pairs. Ask them to find out what events happened in each country on the date given. Students should use their texts and make notes. Discuss their answers as a class.

COOPERATIVE LEARNING

CLOSE

Lead a class discussion about the role nationalism has played since 1945 in the development of countries in Asia, Africa, and the Middle East. Ask students to provide examples.

History Maker

NELSON MANDELA. Born in 1918, Nelson Mandela was the son of a tribal chief. Instead of claiming his chieftainship, he became a lawyer and a leader of the African National Congress. He was jailed in 1962 for his activities against apartheid in South Africa. He spent the next 28 years in prison. During his long imprisonment his fame spread around the world.

The South African government released Mandela from prison in 1990. He and President F.W. de Klerk worked together to bring nonracial democracy to South Africa. In 1993 they were awarded the Nobel Prize for Peace for their efforts. After one term as president (1994–1999), Mandela retired from active politics.

internet connect

TOPIC: Apartheid
GO TO: go.hrw.com
KEYWORD: SP3 WHEP

Have students access the Internet through the HRW Go site to conduct research of apartheid in South Africa. Ask students to create a time line sequencing the major events of apartheid in South Africa. Ask them to include information on the origins, growth, opposition, and policy changes of apartheid.

CONNECTING TO GEOGRAPHY ANSWER
It unifies people of African descent throughout the world.

CONNECTING TO GEOGRAPHY

Pan-Africanism

Pan-Africanism refers to the movement whose goal has been to improve the lives of all people of African descent. The word *Pan-Africanism* was chosen to describe the movement because it means "all African." American intellectual W. E. B. Du Bois and Jamaican Marcus Garvey were leaders of the movement. While Pan-Africanism sought to end colonial control of Africa, it had as its larger goal the unification of people of African descent throughout the world. It was, then, a movement that went beyond geographical boundaries. The Organization of African Unity (OAU) was founded in 1963 to promote Pan-Africanism. It had 53 member nations by the end of the 1900s.

Understanding Geography

How is Pan-Africanism different from a single nation's independence movement?

Africa and the Middle East Since 1945

The African and Middle Eastern nations that became independent in the years after World War II often faced drought, famine, and disease. As the colonial era faded, ethnic and political divisions throughout the region reemerged. Britain's West African colony of the Gold Coast achieved independence in 1957. Leader Kwame Nkrumah changed the country's name to Ghana. Kenya, Zambia, Malawi, and Rhodesia—later called Zimbabwe—followed Ghana's lead. Although methods for gaining independence varied, a combination of guerrilla tactics and constitutional change was common.

The road to independence for the Belgian Congo was much more violent. Many ethnic groups in the region did not have one clear leader. In the 1960s Colonel Joseph Mobutu established a military dictatorship that lasted for some 30 years. In 1971 he changed the name of the country to Zaire.

In South Africa a policy of **apartheid,** or total racial segregation, enabled whites to dominate the country. Segregation became the law in 1948. People were classified by race and forced to live in particular areas based on their racial classification. Marriage between people of different races was banned, and nonwhites had to carry identity cards.

An organization called the African National Congress used civil disobedience to protest apartheid during the 1950s. The South African government violently suppressed all opposition, arresting leaders such as **Nelson Mandela** and sentencing them to life in prison. In 1989, however, President F.W. de Klerk lifted many restrictions. In 1994 South Africa held its first all-race elections. Mandela was elected president.

Many African nations turned to either the Soviet Union or the United States for economic assistance. Both superpowers became involved in the civil war in Angola during the mid-1970s. Even after the end of the Cold War, tensions persisted in Angola. In Ethiopia and Somalia, guerrilla fighting and conflict continued long after the two superpowers had withdrawn.

Ethnic violence proved a problem in Africa as well. In Rwanda conflicts between the two major ethnic groups, the Tutsi and the Hutu, exploded into violence. Some 2 million people left Rwanda for refugee camps in neighboring countries. Zaire, which housed many refugees, became unstable as people flooded into the country. After ousting Mobutu in 1997, Laurent Kabila took control and renamed Zaire the Democratic Republic of the Congo.

Drought and disease also took their toll on Africa. As the African population expanded, farmers overused the land. They planted in dry or flat areas where fierce winds often stripped away the topsoil. In addition, people in many parts of Africa cut down trees for firewood. As a result of these practices, the spread of deserts in Africa became common. The emergence of diseases such as AIDS and the Ebola virus also brought suffering to the peoples of Africa. In spite of these and other hardships, independence brought many Africans a sense of ethnic and cultural pride. New literary and artistic traditions have developed alongside ancient traditions.

✔ **READING CHECK: Identifying Bias** How have ethnic differences affected the development of nations in Africa? often led to suppression of some groups by others, to ethnic divisions and conflicts

Nationalism in North Africa and the Middle East

During World War II the British reestablished their control over strategic countries such as Egypt and Iran. British control angered these countries and fueled nationalist

REVIEW

Have students complete the Section 4 Review on p. 473.

ASSESS

Have students complete Daily Quiz Epilogue 4. As Alternative Assessment, you may want to use the charts in this section's lessons.

RETEACH

Have students complete Main Idea Activity for English Language Learners and Special-Needs Students Epilogue 4. Then have stu-dents write a main idea question and answer for each subsection in the section. **ENGLISH LANGUAGE LEARNERS**

EXTEND

Organize the class into small groups. Have each group research, prepare, and present a short "newscast" about one of these conflicts: Vietnam War, Six-Day War, or Persian Gulf War.
BLOCK SCHEDULING , COOPERATIVE LEARNING

---

sentiments in the region. In Egypt a coup overthrew the monarchy and established a republic in 1952. Egyptian leader Gamal Abdel Nasser emphasized industrialization, government economic control, and more rights for women.

The British also faced nationalist challenges in Palestine. In 1947 the United Nations voted to divide Palestine into separate Jewish and Arab states. When the last British troops left in 1948, Jewish leaders proclaimed the Republic of Israel. This move angered Palestinian Arabs and neighboring Arab nations, who quickly moved against Israel. Israel survived, but found itself at war again in 1956 and 1967. The so-called Six-Day War of 1967 ended with the Israelis acquiring territory. In response to Israel's land gains, Palestinians formed the Palestine Liberation Organization (PLO), led by Yasser Arafat.

Israel and its neighbors were again at war in 1973. A peace process began in 1979 with the signing of the **Camp David Accords.** Another peace agreement was reached in 1993, but violence between Palestinians and Israelis flared up again in late 1999 and continued into the 2000s.

Iran also faced unrest. In 1979 a revolution toppled the monarchy and established an Islamic republic. In November of that year, Iranian militants captured the U.S. embassy in Tehran. They took more than 60 Americans hostage. Despite an international outcry, the hostages were not released until 1981.

Iran also faced pressure from its neighbor Iraq. In 1980 Iraq tried to take control of the waterway that divided the two countries in the south. War raged for eight years. The war caused international concern because of the region's importance as a source of oil. Iran and Iraq were both members of the Organization of Petroleum Exporting Countries (**OPEC**), founded in 1960 to set oil prices.

In 1990 Iraq attacked Kuwait, its tiny neighbor to the south, in a dispute over oil. In response, a U.S.-led coalition of about 30 nations opposed Iraq in what became known as the Persian Gulf War. After an air attack that lasted nearly 40 days, ground forces quickly liberated Kuwait. Iraqi leader Saddam Hussein, however, remained in power, but the UN imposed numerous restrictions on his government. In 2003, Hussein was toppled by another U.S.-led coalition that invaded Iraq, in part, for its repeated violations of these restrictions.

✔ **READING CHECK: Making Generalizations** What issues affected the Middle East in the postwar period? rise of nationalist movements; conflict between Israel and Arab states; religious unrest

INTERPRETING THE VISUAL RECORD

The hostage crisis Images of the Ayatollah Khomeini were posted outside the U.S. embassy in Tehran, where Iranian revolutionaries held 60 Americans hostage. *What does this picture tell you of the Iranian revolutionaries' view of Khomeini?*

VISUAL RECORD ANSWER
He was revered as their leader.

SECTION 4 REVIEW ANSWERS

❶ **Define**
• apartheid, p. 472

❷ **Identify**
• Great Leap Forward, p. 469
• Deng Xiaoping, p. 469
• Corazon Aquino, p. 470
• Ho Chi Minh, p. 470
• Jawaharlal Nehru, p. 471
• Indira Gandhi, p. 471
• Benazir Bhutto, p. 471
• Nelson Mandela, p. 472
• Camp David Accords, p. 473
• OPEC, p. 473

❸ Students' answers should include Cold War politics, communism, and religious influences.

❹ **a.** Japan became Asia's leading economic power. China's economy grew weaker.

b. Israeli-Palestinian conflicts, revolution in Iran, Iran-Iraq War, concerns over oil

❺ Students' reports should include the results of five-year plans, Cultural Revolution, Red Guards, Tiananmen Square

---

SECTION 4 REVIEW

1. **Define** and explain the significance:
   apartheid

2. **Identify** and explain the significance:
Great Leap Forward	Indira Gandhi
Deng Xiaoping	Benazir Bhutto
Corazon Aquino	Nelson Mandela
Ho Chi Minh	Camp David Accords
Jawaharlal Nehru	OPEC

3. **Finding the Main Idea** Copy the web diagram below. Use it to show factors that influenced the development of nations in Asia, Africa, and the Middle East after World War II.

   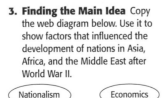

4. **Finding the Main Idea**
   a. How did economic development in China and Japan differ after World War II?
   b. Why was peace in the Middle East so difficult to achieve?

5. **Writing and Critical Thinking**
   Evaluating Write a brief report to assess the effectiveness of communist rulers in China after World War II.
   Consider:
   • efforts at economic development
   • human rights issues

Homework Practice Online
keyword: SP3 HPEP

OBJECTIVES

1 **Describe how the superpowers dealt with a changing world.**

2 **Explain how technological developments affected health, the environment, and entertainment.**

SECTION 5 RESOURCES

SECTION 5

READ TO DISCOVER

❶ How did superpowers deal with a changing world?

❷ How did technological developments affect health, the environment, and entertainment?

DEFINE

perestroika
glasnost
miniaturization

IDENTIFY

Ronald Reagan
Bill Clinton
George W. Bush
Mikhail Gorbachev
Boris Yeltsin
Yury Gagarin
Neil Armstrong

WHY IT MATTERS TODAY

European unification remained an important global issue during the early 2000s. Use **CNNfyi.com** or other **current event** sources to learn more about unification efforts. Record your findings in your journal.

CNNfyi.com

The Modern Era and Beyond

The Main Idea
The collapse of communism and technological developments dramatically changed life in the late 1900s.

The Story Continues *United States president Ronald Reagan stood in West Berlin near the Berlin Wall. Reagan told the crowd, "There is one sign the Soviets can make that would be unmistakable, that would advance dramatically the cause of freedom and peace. . . . Mr. Gorbachev, tear down this wall!"*

Superpowers in the Modern Era

The world changed dramatically in the 1980s and 1990s. The Cold War ended, but new crises and conflicts arose. The United States faced new challenges in the world's changing political structure. The Vietnam War had deeply divided Americans. The failure to prevent the fall of South Vietnam to the Communists disillusioned many people. This disillusionment extended to domestic matters with the Watergate scandal, which led to President Richard Nixon's resignation in 1974.

Politics in North America. In the wake of the Watergate scandal, many Americans believed that politicians could not be trusted. In 1976 James "Jimmy" Carter, former governor of Georgia, was elected president. Carter proved to be a man of integrity, but his presidency suffered from serious problems. A sluggish economy and the Iranian hostage crisis weakened public approval of Carter's presidency.

In 1980 **Ronald Reagan,** the former governor of California, was elected president. Reagan's optimistic view of the future inspired many Americans, although a scandal marred his final years in office. Reagan's vice president, George Bush, won the presidency in 1988, but lost his reelection bid in 1992 to **Bill Clinton,** the governor of Arkansas. Although he easily won reelection in 1996, in 1999 Clinton became the second president to be impeached by the House of Representatives, for lying to a grand jury. The Senate did not convict Clinton, however, and he finished his term in office. Clinton's successor in the White House, **George W. Bush** of Texas, was the son of former President Bush.

The sluggish economy that weakened Carter's administration began to improve during Reagan's presidency. In the 1980s and 1990s American products dominated such important industries as aerospace engineering. American companies pioneered the global revolution in computers and information technology.

Dependence on fossil fuels such as coal, natural gas, and oil caused some people to search for alternative energy sources in the 1970s. One popular alternative was nuclear power. Critics worried, however, about safety issues. Accidents at nuclear power plants in Pennsylvania and the Soviet Union reinforced the growing popular dissatisfaction with nuclear energy.

Relations between the United States and the Soviet Union remained tense for much of the 1970s and 1980s. President Nixon attempted to improve relations through treaties that limited the spread of nuclear weapons. During the late 1970s relations again cooled as President Carter made human rights a priority in foreign

TEACH OBJECTIVE 1

ALL LEVELS: Have students fill in the graphic organizer that follows to summarize political and economic changes in the 1980s and 1990s. Discuss the organizers in class. **ENGLISH LANGUAGE LEARNERS**

HOMEWORK Have students find a contemporary news event that is related to changes that occurred in North America, Europe, or the Soviet Union in the 1980s or 1990s. Have students write a brief report explaining how the news event is related to the past.

Changes in the 1980s and 1990s

North America	Europe	Soviet Union
U.S. products dominate important industries	Germany unifies	Soviet Union breaks up
U.S. foreign policy changes	European Union forms, drops trade barriers, and creates currency	Russia has economic problems
Quebec seeks separation from Canada		Russia fights civil war in Chechnya

relations. During the 1990s U.S. foreign policy shifted toward threats posed by smaller nations as well as continued efforts to renew relations with China.

In Canada political and economic challenges led to reforms in the 1980s. At the same time, many people living in the French-speaking province of Quebec sought special recognition for their heritage and language. On several occasions referendums were held to determine whether Quebec would formally separate from the rest of Canada.

Europe. Germany remained divided for decades after the end of World War II. By the late 1960s West Germany had become a major economic power in Western Europe. In 1990 East and West Germany were reunified. High unemployment and other economic problems, however, placed heavy burdens on the unified nation.

During the 1970s and 1980s the European Economic Community (EEC) expanded to include 12 nations. With the signing of the Maastricht Treaty in 1993, the EEC evolved into the more closely knit European Union (EU). Member nations dropped trade barriers among themselves and agreed to adopt a common currency.

The fall of communism. One of the most dramatic changes in world politics was the breakup of the Soviet Union. A new generation of Communist Party leaders came to power when Mikhail Gorbachev became the leader of the Soviet Union in 1985. Gorbachev introduced a series of dramatic political and economic reforms known as **perestroika** (per·uh·STROY·kuh), or restructuring, and **glasnost,** (GLAZ·nohst) or openness. As Gorbachev's reforms took effect, communist nations in Eastern Europe moved toward freedom. Democratic movements swept communist governments from power. In 1989 protesters tore down the Berlin Wall. Gorbachev's reforms led to a coup in the Soviet Union in 1991. Although the coup was unsuccessful, Gorbachev never regained his earlier popularity. He stepped down in 1991. Within a few months, the Soviet Union ceased to exist.

With the collapse of the Soviet Union, Russia and other independent republics emerged. Economic troubles weakened the power base of Russian president **Boris Yeltsin,** and a brutal civil war in the region of Chechnya led to international criticism. Some observers feared that Yeltsin's successor, Vladimir Putin, would suppress dissent and strengthen the central government at the expense of civil rights.

✔ **READING CHECK: Contrasting** How did postwar changes in Western Europe differ from those in Eastern Europe and the Soviet Union? Western Europe moved toward economic and political unification, while Eastern Europe and the Soviet Union broke into smaller units

INTERPRETING THE VISUAL RECORD

Independence for Quebec
Despite the failure of the Meech Lake Accord, many people in Quebec continue to push for separation from Canada. *How do the flags in this photo reveal Quebec's French-based culture?*

Government

When protesters tore down the Berlin Wall in 1989, they were tearing down the symbol of the Cold War. The barrier had gone up in 1961 to keep East Germans from fleeing to West Germany.

By the 1980s, the system of concrete walls, electrified fences, and fortifications extended for 28 miles through Berlin. It extended another 75 miles around West Berlin to separate it from the rest of East Germany.

Critical Thinking

Why did East Germans want to flee into West Germany?

ANSWER: They did not want to live under the communist regime in East Germany.

VISUAL RECORD ANSWER

The stylized fleur-de-lis is the emblem of the kings of France.

LEVEL 3: Divide the class into two groups representing the United States and the Soviet Union. Have members of each group write newspaper articles describing their country's response to the changes in the 1980s and 1990s. Ask volunteers from each group to read their article for the class to discuss.

TEACH OBJECTIVE 2

LEVEL 1: Ask students to list developments in the 1980s and 1990s in technology, health, the environment, and entertainment. *(technology: miniaturization, computers, Internet, cellular phones, space shuttle; health: smallpox eliminated, genetic research; the* *environment: pollution, ozone layer damage, global warming, loss of habitat; entertainment: music synthesizers, computer-generated special effects for films)* Then ask students how these changes affect their own lives. **ENGLISH LANGUAGE LEARNERS**

Interdisciplinary Connection

DRAMA. Science fiction became increasingly popular in the 1990s. What had started in the 1800s with a small group of writers—such as Jules Verne and H.G. Wells—had become an important part of the entertainment business. Science fiction novels, movies, television shows, and a Sci-Fi cable channel indicated the growing popularity of the genre.

Part of the reason for this popularity was that it reflected the scientific possibilities of the rapidly advancing technological world. It reminded people that there were no bounds to human imagination and exploration.

ACTIVITY: Ask students to suggest plots for science fiction stories that are based on real science or technology.

This painting by Jackson Pollock, Silver Over Black, White, Yellow, and Red *(1948), exemplifies the abstract expressionist style.*

On July 20, 1969, the United States won the intense race to put the first person on the moon.

Analyzing Primary Sources

What did Rheingold regard as the main benefit of the Internet?
increased communication and ease of contact

The World in the Twenty-First Century

Many developments marked the 1900s, including changes in political structures, economic systems, and attitudes toward human rights. The people of the twenty-first century will continue to face many of these same challenges.

The arts and literature. Many new styles of painting and sculpture developed as artists looked for new ways to work with ideas, images, and color. New materials and techniques also developed in architecture, as architects emphasized smoothness, polish, and shapes.

Experimentation was also important in the world of music. New uses of instruments, rhythm, harmony, and melody were introduced. Experimenters soon found that computers could produce sounds, and innovative composers wrote music for synthesizers as well as traditional instruments.

New filmmaking technology provided moviegoers with a variety of experiences. Computers became central to the development of movies such as *Twister* (1996) and *A.I.* (2001). Some moviemakers examined key social issues such as racism and violence.

Some of the influential writers after World War II were known as the Beat Generation. This group of poets and novelists attacked the conventions of the American way of life. Other writers used their work to explore themes such as the lives of minority groups in the United States, the effects of colonial rule in Africa, and the impact of Hitler on Germany. Science fiction became increasingly important after World War II, as writers became interested in the opportunities and dangers that technological advances posed.

Science and technology. Transportation became faster, more reliable, and more accessible during the 1900s. By the mid-1960s jet travel had become commonplace. Other transportation advances included trains that could travel at more than 150 miles per hour. Automobile use and automobile production increased throughout the world.

In 1957 the Soviet Union launched the world's first space satellite, called *Sputnik I,* into orbit. In 1961 a Soviet named **Yury Gagarin** became the first person to orbit Earth. One month later Alan Shepard became the first American in space. In 1969 American **Neil Armstrong** became the first person to walk on the surface of the moon. Both the Soviet Union and the United States constructed space stations. The United States, however, concentrated on building reusable spacecraft. Introduced in 1981, the space shuttle allows scientists to conduct experiments in space.

One of the most important developments in technology has been miniaturization, the building of machines that are quite small. Researchers developed lighter, more durable materials that made **miniaturization** possible. Computers were one of the machines that became smaller. In addition, computers became much faster. The development of the Internet, a global network of computers, made communications easier. A computer communications expert explained the widespread popularity of the Internet.

 ❝[The Internet] allows many people to reach other people. . . . It also allows you to communicate very easily with those who share your personal or professional interests, no matter where they are in the world or what time it is. It crosses a lot of barriers. If you have an interest in photography or raising roses, there might be a grandmother in Prague or a 14-year-old kid in St. Louis or someone in Tokyo with similar interests. Now you can all communicate.❞

Howard Rheingold, from *What They Said in 1995*

CLOSE

Ask students to list one positive effect and one negative effect of the technological developments of the last twenty years.

REVIEW

Have students complete the Section 5 Review on p. 477.

ASSESS

Have students complete Daily Quiz Epilogue 5. As Alternative Assessment, you may want to use the graphic organizer in this section's lessons.

RETEACH

Have students complete Main Idea Activity for English Language Learners and Special-Needs Students Epilogue 5. Then have students write a two-paragraph summary of the section.
ENGLISH LANGUAGE LEARNERS

EXTEND

Have students identify two technological devices that they use every day. Then have them write a brief paper explain how their lives would be different if they did not have those devices.
BLOCK SCHEDULING

Other communications innovations included cellular phones, fax machines, fiber-optic cables, and photocopiers. These advances have helped to link people and societies around the world.

Health and human rights. Biologists made breakthroughs during the 1900s. Penicillin and other antibiotics, which destroy or limit bacterial growth, were developed to fight diseases. Polio vaccines largely eliminated polio in developed countries. A worldwide campaign against smallpox virtually eliminated that disease by the 1980s. Although today there is no cure or vaccine for AIDS, researchers had had some success in fighting that disease. Some scientists studied genetics to understand how chromosomes affect development. Their research provided insights into bacteria, human cells, viruses, and diseases such as cancer. A major development in the field of genetics took place in 1997, when researchers successfully cloned a sheep.

Medical advances allowed people to live longer. This development contributed to tremendous population growth. Large-scale migration also affected population size. Overcrowding in cities strained many governments' ability to provide adequate health and human services. Jobs and housing sometimes became scarce. Some cities experienced water shortages.

Population growth and industrialization led to increased use of land and natural resources. Some natural habitats were destroyed, and many plants and animal species were threatened. Industrialization led to some pollution problems. Some scientists argued that increased pollution damaged the Earth's ozone layer and contributed to a worldwide rise in temperatures. People around the world worked to combat these environmental problems through recycling and reuse of materials.

Many people also became involved in the issue of human rights. In many parts of the world, repressive governments imprisoned, tortured, and executed people who spoke out against them. International organizations such as the United Nations, the Council of Europe, and Amnesty International investigated and reported on human rights violations around the world.

✔ **READING CHECK: Summarizing** How did technological advances change life during the 1900s? improved transportation, communication; led to advances in space exploration, miniaturization

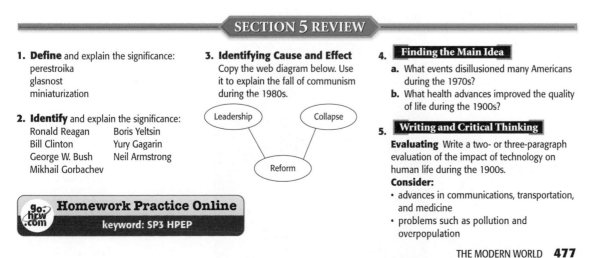

SECTION 5 REVIEW

1. **Define** and explain the significance:
   perestroika
   glasnost
   miniaturization

2. **Identify** and explain the significance:
   Ronald Reagan   Boris Yeltsin
   Bill Clinton   Yury Gagarin
   George W. Bush   Neil Armstrong
   Mikhail Gorbachev

3. **Identifying Cause and Effect**
   Copy the web diagram below. Use it to explain the fall of communism during the 1980s.

   Leadership   Collapse

   Reform

4. **Finding the Main Idea**
   a. What events disillusioned many Americans during the 1970s?
   b. What health advances improved the quality of life during the 1900s?

5. **Writing and Critical Thinking**
   Evaluating Write a two- or three-paragraph evaluation of the impact of technology on human life during the 1900s.
   Consider:
   • advances in communications, transportation, and medicine
   • problems such as pollution and overpopulation

Homework Practice Online
go. hrw .com
keyword: SP3 HPEP

SECTION
5 REVIEW ANSWERS

❶ **Define**
• perestroika, p. 475
• glasnost, p. 475
• miniaturization, p. 476

❷ **Identify**
• Ronald Reagan, p. 474
• Bill Clinton, p. 474
• George W. Bush, p. 474
• Mikhail Gorbachev, p. 475
• Boris Yeltsin, p. 475
• Yury Gagarin, p. 476
• Neil Armstrong, p. 476

❸ Leadership: Mikhail Gorbachev; Reform: perestroika, glasnost; Collapse: Russia and independent republics emerged

❹ **a.** Vietnam War, Watergate scandal

b. penicillin and other antibiotics, polio vaccines, smallpox eliminated, genetic research

❺ Students should include the problems associated with every advance they mention.

SECTION 6

OBJECTIVES

1 **Describe how the United States was attacked on September 11, 2001, and how people responded.**

2 **Explain how the events of September 11, 2001, affected the U.S. economy.**

3 **Identify the immediate steps U.S. leaders and their allies took to find those responsible for the attacks and bring them to justice.**

📻 LET'S GET STARTED!

As students enter the classroom, ask them to list the buildings, monuments, or objects that symbolize the United States. *(U.S. Capitol, White House, Washington Monument, Statue of Liberty, Liberty Bell)* Have any students who have visited these places to describe them. Tell students that in Section 6 they will learn about a devastating terrorist attack on buildings in the United States in 2001 and how the attack changed the world.

SECTION 6

READ TO DISCOVER

1 How was the United States attacked on September 11, 2001, and how did people respond?

2 How did the events of September 11, 2001 affect the U.S. economy?

3 What immediate steps did U.S. leaders and their allies take to find those responsible for the attacks and bring them to justice?

IDENTIFY

World Trade Center
Pentagon
Rudolph Giuliani
Tom Ridge
Donald Rumsfeld
Colin Powell

WHY IT MATTERS TODAY

The terrorist attacks of September 11, 2001, continue to affect American life and U.S. foreign policy. Use **CNNfyi.com** or other **current events** sources to learn about the latest issues and events stemming from this national tragedy.

CNNfyi.com

A Day That Changed the World

The Main Idea
The United States suffered a devastating terrorist attack by Islamic extremists on September 11, 2001.

The Story Continues *On Tuesday morning, September 11, 2001, it was business as usual in the downtown financial district of New York City. In the World Trade Center complex, some of the 50,000 employees were starting their workday, most of them within the Twin Towers that dominated the Manhattan skyline. Others were still on their way to work. On Fifth Avenue a group of pedestrians noticed a large airplane pass by. "We all looked up," recalled one man. "We all thought it would be unusual for a plane to be flying so low over the city." Moments later they witnessed a terrible disaster unfold.*

The Attack

At 8:45 A.M., the daily routine of a city and a nation was shattered when an American Airlines passenger jet crashed into the north tower of the **World Trade Center.** The impact was devastating, as though a bomb had struck the 110-story building. Lynn Simpson, who was working on the 89th floor, recalled, "I heard an enormous crash. The ceiling fell in, the lights went out and the sprinklers went on. . . . I told everyone to get out." Stunned men and women began evacuating the building as emergency crews rushed to the scene. Then at about 9:00 A.M. a second plane—United Airlines Flight 175—slammed into the south tower of the WTC complex.

Shocked Americans began to realize that these were deliberate attacks when it was learned that both planes had been hijacked by terrorists. Moreover, it was soon clear that New York was not the terrorists' only target. At approximately 9:40 A.M. a third plane, American Airlines Flight 77, hit the west side of the Pentagon. Located just outside Washington, D.C., the **Pentagon** is the headquarters of the U.S. military leadership. The impact of the crash caused massive damage and started fires deep within the huge, five-sided building. Hundreds of military personnel and civilians were killed.

At the World Trade Center complex, hundreds of rescue workers struggled to aid victims and firefighters tried to control the raging fires. In the midst of their efforts, further disaster struck. At 10:00 A.M. the south tower suddenly collapsed, followed half an hour later by the fall of the north tower. "It [the south tower] just fell down in perfect symmetry, one floor, then another

Columns of thick smoke billow from the wreckage of the World Trade Center's twin towers on September 11, 2001, after hijacked commercial airliners piloted by Islamic extremists dove into the buildings, killing thousands.

TEACH OBJECTIVE 1

LEVEL 1: Help students complete a timetable of the terrorist attack of September 11, 2001, similar to the one on the right. Lead a class discussion of the events.

ENGLISH LANGUAGE LEARNERS

September 11, 2001

8:45 A.M.	Hijacked American Airlines plane crashes into WTC north tower.
9:00 A.M.	Hijacked United Airlines plane crashes into WTC south tower.
9:40 A.M.	Hijacked American Airlines plane crashed into Pentagon.
10:00 A.M.	WTC south tower collapses.
10:30 A.M.	WTC north tower collapses.
c. 10:30 A.M.	Hijacked United Airlines plane crashes near Pittsburgh, PA.

floor, then another," said a stunned witness. The collapse of the massive buildings killed or trapped thousands of people still inside or near the towers, including hundreds of firefighters, police officers, and other rescuers.

A fourth plane—United Airlines Flight 93—was also hijacked and still in the air over southern Pennsylvania. Cell phone calls from passengers aboard the plane indicate that they learned of the other attacks and decided to stop the terrorists on board from hitting their next target. Flight 93 crashed southeast of Pittsburgh sometime around the time of the collapse of the World Trade Center's towers.

In downtown New York City, clouds of smoke, dust, and ash drifted through the streets along with thousands of battered and dazed survivors. Thousands more people were unaccounted for in the wreckage. Meanwhile, emergency teams battling fires in the Pentagon were unable to search for survivors. As many as 266 passengers and crew aboard the four hijacked flights had been killed. Americans everywhere were shocked, wondering what was to come.

✔ **READING CHECK: Sequencing** In what order did the events of the morning of September 11, 2001, take place?

The World Responds

Government officials raced to mount rescue efforts and placed the U.S. military on full alert. The Federal Aviation Administration temporarily grounded air traffic nationwide and closed airports. Key government centers, such as the White House, were briefly evacuated.

Rescue and relief. New York hospitals mobilized hundreds of doctors but found, tragically, that there were relatively few survivors to care for. Within hours, firefighters and other rescue workers from across the nation came to New York to join state and city emergency personnel searching the rubble for survivors. Their efforts were hampered by the tons of unstable debris and by the intense heat from underground fires. Three weeks after the attack there were still more than 5,900 people missing, all presumed dead. New York mayor **Rudolph Giuliani** said of the final death toll, "It will be more than we can bear." In all, about 2,500 people were killed at the World Trade Center, including more than 300 firefighters and many other rescue workers. At the Pentagon, 184 military and civilian personnel, including those on the hijacked plane, had been killed.

Congress swiftly approved a $40 billion relief package to help the nation recover from the attacks. The money would fund emergency assistance and national security measures. The government also passed legislation that provided compensation to the families of victims. Democrats and Republicans displayed an unusual degree of cooperation in pushing through such measures. "I think the message is very simply we are united . . . when it comes to a national threat as great as this," said Senate Majority Leader Tom Daschle of South Dakota.

People unite. Political leaders also tried to rally Americans' spirit on the day of the attack. Mayor Giuliani assured fellow New Yorkers, "We're going to rebuild and rebuild stronger." President George W. Bush, who had been in Florida visiting an elementary school, was moved to a safe location. From there, he

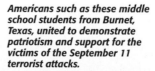

In the aftermath of the terrorist attacks, members of New York City's fire and police departments mounted a heroic effort to rescue victims trapped in the rubble of the World Trade Center.

Americans such as these middle school students from Burnet, Texas, united to demonstrate patriotism and support for the victims of the September 11 terrorist attacks.

TEACH OBJECTIVE 1

ALL LEVELS: Ask students to describe how the U.S. government, the American people, and the rest of the world responded to the attack. *(Government: military on full alert, planes grounded, airports closed, buildings evacuated, $40 billion in relief, FBI investigation started, suspects detained; American people: on-site rescue efforts, donated money and blood, showed patriotism; the world: EU declared day of mourning, other world leaders expressed sympathy and provided support)* **ENGLISH LANGUAGE LEARNERS**

TEACH OBJECTIVE 2

LEVEL 3: Have students study the information in Section 6 about the economic impact of the attack. Then ask them to summarize the areas of concern. *(actual damage costs; effects on stock markets in the United States, Europe, and Asia; impact on airline and tourism industries; consumer confidence)*

In the days following the terrorist attacks, Americans across the nation came together in a series of interfaith memorial services to honor the victims and to demonstrate unity and faith.

gave a brief speech to the nation. "Freedom itself was attacked this morning by a faceless coward," he declared. Republican and Democratic members of Congress issued a joint declaration to the country from the Capitol steps. They said that the United States would not be intimidated by terrorism. The members then sang a chorus of "God Bless America."

The tragic events of September 11, 2001, drew sympathy and support from around the world. Citizens of more than 40 countries were among the missing. The European Union declared September 14 a day of mourning throughout its 15 member states. British prime minister Tony Blair called the terrorist acts "an attack on the free and democratic world everywhere." The French newspaper *Le Monde* ran a headline saying, "WE ARE ALL AMERICANS." Russian and Chinese leaders gave their condolences. Even traditional opponents of the United States, such as Cuba and Iran, expressed their sympathy and regret. U.S. leaders gave thanks for these gestures and worked to form an active coalition against terrorism.

Perhaps the greatest show of unity came from the American people themselves. Many were inspired to displays of charity and patriotism. Within two days Wal-Mart, the nation's largest retail chain, had sold its entire stock of half a million American flags. Charitable groups across the country moved swiftly to raise funds for relief efforts. Thousands of people went to Red Cross centers to donate blood. "It's just amazing," said one nurse in New York. "There'll be a three- or four-hour wait, and just look at all of these people standing here." Actors and musicians held a special telethon, "America: A Tribute to Heroes," on September 21. The effort raised some $150 million to benefit the families who had lost loved ones in the attacks.

People also came together in public to heal their wounds and show their strength. When professional sports leagues resumed their schedules, stadiums were filled with patriotic tributes and fans waving flags. Actor James Earl Jones drew cheers as he opened a mass prayer service held in New York City's Yankee Stadium.

"Our spirit is unbroken. In fact, it is stronger than ever. Today we reaffirm our faith in the essential dignity of every individual. What we share as Americans and as human beings is far greater than what divides us."

James Earl Jones, September 23, 2001

Spiritual leaders representing many faiths led prayers for the victims and called for unity as a nation. The Boys and Girls Choir of Harlem sang a stirring rendition of "We Shall Overcome," with its refrain, "We are not afraid. . . . We shall live in peace."

✔ **READING CHECK: Finding the Main Idea** In what ways did Americans first respond to the terrorist attacks? shock, followed by displays of patriotism, charity, and unity

The Investigation

Immediately after the attacks, the largest criminal investigation in U.S. history began. Within 48 hours the Federal Bureau of Investigation (FBI) placed more than 4,000 special agents on the case. The FBI soon released the names of 19 suspected hijackers from several Middle Eastern nations. Investigators gathered evidence suggesting that

LEVEL 2: Have students work in pairs to create a chart showing the steps U.S. leaders took in response to the terrorist attacks. The chart might include international actions and domestic actions. *(international actions: created a coalition, froze suspects' assets, mobilized military, singled out Taliban regime, started air strikes on Afghanistan, dropped food and medicine for civilians; domestic actions: created Office of Homeland Security, increased airport security, protected transportation and power networks, expanded law-enforcement powers)* **COOPERATIVE LEARNING**

each group of hijackers included trained pilots and that some of these men had been living and training in the United States for months. Even more crucial was the identity of those who had planned these acts of terror.

A prime suspect surfaced almost immediately—Osama bin Laden. This wealthy Saudi Arabian exile was already wanted for his suspected role in earlier terrorist attacks against U.S. forces overseas. A supporter of an extreme form of Islamic fundamentalism, bin Laden had publicly called for attacks on the United States, which he claimed had corrupted and oppressed Muslims. Officials believed that bin Laden's global terrorism network, known as al Qaeda, or "the Base," was one of the few terrorist groups with the resources and organizational structure to have carried out the attacks.

Experts also agreed that the attacks of September 11 probably involved the cooperation of more than one terrorist group. Investigators from a broad range of federal agencies, with assistance from other nations, began a global manhunt for anyone with knowledge of the attacks. They sifted through debris at the crash sites to find physical evidence and tracked airline, telephone, credit card, and other financial records to trace terrorists' movements. Several hundred suspects were detained at home and abroad for questioning. Although the complexity of the task and the need to protect security and sources forced officials to be cautious, the Bush administration pledged to release conclusive evidence about the attacks as soon as it was feasible to do so.

✔ **READING CHECK: Summarizing** What early conclusions did investigators draw about the source of the attacks, and how did they investigate them? FBI investigators analyzed physical evidence and telephone, airline, and financial records to conclude that Osama bin Laden's al Qaeda network was responsible.

The Economic Impact

The terrorist strikes on the World Trade Center had a high cost in economic terms as well as in lives. The costs related to the immediate physical damage were estimated at $25 billion. In addition, the New York Stock Exchange (NYSE) had to shut down operations for four days following the attack. When the stock market reopened, concerns about a potential war and poor economic indicators combined to cause one of the worst weeks in the history of the NYSE. European and Asian stock markets also suffered heavy losses. Although stock prices made a modest rally the following week, concerns about the health of the national and global economy remained. "The insecurity is still there," commented one German trader. "There is no way to tell what is going to happen," explained an American trader. The Federal Reserve quickly cut interest rates in an effort to help the economy.

One area of particular concern was the airline industry. Forced to shut down operations for days and facing greatly increased security expenses and a public reluctance to fly, major airlines took heavy financial losses. They laid off thousands of workers, and at least one smaller carrier went out of business. The air-travel crisis caused wider problems as well. Tourism declined severely around the nation, and companies relying on supplies shipped by air endured shortages. Congress and the president rushed to pass a $15 billion bail-out package to help keep the nation's airlines operating.

One of the most difficult economic problems for the government to address was falling consumer confidence. Many Americans had been concerned by the weakness of the economy before the terrorist attacks. Uncertainty and fear raised by

The stock market tumbled sharply when exchanges such as the NASDAQ, pictured here, reopened six days after the September 11 terrorist attacks. National economies around the world were hard hit by the attacks and the threats they posed to global peace.

Linking Past to Present

The September 11, 2001, attack on the World Trade Center in New York City was not the first time the complex had been attacked. On February 26, 1993, a terrorist bomb exploded in the underground parking garage of the WTC. The massive explosion caused a 100– by 100-foot opening in the garage and scattered debris throughout the adjacent subway station. All 110 floors of the north tower filled with smoke. Six people were killed and 1,000 were injured. In 1994 four Islamic militants were found guilty of the bombing. Two were convicted in 1997.

ACTIVITY: Have students find and compare news reports about the attacks on the World Trade Center in 1993 and 2001.

HOMEWORK Have students research the hijacking and crash in Pennsylvania of United Airlines Flight 93 on September 11, 2001. Then have students write a paragraph expressing their opinion of the actions of the passengers.

CLOSE

Lead a class discussion about global terrorism, the reasons for it, and how the United States and other countries that have been attacked should respond to it.

REVIEW

Have students complete the Section 6 Review on p. 483.

Government

Members of the Taliban regime were Islamic fundamentalists who became active in Afghanistan around 1994. *Taliban* is the Persian word for "students." Taliban members were recruited from schools set up among Afghan refugees in Pakistan during the time when Afghanistan was ruled by a Soviet-backed government. Many Afghans supported them at first, but support soon disappeared. The Taliban enforced a rigorous Islamic social order. All men had to grow beards, schools for girls were closed, and women were forbidden to work outside their homes. Islamic law was enforced by amputations and public executions.

Critical Thinking

Ask students why they think the Afghan people welcomed the Taliban at first.

ANSWER: They wanted their country to be Islamic, not communist.

President George W. Bush addressed a joint session of Congress on September 20, 2001, during which he pledged to utilize the full might of the nation in a war on international terrorism.

Analyzing Primary Sources

Identifying a Point of View
What did President Bush call on other nations to do? determine if they supported the U.S. or the terrorists

the events of September 11 made many Americans believe the country was headed for a recession. "We do have to fear fear itself, it matters, it affects consumer spending," stated one economist. Government officials responded to such concerns by emphasizing that the long-term health of the economy was strong, even if difficult times lay ahead.

✔ **READING CHECK: Identifying Cause and Effect** What immediate effect did the terrorist attacks have on the U.S. economy? huge costs of damage, falling stock prices, declining consumer confidence

A Call to Action

In a national address on September 20, President George W. Bush called the attacks on the World Trade Center and the Pentagon "an act of war." He promised that the United States would bring those responsible to justice.

A war on terrorism. The president also declared that the United States would wage war on terrorism itself. Bush emphasized that U.S. efforts would be aimed not only against terrorist organizations but also against national governments that supported and protected terrorists. "Either you are with us, or you are with the terrorists," he declared.

 "Tonight we are a country awakened to danger and called to defend freedom. Our grief has turned to anger, and anger to resolution. Whether we bring our enemies to justice, or bring justice to our enemies, justice will be done. . . . The enemy of America is not our many Muslim friends; it is not our many Arab friends. Our enemy is a radical network of terrorists, and every government that supports them. . . . Every nation, in every region, now has a decision to make. Either you are with us, or you are with the terrorists. From this day forward, any nation that continues to harbor or support terrorism will be regarded by the United States as a hostile regime. . . . Great harm has been done to us. We have suffered great loss. And in our grief and anger we have found our mission and our moment. Freedom and fear are at war. The advance of human freedom—the great achievement of our time, and the great hope of every time—now depends on us. Our nation—this generation—will lift a dark threat of violence from our people and our future. We will rally the world to this cause by our efforts, by our courage. We will not tire, we will not falter, and we will not fail."

George W. Bush, September 20, 2001

In his speech the president singled out one government—the Taliban regime of Afghanistan—as a key sponsor of terror. The Taliban emerged in the mid-1990s as a splinter group of fundamentalist Muslims. Many members had fought against the Soviets during their occupation of Afghanistan. Its leaders had developed ties to Osama bin Laden, whom they later sheltered.

Domestic security. President Bush appointed Governor **Tom Ridge** of Pennsylvania to head the Office of Homeland Security. This office was created to coordinate the domestic national security efforts of various government agencies.

Key goals included improving airport security and protecting vital systems such as transportation and power networks from attack. Proposed airline security measures included background checks on passengers and employees, more-thorough

ASSESS

Have students complete Daily Quiz Epilogue 6. As Alternative Assessment, you may want to use the chart in this section's lessons.

RETEACH

Have students complete Main Idea Activity for English Language Learners and Special-Needs Students Epilogue 6. Then have students create an outline of the section's main ideas and supporting details. **ENGLISH LANGUAGE LEARNERS**

EXTEND

Ask students to research the history of the Pentagon building and write a brief report of their findings. **BLOCK SCHEDULING**

baggage searches, and restricted access to airport facilities. Political leaders such as U.S. Attorney General John Ashcroft also called for expanded law-enforcement powers to combat terrorism.

A difficult mission. Administration officials, including Secretary of Defense **Donald Rumsfeld,** agreed that striking at terrorists outside the United States would be a lengthy and difficult task. Success would require identifying the proper targets as well as finding ways to destroy them.

The Bush administration sought to fight terrorism using economic, diplomatic, and military means. The president froze the assets of individuals, groups, and companies with suspected terrorist ties. Secretary of State **Colin Powell** led U.S. efforts to build an international coalition against terrorism and to isolate the Taliban regime. The leaders of nations such as Great Britain and Russia pledged their support of antiterrorist efforts. For the first time in its existence, NATO invoked Article 5 of its original treaty, under which NATO members are required to come to the defense of an alliance member under attack. Even former allies of the Taliban regime, such as Pakistan and Saudi Arabia, were convinced to support U.S. efforts.

The United States also began mobilizing military forces such as aircraft carrier groups and ground troops in preparation for attacks on terrorism. Less than one month after the terrorists' attacks, the United States and its allies began their offensive. On October 7, the first in a series of powerful air strikes hit al Qaeda bases and Taliban sites in Afghanistan. At the same time, food, medicine, and other supplies were air-dropped to the country's impoverished civilian population. The Northern Alliance, an Afghan group that had fought against the Taliban since the early 1990s, provided ground support. The United States and Great Britain also sent troops. The troops slowly drove out the Taliban and captured members of al Qaeda. On December 17, the American flag was raised at the U.S. embassy in Kabul for the first time since 1989. Four days later a new Afghan government was established.

✔ **READING CHECK: Summarizing** What early steps did U.S. leaders take to respond to the terrorist attacks on the United States?

In the days immediately following the attacks of September 11, 2001, the United States began deploying its military arsenal in preparation for a long and difficult struggle against global terrorism. Pictured here is the U.S. aircraft carrier Theodore Roosevelt.

SECTION 6 REVIEW ANSWERS

❶ **Define**
• World Trade Center, p. 478
• Pentagon, p. 478
• Rudolph Giuliani, p. 479
• Tom Ridge, p. 482
• Donald Rumsfeld, p. 483
• Colin Powell, p. 483

❷ Economic: froze assets of terrorists; Social: improved domestic security; Military: attacked Taliban sites in Afghanistan; Diplomatic: built coalition against terrorism

❸ **a.** suspected hijackers from the Middle East and Osama bin Laden; sifted through debris at crash sites, tracked financial records, detained suspects for questioning

b. $25 billion damage costs, markets suffered heavy losses, airlines laid off workers, tourism declined, consumer confidence fell

❹ Paragraphs should include actions students could take, such as fundraising drives for donations, writing letters of support, or volunteering at relief agencies.

SECTION 6 REVIEW

1. Identify and explain:
World Trade Center
Pentagon
Rudolph Giuliani
Tom Ridge
Donald Rumsfeld
Colin Powell

2. Analyzing Information Copy the graphic organizer below. Use it to explain some of the ways in which the U.S. government responded to protect the United States and bring its attackers to justice.

Economic — Government Actions — Military
Social — Government Actions — Diplomatic

3. ### Finding the Main Idea

a. Who did investigators initially suspect of carrying out the terrorist attacks of September 11, 2001, and how did they pursue the investigation?
b. How did the attacks affect the economy?

4. ### Writing and Critical Thinking

Evaluating Imagine that you are first learning of the attacks on September 11, 2001, and want to help however you can. Write a paragraph describing possible actions you could take to assist those in need.
Consider the following:
• the efforts of relief agencies to help victims
• the need for national unity
• the importance of tolerance

Homework Practice Online
keyword: SP3 HPEP

CHAPTER

REVIEW AND ASSESSMENT RESOURCES

REPRODUCIBLE RESOURCES
▸ Vocabulary Activity Epilogue

TECHNOLOGY RESOURCES
▸ Epilogue Test Generator (on the One-Stop Planner)
▸ Global Skill Builder CD-ROM
▸ HRW Web Site

REINFORCEMENT, REVIEW, and ASSESSMENT
▸ Epilogue Review, pp. 484–485
▸ Epilogue Tutorial for Students, Parents, Mentors, and Peers
▸ Epilogue Test (Form A or B)
▸ Alternative Assessment Handbook
▸ Epilogue Test for English Language Learners and Special-Needs Students

Have students complete the Epilogue Review on pages 484–485.

ASSESS

Use one of the chapter tests to assess students' understanding of content. For Alternative Assessment, see the Portfolio Activities and Alternative Assessment Handbook.

CHAPTER

REVIEW ANSWERS

Understanding Main Ideas

1. strengthened governments and economies, built empires

2. equality, representative government, limited government power

3. improved quality of life, new forms of entertainment and art

4. labor should control production and profits

5. political philosophy that places the needs of the state above the needs of the individual

6. Japan invaded Manchuria, Italy invaded Ethiopia, Germany invaded Austria and Sudetenland

7. U.S. pledge to help other countries resist communism; purpose was containment

8. political and economic instability, drugs, violence

9. built up industry, developed advanced technology

10. apartheid ended

11. pollution, ozone layer damage, AIDS

12. terrorist attacks on World Trade Center and Pentagon

Reviewing Themes

1. There were no laws to protect workers.

2. Hindu and Muslim differences were so great that two countries—India and Pakistan—were formed.

484

Review

Creating a Time Line

Copy the time line below on to a sheet of paper. Complete the time line by filling in the events, individuals, and dates from the chapter that you think were significant. Pick three events and explain why you think they were significant.

| 1500 | 1800 | present |

Writing a Summary

Using standard grammar, spelling, sentence structure, and punctuation, write an overview of the events in the chapter.

Identifying People and Ideas

Identify the following terms or individuals and explain their significance:

1. Karl Marx
2. imperialism
3. Mao Zedong
4. League of Nations
5. Marshall Plan
6. NAFTA
7. Deng Xiaoping
8. apartheid
9. Mikhail Gorbachev
10. World Trade Center

Understanding Main Ideas

Section 1 *(pp. 450–457)*
Revolution to Imperialism
1. How did monarchies in Europe change after 1500?
2. What new ideas about government affected England, the United States, and France?
3. How did the Industrial Revolution affect society?
4. What changes did communists such as Karl Marx demand?

Section 2 *(pp. 458–463)*
World War in the Twentieth Century
5. What is fascism?
6. What aggressive actions did Japan, Italy, and Germany carry out in the 1930s?

Section 3 *(pp. 464–467)*
Europe and the Americas Since 1945
7. What was the Truman Doctrine, and how was it related to the concept of containment?
8. What issues affected Latin America in the 1900s?

484 EPILOGUE

Section 4 *(pp. 468–473)*
Asia, Africa, and the Middle East Since 1945
9. How did Japan's postwar economy develop?
10. What changes took place in South African politics?

Section 5 *(pp. 474–477)*
The Modern Era and Beyond
11. What global problems were of concern in the late 1900s?

Section 6 *(pp. 478-483)*
A Day That Changed the World
12. What events took place in the United States on September 11, 2001?

Reviewing Themes

1. Economics Why did the working class endure harsh conditions at the beginning of the Industrial Revolution?
2. Culture How did religious differences influence the Indian independence movement?
3. Science, Technology & Society How did healthcare improvements lead to problems in the late 1900s?

Thinking Critically

1. Sequencing What were the major events affecting czarist Russia and the Soviet Union during the 1900s?
2. Analyzing Information What problems did the containment policy create for the United States?
3. Making Predictions What conflicts and debates might arise in the future regarding cloning?
4. Finding the Main Idea What problems did African nations face at the end of the 1900s?

Writing About History

Summarizing The 1800s saw great changes in the sciences and arts and in where and how people lived. Write a page from a memoir of a person who has lived through some of these significant changes. Use the following chart to organize your thoughts before you begin writing.

Advances of the Industrial Age	Technology	Medicine	Social sciences	Arts
Effect on daily life				

CLOSE

Ask students to make a two-column chart. One column should show positive developments from 1500 to the present. The other column should show negative developments.

RETEACH

Have students who had difficulty with the test create flash cards based on the chapter content. Have them take turns reviewing the cards with a partner. Then have students take the Form B Test to assess their mastery of the material.

ENGLISH LANGUAGE LEARNERS, COOPERATIVE LEARNING

Portfolio Extensions

1. Ask students to imagine they are historians trying to investigate the effects of World War II on the Western European countries. Have them create a bibliography of sources about the topic, categorize the sources, and identify each source as a primary or secondary source.

2. Assign groups of students to investigate a technological advance that has occurred in the past decade. Have group members research how the new technology was created, who created it, and how and where it is being used.

3. Have students evaluate the long-term impact of the terrorist attacks of September 11, 2001. Their evaluations should include local, national, and global effects.

Building Social Studies Skills

Interpreting a Graph

Study the graph below. Then use the information on the graph to answer the questions that follow.

Nuclear Electricity Generation in Selected Countries (2003)

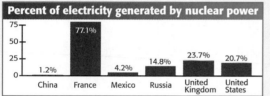

Percent of electricity generated by nuclear power

China 1.2% | France 77.1% | Mexico 4.2% | Russia 14.8% | United Kingdom 23.7% | United States 20.7%

1. Which of the following is a correct general statement about the data shown on the graph?

  a. The more lakes and rivers a country has, the more nuclear power it uses.

  b. The amount of electricity generated by nuclear power has no relationship to the size of the country.

  c. Electricity generated by nuclear power is expensive.

  d. Some nuclear reactors generate more electricity than can be used by customers.

2. Of the 32 countries that use nuclear power, most have cut back on their nuclear energy programs. Why do you think the countries cut back? Give specific reasons to support your view.

Understanding Frames of Reference

Read the following excerpt from a speech given by historian Barbara Tuchman in 1966. Then answer the questions.

> "I know very little . . . about laboratory science, but I have the impression that . . . from a given set of circumstances a predictable result should follow. The trouble is that in human behavior and history it is impossible to isolate or repeat a given set of circumstances. . . . Tides are so obedient to schedule that a timetable for them can be printed like that for trains, though more reliable. In fact, tides and trains sharply illustrate my point: One depends on the moon and is certain; the other depends on man and is uncertain."

3. Which of the following probably best describes Tuchman's approach to understanding human behavior?

  a. Tuchman sees little difference between the study of history and the study of science.

  b. Patterns of human behavior are predictable.

  c. Tuchman believes that history repeats itself.

  d. Tuchman follows a historical—rather than a purely scientific—approach toward understanding human behavior.

4. Explain your choice of statements in question 3. Give specific examples to support your point of view.

Alternative Assessment

Building Your Portfolio

Government

Political systems of the superpowers are based on philosophies and ideas developed throughout history. Use the library and other sources to compile a list of such ideas, including Judeo-Christian ethics and the rise of secularism and individualism in Western civilization, beginning with the Enlightenment. Then write a report that analyzes how at least one of these ideas has influenced governments, institutions, or societies.

internet connect

Internet Activity: go.hrw.com
KEYWORD: SP3 WHEP

Choose a topic on the Modern World to:

• write a biography of Louis XIV, the "Sun King."

• research the Cold War and look for elements of popular culture that reflect Cold War anxieties.

• create a time line sequencing the major events of apartheid in South Africa.

---

3. Improved healthcare meant more people were living longer. This led to overpopulation, and in some places shortages of jobs, housing, and water.

Thinking Critically

1. Answers should include abdication of Czar Nicholas II, establishment of Soviet Union, Joseph Stalin's policies, Cold War, and Mikhail Gorbachev's reforms.

2. threat of nuclear war, Cuban missile crisis

3. overpopulation, rights of the individual, ethical and religious questions

4. population growth, disease, famine, land overuse, political conflicts

Writing About History

Students' memoirs should include at least one change in technology, medicine, and art.

Building Social Studies Skills

1. b

2. concern about safety after accidents at Three Mile Island and Chernobyl

3. d

4. Answers will vary.

Building Your Portfolio

Students should express a connection between the philosophical idea and the government or institution it influenced.

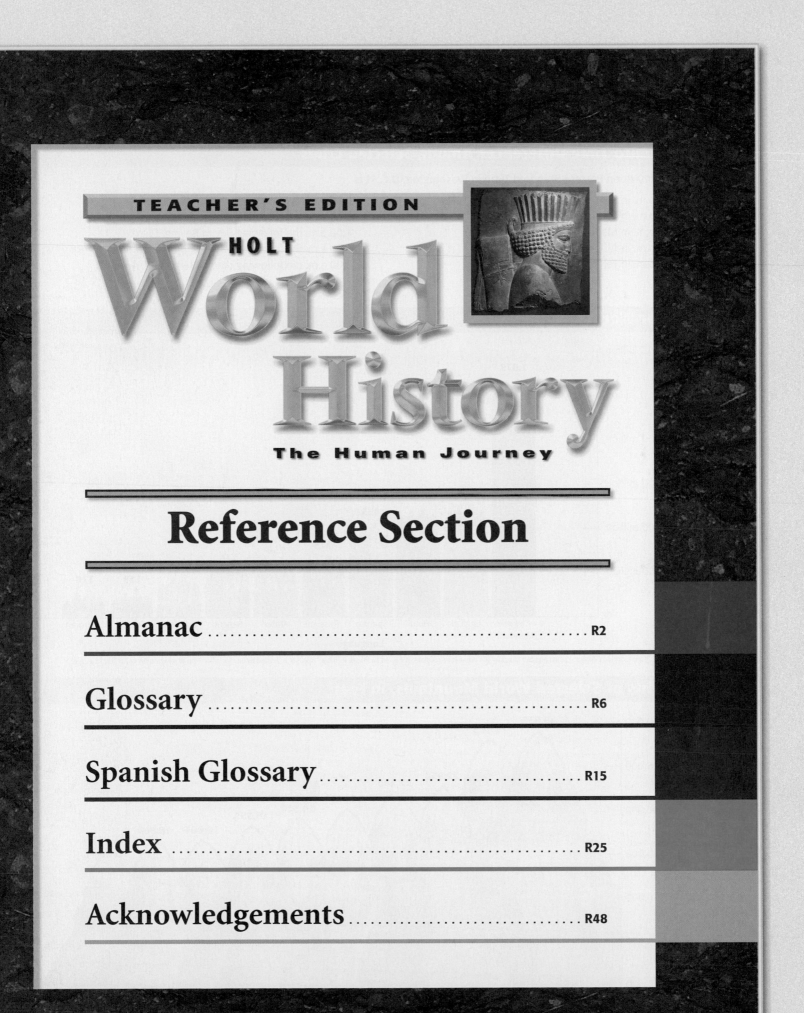

TEACHER'S EDITION

HOLT

World History

The Human Journey

Reference Section

Almanac

Standard Time Differences Among Selected Cities

At 12:00 noon Eastern Standard Time in Washington, D.C., it is . . .

1:00 p.m. in Santiago, Chile
5:00 p.m. in London, United Kingdom
6:00 p.m. in Madrid, Spain
7:00 p.m. in Athens, Greece
7:00 p.m. in Tel Aviv, Israel

8:00 p.m. in Moscow, Russian Republic
8:00 p.m. in Nairobi, Kenya
1:00 a.m. the following day in Beijing, China
2:00 a.m. the following day in Seoul, Korea
3:00 a.m. the following day in Melbourne, Australia

Major World Languages[1]

Number of Speakers

Language	Speakers (millions)
Chinese (Mandarin)	1,075
English	514
Hindi	496
Spanish	425
Russian	275
Arabic	256
Bengali	215
Portuguese	194
French	129
German	128

[1]Figures include estimated total number of native and non-native speakers of a given language. A "native" speaker is defined as one for whom the language is his or her first language.

Heights of Selected World Mountains, in Feet

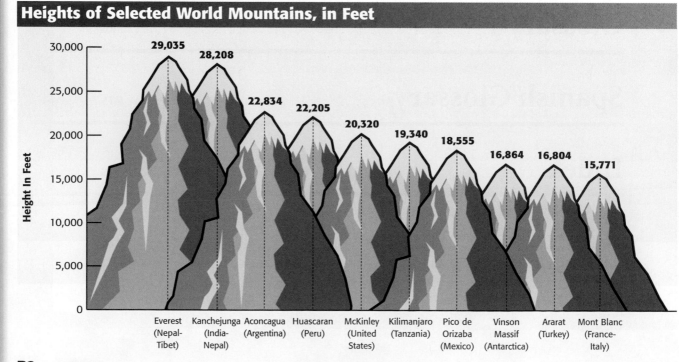

Mountain	Height In Feet
Everest (Nepal-Tibet)	29,035
Kanchejunga (India-Nepal)	28,208
Aconcagua (Argentina)	22,834
Huascaran (Peru)	22,205
McKinley (United States)	20,320
Kilimanjaro (Tanzania)	19,340
Pico de Orizaba (Mexico)	18,555
Vinson Massif (Antarctica)	16,864
Ararat (Turkey)	16,804
Mont Blanc (France-Italy)	15,771

Selected Major Rivers of the World

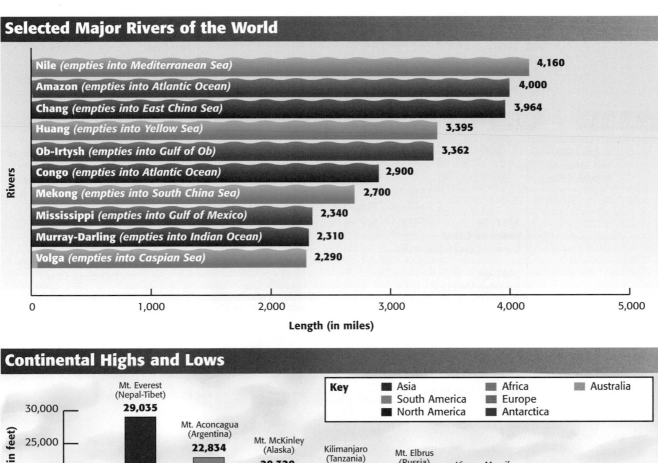

Rivers	Length (in miles)
Nile *(empties into Mediterranean Sea)*	4,160
Amazon *(empties into Atlantic Ocean)*	4,000
Chang *(empties into East China Sea)*	3,964
Huang *(empties into Yellow Sea)*	3,395
Ob-Irtysh *(empties into Gulf of Ob)*	3,362
Congo *(empties into Atlantic Ocean)*	2,900
Mekong *(empties into South China Sea)*	2,700
Mississippi *(empties into Gulf of Mexico)*	2,340
Murray-Darling *(empties into Indian Ocean)*	2,310
Volga *(empties into Caspian Sea)*	2,290

Continental Highs and Lows

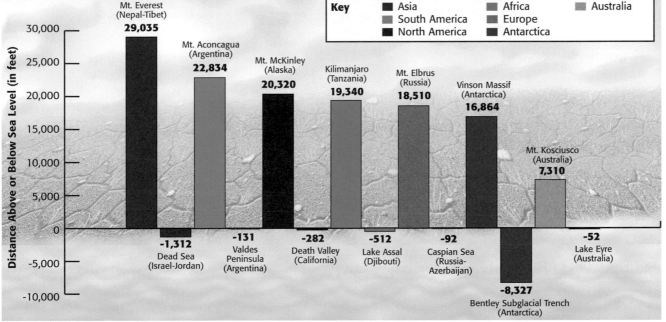

Key
- Asia
- South America
- North America
- Africa
- Europe
- Antarctica
- Australia

Distance Above or Below Sea Level (in feet)

- Mt. Everest (Nepal-Tibet) **29,035**
- Mt. Aconcagua (Argentina) **22,834**
- Mt. McKinley (Alaska) **20,320**
- Kilimanjaro (Tanzania) **19,340**
- Mt. Elbrus (Russia) **18,510**
- Vinson Massif (Antarctica) **16,864**
- Mt. Kosciusco (Australia) **7,310**

- **-1,312** Dead Sea (Israel-Jordan)
- **-131** Valdes Peninsula (Argentina)
- **-282** Death Valley (California)
- **-512** Lake Assal (Djibouti)
- **-92** Caspian Sea (Russia-Azerbaijan)
- **-8,327** Bentley Subglacial Trench (Antarctica)
- **-52** Lake Eyre (Australia)

The World's Largest Natural Lakes

Sea or Lake (Continent)	Area (Sq. Mi.)	Max. Depth (ft.)	Sea or Lake (Continent)	Area (Sq. Mi.)	Max. Depth (ft.)
Caspian Sea (Asia-Europe)	143,244	3,363	Lake Michigan (North America)	22,300	923
Lake Superior (North America)	31,700	1,330	Lake Tanganyika (Africa)	12,700	4,823
Lake Victoria (Africa)	26,828	270	Lake Baikal (Asia)	12,162	5,315
Aral Sea (Asia)	24,904 (est.)	220	Great Bear Lake (North America)	12,096	1,463
Lake Huron (North America)	23,000	750	Lake Malawi (Africa)	11,150	2,280

Some Early Explorers of the Western Hemisphere

1513
Vasco Núñez de Balboa
Panama, Pacific Ocean

1492–1502
Christopher Columbus
West Indies

1539–41
Hernando de Soto
Mississippi River

1576
Sir Martin Frobisher
Frobisher's Bay, Canada

1603–09
Samuel de Champlain
Canadian interior

A.D. 1000 | **1500** | **1550** | **1600**

C. A.D. 1000
Leif Ericsson
Newfoundland

1534
Jacques Cartier
Canada, Gulf of St. Lawrence

1609–10
Henry Hudson
Hudson River, Hudson Bay

1519–20
Ferdinand Magellan
Straits of Magellan

1497–98
Vasco da Gama
Cape of Good Hope, India

1595
Sir Walter Raleigh
Orinoco River

1497–99
Amerigo Vespucci
Coastal South America

Ferdinand Magellan

World Energy Facts

Estimated World Crude Oil Reserves by Region, January 2002
(Expressed as approximate percent of estimated world total, rounded)

Africa 8%

Far East and Oceania 4%

North America 5%

Central & South America 9%

WORLD TOTAL 100%

Middle East 66%

Western Europe 2%

Eastern Europe and Former Soviet Union 6%

Some Great Milestones in Medicine

1890
Robert Koch
Tuberculin diagnosis

1909
Charles Nicolle
Typhus transmission

1842
Crawford Long
Ether (anesthesia)

1867
Joseph Lister
Antiseptic surgery

1892
Emil von Behring
Diptheria antitoxin

1650 | **1850** | **1900**

1676
Antoni van Leeuwenhoek
Description of bacteria

1885
Louis Pasteur
Anti-rabies treatment

1909
Paul Ehrlich
Chemotherapy

1895
Wilhelm Röntgen
X–ray

Louis Pasteur

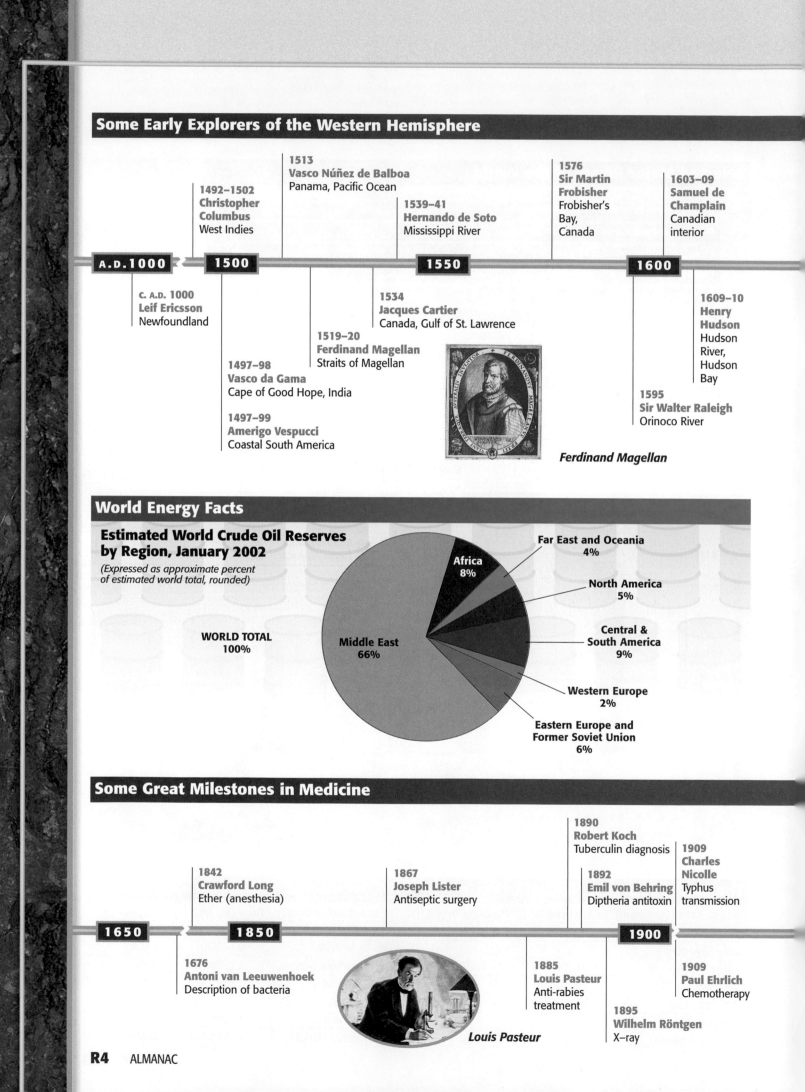

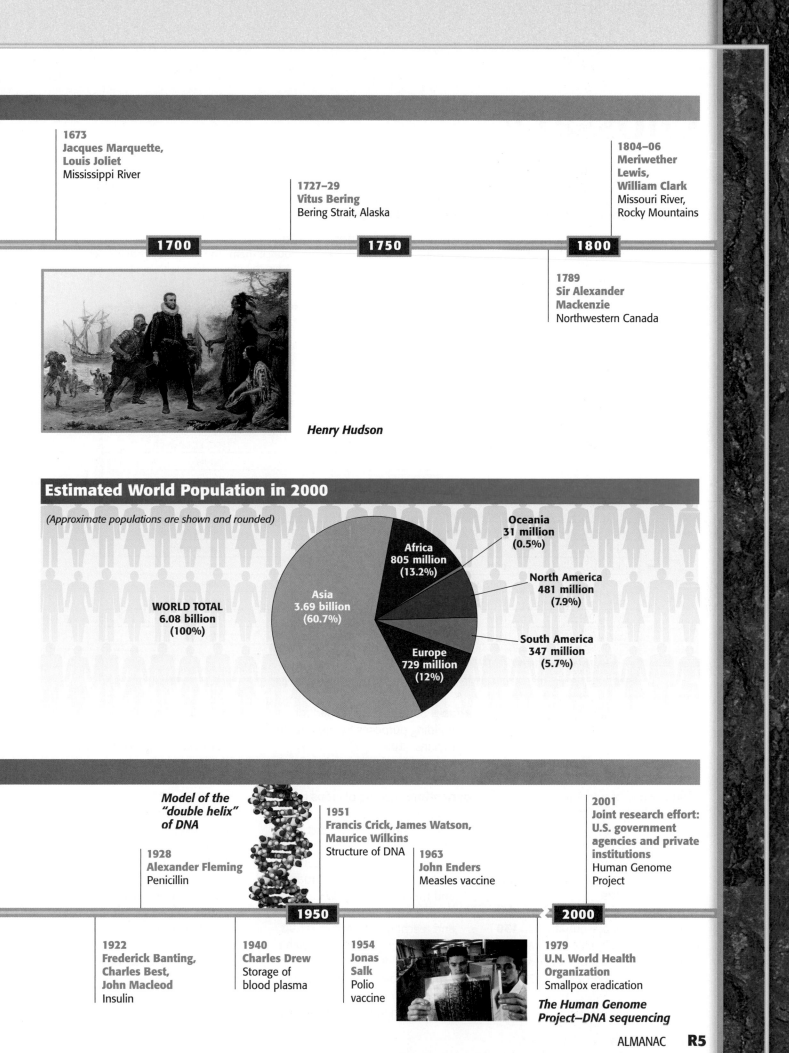

1673
Jacques Marquette, Louis Joliet
Mississippi River

1727–29
Vitus Bering
Bering Strait, Alaska

1804–06
Meriwether Lewis, William Clark
Missouri River, Rocky Mountains

1700 **1750** **1800**

1789
Sir Alexander Mackenzie
Northwestern Canada

Henry Hudson

Estimated World Population in 2000

(Approximate populations are shown and rounded)

WORLD TOTAL
6.08 billion
(100%)

Asia
3.69 billion
(60.7%)

Africa
805 million
(13.2%)

Oceania
31 million
(0.5%)

North America
481 million
(7.9%)

South America
347 million
(5.7%)

Europe
729 million
(12%)

Model of the "double helix" of DNA

1951
Francis Crick, James Watson, Maurice Wilkins
Structure of DNA

1963
John Enders
Measles vaccine

2001
Joint research effort:
U.S. government agencies and private institutions
Human Genome Project

1928
Alexander Fleming
Penicillin

1950 **2000**

1922
Frederick Banting, Charles Best, John Macleod
Insulin

1940
Charles Drew
Storage of blood plasma

1954
Jonas Salk
Polio vaccine

1979
U.N. World Health Organization
Smallpox eradication

The Human Genome Project–DNA sequencing

Glossary

This Glossary contains many of the terms you need to understand as you study world history. After each term there is a brief definition or explanation of the meaning of the term as it is used in world history. The boldfaced page number after each definition refers to the page on which the term is boldfaced in the textbook. A phonetic respelling is provided to help you pronounce many of the terms.

Phonetic Respelling Guide

Many of the key terms in the textbook have been respelled to help readers pronounce them. The following Phonetic Respelling and Pronunciation Guide has been adapted from several common dictionaries. Using the guide along with the text respellings will allow readers to pronounce difficult terms, including biographical and place names.

Mark	As In	Respelling	Example
a	alphabet	a	*AL·fuh·bet
ā	Asia	ay	AY·zhuh
ä	cart, top	ah	KAHRT, TAHP
e	let, ten	e	LET, TEN
ē	even, leaf	ee	EE·vuhn, LEEF
i	it, tip, British	i	IT, TIP, BRIT·ish
ī	site, buy, Ohio	y	SYT, BY, oh·HY·oh
	iris	eye	EYE·ris
k	card	k	KAHRD
kw	quest	kw	KWEHST
ō	over, rainbow	oh	OH·vuhr, RAYN·boh
ū	book, wood	ooh	BOOHK, WOOHD
ō	all, orchid	aw	AWL, AWR·kid
aù	out	ow	OWT
ə	cup, butter	uh	KUHP, BUHT·uhr
ü	rule, food	oo	ROOL, FOOD
yü	few	yoo	FYOO
zh	vision	zh	VIZH·uhn

*A syllable printed in small capital letters receives heavier emphasis than other syllables in a word.

A

abbess Head of a convent who served a role similar to an abbot. **302**

abbot Head of a monastery who controlled and distributed all property. **302**

acropolis Hill or mountain in Greece that included a fort as well as temples and other public buildings. **109**

Acropolis A high hill that marked the center of ancient Athens. **130**

acupuncture Chinese medical practice of inserting needles into certain areas of the body. **95**

adobe Sun-dried brick used for building purposes by the Pueblo Indians. **205**

agora Marketplace in a city-state in Greece. **109**

agriculture Raising of crops for food. **9**

almanacs Books that predict the weather and the prospects for growing crops, and also contain such things as calendars, maps, and medical advice. **375**

Analects Collection of the ideas and teachings of Confucius. **90**

animism Belief that spirits inhabit everything. **82**

apartheid Government policy of segregation and economic exploitation in South Africa. **472**

apprentice One who learns a skill under a master. **328**

aqueducts Bridgelike structures that carry water. **166**

arch Curved structure over an opening. **32**

archons Rulers in ancient Athens who served one-year terms. **115**

aristocracies Greek city-states controlled by nobles. **111**

aristocracy Government ruled by an upper class. **134**

artifacts Objects made and used by early humans. **6**

artisans Skilled workers. **12**

Ashikaga Family of shoguns who ruled in Japan for nearly 250 years. **278**

astrolabe Instrument used to calculate latitude by looking at stars. **251**

autocracy Government in which the ruler holds absolute power. **86**

Aztec Wandering warriors who gradually came to rule central Mexico. **210**

Babylonian Captivity Years that the pope lived in Avignon, France, instead of Rome, Italy (1309–1377). **342**

Bantu Family of closely related African languages. **184**

barter Exchange of one good or service for another. **43**

barter economy Economy of exchanging goods and services for other goods and services without using money. **325**

Battle of Marathon Battle during the Persian Wars when Persia invaded Greece. **121**

Battle of Thermopylae Battle during the Persian Wars in which Spartan troops fought to the death against a much larger Persian force. **121**

bedouins Nomadic Arab herders of sheep and camel. **240**

Beringia Land bridge during the Ice Age that provided the means for Asians to travel to the Americas. **200**

Bhagavad Gita Last 18 chapters of the Mahabharata, stressing the idea of proper conduct for one's status. **60**

bishops Heads of the Catholic Church in major cities. **171**

Black Death Terrible plague that swept through Europe, beginning in 1347. **330**

Bolsheviks Radical faction of Russia who won over the Mensheviks for control, led by Lenin. **459**

boyars Nobles who advised the prince in each Kievan city. **231**

Brahmins Special priests of the Indo-Aryan society who knew the proper forms and rules of their complicated religious rituals. **57**

broadsides Single printed news sheets sold to the public. **375**

buffalo Primary animal that roamed the Great Plains of the United States; hunted by the Plains people. **205**

bureaucracy Government organized into different levels and tasks. **81**

Bushido "Way of the warrior"; code of behavior of the samurai, stressing bravery, loyalty, and honor. **278**

caliph Title meaning "successor to the Prophet" used in government and religion in Islamic society. **243**

calligraphy Chinese art of writing. **83**

Camp David Accords Peace agreement between Egypt and Israel, mediated by the United States. **473**

canon law The code of law in the Catholic Church. **302**

capital Wealth that is earned, saved, and invested to make profits. **326**

capitalism Economic system in which individuals, rather than governments, control the factors of production. **454**

caravans Groups of people traveling together for safety over long distances. **29**

cardinals Catholic officials ranking next below the pope. **301**

Carolingians Line of Frankish rulers established by Pepin III's coronation in A.D. 751. **289**

caste system Complex form of social organization that began to take shape after the Indo-Aryan migration. **61**

censors Roman officials who registered citizens according to their wealth. **152**

Chavín Earliest people of Andean South America. **209**

checks and balances System of government that prevents any

one part of the government from becoming too powerful. **152**

Children's Crusade Short-lived failed crusade in 1212 by young people from Europe who marched on the Holy Land to regain it for Christianity. **321**

chinampas Raised fields made by the Aztec with mud taken from the bottoms of lakes. **210**

chivalry Code of conduct that dictated knights' behavior toward others. **298**

citadel Strong central fortress of a city. **53**

city-state Form of government that includes a town or city and the surrounding land controlled by it. **32**

civil service Centralized system that runs the day-to-day business of government. **87**

civilization Complex culture that can produce a surplus of food, establish large towns with a government, and has people who perform different jobs. **11**

Columbian Exchange Massive exchange of goods, plants, animals, and diseases that took place between the Western and Eastern Hemispheres following Columbus's voyage. **394**

command economy Economy in which the government controls all economic decisions. **465**

Commercial Revolution Era between 1400 and 1750 when Europeans made major changes to their economies due to new exploration. **389**

commodities Goods that have value, especially relating to barter economies. **43**

common law Law based upon customs and judges' decisions rather than upon written codes. **307**

compass Navigational instrument created in the 1300s that uses a magnetized piece of metal that points to the north. **388**

consulates Foreign diplomatic offices headed by consuls. **427**

consuls Chief executives elected to run the government in ancient Rome. **152**

Council of Trent Meeting of church leaders in the 1500s to clearly define Catholic doctrines for the Counter-Reformation. **369**

Counter-Reformation Attempt by the Catholic Church, following the Reformation, to return the church to an emphasis on spiritual matters. **368**

covenant Solemn agreement. **45**

craft guilds Associations of skilled workers that set standards for working conditions. **328**

Cro-Magnons Group of early people appearing about 35,000 years ago in Europe. **8**

Crusades Expeditions by Christians to regain the Holy Land from the Muslims. **318**

Cuban missile crisis Situation during the Cold War in which the Soviet Union built nuclear missile sites in Cuba. **466**

cultural diffusion Spread of culture from one area of the world to another. **12**

culture Beliefs, knowledge, and patterns of living that a group of people acquire by living together. **6**

cuneiform (kyoo·NEE·uh·fawrm) Sumerian writing made by pressing a wedge-shaped tool into clay tablets. **31**

curia Group of advisers to the pope drawn from the highest ranks of clergy. **301**

czar Title taken by Ivan the Terrible; Russian for "caesar." **234**

daimyo (dy·mee·oh) Powerful local lords in feudal Japan. **280**

Dao De Jing Compilation of Laozi's teachings on Daoism. **91**

D-Day June 6, 1944, the day Allied troops began the invasion on France's Normandy coast. **462**

Delian League Alliance of city-states in ancient Greece, with Athens as a leader. **123**

democracy Government in which citizens take part. **112**

dialects Variations of a language. **82**

Diamond Sutra World's first known printed book, a Buddhist text produced in China in A.D. 868. **270**

dictator Absolute ruler. **151**

dikes Earthen walls built along a river to protect from floods. **78**

direct democracy Form of democracy in which all citizens participate directly in making decisions. **117**

division of labor Characteristic of civilizations in which different people perform different jobs. **12**

domestic system Method of production that takes place in the worker's home rather than in a shop or factory. **325**

domestication Taming of animals such as cattle, goats, sheep, and pigs. **9**

dowry Money or goods a wife brings to a marriage. **222**

dramas Plays containing action or dialogue and usually involving conflict and emotion. **136**

dynasty Family of rulers whose right to rule is hereditary. **22**

empire Form of government that unites different territories and peoples under one ruler. **24**

English Bill of Rights Document in 1689 that declared the powers of Parliament and protected private citizens. **452**

Enlightenment Period in the 1700s when philosophers believed that they could apply the scientific method and use reason to explain human nature logically. **452**

ephors Five officials in ancient Sparta who were elected for one-year terms to make sure the king stayed within the law. **114**

epics Long poems based on historical or religious themes. **60**

equites Class of business people and landowners in ancient Rome who had wealth and power. **157**

ethical monotheism Religion believing in one god, emphasizing ethics. **47**

ethics Study of what is good and bad, and of moral duty. **120**

excommunication Official edict that bars a person from church membership. **226**

Exodus Escape of the Hebrews from Egypt. **44**

export Good or service sold to another country or region. **118**

extraterritoriality Exemption of foreigners from the laws of the country in which they live or do business. **419**

fascism Governmental doctrine that relies on dictatorial rule and a totalitarian regime, in which the state maintains rigid control of the people through force and censorship. **460**

favorable balance of trade Situation that exists when a country sells more goods than it buys. **390**

federal system of government System of government in which power is divided between a central, or federal, government and individual states. **453**

feudalism Political system of local government based on the granting of land in return for loyalty, military assistance, and other services. **294**

fief Grant of land given to a vassal from a lord. **294**

Five Classics Texts used to train scholars and civil servants in ancient China. **94**

Five Good Emperors Five rulers who led Rome for almost 100 years during the Pax Romana. **161**

Flemish school Group of painters who perfected the technique of oil painting on canvas. **361**

free trade Practice based on the belief that government should not restrict or interfere with international trade. **418**

frescoes Paintings done on wet plaster walls. **107**

Fujiwara First family to gain control over the central government in Japan; had power from the mid-800s to the mid-1100s. **278**

genealogy Record of a family history. **93**

geocentric theory Theory according to Hellenistic thinker Ptolemy that Earth is the center of the universe. **383**

ghazis Warriors for Islam; Turkish soldiers who were the first Ottomans. **432**

gladiators Trained fighters, usually slaves, who fought in arenas as entertainment. **165**

glasnost (GLAZ·nohst) Soviet policy of openness under which government controls on the economy were relaxed and restrictions on dissent were eased. **475**

golden age Era of cultural progress in Greece in the 400s B.C. **130**

Golden Horde Name given by Europeans to the Mongol invaders of the 1200s due to the golden color of their tents. **273**

Gothic Style of church architecture characterized by tall spires and flying buttresses that was developed by master builders during the mid-1100s. **334**

Goths One of a group of Germanic tribes who flooded into the Roman Empire and later revolted, weakening the empire. **174**

Gracchi, the Two brothers, Tiberus and Gaius Gracchus, who saw the need for reform in the Roman Republic. **158**

Grand Canal Canal constructed during the Sui dynasty that linked northern and southern China for the first time. **266**

Great Leap Forward Mao Zedong's second Five-Year Plan for China in 1958, intended to speed progress. **469**

Great Schism Period of church history from 1378 to 1417 when the church was divided into opposing groups. **342**

Great Wall of China Wall built and expanded upon by early rulers of China to protect from invasions. **86**

Greek fire Flammable liquid used as a weapon by the Byzantine navy. **224**

guerrilla warfare Military technique relying on swift raids by small bands of soldiers. **403**

Habsburg Powerful family of European rulers in the 1200s. **340**

Hagia Sophia Great, decorative Byzantine church in Constantinople. **227**

Han Dynasty of rulers that ruled a centralized and growing empire in China. **84**

heliocentric theory Theory developed by Copernicus that the sun is the center of the universe. **383**

Hellenistic culture "Greek-like" way of life that combined ideas and values drawn from the Mediterranean and Asia. **141**

helots (HEL·uhts) Conquered people of the Peloponnesus, who became the lowest class in Spartan society. **113**

heresy Opinion that conflicts with official church beliefs. **226**

heretics People who denied the truth of the official church's principles or who preached beliefs not approved by the church. **302**

hieroglyphics (hy·ruh·GLI·fiks) Form of ancient writing developed by Nile River valley people by about 3000 B.C. **22**

hijrah (hi·JY·ruh) Migration of Muhammad and his followers in A.D. 622, marking the first year in the Muslim calendar. **241**

Hohokam Group of people who lived in the southwestern United States who abandoned their communities in the 1300s or 1400s. **203**

hominids Early humans and other humanlike creatures. **6**

Hopewell Group of people who settled in the Ohio Valley region sometime from about 300 B.C. to 200 B.C. **207**

hoplites Heavily armed Greek infantry who carried long spears and fought in closely spaced rows. **112**

Huguenots French people, including high-ranking nobles, who converted to Calvinism. **367**

humanists People who specialize in studying the humanities, which includes grammar, history, poetry, and rhetoric. **355**

Hundred Years' War War between France and England f or the French throne that continued from 1337 to 1453, and introduced the use of new weapons. **336**

Huns Nomadic people from Asia who attacked the Roman Empire. **175**

hunter-gatherers Early people who lived by hunting animals and gathering plants for food. **10**

Hyksos Group of people who arrived in ancient Egypt from Asia and introduced new war tools. **23**

icon Holy picture of Jesus, the Virgin Mary, or a saint. **224**

Iconoclastic Controversy Debate between opponents and defenders of icons in the Byzantine Church; one of the issues that led to the split of the Christian church in 1054. **226**

iconoclasts People who opposed the use of icons in worship. **224**

Iliad Homer's great epic that tells the story of the Trojan War. **110**

imams Spiritual leaders who, according to some Shi'ah Muslims, should be direct descendants of Muhammad. **244**

imperialism Ambition of a powerful nation to dominate the political, economic, and cultural affairs of another nation or region. **456**

import Good or service bought from another country or region. **118**

Inca Civilization in the Andes Mountains in South America that by the end of the 1400s included much of what is now Peru, Ecuador, Bolivia, and Chile. **211**

Indo-Aryans Indo-European tribes who moved in slow waves into India in about 1750 B.C. **56**

indulgences Paid pardons from punishment for sin. **363**

Industrial Revolution Term for changes beginning in the 1700s, when power-driven machines began to do much of the work that people had done before. **454**

inflation Rise in prices caused by a decrease in the value of the medium of exchange. **172**

inoculation Practice of infecting people with a mild form of a disease to protect them from more serious illness. **71**

Inquisition Institution of the Roman Catholic Church that sought to eliminate heresy by seeking out and punishing heretics. **303**

interdict The Catholic Church's punishment of a region, involving closing churches and withholding sacraments. **302**

irrigation System of ditches and canals that transports water from a source into an agricultural field. **12**

Islam Religion based on Muhammad's teachings and ideas that began spreading throughout Arab tribes in the A.D. 600s. **241**

Janissaries Highly trained troop of slave soldiers for Ottoman sultans. **432**

Jesuits Catholic religious order founded by Ignatius de Loyola in 1534. **369**

jihad (ji-HAHD) Teaching of Islam to defend the faith. **242**

joint-stock company Business organization developed during the Commercial Revolution in which owners raised money by selling shares, or stock, in the company. **389**

journeyman Skilled worker who was paid wages by a master. **328**

Judeo-Christian ethics Values first established by the Hebrews that contribute greatly to Western civilization. **47**

Julio-Claudian Emperors Relatives of Caesar who ruled for 54 years of the Pax Romana following the death of Augustus. **160**

jungle Thick growth of plants found in a tropical rain forest. **182**

junks Large Chinese ships. **412**

Justinian Code Collection of laws that formed the basis for Byzantine law under Emperor Justinian. **222**

kami Japanese gods or nature spirits. **277**

kizilbash Military army developed by the Safavids to fight for political power. **436**

League of Nations World organization formed after World War I to maintain peace. **459**

Legalism School of Chinese philosophy concerned with politics. **91**

leveling Policy in which government uses price controls to balance the economic effects of farm surpluses or shortages. **87**

limited evidence Evidence, such as artifacts, about which little information is given, requiring scientists to make educated guesses. **6**

linguists Scholars who study languages. **184**

loess (les) Fertile yellow soil. **78**

Magna Carta "Great Charter," English document that made the law the supreme power and became a cornerstone of constitutional government. **306**

Magyars Nomadic group who invaded Europe; eventually settled in what is now Hungary. **292**

manorialism Economic system during the Middle Ages that revolved around self-sufficient farming estates where lords and peasants shared the land. **297**

market economy Economy in which land, labor, and capital are controlled by individual persons. **326**

Marshall Plan Massive economic assistance program to European countries by the United States. **465**

martyrs Persons put to death for their beliefs. **170**

matrilineal Describes a society in which people trace their ancestors and inherited property through their mothers rather than through their fathers. **186**

Maya One of the most advanced early people in the Americas, occupying most of the Yucatán Peninsula. **209**

maya Illusory world of the senses, according to Hinduism. **61**

medieval Term that describes the period of western European history known as the Middle Ages. **288**

mercantilism Economic theory stating that there is a fixed amount of wealth in the world and that in order to receive a larger share, one country has to take some wealth away from another country. **390**

merchant guild Association of merchants and workers created to protect their rights to trade and to help out members and their families. **327**

Merovingians Clovis and his successors, who were generally weak Frankish rulers who left the job of governing to palace officials. **288**

metics People living in Athens who were not Athenian citizens, who could work and who paid taxes but were not allowed to own land or take part in government. **115**

Middle Ages Period in western European history between the collapse of the Roman Empire and the Renaissance. **288**

middle class Class of skilled workers between the upper class and the poor and unskilled workers. **328**

Middle Passage Second stage of the triangular trade system, which involved the shipping of slaves across the Atlantic to the Americas. **398**

millets Separate, self-governed religious minorities within the Ottoman Empire. **434**

Minamoto Clan reigning in Japan beginning in 1156; changed the way governments were run by introducing the shogun control. **278**

minaret Tower attached to the outside of a mosque, from where a crier would call Muslims to worship. **253**

miniaturization Process of making machines smaller and lighter. **476**

Minoans Earliest Greek civilization that had developed on the island of Crete by 2000 B.C. **107**

Mississippians Group that lived in the Eastern Woodlands of North America from about A.D. 700 to A.D. 1550. **207**

monasticism Way of life in convents and monasteries where nuns and monks withdraw from the world and its temptations. **301**

money economy Economic system based on the use of money as a measure of value and a unit of account. **43**

monism Belief in the unity of God and creation. **61**

monotheism Belief in one god. **25**

monsoons Winds that mark the seasons in India. **52**

Moors Muslims who made Spain their home in the A.D. 700s. **245**

mosaic Picture or design made from small pieces of enamel, glass, or stone. **227**

mosques Muslim places of worship. **242**

mummification Process of preserving the body with chemicals after death. **28**

Muslims Followers of the religion of Islam. **242**

Mycenaeans Civilization on the Greek mainland that conquered the Minoans in Crete in about 1400 B.C. **107**

myths Traditional stories about gods, goddesses, and heroes. **111**

NAFTA North American Free Trade Agreement, linking Mexico, Canada, and the United States in a large free-trade zone. **467**

Nalanda Famous Buddhist university of ancient India. **71**

NATO North Atlantic Treaty Organization; an alliance of twelve Western nations formed in 1949. **465**

Neanderthals Early people who lived during the Old Stone Age. **8**

Neolithic agricultural revolution Shift in human history from food gathering to food producing. **10**

New Deal Programs by President Franklin D. Roosevelt in which the federal government established public works to create jobs and granted money to each state to provide for the needy. **460**

nirvana Perfect spiritual peace, as taught in Hinduism. **62**

nomads People who wander from place to place. **9**

Odyssey Homer's epic that tells the story of the Greek hero Odysseus on his way home from the Trojan War. **110**

Olmec Earliest culture of Mexico, beginning in about 1200 B.C. **209**

Olympic Games Originally, ancient Greek festival including contests of sports, music, and literature; the modern revival of these games as international athletic competitions. **111**

OPEC Organization of Petroleum Exporting Countries, created in 1960 to set oil prices and world oil production levels. **473**

Opium War Conflict from 1839 to 1842 between China and Britain that arose due to Britain's export of opium to China. **419**

oracle bones Cattle bones or tortoise shells on which Chinese priests would write questions and then interpret answers from the cracks that formed when the bones were heated. **82**

oracles Special places where the ancient Greeks believed gods spoke through priests and priestesses. **111**

oral traditions Poems, songs, and stories passed by word of mouth from one generation to another. **184**

orators Public speakers. **139**

Ottoman Turks Asian people who conquered Constantinople in the 1300s and established a large empire. **228**

Panchatantra Fables from the Gupta period of ancient India. **70**

papyrus Kind of paper made by Egyptians from the stem of the papyrus plant. **22**

Parthenon White marble temple built in ancient Athens in honor of Athena. **130**

patriarchs Bishops of the administrative centers for the church in the last years of the Roman Empire. **171**

patricians Powerful landowners who controlled Roman government and society. **153**

Pax Romana Period of Roman peace from the beginning of

Augustus's reign until the death of Marcus Aurelius. **160**

pedagogue In ancient Greece, a male slave who taught a young boy manners. **119**

Peloponnesian War War between Sparta and Athens that broke out in 431 B.C. and lasted for 27 years. **124**

Pentagon Headquarters of the United States military leadership, located near Washington, D.C., and the scene of a terrorist attack on September 11, 2001. **478**

perestroika (per·uh·STROY·kuh) Soviet restructuring policy designed to overhaul the Soviet political and economic systems. **475**

Persian Wars Conflicts between Greece and Persia. **121**

perspective Art technique that involves making distant objects smaller than those in the foreground and arranging them to create the illusion of depth on a flat canvas. **356**

phalanx (FAY·langks) Military formation composed of rows of soldiers standing shoulder to shoulder, carrying pikes or heavy spears. **138**

pharaoh "Great House"; Egyptian ruler's title. **22**

philology History of literature and language. **415**

philosophy Study of basic questions of reality and human existence. **133**

Phoenician alphabet Alphabet developed by the Phoenicians that became the model for later Western alphabets. **42**

plebeians Farmers and workers who made up most of the Roman population. **153**

polis Greek word for city-state, which developed around a central fort. **108**

Polovtsy Turkish people who after 1055 controlled the area south of Kiev in Russia. **233**

polygamy Practice in which a man is allowed to have more than one wife. **69**

polytheism Belief that many gods exist. **25**

polytheistic Based on a belief in many gods. **62**

pope Title assumed by the patriarch of Rome and head of the Catholic Church; from the Latin word meaning "father." **171**

popular government Idea that people can and should rule themselves. **112**

potlatches Ceremonial gatherings of Native Americans of the Pacific Northwest. **203**

praetors (PREET·uhrz) Elected Roman officials who helped the consuls. **152**

Pravda Russkia Russia's first law code, created by Yaroslav I. **231**

predestination Belief that at the beginning of time God decided who would be saved. **366**

primogeniture (pry·moh·JE·nuh·choohr) System of inheritance from father to eldest son for ownership or possession of land. **294**

Pueblo Group of people who lived in permanent settlements in the southwestern United States. **205**

Punic Wars Three costly conflicts between Romans and Carthaginians over control of the Mediterranean and overseas expansion. **155**

Qin Dynasty that came to power in China in 221 B.C. under which the first true empire of China was created. **84**

Quechua Inca language, still spoken today by millions in South America. **211**

queue Single braid that characterized the hairstyle that all Chinese men were required to wear during the Qing dynasty. **414**

quipu (KEE·poo) Kind of knotted string used as a memory aid by the Inca. **211**

Qur'an Holy book of Islam. **242**

rabbis Religious scholars of Judaism. **168**

raja Prince who ruled an Indo-Aryan city-state. **57**

Rajputs Indian warrior princes who began challenging Turkish Muslim control in India in the 1500s. **439**

reaya Masses of ordinary subjects in Ottoman society. **434**

Reformation Religious revolution that split the church in western Europe and created a number of new churches. **363**

reincarnation Belief in the rebirth of souls. **61**

Renaissance Movement following the Middle Ages that centered on revival of interest in the classical learning of Greece and Rome; French word meaning "rebirth." **354**

representative democracy Form of government in which citizens elect representatives to run the government for them, rather than each citizen serving directly in the government. **117**

republic Form of government in which voters elect officials to run the state. **151**

rhetoric Study of public speaking and debating. **120**

Rosetta Stone Black basalt stone found in 1799 that bears an inscription in hieroglyphics, demotic characters, and Greek; gave the first clue to deciphering Egyptian hieroglyphics. **22**

Rus People led by Rurik who came to rule Keiv and the Slavic tribes along the Dnieper River. **230**

sacraments Ceremonies at which participants receive God's direct favor, or grace, to ward off the consequences of sin. **300**

samurai Japanese warriors hired for protection by wealthy landlords in feudal Japan. **278**

Sanskrit Indo-Aryan language. **56**

savannas Dry grasslands south of the Sahara Desert in Africa. **182**

scholasticism Medieval philosophy attempting to bring together faith and reason. **334**

scientific method Method of inquiry that includes carefully conducted experiments and mathematical calculations to verify the results of experiments. **383**

Scientific Revolution Transformation in thinking that occurred during the 1500s and 1600s caused by scientific observation, experimentation, and the questioning of traditional opinions. **382**

scribes Egyptian clerks who read or wrote for those who could not do so for themselves. **27**

sects Religious societies of a few people, usually with a preacher as their leader. **365**

Seljuq Turks Muslim people from central Asia who gained control of Palestine, or the Holy Land to Christians, during the late 1000s. **318**

seppuku (SE·poo·koo) Form of ceremonial suicide of defeated or disloyal samurai to avoid dishonor; also known in the West as hari-kari. **278**

serfs Peasants who were bound to the land where they worked for a lord. **298**

Shang Invaders of the Huang River valley who came to power sometime between 1750 B.C. and 1500 B.C. and established the first dynasty in China. **81**

Shi'ah Branch of Islam formed in the A.D. 600s that believed only imams should decide religious and worldly matters. **244**

Shinto "Way of the kami"; indigenous religion of Japan involving rituals and prayers to appease nature spirits, and veneration of the emperor. **277**

shires Governmental districts in early England; governed by a shire-reeve (sheriff). **304**

shogun Chief military and governmental officer in feudal Japan. **278**

Shona People who migrated onto the plateau of what is known today as Zimbabwe. **192**

Sikh Religion based on the teachings of Nānak, an Indian mystic in the 1500s, who tried to unite the Hindu and Muslim religions. **441**

Silk Road Trade route stretching from China to the Mediterranean. **88**

simony (SY·moh·nee) Practice of buying high positions in the Catholic Church, common during the Middle Ages. **303**

socialism Political and economic system in which the government owns the means of production. **455**

Sophists Athenian men who opened schools for boys to study government, mathematics, ethics, and rhetoric. **120**

standard of living Measure of the quality of life. **376**

steppe Large, grassy plain stretching across eastern Europe and central Asia that is ideal for agriculture. **229**

strait Narrow strip of water that connects two larger bodies of water. **200**

subsidies Government grants of money. **390**

Sufi Muslim mystics who tried to live simple lives. **245**

sultan Ruler of the Turks who claimed to serve the Muslim caliph. **247**

Sunni Branch of Islam formed in the A.D. 600s who believed agreement among Muslim people should settle religious and worldly matters. **244**

suttee Ancient Indian practice of a woman committing suicide after her husband's death. **69**

Swahili African society that emerged in the late 1100s along the East African coast and combined elements of African, Asian, and Islamic cultures. **191**

taiga (TY·gah) Russian region north of the steppe having great forests, much rainfall, and cold, long winters. **231**

Taiping Rebellion Revolt in China from 1850 to 1864, led by Hong Xiuquan who, influenced by Christian teachings, declared a mission to establish a new dynasty. **421**

Taj Mahal Building constructed under Shah Jahan as a tomb for his wife, which remains one of the architectural wonders of the world. **441**

Tale of Genji, The Story of courtly life in Japan written by Murasaki Shikibu in about A.D. 1000; generally considered the world's first novel. **278**

tariffs Import taxes on foreign goods. **390**

tepees Cone-shaped tents made of buffalo hide. **205**

terracing Carving small, flat plots of land from hillsides to use for farming. **118**

theocracy Government ruled by religious leaders claiming God's authority. **367**

third Rome Moscow; Russian Orthodox interpretation of the city's leading role in bringing spiritual light to the world. **235**

Thirty Years' War War beginning in Prague in 1618 as a Protestant rebellion against the Holy Roman Empire. **455**

Thousand and One Nights, The Popular collection of Muslim folktales. **253**

tithe Church tax collected from Christians in early times that represented one tenth of their income; later became a gift to the church representing one tenth of a person's income. **302**

Toltec People who invaded central Mexico from the north in about A.D. 800. **210**

Torah Jewish scriptures that include the first five books of the Old Testament of the Bible. **46**

tragedies Forms of Greek drama in which the main character struggles against fate or events. **137**

Treaty of Kanagawa Negotiations between Matthew Perry and Japan in 1854 that permitted trade between the two countries. **427**

Treaty of Nanjing Treaty following the Opium War in which China gave Hong Kong to Britain and opened ports to British trade. **419**

Treaty of Tordesillas Agreement between Spain and Portugal that moved west the line determining the land each country could claim in the Atlantic. **394**

triangular trade System of trade involving three stages, one of which was the transatlantic slave trade. **398**

tribunes Officials elected by Rome's popular assemblies. **152**

triumvirate Political alliance of three rulers. **159**

tropical rain forests Vast forests that have a great amount of rainfall and vegetation. **182**

troubadours Traveling singers who entertained people during the Middle Ages. **332**

Truman Doctrine Policy declaring that the United States must consider the continued spread of communism as a threat to democracy. **465**

Twelve Tribes of Israel Twelve sons of Abraham's grandson Jacob (Israel), from whom modern Jews trace their heritage. **44**

tyrants In ancient Greece, rulers who seized power by force but who ruled with the people's support; later came to refer to rulers who exercise brutal and oppressive power. **112**

"unequal" treaties Trade treaties that China signed under pressure of invasion, giving Western powers trade benefits. **419**

United Nations Organization of nations to keep peace through collective security arrangements. **464**

Upanishads Written explanations of the Vedic religion. **60**

usury (YOO-zhuh-ree) Policy of charging high interest on loans. **326**

Vandals One of a group of Germanic tribes who invaded and destroyed territory in the Roman Empire. **174**

varnas Social classes in Indian society. **61**

vassal Person granted land from a lord in return for services. **294**

Vedas Great literature of the Indo-Aryan religion. **56**

Vedic Age Period of India's history from 1500 B.C. to 1000 B.C. **56**

vernacular languages Everyday speech that varies from place to place. **331**

veto Refuse to approve, as in a bill or law. **152**

viceroys Spanish officials who represented the monarchy in Spain's colonial empire. **401**

Vikings Germanic people from Scandinavia who often raided western Europe during the A.D. 800s and 900s. **292**

War of the Roses War between the York and Lancaster families of England in 1455. **337**

White Lotus Rebellion Peasant rebellion against the Qing dynasty led by the Buddhist cult known as the White Lotus Society. **416**

World Trade Center New York City office complex that was struck by a devastating terrorist attack on September 11, 2001. **478**

Xia Line of kings ruling over a late Neolithic people in the Huang River region of China starting in about 2000 B.C. **80**

yang Force that is male, bright, and active; part of the Chinese belief of dualism or balance in life. **89**

Yi Korean dynasty founded in 1392 when Koreans drove out the Mongols; lasted until Korea was annexed by Japan in 1910. **281**

yin Force that is female, dark, and passive; part of the Chinese belief of dualism or balance in life. **89**

Zen Sect of Buddhism that stresses meditation as a means of enlightenment. **269**

Zhou People who overthrew the Shang dynasty of China in 1122 B.C. **83**

ziggurats Sumerian temples made of sun-dried brick. **32**

Glosario

Este GLOSARIO contiene muchos de los términos que necesitas entender cuando estudias la historia mundial. Cada palabra tiene una breve definición o explicación de su significado, según su uso en historia mundial. El número entre paréntesis al lado de cada definición, se refiere al número de página en la cual esa palabra está marcada en el libro de texto.

abbess/Abadesa Dirigente de un convento, quien ejerce un rol similar al de un abad. **302**

abbot/abad Dirigente de un monasterio, quien controla y distrubuye la propiedad. **302**

acropolis/acrópolis Monte o montaña en Grecia, que incluye un fuerte, así como también templos y otros edificios públicos. **109**

Acropolis/Acrópolis Monte alto que marcó el centro de la antigua Atenas. **130**

acupuncture/acupunctura Práctica medicinal china que consiste en insertar agujas en ciertas partes del cuerpo. **95**

adobe/adobe Ladrillo de barro secado al aire, usado para la construcción por los Pueblos Indígenas. **205**

agora/ágora Plaza pública en las ciudades griegas. **109**

agriculture/agricultura Cultivo y cosecha de alimentos. **9**

almanacs/almanaques Libros que pronostican el tiempo y las probabilidades de crecimiento de los cultivos, y también contienen cosas como calendarios, mapas, y consejos médicos. **375**

Analects/Analectas, Las Colección de ideas y enseñanzas de Confucio. **90**

animism/animismo Creencia de que los espíritus habitan todas las cosas. **82**

apartheid/apartheid Política de gobierno, de segregación y explotación económica en Sudáfrica. **472**

apprentice/aprendiz El que aprende alguna destreza de su maestro. **328**

aqueducts/acueductos Construcciones para la conducción de agua. **166**

arch/arco Estructura curva que está sobre una entrada. **32**

archons/arcontes Dirigentes en la antigua Grecia, que servían durante períodos de un año. **115**

aristocracies/aristocracias Ciudades griegas controladas por nobles. **111**

aristocracy/aristocracia gobierno controlado por la clase alta. **134**

artifacts/artefactos Objetos fabricados y utilizados por los primeros humanos. **6**

artisans/artesano Los que trabajan alguna técnica o arte manual. **12**

Ashikaga/Ashikaga Familias de shogunes quienes gobernaron Japón durante cerca de 250 años. **278**

astrolabe/astrolabio Instrumento usado para calcular la latitud, por medio de la observación de estrellas. **251**

autocrat/Autocracia gobierno en el cual la persona al mando tiene el poder absoluto. **86**

Aztec/Aztecas Guerreros viajantes quienes gradualmente llegaron a gobernar el centro de México. **210**

---B---

Babylonian Captivity/Cautiverio Babilónico Años durante los cuales El Papa vivió en Avignon, Francia, en lugar de Roma, Italia. (1309–1377) **342**

Bantu/Bantú Familia de lenguas africanas. Relativo bantúes, pueblos del centro y sur de África. **184**

barter/trueque Intercambio de un bien y servicio por otro. **43**

barter economy/economía de trueque Economía basada en el intercambio de bienes y servicios, sin usar dinero. **325**

Battle of Marathon/Batalla de Maratón Batalla durante la guerra persa, cuando Persia invadió Grecia. **121**

Battle of Thermopylae/Batalla de Termópilas Batalla durante las Guerras Persas en la cual un reducido ejército espartano peleó hasta la muerte contra fuerzas persas mucho más grandes que ellos. **121**

bedouins/beduinos Árabes nómadas del desierto, que llevan manadas de camellos y ovejas. **240**

Beringia/Estrecho de Bering Camino o puente que permitía el paso entre Asia y América durante la Edad de Hielo. **200**

Bhagavad Gita/Bhagavad Gita Últimos 18 capítulos del Mahabharata, que enfatizan la idea de conducta apropiada según la posición o status de uno. **60**

bishops/obispo Dirigente de la Iglesia Católica en una ciudad importante. **171**

Black Death/muerte negra Terrible plaga que devastó Europa a principios de 1347 **330**

Bolsheviks/bolcheviques Facción radical de Rusia dirigida por Lenin, que ganaron el control contra los Mencheviques. **459**

boyars/boyardos Nobles que aconsejaban al príncipe en cada ciudad Kievan. **231**

Brahmins/Brahmins Sacerdote especial de la sociedad Indoaria, quien sabía las formas y reglas apropiadas de sus complicados rituales religiosos. **57**

broadsides/broadsides Hojas de papel impreso con noticias, vendidos al público. **375**

buffalo/búfalo Animal que andaba en las Grandes Planicies de los Estados Unidos, y eran cazados por la gente de las planicies. **205**

bureaucracy/burocracia gobierno organizado en diferentes niveles y tareas. **81**

Bushido/Bushido Código de conducta del samurai,que enfatiza valentía, lealtad y honor. **278**

C

caliph/califa Título que significa "sucesor del Profeta" usado en el gobierdo y religión de la sociedad Islámica. **243**

calligraphy/caligrafía Arte de escritura china. **83**

Camp David Accords/Acuerdos de Campo David Acuerdo de paz entre Egipto e Israel, mediadas por los Estados Unidos. **473**

canon law/ley canónica Código de derecho de la Iglesia Católica. **302**

capital/capital Dinero ganado, ahorrado e invertido para conseguir ganancias. **326**

capitalism/capitalismo Sistema ecónomico en el cual los individuos, en vez del gobierno, son quienes controlan los factores de la producción. **454**

caravans/caravanas Grupos de personas que por seguridad viajaban juntos, recorriendo largas distancias. **29**

cardinals/cardenales Rangos oficiales de la Iglesia Católica, que siguen detrás del Papa. **301**

Carolingians/Carolingios Dinastía relativa a Carlomagno, establecida con la coronación de Pipino III como"rey por la gracia de Dios" desde el 751 D.C. **289**

caste system/sistema de castas Compleja forma de organización social que comienza a tomar forma después de la migración Indoaria. **61**

censors/censores Oficiales romanos que registraban a los ciudadanos de acuerdo con su fortuna. **152**

Chavín/Chavín Primeros habitantes andinos en Suramérica. **209**

checks and balances/revisión y balance Sistema de gobierno que impide que alguna parte del gobierno se convierta demasiado poderosa. **152**

Children's Crusade/Cruzada de los Niños Efímera cruzada en 1212, donde jóvenes de Europa marcharon en la Tierra Santa para recuperar el Cristianismo. **321**

chinampas/chinampas Terrenos levantados construidos por los Aztecas, hechos con barro tomado del fondo de los lagos. **210**

chivalry/Caballería Código o sistema medieval de caballería. **298**

citadel/ciudadela Fortaleza central en una ciudad. **53**

city-state/ciudad-estado Forma de gobierno que incluye una ciudad o pueblo, y las áreas que la rodean y que son controladas por ella. **32**

civil servant/servicio civil Sistema centralizado que se encarga de los asuntos del gobierno día a día. **87**

civilization/civilización Cultura compleja que puede producir un excedente de comida, establecer grandes poblaciones con un gobierno, y tener personas que realizan diferentes labores. **11**

Columbian Exchange/intercambio colonista Intercambio masivo de bienes, plantas, animales, y enfermedades, que tuvo lugar entre los hemisferios Oriente y Occidente, que siguieron a los viajes de Colón. **394**

command economy/economía de mando Economía en la cual el gobierno controla todas las decisiones económicas. **465**

Commercial Revolution/Revolución Comercial Época entre 1400 y 1750 cuando los europeos hicieron cambios ma

yores a sus economías debido a las nuevas exploraciones. **389**

commodities/mercancías Bienes que tienen valor, especialmente relacionados con economías de trueque. **43**

common law/ley común Ley basada en las costumbres y decisiones de jueces, en vez de lo escrito en los códigos. **307**

compass/brújula Instrumento de navegación creado en 1930, que utiliza una pieza de metal magnetizada que apunta al norte. **388**

consulates/consulados Oficinas diplomáticas en el extranjero, dirigidas por un cónsul. **427**

consuls/cónsul Jefes ejecutivos elegidos para dirigir el gobierno en la antigua Roma. **152**

Council of Trent/Concilio de Trento Reunión de líderes de la Iglesia en los años 1500, para definir claramente las doctrinas católicas para la Contrareforma. **369**

Counter-Reformation/Contrareforma Intento de la Iglesia Católica, luego de la Reforma, por devolver a la Iglesia a un énfasis en asuntos espirituales. **368**

covenant/alianza Acuerdo solemne. **45**

craft guilds/gremios de artesanos Asociación de trabajadores manuales para establecer las condiciones de trabajo. **328**

Cro-Magnons/Cromañones Grupo de los primeros hombres aparecidos hace cerca de 35,000, en Europa. **8**

Crusades/Cruzadas Expediciones hechas por los cristianos para recuperar la Tierra Santa de los musulmanes. **318**

Cuban missile crisis/Crisis de los misiles Cuba Situación durante la Guerra Fría en la cual la Unión Soviética construyó zonas de misiles nucleares en Cuba. **466**

cultural diffusion/difusión cultural Expansión de una cultura de un área del mundo a otra. **12**

culture/cultura Creencias, conocimiento, y patrones de vida, que un grupo de personas adquiere al vivir juntas. **6**

cuneiforme/cuneiforme Escritura sumeria en forma de cuñas. **31**

curia/curia Grupo de consejeros del Papa, llevados desde los más altos rangos del clero. **301**

czar/zar Título tomado por Iván el Terrible; palabra rusa para "caesar" o "césar". **234**

daimyo/daimyo señores o amos feudales en Japón. **280**

Dao De Jing/Dao de Jing Compilación de las enseñanzas de Laozi en el Daoismo. **91**

D-Day/día D 6 de junio, 1944, el día que las tropas aliadas iniciaron la invasión de la costa de Normandía. **462**

Delian League/Liga Delian Alianza de ciudades y estados en la antigua Grecia, con Atenas como líder. **123**

democracy/democracia Gobierno en el cual los ciudadanos forman parte de él. **112**

dialects/dialectos Variaciones de un lenguaje. **82**

Diamond Sutra/Diamond Sutra Primer libro impreso del mundo, un texto Budista producido en China en el año 868 A.C. **270**

dictator/dictador Gobernante absoluto. **151**

dikes/diques Muros de tierra construidos a lo largo de un río para evitar innundaciones. **78**

direct democracy/democracia directa Forma de democracia en la que todos los ciudadadanos participan directamente en la toma de decisiones. **117**

division of labor/división de labores Característica de las civilizaciones en la cual diferentes personas rea-lizan diferentes trabajos. **12**

domestic system/sistema doméstico Método de producción que tiene lugar en la casa del trabajador, y no en una tienda o fábrica. **325**

domestication/domesticación Amansar animales como cabras, ovejas y cerdos. **9**

dowry/dote Dinero y bienes que una esposa brinda al matrimonio. **222**

dramas/dramas Piezas o representaciones de teatro que contienen acciones y diálogos y que usualmente involucran conflicto y emoción. **136**

dynasty/dinastía Familia de gobernantes que reinan en forma hereditaria. **22**

empire/imperio Forma de gobierno que une diferentes territorios y poblaciones, bajo el mando de un mismo gobernante. **24**

English Bill of Rights/Cesión Inglesa de Derechas Documento en 1689 que declaró los poderes del Parlamento y protegía a los ciudadanos particulares. **452**

Enlightenment/Ilustración Período en los años 1700, cuando los filósofos creían que podían aplicar el método científico y el uso de la razón para explicar de ma-nera lógica la naturaleza humana. **452**

ephors/éforos Cada uno de los cinco magistrados que elegía el pueblo todos los años en Esparta. **114**

epics/épicas Largos poemas basados en temas históricos o religiosos. **60**

equites/équites Clase de gente de negocios y dueños de propiedades que tenían el poder en la Antigua Roma. **157**

ethical monotheism/monoteísmo ético Religión que cree en un sólo Dios, y enfatiza la ética. **47**

ethics/ética Estudio de lo que es bueno y malo, y del deber moral. **120**

excommunication/excomulgación Edicto oficial que expulsa a una persona como miembro de la Iglesia. **226**

Exodus/éxodo Escape de los hebreos de Egipto. **44**

export/exportación Bienes y servicios vendidos a otro país. **118**

extraterritoriality/inmunidad Exoneración de extranjeros de las leyes del país en el cual viven o trabajan. **419**

fascism/fascismo Doctrina gubernamental que se basa en reglas dictatoriales y en un régimen totalitario, en el cual el Estado mantiene control rígido de la población, por medio de la fuerza y de censura. **460**

balance de comercio Situación favorable que existe cuando un país vende más bienes de los que compra. **390**

federal system of government/ sistema de gobierno federal Sistema de gobierno en el cual el poder está dividido entre un poder central, uno federal, gobierno, y estados individuales. **453**

feudalism/feudalismo Sistema de gobierno local basado en la concesión de tierras como pago por lealtad, ayuda militar y otros servicios. **294**

fief/feudo Concesión de tierras de un amo a su vasayo. **294**

Five Classics/Cinco Clásicos Textos usados para entrenar alumnos y servidores civiles en la antigua China. **94**

Five Good Emperors/Cinco Emperadores Buenos Cinco gobernantes que dirigieron Roma por casi 100 años durante la Pax Romana. **161**

Flemish school/escuela Flamenca Grupo de pintores que perfeccionaron la técnica de pintura sobre lienzo. **361**

free trade/libre comercio Práctica basada en la creencia de que el gobierno no debe restringir o interferir con el comercio internacional. **418**

frescoes/frescos Pinturas en paredes y muros hechas con yeso mojado. **107**

Fujiwara/Fujiwara Primer familia en ganar control sobre el gobierno central en Japón, desde mediados de los años 800 hasta mediados de los 1100. **278**

genealogy/genealogía Récord de la historia de una familia. **93**

geocentric theory/teoría geocéntrica Teoría de acuerdo con el pensador Helenístico Tolomeo, de que la Tierra es el centro del universo. **383**

ghazis/ghazis Guerreros del Islam; soldados turcos quienes fueron los primeras Otomanos. **432**

gladiators/gladiadores Luchadores entrenados, usualmente esclavos, que peleaban en arenas para entretenimiento. **165**

glasnost/glásnost Política soviética de apertura bajo el cual el gobierno controla que la economía fuera desahogada y las restricciones en desacuerdo fueran disminuidas. **475**

golden age/epoca dorada Era de progreso cultural en Grecia en los años 400 A.C. **130**

Golden Horde/Horda Dorada Nombre dado por los europeos a los invasores mongoles de 1200, debido al color dorado de sus tiendas. **273**

Gothic/gótico Estilo arquitectónico de iglesias, caracterizado por arcos apuntados y la bóveda sobre crucería de ojivas. Este estilo fué desarrollado por los maestros constructores de mediados de los 1100. **334**

Goths/Godos Individuos de un antiguo pueblo germano, que se estableció en la desembocadura del Vístula en el siglo I A.C. **174**

Gracchi, the/Gracchi, los Dos hermanos, Tiberus y Gaius Gracchus, quienes vieron la necesidad de reforma en la República Romana. **158**

Grand Canal/Gran Canal Canal construido durante la dinastía Sui que unió el norte con el sur de China por primera vez. **266**

Great Leap Forward/Gran Salto Adelante Segundo Plan Quiquenal de Mao Zedong para China, en 1958, para ace-lerar el progreso. **469**

Great Schism/Gran Escición Período de la historia de la Iglesia, de 1378 a 1417 cuando ésta fué dividida en dos grupos opuestos. **342**

Great Wall of China/Gran Muralla China Muro construido y expandido alrededor de China, construido por antiguos gobernantes para proteger a China de las invasiones. **86**

Greek Fire/combustible Griego Líquido inflamable usado como arma por la marina bizantina. **224**

guerilla warfare/guerrilla Técnica que cuenta de invasiones repentinas por parte de pequeñas bandas de soldados. **403**

Habsburg/Habsburg Poderosa familia de gobernantes europeos en los años 1200. **340**

Hagia Sophia/Hagia Sophia Iglesia decorativa Bizantina en Constantinopla. **227**

Han/Han Dinastía de gobernantes que dirigieron un imperio creciente y centralizado en China. **84**

heliocentric theory/teoría heliocentrista Teoría desarrollada por Copérnico, que dice que el Sol es el centro del universo. **383**

Hellenistic culture/cultura Helénica Cultura que mezcló ideas griegas con características de otras culturas de la región Mediterránea. **141**

helots/helots Pueblos conquistados del Peloponeso, que se convirtieron en la clase más baja de la sociedad Espartana. **113**

heresy/herejía Opinión que la Iglesia considera contra la fé católica. **226**

heretics/herejes Personas que negaban la veracidad de los principios de la Iglesia, o que predicaban creencias que la Iglesia no aprobaba. **302**

hieroglyphics/hieroglíficos Forma antigua de escritura, desarrollada por los habitantes del valle del Río Nilo, alrededor de los 3000 B.C. **22**

hijrah/hijrah Migración de Muhammad y sus seguidores en 622 D.C., marcando el primer año en el calendario Musulmán. **241**

Hohokam/Hohokam Grupo de personas que habitaron en el suroeste de Estados Unidos, y que abandonaron sus comunidades en 1300 o 1400. **203**

hominids/homínidos Primeras criaturas similares al hombre. **6**

Hopewell/Hopewell Grupo de personas asentados en el Valle de Ohio, aproximadamente entre los años 300 y 200 A.C. **207**

hoplites/hoplites Infantería griega fuertemente armada, que llevaban largas lanzas, y peleaban formados en líneas muy estrechas. **112**

Huguenots/Hugonotes Franceses, entre ellos nobles de alto rango, que se convirtieron al Calvinismo. **367**

humanists/humanistas Personas que se especializan en el estudio del Humanismo. Este incluye gramática, historia, poesía y retórica. **355**

Hundred Years' War/Guerra de los Cien Años Guerra entre Francia e Inglaterra por el trono francés, que continuó desde 1337 a 1435, e introdujo el uso de nuevas armas. **336**

Huns/Hunos Población nómada de Asia, que atacó el Imperio Romano. **175**

hunters-gatherers/cazadores-recolectores Pobladores tempranos que vivían de la caza. **10**

Hyksos/Hyksos Grupo de personas que llegaron de Asia al antiguo Egipto, e introdujeron nuevas herramientas de guerra. **23**

icon/ícono Imagen sacra de Jesús, la Virgen María, o de algún santo. **224**

Iconoclastic Controversy/Controversia Iconoclástica Debate entre oponentes y defensores de iconos en la Iglesia Bizantina. Uno de los motivos que llevó a la división de la Iglesia Cristiana en 1054. **226**

martyrs/mártires Personas que han padecido muerte, persecución o torturas por mantenerse fiel a sus ideas o creencias. **170**

matrilineal/materno Describe la forma de transmitir la propiedad, la herencia o el nombre por línea materna. **186**

Maya/Maya Una de las más avazadas poblaciones de las Américas, que ocuparon gran parte la Península de Yucatán. **209**

maya/maya Mundo ilusorio de los sentidos, de acuerdo con el hinduismo. **61**

medieval/medieval Término que describe el período de la historia de Europa occidental, conocido como la Edad Media. **288**

merchantilism/mercantilismo Sistema económico vigente en los siglos XVII y XVIII que atiende en primer término al desarrollo del comercio con intervención del Estado, y que considera la posesión de metales preciosos como signo de riqueza. **390**

merchant guild/gremio mercantilista Asociación de mercaderes y trabajadores, para proteger sus derechos de comerciar y para ayudar a los miembros de su familia. **327**

Merovingians/Merovingios Dinastía de los primeros reyes de Francia. Clodoveo, hijo de Meroveo extendió sus dominios a casi toda la Galia. **288**

metics/meticos Personas que vivían en Atenas pero no eran ciudadanos atenienses, que podían trabajar y pagaban impuestos, pero no tenían derecho de poseer tierra propia ni a formar parte del gobierno. **115**

Middle Ages/edad media Período de la historia occidental de Europa, comprendido entre la caída del Imperio Romano y el Renacimiento. **288**

middle class/clase media Clase formada por comerciantes, patronos de pequeña y mediana industria y profesiones liberales. Está entre la clase noble y la clase campesina en la Edad Media. **328**

Middle Passage/Pasaje Medio Travesía. Segunda etapa del sistema de comercio triangular, el cual envolvía el transporte de esclavos a las Américas a través del Atlántico. **398**

millets/millets Minorías religiosas separadas y autogobernadas en el Imperio Otomano. **434**

Minamoto/Minamoto Clan que reinaba en Japón en 1156; introdujo el control shogun, y cambió el la forma en que el gobierno era llevado. **278**

minaret/minarete Alminar, torre de la mezquita. **253**

miniaturization/miniaturización Proceso de hacer máquinas más pequeñas y livianas. **476**

Minoans/Minóicas La más temprana civilización griega, que se desarrolló en la isla de Creta alrededor del 2000 A.C. **107**

Mississippians/Mississippianos Grupo que vivía en los bosques del Este en Norteamérica alrededor del 700 al 1500 D.C. **207**

monasticism/monasticismo Modo de vida en conventos y monasterios donde las monjas y monjes eran alejados del mundo y sus tentaciones. **301**

money economy/sistema monetario Sistema económico basado en el uso de la moneda como una medida de valor y una unidad de cuentas. **43**

monism/monismo Creencia en la unidad de Dios y la creación. **61**

monotheism/monoteísmo Que cree en un solo Dios. **25**

monsoons/monzones Vientos que marcan las estaciones en la India. **52**

Moors/Moros Musulmanes que hicieron de España su hogar en los años 700 D.C. **245**

mosaic/mosaico Pintura o diseño hecho de pequeñas piezas de esmalte, vidrio o piedra. **227**

mosques/mezquita Edificio que los mahometanos usaban para la oración y las ceremonias religiosas. **242**

mummification/momificación Proceso de preservar con el uso de químicos, un cuerpo después de la muerte. **28**

Muslims/Musulmánes Seguidores de la religión islámica. **242**

Mycenaeans/Micenas Civilización en tierras griegas, que conquistaron loa Micens en Creta alrededor de 1400 A.C. **107**

myths/mitos Historias tradicionales sobre dioses, diosas y héroes. **111**

NAFTA/NAFTA Acuerdo Norteamericano de Libre Comercio. Grupo que trabajaba por los derechos civiles. Este une a México, Canadá y los Estados Unidos, como una sola zona de comercio. **912**

Nalanda/Nalanda Famoso universo Budista en la antigua India. **71**

NATO/NATO Tratado de Organización Norte Atlántica. Alianza de doce naciones occidentales, formada en 1949. **465**

Neanderthals/neandertals Hombres que vivieron el la Era de Piedra, encontrados en Europa, Africa y Asia. **8**

Neolithic agricultural revolution/revolución agrícola del Neolítico Cambio en la historia humana, de la caza a la agricultura. **10**

New Deal/New Deal Programa del presidente Franklin D. Roosevelt en el que el gobierno federal estableció un amplio programa de obras públicas para crear empleo y conceder dinero a cada estado para sus necesidades. **460**

nirvana/nirvana Perfecta paz espiritual, según lo enseña el Hinduismo. **62**

nomads/nómadas Antiguos pueblos que viajaban de un lugar. **9**

Odyssey/La Odisea La épica de Homero que cuenta la historia de Ulises Odiseo en su camino a casa de vuelta de la guerra troyana. **110**

Olmec/olmeca Cultura temprana de México alrededor de 1200 A.C. **209**

Olympic Games/Juegos Olímpicos Festival en la antigua Grecia, de competencias de deportes, música y lite-ratura; la versión moderna de estos juegos, son competencias deportivas internacionales. **111**

OPEC/OPEC Organización de Países Exportadores de Petróleo, creada en 1960 para establecer los precios del petróleo y los niveles de producción de petróleo en el mundo. **473**

Opium War/guerra del opio Conflicto entre China e Inglaterra entre 1839 y 1842 que surgió por la oposición china al comercio de opio por los ingleses. **419**

oracle bones/huesos oráculos Huesos de ganado o caparazones de tortugas en las que los sacerdotes chinos escribían preguntas y luego interpretaban las respuestas basados en la quebraduras del hueso cuando éste era calentado. **82**

oracles/oráculos Lugares especiales donde los antiguos griegos creían que los dioses hablaban a través de los sacerdotes y pitonisas. **111**

oral traditions/tradición oral Poemas, canciones, y historias, transmitidas de boca en boca, de generación en generación. **184**

orators/oradores Habladores públicos. **139**

Ottoman Turks/Otomanos Pueblos asiáticos que conquistaron Constantinopla en 1300 y establecieron un gran imperio. **228**

Panchatantra/Panchatantra Fábulas del período Gupta en la antigua India. **70**

papyrus/papiro Tipo de papel hecho por los egipcios, extraído del tallo de la planta del mismo nombre. **22**

Parthenon/Partenón Templo de mármol en honor a la diosa Atenea, en Atenas. **130**

patriarchs/patriarcado Obispos de los centros administrativos para la Iglesia, en los últimos años del Imperio Romano. **171**

patricians/patricios Clase aristocrática te-rrateniente que controló el gobierno y la sociedad romana. **153**

Pax Romana/Pax Romana Período de paz romana desde el principio del reinado de Augusto hasta la muerte de Marco Aurelio. **160**

pedagogue/pedagogo Hombre que enseñaba modales en la Antigua Grecia. Esclavo que enseñaba a alguien más jóven que él. **119**

Peloponnesian War/Guerra del Peloponeso Guerra entre Esparta y Atenas, que estalló en 431 A.C. y duró por 27 años. **124**

Pentagon/Pentágono Sede de los jefes mi-litares de los Estados Unidos, localizado en Washington, D.C. Fué escenario de un ataque te-rrorista el 11 de septiembre, 2001. **478**

perestroika/perestroika Política de restructuración soviética diseñada para revisar el sistema político y económico. **475**

Persian Wars/Guerras Persas Conflictos entre Grecia y Persia. **121**

perspective/perspectiva Técnica de arte que envuelve hacer los objetos distantes más pequeños que los que están al frente, y acomodarlos de manera que se cree la ilusión de profundidad en un lienzo plano. **356**

phalanx/falanges Formación militar compuesta por líneas de soldados, que marchaban hombro con hombro, cargando lanzas. **138**

pharaoh/faraón Título del emperador egipcio. **22**

philology/filología Estudio de literatura y lenguaje. **415**

philosophy/filosofía Estudio de cuestio-namientos básicos sobre la realidad y la existencia humana. **133**

Phoenician alphabet/alfabeto Fenicio Alfabeto desarrollado por los fenicios, que fué el modelo de futuros alfabetos occidentales. **42**

plebeians/plebeyos Campesinos y trabajadores que constituyeron la mayoría de la población romana. **153**

polis/polis Palabra griega para estadociudad. **108**

Polovtsy/Polovtsios Pueblo turco que después de 1055 controló el área del sur del Kiev en Rusia. **233**

polygymy/poligamia Práctica en la cual a un hombre se le permite tener más de una esposa. **69**

polytheism/politeísmo Creencia en más de un Dios. **25**

polytheistic/politeísta Que practica el politeísmo, o la creencia en muchos dioses. **62**

pope/Papa Título asumido por el patriarca de Roma y cabeza de la Iglesia Católica. Palabra latina que significa "padre". **171**

popular government/gobierno popular Idea de que el pueblo debe gobernarse a sí mismo. **112**

potlatches/potlatches Asambleas ceremoniales de los nativos americanos, en la costa Noroeste del Pacífico. **203**

praetors/praetors Oficiales romanos que ayudaban a los cónsules. **152**

Pravda Russkia/Pravda Russkia Primer código de leyes ruso, creado por Yaroslav I. **231**

predestination/predestinación Creencia de que al principio del tiempo, Dios decidió quienes iban a salvarse. **366**

primogeniture/primogenitura Sistema de heredar poseciones y tierra de un padre a su hijo mayor. **294**

Pueblo/Pueblo Grupo de personas que vivían en asentamientos permanentes en el suroeste de Estados Unidos. **205**

Punic Wars/Guerras Púnicas Conflictos entre Romanos y Cartagos, por el control del Mediterráneo y la expansión marítima. **155**

Qin/Qin Dinastía que llegó al poder en China en 221 A.C., bajo la cual el primer imperio chino verdadero fué creado. **84**

Quechua/Quechua Lenguaje Inca, aún hablado hoy día por millones de personas en América del Sur. **211**

queue/queue Trenza de cabello que caracterizaba el estilo de peinado que todos los hombres chinos debían usar durante la dinastía Qing. **414**

quipu/quipu tipo de cuerdas con nudos y de colores usados para suplir la falta de escritura por los Incas. **211**

Qur'an/Corán libro sagrado del Islam. **242**

rabbis/rabinos Religiosos expertos del Judaísmo. **168**

raja/rajá Príncipe que reinaba en una ciudad indoaria. **57**

Rajputs/Rajputas Príncipes guerreros indios que empezaron a retar el control turco musulmano en la India en 1500. **439**

reaya/reaya Masas de sujetos ordinarios en la sociedad Otomana. **434**

Reformation/Reforma Revolución religiosa que dividió la Iglesia en Europa occidental, y creó una cantidad de iglesias nuevas. **363**

reincarnation/reencarnación Creencia del renacimiento de las almas. **61**

Renaissance/Renacimiento Movimiento que precedió a la Edad Media, es el renacer del interés en las enseñanzas clásicas de Grecia y Roma. **354**

representative democracy/ democracia representativa Forma de gobierno en el que los ciudadanos eligen el representante para llevar el gobierno, en vez de que cada ciudadano le sirva directamente al gobierno. **117**

republic/república Forma de gobierno representativo en que la soberania reside en el pueblo. **151**

rhetoric/retórica Estudio de debates y discursos públicos. **120**

Rosetta Stone/Roseta Piedra negra encontrada en 1799 cuya inscripción trilingue fué el punto de partida de la egiptología. **22**

Rus/Rus Región bajo el control de Rurik quines llegaron a go-bernar Kiev y las tribus Eslavas a lo largo del Río Dneiper. **230**

sacraments/sacramentos Ceremonias en las que los participantes reciben la gracia de Dios para salvarse de las consecuencias de pecar. **300**

samurai/sanyrau Guerreros japoneses contratados para proteger el bienestar de los terratenientes en Japón feudalista. **278**

Sanskrit/Sánscrito Lenguaje indo-ario. **56**

savannas/sabanas Llanuras secas al sur del desierto del Sahara en África. **182**

scholasticism/escolasticismo Filosofía medieval que intentara juntar la fé y la razón. **334**

scientific method/método científico Método de investigación que incluye cuidadosos experimentos conducidos y cálculos matemáticos para verificar el resultado de los experimentos. **383**

Scientific Revolution/Revolución Científica Transformación de pensamiebnto ocu-rrido durante 1500 y 1600, causada por la observación científica, la experimentación, y el cuestionamiento de las opi-niones tradicionales. **382**

scribes/escriba Clérico egipcio que leía y escribía para aquellos que no podían hacerlo por sí mismos. **27**

sects/sectas Sociedades religiosas de pocas personas, usualmente con un sacerdote como líder. **365**

Seljuq Turks/turcos Seljuq Musulmanes de Asia central quienes le ganaron el control de Palestina o Jerusalem a los cristianos, a finales de los 1000. **318**

seppuku/seppuku Forma ceremonial de suicidio de samurais derrotados o desleales, para salvar el honor. También conocidos en Occidente como hari-kari. **278**

serfs/siervos Campesinos que debían vivir en la tierra en la que trabajaban para un amo. **298**

Shang/Shang Invasores del valle del río Huang que llegaron al poder entre 1750 y 1500 A.C., y establecieron la primer dinastía China. **81**

Shi'ah/Shi'ah Rama del Islam formada en los 600 D.C., que creía que solo los imams deberían decidir sobre asuntos religiosos y terrenales. **244**

Shinto/Shintoísmo o Sintoísmo Religión indígena de Japón que envuelve rituales y oraciones para apaciguar espítitus de la naturaleza y venerar al emperador. **277**

shires/condados Distritos gubernamentales en la vieja Inglaterra. **304**

shogun/shogun Jefe militar y oficial gubernamental en Japón feudal. **278**

Shona/Shona Pueblo que emigró al lugar que hoy día es conocido como Zimbabwe. **192**

Sikh/Sikh Religión basada en las enseñanzas de Nañak, un místico hindú en 1500, quien trató de unir las religiones hinduista y la musulmana. **441**

Silk Road/Ruta de seda Ruta de comercio que se extiende desde China hasta el Mediterráneo. **88**

simony/simonía Práctica de comprar altos puestos en la Iglesia, actividad común en la Edad Media. **303**

socialism/socialismo Sistema político y económico en el que el gobierno posee los medios de producción. **455**

sophists/Sofistas Hombres atenienses que abrieron escuelas para que jóvenes estudiaran política, matemática, ética y retórica. **120**

standard of living/Estándares de vida Medición de la calidad de vida. **376**

steppe/estepa Llanura muy extensa ideal para la agricultura, en el este de Europa y el centro de Asia. **229**

strait/estrecho Angosta faja de agua que conecta dos masas de agua más grandes. **200**

subsidies/subsidios Concesiones de dinero del gobierno. **390**

Sufi/Sufi Místicos mahometanos que trataban de vivir una vida simple. **245**

sultan/sultán Título del emperador de los Turcos. Príncipe o gobernador mahometano. **247**

Sunni/Sunní Nombre que se le da en el islamismo a los ortodoxos seguidores de la Sunna. **244**

suttee/suttee Antigua práctica hindú en que una mujer cometía suicidio después de la muerte de su marido. **69**

Swahili/Swahili Sociedad africana que emergió a finales de los años 1100 a lo largo de la costa Este africana. Combinaba elementos de las culturas africana, asiática e islámica. **191**

taiga/taiga Región rusa muy lluviosa, al norte de las estapas, con largos y fríos inviernos. **231**

Taiping Rebellion/Rebelión de Taiping Revuelta en China entre 1850 a 1864, guiada por Hong Xiuquan, quien influenciado por las enseñanzas del cristianismo, declaró una misión para establecer una nueva dinastía. **421**

Taj Mahal/Taj Mahal Palacio construido bajo Shah Jahan, como una tumba para su esposa. Actualmente es una de las maravillas arquitectónicas del mundo. **441**

Tale of Genji, The/La Aventura de Genji Historia escrita por Murasaki Shikibu, en Japón, alrededor del año 1000 D.C. Considerada generalmente como la primer novela en el mundo. **278**

tariffs/tarifas Impuestos a la importación de productos extranjeros. **390**

tepees/tepees Tiendas de forma cónica, hechas de piel de búfalo. **205**

terracing/parcelar Cavar pequeñas parcelas de tierra en las colinas, para la agricultura. **118**

theocracy/teocracia Gobierno dirigido por líderes religiosos, que proclaman la autoridad de Dios. **367**

third Rome/tercera Romana Interpretación rusa ortodoxa de su rol principal de traer la luz espiritual al mundo. **235**

Thirty Years' War/Guerra de los Treinta Años Guerra iniciada en Praga en 1618, como una rebelión de los Protestantes contra el Santo Imperio Romano. **455**

Thousand and One Nights, The/Las Mil y Una Noches Colección de cuentos populares musulmanes. **253**

tithe/diezmo Impuesto recogido por los cristianos para la Iglesia en los viejos tiempos, que representaba una décima parte de sus ganancias. **302**

Toltec/tolteca Pueblo que invadió el centro de México desde el norte, alrededor de los 800 D.C. **210**

Torah/Torá Escrituras judías que incluyen los primeros cinco libros del Viejo Testamento de la Biblia, que incluyen el libro de las leyes hebreas. **46**

tragedies/tragedia Forma de drama griego en el cual el personaje principal luchaba contra el destino y los eventos. **137**

Treaty of Kanagawa/Tratado de Kanagawa Negociaciones entre Matthew Perry y Japón en 1854 que permitió comerciar entre los dos países. **427**

Treaty of Nanjing/Tratado de Nanjing Tratado que siguió la Guerra del Opio en la cual China cedió Hong Kong a los británicos y abrieron puertos para el comercio británico. **419**

Treaty of Tordesillas/Tratado de Tordesillas Acuerdo entre

España y Portugal que movió hacia el oeste el límite del territorio que cada país podía reclamar en el Atlántico. **394**

triangular trade/comercio triangular Sistema de comercio que involucra tres etapas, una de las cuales es la trata de esclavos a traves del Atlántico. **398**

tribunes/tribuna Oficiales elegidos por las asambleas populares romanas. **152**

triumvirate/triunvirato Alianza política de tres dirigentes. **159**

tropical rain forests/bosque tropical lluvioso Bosques de vasta vegetación donde llueve mucho. **182**

troubadours/trovadores Cantantes que viajaban enteniéndo gente en la Edad Media. **332**

Truman Doctrine/Doctrina Truman Política que declara que los Estados Unidos considera que el continuar con la expansión del comunismo es una amenaza a la democracia. **465**

Twelve Tribes of Israel/Las Doce Tribus de Israel Doce hijos de Israel, nieto de Abraham, de quienes los judíos modernos siguieron su herencia. **44**

tyrants/tiranos En la Grecia antigua, go-bernantes que medían el poder por la fuerza, pero eran gobernantes con el apoyo del pueblo; más adelante este término se refería a gobernantes que ejercían poder brutal y opresivo. **112**

"unequal" treaties/trueque desigual Intercambio de bienes que China firmó bajo amenaza de invasión, dándole a las potencias Occidentales los beneficios del intercambio. **419**

United Nations/Organización de las Naciones Unidas Organización de naciones para mantener la paz a traves de acuerdos colectivos. **464**

Upanishads/Upanishad Escritura sagrada que explica la religión Védica. **60**

usury/usura Política de cobrar altos intereses por un préstamo. **326**

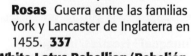

Vandals/Vándalos Que pertenece a un grupo de tribus germánicas que invadieron y destruyeron territorio en el Imperio Romano. **174**

varnas/varnas Clases sociales en la sociedad de la India. **61**

vassal/vasallo Persona a la que un amo le concedía tierras, como pago por sus servicios. **294**

Vedas/Vedas Los más antiguos textos religiosos de la India. **56**

Vedic Age/Edad Védica Período histórico de India, de 1500 al 1000 A.C. **56**

vernacular language/lenguaje vernácular Lenguaje doméstico, nativo, propio de un país. **331**

veto/veto Derecho de vedar o impedir una cosa, tal como un proyecto de ley. **152**

viceroys/virrey El que con ese título gobierna en nombre y con autoridad del rey. Oficiales españoles que representaban a la monarquía en el imperio colonial español. **401**

Vikings/Vikingos Pueblo germánico de Escandinavia que atacaban frecuentemente el oeste de Europa durante los años 800 y 900. **292**

War of the Roses/Guerra de las Rosas Guerra entre las familias York y Lancaster de Inglaterra en 1455. **337**

White Lotus Rebellion/Rebelión de Lotos Blancos Rebelión campesina contra la dinastía Qing, liderada por el culto budista conocido como la Sociedad de Lotos. **416**

World Trade Center/Centro de Comercio Internacional (WTC) Complejo de oficinas en la ciudad de Nueva York, que fué destruido por un devastador ataque terrorista el 11 de septiembre del 2001. **478**

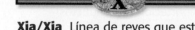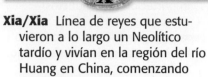

Xia/Xia Línea de reyes que estuvieron a lo largo un Neolítico tardío y vivían en la región del río Huang en China, comenzando alrededor del 2000 antes de cristo. **80**

yang/yang Fuerza masculina. Brillante y activa, y es parte de la creencia china de dualismo o balance en la vida. **89**

Yi/Yi Dinastía coreana en 1392, cuando los coreanos sacaron a los mongoles, y duró hasta que Corea se anexó a Japón en 1910. **281**

yin/yin Fuerza femenina, oscura y pasiva, y es parte de la creencia del dualismo o balance en la vida. **89**

Zen/Zen Secta del Budismo que se enfoca en la meditación como método de ilustración. **269**

Zhou/Zhou Los que derrocaron la dinastía china Shang, en 1122 A.C. **83**

ziggurats/zigurats Templos sumerios hechos de ladrillo secado al sol. **32**

Index

Amytis, 38
An, 34
Analects (Confucius), 90 *p*260
Anasazi civilization, 203
Anatolia, 432, 434
anatomy, 145, 383
ancestor worship, 82, 231
Andes Mountains, 200, 211
Angkor Wat, 283, *p*283
Angles, 304
Anglican Church, 365–366, 451. *See also* Reformation
Angola, *m*A2, *m*A10, 399
animals: in agriculture, 15; domestication of, 5, 9, 81; in zoos, 74
animism, 82
Ankara, Battle of, 432
Anna (wife of Vladimir I), 231
Annals (Tacitus), 167
Annam, 282. *See also* Vietnam
Anne (queen of England), 488
Anne of Denmark, *p*473. *See also* James I
Anthology of Chinese Literature, 81, 94
anthropologists, 6
Antioch, 171, 319
Antony, Marc, 160
Anyang, 74, 81
apartheid, 472
Apennine Mountains, 150
Apollo (Greek god), 111
apprentice, 328
aqueducts, *p*166
Aquinas, Thomas, 334, *f*334
Aquino, Corazon, 470, *f*470
Arabia, 240–241
Arabian peninsula, *m*240
Arafat, Yasser, 473
archaeologists, 6, 33, 185

archaeology, 53, 58, *f*58, 192; sources of evidence in, *f*33
archbishop, 301
Archbishop of Canterbury, 302, 306
archdiocese, 301
Archimedes, *f*143, *p*143, 144
Archimedes screw, 143–144, *f*144, *p*144
architecture, 476; of ancient Egypt, 26–27; of ancient Greece, 111, 130, 132; of ancient India, 70; of ancient Sumeria, 32; Byzantine, *p*227; Gothic, 316, 334–335, *p*335; of Harappan civilization, 54; Islamic, 252–253; Maya, 198; of Middle Ages, 219, *p*219, *f*331, 334–335, *p*335, *p*347; modern, *f*26; Mughal Empire and, 440; of Roman Empire, 166; Romanesque, 334; Russian Orthodox, *p*235; Vatican, 286
archons, 115
Argentina, *m*A1, *m*A8, 467
Aristarchus, 145
aristocracy, 111–112, 134
Aristophanes, 137
Aristotle: influence of philosophies, 333, 334, 382, 385; musical theory and, 128; 129; teachings of, 134–135
Ark of the Covenant, 45
armor, 295
Armstrong, Neil, 476
army, first professional, 138–139
Arno River, *m*354
Arouet, Francois-Marie. *See* Voltaire
art, 476; in ancient China, *p*99; in ancient Egypt, 26–27, *p*27; in ancient Greece, *p*128, 130–132; in ancient India, 70; Byzantine,

227; Flemish school, 361; Islamic, *p*217, 252–253, *f*253, *p*347; Italian Renaissance painting, 356–358; medieval, *p*286–287; Northern Renaissance artists, 361–362; Olmec, 198; prehistoric, *pv*–1, *p*4, *p*5, *p*8, *p*17; understanding history and, 17
Articles of Confederation, 453
artifacts, 6, *f*6, 50; as historical evidence, 189; interpreting, 127; Mycenaean, *p*104, *p*108
artisans, 12; ancient Chinese, 81; Greek, *p*119; in Sparta, 113; Sumerian, 34
Aryabhata, 71
Ashcroft, John, 483
Ashikaga shogunate, 278, 280, 422, 423
Ashikaga Takauji, 278
Ashur (city), 37
Ashur (god), 38
Asia, *m*A2, *m*A11; influence on Muslim culture, 250; in transition, *f*429. *See also under specific countries of Asia*
Asia Minor: capture by Seljuq Turks, 228; conquered by Alexander the Great, 140; crusaders and, 319; Muslim conquest of, 247; Turkish conquest of, 221
Askia Mohammed I, 195, *f*195
Aśoka (Mauryan ruler), 51, 67, *f*67
assemblies, Roman, 152
Assumption of the Virgin (Titian), 358
Assyrian Empire, 19, 25, 37–38, *m*38, 44, 46
astrolabe, *p*251, 389, *f*389
astrologers, 382
Astronomer (Vermeer), 388

astronomy, 386; in ancient China, 74, 75, 82; in ancient Rome, 166; Chaldeans and, 38; Galileo and, 384–385, *p*385; the Maya and, 199, 209, *f*209, 213; Muslims and, 239, 251
Atatürk. *See* Kemal, Mustafa
Athena (Greek goddess), 111, 130–131, 132
Athens: decline in power, 138; democracy, *p*102, *f*116, 117; early government of, 115; economy of, 118; education and military service in, 120; home and family life in, 119; Peloponnesian War, 124–125; siege of, 125; size of, 109; society, 115
Atman, 61
Atomic Energy Community, 465
Aton, 25
Attic peninsula, 115, 125
Attila (the Hun), 175
Augustine, Saint, 302
Augustulus, Romulus, 175
Augustus, 160
Aurangzeb, 431, 442, *p*442, 443
Aurelius, Marcus (Roman emperor), 161, *p*161, 172
Australia, *m*A2, *m*A11, *m*A12, 461
Australopithecus, 7
Austria, *m*A2, *m*A9; Congress of Vienna in, 454; German invasion of, 462; post–World War I, 460
Austria-Hungary, 456; in Triple Alliance, 458; in World War I, 458–459
Austrian Empire, Dual Monarchy and, 448, 456
autocracy, 86

461; natural resources in, 3; northern frontier of, 413; opium trade and, 418–419; paper in, 75, 95; physical setting, 76–79; popular culture in, 415; population of, 416; Portugal and, 395, 410, 417; Qin dynasty, 75, 85–86, m85, 91, 94, 95; Qing dynasty, 411, 414–416, m415; as a sea power, f413; Shang dynasty, 80–83, m80; ships and, 412; Silk Road and, 75, 88, 94; Sui dynasty, 264, 266, 281; Sung dynasty, 217, 264, 269–271, m270; Taiping Rebellion, 421; Taiwan and Korea and, 470; Tang dynasty, 266–269, m268; trade and, f412, 413; Treaty of Nanjing and, 419; in United Nations, 464; "unequal" treaties, 419; and United States, 475; Vietnam and, 282; White Lotus Rebellion, 411, 416; women in, 93, 271; writing in, 82–83; yin and yang and, 89, 260; Zhou dynasty, 84–85, m85, 89–90

China Proper, 76
chinampas, 210
Chinese Communist Party, 468
Chinese Nationalist Party, 461, 468
chivalry, 298–299
chocolate, 198
Chosŏn, 280–281
Christian church: division of, 221, 224, 226, 231, 316; Franks and, 288, 290; reform of, 343. *See also* Christianity
Christianity, 40, 261, f363; Abraham and, 257; in Aksum, 190; in Anglo-Saxon England, 305; beginnings of,

168–169; Byzantine Empire and, 224, 226; Charlemagne and, 290; Crusades and, 318–322; European exploration and, 392, 401; 'Ēzānā conversion to, 190; humanism and, 363; hymns and, 149; Jesus and, 169; in Kievan Russia, 231; martyrs of, 170; in Renaissance and, 360, 362; Roman Empire and, 169–171; spread of, 169–170, m170; Trinity as central belief of, 171

Church of England. *See* Anglican Church
Churchill, Winston, 464
cinnamon, p391
Circus Maximus, 165
citadel, 53
cities: as characteristic of civilization, 11, 12; changes in, 377; development of, 5; in Indus River valley, 50, 55; in Middle Ages, 323, 328, 330; and rural life, f266
citizenship, 127; in Greek city-states, 109
City of God (Saint Augustine), 290
city-states, 32, 41; African, 191; ancient Greek, 104, 108–109, f127, 132; concept of, 108; Greek colonies in Italy, 151, 154; Italian, 323; Sumerian, 32
civil service system, in ancient China, f87, p87, 270
civil war: in Angola, 472; in Central America, 467; in Chechnya, 475; in England, 451–452; in Japan, 427; in United States, 475
civilization: characteristics of, 11–13, f11; 54; defined, 11; emergence of, 4–15, f17;

river valley civilizations, 11–12, m12, 15
clans, 108
Classic Period, 103
Cleisthenes, 117
Clement V (pope), 309
Cleopatra, 159, 160
Clermont, 448
Clermont (in France), 318
cliff dwellings, p203
climate, f200
Clinton, Bill, 470, 474
cloning, 477
Clouds (Aristophanes), 137
Clovis (Frankish king), 288–289
Clovis points, 202
coal, 558
coats of arms, 299, p299
Code of Hammurabi, 36
code of the Twelve Tables, 162
coffee, 431
coined money, 43, 115; ancient Chinese, 74, p74, 275, p275; Greek, p104; Roman, 148, p149; standardization of, 317, 389
Cold War, 464–465
collective farms, 469
Colombia, mA1, mA8, 467
colonization. *See* European age of colonization
colonnade, 131
Colosseum, 165
Columbian Exchange, 394
Columbus, Christopher, 380, 393, 400; crossing the Atlantic, p348–349
comedies (theater), ancient Greek, 137
command economy, 465
Commercial Revolution, 389
commodities, 43
Commodus (emperor of Rome), 172
Common Market, 465. *See also* European Economic Community (EEC)

communications, f14, 274, 387, 476
communism, 455, 459, 461, 470, 475
Communist Manifesto (Marx and Engels), 455
compass, 287, 388, 412
compurgation, 295, 297
Concord, Massachusetts, 452
Concordat of Worms, 311–312
Confederate States of America, 455
Conflict of the Orders, 153
Confucianism, 90, f90, 91, 92, 256, 260, 269, 281; four classes under, 413; restored in China, 413; Vietnam and, 282
Confucius (K'ung Ch'iu), 90, f90, p90, 260, f260, p260, 267, 269, 282
Congo River, 182
Congress of Vienna, 454
Conrad III (king of Germany), 320
conservation of matter, law of, 387
Constantine (emperor of Rome), 149, 171, 173–174
Constantinople, 173, p173, p220, 221, f222, 224, m224, 430; captured by Crusaders, 221; as center of Christian church, 171; Muslim attempted conquest of, 243; Ottoman conquest of, 221, 433, 434; Russian attack of, 229
Constantius (Roman emperor), 173
constitution, changes in Europe, f450
consulates, 427
consuls, Roman, 152
containment, 465
Continental Congress, 452–453
Copernicus, Nicolaus, 380, 383, f383, p383

earthen mounds, 207

earthquakes, 95

East Africa, 181, 191–192

East Berlin, 465

East Germany, 465, 475

East Indies, 395, 400

East Pakistan, 471. *See also* Bangladesh

Eastern Europe: Catholicism and, 371; Slavic settlement of, 229

Eastern Ghats, 52

Eastern Orthodox Church, 226, 231

Ebola virus, 472

economic leveling, 87–88

economics, *f*155, *f*350

economy: commercial, *f*391; conflict in, *f*233; Great Depression, 460; in modern era, 474; NAFTA, 449, 467; post–World War II, 468

Ecuador, *m*A1, *m*A8, 211, 401

Edgar, Blake, 7

Edict of Nantes, 367

Edo, 423, 427

education: in ancient China, 87, 94; in ancient Egypt, 27; in ancient India, 71; in ancient Rome, 165; ancient Sumerians and, 34; Charlemagne and, 290; humanists and, 355; Inca civilization and, 211; Jesuits and, 370, 371; in Middle Ages, 333; Muslim Empire and, 249

Edward I (king of England), 287, 307

Edward VI (king of England), 366

Edward the Confessor (king of England), 305

Egypt, *m*A2, *m*A10, 461, 472–473

Egypt: ancient, *m*21, *m*24, 44, *f*49; Alexander the Great and, 140, 141; archaeology and, 33; architecture and the arts in, 26–27; artifacts of, *p*99; cultural exchange with Karmah, 187; decline of, 25; early civilization of, 18; education and religion in, 27–28; eras of, *c*25; escape of Hebrews from, 19, 44; farming and transportation, 2; geography of, 20–21; gods of, 27–28; kingdoms of, 22–25; Middle Kingdom period, 23; natural resources of, 20–21; New Kingdom period, 19, 24–25; Old Kingdom period, 18, 23; science, math, and medicine in, 27, 135; society and economy in, 28–29; trade and, 21, 22, 104; writing and hieroglyphics in, 22

Egypt, Greece and Rome (Freeman), 165

Eightfold Path, 64

El Salvador, *m*A1, *m*A7, 467

El Escorial, 402

Eleanor of Aquitaine (queen of France, queen of England), 306, *f*306, *p*306

"elect, the", 366, 367

Elements (Euclid), 129, 143

Elizabeth I (queen of England), 431, 448, 450, 451, *f*451

ellipses, 384

embalming, 145

Empedocles, 105

empire, 24

energy, alternative, 474

Engels, Friedrich, 455

England, *m*A2, *m*A9; Alfred the Great and, 304; Anglo-Saxon, 304–305; British East India Company, 411, 418, 431; civil war in, 451–452; colonial expansion, 452; colonies in North America, 367; common law, 307; Danish rule of, 305; Edict of Nantes, 367; English Bill of Rights, 452; House of Commons, 307, 337; House of Lords, 307, 337; Hundred Years' War in, 317, 336–337; invasion by Vikings, 286; Magna Carta and, 239, 306–307; Norman, 305; Parliament, 307, 337, 451; Restoration, 451; Scotland and, 287; slave trade and, 395; trade and, 324–325; Tudor dynasty, 317; Tudor monarchy and, 451; War of the Roses, 337. *See also* Great Britain

English Bill of Rights, 452

English pirates, 401

Enki, 34

Enlightenment, 452, 453

enlightenment (Buddhism), 63

Enlil, 34

entertainment, 455, 456

environmental issues, 477

ephors, 114

epic, 60, 98, 110, 346

Epic of Gilgamesh, 37, 38, *f*98

Epicurean philosophy, 143

Epicurus, 143

Equiano, Olaudah, *f*399

equites, 157

Erasmus, Desiderius, 360, 363, 366, 368

Eratosthenes, 145, *f*145

Ericsson, Leif, 239

Eṣfahān, 351, 431, 438

Esmā'īl, 436

Estates General, 309, 341

d'Este, Isabella, 355, *f*355, *p*355

Estonia, *m*A2, *m*A9, 459

ethical monotheism, 47

ethics, 46, 47, 120, 143

Ethics (Aristotle), 134

Ethiopia, *m*A2, *m*A10, 6, 188, 462, 472; Indian traders in, 51

Ethiopian Church, 190

Ethiopian Plateau, 184

Etruscans, 148, 151

Euclid, 129, 143

Eunomy (Solon), 115

Euphrates River, 11, 31

Eurasia, 229

Euripides, 137

Europe, *m*A2, *m*A9; colonial empires of, *m*404–405; economic growth during Renaissance, 350; imperialism and, 457; Marshall Plan and, 465; nationalism in, 456–457; Soviet Union and, 464–466; trade and, 323–325; unification of, *f*474; Western Europe, *f*336. *See also under specific countries of Europe*

European age of colonization, *f*400; causes of, 391; France and, 389; mercantilism and, 390; Netherlands and, 403; Portugal and, 389, 392–393, 395, 399; Spain and, 400–401

European Coal and Steel Community (ECSC), 465

European Community (EC), 465

European Economic Community (EEC), 465, 475

European Recovery Plan, 465

European Union (EU), 449, 475

Eusebius, 173

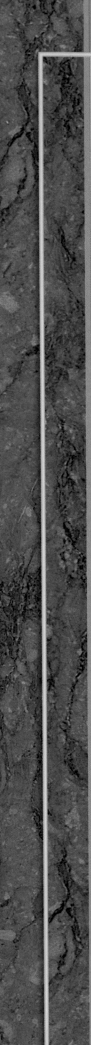

ization and, 462; since 1945, 466–467
Latium, 151
Latvia, mA2, mA9, 459
Lavoisier, Antoine-Laurent, 387
law: Code of Hammurabi, 36; English civil law, 222; Judaism, 46; juror's token, p115; Justinian Code, 222; Magna Carta, 306; proposal of, f35; Roman Republic, 153
Laws of Manu, 69
lay investiture, 303, 311
League of Nations, 459
Leakey, Mary, 4, p4, 7, f8
Lebanon, mA2, mA11, 41
Lee Kwan Yew, 471
Leeuwenhoek, Antoni van, 381, 386–387
Legalism, 91–92
legionnaires, 153, p153
Leo III (pope), 218, 226, 289–290, p290
Leo X (pope), 363, 364
Lenin, Vladimir Ilyich, 460
Lepanto, Battle of, 435
leprosy, 221
leveling (economic), 87–88
Lexington, Massachusetts, 452
Li Bo (Li Po), 267
library at Alexandria, 142
Libya, mA2, mA10, 462
Liebnitz, Gottfried, 386
Liliuokalani (queen of Hawaiian Islands), 457, f457, p457
limited constitutional monarchy, 452
limited evidence, 6
Lincoln, Abraham, 448
Lindisfarne Gospels, 301, f301, p301
linear B, 108
linen, 287
linguists, 184
Lion Temple (Kush), p187
Lisbon, 390, p390

literature, 476, ancient Greek, 136–137; drama, 332; fabliaux, 332; Indian, 56, 60, 70; of Islamic Empire, 253, 440; Italian Renaissance writers, 355–356; of Roman Empire, 167; of Tang dynasty, 267–268; troubadours and, 332; vernacular, 332–333
Lithuania, mA2, mA9, 234, 459
Liu Bang, 86–87
Liu Ch'e, 75, 87–88, f88, p88
Livy, 151
Loeffler, Reinhold, 245
loess, 78
Lombard League, 312
Lombards, 228, 289
Lombardy, 312
London, 328
Long March, 461
longbows, 336–337, p336
lord, 294–295, p294
Lorris, Guillaume de, 316
Lothair, 291
Louis VII (king of France), 306, 320
Louis XI (king of France), 338
Louis XIV (king of France), 450
Louis XVI (king of France), 453
Louis XVIII (king of France), 454
Louis the German, 291
Louis the Pious, 291
Lower Egypt, 22. See also Egypt, ancient
Loyola, Ignatius de, 368, 369–370
Lübeck, 323
Lucy, 7, f7
Luther, Martin, 353, 363, 364–365, f364, p364
Lutheran Church, 365
Lutheranism, 364–365
Luxembourg, mA2, mA9, 465

Lycurgus, 114
Lydians, 19, 43

Maastricht Treaty, 475
Macao, 417
MacArthur, Douglas, 468
Macbeth (Shakespeare), 361
Macedon, 121, 138–139, 141, 157
Machiavelli, Niccolò, 353, p353, 356
Madagascar, mA2, mA10, 185, 191
Madame Bovary (Flaubert), 448
Magadha, 68
Magellan, Ferdinand, 395, f395, p395, m396–397, p447
magistrates, Roman, 152
Magna Carta, 239, 306–307, f307
Magyars, 229, 292
Mahabharata, 60
Mahal, Mumtāz, 441
Mahavira, 258, p258. See also Vardhamana
Mahayana Buddhism, 65, 92, 282
Mahfouz, Naguib, 449
Malacca, 395
Malagasy, 185
Malawi, mA2, mA10, 472
Malay Peninsula, 395
Malaya, 471. See also Malaysia
Malaysia, mA2, mA11, 282, 470, 471
Mali, mA1, mA10, 181, 193, 194
Malinke, 194, 195
mammoths, 202
Manchu, 414
Manchuria, 76, 266, 269, 414, 461, 462
"Mandate of Heaven", 84
Mandela, Nelson, 472
Manetho, 23
Manhattan Island, 381, 403
manorial system, 297–299, 376; major characteristics of, 297

manorialism, 297. See also manorial system
Mansa Mūsā, 181, 194, f194
Manzikert, Battle of, 239, 247
Mao Zedong, 461, 469, p469
maps: basics of, 77; interpreting, 179; mapmaking, 388; Mercator projection map, 380, Muslims and, 251
Marcos, Ferdinand, 470
market economy, 465
Marshall Plan, 465
Marx, Karl, 455
Muslims, 251
Marathon, Battle of, p105, 121
Marcellinus, Ammianus, 164, 175
market days, 325
market economy, 326
markets, 325
Marlowe, Christopher, 361
marriage: arranged Muslim, 249; dowries and, 222; Indo-Aryan, 57
Marsalis, Wynton, p185
Martel, Charles, 289
martyrs, 170
Mary I (queen of England), 451, f451
Mary II (queen of England), 452
Mary Queen of Scots, 451
Masaccio, 358
masks: funeral, f22; queen mother of Benin, p181; theatrical, p137
mathematics: in ancient Egypt, 27; in ancient India, 71; Chaldeans and, 38; the Maya and, 209; in Middle Ages, 333–334; Muslims and, 252
Matilda of Tuscany, 311
matrilineal, 186
Mauritania, mA1, mA10, 193

Moscow, 234–235

Moses, *p*19, 44

Mosque of Córdoba, 238, *p*252

mosques, *p*194, *p*238, *p*241, 242, *p*245, 252–253, *p*431

motion, laws of, 385

Mount Kenya, 184

Mount Kilimanjaro, 184

Mount Sinai, *p*44

Mount Vesuvius, 149

movable type, 265, 270, 353, 359

Mozart, Wolfgang Amadeus, 381

Mu'awiyah, 244–245

Mughal Empire, 351, 431, 439–443, *m*440

Muhammad, 238, 241–243, *f*241, 246, 248, 252, 262, *f*262

mummification, 28

al-Muqaddasī, 322

Murad II (Ottoman sultan), 433

Murasaki Shikibu, Lady, 265, *p*265, 278

murex, 42

music, 476; African, 185, *f*185; Arab influence in Europe, 239; in Japan, 426; "troubadour" tradition in France, 287

Muslim Empire, *f*250, conquest of Syria, Palestine, and North Africa, 228

Muslim League, 471

Muslims, 242–255, *f*243, *f*248, 318–322, 338, 482

Mussolini, Benito, 460, *f*460

Myanmar, *m*A2, *m*A11, 65, 282, 470, 471. *See also* Burma

Mycenaeans, 104, 107–108, *p*108

Myron, 131

mystery plays, 332

mystery religions, 143

myths, *f*80, 98, 111, 214; creation myths, 200, 201

 **N**

NAFTA (North American Free Trade Agreement), 449, *p*449, 467, *f*467

Nagasaki, 403, 463

Nalanda, 71, *p*71

Namib Desert, 183

Nānak, 441

Nanjing, 413

Nanjing, Treaty of, 419

Nanna, 34

Napata, 187, 188

Naples, 355

Napoléon I. *See* Bonaparte, Napoléon (Napoléon I)

NASDAQ, 481

Nasser, Gamal Abdel, 473

National Socialist German Workers Party. *See* Nazi Party

nationalism, 461–462; in Africa, 472–473; Europe, 456, *f*456, 458; in Middle East, 472–473; Serbia and, 458

NATO (North Atlantic Treaty Organization), 465, 483

Native Americans: attempted enslavement of, 395; children, *f*205; creation myths of, 200, 201, *f*214; diseases from Europe, 401; European explorers and, 394; Spanish missionaries and, *p*406

natural philosophers, 382

nature gods, 231

navigation instruments, 388–389

navigation map, 380

Nazi Party, 460, 464

Neanderthals, 8

Nebuchadnezzar, 19, 38

Nehru, Jawaharlal, 471, *p*471

Neither Gods nor Emperors (Shen Tong), 469

Neman River, 229

Neo-Confucianism, 269

Neolithic Age, *p*4, 9, 10, 182. *See also* New Stone Age

Neolithic agricultural revolution, 8–10

Netherlands, *m*A2, *m*A9, 323; Calvinists and, 367, 403; colonial empire of, 403; Dutch East India Company, 403; economy and, 465; in Europe, 456, 458; in Indonesia, 470; in Middle East, 472–473; religious wars in, 371; revolt against Spain, 403; Serbia and, 458; society of, 403; stock exchange opens in, 353; war with France, 454

New Amsterdam, 403

New Deal, 460

New Economic Policy, 460

New Kingdom (Egypt), 24–25, *m*24

New Stone Age, 8, 9. *See also* Neolithic Age

New Testament, 169

New York City, 478, *p*478

New York Stock Exchange (NYSE), 449, 482

New Zealand, 461

Newton, Isaac, 385, 386

Nibelungenlied, *f*346

Nicaea, 171

Nicaragua, 467

Nicolas I (czar of Russia), 456

Nicolas II (czar of Russia), 456, 459

Niger River, 182

Nigeria, *m*A2, *m*A10, 184

Nika Revolt, 223

Nile River, 2, 20–21, *p*20, *m*21, 184, 200

Nile River valley: annual flooding of, 11, *p*11, 21, *m*21; natural resources of, 21. *See also* Egypt, ancient

Niña, 393

95 Theses, 353, 364, 366

Nineveh, 38

Nippur, 34

nirvana, 64, 65

Nixon, Richard, 474

Nkrumah, Kwame, 472

Nobel Peace Prize, 466

Nobel Prize for literature, 449

noblewoman, *f*298, *p*298

Noh play, 265, 280

nomads, 9, *p*79, 202

Noriega, Manuel, 467

Normandy, 293

North Africa, 174, 228, 243, 462, 472–473

North America, *m*A2, *m*A10; American Revolution, 452; Dutch colonization in, 403; Eastern Woodlands, 207; English colonial expansion in, 452; Great Plains, 199, 205; Northwest, 203; peoples of, *m*204, 206; Southwest, *c*203; Spanish settlements in, 401; Vikings and, 293. *See also* Americas.

North American Free trade Agreement. *See* NAFTA

North Atlantic Treaty Organization. *See* NATO

North Borneo, 471

North Korea, *m*A2, *m*A11, 470

northern Vietnam, 282, 470

Northumbria, 304, 305

Norway, *m*A2, *m*A9, 292

Notre Dame Cathedral, *p*317, 335, *p*335

Novgorod, 221, 230, 234

Novum Organum (Bacon), 386

Noye's Fludde, 332

Nubia, 24, 187

Nubians, 180

nuclear power, 474

numbers system: ancient Egyptian, 27; Arabic, 252

Nurhachi, 414

observatory, Maya, 199
Octavian (Augustus Caesar), 160, *f*160
Oda Nobunaga, 423, *f*423, 424
Odyssey (Homer), 110, 120
Oedipus Rex (Sophocles), 137
Office of Homeland Security, 482
Old Kingdom (Egypt), 18, 23
Old Stone Age, 7, 8
Olduvai Gorge, *p*4
Olmec, 198, 209
Olympic Games, 104, 111
On the Fabric of the Human Body (Vesalius), 385
OPEC (Organization of Petroleum Exporting Countries), 449, 473
opium trade, 418
Opium War, 419
oprichniki, 234
optics, 334
oracle bones, 82
oracles, 111
oral traditions, 184
orators, 139
Organization of African Unity, 472
Organization of Petroleum Exporting Countries. *See* OPEC
Orléans, House of, 337
Orthodox Christianity, 231
Orthodox Church, 234–235
Osaka, 427
Osiris, 27–28
Osman, 432
Ostrogoth kingdom, 220
Otto I (Otto the Great), 310
Ottoman Empire, 457; campaigns in Eastern and Central Europe, *m*445; decline of, 434–435; expansion of, 433, *m*433; govern-ment and society of, 434–435; Janissaries and, 432; millet sys-tem and, 434; rise of the Ottomans, 432–433; Spain and, 402; in World War I, 458, 459
Ottoman Turks: besiege Vienna, 453; building empire, 436, 447; con-quest of Constantinople, 228, *p*228; rise of, 228, 432. *See also* Ottoman Empire; Turks
overcrowding, 476
Ovid, 149, *p*149, 167, 214
Oxford, in Middle Ages, 333
oxygen, 387

Pacal, 199
Pacific Ocean, 395
Padua, 312
Paekche, 280
painting, *f*403; in ancient Greece, 131
Pakistan, 471, 483. See also Bangladesh; East Pakistan; West Pakistan
Palace of Chihil Soutoun, 351
Paleolithic Age, 7. *See also* Old Stone Age
Palestine, 169, 459, 473; conquest by Muslim Empire, 228; Crusades and, 318–322
Palestine Liberation Organization. *See* PLO
Pali Canon, 259
Pan-Africanism, *f*472
Panama, 467
Panchatantra ("Five Books"), 70
Panipat, 439
papacy, 171, 224, 371; Crusades and, 322; Holy Roman Empire and, 311; power in Middle Ages, *f*300, 301. *See also under specific popes*
Papal States, 289
paper, Chinese invention of, 75, 88, 95
papyrus, 95, *p*145
Parallel Lives (Plutarch), 114, 167
Pariahs, 61
Paris, in Middle Ages, 328, 333
Paris Peace Conference, 459
parish church, 300, 303, *f*303
Parliament, 307
Parliament of Paris, 308
Parmenides of Elea, 133
Parthenon, 130–131, *p*130, 132
Pataliputra, 67
Pate, 191
patriarch of Constantinople, 224, 226
patriarchs, 171
patricians, 153
Patrick, Saint, 302
Paul (Christian martyr), *p*170
Paul III (pope), 368–369, *p*368, 369
Paul IV (pope), 353, 368
Pax Romana, 160–161, 162–164
Peace of Augsburg, 353, 365
Pearl Harbor, 462, *p*462
peasants: Japanese, 280; Korean, 282; in medieval Europe, 297–298; Russian, 232, 233
pedagogue, 119
Peisistratus, 105, 117
Peloponnesian War, 124–125, *m*124
Peloponnesus, 108, 113
Pennsylvania: nuclear power accident in, 474; plane crash in 2001, 479
Pentagon, 478, 479
People's Action Party, 471
Pepin II (ruler of Franks), 289

Pepin III (Pepin the Short, king of Franks), 289
perestroika, 475
Pericles, 116, 117, 123–124, *f*123, *p*123, 125, 130
Perry, Matthew, 411, 426–427
persecution, coloniza-tion and, 391
Persia, 141, 243, 436–438, *m*437, 441, 461. *See also* Iran
Persian Empire, 39–40, *m*39, 44; attack of Egypt by, 25; decline of, 40; destruction by Alexander the Great, 140; government in, 39–40; Islamic con-quest of, 243; money economy, 43; Peloponnesian War, 125; Persian migration to East Africa, 191; Red Sea trade and, 190; religion in, 19, 40
Persian Gulf War, 473
Persian rugs, 438
Persian Wars, 105, 121–123, *m*122
perspective, in art, 356, 362
Peru: *m*A1, *m*A8; agricul-ture and, 202; Inca Empire and, 211, 401
Peter (Christian disciple), 171
Peter the Great (czar of Russia), 450
Petrarch, Francesco, 355–356, *f*355
phalanx, 138, *p*138
pharaohs, 22–25, 33. *See also under spe-cific names*
Pharaoh's People, 29
Phidias, 131
Philip (Habsburg emperor), 340
Philip II (king of France), 304, 308, 320–321
Philip II (king of Spain), 402, 435
Philip II of Macedon, 138–139

Forum and, *p*152; founding of, 148, 150–154; government of, 102, 151–152, 157; physical setting of, 150, *m*150; Punic Wars, 148, 155–157; slavery in, 157, 164; Twelve Tables of, 153; weakening of, 158–59

Romanesque architecture, 334

Romanov, Michael (czar of Russia), 450

Rome, 151, 355; as center of Christian church, 171; city of, 148; Germanic settlement in provinces of, 220; influence on Muslim culture, 250; Inquisition and, 368–369

Romeo and Juliet (Shakespeare), 361

Romulus and Remus, 151, *f*151

Roosevelt, Franklin D., 460

Rosetta Stone, 22

Rousseau, Jean-Jacques, 452

Royal Road, 40

rubber, 199

ruler-worship, 143

Rumsfeld, Donald, 483

Rurik, 230, *f*230

Rus, 230

Russia, *m*A2, *m*A11, 229–235; after collapse of Soviet Union, 475; China and, 419; Communist Party and, 459; economy of, *f*229; government in, *f*711; Kievan Russia, 230–232, *m*230, 233–234; Mongols and, 233–235, 273; Moscow, 234–235; nationalist movement in, 456; Romanov dynasty in, 450; setting and people, 229–230; in Triple Entente, 458; in World War I, 458–459. *See also* Soviet Union

Russian Orthodox Church, 234–235

Rwanda, 472

Sabah, 471. *See also* North Borneo

sacraments, 300

Sacred Books of the East, The (Mueller, ed.), 65

sacrifice, human, 42

Safavid Empire, 351, 431, 436–438

Safī od-Dīn, 436

Sahara, 181, 182, 183

Sahel, 182, 185

Sakaguchi Ango, 468

Saladin, 320, 321

salt, 193, 376

samurai, 219; feudal society and, 278, *p*278, 280; Tokugawa shogunate and, 424, *p*424, 425–426, 427; training of, *f*278

San Salvador, 393

Sanchi Stupa, *p*50, 51

Sanskrit, 56, 283

Santa Maria, 393

Sappho, 105, 119, *f*119, *p*119

Sappho: A New Translation (Bernard), 119

Sarawak, 471

Sardis, 40

Sargon, 18, 35

Saudi Arabia, *m*A2, *m*A11, *f*240, 483

Saul, 45

savannas, 182, 183

Saxons, 289, 304

Scandinavia, Vikings and, 292

scarab beetles, *p*18

Scheherazade, 253

scholar-gentry, 413

scholasticism, 334

science, 476; in ancient Egypt, 27; astronomy, 145; discoveries, *f*382; geography, 145; Islamic civilization and, 248; medical science, 145; in Middle Ages,

334; physics, 143–144; scientific method, 383, 386. *See also* Scientific Revolution

Science and Civilisation in China, 78

science fiction, 476

scientific method, 383

Scientific Revolution, 382–387, 542; anatomy, 385; astronomy, 383–385; chemistry, 387; mathematics, 383, 386; microscope, 386–387; nature study, 383; printing press and, 386, 387; scientific method and, 383, 386

scientific societies, 387

scientific thought, 135

Scipio (Roman general), 156

Scotland, *m*A9; Calvinists and, 367; independence from England, 287

scribes, 27, 359

sculpture, 131, *p*180, *p*181, *p*193

Sea Peoples, 25

sea traders, 115

Second Temple, *p*168

Secret History, The (Procopius), 225, 227

sects, 365

secular clergy, 301

Security Council (United Nations), 464

seismography, in ancient China, 95

Sejong (Korean emperor), *f*282, 284

Seljuq Turks, 228; and Crusades, 318–321

Senate, Roman, 102–103, 151

Seneca (Roman senator), 165

seppuku, 278

September 11 attacks, 478–482

sequence, understanding, 246

Serbia: nationalism and, 458; in World War I, 458

serfs, 328, 376

serpent mound, *p*207

Shah-nameh (Firdausi), *f*446

Shah's Peacock Throne, 443

Shakespeare, William, 359, *f*359, 361, *p*361, 381, *f*446, *p*446

Shang dynasty: area of rule, *m*80; astronomy and, 82; bronze casting in, *p*81; calendars in, 82; economy of, 81; fall of, 83; as first Chinese dynasty, 81; handicrafts of, 81; invasion of Huang River valley, 81; language and writing in, 82–83; religion in, 82; silk and, 81

Shangdi, 82

Shanghai, 414

sheikh, 240

Shen Tong, 469

Shepard, Alan, 476

Shi'ah, 244–245, 436, 443

Shinto religion, 277–278

Shipman, Pat, 17

ships: ancient Egyptian, 29; ancient Roman, *p*155; Arab, *p*248; European exploration and, 389; Korean, 410; Phoenician, *p*42; slave ships, 398, *p*398; Viking, 220, 229–230, *p*229

shires, 304

shogun, 219, 278–279

Shona, 192

Siam, 65, 282

Siberia, 234

Sic et Non (Abelard), 334

Sicily, 248, 310

Siddhartha (Hesse), 73

Siddhartha Gautama (Buddha), 51, 63–65, *f*63, 259, *f*259

Sidon, 41, 42

Sikh, 441

silk, 81, 220, 414, 416, *p*416, 435

Silk Road, 75, 88, 94

and, 140–141; conquest by Muslim Empire, 228, 247
Syrians, 44

table customs, 377
Tabrīz, 436
Tacitus, 167
Tahmāsp (shah of Safavid Empire), 437
taiga, 231
Taiping Rebellion, 421
Taiwan, *m*A2, *m*A11, 470
Taj Mahal, 431, 439, *f*439, 441, *p*441
Tale of Genji, The (Lady Murasaki Shikibu), 265, 278
Taliban regime, 482, 483
Tang (Shang leader), 81
Tang dynasty, 266–269, *m*268; art of, *p*264, *p*266; decline of, 269; influence on Japan, 278; Korea and, 281; literature and, 267–268; religion in, 269; Xi-an as capital of, 267
Tanzania, *m*A2, *m*A10, 4, 7, 191
tariffs, 390
Tāriq, 238, 245–246
Tartars, 272
taxation without representation, 452
tea: in China, 270, 411, 414; tea ceremony in Japan, 219, *p*219, 265, 280
technology, 476; exploration and, 388–389
telescope, *p*380, 383–384
Temple of Athena Nike, *p*215
Temple of the Great Jaguar, 199
Temple of Olympia, 131
Temujin. *See* Genghis Khan
Ten Commandments, *f*44, 45, 47
Tenochtitlán, 210, 400

Teotihuacán, 213
tepees, 205
terracing, 118
terra-cotta warriors, *p*75
terrorism, *f*478, 482–483
Tetzel, Johann, 363–364
texts, prehistoric, 5
Thailand, *m*A2, *m*A11, 65, 285, 470
Thales of Miletus, 133
theater: in ancient Greece, 136–137, *p*136; in ancient India, 70; in ancient Rome, 148, 165; Kabuki, 425; Noh play, 280
Thebes, 24, 125
Themistocles, 122
theocracy, 367
Theodora, 222–223, *f*223, *f*224, *p*224, 225, *p*225
Theodore Roosevelt (U.S. aircraft carrier), 483, *p*483
Theodosius (Roman emperor), 171
"Theory of Forms" (Plato), 134
Theravada, 65
Theravada Buddhism, 65, 283
thermometer, 383
Thermopylae, Battle of, 121
"third Rome", 235
Thirty Years' War, 450
Thousand and One Nights, The, 239, *p*239, 253
Thrace, 121
Thucydides, 116, 124, 136, *f*136
Thutmose III, 24
Tiananmen Square, 469, *p*469
Tiber River, 151
Tibet, 76, 269, 273
Tigris River, 11, 31
Tigris-Euphrates River valley, 31, 55
Tikal, 199
Timbuktu, 194–195
Timur (Turko-Mongol leader), 430, 432–433, 439

tithe, 302
Titian, 358, 369
tobacco, 350
Tokugawa Ieyasu, 423, *f*423
Tokugawa shogunate, 422–427, *m*422, 457
Tokyo, 423
Toledo, Spain, 248
toll roads, in England, 287
Toltec, 199, 210
Tonatiuh (Aztec sun god), 210
tools, 4, 7, 8, 10, 15, 202
Torah, 46, *p*46, 243, 257, *p*257
Tordesillas, Treaty of, 394
Toreador Fresco, The, *p*106
Tories, 451
totem poles, 203
Totman, Conrad, 278
Tours, Battle of, 238, 245
towns, 11, 50, *f*231, 323, 327–330
Toyotomi Hideyoshi (overlord of Japan), 423, *f*423
trade: Africa, 187, *f*187; in Aksum, 188; in Americas, 207; in ancient China, 75, 88, 94; in ancient Egypt, 29; in ancient Greece and East Africa, 181, 190, 191; in ancient Israel, 46; in ancient Japan, 280; in ancient Sumer, 34; in ancient world, *m*118; in Arabia, 238; articles of, 324; in Athens, 115; Babylonians and, 36, 38; banking and, 326; barter economy and, 325; British East India Company, 411, 418; Byzantine, 224; Crusades and, 320; culture and, 49; diet and, 376; during Hellenistic age, 142; European exploration and, 388, 393; favor-

able balance of trade, 390, 409; gold-for-salt, 193; India and, 51; Indo-Aryans, 50, 55, 59; international, *f*41; investing and, 326; Islamic culture of, 248; Kiev and Byzantine Empire, 230, *p*232; Kublai Khan and, 274; manufacturing and, 325; market days, 325; in Middle Ages, 312, 323–325, *f*325, 327; Mughal Empire and, 440; Persians and, 190; Phoenicians and, 41–42, *f*42; plague and, 330; Russian, 229; southern India and Rome, 51; Red Sea, 190; routes, 193, 230, 243, 323–324, *m*324; Silk Road and, 75, 88, 94; trading empires, 391; triangular trade, 398
tragedies (drama), in ancient Greece, 137
Transjordan, 459
transportation, 476
Travels of Marco Polo, The (Latham), 275
Treaty of Versailles, 459
triangular trade, 398
tribes, Mycenaean, 108
tribunes, 152
Trinity, 171
Triple Alliance, 458
Triple Entente, 458
triumvirate, 149, 159–160
Trojan War legend, 110
Trojan Women, The (Euripides), 137
tropical rain forests, 182–183. *See also* rain forests
troubadours, 287, 332
Troyes, Chrétien de, 287
Truman Doctrine, 465
Truman, Harry S., 463, 465
Tuareg, 195
Tudor dynasty, 317, *p*452. *See also under* specific monarchs

Acknowledgements

For permission to reprint copyrighted material, grateful acknowledgment is made to the following sources:

American Heritage Magazine, a division of Forbes Inc.: Quotes by Al-Bakri and Ibn Battuta from *The Horizon History of Africa*, edited by Alvin M. Josephy, Jr. Copyright © 1971 by American Heritage Publishing Co. Inc.

Columbia University Press: From "The Russian Law" from *Medieval Russian Laws*, translated by George Vernadsky. Copyright 1947 by Columbia University Press.

Grove/Atlantic, Inc.: From "A Song of War Chariots" by Du Fu, translated by Witter Bynner, and from "The Book of Songs" from *Anthology of Chinese Literature: From Early Times to the Fourteenth Century*, edited by Cyril Birch. Copyright © 1965 by Grove Press. Inc.

HarperCollins Publishers, Inc.: "No. 47. Without Even Going out the Door" from *The Essential Tao: An Initiation into the Heart of Taoism Through the Authentic Tao Te Ching and the Inner Teachings of Chuang-tzu*, translated by Thomas Cleary. Copyright © 1991 by Thomas Cleary.

David Higham Associates Ltd.: From *The Song of Roland*, translated by Dorothy L. Sayers (Penguin Classics, 1937). Copyright © 1957 by Executors of Dorothy L. Sayers. Originally published by Penguin Books Ltd.

National Geographic Society: From "Viking Trail East" by R. P. Jordan from *National Geographic*, March 1985. Copyright © 1985 by National Geographic Society.

Oxford University Press: From "The Period of Civil Wars" from *The Sumerians* by C. Leonard Woolley. Copyright 1928 by Oxford University Press.

Pantheon Books, a division of Random House, Inc.: From "The Jicarilla Genesis" from *American Indian Myths and Legends*, edited by Richard Erdoes and Alfonso Ortiz. Copyright © 1984 by Richard Erdoes and Alfonso Ortiz.

Penguin Books Ltd.: From *Utopia* by Thomas More, translated by Paul Turner. Copyright © 1965 by Paul Turner. From *The Peloponnesian War* by Thucydides, translation by Rex Warner (Penguin Classics, 1954). English translation copyright 1954 by Rex Warner. From "Julius Caesar" from *The Twelve Caesers* by Gaius Suetonius Tranquillus, translated by Robert Graves, revised with an introduction by Michael Grant. Copyright © 1957 by Robert Graves; copyright © 1979 by Michael Grant Publication Limited. From *Procopius: The Secret History*, translated by G. A. Williamson (Penguin Classics, 1966). Copyright © 1966 by G. A. Williamson.

University of California Press: From "Sleep, darling" from *Sappho: A New Translation* by Mary Barnard. Copyright © 1958 by The Regents of the University of California; copyright renewed © 1984 by Mary Barnard. From Part III, Chapter B "Sacrifice" from *The Vedic Experience*, edited and translated with introductions and commentary by Raimon Panikkar. Copyright © 1977 by the University of California Press.

The University of Chicago Press: From "The Fundamental Characteristics of European Feudalism" from *Feudal Society* by Marc Bloch, translated by L. A. Manyon. Copyright © 1961 by The University of Chicago Press. From "Eunomy" by Solon from *History of Western Civilization, Topic II*, pp. 5-9 by the University of Chicago College History Staff.

Sources Cited:

From "The Bucolic Mode" from *Pharaoh's People* by T. G. H. James. Published by Bodley Head Ltd., London, 1984.

From *The Tomb of Tutankhamen* by Howard Carter. Published by Cassell and Company Ltd., London, 1923.

From "Eastern Asia and Oceania: Mohenjo-Daro, Pakistan" from *The Atlas of Past Worlds: A Comparative Chronology of Human History 2000 BC-AD 1500* by John Manley. Published by Cassell Publishers Limited, London, 1993.

From "To Feed My People: The Coming of Corn—Zuñi" from *American Indian Mythology* by Alice Marriott and Carol K. Rachlin. Published by Thomas Y. Crowell Publishers, a division of HarperCollins Publishers, Inc, New York, 1968.

Quote by Carmelite cleric from "Half the World (1450-1750)" from *Crossroads of Civilization: 3000 Years of Persian History* by Clive Irving. Published by HarperCollins Publishers, Inc., New York, 1979.

From "Poets, Scholars, and Physicians" from *Islam, from the Prophet Mohammad to the Capture of Constaninople, Part II: Religion and Society*, edited and translated by Bernard Lewis. Published by HarperCollins Publishers, Inc., New York, 1974.

Quote from Bernabe Cobe's account regarding worship of the sun god from *Latin American Civilization: The Colonial Origins, Vol. 1, Third Edition* edited by Benjamin Keen. Published by Houghton Mifflin Company, Boston, 1974.

From granite inscription by Ezana, King of Aksum, from *An Introduction to the Economic History of Ethiopia from Early Times to 1800* by Richard Pankhurst. Published by Lalibela House, London, 1961.

From military account from "Events of the Year 932" from *The Baburnama: Memoirs of Babur, Prince and Emperor*, edited, translated and annotated by Wheeler M. Thackston. Published by Oxford University Press, New York, 1996.

From "Book One" from *Livy, The History of Early Rome*, translated by Aubrey de Sélincourt. Published by Penguin Books Ltd., London, 1960.

Quote by Ammianus Marcellinus, translated by W. Hamilton from "The Huns" from *Readings in the Classical Historians*, selected and introduced by Michael Grant. Published by Scribner, a division of Simon & Schuster, New York, 1992.

From Native American myth regarding the disappearance of the Paleo-Indians from "The Big Game Vanishes" from *Kingdoms of Gold, Kingdoms of Jade: The Americas Before Columbus* by Brian M. Fagan. Published by Thames & Hudson Ltd., London, 1991.

From *Dao de Jing* by Laozi and quote by Legalist Han Fei Tzu from *Chinese Thought: From Confucius to Mao Tso-Tung* by Herrlee G. Creel. Published by The University of Chicago Press, 1953.

From writing on an ancient clay tablet from "The First Case of Juvenile Delinquency" from *The Sumerians* by Samuel Noah Kramer. Published by The University of Chicago Press, 1963.

From "Paris During the Hundred Years' War" from *The Portable Medieval Reader*, edited by James Bruce Ross and Mary M. McLaughlin. Published by Viking Penguin, a division of Penguin Putnam Inc., New York, 1949.

From poem from *Shang Civilization* by Kwang-Chih Chang. Published by Yale University Press, New Haven, 1980.

Exodus 20:1–7, Ezekiel 27:32–33, and *Luke 6:20-22* from *The Holy Bible, New International Version.* Published by Zondervan Bible Publishers, Grand Rapids, MI, 1984.

Photo Credits

Positions are shown in abbreviated form as follows: t-top, b-bottom, c-center, l-left, r-right.

v (l) Erich Lessing/Art Resource, NY, (r) Dilip Mehta/Woodfin Camp & Associates; vi (l) George Grigoriou/Stone, (c) The Michael C. Rockefeller Memorial Collection/Gift of Nelson A. Rockefeller, 1972/Metropolitan Museum of Art; vi-vii Leo Keeler/Animals Animals; vii (c) Paul Dupuy Museum, Toulouse, France/Lauros-Giraudon, Paris/ SuperStock, (r) Bildarchiv Steffens/Bridgeman Art Library; viii (l) Gail Mooney/Corbis, (c) Alinari/Art Resource, NY; viii-ix Werner Forman Archive/Art Resource, NY; ix (cl) Bonhams, London, UK/Bridgeman Art Library, (cr) Magdalen College, Oxford/Bridgeman Art Library, (r) Dave G. Houser/Corbis; x (t) Palubniak Studios, (c) Salim Amin/Camerapix Ltd, Kenya, (b) Scala/Art Resource, NY; xi Gianni Dagli Orti/Corbis; xii Gable/Sylvia Cordaiy Photo Library; xiii (tl) Bojan Brecelj/Corbis, (tr) The British Museum, (cr) Dagli Orti/Musee du Chateau de Versailles/The Art Archive, (bl) Eileen Tweedy/Victoria & Albert Museum London/The Art Archive, (br) Werner Forman Archive/Art Resource, NY; xiv (l) Pix 2000/FPG International, (r) Werner Forman Archive/Art Resource, NY; xvi Elio Ciol/Corbis; xix HRW Photo; xxiii (t) Michael Dibari Jr./AP/Wide World Photo, (b) E. Rooraid/PhotoEdit, (frame) MetaTools; xxiv (t) Erich Lessing/Art Resource, NY, (bl) Réunion des Musées Nationaux/Bridgeman Art Library, (br) Werner Forman Archive/Treasury of St. Mark's, Venice/Art Resource, NY; xxv (t) Réunion des Musées Nationaux/Art Resource, NY, (b) HRW Photo; xxvi Hugh Sitton/Stone; S01 (l) Dagli Orti/Musée du Chateau de Versailles/The Art Archive, (r) David Parker/Science Photo Library/Photo Researchers; S02 (t) Scala/Art Resource, NY, (b) Laurie Platt Winfrey/Woodfin Camp & Associates; S03 (t) North Wind Picture Archives, (bl) Bettmann/Corbis, (br) HRW Photo; S04, S05, S06 (t, b), S08 (t, c) HRW Photo; S08 (b) AKG London; S09 S12, S14 HRW Photo; v-1 Sisse Brimberg/NGS Image Collection, (b) Corbis; 2 (l) Courtesy Mammoth Site Museum, Hot Springs, SD, (r) Scala/Art Resource, NY; 3 (tl) Scala/Art Resource, NY, (tr) Werner Forman Archive/Art Resource, NY, (bl) Joseph Needham (Science and Civilisation in China, Vols 1-6, Cambridge University Press), (br) Genius of China Exhibition/ The Art Archive; 4 (tr) Shelly Grossman/Woodfin Camp & Associates, (rc) Archivo Iconographico, S.A./Corbis, (bl) Robert Campbell/ NGS Image Collection, (br) Martha Avery/Asian Art & Archaeology, Inc./Corbis; 5 (tl) Erich Lessing/Art Resource, NY, (tr) Erich Lessing/Art Resource, NY, (b) Richard T. Nowitz/Corbis; 6 Nik Wheeler/Corbis; 7 Dr. Owen Lovejoy and students, Kent State University. Photo © 1985 David L. Brill; 8 R. Sheridan/Ancient Art & Architecture Collection; 10 Zafer Kizilkaya/Atlas Geographic; 11 Paul Almasy/Corbis; 14 Winfield I. Parks/NGS Image Collection; 15 Sisse Brimberg/NGS Image Collection; 17 Gianni Dagli Orti/Corbis; 18 (tl) Gianni Dagli Orti/Corbis, (tr) Erich Lessing/ Art Resource, NY, (b) Gianni Dagli Orti/Corbis;19 (t) Dagli Orti/Archaeological Museum Spalato/The Art Archive, (bl) AKG London, (br) Gianni Dagli Orti/Corbis; 20 Robert Caputo/Stock Boston/ PictureQuest; 22 Pix 2000/FPG International; 23 Jim Zuckerman/Corbis; 24 (t) Carmen Redondo/Corbis, (b) Erich Lessing/Art Resource, NY; 25 Erich Lessing/Art Resource, NY, 26 Hugh Sitton/Stone; 27 (t) Zefa/H. Armstrong Roberts, (b) Scala/Art Resource, NY; 28 (l) The British Museum/DK Images, (r) Harvey Lloyd/FPG International; 29 Erich Lessing/Art Resource, NY; 31 Gianni Dagli

Orti/Corbis; 32 Nik Wheeler; 33 (t) Hulton-Deutsch Collection/ Corbis, (b) Ronald Sheridan/Ancient Art & Architecture Collection; 34 (t) The British Museum/Compass, (b) Gianni Dagli Orti/Corbis; 36 Gianni Dagli Orti/Corbis; 37 Dagli Orti/Musée du Louvre, Paris/The Art Archive; 40 Hulton Archive by Getty Images; 42 (t) Dagli Orti/The British Museum/The Art Archive, (b) Ronald Sheridan/Ancient Art & Architecture Collection; 43 (l, c) Scala/Art Resource, NY, (r) Erich Lessing/Art Resource, NY; 44 O. Alamany & E. Vicens/Corbis; 46 Gene Plaisted, OSC, The Crosiers; 47 R. Sheridan/Ancient Art & Architecture Collection; 50 (t) Angelo Hornak/ Corbis, (bl) Archivo Iconografico, S.A./Corbis; 50-51 Christophe Boisvieux/Corbis; 51 (tl) Victoria & Albert Museum, London/Art Resource, NY, (tr) Jeremy Horner/Corbis; 53 Paul Almasy/Corbis; 54 (t) Archivo Iconografico, S.A./Corbis, (b) Robert Harding/Corbis; 55 Dilip Mehta/Woodfin Camp & Associates; 57 Scala/Art Resource, NY; 59 Gable/Sylvia Cordaiy Photo Library; 60 Luca I. Tettoni/Corbis; 61 Peter Baker/Leo de Wys ; 62 (t) Erich Lessing/Art Resource, NY, (b) Reuters NewMedia Inc./Corbis; 64 Bill Gallery/Viesti Associates; 67 Hulton Archive by Getty Images; 69 Dagli Orti/Biblioteca Nazionale Marciana Venice/The Art Archive; 70 Alison Wright/The Image Works; 71 (b) Imtiaz Dharkas/The Image Works, (t) Lindsay Hebberd/Woodfin Camp & Associates; 73 Diego Lezama Orezzoli/Corbis; 74 (tl) Philadelphia Museum of Art/Corbis, (tr) Dagli Orti/The Art Archive, (b) O. Louis Mazzatenta/NGS Image Collection; 75 (b) Dennis Cox/ChinaStock, (tl) Werner Forman Archive/Art Resource, NY, (tr) Werner Forman Archive/Art Resource, NY, (c) Martha Avery/Asian Art & Archaelology, Inc./Corbis; 76 Wang Lu/ChinaStock; 77 Dennis Cox/ChinaStock; 78 Julia Waterlow/Eye Ubiquitous/Corbis; 79 Michel Setboun/Stone; 81 Freer Gallery of Art, Smithsonian Institution, Washington, D.C.; 82 The British Museum/ Bridgeman Art Library; 83 British Museum/ Bridgeman Art Library; 84 Wang Lu/ChinaStock; 86 Bibliothèque Nationale, Paris/The Art Archive; 87 Giraudon/Art Resource, NY; 88 (l) Wan-go Weng/National Palace Museum, Taipei, (r) Ancient Art & Architecture Collection; 89 The British Museum/The Art Archive; 90 Bibliothèque Nationale, Paris/Bridgeman Art Library, London/ SuperStock; 91 Giraudon/Art Resource, NY; 92 Dennis Cox/ChinaStock; 93 Keren Su/Corbis; 94 Bob Rowan/ Progressive Image/Corbis; 95 Dennis Cox/ChinaStock; 98 (l) Dagli Orti/ Archaeological Museum Aleppo/The Art Archive, (r) Angelo Hornak/Corbis; 99(t) Robert E. Murowchick/Photo Researchers, (bowl) Erich Lessing/Art Resource, NY, (tools) Gianni Dagli Orti/Corbis; 100-101 Scala/Art Resource, NY; 101 (b) Borromeo/Art Resource, NY; 102 (tl) Araldo de Luca/Corbis, (tr) John Hios/AKG London; 102-103 (b) Scala/Art Resource, NY; 103 (t) Fitzwilliam Museum, University of Cambridge, UK/Bridgeman Art Library, (cr) North Carolina Museum of Art/Corbis, (cl) Werner Forman Archive/Art Resource, NY; 104 (tl) Archaeological Museum of Heraklion, Crete, Greece/ Bridgeman Art Library, (tc, tr) Ashmolean Museum, Oxford, UK/Bridgeman Art Library, (b) National Archaeological Museum, Athens, Greece/Bridgeman Art Library; 105 (tl) Scala/Art Resource, NY, (tr) Scala/Art Resource, NY, (b) Erich Lessing/Art Resource, NY; 106 National Archaeological Museum, Athens, Greece/Bridgeman Art Library; 108 (l) National Archaeological Museum, Athens, Greece/Bridgeman Art Library, (r) Archaeological Museum of Chora, Greece/Bridgeman Art Library; 109 SEF/Art Resource, NY; 111 (t) SuperStock, (b) Walter Schmid/Stone; 112 Gianni Dagli Orti/Corbis; 113 Gian Berto Vanni/Art Resource, NY; 114 Robert Harding/ Corbis; 115 The Brooklyn Museum, Charles Wilbour Fund; 116 Phyllis Picardi/ Stock South/PictureQuest; 119 Erich Lessing/ Art Resource, NY; 120 The British Museum, London, UK/Bridgeman Art Library; 121 Wolfgang Kaehler; 123 (t) Scala/Art Resource, NY, (b) George Grigoriou/Stone; 125 Nimatallah/Art Resource, NY ; 127 Ashmolean Museum, Oxford, UK/Bridgeman Art Library; 128 (t) Private Collection, Milan/Canali PhotoBank Milan/SuperStock, (bl) Gian Berto Vanni/Corbis, (br) Yann Arthus-Bertrand/Corbis; 129 (tl) Réunion des Musées Nationaux/Art Resource, NY, (tr) Erich Lessing/Art Resource, NY, (b) Jeremy Horner/Corbis; 130 Charles O'Rear/Corbis; 131 National Museum, Athens/Art Resource, NY; 132 Scala/Art Resource, NY; 134 (t) Museo Archeologico Nazionale, Naples/Bridgeman Art Library, (b) Roger-Viollet, Paris/Bridgeman Art Library; 136 Scala/Art Resource, NY; 137 The Lowe Art Museum, The University of Miami/SuperStock; 138 Bettmann/Corbis; 139 Fitzwilliam Museum, University of Cambridge/ Bridgeman Art Library; 140 Erich Lessing/Art Resource, NY; 141 (t) Art Resource, NY, (b) Staatliche Glypothek, Munich, Germany/ET Archive, London/ SuperStock; 142 Michael Holford; 143 Erich Lessing/Art Resource, NY; 145 Réunion des Musées Nationaux/Art Resource, NY; 151 AKG London; 152 VCG/FPG International; 153 (t) Erich Lessing/Art Resource, NY, (b) Erich Lessing/Art Resource, NY; 154 Erich Lessing/Art Resource, NY; 155 Scala/Art Resource, NY; 157 Réunion des Musées Nationaux/Art Resource, NY; 159 Giraudon/Art Resource, NY; 160 Robert Emmett Bright/Photo Researchers; 161 Bettmann/Corbis; 162 (t) Florence Bargello/ Bridgeman Art Library, (bl) National Musems of Scotland/Bridgeman Art Library, (br) Victoria & Albert Museum, London/Art Resource, NY; 164 Archivo Iconografico, S.A./Corbis; 165 Roger Wood/Corbis; 166 Jose Fuste Raga/Corbis Stock Market; 167 Index/Bridgeman Art Library; 168 Scala/Art Resource, NY; 169, 170, 171 Gene Plaisted, OSC/The Crosiers; 172 Scala/Art Resource, NY; 173 Robert Frerck/Stone; 175 Courtesy The Bancroft Library; 176 (t) Archäologisches Landesmuseum der Christian-Albrechts-Universität, Schloss Gottorf, Schleswig, Germany, (b) Elio Ciol/Corbis; 177 Dallas

and John Heaton/Corbis; 180 (t) Mike Yamashita/Woodfin Camp & Associates, (bl) Stephen Studd/Stone, (br) The British Museum, London/Bridgeman Art Library/SuperStock; 181 (tl) MIT Collection/Corbis, (tr) The Michael C. Rockefeller Memorial Collection/Gift of Nelson A. Rockefeller, 1972, Metropolitan Museum of Art, (b) Réunion des Musées Nationaux/Art Resource, NY; 184 (t) Gallo Images/Corbis, (b) M & E Bernheim/ Woodfin Camp & Associates; 185 (t) Boltin Picture Library, (b) Ebet Roberts; 186 Trip/M Jelliffe/The Viesti Collection; 187 Mike Yamashita/Woodfin Camp & Associates; 189 (l, c, r) Werner Forman Archive/Art Resource, NY; 190 Salim Amin/Camerapix Ltd, Kenya; 191 Cordaiy Photo Library Ltd./Corbis; 192 Barbara Maurer/Stone; 193 Museum of Mankind, London/Bridgeman Art Library; 194 (t) Giraudon/Art Resource, NY, (b) Sandro Vannini/Corbis; 195 Dagli Orti/Musée des Arts Africains et Océaniens/The Art Archive; 198 (t) Kevin Schafer/Corbis, (bl) Runk/Schoenberger/Grant Heilman Photography, (br) PhotoDisc, Inc.; 199 (t) Dr. S. Coyne/ Ancient Art & Architecture Collection, (bl) Patti Murray/Earth Scenes, (br) Courtesy, National Museum of the American Indian, Smithsonian Institution (T189306). Photo by David Heald.; 200 Tom McHugh/Photo Researchers; 202 Werner Forman Archive/Art Resource, NY; 203 Wild Country/Corbis; 205 Leo Keeler/Animals Animals; 206 (totem pole) HRW Photo, (salmon, evergreens) Corbis, (buffalo) Courtesy Department of Library Services, American Museum of Natural History, (cactus, acorns) PhotoDisc, Inc., (clovis points) Steve Elmore/Tony Stone/AllStock, (corn) HRW Photo by Sam Dudgeon, (r) Johan Adlercreutz/Ancient Art & Architecture Collection; 207 Richard A. Cooke/Corbis; 209 Jose Fuste Raga/Corbis Stock Market; 210 (t) Werner Forman Archive/National Museum of Anthropology, Mexico City/Art Resource, NY, (b) Ancient Art & Architecture Collection; 211 Stephen L. Alvarez/NGS Image Collection; 213 Bettmann/Corbis; 214 (l) AKG London, (r) Werner Forman Archive/Art Resource, NY; 215 (r) Werner Forman Archive/Art Resource, NY, (l) Erich Lessing/Art Resource, NY; 216-217 Burstein Collection/Corbis; 217 (b) Victoria & Albert Museum, London/Art Resource, NY; 218 (l) Andrea Jemolo/Corbis, (bl) Bojan Brecelj/Corbis, (cr) The British Museum; 219 (t) Peter M. Wilson/Corbis, (bl) Dagli Orti/The Art Archive, (br) Paul Almasy/Corbis; 220 (l) Church of San Vitale, Ravenna, Italy/Canali PhotoBank, Milan/SuperStock, (r) British Library, London, UK/Bridgeman Art Library; 221 (tl) The British Museum, London, UK/Bridgeman Art Library, (tr) Scala/Art Resource, NY, (b) Erich Lessing/Art Resource, NY; 222 Werner Forman Archive/Treasury of St. Mark's, Venice/Art Resource, NY; 224 Scala/Art Resource, NY; 225 (t) Church of San Vitale, Ravenna, Italy/Canali PhotoBank, Milan/SuperStock, (b) Church of San Vitale, Ravenna, Italy/Canali PhotoBank, Milan/SuperStock; 226 Jose F. Poblete/ Corbis; 227 Robert Frerck/Stone; 228 Scala/Art Resource, NY; 229 Werner Forman Archive/Art Resource, NY; 231 Bridgeman Art Library; 232 Giraudon/Art Resource, NY; 233 Art Resource, NY; 234 Tretjakov Gallery, Moscow/AKG London; 235 Geoff Johnson/Stone; 238 (tl) Giraudon/Art Resource, NY, (tr) Owen Franken/ Corbis, (b) Sylvain Grandadam/Stone; 239 (tl) AKG London, (tr) Dagli Orti/National Museum Damascus, Syria/The Art Archive, (b) Réunion des Musées Nationaux/Art Resource, NY; 241 Nabeel Turner/Stone; 245 (t) Printed by permission from the International Association of Sufism, (b) SuperStock; 246 (t, l) AKG London, (r) Werner Forman Archive/Art Resource, NY; 246 (b) Reprinted courtesy the Rare Book Department, The Free Library of Philadelphia, Philadelphia, PA; 247 Bibliothèque Nationale, Paris, France/Bridgeman Art Library; 248 Sonia Halliday Photographs; 249 Bibliothèque Nationale, Paris/AKG Berlin/SuperStock; 250 (t) Giraudon/Art Resource, NY, (b) Roland & Sabrina Michaud/Woodfin Camp & Associates; 251 (l) Roland & Sabrina Michaud/Woodfin Camp & Associates, (r) Paul Dupuy Museum, Toulouse, France/Lauros-Giraudon, Paris/SuperStock; 252 (t) Bridgeman Art Library, (b) Index/ Bridgeman Art Library; 253 Dreweatt Neate Fine Art Auctioneers, Newbury, Berkshire, UK/Bridgeman Art Library; 255 Archivo Iconografico, S. A./Corbis; 257 (tl) Lisa Quinones/Black Star Publishing/ PictureQuest, (tc) Jewish Museum, London/Bridgeman Art Library, (tr) Scala/Art Resource, NY, (c) Richard Nowitz/Words & Pictures/ PictureQuest, (b) Annie Griffiths Belt/Corbis; 258 (tl) Dinodia/Trip Photo Library, (tc) Milind A. Ketkar/ Dinodia Picture Agency, (tr) Mark Downey/Viesti Associates, Inc., (c) Lindsay Hebberd/Corbis, (b) Gian Berto Vanni/Corbis; 259 (tl) AFP/Corbis, (tc) Luca I. Tettoni/Corbis, (tr) Josef Beck/FPG International, (cl) SOA/Dinodia, (b) ML Sinibaldi/Corbis Stock Market; 260 (tl) Bridgeman Art Library, (tc) Bohemian Nomad Picturemakers/Corbis, (tr) Courtesy of Information Division, Taipei Economic and Cultural Office in Chicago, (c) Alan Thornton/ Stone, (b) Courtesy of Information Division, Taipei Economic and Cultural Office in Chicago; 261 (tl) Scala/Art Resource, NY, (tc) PhotoDisc, Inc., (tr) Erich Lessing/Art Resource, NY, (c) Elio Ciol/Corbis, (b) Mark Thiessen/Corbis; 262 (tl) Ronald Sheridan/Ancient Art & Architecture Collection, (tc) Werner Forman Archive/Art Resource, NY, (tr) Bonhams, London/Bridgeman Art Library, (c) AFP/Corbis, (b) Reuters NewMedia Inc./Corbis; 263 Gael Cornier/ AP/Wide World Photos; 264 (t) Erich Lessing/Art Resource, NY, (bl) Victoria & Albert Museum, London/Art Resource, NY, (br) British Library, London/Bridgeman Art Library; 265 (t) Sakamoto Photo Research Laboratory/ Corbis, (bl) The Art Archive, (br) Michael Bodycomb/Kimbell Art Museum/Corbis; 266 Musée Guimet, Paris, France/Lauros-Giraudon, Paris/SuperStock; 267 Liu Xiasyang/ChinaStock; 269 The British Library/The Art Archive; 271 (t) The Metropolitan Museum of Art,

A.W. Bahr Collection, Fletcher Fund, 1947. (47.18.1) Photography © 1978 The Metropolitan Museum of Art, (b) Photograph Courtesy Peabody Essex Museum; 272 Werner Forman Archive/ Art Resource, NY; 274 (t) National Palace Museum, Taiwan/ET Archive, London/SuperStock, (b) Giraudon/ Art Resource, NY; 275 Bibliothèque Nationale, Paris, France/Bridgeman Art Library; 276 Janette Ostier Gallery, Paris, France/Giraudon, Paris/SuperStock; 278 Werner Forman Archive/ Victoria & Albert Museum, London/Art Resource, NY; 280 Chris Lisle/Corbis; 281 Ronald Sheridan/Ancient Art & Architecture Collection; 282 Boltin Picture Library; 283 (t) Dan McCoy/Rainbow/PictureQuest, (b) Pictor International/Pictor International, Ltd./PictureQuest; 286 (t) Dagli Orti/University Library Heidelberg/ The Art Archive, (bl) Eirik Irgens Johnsen/University Museum of National Antiquities, Oslo, Norway, (br) The Pierpont Morgan Library/Art Resource, NY; 287 (t) Musée de la Tapisserie, Bayeux, France/Bridgeman Art Library, (bl) Bibliothèque Nationale, Paris/AKG London, (br) Erich Lessing/Art Resource, NY; 288 Pierre Belzeaux/Photo Researchers; 289 (t) AKG London, (b) Bildarchiv Steffens/ Bridgeman Art Library; 290 Giraudon/Bridgeman Art Library; 293 Knudsens-Giraudon/Art Resource, NY; 294 Bettmann/Corbis; 295 (t) AKG London, (b) Robert W. Madden/National Geographic Image Collection; 297 Bridgeman Art Library/SuperStock; 298 Bibliothèque Nationale, Paris/AKG London; 299 (l) The Pierpont Morgan Library/Art Resource, NY, (r) New York Public Library/Art Resource, NY; 300 AKG London; 301 British Library/Bridgeman Art Library; 302 Michael Teller/AKG London; 303 Dagli Orti/The Art Archive; 304 Winchester Cathedral, Hampshire, UK/Bridgeman Art Library; 305 Michael Freeman/Corbis; 306 Bettmann/Corbis; 309 AKG London; 310 Erich Lessing/Art Resource, NY; 311, 312 AKG London; 313 Harper Collins Publishers/The British Library/The Art Archive; 316 (t) Archivo Iconografico, S.A./Corbis, (bl) Erich Lessing/Art Resource, NY, (br) The British Library/The Art Archive; 317 (tl) Bibliothèque Royale de Belgique, Brussels, Belgium/Bridgeman Art Library, (tr) Réunion des Musées Nationaux/Art Resource, NY, (b) Bill Bachmann/Index Stock Imagery/PictureQuest; 318 Bridgeman Art Library; 320 Bibliothèque Nationale, Paris, France/Bridgeman Art Library; 322 Ancient Art & Architecture Collection; 325 Giraudon/Art Resource, NY; 326 British Library, London/ Bridgeman Art Library, London/SuperStock; 328 Victoria & Albert Museum, London/Art Resource, NY; 329 Mary Evans Picture Library; 330 Giraudon/Art Resource, NY; 331 Giraudon/Art Resource, NY; 332 Archivo Iconografico, S.A./Corbis; 333 (t) Mary Evans Picture Library, (b) Archivo Iconografico, S.A./Corbis; 334 Archivo Iconografico, S.A./Corbis; 335 (t) Mimmo Jodice/Corbis, (b) Massimo Listri/Corbis; 336 Bibliothèque Nationale, Paris/AKG London; 338 Christie's Images/Corbis; 340 Dagli Orti/Musée du Chateau de Versailles/The Art Archive; 341 Giraudon/Art Resource, NY; 342 Gail Mooney/Corbis; 343 Dagli Orti/University Library Prague/The Art Archive; 346 (l) Archivo Iconografico, S.A./Corbis, (r) Eileen Tweedy/Victoria & Albert Museum London/The Art Archive; 347 (t) Dagli Orti/Tiroler Landesmuseum, Innsbruck/The Art Archive, (cl) von Linden/AKG London, (cr) Dagli Orti/The Art Archive; 348-349 Library of Congress, Washington D.C./Bridgeman Art Library; 349 Eileen Tweedy/The Art Archive; 350 (tl) Alinari/Art Resource, NY, (tr) Victoria & Albert Museum/Art Resource, NY, (b) Erich Lessing/Art Resource, NY; 351 (t) Royal Ontario Museum/Corbis, (bl) Dagli Orti/Palace of Chihil Soutoun Isfahan/The Art Archive, (br) Victoria & Albert Museum, London/Bridgeman Art Library; 352 (t) Dagli Orti/Galleria degli Uffizi Florence/The Art Archive, (b) Gary Yeowell/Stone; 353 (tl) Bettmann/Corbis, (tr) Réunion des Musées Nationaux/Art Resource, NY, (b) Scala/Art Resource, NY; 355 Ali Meyer/Bridgeman Art Library; 356 Musée Des Beaux-Arts de Lille, Jardin du Muss/Giraudon/Art Resource, NY; 357 (t) Scala/Art Resource, NY, (b) Araldo de Luca/Corbis; 358 Réunion des Musées Nationaux/Art Resource, NY; 359 The Pierpont Morgan Library/Art Resource, NY; 360 Erich Lessing/Art Resource, NY; 361 (t) Art Resource, NY, (bl, br) Scala/Art Resource, NY; 362 Erich Lessing/Art Resource, NY; 363 The Art Archive; 364 Scala/Art Resource, NY; 365 Index/ Bridgeman Art Library; 366 Belvoir Castle, Leicestershire/Bridgeman Art Library; 367 British Library, London/Bridgeman Art Library; 368 Erich Lessing/Art Resource, NY; 369 Giraudon/Art Resource, NY; 371 Bridgeman Art Library; 372 Peter Willi/Bridgeman Art Library; 373 Bridgeman Art Library; 374 Kunsthistorisches Museum, Vienna, Austria/Bridgeman Art Library; 376 (t) Phillips, The International Fine Art Auctioneers, UK/Bridgeman Art Library, (b) Francis G. Mayer/Corbis; 377 Giraudon/Art Resource, NY; 379 Eilo Ciol/Corbis; 380 (tl) Corbis, (tr) Dagli Orti/The Art Archive, (b) Scala/Art Resource, NY; 381 (tl) Dave Bartruff/Corbis, (tr) Bettmann/Corbis, (bl) Library of Congress, Washington D.C., USA/Bridgeman Art Library, (br) Bettmann/Corbis; 382 Scala/Art Resource, NY; 383 (t) Erich Lessing/Art Resource, NY, (b) Alinari/Art Resource, NY; 384 Scala/Art Resource, NY; 385 Nimatallah/Art Resource, NY; 386 Sheila Terry/Science Photo Library/Photo Researchers; 387 Giraudon/Art Resource, NY; 388 Réunion des Musées Nationaux/Bridgeman Art Library; 389 David Parker/Science Photo Library/Photo Researchers; 390 Lauros-Giraudon/Bridgeman Art Library; 391 PhotoDisc, Inc.; 393 (l) Bettmann/Corbis; 393 (r) Bridgeman Art Library; 395 Royal Geographical Society, London/Bridgeman Art Library; 398 Bettmann/Corbis; 400 Historical Picture Archive/Corbis; 401 Bettmann/Corbis; 402 Francis G. Mayer/Corbis; 403 Francis G. Mayer/Corbis; 406 (l) Art Resource, NY, (r) Museum of the City of New York/Corbis; 407 Archivo Iconografico,

S.A./Corbis; 410 (t) Grafica/Pacific Stock, (b) Werner Forman Archive/Art Resource, NY; 411 (tl) Richard Powers/Corbis, (tr) Paul Freeman/Bridgeman Art Library, (b) Fitzwilliam Museum/ University of Cambridge, UK/Bridgeman Art Library; 413 Pierre Colombel/Corbis; 414 Stock Montage; 415 Victoria & Albert Museum, London/Art Resource, NY; 416 Archivo Iconografico, S.A./Corbis; 417 Royal Geographical Society, London/Bridgeman Art Library; 418 (t) AKG London, (b) Paul Freeman/Bridgeman Art Library; 419 Hulton-Deutsch Collection/Corbis; 421 Historical Picture Archive/Corbis; 423 (t) The Art Archive, (b) Palubniak Studios; 424 Victoria & Albert Museum, London/Art Resource, NY; 425 Réunion des Musées Nationaux/Art Resource, NY; 426 Palubniak Studios; 427 The British Museum/Bridgeman Art Library; 430 (t) Victoria & Albert Museum, London/Art Resource, NY, (bl) Eileen Tweedy/Victoria & Albert Museum, London/The Art Archive; 430 (br) Erich Lessing/Art Resource, NY; 431 (tl) Magdalen College, Oxford/Bridgeman Art Library, (tr) Bonhams, London, UK/Bridgeman Art Library, (bl) Madar-i-Shah Madrasa, Isfahan, Iran/Bridgeman Art Library, (br) Bibliothèque Nationale, Paris, France/ Bridgeman Art Library; 432 Dagli Orti/Topkapi Museum Istanbul/The Art Archive; 434 (t) Erich Lessing/AKG London, (b) Giraudon/Art Resource, NY; 435, 436 Ronald Sheridan/Ancient Art & Architecture Collection; Ronald Sheridan/Ancient Art & Architecture Collection; 438 Bonhams, London, UK/Bridgeman Art Library; 439 The British Library/The Art Archive; 441 Chris Haigh/Stone; 442 Chester Beatty Library & Gallery of Oriental Art, Dublin/ Bridgeman Art Library; 443 Metropolitan Museum of Art, New York/Bridgeman Art Library; 446 (l) Werner Forman Archive/Art Resource, NY, (r) Dagli Orti/Musée du Chateau de Versailles/The Art Archive; 447 (l) Dagli Orti/Musée Ceramique Sevres/The Art Archive, (r) Bjorn Landstrom/NGS Image Collection; 448 (tl) Victoria & Albert Museum, London/The Art Archive, (tr) Francis G. Mayer/ Corbis, (b) Palubniak Studios; 449 (tl) Hulton Archive by Getty Images, (tr) Bettmann/Corbis, (bl) Brown Brothers, (br) Stuart Ramson/AP/Wide World Photos; 450 Dagli Orti/Russian Historical Museum, Moscow/The Art Archive; 451 Houses of Parliament, Westminster, London, UK/Bridgeman Art Library; 452 Erich Lessing/Art Resource, NY; 453 Giraudon/Art Resource, NY; 454 Réunion des Musées Nationaux/Art Resource, NY; 455 Steidle Collection, College of Earth and Mineral Sciences, Pennsylvania State University/Steidle Art Collection/ SuperStock; 456 (t) AKG London, (b) A. Liebert/Hulton-Deutsch Collection/ Corbis; 457 Bettmann/Corbis; 458 Leonard de Selva/Corbis; 459 Culver Pictures; 460 AP/Wide World Photos; 461 AKG London; 462 (t) American Stock/Hulton Archive by Getty Images, (c, b) Hulton Archive by Getty Images; 463 Division of Political History, Smithsonian Institution, Washington, D.C.; 465 Leonard de Selva/Corbis; 466 AP/Wide World Photos; 467 Kelly Gillin/The Wenatchee World/AP/Wide World Photos; 469 (t) Macduff Everton/Corbis, (b) Michael Coyne/Black Star Publishing/PictureQuest; 470 Bettmann/Corbis; 471 AP/Wide World Photos; 473 Reza/SIPA Press; 475 Steve Liss/TimePix; 476 (t) © 1999 Pollock-Krasner Foundation/Artists Rights Society (ARS) New York/Musée National d'Art Moderne, Paris, France/Giraudon/Art Resource, NY (b) Courtesy NASA; 478 Daniel Hulshizer/AP/Wide World Photos; 479 (t) Victoria Smith/HRW, (b) Bob Daemmrich/Corbis Sygma; 480 AFP/Corbis; 481 Spencer Platt/Getty News Services; 482 Mark Wilson/Getty News Services; 483 Adrin Snider/Daily Press/Corbis Sygma; R1 spread (verso) Kunsthistorisches Museum, Vienna, Austria/Bridgeman Art Library, (recto) Bursteun Collection/Corbis; R4 Royal Geographical Society, London/Bridgeman Art Library, (b) Bettmann/Corbis; R5 (t) SuperStock, (bl) Ken Eward/Biografx/Science Source/Photo Researchers, (br) H. Raguet/ Phototake.

Maps
Maps provided by MapQuest, Inc.

Illustrations
58, 144, 209, 279, 296 Nenad Jakesevic; 375 UHL Studios.